DK ULTIMATE VISUAL DICTIONARY 2000

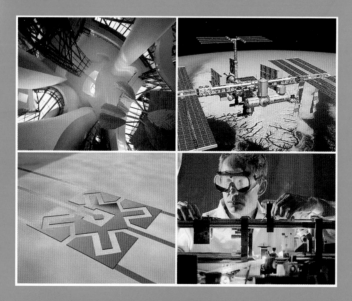

DK

DK PUBLISHING, INC.
New York
www.dk.com

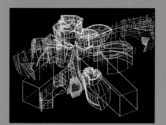

ANIMATED MODEL OF THE
GUGGENHEIM MUSEUM, BILBAO

CONTENTS

IRIDIUM HANDSET

EXTERIOR VIEW OF
OYSTER HOUSE

GALILEO'S PENDULUM CLOCK

INTERNAL STRUCTURE
OF THE HAND

INTERNATIONAL SPACE STATION

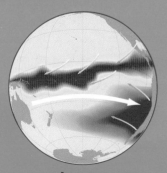

EL NIÑO CLIMATE CYCLE

LEFT: SUBATOMIC PARTICLE TRACKS

VERY LARGE TELESCOPE

Hubble Space Telescope

ORBITING 360 MILES ABOVE the Earth, the Hubble Space Telescope bypasses the blurring effects of the atmosphere to give astronomers some of the clearest and deepest views of space ever witnessed. During 1995, Hubble sent back images that significantly improved our understanding of the Universe. Scientists believed that there were about 10 billion galaxies in the Universe, until studies of Hubble's deep field view enabled them to calculate that this figure is closer to 50 billion. Details of the stunning photographs of the interstellar cloud and dust columns found in the Eagle Nebula have documented, for the first time, the way in which newly-formed stars are revealed by a process called "photo-evaporation," where ultraviolet light from nearby stars erodes surrounding clouds of gas into space. Close-ups of the Orion Nebula provide the best evidence so far that the dark "splotches" found within it are discs of dust swirling around protostars (baby stars). These are believed to be solar systems in the making, which increases the chance of finding life elsewhere in the Universe.

HUBBLE SPACE TELESCOPE
When Hubble was first launched from the Space Shuttle in April 1990, NASA scientists discovered several structural flaws, including a fault with the 2.4 m mirror. A repair mission was successfully performed by astronauts in December 1993.

DEEP FIELD VIEW
In December 1995, a team of astronomers studied this section of sky, which begins near the handle of the Big Dipper and stretches as far as the visible horizon of the Universe. At least 1,500 galaxies in total were counted. Extrapolating from this figure, they calculated that there is probably a total of 50 billion galaxies in the Universe.

Light has left the oldest, most distant galaxies (shown in red) up to 9 billion years ago

This view, assembled from separate images taken in blue, red, and infrared light, approximates true color

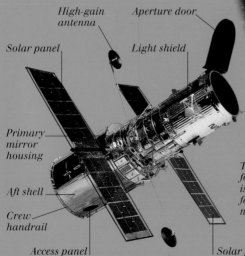

High-gain antenna

Aperture door

Solar panel

Light shield

Primary mirror housing

Aft shell

Crew handrail

Access panel

Solar panel

This apparently foreground star is 400,000 times fainter than the naked eye limit

Bluer galaxies contain young stars and are relatively close

The farthest galaxies are up to 4 billion times fainter than the limits of human vision

ORION NEBULA

A sequence of close-up images of the Orion Nebula (a cloud of dust and gas within our Galaxy) revealed that the mysterious set of dark "splotches" are, in fact, dust clouds swirling around very young stars. Scientists believe that these could be embryonic solar systems.

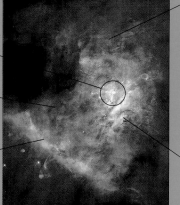

Four massive young stars known as "The Trapezium"

Molecular cloud

The "Great Wall" or "Bright Bar," made up of luminous gas

The Orion Nebula is 1,500 light years away, and spreads across 90 million million miles

Ultraviolet radiation from stars ionizes gas, causing it to glow

STAR DEATH (MYCN18)

The fine detail shown in Hubble images of the star MYCN18 has helped scientists understand how a star like the sun will die. Over several thousands of years, a dying star expands, becoming cooler and redder, and gently puffs its layers of gas into space.

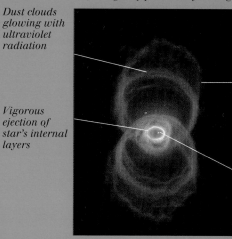

Dust clouds glowing with ultraviolet radiation

Vigorous ejection of star's internal layers

Episodic ejections of star's outer layers produces concentric shells

Hot central core cools off to become a white dwarf (a collapsed, cooling star)

INTERSTELLAR GAS AND DUST IN THE EAGLE NEBULA

Over six million million miles high and 7,000 light years away (one light year equals 6 million million miles), these columns of interstellar dust and gas are found in the Eagle Nebula. Projecting from their surfaces are small fingerlike projections called EGGs (Evaporating Gas Globules). Within these extra-dense regions of gas – which are approximately the size of our solar system – young stars develop. Over millions of years, the surrounding gas globules evaporate to reveal the newly formed stars.

Dramatic illumination is caused by nearby stars

EGGs appear as tiny bumps on the column surface

Foreground star

Smaller columns form, protected from photoevaporation by the shadow of EGGs

Molecular hydrogen gas dispersing into space

PHOTOEVAPORATION

The whiteish haze surrounding each column represents the dispersal of hydrogen into space. This process of erosion, called photoevaporation, is caused by UV light from nearby stars.

Columns are formed by very dense clouds of gas and dust that will eventually erode away

An EGG that has been eroded from the main surface of column

Galileo spacecraft

IN DECEMBER 1995, the Galileo spacecraft finally arrived at the planet Jupiter. More than six years after it had been launched by NASA, the spacecraft's atmospheric probe, which had separated from the orbiter four months earlier, plunged through the gas giant's intense radiation belts and deep into its atmosphere. The onboard electronic systems had to be heavily shielded to protect them against the radiation and temperatures twice as hot as the Sun's surface. As the probe parachuted into Jupiter's atmosphere, pulled in by the enormous gravity, the orbiter passed close to the planet, receiving and storing information for later relay back to Earth. This was just the start of the Galileo mission – since 1995, the orbiter has been circling Jupiter and recording information about its weather and its planet-sized moons. Before arriving at Jupiter, Galileo photographed the impact of Comet P/Shoemaker-Levy 9 with Jupiter, the largest explosion ever seen in the Solar System. More recently, the spacecraft has photographed volcanic activity on the moon Io, and found evidence of water beneath the icy crust of another moon, Europa.

PLANET JUPITER

GALILEO'S JOURNEY

As it began its six-year flight, Galileo moved away from Earth towards Venus, then doubled back, using the gravitational fields of Venus and Earth to propel it toward Jupiter.

Jupiter

Jupiter's orbit

LIFE ON MARS?

Organic molecules thought to be from Mars were recently found in a 4.5 billion-year-old rock that fell into the Antarctic 13,000 years ago. Mineral features suggesting biological activity and possible microscopic fossils of bacterialike organisms were discovered.

Composition matches Martian rock

Water-penetrated cracks

MARTIAN METEORITE

Hydrocarbon deposits

Possible microfossil

Rock structure

MICROSCOPIC VIEW OF METEORITE

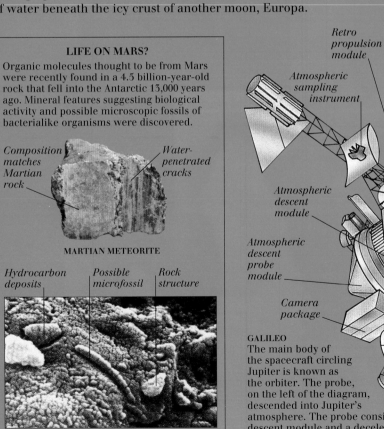

Long boom carrying magnetic sensors

Low-gain antenna

Retro propulsion module

Double-dish antenna

Atmospheric sampling instrument

Atmospheric descent module

Atmospheric descent probe module

Camera package

GALILEO
The main body of the spacecraft circling Jupiter is known as the orbiter. The probe, on the left of the diagram, descended into Jupiter's atmosphere. The probe consists of a descent module and a deceleration module; the latter protects the former from excessive heat, separating off and slowing the probe's descent.

Instruments package

Radioisotope thermoelectric generator

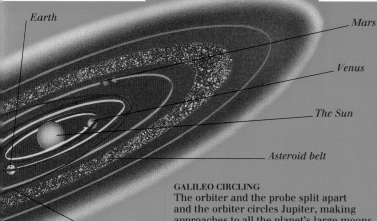

Earth

Mars

Venus

The Sun

Asteroid belt

Galileo's flight path

GALILEO CIRCLING
The orbiter and the probe split apart and the orbiter circles Jupiter, making approaches to all the planet's large moons. It uses their gravity to change course and pick up speed with very little fuel.

COMET SHOEMAKER-LEVY 9
From July 16 to 22, 1994, pieces of a comet designated P/Shoemaker-Levy 9 collided with the planet Jupiter. This was the first collision of two Solar System bodies ever to be observed. While other comets revolve around the Sun, Shoemaker-Levy 9 – named after its discoverers, Eugene and Carolyn Shoemaker and David Levy – moved around Jupiter in a very unusual elongated orbit within a period of just over two years. It became clear that the comet had recently been "captured" by the gravitational field of the planet and would soon collide with it.

Close encounter with Jupiter in 1992 broke comet apart

The gravities of Jupiter and the Sun string fragments out

Pieces consist of fragments of ice and dust

Fragment up to two kilometers in diameter

Surrounding debris cloud

Fragment a few hundred meters in diameter

TRAVELLING COMET
The comet consisted of at least 21 discernible icy fragments with diameters estimated at up to two kilometers. The fragments stretched across 710,000 miles (1.1 million km) of space, almost three times the distance between Earth and the Moon.

Antenna transmits data back to Earth

Erupting volcano on the moon Io

Io, Jupiter's largest moon

Jupiter

Scars formed by dark gases rising to Jupiter's surface

Impact scars larger than Earth

Light cloud zones

Darker cloud belts

Main parachute

Descent module

Protective shield of deceleration module

THE PROBE DESCENDING
The probe descended through Jupiter's atmosphere gathering data. The descent module split from the deceleration module and a parachute slowed its rate of descent. The module descended for 57 minutes before burning out.

POINT OF IMPACT
The impacts of the comet on Jupiter's atmosphere have been spectacular, with plumes thousands of miles high, hot "bubbles" of gas in the atmosphere, and large dark "scars."

Very Large Telescope

THE WORLD'S LARGEST telescope system, the Very Large Telescope (VLT), is located at Cerro Paranal in the Atacama desert, Chile. It is used to study visible light and to collect and analyze infrared heat energy and ultraviolet radiation. During a one hour exposure, each telescope can photograph objects that are four billion times fainter than can be seen with the naked eye. The VLT consists of four telescope units, each with a mirror of 27 ft (8.2 m) in diameter. These units can be used individually or in parallel; together they simulate one large telescope with a mirror of 52 ft (16 m) in diameter. Working in parallel, a process known as interferometry, the VLT allows celestial objects to be seen in much finer detail than with the Hubble Space Telescope. On May 22, 1998, one of the telescope units took its first photograph of a celestial object, an event that astronomers call "first light." The VLT will be used principally to search for small, Earthlike planets around other stars.

SPACE PROBES

In addition to telescopes, new space probes continue to explore the Solar System. In 1997, the Mars Pathfinder successfully surveyed an ancient flood plain on Mars. In the same year, the Galileo space probe discovered strong evidence for a global ocean under the ice sheets of Europa, one of Jupiter's 16 moons. Future space probes will investigate the possible existence of alien microbes on both Mars and Europa.

Ramp from the Pathfinder *Research buggy inspects the rock, Yogi*

MARS PATHFINDER MISSION

Natural color of ice floes *Enhanced color shows ice composition*

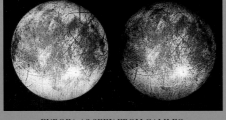

EUROPA AS SEEN FROM GALILEO

TELESCOPE UNIT
The four telescopes of the VLT are precisely engineered structures. Each individual telescope was assembled and tested in Europe, before being taken apart and carefully transported to Chile. Final assembly took place inside the telescope enclosures on the mountain.

Small secondary mirror used to focus starlight

Tilting mechanism adjusts altitude of telescope

Primary mirror sits horizontally

Adjustable structure allows telescope to rotate

Flaw exaggerated by computer

REOSC
OPTIQUE

17/06/97
14:07:58

406.0
nm

COMPUTER MAPPING OF MIRROR DEFECT
The four mirrors of the VLT were cast in Germany and polished in France. The shape of each mirror was checked at regular intervals using laser beams, and laser data was formulated into a map of the mirror's surface. Defects (see right), perhaps only a millionth of a millimeter in diameter, were exaggerated by the computer so that they could be located and corrected.

TELESCOPE SITE

The VLT is located at the summit of Cerro Paranal, a mountain in the Atacama desert, Chile. At 8,635 ft (2,632 m) above sea level, the site is one of the driest places on Earth, despite being situated only 7.5 miles (12 km) from the Pacific coast. The mountaintop site provides remarkable conditions for observation and photography. There are up to 350 cloud-free nights per year, and images are stable owing to the lack of water vapor in the atmosphere.

Telescope unit

Telescope enclosure

Surface of mirror

IMAGE QUALITY

The atmosphere of the Earth blurs light from distant celestial objects. The VLT is able to compensate for this using a computerized system known as adaptive optics. Every one hundredth of a second, a computer analyzes a tiny fraction of light from a star being observed by the VLT. It then measures the effect that the Earth's atmosphere is having on the light, and calculates how to compensate for that effect. The computer sends signals to a set of activators, which support the flexible mirror. This then refocuses the light from the telescope. The worst effects of the atmosphere are eliminated and sharp images, comparable with those taken by the Hubble Space Telescope, are produced. Images taken by a ground-based telescope (above right) and the VLT (right), show different views of the same planetary nebula.

PLANETARY NEBULA I
This image of the Dumbbell Nebula shows the cloud of gas that has drifted away into space from the remains of a dead star. It was taken by a ground-based telescope.

Dust and gas of the nebula

PLANETARY NEBULA II
Taken by the VLT, this view of the Dumbbell Nebula shows the center of the gas cloud in far more detail. Complex patterns can reveal the way that gas is moving within the cloud.

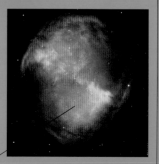

Colors indicate the types of gas

International Space Station

IN 1998, THE FIRST components of the International Space Station (ISS) were launched from Russia and the US. The ISS will provide a unique place to study the Earth, and to see how the Sun's violent eruptions affect the operation of communications satellites, and the weather on Earth. The effects of gravity inside the station will be minuscule and scientists will be able to study a myriad of subtle biological, physical, and chemical reactions which are impossible to duplicate on Earth. Complete construction will require a total of 45 space missions and many hours of space-walking by astronauts. The station is scheduled to be permanently crewed from the eighth mission onward, due to take place in January 2000. Astronauts will spend many months at a time on the station, testing equipment for future space exploration missions.

MIR SPACE STATION
Now referred to as Phase One of the International Space Station, Mir was home to American, Russian, and European astronauts as they learned to work together in space.

ARTIST'S IMPRESSION OF THE ISS
The most ambitious space project since the Apollo missions to land man on the Moon, the ISS is the next step in the human exploration of the Solar System. It is a joint venture between 16 nations, and the largest scientific cooperative program in history. All power on the space station will be generated by the large arrays of solar panels connected to the main structure of the station. Also attached to this framework are corrugated panels, which act as radiators dispersing excess heat from the station into space. Astronauts will live and work in the cylindrical modules between the solar panel arrays, and will eventually be able to spend many years at a time in space.

SPACE HAZARDS

Dust grains traveling through space at speeds of up to 230 ft (70 m) per second can "sandblast" spacecraft and astronauts. Subatomic particles travel close to the speed of light, and can cause severe damage to living cells. Space stations therefore provide shields to protect astronauts from dust and particle storms and solar flares.

DAMAGE CRATER
This tiny crater in a window of the Space Shuttle was caused by a fleck of paint. It is 0.64mm wide and 0.63mm deep.

SOLAR FLARE
These violent eruptions from the photosphere (the visible surface of the Sun) cause major disruptions to communications satellites that orbit the Earth.

Solar panels provide energy

Zaraya control module

Russian Soyuz spacecraft

US MODULES
The US modules of the ISS were built in Alabama. Astronauts will eat and sleep in the habitat module and work in the laboratory module. A connecting unit called Node 1 will join these two modules together.

Laboratory module

Node 1 connecting unit

Habitat module

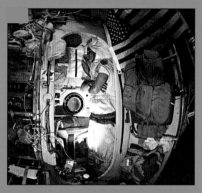

SLEEPING IN SPACE
Astronauts sleep in an upright position so that they receive a constant flow of air. If they slept horizontally, the effects of weightlessness could result in suffocation from exhaled carbon dioxide. This astronaut remains stationary by crossing his arms and using straps to anchor himself to the wall of the module.

Radiators for cooling

Exposure platform

LABORATORY MODULES
The European Columbus Orbital Facility is one of many laboratory modules that contain computer and scientific equipment for running a vast range of experiments. Some modules have access to robotic arms that will be able to conduct experiments on exposure platforms outside the station.

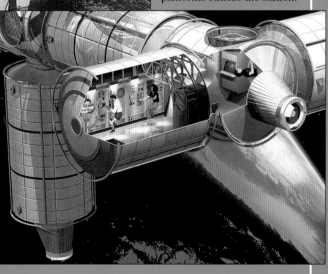

European Columbus Orbital Facility

Connecting module

Japanese Experiment Module

Giganotosaurus

THE BONES OF A GIANT new dinosaur, *Giganotosaurus carolinii*, were recently excavated by two scientists in Argentina. *Giganotosaurus* ("giant reptile of the south") is believed to be one of the largest carnivorous dinosaurs ever found. With a body length of 42 ft (12.5 m) and an estimated weight of between 6 and 8 tons, it is believed to have been even larger than the *Tyrannosaurus rex*. Like T-Rex, the *Giganotosaurus* is classified in the *Theropoda* – a suborder of the Saurischia (lizard-hipped) group of dinosaurs that were characterized by short forelimbs and an S-shaped neck. It existed an estimated 100 million years ago during the Cretaceous period, and appears to be quite closely related to a theropod that lived 50 million years previously, *Allosaurus*.

CARCHARODONTOSAURUS SAHARICUS

Another theropod rivaling the great size of T-Rex is the Moroccan-found *Carcharodontosaurus saharicus* ("shark-toothed reptile from the Sahara"). In May 1996 the discovery of a 5.4 ft (1.65 m) skull was announced by scientists from the University of Chicago. The dinosaur is estimated at being 45 ft (13.7 m) long, 12 ft (3.65 m) high, and weighing 8.3 tons. The skull reveals razor-sharp teeth that would have enabled this formidable dinosaur to slash and slice its prey with the greatest of ease.

Long heavy tail

Hind limb

RECONSTRUCTING THE SKELETON

The skeleton was actually discovered in 1993 by Ruben D. Carolini, who is credited within the full name of the dinosaur, *Giganotosaurus carolinii*. Paleontologists Rodolfo A. Coria and Leonardo Salgado then began the work of excavating, piecing together, and studying the bones. They waited until they had completed a full examination before announcing their findings in the September 1995 issue of the journal *Nature*.

ARTIST'S IMPRESSION OF THE FULL SKELETON
More than 70 percent of the skeleton has been unearthed so far and a clear idea of the full skeleton can be gained from this artist's impression.

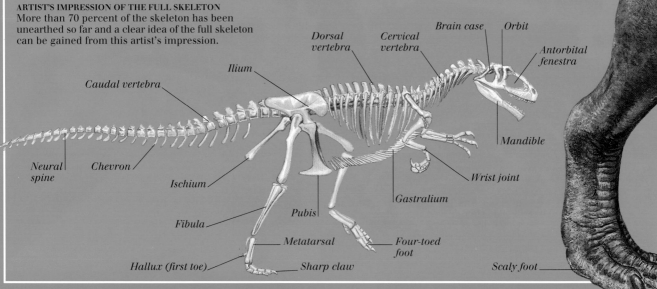

Dorsal vertebra

Cervical vertebra

Brain case

Orbit

Antorbital fenestra

Ilium

Caudal vertebra

Mandible

Wrist joint

Neural spine

Chevron

Ischium

Gastralium

Fibula

Pubis

Metatarsal

Four-toed foot

Hallux (first toe)

Sharp claw

Scaly foot

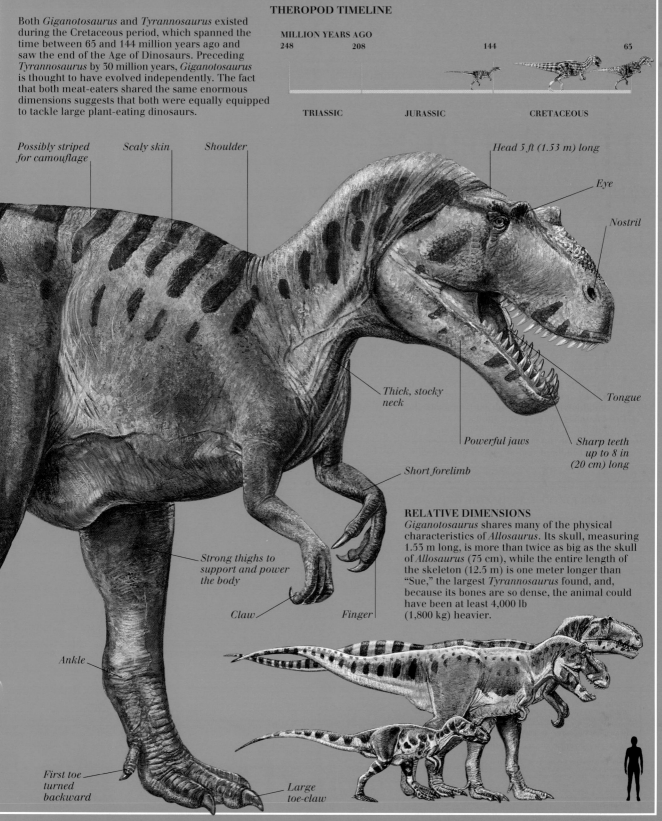

Both *Giganotosaurus* and *Tyrannosaurus* existed during the Cretaceous period, which spanned the time between 65 and 144 million years ago and saw the end of the Age of Dinosaurs. Preceding *Tyrannosaurus* by 30 million years, *Giganotosaurus* is thought to have evolved independently. The fact that both meat-eaters shared the same enormous dimensions suggests that both were equally equipped to tackle large plant-eating dinosaurs.

THEROPOD TIMELINE

MILLION YEARS AGO

248   208   144   65

TRIASSIC   JURASSIC   CRETACEOUS

Possibly striped for camouflage

Scaly skin

Shoulder

Head 5 ft (1.53 m) long

Eye

Nostril

Thick, stocky neck

Powerful jaws

Tongue

Sharp teeth up to 8 in (20 cm) long

Short forelimb

Strong thighs to support and power the body

Claw

Finger

RELATIVE DIMENSIONS

Giganotosaurus shares many of the physical characteristics of *Allosaurus*. Its skull, measuring 1.53 m long, is more than twice as big as the skull of *Allosaurus* (75 cm), while the entire length of the skeleton (12.5 m) is one meter longer than "Sue," the largest *Tyrannosaurus* found, and, because its bones are so dense, the animal could have been at least 4,000 lb (1,800 kg) heavier.

Ankle

First toe turned backward

Large toe-claw

Medical Research

SOME SIGNIFICANT BREAKTHROUGHS have recently been made in DNA research, with enormous implications for controlling and curing diseases, reproducing identical organisms (cloning), and "decoding," or listing, the sequence of the genes that compose an organism's DNA ("genome sequencing"). In May 1996, Oxford University scientists announced that they had identified the regulatory "switch" for the gene CFTR, which, when defective, causes cystic fibrosis. The discovery will potentially enable healthy copies of the gene to be introduced into a patient's body and activated in relevant cells. Geneticists have, for the first time, sequenced the genome of an organism larger than a bacterium, with enormous consequences for the future study into human genetics. Other areas of development include the use of highly specialized computer technology to provide long-distance medical care, and virtual-reality environments for medical practice, training, and research.

THE COMPOSITION OF DNA (DEOXYRIBONUCLEIC ACID)

Human cell

Nucleus

Nucleolus

GENETIC CODING

A chromosome is a condensed strand of DNA. There are 23 pairs of chromosomes in the human cell and together they contain about 100,000 genes. Every gene is a tiny segment of DNA, made up of paired nucleotide bases arranged in triplets. The above computer display shows the base-pair structure of adjacent genes. The entire sequence of these bases forms the specific genetic code (genome) of an organism. A world-wide research effort, known as the Human Genome Project, has been set up to identify and code all of the genes in human DNA.

Nucleosome

Sugar phosphate backbone

Chromosome (human cells have 23 pairs)

DNA wraps around a core of binding proteins

Unraveled double helix of DNA

DNA GENOME SEQUENCING

Saccharomyces cerevisiae, or brewer's yeast, is the first organism more complex than a bacterium to have its entire genome sequenced. Three hundred scientists worked over a period of six years to sequence the 12,071 base pairs. Their achievement was announced at the European Commission in April 1996.

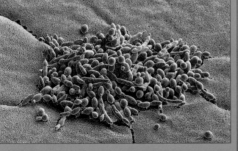

YEAST CELLS

NEMATODE WORM

WORM DNA

Another subject of genetic research is the *Caenorhabditis elegans*, a soil-dwelling nematode worm. Scientists have already mapped out its genes and have embarked on identifying the specific sequence of the 100 million base pairs in its genome.

A DNA SEGMENT

This computer representation shows the double helix (blue) of the DNA linked together by the base pairs (yellow and red).

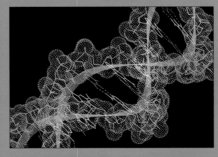

KEY TO BASES

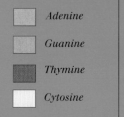

☐ *Adenine*

☐ *Guanine*

☐ *Thymine*

☐ *Cytosine*

CLONING

A breakthrough in efforts to genetically engineer species of animals was announced in March 1996. Pictured here at nine months old, these two Welsh mountain sheep were successfully cloned by using an electric current to fuse a lab-cultured cell with an unfertilized egg (one emptied of all its chromosomes). This stimulus also fertilized the cell, which then divided, developed into an embryo, and was transferred to a surrogate mother.

CLONED SHEEP, MEGAN AND MORAG

BASE PAIRS

The four chemical compounds or bases, are paired in "rungs" and grouped in triplets, forming the double helix "ladder". The sequence of these base pairs contains the inherited coded instructions (genes) responsible for the development of an organism.

Nucleotide base

Paired nucleotide base

Gene is made up of sections of base triplets (3 successive pairs of bases)

TISSUE ENGINEERING

An artificial human ear, developed by growing human cartilage in a biodegradable polyester scaffold mold, was grafted onto the back of a mouse to see whether outer skin would form and the blood would circulate. This experiment, successfully carried out at the Massachusetts Institute of Technology by Dr. C. Vacanti, is a vital step towards using such structures in future human transplant surgery.

COMPUTER TECHNOLOGY AND MEDICINE

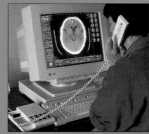

TELEMEDICAL ANALYSIS OF BRAIN SCAN

TELEMEDICINE

Telemedicine – the practice of medicine at a distance using computer networks – was pioneered by NASA to provide medical support to astronauts. Not only can it be used for consulting with patients in rural or widespread geographical areas but it can also provide emergency care in remote and disaster situations.

VIRTUAL REALITY

Virtual reality environments are being developed to provide realistic training for certain surgical procedures, much as flight simulators are used to train pilots to fly. The highly specialized techniques

Surgeon's eyepiece

Keyhole surgery instruments feed back video images

Controls

GASTROSCOPE

performed in minimally invasive "keyhole" surgery, using such instruments as the gastroscope (above), can be practiced using a virtual environment that simulates tissue properties. A virtual environment developed to simulate eye surgery is shown below. The surgeon is able to experience both the visual and mechanical sensations associated with performing the operation.

VIRTUAL ENVIRONMENT FOR SIMULATION OF EYE SURGERY

STRESS CONTOURS SHOWN AS INCISION IS MADE IN CORNEA

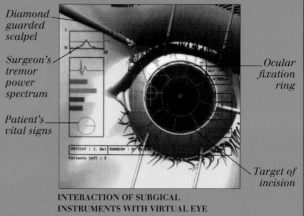

Diamond guarded scalpel

Surgeon's tremor power spectrum

Patient's vital signs

Ocular fixation ring

Target of incision

INTERACTION OF SURGICAL INSTRUMENTS WITH VIRTUAL EYE

Genetic advances

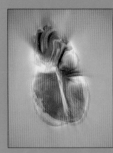

HUMAN HEART

DEVELOPMENTS IN CLONING are among the most important advances in recent genetic science. A clone is a group of genes, cells, or complete organisms in which all of the group's members have the same genetic constitution. The term is also used to refer to individual members of a clone. Clones occur in nature, especially in the case of simple organisms, such as bacteria and viruses, which reproduce merely by splitting (asexual reproduction) after their DNA has replicated itself. They also occur in humans and other animals when a single fertilized egg divides and separates to form two or more identical individuals. Artificial cloning of selected genes is one of the most significant breakthroughs ever made in biology and has powerful implications for both science and industry. Once the desired gene is obtained, the cloning can be left to organisms such as bacteria, which, under suitable conditions, reproduce almost indefinitely. In this way, enormous quantities of the particular gene may be produced. Gene cloning is most commonly done in the laboratory by means of the polymerase chain reaction (PCR), which can produce millions of copies of a single gene in a matter of hours. Far more daunting an enterprise than gene cloning is the cloning of whole animals (see below right), only recently shown to be practicable. A further key genetic advance is the creation of transgenic animals, in particular pigs, which are currently being used for the "manufacture" of human-compatible organs, such as hearts.

CREATING A TRANSGENIC ANIMAL

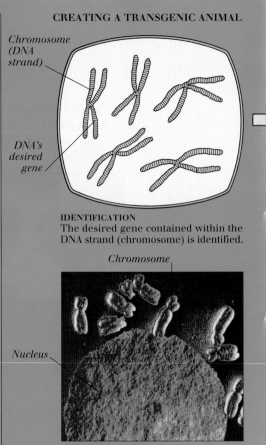

Chromosome (DNA strand)

DNA's desired gene

IDENTIFICATION
The desired gene contained within the DNA strand (chromosome) is identified.

Chromosome

Nucleus

HUMAN CELL
After cell division, perfect copies of each of its chromosomes are passed to each of the daughter cells.

BSE

Among the more worrying aspects of biological research is the discovery that the brain disease bovine spongiform encephalopathy (BSE) is identical to the fatal human condition Creutzfeldt-Jakob disease (CJD). There is general agreement that the introduction of bovine tissue from affected animals into the food chain was the cause of the recent BSE epidemic. Although the genetic modification of animals is unlikely to involve the genes active in BSE, the number of unanswered questions has caused much concern about the propriety of the procedure.

GENETICALLY MODIFIED FOODS

An increasingly common practice in the food industry is the genetic modification of foodstuffs in order to extend their shelf life. This means that not only foods, for example fruit and vegetables, but also food ingredients and additives that contain genes derived from animals, fish, insects, and viruses, will appear in stores unlabeled as such.

A little decay is apparent

Rotting is far more visible

GENETICALLY MODIFIED TOMATO

"NATURAL" TOMATO OF THE SAME AGE

ANIMAL CLONING

To produce a clone of an animal, a sample of its DNA must be used. Since each body cell contains a complete DNA genome, this is easily obtained. This DNA has to be introduced into an ovum (egg) of another animal of the same species after the ovum's original DNA is extracted. The egg is then inserted into a surrogate animal's womb and the pregnancy proceeds as normal. Although every body cell contains a complete genome, it will normally activate only those genes necessary for its own body part – for example kidney, brain, or bone. The other genes are not needed and are not "switched on." However, if the cell is starved of nutrients, development can be stopped at an early stage, at which point all the genes can be operative. The ovum into which the DNA is inserted will then behave as if the DNA were its own.

A donor provides the cell for cloning, e.g. mammary cell

CELL DONOR

A ewe provides an egg

EGG DONOR

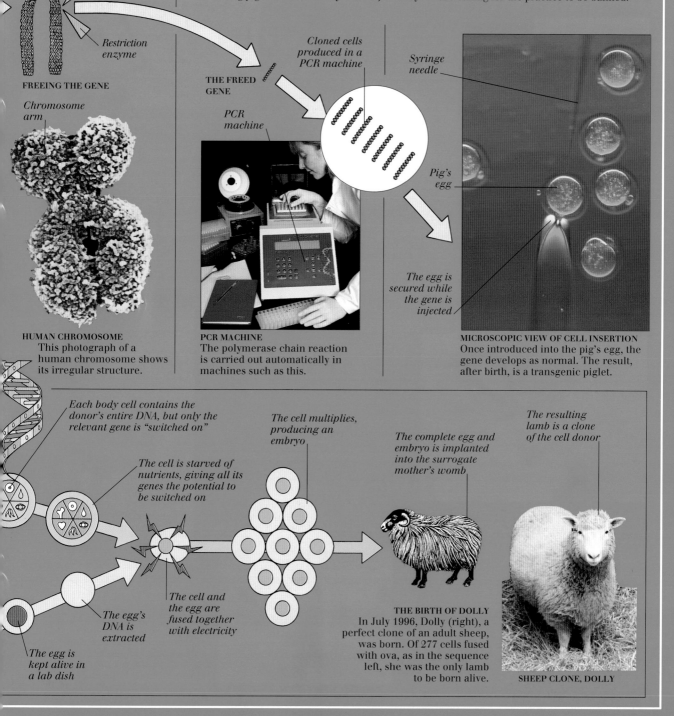

Special enzymes called restriction enzymes snip the DNA at specific points to isolate and free the gene

Restriction enzyme

FREEING THE GENE

Chromosome arm

HUMAN CHROMOSOME
This photograph of a human chromosome shows its irregular structure.

TRANSGENIC ANIMALS
A transgenic animal is not a clone, but an animal whose genes contain DNA taken from another source. It is now possible to create transgenic pigs in order to provide organs for human transplant. If, for example, a human gene is introduced at the one-cell stage of pig embryo development, the organ taken from the resulting pig will be less likely to be rejected by the human. The gene must be introduced at the one-cell stage so that it is incorporated into all of the grown specimen's cells. The diagram (left) shows the commonest way to create a transgenic pig. However, following a recent discovery that pigs carry a virus that can infect human cells, some researchers are calling for the practice to be banned.

THE FREED GENE

Cloned cells produced in a PCR machine

PCR machine

PCR MACHINE
The polymerase chain reaction is carried out automatically in machines such as this.

Syringe needle

Pig's egg

The egg is secured while the gene is injected

MICROSCOPIC VIEW OF CELL INSERTION
Once introduced into the pig's egg, the gene develops as normal. The result, after birth, is a transgenic piglet.

Each body cell contains the donor's entire DNA, but only the relevant gene is "switched on"

The cell is starved of nutrients, giving all its genes the potential to be switched on

The cell multiplies, producing an embryo

The complete egg and embryo is implanted into the surrogate mother's womb

The resulting lamb is a clone of the cell donor

The cell and the egg are fused together with electricity

The egg's DNA is extracted

The egg is kept alive in a lab dish

THE BIRTH OF DOLLY
In July 1996, Dolly (right), a perfect clone of an adult sheep, was born. Of 277 cells fused with ova, as in the sequence left, she was the only lamb to be born alive.

SHEEP CLONE, DOLLY

Modern surgery

WITH NEW DISCOVERIES AND advancing technology, medicine is constantly evolving. Developments in technical expertise have resulted in a successful hand transplant and the repair of a congenital defect in a fetus while still in the womb. Advances in technology have also been far-reaching, providing a glimpse of what might be achieved in the future. The application of virtual reality in medicine has already enabled progress in both the teaching and practice of surgery, and may soon be used in the treatment of eating disorders and agoraphobia. Minimally invasive and robot- and computer-aided surgery allow delicate and complex surgical procedures to be carried out with the precision of a thousandth of a millimeter. This means that surgery has become safer, and patient pain and recovery time have been reduced.

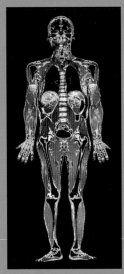

MRI SCAN OF A FEMALE BODY
This color-enhanced Magnetic Resonance Image (MRI) is the product of a number of MRI scans made along the length of the body, which have been collated by the scanner's computer.

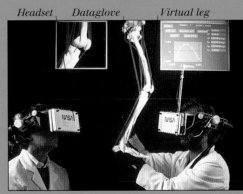

Headset   Dataglove   Virtual leg

VIRTUAL SURGERY
Medical imaging such as X-ray, Computerized Tomography (CT), and Magnetic Resonance Imaging (MRI), allows visual access to the internal anatomy and functions of the human body. The precise anatomical information provided by these images can be used to create a virtual patient, on which surgeons and medical students can practice procedures. To study the anatomy of the human leg, these surgeons wear headsets equipped with a 3-D video display to view an image, and a black rubber glove (dataglove) that has woven optical fiber sensors. The glove relays details of the body part to the computer, which then generates the image.

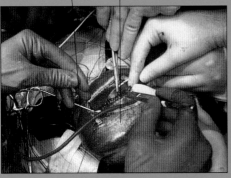

Surgical clamp   Muscular wall of mother's womb

INTRAUTERINE SURGERY
The repair of birth defects through fetal surgery has so far been mostly experimental. However, groundbreaking advances were made in 1998 with the treatment of a case of spina bifida, a developmental defect in the posterior wall of the spinal canal. With this condition, the delicate tissue of the spinal cord may be exposed to varying degrees of damage, depending on the severity of the defect. This can result in paralysis of the lower limbs and incontinence. A team of surgeons in the US corrected the defect in a 23-week-gestation fetus, after the condition had been detected during a routine ultrasound. Follow-up at the walking and toilet-training stages will be necessary to judge the success of the operation.

ROBOTS IN SURGERY

Recent advances in biomedical engineering have led to the increasing use of robots in surgery. Once a robot has been correctly programmed, it will be more accurate than a human in performing many precise but repetitive tasks. Robots may soon act as surgeons' assistants during operations, holding instruments such as an endoscope (for viewing internal parts of the body), and making incisions when required.

ROBOT-AIDED BRAIN SURGERY
A robot performs simulated brain surgery on a model head (right). The surgeon views the operation on a large screen and uses a joystick to control the robot's movements.

Robotic arm   Model head

COMPUTER-AIDED BRAIN SURGERY
A surgeon uses a computer-assisted microscope to locate a brain tumour in a patient. The microscope uses MRI scans to plot the position of the tumor, and maps it in 3-D virtual reality. The surgeon can then locate and destroy the tumor using a laser integrated into the microscope.

Digital
artery

Blood
capillary
network

Distal
flexor
tendon

Nerve to
finger

Vein

Flexed finger

Muscle

Flexor
retinaculum

Deep flexor
tendons

Superficial
flexor tendon

Pronator
muscle

Radial
artery

Radius

Median
nerve

Palmaris
longus tendon

Ulnar
nerve

Ulnar
artery

Ulna

Skin

Fatty layer

ROBOTIC HAND

This battery-operated robotic hand needs only three fingers to perform 85 percent of the functions of a normal hand. The hand will be covered in artificial skin that contains tiny pressure sensors to aid use (see below). Artificial hands will eventually be powered by energy generated by the movement of tendons in the upper arm.

Adjustable
finger
manipulation

ROBOT SENSOR CHIP

Sensors built into artificial skin react to pressure on the fingertips caused by the manipulation of objects. The sensors enable the hand to maintain a grip on objects of all shapes and sizes.

HAND TRANSPLANT

In 1998, a multinational team of surgeons performed the first successful hand transplant in France. The transplant recipient had lost his hand in a circular saw accident nine years previously. Arteries and veins in the arm and hand were connected to supply vital nutrients to, and remove waste products from, the skin and tissues of the hand. Regeneration of nerve tissue, even after reconstruction, was more gradual and, three months after the operation, the patient started to regain sensation in his fingertips.

Bursa protecting tendons

Superficial flexor tendons

Deep flexor tendons

Median nerve

Radial artery

Pronator
muscle

Radius

Tendons
stabizing radial
and ulnar bones

Ulnar artery

Ulna

Ulnar
nerve

TRANSVERSE SECTION THROUGH WRIST

This diagram shows the arteries, veins, and nerves that travel through the arm and hand. At the wrist joint, bones in the arm articulate with bones in the hand to allow movement.

El Niño and La Niña

ALSO REFERRED TO AS the El Niño-Southern Oscillation (ENSO) Cycle, El Niño and La Niña are extreme instances of the natural climate cycle of the tropical Pacific. Although scientists have been aware of the oscillation for several decades, the public has only become aware of its increasingly destructive effects in more recent years. These warm and cold seasonal variations occur due to interaction between the ocean surface, the atmosphere, and trade winds (general wind patterns). The resulting rise and fall in ocean temperature has been linked with severe weather conditions in parts of South America, Indonesia, and Australia. The cycle oscillates between warm (El Niño) to neutral or cold (La Niña) conditions every 3–7 years. Meteorologists use information provided by weather satellites in the prediction and tracking of these events, which have had a dramatic effect on climate patterns around the world since at least the last century. It is not known how the ENSO Cycle will be affected if the global climate grows warmer.

NORMAL CONDITIONS

Normally, southeasterly trade winds drive water westward across the equatorial South Pacific, causing warm surface water to form a deep pool near Indonesia. The Peru Current flows northward along the South American coast, and cold water wells up to the surface, carrying oxygen and nutrients that sustain fish and birds.

INTERPRETING INFORMATION

Weather forecasts in newspapers and on radio and television begin as observations. Thousands of surface stations on land and hundreds of weather ships at sea – many of them are fully automated – monitor visibility, air pressure, wind direction and speed, temperature, humidity, and the amount, type, and height of cloud. Together with information received from weather balloons and satellites, data is collated at weather centers to produce synoptic charts (see below). These enable meteorologists to prepare forecasts.

FORECAST PREPARATION

Trade winds slacken

Cool water is suppressed

Pacific

Ocean

Center of low pressure   *Isobar*

Sea current changes direction and flows east

Warm surface water

SYNOPTIC WEATHER CHART

EL NIÑO CONDITIONS

During an El Niño episode, trade winds slacken or even reverse. Warm surface water flows from west to east, increasing the depth of warm water off the South American coast. Heavy rainfall follows the warm water, leading to flooding in Peru and drought in parts of Indonesia and Australia.

EL NIÑO SEA CURRENTS

The normal sea current reverses and warm water forms a pool near South America. This pool suppresses the nutrient-rich water of the Peru Current and, starved of nutrients, fish and sea birds move away or die.

Trade winds drive warm water toward Asia

Current carries water westward

Cool water of Peru Current wells to the surface

Pacific

Ocean

Warm water

South America

NORMAL SEA CURRENTS
Sea currents flow westward and carry warm water across the ocean. The body of water near South America remains relatively cool.

WEATHER SATELLITE
Five satellites in equally spaced geostationary orbits about 22,000 miles (35,400 km) above the equator, observe the whole of the Earth. They transmit data that is shared under the supervision of the World Meteorological Organization. Satellites in lower orbits pass over the poles every 90 minutes.

Casing encloses transmission equipment

Pool of warm water grows larger and deeper

A tiny spark can cause fierce flames

LA NIÑA CONDITIONS
During a La Niña episode, trade winds strengthen and warm surface water accumulates in a deep pool near Asia. Rainfall follows the warm water, bringing heavy rain to parts of Australia and Indonesia. The upwelling of the Peru Current increases and cool water flows north and then west, flowing as a surface current part of the way across the ocean.

Pacific

Ocean

Cool surface water

South America

BUSH FIRE
El Niño episodes affect weather over a large area. They have been linked to droughts in Indonesia and Australia, where vegetation becomes so dry that the smallest spark can ignite it. The result is a fierce bush fire, as shown above.

Storm surge at high tide

Sea level rises due to low pressure

Cool ocean current

LA NIÑA SEA CURRENTS
The cold upwelling intensifies and sea-surface temperatures drop by up to 4°C. This brings nutrients and improves fishing across a wide area.

Trade winds strengthen

HURRICANE AND FLOODING
Hurricanes have been linked to La Niña episodes. As well as ferocious winds and torrential rain, hurricanes can cause coastal flooding. The sea level rises due to very low pressure, and strong winds drive water toward the shore. If the hurricane coincides with a high tide, the resulting storm surge can cause severe damage.

21A

House of the future

IN THE LAST FEW decades, the environmentally friendly or sustainable house has been associated with green enthusiasts who built homes to both blend in with the natural landscape and harness renewable energy resources. As we enter the new millennium, environmental concerns will become a matter of expediency. Architects, developers, and homeowners will be pressed to take a more pragmatic approach to where they build, and the more economic use of space and energy supplies. Extreme climates currently present architects with the greatest challenge in energy conservation. In urban areas, there is a growing trend for disused buildings that can be converted into housing, and for dwellings that can be easily adapted to accommodate different types of residents.

SOHO TRANSFORMABLE APARTMENT
This Central London flat can be used as one large living space, or partitioned with freestanding boxes to provide bedrooms. It was designed by architect Mark Guard.

CONVERTED WATER TOWER
This structure on the outskirts of Antwerp, Belgium, was originally built in the early 20th century. It was converted into a dramatic and unusual dwelling by architect Jo Crepain in 1998.

Platform of original tower

Drum where water originally collected

Winter garden

Columns form main structure of house

Opaque glass

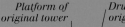

MEZZANINE VIEW
A mezzanine level in the base of the tower overlooks the living room and creates a cosy space for watching television. The natural, wooded setting of the tower is emphasized by the great expanse of glass.

TOP-FLOOR WINTER GARDEN
The use of buildings that were not originally intended for domestic purposes often results in an unconventional house layout. Here, rooms inside the glass-encased water tower are stacked on top of one other. The winter garden is located below the disused water drum.

INTERIOR OF THE BASE
The architect used the original structure to divide the concrete base of the tower. The sitting area is located at the rear, and the kitchen on the street front.

OYSTER HOUSE

Nigel Coates' Oyster House was the winning entry in the Concept House competition at the 1998 *Daily Mail* Ideal Home Exhibition in London. It was designed to provide a new model for the speculative home in a typical suburban community. With this design, Coates extended the idea of loft living to the family home. The ground floor is open plan with flexible partitions, enabling the living space to adapt as children grow up, and to incorporate friends, work, and guests. There are two staircases, which allow for separation and privacy upstairs. Each stairway leads to a bathroom, with a double bedroom on each side of the house.

EXTERIOR VIEW

INTERIOR VIEW OF GROUND FLOOR

WENDELL BURNETTE HOUSE

This house and studio were built by the architect Wendell Burnette in 1995. The house is situated in a desert landscape on the west face of the Phoenix Mountain Preserve in Arizona. Burnette's innovative design takes a truly inspired approach to environmental concerns. It proposes imaginative solutions to both the extreme desert climate, and the existence of unsightly housing in the surrounding area.

MONOLITHIC WALLS
Among the most distinctive features of the Burnette house are its concrete walls with narrow glass slits. These walls filter the sun on the north and south walls, while the glass slits act as a giant sundial that charts the movement of the sun throughout the day.

Glass front of east elevation has low-emissivity surface

Narrow glass slit

East block contains living spaces

Fully shaded evaporative pool

Internal court divides living area and studio

Carport

Stairway to terrace

MICROCLIMATE IN THE INTERNAL COURT
Burnette's inspiration for a water-cooling system was drawn from the naturally occurring "canyon seats" or springs found in the Arizona desert. Here, his water-cooled internal court supports a lush microclimate at the entrance to the house, and divides the east and west blocks. A fully shaded evaporative pool located below the studio floor overflows into a trough. Water runs down the natural slope of the site, cooling the internal court and improving ventilation throughout the house.

Tilting trains

ALTHOUGH TILTING TRAINS have been in use since the 1960s, it is only recent technological developments that have been able to prevent much of the passenger discomfort caused by cornering at high speeds. As a train goes into a curve, it produces substantial centrifugal force toward the outside of the curve. By tilting the train (the equivalent of leaning into a curve on a bicycle), this centrifugal force is balanced by a force into the inner curve, and passenger discomfort is reduced. Current computer-controlled active tilting systems operate from self-steering trucks (the wheeled undercarriage of the train). Improvements in design enhance the operation of the train by reducing track forces, and radial self-steering trucks with "soft" suspension have been introduced. Modern tilting trains allow operators to achieve higher speeds on existing curved routes without costly track improvements or the need to consider completely new high-speed lines.

SWEDISH TILTING TRAIN (1990)

NORMAL TRAIN CARRIAGE

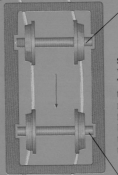

Centrifugal force pushes the car contents toward the outside of the curve

CENTRIFUGAL FORCE

As the train enters the curve, a strong centrifugal force is produced

Banking is limited to 6°

NORMAL TRAIN ON CURVE
The normal train is "banked" slightly and slows as it goes into the bend, but the car body does not tilt.

Train approaches at an angle

Track

Strong sideways force outward

STIFF-WHEEL AXLES
The inability of the axles to move means that high forces are taken by the axles themselves and then by the track.

Axle

Fiat's Pendolino – "Little Pendulum" – tilting train

PENDOLINO
Fiat's Pendolino is the prototype for most recent European tilting trains. The French tilting train shown in the main diagram (opposite) will be based on similar technology.

HIGH-SPEED TRAINS

The Japanese pioneered modern high-speed rail travel with their *Shinkansen* (High-Speed Line) trains, which entered service in 1964. On a special new line between Tokyo and Osaka, they achieved speeds of up to 130 mph (210 km/h). The line was reserved for high-speed trains, so there was no slower moving, conflicting traffic to interfere with operations. The latest Bullet Train, *Nozomi*, pictured here, has also broken speed records. Since the early 1980s, similar trains have been developed in France, intitially running between Paris and Lyon and, like the Japanese train, running on priority "dedicated" tracks. German Railways have also developed high-speed links since 1991.

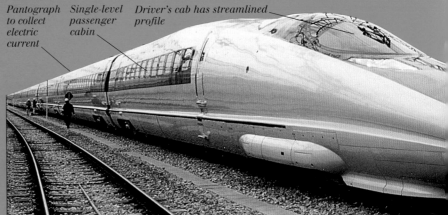

Pantograph to collect electric current

Single-level passenger cabin

Driver's cab has streamlined profile

TILTING TRAIN CARRIAGE

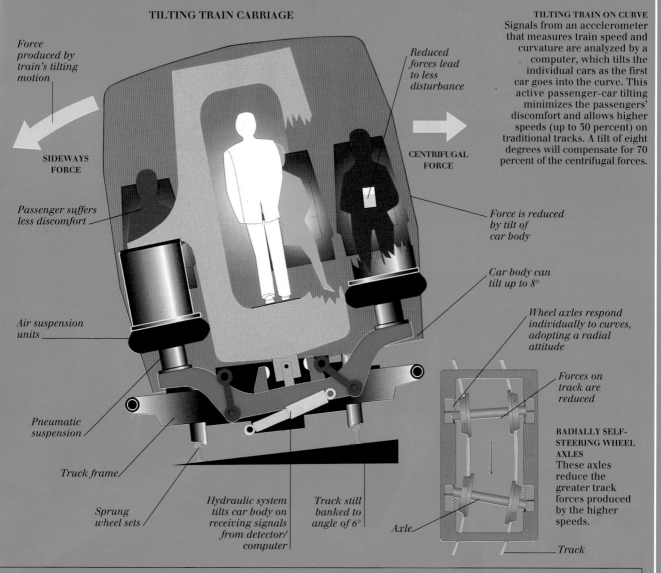

Force produced by train's tilting motion

SIDEWAYS FORCE

Passenger suffers less discomfort

Reduced forces lead to less disturbance

CENTRIFUGAL FORCE

Force is reduced by tilt of car body

Car body can tilt up to 8°

Wheel axles respond individually to curves, adopting a radial attitude

Air suspension units

Pneumatic suspension

Truck frame

Sprung wheel sets

Hydraulic system tilts car body on receiving signals from detector/ computer

Track still banked to angle of 6°

Axle

Track

TILTING TRAIN ON CURVE
Signals from an accelerometer that measures train speed and curvature are analyzed by a computer, which tilts the individual cars as the first car goes into the curve. This active passenger-car tilting minimizes the passengers' discomfort and allows higher speeds (up to 30 percent) on traditional tracks. A tilt of eight degrees will compensate for 70 percent of the centrifugal forces.

Forces on track are reduced

RADIALLY SELF-STEERING WHEEL AXLES
These axles reduce the greater track forces produced by the higher speeds.

Electronic signal/speed detection equipment in train nose

BULLET TRAIN
The train can carry 1,324 passengers and features 64 separate traction motors, each producing 285kw of power. The body shells are made of aluminum alloy.

RECORD BREAKER
The latest prototype Bullet Train has reached speeds of 214 mph (345 km/h), but the French TGV holds the world railspeed record of 320 mph (515 km/h).

Electric Car / Le Shuttle

IN 1995, PEUGEOT LAUNCHED their first electrically powered vehicle designed for the private motorist – the Peugeot 106 Electric. Unlike conventional gas-driven cars, the electric car has the advantage of being a "zero emission" vehicle that does not pollute or damage the environment. Other advantages include an engine that is durable, quiet, and mechanically almost trouble-free. With a top speed of 56 mph (90 km/h) and a capacity of 50 miles (80 km) per battery, the 106 Electric goes a long way toward overcoming the customary disadvantages of the electric car (low speeds and short range of distance), which had limited its use to specific commercial applications. This new vehicle represents a significant step towards the development of an alternative to petrol-driven cars. Other "zero-emission" vehicles, such as solar-powered cars (top right), are still in the experimental stages of development.

THE PEUGEOT 106 ELECTRIC
After a series of trials held throughout France, the Peugeot 106 Electric went on sale to the public. Using the body of an existing Peugeot model, it looks no different to other cars and is suited to motorists who use their vehicles for short urban journeys.

THE BATTERY
The 20-battery pack has a combined acceleration rate of 30 mph (0–50 km/h) in 8.3 seconds, a top speed of 56 mph (90 km/h) and a maximum mileage of 50 miles (80 km).

RECHARGING
The battery can be recharged from any 220v/16-amp socket. It takes up to 6 hours to fully recharge the battery, at a rate of 1 hour for every 12.5 miles (20 km).

Block of 11 batteries

Tinted electric window

Wheel shaft

Fiberglass body

Connects to 220v/16-amp socket

Plugs into connector on side of car

Connector for charge plug

THE CHARGING PLUG

SOLAR-POWERED CARS

Solar power is an even better solution to the problem of air pollution than is the electric car. It represents a renewable source of energy and, unlike fossil fuels, can be generated without seriously depleting the world's finite resources. Solar-powered vehicles have external solar cell panels that can absorb sunlight and convert its energy into electricity. This prototype of a solar-powered racing car, the "Swatchmobile," was recently developed in Switzerland by the Biel Engineering School .

THE "SWATCHMOBILE"

THE SHUTTLE

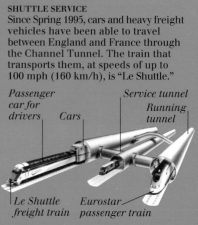

SHUTTLE SERVICE
Since Spring 1995, cars and heavy freight vehicles have been able to travel between England and France through the Channel Tunnel. The train that transports them, at speeds of up to 100 mph (160 km/h), is "Le Shuttle."

Passenger car for drivers   *Cars*   *Service tunnel*   *Running tunnel*

Le Shuttle freight train   *Eurostar passenger train*

LOADING THE CARS
Cars, buses, and trucks are loaded onto freight wagons at terminals in Folkestone, England, and Coquelles, France. Once inside, the drivers move to passenger cars at the front of Le Shuttle for the 35-minute journey.

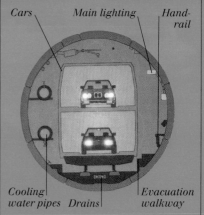

CROSS-SECTION OF THE TUNNEL
Construction of the 32 mile- (51.8 km-) long tunnels housing the rail link was completed in 1994. They are lined with reinforced concrete rings and equipped with complex draining, cooling, and ventilation systems.

Cars   *Main lighting*   *Hand-rail*

Cooling water pipes   *Drains*   *Evacuation walkway*

Cooling system

Box containing 3 batteries

Electric motor

Electrical unit

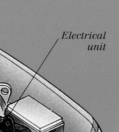

Fan

Radiator

Drive shaft

Batteries stored below

Raising Alexandria

MAP OF ALEXANDRIA HARBOR
(ANCIENT CITY IN RED)

IN NOVEMBER 1996, the stunning revelation was made that marine archaeologists had discovered remains of the vanished royal quarter of the ancient city of Alexandria. Founded by Alexander the Great in 331BC, Alexandria was a celebrated center of culture and learning in ancient times, as well as the scene of legendary events involving Cleopatra, Mark Antony, and the Caesars. The discovery was made just 20–26 ft (6–8 m) under the Mediterranean Sea on the eastern side of modern Alexandria's harbor. A team of 16 divers made 3,500 dives over a period of four months and discovered some 9,000 blocks and pieces, including material from pavements, quays, columns, and statues. Using a satellite-based global positioning system (GPS), the team mapped out a two-acre area. Selected finds were then hoisted to the surface using air-filled balloons and cables lowered by cranes. Among the pieces raised were portions of the mighty Pharos lighthouse, once the tallest building on earth and one of the Seven Wonders of the ancient world.

MARINE ENCRUSTATION
Underwater archaeologists often remove marine encrustation from material while it is still on the seabed. Here, the diver begins the task of uncovering an engraved stone.

Specially adapted underwater scraping tool

A huge concave mirror reflected light up to 31 miles (50 km) out to sea

Airlift hose

The total height of the building was 384 ft (117 m)

The lighthouse was covered in white marble

RECONSTRUCTION OF PHAROS LIGHTHOUSE
Although the lighthouse was toppled by an earthquake in the 14th century, it is possible to combine historical information with the results of the search campaign to render three-dimensional computer images of its structure.

AIRLIFT HOSE
Among the specialized equipment used in the project was this airlift hose. Here, the sand is sucked away to unearth a magnificent sphinx statue.

MEASURING ON SITE
The puzzle of the sunken city was pieced together without the excavation of every find. The team precisely drew and measured material on site, before transferring the information to computer.

The diver records the exact dimensions of the find

Scale bar

Two-ton sphinx

Block inscribed with hieroglyphics

Underwater breathing apparatus

Rose granite statue head

POSITIONING THE HARNESS
Using harness equipment, the diver prepares this statue head for removal to the surface.

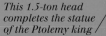

This 1.5-ton head completes the statue of the Ptolemy king

THE STATUE OF THE PTOLEMY KING
The colossal bust of the Ptolemy king is one of the great discoveries of sunken Alexandria. The dynasty ruled Egypt from the death of Alexander the Great (323BC) until the death of Cleopatra (30BC).

FROM WATER TO DRY LAND
The mighty granite bust is hoisted clear of the water and transported to the dock using cables lowered from a crane.

SECURING THE STATUE
Even when stationary on the dock, the priceless statue must be kept carefully secured with sturdy ropes and cables.

EXAMINING THE STONE
Before the process of desalinization takes place, archaeologists make an initial examination of the stone's surface.

Kansai Airport

AERIAL VIEW OF KANSAI

OPEN FOR BUSINESS since 4 September 1994, Kansai International Airport (KIX) is one of only two artificial structures visible from space – the other is the Great Wall of China. The purpose of this project was to build Japan's first 24-hour international airport, in order to respond to the increased demand for air transport not only in Kansai but in the whole of the country. Three mountains in the southeastern part of Japan's Osaka Bay had to be leveled to provide the landmass, and transport bridges from the harbor 3 miles (5 km) away also had to be built. The cost and constructional difficulties of this ambitious undertaking were outweighed by the ideal of an isolated flight-site with future expansion possibilities and without the need for noise restrictions. Although the island is fully operational, this is only the end of Phase 1. Plans for Phase 2 include increasing the size of the island and adding a further two runways.

Each year, the runway handles 160,000 takeoffs and landings

Taxiing area

Passenger boarding bridge

Check-in points

The roof comprises 90,000 stainless-steel panels – all identical in size

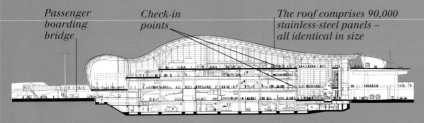

CROSS-SECTION OF THE TERMINAL
In the cross-section above, the aerodynamic shape of the terminal building's roof is clearly defined. Italian architect Renzo Piano developed this design to combat the local hazard – hurricanes. The central terminal uses a tiered system, which allows passengers quick and easy transfers between flights.

The island measures ¾ x 2¾ miles (1.25 x 4.37 km)

The transport bridge from the mainland has a six-lane highway and a two-way rail link

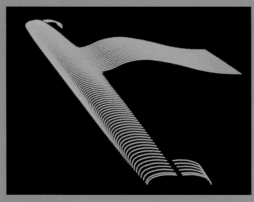

AIR CIRCULATION
This computer-rendered image illustrates the gentle, aerodynamic curve of the building's roof. This design is echoed on the ceiling inside the building, allowing the fresh air, introduced through vents, to move around freely.

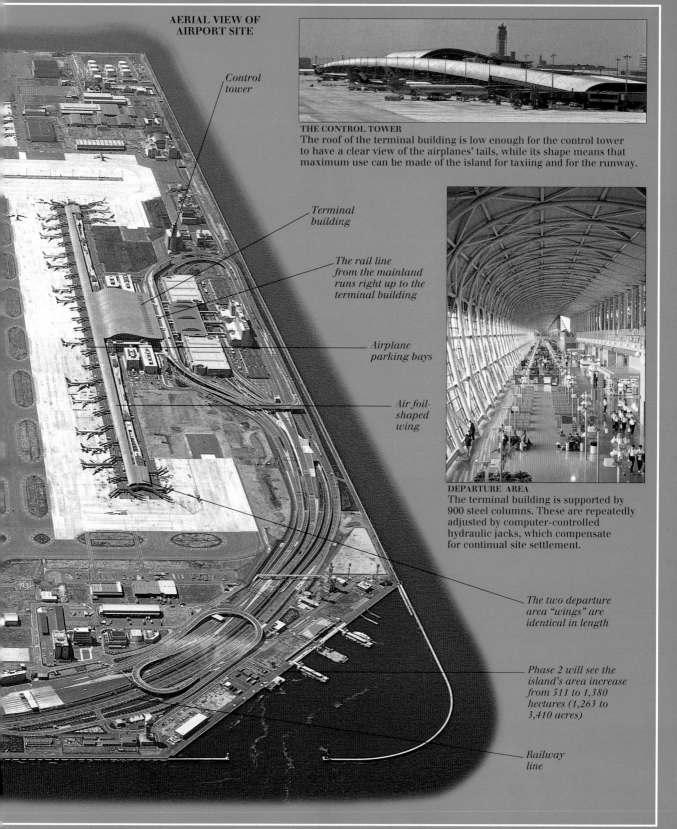

**AERIAL VIEW OF
AIRPORT SITE**

*Control
tower*

*Terminal
building*

*The rail line
from the mainland
runs right up to the
terminal building*

*Airplane
parking bays*

*Air foil-
shaped
wing*

THE CONTROL TOWER
The roof of the terminal building is low enough for the control tower
to have a clear view of the airplanes' tails, while its shape means that
maximum use can be made of the island for taxiing and for the runway.

DEPARTURE AREA
The terminal building is supported by
900 steel columns. These are repeatedly
adjusted by computer-controlled
hydraulic jacks, which compensate
for continual site settlement.

*The two departure
area "wings" are
identical in length*

*Phase 2 will see the
island's area increase
from 511 to 1,380
hectares (1,263 to
3,410 acres)*

*Railway
line*

Pont de Normandie

THE PONT DE NORMANDIE, which spans the estuary of the Seine River, was officially opened in January 1995. Built using state-of-the-art engineering, this stunning cable-stayed bridge is the longest of its kind in the world. Its central span, measuring 2,808 ft (856 m), crosses the estuary at 170.6 ft (52 m) above water level to enable shipping traffic to pass beneath it. The team of engineers, led by Michel Virlogeux of the French road administration, SETRA, designed every aspect of the bridge to withstand fierce coastal winds, which can reach 112 mph (180 km/h). Carrying an average of 6,000 vehicles a day, the bridge cuts 31 miles (50 km) from the journey between Le Havre and Honfleur, and forms part of "The Road of the Estuaries" motorway project, designed to link Belgium with Spain.

THE FOUNDATION

At the foundation of each tower are 28 piles, bored to a depth of between 164–197 ft (50–60 m). Layers of clay and large boulders caused major problems during construction.

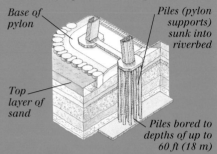

Base of pylon

Top layer of sand

Piles (pylon supports) sunk into riverbed

Piles bored to depths of up to 60 ft (18 m)

CABLE-STAYED BRIDGE DESIGN

The deck of cable-stayed bridges is supported by straight cables attached to both sides of one or more towers (pylons). The side spans may have additional suport from piers. One of the reasons why this design was chosen is because the marshy banks of the Seine estuary could not support the huge anchorage needed for a suspension bridge.

Inverted "Y" shape of pylons increases structural capacity to reduce wind forces

Cables anchored to pylon crest

23 pairs of cables attached to either side of each pylon

Artificial island created to support northern shore pylon

4 lanes of traffic

Piers support side spans

DESIGN OF THE VEHICLE DECK

The deck is aerodynamic in design, tapering at either edge. It is made of reinforced concrete, covering the outer sectional steel box-girders of the central span. This streamlined design reduced the weight and increased the stability of the Pont de Normandie, enabling it to exceed other cable-stayed bridges by 40 percent.

75 ft (23 m) wide vehicle deck

Tapered edges minimize the force of wind

10 ft (3 m) deep

Aerodynamic design was developed for the construction of the first Severn Bridge in the UK

Steel box-girder

BASIC PRINCIPLES OF BRIDGE ENGINEERING

BEAM (OR GIRDER) BRIDGE
The most basic bridge type has compression (pushing together) and tension (pulling apart) balanced within a single rigid beam, or girder, supported at each end.

ARCH BRIDGE
As heavy loads put all the material of an arch into compression, the forces have to be channeled downward and outward into the supporting abutments.

CANTILEVER BRIDGE
This develops the principle of the beam bridge by using balanced supports that extend and rise from both sides of the piers, attached to the central span.

SUSPENSION BRIDGE
This type of bridge principally exploits tension. The deck is hung from hanger cables or chains that are draped over the towers and anchored at each end.

BRIDGE DIMENSIONS

2,810 ft (856 m) from pylon to pylon

2,047 ft (624 m) steel box-girder

7,025 ft (2141.25 m) length of entire bridge

Aerodynamic vehicle deck

Ships can pass beneath the deck, which is 170 ft (52 m) above water level

Southern shore pylon

23 pairs of cables

THE CABLES
Each one of the 184 cables is made up of between 30 and 51 steel strands. The cables are protected from corrosion by polypropylene sheaths. Designed to prevent the collection of rain droplets, they also create additional wind resistance.

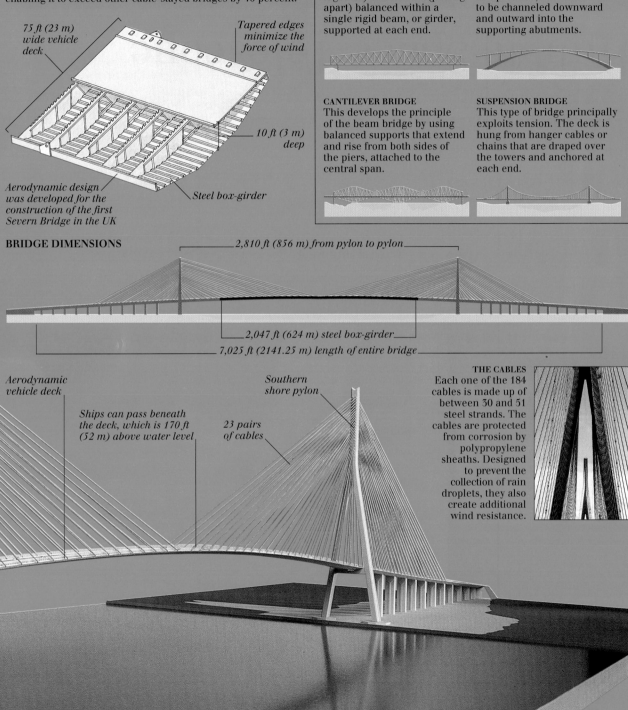

Guggenheim, Bilbao

AT THE BEGINNING OF the 20th century, modern architects hailed the coming of a new "age of the machine" when buildings would become as innovative as the most technically advanced cars, ships, and planes. As we enter the new millennium, computer technology, rather than engineering, is having the most impact on the form of buildings and the way that they are used. The fantastic curves and fractured planes of Frank Gehry's Guggenheim Museum in Bilbao, Spain (1997) would have been impossible to realize without the aid of computers in the design and construction processes. Technology has allowed the architect to realize what is, effectively, an enormous sculpture. Like an artist, Gehry made models out of sheets of paper and tape, which were then translated on screen into working drawings for the building's construction. Not all futuristic architectural designs have a sculptural look. Sir Norman Foster's proposal for the Millennium Tower in Tokyo, Japan (1989) brings together all the features of a city in one megastructure that was to be the highest in the world.

MILLENNIUM TOWER
In contrast to the sculptural curves of the Guggenheim, the complex structure of Sir Norman Foster's proposal for the Millennium Tower resembles a rocket.

"Sky centers" were to house public areas

GUGGENHEIM MUSEUM
Los Angeles architect Frank Gehry is well known for his striking and inventive creations. For Bilbao, he has designed a truly iconic building that now represents the city on postcards and in photographs around the world. The decision to locate the Guggenheim Foundation's modern art collection in Bilbao was part of a conscious attempt by the authorities to revitalize the city.

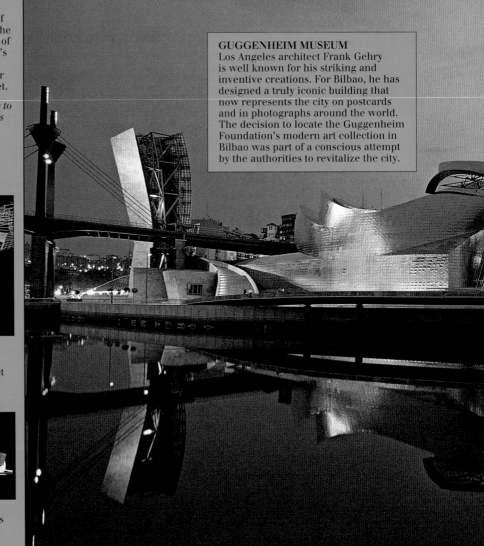

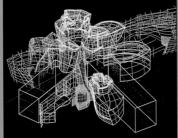

GUGGENHEIM ANIMATED MODEL
Gehry's office used a computer program called CATIA to construct onscreen models that could be worked on in an animated form.

COMPUTER RENDERING
Geometric mathematical formulas were used to define each of the building's surfaces and elements.

MONUMENTAL FISH SCULPTURE

The monumental fish sculpture was designed by Gehry's practice for a hotel in Barcelona, Spain. It was the first structure the office completed using the CATIA program, a specialized computer application developed by the French aeronautical industry. Like the Guggenheim Museum, the fish sculpture was developed directly on screen from a model. It also has a curvilinear surface with metal cladding. The CATIA computer model was the principal reference for its development, and there was little need for traditional architectural or technical drawings. The program enabled the 180 ft- (55 m-) long and 115 ft- (35 m-) high sculpture to be designed and built in just over eight months.

Curvilinear surface

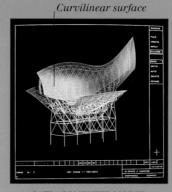

CATIA COMPUTER MODEL

Exposed structure　　*Metal cladding*

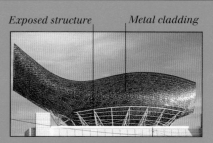

WATERFRONT MONUMENT
For many years, Frank Gehry has explored movement in architecture, often using fishlike shapes. Located on the waterfront, this sculpture may also be a reference to Barcelona as a port city.

The structure crowning the museum resembles an artichoke heart

The titanium sheets were milled on site

A slight pillow effect softens the appearance of the building

INTERIOR VESTIBULE
The large central atrium connects the main entrance with three floors of galleries via a system of curvilinear bridges, glass elevators, and stair towers. A soaring space over 164 ft (50 m) high, it has a sculptural roof with forms that have been likened to the billowing shapes of Marilyn Monroe's skirt.

Global telecommunications

CONSTELLATIONS OF LOW-ORBITING satellites hold the key to today's flexible global telephone networks. These systems integrate satellite communications with existing land-line and cellular networks to provide truly global coverage from a mobile phone. This enables people in remote areas, even those on tiny Pacific islands or high in the Himalayas, to keep in touch with the rest of the world. Satellite systems are the next logical step in the mobile-phone revolution that swept the world in the late 1990s. Iridium® was the first system to offer a commercial service. It was conceived and developed by the US electronics company Motorola, and began operation on November 1, 1998. The system was named after the 77th chemical element in the Periodic Table, as there were originally to be 77 satellites in the network. Other networks offering a similar service include Globalstar, which operates with a constellation of 48 satellites.

Communication antenna receives and transmits signals

IRIDIUM HANDSET
Early satellite phones required briefcase-sized units to receive and process signals from communication satellites. The Iridium handset has similar features to a conventional mobile phone but is slightly larger in size. It is also more expensive to purchase and operate but, unlike an ordinary mobile phone, can be used in any location on Earth.

LCD display panel

Lightweight main body

Processing unit

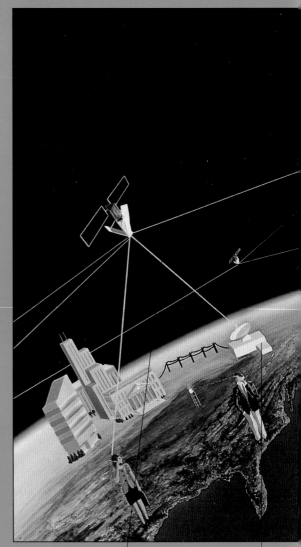

Satellite sends signal to ground-based gateway

Gateway connects with land-line system

IRIDIUM SATELLITE ORBITAL NETWORK
The Iridium network consists of 66 satellites, each providing a coverage of 6 million square miles (16 million square km). It offers a constant service, as there will always be one or more satellites over the horizon. The network operates as a constellation, which means that a failed or malfunctioning satellite will not impede the system's ability to provide global coverage. When a call is made it is routed to the nearest satellite, and then relayed around the world to its destination. If the destination is a land-based telephone, the last satellite in the chain feeds the signal to a "gateway" ground station. This gateway then connects with the existing land-line telephone system.

Connection is achieved in remote location

Message is relayed between satellites

Call is routed to nearest satellite

MICROWAVE RELAY TOWER
The Iridium communications system can route calls through an ordinary mobile telephone network, if available, and also interconnect with conventional telephone networks. Land links, such as this microwave relay tower, are often needed to route calls to their final destination.

Satellites pass over the Poles

Satellite orbits the Earth

ORBITAL PLANES
The 66 satellites of the Iridium network circle the Earth in six different orbital planes. They pass over the North and South Poles at a height of 485 miles (780 km), circling the Earth once every 100 minutes.

ENVIRONMENTAL CONCERNS

Mobile phones operate using radio signals. They have a transmitter that sends a signal to an antenna, which is part of a nationwide communications network. These radios work at low power, so mobile phone users need to be within a few miles of an antenna for their signal to be received. The mobile-phone revolution of the late 1990s has resulted in hundreds of millions of users worldwide, and thousands of antennas have been built, both in town and country, to receive the ever-increasing number of signals. In environmentally sensitive areas, unsightly antenna masts are sometimes disguised as trees (right) or flagpoles. They have also been sited on buildings and church towers, and then camouflaged.

APS and Digital Photography

THE ADVANCED PHOTO SYSTEM was announced in 1995 as a breakthrough in photographic technology. Developed over five years by a consortium of film and camera manufacturers (Kodak, Nikon, Fuji, Canon, Minolta), the APS was designed to maximize the quality of images taken by amateur photographers, and to overcome some of the most common problems encountered. The key to this new system is the "smart" film with its drop-in and automatic-load cassette. The film contains a magnetic strip, which records information specific to each shot, such as lighting conditions, magnification, date and time, and communicates this data to the processing equipment in the minilab. Once processed, the photographer receives a set of index prints, the photographs in any one of three different print sizes, and the developed film stored within the original cassette. APS film can be directly scanned and digitized, allowing the new system to bridge the gap between conventional 35mm film and digital photography.

PRINT FORMATS

A great advantage of APS is the variety it allows in the format of the print. When taking a picture there are three different formats which can be selected: C (Classic) gives a normal 35mm print, H (HDTV) is for a wider view and P (Panorama) provides the extra-wide landscape shot.

H and P
C
P
H and C

PRINT FORMATS

INFORMATION EXCHANGE ("IX")

Information about each frame – such as lighting conditions, selected print format, and exposure speed – is recorded on magnetic data strips. In a process called "information exchange" this data is read by processing equipment, which adjusts itself to produce the best results for each individual picture.

IX DATA TRACKS

Photofinishing magnetic data

Manufacturer's optical leader data   *Camera optical data*   *Camera magnetic data*   *Manufacturer's optical frame data*

THE MINOLTA VECTIS-40

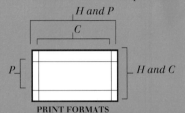

View finder

Diopter adjuster

Subject program pointer

PRINT

SEL   TITLE

ADJ   DATE

For title backprinting

For date and time imprinting

Flash mode indicator

Fill-flash

APS FILM AND CARTRIDGE

To avoid misfeeding, the cassette loads, advances, and retracts the film automatically, and is also used to store processed film. A data disc tells the camera the film speed, type, and exposure length.

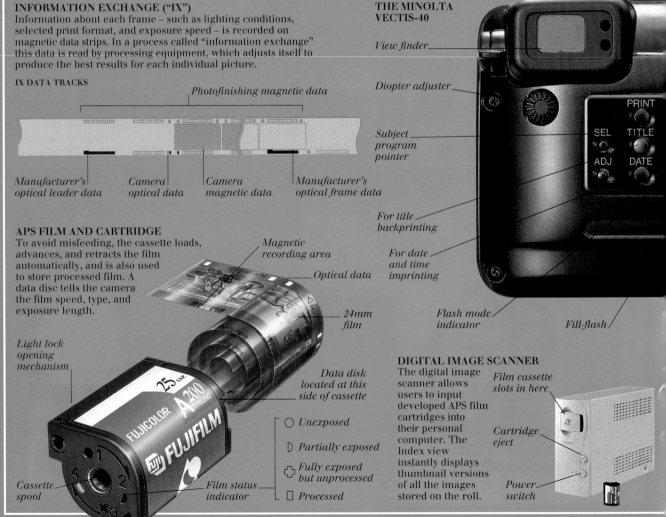

Magnetic recording area

Optical data

24mm film

Light lock opening mechanism

Data disk located at this side of cassette

FUJICOLOR A200   25   FUJIFILM

Cassette spool

Film status indicator

○ *Unexposed*

D *Partially exposed*

✚ *Fully exposed but unprocessed*

☐ *Processed*

DIGITAL IMAGE SCANNER

The digital image scanner allows users to input developed APS film cartridges into their personal computer. The Index view instantly displays thumbnail versions of all the images stored on the roll.

Film cassette slots in here

Cartridge eject

Power switch

INFORMATIVE DATA AND INDEX PRINTS

IX allows a variety of information to be imprinted on the back of each photo. Not only is the date and time given, but a title for each shot can be chosen. At-a-glance index prints are also provided showing the C, H, or P format of each frame plus the print number.

INDEX PRINT

Individual index print

Frame type

Frame number

Barcode

Frame number

Subject program selection

Date/time

Cartridge ID

Automatic flash

LCD panel

Frame counter

Drop-in loading and film chamber

Film chamber door below

Self-timer

Close-ups

Film cartridge loaded

DIGITAL IMAGE WORKSTATION

Photographs are digitized and placed on templates for printing out on a color printer. The workstation can also store the images on floppy disks or send them online to other locations.

Monitor

Floppy disk drive

2 Gigabyte hard disk drive

Cartridge slots in here

100-Megabyte Zip™ disk drive

DIGITAL CAMERA

NO FILM OR PROCESSING REQUIRED

Filmless digital cameras are a technological advancement in the photography world. Within minutes a picture can be taken and transmitted anywhere in the world, via email or the World Wide Web. Digital cameras are also ideal for desktop publishing, business presentations, and a variety of scientific or industrial applications.

KODAK DC50

CANON EOS-1 WITH KODAK DCS 3C

Accessory shoe for flash

Shutter release button

Lens release button

Zoom lens

PCMCIA card slots in back

TRANSMITTING LIGHT INTO DIGITAL DATA

Electronic sensors inside the camera transmit the different levels of light, which enter through the red, green, and blue filters (seen in this order below), onto a CCD (photosensitive semiconductor). The CCD digitally records the image and stores it onto a PCMCIA card – a tiny disk drive.

Red filter

Green filter

Green filter

Blue filter

FROM DATA TO ON-SCREEN IMAGE

Digital cameras can be plugged into a computer's serial port and the pictures can be instantly transferred from the camera's hard disk into popular graphics or publishing applications.

Interactive television

THE FUTURE OF TELEVISION is undoubtedly digital. Television or video signals can be converted from their normal analog form (continuously varying) into a digital form, which consists of a series of definite pulses. Digital signals can be transmitted, compressed, and manipulated by computers without any unwanted "noise" affecting the data. One of the advantages of digital technology is that video data can be manipulated to make interactive television possible. Interactive "video-on-demand" (VOD) services allow users to watch the material of their choice from a large central video "vault." A digital server enables many users to watch the same film, starting at different times, by sending the video data in small "packets" to them. Other services include news programs, games, music, and electronic shopping. With the latter, the user "strolls" through a virtual store and uses a credit card to buy items, which are then delivered to the home within days.

VIDEO-ON-DEMAND

Allowing viewers to choose a film or television program from a vast selection whenever desired, video-on-demand comes complete with all the flexibility of a video recorder (including fast-forward, rewind, and pause facilities). A typical VOD system consists of video vaults containing compressed digital video data, a sophisticated digital server that sends the requested material to the correct destination, and decoder and remote control units in the home.

REMOTE CONTROL

As well as offering the standard features, the remote control enables the user to operate the VOD, play games, and buy goods from home-shopping services.

The Fin button returns the viewer to normal cable television service

Video-on-demand button

Select button

Remote controls for interactive television are simple and user-friendly in format

SET-TOP BOX

The set-top box sends the user's choices to the digital server and decodes video data entering the home system. Depending on the system used, the digital video data from the server is converted to an analog signal for the television either by a junction box outside the home or by the set-top box.

Direction buttons for navigating on-screen menus

These keys allow quick selection of color-coded, on-screen choices

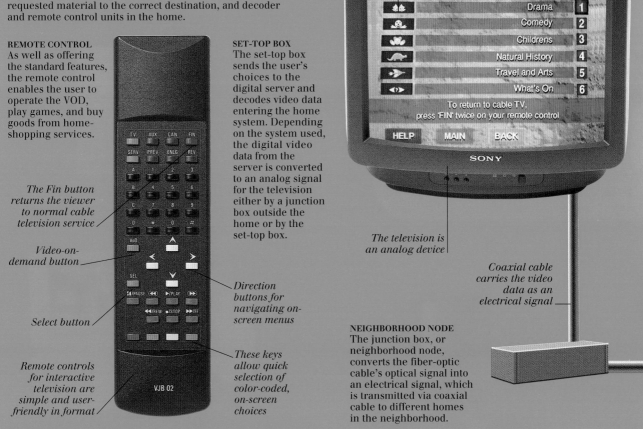

On-screen menus

Many new set-top boxes have considerable computing power

CATEGORIES

Drama	1
Comedy	2
Childrens	3
Natural History	4
Travel and Arts	5
What's On	6

To return to cable TV, press 'FIN' twice on your remote control

HELP   MAIN   BACK

SONY

The television is an analog device

Coaxial cable carries the video data as an electrical signal

NEIGHBORHOOD NODE

The junction box, or neighborhood node, converts the fiber-optic cable's optical signal into an electrical signal, which is transmitted via coaxial cable to different homes in the neighborhood.

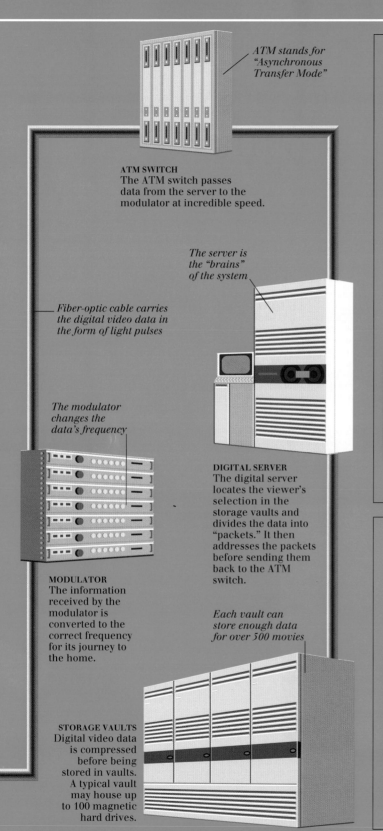

ATM stands for "Asynchronous Transfer Mode"

ATM SWITCH
The ATM switch passes data from the server to the modulator at incredible speed.

The server is the "brains" of the system

Fiber-optic cable carries the digital video data in the form of light pulses

The modulator changes the data's frequency

DIGITAL SERVER
The digital server locates the viewer's selection in the storage vaults and divides the data into "packets." It then addresses the packets before sending them back to the ATM switch.

MODULATOR
The information received by the modulator is converted to the correct frequency for its journey to the home.

Each vault can store enough data for over 500 movies

STORAGE VAULTS
Digital video data is compressed before being stored in vaults. A typical vault may house up to 100 magnetic hard drives.

DIGITAL VIDEO DISC

The video format set to replace tapes and laserdiscs in the home looks exactly like an audio compact disc (CD) – a silver platter 4¾ in (12 cm) in diameter. (To avoid a repetition of the 1980s VHS/Beta videocassette war, electronics companies involved have agreed on one format.) However, the digital video disc can hold up to 9 hours of data on its 2 sides, with each side containing 133 minutes of program time. This is compared with the 74 minutes held by a CD. In addition, DVD's interactivity means that certain programs can be viewed from a variety of camera angles.

COMPACT DISC

DIGITAL VIDEO DISC

CD "tracks"

DVD tracks are packed more tightly

CD CROSS-SECTION

DVD CROSS-SECTION

CD has one layer of data

DVD has two layers of data on each side

MOVIES BY COMPUTER

Disney Productions' *Toy Story* (1995) was the world's first feature film to be generated entirely on computer. A team of 27 animators worked on the film, producing an average of 3½ minutes of footage per week. Some of the characters and scenes were created solely on computer, while others were set up with models and props before being scanned into the computer for digitization.

BUZZ LIGHTYEAR AND WOODY IN *TOY STORY*

Measuring time

ALL TIMEKEEPING DEVICES depend on counting a regularly repeated phenomenon. The earliest timekeeping devices were based on daily, monthly, or yearly cycles of the sun or moon. Most modern clocks are based on repeated mechanical or electronic oscillations (vibrations). The more frequent the vibrations, the greater the potential accuracy of the clock. The crystal in a quartz watch typically vibrates at 32,768 hertz (32,768 times a second), so it keeps better time than a pendulum clock, whose pendulum typically swings twice a second.

The most accurate timekeeping devices are atomic fountains, which are based on oscillations of cesium atoms. Global communication technologies, such as computer networks and broadcasting, rely on the world using one accurate time standard. This is called UCT (Universal Coordinated Time), and is based on the average time signal received from over 200 atomic clocks worldwide. The more we rely on high technology for precise timekeeping, the more vulnerable we become to problems with that technology – for example, the bug that threatens to strike at the beginning of the new millennium.

Microwave cavity

E

Trapping coils help keep the ball of atoms together

Mechanism advances the hands

Pendulum swings back and forth

PENDULUM CLOCK
In the 16th century, Italian scientist Galileo Galilei used the regular swing of a pendulum to measure periods of time. He suggested that a pendulum could be connected to the hands of a clock to turn them in regular steps.

THE ATOMIC FOUNTAIN
At present, the most accurate time-keeping device is the atomic fountain. It was developed by Nobel prize-winning scientists in the early 1990s and is far more accurate than a standard atomic clock, such as NIST-7 (see below, left). The atomic fountain enables us to measure time with greater accuracy, mainly because it uses cooler, slower-moving atoms than an atomic clock. Atomic fountain devices are accurate to within one ten-billionth of a second per day.

C

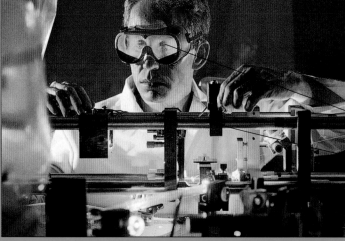

Goggles protect eyes from radiation

Laser components held in place by an optical bench

NIST-7 ATOMIC CLOCK
This laser forms part of an early 1990s atomic clock developed by the US National Institute of Standards and Technology. At that time, the clock was the most accurate timekeeping device in the world, precise to within one billionth of a second per day (one second in three million years). Above, a scientist observes the laser as it "excites" cesium atoms. The atoms oscillate between two energy states, and the clock counts the oscillations.

Detector laser source

Detector laser

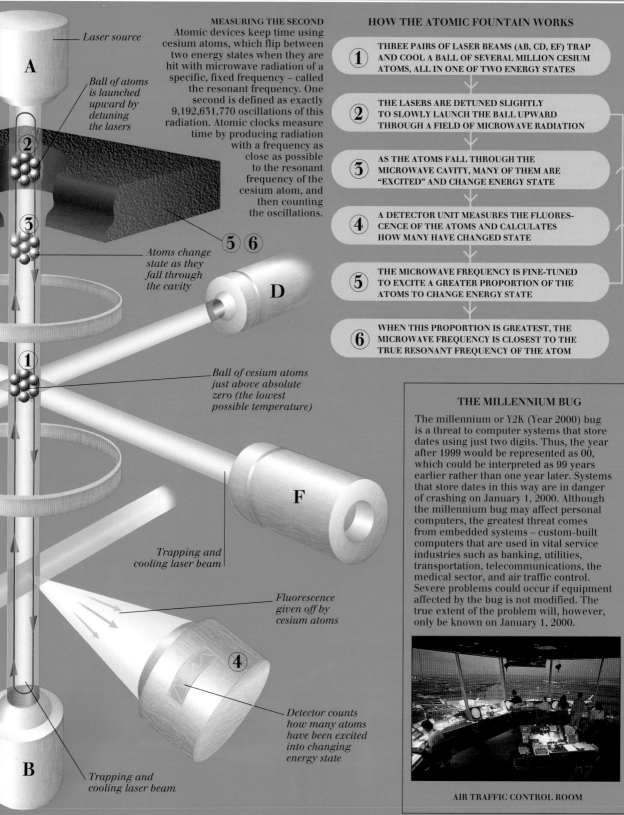

Laser source

A

Ball of atoms is launched upward by detuning the lasers

② Ball of atoms

③

Atoms change state as they fall through the cavity

D

① Ball of cesium atoms just above absolute zero (the lowest possible temperature)

Trapping and cooling laser beam

F

Fluorescence given off by cesium atoms

④ Detector counts how many atoms have been excited into changing energy state

B

Trapping and cooling laser beam

MEASURING THE SECOND
Atomic devices keep time using cesium atoms, which flip between two energy states when they are hit with microwave radiation of a specific, fixed frequency – called the resonant frequency. One second is defined as exactly 9,192,631,770 oscillations of this radiation. Atomic clocks measure time by producing radiation with a frequency as close as possible to the resonant frequency of the cesium atom, and then counting the oscillations.

⑤ ⑥

HOW THE ATOMIC FOUNTAIN WORKS

① THREE PAIRS OF LASER BEAMS (AB, CD, EF) TRAP AND COOL A BALL OF SEVERAL MILLION CESIUM ATOMS, ALL IN ONE OF TWO ENERGY STATES

② THE LASERS ARE DETUNED SLIGHTLY TO SLOWLY LAUNCH THE BALL UPWARD THROUGH A FIELD OF MICROWAVE RADIATION

③ AS THE ATOMS FALL THROUGH THE MICROWAVE CAVITY, MANY OF THEM ARE "EXCITED" AND CHANGE ENERGY STATE

④ A DETECTOR UNIT MEASURES THE FLUORESCENCE OF THE ATOMS AND CALCULATES HOW MANY HAVE CHANGED STATE

⑤ THE MICROWAVE FREQUENCY IS FINE-TUNED TO EXCITE A GREATER PROPORTION OF THE ATOMS TO CHANGE ENERGY STATE

⑥ WHEN THIS PROPORTION IS GREATEST, THE MICROWAVE FREQUENCY IS CLOSEST TO THE TRUE RESONANT FREQUENCY OF THE ATOM

THE MILLENNIUM BUG

The millennium or Y2K (Year 2000) bug is a threat to computer systems that store dates using just two digits. Thus, the year after 1999 would be represented as 00, which could be interpreted as 99 years earlier rather than one year later. Systems that store dates in this way are in danger of crashing on January 1, 2000. Although the millennium bug may affect personal computers, the greatest threat comes from embedded systems – custom-built computers that are used in vital service industries such as banking, utilities, transportation, telecommunications, the medical sector, and air traffic control. Severe problems could occur if equipment affected by the bug is not modified. The true extent of the problem will, however, only be known on January 1, 2000.

AIR TRAFFIC CONTROL ROOM

Network computers

THE INTERNET LINKS MILLIONS of computers worldwide, and anybody with a personal computer (PC) and basic communication tools can become a part of it. The ever-expanding "Net" is becoming a vital resource for business, education, and entertainment. The huge multimedia database of the World Wide Web, which is one aspect of the Net, is so sophisticated that users can meet in "virtual worlds." As the Net evolves, so new ways of computing are made possible. Network computing is one possible development which promises greater compatibility and efficiency than personal computing. At present, the Net consists mainly of PCs with large amounts of processing power and disk space (called "fat client computers") connected to servers (other computers that distribute data). The idea behind network computing is to replace the PC, or fat client, with a network computer (NC), or "thin client." A thin client computer has a processor, like a PC, but less memory and no disk storage, and so is much cheaper. Instead of storing application programs and data on a local hard disk (as a PC does), an NC simply downloads programs and data from a server into its RAM as needed. Network computing promises economies of scale and centralization, since all the data is stored on a few servers, and any software developments that need to be made apply to these servers only.

DATA SERVER

Data server stores data from many users

JAVA APPLET SERVER

Java applet server stores a wide range of compact, downloadable programs

MODEM

High-speed Internet links via modems and other devices

THIN CLIENT COMPUTER
The thin client NC is halfway between a PC and a dumb terminal, used on mainframe computers. A dumb terminal consists only of a keyboard and a monitor – all processing and data storage is carried out centrally by the mainframe. Like dumb terminals, NCs have no local disk storage, but like PCs, they do have a processor. In addition to being smaller and cheaper than PCs, NCs should be more reliable, since they do not have complex peripherals with moving parts, such as disk drives.

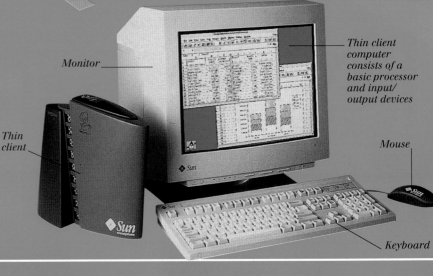

Monitor

Thin client

Thin client computer consists of a basic processor and input/ output devices

Mouse

Keyboard

Monitor

Applet developers write software for the servers

Server

APPLET DEVELOPERS' SYSTEM

Different regions of the network are separated for security purposes by firewalls

FIREWALL

Firewalls limit access to authorized users

DISTRIBUTED COMPUTING

Network computing has been made possible because the computer industry has agreed hardware and software standards, including a new language, Java. When a thin client – or a fat client acting as a Java station – is switched on, its basic boot-up software connects to a network and downloads the full Java operating system. The user can then download Java application programs (called applets) and data required, paying any fee with a smart card. High-speed links between client and server mean that processing tasks can be distributed between computers, so the applets can be relatively small. In network computing, the main burden falls not on the client machines but on the network. Whether the present Internet infrastructure (phone lines, cables, etc.) has the required capacity, speed, and reliability to support network computing remains to be seen.

VIRTUAL WORLDS ON THE NET

The World Wide Web has brought multimedia – graphics, animations, sound, and hyperlinking – to the Internet. The Virtual World Wide Web (VWWW), with virtual environments, is a further development where users can interact graphically with each other. Typical VWWW environments are spread across sites on the Net and on a CD-ROM. The basic program runs from the CD, but "interactions" between users occur at VWWW sites.

VIRTUAL PARIS

3D ENVIRONMENTS
All three-dimensional virtual worlds must first be rendered in ink, as shown below, after which the illustrations are digitized by a computer.

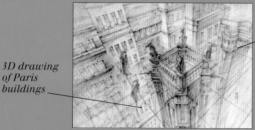

3D drawing of Paris buildings

The CD-ROM is based on a series of detailed sketches

CITIZENS OF A VIRTUAL WORLD
When a user logs on to a virtual world, he or she chooses a graphical identity; this is how they will appear on other users' screens around the world. These virtual people stroll around and meet in virtual streets – although the real users might be thousands of miles apart.

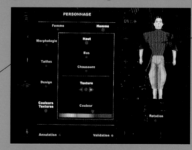

Style and measure- ment categories

Users can choose their appearance and their personality

REAL SERVICES IN A VIRTUAL SOCIETY
Some features of a virtual world are purely fictional, like a user's graphical identity, while the streets or environment may be based on a real place. But, as in the real Paris, you can "walk" into a store, shop using your real credit card, and have the real goods delivered.

Virtual transport takes the user to other worlds

Home shopping services are located around the virtual city

World Wide Web

Sɪɴᴄᴇ 1993, THE WORLD WIDE WEB (WWW) has become one of the fastest growing communication systems in history. Consisting of an expanding pool of "pages" created by companies, associations, and individuals, it is accessible to anyone connected to the Internet. Two features of the Web make it appealing. The first is the nonlinear method of presenting information known as "hypertext." This enables users to jump between documents of subject-related material at the click of the mouse. The second is the multimedia format of Web pages, which can be designed using sophisticated graphics, sound, and animation, and displayed on-screen by a program called a browser. Since the development of the browser, the Web has become more sophisticated and easier to use and interest in the WWW has exploded.

THE INTERNET AND THE WEB

Tim Berners-Lee, the physics researcher who first conceived the Web in 1989, compared the Internet and the Web to the difference between the brain and the mind; where the Internet is the physical method of communication and the Web is the information itself.

1. Web page broken down into packets of binary data for transmission

5. Web page is downloaded onto user's screen

4. Packets of binary data are translated into a readable message

3. Analog audio signal received and converted into binary data via modem

Web site

Original Web page

2. Data is sent to destination via the Internet

WEB SITES

A web site is a collection of linked documents stored on a single computer, anywhere in the world. Sites can be linked up to each other using hyperlinks.

NAVIGATING THE WEB

WELCOME PAGE

There are millions of pages available on the Web and graphical browsers, such as Netscape Navigator, provide a window in the computer screen on which these pages are displayed in fine detail. Keyword searches can be performed using a facility called a search engine; particular topics can be explored using directories called subject trees; and specific pages can be accessed by typing the exact address, or URL (Universal Resource Locator). Other browser tools include history lists, hot lists, and bookmarks.

UNIVERSAL RESOURCE LOCATOR (URL)

Prefix "http://" (hyper-text transfer protocol) indicates a Web site or page is being accessed

Locates particular folder and file

http:// | www.astro.uva.nl | / | michielb/sun | / | kaft.htm.

Commands browser to look for Web pages stored at this computer

Indicates name of document to be retrieved

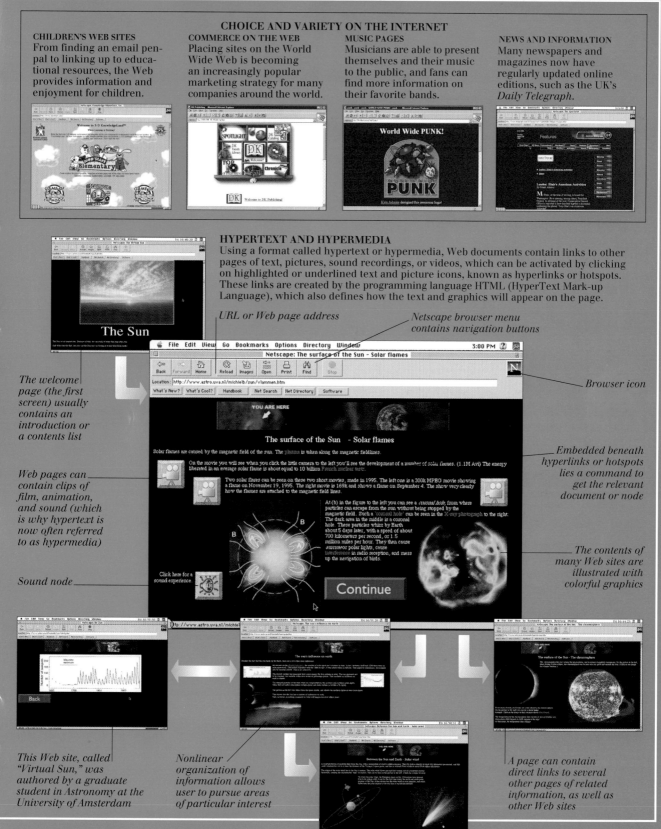

CHOICE AND VARIETY ON THE INTERNET

CHILDREN'S WEB SITES
From finding an email pen-pal to linking up to educational resources, the Web provides information and enjoyment for children.

COMMERCE ON THE WEB
Placing sites on the World Wide Web is becoming an increasingly popular marketing strategy for many companies around the world.

MUSIC PAGES
Musicians are able to present themselves and their music to the public, and fans can find more information on their favorite bands.

NEWS AND INFORMATION
Many newspapers and magazines now have regularly updated online editions, such as the UK's *Daily Telegraph.*

HYPERTEXT AND HYPERMEDIA
Using a format called hypertext or hypermedia, Web documents contain links to other pages of text, pictures, sound recordings, or videos, which can be activated by clicking on highlighted or underlined text and picture icons, known as hyperlinks or hotspots. These links are created by the programming language HTML (HyperText Mark-up Language), which also defines how the text and graphics will appear on the page.

URL or Web page address

Netscape browser menu contains navigation buttons

The welcome page (the first screen) usually contains an introduction or a contents list

Browser icon

Web pages can contain clips of film, animation, and sound (which is why hypertext is now often referred to as hypermedia)

Embedded beneath hyperlinks or hotspots lies a command to get the relevant document or node

Sound node

The contents of many Web sites are illustrated with colorful graphics

This Web site, called "Virtual Sun," was authored by a graduate student in Astronomy at the University of Amsterdam

Nonlinear organization of information allows user to pursue areas of particular interest

A page can contain direct links to several other pages of related information, as well as other Web sites

47A

Index

ACKNOWLEDGMENTS

Project Editors Kirstie Hills, Julie Oughton, Nichola Thomasson
Art Editors Paul Greenleaf, Sasha Howard, Joanne Mitchell, Dawn Terrey
Editors Caroline Hunt, David Tombesi-Walton
DTP Designers Mark Bracey, Rob Campbell

Consultants
Michael Allaby (El Niño and La Niña), Anita Bardhan-Roy (World Wide Web), David Brown
(Pont de Normandie), Helen Castle (Guggenheim, Bilbao; House of the future), Stuart Clarke
(International Space Station; Very Large Telescope), John Coiley (Tilting trains), Heather
Couper (Hubble Space Telescope), Robin Kerrod (Global telecommunications), David Lambert
(Giganotosaurus), Michael Langford (APS and Digital Photography), Colin Lewis (Electric Car/
Le Shuttle), Angela Marlow (Medical research), Dr. Gabrielle Murphy (Modern surgery), Mukul
Patel (Interactive television; Measuring time; Network computers), Dr. Tony Smith (Medical
research), Giles Sparrow (Galileo spacecraft), Dr. Robert Youngsen (Genetic advances)

Senior Editors Louise Candlish, Peter Jones
Senior Art Editors Tracy Hambleton-Miles, Heather McCarry
Managing Editors Gwen Edmonds, Christine Winters
Senior Managing Editor Anna Kruger
Senior Managing Art Editor Steve Knowlden
Deputy Art Director Tina Vaughan
Category Publisher Sean Moore

Illustrations
Andy Burton, Rob Campbell, Geoff Denney, Mick Gillah, Tony Graham,
Nicholas H. T. Hall, Steve Kirk, Matthew Wallis, John Woodcock

Photography Andy Crawford, Bob Gathany
Picture Research Angela Anderson, Katherine Mesquita, Sam Ruston, Mariana Sonnenberg
Production Sarah Coltman, David Proffit, Meryl Silbert

Copyright © 1999 Dorling Kindersley Limited, London

DK Publishing would like to thank:
Christine Baker, Jonathan Biggington, Laura Buller, Brian Cooper, Nicola Erdpresser, Mike
Flynn, Alan Greenwood, Steve Howard, Neil Lockley, Tim Mann, Simon Murrell, Eric Pierrat
(Gallimard), Nicola Powling, Clare Ryder, Richard Shellabear, Richard Sinclair, Nigel Spencer
(British Library/Holborn Reading Room), Sylvia Tombesi

The publisher would like to thank the following for their kind permission to reproduce
photographs and artworks:

(a=above, b=bottom, c=center, l=left, r=right, t=top)

Adtranz: 24a tl; *Amateur Photographer:* 39a bl; **1996 American Association for the
Advancement of Science:** Excerpt from *Science* reprinted with permission: 12a cl; **BBC
Tomorrow's World:** 15a bc; **Michiel Berger (Astronomical Institute, University of
Amsterdam):** 45a br, 47a c, cla, bl, bc, br; **Wendell Burnette Architects:** 23a cr, 23a tr,
23a bc; **Canal Plus:** 45a tr, tcr, bcr, br; **Canon (UK) Limited:** 39a cra; **Branson Coates
Architecture:** Branson Coates 23a cla, Philip Vile 23a cl; **Eumestat (European
Organisation for the Exploitation of Meteorological Satellites):** 21a tr, 21a tr; **Fuji Photo
Film:** 38a cl, bl, br, 39a t, bc; **Galaxy Picture Library:** 6a tl, 7a br; **Galaxy Picture Library:**
9a crb, 9a br; **Victor Gedris / Ken Adams:** 47a tc; **Genesis Space Photo Library:** 12-13a ca;
Mark Guard Associates: 22a tl; **Guggenheim Museum, Bilbao:** Erika Barahona Ede 54-35a,
35a br; **K. Hiwatashi:** 30a tl; **Institut Amatller D'Art Hispanic:** 35a tr; **Shunji Ishiba** 30-31a
cr; **Kansai International Airport Co. Ltd:** 30-31a c, 31a tr; **KeyMed (Medical & Industrial
Equipment) Ltd:**15a cra; **1996 Knowledge Adventure Inc.** all rights reserved. JumpStart,
Knowledge Land and Knowledge Adventure are trademarks of Knowledge Adventure, Inc:
47a tl; **The Kodak Library:** 39a tr; **Magnum Photos:** Jean Gaumy 52a tl, 55a br; **Michelin:**
27a tl, tr; **Minolta (UK) Ltd:** 38a tl, 38-39a c; **NASA:** 4a tl, 6a bl, 6-7a tc, cr, bc, bcl, bl; 8a bl,
10a bc, tl, 10-11a, 11a tl, tr; **Netscape Communications Corporation:** Netscape and
Netscape Navigator are trademarks of Netscape Communications, all rights reserved 46a bl;
Panasonic UK Ltd: 41a tr; **Peugeot:** 26a tl, cl, bl, 26-27a; **Press Association:** 17a br; **Profile
Public Relations:** 36a l; **QA Photos Ltd:** 27a tr, crb, Channel Tunnel Group Ltd. 27a cra, br;
Renzo Piano Building Workshop: 30a l; **Rex Features:** Paul Felix 37a br; **SNCF:** 24a tr,
25a tl; **Mark Sagar:** 15a c, crb, br; **Science Museum:** 3a crb; **Science Photo Library:** 16-17a
cr, cl, crb, c, 8-9a, David Ducros 11a br, Simon Fraser 15a tr, Carlos Goldin 12a tl, tr, Patrice
Loiez 2a c, Will & Deni McIntryre 14a br, Peter Menzel 45a br, Motorola 36-37a, 37a bl,
Carlos Munoz-Yague 20a bl, N.A.S.A: 8a clb, 10a clb, David Parker 20a clb, 37a tr, JC Revy
14a tr, David Scharf 14a bc, Space Telescope Science Institute 4a cr, 5a b, tl, tr, cl, r, Sinclair
Stammers 14a bl; Alexander Tsiaras 42a bl; **Frank Spooner Pictures / Gamma:** Clare Aaron
15a cla, 21a cr, 40a br; **Tony Stone Images:** 16a tl; **Sun Microsystems:** 44a bl, 44/45a lc;
Sygma 21a br, 28-29a (all except Stephanie Compoint 28a bl © Gedeon-Exmachina) Warren
Winter 16a bl; © **The Telegraph plc. London 1996:** 47a tr. **Verne Fotografie:** 22a clb, br, c,
cra; **West Japan Railways:** 24a bl, 25a br, 24-25a clb; **Westminster Cable:** 40a bl, 40-41a cl.

DORLING KINDERSLEY
ULTIMATE
VISUAL
DICTIONARY

**EXTERNAL FEATURES
OF A BUTTERFLY**

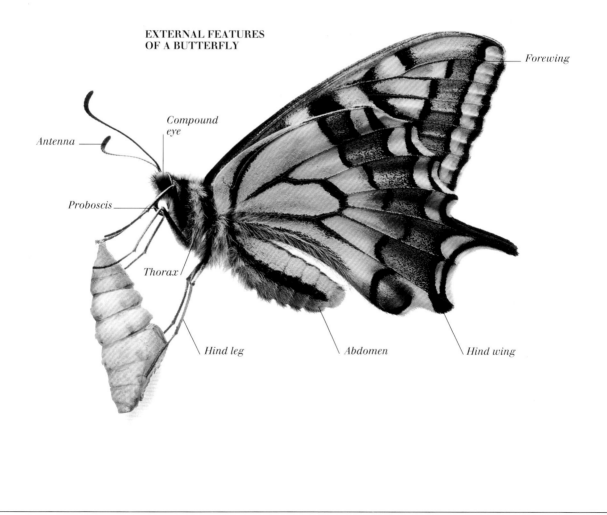

Forewing

*Compound
eye*

Antenna

Proboscis

Thorax

Hind leg

Abdomen

Hind wing

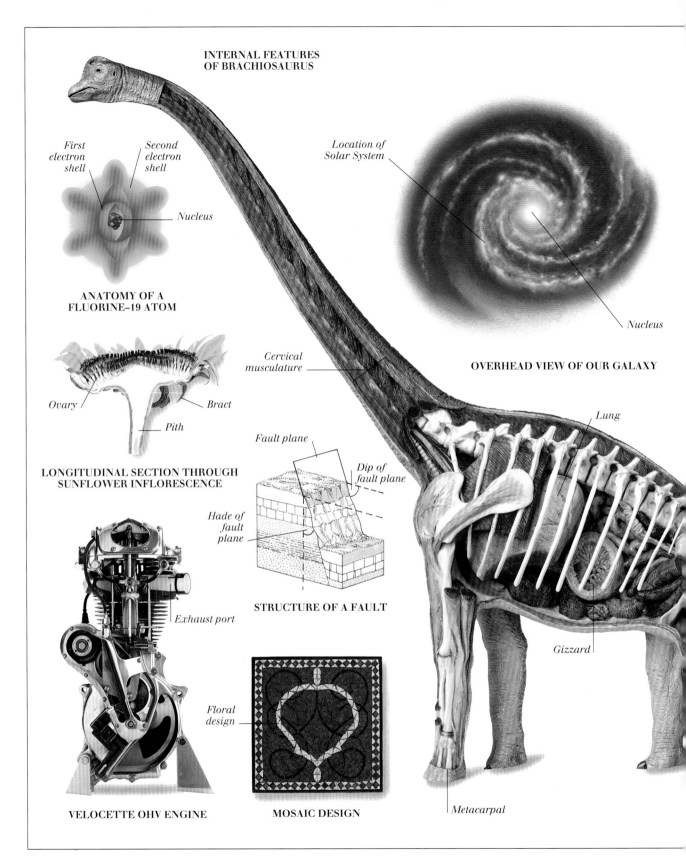

**INTERNAL FEATURES
OF BRACHIOSAURUS**

*First
electron
shell*

*Second
electron
shell*

Nucleus

**ANATOMY OF A
FLUORINE–19 ATOM**

*Location of
Solar System*

Nucleus

OVERHEAD VIEW OF OUR GALAXY

*Cervical
musculature*

Lung

Ovary

Bract

Pith

**LONGITUDINAL SECTION THROUGH
SUNFLOWER INFLORESCENCE**

Fault plane

*Dip of
fault plane*

*Hade of
fault
plane*

STRUCTURE OF A FAULT

Gizzard

Exhaust port

*Floral
design*

VELOCETTE OHV ENGINE

MOSAIC DESIGN

Metacarpal

DORLING KINDERSLEY
ULTIMATE
VISUAL
DICTIONARY

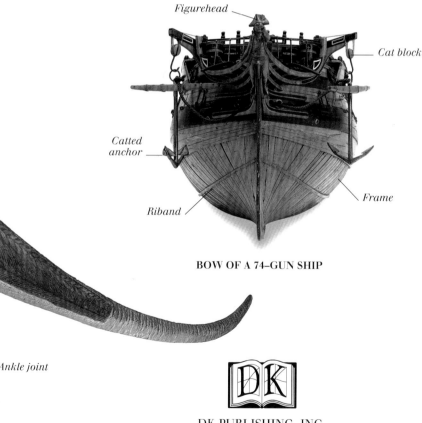

Figurehead

Cat block

Catted anchor

Frame

Riband

BOW OF A 74–GUN SHIP

Ankle joint

DK

DK PUBLISHING, INC.
New York
www.dk.com

A DK PUBLISHING BOOK
www.dk.com

PROJECT ART EDITORS HEATHER MCCARRY, JOHNNY PAU, CHRIS WALKER, KEVIN WILLIAMS
DESIGNER SIMON MURRELL
PROJECT EDITORS LUISA CARUSO, PETER JONES, JANE MASON, GEOFFREY STALKER
EDITOR JO EVANS
U.S. EDITOR JULEE BINDER

DTP DESIGNER ZIRRINIA AUSTIN
PICTURE RESEARCHER CHARLOTTE BUSH

MANAGING ART EDITOR TONI KAY
SENIOR EDITOR ROGER TRITTON
MANAGING EDITOR SEAN MOORE

PRODUCTION MANAGER HILARY STEPHENS

ANATOMICAL AND BOTANICAL MODELS SUPPLIED BY SOMSO MODELLE, COBURG, GERMANY

Sound hole

Hollow body

Bridge

Headstock

ACOUSTIC GUITAR

REVISED AMERICAN EDITION © 1999
2 4 6 8 10 9 7 5 3
PUBLISHED IN THE UNITED STATES BY
DORLING KINDERSLEY PUBLISHING, INC., 95 MADISON AVENUE,
NEW YORK, NEW YORK 10016

COPYRIGHT © 1994 DORLING KINDERSLEY LIMITED, LONDON

LIBRARY OF CONGRESS CATALOGING-IN-PUBLICATION DATA

DORLING KINDERSLEY ULTIMATE VISUAL DICTIONARY. - - REVISED AMERICAN ED.
INCLUDES INDEX
ISBN 0–7894–4619–7
1. PICTURE DICTIONARIES, ENGLISH. I. DORLING KINDERSLEY. INC.
PE 1629.D67 1994   94-11173
423 ' . 1- -dc20   CIP

REPRODUCED BY COLOURSCAN, SINGAPORE
PRINTED AND BOUND IN ITALY BY GRAPHICOM

Prosoma (cephalothorax)

Spinneret

Leg

EXTERNAL FEATURES OF A SPIDER

Canopy

Fin

G-BNHB

Main landing gear

SIDE VIEW OF ARV SUPER 2 AIRPLANE

Brachialis

Frontalis

Deltoid

Rectus femoris

SUPERFICIAL SKELETAL MUSCLES

Barrel

Permanent black ink

FOUNTAIN PEN AND INK

Architrave

Podium

TEMPLE OF VESTA, TIVOLI, ITALY, c.80 BC

Low pressure gases

Central electrode

BALL CONTAINING HIGH TEMPERATURE GAS (PLASMA)

Sepal

Pedicel (flower stalk)

Swollen fleshy tissues of receptacle

LONGITUDINAL SECTION THROUGH A STRAWBERRY

Nonbreakable plastic

Shock absorber

FOOTBALL HELMET

CONTENTS

Introduction

T HE ULTIMATE VISUAL DICTIONARY
is a completely new kind of reference
book. It provides a link between pictures
and words in a way that no ordinary
dictionary ever has. Most dictionaries
simply tell you what a word means, but
the *Ultimate Visual Dictionary* shows
you — through a combination of detailed annotations, explicit photographs,
and illustrations. In the *Ultimate Visual
Dictionary*, pictures define the annotations
around them. You do not read definitions
of the annotated words, you see them.
The highly accessible format of the
Ultimate Visual Dictionary, the thoroughness
of its annotations, and the range of its
subject matter make it a unique
and helpful reference tool.

How to use the ULTIMATE VISUAL DICTIONARY
You will find the *Ultimate Visual Dictionary* simple
to use. It is divided by subject into 14 sections—
THE UNIVERSE, PREHISTORIC EARTH, PLANTS, ANIMALS,
THE HUMAN BODY, etc. Each section begins with a
table of contents listing the major entries within
that section. For example, THE VISUAL ARTS section
contains entries on *Drawing, Tempera, Fresco,
Oils, Watercolor, Pastels, Acrylics, Calligraphy,
Printmaking, Mosaic,* and *Sculpture.* Every entry
includes a short introduction explaining the
purpose of the photographs and illustrations,
and the significance of the annotations.

If you know what something looks like, but don't
know its name, turn to the annotations surrounding
the pictures; if you know a word, but don't know
what it refers to, use the comprehensive index
to direct you to the appropriate page.

Suppose you want to know what the bone at the
end of your little finger is called. With a standard
dictionary, you wouldn't know where to begin. But
with the *Ultimate Visual Dictionary* you simply turn
to the entry called *Hands*—within THE HUMAN BODY
section—and you will find four fully annotated color
photographs showing the skin, muscles, and bones

of the human hand. In this entry you will quickly
find that the bone you are searching for is called the
distal phalanx. In addition, you will discover that it
is attached to the middle phalanx by the distal
interphalangeal joint.

Perhaps you want to know what a catalytic converter
looks like. If you look up "catalytic converter" in an
ordinary dictionary, you will be told what it is and
possibly what it does—but you will not be able to
tell what shape it is or what it is made of. However,
if you look up "catalytic converter" in the index of
the *Ultimate Visual Dictionary*, you will be directed
to the *Modern engines* entry on page 344—where
the introduction gives you basic information
about what a catalytic converter is—and to page
350—where there is a spectacular exploded-view
photograph of the mechanics of a Renault Clio.
From these pages you will find out not only what
a catalytic converter looks like, but also that it is
attached at one end to an exhaust downpipe
and at the other to a silencer.

Whatever it is that you want to find a name for, or
whatever name you want to find a picture for, you
will find it quickly and easily in the *Ultimate Visual
Dictionary*. Perhaps you need to know where the
vamp on a shoe is; or how to tell obovate and
lanceolate leaves apart; or what a spiral galaxy
looks like; or whether birds have nostrils.
With the *Ultimate Visual Dictionary* close by,
the answers to each of these questions, and
thousands more, are readily available.

The *Ultimate Visual Dictionary* does not just
tell you what the names of the different parts
of an object are. The photographs, illustrations,
and annotations are all specially arranged to
help you understand which parts relate
to one another and how objects function.

With the *Ultimate Visual Dictionary*, in seconds
you can find the words or pictures that you
are looking for; or you can simply browse.
The *Ultimate Visual Dictionary* is not intended to
replace a standard dictionary or encyclopedia, but
is instead a stimulating and valuable companion
to ordinary reference volumes. Giving you access
to the language that is used by astronomers and
architects, musicians and mechanics, pilots and
professional athletes, it is the ideal reference
book for experts and novices of all ages.

Sections of the ULTIMATE VISUAL DICTIONARY
The 14 sections of the *ULTIMATE VISUAL DICTIONARY* contain a total of more than 30,000 terms, encompassing a wide range of topics:

●In the first section, THE UNIVERSE, spectacular photographs and illustrations are used to show the names of the stars and planets and to explain the structure of solar systems, galaxies, nebulae, comets, and black holes.

●PREHISTORIC EARTH tells the story of how our own planet has evolved since its formation. It includes examples of prehistoric flora and fauna, and fascinating dinosaur models— some with parts of the body stripped away to show anatomical sections.

●PLANTS covers a huge range of species— from the familiar to the exotic. In addition to the color photographs of plants included in this section, there is a series of micrographic photographs illustrating plant details—such as pollen grains, spores, and cross-sections of stems and roots.

●In the ANIMALS section, skeletons, anatomical diagrams, and different parts of animals' bodies have been meticulously annotated. This section provides a comprehensive guide to the vocabulary of zoological classification and animal physiology.

●The structure of the human body, its parts, and its systems are presented in THE HUMAN BODY. The section includes lifelike, three-dimensional models and the latest false-color images. Clear and authoritative annotations indicate the correct anatomical terms.

●GEOLOGY, GEOGRAPHY, AND METEOROLOGY describes the structure of the Earth—from the inner core to the exosphere—and the physical phenomena, such as volcanoes, rivers, glaciers, and climate, that shape its surface.

●PHYSICS AND CHEMISTRY is a visual journey through the fundamental principles underlying the physical universe, that provides the essential vocabulary of these sciences.

●In RAIL AND ROAD, a wide range of trains, trolleys and buses, cars, bicycles, and motorcycles are described. Exploded-view photographs show mechanical details with striking clarity.

●SEA AND AIR illustrates hundreds of parts of ships and airplanes. The section includes civil and fighting craft, both historical and modern.

●THE VISUAL ARTS shows the equipment and materials used by painters, sculptors, printers, and other artists. Well-known compositions have been chosen to illustrate specific artistic techniques and effects.

●ARCHITECTURE includes photographs of exemplary architectural models and illustrates dozens of additional features such as columns, domes, and arches.

●MUSIC provides a visual introduction to the special language of music and musical instruments. It includes clearly annotated photographs of each of the major groups of traditional instruments—brass, woodwind, strings, and percussion—together with modern electronic instruments.

●The SPORTS section is a guide to the playing areas, formations, equipment, and techniques needed for many of today's most popular sports.

●In EVERYDAY THINGS, familiar objects, such as shoes, clocks, and toasters, are taken apart—down to the very last screw or length of thread—to show their inner workings and to give a special insight into the language that is used by their manufacturers.

THE UNIVERSE

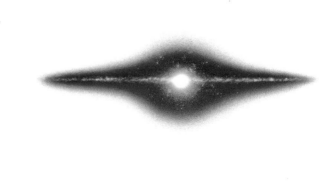

Anatomy of the Universe

Fireball of rapidly expanding, extremely hot gas lasting about one million years

THE UNIVERSE CONTAINS EVERYTHING that exists, from the tiniest subatomic particles to galactic superclusters (the largest structures known). Nobody knows how big the Universe is, but astronomers estimate that it contains about 100 billion galaxies, each comprising an average of 100 billion stars. The most widely accepted theory about the origin of the Universe is the Big Bang theory, which states that the Universe came into being in a huge explosion—the Big Bang—that took place between 10 and 20 billion years ago. The Universe initially consisted of a very hot, dense fireball of expanding, cooling gas. After about one million years, the gas probably began to condense into localized clumps called protogalaxies. During the next five billion years, the protogalaxies continued condensing, forming galaxies in which stars were being born. Today, billions of years later, the Universe as a whole is still expanding, although there are localized areas in which objects are held together by gravity; for example, many galaxies are found in clusters. The Big Bang theory is supported by the discovery of faint, cool background radiation coming evenly from all directions. This radiation is believed to be the remnant of the radiation produced by the Big Bang. Small "ripples" in the temperature of the cosmic background radiation are thought to be evidence of slight fluctuations in the density of the early Universe, which resulted in the formation of galaxies. Astronomers do not yet know if the Universe is "closed," which means it will eventually stop expanding and begin to contract, or if it is "open," which means it will continue expanding forever.

COMPUTER-ENHANCED MICROWAVE MAP OF COSMIC BACKGROUND RADIATION

Pink indicates "warm ripples" in background radiation

Pale blue indicates "cool ripples" in background radiation

Deep blue indicates background radiation corresponding to -454.5°F (remnant of the Big Bang)

Red and pink band indicates radiation from our galaxy

Low-energy microwave radiation corresponding to about -454°F

High-energy gamma radiation corresponding to about 5,400°F

ORIGIN AND EXPANSION OF THE UNIVERSE

Quasar (probably the center of a galaxy containing a massive black hole)

Universe one to five billion years after Big Bang

Protogalaxy (condensing gas cloud)

Galaxy spinning and flattening to become spiral shaped

Dark cloud (dust and gas condensing to form a protogalaxy)

Elliptical galaxy in which stars form rapidly

Universe today (10–20 billion years after Big Bang)

Cluster of galaxies held together by gravity

Elliptical galaxy containing old stars and little gas and dust

Irregular galaxy

Spiral galaxy containing gas, dust, and young stars

OBJECTS IN THE UNIVERSE

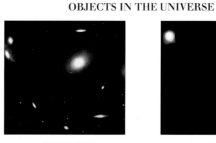

CLUSTER OF GALAXIES IN VIRGO

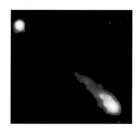

COLOR-ENHANCED IMAGE OF 3C273 (QUASAR)

NGC 4406 (ELLIPTICAL GALAXY)

NGC 5236 (SPIRAL GALAXY)

NGC 6822 (IRREGULAR GALAXY)

THE ROSETTE NEBULA (EMISSION NEBULA)

THE JEWEL BOX (STAR CLUSTER)

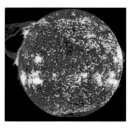

THE SUN (MAIN SEQUENCE STAR)

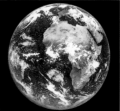

EARTH

THE MOON

Galaxies

**SOMBRERO,
A SPIRAL GALAXY**

A GALAXY IS A HUGE MASS OF STARS, nebulae, and interstellar material. The smallest galaxies contain about 100,000 stars, while the largest contain up to 3,000 billion stars. There are three main types of galaxy, classified according to their shape: elliptical, which are oval shaped; spiral, which have arms spiraling outward from a central bulge; and irregular, which have no obvious shape. Sometimes, the shape of a galaxy is distorted by a collision with another galaxy. Quasars (quasi-stellar objects) are thought to be galactic nuclei but are so far away that their exact nature is still uncertain. They are compact, highly luminous objects in the outer reaches of the known Universe; while the farthest known "ordinary" galaxies are about 10 billion light-years away, the farthest known quasar is about 15 billion light-years away. Active galaxies, such as Seyfert galaxies and radio galaxies, emit intense radiation. In a Seyfert galaxy, this radiation comes from the galactic nucleus; in a radio galaxy, it also comes from huge lobes on either side of the galaxy. The radiation from active galaxies and quasars is thought to be caused by black holes (see pp. 28-29).

**OPTICAL IMAGE OF NGC 4486
(ELLIPTICAL GALAXY)**

Globular cluster
containing very
old red giants

Central region
containing old
red giants

Less densely
populated region

Neighboring galaxy

**OPTICAL IMAGE OF LARGE MAGELLANIC
CLOUD (IRREGULAR GALAXY)**

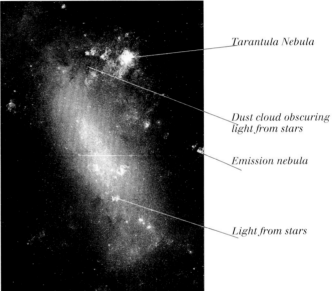

Tarantula Nebula

Dust cloud obscuring
light from stars

Emission nebula

Light from stars

OPTICAL IMAGE OF NGC 2997 (SPIRAL GALAXY)

Glowing nebula
in spiral arm

Spiral arm
containing
young stars

Galactic nucleus
containing
old stars

Dust in spiral
arm reflecting
blue light from
hot young stars

Hot, ionized
hydrogen gas
emitting red light

Dust lane

OPTICAL IMAGE OF CENTAURUS A (RADIO GALAXY)

Dust lane crossing elliptical galaxy

Galactic nucleus containing powerful source of radiation

Light from old stars

COLOR-ENHANCED RADIO IMAGE OF CENTAURUS A

Radio lobe

Red indicates high-intensity radio waves

Blue indicates low-intensity radio waves

Radiation from galactic nucleus

Outline of optical image of Centaurus A

Radio lobe

Yellow indicates medium-intensity radio waves

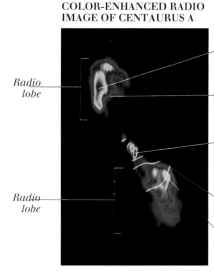

COLOR-ENHANCED RADIO IMAGE OF 3C273 (QUASAR)

Radiation from jet of high-energy particles moving away from quasar

Quasar nucleus

Blue indicates low-intensity radio waves

White indicates high-intensity radio waves

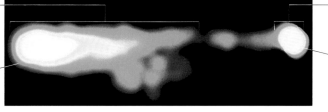

OPTICAL IMAGE OF NGC 1566 (SEYFERT GALAXY)

Nebula in spiral arm

Compact nucleus emitting intense radiation

Spiral arm

COLOR-ENHANCED OPTICAL IMAGE OF NGC 5754 (TWO COLLIDING GALAXIES)

Blue indicates low-intensity radiation

Red indicates medium-intensity radiation

Spiral arm distorted by gravitational influence of smaller galaxy

Large spiral galaxy

Smaller galaxy colliding with larger galaxy

Yellow indicates high-intensity radiation

The Milky Way

**VIEW TOWARD
GALACTIC CENTER**

THE MILKY WAY IS THE NAME GIVEN TO THE FAINT BAND OF LIGHT that stretches across the night sky. This light comes from stars and nebulae in our galaxy, known as the Milky Way Galaxy or simply as "the Galaxy." The Galaxy is shaped like a spiral, with a dense central bulge that is encircled by four arms spiraling outward and surrounded by a less dense halo. We cannot see the spiral shape because our Solar System is in one of the spiral arms, the Orion Arm (also called the Local Arm). From our position, the center of the Galaxy is completely obscured by dust clouds; as a result, optical maps give only a limited view of the Galaxy. However, a more complete picture can be obtained by studying radio, infrared, and other radiation. The central bulge of the Galaxy is a relatively small, dense sphere that contains mainly older red and yellow stars. The halo is a less dense region in which the oldest stars are situated; some of these stars may be as old as the Galaxy itself (possibly 15 billion years). The spiral arms contain mainly hot, young, blue stars, as well as nebulae (clouds of dust and gas, inside which stars are born). The Galaxy is vast—about 100,000 light-years across (a light-year is about 5,879 billion miles); in comparison, the Solar System seems small, at about 12 light-hours across (about 8 billion miles). The entire Galaxy is rotating in space, although the inner stars travel faster than those further out. The Sun, which is about two-thirds out from the center, completes one lap of the Galaxy about every 220 million years.

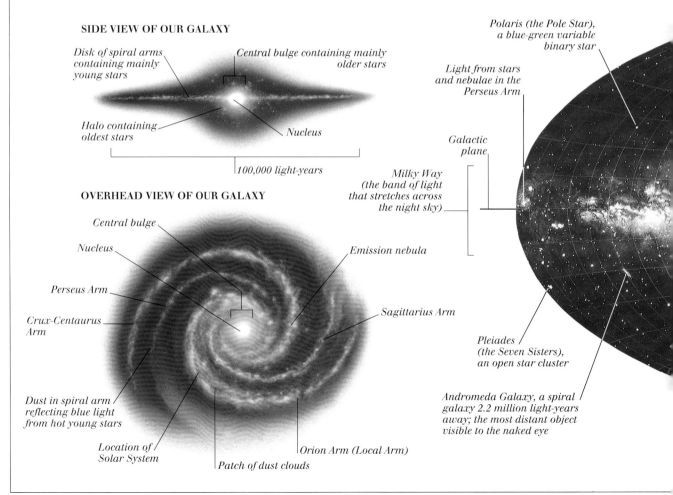

SIDE VIEW OF OUR GALAXY

Disk of spiral arms
containing mainly
young stars

Central bulge containing mainly
older stars

Halo containing
oldest stars

Nucleus

100,000 light-years

OVERHEAD VIEW OF OUR GALAXY

Central bulge

Nucleus

Perseus Arm

Crux-Centaurus
Arm

Dust in spiral arm
reflecting blue light
from hot young stars

Location of
Solar System

Patch of dust clouds

Emission nebula

Sagittarius Arm

Orion Arm (Local Arm)

**PANORAMIC OPTICAL MAP OF OUR
GALAXY AND NEARBY GALAXIES**

Polaris (the Pole Star),
a blue-green variable
binary star

Light from stars
and nebulae in the
Perseus Arm

Galactic
plane

Milky Way
(the band of light
that stretches across
the night sky)

Pleiades
(the Seven Sisters),
an open star cluster

Andromeda Galaxy, a spiral
galaxy 2.2 million light-years
away; the most distant object
visible to the naked eye

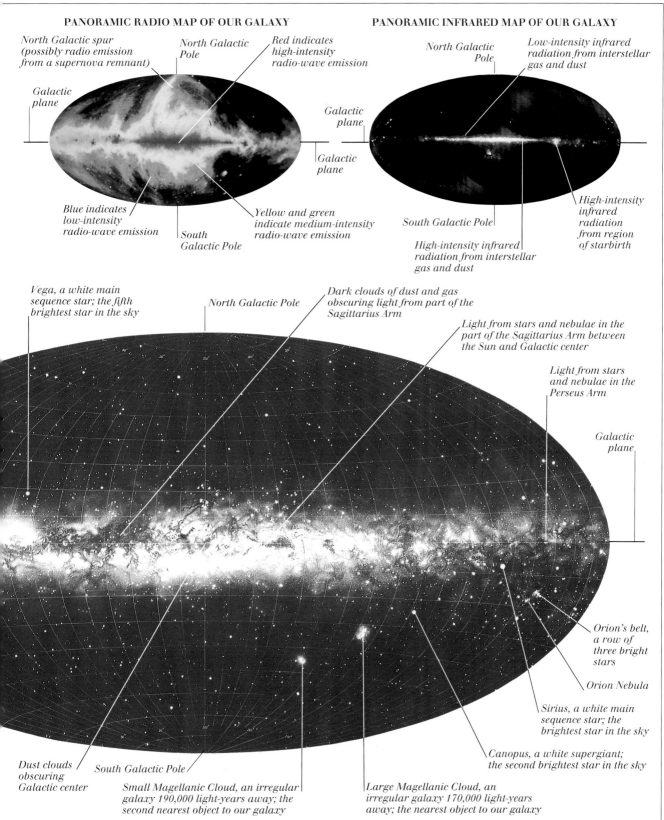

PANORAMIC RADIO MAP OF OUR GALAXY

North Galactic spur
(possibly radio emission
from a supernova remnant)

North Galactic
Pole

Red indicates
high-intensity
radio-wave emission

Galactic
plane

Blue indicates
low-intensity
radio-wave emission

South
Galactic Pole

Yellow and green
indicate medium-intensity
radio-wave emission

PANORAMIC INFRARED MAP OF OUR GALAXY

North Galactic
Pole

Low-intensity infrared
radiation from interstellar
gas and dust

Galactic
plane

Galactic
plane

South Galactic Pole

High-intensity infrared
radiation from interstellar
gas and dust

High-intensity
infrared
radiation
from region
of starbirth

Vega, a white main
sequence star; the fifth
brightest star in the sky

North Galactic Pole

Dark clouds of dust and gas
obscuring light from part of the
Sagittarius Arm

Light from stars and nebulae in the
part of the Sagittarius Arm between
the Sun and Galactic center

Light from stars
and nebulae in the
Perseus Arm

Galactic
plane

Orion's belt,
a row of
three bright
stars

Orion Nebula

Sirius, a white main
sequence star; the
brightest star in the sky

Canopus, a white supergiant;
the second brightest star in the sky

Dust clouds
obscuring
Galactic center

South Galactic Pole

Small Magellanic Cloud, an irregular
galaxy 190,000 light-years away; the
second nearest object to our galaxy

Large Magellanic Cloud, an
irregular galaxy 170,000 light-years
away; the nearest object to our galaxy

Nebulae and star clusters

A NEBULA IS A CLOUD OF DUST AND GAS inside a galaxy. Nebulae become visible if the gas glows or if the cloud reflects starlight or obscures light from more distant objects. Emission nebulae shine because their gas emits light when it is stimulated by radiation from hot young stars. Reflection nebulae shine because their dust reflects light from stars in or around the nebula. Dark nebulae appear as silhouettes because they block light from shining nebulae or stars behind them. Two types of nebula are associated with dying stars: planetary nebulae and supernova remnants. Both consist of expanding shells of gas that were once the outer layers of a star. A planetary nebula is a gas shell drifting away from a dying stellar core. A supernova remnant is a gas shell moving away from a stellar core at great speed following a violent explosion called a supernova (see pp. 26-27). Stars are often found in groups known as clusters. Open clusters are loose groups of a few thousand young stars that were born in the same cloud and are drifting apart. Globular clusters are densely packed, roughly spherical groups of hundreds of thousands of older stars.

TRIFID NEBULA (EMISSION NEBULA)

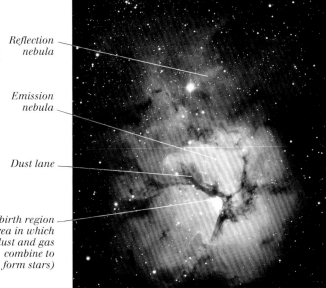

Reflection nebula

Emission nebula

Dust lane

Starbirth region (area in which dust and gas combine to form stars)

PLEIADES (OPEN STAR CLUSTER) WITH A REFLECTION NEBULA

Wisps of dust and hydrogen gas remaining from cloud in which stars formed

Young star in an open cluster of 300–500 stars

Reflection nebula

HORSEHEAD NEBULA (DARK NEBULA)

Glowing filament of hot, ionized hydrogen gas

Alnitak (star in Orion's belt)

Dust lane

Emission nebula

Star near southern end of Orion's belt

Emission nebula

Horsehead Nebula

Reflection nebula

Dark nebula obscuring light from distant stars

ORION NEBULA (DIFFUSE EMISSION NEBULA)

Glowing cloud of dust and hydrogen gas forming part of Orion Nebula

Gas cloud emitting light because of ultraviolet radiation from the four young Trapezium stars

Dust cloud

Trapezium (group of four young stars)

Green light from hot, ionized oxygen gas

Glowing filament of hot, ionized hydrogen gas

Red light from hot, ionized hydrogen gas

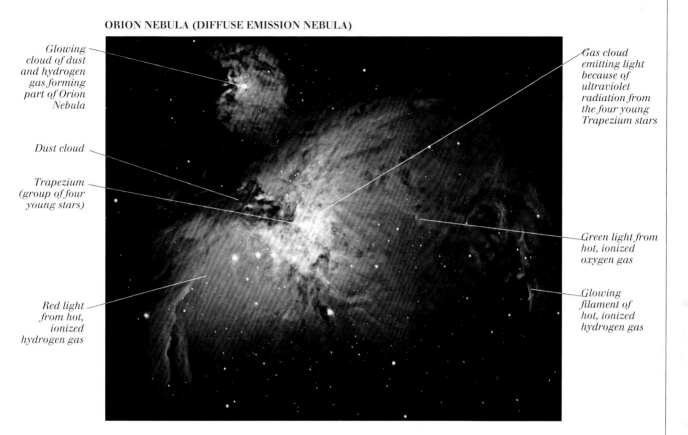

HELIX NEBULA (PLANETARY NEBULA)

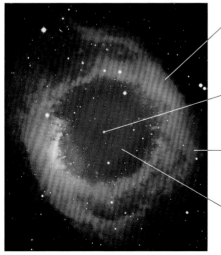

Planetary nebula (gas shell expanding outward from dying stellar core)

Stellar core at a temperature of about 180,000°F

Red light from hot, ionized hydrogen gas

Blue-green light from hot, ionized oxygen and nitrogen gases

VELA SUPERNOVA REMNANT

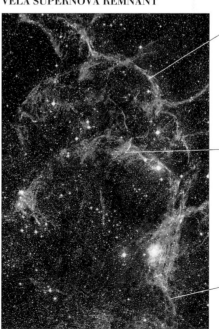

Supernova remnant (gas shell consisting of outer layers of star thrown off in supernova explosion)

Hydrogen gas emitting red light due to being heated by supernova explosion

Glowing filament of hot, ionized hydrogen gas

Stars of northern skies

WHEN YOU LOOK AT THE NORTHERN SKY, you look away from the densely populated Galactic center, so the northern sky generally appears less bright than the southern sky (see pp. 20-21). Among the best-known sights in the northern sky are the constellations Ursa Major (the Great Bear) and Orion. Some ancient civilizations believed that the stars were fixed to a celestial sphere surrounding the Earth, and modern maps of the sky are based on a similar idea. The North and South Poles of this imaginary celestial sphere are directly above the North and South Poles of the Earth, at the points where the Earth's axis of rotation intersects the sphere. The celestial North Pole is at the center of the map shown here, and Polaris (the Pole Star) lies very close to it. The celestial equator marks a projection of the Earth's equator on the sphere. The ecliptic marks the path of the Sun across the sky as the Earth orbits the Sun. The Moon and planets move against the background of the stars because the stars are much more distant; the nearest star outside the Solar System (Proxima Centauri) is more than 50,000 times farther away than the planet Jupiter.

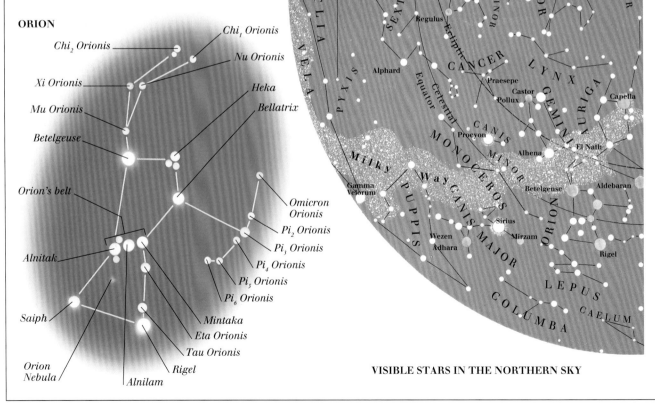

ORION

- Chi₂ Orionis
- Chi₁ Orionis
- Nu Orionis
- Xi Orionis
- Heka
- Mu Orionis
- Bellatrix
- Betelgeuse
- Orion's belt
- Omicron Orionis
- Pi₂ Orionis
- Pi₃ Orionis
- Pi₄ Orionis
- Pi₅ Orionis
- Pi₆ Orionis
- Alnitak
- Saiph
- Mintaka
- Eta Orionis
- Tau Orionis
- Orion Nebula
- Rigel
- Alnilam

VISIBLE STARS IN THE NORTHERN SKY

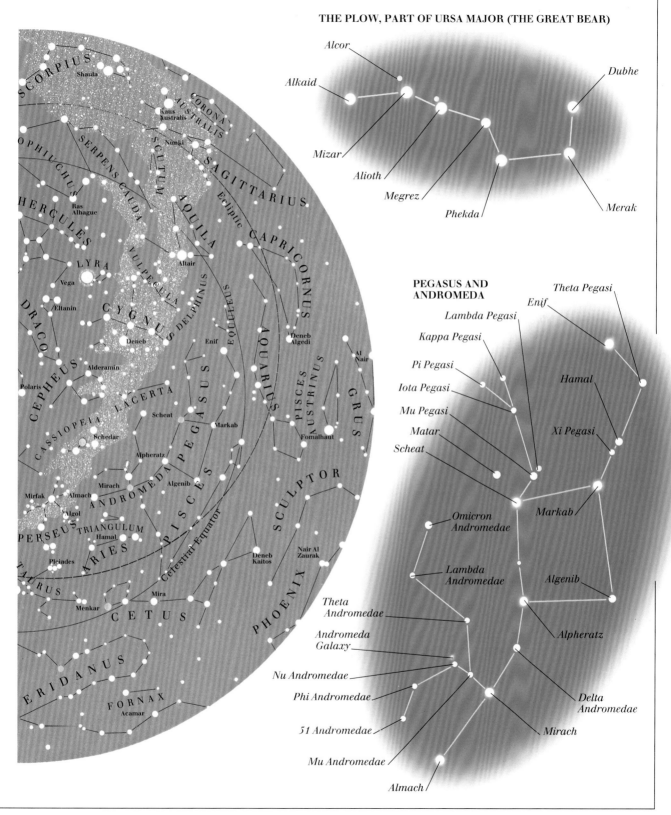

THE PLOW, PART OF URSA MAJOR (THE GREAT BEAR)

Alcor
Alkaid
Dubhe
Mizar
Alioth
Megrez
Phekda
Merak

PEGASUS AND ANDROMEDA

Theta Pegasi
Enif
Lambda Pegasi
Kappa Pegasi
Hamal
Pi Pegasi
Iota Pegasi
Mu Pegasi
Xi Pegasi
Matar
Scheat
Markab
Omicron Andromedae
Lambda Andromedae
Algenib
Alpheratz
Theta Andromedae
Andromeda Galaxy
Delta Andromedae
Nu Andromedae
Phi Andromedae
Mirach
51 Andromedae
Mu Andromedae
Almach

SCORPIUS
Shaula
CORONA AUSTRALIS
Kaus Australis
Nunki
OPHIUCHUS
SERPENS CAUDA
SCUTUM
SAGITTARIUS
Ecliptic
AQUILA
Ras Alhague
CAPRICORNUS
HERCULES
VULPECULA
Altair
LYRA
Vega
DELPHINUS
EQUULEUS
Deneb Algedi
Eltanin
CYGNUS
Enif
AQUARIUS
Al Nair
DRACO
Deneb
PEGASUS
PISCES AUSTRINUS
GRUS
CEPHEUS
Alderamin
LACERTA
Scheat
Markab
Polaris
Fomalhaut
CASSIOPEIA
Schedar
Alpheratz
ANDROMEDA
PEGASUS
Algenib
SCULPTOR
Mirfak
Almach
Mirach
PISCES
Algol
TRIANGULUM
Nair Al Zaurak
PERSEUS
Hamal
ARIES
Celestial Equator
Deneb Kaitos
PHOENIX
Pleiades
TAURUS
Mira
Menkar
CETUS
ERIDANUS
FORNAX
Acamar

Stars of southern skies

When you look at the southern sky, you look toward the Galactic center, which has a huge population of stars. As a result, the Milky Way appears brighter in the southern sky than in the northern sky (see pp. 18-19). The southern sky is rich in nebulae and star clusters. It contains the Large and Small Magellanic Clouds, which are the two nearest galaxies to our own. Stars make fixed patterns in the sky called constellations. The constellations, however, are only apparent groupings of stars, because the distances to the stars in a constellation may vary enormously. The shapes of constellations may change over many thousands of years because of the relative motions of stars. The apparent movement of entire constellations across the sky is due to the Earth's motion in space. The daily rotation of the Earth causes the constellations to move across the sky from east to west, and the orbit of the Earth around the Sun causes different areas of sky to be visible in different seasons. The visibility of areas of sky also depends on the location of the observer. For instance, stars near the celestial equator may be seen from either hemisphere at some time during the year, while stars close to the celestial poles (the celestial South Pole is at the center of the map shown here) can never be seen from the opposite hemisphere.

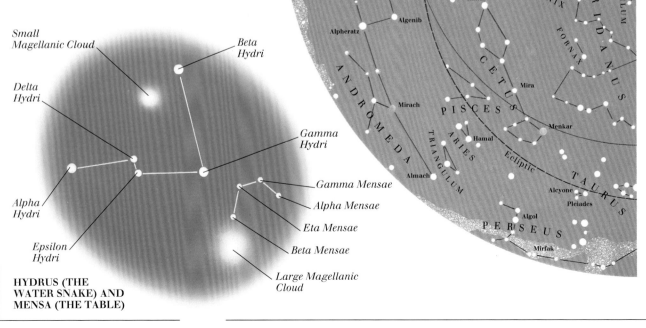

Small Magellanic Cloud

Beta Hydri

Delta Hydri

Gamma Hydri

Alpha Hydri

Epsilon Hydri

Gamma Mensae

Alpha Mensae

Eta Mensae

Beta Mensae

Large Magellanic Cloud

HYDRUS (THE WATER SNAKE) AND MENSA (THE TABLE)

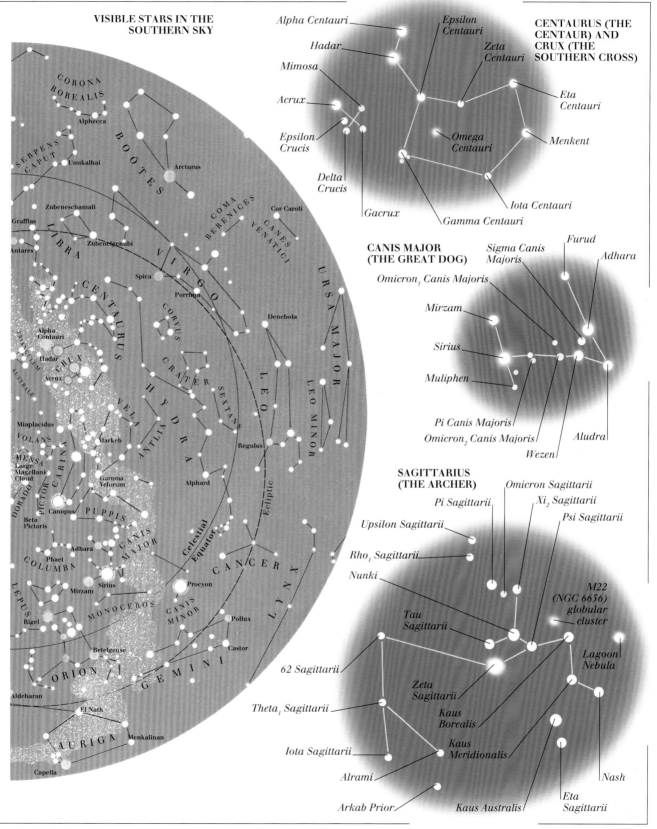

VISIBLE STARS IN THE SOUTHERN SKY

CORONA BOREALIS
Alphecca
SERPENS CAPUT
Unukalhai
BOÖTES
Arcturus
COMA BERENICES
CANES VENATICI
Cor Caroli
Graffias
Zubeneschamali
LIBRA
Zubenelgenubi
Antares
Spica
VIRGO
Porrhua
URSA MAJOR
Denebola
CENTAURUS
CORVUS
Alpha Centauri
CRUX
Hadar
Acrux
HYDRA
CRATER
SEXTANS
LEO
LEO MINOR
TRIANGULUM AUSTRALE
VELA
ANTLIA
Ecliptic
Miaplacidus
VOLANS
Markeb
Gamma Velorum
Alphard
Regulus
MENSA
Large Magellanic Cloud
CARINA
PICTOR
PUPPIS
Celestial Equator
DORADO
Canopus
Beta Pictoris
CANIS MAJOR
CANCER
LYNX
Adhara
COLUMBA
Phaet
Mirzam
Sirius
MONOCEROS
CANIS MINOR
Procyon
Pollux
LEPUS
Rigel
Betelgeuse
ORION
Castor
GEMINI
Aldebaran
El Nath
Menkalinan
AURIGA
Capella

CENTAURUS (THE CENTAUR) AND CRUX (THE SOUTHERN CROSS)

Alpha Centauri
Epsilon Centauri
Hadar
Zeta Centauri
Mimosa
Acrux
Eta Centauri
Epsilon Crucis
Omega Centauri
Menkent
Delta Crucis
Gacrux
Gamma Centauri
Iota Centauri

CANIS MAJOR (THE GREAT DOG)

Furud
Sigma Canis Majoris
Adhara
Omicron₁ Canis Majoris
Mirzam
Sirius
Muliphen
Pi Canis Majoris
Omicron₂ Canis Majoris
Aludra
Wezen

SAGITTARIUS (THE ARCHER)

Pi Sagittarii
Omicron Sagittarii
Xi₂ Sagittarii
Psi Sagittarii
Upsilon Sagittarii
Rho₁ Sagittarii
Nunki
M22 (NGC 6656) globular cluster
Lagoon Nebula
Tau Sagittarii
62 Sagittarii
Zeta Sagittarii
Kaus Borealis
Theta₁ Sagittarii
Kaus Meridionalis
Iota Sagittarii
Alrami
Kaus Australis
Nash
Eta Sagittarii
Arkab Prior

21

Stars

OPEN STAR CLUSTER AND DUST CLOUD

STARS ARE BODIES of hot glowing gas that are born in nebulae (see pp. 24-27). They vary enormously in size, mass, and temperature: diameters range from about 450 times smaller to over 1,000 times bigger than that of the Sun; masses range from about a twentieth to over 50 solar masses; and surface temperatures range from about 5,500°F to over 90,000°F. The color of a star is determined by its temperature: the hottest stars are blue and the coolest are red. The Sun, with a surface temperature of 10,000°F, is between these extremes and appears yellow. The energy emitted by a shining star is produced by nuclear fusion in the star's core. The brightness of a star is measured in magnitudes—the brighter the star, the lower its magnitude. There are two types of magnitude: apparent magnitude, which is the brightness seen from Earth, and absolute magnitude, which is the brightness that would be seen from a standard distance of 10 parsecs (32.6 light-years). The light emitted by a star may be split to form a spectrum containing a series of dark lines (absorption lines). The patterns of lines indicate the presence of particular chemical elements, enabling astronomers to deduce the composition of the star's atmosphere. The magnitude and spectral type (color) of stars may be plotted on a graph called a Hertzsprung-Russell diagram, which shows that stars tend to fall into several well-defined groups. The principal groups are main sequence stars (those which are fusing hydrogen to form helium), giants, supergiants, and white dwarfs.

STAR SIZES

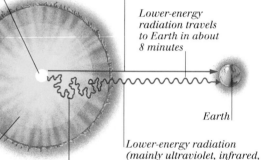

Red giant (diameters between about 10 million and 100 million miles)

The Sun (main sequence star with diameter about 870,000 miles)

White dwarf (diameters between about 2,000 and 30,000 miles)

ENERGY EMISSION FROM THE SUN

Nuclear fusion in core produces gamma rays and neutrinos

Neutrinos travel to Earth directly from Sun's core in about 8 minutes

Lower-energy radiation travels to Earth in about 8 minutes

Earth

Lower-energy radiation (mainly ultraviolet, infrared, and light rays) leaves surface

Sun

High-energy radiation (gamma rays) loses energy while traveling to surface over 2 million years

STAR MAGNITUDES

APPARENT MAGNITUDE

ABSOLUTE MAGNITUDE

Brighter stars

-9

0

+9

Fainter stars

Sirius: apparent magnitude of -1.46

Rigel: apparent magnitude of +0.12

Objects of magnitude higher than about +5.5 cannot be seen by the naked eye

Rigel: absolute magnitude of -7.1

Sirius: absolute magnitude of +1.4

NUCLEAR FUSION IN MAIN SEQUENCE STARS LIKE THE SUN

Positron

Deuterium nucleus

Proton

Neutron

Proton (hydrogen nucleus)

Neutrino

Gamma rays

Helium-3 nucleus

Helium-4 nucleus

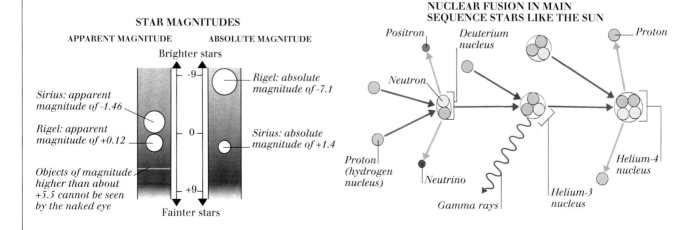

HERTZSPRUNG-RUSSELL DIAGRAM

Hotter stars   **TEMPERATURE (°F)**   Cooler stars

65,000   18,000   9,000   6,500   4,500

Brighter stars −7
−6
Deneb (blue supergiant) −5 SUPERGIANTS   Betelgeuse (red supergiant)
−4
−3
−2
−1
0 GIANTS   Arcturus (red giant)
Sirius A (massive +1
main sequence star) +2 MAIN SEQUENCE STARS
+3
+4
ABSOLUTE +5   The Sun (yellow main
VISUAL +6   sequence dwarf)
MAGNITUDE +7
+8
+9
+10
Sirius B (white dwarf) +11
+12
+13 WHITE DWARFS
+14   Barnard's Star (main
+15   sequence red dwarf)
Fainter stars +16

O5 B0   A0   F0   G0   K0   M0 M5

SPECTRAL TYPE

STELLAR SPECTRAL ABSORPTION LINES

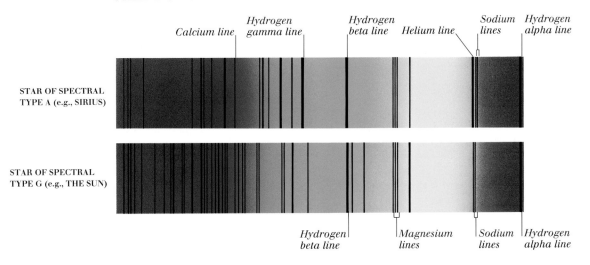

Calcium line | Hydrogen gamma line | Hydrogen beta line | Helium line | Sodium lines | Hydrogen alpha line

STAR OF SPECTRAL TYPE A (e.g., SIRIUS)

STAR OF SPECTRAL TYPE G (e.g., THE SUN)

Hydrogen beta line | Magnesium lines | Sodium lines | Hydrogen alpha line

Small stars

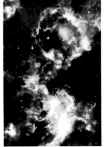

REGION OF STAR FORMATION IN ORION

SMALL STARS HAVE A MASS of up to about one and a half times that of the Sun. They begin to form when a region of higher density in a nebula condenses into a huge globule of gas and dust that contracts under its own gravity. Within a globule, regions of condensing matter heat up and begin to glow, forming protostars. If a protostar contains enough matter, the central temperature reaches about 27 million °F. At this temperature, nuclear reactions in which hydrogen fuses to form helium can start. This process releases energy, which prevents the star from contracting further, and also causes it to shine; it is now a main sequence star. A star of about one solar mass remains in the main sequence for about 10 billion years, until the hydrogen in the star's core has been converted into helium. The helium core then contracts again, and nuclear reactions continue in a shell around the core. The core becomes hot enough for helium to fuse to form carbon, while the outer layers of the star expand, cool, and shine less brightly. The expanding star is known as a red giant. When the helium in the core runs out, the outer layers of the star may drift off as an expanding gas shell called a planetary nebula. The remaining core (about 80 percent of the original star) is now in its final stages. It becomes a white dwarf star that gradually cools and dims. When it finally stops shining altogether, the dead star will become a black dwarf.

STRUCTURE OF A MAIN SEQUENCE STAR

Core containing hydrogen fusing to form helium

Radiative zone

Convective zone

Surface temperature about 10,000°F

Core temperature about 27 million °F

STRUCTURE OF A NEBULA

Young main sequence star

Dense region of dust and gas (mainly hydrogen) condensing under gravity to form globules

Hot, ionized hydrogen gas emitting red light due to stimulation by radiation from hot young stars

Dark globule of dust and gas (mainly hydrogen) contracting to form protostars

LIFE OF A SMALL STAR OF ABOUT ONE SOLAR MASS

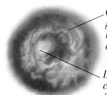

Cool cloud of gas (mainly hydrogen) and dust

Dense globule condensing to form protostars

NEBULA

Glowing ball of gas (mainly hydrogen)

Natal cocoon (shell of dust blown away by radiation from protostar)

PROTOSTAR
Duration: 50 million years

About 870,000 miles

Star producing energy by nuclear fusion in core

MAIN SEQUENCE STAR
Duration: 10 billion years

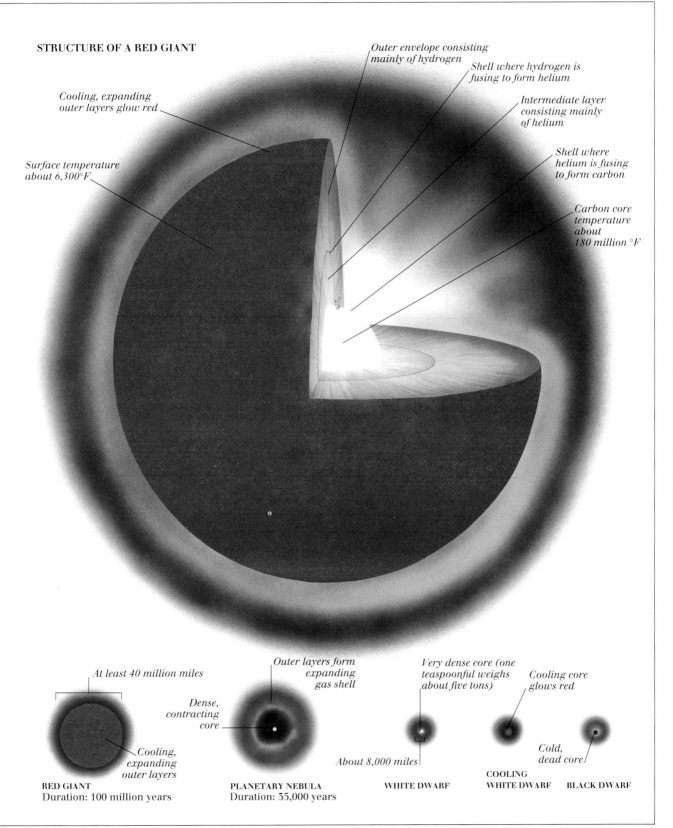

STRUCTURE OF A RED GIANT

Outer envelope consisting
mainly of hydrogen

Shell where hydrogen is
fusing to form helium

Intermediate layer
consisting mainly
of helium

Shell where
helium is fusing
to form carbon

Carbon core
temperature
about
180 million °F

Cooling, expanding
outer layers glow red

Surface temperature
about 6,300°F

At least 40 million miles

Outer layers form
expanding
gas shell

Very dense core (one
teaspoonful weighs
about five tons)

Cooling core
glows red

Dense,
contracting
core

Cooling,
expanding
outer layers

About 8,000 miles

Cold,
dead core

RED GIANT
Duration: 100 million years

PLANETARY NEBULA
Duration: 35,000 years

WHITE DWARF

**COOLING
WHITE DWARF**

BLACK DWARF

Massive stars

MASSIVE STARS HAVE A MASS AT LEAST THREE TIMES that of the Sun, and some stars are as massive as about 50 Suns. A massive star evolves in a similar way to a small star until it reaches the main sequence stage (see pp. 24-25). During the main sequence, a star shines steadily until the hydrogen in its core has fused to form helium. This process takes billions of years in a small star, but only millions of years in a massive star. A massive star then becomes a red supergiant, which initially consists of a helium core surrounded by outer layers of cooling, expanding gas. Over the next few million years, a series of nuclear reactions form different elements in shells around an iron core. The core eventually collapses in less than a second, causing a massive explosion called a supernova, in which a shock wave blows away the outer layers of the star. Supernovae shine brighter than an entire galaxy for a short time. Sometimes, the core survives the supernova explosion. If the surviving core is between about one and a half and three solar masses, it contracts to become a tiny, dense neutron star. If the core is considerably greater than three solar masses, it contracts to become a black hole (see pp. 28-29).

SUPERNOVA

TARANTULA NEBULA BEFORE SUPERNOVA

STRUCTURE OF A RED SUPERGIANT

Outer envelope consisting mainly of hydrogen

Layer consisting mainly of helium

Layer consisting mainly of carbon

Layer consisting mainly of oxygen

Layer consisting mainly of silicon

Shell of hydrogen fusing to form helium

Shell of helium fusing to form carbon

Shell of carbon fusing to form oxygen

Shell of oxygen fusing to form silicon

Shell of silicon fusing to form iron core

Surface temperature about 5,500°F

Cooling, expanding outer layers glow red

Core of mainly iron at a temperature of 5.4–9 billion °F

LIFE OF A MASSIVE STAR OF ABOUT 10 SOLAR MASSES

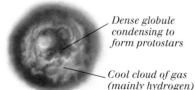

Dense globule condensing to form protostars

Cool cloud of gas (mainly hydrogen) and dust

NEBULA

Glowing ball of gas (mainly hydrogen)

Natal cocoon (shell of dust blown away by radiation from protostar)

PROTOSTAR
Duration: a few hundred thousand years

About 2 million miles

Star producing energy by nuclear fusion in core

MAIN SEQUENCE STAR
Duration: 10 million years

FEATURES OF A SUPERNOVA

**TARANTULA NEBULA SHOWING
SUPERNOVA IN 1987**

*Ejecta (outer layers of star
thrown off during explosion)
travels at speeds of up to
6,000 miles/sec*

*Shock wave travels outward
from core at speeds of up to
20,000 miles/sec*

*Reverse shock wave
moves inward and
heats ejecta, causing
it to shine*

*Heavy chemical
elements are
scattered through
space by explosion*

*Contracting
core consisting
mainly of neutrons
remains after explosion*

*Central
temperature
more than
18 billion °F*

*Light energy
of a billion Suns
emitted during explosion*

*Extremely dense core
(one teaspoonful
weighs about a
billion tons)*

About 6 miles

*Core mass of
less than three
solar masses*

NEUTRON STAR

About 60 million miles

*Cooling,
expanding
outer layers*

*Outer layers of
star blown off
in explosion*

*Contracting
stellar core may
remain after
supernova*

*Core of mass greater
than three solar masses
continues contracting
to become black hole*

*Accretion
disk*

RED SUPERGIANT
Duration: 4 million years

SUPERNOVA
Duration of
visibility: 1–2 years

BLACK HOLE

Neutron stars and black holes

NEUTRON STARS AND BLACK HOLES form from the stellar cores that remain after stars have exploded as supernovae (see pp. 26-27). If the remaining core is between about one and a half and three solar masses, it contracts to form a neutron star. If the remaining core is considerably greater than about three solar masses, it contracts to form a black hole. Neutron stars are typically only about six miles in diameter and consist almost entirely of subatomic particles called neutrons. These stars are so dense that a teaspoonful would weigh about a billion tons. Neutron stars are observed as pulsars, so-called because they rotate rapidly and emit two beams of radio waves, which sweep across the sky and are detected as short pulses. Black holes are characterized by their extremely strong gravity, which is so powerful that not even light can escape; as a result, black holes are invisible. However, they may be detected if they have a close companion star. The gravity of the black hole pulls gas from the other star, forming an accretion disk that spirals around the black hole at high speed, heating up and emitting radiation. Eventually, the matter spirals in to cross the event horizon (the boundary of the black hole), finally disappearing from the visible Universe.

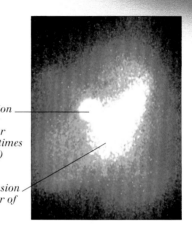

X-ray emission from pulsar (neutron star rotating 30 times each second)

X-ray emission from center of nebula

X-RAY IMAGE OF THE CRAB NEBULA (SUPERNOVA REMNANT)

PULSAR (ROTATING NEUTRON STAR)

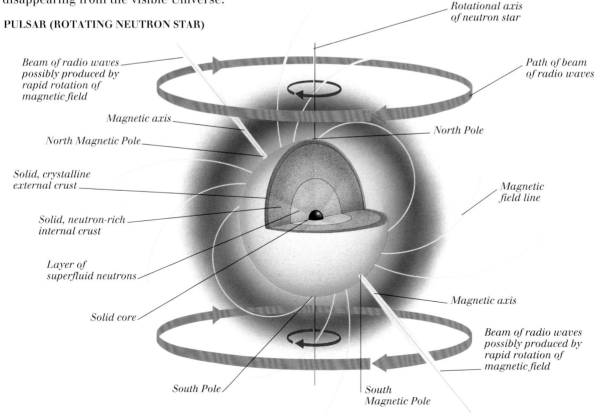

Rotational axis of neutron star

Beam of radio waves possibly produced by rapid rotation of magnetic field

Path of beam of radio waves

Magnetic axis

North Magnetic Pole

North Pole

Solid, crystalline external crust

Magnetic field line

Solid, neutron-rich internal crust

Layer of superfluid neutrons

Solid core

Magnetic axis

Beam of radio waves possibly produced by rapid rotation of magnetic field

South Pole

South Magnetic Pole

STELLAR BLACK HOLE

Blue supergiant star

Gas current (outer layers of nearby blue supergiant pulled toward black hole by gravity)

Singularity (theoretical region of infinite density, pressure, and temperature)

Hot spot (region of intense friction where gas current joins accretion disk)

Gas in outer part of accretion disk emitting low-energy radiation

Event horizon (boundary of black hole)

Accretion disk (matter spiraling around black hole)

Hot gas in inner part of accretion disk emitting high-energy X-rays

Black hole

Gas at temperatures of millions °F spiraling at close to the speed of light

FORMATION OF A BLACK HOLE

Stellar core remains after supernova explosion

Light rays increasingly bent by gravity as core collapses

Core shrinks beyond its event horizon to become a black hole

Light rays cannot escape because gravity is so strong

Core greater than three solar masses collapses under its own gravity

Density, pressure, and temperature of core increase as core collapses

Event horizon

Outer layers of massive star thrown off in explosion

Singularity (theoretical region of infinite density, pressure, and temperature)

SUPERNOVA

COLLAPSING STELLAR CORE

BLACK HOLE

The Solar System

THE SUN

THE SOLAR SYSTEM consists of a central star (the Sun) and the bodies that orbit it. These bodies include nine planets and their 61 known moons, asteroids, comets, and meteoroids. The Solar System also contains interplanetary gas and dust. Most of the planets fall into two groups: four small rocky planets near the Sun (Mercury, Venus, Earth, and Mars), and four planets farther out, the gas giants (Jupiter, Saturn, Uranus, and Neptune). Pluto belongs to neither group—it is very small, solid, and icy. Pluto is the outermost planet, except when it passes briefly inside Neptune's orbit. Between the rocky planets and gas giants is the asteroid belt, which contains thousands of chunks of rock orbiting the Sun. Most of the bodies in the Solar System move around the Sun in elliptical orbits located in a thin disk around the Sun's equator. All the planets orbit the Sun in the same direction (counterclockwise when viewed from above) and all but Venus, Uranus, and Pluto also spin around their axes in this direction. Moons also spin as they, in turn, orbit their planets. The entire Solar System orbits the center of our galaxy, the Milky Way (see pp. 14-15).

Perihelion (orbital point closest to Sun)

Sun

Elliptical orbit

Planet orbiting Sun

Direction of planetary rotation

Aphelion (orbital point farthest from Sun)

Aphelion of Neptune: 2,819 million miles

ORBITS OF INNER PLANETS

Average orbital speed of Venus: 21.8 miles/sec
Average orbital speed of Mercury: 29.8 miles/sec
Average orbital speed of Earth: 18.5 miles/sec
Average orbital speed of Mars: 15 miles/sec

Mercury

Perihelion of Mercury: 28.5 million miles
Perihelion of Venus: 66.7 million miles
Perihelion of Earth: 91.4 million miles

Mars

Perihelion of Mars: 128.4 million miles

Earth

Venus

Sun

Aphelion of Mercury: 43.3 million miles

Asteroid belt

Aphelion of Venus: 67.7 million miles

Aphelion of Earth: 94.5 million miles

Aphelion of Mars: 154.8 million miles

Aphelion of Pluto: 4,583 million miles

MERCURY
Year: 87.97 Earth days
Mass: 0.055 Earth masses
Diameter: 3,031 miles

VENUS
Year: 224.7 Earth days
Mass: 0.81 Earth masses
Diameter: 7,521 miles

EARTH
Year: 365.26 days
Mass: 1 Earth mass
Diameter: 7,926 miles

MARS
Year: 1.88 Earth years
Mass: 0.11 Earth masses
Diameter: 4,217 miles

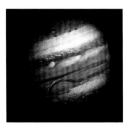

JUPITER
Year: 11.86 Earth years
Mass: 318 Earth masses
Diameter: 88,850 miles

ORBITS OF OUTER PLANETS

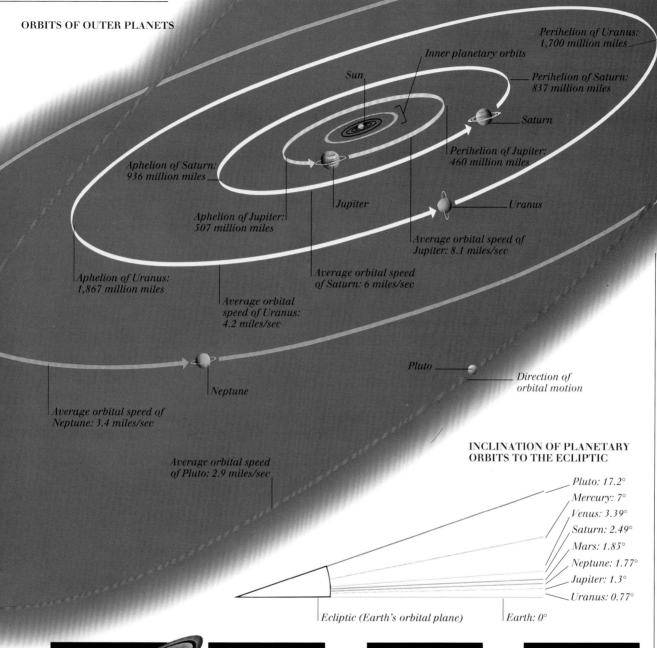

Perihelion of Uranus: 1,700 million miles

Inner planetary orbits

Sun

Perihelion of Saturn: 837 million miles

Saturn

Perihelion of Jupiter: 460 million miles

Aphelion of Saturn: 936 million miles

Jupiter

Uranus

Average orbital speed of Jupiter: 8.1 miles/sec

Aphelion of Jupiter: 507 million miles

Aphelion of Uranus: 1,867 million miles

Average orbital speed of Saturn: 6 miles/sec

Average orbital speed of Uranus: 4.2 miles/sec

Pluto

Direction of orbital motion

Neptune

Average orbital speed of Neptune: 3.4 miles/sec

Average orbital speed of Pluto: 2.9 miles/sec

INCLINATION OF PLANETARY ORBITS TO THE ECLIPTIC

Pluto: 17.2°
Mercury: 7°
Venus: 3.39°
Saturn: 2.49°
Mars: 1.85°
Neptune: 1.77°
Jupiter: 1.3°
Uranus: 0.77°

Ecliptic (Earth's orbital plane)

Earth: 0°

SATURN
Year: 29.46 Earth years
Mass: 95.18 Earth masses
Diameter: 74,901 miles

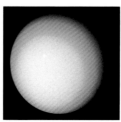

URANUS
Year: 84.01 Earth years
Mass: 14.5 Earth masses
Diameter: 31,765 miles

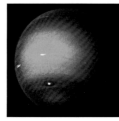

NEPTUNE
Year: 164.79 Earth years
Mass: 17.14 Earth masses
Diameter: 30,777 miles

PLUTO
Year: 248.54 Earth years
Mass: 0.0022 Earth masses
Diameter: 1,429 miles

The Sun

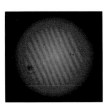

SOLAR
PHOTOSPHERE

THE SUN IS THE STAR AT THE CENTER of our Solar System. It is about five billion years old and will probably continue to shine as it does now for about another five billion years. The Sun is a yellow main sequence star (see pp. 22-23) about 870,000 miles in diameter. It consists almost entirely of hydrogen and helium. In the Sun's core, hydrogen is converted to helium by nuclear fusion, releasing energy in the process. The energy travels from the core through the radiative and convective zones to the photosphere (visible surface), where it leaves the Sun in the form of heat and light. On the photosphere there are often dark, relatively cool areas called sunspots. These usually appear in pairs or groups and are thought to be caused by magnetic fields. Other types of solar activity are flares, which are usually associated with sunspots, and prominences. Flares are sudden discharges of high-energy radiation and atomic particles. Prominences are huge loops or filaments of gas extending into the solar atmosphere; some last for hours, others for months. Beyond the photosphere is the chromosphere (inner atmosphere) and the extremely rarified corona (outer atmosphere), which extends millions of miles into space. Tiny particles that escape from the corona give rise to the solar wind, which streams through space at hundreds of miles per second. The chromosphere and corona can be seen from Earth when the Sun is totally eclipsed by the Moon.

Sun

Moon passes between Sun and Earth

Umbra (inner, total shadow) of Moon

Region of Earth from which total eclipse is visible

Penumbra (outer, partial shadow) of Moon

Region of Earth from which partial eclipse is visible

Umbra (inner, total shadow) of Earth

Earth

Penumbra (outer, partial shadow) of Earth

SURFACE FEATURES

Gas loop (looped prominence)

Prominence (jet of gas at edge of Sun's disk up to hundreds of thousands of miles high)

Spicule (vertical jet of gas)

Photosphere (visible surface)

Chromosphere (inner atmosphere)

TOTAL SOLAR ECLIPSE

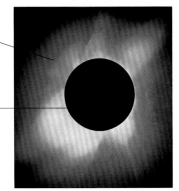

Corona (outer atmosphere of extremely hot diffuse gas)

Moon covers Sun's disk

SUNSPOTS

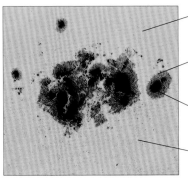

Granulated surface of Sun

Penumbra (lighter, outer region) containing radial fibril

Umbra (darker, inner region) temperature about 7,200°F

Photosphere temperature about 9,900°F

**EXTERNAL FEATURES AND
INTERNAL STRUCTURE OF THE SUN**

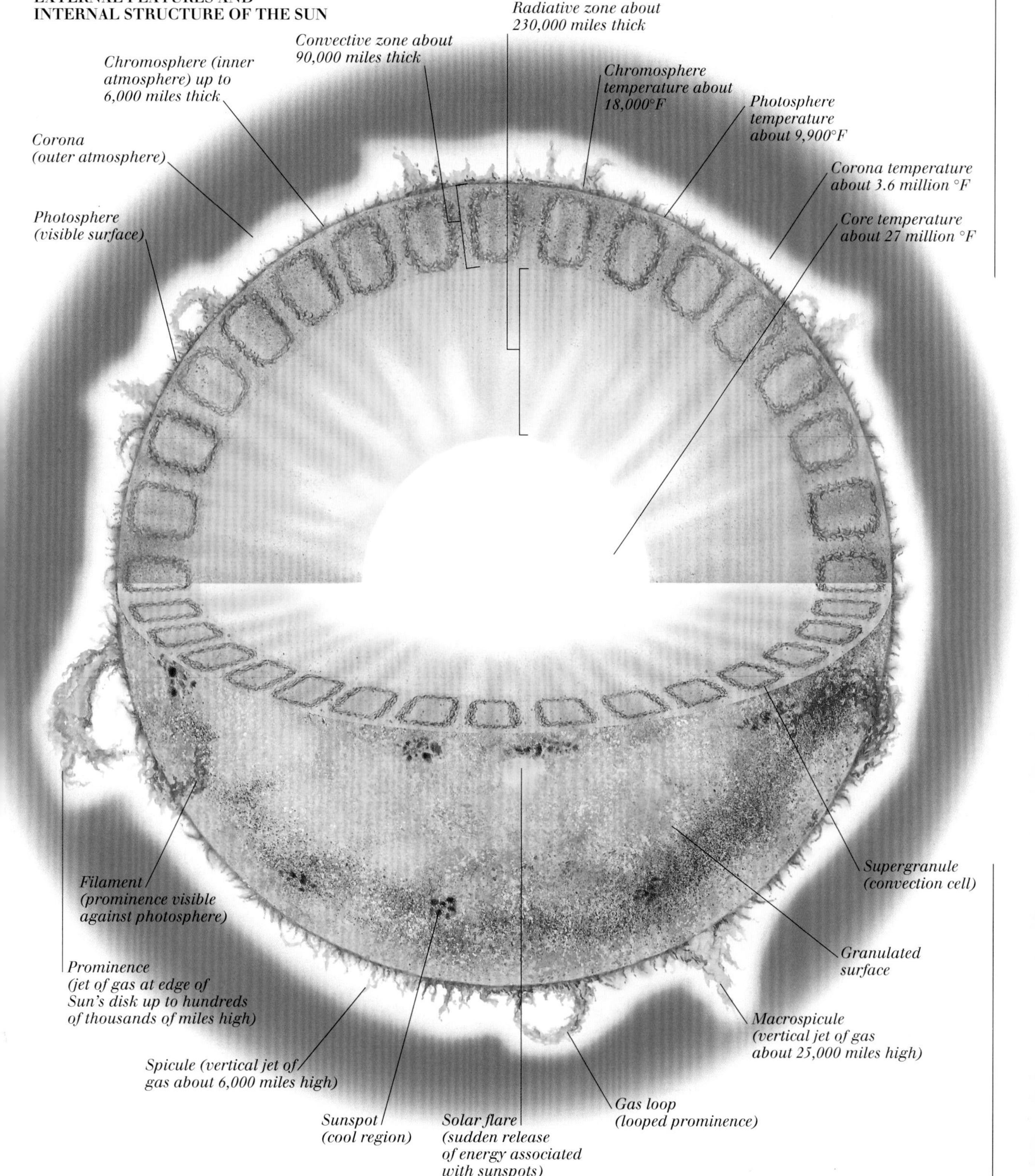

Chromosphere (inner
atmosphere) up to
6,000 miles thick

Convective zone about
90,000 miles thick

Radiative zone about
230,000 miles thick

Chromosphere
temperature about
18,000°F

Photosphere
temperature
about 9,900°F

Corona
(outer atmosphere)

Corona temperature
about 3.6 million °F

Core temperature
about 27 million °F

Photosphere
(visible surface)

Supergranule
(convection cell)

Granulated
surface

Filament
(prominence visible
against photosphere)

Macrospicule
(vertical jet of gas
about 25,000 miles high)

Prominence
(jet of gas at edge of
Sun's disk up to hundreds
of thousands of miles high)

Spicule (vertical jet of
gas about 6,000 miles high)

Sunspot
(cool region)

Solar flare
(sudden release
of energy associated
with sunspots)

Gas loop
(looped prominence)

Mercury

MERCURY IS THE NEAREST PLANET to the Sun, orbiting at an average distance of about 36 million miles. Because Mercury is the closest planet to the Sun, it moves faster than any other planet, traveling at an average speed of nearly 30 miles per second and completing an orbit in just under 88 days. Mercury is very small (only Pluto is smaller) and rocky. Most of the surface has been heavily cratered by the impact of meteorites, although there are also smooth, sparsely cratered plains. The Caloris Basin is the largest crater, measuring about 800 miles across. It is thought to have been formed when a rock the size of an asteroid hit the planet and is surrounded by concentric rings of mountains thrown up by the impact. The surface also has many ridges, called rupes, that are thought to have been formed when the hot core of the young planet cooled and shrank about four billion years ago, buckling the planet's surface in the process. The planet rotates about its axis very slowly, taking nearly 59 Earth days to complete one rotation. As a result, a solar day (sunrise to sunrise) on Mercury is about 176 Earth days—twice as long as the 88-day Mercurian year. Mercury has extreme surface temperatures, ranging from a maximum of 800°F on the sunlit side to -270°F on the dark side. At nightfall, the temperature drops very quickly because the planet's atmosphere is almost nonexistent. It consists only of minute amounts of helium and hydrogen captured from the solar wind, plus traces of other gases.

MERCURY

TILT AND ROTATION OF MERCURY

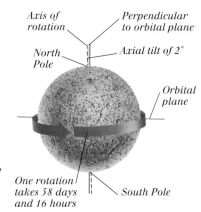

Axis of rotation

Perpendicular to orbital plane

North Pole

Axial tilt of 2°

Orbital plane

One rotation takes 58 days and 16 hours

South Pole

DEGAS AND BRONTË (RAY CRATERS)

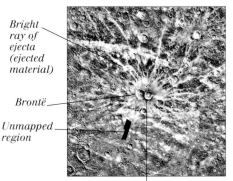

Bright ray of ejecta (ejected material)

Brontë

Unmapped region

Degas with central peak

FORMATION OF A RAY CRATER

Debris thrown out by impact

Path of meteorite colliding with planet

Wall of rock thrown up around crater

Impact forms saucer-shaped crater

Fractured rock

METEORITE IMPACT

Path of rocky ejecta (ejected material)

Ejecta forms secondary craters

Loose debris on crater floor

SECONDARY CRATERING

Wall of rock forms ring of mountains

Ray of ejecta (ejected material)

Small secondary crater

Loose ejected rock

Central mountain rings form if floor of large crater recoils from meteorite impact

Falling debris forms ridges on side of wall

RAY CRATER

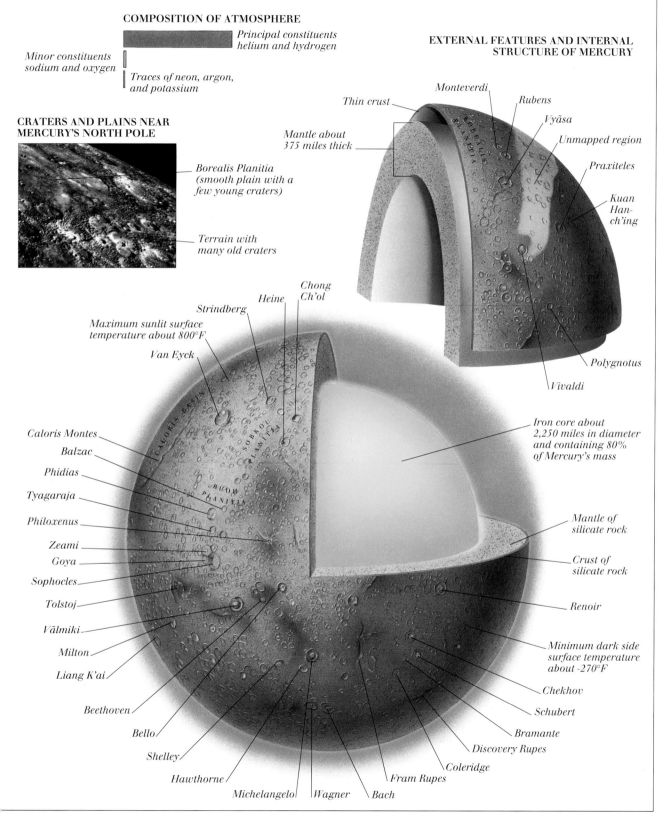

COMPOSITION OF ATMOSPHERE

Principal constituents
helium and hydrogen

Minor constituents
sodium and oxygen

Traces of neon, argon,
and potassium

**CRATERS AND PLAINS NEAR
MERCURY'S NORTH POLE**

**EXTERNAL FEATURES AND INTERNAL
STRUCTURE OF MERCURY**

Monteverdi
Rubens
Vyāsa
Thin crust
Unmapped region
Praxiteles
Mantle about
375 miles thick
Kuan
Han-
ch'ing

Borealis Planitia
(smooth plain with a
few young craters)

Terrain with
many old craters

Polygnotus

Vivaldi

Chong
Ch'ol
Heine
Strindberg

Maximum sunlit surface
temperature about 800°F

Van Eyck

Caloris Montes
Balzac
Phidias
Tyagaraja
Philoxenus
Zeami
Goya
Sophocles
Tolstoj
Vālmiki
Milton
Liang K'ai

Beethoven

Bello

Shelley

Hawthorne

Michelangelo   Wagner   Bach

Fram Rupes

Coleridge

Discovery Rupes

Bramante

Schubert

Chekhov

Minimum dark side
surface temperature
about -270°F

Renoir

Crust of
silicate rock

Mantle of
silicate rock

Iron core about
2,250 miles in diameter
and containing 80%
of Mercury's mass

CALORIS BASIN

SOBKOU
PLANITIA

BUDH
PLANITIA

Venus

RADAR IMAGE OF
VENUS

VENUS IS A ROCKY PLANET and the second planet from the Sun. Venus spins slowly backward as it orbits the Sun, causing its rotational period to be the longest in the Solar System, at about 243 Earth days. It is slightly smaller than Earth and probably has a similar internal structure, consisting of a semisolid metal core surrounded by a rocky mantle and crust. Venus is the brightest object in the sky after the Sun and Moon because its atmosphere reflects sunlight strongly. The main component of the atmosphere is carbon dioxide, which traps heat in a greenhouse effect far stronger than that on Earth. As a result, Venus is the hottest planet, with a maximum surface temperature of about 900°F. The thick cloud layers contain droplets of sulfuric acid and are driven around the planet by winds at speeds of up to 220 miles per hour. Although the planet takes 243 Earth days to rotate once, the high-speed winds cause the clouds to circle the planet in only four Earth days. The high temperature, acidic clouds, and enormous atmospheric pressure (about 90 times greater at the surface than that on Earth) make the environment extremely hostile. However, orbiting satellites have managed to land on Venus and photograph its dry, dusty surface. The Venusian surface has also been mapped by probes with radar equipment that can "see" through the cloud layers. Such radar maps reveal a terrain with craters, mountains, volcanoes, and areas where craters have been covered by plains of solidified volcanic lava. There are two large highland regions called Aphrodite Terra and Ishtar Terra.

TILT AND ROTATION OF VENUS

Axis of rotation
Perpendicular to orbital plane
North Pole
Axial tilt of 2°
Orbital plane
One rotation takes 243 days and 14 minutes
South Pole

CLOUD FEATURES

Polar hood
Dark, mid-latitude band
Cloud features swept around planet by winds of up to 220 mph
Dirty yellow hue due to sulfuric acid in atmosphere
Bright polar band

VENUSIAN CRATERS

Danilova
Ejecta (ejected material)
Central peak
Howe

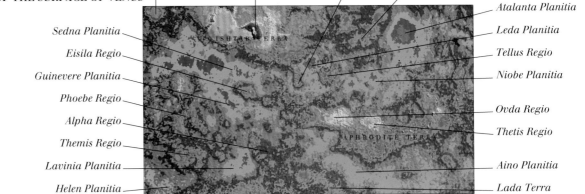

COMPUTER-ENHANCED RADAR MAP OF THE SURFACE OF VENUS

Metis Regio
Maxwell Montes
Bell Regio
Tethus Regio
Atalanta Planitia
Sedna Planitia
Leda Planitia
Eisila Regio
Tellus Regio
Guinevere Planitia
Niobe Planitia
Phoebe Regio
Alpha Regio
Ovda Regio
Themis Regio
Thetis Regio
Lavinia Planitia
Aino Planitia
Helen Planitia
Lada Terra

ISHTAR TERRA
APHRODITE TERRA

**EXTERNAL FEATURES AND
INTERNAL STRUCTURE OF VENUS**

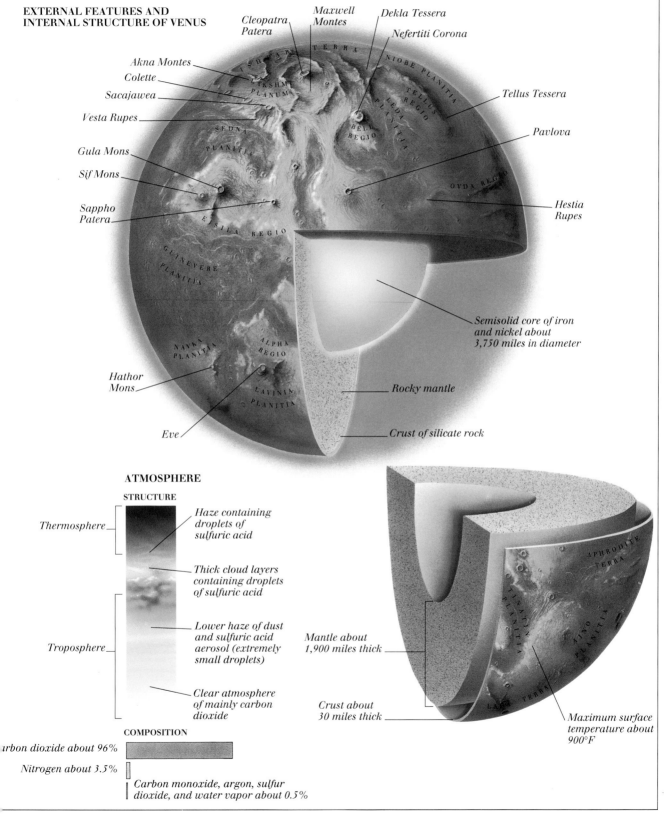

Cleopatra Patera

Maxwell Montes

Dekla Tessera

Nefertiti Corona

Akna Montes

Colette

Sacajawea

Vesta Rupes

Gula Mons

Sif Mons

Sappho Patera

Tellus Tessera

Pavlova

Hestia Rupes

Semisolid core of iron and nickel about 3,750 miles in diameter

Rocky mantle

Crust of silicate rock

Hathor Mons

Eve

ATMOSPHERE

STRUCTURE

Thermosphere

Troposphere

Haze containing droplets of sulfuric acid

Thick cloud layers containing droplets of sulfuric acid

Lower haze of dust and sulfuric acid aerosol (extremely small droplets)

Clear atmosphere of mainly carbon dioxide

Mantle about 1,900 miles thick

Crust about 30 miles thick

Maximum surface temperature about 900°F

COMPOSITION

Carbon dioxide about 96%

Nitrogen about 3.5%

Carbon monoxide, argon, sulfur dioxide, and water vapor about 0.5%

The Earth

THE EARTH

THE EARTH IS THE THIRD of the nine planets that orbit the Sun. It is the largest and densest rocky planet, and the only one known to support life. About 70 percent of the Earth's surface is covered by water, which is not found in liquid form on the surface of any other planet. There are four main layers: the inner core, the outer core, the mantle, and the crust. At the heart of the planet the solid inner core has a temperature of about 7,230°F. The heat from this inner core causes material in the molten outer core and mantle to circulate in convection currents. It is thought that these convection currents generate the Earth's magnetic field, which extends into space as the magnetosphere. The Earth's atmosphere helps screen out some of the harmful radiation from the Sun, stops meteorites from reaching the planet's surface, and traps enough heat to prevent extremes of cold. The Earth has one natural satellite, the Moon, which is large enough for both bodies to be considered a double-planet system.

TILT AND ROTATION OF THE EARTH

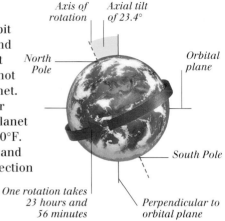

Axis of rotation

Axial tilt of 23.4°

North Pole

Orbital plane

South Pole

One rotation takes 23 hours and 56 minutes

Perpendicular to orbital plane

THE FORMATION OF THE EARTH

The heat of the collisions caused the planet to glow red

The cloud broke up into particles of ice and rock, which stuck together to form planets

Microorganisms began to photosynthesize, creating a supply of oxygen

4,600 YEARS AGO, THE SOLAR SYSTEM FORMED FROM A CLOUD OF GAS AND DUST

THE EARTH WAS FORMED FROM COLLIDING ROCKS

4,500 YEARS AGO THE SURFACE COOLED TO FORM THE CRUST

THE CONTINENTS BROKE UP AND REFORMED, GRADUALLY TAKING THEIR PRESENT POSITIONS

Solar wind enters atmosphere and produces aurora

Magnetosphere (magnetic field)

Solar wind (stream of electrically charged particles)

THE EARTH'S MAGNETOSPHERE

Van Allen radiation belt

Earth

Axis of geographic poles

Axis of magnetic poles

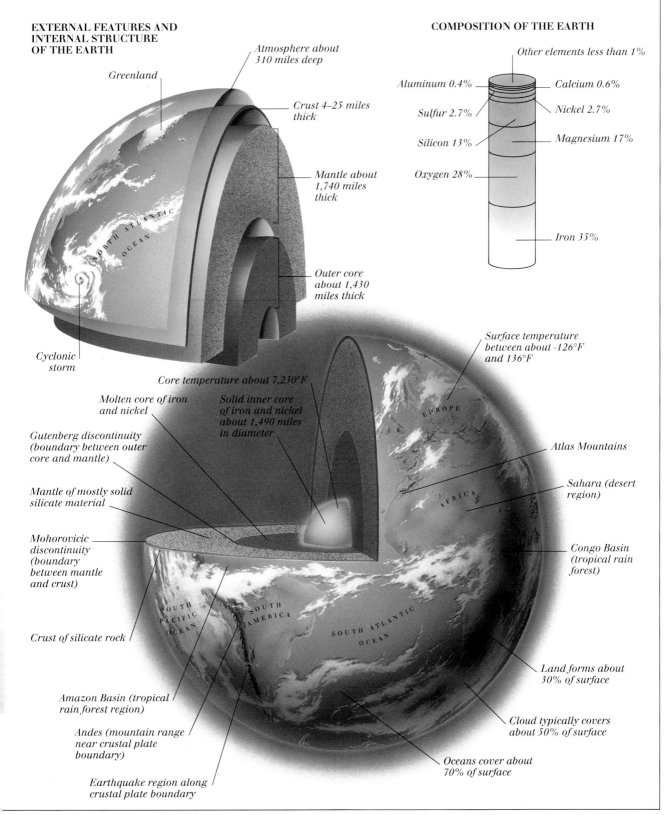

EXTERNAL FEATURES AND INTERNAL STRUCTURE OF THE EARTH

Greenland

Atmosphere about 310 miles deep

Crust 4–25 miles thick

Mantle about 1,740 miles thick

Outer core about 1,430 miles thick

NORTH ATLANTIC OCEAN

Cyclonic storm

COMPOSITION OF THE EARTH

Other elements less than 1%

Aluminum 0.4%

Calcium 0.6%

Sulfur 2.7%

Nickel 2.7%

Silicon 13%

Magnesium 17%

Oxygen 28%

Iron 35%

Core temperature about 7,230°F

Molten core of iron and nickel

Solid inner core of iron and nickel about 1,490 miles in diameter

Gutenberg discontinuity (boundary between outer core and mantle)

Mantle of mostly solid silicate material

Mohorovicic discontinuity (boundary between mantle and crust)

Crust of silicate rock

Amazon Basin (tropical rain forest region)

Andes (mountain range near crustal plate boundary)

Earthquake region along crustal plate boundary

SOUTH PACIFIC OCEAN

SOUTH AMERICA

SOUTH ATLANTIC OCEAN

EUROPE

AFRICA

Surface temperature between about -126°F and 136°F

Atlas Mountains

Sahara (desert region)

Congo Basin (tropical rain forest)

Land forms about 30% of surface

Cloud typically covers about 50% of surface

Oceans cover about 70% of surface

The Moon

THE MOON FROM EARTH

THE MOON IS THE EARTH'S only natural satellite. It is relatively large for a moon, with a diameter of about 2,155 miles—just over a quarter that of the Earth. The Moon takes the same time to rotate on its axis as it takes to orbit the Earth (27.3 days), and so the same side (the near side) always faces us. However, the amount of the surface we can see—the phase of the Moon—depends on how much of the near side is in sunlight. The Moon is dry and barren, with no atmosphere or water. It consists mainly of solid rock, although its core may contain molten rock or iron. The surface is dusty, with highlands covered in craters caused by meteorite impacts, and lowlands in which large craters have been filled by solidified lava to form dark areas called maria or "seas." Maria occur mainly on the near side, which has a thinner crust than the far side. Many of the craters are rimmed by mountain ranges that form the crater walls and can be thousands of feet high.

TILT AND ROTATION OF THE MOON

Axis of rotation
Perpendicular to orbital plane
Axial tilt of 6.7°
North Pole
Orbital plane
One rotation takes 27 Earth days and 8 hours
South Pole

CRATERS ON OCEANUS PROCELLARUM

Aristarchus
Cobra Head (head of Schröter's Valley)
Herodotus

NEAR SIDE OF THE MOON

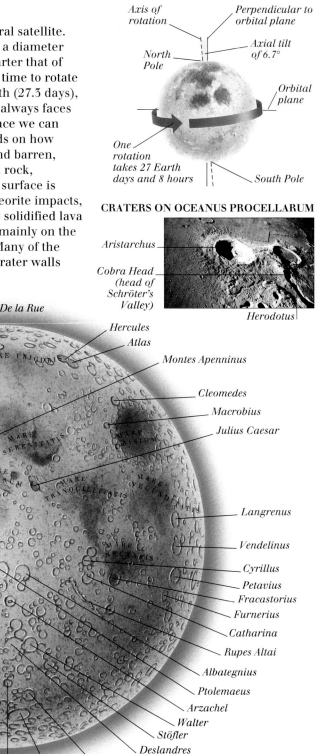

Aristoteles *De la Rue*
Aristillus *Hercules*
Plato *Atlas*
Archimedes *Montes Apenninus*
Montes Jura *Cleomedes*
Sinus Iridum *Macrobius*
Bright rays of ejected material *Julius Caesar*
Copernicus
Aristarchus
Langrenus
Kepler *Vendelinus*
Encke *Cyrillus*
Flamsteed *Petavius*
Fra Mauro *Fracastorius*
Grimaldi *Furnerius*
Letronne *Catharina*
Gassendi *Rupes Altai*
Mersenius *Albategnius*
Ptolemaeus
Arzachel
Walter
Pitatus *Stöfler*
Schickard *Deslandres*
Alphonsus *Bailly* *Tycho* *Clavius* *Maginus*

MARE FRIGORIS
MARE IMBRIUM
MARE SERENITATIS
MARE CRISIUM
MARE VAPORUM
MARE TRANQUILLITATIS
MARE FECUNDITATIS
OCEANUS PROCELLARUM
MARE NECTARIS
MARE HUMORUM
MARE NUBIUM

PHASES OF THE MOON

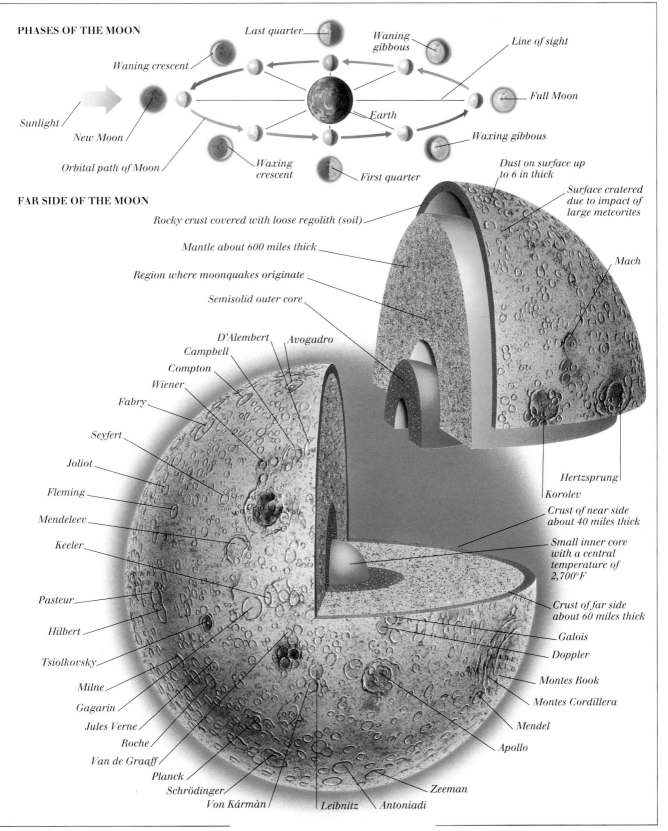

Last quarter

Waning gibbous

Waning crescent

Line of sight

Full Moon

Sunlight

Earth

New Moon

Waxing gibbous

Orbital path of Moon

Waxing crescent

First quarter

FAR SIDE OF THE MOON

Dust on surface up to 6 in thick

Surface cratered due to impact of large meteorites

Rocky crust covered with loose regolith (soil)

Mantle about 600 miles thick

Region where moonquakes originate

Semisolid outer core

Mach

D'Alembert

Avogadro

Campbell

Compton

Wiener

Fabry

Seyfert

Joliot

Fleming

Mendeleev

Keeler

Hertzsprung

Korolev

Crust of near side about 40 miles thick

Small inner core with a central temperature of 2,700°F

Crust of far side about 60 miles thick

Pasteur

Galois

Hilbert

Doppler

Tsiolkovsky

Milne

Montes Rook

Gagarin

Montes Cordillera

Jules Verne

Mendel

Roche

Van de Graaff

Apollo

Planck

Schrödinger

Zeeman

Von Kármàn

Leibnitz

Antoniadi

Mars

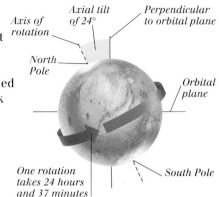

TILT AND ROTATION OF MARS

Axis of rotation

Axial tilt of 24°

Perpendicular to orbital plane

North Pole

Orbital plane

One rotation takes 24 hours and 37 minutes

South Pole

MARS

MARS, KNOWN AS THE RED PLANET, is the fourth planet from the Sun and the outermost rocky planet. In the 19th century, astronomers first observed what were thought to be signs of life on Mars. These signs included apparent canal-like markings on the surface, and dark patches that were thought to be vegetation. It is now known that the canals are an optical illusion and the dark patches are areas where the red dust that covers most of the planet has blown away. The fine dust particles are often whipped up by winds into dust storms that occasionally obscure almost all Mars's surface. Residual dust in the atmosphere gives the Martian sky a pinkish hue. The northern hemisphere of Mars has many large plains formed of solidified volcanic lava, while the southern hemisphere has many craters and large impact basins. There are also several huge, extinct volcanoes, including Olympus Mons, which at 370 miles wide and 15 miles high is the largest known volcano in the Solar System. The surface also has many canyons and branching channels. The canyons were formed by movements of the surface crust, but the channels are thought to have been formed by flowing water that has now vaporized almost completely and escaped from the atmosphere. The Martian atmosphere is much thinner than Earth's, with only a few clouds and morning mists. Mars has two tiny irregularly shaped moons, Phobos and Deimos. Their small size indicates that they may be asteroids that have been captured by the gravity of Mars.

SURFACE FEATURES OF MARS

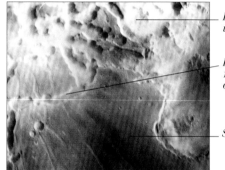

Bright water-ice fog

Fog in canyon about 12 miles wide at end of Valles Marineris

Syria Planum

NOCTIS LABYRINTHUS (CANYON SYSTEM)

Summit caldera consisting of overlapping collapsed volcanic craters

Crater

Gentle slope produced by lava flow

Cloud formation

OLYMPUS MONS (EXTINCT SHIELD VOLCANO)

THE SURFACE OF MARS

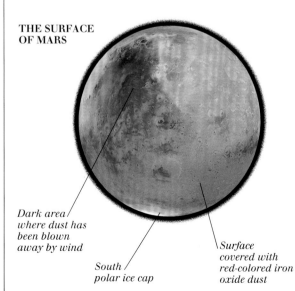

Dark area where dust has been blown away by wind

South polar ice cap

Surface covered with red-colored iron oxide dust

MOONS OF MARS

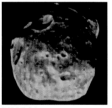

PHOBOS
Average diameter: 14 miles
Average distance from planet: 5,800 miles

DEIMOS
Average diameter: 8 miles
Average distance from planet: 14,600 miles

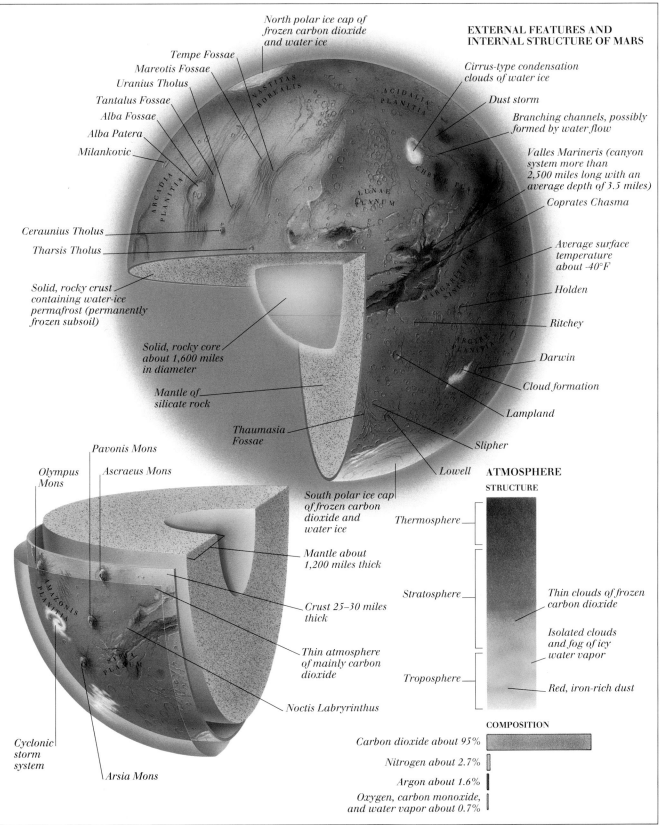

North polar ice cap of frozen carbon dioxide and water ice

EXTERNAL FEATURES AND INTERNAL STRUCTURE OF MARS

Tempe Fossae

Mareotis Fossae

Uranius Tholus

Tantalus Fossae

Alba Fossae

Alba Patera

Milankovic

Ceraunius Tholus

Tharsis Tholus

Cirrus-type condensation clouds of water ice

Dust storm

Branching channels, possibly formed by water flow

Valles Marineris (canyon system more than 2,500 miles long with an average depth of 3.5 miles)

Coprates Chasma

Average surface temperature about -40°F

Holden

Ritchey

Darwin

Cloud formation

Lampland

Slipher

Lowell

Solid, rocky crust containing water-ice permafrost (permanently frozen subsoil)

Solid, rocky core about 1,600 miles in diameter

Mantle of silicate rock

Thaumasia Fossae

South polar ice cap of frozen carbon dioxide and water ice

Olympus Mons

Pavonis Mons

Ascraeus Mons

Mantle about 1,200 miles thick

Crust 25–30 miles thick

Thin atmosphere of mainly carbon dioxide

Noctis Labryrinthus

Cyclonic storm system

Arsia Mons

ATMOSPHERE

STRUCTURE

Thermosphere

Stratosphere

Troposphere

Thin clouds of frozen carbon dioxide

Isolated clouds and fog of icy water vapor

Red, iron-rich dust

COMPOSITION

Carbon dioxide about 95%

Nitrogen about 2.7%

Argon about 1.6%

Oxygen, carbon monoxide, and water vapor about 0.7%

Jupiter

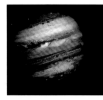

JUPITER

JUPITER IS THE FIFTH PLANET from the Sun and the first of the four gas giants. It is the largest and the most massive planet, with a diameter about 11 times that of the Earth and a mass about 2.5 times the combined mass of the eight other planets. Jupiter is thought to have a small rocky core surrounded by an inner mantle of metallic hydrogen (liquid hydrogen that acts like a metal). Outside the inner mantle is an outer mantle of liquid hydrogen and helium that merges into the gaseous atmosphere. Jupiter's rapid rate of rotation causes the clouds in its atmosphere to form belts and zones that encircle the planet parallel to the equator. Belts are dark, low-lying, relatively warm cloud layers. Zones are bright, high-altitude, cooler cloud layers. Within the belts and zones, turbulence causes the formation of cloud features such as white ovals and red spots, both of which are huge storm systems. The most prominent cloud feature is a storm called the Great Red Spot, which consists of a spiraling column of clouds three times wider than the Earth that rises about five miles above the upper cloud layer. Jupiter has one thin, faint, main ring, inside of which is a halo ring of tiny particles extending toward the planet. There are 16 known Jovian moons. The four largest moons (called the Galileans) are Ganymede, Callisto, Io, and Europa. Ganymede and Callisto are cratered and probably icy. Europa is smooth and icy and may contain water. Io is covered in bright red, orange, and yellow splotches. This coloring is caused by sulfurous material from active volcanoes that shoot plumes of lava hundreds of miles above the surface.

TILT AND ROTATION OF JUPITER

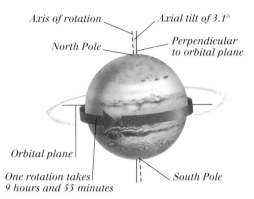

Axis of rotation
Axial tilt of 3.1°
North Pole
Perpendicular to orbital plane
Orbital plane
One rotation takes 9 hours and 55 minutes
South Pole

GREAT RED SPOT AND WHITE OVAL

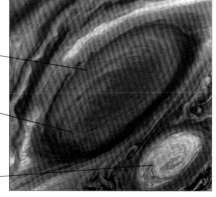

Great Red Spot (anticyclonic storm system)

Red color probably due to phosphorus

White oval (temporary anticyclonic storm system)

GALILEAN MOONS OF JUPITER

EUROPA
Diameter: 1,950 miles
Average distance from planet: 416,900 miles

CALLISTO
Diameter: 2,983 miles
Average distance from planet: 1,168,200 miles

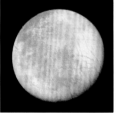

GANYMEDE
Diameter: 3,270 miles
Average distance from planet: 664,900 miles

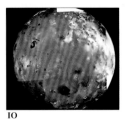

IO
Diameter: 2,263 miles
Average distance from planet: 262,100 miles

RINGS OF JUPITER

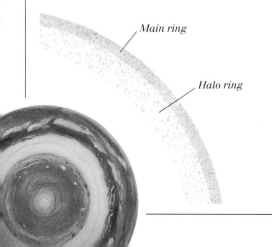

Main ring

Halo ring

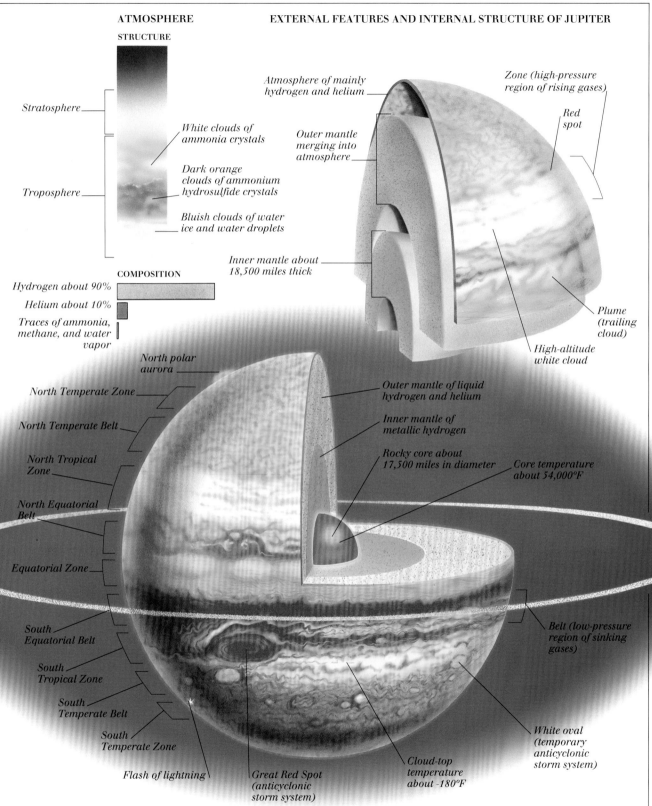

ATMOSPHERE

STRUCTURE

Stratosphere

Troposphere

White clouds of
ammonia crystals

Dark orange
clouds of ammonium
hydrosulfide crystals

Bluish clouds of water
ice and water droplets

COMPOSITION

Hydrogen about 90%

Helium about 10%

Traces of ammonia,
methane, and water
vapor

EXTERNAL FEATURES AND INTERNAL STRUCTURE OF JUPITER

Atmosphere of mainly
hydrogen and helium

Outer mantle
merging into
atmosphere

Inner mantle about
18,500 miles thick

Zone (high-pressure
region of rising gases)

Red
spot

Plume
(trailing
cloud)

High-altitude
white cloud

North polar
aurora

North Temperate Zone

North Temperate Belt

North Tropical
Zone

North Equatorial
Belt

Equatorial Zone

South
Equatorial Belt

South
Tropical Zone

South
Temperate Belt

South
Temperate Zone

Flash of lightning

Great Red Spot
(anticyclonic
storm system)

Outer mantle of liquid
hydrogen and helium

Inner mantle of
metallic hydrogen

Rocky core about
17,500 miles in diameter

Core temperature
about 54,000°F

Belt (low-pressure
region of sinking
gases)

White oval
(temporary
anticyclonic
storm system)

Cloud-top
temperature
about -180°F

45

Saturn

COLOR-ENHANCED IMAGE OF SATURN

SATURN IS THE SIXTH PLANET from the Sun. It is a gas giant almost as big as Jupiter, with an equatorial diameter of about 74,900 miles. Saturn is thought to consist of a small core of rock and ice surrounded by an inner mantle of metallic hydrogen (liquid hydrogen that acts like a metal). Outside the inner mantle is an outer mantle of liquid hydrogen that merges into a gaseous atmosphere. Saturn's clouds form belts and zones similar to those on Jupiter, but obscured by overlying haze. Storms and eddies, seen as red or white ovals, occur in the clouds. Saturn has an extremely thin but wide system of rings that is less than one mile thick but extends outward to about 260,000 miles from the planet's surface. The main rings comprise thousands of narrow ringlets, each made of icy lumps that range in size from tiny particles to chunks several yards across. The D, E, and G rings are very faint, the F ring is brighter, and the A, B, and C rings are bright enough to be seen from Earth with binoculars. Saturn has 18 known moons, some of which orbit inside the rings and are thought to exert a gravitational influence on the shapes of the rings. Unusually, seven of the moons are co-orbital—they share an orbit with another moon. Astronomers believe that such co-orbital moons may have originated from a single satellite that broke up.

TILT AND ROTATION OF SATURN

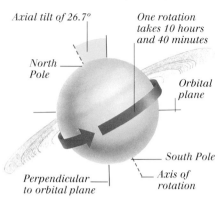

Axial tilt of 26.7°

One rotation takes 10 hours and 40 minutes

North Pole

Orbital plane

South Pole

Axis of rotation

Perpendicular to orbital plane

COLOR-ENHANCED IMAGE OF SATURN'S CLOUD FEATURES

Ribbon-shaped striation caused by winds of up to 335 mph

Oval (rotating storm system)

INNER RINGS OF SATURN

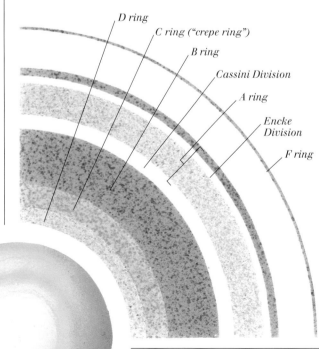

D ring

C ring ("crepe ring")

B ring

Cassini Division

A ring

Encke Division

F ring

MOONS OF SATURN

ENCELADUS
Diameter: 309 miles
Average distance from planet: 148,000 miles

TETHYS
Diameter: 652 miles
Average distance from planet: 183,000 miles

DIONE
Diameter: 695 miles
Average distance from planet: 234,000 miles

MIMAS
Diameter: 247 miles
Average distance from planet: 115,600 miles

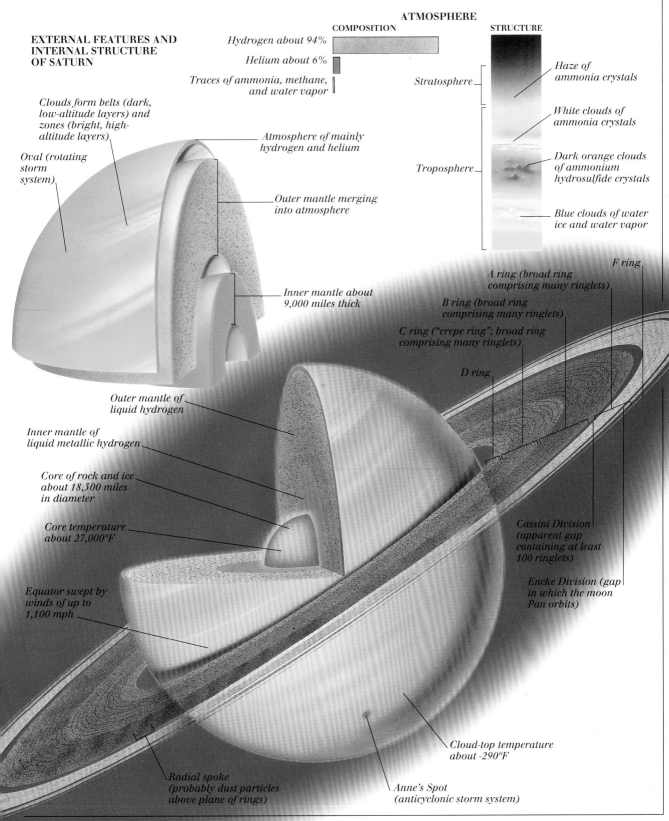

ATMOSPHERE

EXTERNAL FEATURES AND
INTERNAL STRUCTURE
OF SATURN

COMPOSITION

Hydrogen about 94%

Helium about 6%

Traces of ammonia, methane,
and water vapor

STRUCTURE

Stratosphere

Troposphere

Haze of
ammonia crystals

White clouds of
ammonia crystals

Dark orange clouds
of ammonium
hydrosulfide crystals

Blue clouds of water
ice and water vapor

Clouds form belts (dark,
low-altitude layers) and
zones (bright, high-
altitude layers)

Oval (rotating
storm
system)

Atmosphere of mainly
hydrogen and helium

Outer mantle merging
into atmosphere

Inner mantle about
9,000 miles thick

Outer mantle of
liquid hydrogen

Inner mantle of
liquid metallic hydrogen

Core of rock and ice
about 18,500 miles
in diameter

Core temperature
about 27,000°F

Equator swept by
winds of up to
1,100 mph

A ring (broad ring
comprising many ringlets)

B ring (broad ring
comprising many ringlets)

C ring ("crepe ring"; broad ring
comprising many ringlets)

D ring

F ring

Cassini Division
(apparent gap
containing at least
100 ringlets)

Encke Division (gap
in which the moon
Pan orbits)

Cloud-top temperature
about -290°F

Radial spoke
(probably dust particles
above plane of rings)

Anne's Spot
(anticyclonic storm system)

47

Uranus

COLOR-ENHANCED IMAGE OF URANUS

URANUS IS THE SEVENTH PLANET from the Sun and the third largest, with a diameter of about 32,000 miles. It is thought to consist of a dense mixture of different types of ice and gas around a solid core. Its atmosphere contains traces of methane, giving the planet a blue-green hue, and the temperature at the cloud tops is about -350°F. Uranus is the most featureless planet to have been closely observed: only a few icy clouds of methane have been seen so far. Uranus is unique among the planets in that its axis of rotation lies close to its orbital plane. As a result of its strongly tilted rotational axis, Uranus rolls on its side along its orbital path around the Sun, while other planets spin more or less upright. Uranus is encircled by 11 rings that consist of rocks interspersed with dust lanes. The rings contain some of the darkest matter in the Solar System. They are extremely narrow, making them difficult to detect: nine of them are less than six miles wide, whereas most of Saturn's rings are thousands of miles in width. There are 15 known Uranian moons, all of which are icy and most of which are farther out than the rings. The 10 inner moons are small and dark, with diameters of less than 100 miles, and the five outer moons are between about 290 and 1,000 miles in diameter. The outer moons have a wide variety of surface features. Miranda has the most varied surface, with cratered areas broken up by huge ridges and cliffs 12 miles high.

TILT AND ROTATION OF URANUS

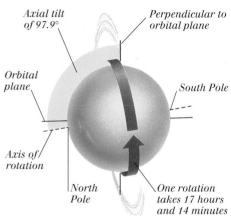

Axial tilt of 97.9°

Perpendicular to orbital plane

Orbital plane

South Pole

Axis of rotation

North Pole

One rotation takes 17 hours and 14 minutes

OUTER MOONS

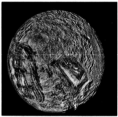

MIRANDA
Diameter: 293 miles
Average distance from planet: 80,700 miles

RINGS OF URANUS

Epsilon ring

Ring 1986 U1R

Delta ring

Gamma ring

Eta ring

Beta ring

Alpha ring

Rings 4 and 5

Ring 6

Ring 1986 U2R

RINGS AND DUST LANES

ARIEL
Diameter: 720 miles
Average distance from planet: 118,800 miles

TITANIA
Diameter: 981 miles
Average distance from planet: 270,900 miles

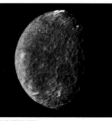

UMBRIEL
Diameter: 726 miles
Average distance from planet: 165,300 miles

OBERON
Diameter: 946 miles
Average distance from planet: 362,000 miles

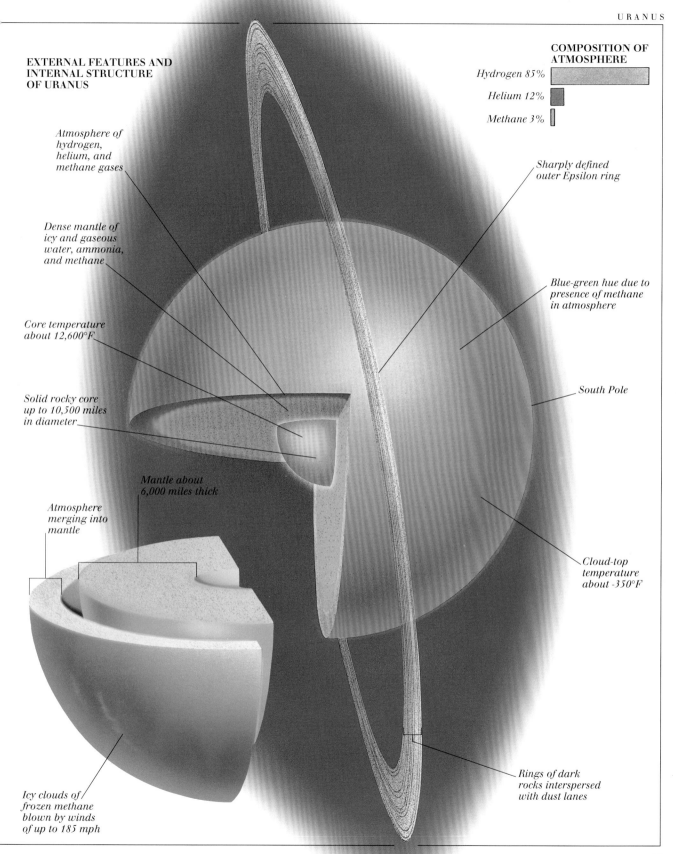

EXTERNAL FEATURES AND
INTERNAL STRUCTURE
OF URANUS

COMPOSITION OF
ATMOSPHERE

Hydrogen 85%

Helium 12%

Methane 3%

Atmosphere of
hydrogen,
helium, and
methane gases

Dense mantle of
icy and gaseous
water, ammonia,
and methane

Core temperature
about 12,600°F

Solid rocky core
up to 10,500 miles
in diameter

Mantle about
6,000 miles thick

Atmosphere
merging into
mantle

Icy clouds of
frozen methane
blown by winds
of up to 185 mph

Sharply defined
outer Epsilon ring

Blue-green hue due to
presence of methane
in atmosphere

South Pole

Cloud-top
temperature
about -350°F

Rings of dark
rocks interspersed
with dust lanes

Neptune and Pluto

**COLOR-ENHANCED
IMAGE OF NEPTUNE**

NEPTUNE AND PLUTO are the two farthest planets from the Sun, at an average distance of about 2,800 million miles and 3,700 million miles, respectively. Neptune is a gas giant and is thought to consist of a small rocky core surrounded by a mixture of liquids and gases. The atmosphere contains several prominent cloud features. The largest of these are the Great Dark Spot, which is as wide as the Earth, the Small Dark Spot, and the Scooter. The Great and Small Dark Spots are huge storms that are swept around the planet by winds of about 1,200 miles per hour. The Scooter is a large area of cirrus cloud. Neptune has four tenuous rings and eight known moons. Triton is the largest Neptunian moon and the coldest object in the Solar System, with a temperature of -391°F. Unlike most moons in the Solar System, Triton orbits its mother planet in the opposite direction to the planet's rotation. Pluto is usually the outermost planet, but its elliptical orbit causes it to pass inside the orbit of Neptune for 20 years of its 248-year orbit. Pluto is so small and distant that little is known about it. It is a rocky planet, probably covered with ice and frozen methane. Pluto's only known moon, Charon, is large for a moon, at half the size of its parent planet. Because of the small difference in their sizes, Pluto and Charon are sometimes considered to be a double-planet system.

TILT AND ROTATION OF NEPTUNE

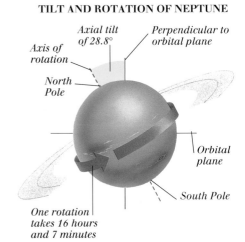

Axial tilt of 28.8°

Perpendicular to orbital plane

Axis of rotation

North Pole

Orbital plane

South Pole

One rotation takes 16 hours and 7 minutes

CLOUD FEATURES OF NEPTUNE

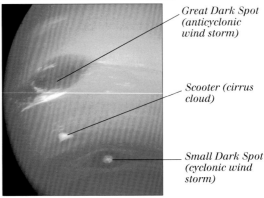

Great Dark Spot (anticyclonic wind storm)

Scooter (cirrus cloud)

Small Dark Spot (cyclonic wind storm)

HIGH-ALTITUDE CLOUDS

Methane cirrus clouds 25 miles above main cloud deck

Cloud shadow

Main cloud deck blown by winds at speeds of about 1,200 mph

RINGS OF NEPTUNE

Adams ring

Plateau

Le Verrier ring

Galle ring

MOONS OF NEPTUNE

TRITON
Diameter: 1,681 miles
Average distance from planet: 220,500 miles

PROTEUS
Diameter: 259 miles
Average distance from planet: 73,100 miles

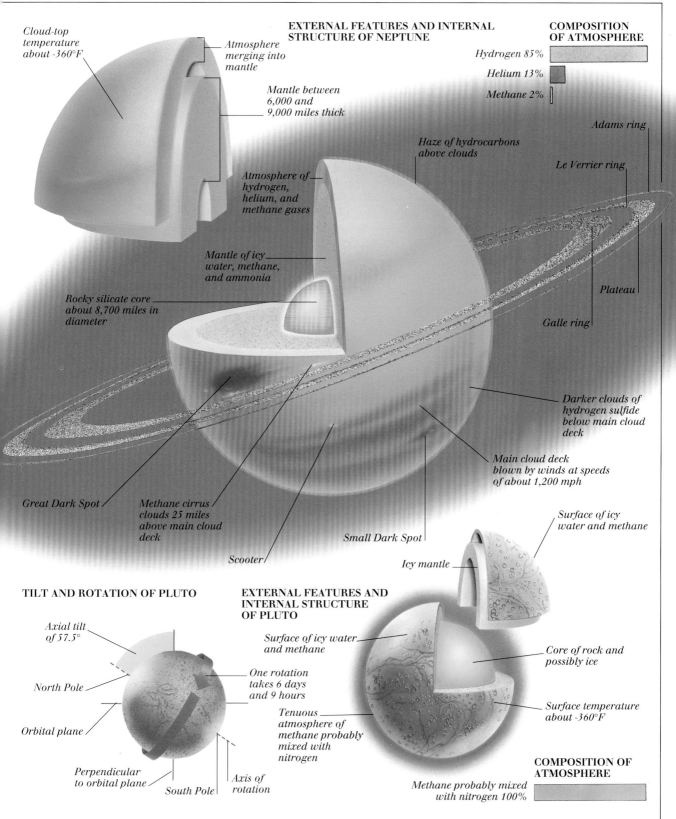

EXTERNAL FEATURES AND INTERNAL STRUCTURE OF NEPTUNE

COMPOSITION OF ATMOSPHERE

Hydrogen 85%

Helium 13%

Methane 2%

Cloud-top temperature about -360°F

Atmosphere merging into mantle

Mantle between 6,000 and 9,000 miles thick

Haze of hydrocarbons above clouds

Adams ring

Le Verrier ring

Atmosphere of hydrogen, helium, and methane gases

Mantle of icy water, methane, and ammonia

Rocky silicate core about 8,700 miles in diameter

Plateau

Galle ring

Darker clouds of hydrogen sulfide below main cloud deck

Main cloud deck blown by winds at speeds of about 1,200 mph

Great Dark Spot

Methane cirrus clouds 25 miles above main cloud deck

Scooter

Small Dark Spot

Surface of icy water and methane

Icy mantle

TILT AND ROTATION OF PLUTO

EXTERNAL FEATURES AND INTERNAL STRUCTURE OF PLUTO

Axial tilt of 57.5°

North Pole

Orbital plane

Perpendicular to orbital plane

South Pole

Axis of rotation

One rotation takes 6 days and 9 hours

Surface of icy water and methane

Tenuous atmosphere of methane probably mixed with nitrogen

Core of rock and possibly ice

Surface temperature about -360°F

COMPOSITION OF ATMOSPHERE

Methane probably mixed with nitrogen 100%

Asteroids, comets, and meteoroids

ASTEROID 951 GASPRA

ASTEROIDS, COMETS, AND METEOROIDS are all debris remaining from the nebula in which the Solar System formed 4.6 billion years ago. Asteroids are rocky bodies up to several hundred miles in diameter, although most are much smaller. Most of them orbit the Sun in the asteroid belt, which lies between the orbits of Mars and Jupiter. Comets may originate in a huge cloud, called the Oort Cloud, that is thought to surround the Solar System. They are made of frozen gases and dust, and are a few miles in diameter. Occasionally, a comet is deflected from the Oort Cloud to orbit the Sun in a long, elliptical path. As the comet approaches the Sun, the comet's surface starts to vaporize in the heat, producing a brightly shining coma (a huge sphere of gas and dust around the nucleus), a gas tail, and a dust tail. Meteoroids are small chunks of stone or stone and iron, some of which are fragments of asteroids or comets. Meteoroids range in size from tiny dust particles to objects tens of yards across. If a meteoroid enters the Earth's atmosphere, it is heated by friction and appears as a glowing streak of light called a meteor (also known as a shooting star). Meteor showers occur when the Earth passes through the trail of dust particles left by a comet. Most meteors burn up in the atmosphere. The few that are large enough to reach the Earth's surface are termed meteorites.

OPTICAL IMAGE OF HALLEY'S COMET

COLOR-ENHANCED IMAGE OF HALLEY'S COMET

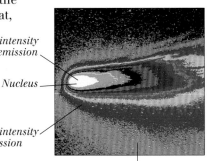

High-intensity light emission

Nucleus

Medium-intensity light emission

Low-intensity light emission

COLOR-ENHANCED IMAGE OF A LEONID METEOR SHOWER

METEORITES

DEVELOPMENT OF COMET TAILS

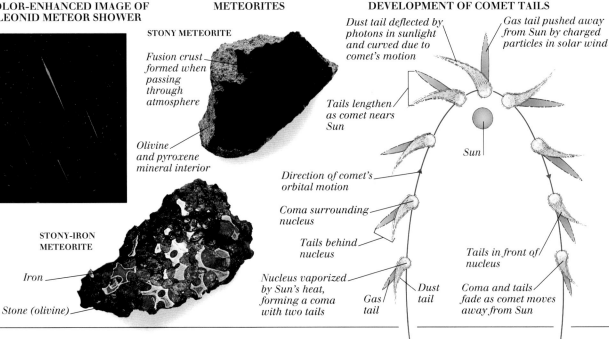

STONY METEORITE

Fusion crust formed when passing through atmosphere

Olivine and pyroxene mineral interior

STONY-IRON METEORITE

Iron

Stone (olivine)

Dust tail deflected by photons in sunlight and curved due to comet's motion

Gas tail pushed away from Sun by charged particles in solar wind

Tails lengthen as comet nears Sun

Sun

Direction of comet's orbital motion

Coma surrounding nucleus

Tails behind nucleus

Nucleus vaporized by Sun's heat, forming a coma with two tails

Gas tail

Dust tail

Tails in front of nucleus

Coma and tails fade as comet moves away from Sun

FEATURES OF A COMET

Thin, straight
gas tail

Broad, curved
dust tail

Gas molecules
heated by Sun
and emitting
light

Comet tails up to
62 million miles long

Thin, straight gas
tail blown by
solar wind

Head (coma and nucleus)

Coma
surrounding
nucleus

Nucleus a few
miles across

**STRUCTURE OF
A COMET**

Glowing coma
up to 600,000
miles across
surrounding
nucleus

Possible
core of
silicate
dust

Crust
with active
areas emitting
jets of gas
and dust

Jet of gas
and dust produced
by vaporization on
sunlit side of nucleus

Ices, including
water ice, and frozen carbon
dioxide, methane, and ammonia

Broad dust
tail curved along
comet's orbital path

Dust particles
reflecting sunlight

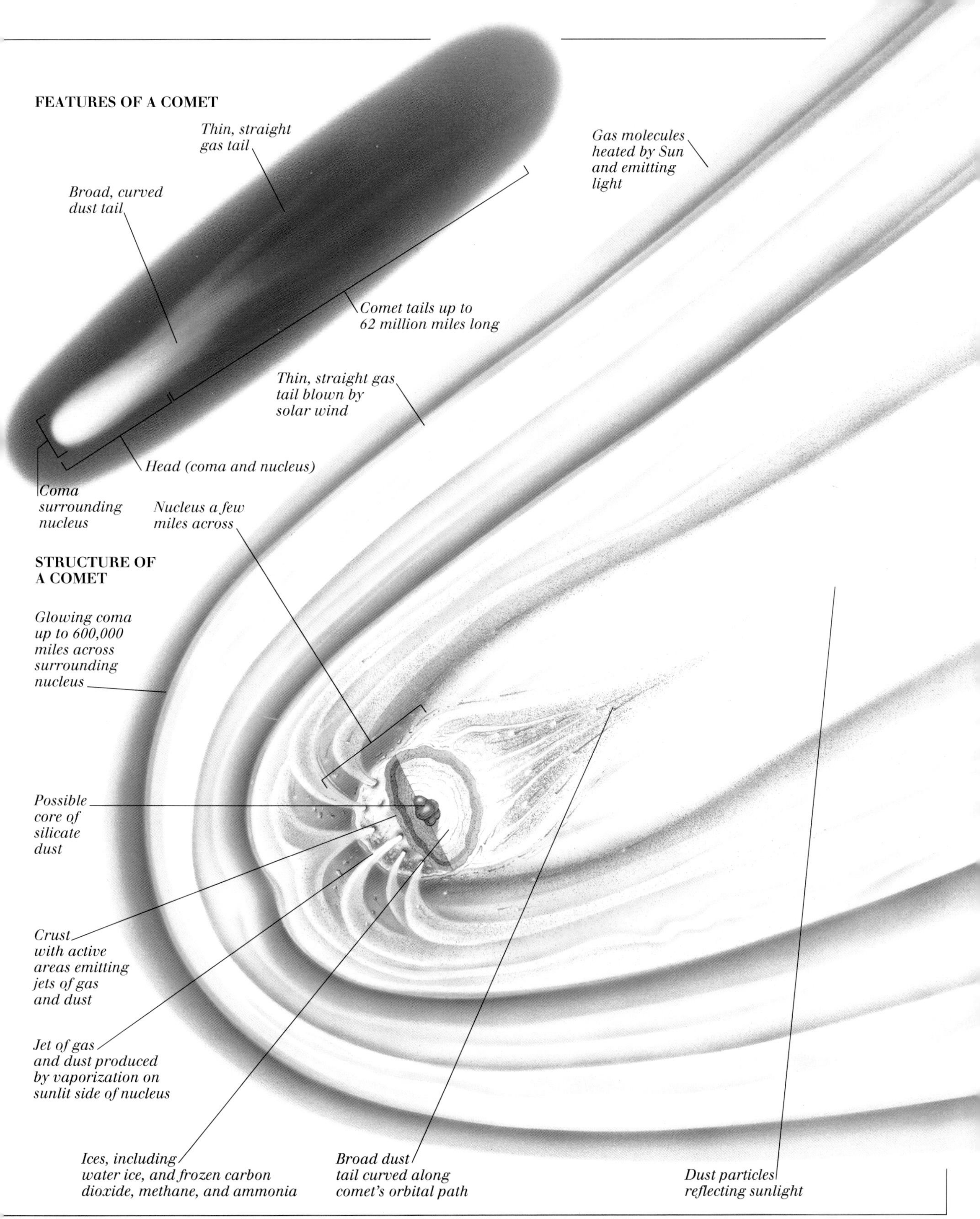

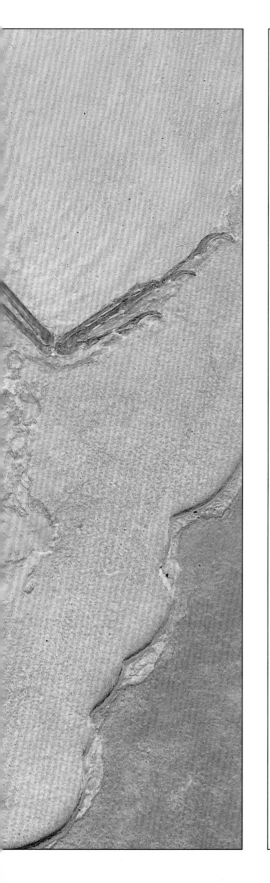

PREHISTORIC EARTH

The changing Earth

THE EARTH FORMED FROM A CLOUD OF DUST and gas drifting through space about 4,600 million years ago. Dense minerals sank to the center while lighter ones formed a thin rocky crust. However, the first known life forms—bacteria and blue-green algae—did not appear until about 3,400 million years ago, and it was only about 700 million years ago that more complex plants and animals began to develop. Since then, thousands of animal and plant species have evolved. Some, such as the dinosaurs, survived for millions of years, while others died out quickly. The Earth itself is continually changing. Although continents neared their present locations about 50 million years ago, they are still drifting slowly over the planet's surface, and mountain ranges such as the Himalayas—which began to form 40 million years ago—are continually being built up and worn away. Climate is also subject to change: the Earth has undergone a series of ice ages interspersed with warmer periods (the most recent ice age was at its height about 20,000 years ago).

Small mammals appeared (e.g., Crusafontia)

Dinosaurs became extinct

Global mountain building occurred

Multicellular soft-bodied animals appeared (e.g., worms and jellyfish)

Shelled invertebrates appeared (e.g., trilobites)

Marine plants flourished

Land plants appeared (e.g., Cooksonia)

Unicellular organisms appeared (e.g., blue-green algae)

CRETACEOUS

ORDOVICIAN

CAMBRIAN

PRECAMBRIAN TIME

SILURIAN

DEVONIAN

Earth formed

Coral reefs appeared

Vertebrates appeared (e.g., Hemicyclaspis)

More complex types of algae appeared

Amphibians appeared (e.g., Ichthyostega)

GEOLOGICAL TIMESCALE

MILLIONS OF
YEARS AGO (MYA)

4,600	570	510	439	409	363	323	290

					MISSISSIPPIAN (NORTH AMERICA)	PENNSYLVANIAN (NORTH AMERICA)
	CAMBRIAN	ORDOVICIAN	SILURIAN	DEVONIAN	CARBONIFEROUS	
PRECAMBRIAN TIME	PALEOZOIC					

EVOLUTION OF THE EARTH

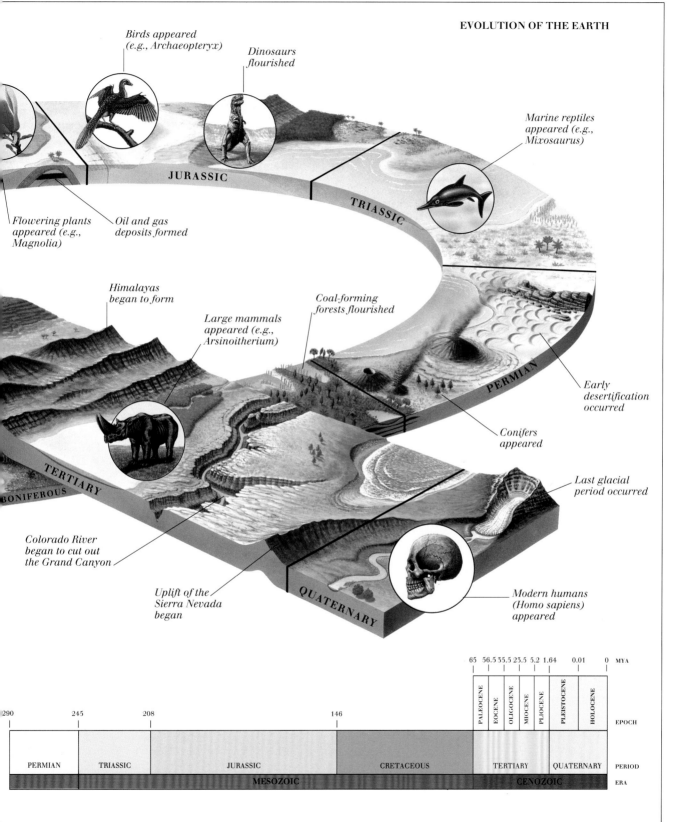

Birds appeared
(e.g., Archaeopteryx)

Dinosaurs
flourished

Marine reptiles
appeared (e.g.,
Mixosaurus)

JURASSIC

TRIASSIC

Flowering plants
appeared (e.g.,
Magnolia)

Oil and gas
deposits formed

Himalayas
began to form

Large mammals
appeared (e.g.,
Arsinoitherium)

Coal-forming
forests flourished

PERMIAN

Early
desertification
occurred

Conifers
appeared

TERTIARY

BONIFEROUS

Last glacial
period occurred

Colorado River
began to cut out
the Grand Canyon

Uplift of the
Sierra Nevada
began

QUATERNARY

Modern humans
(Homo sapiens)
appeared

	65	56.5	35.5	23.5	5.2	1.64		0.01	0	MYA
	PALEOCENE	EOCENE	OLIGOCENE	MIOCENE	PLIOCENE	PLEISTOCENE		HOLOCENE		EPOCH

290	245	208	146				
PERMIAN	TRIASSIC	JURASSIC	CRETACEOUS	TERTIARY	QUATERNARY		PERIOD
	MESOZOIC			CENOZOIC			ERA

The Earth's crust

THE EARTH'S CRUST IS THE SOLID outer shell of the Earth. It includes continental crust (about 25 miles thick) and oceanic crust (about four miles thick). The crust and the topmost layer of the mantle form the lithosphere. The lithosphere consists of semi-rigid plates that move relative to each other on the underlying asthenosphere (a partly molten layer of the mantle). This movement is known as plate tectonics and helps explain continental drift. Where two plates move apart, there are rifts in the crust. In mid-ocean, this movement results in seafloor spreading and the formation of ocean ridges; on continents, crustal spreading can form rift valleys. When plates move toward each other, one may be subducted beneath (forced under) the other. In mid-ocean, this causes ocean trenches, seismic activity, and arcs of volcanic islands. Where oceanic crust is subducted beneath continental crust or where continents collide, land may be uplifted and mountains formed (see pp. 62–63). Plates may also slide past each other—along the San Andreas fault, for example. Crustal movement on continents may result in earthquakes, while movement under the seabed can lead to tidal waves.

ELEMENTS IN THE EARTH'S CRUST

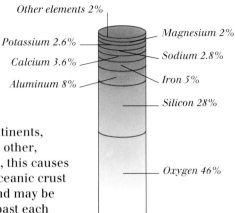

Other elements 2%
Potassium 2.6%
Calcium 3.6%
Aluminum 8%
Magnesium 2%
Sodium 2.8%
Iron 5%
Silicon 28%
Oxygen 46%

FEATURES OF PLATE MOVEMENTS

Ridge where magma is rising to form new oceanic crust

Region of seafloor spreading

Ocean trench formed where oceanic crust is forced under continental crust

Subduction zone

Rift formed where two plates are moving apart

Magma (molten rock) erupts at rift

Magma rises to form a hot spot

Volcano develops over hot spot and builds up to form an island

Volcanic island that originally formed over hot spot

Oceanic crust melts

Magma rises to form a volcano

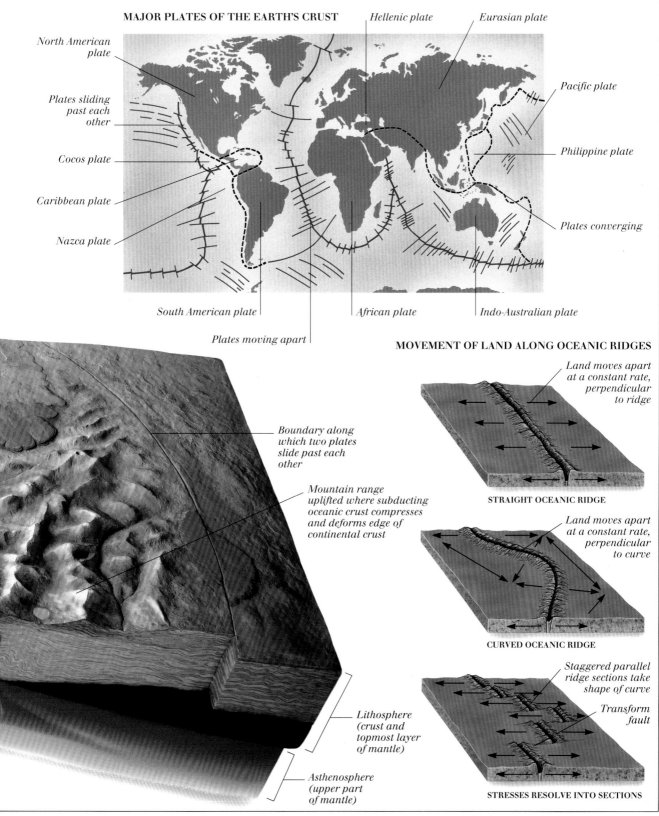

MAJOR PLATES OF THE EARTH'S CRUST

Hellenic plate

Eurasian plate

North American plate

Plates sliding past each other

Cocos plate

Caribbean plate

Nazca plate

Pacific plate

Philippine plate

Plates converging

South American plate

African plate

Indo-Australian plate

Plates moving apart

Boundary along which two plates slide past each other

Mountain range uplifted where subducting oceanic crust compresses and deforms edge of continental crust

Lithosphere (crust and topmost layer of mantle)

Asthenosphere (upper part of mantle)

MOVEMENT OF LAND ALONG OCEANIC RIDGES

Land moves apart at a constant rate, perpendicular to ridge

STRAIGHT OCEANIC RIDGE

Land moves apart at a constant rate, perpendicular to curve

CURVED OCEANIC RIDGE

Staggered parallel ridge sections take shape of curve

Transform fault

STRESSES RESOLVE INTO SECTIONS

Faults and folds

THE CONTINUOUS MOVEMENT of the Earth's crustal plates (see pp. 58–59) can squeeze, stretch, or break rock strata, deforming them and producing faults and folds. A fault is a fracture in a rock along which there is movement of one side relative to the other. The movement can be vertical, horizontal, or oblique (vertical and horizontal). Faults develop when rocks are subjected to compression or tension. They tend to occur in hard, rigid rocks, which are more likely to break than bend. The smallest faults occur in single mineral crystals and are microscopically small, while the largest —the Great Rift Valley in Africa, which formed between 5 million and 100,000 years ago—is more than 6,000 miles long. A fold is a bend in a rock layer caused by compression. Folds occur in elastic rocks, which tend to bend rather than break. The two main types of fold are anticlines (upfolds) and synclines (downfolds). Folds vary in size from a few millimeters long to folded mountain ranges hundreds of miles long, such as the Himalayas (see pp. 62–63) and the Alps, which are repeatedly folding. In addition to faults and folds, other features associated with rock deformations include boudins, mullions, and *en échelon* fractures.

STRUCTURE OF A FOLD

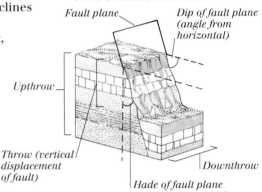

Axial plane

Crest

Limb

Angle of plunge

Hingeline

STRUCTURE OF A FAULT

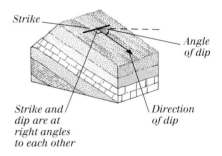

Fault plane

Dip of fault plane (angle from horizontal)

Upthrow

Throw (vertical displacement of fault)

Downthrow

Hade of fault plane (angle from vertical)

STRUCTURE OF A SLOPE

Strike

Angle of dip

Strike and dip are at right angles to each other

Direction of dip

FOLDED ROCK

Steeply dipping limbs

Crest of anticline

Plunge

SECTION THROUGH FOLDED ROCK STRATA THAT HAVE BEEN ERODED

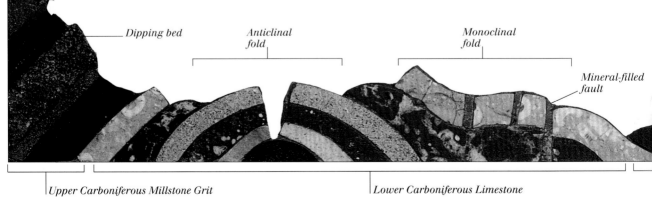

Dipping bed

Anticlinal fold

Monoclinal fold

Mineral-filled fault

Upper Carboniferous Millstone Grit

Lower Carboniferous Limestone

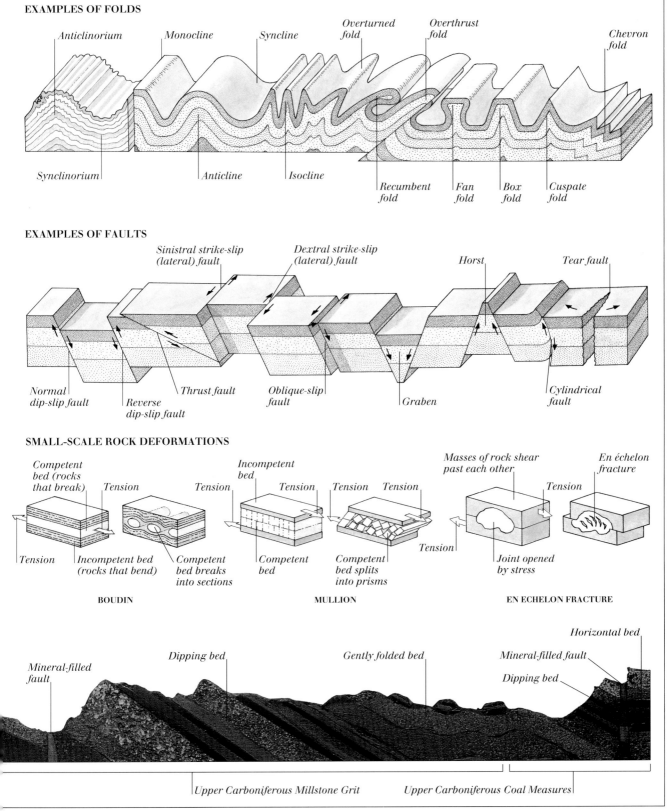

EXAMPLES OF FOLDS

Anticlinorium
Monocline
Syncline
Overturned fold
Overthrust fold
Chevron fold

Synclinorium
Anticline
Isocline
Recumbent fold
Fan fold
Box fold
Cuspate fold

EXAMPLES OF FAULTS

Sinistral strike-slip (lateral) fault
Dextral strike-slip (lateral) fault
Horst
Tear fault

Normal dip-slip fault
Reverse dip-slip fault
Thrust fault
Oblique-slip fault
Graben
Cylindrical fault

SMALL-SCALE ROCK DEFORMATIONS

Competent bed (rocks that break)
Tension
Incompetent bed
Tension
Tension
Masses of rock shear past each other
En échelon fracture
Tension

Tension
Incompetent bed (rocks that bend)
Competent bed breaks into sections
Competent bed
Competent bed splits into prisms
Tension
Joint opened by stress

BOUDIN
MULLION
EN ECHELON FRACTURE

Mineral-filled fault
Dipping bed
Gently folded bed
Horizontal bed
Mineral-filled fault
Dipping bed

Upper Carboniferous Millstone Grit
Upper Carboniferous Coal Measures

61

Mountain building

THE PROCESSES INVOLVED in mountain building—termed orogenesis—occur
as a result of the movement of the Earth's crustal plates (see pp. 58-59).
There are three main types of mountains: volcanic mountains, fold mountains,
and block mountains. Most volcanic mountains have been formed along plate
boundaries where plates have come together or moved apart and
lava and other debris have been ejected onto the Earth's surface.
The lava and debris may have built up to form a dome around the
vent of a volcano. Fold mountains are formed where plates push
together and cause the rock to buckle
upward. Where oceanic crust meets
less dense continental crust, the oceanic
crust is forced under the continental
crust. The continental crust is buckled by the
impact. This is how folded mountain ranges,
such as the Appalachian Mountains in North
America, were formed. Fold mountains are also
formed where two areas of continental crust meet.
The Himalayas, for example, began to form when
India collided with Asia, buckling the sediments
and parts of the oceanic crust between them. Block mountains are formed
when a block of land is uplifted between two faults as a result of compression or tension
in the Earth's crust (see pp. 60-61). Often, the movement along faults has taken place
gradually over millions of years. However, two plates may cause an earthquake by
suddenly sliding past each other along a faultline.

**BHAGIRATHI PARBAT,
HIMALAYAS**

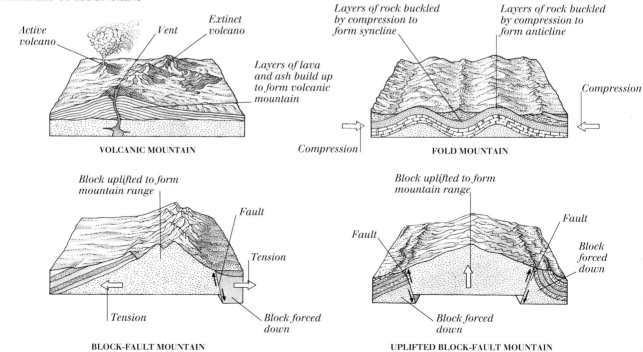

Asia

*Himalayas
formed by
buckling of
sediment and
part of the
oceanic crust
between two
colliding
continents*

*India moves
north*

*India collides
with Asia about 40
million years ago*

EXAMPLES OF MOUNTAINS

*Active
volcano*

Vent

*Extinct
volcano*

*Layers of lava
and ash build up
to form volcanic
mountain*

VOLCANIC MOUNTAIN

*Layers of rock buckled
by compression to
form syncline*

*Layers of rock buckled
by compression to
form anticline*

Compression

Compression

FOLD MOUNTAIN

*Block uplifted to form
mountain range*

Fault

Tension

Tension

*Block forced
down*

BLOCK-FAULT MOUNTAIN

*Block uplifted to form
mountain range*

Fault

Fault

*Block
forced
down*

*Block forced
down*

UPLIFTED BLOCK-FAULT MOUNTAIN

STAGES IN THE FORMATION OF THE HIMALAYAS

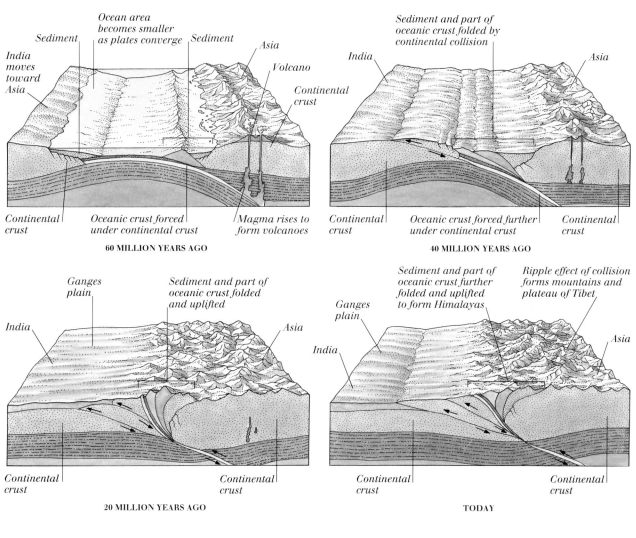

Sediment

Ocean area
becomes smaller
as plates converge

Sediment

Asia

India
moves
toward
Asia

Volcano

Continental
crust

Continental
crust

Oceanic crust forced
under continental crust

Magma rises to
form volcanoes

60 MILLION YEARS AGO

Sediment and part of
oceanic crust folded by
continental collision

India

Asia

Continental
crust

Oceanic crust forced further
under continental crust

Continental
crust

40 MILLION YEARS AGO

Ganges
plain

Sediment and part of
oceanic crust folded
and uplifted

India

Asia

Continental
crust

Continental
crust

20 MILLION YEARS AGO

Sediment and part of
oceanic crust further
folded and uplifted
to form Himalayas

Ripple effect of collision
forms mountains and
plateau of Tibet

Ganges
plain

India

Asia

Continental
crust

Continental
crust

TODAY

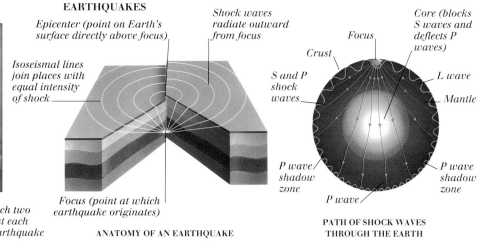

SAN ANDREAS FAULT

Faultline along which two
plates may slide past each
other, causing an earthquake

EARTHQUAKES

Epicenter (point on Earth's
surface directly above focus)

Shock waves
radiate outward
from focus

Isoseismal lines
join places with
equal intensity
of shock

Focus (point at which
earthquake originates)

ANATOMY OF AN EARTHQUAKE

Core (blocks
S waves and
deflects P
waves)

Focus

Crust

L wave

S and P
shock
waves

Mantle

P wave
shadow
zone

P wave
shadow
zone

P wave

**PATH OF SHOCK WAVES
THROUGH THE EARTH**

Precambrian to Devonian periods

WHEN THE EARTH FORMED about 4,600 million years ago, its atmosphere consisted of volcanic gases with little oxygen, making it hostile to most forms of life. One large supercontinent, Gondwanaland, was situated over the southern polar region, while other smaller continents were spread over the rest of the world. Constant movement of the earth's crustal plates carried continents across the earth's surface. The first primitive life-forms emerged around 3,400 million years ago in shallow, warm seas. The build up of oxygen began to form a shield of ozone around the earth, protecting living organisms from the sun's harmful rays and helping to establish an atmosphere in which life could sustain itself. The first vertebrates appeared about 470 million years ago, during the Ordovician period (510–439 million years ago), the first land plants appeared around 400 million years ago during the Devonian period (409–363 million years ago), and the first land animals about 30 million years later.

MIDDLE ORDOVICIAN POSITIONS OF PRESENT-DAY LANDMASSES

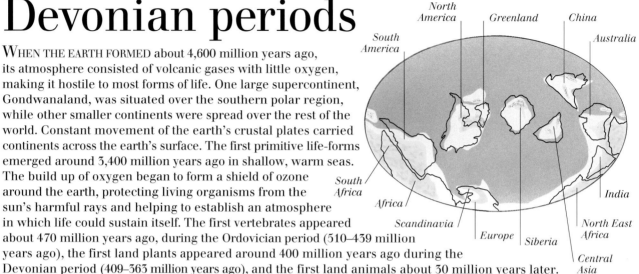

North America · Greenland · China · South America · Australia · South Africa · Africa · Scandinavia · Europe · Siberia · India · North East Africa · Central Asia

EXAMPLES OF PRECAMBRIAN TO DEVONIAN PLANT GROUPS

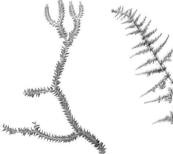

A PRESENT-DAY CLUBMOSS
(*Lycopodium sp.*)

A PRESENT-DAY LAND PLANT
(*Asparagus setaceous*)

FOSSIL OF AN EXTINCT LAND PLANT
(*Cooksonia hemisphaerica*)

FOSSIL OF AN EXTINCT SWAMP PLANT
(*Zosterophyllum llanoveranum*)

EXAMPLES OF PRECAMBRIAN TO DEVONIAN TRILOBITES

ACADAGNOSTUS
Family: Agnostidae
Length: $\frac{1}{3}$ in (8 mm)

PHACOPS
Family: Phacopidae
Length: $1\frac{3}{4}$ in (4.5 cm)

OLENELLUS
Family: Olenellidae
Length: $2\frac{1}{2}$ in (6 cm)

ELRATHIA
Family: Ptychopariidae
Length: $\frac{3}{4}$ in (2 cm)

THE EARTH DURING THE MIDDLE ORDOVICIAN PERIOD

EXAMPLES OF EARLY MARINE INVERTEBRATES

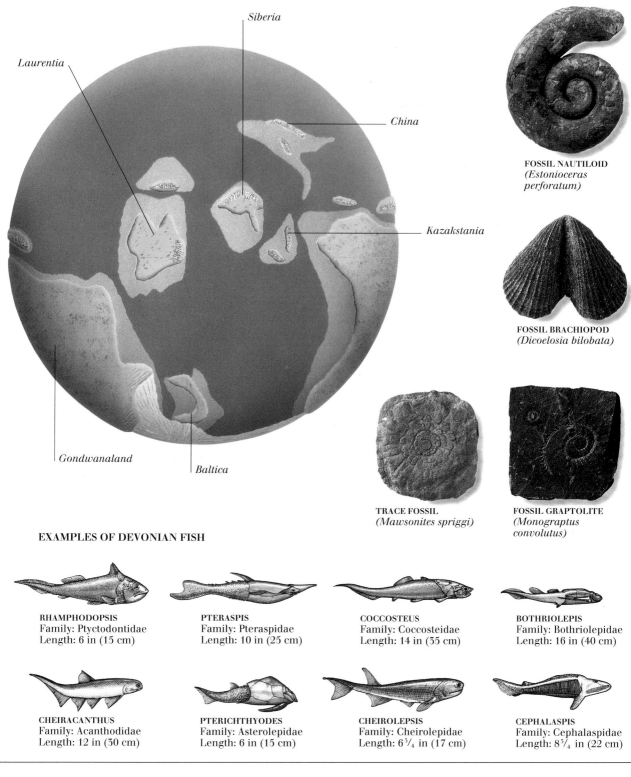

Siberia

Laurentia

China

Kazakstania

Gondwanaland

Baltica

FOSSIL NAUTILOID
(*Estonioceras perforatum*)

FOSSIL BRACHIOPOD
(*Dicoelosia bilobata*)

TRACE FOSSIL
(*Mawsonites spriggi*)

FOSSIL GRAPTOLITE
(*Monograptus convolutus*)

EXAMPLES OF DEVONIAN FISH

RHAMPHODOPSIS
Family: Ptyctodontidae
Length: 6 in (15 cm)

PTERASPIS
Family: Pteraspidae
Length: 10 in (25 cm)

COCCOSTEUS
Family: Coccosteidae
Length: 14 in (35 cm)

BOTHRIOLEPIS
Family: Bothriolepidae
Length: 16 in (40 cm)

CHEIRACANTHUS
Family: Acanthodidae
Length: 12 in (30 cm)

PTERICHTHYODES
Family: Asterolepidae
Length: 6 in (15 cm)

CHEIROLEPIS
Family: Cheirolepidae
Length: 6³/₄ in (17 cm)

CEPHALASPIS
Family: Cephalaspidae
Length: 8³/₄ in (22 cm)

Carboniferous to Permian periods

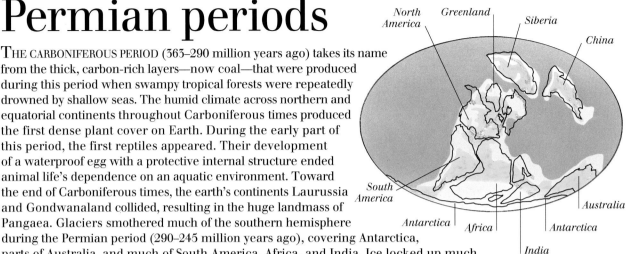

North America
Greenland
Siberia
China
South America
Antarctica
Africa
India
Australia
Antarctica

THE CARBONIFEROUS PERIOD (363–290 million years ago) takes its name from the thick, carbon-rich layers—now coal—that were produced during this period when swampy tropical forests were repeatedly drowned by shallow seas. The humid climate across northern and equatorial continents throughout Carboniferous times produced the first dense plant cover on Earth. During the early part of this period, the first reptiles appeared. Their development of a waterproof egg with a protective internal structure ended animal life's dependence on an aquatic environment. Toward the end of Carboniferous times, the earth's continents Laurussia and Gondwanaland collided, resulting in the huge landmass of Pangaea. Glaciers smothered much of the southern hemisphere during the Permian period (290–245 million years ago), covering Antarctica, parts of Australia, and much of South America, Africa, and India. Ice locked up much of the world's water and large areas of the northern hemisphere experienced a drop in sea-level. Away from the poles, deserts and a hot dry climate predominated. As a result of these conditions, the Permian period ended with the greatest mass extinction of life on earth ever.

EXAMPLES OF CARBONIFEROUS AND PERMIAN PLANT GROUPS

A PRESENT-DAY FIR
(Abies concolor)

FOSSIL OF AN EXTINCT FERN
(Zeilleria frenzlii)

**FOSSIL OF AN
EXTINCT HORSETAIL**
(Equisetites sp.)

**FOSSIL OF AN
EXTINCT CLUBMOSS**
(Lepidodendron sp.)

EXAMPLES OF CARBONIFEROUS AND PERMIAN TREES

PECOPTERIS
Family: Marattiaceae
Height: 13 ft (4 m)

PARIPTERIS
Family: Medullosaceae
Height: 16 ft 6 in (5 m)

MARIOPTERIS
Family: Unclassified
Height: 16 ft 6 in (5 m)

MEDULLOSA
Family: Medullosaceae
Height: 16 ft 6 in (5 m)

THE EARTH DURING THE LATE CARBONIFEROUS PERIOD

EXAMPLES OF CARBONIFEROUS AND PERMIAN ANIMALS

Siberia

Laurussia

China

Ural Mountains

Caledonian Mountains

Appalachian Mountains

Gondwanaland

SKULL OF AN EXTINCT SYNAPSID REPTILE
(Dimetrodon loomisi)

FOSSIL TEETH OF AN EXTINCT SHARK
(Helicoprion bessonowi)

MODEL OF AN EXTINCT CARBONIFEROUS REPTILE
(Westlothiana lizziae)

LEPIDODENDRON
Family: Lepidodendraceae
Height: 100 ft (30 m)

CORDAITES
Family: Cordaitacea
Height: 33 ft (10 m)

GLOSSOPTERIS
Family: Glossopteridaceae
Height: 26 ft (8 m)

ALETHOPTERIS
Family Medullosaceae
Height: 16 ft 6 in (5 m)

Triassic period

THE TRIASSIC PERIOD (245–208 million years ago) marked the beginning of what is known as the Age of the Dinosaurs (the Mesozoic era). During this period, the present-day continents were massed together, forming one huge continent known as Pangaea. This landmass experienced extremes of climate, with lush green areas around the coast or by lakes and rivers, and arid deserts in the interior. The only forms of plant life were nonflowering plants, such as conifers, ferns, cycads, and ginkgos; flowering plants had not yet evolved. The principal forms of animal life included primitive amphibians, rhynchosaurs ("beaked lizards"), and primitive crocodilians. Dinosaurs first appeared about 230 million years ago, at the beginning of the Late Triassic period. The earliest known dinosaurs were the carnivorous (flesh-eating) herrerasaurids and staurikosaurids, such as *Herrerasaurus* and *Staurikosaurus*. Early herbivorous (plant-eating) dinosaurs first appeared in Late Triassic times and included *Plateosaurus* and *Technosaurus*. By the end of the Triassic period, dinosaurs dominated Pangaea, possibly contributing to the extinction of many other reptiles.

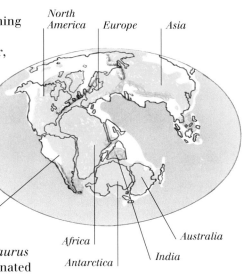

North America
Europe
Asia
South America
Africa
Antarctica
India
Australia

EXAMPLES OF TRIASSIC PLANT GROUPS

A PRESENT-DAY CYCAD
(*Cycas revoluta*)

A PRESENT-DAY GINKGO
(*Ginkgo biloba*)

A PRESENT-DAY CONIFER
(*Araucaria araucana*)

FOSSIL OF AN EXTINCT FERN
(*Pachypteris* sp.)

FOSSIL LEAF OF AN EXTINCT CYCAD
(*Cycas* sp.)

EXAMPLES OF TRIASSIC DINOSAURS

MELANOROSAURUS
A melanorosaurid
Length: 40 ft (12.2 m)

MUSSAURUS
A plateosaurid
Length: 6 ft 6 in–10 ft (2–3 m)

HERRERASAURUS
A herrerasaurid
Length: 10 ft (3 m)

PISANOSAURUS
A primitive ornithischian
Length: 3 ft (90 cm)

THE EARTH DURING THE TRIASSIC PERIOD

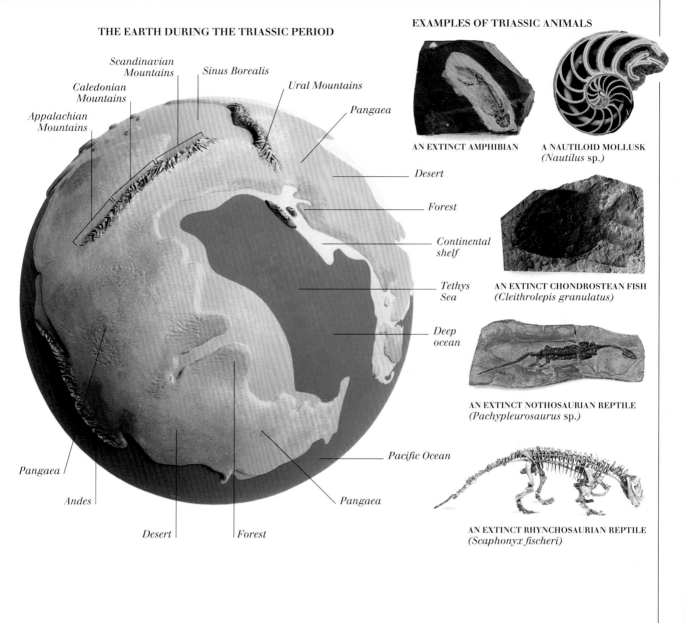

Scandinavian Mountains

Caledonian Mountains

Appalachian Mountains

Sinus Borealis

Ural Mountains

Pangaea

Desert

Forest

Continental shelf

Tethys Sea

Deep ocean

Pacific Ocean

Pangaea

Pangaea

Andes

Desert

Forest

EXAMPLES OF TRIASSIC ANIMALS

AN EXTINCT AMPHIBIAN

A NAUTILOID MOLLUSK
(*Nautilus* sp.)

AN EXTINCT CHONDROSTEAN FISH
(*Cleithrolepis granulatus*)

AN EXTINCT NOTHOSAURIAN REPTILE
(*Pachypleurosaurus* sp.)

AN EXTINCT RHYNCHOSAURIAN REPTILE
(*Scaphonyx fischeri*)

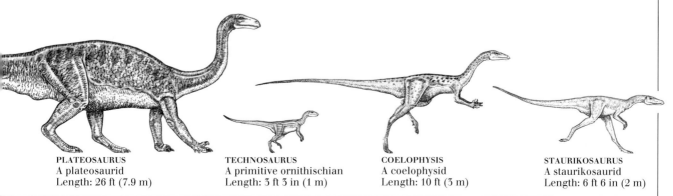

PLATEOSAURUS
A plateosaurid
Length: 26 ft (7.9 m)

TECHNOSAURUS
A primitive ornithischian
Length: 3 ft 3 in (1 m)

COELOPHYSIS
A coelophysid
Length: 10 ft (3 m)

STAURIKOSAURUS
A staurikosaurid
Length: 6 ft 6 in (2 m)

Jurassic period

THE JURASSIC PERIOD, the middle part of the Mesozoic era, lasted from 208 to 146 million years ago. During the Jurassic period, the landmass of Pangaea broke up into the continents of Gondwanaland and Laurasia, and sea-levels rose, flooding areas of lower land. The Jurassic climate was warm and moist. Plants such as ginkgos, horsetails, and conifers thrived, and giant redwood trees appeared, as did the first flowering plants. The abundance of plant food coincided with the proliferation of herbivorous (plant-eating) dinosaurs, such as the large sauropods (e.g., *Diplodocus*) and stegosaurs (e.g., *Stegosaurus*). Carnivorous (flesh-eating) dinosaurs, such as *Compsognathus* and *Allosaurus,* also flourished by hunting the many animals that existed—among them other dinosaurs. Further Jurassic animals included shrewlike mammals, and pterosaurs (flying reptiles), as well as plesiosaurs and ichthyosaurs (both marine reptiles).

JURASSIC POSITIONS OF PRESENT-DAY LANDMASSES

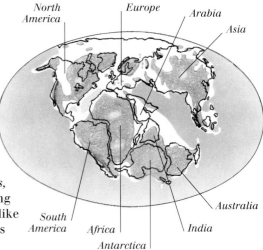

North America
Europe
Arabia
Asia
Australia
India
Antarctica
Africa
South America

EXAMPLES OF JURASSIC PLANT GROUPS

A PRESENT-DAY FERN
(Dicksonia antarctica)

A PRESENT-DAY HORSETAIL
(Equisetum arvense)

A PRESENT-DAY CONIFER
(Taxus baccata)

FOSSIL LEAF OF AN EXTINCT CONIFER
(Taxus sp.)

FOSSIL LEAF OF AN EXTINCT REDWOOD
(Sequoiadendron affinis)

EXAMPLES OF JURASSIC DINOSAURS

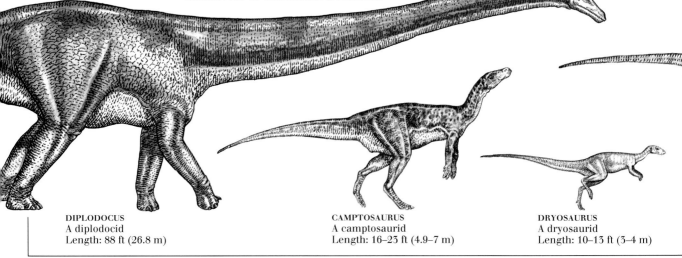

DIPLODOCUS
A diplodocid
Length: 88 ft (26.8 m)

CAMPTOSAURUS
A camptosaurid
Length: 16–23 ft (4.9–7 m)

DRYOSAURUS
A dryosaurid
Length: 10–13 ft (3–4 m)

THE EARTH DURING THE JURASSIC PERIOD

EXAMPLES OF JURASSIC ANIMALS

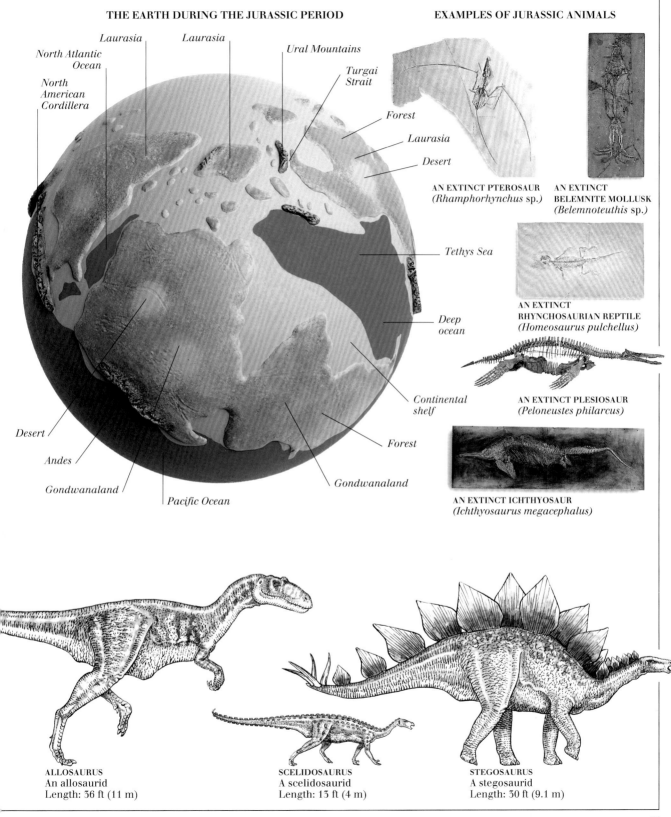

Laurasia

Laurasia

North Atlantic Ocean

North American Cordillera

Ural Mountains

Turgai Strait

Forest

Laurasia

Desert

Tethys Sea

Deep ocean

Continental shelf

Forest

Desert

Andes

Gondwanaland

Gondwanaland

Pacific Ocean

AN EXTINCT PTEROSAUR
(*Rhamphorhynchus* sp.)

AN EXTINCT BELEMNITE MOLLUSK
(*Belemnoteuthis* sp.)

AN EXTINCT RHYNCHOSAURIAN REPTILE
(*Homeosaurus pulchellus*)

AN EXTINCT PLESIOSAUR
(*Peloneustes philarcus*)

AN EXTINCT ICHTHYOSAUR
(*Ichthyosaurus megacephalus*)

ALLOSAURUS
An allosaurid
Length: 36 ft (11 m)

SCELIDOSAURUS
A scelidosaurid
Length: 13 ft (4 m)

STEGOSAURUS
A stegosaurid
Length: 30 ft (9.1 m)

Cretaceous period

THE MESOZOIC ERA ENDED WITH the Cretaceous period, which lasted from 146 to 65 million years ago. During this period, Gondwanaland and Laurasia were breaking up into smaller landmasses that more closely resembled those of the modern continents. The climate remained mild and moist, but the seasons became more marked. Flowering plants, including deciduous trees, replaced many cycads, seed ferns, and conifers. Animal species became more varied, with the evolution of new mammals, insects, fish, crustaceans, and turtles. Dinosaurs evolved into a wide variety of species during Cretaceous times; more than half of all known dinosaurs—including *Iguanodon*, *Deinonychus*, *Tyrannosaurus*, and *Hypsilophodon* —lived during this period. At the end of the Cretaceous period, however, large dinosaurs became extinct. The reason for this mass extinction is unknown but it is thought to have been caused by climatic changes due to either a catastrophic meteor impact with the Earth or extensive volcanic eruptions.

CRETACEOUS POSITIONS OF PRESENT-DAY LANDMASSES

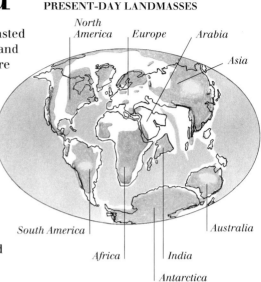

North America
Europe
Arabia
Asia
South America
Australia
Africa
India
Antarctica

EXAMPLES OF CRETACEOUS PLANT GROUPS

A PRESENT-DAY CONIFER
(*Pinus muricata*)

A PRESENT-DAY DECIDUOUS TREE
(*Magnolia* sp.)

FOSSIL OF AN EXTINCT FERN
(*Sphenopteris latiloba*)

FOSSIL OF AN EXTINCT GINKGO
(*Ginkgo pluripartita*)

FOSSIL LEAVES OF AN EXTINCT DECIDUOUS TREE
(*Cercidyphyllum* sp.)

EXAMPLES OF CRETACEOUS DINOSAURS

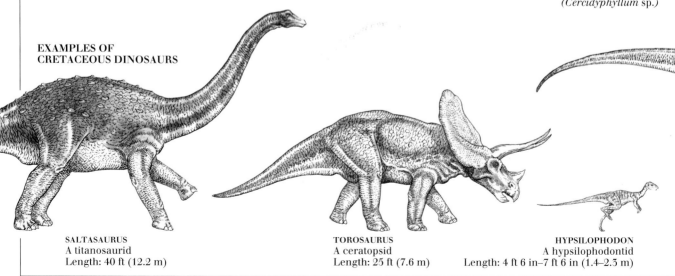

SALTASAURUS
A titanosaurid
Length: 40 ft (12.2 m)

TOROSAURUS
A ceratopsid
Length: 25 ft (7.6 m)

HYPSILOPHODON
A hypsilophodontid
Length: 4 ft 6 in–7 ft 6 in (1.4–2.3 m)

THE EARTH DURING THE CRETACEOUS PERIOD

EXAMPLES OF CRETACEOUS ANIMALS

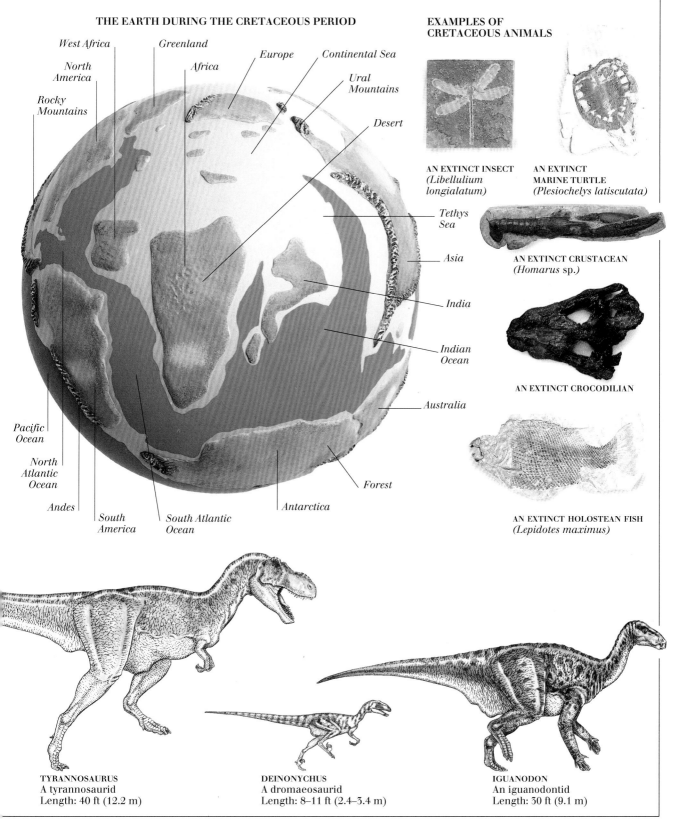

West Africa

Greenland

North America

Africa

Europe

Continental Sea

Rocky Mountains

Ural Mountains

Desert

Tethys Sea

Asia

India

Indian Ocean

Australia

Pacific Ocean

North Atlantic Ocean

Andes

South America

South Atlantic Ocean

Antarctica

Forest

AN EXTINCT INSECT
(*Libellulium longialatum*)

AN EXTINCT MARINE TURTLE
(*Plesiochelys latiscutata*)

AN EXTINCT CRUSTACEAN
(*Homarus* sp.)

AN EXTINCT CROCODILIAN

AN EXTINCT HOLOSTEAN FISH
(*Lepidotes maximus*)

TYRANNOSAURUS
A tyrannosaurid
Length: 40 ft (12.2 m)

DEINONYCHUS
A dromaeosaurid
Length: 8–11 ft (2.4–3.4 m)

IGUANODON
An iguanodontid
Length: 30 ft (9.1 m)

Tertiary period

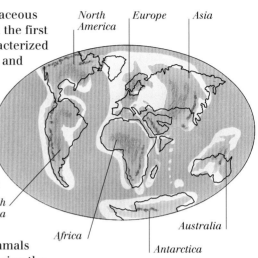

FOLLOWING THE DEMISE OF THE DINOSAURS at the end of the Cretaceous period, the Tertiary period (65–1.6 million years ago), which formed the first part of the Cenozoic era (65 million years ago–present), was characterized by a huge expansion of mammal life. Placental mammals nourish and maintain their young in the mother's uterus; only three orders of placental mammals existed during Cretaceous times, compared with 25 orders during the Tertiary period. One of these 25 included the first hominid (see pp.108–109), *Australopithecus*, which appeared in Africa. By the beginning of the Tertiary period, the continents had almost reached their present position. The Tethys Sea, which had separated the northern continents from Africa and India, began to close up, forming the Mediterranean Sea and allowing the migration of terrestrial animals between Africa and western Europe. India's collision with Asia led to the formation of the Himalayas. During the middle part of the Tertiary period, the forest-dwelling and browsing mammals were replaced by mammals such as the horse, better suited to grazing the open savannahs that began to dominate. Repeated cool periods throughout the Tertiary period established the Antarctic as an icy island continent.

North America

Europe

Asia

South America

Africa

Australia

Antarctica

EXAMPLES OF TERTIARY PLANT GROUPS

A PRESENT-DAY OAK
(Quercus palustris)

A PRESENT-DAY BIRCH
(Betula grossa)

**FOSSIL LEAF OF AN
EXTINCT BIRCH**
(Betulites sp.)

**FOSSIL STEM OF AN
EXTINCT PALM**
(Palmoxylon)

EXAMPLES OF TERTIARY ANIMAL GROUPS

HYAENODON
An hyaenodontid
Length: 6 ft 6 in (2 m)

TITANOHYRAX
A pliohyracid
Length: 6 ft 6 in (2 m)

PHORUSRHACUS
A phorusrhacid
Length: 5 ft (1.5 m)

SAMOTHERIUM
A giraffid
Length: 10 ft (3 m)

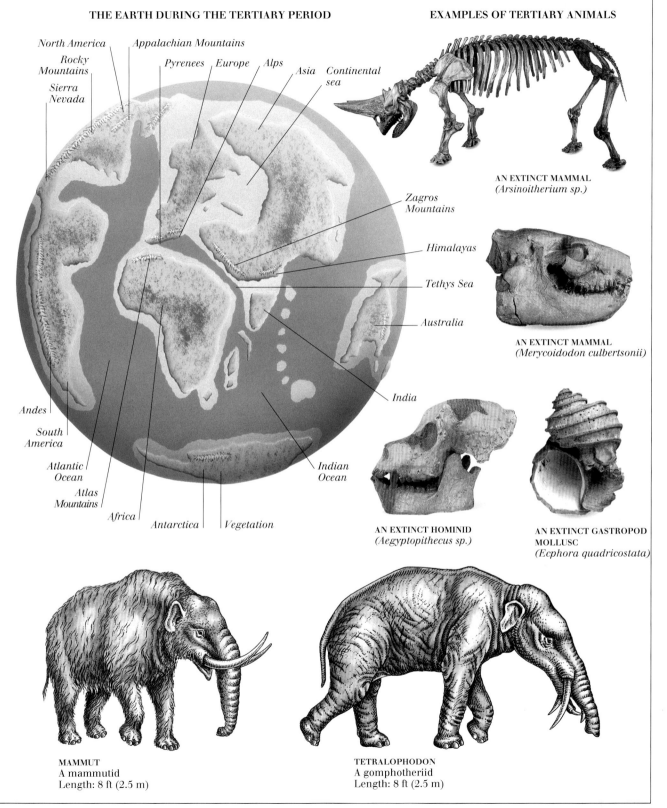

THE EARTH DURING THE TERTIARY PERIOD

North America
Rocky Mountains
Sierra Nevada
Appalachian Mountains
Pyrenees
Europe
Alps
Asia
Continental sea
Zagros Mountains
Himalayas
Tethys Sea
Australia
India
Andes
South America
Atlantic Ocean
Atlas Mountains
Africa
Antarctica
Vegetation
Indian Ocean

EXAMPLES OF TERTIARY ANIMALS

AN EXTINCT MAMMAL
(*Arsinoitherium sp.*)

AN EXTINCT MAMMAL
(*Merycoidodon culbertsonii*)

AN EXTINCT HOMINID
(*Aegyptopithecus sp.*)

AN EXTINCT GASTROPOD
MOLLUSC
(*Ecphora quadricostata*)

MAMMUT
A mammutid
Length: 8 ft (2.5 m)

TETRALOPHODON
A gomphotheriid
Length: 8 ft (2.5 m)

Quaternary period

THE QUATERNARY PERIOD (1.6 million years ago–present) forms the second part of the Cenozoic era (65 million years ago–present): it has been characterized by alternating cold (glacial) and warm (interglacial) periods. During cold periods, ice sheets and glaciers have formed repeatedly on northern and southern continents. The cold environments in North America and Eurasia, and to a lesser extent in southern South America and parts of Australia, have caused the migration of many life forms toward the Equator. Only the specialized ice-age mammals such as *Mammuthus* and *Coelodonta*, with their thick wool and fat insulation, were suited to life in very cold climates. Humans developed throughout the Pleistocene period (1.6 million–10,000 years ago) in Africa and migrated northward into Europe and Asia. Modern humans, *Homo sapiens*, lived on the cold European continent 30,000 years ago and hunted mammals. The end of the last ice age and the climatic changes that occurred about 10,000 years ago brought extinction to many Pleistocene mammals, but enabled humans to flourish.

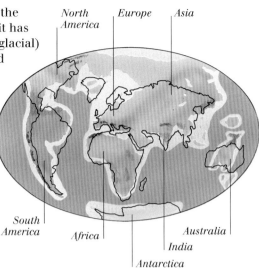

North America   Europe   Asia

South America   Africa   Australia   India   Antarctica

EXAMPLES OF QUATERNARY PLANT GROUPS

A PRESENT-DAY BIRCH
(Betula lenta)

A PRESENT-DAY SWEETGUM
(Liquidambar styraciflua)

FOSSIL LEAF OF A SWEETGUM
(Liquidambar europeanum)

FOSSIL LEAF OF A BIRCH
(Betula sp.)

EXAMPLES OF QUATERNARY ANIMAL GROUPS

PROCOPTODON
A macropodid
Length: 10 ft (3 m)

DIPROTODON
A diprotodontid
Length: 10 ft (3 m)

TOXODON
A toxodontid
Length: 10 ft (3 m)

MAMMUTHUS
An elephantid
Length: 10 ft (3 m)

THE EARTH DURING THE QUATERNARY PERIOD

EXAMPLES OF QUATERNARY ANIMALS

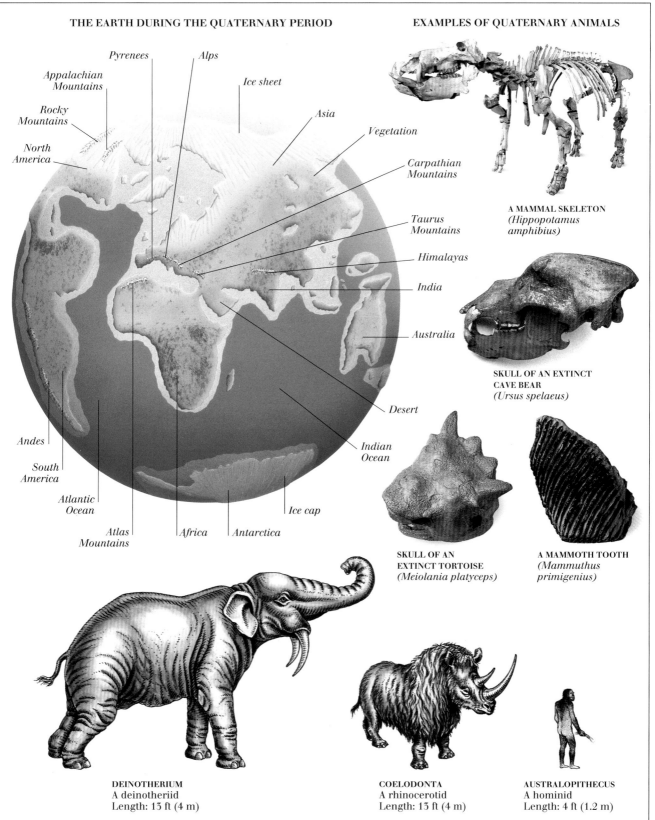

Appalachian Mountains

Rocky Mountains

North America

Pyrenees

Alps

Ice sheet

Asia

Vegetation

Carpathian Mountains

Taurus Mountains

Himalayas

India

Australia

Desert

Indian Ocean

Andes

South America

Atlantic Ocean

Atlas Mountains

Africa

Antarctica

Ice cap

A MAMMAL SKELETON
(Hippopotamus amphibius)

SKULL OF AN EXTINCT CAVE BEAR
(Ursus spelaeus)

SKULL OF AN EXTINCT TORTOISE
(Meiolania platyceps)

A MAMMOTH TOOTH
(Mammuthus primigenius)

DEINOTHERIUM
A deinotheriid
Length: 13 ft (4 m)

COELODONTA
A rhinocerotid
Length: 13 ft (4 m)

AUSTRALOPITHECUS
A hominid
Length: 4 ft (1.2 m)

Early signs of life

FOR ALMOST A THOUSAND MILLION YEARS after its formation, there was no known life on Earth. The first simple, sea-dwelling organic structures appeared about 3,400 years ago; they may have formed when certain chemical molecules joined together. Prokaryotes, single-celled micro-organisms such as blue-green algae, were able to photosynthesize (see pp. 138–139), and thus produce oxygen. A thousand million years later, sufficient oxygen had built up in the earth's atmosphere to allow multicellular organisms to proliferate in the Precambrian seas (before 570 million years ago). Soft-bodied jellyfish, corals, and seaworms flourished about 700 million years ago. Trilobites, the first animals with hard body frames, developed during the Cambrian period (570–510 million years ago). However, it was not until the beginning of the Devonian period (409–363 million years ago) that early land plants, such as *Asteroxylon*, formed a water-retaining cuticle, which ended their dependence on an aquatic environment. About 363 million years ago, the first amphibians (see pp. 80–81) crawled onto the land, although they still returned to the water to lay their soft eggs. Not until the emergence of the first reptiles would animals appear that were not dependent on water in this way.

STROMATOLITIC LIMESTONE

Alternate layers of mud and sand

Layers bound by algae

Layered structure

Limestone

Glabella

Eye

Long, beaklike snout

Growth line

Thoracic pleurae

Dorsal plate

Fixed lateral plate

Bony dorsal shield

Dorsal spine base

Tail shield

Tail area

FOSSILIZED JAWLESS FISH

FOSSILIZED TRILOBITE

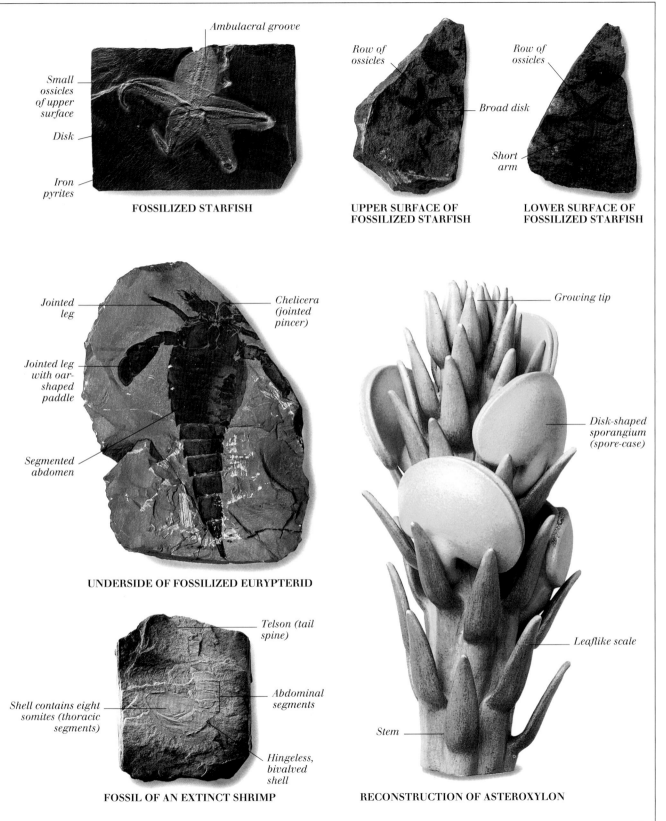

FOSSILIZED STARFISH

Ambulacral groove

Small ossicles of upper surface

Disk

Iron pyrites

Row of ossicles

Broad disk

UPPER SURFACE OF FOSSILIZED STARFISH

Row of ossicles

Short arm

LOWER SURFACE OF FOSSILIZED STARFISH

Jointed leg

Chelicera (jointed pincer)

Jointed leg with oar-shaped paddle

Segmented abdomen

UNDERSIDE OF FOSSILIZED EURYPTERID

Growing tip

Disk-shaped sporangium (spore-case)

Leaflike scale

Stem

Telson (tail spine)

Abdominal segments

Shell contains eight somites (thoracic segments)

Hingeless, bivalved shell

FOSSIL OF AN EXTINCT SHRIMP

RECONSTRUCTION OF ASTEROXYLON

Amphibians and reptiles

THE EARLIEST KNOWN AMPHIBIANS, such as *Acanthostega* and *Ichthyostega*, lived about 363 million years ago at the end of the Devonian period (409–363 million years ago). Their limbs may have evolved from the muscular fins of lungfish. These fish can use their fins to push themselves along the bottom of lakes and some can breathe at the water's surface. While amphibians (see pp. 182–183) can exist on land, they are dependent on a wet environment because their skin does not retain moisture and they must return to the water to lay their eggs. Evolving from amphibians, reptiles (see pp. 184–187) first appeared during the Carboniferous period (363–290 million years ago): *Westlothiana*, the earliest known reptile, lived on land 338 million years ago. The development of the amniotic egg, with an embryo enclosed in its own wet environment (the amnion) and protected by a waterproof shell, freed reptiles from the amphibian's dependence on a wet habitat. A scaly skin protected the reptile from desiccation on land and enabled it to exploit ways of life closed to its amphibian ancestors. Reptiles include the dinosaurs, which came to dominate life on land during the Mesozoic era (245–65 million years ago).

Orbit

Sculpted or pitted bone surface

Pocket enclosing nostril

Spiracle to draw in water

Mandible

Small tooth

FOSSIL SKULL OF ACANTHOSTEGA

Muscular back

Shoulder girdle

Scaly skin

Finned tail

Hip girdle

MODEL OF ICHTHYOSTEGA

Dorsal vertebra

Scapula

Cleithrum

Cervical vertebra

Cranium

Orbit

Maxilla

Naris

Rib

Glenoid cavity

Humerus

Elbow joint

Mandible

Clavicle

Radius

Ulna

Metacarpals

Sharp tooth

Phalanges

SKELETON OF ERYOPS

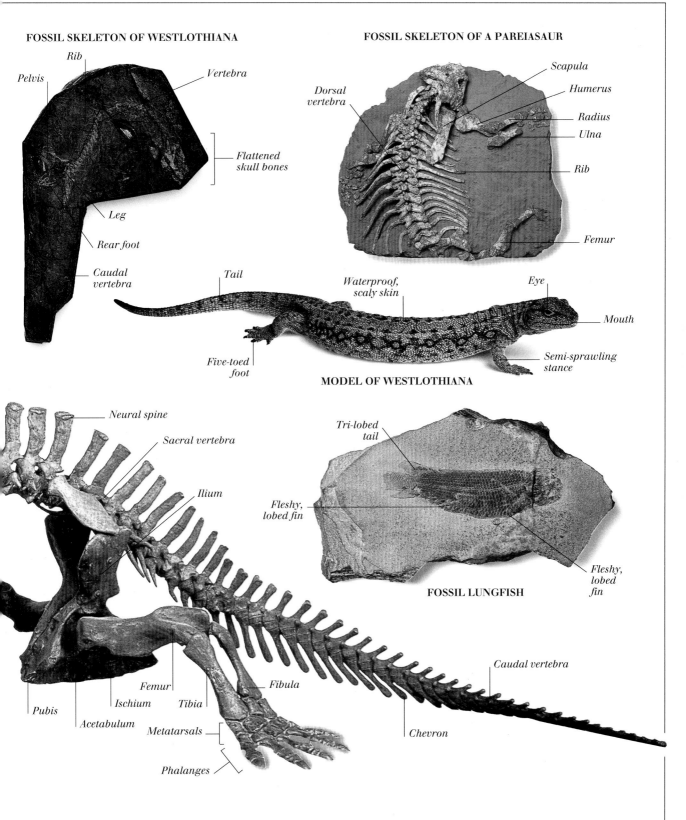

FOSSIL SKELETON OF WESTLOTHIANA

Rib

Vertebra

Pelvis

Flattened
skull bones

Leg

Rear foot

Caudal
vertebra

FOSSIL SKELETON OF A PAREIASAUR

Scapula

Humerus

Dorsal
vertebra

Radius

Ulna

Rib

Femur

Tail

Waterproof,
scaly skin

Eye

Mouth

Five-toed
foot

Semi-sprawling
stance

MODEL OF WESTLOTHIANA

Neural spine

Sacral vertebra

Tri-lobed
tail

Ilium

Fleshy,
lobed fin

Fleshy,
lobed
fin

FOSSIL LUNGFISH

Caudal vertebra

Femur

Fibula

Pubis

Ischium

Tibia

Acetabulum

Metatarsals

Chevron

Phalanges

The dinosaurs

THE DINOSAURS WERE A LARGE GROUP of reptiles that were the dominant land vertebrates (animals with backbones) for most of the Mesozoic era (245–65 million years ago). They appeared some 230 million years ago and were distinguished from other scaly, egg-laying reptiles by an important feature: dinosaurs had an erect limb stance. This enabled them to keep their bodies well above the ground, unlike the sprawling and semi-sprawling stance of other reptiles. The head of the dinosaur's femur (thighbone) fits into a socket in its pelvis (hipbone), producing efficient and mobile locomotion. Dinosaurs are categorized into two groups according to the structure of their pelvis: saurischian (lizard-hipped) and ornithischian (bird-hipped) dinosaurs. In the case of most saurischians, the pubis (part of the pelvis) jutted forward, while in ornithischians it slanted back, parallel to the ischium (another part of the pelvis). The enormous variety of dinosaur species equals that of mammals. The Dinosauria were the most successful land vertebrates ever, and survived for 165 million years, until their extinction 65 million years ago.

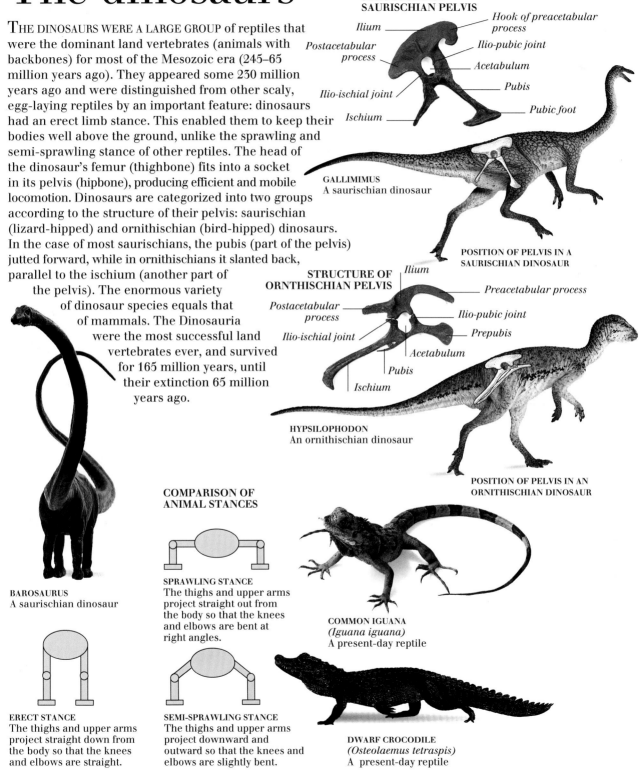

STRUCTURE OF SAURISCHIAN PELVIS

Ilium

Postacetabular process

Ilio-ischial joint

Ischium

Hook of preacetabular process

Ilio-pubic joint

Acetabulum

Pubis

Pubic foot

GALLIMIMUS
A saurischian dinosaur

POSITION OF PELVIS IN A SAURISCHIAN DINOSAUR

STRUCTURE OF ORNITHISCHIAN PELVIS

Ilium

Postacetabular process

Ilio-ischial joint

Acetabulum

Pubis

Ischium

Preacetabular process

Ilio-pubic joint

Prepubis

HYPSILOPHODON
An ornithischian dinosaur

POSITION OF PELVIS IN AN ORNITHISCHIAN DINOSAUR

BAROSAURUS
A saurischian dinosaur

COMPARISON OF ANIMAL STANCES

SPRAWLING STANCE
The thighs and upper arms project straight out from the body so that the knees and elbows are bent at right angles.

COMMON IGUANA
(Iguana iguana)
A present-day reptile

ERECT STANCE
The thighs and upper arms project straight down from the body so that the knees and elbows are straight.

SEMI-SPRAWLING STANCE
The thighs and upper arms project downward and outward so that the knees and elbows are slightly bent.

DWARF CROCODILE
(Osteolaemus tetraspis)
A present-day reptile

EXAMPLES OF DINOSAUR CLAWS

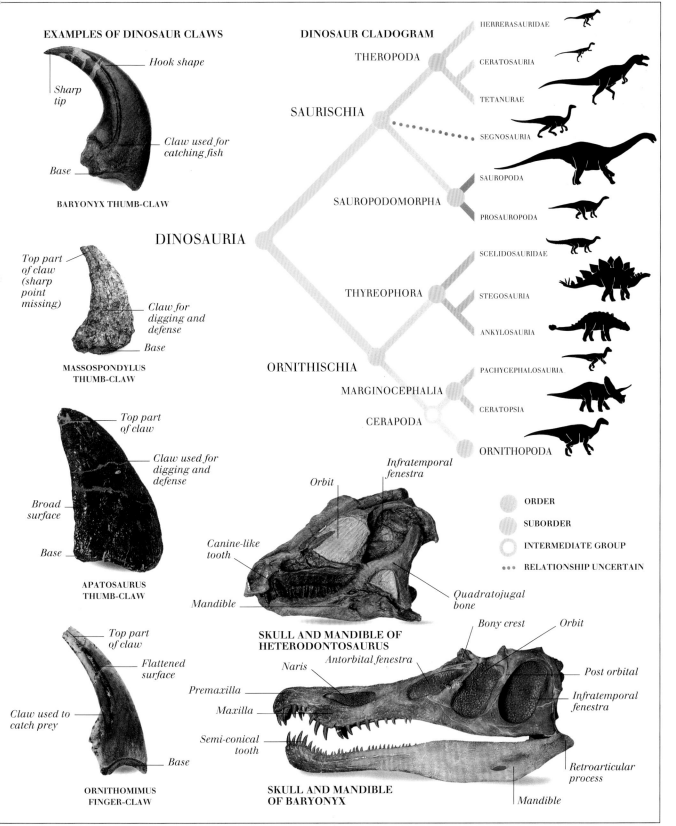

Hook shape

Sharp tip

Claw used for catching fish

Base

BARYONYX THUMB-CLAW

Top part of claw (sharp point missing)

Claw for digging and defense

Base

MASSOSPONDYLUS THUMB-CLAW

Top part of claw

Claw used for digging and defense

Broad surface

Base

APATOSAURUS THUMB-CLAW

Top part of claw

Flattened surface

Claw used to catch prey

Base

ORNITHOMIMUS FINGER-CLAW

DINOSAUR CLADOGRAM

HERRERASAURIDAE

THEROPODA

CERATOSAURIA

TETANURAE

SAURISCHIA

SEGNOSAURIA

SAUROPODA

SAUROPODOMORPHA

PROSAUROPODA

DINOSAURIA

SCELIDOSAURIDAE

THYREOPHORA

STEGOSAURIA

ANKYLOSAURIA

ORNITHISCHIA

PACHYCEPHALOSAURIA

MARGINOCEPHALIA

CERATOPSIA

CERAPODA

ORNITHOPODA

ORDER

SUBORDER

INTERMEDIATE GROUP

RELATIONSHIP UNCERTAIN

Infratemporal fenestra

Orbit

Canine-like tooth

Mandible

Quadratojugal bone

SKULL AND MANDIBLE OF HETERODONTOSAURUS

Bony crest

Orbit

Antorbital fenestra

Naris

Post orbital

Premaxilla

Infratemporal fenestra

Maxilla

Semi-conical tooth

Retroarticular process

SKULL AND MANDIBLE OF BARYONYX

Mandible

83

Theropods 1

AN ENORMOUSLY SUCCESSFUL SUBORDER of the Saurischia, the bipedal (two-footed) theropods ("beast feet") emerged 230 million years ago in Late Triassic times; the oldest known example comes from South America. Theropods spanned the whole of the Age of the Dinosaurs (230–65 million years ago) and included most known predatory dinosaurs. The typical theropod had small arms with sharp, clawed fingers; powerful jaws lined with sharp teeth; an S-shaped neck; long, muscular hind limbs; and clawed, usually four-toed feet. Many theropods may have been warm-blooded; most were exclusively carnivorous. Theropods ranged from animals no larger than a chicken to huge creatures, such as *Tyrannosaurus* and *Baryonyx*. The group also included ostrichlike omnivores and herbivores with toothless beaks, such as *Struthiomimus* and *Gallimimus*. Many scientists believe that birds are the closest living relatives to the dinosaurs, and share a common ancestor with the theropods. *Archaeopteryx*, small and feathered, was the first known bird and lived alongside its dinosaur relatives.

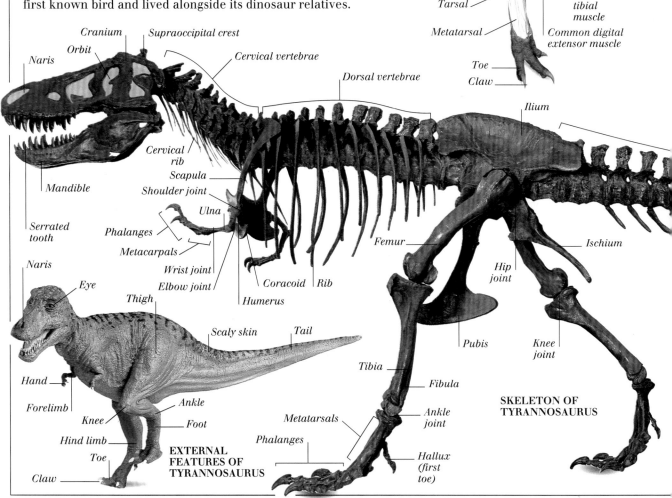

INTERNAL ANATOMY OF ALBERTOSAURUS LEG

Iliotibial muscle
Iliofemoral muscle
Femorotibial muscle
Internal tibial flexor muscle
Femur
Iliofibular muscle
Gastrocnemius muscle
Digital flexor muscle
Fibula
Tarsal
Metatarsal
Ambiens muscle
Femoro-tibial muscle
Anterior tibial muscle
Common digital extensor muscle
Toe
Claw

Cranium
Orbit
Naris
Supraoccipital crest
Cervical vertebrae
Dorsal vertebrae
Ilium
Cervical rib
Scapula
Shoulder joint
Ulna
Mandible
Serrated tooth
Phalanges
Metacarpals
Wrist joint
Elbow joint
Coracoid Rib
Humerus
Femur
Ischium
Hip joint
Knee joint
Pubis

SKELETON OF TYRANNOSAURUS

Naris
Eye
Thigh
Scaly skin
Tail
Hand
Forelimb
Knee
Hind limb
Toe
Claw
Ankle
Foot
Metatarsals
Phalanges
Tibia
Fibula
Ankle joint
Hallux (first toe)

EXTERNAL FEATURES OF TYRANNOSAURUS

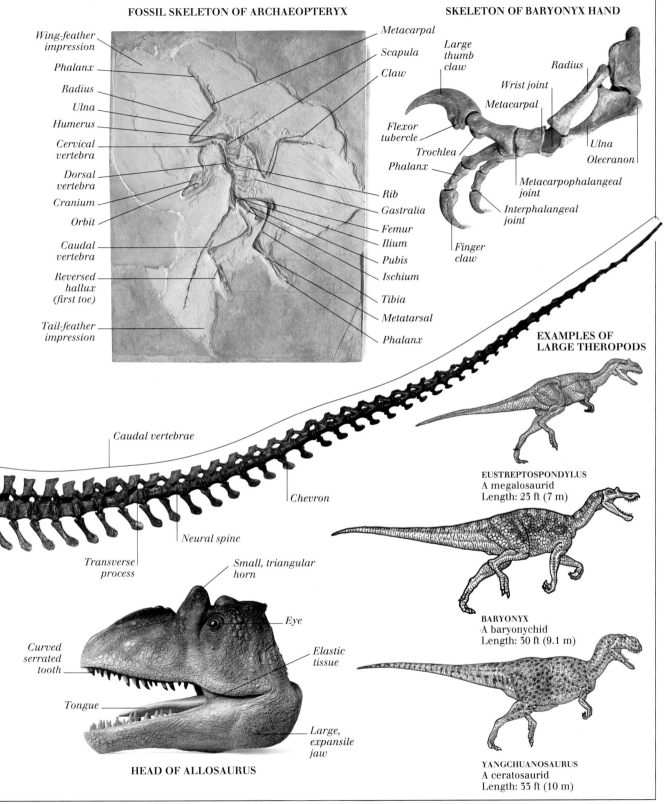

FOSSIL SKELETON OF ARCHAEOPTERYX

Wing-feather impression
Phalanx
Radius
Ulna
Humerus
Cervical vertebra
Dorsal vertebra
Cranium
Orbit
Caudal vertebra
Reversed hallux (first toe)
Tail-feather impression

Metacarpal
Scapula
Claw
Rib
Gastralia
Femur
Ilium
Pubis
Ischium
Tibia
Metatarsal
Phalanx

SKELETON OF BARYONYX HAND

Large thumb claw
Flexor tubercle
Trochlea
Phalanx
Finger claw
Wrist joint
Metacarpal
Radius
Ulna
Olecranon
Metacarpophalangeal joint
Interphalangeal joint

Caudal vertebrae
Chevron
Neural spine
Transverse process

EXAMPLES OF LARGE THEROPODS

EUSTREPTOSPONDYLUS
A megalosaurid
Length: 23 ft (7 m)

BARYONYX
A baryonychid
Length: 30 ft (9.1 m)

YANGCHUANOSAURUS
A ceratosaurid
Length: 33 ft (10 m)

Small, triangular horn
Eye
Elastic tissue
Curved serrated tooth
Tongue
Large, expansile jaw

HEAD OF ALLOSAURUS

Theropods 2

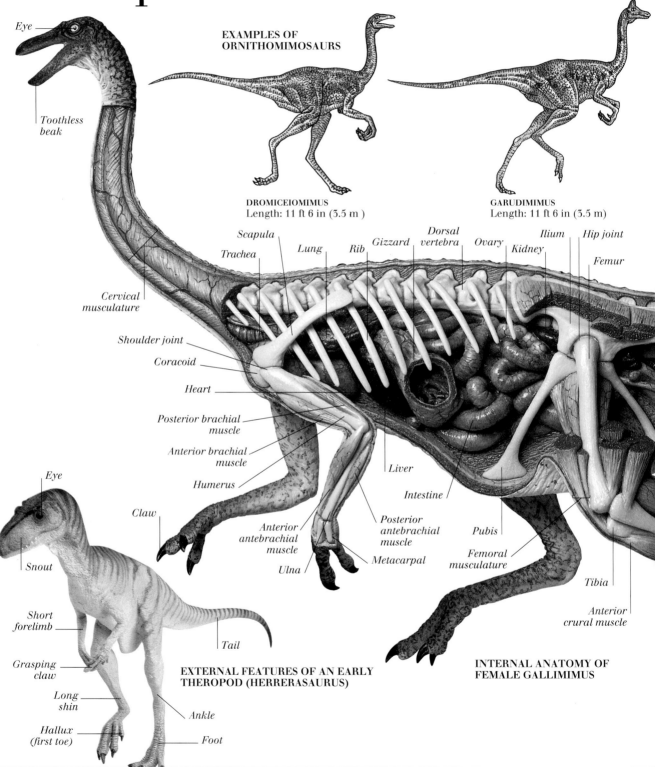

Eye

Toothless beak

EXAMPLES OF ORNITHOMIMOSAURS

DROMICEIOMIMUS
Length: 11 ft 6 in (3.5 m)

GARUDIMIMUS
Length: 11 ft 6 in (3.5 m)

Cervical musculature

Scapula

Trachea

Lung

Rib

Gizzard

Dorsal vertebra

Ovary

Kidney

Ilium

Hip joint

Femur

Shoulder joint

Coracoid

Heart

Posterior brachial muscle

Anterior brachial muscle

Humerus

Eye

Claw

Snout

Anterior antebrachial muscle

Ulna

Posterior antebrachial muscle

Metacarpal

Liver

Intestine

Pubis

Femoral musculature

Tibia

Anterior crural muscle

Short forelimb

Grasping claw

Long shin

Hallux (first toe)

Ankle

Foot

Tail

EXTERNAL FEATURES OF AN EARLY THEROPOD (HERRERASAURUS)

INTERNAL ANATOMY OF FEMALE GALLIMIMUS

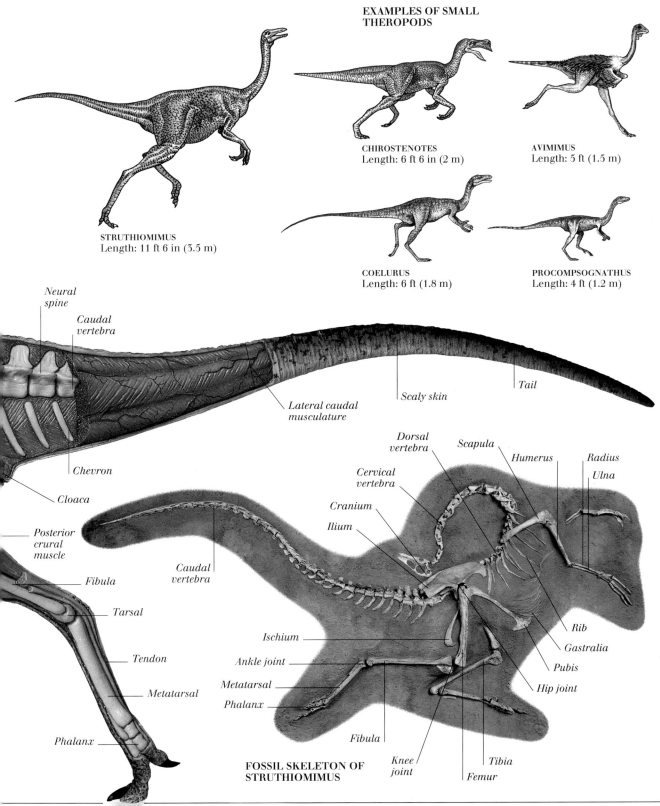

EXAMPLES OF SMALL THEROPODS

CHIROSTENOTES
Length: 6 ft 6 in (2 m)

AVIMIMUS
Length: 5 ft (1.5 m)

STRUTHIOMIMUS
Length: 11 ft 6 in (3.5 m)

COELURUS
Length: 6 ft (1.8 m)

PROCOMPSOGNATHUS
Length: 4 ft (1.2 m)

Neural spine

Caudal vertebra

Scaly skin

Tail

Lateral caudal musculature

Dorsal vertebra

Scapula

Humerus

Radius

Cervical vertebra

Ulna

Cranium

Chevron

Ilium

Cloaca

Posterior crural muscle

Fibula

Caudal vertebra

Rib

Tarsal

Gastralia

Pubis

Tendon

Ischium

Hip joint

Ankle joint

Metatarsal

Metatarsal

Phalanx

Phalanx

Fibula

Tibia

FOSSIL SKELETON OF STRUTHIOMIMUS

Knee joint

Femur

Sauropodomorphs 1

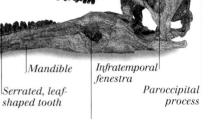

**SKULL AND MANDIBLE OF
PLATEOSAURUS**

Naris

*Antorbital
fenestra*

Orbit

Mandible

*Infratemporal
fenestra*

*Paroccipital
process*

*Serrated, leaf-
shaped tooth*

*Mandibular
fenestra*

THECODONTOSAURUS

THE SAUROPODOMORPHA ("lizard-feet forms") were herbivorous, usually quadrupedal (four-footed) dinosaurs. A suborder of the Saurischia, they were characterized by small heads, bulky bodies, and long necks and tails. There were two infraorders: prosauropods and sauropods. Prosauropods lived from Late Triassic to Early Jurassic times (225–180 million years ago) and included beasts such as the small *Anchisaurus* and one of the first very large dinosaurs, *Melanosaurus*. By Middle Jurassic times (about 165 million years ago), sauropods had replaced prosauropods and spread worldwide. They included the heaviest and longest land animals ever, such as *Diplodocus* and *Brachiosaurus*. Sauropods persisted to the end of the Cretaceous period (65 million years ago). Many of these dinosaurs moved in herds, protected from predatory theropods by their huge bulk and powerful tails, which they could use to lash out at attackers. Sauropodomorphs were the most common large herbivores until Late Jurassic times (about 145 million years ago), and appear to have survived in southern continents long after they had disappeared from the north.

**SKELETON OF
PLATEOSAURUS**

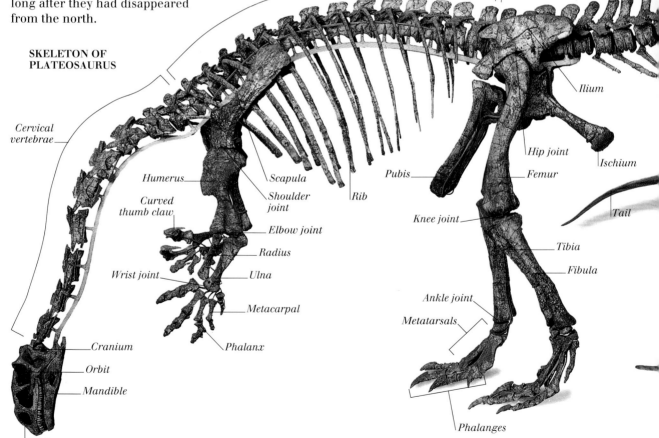

Dorsal vertebrae

Sacral vertebrae

Ilium

*Cervical
vertebrae*

Humerus

Scapula

*Shoulder
joint*

Rib

Hip joint

Pubis

Femur

Ischium

*Curved
thumb claw*

Elbow joint

Radius

Knee joint

Tail

Wrist joint

Ulna

Tibia

Metacarpal

Fibula

Cranium

Phalanx

Ankle joint

Orbit

Metatarsals

Mandible

Naris

Phalanges

THUMB CLAW OF MASSOSPONDYLUS

Top part of claw (sharp point missing)

Curved body of claw

Base of claw

Caudal vertebrae

Neural spine

Chevron

Transverse process

EXAMPLES OF PROSAUROPODS

MASSOSPONDYLUS
A massospondylid
Length: 13 ft (4 m)

LUFENGOSAURUS
A plateosaurid
Length: 20 ft (6.1 m)

RIOJASAURUS
A melanorosaurid
Length: 36 ft (11 m)

MELANOROSAURUS
A melanorosaurid
Length: 40 ft (12.2 m)

EXTERNAL FEATURES OF ANCHISAURUS

Naris

Eye

Leaf-shaped tooth

Long, flexible neck

Shoulder

Forelimb

Elbow

Hand

Large, curved thumb claw

Toe

Thigh

Claw

Forelimb

Hind limb

TOP VIEW OF ANCHISAURUS

Slender snout

Long body

Hip

Scaly skin

Thigh

Tail

Knee

Ankle

Hind limb

Hallux (first toe)

Finger

Foot

Toe

Claw

SIDE VIEW OF ANCHISAURUS

Sauropodomorphs 2

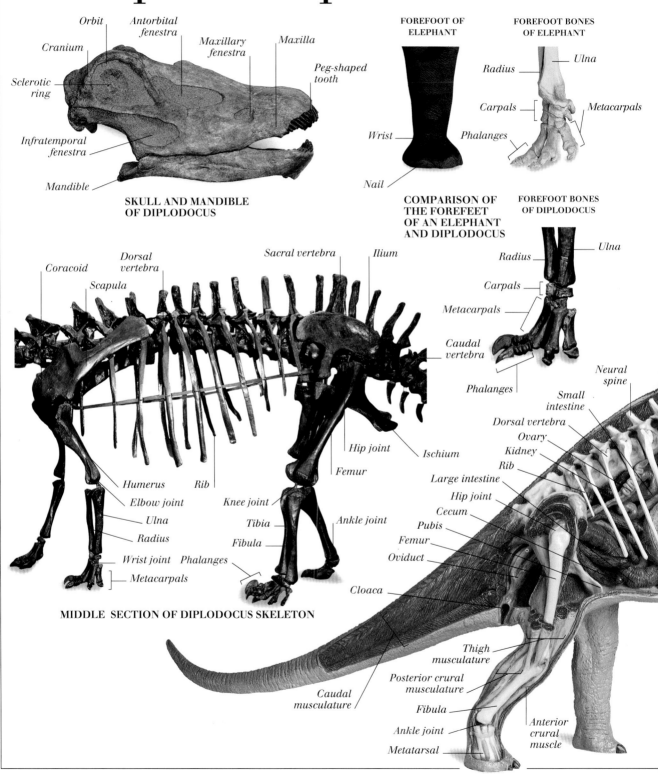

FOREFOOT OF ELEPHANT

FOREFOOT BONES OF ELEPHANT

Orbit

Antorbital fenestra

Maxillary fenestra

Maxilla

Cranium

Peg-shaped tooth

Sclerotic ring

Radius

Ulna

Infratemporal fenestra

Carpals

Metacarpals

Wrist

Phalanges

Mandible

Nail

SKULL AND MANDIBLE OF DIPLODOCUS

COMPARISON OF THE FOREFEET OF AN ELEPHANT AND DIPLODOCUS

FOREFOOT BONES OF DIPLODOCUS

Radius

Ulna

Coracoid

Dorsal vertebra

Sacral vertebra

Ilium

Carpals

Scapula

Metacarpals

Caudal vertebra

Phalanges

Neural spine

Small intestine

Dorsal vertebra

Ovary

Kidney

Rib

Large intestine

Hip joint

Cecum

Humerus

Rib

Pubis

Elbow joint

Knee joint

Femur

Ulna

Ankle joint

Oviduct

Radius

Tibia

Hip joint

Wrist joint

Phalanges

Fibula

Ischium

Cloaca

Metacarpals

Femur

MIDDLE SECTION OF DIPLODOCUS SKELETON

Thigh musculature

Posterior crural musculature

Caudal musculature

Fibula

Anterior crural muscle

Ankle joint

Metatarsal

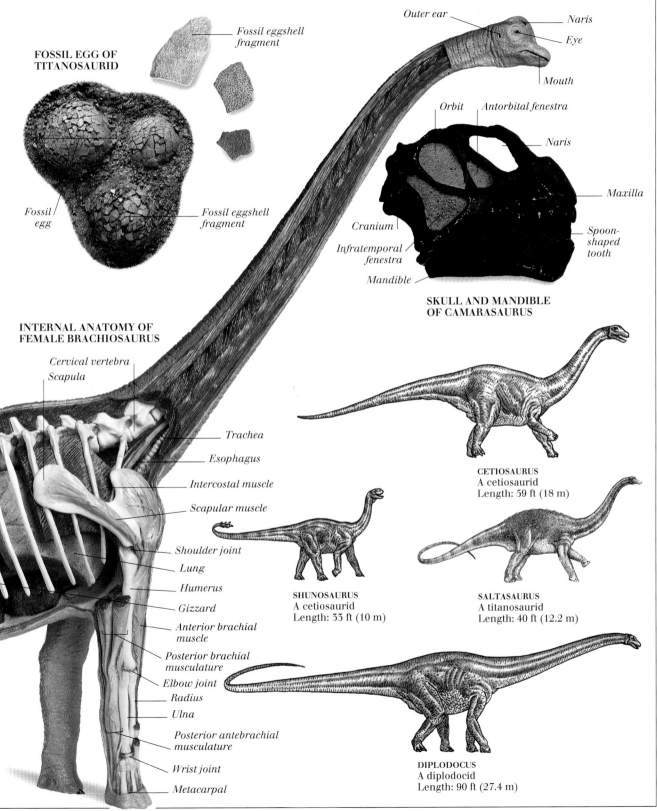

**FOSSIL EGG OF
TITANOSAURID**

Fossil eggshell
fragment

Fossil
egg

Fossil eggshell
fragment

Outer ear

Naris

Eye

Mouth

Orbit

Antorbital fenestra

Naris

Maxilla

Cranium

Infratemporal
fenestra

Mandible

Spoon-
shaped
tooth

**SKULL AND MANDIBLE
OF CAMARASAURUS**

**INTERNAL ANATOMY OF
FEMALE BRACHIOSAURUS**

Cervical vertebra
Scapula

Trachea

Esophagus

Intercostal muscle

Scapular muscle

Shoulder joint

Lung

Humerus

Gizzard

Anterior brachial
muscle

Posterior brachial
musculature

Elbow joint

Radius

Ulna

Posterior antebrachial
musculature

Wrist joint

Metacarpal

CETIOSAURUS
A cetiosaurid
Length: 59 ft (18 m)

SHUNOSAURUS
A cetiosaurid
Length: 33 ft (10 m)

SALTASAURUS
A titanosaurid
Length: 40 ft (12.2 m)

DIPLODOCUS
A diplodocid
Length: 90 ft (27.4 m)

Thyreophorans 1

THYREOPHORANS ("SHIELD BEARERS") were a group
of quadrupedal armored dinosaurs. A suborder of the
Ornithischia (bird-hipped dinosaurs), they were characterized
by rows of bony studs, plates, or spikes along the back, which
protected some from predators and may have helped others regulate
body temperature. Up to 30ft (9m) long, with a small head and small cheek
teeth, Thyreophorans had shorter forelimbs than hind limbs and probably
browsed on low-level vegetation. The earliest thyreophorans were
small and lived in Early Jurassic times (about 200 million
years ago) in Europe, North America, and
China. Stegosaurs, such as *Stegosaurus*
and *Kentrosaurus*, replaced these older
forms. The earliest stegosaur remains
come from England and China. Several genera
of stegosaurs survived into the Early Cretaceous period
(146–100 million years ago), but only in India did they persist
into Late Cretaceous times (97–65 million years ago).
Ankylosaurs, with their toothless beaks and cheek
teeth adapted for cropping vegetation,
appeared later than stegosaurs.
They originated in the Late
Jurassic period (155 million
years ago) and in North
America survived until the
extinction of the dinosaurs,
65 million years ago.

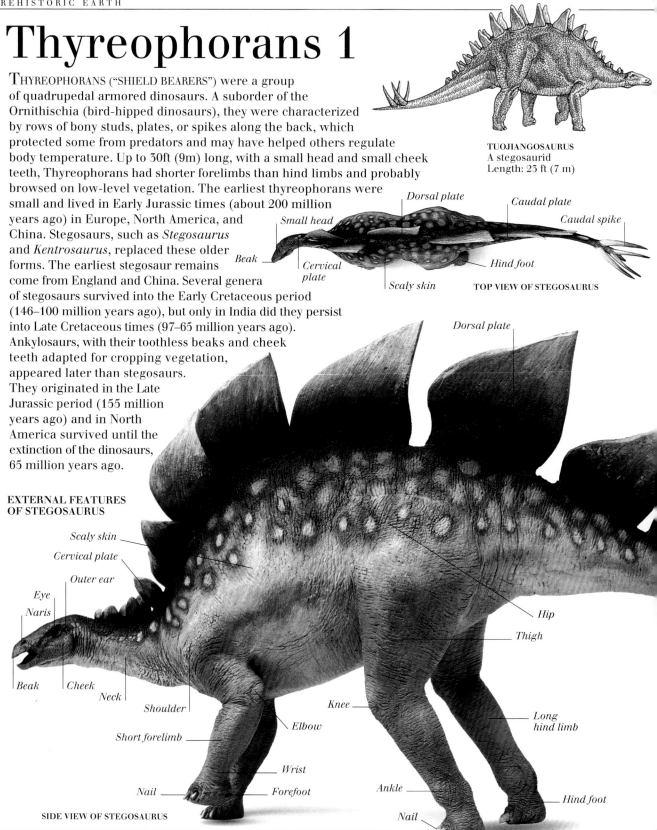

TUOJIANGOSAURUS
A stegosaurid
Length: 23 ft (7 m)

Dorsal plate

Caudal plate

Caudal spike

Small head

Beak

Cervical plate

Scaly skin

Hind foot

TOP VIEW OF STEGOSAURUS

Dorsal plate

**EXTERNAL FEATURES
OF STEGOSAURUS**

Scaly skin

Cervical plate

Outer ear

Eye

Naris

Beak

Cheek

Neck

Shoulder

Short forelimb

Elbow

Wrist

Nail

Forefoot

Knee

Hip

Thigh

Long
hind limb

Ankle

Nail

Hind foot

SIDE VIEW OF STEGOSAURUS

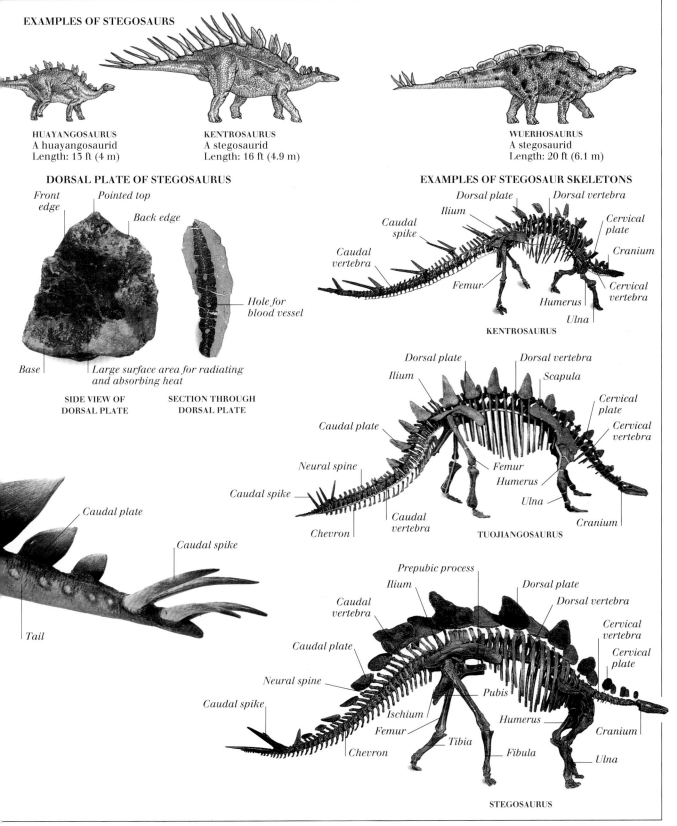

EXAMPLES OF STEGOSAURS

HUAYANGOSAURUS
A huayangosaurid
Length: 13 ft (4 m)

KENTROSAURUS
A stegosaurid
Length: 16 ft (4.9 m)

WUERHOSAURUS
A stegosaurid
Length: 20 ft (6.1 m)

DORSAL PLATE OF STEGOSAURUS

Front edge

Pointed top

Back edge

Hole for blood vessel

Base

Large surface area for radiating and absorbing heat

SIDE VIEW OF DORSAL PLATE

SECTION THROUGH DORSAL PLATE

EXAMPLES OF STEGOSAUR SKELETONS

Dorsal plate

Ilium

Caudal spike

Caudal vertebra

Dorsal vertebra

Cervical plate

Cranium

Femur

Humerus

Cervical vertebra

Ulna

KENTROSAURUS

Dorsal plate

Ilium

Dorsal vertebra

Scapula

Caudal plate

Cervical plate

Cervical vertebra

Neural spine

Caudal spike

Femur

Humerus

Chevron

Caudal vertebra

Ulna

Cranium

TUOJIANGOSAURUS

Caudal plate

Caudal spike

Tail

Prepubic process

Ilium

Caudal vertebra

Dorsal plate

Dorsal vertebra

Cervical vertebra

Cervical plate

Caudal plate

Neural spine

Pubis

Caudal spike

Ischium

Humerus

Femur

Chevron

Tibia

Cranium

Fibula

Ulna

STEGOSAURUS

Thyreophorans 2

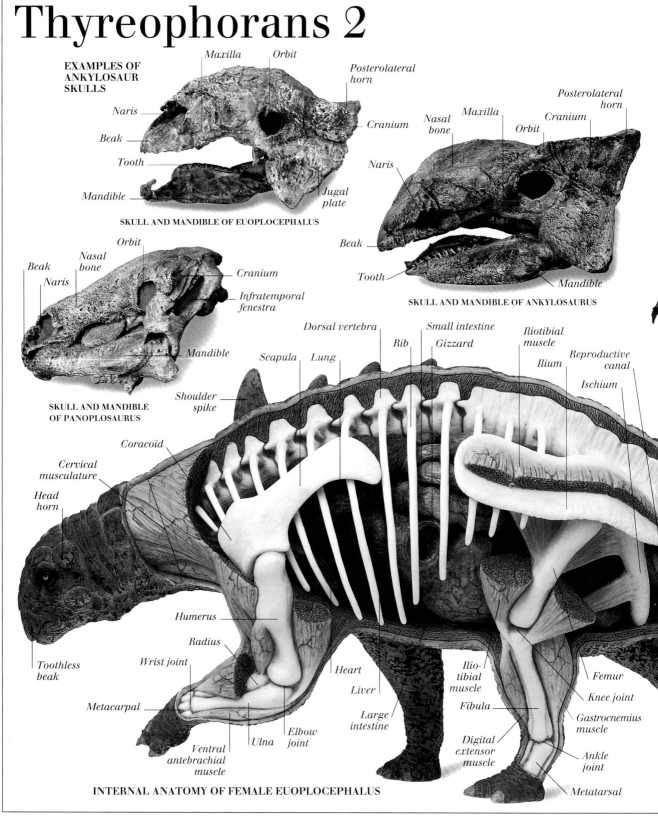

EXAMPLES OF ANKYLOSAUR SKULLS

Maxilla

Orbit

Posterolateral horn

Naris

Cranium

Beak

Tooth

Mandible

Jugal plate

SKULL AND MANDIBLE OF EUOPLOCEPHALUS

Posterolateral horn

Nasal bone

Maxilla

Cranium

Orbit

Naris

Beak

Tooth

Mandible

SKULL AND MANDIBLE OF ANKYLOSAURUS

Orbit

Nasal bone

Beak

Cranium

Naris

Infratemporal fenestra

Mandible

SKULL AND MANDIBLE OF PANOPLOSAURUS

Dorsal vertebra

Rib

Small intestine

Gizzard

Iliotibial muscle

Ilium

Reproductive canal

Ischium

Scapula

Lung

Shoulder spike

Coracoid

Cervical musculature

Head horn

Humerus

Radius

Wrist joint

Toothless beak

Metacarpal

Ventral antebrachial muscle

Ulna

Elbow joint

Heart

Liver

Large intestine

Ilio-tibial muscle

Fibula

Digital extensor muscle

Femur

Knee joint

Gastrocnemius muscle

Ankle joint

Metatarsal

INTERNAL ANATOMY OF FEMALE EUOPLOCEPHALUS

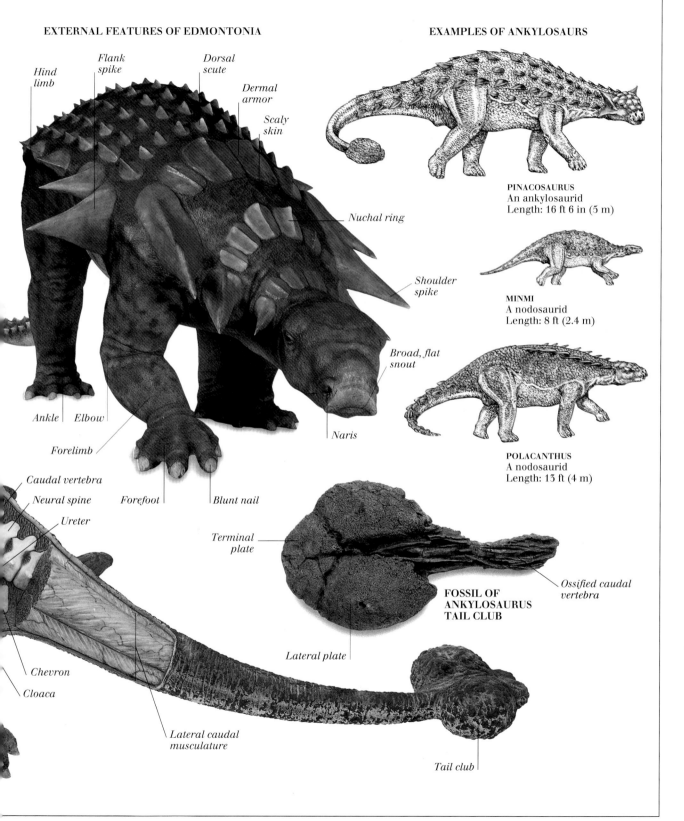

EXTERNAL FEATURES OF EDMONTONIA

Hind limb

Flank spike

Dorsal scute

Dermal armor

Scaly skin

Nuchal ring

Shoulder spike

Broad, flat snout

Naris

Ankle

Elbow

Forelimb

Forefoot

Blunt nail

Caudal vertebra

Neural spine

Ureter

Chevron

Cloaca

Terminal plate

Lateral plate

Lateral caudal musculature

Tail club

EXAMPLES OF ANKYLOSAURS

PINACOSAURUS
An ankylosaurid
Length: 16 ft 6 in (5 m)

MINMI
A nodosaurid
Length: 8 ft (2.4 m)

POLACANTHUS
A nodosaurid
Length: 13 ft (4 m)

Ossified caudal vertebra

FOSSIL OF ANKYLOSAURUS TAIL CLUB

Ornithopods 1

IGUANODON TOOTH

ORNITHOPODS ("BIRD FEET") were a group of ornithischian ("bird-hipped") dinosaurs. These bipedal and quadrupedal herbivores had a horny beak, plant-cutting or grinding cheek teeth, and a pelvic and tail region stiffened by bony tendons. They evolved teeth and jaws adapted to pulping vegetation and flourished from the Middle Jurassic to the Late Cretaceous period (165–65 million years ago) in North America, Europe, Africa, China, Australia, and Antarctica. Some ornithopods were no larger than a dog, while others were immense creatures up to 49 ft (15 m) long. Iguanodonts, an ornithopod group, had a broad, toothless beak at the end of a long snout, large jaws with long rows of ridged, closely packed teeth for grinding vegetation, a bulky body, and a heavy tail. *Iguanodon* and some other iguanodonts had large thumb-spikes that were strong enough to stab attackers. Another group, the hadrosaurs, such as *Gryposaurus* and *Hadrosaurus,* lived in Late Cretaceous times (97–65 million years ago) and with their broad beaks are sometimes known as "duckbills." They were characterized by their deep skulls and closely packed rows of teeth, while some, such as *Corythosaurus* and *Lambeosaurus,* had tall, hollow, bony head crests.

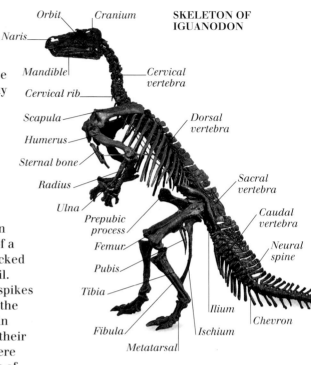

SKELETON OF IGUANODON

Orbit
Cranium
Naris
Mandible
Cervical vertebra
Cervical rib
Scapula
Dorsal vertebra
Humerus
Sternal bone
Radius
Sacral vertebra
Ulna
Caudal vertebra
Prepubic process
Neural spine
Femur
Pubis
Tibia
Ilium
Chevron
Fibula
Ischium
Metatarsal

Thigh

Heavy, stiff tail

SKULL AND MANDIBLE OF YOUNG IGUANODON

Cheek tooth
Maxilla
Orbit
Cranium
Premaxilla
Paroccipital process
Jugal bone
Coronoid process
Predentary bone
Dentary bone
Mandible

Knee
Hind limb
Ankle
Toe
Foot
Hooflike nail

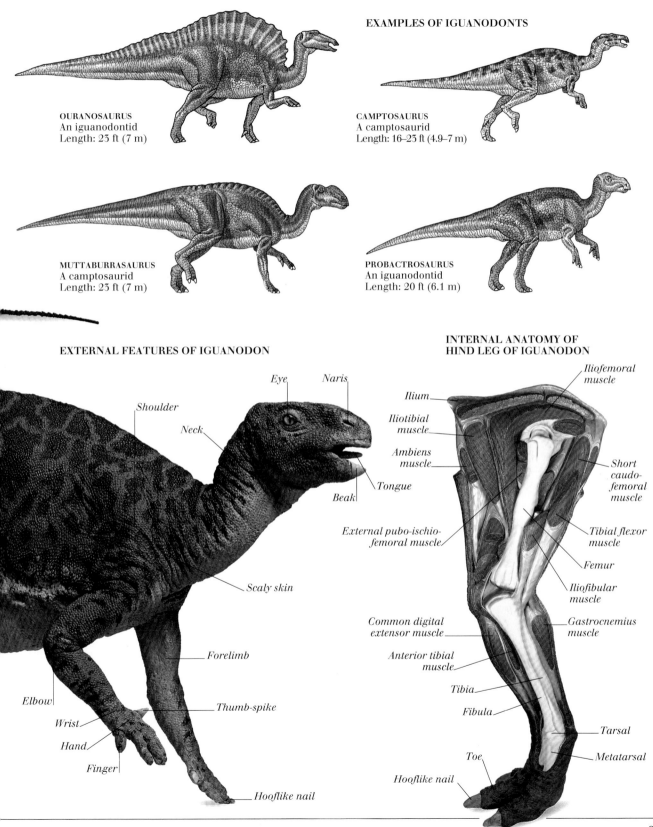

EXAMPLES OF IGUANODONTS

OURANOSAURUS
An iguanodontid
Length: 23 ft (7 m)

CAMPTOSAURUS
A camptosaurid
Length: 16–23 ft (4.9–7 m)

MUTTABURRASAURUS
A camptosaurid
Length: 23 ft (7 m)

PROBACTROSAURUS
An iguanodontid
Length: 20 ft (6.1 m)

EXTERNAL FEATURES OF IGUANODON

Eye

Naris

Shoulder

Neck

Tongue

Beak

Scaly skin

Forelimb

Elbow

Wrist

Hand

Thumb-spike

Finger

Hooflike nail

INTERNAL ANATOMY OF HIND LEG OF IGUANODON

Iliofemoral muscle

Ilium

Iliotibial muscle

Ambiens muscle

Short caudo-femoral muscle

External pubo-ischio-femoral muscle

Tibial flexor muscle

Femur

Iliofibular muscle

Common digital extensor muscle

Gastrocnemius muscle

Anterior tibial muscle

Tibia

Fibula

Tarsal

Metatarsal

Toe

Hooflike nail

Ornithopods 2

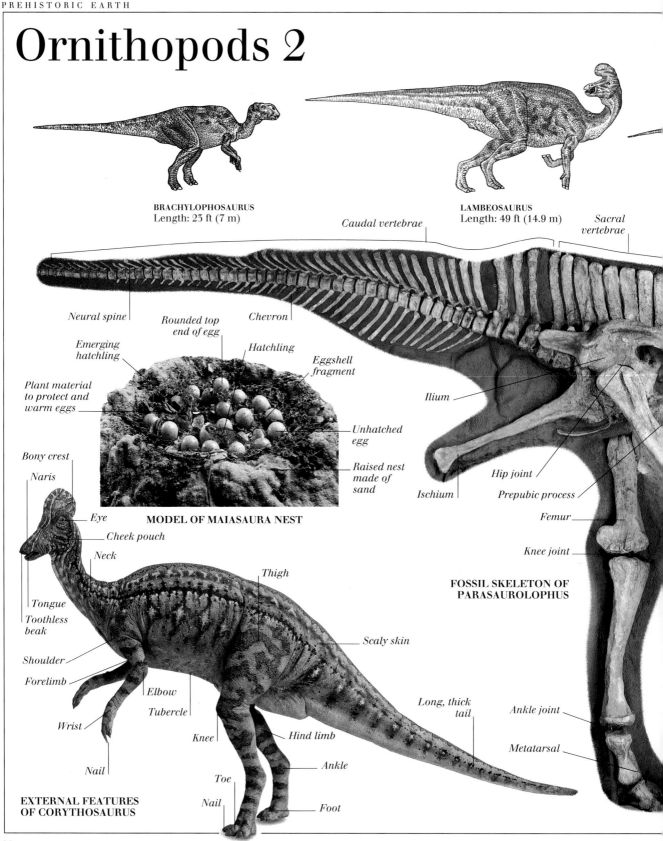

BRACHYLOPHOSAURUS
Length: 23 ft (7 m)

LAMBEOSAURUS
Length: 49 ft (14.9 m)

Caudal vertebrae

Sacral vertebrae

Neural spine

Rounded top end of egg

Chevron

Emerging hatchling

Hatchling

Eggshell fragment

Plant material to protect and warm eggs

Ilium

Hip joint

Unhatched egg

Ischium

Prepubic process

Raised nest made of sand

Femur

Bony crest

Naris

MODEL OF MAIASAURA NEST

Knee joint

Eye

FOSSIL SKELETON OF PARASAUROLOPHUS

Cheek pouch

Neck

Thigh

Tongue

Toothless beak

Scaly skin

Shoulder

Forelimb

Elbow

Tubercle

Long, thick tail

Ankle joint

Wrist

Knee

Hind limb

Metatarsal

Nail

Ankle

Toe

EXTERNAL FEATURES OF CORYTHOSAURUS

Nail

Foot

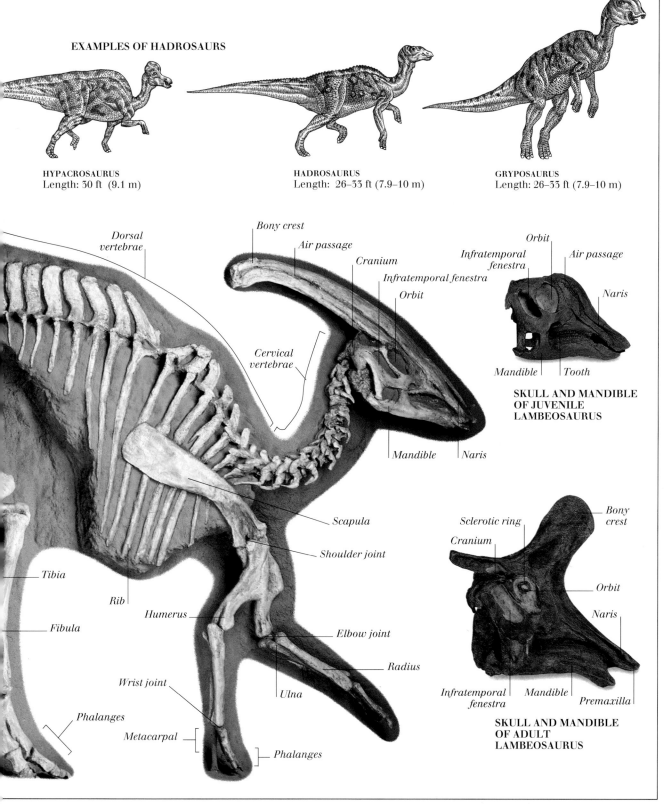

EXAMPLES OF HADROSAURS

HYPACROSAURUS
Length: 30 ft (9.1 m)

HADROSAURUS
Length: 26–33 ft (7.9–10 m)

GRYPOSAURUS
Length: 26–33 ft (7.9–10 m)

Dorsal vertebrae

Bony crest

Air passage

Cranium

Infratemporal fenestra

Orbit

Cervical vertebrae

Orbit

Infratemporal fenestra

Air passage

Naris

Mandible

Naris

Mandible

Tooth

SKULL AND MANDIBLE OF JUVENILE LAMBEOSAURUS

Scapula

Shoulder joint

Tibia

Rib

Humerus

Fibula

Elbow joint

Radius

Wrist joint

Ulna

Phalanges

Metacarpal

Phalanges

Sclerotic ring

Bony crest

Cranium

Orbit

Naris

Infratemporal fenestra

Mandible

Premaxilla

SKULL AND MANDIBLE OF ADULT LAMBEOSAURUS

Marginocephalians 1

HEAD-BUTTING PRENOCEPHALES

MARGINOCEPHALIA ("margined heads") were a group of bipedal and quadrupedal ornithischian dinosaurs with a narrow shelf or deep, bony frill at the back of the skull. Marginocephalians were probably descended from the same ancestor as the ornithopods and lived in what are now North America, Africa, Asia, and Europe during the Cretaceous period (146–65 million years ago). They were divided into two infraorders: Pachycephalosauria ("thick-headed lizards"), such as *Pachycephalosaurus* and *Stegoceras*, and Ceratopsia ("horned faces"), such as *Triceratops* and *Psittacosaurus*. The thick skulls of Pachycephalosauria protected their brains during head-butting contests fought to win territory and mates; their hips and spines were also strengthened to withstand the shock. The bony frill of Ceratopsia would have added to their frightening appearance when charging; the neck was strengthened for impact and to support the huge head, with its snipping beak and powerful slicing toothed jaws. A charging ceratops would have been a formidable opponent for even the largest predators. Ceratopsia were among the most abundant herbivorous dinosaurs of the Late Cretaceous period (97–65 million years ago).

Thick, high-domed cranium
Supraorbital ridge
Orbit
Naris
Mandible
Neural spine
Cervical rib
Humerus
Ulna
Radius
Prepubis
Wrist joint
Metacarpal
Phalanx
Ilium
Ischium
Metatarsals
Phalanges

EXAMPLES OF SKULLS OF PACHYCEPHALOSAURS

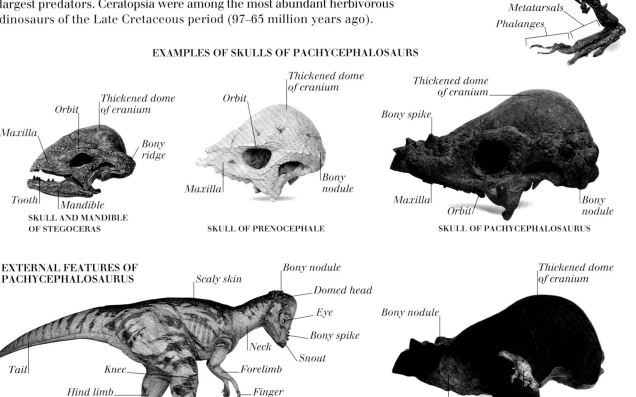

Orbit
Thickened dome of cranium
Maxilla
Bony ridge
Tooth
Mandible

SKULL AND MANDIBLE OF STEGOCERAS

Orbit
Thickened dome of cranium
Maxilla
Bony nodule

SKULL OF PRENOCEPHALE

Thickened dome of cranium
Bony spike
Maxilla
Orbit
Bony nodule

SKULL OF PACHYCEPHALOSAURUS

EXTERNAL FEATURES OF PACHYCEPHALOSAURUS

Scaly skin
Bony nodule
Domed head
Eye
Bony spike
Neck
Snout
Forelimb
Finger
Hand
Claw
Toe
Foot
Claw
Ankle
Hind limb
Knee
Tail

Thickened dome of cranium
Bony nodule
Buccal cavity
Brain cavity

SECTION THROUGH SKULL OF PACHYCEPHALOSAURUS

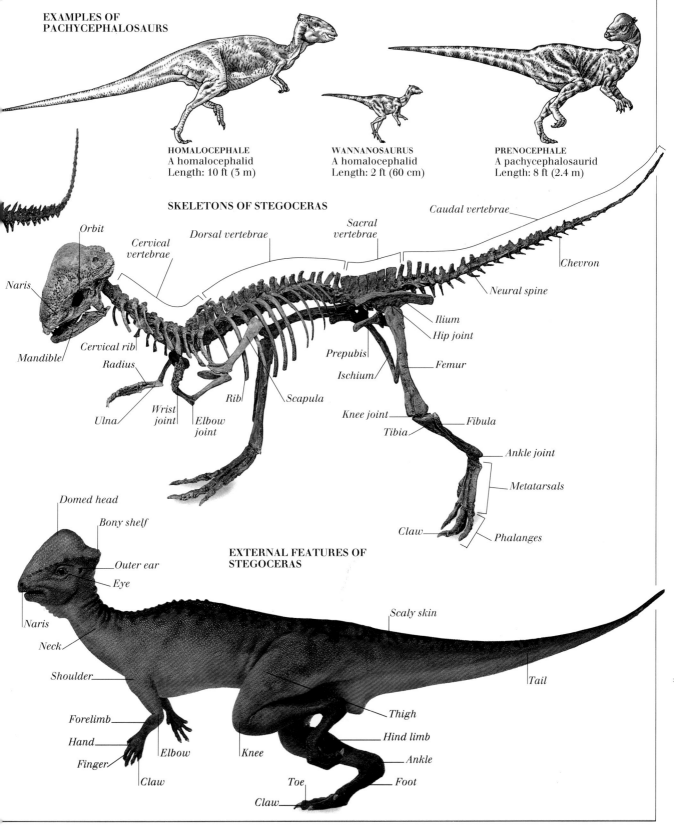

**EXAMPLES OF
PACHYCEPHALOSAURS**

HOMALOCEPHALE
A homalocephalid
Length: 10 ft (3 m)

WANNANOSAURUS
A homalocephalid
Length: 2 ft (60 cm)

PRENOCEPHALE
A pachycephalosaurid
Length: 8 ft (2.4 m)

SKELETONS OF STEGOCERAS

Caudal vertebrae

Sacral
vertebrae

Dorsal vertebrae

Orbit

Cervical
vertebrae

Chevron

Naris

Neural spine

Ilium

Hip joint

Mandible

Cervical rib

Prepubis

Femur

Radius

Ischium

Rib

Scapula

Wrist
joint

Elbow
joint

Ulna

Knee joint

Fibula

Tibia

Ankle joint

Metatarsals

Claw

Phalanges

Domed head

Bony shelf

**EXTERNAL FEATURES OF
STEGOCERAS**

Outer ear

Eye

Scaly skin

Naris

Neck

Tail

Shoulder

Thigh

Forelimb

Hand

Hind limb

Elbow

Knee

Ankle

Finger

Foot

Claw

Toe

Claw

Marginocephalians 2

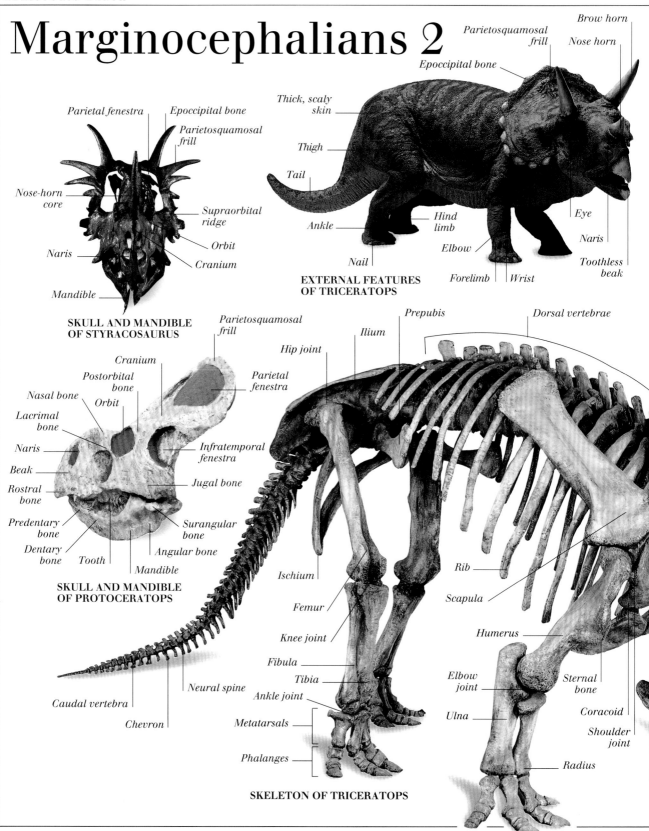

SKULL AND MANDIBLE OF STYRACOSAURUS

Parietal fenestra
Epoccipital bone
Parietosquamosal frill
Nose-horn core
Supraorbital ridge
Orbit
Naris
Cranium
Mandible

EXTERNAL FEATURES OF TRICERATOPS

Parietosquamosal frill
Brow horn
Nose horn
Epoccipital bone
Thick, scaly skin
Thigh
Tail
Ankle
Nail
Hind limb
Elbow
Forelimb
Wrist
Eye
Naris
Toothless beak

SKULL AND MANDIBLE OF PROTOCERATOPS

Cranium
Postorbital bone
Nasal bone
Orbit
Lacrimal bone
Naris
Beak
Rostral bone
Predentary bone
Dentary bone
Tooth
Mandible
Angular bone
Surangular bone
Jugal bone
Infratemporal fenestra
Parietal fenestra
Parietosquamosal frill

SKELETON OF TRICERATOPS

Prepubis
Ilium
Hip joint
Dorsal vertebrae
Ischium
Femur
Knee joint
Fibula
Tibia
Ankle joint
Metatarsals
Phalanges
Caudal vertebra
Chevron
Neural spine
Rib
Scapula
Humerus
Elbow joint
Ulna
Sternal bone
Coracoid
Shoulder joint
Radius

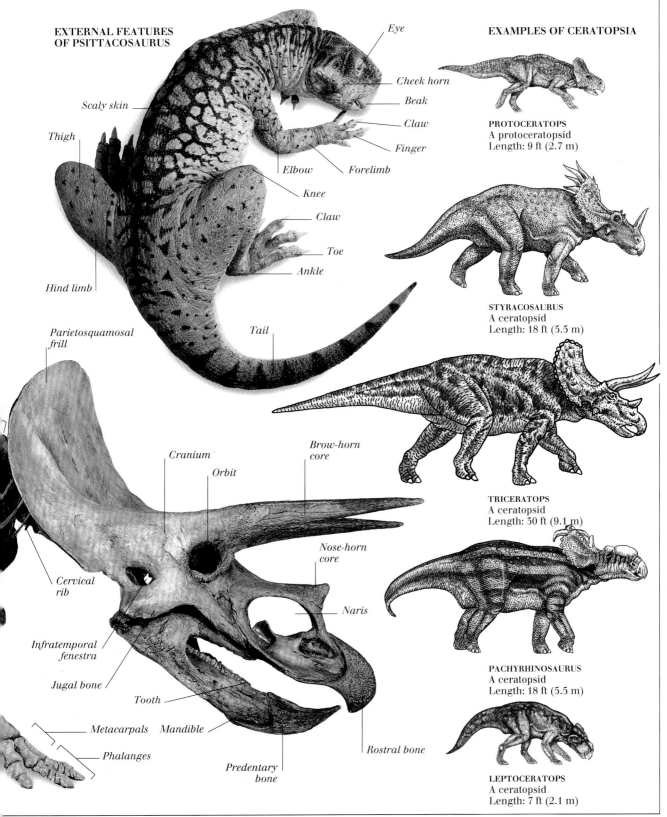

EXTERNAL FEATURES OF PSITTACOSAURUS

Eye

Cheek horn

Beak

Claw

Finger

Scaly skin

Thigh

Elbow

Forelimb

Knee

Claw

Toe

Ankle

Hind limb

Parietosquamosal frill

Tail

Cranium

Orbit

Brow-horn core

Cervical rib

Nose-horn core

Naris

Infratemporal fenestra

Jugal bone

Tooth

Metacarpals

Mandible

Phalanges

Predentary bone

Rostral bone

EXAMPLES OF CERATOPSIA

PROTOCERATOPS
A protoceratopsid
Length: 9 ft (2.7 m)

STYRACOSAURUS
A ceratopsid
Length: 18 ft (5.5 m)

TRICERATOPS
A ceratopsid
Length: 30 ft (9.1 m)

PACHYRHINOSAURUS
A ceratopsid
Length: 18 ft (5.5 m)

LEPTOCERATOPS
A ceratopsid
Length: 7 ft (2.1 m)

Mammals 1

**TETRALOPHODON
CHEEK TEETH**

SINCE THE EXTINCTION of the dinosaurs 65 million years ago, mammals have been the dominant vertebrates on Earth and include terrestrial, aerial, and aquatic forms. Having developed from the reptilian Therapsids, the first true mammals—small, nocturnal, rodentlike creatures, such as *Megazostrodon*—appeared over 200 million years ago during the Triassic period (245–208 million years ago). Mammals had several features that improved on those of their reptilian ancestors: an efficient four-chambered heart allowed these warm-blooded animals to sustain high levels of activity; a covering of hair helped them maintain a constant body temperature; an improved limb structure gave them more efficient locomotion; and the birth of live young and the immediate supply of food from the mother's milk aided their rapid growth. Since the end of the Mesozoic era (65 million years ago), the number of different mammal orders and the abundance of species in each order have varied dramatically. For example, the Perissodactyla (the order that includes *Coelodonta* and modern horses) was the most common group during the Early Tertiary period (about 54 million years ago). Today, the mammalian orders with the most populous species are the Rodentia (rats and mice), the Carnivora (bears, cats, and dogs), and the Artiodactyla (cattle, deer, and pigs), while the Proboscidea order, which included many genera, such as *Phiomia, Moeritherium, Tetralophodon,* and *Mammuthus*, now has only one member: the modern elephant. In Australia and South America, millions of years of continental isolation led to the development of the marsupials, a group of mammals distinct from the placentals (see p. 74) that existed elsewhere.

*Long tail aids
balance*

*Insulating
hair*

*Neural
spine*

Scapula

*Cervical
vertebra*

Humerus

Nasal horn

Naris

Orbit

Mandible

Radius

*Predentary
bone*

Ulna

*Chisel-edged
molar*

Metacarpal

Phalanx

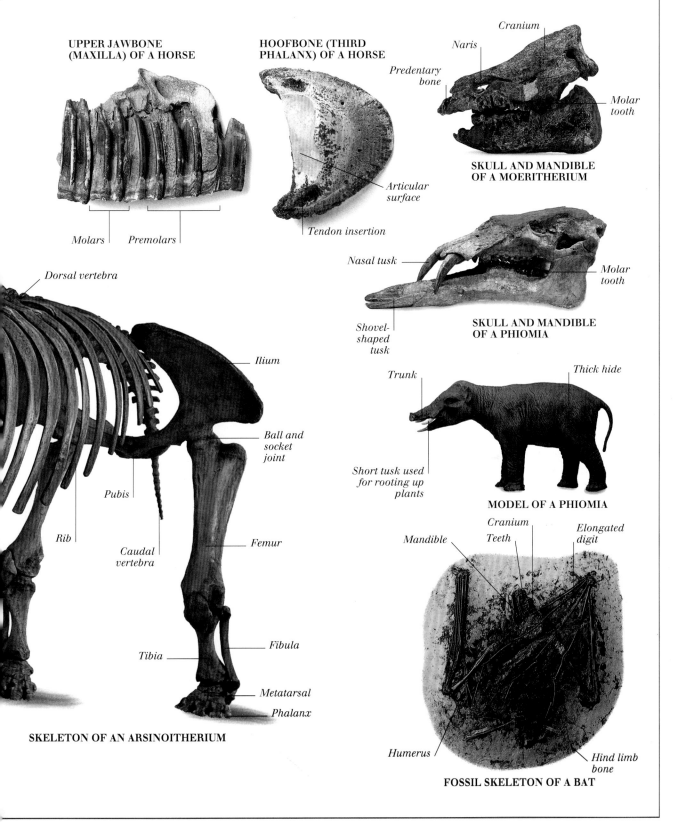

UPPER JAWBONE (MAXILLA) OF A HORSE

Molars Premolars

HOOFBONE (THIRD PHALANX) OF A HORSE

Articular surface

Tendon insertion

Cranium

Naris

Predentary bone

Molar tooth

SKULL AND MANDIBLE OF A MOERITHERIUM

Nasal tusk

Molar tooth

Shovel-shaped tusk

SKULL AND MANDIBLE OF A PHIOMIA

Trunk

Thick hide

Short tusk used for rooting up plants

MODEL OF A PHIOMIA

Dorsal vertebra

Ilium

Ball and socket joint

Pubis

Rib

Caudal vertebra

Femur

Tibia

Fibula

Metatarsal

Phalanx

SKELETON OF AN ARSINOITHERIUM

Mandible

Cranium

Teeth

Elongated digit

Humerus

Hind limb bone

FOSSIL SKELETON OF A BAT

Mammals 2

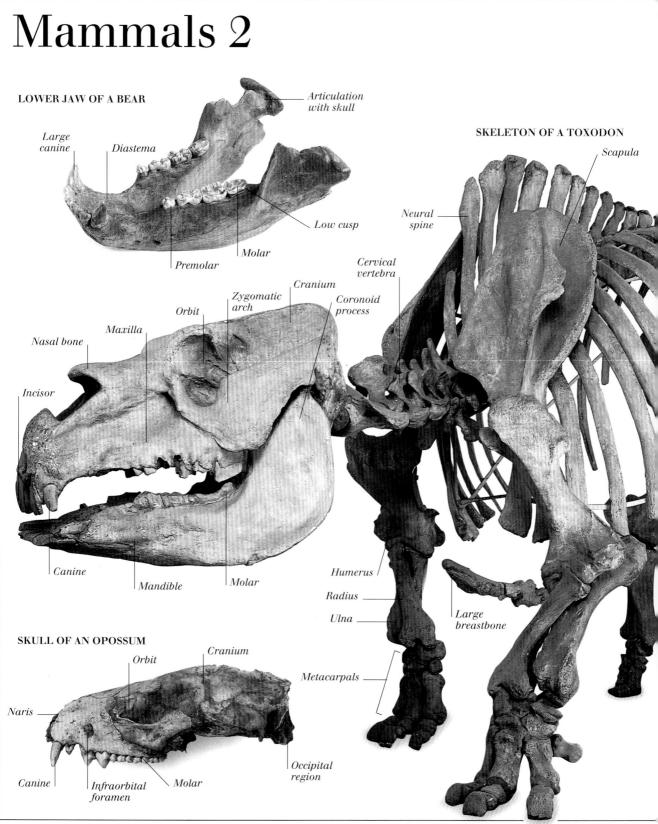

LOWER JAW OF A BEAR

Articulation
with skull

Large
canine

Diastema

Low cusp

Molar

Premolar

SKELETON OF A TOXODON

Scapula

Neural
spine

Cervical
vertebra

Cranium

Coronoid
process

Zygomatic
arch

Orbit

Maxilla

Nasal bone

Incisor

Canine

Mandible

Molar

Humerus

Radius

Ulna

Large
breastbone

SKULL OF AN OPOSSUM

Orbit

Cranium

Naris

Metacarpals

Occipital
region

Canine

Infraorbital
foramen

Molar

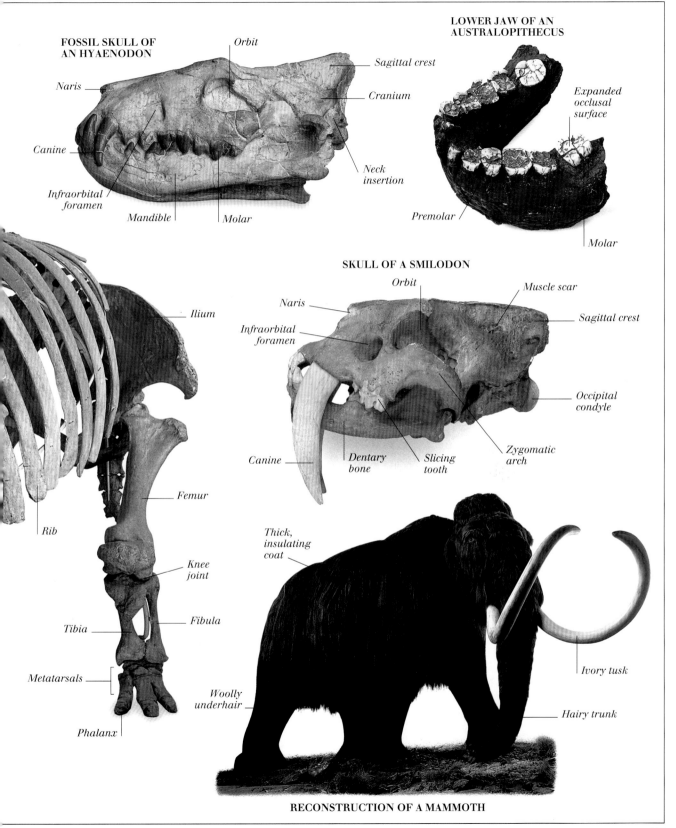

FOSSIL SKULL OF AN HYAENODON

Orbit

Naris

Canine

Infraorbital foramen

Mandible

Molar

Sagittal crest

Cranium

Neck insertion

LOWER JAW OF AN AUSTRALOPITHECUS

Expanded occlusal surface

Premolar

Molar

SKULL OF A SMILODON

Orbit

Naris

Infraorbital foramen

Canine

Dentary bone

Slicing tooth

Muscle scar

Sagittal crest

Occipital condyle

Zygomatic arch

Ilium

Rib

Femur

Knee joint

Tibia

Fibula

Metatarsals

Phalanx

RECONSTRUCTION OF A MAMMOTH

Thick, insulating coat

Woolly underhair

Ivory tusk

Hairy trunk

The first hominids

MODERN HUMANS BELONG TO THE MAMMALIAN order of primates (see pp. 202–203), which originated about 55 million years ago; they comprise the only extant hominid species. The earliest hominid was *Australopithecus* ("southern ape"), a small-brained intermediate between apes and humans that was capable of standing and walking upright. *Homo habilis*, the first known human appeared at least 2 million years ago. This larger-brained "handy man" began making tools for hunting. *Homo erectus* first appeared in Africa about 1.8 million years ago and spread into Asia about 800,000 years later. Smaller toothed than *Homo habilis*, it developed fire as a tool, which enabled it to cook food. Neanderthals, a near relative of modern humans, originated about 200,000 years ago, and *Homo sapiens* (modern humans) appeared in Africa about 100,000 years later. The two coexisted for thousands of years, but by 30,000 years ago, *Homo sapiens* had become dominant and the Neanderthals had died out. Classification of *Homo sapiens* in relation to its ancestors is enormously problematic: modern humans must be classified not only by bone structure, but also by specific behavior—the ability to plan future action; to follow traditions; and to use symbolic communication, including complex language and the ability to use and recognize symbols.

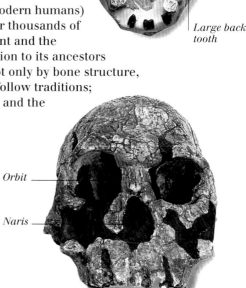

JAWBONE OF AUSTRALOPITHECUS (SOUTHERN APE)

Larger jawbone than modern human

Large back tooth

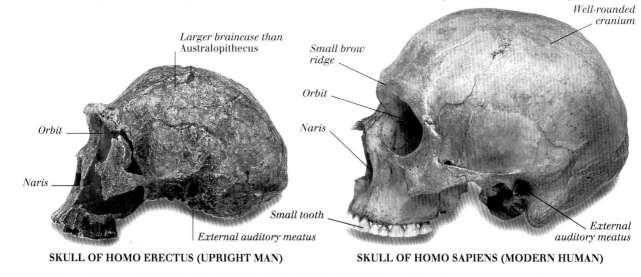

Jutting brow ridge

Cranium

Orbit

Naris

Jutting jawbone

SKULL OF AUSTRALOPITHECUS (SOUTHERN APE)

Orbit

Naris

SKULL OF HOMO HABILIS (FIRST KNOWN HUMAN)

Larger braincase than Australopithecus

Orbit

Naris

External auditory meatus

SKULL OF HOMO ERECTUS (UPRIGHT MAN)

Well-rounded cranium

Small brow ridge

Orbit

Naris

Small tooth

External auditory meatus

SKULL OF HOMO SAPIENS (MODERN HUMAN)

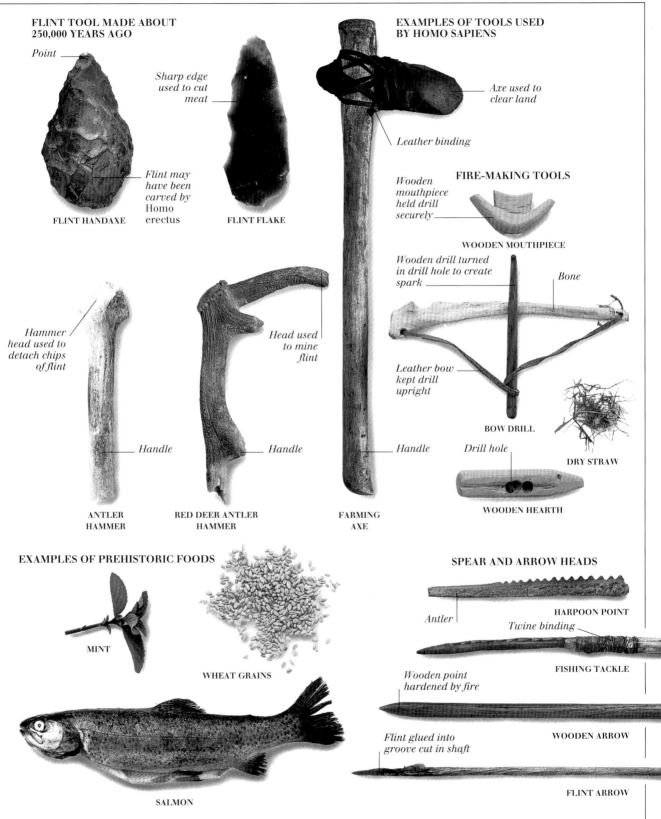

FLINT TOOL MADE ABOUT 250,000 YEARS AGO

Point

Sharp edge used to cut meat

Flint may have been carved by Homo erectus

FLINT HANDAXE

FLINT FLAKE

EXAMPLES OF TOOLS USED BY HOMO SAPIENS

Axe used to clear land

Leather binding

FIRE-MAKING TOOLS

Wooden mouthpiece held drill securely

WOODEN MOUTHPIECE

Wooden drill turned in drill hole to create spark

Bone

Leather bow kept drill upright

BOW DRILL

Drill hole

DRY STRAW

WOODEN HEARTH

Hammer head used to detach chips of flint

Head used to mine flint

Handle

Handle

Handle

ANTLER HAMMER

RED DEER ANTLER HAMMER

FARMING AXE

EXAMPLES OF PREHISTORIC FOODS

MINT

WHEAT GRAINS

SALMON

SPEAR AND ARROW HEADS

Antler

HARPOON POINT

Twine binding

FISHING TACKLE

Wooden point hardened by fire

WOODEN ARROW

Flint glued into groove cut in shaft

FLINT ARROW

PLANTS

Plant varieties

FLOWERING PLANT
Bromeliad
(*Acanthostachys strobilacea*)

Leaf

THERE ARE MORE THAN 300,000 SPECIES of plants. They
show a wide diversity of forms, ranging from delicate liverworts, adapted for life
in a damp habitat, to cacti, capable of surviving in the desert. The plant kingdom includes
herbaceous plants, such as corn, which completes its life cycle in one year, to the giant redwood tree, which
can live for thousands of years. This diversity reflects the adaptations of plants to survive in a wide range of
habitats. This is seen most clearly in the flowering plants (phylum Angiospermophyta), which are the most
numerous, with over 250,000 species. They are also the most widespread, being found from the tropics to the
arctic. Despite their diversity, plants share certain characteristics. Typically, plants are green, and make their
food by photosynthesis. Most plants live in or on a substrate, such as soil, and do not actively move. Algae
(kingdom Protista) and fungi (kingdom Fungi) have some plantlike characteristics and are
often studied alongside plants, although they are not true plants.

GREEN ALGA
Micrograph of desmid
(*Micrasterias sp.*)

FERN
Tree fern
(*Dicksonia antarctica*)

*Pyrenoid
(small protein
body)*

Chloroplast

*Sinus
(division between
two halves of cell)*

Cell wall

*Rachis
(main axis
of pinnate leaf)*

BRYOPHYTE
Moss
(*Bryum sp.*)

*Seta
(stalk)*

Immature capsule

*Petiole
(leaf stalk)*

*Ramentum
(brown scale)*

*Sporophyte
(spore-
producing
plant)*

*Capsule
(site of spore
production)*

*Base of dead
frond (leaf)*

Trunk

"Leaf"

*Gametophyte
(gamete-producing
plant)*

*Adventitious
root*

*Epiphytic
fern growing
at base*

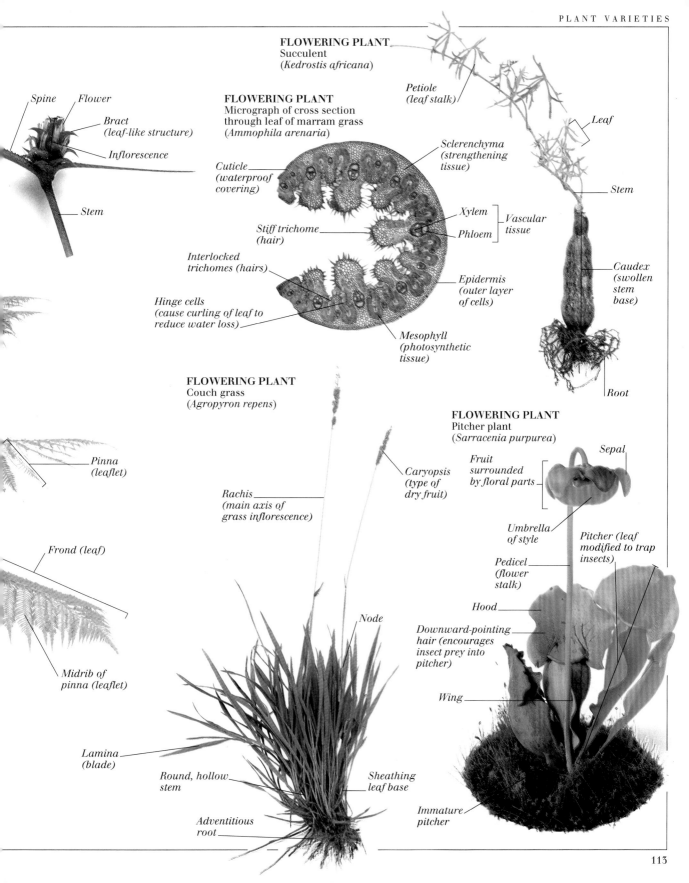

FLOWERING PLANT
Succulent
(*Kedrostis africana*)

*Petiole
(leaf stalk)*

Leaf

Stem

*Caudex
(swollen
stem
base)*

Root

Spine *Flower*

*Bract
(leaf-like structure)*

Inflorescence

Stem

FLOWERING PLANT
Micrograph of cross section
through leaf of marram grass
(*Ammophila arenaria*)

*Cuticle
(waterproof
covering)*

*Sclerenchyma
(strengthening
tissue)*

Xylem

Phloem

*Vascular
tissue*

*Stiff trichome
(hair)*

*Interlocked
trichomes (hairs)*

*Hinge cells
(cause curling of leaf to
reduce water loss)*

*Epidermis
(outer layer
of cells)*

*Mesophyll
(photosynthetic
tissue)*

*Pinna
(leaflet)*

Frond (leaf)

*Midrib of
pinna (leaflet)*

FLOWERING PLANT
Couch grass
(*Agropyron repens*)

*Rachis
(main axis of
grass inflorescence)*

*Caryopsis
(type of
dry fruit)*

Node

*Lamina
(blade)*

*Round, hollow
stem*

*Sheathing
leaf base*

*Adventitious
root*

FLOWERING PLANT
Pitcher plant
(*Sarracenia purpurea*)

Sepal

*Fruit
surrounded
by floral parts*

*Umbrella
of style*

*Pitcher (leaf
modified to trap
insects)*

*Pedicel
(flower
stalk)*

Hood

*Downward-pointing
hair (encourages
insect prey into
pitcher)*

Wing

*Immature
pitcher*

Fungi and lichens

FUNGI WERE ONCE THOUGHT OF AS PLANTS but are now classified as a separate kingdom. This kingdom includes not only the familiar mushrooms, puffballs, stinkhorns, and molds, but also yeasts, smuts, rusts, and lichens. Most fungi are multicellular, consisting of a mass of thread-like hyphae that together form a mycelium. However, the simpler fungi, like yeasts, are microscopic, single-celled organisms. Typically, fungi reproduce by means of spores. Most fungi feed on dead or decaying matter or on living organisms. A few fungi obtain their food from plants or algae, with which they have a symbiotic (mutually advantageous) relationship. Lichens are a symbiotic partnership between algae and fungi. Of the six types of lichens the three most common are crustose (flat and crusty), foliose (leafy), and fruticose (shrub-like). Some lichens (such as *Cladonia floerkeana*) are a combination of types. Lichens reproduce by means of spores or soredia (powdery vegetative fragments).

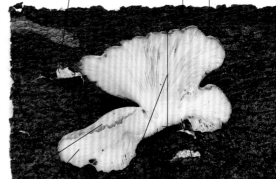

Emerging sporophore (spore-bearing structure)

Pileus (cap) continuous with stipe (stalk)

Bark of dead beech tree

Inrolled margin of pileus (cap)

Gill (site of spore production)

Sporophore (spore-bearing structure)

Stipe (stalk)

Hyphae (fungal filaments)

OYSTER FUNGUS
(*Pleurotus pulmonarius*)

EXAMPLES OF LICHENS

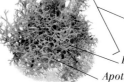

Secondary fruticose thallus

Branched, hollow stem

Apothecium (spore-producing body)

FRUTICOSE
Cladonia portentosa

Soredia (powdery vegetative fragments) produced at end of lobe

Tree bark

Foliose thallus

FOLIOSE
Hypogymnia physodes

Gleba (spore-producing tissue found in this type of fungus)

Sporophore (spore-bearing structure)

Porous stipe (stalk)

Volva (remains of universal veil)

STINKHORN
(*Phallus impudicus*)

Toothed branchlet

Branch

Sporophore (spore-bearing structure)

Stipe (stalk)

RAMARIA FORMOSA

Soredia (powdery vegetative fragments) released onto surface of squamulose thallus

Apothecium (spore-producing body)

Basal scale of primary squamulose thallus

Podetium (granular stalk) of secondary fruticose thallus

Moss

SQUAMULOSE (SCALY) AND FRUTICOSE THALLUS
Cladonia floerkeana

SECTION THROUGH FOLIOSE LICHEN SHOWING REPRODUCTION BY SOREDIA

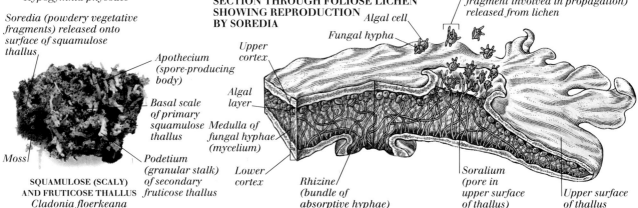

Algal cell

Fungal hypha

Soredium (powdery vegetative fragment involved in propagation) released from lichen

Upper cortex

Algal layer

Medulla of fungal hyphae (mycelium)

Lower cortex

Rhizine (bundle of absorptive hyphae)

Soralium (pore in upper surface of thallus)

Upper surface of thallus

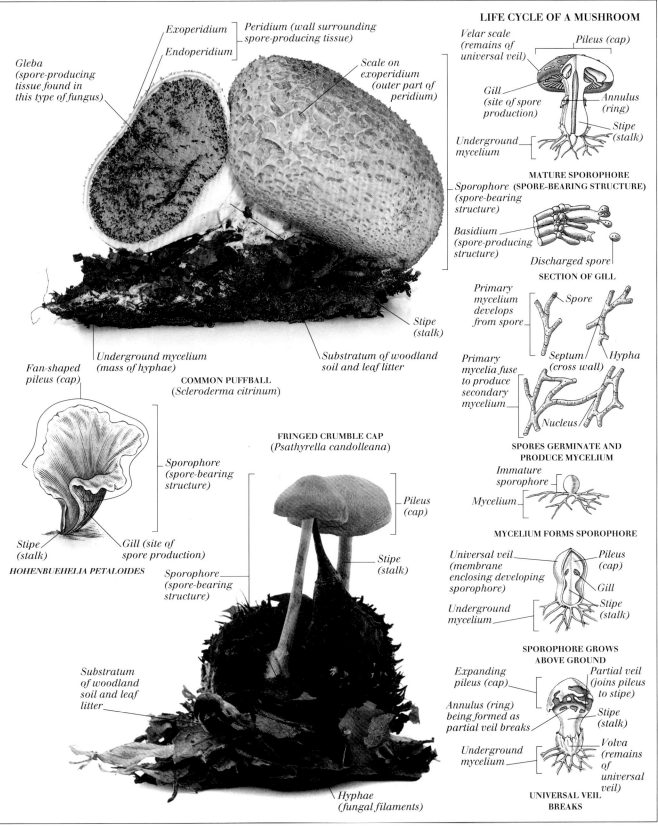

LIFE CYCLE OF A MUSHROOM

Exoperidium

Endoperidium

Peridium (wall surrounding spore-producing tissue)

Gleba (spore-producing tissue found in this type of fungus)

Scale on exoperidium (outer part of peridium)

Velar scale (remains of universal veil)

Pileus (cap)

Gill (site of spore production)

Annulus (ring)

Stipe (stalk)

Underground mycelium

MATURE SPOROPHORE (SPORE-BEARING STRUCTURE)

Sporophore (spore-bearing structure)

Basidium (spore-producing structure)

Discharged spore

SECTION OF GILL

Primary mycelium develops from spore

Spore

Septum (cross wall)

Hypha

Primary mycelia fuse to produce secondary mycelium

Nucleus

SPORES GERMINATE AND PRODUCE MYCELIUM

Stipe (stalk)

Underground mycelium (mass of hyphae)

Substratum of woodland soil and leaf litter

COMMON PUFFBALL
(*Scleroderma citrinum*)

Immature sporophore

Mycelium

MYCELIUM FORMS SPOROPHORE

Fan-shaped pileus (cap)

Sporophore (spore-bearing structure)

FRINGED CRUMBLE CAP
(*Psathyrella candolleana*)

Pileus (cap)

Stipe (stalk)

Universal veil (membrane enclosing developing sporophore)

Pileus (cap)

Gill

Stipe (stalk)

Underground mycelium

Stipe (stalk)

Gill (site of spore production)

Sporophore (spore-bearing structure)

HOHENBUEHELIA PETALOIDES

SPOROPHORE GROWS ABOVE GROUND

Expanding pileus (cap)

Partial veil (joins pileus to stipe)

Annulus (ring) being formed as partial veil breaks

Stipe (stalk)

Substratum of woodland soil and leaf litter

Underground mycelium

Volva (remains of universal veil)

Hyphae (fungal filaments)

UNIVERSAL VEIL BREAKS

Algae and seaweed

ALGAE ARE NOT TRUE PLANTS. They form a diverse group of plantlike organisms that belong to the kingdom Protista. Like plants, algae possess the green pigment chlorophyll and make their own food by photosynthesis (see pp. 138-139). Many algae also possess other pigments by which they can be classified. For example, the brown pigment fucoxanthin is found in brown algae. Some of the ten phyla of algae are exclusively unicellular (single-celled); others also contain aggregates of cells in filaments or colonies. Three phyla—the Chlorophyta (green algae), Rhodophyta (red algae), and Phaeophyta (brown algae)—contain larger, multicellular, thalloid (flat), marine organisms commonly known as seaweed. Most algae can reproduce sexually. For example, in brown seaweed *Fucus vesiculosus*, gametes (sex cells) are produced in conceptacles (chambers) in the receptacles (fertile tips of fronds); after their release into the sea, antherozoids (male gametes) and oospheres (female gametes) fuse. The resulting zygote settles on a rock and develops into a new seaweed.

BROWN SEAWEED
Channeled wrack
(*Pelvetia canaliculata*)

Thallus (plant body)

Receptacle (fertile tip of frond)

Apical notch

Margin of lamina (blade) rolled inwards to form channel

Hapteron (holdfast)

BROWN SEAWEED
Spiral wrack
(*Fucus spiralis*)

Apical notch

Conceptacle (chamber)

Receptacle (fertile tip of frond)

Lamina (blade)

Smooth margin

Midrib

Thallus (plant body)

Hapteron (holdfast)

EXAMPLES OF ALGAE

Reproductive chamber

Cap

Sterile whorl

Cell wall

Stalk

Rhizoid

GREEN ALGA
Acetabularia sp.

Flagellum

Eyespot

Contractile vacuole

Cytoplasm

Nucleus

Cell wall

Chloroplast

Pyrenoid (small protein body)

Starch grain

GREEN ALGA
Chlamydomonas sp.

Coenobium (colony of cells)

Daughter coenobium

Girdle

Gelatinous sheath

Nucleus

Biflagellate cell

GREEN ALGA
Volvox sp.

Spine

Cytoplasm

Vacuole

Plastid (photosynthetic organelle)

Nucleus

DIATOM
Thalassiosira sp.

Apical notch

Receptacle (fertile tip of frond)

Conceptacle (chamber) containing reproductive structures)

Lamina (blade)

Midrib

RECEPTACLE
Spiral wrack
(*Fucus spiralis*)

BROWN SEAWEED
Oarweed
(*Laminaria digitata*)

Thallus (plant body)

Lamina (blade) palmately divided

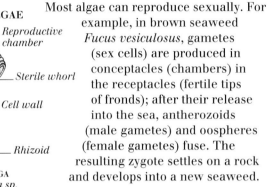
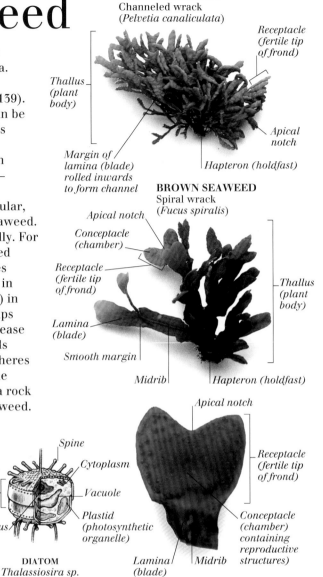

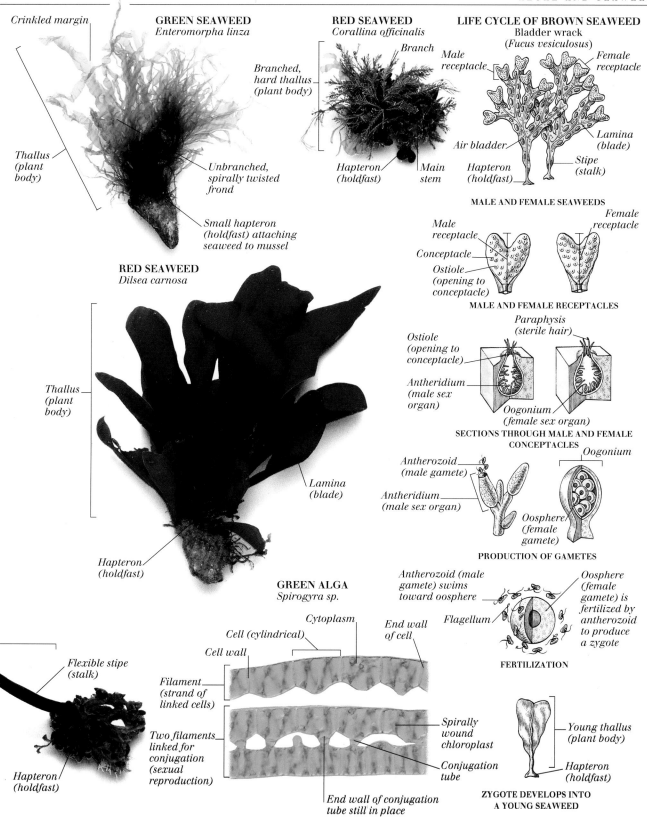

GREEN SEAWEED
Enteromorpha linza

Crinkled margin

Thallus
(plant
body)

Unbranched,
spirally twisted
frond

Small hapteron
(holdfast) attaching
seaweed to mussel

RED SEAWEED
Corallina officinalis

Branch

Branched,
hard thallus
(plant body)

Hapteron
(holdfast)

Main
stem

LIFE CYCLE OF BROWN SEAWEED
Bladder wrack
(*Fucus vesiculosus*)

Male
receptacle

Female
receptacle

Air bladder

Lamina
(blade)

Hapteron
(holdfast)

Stipe
(stalk)

MALE AND FEMALE SEAWEEDS

Male
receptacle

Female
receptacle

Conceptacle

Ostiole
(opening to
conceptacle)

MALE AND FEMALE RECEPTACLES

Paraphysis
(sterile hair)

Ostiole
(opening to
conceptacle)

Antheridium
(male sex
organ)

Oogonium
(female sex organ)

**SECTIONS THROUGH MALE AND FEMALE
CONCEPTACLES**

Antherozoid
(male gamete)

Oogonium

Antheridium
(male sex
organ)

Oosphere
(female
gamete)

PRODUCTION OF GAMETES

RED SEAWEED
Dilsea carnosa

Thallus
(plant
body)

Lamina
(blade)

Hapteron
(holdfast)

Antherozoid (male
gamete) swims
toward oosphere

Flagellum

Oosphere
(female
gamete) is
fertilized by
antherozoid
to produce
a zygote

FERTILIZATION

GREEN ALGA
Spirogyra sp.

Cytoplasm

Cell (cylindrical)

End wall
of cell

Cell wall

Filament
(strand of
linked cells)

Two filaments
linked for
conjugation
(sexual
reproduction)

Spirally
wound
chloroplast

Conjugation
tube

End wall of conjugation
tube still in place

Young thallus
(plant body)

Hapteron
(holdfast)

**ZYGOTE DEVELOPS INTO
A YOUNG SEAWEED**

Flexible stipe
(stalk)

Hapteron
(holdfast)

Liverworts and mosses

LIVERWORTS AND MOSSES ARE SMALL, LOW-GROWING PLANTS that belong to the phylum Bryophyta. Bryophytes do not have true stems, leaves, or roots (they are anchored to the ground by rhizoids), nor do they have the vascular tissues (xylem and phloem) that transport water and nutrients in higher plants. With no outer, waterproof cuticle, bryophytes are susceptible to dehydration, and most grow in moist habitats. The bryophyte life cycle has two stages. In stage one, the green plant (gametophyte) produces male and female gametes (sex cells), which fuse to form a zygote. In stage two, the zygote develops into a sporophyte that remains attached to the gametophyte. The sporophyte produces spores, which are released and germinate into new green plants. Liverworts (class Hepaticae) grow horizontally and may be thalloid (flat and ribbon-like) or "leafy." Mosses (class Musci) typically have an upright "stem" with spirally arranged "leaves."

A LEAFY LIVERWORT
Scapania undulata

"Stem"

"Leaf"

Rhizoid

A THALLOID LIVERWORT
Marchantia polymorpha

Gemma cup

Gemma (detachable tissue that produces new plants)

Thallus (plant body)

Toothed margin of cup

DETAIL OF GEMMA CUP

Archegoniophore (stalked structure carrying archegonia)

Disk

Lobe

Stalk

Thallus (plant body)

Apical notch

Rhizoid

FEMALE GAMETOPHYTE

Disk

Lobe

Stalk

Rhizoid

SIDE VIEW OF ARCHEGONIOPHORE

Lobe

Disk

Ray (radial groove)

Stalk

ARCHEGONIOPHORE FROM BELOW

Pore

Ray (radial groove)

MICROGRAPH OF LOBE

Gemma cup

Thallus (plant body)

Midrib

Archegoniophore (stalked structure carrying archegonia)

MICROGRAPH OF THALLUS
Conocephalum conicum

Position of air chamber

Pore for exchange of gases

Upper surface

Rhizoid

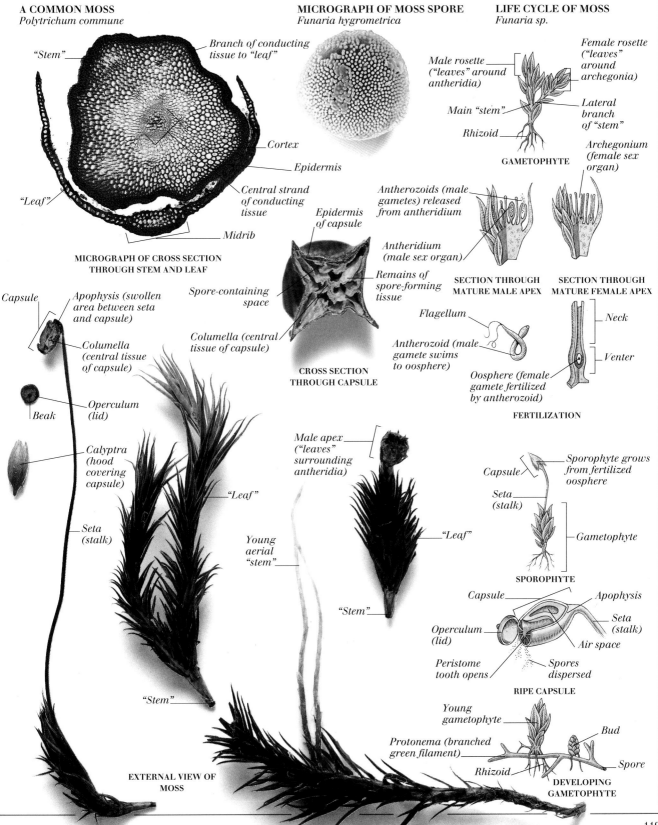

A COMMON MOSS
Polytrichum commune

"Stem"

Branch of conducting
tissue to "leaf"

Cortex

Epidermis

Central strand
of conducting
tissue

"Leaf"

Midrib

**MICROGRAPH OF CROSS SECTION
THROUGH STEM AND LEAF**

MICROGRAPH OF MOSS SPORE
Funaria hygrometrica

LIFE CYCLE OF MOSS
Funaria sp.

Male rosette
("leaves" around
antheridia)

Female rosette
("leaves"
around
archegonia)

Main "stem"

Lateral
branch
of "stem"

Rhizoid

GAMETOPHYTE

Archegonium
(female sex
organ)

Epidermis
of capsule

Spore-containing
space

Columella (central
tissue of capsule)

Remains of
spore-forming
tissue

**CROSS SECTION
THROUGH CAPSULE**

Antherozoids (male
gametes) released
from antheridium

Antheridium
(male sex organ)

**SECTION THROUGH
MATURE MALE APEX**

**SECTION THROUGH
MATURE FEMALE APEX**

Neck

Flagellum

Antherozoid (male
gamete swims
to oosphere)

Oosphere (female
gamete fertilized
by antherozoid)

Venter

FERTILIZATION

Capsule

Apophysis (swollen
area between seta
and capsule)

Columella
(central tissue
of capsule)

Operculum
(lid)

Beak

Calyptra
(hood
covering
capsule)

Seta
(stalk)

"Leaf"

"Stem"

Young
aerial
"stem"

Male apex
("leaves"
surrounding
antheridia)

"Leaf"

"Stem"

**EXTERNAL VIEW OF
MOSS**

Sporophyte grows
from fertilized
oosphere

Capsule

Seta
(stalk)

Gametophyte

SPOROPHYTE

Capsule

Apophysis

Operculum
(lid)

Seta
(stalk)

Air space

Peristome
tooth opens

Spores
dispersed

RIPE CAPSULE

Young
gametophyte

Bud

Protonema (branched
green filament)

Spore

Rhizoid

**DEVELOPING
GAMETOPHYTE**

Horsetails, club mosses, and ferns

HORSETAILS, CLUB MOSSES, AND FERNS are primitive land plants, which, like higher plants, have stems, roots, leaves, and vascular systems that transport water, minerals, and food. Unlike higher plants, however, they do not produce seeds when reproducing. Their life cycles involve two stages. In stage one, the sporophyte (green plant) produces spores in sporangia. In stage two, the spores germinate, developing into small, short-lived gametophyte plants that produce male and female gametes (sex cells). The gametes fuse to form a zygote from which a new sporophyte plant develops. Horsetails (phylum Sphenophyta) have erect green stems with branches arranged in whorls. Some stems are fertile and have a single spore-producing strobilus (group of sporangia) at the tip. Club mosses (phylum Lycopodophyta) typically have small leaves arranged spirally around the stem, with spore-producing strobili at the tip of some stems. Ferns (phylum Filicinophyta) usually have large, pinnate leaves called fronds. Sporangia, grouped together in sori, develop on the underside of fertile fronds.

FROND
Male fern
(*Dryopteris filix-mas*)

CLUB MOSS
Lycopodium sp.

Stem with spirally arranged leaves

Branch

Strobilus (group of sporangia)

CLUB MOSS
Selaginella sp.

Shoot apex

Branch

Rhizophore (leafless branch)

Creeping stem with spirally arranged leaves

Epidermis (outer layer of cells)

Cortex (layer between epidermis and vascular tissue)

Vascular tissue — Phloem / Xylem

Lacuna (air space)

Root

MICROGRAPH OF CROSS SECTION THROUGH CLUB MOSS STEM

HORSETAIL
Common horsetail
(*Equisetum arvense*)

Apex of sterile shoot

Sporangiophore (structure carrying sporangia)

Strobilus (group of sporangia)

Non-photosynthetic fertile stem

Collar of small brown leaves

Young shoot

Lateral branch

Photosynthetic sterile stem

Node

Internode

Node

Tuber

Rhizome

Adventitious root

Endodermis (inner layer of cortex)

Vascular tissue

Sclerenchyma (strengthening tissue)

Chlorenchyma (photosynthetic tissue)

Epidermis (outer layer of cells)

Parenchyma (packing tissue)

Cortex (layer between epidermis and vascular tissue)

Hollow pith cavity

Vallecular canal (longitudinal channel)

Carinal canal (longitudinal channel)

MICROGRAPH OF CROSS SECTION THROUGH HORSETAIL STEM

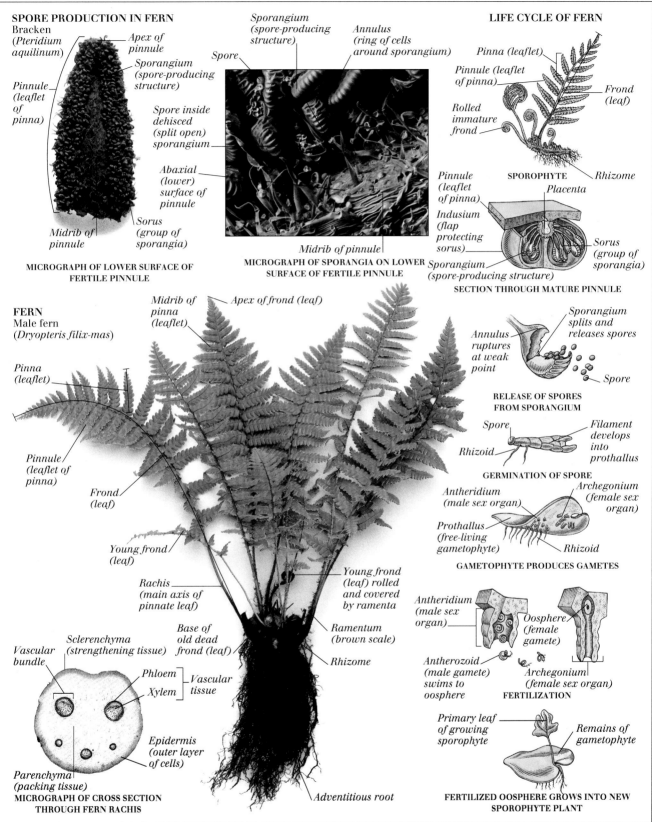

SPORE PRODUCTION IN FERN

Bracken
(*Pteridium aquilinum*)

Apex of pinnule

Sporangium (spore-producing structure)

Pinnule (leaflet of pinna)

Spore inside dehisced (split open) sporangium

Abaxial (lower) surface of pinnule

Midrib of pinnule

Sorus (group of sporangia)

MICROGRAPH OF LOWER SURFACE OF FERTILE PINNULE

Sporangium (spore-producing structure)

Spore

Annulus (ring of cells around sporangium)

Midrib of pinnule

MICROGRAPH OF SPORANGIA ON LOWER SURFACE OF FERTILE PINNULE

LIFE CYCLE OF FERN

Pinna (leaflet)

Pinnule (leaflet of pinna)

Frond (leaf)

Rolled immature frond

SPOROPHYTE

Rhizome

Pinnule (leaflet of pinna)

Placenta

Indusium (flap protecting sorus)

Sporangium (spore-producing structure)

Sorus (group of sporangia)

SECTION THROUGH MATURE PINNULE

FERN

Male fern
(*Dryopteris filix-mas*)

Midrib of pinna (leaflet)

Apex of frond (leaf)

Pinna (leaflet)

Pinnule (leaflet of pinna)

Frond (leaf)

Young frond (leaf)

Rachis (main axis of pinnate leaf)

Young frond (leaf) rolled and covered by ramenta

Ramentum (brown scale)

Rhizome

Base of old dead frond (leaf)

Vascular bundle

Sclerenchyma (strengthening tissue)

Phloem

Xylem

Vascular tissue

Epidermis (outer layer of cells)

Parenchyma (packing tissue)

MICROGRAPH OF CROSS SECTION THROUGH FERN RACHIS

Adventitious root

Sporangium splits and releases spores

Annulus ruptures at weak point

Spore

RELEASE OF SPORES FROM SPORANGIUM

Spore

Filament develops into prothallus

Rhizoid

GERMINATION OF SPORE

Antheridium (male sex organ)

Archegonium (female sex organ)

Prothallus (free-living gametophyte)

Rhizoid

GAMETOPHYTE PRODUCES GAMETES

Antheridium (male sex organ)

Oosphere (female gamete)

Antherozoid (male gamete) swims to oosphere

Archegonium (female sex organ)

FERTILIZATION

Primary leaf of growing sporophyte

Remains of gametophyte

FERTILIZED OOSPHERE GROWS INTO NEW SPOROPHYTE PLANT

121

Gymnosperms 1

THE GYMNOSPERMS ARE FOUR RELATED PHYLA of seed-producing
plants: Their seeds, however, lack the protective outer covering
which surrounds the seeds of flowering plants. Typically,
gymnosperms are woody, perennial shrubs or trees, with stems,
leaves, roots, and a well-developed vascular (transport) system.
The reproductive structures in most gymnosperms are cones. Male
cones produce microspores in which male gametes (sex cells) develop;
female cones produce megaspores in which female gametes develop.
Microspores are blown by the wind to female cones, male and female
gametes fuse during fertilization, and a seed develops. The four
gymnosperm phyla are the conifers (phylum Coniferophyta), mostly
tall trees; cycads (phylum Cycadophyta), small palm-like
trees; the ginkgo or maidenhair tree
(phylum Ginkgophyta), a tall tree with
bilobed leaves; and gnetophytes
(phylum Gnetophyta), a diverse
group of plants, mainly shrubs,
but also including the
horizontally growing
welwitschia.

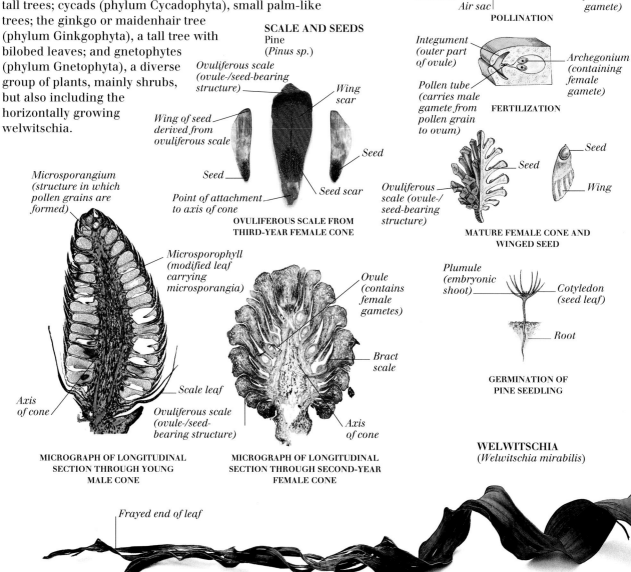

LIFE CYCLE OF SCOTS PINE
(Pinus sylvestris)

Needle *(foliage leaf)*

Cone

Ovuliferous scale *(ovule-/seed-bearing structure)*

MALE CONES   **YOUNG FEMALE CONE**

Pollen grain in micropyle *(entrance to ovule)*   Ovuliferous scale

Pollen grain

Nucleus

Air sac

Ovule *(contains female gamete)*

POLLINATION

Integument *(outer part of ovule)*

Pollen tube *(carries male gamete from pollen grain to ovum)*

Archegonium *(containing female gamete)*

FERTILIZATION

SCALE AND SEEDS
Pine
(Pinus sp.)

Ovuliferous scale *(ovule-/seed-bearing structure)*

Wing of seed derived from ovuliferous scale

Seed

Point of attachment to axis of cone

Wing scar

Seed

Seed scar

OVULIFEROUS SCALE FROM THIRD-YEAR FEMALE CONE

Seed

Ovuliferous scale *(ovule-/seed-bearing structure)*

Seed

Wing

MATURE FEMALE CONE AND WINGED SEED

Plumule *(embryonic shoot)*

Cotyledon *(seed leaf)*

Root

GERMINATION OF PINE SEEDLING

Microsporangium *(structure in which pollen grains are formed)*

Microsporophyll *(modified leaf carrying microsporangia)*

Ovule *(contains female gametes)*

Bract scale

Scale leaf

Ovuliferous scale *(ovule-/seed-bearing structure)*

Axis of cone

Axis of cone

MICROGRAPH OF LONGITUDINAL SECTION THROUGH YOUNG MALE CONE

MICROGRAPH OF LONGITUDINAL SECTION THROUGH SECOND-YEAR FEMALE CONE

WELWITSCHIA
(Welwitschia mirabilis)

Frayed end of leaf

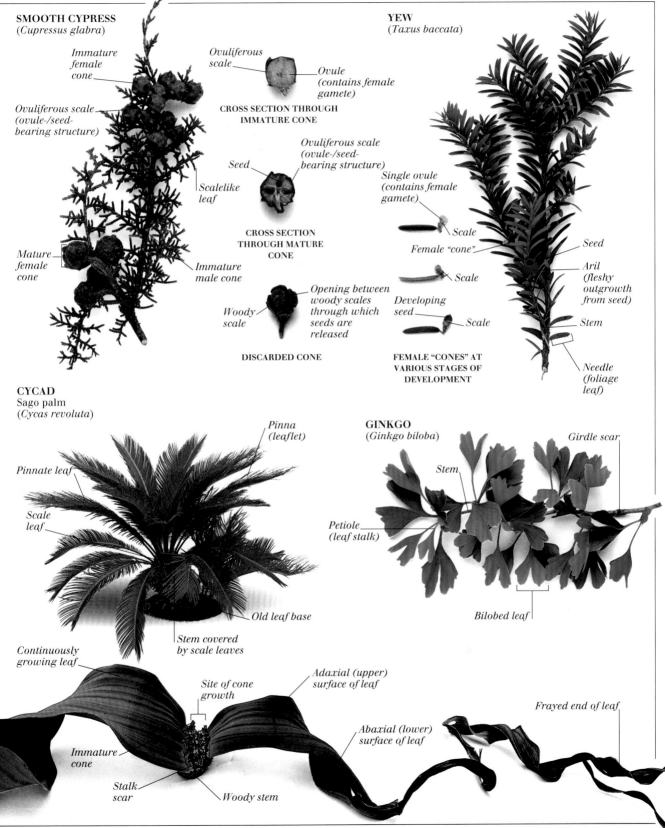

SMOOTH CYPRESS
(*Cupressus glabra*)

Immature female cone

Ovuliferous scale (ovule-/seed-bearing structure)

Mature female cone

Immature male cone

Scalelike leaf

Ovuliferous scale

Ovule (contains female gamete)

CROSS SECTION THROUGH IMMATURE CONE

Ovuliferous scale (ovule-/seed-bearing structure)

Seed

CROSS SECTION THROUGH MATURE CONE

Opening between woody scales through which seeds are released

Woody scale

DISCARDED CONE

YEW
(*Taxus baccata*)

Single ovule (contains female gamete)

Scale

Female "cone"

Scale

Developing seed

Scale

FEMALE "CONES" AT VARIOUS STAGES OF DEVELOPMENT

Seed

Aril (fleshy outgrowth from seed)

Stem

Needle (foliage leaf)

CYCAD
Sago palm
(*Cycas revoluta*)

Pinna (leaflet)

Pinnate leaf

Scale leaf

Old leaf base

Stem covered by scale leaves

GINKGO
(*Ginkgo biloba*)

Girdle scar

Stem

Petiole (leaf stalk)

Bilobed leaf

Continuously growing leaf

Site of cone growth

Adaxial (upper) surface of leaf

Abaxial (lower) surface of leaf

Frayed end of leaf

Immature cone

Stalk scar

Woody stem

Gymnosperms 2

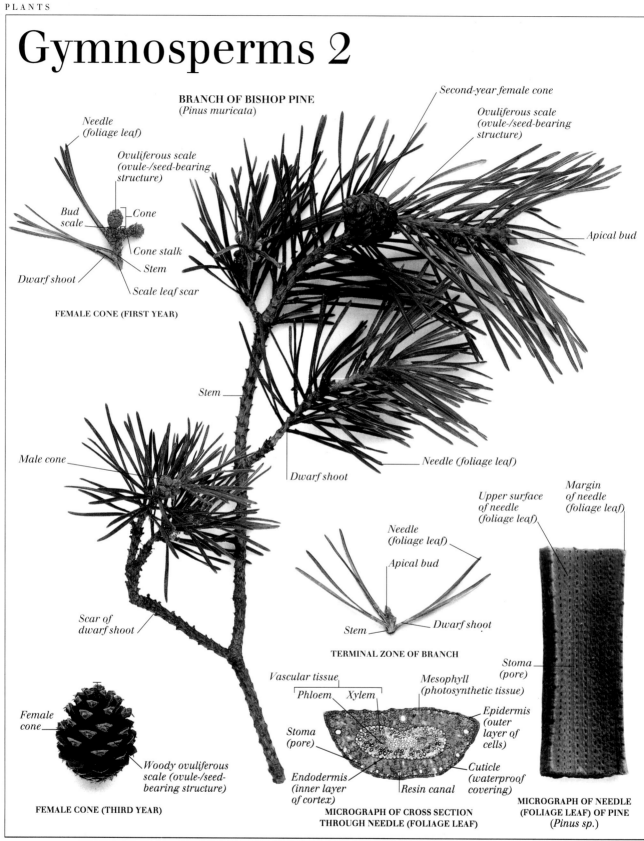

BRANCH OF BISHOP PINE
(*Pinus muricata*)

Second-year female cone

*Ovuliferous scale
(ovule-/seed-bearing
structure)*

*Needle
(foliage leaf)*

*Ovuliferous scale
(ovule-/seed-bearing
structure)*

*Bud
scale*

Cone

Cone stalk

Stem

Scale leaf scar

Dwarf shoot

FEMALE CONE (FIRST YEAR)

Apical bud

Stem

Dwarf shoot

Needle (foliage leaf)

Male cone

*Upper surface
of needle
(foliage leaf)*

*Margin
of needle
(foliage leaf)*

*Needle
(foliage leaf)*

Apical bud

*Scar of
dwarf shoot*

Stem

Dwarf shoot

TERMINAL ZONE OF BRANCH

*Stoma
(pore)*

*Female
cone*

Vascular tissue

Phloem   *Xylem*

*Mesophyll
(photosynthetic tissue)*

*Stoma
(pore)*

*Epidermis
(outer
layer of
cells)*

*Woody ovuliferous
scale (ovule-/seed-
bearing structure)*

*Endodermis
(inner layer
of cortex)*

Resin canal

*Cuticle
(waterproof
covering)*

FEMALE CONE (THIRD YEAR)

**MICROGRAPH OF CROSS SECTION
THROUGH NEEDLE (FOLIAGE LEAF)**

**MICROGRAPH OF NEEDLE
(FOLIAGE LEAF) OF PINE
(*Pinus sp.*)**

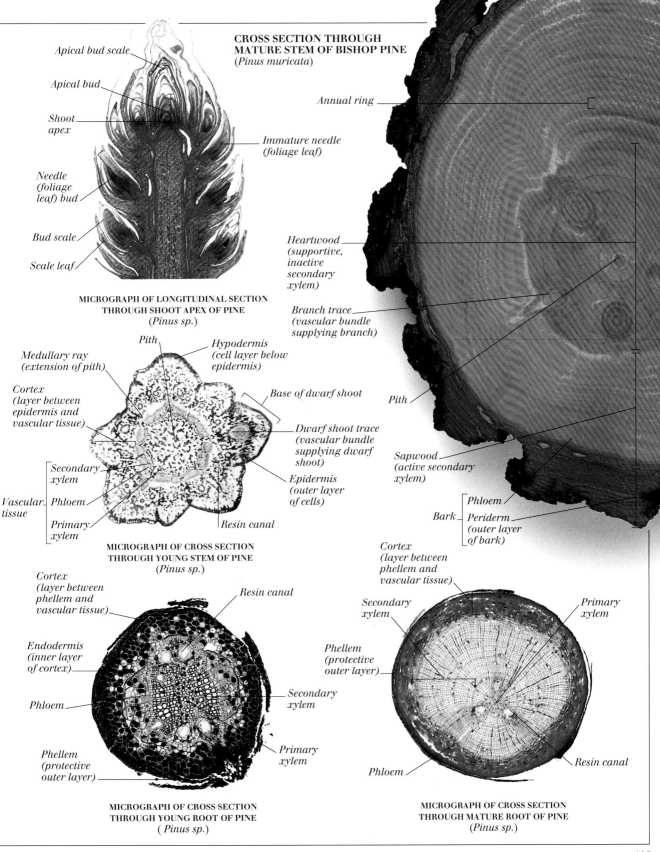

CROSS SECTION THROUGH MATURE STEM OF BISHOP PINE
(*Pinus muricata*)

Apical bud scale

Apical bud

Shoot apex

Immature needle (foliage leaf)

Needle (foliage leaf) bud

Bud scale

Scale leaf

MICROGRAPH OF LONGITUDINAL SECTION THROUGH SHOOT APEX OF PINE
(*Pinus sp.*)

Annual ring

Heartwood (supportive, inactive secondary xylem)

Branch trace (vascular bundle supplying branch)

Pith

Sapwood (active secondary xylem)

Phloem

Bark

Periderm (outer layer of bark)

Medullary ray (extension of pith)

Pith

Hypodermis (cell layer below epidermis)

Cortex (layer between epidermis and vascular tissue)

Base of dwarf shoot

Dwarf shoot trace (vascular bundle supplying dwarf shoot)

Epidermis (outer layer of cells)

Secondary xylem

Phloem

Vascular tissue

Primary xylem

Resin canal

MICROGRAPH OF CROSS SECTION THROUGH YOUNG STEM OF PINE
(*Pinus sp.*)

Cortex (layer between phellem and vascular tissue)

Resin canal

Endodermis (inner layer of cortex)

Phloem

Phellem (protective outer layer)

Secondary xylem

Primary xylem

MICROGRAPH OF CROSS SECTION THROUGH YOUNG ROOT OF PINE
(*Pinus sp.*)

Cortex (layer between phellem and vascular tissue)

Secondary xylem

Phellem (protective outer layer)

Primary xylem

Phloem

Resin canal

MICROGRAPH OF CROSS SECTION THROUGH MATURE ROOT OF PINE
(*Pinus sp.*)

Monocotyledons and dicotyledons

FLOWERING PLANTS (PHYLUM ANGIOSPERMOPHYTA) are divided into two classes: monocotyledons (class Monocotyledoneae) and dicotyledons (class Dicotyledoneae). Typically, monocotyledons have seeds with one cotyledon (seed leaf); their foliage leaves are narrow with parallel veins; the flower components occur in multiples of three; sepals and petals are indistinguishable and are known as tepals; vascular (transport) tissues are scattered in random bundles throughout the stem; and, because they lack stem cambium (actively dividing cells that produce wood), most monocotyledons are herbaceous (see pp. 128-129). Dicotyledons have seeds with two cotyledons; leaves are broad with a central midrib and branched veins; flower parts occur in multiples of four or five; sepals are generally small and green; petals are large and colorful; vascular bundles are arranged in a ring around the edge of the stem; and, because many dicotyledons possess wood-producing stem cambium, there are woody forms (see pp. 130-131) as well as herbaceous ones.

CROSS SECTION THROUGH MONOCOTYLEDONOUS LEAF BASES

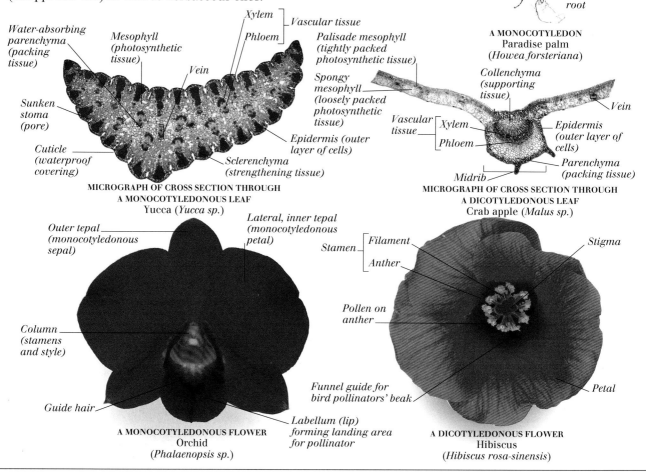

Vein (parallel venation)

Leaflet

Petiole (leaf stalk)

Emerging leaf

Leaf base

Adventitious root

A MONOCOTYLEDON
Paradise palm
(*Howea forsteriana*)

Water-absorbing parenchyma (packing tissue)

Mesophyll (photosynthetic tissue)

Xylem

Phloem

Vascular tissue

Vein

Sunken stoma (pore)

Cuticle (waterproof covering)

Sclerenchyma (strengthening tissue)

Epidermis (outer layer of cells)

MICROGRAPH OF CROSS SECTION THROUGH A MONOCOTYLEDONOUS LEAF
Yucca (*Yucca sp.*)

Palisade mesophyll (tightly packed photosynthetic tissue)

Spongy mesophyll (loosely packed photosynthetic tissue)

Collenchyma (supporting tissue)

Vein

Vascular tissue

Xylem

Phloem

Epidermis (outer layer of cells)

Parenchyma (packing tissue)

Midrib

MICROGRAPH OF CROSS SECTION THROUGH A DICOTYLEDONOUS LEAF
Crab apple (*Malus sp.*)

Outer tepal (monocotyledonous sepal)

Lateral, inner tepal (monocotyledonous petal)

Stamen

Filament

Anther

Stigma

Column (stamens and style)

Pollen on anther

Guide hair

Funnel guide for bird pollinators' beak

Labellum (lip) forming landing area for pollinator

Petal

A MONOCOTYLEDONOUS FLOWER
Orchid
(*Phalaenopsis sp.*)

A DICOTYLEDONOUS FLOWER
Hibiscus
(*Hibiscus rosa-sinensis*)

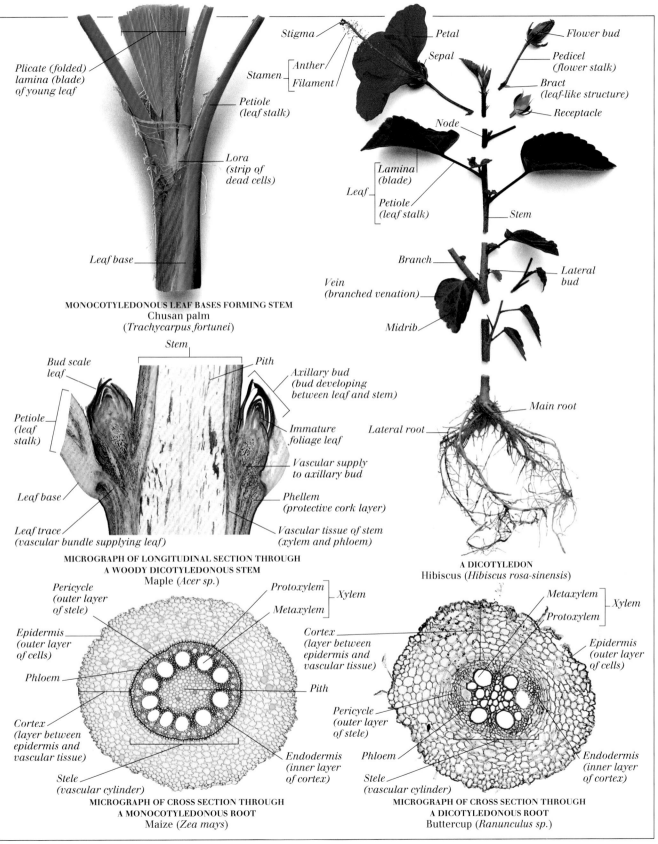

Plicate (folded) lamina (blade) of young leaf

Petiole (leaf stalk)

Lora (strip of dead cells)

Leaf base

MONOCOTYLEDONOUS LEAF BASES FORMING STEM
Chusan palm
(*Trachycarpus fortunei*)

Stigma

Stamen { Anther / Filament }

Petal

Sepal

Flower bud

Pedicel (flower stalk)

Bract (leaf-like structure)

Receptacle

Node

Leaf { Lamina (blade) / Petiole (leaf stalk) }

Stem

Branch

Vein (branched venation)

Midrib

Lateral bud

Bud scale leaf

Stem

Pith

Axillary bud (bud developing between leaf and stem)

Petiole (leaf stalk)

Immature foliage leaf

Vascular supply to axillary bud

Phellem (protective cork layer)

Leaf base

Leaf trace (vascular bundle supplying leaf)

Vascular tissue of stem (xylem and phloem)

MICROGRAPH OF LONGITUDINAL SECTION THROUGH A WOODY DICOTYLEDONOUS STEM
Maple (*Acer sp.*)

Main root

Lateral root

A DICOTYLEDON
Hibiscus (*Hibiscus rosa-sinensis*)

Pericycle (outer layer of stele)

Epidermis (outer layer of cells)

Phloem

Cortex (layer between epidermis and vascular tissue)

Stele (vascular cylinder)

Protoxylem } Xylem
Metaxylem

Pith

Endodermis (inner layer of cortex)

MICROGRAPH OF CROSS SECTION THROUGH A MONOCOTYLEDONOUS ROOT
Maize (*Zea mays*)

Cortex (layer between epidermis and vascular tissue)

Metaxylem } Xylem
Protoxylem

Epidermis (outer layer of cells)

Pericycle (outer layer of stele)

Phloem

Stele (vascular cylinder)

Endodermis (inner layer of cortex)

MICROGRAPH OF CROSS SECTION THROUGH A DICOTYLEDONOUS ROOT
Buttercup (*Ranunculus sp.*)

Herbaceous flowering plants

HERBACEOUS FLOWERING PLANTS TYPICALLY HAVE GREEN NON-WOODY STEMS, and tend to be relatively short-lived. Many herbaceous plants live for only one or two years. Annuals (such as sweet peas) grow from seed, produce flowers and then seeds, and die within a single year. Biennials (like carrots) have a two-year life cycle. In the first year, seeds grow into plants, which produce leaves and store food in underground storage organs; the stems and foliage then die in winter. In the second year, new stems grow from the storage organs, produce leaves, flowers, and seeds, and then die. Some herbaceous plants (such as potatoes) are perennial. They grow back year after year, producing shoots and flowers in spring, storing food in underground tubers or rhizomes during summer, dying in autumn, and surviving underground during winter.

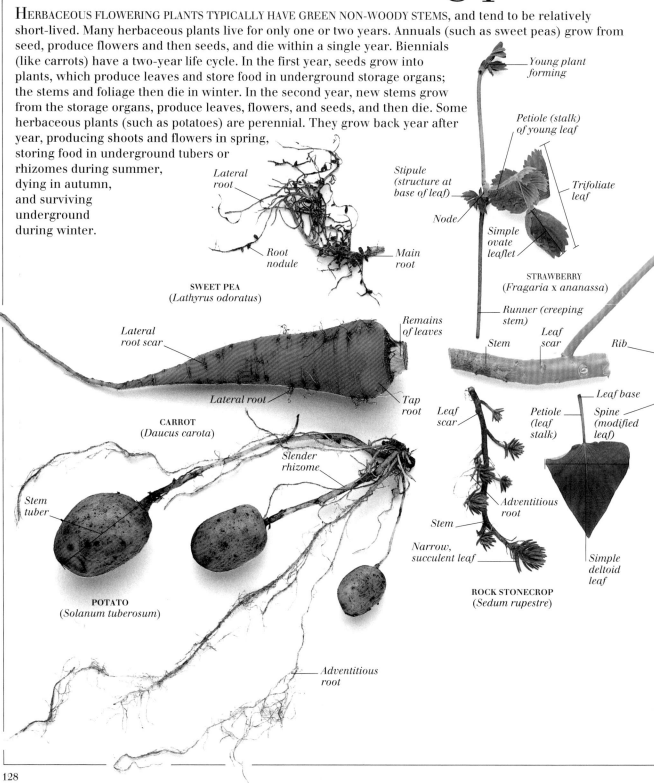

Young plant forming

Petiole (stalk) of young leaf

Stipule (structure at base of leaf)

Trifoliate leaf

Node

Simple ovate leaflet

Lateral root

Root nodule

Main root

SWEET PEA
(*Lathyrus odoratus*)

STRAWBERRY
(*Fragaria* x *ananassa*)

Runner (creeping stem)

Remains of leaves

Lateral root scar

Stem

Leaf scar

Rib

Lateral root

Tap root

CARROT
(*Daucus carota*)

Leaf scar

Petiole (leaf stalk)

Leaf base

Spine (modified leaf)

Slender rhizome

Stem tuber

Adventitious root

Stem

Narrow, succulent leaf

Simple deltoid leaf

POTATO
(*Solanum tuberosum*)

ROCK STONECROP
(*Sedum rupestre*)

Adventitious root

PARTS OF HERBACEOUS FLOWERING PLANTS

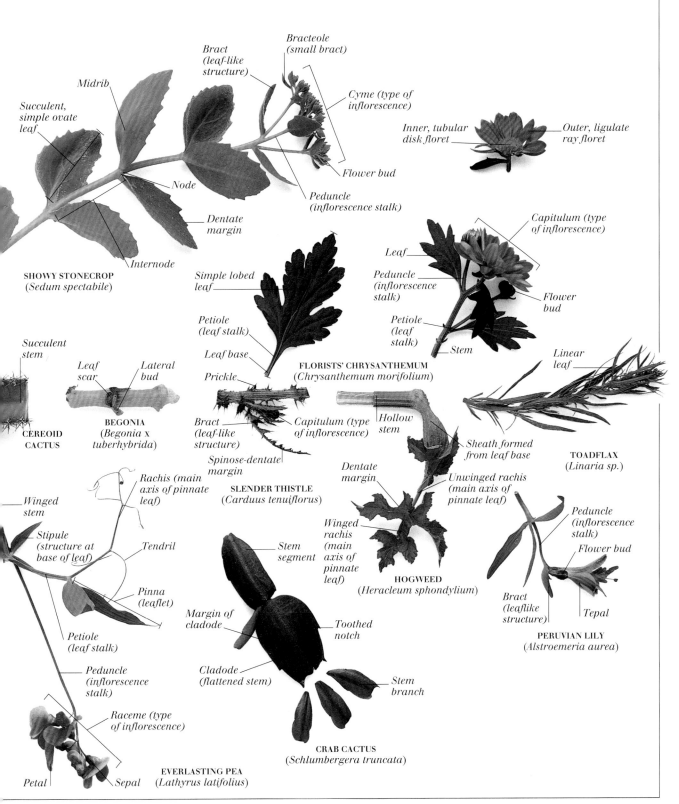

Bract
(leaf-like
structure)

Bracteole
(small bract)

Midrib

Cyme (type of
inflorescence)

Succulent,
simple ovate
leaf

Inner, tubular
disk floret

Outer, ligulate
ray floret

Node

Flower bud

Dentate
margin

Peduncle
(inflorescence stalk)

Internode

SHOWY STONECROP
(*Sedum spectabile*)

Simple lobed
leaf

Capitulum (type
of inflorescence)

Leaf

Peduncle
(inflorescence
stalk)

Flower
bud

Petiole
(leaf stalk)

Leaf base

Petiole
(leaf
stalk)

Stem

Succulent
stem

Leaf
scar

Lateral
bud

Prickle

FLORISTS' CHRYSANTHEMUM
(*Chrysanthemum morifolium*)

Linear
leaf

**CEREOID
CACTUS**

BEGONIA
(*Begonia* x
tuberhybrida)

Bract
(leaf-like
structure)

Capitulum (type
of inflorescence)

Hollow
stem

Sheath formed
from leaf base

TOADFLAX
(*Linaria sp.*)

Spinose-dentate
margin

Dentate
margin

Unwinged rachis
(main axis of
pinnate leaf)

Rachis (main
axis of pinnate
leaf)

SLENDER THISTLE
(*Carduus tenuiflorus*)

Winged
stem

Tendril

Stem
segment

Winged
rachis
(main
axis of
pinnate
leaf)

Peduncle
(inflorescence
stalk)

Stipule
(structure at
base of leaf)

Flower bud

Pinna
(leaflet)

HOGWEED
(*Heracleum sphondylium*)

Petiole
(leaf stalk)

Margin of
cladode

Toothed
notch

Bract
(leaflike
structure)

Peduncle
(inflorescence
stalk)

Tepal

Cladode
(flattened stem)

Stem
branch

PERUVIAN LILY
(*Alstroemeria aurea*)

Raceme (type
of inflorescence)

Petal

Sepal

EVERLASTING PEA
(*Lathyrus latifolius*)

CRAB CACTUS
(*Schlumbergera truncata*)

Woody flowering plants

Woody flowering plants are perennial: They continue to grow and reproduce for many years. They have one or more permanent stems above ground and numerous smaller branches. The stems and branches have a strong woody core that supports the plant and contains vascular tissue for transporting water and nutrients. Outside the woody core is a layer of tough, protective bark, which has lenticels (tiny pores) to allow gases to pass through. Woody flowering plants may be shrubs, which have several stems rising from the soil; bushes, which are shrubs with dense branching and foliage; or trees, which typically have a single upright stem (the trunk) that bears branches. Deciduous woody plants (like roses) shed all their leaves once a year and remain leafless during winter. Evergreen woody plants (such as holly) shed their leaves gradually, so they retain full leaf cover throughout the year.

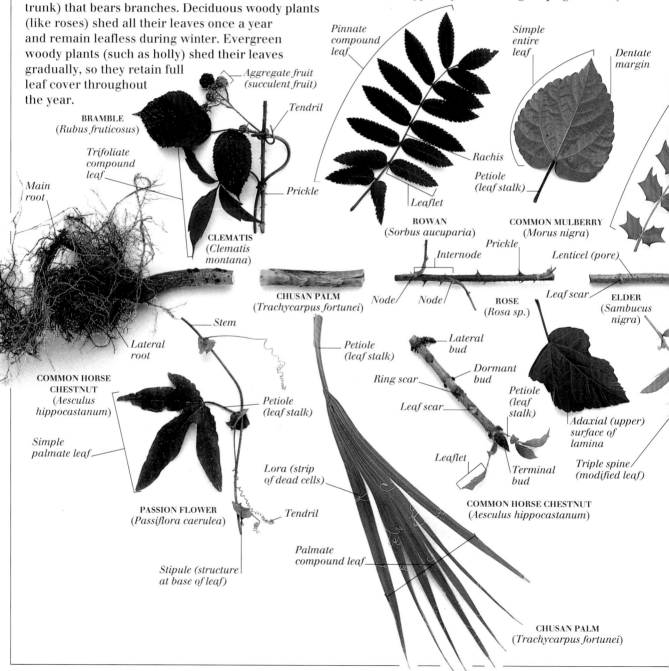

Aggregate fruit (succulent fruit)

BRAMBLE (*Rubus fruticosus*)

Trifoliate compound leaf

Tendril

Prickle

CLEMATIS (*Clematis montana*)

Main root

Lateral root

Stem

COMMON HORSE CHESTNUT (*Aesculus hippocastanum*)

Simple palmate leaf

Pinnate compound leaf

Rachis

Petiole (leaf stalk)

Leaflet

ROWAN (*Sorbus aucuparia*)

Simple entire leaf

Dentate margin

COMMON MULBERRY (*Morus nigra*)

Prickle

Internode

Node   *Node*

ROSE (*Rosa sp.*)

Lenticel (pore)

Leaf scar   **ELDER** (*Sambucus nigra*)

CHUSAN PALM (*Trachycarpus fortunei*)

Petiole (leaf stalk)

Petiole (leaf stalk)

Lateral bud

Dormant bud

Ring scar

Leaf scar

Petiole (leaf stalk)

Adaxial (upper) surface of lamina

Leaflet

Terminal bud

Triple spine (modified leaf)

COMMON HORSE CHESTNUT (*Aesculus hippocastanum*)

Lora (strip of dead cells)

PASSION FLOWER (*Passiflora caerulea*)

Tendril

Stipule (structure at base of leaf)

Palmate compound leaf

CHUSAN PALM (*Trachycarpus fortunei*)

PARTS OF WOODY FLOWERING PLANTS

DURMAST OAK
(*Quercus petraea*)

Simple lobed obovate leaf

Midrib

Remains of bracts

Nut (dry fruit)

Immature acorn

Pinnate compound leaf

Spine

Pinna (leaflet)

MAHONIA
(*Mahonia lomariifolia*)

Axillary bud

Pome (succulent fruit)

Pedicel (flower stalk)

Peduncle (inflorescence stalk)

Stipule (structure at base of leaf)

Variegated lamina (blade)

Adventitious root

Stem

Remains of style

COMMON ENGLISH IVY
(*Hedera helix* 'Goldheart')

Node

MOUNTAIN ASH
(*Sorbus aucuparia*)

Lateral bud

Ring scar

MOUNTAIN ASH
(*Sorbus aucuparia*)

Flower bud

Sepal

Receptacle

Pedicel (flower stalk)

Bract

Stamen

Petal

Sepal

Ovary

ROSE
(*Rosa sp.*)

Leaflet

ROSE
(*Rosa sp.*)

Petiole (leaf stalk)

Sepal

Flower bud

Pedicel (flower stalk)

CLEMATIS
(*Clematis sp.*)

Culm (jointed stem)

BAMBOO
(*Arundinaria nitida*)

Petiole (leaf stalk)

Vein

Adaxial (upper) surface of lamina (blade)

TREE MALLOW
(*Lavatera arborea*)

Stem

Leaf

Pedicel (flower stalk)

Wing

Double samara (winged dry fruit)

Pericarp (fruit wall) enclosing seed

Triple spine (modified leaf)

SYCAMORE MAPLE
(*Acer pseudoplatanus*)

Stem

Petiole (leaf stalk)

Simple lanceolate leaf

Peduncle (inflorescence stalk)

Drupe (succulent fruit)

PEACH
(*Prunus persica*)

Peduncle (inflorescence stalk)

Pedicel (flower stalk)

Compound inflorescence (panicle)

SILVER LACE VINE
(*Polygonum baldschuanicum*)

BARBERRY
(*Berberis sp.*)

Roots

ROOTS ARE THE UNDERGROUND PARTS OF PLANTS. They have three main functions. First, they anchor the plant in the soil. Second, they absorb water and minerals from the spaces between soil particles. The roots' absorptive properties are increased by root hairs, which grow behind the root tip, allowing maximum absorption of vital substances. Third, the root is part of the plant's transport system. Xylem carries water and minerals from the roots to the stem and leaves, and phloem carries nutrients from the leaves to all parts of the root system. In addition, some roots (like carrots) are food stores. Roots have an outer epidermis covering a cortex of parenchyma (packing tissue), and a central cylinder of vascular tissue. This arrangement helps the roots resist the forces of compression as they grow through the soil.

MICROGRAPH OF PRIMARY ROOT DEVELOPMENT
Cabbage (*Brassica sp.*)

Split in testa as seed germinates
Cotyledon (seed leaf)
Primary root
Testa (seed coat)
Root hair
Root tip (region of cell division)

CARROT (*Daucus carota*)

FEATURES OF A TYPICAL ROOT
Buttercup (*Ranunculus sp.*)

Pericycle (outer layer of stele)
Root hair
Air space (allowing gas diffusion in the root)
Stele (vascular cylinder)
Phloem sieve tube (through which nutrients are transported)
Companion cell (cell associated with phloem sieve tube)
Cortex (layer between epidermis and vascular tissue)
Root hair

Epidermis (outer layer of cells)
Xylem vessel (through which water and minerals are transported)
Endodermis (inner layer of cortex)
Cell wall
Nucleus
Cytoplasm
Parenchyma (packing) cell

PRIMARY ROOT AND MICROGRAPHS OF SECTIONS THROUGH ROOTS

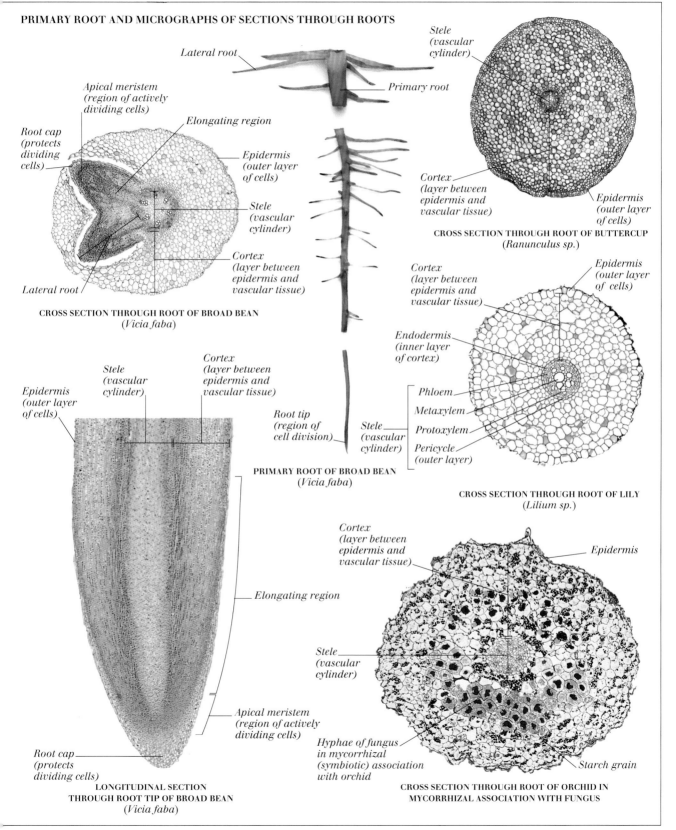

Lateral root

Primary root

Stele
(vascular
cylinder)

Apical meristem
(region of actively
dividing cells)

Elongating region

Root cap
(protects
dividing
cells)

Epidermis
(outer layer
of cells)

Stele
(vascular
cylinder)

Cortex
(layer between
epidermis and
vascular tissue)

Lateral root

CROSS SECTION THROUGH ROOT OF BROAD BEAN
(*Vicia faba*)

Cortex
(layer between
epidermis and
vascular tissue)

Epidermis
(outer layer
of cells)

CROSS SECTION THROUGH ROOT OF BUTTERCUP
(*Ranunculus sp.*)

Cortex
(layer between
epidermis and
vascular tissue)

Epidermis
(outer layer
of cells)

Endodermis
(inner layer
of cortex)

Phloem

Metaxylem

Protoxylem

Pericycle
(outer layer)

Stele
(vascular
cylinder)

CROSS SECTION THROUGH ROOT OF LILY
(*Lilium sp.*)

Epidermis
(outer layer
of cells)

Stele
(vascular
cylinder)

Cortex
(layer between
epidermis and
vascular tissue)

Root tip
(region of
cell division)

Stele
(vascular
cylinder)

PRIMARY ROOT OF BROAD BEAN
(*Vicia faba*)

Elongating region

Apical meristem
(region of actively
dividing cells)

Root cap
(protects
dividing
cells)

**LONGITUDINAL SECTION
THROUGH ROOT TIP OF BROAD BEAN**
(*Vicia faba*)

Cortex
(layer between
epidermis and
vascular tissue)

Epidermis

Stele
(vascular
cylinder)

Hyphae of fungus
in mycorrhizal
(symbiotic) association
with orchid

Starch grain

**CROSS SECTION THROUGH ROOT OF ORCHID IN
MYCORRHIZAL ASSOCIATION WITH FUNGUS**

Stems

THE STEM IS THE MAIN SUPPORTIVE PART OF A PLANT that grows above ground. Stems bear leaves (organs of photosynthesis), which grow at nodes; buds (shoots covered by protective scales), which grow at the stem tip (apical or terminal buds) and in the angle between a leaf and the stem (axillary or lateral buds); and flowers (reproductive structures). The stem forms part of the plant's transport system. Xylem tissue in the stem transports water and minerals from the roots to the aerial parts of the plant, and phloem tissue transports nutrients manufactured in the leaves to other parts of the plant. Stem tissues are also used for storing water and food. Herbaceous (nonwoody) stems have an outer protective epidermis covering a cortex that consists mainly of parenchyma (packing tissue) but also has some collenchyma (supporting tissue). The vascular tissue of such stems is arranged in bundles, each of which consists of xylem, phloem, and sclerenchyma (strengthening tissue). Woody stems have an outer protective layer of tough bark, which is perforated with lenticels (pores) to allow gas exchange. Inside the bark is a ring of secondary phloem, which surrounds an inner core of secondary xylem.

MICROGRAPH OF LONGITUDINAL SECTION THROUGH APEX OF STEM
Coleus sp.

Apical meristem (region of actively dividing cells)

Procambial strand (cells that produce vascular tissue)

Leaf primordium (developing leaf)

Developing bud

Cortex (layer between epidermis and vascular tissue)

Vascular tissue

Epidermis (outer layer of cells)

Pith

YOUNG WOODY STEM
Linden
(*Tilia sp.*)

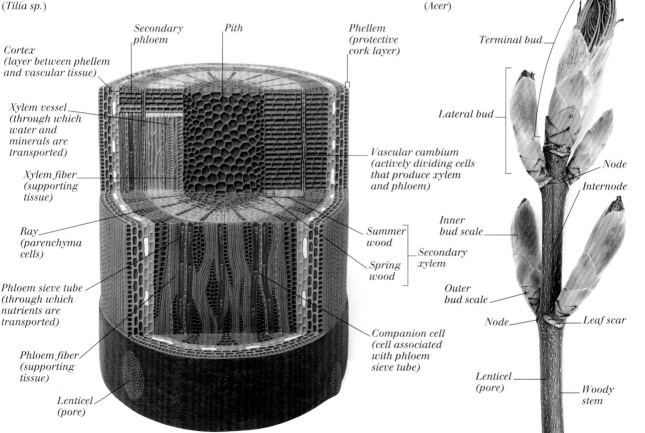

Cortex (layer between phellem and vascular tissue)

Secondary phloem

Pith

Phellem (protective cork layer)

Xylem vessel (through which water and minerals are transported)

Xylem fiber (supporting tissue)

Vascular cambium (actively dividing cells that produce xylem and phloem)

Ray (parenchyma cells)

Summer wood

Secondary xylem

Spring wood

Phloem sieve tube (through which nutrients are transported)

Phloem fiber (supporting tissue)

Companion cell (cell associated with phloem sieve tube)

Lenticel (pore)

EMERGENT BUDS
Maple
(*Acer*)

Young leaves emerging

Terminal bud

Lateral bud

Node

Internode

Inner bud scale

Outer bud scale

Node

Leaf scar

Lenticel (pore)

Woody stem

MICROGRAPHS OF CROSS SECTIONS THROUGH VARIOUS STEMS

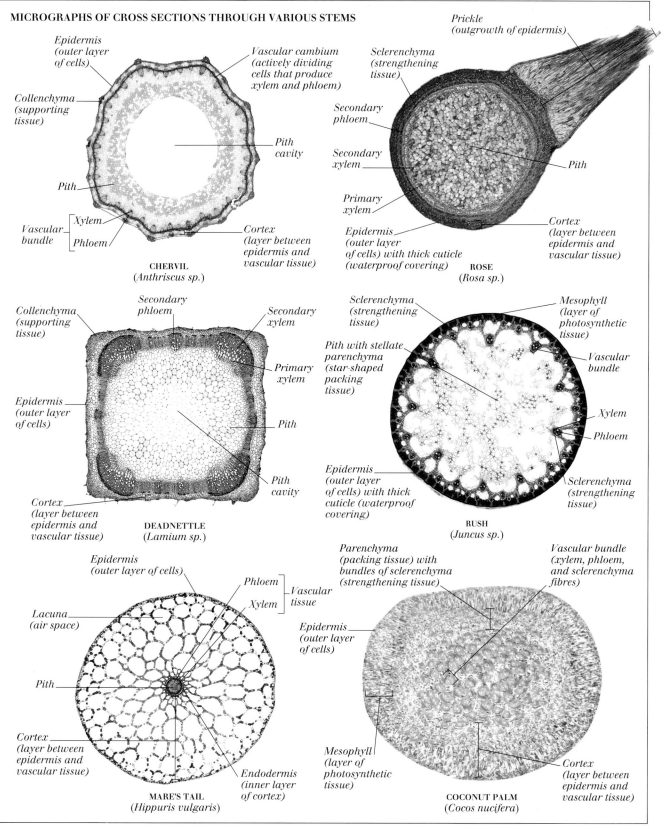

Epidermis (outer layer of cells)

Vascular cambium (actively dividing cells that produce xylem and phloem)

Collenchyma (supporting tissue)

Pith cavity

Pith

Vascular bundle { *Xylem* *Phloem* }

Cortex (layer between epidermis and vascular tissue)

CHERVIL
(Anthriscus sp.)

Prickle (outgrowth of epidermis)

Sclerenchyma (strengthening tissue)

Secondary phloem

Secondary xylem

Primary xylem

Pith

Epidermis (outer layer of cells) with thick cuticle (waterproof covering)

Cortex (layer between epidermis and vascular tissue)

ROSE
(Rosa sp.)

Collenchyma (supporting tissue)

Secondary phloem

Secondary xylem

Primary xylem

Epidermis (outer layer of cells)

Pith

Pith cavity

Cortex (layer between epidermis and vascular tissue)

DEADNETTLE
(Lamium sp.)

Sclerenchyma (strengthening tissue)

Mesophyll (layer of photosynthetic tissue)

Pith with stellate parenchyma (star-shaped packing tissue)

Vascular bundle

Xylem

Phloem

Epidermis (outer layer of cells) with thick cuticle (waterproof covering)

Sclerenchyma (strengthening tissue)

RUSH
(Juncus sp.)

Epidermis (outer layer of cells)

Phloem

Xylem } *Vascular tissue*

Lacuna (air space)

Pith

Cortex (layer between epidermis and vascular tissue)

Endodermis (inner layer of cortex)

MARE'S TAIL
(Hippuris vulgaris)

Parenchyma (packing tissue) with bundles of sclerenchyma (strengthening tissue)

Vascular bundle (xylem, phloem, and sclerenchyma fibres)

Epidermis (outer layer of cells)

Mesophyll (layer of photosynthetic tissue)

Cortex (layer between epidermis and vascular tissue)

COCONUT PALM
(Cocos nucifera)

Leaves

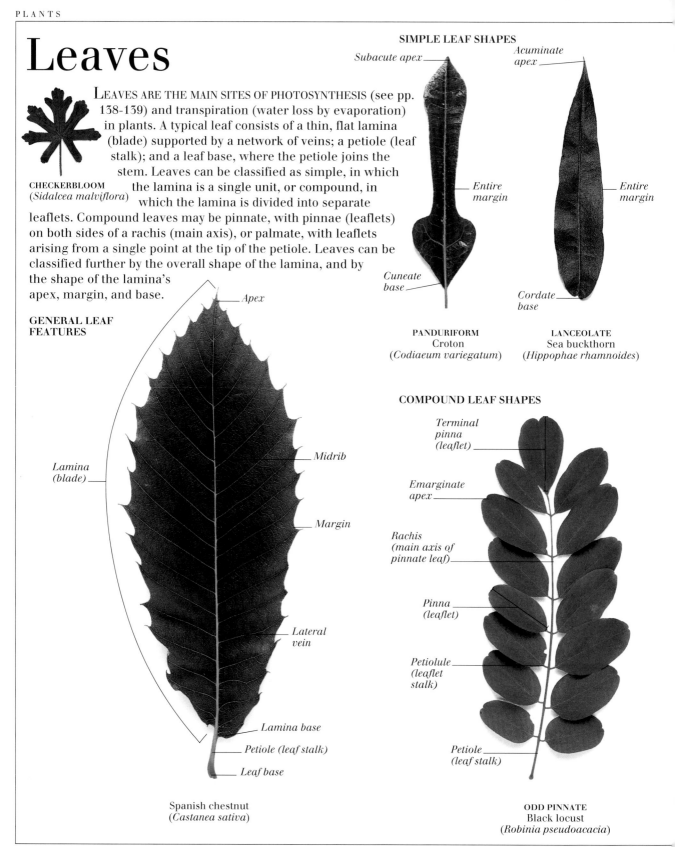

LEAVES ARE THE MAIN SITES OF PHOTOSYNTHESIS (see pp. 138-139) and transpiration (water loss by evaporation) in plants. A typical leaf consists of a thin, flat lamina (blade) supported by a network of veins; a petiole (leaf stalk); and a leaf base, where the petiole joins the stem. Leaves can be classified as simple, in which the lamina is a single unit, or compound, in which the lamina is divided into separate leaflets. Compound leaves may be pinnate, with pinnae (leaflets) on both sides of a rachis (main axis), or palmate, with leaflets arising from a single point at the tip of the petiole. Leaves can be classified further by the overall shape of the lamina, and by the shape of the lamina's apex, margin, and base.

CHECKERBLOOM
(*Sidalcea malviflora*)

SIMPLE LEAF SHAPES

Subacute apex

Acuminate apex

Entire margin

Entire margin

Cuneate base

Cordate base

PANDURIFORM
Croton
(*Codiaeum variegatum*)

LANCEOLATE
Sea buckthorn
(*Hippophae rhamnoides*)

GENERAL LEAF FEATURES

Apex

Lamina (blade)

Midrib

Margin

Lateral vein

Lamina base

Petiole (leaf stalk)

Leaf base

Spanish chestnut
(*Castanea sativa*)

COMPOUND LEAF SHAPES

Terminal pinna (leaflet)

Emarginate apex

Rachis (main axis of pinnate leaf)

Pinna (leaflet)

Petiolule (leaflet stalk)

Petiole (leaf stalk)

ODD PINNATE
Black locust
(*Robinia pseudoacacia*)

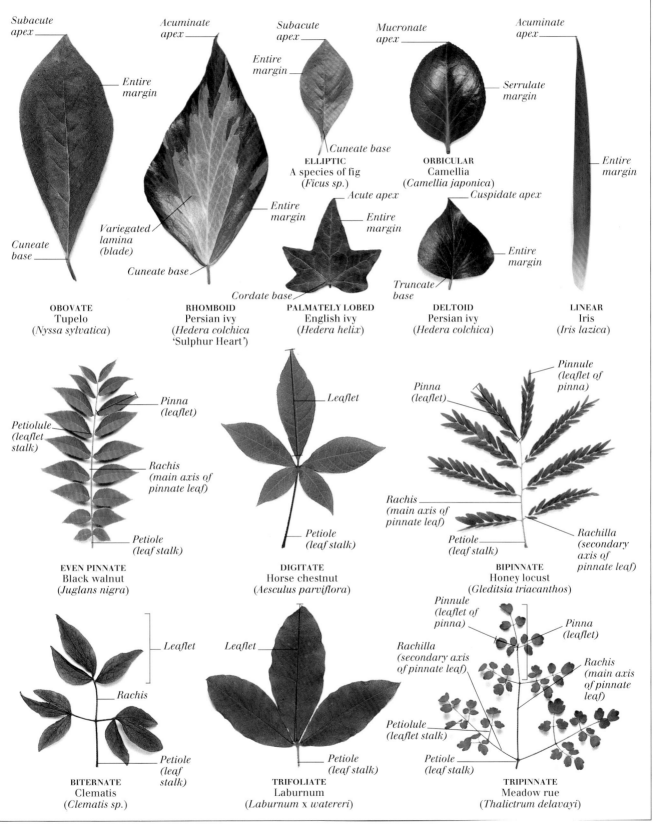

Subacute apex

Entire margin

Cuneate base

OBOVATE
Tupelo
(*Nyssa sylvatica*)

Acuminate apex

Variegated lamina (blade)

Entire margin

Cuneate base

RHOMBOID
Persian ivy
(*Hedera colchica* 'Sulphur Heart')

Subacute apex

Entire margin

Cuneate base

ELLIPTIC
A species of fig
(*Ficus sp.*)

Acute apex

Entire margin

Cordate base

PALMATELY LOBED
English ivy
(*Hedera helix*)

Mucronate apex

Serrulate margin

ORBICULAR
Camellia
(*Camellia japonica*)

Cuspidate apex

Entire margin

Truncate base

DELTOID
Persian ivy
(*Hedera colchica*)

Acuminate apex

Entire margin

LINEAR
Iris
(*Iris lazica*)

Pinna (leaflet)

Petiolule (leaflet stalk)

Rachis (main axis of pinnate leaf)

Petiole (leaf stalk)

EVEN PINNATE
Black walnut
(*Juglans nigra*)

Leaflet

Petiole (leaf stalk)

DIGITATE
Horse chestnut
(*Aesculus parviflora*)

Pinna (leaflet)

Pinnule (leaflet of pinna)

Rachis (main axis of pinnate leaf)

Petiole (leaf stalk)

Rachilla (secondary axis of pinnate leaf)

BIPINNATE
Honey locust
(*Gleditsia triacanthos*)

Leaflet

Rachis

Petiole (leaf stalk)

BITERNATE
Clematis
(*Clematis sp.*)

Leaflet

Petiole (leaf stalk)

TRIFOLIATE
Laburnum
(*Laburnum* x *watereri*)

Pinnule (leaflet of pinna)

Rachilla (secondary axis of pinnate leaf)

Petiolule (leaflet stalk)

Petiole (leaf stalk)

Pinna (leaflet)

Rachis (main axis of pinnate leaf)

TRIPINNATE
Meadow rue
(*Thalictrum delavayi*)

Photosynthesis

PHOTOSYNTHESIS IS THE PROCESS by which plants make their food using sunlight, water, and carbon dioxide. It takes place inside special structures in leaf cells called chloroplasts. The chloroplasts contain chlorophyll, a green pigment that absorbs energy from sunlight. During photosynthesis, the absorbed energy is used to join together carbon dioxide and water to form the sugar glucose, which is the energy source for the whole plant. Oxygen, a waste product, is released into the air. Leaves are the main sites of photosynthesis and have various adaptations for that purpose. Flat laminae (blades) provide a large surface for absorbing sunlight; stomata (pores) in the lower surface of the laminae allow gases (carbon dioxide and oxygen) to pass into and out of the leaves; and an extensive network of veins brings water into the leaves and transports the glucose produced by photosynthesis to the rest of the plant.

MICROGRAPH OF LEAF
Lily (*Lilium sp.*)

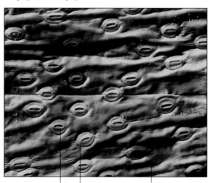

Stoma
(pore)

Guard cell
(controls
opening
and closing
of stoma)

Lower
surface of
lamina
(blade)

THE PROCESS OF PHOTOSYNTHESIS

Glucose molecule

Oxygen
atom

Carbon
atom

Hydrogen
atom

Glucose is a high-energy
product of photosynthesis.
It travels to all parts of the
plant through the phloem

Sunlight, which is absorbed
by chloroplasts in the leaf,
provides the energy for
photosynthesis

The leaf is the main site of
photosynthesis. Its broad,
thin lamina (blade) is an
adaptation for this process

Hydrogen atom

Oxygen atom — Water
molecule

Hydrogen atom

Oxygen
atom

Oxygen
atom — Oxygen
molecule

Carbon dioxide
molecule

Oxygen atom

Carbon atom

Oxygen atom

Water, a raw material
in the soil, travels to the
leaf from the roots via
the xylem

Carbon dioxide, a raw
material in the air, enters
the leaf through stomata
on the lower surface of the
lamina (blade)

Oxygen, a waste product
of photosynthesis, leaves
the leaf through stomata
on the lower surface of
the lamina (blade)

CROSS SECTION THROUGH LEAF
Christmas rose
(*Helleborus niger*)

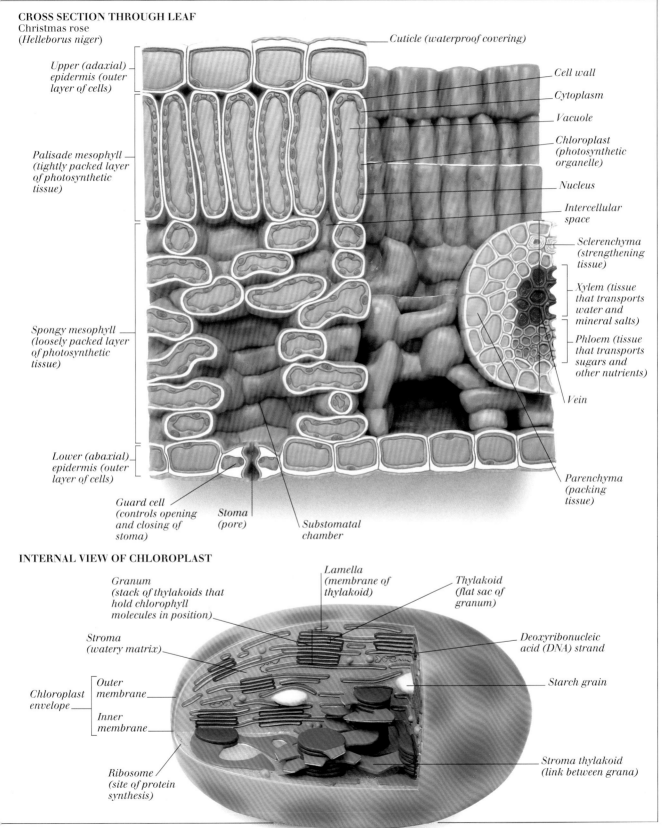

Cuticle (waterproof covering)

Upper (adaxial)
epidermis (outer
layer of cells)

Cell wall

Cytoplasm

Vacuole

Palisade mesophyll
(tightly packed layer
of photosynthetic
tissue)

Chloroplast
(photosynthetic
organelle)

Nucleus

Intercellular
space

Sclerenchyma
(strengthening
tissue)

Xylem (tissue
that transports
water and
mineral salts)

Spongy mesophyll
(loosely packed layer
of photosynthetic
tissue)

Phloem (tissue
that transports
sugars and
other nutrients)

Vein

Lower (abaxial)
epidermis (outer
layer of cells)

Parenchyma
(packing
tissue)

Guard cell
(controls opening
and closing of
stoma)

Stoma
(pore)

Substomatal
chamber

INTERNAL VIEW OF CHLOROPLAST

Granum
(stack of thylakoids that
hold chlorophyll
molecules in position)

Lamella
(membrane of
thylakoid)

Thylakoid
(flat sac of
granum)

Stroma
(watery matrix)

Deoxyribonucleic
acid (DNA) strand

Chloroplast
envelope

Outer
membrane

Inner
membrane

Starch grain

Ribosome
(site of protein
synthesis)

Stroma thylakoid
(link between grana)

Flowers 1

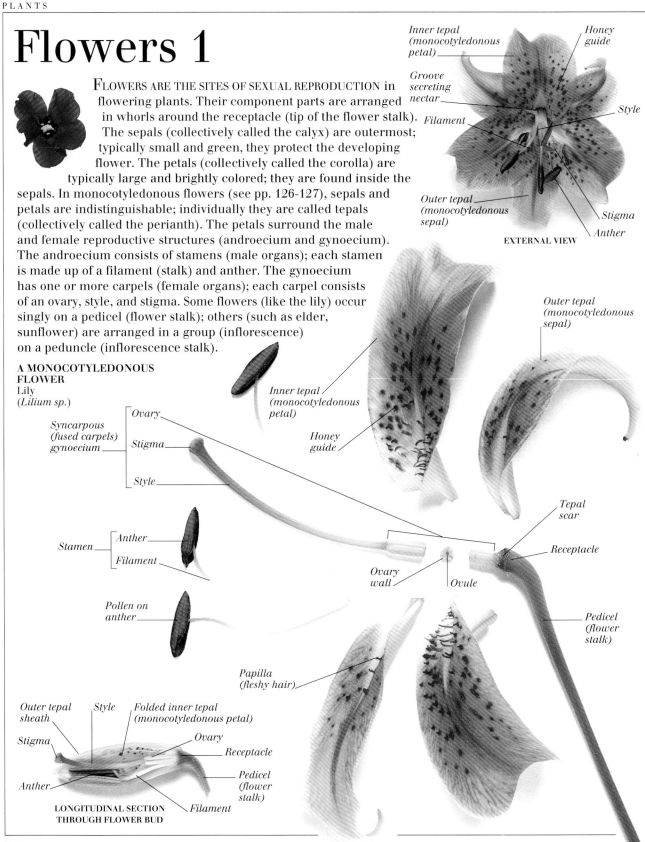

FLOWERS ARE THE SITES OF SEXUAL REPRODUCTION in flowering plants. Their component parts are arranged in whorls around the receptacle (tip of the flower stalk). The sepals (collectively called the calyx) are outermost; typically small and green, they protect the developing flower. The petals (collectively called the corolla) are typically large and brightly colored; they are found inside the sepals. In monocotyledonous flowers (see pp. 126-127), sepals and petals are indistinguishable; individually they are called tepals (collectively called the perianth). The petals surround the male and female reproductive structures (androecium and gynoecium). The androecium consists of stamens (male organs); each stamen is made up of a filament (stalk) and anther. The gynoecium has one or more carpels (female organs); each carpel consists of an ovary, style, and stigma. Some flowers (like the lily) occur singly on a pedicel (flower stalk); others (such as elder, sunflower) are arranged in a group (inflorescence) on a peduncle (inflorescence stalk).

A MONOCOTYLEDONOUS FLOWER
Lily
(*Lilium sp.*)

Syncarpous (fused carpels) gynoecium
Ovary
Stigma
Style

Stamen
Anther
Filament

Pollen on anther

Inner tepal (monocotyledonous petal)

Honey guide

Ovary wall
Ovule

Papilla (fleshy hair)

Outer tepal sheath
Style
Folded inner tepal (monocotyledonous petal)
Ovary
Receptacle
Stigma
Pedicel (flower stalk)
Anther
Filament

LONGITUDINAL SECTION THROUGH FLOWER BUD

Inner tepal (monocotyledonous petal)
Honey guide
Groove secreting nectar
Filament
Style
Outer tepal (monocotyledonous sepal)
Stigma
Anther

EXTERNAL VIEW

Outer tepal (monocotyledonous sepal)

Tepal scar
Receptacle
Pedicel (flower stalk)

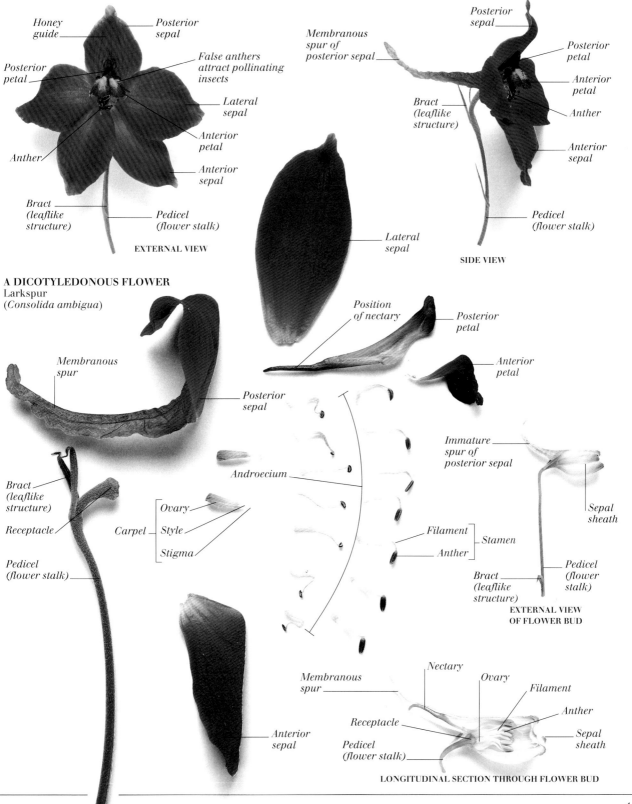

Honey guide

Posterior sepal

False anthers attract pollinating insects

Posterior petal

Lateral sepal

Anterior petal

Anterior sepal

Anther

Bract (leaflike structure)

Pedicel (flower stalk)

EXTERNAL VIEW

Posterior sepal

Membranous spur of posterior sepal

Posterior petal

Anterior petal

Anther

Bract (leaflike structure)

Anterior sepal

Pedicel (flower stalk)

SIDE VIEW

Lateral sepal

A DICOTYLEDONOUS FLOWER
Larkspur
(*Consolida ambigua*)

Membranous spur

Position of nectary

Posterior petal

Anterior petal

Posterior sepal

Immature spur of posterior sepal

Sepal sheath

Bract (leaflike structure)

Receptacle

Androecium

Carpel — Ovary
         Style
         Stigma

Filament
Anther — Stamen

Pedicel (flower stalk)

Bract (leaflike structure)

Pedicel (flower stalk)

EXTERNAL VIEW OF FLOWER BUD

Anterior sepal

Membranous spur

Nectary

Ovary

Filament

Anther

Sepal sheath

Receptacle

Pedicel (flower stalk)

LONGITUDINAL SECTION THROUGH FLOWER BUD

Flowers 2

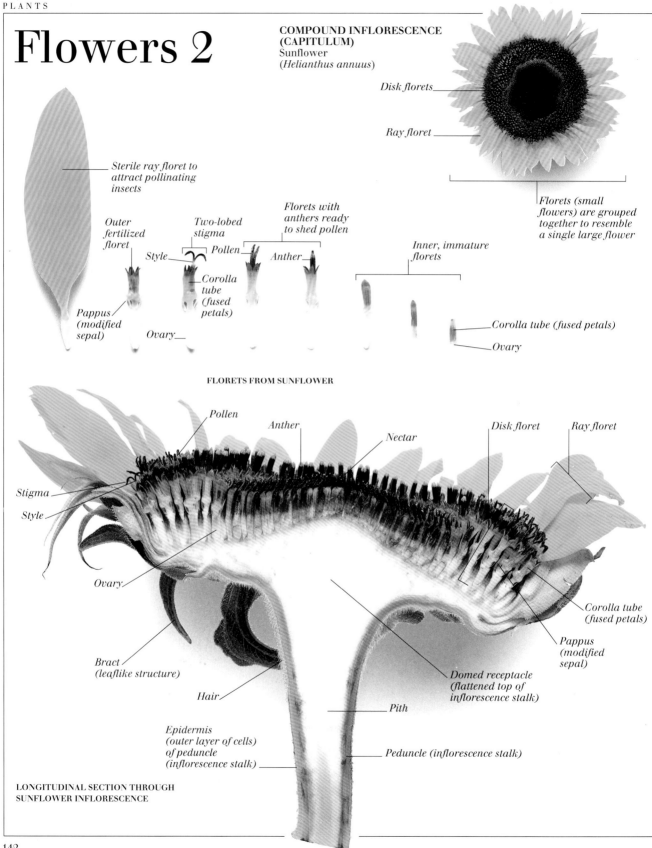

COMPOUND INFLORESCENCE (CAPITULUM)
Sunflower
(*Helianthus annuus*)

Disk florets

Ray floret

Florets (small flowers) are grouped together to resemble a single large flower

Sterile ray floret to attract pollinating insects

Outer fertilized floret

Two-lobed stigma

Florets with anthers ready to shed pollen

Style

Pollen

Anther

Inner, immature florets

Corolla tube (fused petals)

Pappus (modified sepal)

Corolla tube (fused petals)

Ovary

Ovary

FLORETS FROM SUNFLOWER

Pollen

Anther

Nectar

Disk floret

Ray floret

Stigma

Style

Ovary

Corolla tube (fused petals)

Pappus (modified sepal)

Bract (leaflike structure)

Hair

Domed receptacle (flattened top of inflorescence stalk)

Pith

Epidermis (outer layer of cells) of peduncle (inflorescence stalk)

Peduncle (inflorescence stalk)

LONGITUDINAL SECTION THROUGH SUNFLOWER INFLORESCENCE

ARRANGEMENT OF FLOWERS ON STEM

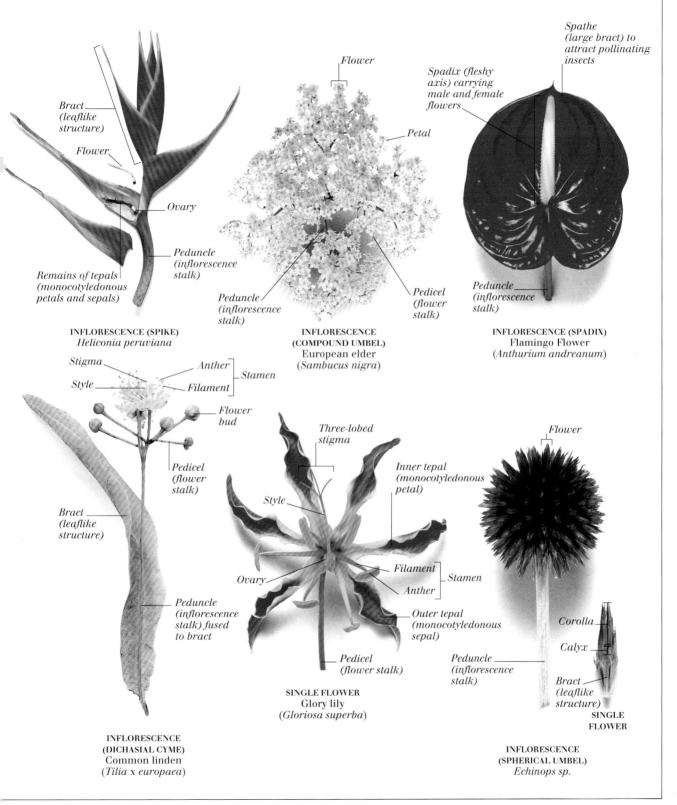

Bract
(leaflike
structure)

Flower

Ovary

Peduncle
(inflorescence
stalk)

Remains of tepals
(monocotyledonous
petals and sepals)

INFLORESCENCE (SPIKE)
Heliconia peruviana

Flower

Petal

Peduncle
(inflorescence
stalk)

Pedicel
(flower
stalk)

**INFLORESCENCE
(COMPOUND UMBEL)**
European elder
(*Sambucus nigra*)

Spathe
(large bract) to
attract pollinating
insects

Spadix (fleshy
axis) carrying
male and female
flowers

Peduncle
(inflorescence
stalk)

INFLORESCENCE (SPADIX)
Flamingo Flower
(*Anthurium andreanum*)

Stigma

Style

Anther

Filament

Stamen

Flower
bud

Pedicel
(flower
stalk)

Bract
(leaflike
structure)

Peduncle
(inflorescence
stalk) fused
to bract

**INFLORESCENCE
(DICHASIAL CYME)**
Common linden
(*Tilia x europaea*)

Three-lobed
stigma

Inner tepal
(monocotyledonous
petal)

Style

Ovary

Filament

Anther

Stamen

Outer tepal
(monocotyledonous
sepal)

Pedicel
(flower stalk)

SINGLE FLOWER
Glory lily
(*Gloriosa superba*)

Flower

Corolla

Calyx

Peduncle
(inflorescence
stalk)

Bract
(leaflike
structure)

**SINGLE
FLOWER**

**INFLORESCENCE
(SPHERICAL UMBEL)**
Echinops sp.

Pollination

POLLINATION IS THE TRANSFER OF POLLEN (which contains the male sex cells) from an anther (part of the male reproductive organ) to a stigma (part of the female reproductive organ). This process precedes fertilization (see pp. 146-147). Pollination may occur within the same flower (self-pollination), or between flowers on separate plants of the same species (cross-pollination). In most plants, pollination is carried out either by insects (entomophilous pollination) or by the wind (anemophilous pollination). Less commonly, birds, bats, or water are the agents of pollination. Insect-pollinated flowers are typically scented and brightly colored. They also produce nectar, on which insects feed. Such flowers also tend to have patterns that are visible only in ultraviolet light, which many insects can see but which humans cannot. These features attract insects, which become covered with the sticky pollen grains when they visit one flower, and then transfer the pollen to the next flower they visit. Wind-pollinated flowers are generally small, relatively inconspicuous, and unscented. They produce large quantities of light pollen grains that are easily blown by the wind to other flowers.

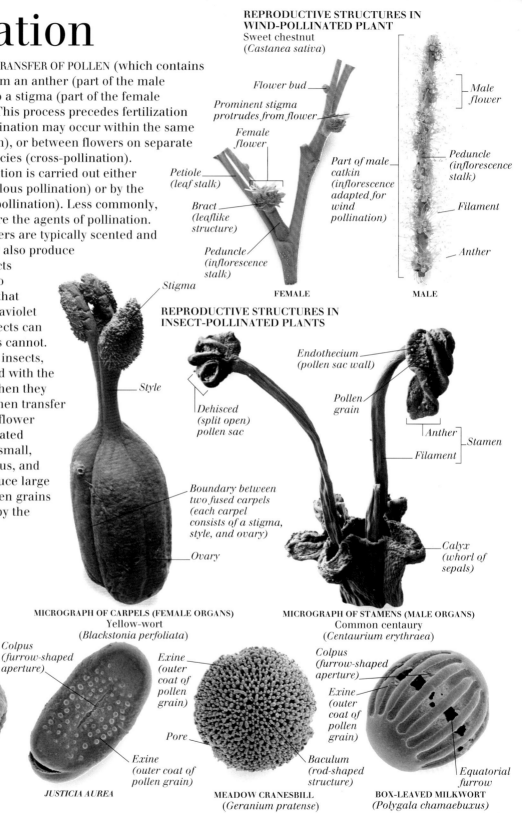

REPRODUCTIVE STRUCTURES IN WIND-POLLINATED PLANT
Sweet chestnut
(*Castanea sativa*)

Flower bud

Prominent stigma protrudes from flower

Female flower

Petiole (leaf stalk)

Bract (leaflike structure)

Peduncle (inflorescence stalk)

Part of male catkin (inflorescence adapted for wind pollination)

Male flower

Peduncle (inflorescence stalk)

Filament

Anther

FEMALE

MALE

REPRODUCTIVE STRUCTURES IN INSECT-POLLINATED PLANTS

Stigma

Style

Dehisced (split open) pollen sac

Boundary between two fused carpels (each carpel consists of a stigma, style, and ovary)

Ovary

Endothecium (pollen sac wall)

Pollen grain

Anther

Filament

Stamen

Calyx (whorl of sepals)

MICROGRAPHS OF POLLEN GRAINS

Exine (outer coat of pollen grain)

Pore

EUROPEAN FIELD ELM
(*Ulmus minor*)

Colpus (furrow-shaped aperture)

Exine (outer coat of pollen grain)

JUSTICIA AUREA

MICROGRAPH OF CARPELS (FEMALE ORGANS)
Yellow-wort
(*Blackstonia perfoliata*)

Exine (outer coat of pollen grain)

Pore

Exine (outer coat of pollen grain)

Baculum (rod-shaped structure)

MEADOW CRANESBILL
(*Geranium pratense*)

MICROGRAPH OF STAMENS (MALE ORGANS)
Common centaury
(*Centaurium erythraea*)

Colpus (furrow-shaped aperture)

Exine (outer coat of pollen grain)

Equatorial furrow

BOX-LEAVED MILKWORT
(*Polygala chamaebuxus*)

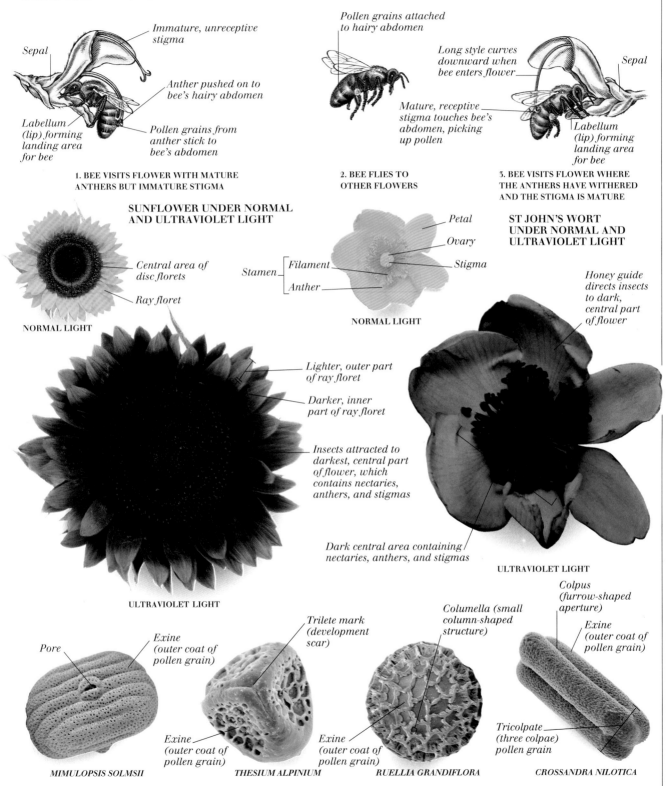

INSECT POLLINATION OF MEADOW SAGE

Immature, unreceptive stigma

Sepal

Anther pushed on to bee's hairy abdomen

Labellum (lip) forming landing area for bee

Pollen grains from anther stick to bee's abdomen

1. BEE VISITS FLOWER WITH MATURE ANTHERS BUT IMMATURE STIGMA

Pollen grains attached to hairy abdomen

Long style curves downward when bee enters flower

Sepal

Mature, receptive stigma touches bee's abdomen, picking up pollen

Labellum (lip) forming landing area for bee

2. BEE FLIES TO OTHER FLOWERS

3. BEE VISITS FLOWER WHERE THE ANTHERS HAVE WITHERED AND THE STIGMA IS MATURE

SUNFLOWER UNDER NORMAL AND ULTRAVIOLET LIGHT

Central area of disc florets

Ray floret

NORMAL LIGHT

Petal

Ovary

Stigma

Stamen { Filament / Anther

NORMAL LIGHT

ST JOHN'S WORT UNDER NORMAL AND ULTRAVIOLET LIGHT

Honey guide directs insects to dark, central part of flower

Lighter, outer part of ray floret

Darker, inner part of ray floret

Insects attracted to darkest, central part of flower, which contains nectaries, anthers, and stigmas

Dark central area containing nectaries, anthers, and stigmas

ULTRAVIOLET LIGHT

ULTRAVIOLET LIGHT

Pore

Exine (outer coat of pollen grain)

Trilete mark (development scar)

Exine (outer coat of pollen grain)

Columella (small column-shaped structure)

Exine (outer coat of pollen grain)

Colpus (furrow-shaped aperture)

Exine (outer coat of pollen grain)

Tricolpate (three colpae) pollen grain

MIMULOPSIS SOLMSH

THESIUM ALPINIUM

RUELLIA GRANDIFLORA

CROSSANDRA NILOTICA

145

Fertilization

FERTILIZATION IS THE FUSION of male and female gametes (sex cells) to produce a zygote (embryo). Following pollination (see pp. 144-145), the pollen grains that contain the male gametes are on the stigma, some distance from the female gamete (ovum) inside the ovule. To enable the gametes to meet, the pollen grain germinates and produces a pollen tube, which grows down and enters the embryo sac (the inner part of the ovule that contains the ovum). Two male gametes, traveling at the tip of the pollen tube, enter the embryo sac. One gamete fuses with the ovum to produce a zygote that will develop into an embryo plant. The other male gamete fuses with two polar nuclei to produce the endosperm, which acts as a food supply for the developing embryo. Fertilization also initiates other changes: the integument (outer part of ovule) forms a testa (seed coat) around the embryo and endosperm; the petals fall off; the stigma and style wither; and the ovary wall forms a layer (called the pericarp) around the seed. Together, the pericarp and seed form the fruit, which may be succulent (see pp. 148-149) or dry (see pp. 150-151). In some species (such as blackberry), apomixis can occur: The seed develops without fertilization of the ovum by a male gamete, but endosperm formation and fruit development take place as in other species.

BANANA
(*Musa 'Lacatan'*)

DEVELOPMENT OF A SUCCULENT FRUIT
Blackberry
(*Rubus fruticosus*)

Petal

Stamen { Filament, Anther }

Carpel { Ovary, Stigma, Style }

1. FLOWER IN FULL BLOOM ATTRACTS POLLINATORS

Abortive seed

Endocarp (inner layer of pericarp)

Remains of style

Carpel

Mesocarp (middle layer of pericarp)

Receptacle

Exocarp (outer layer of pericarp)

Remains of stamen

Sepal

Pedicel (flower stalk)

4. PERICARP FORMS FLESH, SKIN, AND A HARD INNER LAYER (SHOWN IN CROSS SECTION)

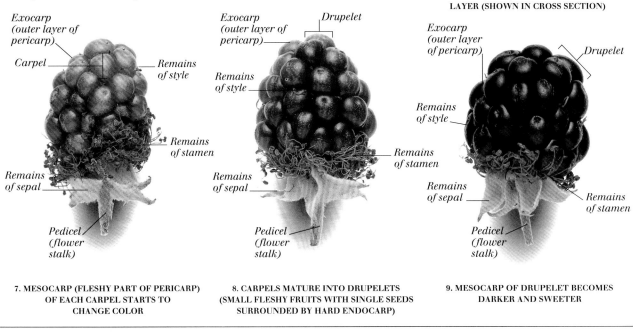

Exocarp (outer layer of pericarp)

Carpel

Remains of style

Remains of stamen

Remains of sepal

Pedicel (flower stalk)

7. MESOCARP (FLESHY PART OF PERICARP) OF EACH CARPEL STARTS TO CHANGE COLOR

Exocarp (outer layer of pericarp)

Drupelet

Remains of style

Remains of stamen

Remains of sepal

Pedicel (flower stalk)

8. CARPELS MATURE INTO DRUPELETS (SMALL FLESHY FRUITS WITH SINGLE SEEDS SURROUNDED BY HARD ENDOCARP)

Exocarp (outer layer of pericarp)

Drupelet

Remains of style

Remains of stamen

Remains of sepal

Pedicel (flower stalk)

9. MESOCARP OF DRUPELET BECOMES DARKER AND SWEETER

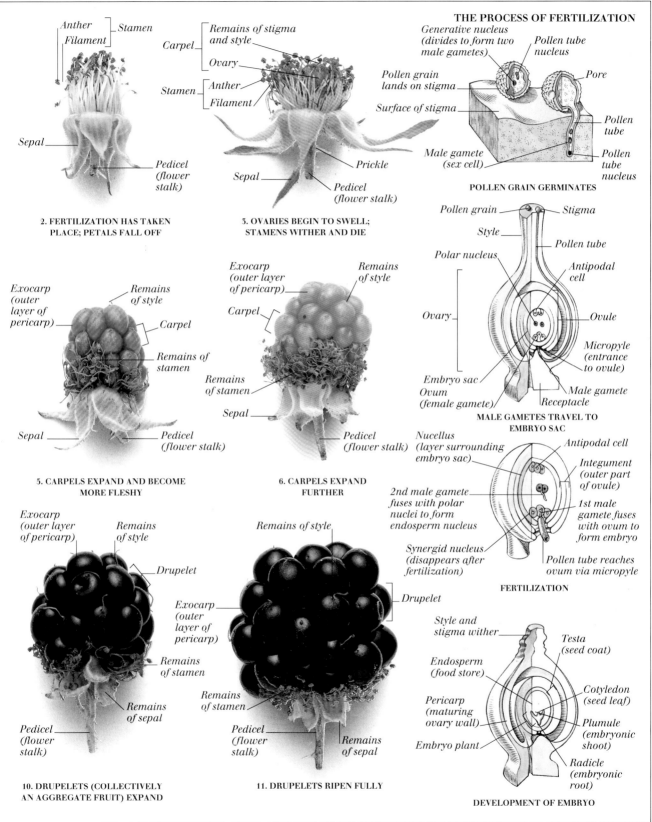

2. FERTILIZATION HAS TAKEN PLACE; PETALS FALL OFF

Anther — Stamen
Filament
Sepal
Pedicel (flower stalk)

3. OVARIES BEGIN TO SWELL; STAMENS WITHER AND DIE

Carpel — Remains of stigma and style
Ovary
Anther — Stamen
Filament
Sepal
Prickle
Pedicel (flower stalk)

THE PROCESS OF FERTILIZATION

Generative nucleus (divides to form two male gametes)
Pollen tube nucleus
Pollen grain lands on stigma
Surface of stigma
Pore
Pollen tube
Pollen tube nucleus
Male gamete (sex cell)

POLLEN GRAIN GERMINATES

5. CARPELS EXPAND AND BECOME MORE FLESHY

Exocarp (outer layer of pericarp)
Remains of style
Carpel
Remains of stamen
Sepal
Pedicel (flower stalk)

6. CARPELS EXPAND FURTHER

Exocarp (outer layer of pericarp)
Remains of style
Carpel
Remains of stamen
Sepal
Pedicel (flower stalk)

Pollen grain
Stigma
Style
Pollen tube
Polar nucleus
Antipodal cell
Ovary
Ovule
Micropyle (entrance to ovule)
Embryo sac
Ovum (female gamete)
Male gamete
Receptacle

MALE GAMETES TRAVEL TO EMBRYO SAC

10. DRUPELETS (COLLECTIVELY AN AGGREGATE FRUIT) EXPAND

Exocarp (outer layer of pericarp)
Remains of style
Drupelet
Remains of stamen
Remains of sepal
Pedicel (flower stalk)

11. DRUPELETS RIPEN FULLY

Remains of style
Drupelet
Exocarp (outer layer of pericarp)
Remains of stamen
Remains of sepal
Pedicel (flower stalk)

Nucellus (layer surrounding embryo sac)
Antipodal cell
Integument (outer part of ovule)
2nd male gamete fuses with polar nuclei to form endosperm nucleus
1st male gamete fuses with ovum to form embryo
Synergid nucleus (disappears after fertilization)
Pollen tube reaches ovum via micropyle

FERTILIZATION

Style and stigma wither
Testa (seed coat)
Endosperm (food store)
Cotyledon (seed leaf)
Pericarp (maturing ovary wall)
Plumule (embryonic shoot)
Embryo plant
Radicle (embryonic root)

DEVELOPMENT OF EMBRYO

Succulent fruits

A FRUIT IS A FULLY DEVELOPED and ripened ovary—the seed-producing part of a plant's female reproductive organs. Fruits may be succulent or dry (see pp. 150-151). Succulent fruits are fleshy and brightly colored, making them attractive to animals, which eat them and disperse the seeds away from the parent plant. The wall (pericarp) of a succulent fruit has three layers: an outer exocarp, a middle mesocarp, and an inner endocarp. These three layers vary in thickness and texture in different types of fruits and may blend into each other. Succulent fruits can be classed as simple (derived from one ovary) or compound (derived from several ovaries). Simple succulent fruits include berries, which typically have many seeds, and drupes, which typically have a single stone or pit (such as cherry and peach). Compound succulent fruits include aggregate fruits, which are formed from many ovaries in one flower, and multiple fruits, which develop from the ovaries of many flowers. Some fruits, known as false fruits or pseudocarps, develop from parts of the flower in addition to the ovaries. For example, the flesh of the apple is formed from the receptacle (the upper end of the flower stalk).

BERRY
Cocoa
(*Theobroma cacao*)

FRUIT WITH FLESHY ARIL
Lychee
(*Litchi chinensis*)

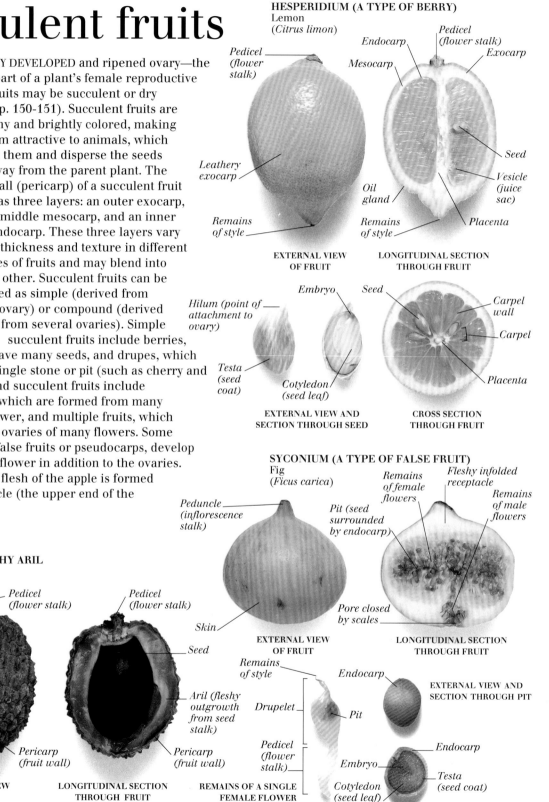

HESPERIDIUM (A TYPE OF BERRY)
Lemon
(*Citrus limon*)

Pedicel (flower stalk)
Endocarp
Mesocarp
Pedicel (flower stalk)
Exocarp
Leathery exocarp
Seed
Vesicle (juice sac)
Oil gland
Remains of style
Remains of style
Placenta

EXTERNAL VIEW OF FRUIT

LONGITUDINAL SECTION THROUGH FRUIT

Embryo
Seed
Carpel wall
Hilum (point of attachment to ovary)
Carpel
Testa (seed coat)
Cotyledon (seed leaf)
Placenta

EXTERNAL VIEW AND SECTION THROUGH SEED

CROSS SECTION THROUGH FRUIT

SYCONIUM (A TYPE OF FALSE FRUIT)
Fig
(*Ficus carica*)

Peduncle (inflorescence stalk)
Remains of female flowers
Fleshy infolded receptacle
Remains of male flowers
Pit (seed surrounded by endocarp)
Skin
Pore closed by scales

EXTERNAL VIEW OF FRUIT

LONGITUDINAL SECTION THROUGH FRUIT

Pedicel (flower stalk)
Pedicel (flower stalk)
Seed
Aril (fleshy outgrowth from seed stalk)
Pericarp (fruit wall)
Pericarp (fruit wall)

EXTERNAL VIEW OF FRUIT

LONGITUDINAL SECTION THROUGH FRUIT

Remains of style
Endocarp
Drupelet
Pit
Pedicel (flower stalk)
Embryo
Cotyledon (seed leaf)
Endocarp
Testa (seed coat)

EXTERNAL VIEW AND SECTION THROUGH PIT

REMAINS OF A SINGLE FEMALE FLOWER

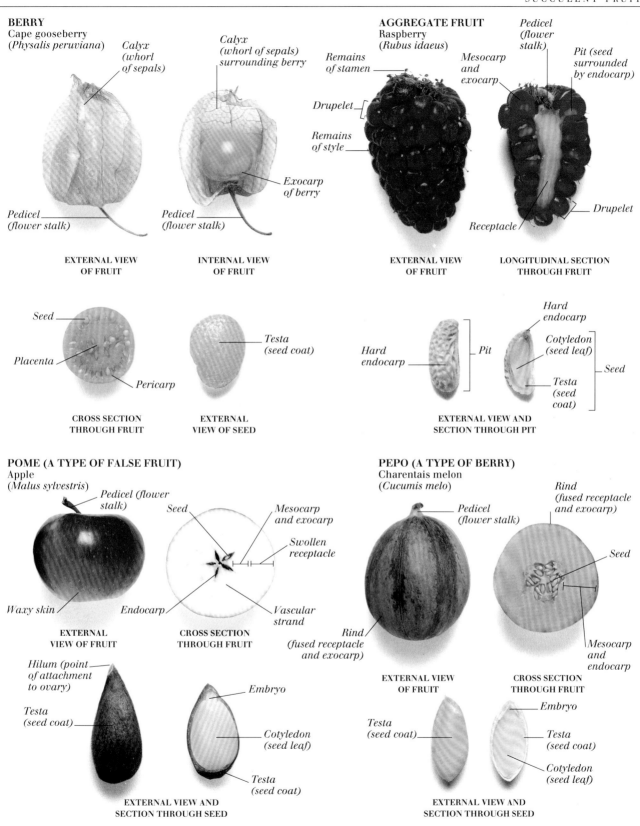

BERRY
Cape gooseberry
(*Physalis peruviana*)

Calyx (whorl of sepals)

Calyx (whorl of sepals) surrounding berry

Exocarp of berry

Pedicel (flower stalk)

Pedicel (flower stalk)

EXTERNAL VIEW
OF FRUIT

INTERNAL VIEW
OF FRUIT

Seed

Placenta

Pericarp

Testa (seed coat)

CROSS SECTION
THROUGH FRUIT

EXTERNAL
VIEW OF SEED

AGGREGATE FRUIT
Raspberry
(*Rubus idaeus*)

Remains of stamen

Drupelet

Remains of style

Mesocarp and exocarp

Pedicel (flower stalk)

Pit (seed surrounded by endocarp)

Receptacle

Drupelet

EXTERNAL VIEW
OF FRUIT

LONGITUDINAL SECTION
THROUGH FRUIT

Hard endocarp

Hard endocarp

Pit

Cotyledon (seed leaf)

Testa (seed coat)

Seed

EXTERNAL VIEW AND
SECTION THROUGH PIT

POME (A TYPE OF FALSE FRUIT)
Apple
(*Malus sylvestris*)

Pedicel (flower stalk)

Seed

Mesocarp and exocarp

Swollen receptacle

Waxy skin

Endocarp

Vascular strand

EXTERNAL
VIEW OF FRUIT

CROSS SECTION
THROUGH FRUIT

Hilum (point of attachment to ovary)

Testa (seed coat)

Embryo

Cotyledon (seed leaf)

Testa (seed coat)

EXTERNAL VIEW AND
SECTION THROUGH SEED

PEPO (A TYPE OF BERRY)
Charentais melon
(*Cucumis melo*)

Pedicel (flower stalk)

Rind (fused receptacle and exocarp)

Seed

Rind (fused receptacle and exocarp)

Mesocarp and endocarp

EXTERNAL VIEW
OF FRUIT

CROSS SECTION
THROUGH FRUIT

Testa (seed coat)

Embryo

Testa (seed coat)

Cotyledon (seed leaf)

EXTERNAL VIEW AND
SECTION THROUGH SEED

Dry fruits

DRY FRUITS HAVE A HARD, DRY PERICARP (fruit wall) around their seeds, unlike succulent fruits, which have fleshy pericarps (see pp. 148-149). Dry fruits are divided into three types: dehiscent, in which the pericarp splits open to release the seeds; indehiscent, which do not split open; and schizocarpic, in which the fruit splits but the seeds are not exposed. Dehiscent dry fruits include capsules (for example, love-in-a-mist), follicles (delphinium), legumes (pea), and silicles (honesty). Typically, the seeds of dehiscent fruits are dispersed by the wind. Indehiscent dry fruits include nuts (sweet chestnut), nutlets (goose grass), achenes (strawberry), caryopses (wheat), samaras (elm), and cypselas (dandelion). Some indehiscent dry fruits are dispersed by the wind, assisted by "wings" (elm) or "parachutes" (dandelion); others (goose grass) have hooked pericarps to aid dispersal on animals' fur. Schizocarpic dry fruits include cremocarps (hogweed), and double samaras (sycamore maple); these are dispersed by the wind.

NUTLET
Goose grass
(*Galium aparine*)

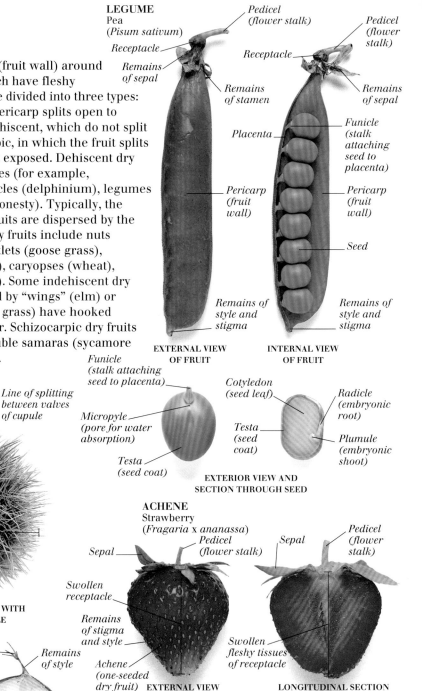

LEGUME
Pea
(*Pisum sativum*)

Pedicel (flower stalk)
Receptacle
Remains of sepal
Remains of stamen
Placenta
Pericarp (fruit wall)
Remains of style and stigma

Pedicel (flower stalk)
Receptacle
Remains of sepal
Funicle (stalk attaching seed to placenta)
Pericarp (fruit wall)
Seed
Remains of style and stigma

EXTERNAL VIEW OF FRUIT

INTERNAL VIEW OF FRUIT

Funicle (stalk attaching seed to placenta)
Micropyle (pore for water absorption)
Testa (seed coat)

Cotyledon (seed leaf)
Testa (seed coat)
Radicle (embryonic root)
Plumule (embryonic shoot)

EXTERIOR VIEW AND SECTION THROUGH SEED

NUT
Spanish chestnut
(*Castanea sativa*)

Peduncle (inflorescence stalk)
Remains of male inflorescence
Nut (indehiscent fruit)
Spiky cupule (husk around fruit formed from bracts)

Line of splitting between valves of cupule

EXTERNAL VIEW OF FRUIT WITH SURROUNDING CUPULE

ACHENE
Strawberry
(*Fragaria* x *ananassa*)

Sepal
Swollen receptacle
Remains of stigma and style
Achene (one-seeded dry fruit)

Pedicel (flower stalk)

Sepal
Pedicel (flower stalk)
Swollen fleshy tissues of receptacle

EXTERNAL VIEW OF FRUIT

LONGITUDINAL SECTION THROUGH FRUIT

Remains of stigma
Remains of style
Nut (indehiscent fruit)
Woody pericarp (fruit wall)

Remains of stigma
Remains of style
Embryo
Cotyledon (seed leaf)
Testa (seed coat)
Woody pericarp (fruit wall)

EXTERNAL VIEW AND SECTION THROUGH FRUIT

Pericarp (fruit wall)

Pericarp (fruit wall)
Cotyledon (seed leaf)
Testa (seed coat)

EXTERNAL VIEW AND SECTION THROUGH SEED

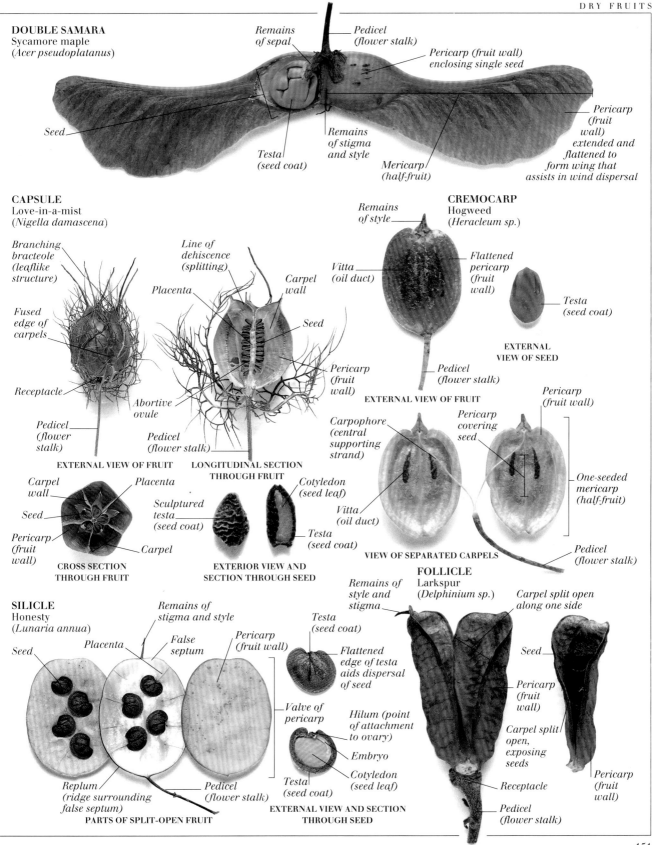

DOUBLE SAMARA
Sycamore maple
(*Acer pseudoplatanus*)

Remains of sepal

Pedicel (flower stalk)

Pericarp (fruit wall) enclosing single seed

Seed

Remains of stigma and style

Testa (seed coat)

Mericarp (half-fruit)

Pericarp (fruit wall) extended and flattened to form wing that assists in wind dispersal

CAPSULE
Love-in-a-mist
(*Nigella damascena*)

Branching bracteole (leaflike structure)

Fused edge of carpels

Receptacle

Pedicel (flower stalk)

EXTERNAL VIEW OF FRUIT

Line of dehiscence (splitting)

Placenta

Carpel wall

Seed

Pericarp (fruit wall)

Abortive ovule

Pedicel (flower stalk)

LONGITUDINAL SECTION THROUGH FRUIT

Carpel wall

Seed

Pericarp (fruit wall)

Placenta

Carpel

CROSS SECTION THROUGH FRUIT

Sculptured testa (seed coat)

Cotyledon (seed leaf)

Testa (seed coat)

EXTERIOR VIEW AND SECTION THROUGH SEED

CREMOCARP
Hogweed
(*Heracleum sp.*)

Remains of style

Vitta (oil duct)

Flattened pericarp (fruit wall)

Testa (seed coat)

EXTERNAL VIEW OF SEED

Pedicel (flower stalk)

EXTERNAL VIEW OF FRUIT

Carpophore (central supporting strand)

Pericarp covering seed

Pericarp (fruit wall)

Vitta (oil duct)

One-seeded mericarp (half-fruit)

Pedicel (flower stalk)

VIEW OF SEPARATED CARPELS

SILICLE
Honesty
(*Lunaria annua*)

Seed

Placenta

Remains of stigma and style

False septum

Pericarp (fruit wall)

Replum (ridge surrounding false septum)

Pedicel (flower stalk)

PARTS OF SPLIT-OPEN FRUIT

Valve of pericarp

Testa (seed coat)

Flattened edge of testa aids dispersal of seed

Hilum (point of attachment to ovary)

Embryo

Cotyledon (seed leaf)

Testa (seed coat)

EXTERNAL VIEW AND SECTION THROUGH SEED

FOLLICLE
Larkspur
(*Delphinium sp.*)

Remains of style and stigma

Carpel split open along one side

Seed

Pericarp (fruit wall)

Carpel split open, exposing seeds

Receptacle

Pericarp (fruit wall)

Pedicel (flower stalk)

Germination

GERMINATION IS THE GROWTH OF SEEDS INTO SEEDLINGS. It starts when seeds become active below ground, and ends when the first foliage leaves appear above ground. A seed consists of an embryo and its food supply, surrounded by a testa (seed coat). The embryo is made up of one or two cotyledons (seed leaves) attached to a central axis. The upper part of the axis consists of an epicotyl, which has a plumule (embryonic shoot) at its tip. The lower part of the axis consists of a hypocotyl and a radicle (embryonic root). After dispersal from the parent plant, the seeds dehydrate and enter a period of dormancy. Germination begins, following this dormant period, as long as the seeds have enough water, oxygen, warmth, and, in some cases, light. In the first stages of germination, the seed takes in water; the embryo starts to use its food store; and the radicle swells, breaks through the testa, and grows downward. Germination then proceeds in one of two ways, depending on the type of seed. In epigeal germination, the hypocotyl lengthens, pulling the plumule and its protective cotyledons out of the soil. In hypogeal germination, the cotyledons remain below ground and the epicotyl lengthens, pushing the plumule upward.

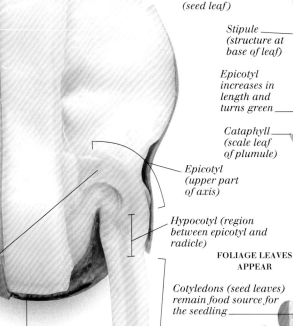

HYPOGEAL GERMINATION
Broad bean
(*Vicia faba*)

Cotyledon
(seed leaf)

Cotyledon
(seed leaf)

Plumule
(embryonic
shoot)

Testa
(seed
coat)

Epicotyl
(upper part
of axis)

Hypocotyl
(region
between
epicotyl and
radicle)

Radicle
(embryonic
root)

**SEED AT START OF
GERMINATION**

Cotyledon
(seed leaf)

Foliage leaf

Cotyledon
(seed leaf)

Stipule
(structure at
base of leaf)

Epicotyl
increases in
length and
turns green

Cataphyll
(scale leaf
of plumule)

Epicotyl
(upper part
of axis)

Hypocotyl (region
between epicotyl and
radicle)

**FOLIAGE LEAVES
APPEAR**

Cotyledons (seed leaves)
remain food source for
the seedling

Primary
root

Radicle
(embryonic
root)

Lateral
root
system

Split in testa
(seed coat) due
to expanding
cotyledons

Young
shoot

Cataphyll
(scale leaf of
plumule)

Testa
(seed coat)

Epicotyl
(upper part
of axis)
lengthens

Plumule
(embryonic
shoot)

Hilum (point of
attachment to ovary)

Cortex

Vascular tissue
(xylem and
phloem)

Epidermis

Root tip
(region of
cell division)

Cotyledons
(seed leaves)
remain within
testa (seed
coat) below
soil's surface

**SHOOT APPEARS
ABOVE SOIL**

Primary
root

Lateral root

**RADICLE BREAKS
THROUGH TESTA**

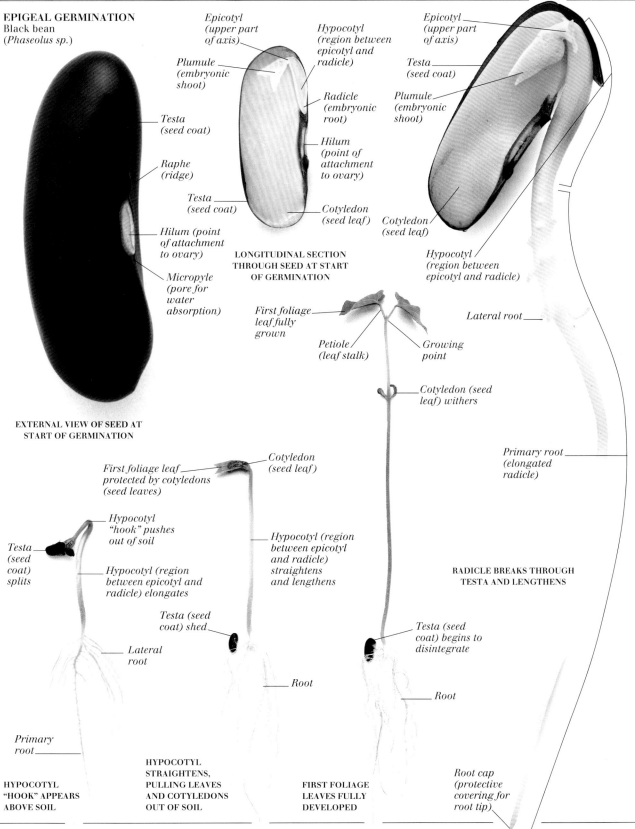

EPIGEAL GERMINATION
Black bean
(*Phaseolus sp.*)

*Testa
(seed coat)*

*Raphe
(ridge)*

*Hilum (point
of attachment
to ovary)*

*Micropyle
(pore for
water
absorption)*

**EXTERNAL VIEW OF SEED AT
START OF GERMINATION**

*Epicotyl
(upper part
of axis)*

*Plumule
(embryonic
shoot)*

*Hypocotyl
(region between
epicotyl and
radicle)*

*Radicle
(embryonic
root)*

*Hilum
(point of
attachment
to ovary)*

*Testa
(seed coat)*

*Cotyledon
(seed leaf)*

**LONGITUDINAL SECTION
THROUGH SEED AT START
OF GERMINATION**

*Epicotyl
(upper part
of axis)*

*Testa
(seed coat)*

*Plumule
(embryonic
shoot)*

*Cotyledon
(seed leaf)*

*Hypocotyl
(region between
epicotyl and radicle)*

*First foliage
leaf fully
grown*

*Petiole
(leaf stalk)*

*Growing
point*

*Cotyledon (seed
leaf) withers*

Lateral root

*Primary root
(elongated
radicle)*

*First foliage leaf
protected by cotyledons
(seed leaves)*

*Cotyledon
(seed leaf)*

*Hypocotyl
"hook" pushes
out of soil*

*Testa
(seed
coat)
splits*

*Hypocotyl (region
between epicotyl and
radicle) elongates*

*Lateral
root*

*Primary
root*

*Hypocotyl (region
between epicotyl
and radicle)
straightens
and lengthens*

*Testa (seed
coat) shed*

Root

**RADICLE BREAKS THROUGH
TESTA AND LENGTHENS**

*Testa (seed
coat) begins to
disintegrate*

Root

*Root cap
(protective
covering for
root tip)*

**HYPOCOTYL
"HOOK" APPEARS
ABOVE SOIL**

**HYPOCOTYL
STRAIGHTENS,
PULLING LEAVES
AND COTYLEDONS
OUT OF SOIL**

**FIRST FOLIAGE
LEAVES FULLY
DEVELOPED**

153

Vegetative reproduction

MANY PLANTS CAN PROPAGATE THEMSELVES by vegetative reproduction. In this process, part of a plant separates, takes root, and grows into a new plant. Vegetative reproduction is a type of asexual reproduction; it involves only one parent and there is no fusion of gametes (sex cells). Plants use various structures to reproduce vegetatively. Some plants use underground storage organs. Such organs include rhizomes (horizontal, underground stems), the branches of which produce new plants; bulbs (swollen leaf bases) and corms (swollen stems), which produce daughter bulbs or corms that separate from the parent; and stem tubers (thickened underground stems) and root tubers (swollen adventitious roots), which also separate from the parent. Other propagative structures include runners and stolons, creeping horizontal stems that take root and produce new plants; bulbils, small bulbs that develop on the stem or in the place of flowers, and then drop off and grow into new plants; and adventitious buds, miniature plants that form on leaf margins before dropping to the ground and growing into mature plants.

CORM
Gladiolus
(*Gladiolus sp.*)

ADVENTITIOUS BUD
Mexican hat plant
(*Kalanchoe daigremontiana*)

Apex of leaf

Lamina (blade) of leaf

Leaf margin

Notch in leaf margin containing meristematic (actively dividing) cells

Adventitious bud (detachable bud with adventitious roots) drops from leaf

Petiole (leaf stalk)

BULBIL IN PLACE OF FLOWER
Orange lily
(*Lilium bulbiferum*)

Scar left by flower

Leaf

Pedicel (flower stalk)

Detachable bulbil formed in place of flower

Peduncle (inflorescence stalk)

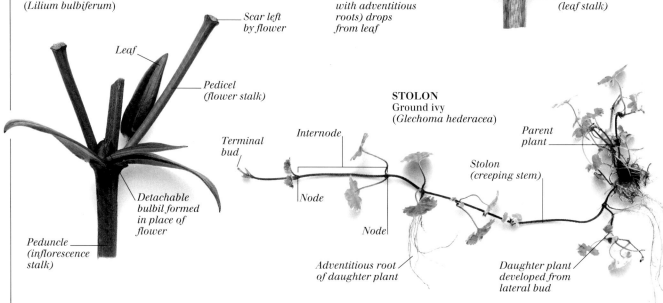

STOLON
Ground ivy
(*Glechoma hederacea*)

Terminal bud

Internode

Node

Node

Parent plant

Stolon (creeping stem)

Daughter plant developed from lateral bud

Adventitious root of daughter plant

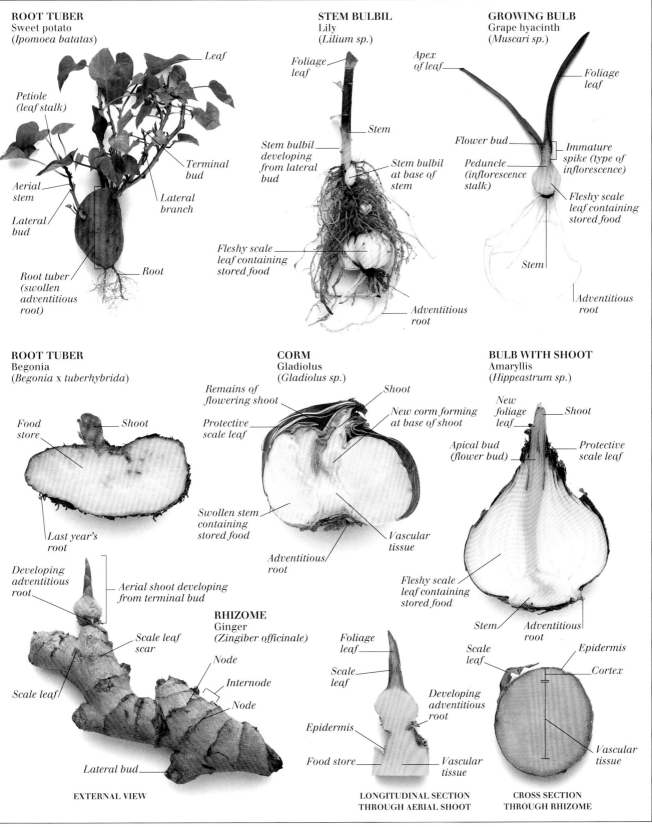

ROOT TUBER
Sweet potato
(*Ipomoea batatas*)

Leaf

Petiole
(leaf stalk)

Terminal
bud

Aerial
stem

Lateral
branch

Lateral
bud

Root tuber
(swollen
adventitious
root)

Root

STEM BULBIL
Lily
(*Lilium sp.*)

Foliage
leaf

Stem

Stem bulbil
developing
from lateral
bud

Stem bulbil
at base of
stem

Fleshy scale
leaf containing
stored food

Adventitious
root

GROWING BULB
Grape hyacinth
(*Muscari sp.*)

Apex
of leaf

Foliage
leaf

Flower bud

Immature
spike (type of
inflorescence)

Peduncle
(inflorescence
stalk)

Fleshy scale
leaf containing
stored food

Stem

Adventitious
root

ROOT TUBER
Begonia
(*Begonia* x *tuberhybrida*)

Food
store

Shoot

Last year's
root

Developing
adventitious
root

Aerial shoot developing
from terminal bud

Scale leaf
scar

Scale leaf

Node

Internode

Node

Lateral bud

EXTERNAL VIEW

CORM
Gladiolus
(*Gladiolus sp.*)

Remains of
flowering shoot

Shoot

Protective
scale leaf

New corm forming
at base of shoot

Swollen stem
containing
stored food

Adventitious
root

Vascular
tissue

RHIZOME
Ginger
(*Zingiber officinale*)

Foliage
leaf

Scale
leaf

Epidermis

Food store

Developing
adventitious
root

Vascular
tissue

**LONGITUDINAL SECTION
THROUGH AERIAL SHOOT**

BULB WITH SHOOT
Amaryllis
(*Hippeastrum sp.*)

New
foliage
leaf

Shoot

Apical bud
(flower bud)

Protective
scale leaf

Fleshy scale
leaf containing
stored food

Stem

Adventitious
root

Scale
leaf

Epidermis

Cortex

Vascular
tissue

**CROSS SECTION
THROUGH RHIZOME**

155

Dryland plants

LEAF SUCCULENT
Lithops sp.

DRYLAND PLANTS (XEROPHYTES) are able to survive in unfavorable habitats. All are found in places where little water is available; some live in high temperatures that cause excessive loss of water from the leaves. Xerophytes show a number of adaptations to dry conditions. These include reduced leaf area, rolled leaves, sunken stomata, hairs, spines, and thick cuticles. One group, succulent plants, stores water in specially enlarged spongy tissues found in leaves, roots, or stems. Leaf succulents have enlarged, fleshy, water-storing leaves. Root succulents have a large underground water-storage organ with short-lived stems and leaves above ground. Stem succulents are represented by the cacti (family Cactaceae). Cacti stems are fleshy, green, and photosynthetic. They are typically ribbed or covered by tubercles in rows, with leaves being reduced to spines or entirely absent.

STEM SUCCULENT
Golden barrel cactus
(*Echinocactus grusonii*)

Areole (modified lateral shoot)

Trichome (hair)

Spine (modified leaf)

Waxy cuticle (waterproof covering)

Water-storing parenchyma (packing tissue)

Tubercle (projection from stem surface)

Vascular cylinder (transport tissue)

Spine (modified leaf)

Tubercle (projection from stem surface)

Root

EXTERNAL VIEW

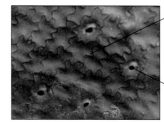

Sinuous (wavy) cell wall

Stoma (pore) controlling exchange of gases

MICROGRAPH OF STEM SURFACE

Spine (modified leaf)

Areole (modified lateral shoot)

Tubercle (projection from stem surface)

Waxy cuticle (waterproof covering)

DETAIL OF STEM SURFACE

Root

LONGITUDINAL SECTION THROUGH STEM

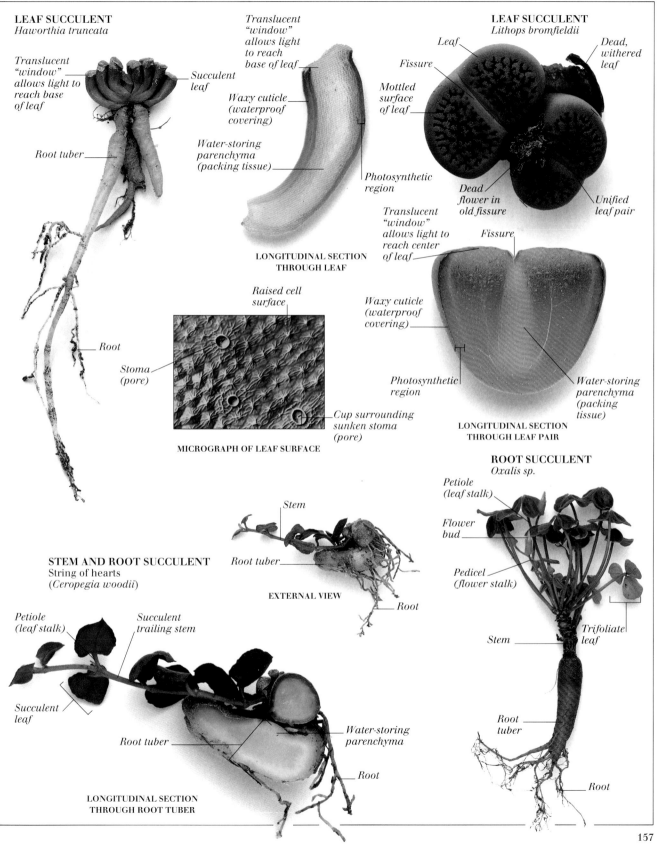

LEAF SUCCULENT
Haworthia truncata

Translucent "window" allows light to reach base of leaf

Succulent leaf

Root tuber

Root

Translucent "window" allows light to reach base of leaf

Waxy cuticle (waterproof covering)

Water-storing parenchyma (packing tissue)

Photosynthetic region

LONGITUDINAL SECTION THROUGH LEAF

Raised cell surface

Stoma (pore)

Cup surrounding sunken stoma (pore)

MICROGRAPH OF LEAF SURFACE

LEAF SUCCULENT
Lithops bromfieldii

Leaf

Fissure

Mottled surface of leaf

Dead, withered leaf

Dead flower in old fissure

Unified leaf pair

Translucent "window" allows light to reach center of leaf

Fissure

Waxy cuticle (waterproof covering)

Photosynthetic region

Water-storing parenchyma (packing tissue)

LONGITUDINAL SECTION THROUGH LEAF PAIR

ROOT SUCCULENT
Oxalis sp.

Petiole (leaf stalk)

Flower bud

Pedicel (flower stalk)

Stem

Trifoliate leaf

Root tuber

Root

STEM AND ROOT SUCCULENT
String of hearts
(*Ceropegia woodii*)

Stem

Root tuber

Root

EXTERNAL VIEW

Petiole (leaf stalk)

Succulent trailing stem

Succulent leaf

Root tuber

Water-storing parenchyma

Root

LONGITUDINAL SECTION THROUGH ROOT TUBER

Wetland plants

WETLAND PLANTS GROW SUBMERGED IN WATER, either partially, like the water hyacinth, or completely, like the pondweeds, and show various adaptations to this habitat. Typically, there are numerous air spaces inside the stems, leaves, and roots; these aid gas exchange and buoyancy. Submerged parts generally have no cuticle (waterproof covering), allowing the plants to absorb minerals and gases directly from the water. Also, because they are supported by the water, wetland plants need little of the supportive tissue found in land plants. Stomata, the gas exchange pores, are absent from plants that are completely submerged. In partially submerged plants with floating leaves, such as water lilies, stomata are found on the upper leaf surfaces, where they cannot be flooded.

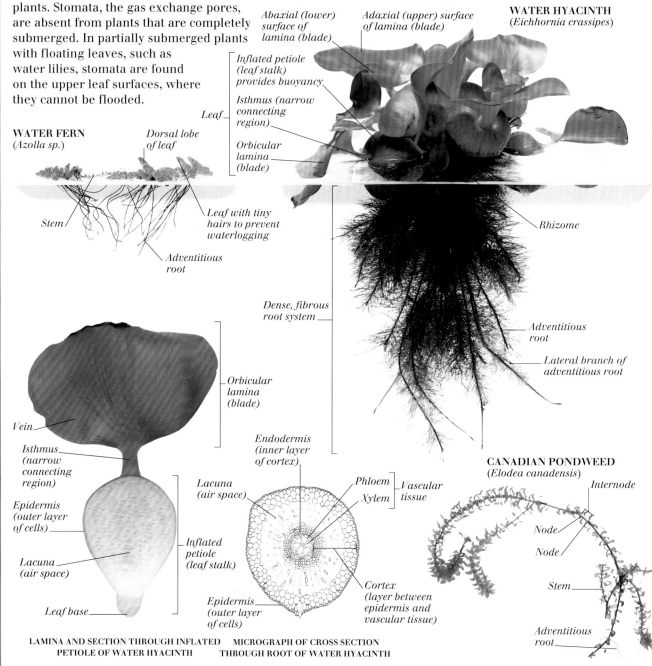

WATER FERN
(*Azolla sp.*)

Dorsal lobe of leaf

Stem

Leaf with tiny hairs to prevent waterlogging

Adventitious root

Abaxial (lower) surface of lamina (blade)

Adaxial (upper) surface of lamina (blade)

WATER HYACINTH
(*Eichhornia crassipes*)

Inflated petiole (leaf stalk) provides buoyancy

Isthmus (narrow connecting region)

Leaf

Orbicular lamina (blade)

Rhizome

Dense, fibrous root system

Adventitious root

Lateral branch of adventitious root

Orbicular lamina (blade)

Vein

Isthmus (narrow connecting region)

Epidermis (outer layer of cells)

Lacuna (air space)

Leaf base

Lacuna (air space)

Inflated petiole (leaf stalk)

Epidermis (outer layer of cells)

Endodermis (inner layer of cortex)

Phloem

Xylem

Vascular tissue

Cortex (layer between epidermis and vascular tissue)

CANADIAN PONDWEED
(*Elodea canadensis*)

Internode

Node

Node

Stem

Adventitious root

LAMINA AND SECTION THROUGH INFLATED PETIOLE OF WATER HYACINTH

MICROGRAPH OF CROSS SECTION THROUGH ROOT OF WATER HYACINTH

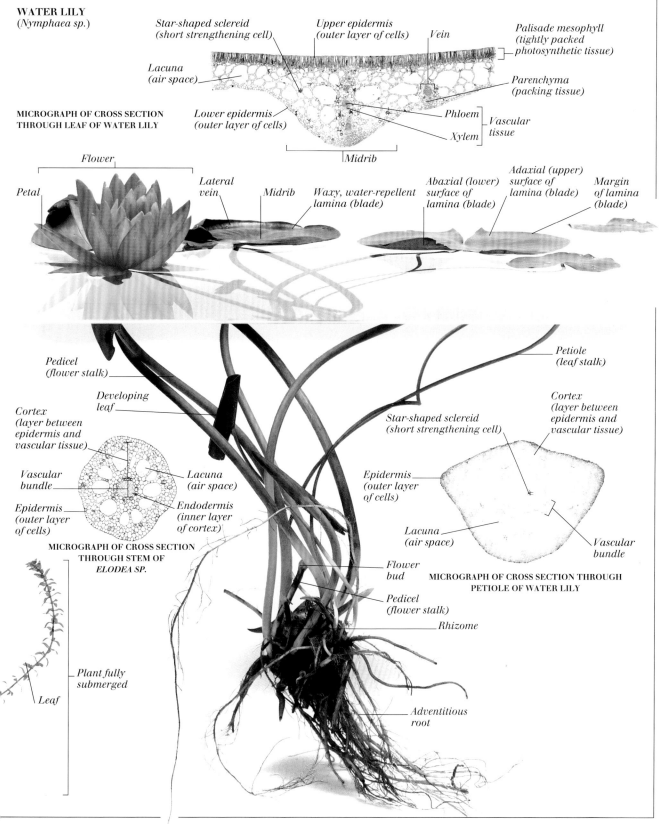

WATER LILY
(*Nymphaea sp.*)

Star-shaped sclereid
(short strengthening cell)

Upper epidermis
(outer layer of cells)

Vein

Palisade mesophyll
(tightly packed
photosynthetic tissue)

Lacuna
(air space)

Parenchyma
(packing tissue)

**MICROGRAPH OF CROSS SECTION
THROUGH LEAF OF WATER LILY**

Lower epidermis
(outer layer of cells)

Phloem

Xylem

Vascular
tissue

Midrib

Flower

Lateral
vein

Midrib

Waxy, water-repellent
lamina (blade)

Abaxial (lower)
surface of
lamina (blade)

Adaxial (upper)
surface of
lamina (blade)

Margin
of lamina
(blade)

Petal

Pedicel
(flower stalk)

Petiole
(leaf stalk)

Developing
leaf

Cortex
(layer between
epidermis and
vascular tissue)

Star-shaped sclereid
(short strengthening cell)

Cortex
(layer between
epidermis and
vascular tissue)

Vascular
bundle

Lacuna
(air space)

Epidermis
(outer layer
of cells)

Epidermis
(outer layer
of cells)

Endodermis
(inner layer
of cortex)

Lacuna
(air space)

Vascular
bundle

**MICROGRAPH OF CROSS SECTION
THROUGH STEM OF
ELODEA SP.**

Flower
bud

Pedicel
(flower stalk)

**MICROGRAPH OF CROSS SECTION THROUGH
PETIOLE OF WATER LILY**

Rhizome

Plant fully
submerged

Leaf

Adventitious
root

Carnivorous plants

Cobra lily (*Darlingtonia californica*)

Areola ("window" of transparent tissue)

Fishtail nectary

Wing

Hood

Pitcher

Tubular petiole (leaf stalk)

Areola ("window" of transparent tissue)

CARNIVOROUS (INSECTIVOROUS) PLANTS FEED ON INSECTS and other small animals in addition to producing food in their leaves by photosynthesis. The nutrients absorbed from trapped insects allow carnivorous plants to thrive in acid, boggy soils that lack essential minerals, especially nitrates, where most other plants could not survive. All carnivorous plants have some leaves modified as traps. Many use bright colors and scented nectar to attract prey, and most use enzymes to digest the prey. There are three types of traps. Pitcher plants, such as the monkey cup and cobra lily, have leaves modified as pitcher-shaped pitfall traps, half-filled with water. Once lured inside the mouth of the trap, insects lose their footing on the slippery surface, fall into the liquid, and either decompose or are digested. Venus fly-traps use a spring-trap mechanism; when an insect touches trigger hairs on the inner surfaces of the leaves, the two lobes of the trap snap shut. Butterworts and sundews entangle prey by sticky droplets on the leaf surface, while the edges of the leaves slowly curl over to envelop and digest the prey.

Smooth surface

Nectar roll

Dome-shaped hood develops

Fishtail nectary appears

Mouth

Immature pitcher

Wing

Downward-pointing hair

DEVELOPMENT OF MODIFIED LEAF IN COBRA LILY

Immature trap

Interlocked teeth

Closed trap

VENUS FLYTRAP
(*Dionaea muscipula*)

Red color of trap attracts insects

Phyllode (flattened petiole)

Summer petiole (leaf stalk)

Nectary zone (glands secrete nectar)

Digestive zone (glands secrete digestive enzymes)

Lobe of trap

Midrib (hinge of trap)

Tooth

Trigger hair

Spring petiole (leaf stalk)

Trap (twin-lobed leaf blade)

Sensory hinge

Trigger hair

Inner surface of trap

Digestive gland

MICROGRAPH OF LOBE OF VENUS FLYTRAP

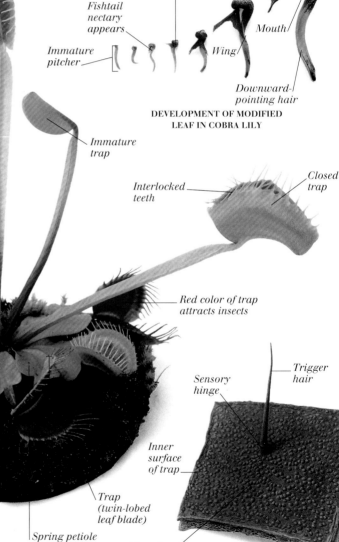

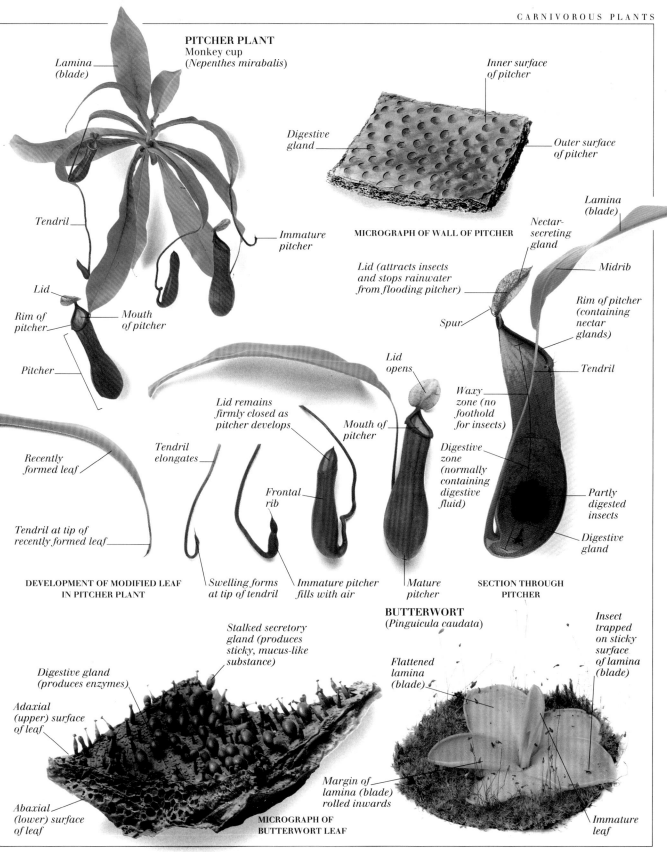

PITCHER PLANT
Monkey cup
(Nepenthes mirabalis)

Lamina
(blade)

Tendril

Immature
pitcher

Lid

Rim of
pitcher

Mouth
of pitcher

Pitcher

Digestive
gland

Inner surface
of pitcher

Outer surface
of pitcher

MICROGRAPH OF WALL OF PITCHER

Lamina
(blade)

Nectar-
secreting
gland

Midrib

Lid (attracts insects
and stops rainwater
from flooding pitcher)

Rim of pitcher
(containing
nectar
glands)

Spur

Tendril

Waxy
zone (no
foothold
for insects)

Digestive
zone
(normally
containing
digestive
fluid)

Partly
digested
insects

Digestive
gland

Recently
formed leaf

Tendril
elongates

Lid remains
firmly closed as
pitcher develops

Lid
opens

Mouth of
pitcher

Frontal
rib

Tendril at tip of
recently formed leaf

Swelling forms
at tip of tendril

Immature pitcher
fills with air

Mature
pitcher

**SECTION THROUGH
PITCHER**

**DEVELOPMENT OF MODIFIED LEAF
IN PITCHER PLANT**

BUTTERWORT
(Pinguicula caudata)

Stalked secretory
gland (produces
sticky, mucus-like
substance)

Insect
trapped
on sticky
surface
of lamina
(blade)

Digestive gland
(produces enzymes)

Flattened
lamina
(blade)

Adaxial
(upper) surface
of leaf

Abaxial
(lower) surface
of leaf

Margin of
lamina (blade)
rolled inwards

**MICROGRAPH OF
BUTTERWORT LEAF**

Immature
leaf

Epiphytic and parasitic plants

EPIPHYTIC AND PARASITIC PLANTS GROW ON OTHER LIVING PLANTS. Typically, epiphytic plants are not rooted in the soil. Instead, they live above ground level on the stems and branches of other plants. Epiphytes obtain water from trapped rainwater and from moisture in the air. They obtain minerals from organic matter that has accumulated on the surface of the plant on which they are growing. Like other green plants, epiphytes produce their food by photosynthesis. Epiphytes include tropical orchids and bromeliads (air plants) and some mosses that live in temperate regions. Parasitic plants obtain all their nutrient requirements from the host plants on which they grow. The parasites produce haustoria, root-like organs that penetrate the stem or roots of the host and grow inward to merge with the host's vascular tissue. These extract water, minerals, and manufactured nutrients. Because they have no need to produce their own food, parasitic plants lack chlorophyll, the green photosynthetic pigment, and they have no foliage leaves. Partial parasitic plants, like mistletoe, obtain water and minerals from the host plant but have green leaves and stems and are therefore able to produce their own food by photosynthesis.

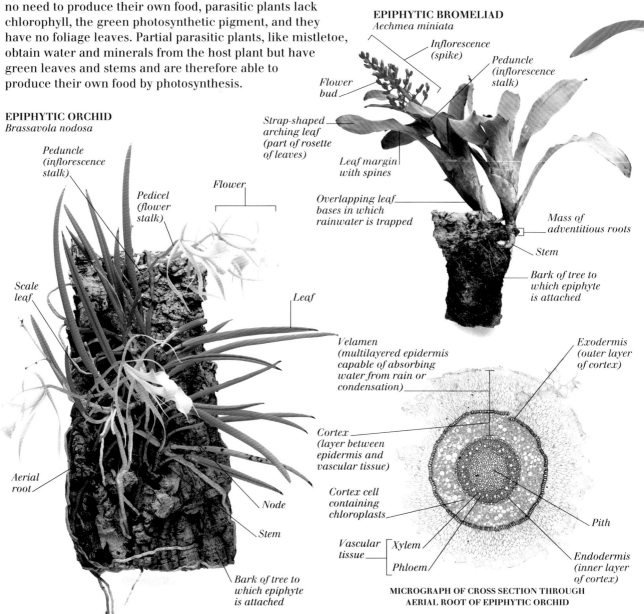

EPIPHYTIC BROMELIAD
Aechmea miniata

Inflorescence (spike)

Peduncle (inflorescence stalk)

Flower bud

Strap-shaped arching leaf (part of rosette of leaves)

Leaf margin with spines

Overlapping leaf bases in which rainwater is trapped

Mass of adventitious roots

Stem

Bark of tree to which epiphyte is attached

EPIPHYTIC ORCHID
Brassavola nodosa

Peduncle (inflorescence stalk)

Pedicel (flower stalk)

Flower

Scale leaf

Leaf

Aerial root

Velamen (multilayered epidermis capable of absorbing water from rain or condensation)

Node

Cortex (layer between epidermis and vascular tissue)

Stem

Cortex cell containing chloroplasts

Vascular tissue — Xylem / Phloem

Exodermis (outer layer of cortex)

Pith

Endodermis (inner layer of cortex)

Bark of tree to which epiphyte is attached

MICROGRAPH OF CROSS SECTION THROUGH AERIAL ROOT OF EPIPHYTIC ORCHID

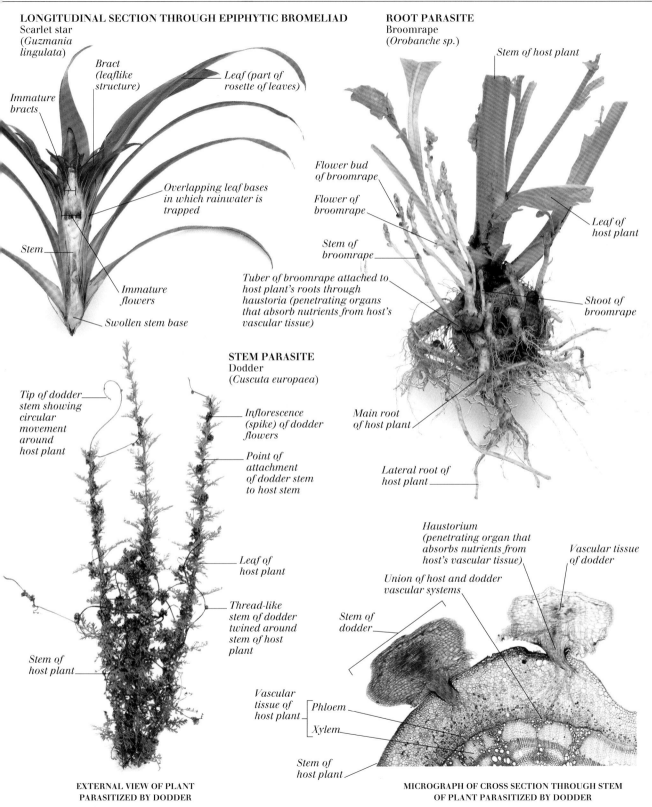

LONGITUDINAL SECTION THROUGH EPIPHYTIC BROMELIAD
Scarlet star
(*Guzmania lingulata*)

Immature bracts

Bract
(leaflike structure)

Leaf (part of rosette of leaves)

Overlapping leaf bases in which rainwater is trapped

Stem

Immature flowers

Swollen stem base

ROOT PARASITE
Broomrape
(*Orobanche sp.*)

Stem of host plant

Flower bud of broomrape

Flower of broomrape

Stem of broomrape

Tuber of broomrape attached to host plant's roots through haustoria (penetrating organs that absorb nutrients from host's vascular tissue)

Leaf of host plant

Shoot of broomrape

Main root of host plant

Lateral root of host plant

STEM PARASITE
Dodder
(*Cuscuta europaea*)

Tip of dodder stem showing circular movement around host plant

Inflorescence (spike) of dodder flowers

Point of attachment of dodder stem to host stem

Leaf of host plant

Thread-like stem of dodder twined around stem of host plant

Stem of host plant

EXTERNAL VIEW OF PLANT PARASITIZED BY DODDER

Haustorium (penetrating organ that absorbs nutrients from host's vascular tissue)

Vascular tissue of dodder

Union of host and dodder vascular systems

Stem of dodder

Vascular tissue of host plant

Phloem

Xylem

Stem of host plant

MICROGRAPH OF CROSS SECTION THROUGH STEM OF PLANT PARASITIZED BY DODDER

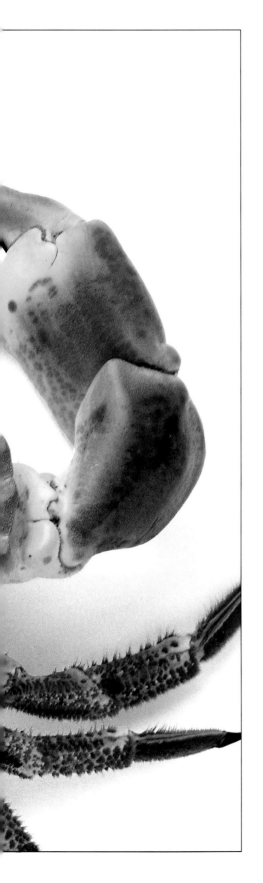

ANIMALS

Sponges, jellyfish, and sea anemones

INTERNAL ANATOMY OF A SPONGE

SPONGES ARE MAINLY MARINE animals that make up the phylum Porifera. They are among the simplest of all animals, having no tissues or organs. Their bodies consist of two layers of cells separated by a jelly-like layer (mesohyal) that is strengthened by mineral spicules or protein fibers. The body is perforated by a system of pores and water channels called the aquiferous system. Special cells (choanocytes) with whip-like structures (flagella) draw water through the aquiferous system, thereby bringing tiny food particles to the sponge's cells. Jellyfish (class Scyphozoa), sea anemones (class Anthozoa), and corals (also class Anthozoa) belong to the phylum Cnidaria, also known as Coelenterata. More complex than sponges, coelenterates have simple tissues, such as nervous tissue; a radially symmetrical body; and a mouth surrounded by tentacles with unique stinging cells (cnidocytes).

Amebocyte

Osculum (excurrent pore)

Choanocyte (collar cell)

Ostium (incurrent pore)

Porocyte (pore cell)

Mesohyal

Spongocoel (atrium; paragaster)

Spicule

Pinacocyte (epidermal cell)

Ostium (incurrent pore)

SKELETON OF A SPONGE

EXTERNAL FEATURES OF A SEA ANEMONE

Protein matrix

Pore

Tentacle

EXAMPLES OF SEA ANEMONES

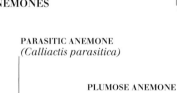

JEWEL ANEMONE
(*Corynactis viridis*)

PARASITIC ANEMONE
(*Calliactis parasitica*)

PLUMOSE ANEMONE
(*Metridium senile*)

MEDITERRANEAN SEA ANEMONE
(*Condylactis sp.*)

GREEN SNAKELOCK ANEMONE
(*Anemonia viridis*)

BEADLET ANEMONE
(*Actinia equina*)

GHOST ANEMONE
(*Actinothoe sphyrodeta*)

Sagartia elegans

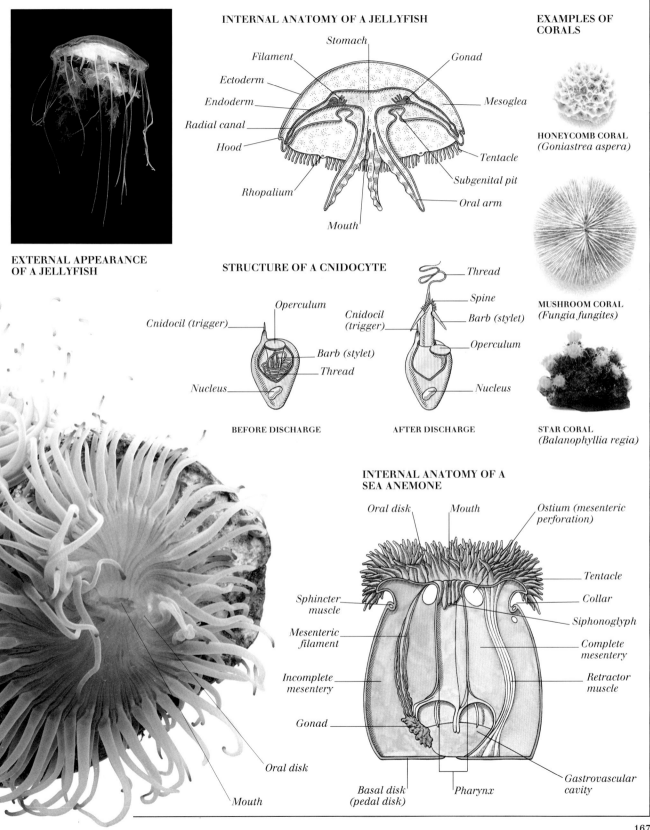

**EXTERNAL APPEARANCE
OF A JELLYFISH**

INTERNAL ANATOMY OF A JELLYFISH

Stomach

Filament

Gonad

Ectoderm

Endoderm

Mesoglea

Radial canal

Hood

Tentacle

Subgenital pit

Rhopalium

Oral arm

Mouth

**EXAMPLES OF
CORALS**

**HONEYCOMB CORAL
(Goniastrea aspera)**

**MUSHROOM CORAL
(Fungia fungites)**

**STAR CORAL
(Balanophyllia regia)**

STRUCTURE OF A CNIDOCYTE

Operculum

Cnidocil (trigger)

Barb (stylet)

Thread

Nucleus

BEFORE DISCHARGE

Thread

Spine

Cnidocil
(trigger)

Barb (stylet)

Operculum

Nucleus

AFTER DISCHARGE

**INTERNAL ANATOMY OF A
SEA ANEMONE**

Oral disk

Mouth

Ostium (mesenteric
perforation)

Sphincter
muscle

Tentacle

Collar

Siphonoglyph

Mesenteric
filament

Complete
mesentery

Incomplete
mesentery

Retractor
muscle

Gonad

Oral disk

Mouth

Basal disk
(pedal disk)

Pharynx

Gastrovascular
cavity

167

Insects

PUPA (CHRYSALIS)

THE WORD INSECT REFERS to small invertebrate creatures, especially those with bodies divided into sections. Insects, including beetles, ants, bees, butterflies, and moths, belong to various orders in the class Insecta, which is a division of the phylum Arthropoda. Features common to all insects are an exoskeleton (external skeleton); three pairs of jointed legs; three body sections (head, thorax, and abdomen); and one pair of sensory antennae. Beetles (order Coleoptera) are the biggest group of insects, with about 300,000 species (about 30 percent of all known insects). They have a pair of hard elytra (wing cases), which are modified front wings. The principal function of the elytra is to protect the hind wings, which are used for flying. Ants, together with bees and wasps, form the order Hymenoptera, which contains about 200,000 species. This group is characterized by a marked narrowing between the thorax and abdomen. Butterflies and moths form the order Lepidoptera, which has about 150,000 species. They have wings covered with tiny scales, hence the name of their order (Lepidoptera means "scale wings"). The separation of lepidopterans into butterflies and moths is largely artificial as there are no features that categorically distinguish one group from the other. In general, however, most butterflies fly by day, whereas most moths are night flyers. Some insects, including butterflies and moths, undergo complete metamorphosis (transformation) during their life cycle. A butterfly metamorphoses from an egg to a larva (caterpillar), then to a pupa (chrysalis), and finally to an imago (adult).

EXAMPLES OF INSECTS

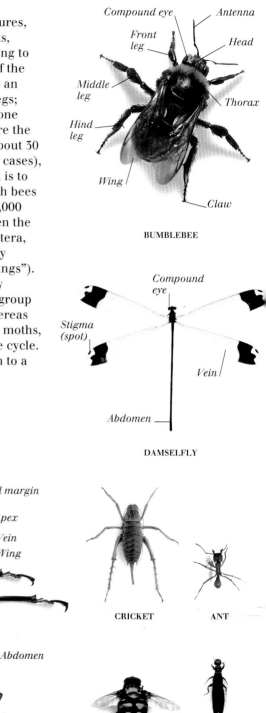

Compound eye · Antenna · Front leg · Head · Middle leg · Thorax · Hind leg · Wing · Claw

BUMBLEBEE

Compound eye · Stigma (spot) · Vein · Abdomen

DAMSELFLY

EXTERNAL FEATURES OF A BEETLE

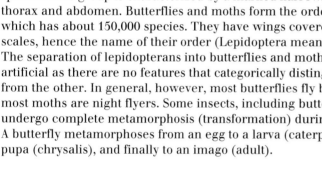

Elytron · Costal margin · Apex · Vein · Wing · Tarsus · Claw · Tibia · Pedicel · Femur · Flagellum · Trochanter · Mandible · Scape · Coxa · Labrum · Labial palpus · Abdomen · Compound eye · Head · Prothorax · Mesothorax · Front leg · Scutellum · Hind leg · Metathorax · Middle leg

CRICKET

ANT

FLY

EARWIG

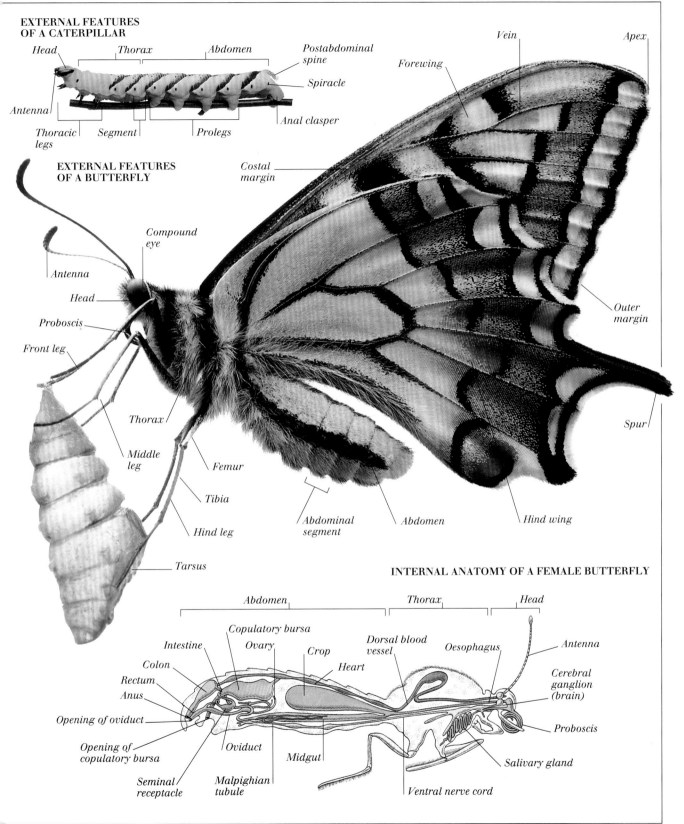

EXTERNAL FEATURES OF A CATERPILLAR

Head
Thorax
Abdomen
Postabdominal spine
Spiracle
Antenna
Thoracic legs
Segment
Prolegs
Anal clasper

Vein
Forewing
Apex

EXTERNAL FEATURES OF A BUTTERFLY

Costal margin

Compound eye
Antenna
Head
Proboscis
Front leg
Thorax
Middle leg
Femur
Tibia
Hind leg
Tarsus

Outer margin

Spur

Abdominal segment
Abdomen
Hind wing

INTERNAL ANATOMY OF A FEMALE BUTTERFLY

Abdomen
Thorax
Head

Intestine
Copulatory bursa
Ovary
Crop
Dorsal blood vessel
Oesophagus
Antenna

Colon
Heart
Cerebral ganglion (brain)

Rectum
Anus
Opening of oviduct
Opening of copulatory bursa
Seminal receptacle
Oviduct
Malpighian tubule
Midgut
Proboscis
Salivary gland
Ventral nerve cord

169

Arachnids

THE CLASS ARACHNIDA INCLUDES SPIDERS (order Araneae) and scorpions (order Scorpiones). The class is part of the phylum Arthropoda, which also includes insects and crustaceans. Spiders and scorpions are characterized by having four pairs of walking legs; a pair of pincer-like mouthparts called chelicerae; another pair of frontal appendages called pedipalps, which are sensory in spiders but used for grasping in scorpions; and a body divided into two sections (a combined head and thorax called a cephalothorax, or prosoma, and an abdomen, or opisthosoma). Unlike other arthropods, spiders and scorpions lack antennae. Spiders and scorpions are carnivorous. Spiders poison prey by biting with the fanged chelicerae, scorpions by stinging with the end of the metasoma (tail).

MEXICAN TRUE RED-LEGGED TARANTULA
(*Euathlus emilia*)

INTERNAL ANATOMY OF A FEMALE SPIDER

Anterior aorta
Ostium
Pumping stomach
Heart
Digestive gland
Posterior aorta
Malpighian tubule
Brain
Intestine
Cloaca
Ovary
Simple eye
Anus
Poison gland
Spinneret
Poison duct
Chelicera
Oviduct
Silk gland
Fang
Vagina
Trachea
Spermatheca (seminal receptacle)
Book lung
Mouth
Gut cecum
Esophagus
Spiracle

EXTERNAL FEATURES OF A SCORPION

Stinger
Metasoma (tail)
Chela (claw of pedipalp)
Pedipalp
Prosoma (cephalothorax)
Opisthosoma (abdomen)
Chelicera
Median eye
Patella
Tibia
Tarsus
Femur
Coxa
3rd walking leg
4th walking leg
1st walking leg
Claw
Metatarsus
Trochanter
2nd walking leg

170

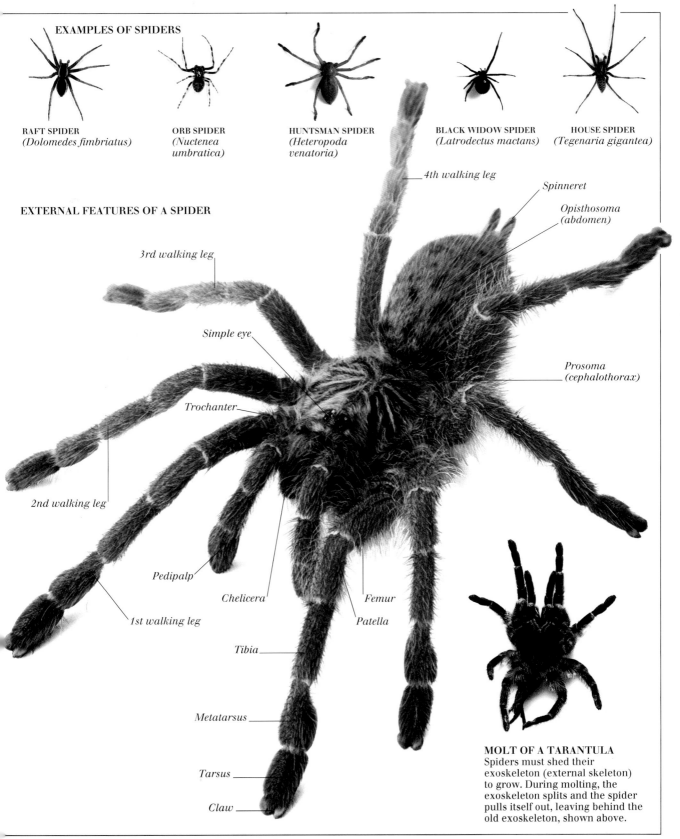

EXAMPLES OF SPIDERS

RAFT SPIDER
(Dolomedes fimbriatus)

ORB SPIDER
(Nuctenea umbratica)

HUNTSMAN SPIDER
(Heteropoda venatoria)

BLACK WIDOW SPIDER
(Latrodectus mactans)

HOUSE SPIDER
(Tegenaria gigantea)

EXTERNAL FEATURES OF A SPIDER

4th walking leg

Spinneret

Opisthosoma (abdomen)

3rd walking leg

Simple eye

Prosoma (cephalothorax)

Trochanter

2nd walking leg

Pedipalp

Chelicera

Femur

1st walking leg

Patella

Tibia

Metatarsus

Tarsus

Claw

MOLT OF A TARANTULA
Spiders must shed their exoskeleton (external skeleton) to grow. During molting, the exoskeleton splits and the spider pulls itself out, leaving behind the old exoskeleton, shown above.

Crustaceans

THE SUBPHYLUM CRUSTACEA is one of the largest groups in the phylum Arthropoda. The subphylum is divided into several classes, the most important of which are Malacostraca and Cirripedia. The class Malacostraca includes crayfish, crabs, lobsters, and shrimps. Typical features of malacostracans include a body divided into two sections (a combined head and thorax called a cephalothorax, and an abdomen); an exoskeleton (external skeleton) with a large plate (carapace) covering the cephalothorax; stalked, compound eyes; and two pairs of antennae. The class Cirripedia includes barnacles, which, unlike other crustaceans, spend their adult lives attached to a surface, such as a rock. Other characteristics of cirripedes include an exoskeleton of overlapping calcareous plates; a body consisting almost entirely of thorax (the abdomen and head are minute); and six pairs of thoracic appendages (cirri) used for filter feeding.

1st swimmeret (1st pleopod)
2nd swimmeret (2nd pleopod)
3rd swimmeret (3rd pleopod)
4th swimmeret (4th pleopod)
5th swimmeret (5th pleopod)
Telson
Abdomen
Endopod
Exopod
Uropod
Abdominal segment

3rd leg (3rd pereopod)
5th leg (5th pereopod)
4th leg (4th pereopod)
2nd leg (2nd pereopod)

EXTERNAL FEATURES OF A CRAB

Carpus
Propodus
Dactylus
Compound eye
Antenna
Cheliped (chela; claw; 1st leg; 1st pereopod)
Carapace (shell)
Merus
Abdomen
2nd leg (2nd pereopod)
3rd leg (3rd pereopod)
5th leg (5th pereopod)
4th leg (4th pereopod)

EXTERNAL FEATURES OF A SHRIMP

Cephalothorax
Compound eye
Abdomen
Antenna
Leg (pereopod)
Swimmeret (pleopod)
Uropod
Exopod
Endopod
Telson

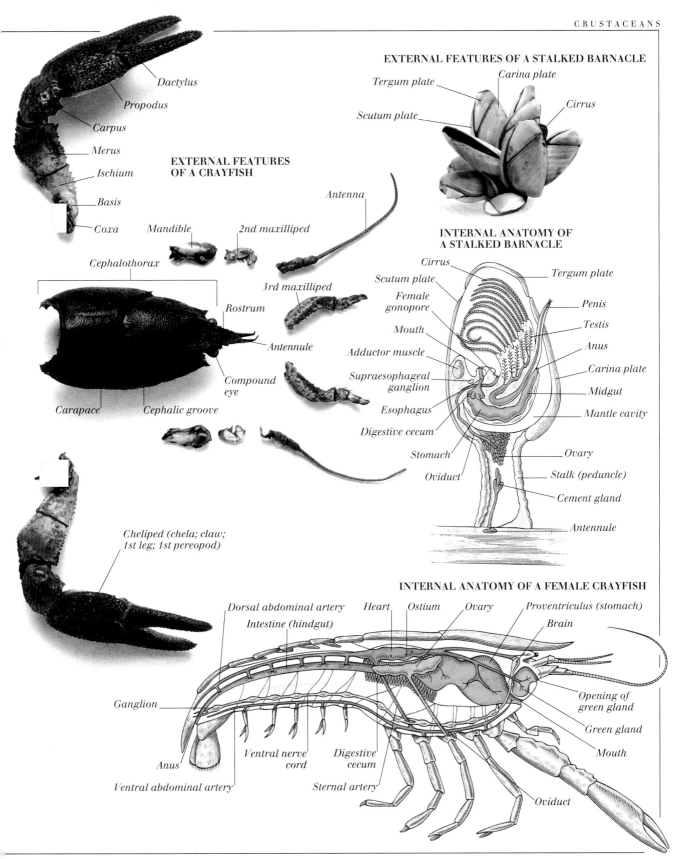

EXTERNAL FEATURES OF A CRAYFISH

Dactylus
Propodus
Carpus
Merus
Ischium
Basis
Coxa

Mandible
2nd maxilliped
Antenna
3rd maxilliped

Cephalothorax
Rostrum
Antennule
Compound eye

Carapace
Cephalic groove

Cheliped (chela; claw; 1st leg; 1st pereopod)

EXTERNAL FEATURES OF A STALKED BARNACLE

Tergum plate
Carina plate
Scutum plate
Cirrus

INTERNAL ANATOMY OF A STALKED BARNACLE

Cirrus
Scutum plate
Female gonopore
Mouth
Adductor muscle
Supraesophageal ganglion
Esophagus
Digestive cecum
Stomach
Oviduct

Tergum plate
Penis
Testis
Anus
Carina plate
Midgut
Mantle cavity
Ovary
Stalk (peduncle)
Cement gland
Antennule

INTERNAL ANATOMY OF A FEMALE CRAYFISH

Dorsal abdominal artery
Intestine (hindgut)
Heart
Ostium
Ovary
Proventriculus (stomach)
Brain

Ganglion
Opening of green gland
Green gland
Mouth

Anus
Ventral nerve cord
Digestive cecum
Oviduct

Ventral abdominal artery
Sternal artery

Starfish and sea urchins

STARFISH, SEA URCHINS, AND THEIR relatives (including feather stars, brittle stars, basket stars, sea daisies, sea lilies, and sea cucumbers) make up the phylum Echinodermata. A unique feature of echinoderms is the water vascular system, which consists of a series of water-filled canals from which protrude thousands of tiny tube feet. The tube feet may be used for movement, feeding, or respiration. Other features include pentaradiate symmetry (that is, the body can be divided into five parts radiating from the center); no head; a diffuse, decentralized nervous system that lacks a brain; and no excretory organs. Typically, echinoderms also have an endoskeleton (internal skeleton) consisting of hard calcite ossicles embedded in the body wall and often bearing protruding spines or tubercles. The ossicles may fit together to form a test (as in sea urchins) or remain separate (as in sea cucumbers).

EXTERNAL FEATURES OF A STARFISH (UPPER, OR ABORAL, SURFACE)

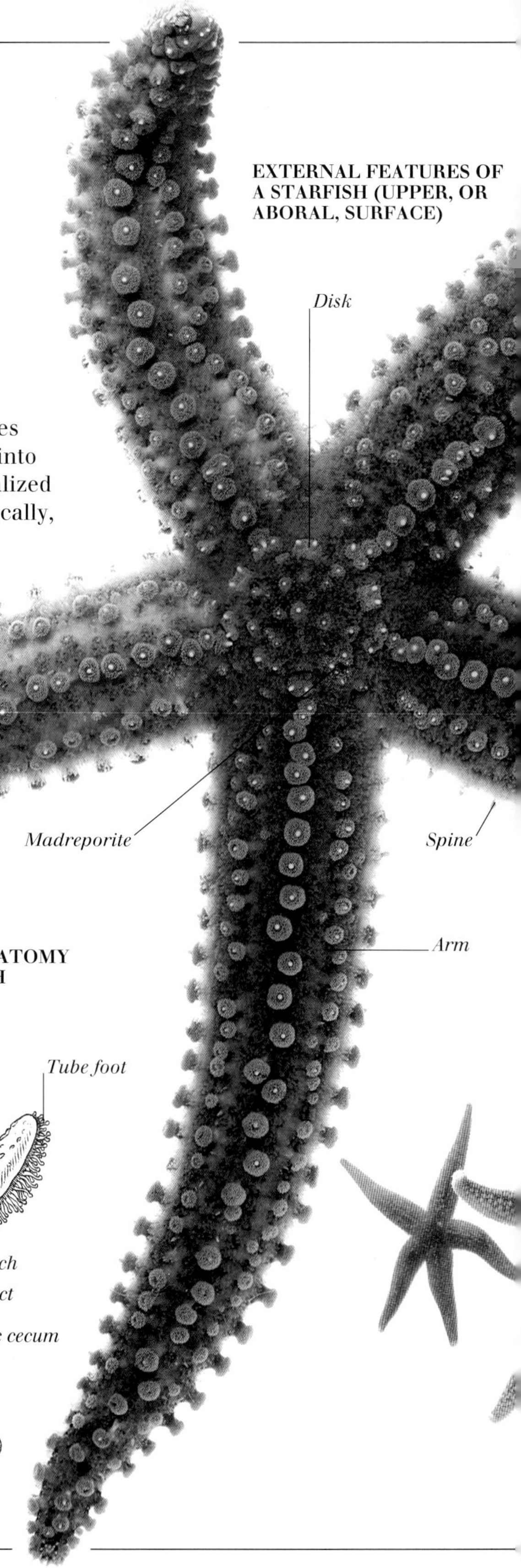

Disk

Madreporite

Spine

Arm

INTERNAL ANATOMY OF A STARFISH

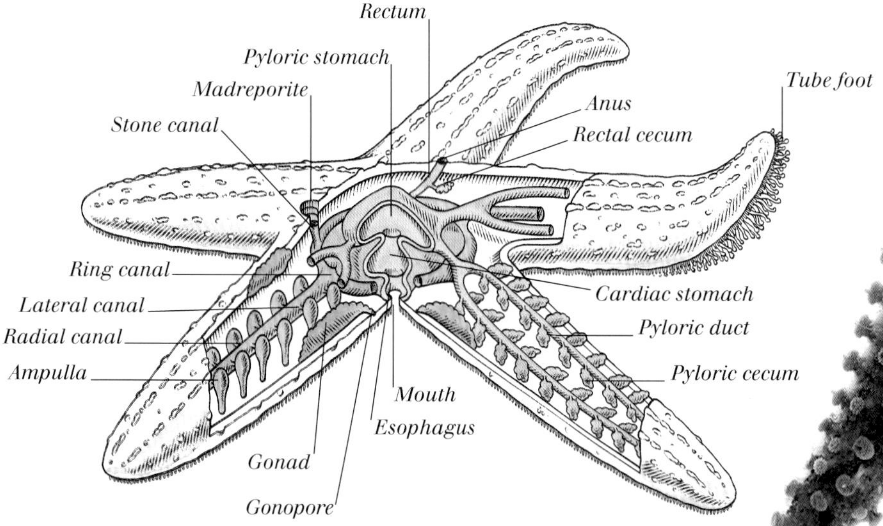

Rectum

Pyloric stomach

Madreporite

Stone canal

Ring canal

Lateral canal

Radial canal

Ampulla

Mouth

Esophagus

Gonad

Gonopore

Anus

Rectal cecum

Tube foot

Cardiac stomach

Pyloric duct

Pyloric cecum

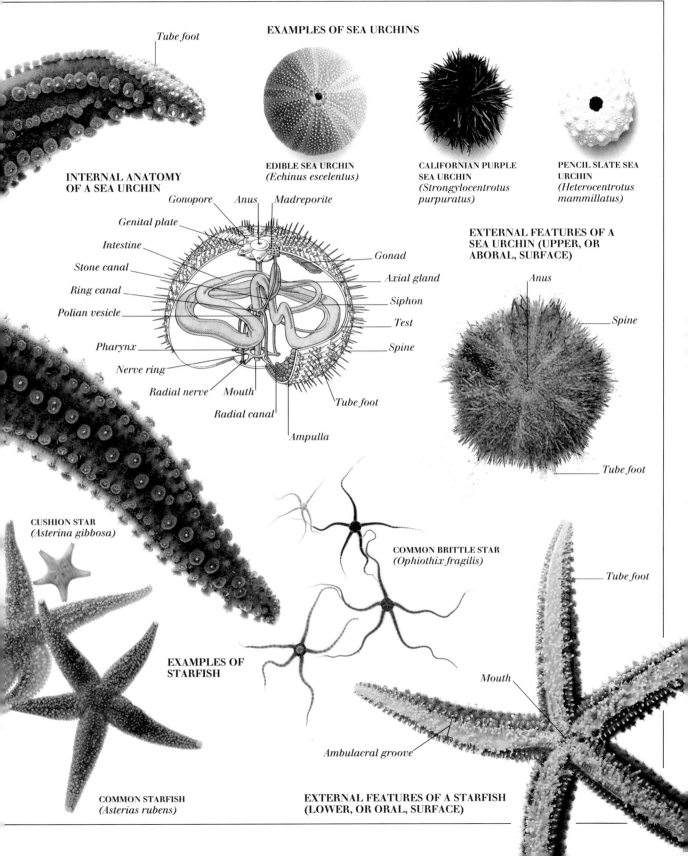

Tube foot

EXAMPLES OF SEA URCHINS

EDIBLE SEA URCHIN
(Echinus escelentus)

**CALIFORNIAN PURPLE
SEA URCHIN**
*(Strongylocentrotus
purpuratus)*

**PENCIL SLATE SEA
URCHIN**
*(Heterocentrotus
mammillatus)*

**INTERNAL ANATOMY
OF A SEA URCHIN**

Gonopore
Anus
Madreporite
Genital plate
Intestine
Stone canal
Gonad
Ring canal
Axial gland
Polian vesicle
Siphon
Test
Pharynx
Spine
Nerve ring
Radial nerve
Mouth
Radial canal
Tube foot
Ampulla

**EXTERNAL FEATURES OF A
SEA URCHIN (UPPER, OR
ABORAL, SURFACE)**

Anus
Spine
Tube foot

CUSHION STAR
(Asterina gibbosa)

COMMON BRITTLE STAR
(Ophiothix fragilis)

Tube foot

**EXAMPLES OF
STARFISH**

Mouth

Ambulacral groove

COMMON STARFISH
(Asterias rubens)

**EXTERNAL FEATURES OF A STARFISH
(LOWER, OR ORAL, SURFACE)**

Mollusks

THE PHYLUM MOLLUSCA (MOLLUSKS) is a large group of animals that includes octopuses, snails, and scallops. Octopuses and their relatives —including squid and cuttlefish—form the class Cephalopoda. Cephalopods typically have a head with a radula (a file-like feeding organ) and beak; a well-developed nervous system; sucker-bearing tentacles; a muscular mantle (part of the body wall) that can expel water through the siphon, enabling movement by jet propulsion; and a small shell or no shell. Snails and their relatives—including slugs, limpets, and abalones—make up the class Gastropoda. Gastropods typically have a coiled external shell, although some, such as slugs, have a small internal shell or no shell; a flat foot; and a head with tentacles and a radula. Scallops and their relatives—including clams, mussels, and oysters—make up the class Bivalvia (also called Pelecypoda). Features of bivalves include a shell with two halves (valves); large gills that are used for breathing and filter feeding; and no radula.

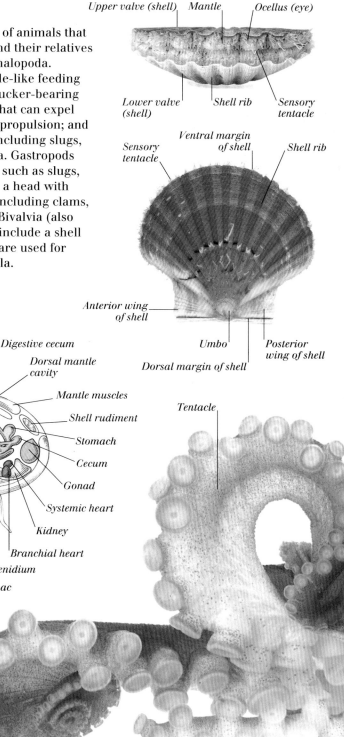

Upper valve (shell) Mantle Ocellus (eye)

Lower valve (shell) Shell rib Sensory tentacle

Sensory tentacle Ventral margin of shell Shell rib

Anterior wing of shell

Umbo Posterior wing of shell

Dorsal margin of shell

INTERNAL ANATOMY OF AN OCTOPUS

Cephalic vein Poison gland

Skull Crop Digestive cecum

Brain Dorsal mantle cavity

Siphon (funnel) Mantle muscles

Buccal mass Shell rudiment

Beak Stomach

Cecum

Gonad

Systemic heart

Kidney

Branchial heart

Anus Ctenidium

Muscular septum Ink sac

Tentacle

Sucker

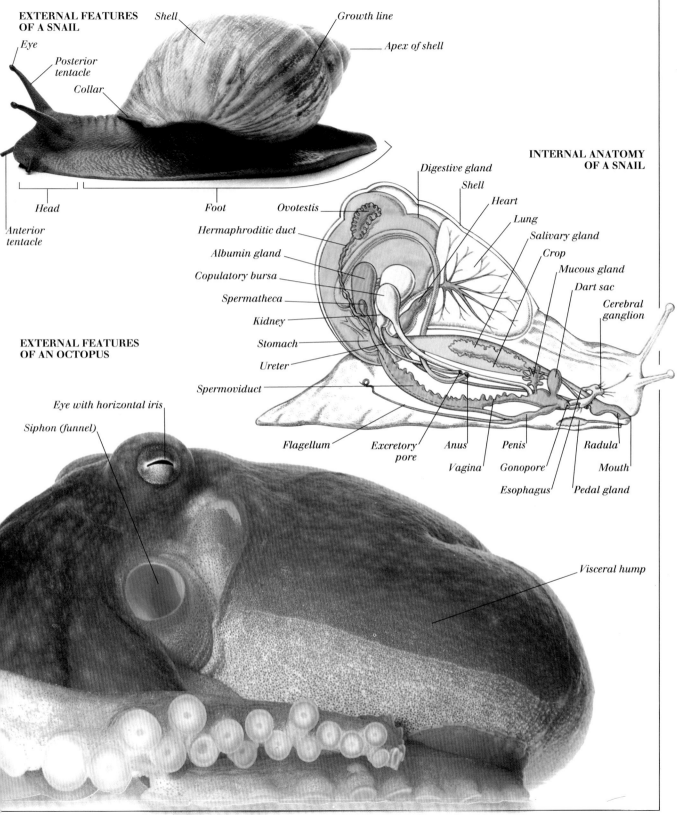

EXTERNAL FEATURES OF A SNAIL

Shell

Growth line

Apex of shell

Eye

Posterior tentacle

Collar

Head

Foot

Anterior tentacle

INTERNAL ANATOMY OF A SNAIL

Digestive gland

Shell

Heart

Lung

Salivary gland

Ovotestis

Crop

Mucous gland

Hermaphroditic duct

Dart sac

Albumin gland

Cerebral ganglion

Copulatory bursa

Spermatheca

Kidney

Stomach

Ureter

Spermoviduct

EXTERNAL FEATURES OF AN OCTOPUS

Flagellum

Excretory pore

Anus

Penis

Radula

Vagina

Gonopore

Mouth

Esophagus

Pedal gland

Eye with horizontal iris

Siphon (funnel)

Visceral hump

Sharks and jawless fish

SHARKS, DOGFISH (WHICH ARE actually small sharks), skates, and rays belong to a class of fish called Chondrichthyes, which is a division of the superclass Gnathostomata (meaning "jawed mouths"). Also sometimes known as elasmobranchs, sharks and their relatives have a skeleton made of cartilage (hence their common name, cartilaginous fish), a characteristic that distinguishes them from bony fish (see pp. 180-181). Other important features of cartilaginous fish are extremely tough, tooth-like scales, and lack of a swim bladder. Jawless fish—lampreys and hagfish—are primitive, eel-like fish that make up the order Cyclostomata (meaning "round mouths"), a division of the superclass Agnatha (meaning "without jaws"). In addition to their characteristic round, sucker-like mouths and lack of jaws, cyclostomes also have smooth, slimy skin without scales, and unpaired fins.

SHARKS' JAWS

Jaws of an adult tiger shark

Jaws of a young tiger shark

EXTERNAL FEATURES OF A DOGFISH

Snout

Eye

Gill slit

Pectoral fin

Anterior dorsal fin

Posterior dorsal fin

FEATURES OF A LAMPREY'S HEAD

Outer lip

Mouth

Tongue

Sucker

Eye

Tooth

Fringed inner lip

EXTERNAL FEATURES OF A LAMPREY

Eye

Gill opening

Sucker

Anal fin

Caudal fin

EXAMPLES OF CARTILAGINOUS FISH

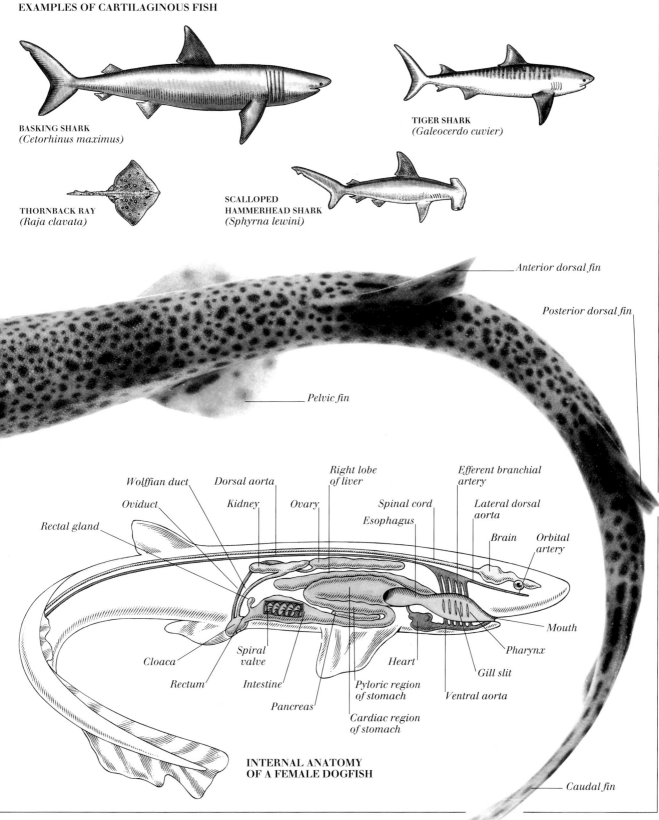

BASKING SHARK
(Cetorhinus maximus)

TIGER SHARK
(Galeocerdo cuvier)

THORNBACK RAY
(Raja clavata)

**SCALLOPED
HAMMERHEAD SHARK**
(Sphyrna lewini)

Anterior dorsal fin

Posterior dorsal fin

Pelvic fin

Wolffian duct

Oviduct

Dorsal aorta

Kidney

Ovary

Right lobe
of liver

Spinal cord

Esophagus

Efferent branchial
artery

Lateral dorsal
aorta

Brain

Orbital
artery

Rectal gland

Mouth

Cloaca

Spiral
valve

Rectum

Intestine

Pancreas

Heart

Pharynx

Gill slit

Ventral aorta

Pyloric region
of stomach

Cardiac region
of stomach

**INTERNAL ANATOMY
OF A FEMALE DOGFISH**

Caudal fin

Bony fish

BONY FISH, SUCH AS CARP, TROUT, SALMON, perch, and cod, are by far the best known and largest group of fish, with more than 20,000 species (over 95 percent of all known fish). As their name suggests, bony fish have skeletons made of bone, in contrast to the cartilaginous skeletons of sharks, jawless fish, and their relatives (see pp. 178-179). Other typical features of bony fish include a swim bladder, which functions as a variable-buoyancy organ, enabling a fish to remain effortlessly at whatever depth it is swimming; relatively thin, bone-like scales; a flap (called an operculum) covering the gills; and paired pelvic and pectoral fins. Scientifically, bony fish belong to the class Osteichthyes, which is a division of the superclass Gnathostomata (meaning "jawed mouths").

HOW FISH BREATHE

Fish "breathe" by extracting oxygen from water through their gills. Water is sucked in through the mouth; simultaneously, the opercula close to prevent the water from escaping. The mouth is then closed, and muscles in the walls of the mouth, pharynx, and opercular cavity contract to pump the water inside over the gills and out through the opercula. Some fish rely on swimming with their mouths open to keep water flowing over the gills.

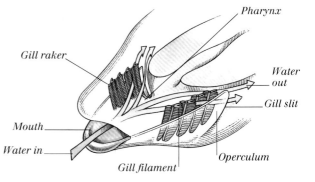

Pharynx

Gill raker

Water out

Gill slit

Mouth

Water in

Operculum

Gill filament

EXAMPLES OF BONY FISH

MANDARINFISH
(*Synchiropus splendidus*)

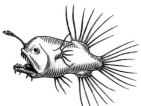

ANGLERFISH
(*Caulophryne jordani*)

LIONFISH
(*Pterois volitans*)

OCEANIC SEAHORSE
(*Hippocampus kuda*)

Vertebra

Neural spine

Hypural

Hemal spine

Caudal fin ray

Anal fin ray

Radial cartilage

STURGEON
(*Acipenser sturio*)

SNOWFLAKE MORAY EEL
(*Echidna nebulosa*)

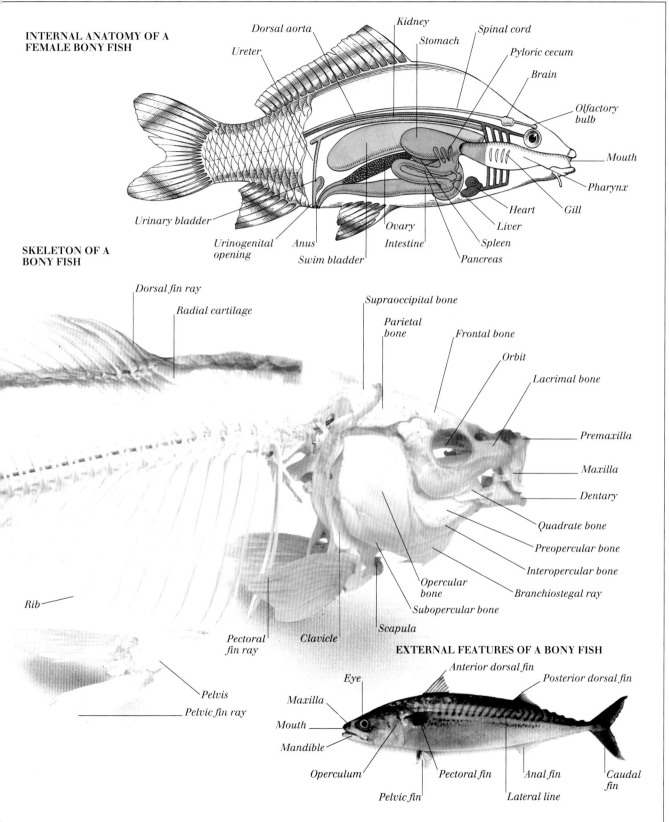

INTERNAL ANATOMY OF A FEMALE BONY FISH

Dorsal aorta

Kidney

Spinal cord

Ureter

Stomach

Pyloric cecum

Brain

Olfactory bulb

Mouth

Pharynx

Heart

Gill

Liver

Urinary bladder

Urinogenital opening

Anus

Ovary

Intestine

Spleen

Swim bladder

Pancreas

SKELETON OF A BONY FISH

Dorsal fin ray

Radial cartilage

Supraoccipital bone

Parietal bone

Frontal bone

Orbit

Lacrimal bone

Premaxilla

Maxilla

Dentary

Quadrate bone

Preopercular bone

Interopercular bone

Branchiostegal ray

Opercular bone

Subopercular bone

Scapula

Rib

Pectoral fin ray

Clavicle

Pelvis

Pelvic fin ray

EXTERNAL FEATURES OF A BONY FISH

Eye

Anterior dorsal fin

Posterior dorsal fin

Maxilla

Mouth

Mandible

Operculum

Pectoral fin

Anal fin

Caudal fin

Pelvic fin

Lateral line

181

Amphibians

THE CLASS AMPHIBIA INCLUDES FROGS and toads (which make up the order Anura) and newts and salamanders (which make up the order Urodela). Amphibians typically have moist, scaleless, hairless skin; lungs; and are cold-blooded. They also undergo complete metamorphosis, from eggs laid in water through various water-living larval stages (such as the tadpole stage) to land-living adults. Typical features of adult frogs and toads include a squat body with no tail; long, powerful hind legs; and large, often bulging, eyes. Adult newts and salamanders typically have a long body with a well-developed tail; and relatively short legs of equal size. However, newts and salamanders show considerable variation; for example, in some species the adults have minute legs, external gills rather than lungs, and spend their entire lives in water.

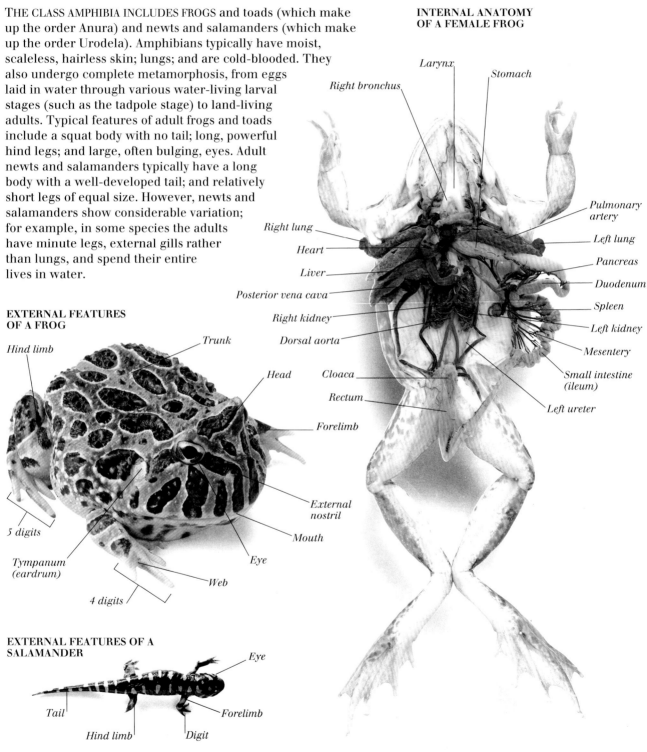

INTERNAL ANATOMY OF A FEMALE FROG

Larynx
Stomach
Right bronchus
Pulmonary artery
Right lung
Left lung
Heart
Pancreas
Liver
Duodenum
Posterior vena cava
Spleen
Right kidney
Left kidney
Dorsal aorta
Mesentery
Cloaca
Small intestine (ileum)
Rectum
Left ureter

EXTERNAL FEATURES OF A FROG

Hind limb
Trunk
Head
Forelimb
5 digits
External nostril
Tympanum (eardrum)
Mouth
Eye
Web
4 digits

EXTERNAL FEATURES OF A SALAMANDER

Eye
Tail
Forelimb
Hind limb
Digit

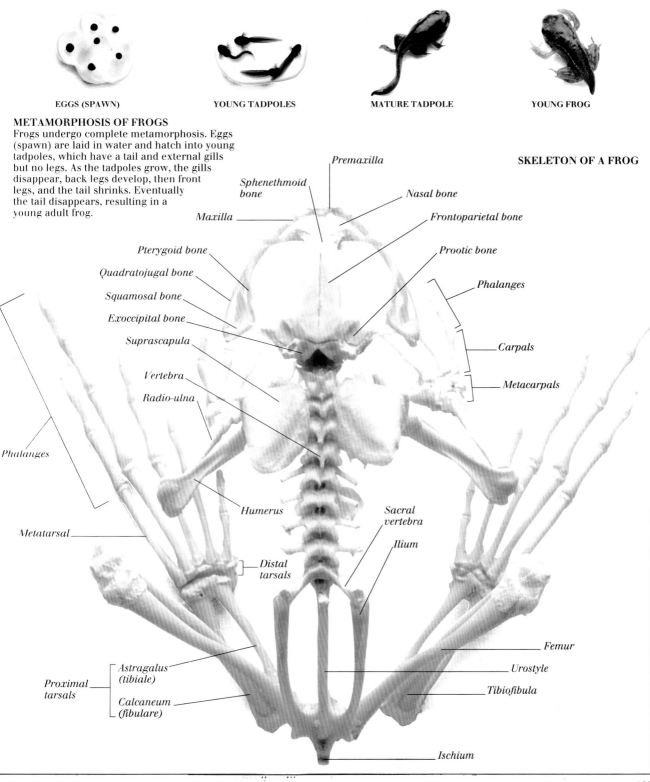

EGGS (SPAWN)

YOUNG TADPOLES

MATURE TADPOLE

YOUNG FROG

METAMORPHOSIS OF FROGS

Frogs undergo complete metamorphosis. Eggs
(spawn) are laid in water and hatch into young
tadpoles, which have a tail and external gills
but no legs. As the tadpoles grow, the gills
disappear, back legs develop, then front
legs, and the tail shrinks. Eventually
the tail disappears, resulting in a
young adult frog.

SKELETON OF A FROG

Premaxilla

Sphenethmoid
bone

Nasal bone

Maxilla

Frontoparietal bone

Pterygoid bone

Prootic bone

Quadratojugal bone

Phalanges

Squamosal bone

Exoccipital bone

Suprascapula

Carpals

Vertebra

Metacarpals

Radio-ulna

Phalanges

Humerus

Sacral
vertebra

Ilium

Metatarsal

Distal
tarsals

Proximal
tarsals

Astragalus
(tibiale)

Femur

Urostyle

Calcaneum
(fibulare)

Tibiofibula

Ischium

Lizards and snakes

LIZARDS AND SNAKES BELONG to the order Squamata, a division of the class Reptilia. Characteristic reptilian features include scaly skin, lungs, and cold-bloodedness. Most reptiles lay leathery-shelled eggs, although some hatch the eggs inside their bodies and give birth to live young. Lizards belong to the suborder Lacertilia. Typically, they have long tails, and shed their skin in several pieces. Many lizards can regenerate a tail if it is lost; some can change color; and some are limbless. Snakes make up the suborder Ophidia (also called Serpentes). All snakes have long, limbless bodies; can dislocate their lower jaw to swallow large prey; and have eyelids that are joined together to form a single transparent covering over the front of the eye. Most snakes shed their skin in a single piece. Constrictor snakes kill their prey by squeezing; venomous snakes poison their prey.

EXAMPLES OF SNAKES

MEXICAN MOUNTAIN KING SNAKE (*Lampropeltis triangulum annulata*)

BANDED MILK SNAKE (*Lampropeltis ruthveni*)

EXTERNAL FEATURES OF A LIZARD

Eye

Mouth

Crest

Eardrum

Masseteric scale

Dorsal scale

External nostril

SKELETON OF A LIZARD

Skull

Orbit

Scapula

Cervical vertebrae

Phalanges

Carpals

Metacarpal

Humerus

Ulna

Radius

Rib

Thoracolumbar vertebrae

Pelvis

Sacrum

Femur

Tibia

Fibula

Tarsals

Metatarsal

Dewlap

Foreleg

Caudal vertebrae

Phalanges

Belly

Ventral scale

Toe

Claw

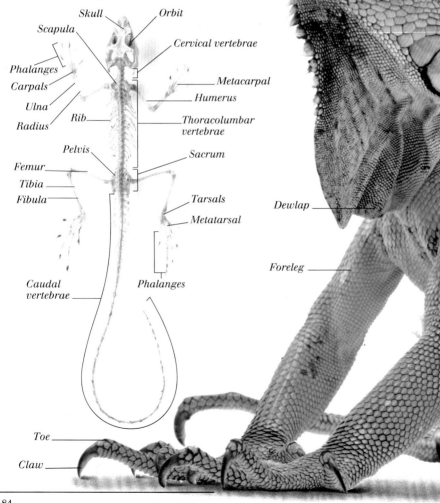

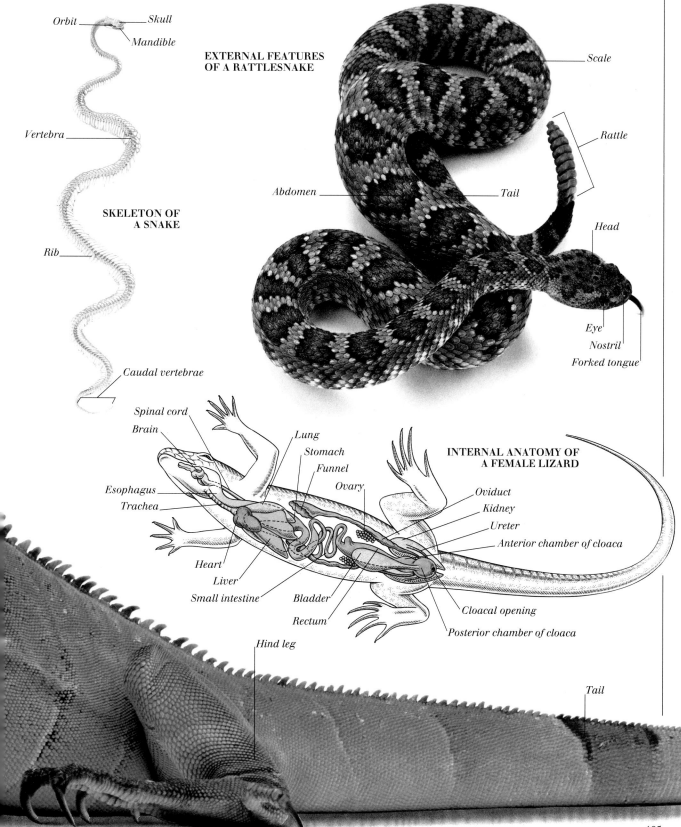

Orbit

Skull

Mandible

EXTERNAL FEATURES OF A RATTLESNAKE

Scale

Vertebra

Rattle

Abdomen

Tail

SKELETON OF A SNAKE

Head

Rib

Eye

Nostril

Forked tongue

Caudal vertebrae

Spinal cord

Brain

Lung

Stomach

Funnel

Ovary

INTERNAL ANATOMY OF A FEMALE LIZARD

Esophagus

Oviduct

Trachea

Kidney

Ureter

Anterior chamber of cloaca

Heart

Liver

Small intestine

Bladder

Cloacal opening

Rectum

Posterior chamber of cloaca

Hind leg

Tail

Crocodilians and turtles

CROCODILIANS AND TURTLES BELONG to different orders in the class Reptilia. The order Crocodilia includes crocodiles, alligators, caimans, and gharials. Typically, crocodilians are carnivores (flesh-eaters), and have a long snout, sharp teeth for gripping prey, and hard, square scales. All crocodilians are adapted to living on land and in water: they have four strong legs for moving on land; a powerful tail for swimming; and their eyes and nostrils are high on the head so that they stay above water while the rest of the body is submerged. The order Chelonia includes marine turtles, freshwater turtles (terrapins), and land turtles (tortoises). Characteristically, chelonians have a short, broad body encased in a bony shell with an outer horny covering, into which the head and limbs can be withdrawn; and a horny beak instead of teeth.

SKULLS OF CROCODILIANS

GHARIAL
(Gavialis gangeticus)

NILE CROCODILE
(Crocodylus niloticus)

MISSISSIPPI ALLIGATOR
(Alligator mississippiensis)

SKELETON OF A CROCODILE

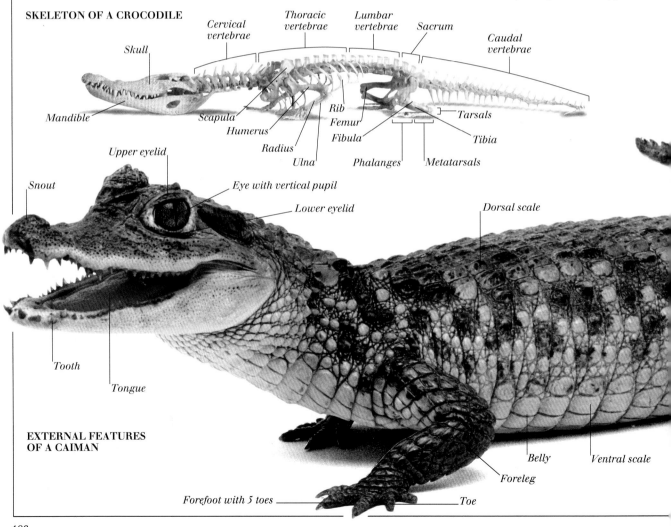

Cervical vertebrae
Thoracic vertebrae
Lumbar vertebrae
Sacrum
Caudal vertebrae
Skull
Mandible
Scapula
Humerus
Radius
Ulna
Rib
Femur
Fibula
Phalanges
Metatarsals
Tarsals
Tibia

EXTERNAL FEATURES OF A CAIMAN

Upper eyelid
Eye with vertical pupil
Lower eyelid
Dorsal scale
Snout
Tooth
Tongue
Belly
Ventral scale
Foreleg
Forefoot with 5 toes
Toe

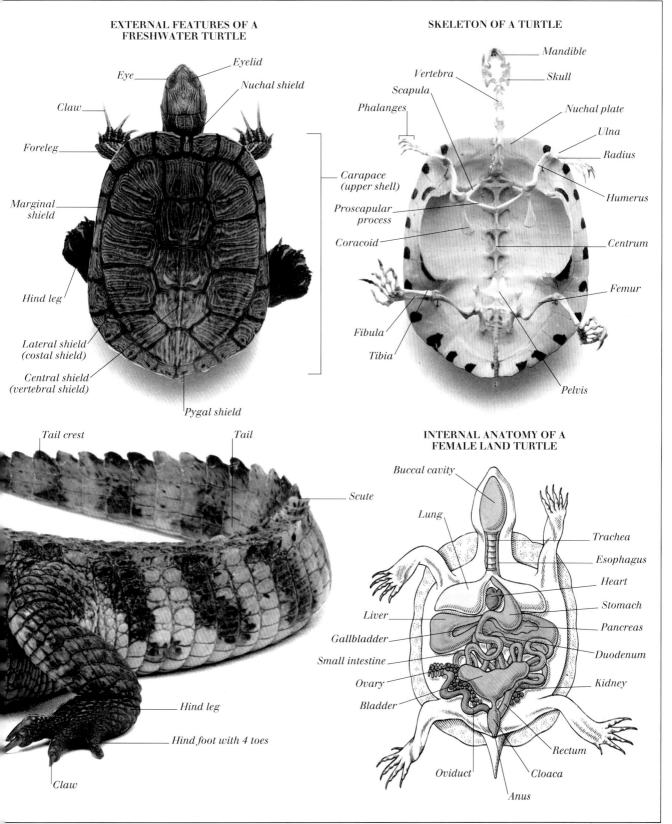

EXTERNAL FEATURES OF A FRESHWATER TURTLE

Eye

Eyelid

Nuchal shield

Claw

Foreleg

Marginal shield

Hind leg

Lateral shield (costal shield)

Central shield (vertebral shield)

Pygal shield

Carapace (upper shell)

SKELETON OF A TURTLE

Mandible

Vertebra

Skull

Scapula

Phalanges

Nuchal plate

Ulna

Radius

Humerus

Carapace (upper shell)

Proscapular process

Coracoid

Centrum

Femur

Fibula

Tibia

Pelvis

Tail crest

Tail

Scute

Hind leg

Hind foot with 4 toes

Claw

INTERNAL ANATOMY OF A FEMALE LAND TURTLE

Buccal cavity

Lung

Trachea

Esophagus

Heart

Stomach

Pancreas

Duodenum

Kidney

Liver

Gallbladder

Small intestine

Ovary

Bladder

Rectum

Oviduct

Cloaca

Anus

Birds 1

BIRDS MAKE UP THE CLASS AVES. There are more than 9,000 species, almost all of which can fly (the only flightless birds are penguins, ostriches, rheas, cassowaries, and kiwis). The ability to fly is reflected in the typical bird features: forelimbs modified as wings, a streamlined body, and hollow bones to reduce weight. All birds lay hard-shelled eggs, which the parents incubate. Birds' beaks and feet vary according to diet and way of life. Beaks range from general purpose types suitable for a mixed diet (those of thrushes, for example), to types specialized for particular foods (such as the large, curved, sieving beaks of flamingos). Feet range from the webbed "paddles" of ducks, to the talons of birds of prey. Plumage also varies widely, and in many species the male is brightly colored for courtship display whereas the female is drab.

EXTERNAL FEATURES OF A BIRD

Forehead

Eye

Crown

Nostril

Nape

Upper mandible

Beak

Lower mandible

Chin

Throat

EXAMPLES OF BIRDS

MALE TUFTED DUCK
(*Aythya fuligula*)

WHITE STORK
(*Ciconia ciconia*)

MALE OSTRICH
(*Struthio camelus*)

Minor coverts

Lesser wing coverts

Median wing coverts

Greater wing coverts
(major coverts)

Secondary flight feathers
(secondary remiges)

Primary flight feathers
(primary remiges)

Breast

Belly

Flank

Thigh

Under tail
coverts

Tarsus

Claw

Toe

Tail feathers (retrices)

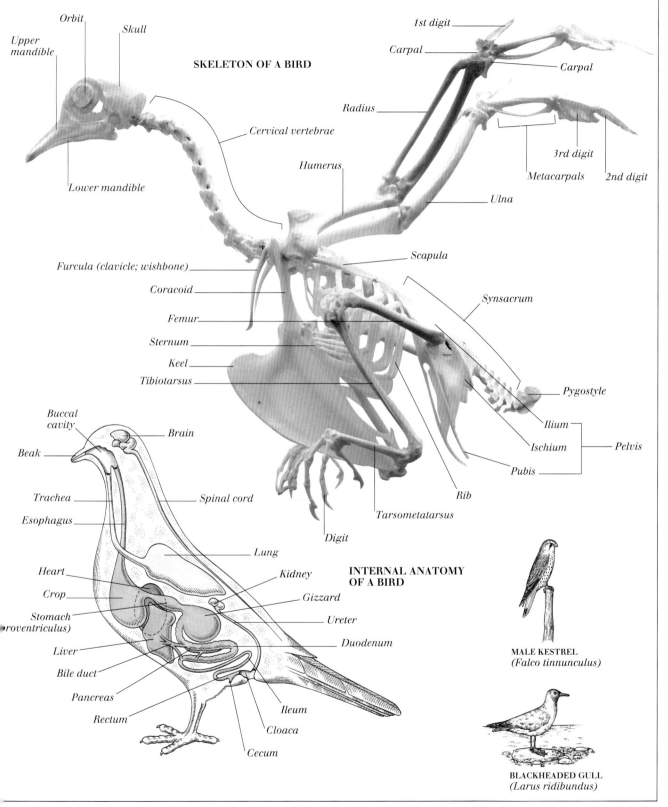

SKELETON OF A BIRD

Orbit

Skull

Upper mandible

1st digit

Carpal

Carpal

Radius

3rd digit

Metacarpals

2nd digit

Cervical vertebrae

Humerus

Ulna

Lower mandible

Scapula

Furcula (clavicle; wishbone)

Synsacrum

Coracoid

Femur

Sternum

Keel

Tibiotarsus

Pygostyle

Ilium

Ischium

Pelvis

Pubis

Rib

Tarsometatarsus

Digit

Buccal cavity

Brain

Beak

Trachea

Spinal cord

Esophagus

Lung

Heart

Kidney

INTERNAL ANATOMY OF A BIRD

Crop

Gizzard

Stomach (proventriculus)

Ureter

Liver

Duodenum

Bile duct

Pancreas

Rectum

Ileum

Cloaca

Cecum

MALE KESTREL (Falco tinnunculus)

BLACKHEADED GULL (Larus ridibundus)

Birds 2

EXAMPLES OF BIRDS' FEET

KITTIWAKE
(Rissa tridactyla)
The webbed feet are
adapted for paddling
through water.

LITTLE GREBE
(Tachybaptus ruficollis)
The lobed, flattened feet
are adapted for swimming
underwater.

TAWNY OWL
(Strix aluco)
The clawed feet are adapted
for gripping prey.

EXAMPLES OF BIRDS' BEAKS

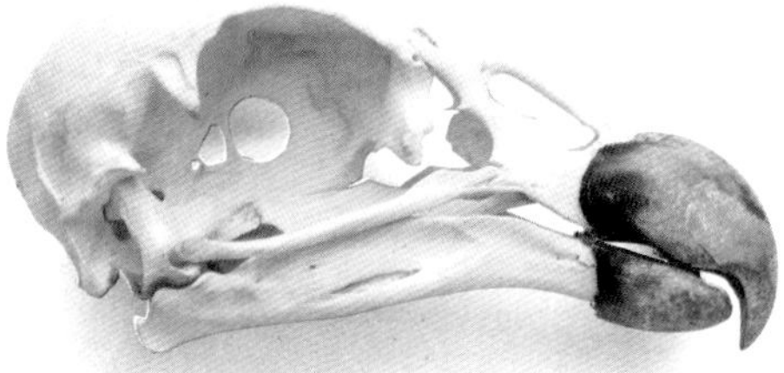

KING VULTURE
(Sarcorhamphus papa)
The hooked beak is adapted
for pulling apart flesh.

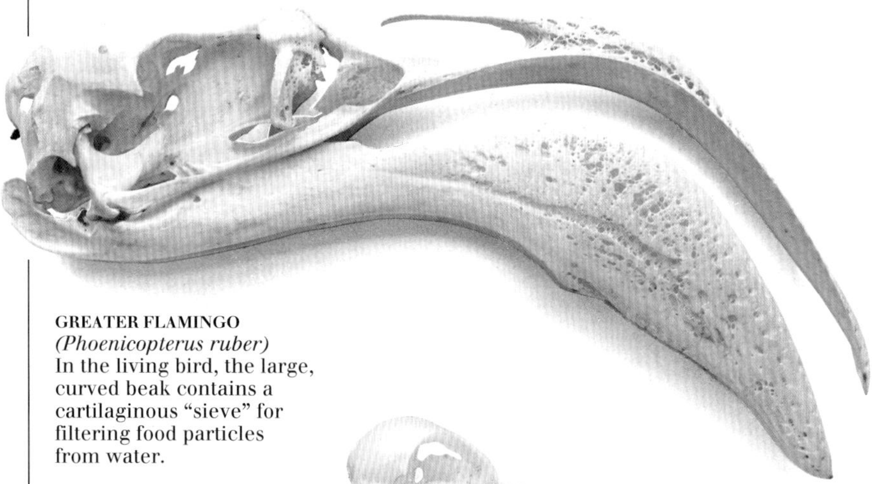

GREATER FLAMINGO
(Phoenicopterus ruber)
In the living bird, the large,
curved beak contains a
cartilaginous "sieve" for
filtering food particles
from water.

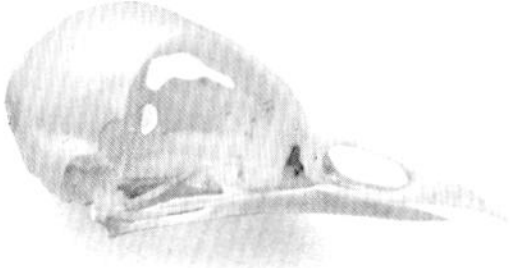

MAVIS, OR MISTLE THRUSH
(Turdus viscivorus)
The all-purpose beak is suitable
for gathering a wide range of
animal and plant foods.

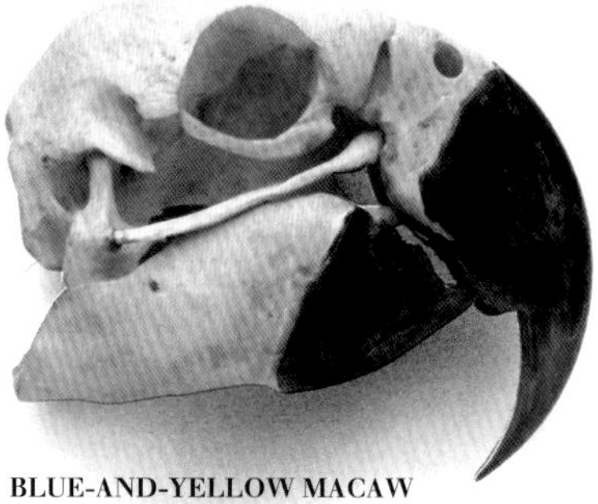

BLUE-AND-YELLOW MACAW
(Ara ararauna)
The broad, powerful, hooked beak
is adapted for crushing seeds and
eating fruit.

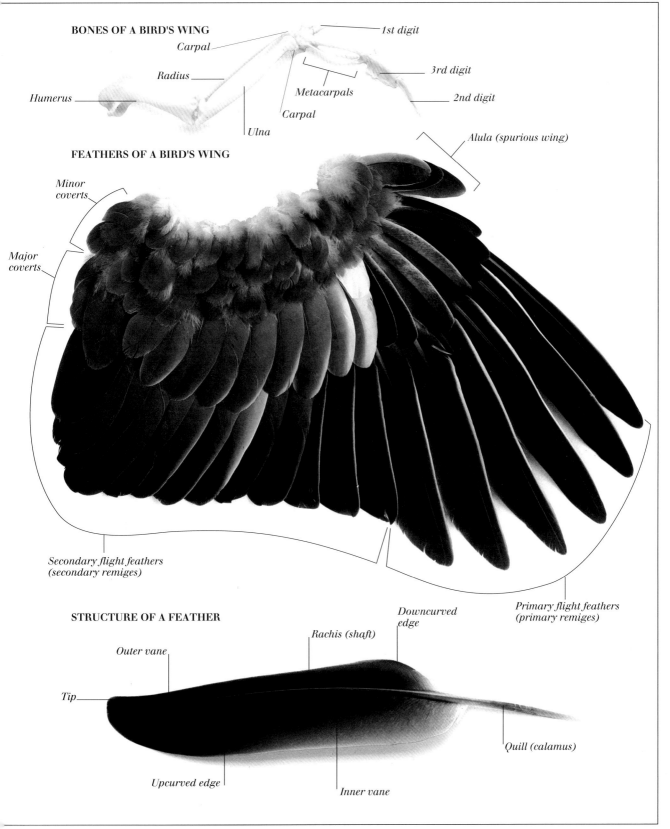

BONES OF A BIRD'S WING

1st digit

Carpal

3rd digit

Radius

2nd digit

Humerus

Metacarpals

Carpal

Ulna

Alula (spurious wing)

FEATHERS OF A BIRD'S WING

Minor coverts

Major coverts

Secondary flight feathers (secondary remiges)

Primary flight feathers (primary remiges)

STRUCTURE OF A FEATHER

Downcurved edge

Rachis (shaft)

Outer vane

Tip

Quill (calamus)

Upcurved edge

Inner vane

Eggs

AN EGG IS A SINGLE CELL, produced by the female, with the capacity to develop into a new individual. Development may take place inside the mother's body (as in most mammals) or outside, in which case the egg has a protective covering such as a shell. Egg yolk nourishes the growing young. Eggs developing inside the mother generally have little yolk, because the young are nourished from her body. Eggs developing outside may also have little yolk if they are produced by animals whose young go through a larval stage (such as a caterpillar) that feeds itself while developing into the adult form. The shelled eggs of birds and reptiles contain enough yolk to sustain the young until it hatches into a juvenile version of the adult.

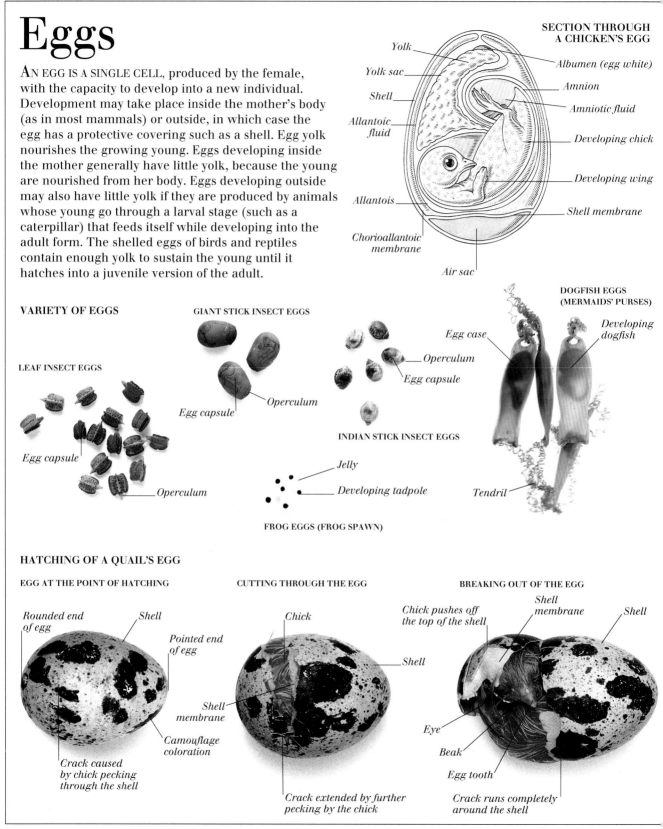

SECTION THROUGH A CHICKEN'S EGG

Yolk
Albumen (egg white)
Yolk sac
Amnion
Shell
Amniotic fluid
Allantoic fluid
Developing chick
Developing wing
Allantois
Shell membrane
Chorioallantoic membrane
Air sac

VARIETY OF EGGS

GIANT STICK INSECT EGGS

LEAF INSECT EGGS

Egg capsule
Operculum
Egg capsule

Egg capsule
Operculum

DOGFISH EGGS (MERMAIDS' PURSES)

Egg case
Developing dogfish
Operculum
Egg capsule

INDIAN STICK INSECT EGGS

Tendril

Jelly
Developing tadpole

FROG EGGS (FROG SPAWN)

HATCHING OF A QUAIL'S EGG

EGG AT THE POINT OF HATCHING

Rounded end of egg
Shell
Pointed end of egg
Shell membrane
Camouflage coloration
Crack caused by chick pecking through the shell

CUTTING THROUGH THE EGG

Chick
Shell
Shell membrane
Crack extended by further pecking by the chick

BREAKING OUT OF THE EGG

Chick pushes off the top of the shell
Shell membrane
Shell
Eye
Beak
Egg tooth
Crack runs completely around the shell

EXAMPLES OF BIRDS' EGGS

BEE HUMMINGBIRD
(Calypte helenae)

GREATER BLACKBACKED GULL
(Larus marinus)

BALTIMORE ORIOLE
(Icterus galbula)

WILLOW GROUSE
(Lagopus lagopus)

COMMON TERN
(Sterna hirundo)

CARRION CROW
(Corvus corone)

CHAFFINCH
(Fringilla coelebs)

OSTRICH
(Struthio camelus)

EMERGING FROM THE EGG

Eye

Beak

Egg tooth

Chick heaves itself out of the egg

Tympanum (eardrum)

Shell

Wet down

Remains of egg membranes (amnion and allantois)

THE NEWLY HATCHED CHICK

Eye

Beak

Egg tooth

Nostril

Tympanum (eardrum)

Chick is dry about an hour after hatching

Dry down

Toe

Claw

Leg

Eggshell

Carnivores

THE MAMMALIAN ORDER CARNIVORA includes cats, dogs, bears, raccoons, pandas, weasels, badgers, skunks, otters, civets, mongooses, and hyenas. The order's name is derived from the fact that most of its members are carnivores (flesh-eaters). Typical carnivore features therefore reflect a hunting lifestyle: speed and agility; sharp claws and well-developed canine teeth for holding and killing prey; carnassial teeth (cheek teeth) for cutting flesh; and forward-facing eyes for good distance judgment. However, some members of the order—bears, badgers, and foxes, for example—have a more mixed diet, and a few are entirely herbivorous (plant-eating), notably pandas. Such animals have no carnassial teeth and tend to be slower-moving than pure flesh-eaters.

EXTERNAL FEATURES OF A MALE LION

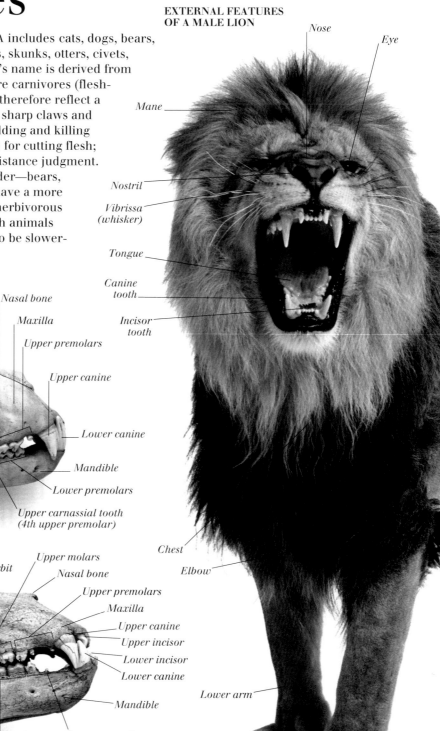

Nose
Eye
Mane
Nostril
Vibrissa (whisker)
Tongue
Canine tooth
Incisor tooth
Chest
Elbow
Lower arm
Toe

SKULL OF A LION

Zygomatic arch
Coronoid process
Sagittal crest
Orbit
Nasal bone
Maxilla
Upper premolars
Upper canine
Lower canine
Mandible
Lower premolars
Occipital condyle
Tympanic bulla
Condyle
Angular process
Upper carnassial tooth (4th upper premolar)

SKULL OF A BEAR

Sagittal crest
Occipital condyle
Zygomatic arch
Orbit
Upper molars
Nasal bone
Upper premolars
Maxilla
Upper canine
Upper incisor
Lower incisor
Lower canine
Mandible
Tympanic bulla
Angular process
Condyle
Lower molars
Lower premolars

EXAMPLES OF CARNIVORES

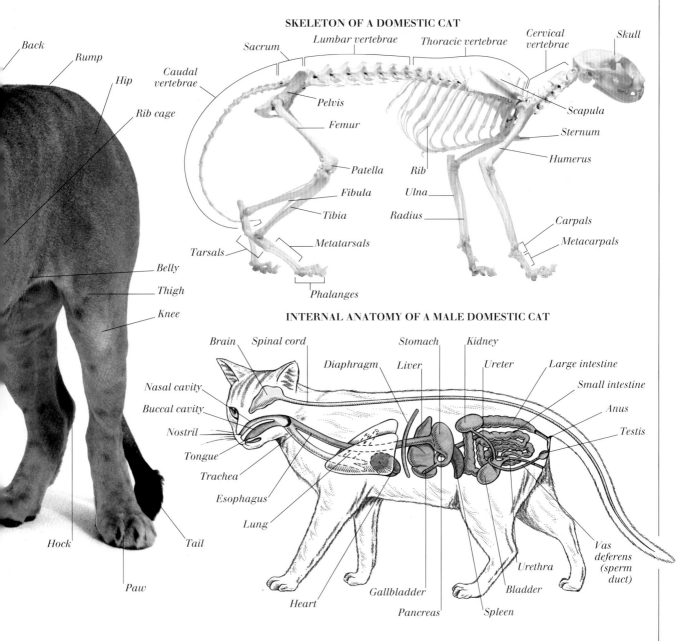

GERMAN SHEPHERD DOG
(Canis familiaris)

MANED WOLF
(Chrysocyon brachyurus)

RACCOON
(Procyon lotor)

AMERICAN BLACK BEAR
(Ursus americanus)

SKELETON OF A DOMESTIC CAT

Back

Rump

Hip

Rib cage

Caudal vertebrae

Sacrum

Lumbar vertebrae

Thoracic vertebrae

Cervical vertebrae

Skull

Pelvis

Femur

Scapula

Sternum

Humerus

Patella

Rib

Fibula

Ulna

Tibia

Radius

Tarsals

Metatarsals

Carpals

Metacarpals

Phalanges

Belly

Thigh

Knee

Hock

Tail

Paw

INTERNAL ANATOMY OF A MALE DOMESTIC CAT

Brain

Spinal cord

Diaphragm

Liver

Stomach

Kidney

Ureter

Large intestine

Small intestine

Anus

Testis

Nasal cavity

Buccal cavity

Nostril

Tongue

Trachea

Esophagus

Lung

Vas deferens (sperm duct)

Heart

Gallbladder

Pancreas

Spleen

Bladder

Urethra

Rabbits and rodents

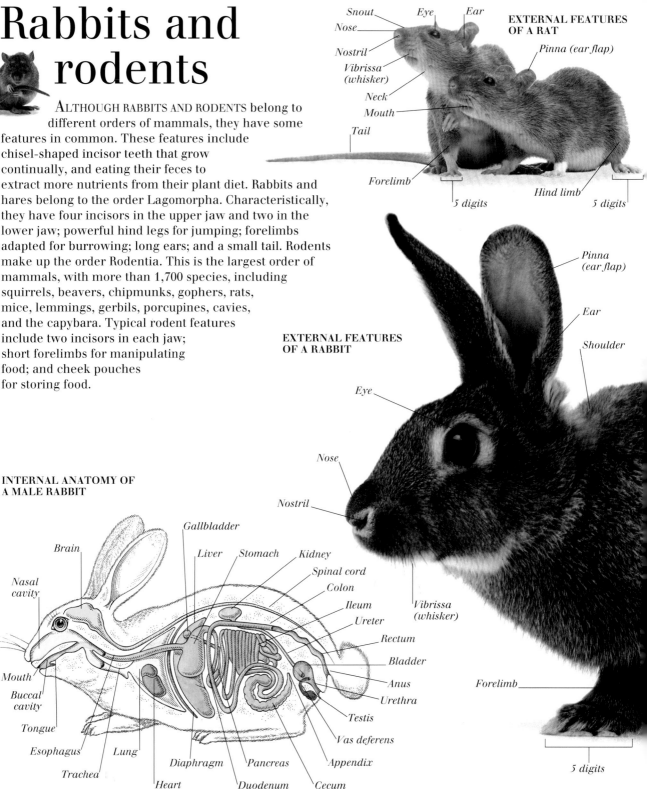

ALTHOUGH RABBITS AND RODENTS belong to different orders of mammals, they have some features in common. These features include chisel-shaped incisor teeth that grow continually, and eating their feces to extract more nutrients from their plant diet. Rabbits and hares belong to the order Lagomorpha. Characteristically, they have four incisors in the upper jaw and two in the lower jaw; powerful hind legs for jumping; forelimbs adapted for burrowing; long ears; and a small tail. Rodents make up the order Rodentia. This is the largest order of mammals, with more than 1,700 species, including squirrels, beavers, chipmunks, gophers, rats, mice, lemmings, gerbils, porcupines, cavies, and the capybara. Typical rodent features include two incisors in each jaw; short forelimbs for manipulating food; and cheek pouches for storing food.

EXTERNAL FEATURES OF A RAT

Snout
Eye
Ear
Nose
Nostril
Pinna (ear flap)
Vibrissa (whisker)
Neck
Mouth
Tail
Forelimb
5 digits
Hind limb
5 digits

EXTERNAL FEATURES OF A RABBIT

Pinna (ear flap)
Ear
Shoulder
Eye
Nose
Nostril
Vibrissa (whisker)
Forelimb
5 digits

INTERNAL ANATOMY OF A MALE RABBIT

Gallbladder
Brain
Liver
Stomach
Kidney
Spinal cord
Nasal cavity
Colon
Ileum
Ureter
Rectum
Bladder
Mouth
Anus
Buccal cavity
Urethra
Testis
Tongue
Vas deferens
Esophagus
Lung
Diaphragm
Pancreas
Appendix
Trachea
Heart
Duodenum
Cecum

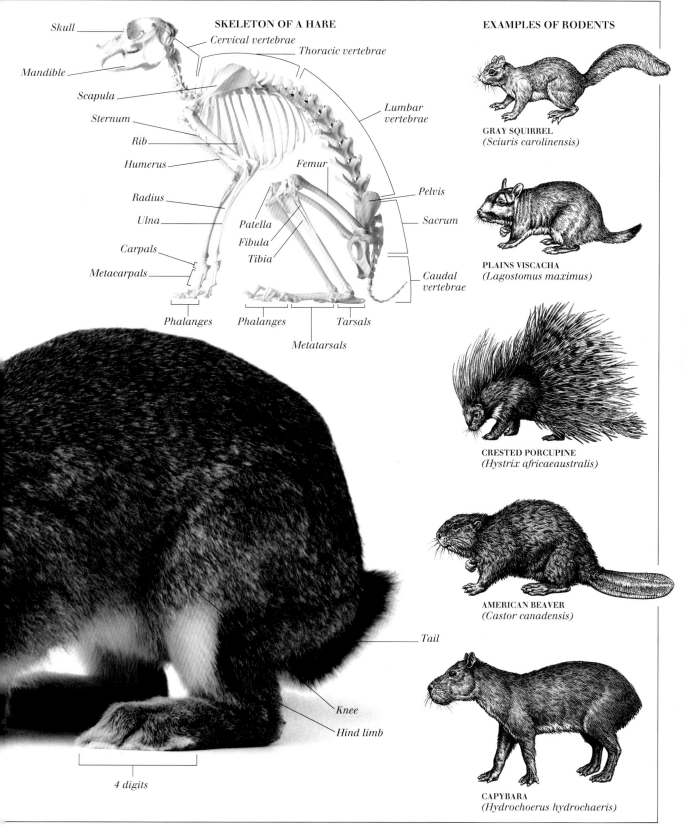

SKELETON OF A HARE

Skull

Mandible

Cervical vertebrae

Thoracic vertebrae

Scapula

Sternum

Lumbar vertebrae

Rib

Humerus

Femur

Radius

Pelvis

Ulna

Sacrum

Patella

Carpals

Fibula

Metacarpals

Tibia

Caudal vertebrae

Phalanges

Phalanges

Tarsals

Metatarsals

Tail

Knee

Hind limb

4 digits

EXAMPLES OF RODENTS

GRAY SQUIRREL
(Sciuris carolinensis)

PLAINS VISCACHA
(Lagostomus maximus)

CRESTED PORCUPINE
(Hystrix africaeaustralis)

AMERICAN BEAVER
(Castor canadensis)

CAPYBARA
(Hydrochoerus hydrochaeris)

Ungulates

UNGULATES IS A GENERAL TERM FOR a large, varied group of mammals that includes horses, cattle, and their relatives. The ungulates are divided into two orders on the basis of the number of toes. Members of the order Perissodactyla (odd-toed ungulates) have one or three toes. Perissodactyls include horses, asses, and zebras (all of which are one-toed), and rhinoceroses and tapirs (which are three-toed). Members of the order Artiodactyla (even-toed ungulates) have two or four toes. Most artiodactyls have two toes, which are typically encased in hooves to give the so-called cloven hoof. Two-toed, cloven-hoofed artiodactyls include cows and other cattle, sheep, goats, antelopes, deer, and giraffes. The other main two-toed artiodactyls are camels and llamas. Most two-toed artiodactyls are ruminants; that is, they have a four-chambered stomach and chew the cud. The principal four-toed artiodactyls are hogs and hippopotamuses.

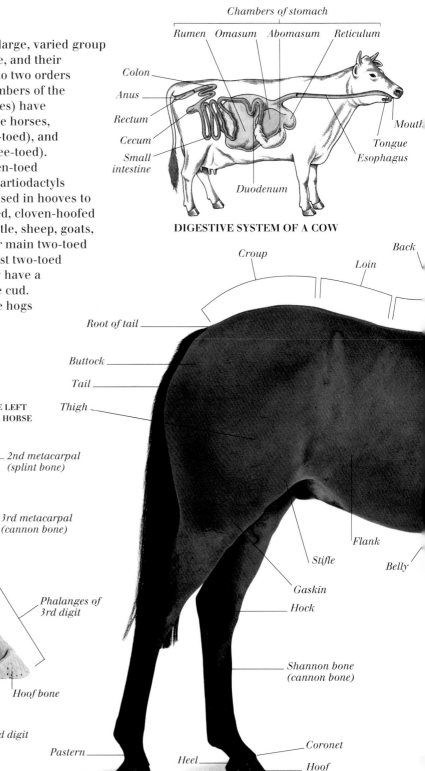

Chambers of stomach

Rumen Omasum Abomasum Reticulum

Colon

Anus

Rectum

Cecum

Small intestine

Duodenum

Mouth

Tongue

Esophagus

DIGESTIVE SYSTEM OF A COW

COMPARISON OF THE FRONT FEET OF A HORSE AND A COW

SKELETON OF THE LEFT FRONT FOOT OF A HORSE

SKELETON OF THE RIGHT FRONT FOOT OF A COW

Fused 3rd and 4th metacarpals

2nd metacarpal (splint bone)

3rd metacarpal (cannon bone)

Sesamoid bone

Sesamoid bone

Phalanges of 3rd digit

Phalanges of 3rd digit

Hoof bone

Phalanges of 4th digit

Hoof bone of 3rd digit

Hoof bone of 4th digit

Croup

Loin

Back

Root of tail

Buttock

Tail

Thigh

Flank

Stifle

Belly

Gaskin

Hock

Shannon bone (cannon bone)

Pastern

Heel

Coronet

Hoof

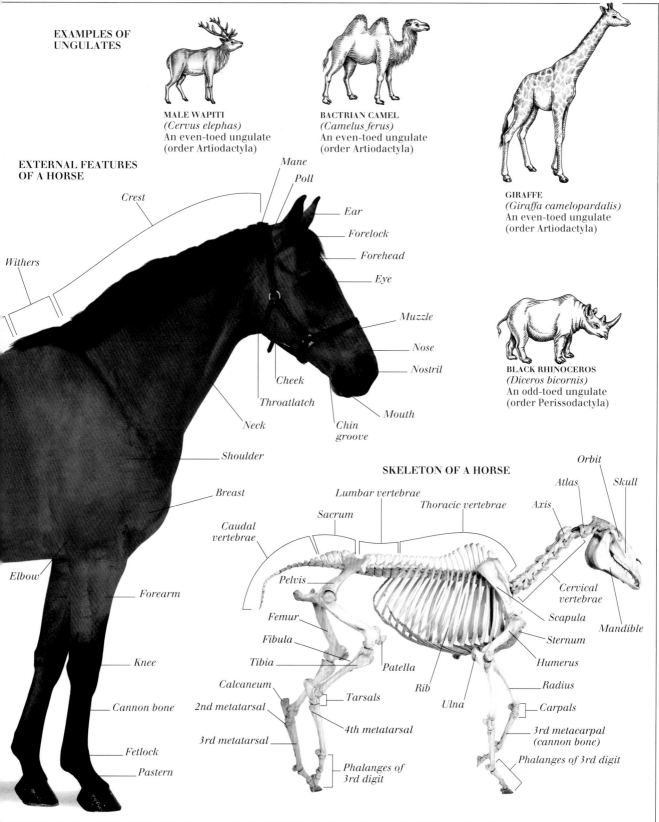

EXAMPLES OF UNGULATES

MALE WAPITI
(Cervus elephas)
An even-toed ungulate
(order Artiodactyla)

BACTRIAN CAMEL
(Camelus ferus)
An even-toed ungulate
(order Artiodactyla)

GIRAFFE
(Giraffa camelopardalis)
An even-toed ungulate
(order Artiodactyla)

BLACK RHINOCEROS
(Diceros bicornis)
An odd-toed ungulate
(order Perissodactyla)

EXTERNAL FEATURES OF A HORSE

Crest

Withers

Mane

Poll

Ear

Forelock

Forehead

Eye

Muzzle

Nose

Nostril

Cheek

Throatlatch

Chin groove

Mouth

Neck

Shoulder

Breast

Elbow

Forearm

Knee

Cannon bone

Fetlock

Pastern

SKELETON OF A HORSE

Orbit

Atlas

Skull

Axis

Lumbar vertebrae

Thoracic vertebrae

Sacrum

Caudal vertebrae

Cervical vertebrae

Pelvis

Scapula

Mandible

Femur

Sternum

Fibula

Humerus

Tibia

Patella

Radius

Calcaneum

Rib

Carpals

2nd metatarsal

Tarsals

Ulna

4th metatarsal

3rd metacarpal (cannon bone)

3rd metatarsal

Phalanges of 3rd digit

Phalanges of 3rd digit

Elephants

THE TWO SPECIES OF elephants—African and Asian—are the only members of the mammalian order Proboscidea. The bigger African elephant is the largest land animal: a fully grown male may be up to 13 ft (4m) tall and weigh as much as 7.7 tons (7 tonnes). A fully grown male Asian elephant may be 11 ft (3.3 m) tall and weigh 6 tons (5.4 tonnes). The muscular trunk—an extension of the nose and upper lip—is the elephant's most obvious feature. It is used for manipulating and lifting, feeding, drinking and spraying water, smelling, touching, and producing trumpeting sounds. Other characteristic features of this mighty plant-eater include a pair of ivory tusks, used for defense and for crushing vegetation; thick, pillar-like legs and broad feet to support the massive body; and large ear flaps that act as radiators to keep the elephant cool.

DIFFERENCES BETWEEN AFRICAN AND ASIAN ELEPHANTS

Flat forehead
Very large ears
2 "lips" at the end of the trunk
4 toenails
Concave back
3 toenails

AFRICAN ELEPHANT
(Loxodonta africana)

Twin-domed forehead
Smaller ears
1 "lip" at the end of the trunk
5 toenails
Arched back
4 toenails

ASIAN ELEPHANT
(Elephas maximus)

INTERNAL ANATOMY OF A FEMALE ELEPHANT

Spinal cord
Heart
Stomach
Duodenum
Kidney
Ureter
Uterus
Rectum
Bladder
Anal flap
Anus
Vagina
Brain
Nasal cavity
Buccal cavity
Mouth
Tongue
Tusk
Epiglottis
Esophagus
Trachea
Lung
Diaphragm
Nasal passage
Nostril
Spleen
Vulva
Small intestine
Rump
Hind leg
Toenail

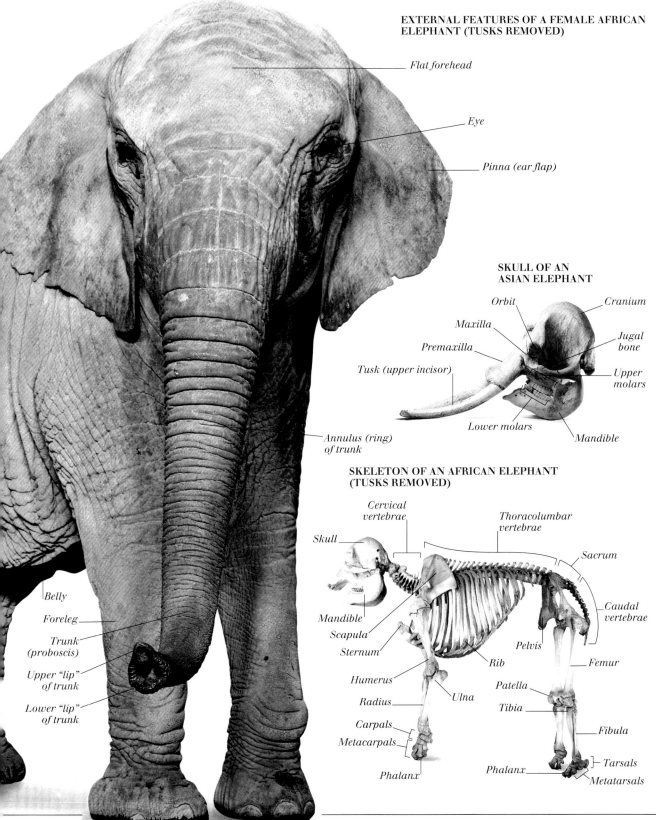

EXTERNAL FEATURES OF A FEMALE AFRICAN ELEPHANT (TUSKS REMOVED)

Flat forehead

Eye

Pinna (ear flap)

Annulus (ring) of trunk

Belly

Foreleg

Trunk (proboscis)

Upper "lip" of trunk

Lower "lip" of trunk

SKULL OF AN ASIAN ELEPHANT

Orbit

Cranium

Maxilla

Jugal bone

Premaxilla

Tusk (upper incisor)

Upper molars

Lower molars

Mandible

SKELETON OF AN AFRICAN ELEPHANT (TUSKS REMOVED)

Cervical vertebrae

Thoracolumbar vertebrae

Skull

Sacrum

Mandible

Caudal vertebrae

Scapula

Sternum

Pelvis

Humerus

Rib

Femur

Radius

Ulna

Patella

Tibia

Carpals

Fibula

Metacarpals

Phalanx

Tarsals

Metatarsals

Phalanx

Primates

THE MAMMALIAN ORDER PRIMATES consists of monkeys, apes, and their relatives (including humans). There are two suborders of primates: Prosimii, the primitive primates, which include lemurs, tarsiers, and lorises; and Anthropoidea, the advanced primates, which include monkeys, apes, and humans. The anthropoids are divided into New World monkeys, Old World monkeys, and hominids. New World monkeys typically have widespread nostrils that open to the side; and long tails, which are prehensile (grasping) in some species. This group of monkeys lives in South America, and includes marmosets, tamarins, and howler monkeys. Old World monkeys typically have close-set nostrils that open forward or downward and nonprehensile tails. This group of monkeys lives in Africa and Asia, and includes langurs, mandrills, macaques, and baboons. Hominids typically have large brains and no tail. This group includes the apes—chimpanzees, gibbons, gorillas, and orangutans—and humans.

**INTERNAL ANATOMY OF
A FEMALE CHIMPANZEE**

Buccal cavity
Brain
Tongue
Nasal cavity
Trachea
Spinal cord
Lung
Esophagus
Liver
Heart
Pancreas
Diaphragm
Small intestine
Stomach
Cecum
Spleen
Appendix
Large intestine
Ovary
Rectum
Uterus
Bladder
Vagina
Urethra

**SKELETON OF A
RHESUS MONKEY**

Skull
Orbit
Cervical vertebrae
Mandible
Thoracic vertebrae
Clavicle
Scapula
Rib
Lumbar vertebrae
Humerus
Sacrum
Radius
Ulna
Femur
Patella
Tibia
Carpals
Fibula
Metacarpals
Pelvis
Caudal vertebrae
Tarsals
Phalanges
Metatarsals
Phalanges

SKULL OF A CHIMPANZEE

Temporal bone
Suture
Frontal bone
Parietal bone
Supraorbital ridge
Orbit
Occipital bone
Maxilla
Premaxilla
Auditory meatus
Incisor tooth
Zygomatic arch
Canine tooth
Mandible
Molar tooth
Premolar tooth

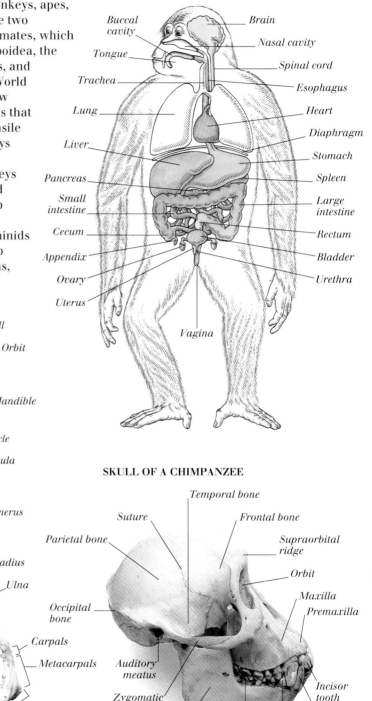

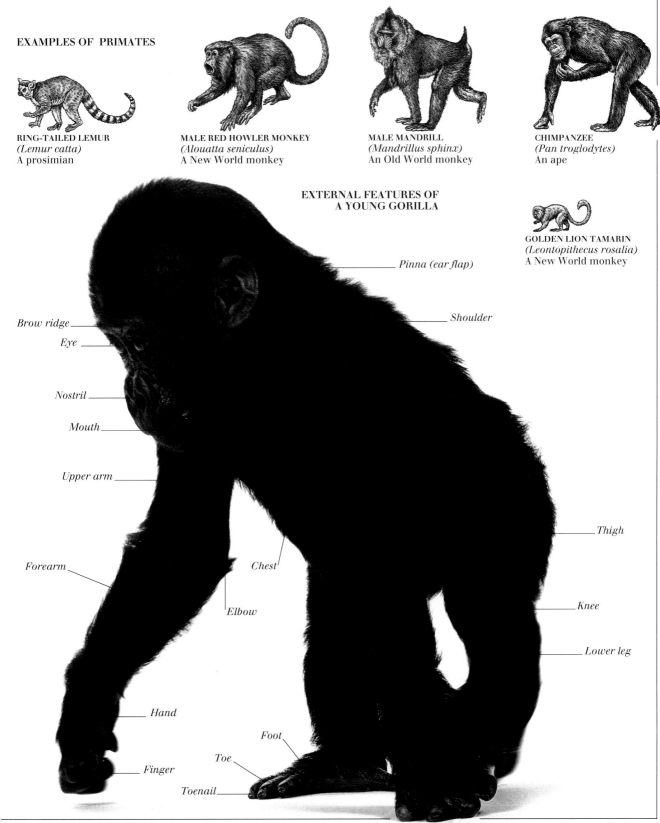

EXAMPLES OF PRIMATES

RING-TAILED LEMUR
(Lemur catta)
A prosimian

MALE RED HOWLER MONKEY
(Alouatta seniculus)
A New World monkey

MALE MANDRILL
(Mandrillus sphinx)
An Old World monkey

CHIMPANZEE
(Pan troglodytes)
An ape

**EXTERNAL FEATURES OF
A YOUNG GORILLA**

GOLDEN LION TAMARIN
(Leontopithecus rosalia)
A New World monkey

Pinna (ear flap)

Brow ridge

Shoulder

Eye

Nostril

Mouth

Upper arm

Thigh

Forearm

Chest

Knee

Elbow

Lower leg

Hand

Foot

Toe

Finger

Toenail

Dolphins, whales, and seals

DOLPHINS, WHALES, AND SEALS belong to
two orders of mammals adapted to living
in water. Dolphins and whales make up the
order Cetacea. Typical cetacean features include
a streamlined, fish-like shape; forelimbs in the form
of flippers; no visible hind limbs; a horizontally flattened
tail; and thick blubber under the skin. There are two groups
of cetaceans: toothed whales, including sperm whales, white whales,
beaked whales, dolphins, and porpoises; and the larger whalebone (baleen)
whales, including rorquals, gray whales, and right whales. The blue whale—a
rorqual—is the largest living animal: an adult may be up to 100 ft (30m) long
and weigh 145 tons (130 tonnes). Seals and their relatives—sea lions and
walruses—make up the order Pinnipedia. Characteristically, they have a
streamlined, torpedo-shaped body; forelimbs and hind limbs modified as
flippers; thick blubber; and no external ears.

Forehead

Rostrum (beak)

Mouth

Gape
(lower jaw)

Eye

Flipper

Belly

Mouth

Gape (lower jaw)

5 digits

Hind flipper

EXTERNAL FEATURES OF A SEAL

Auditory
meatus

Eye

Nostril

Vibrissa
(whisker)

Mouth

Front flipper

5 digits

SKELETON OF A SEAL

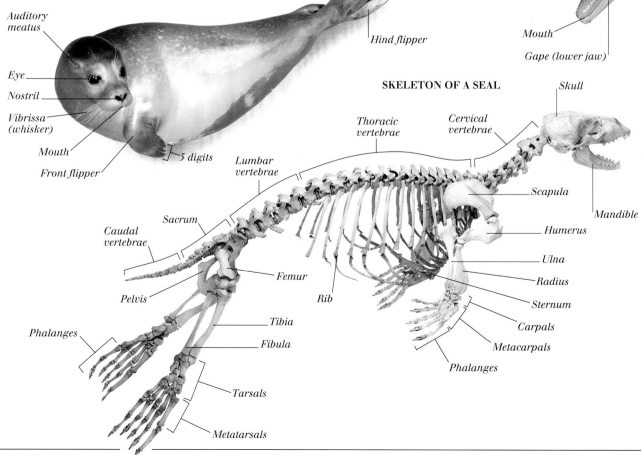

Thoracic
vertebrae

Cervical
vertebrae

Skull

Lumbar
vertebrae

Scapula

Mandible

Sacrum

Humerus

Caudal
vertebrae

Ulna

Femur

Radius

Pelvis

Rib

Sternum

Tibia

Carpals

Phalanges

Fibula

Metacarpals

Phalanges

Tarsals

Metatarsals

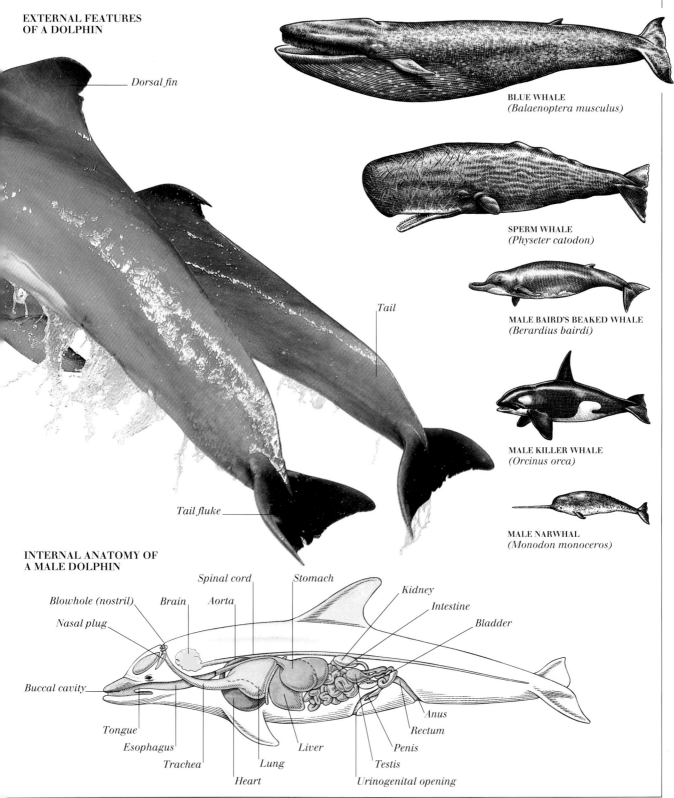

EXAMPLES OF CETACEANS

EXTERNAL FEATURES
OF A DOLPHIN

Dorsal fin

Tail

Tail fluke

BLUE WHALE
(Balaenoptera musculus)

SPERM WHALE
(Physeter catodon)

MALE BAIRD'S BEAKED WHALE
(Berardius bairdi)

MALE KILLER WHALE
(Orcinus orca)

MALE NARWHAL
(Monodon monoceros)

INTERNAL ANATOMY OF
A MALE DOLPHIN

Spinal cord

Stomach

Kidney

Intestine

Bladder

Blowhole (nostril)

Brain

Aorta

Nasal plug

Buccal cavity

Anus

Rectum

Penis

Tongue

Esophagus

Trachea

Heart

Lung

Liver

Testis

Urinogenital opening

Marsupials and Monotremes

MARSUPIALS AND MONOTREMES are two orders of mammals that differ from other mammalian groups in the ways that their young develop. The order Marsupalia, the pouched mammals, is made up of kangaroos and their relatives. Typically, marsupials give birth to their young at a very early stage of development. The young then crawls to the mother's pouch (which is on the outside of her abdomen), where it attaches itself to a nipple and remains until fully developed. Most marsupials live in Australia, although the opossums—which are classified as marsupials despite not having a pouch—live in the Americas. The order Monotremata is made up of the platypus and its relatives (the echidnas, or spiny anteaters). The monotremes are primitive mammals that lay eggs, which the mother incubates. The monotremes are found only in Australia and New Guinea.

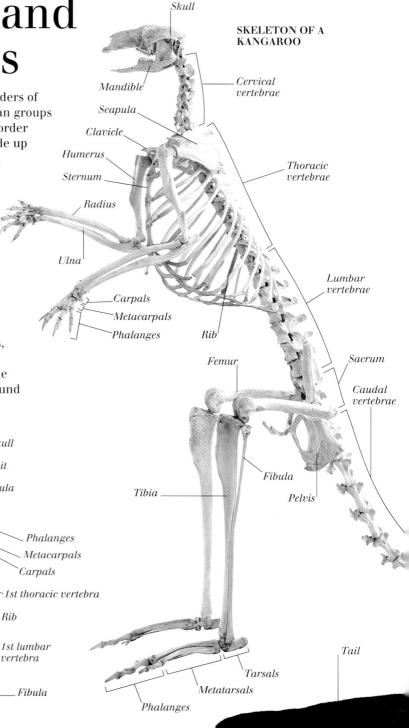

SKELETON OF A KANGAROO

Skull
Mandible
Cervical vertebrae
Scapula
Clavicle
Humerus
Sternum
Radius
Thoracic vertebrae
Ulna
Lumbar vertebrae
Carpals
Metacarpals
Phalanges
Rib
Femur
Sacrum
Caudal vertebrae
Fibula
Tibia
Pelvis
Tail
Tarsals
Metatarsals
Phalanges

SKELETON OF A PLATYPUS

Skull
Orbit
1st cervical vertebra
Scapula
Phalanges
Metacarpals
Carpals
Ulna
Radius
Humerus
1st thoracic vertebra
Rib
Femur
1st lumbar vertebra
Tarsals
Fibula
Metatarsals
Phalanges
Patella
Tibia
Pelvis
1st caudal vertebra

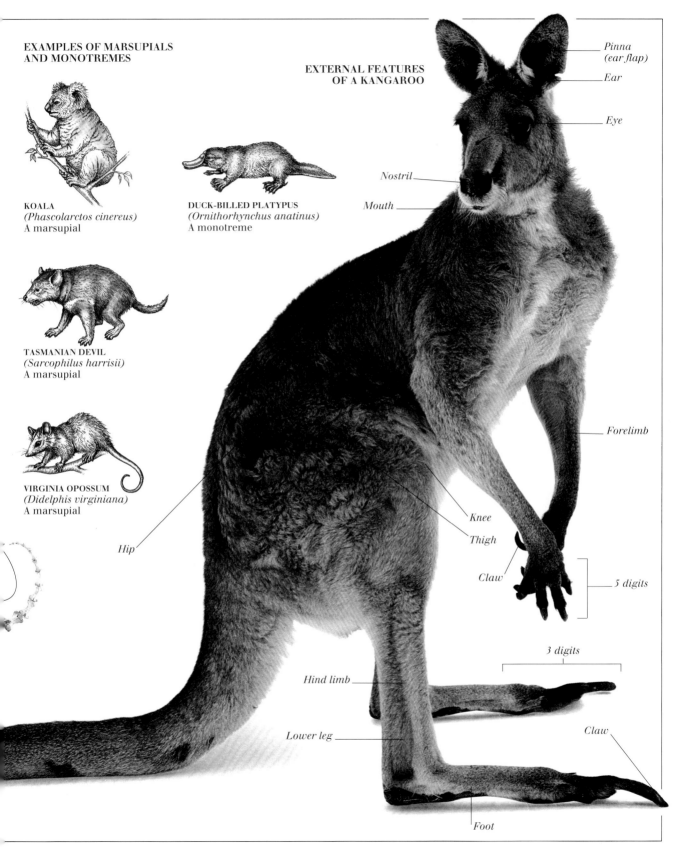

EXAMPLES OF MARSUPIALS AND MONOTREMES

EXTERNAL FEATURES OF A KANGAROO

KOALA
(Phascolarctos cinereus)
A marsupial

DUCK-BILLED PLATYPUS
(Ornithorhynchus anatinus)
A monotreme

TASMANIAN DEVIL
(Sarcophilus harrisii)
A marsupial

VIRGINIA OPOSSUM
(Didelphis virginiana)
A marsupial

*Pinna
(ear flap)*

Ear

Eye

Nostril

Mouth

Forelimb

Hip

Knee

Thigh

Claw

5 digits

3 digits

Hind limb

Lower leg

Claw

Foot

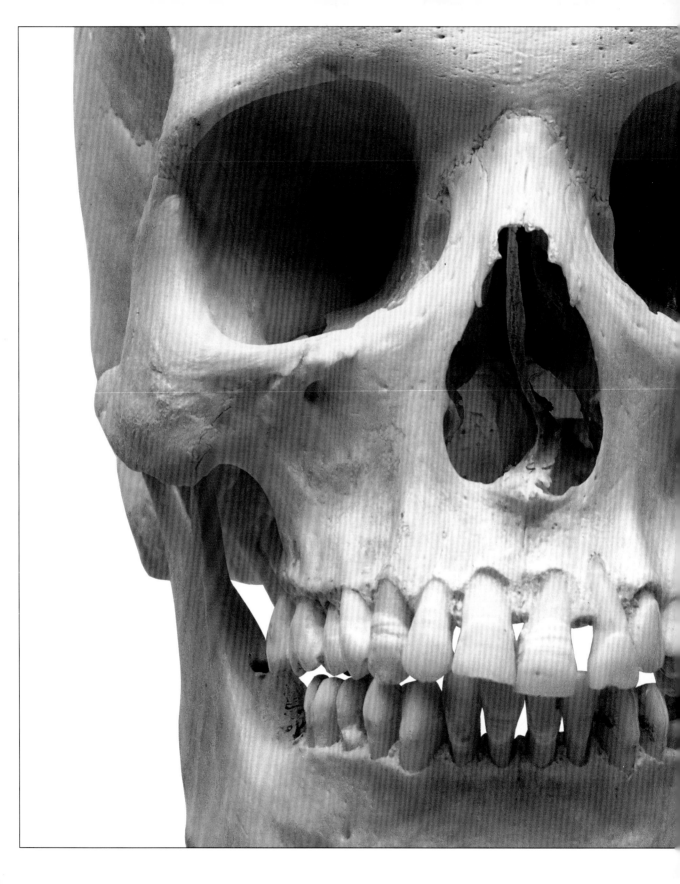

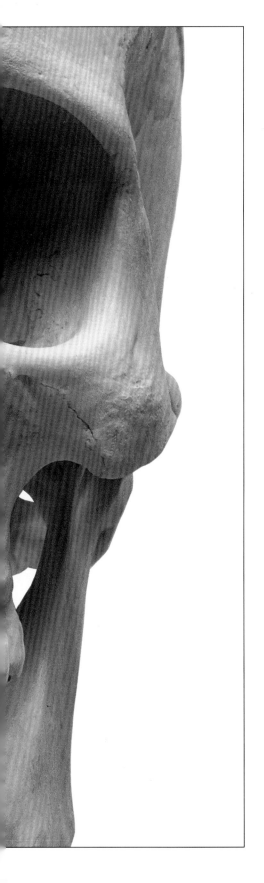

The Human Body

Body features

ALTHOUGH THERE IS enormous variation between the external appearances of humans, all bodies contain the same basic features. The outward form of the human body depends on the size of the skeleton, the shape of the muscles, the thickness of the fat layer beneath the skin, the elasticity or sagginess of the skin, and the person's age and gender. Males tend to be taller than females, with broader shoulders, more body hair, and a different pattern of fat deposits under the skin; the female body tends to be less muscular and has a shallower and wider pelvis to allow for childbirth.

Ear

Nape of neck

Shoulder

Back

Scapula
(shoulder blade)

Upper arm

Elbow

Loin

Waist

Forearm

Natal
cleft

Buttock

Arm

Hand

Gluteal fold

Popliteal fossa

Leg

Calf

Foot

Heel

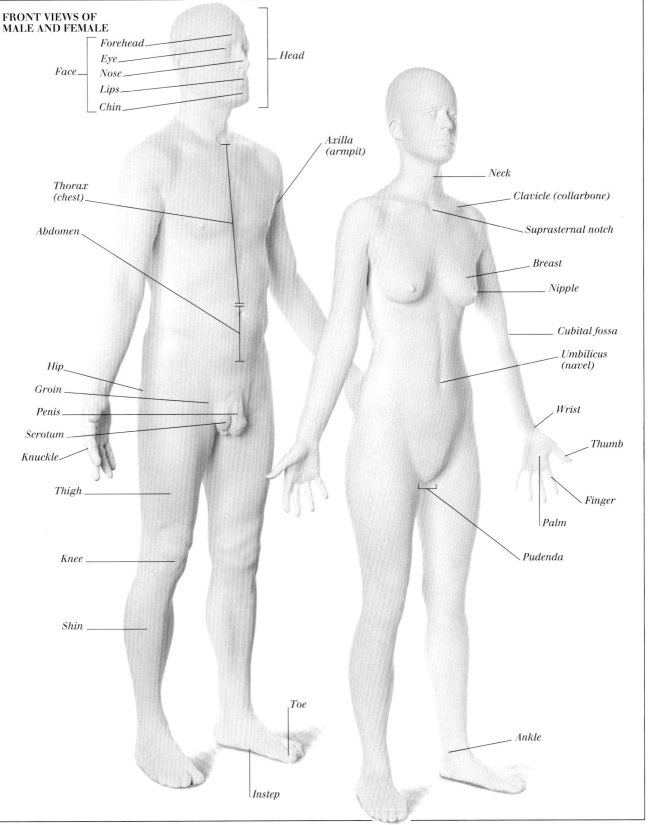

**FRONT VIEWS OF
MALE AND FEMALE**

Forehead

Eye

Face

Nose

Lips

Chin

Head

Axilla
(armpit)

Neck

Clavicle (collarbone)

Suprasternal notch

Thorax
(chest)

Abdomen

Breast

Nipple

Cubital fossa

Umbilicus
(navel)

Hip

Groin

Penis

Scrotum

Knuckle

Wrist

Thumb

Finger

Thigh

Palm

Pudenda

Knee

Shin

Toe

Ankle

Instep

Head

IN A NEWBORN BABY, the head accounts for one quarter of the total body length; by adulthood, the proportion has reduced to one eighth. Contained in the head are the body's main sense organs: eyes, ears, olfactory nerves that detect smells, and the taste buds of the tongue. Signals from these organs pass to the body's great coordination center: the brain, housed in the protective, bony dome of the skull. Hair on the head insulates against heat loss, and adult males also grow thick facial hair. The face has three important openings: two nostrils through which air passes, and the mouth, which takes in nourishment and helps form speech. Although all heads are basically similar, differences in the size, shape, and color of features produce an infinite variety of appearances.

SIDE VIEW OF EXTERNAL FEATURES OF HEAD

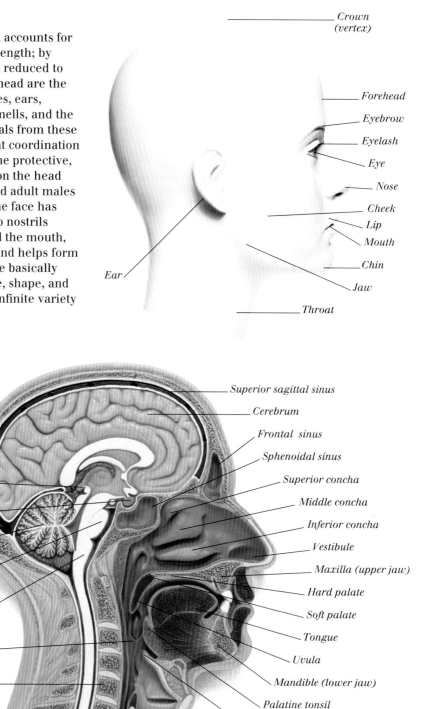

Crown (vertex)

Forehead

Eyebrow

Eyelash

Eye

Nose

Cheek

Lip

Mouth

Chin

Jaw

Ear

Throat

SECTION THROUGH HEAD

Superior sagittal sinus

Cerebrum

Frontal sinus

Sphenoidal sinus

Superior concha

Middle concha

Inferior concha

Vestibule

Maxilla (upper jaw)

Hard palate

Soft palate

Tongue

Uvula

Mandible (lower jaw)

Palatine tonsil

Epiglottis

Trachea

Esophagus

Skull

Pineal body

Pituitary gland

Cerebellum

Pons

Medulla oblongata

Pharynx

Cervical vertebra

Spinal cord

Intervertebral disk

212

**FRONT VIEW OF EXTERNAL
FEATURES OF HEAD**

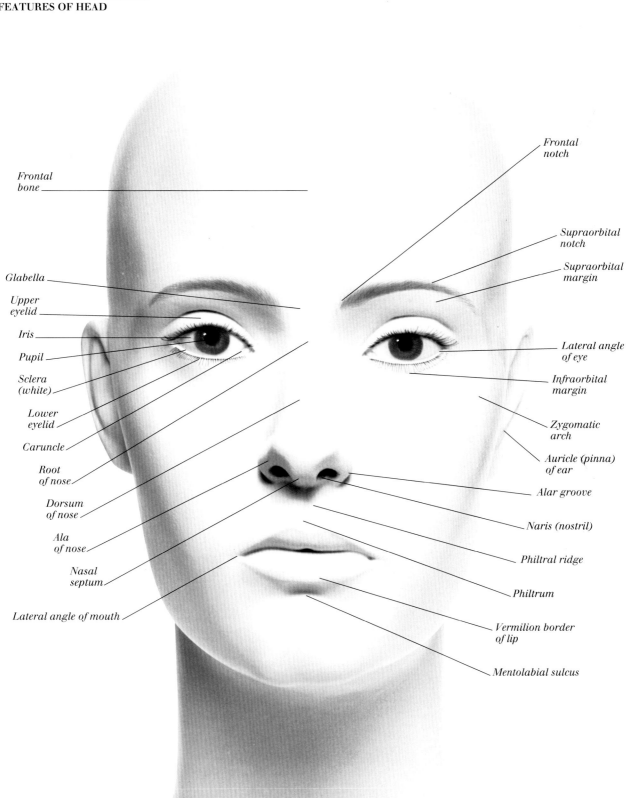

Frontal
notch

Supraorbital
notch

Supraorbital
margin

Frontal
bone

Glabella

Upper
eyelid

Iris

Pupil

Sclera
(white)

Lower
eyelid

Caruncle

Root
of nose

Dorsum
of nose

Ala
of nose

Nasal
septum

Lateral angle of mouth

Lateral angle
of eye

Infraorbital
margin

Zygomatic
arch

Auricle (pinna)
of ear

Alar groove

Naris (nostril)

Philtral ridge

Philtrum

Vermilion border
of lip

Mentolabial sulcus

213

Body organs

ALL THE VITAL BODY ORGANS except for the brain are enclosed within the trunk or torso (the body apart from the head and limbs). The trunk contains two large cavities separated by a muscular sheet called the diaphragm. The upper cavity, known as the thorax or chest cavity, contains the heart and lungs. The lower cavity, called the abdominal cavity, contains the stomach, intestines, liver, and pancreas, which all play a role in digesting food. Also within the trunk are the kidneys and bladder, which are part of the urinary system, and the reproductive organs, which hold the seeds of new human life. Modern imaging techniques, such as contrast X-rays and different types of scans, make it possible to see and study body organs without the need to cut through their protective coverings of skin, fat, muscle, and bone.

MAJOR INTERNAL STRUCTURES

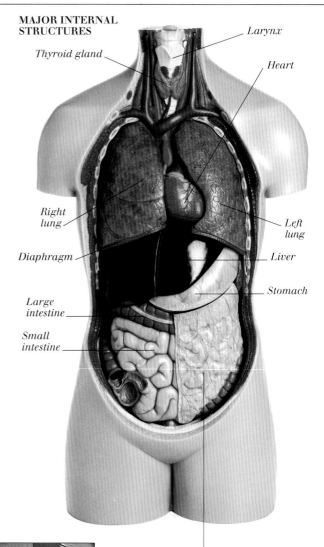

Thyroid gland

Larynx

Heart

Right lung

Left lung

Diaphragm

Liver

Stomach

Large intestine

Small intestine

Greater omentum

IMAGING THE BODY

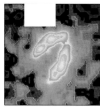

SCINTIGRAM OF HEART CHAMBERS

ANGIOGRAM OF RIGHT LUNG

CONTRAST X-RAY OF GALLBLADDER

SCINTIGRAM OF NERVOUS SYSTEM

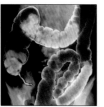

DOUBLE CONTRAST X-RAY OF COLON

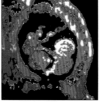

ULTRASOUND SCAN OF TWINS IN UTERUS

ANGIOGRAM OF KIDNEYS

ANGIOGRAM OF ARTERIES OF HEAD

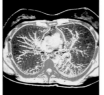

CT SCAN THROUGH FEMALE CHEST

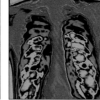

THERMOGRAM OF CHEST REGION

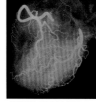

ANGIOGRAM OF ARTERIES OF HEART

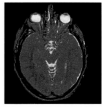

MRI SCAN THROUGH HEAD AT EYE LEVEL

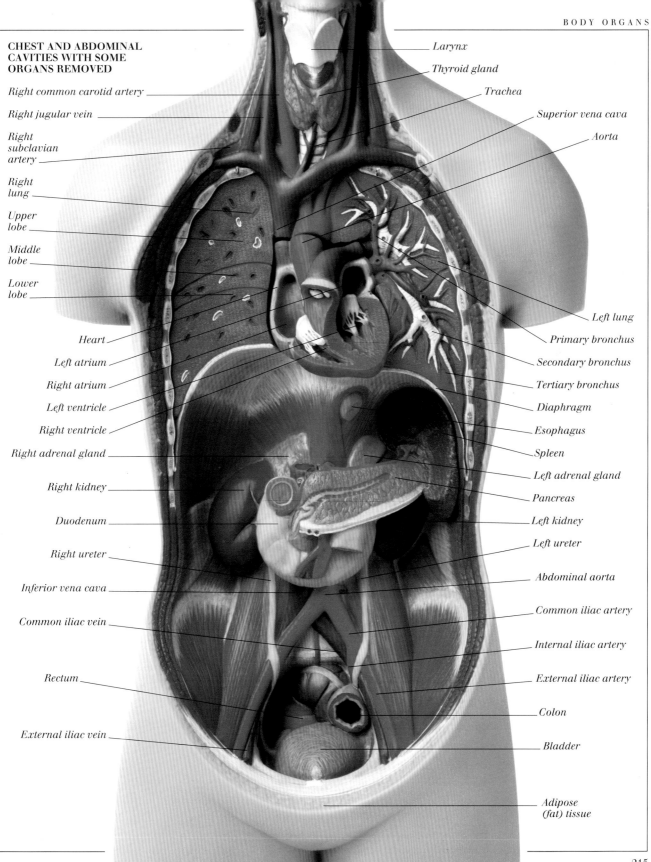

**CHEST AND ABDOMINAL
CAVITIES WITH SOME
ORGANS REMOVED**

Right common carotid artery

Right jugular vein

Right subclavian artery

Right lung

Upper lobe

Middle lobe

Lower lobe

Heart

Left atrium

Right atrium

Left ventricle

Right ventricle

Right adrenal gland

Right kidney

Duodenum

Right ureter

Inferior vena cava

Common iliac vein

Rectum

External iliac vein

Larynx

Thyroid gland

Trachea

Superior vena cava

Aorta

Left lung

Primary bronchus

Secondary bronchus

Tertiary bronchus

Diaphragm

Esophagus

Spleen

Left adrenal gland

Pancreas

Left kidney

Left ureter

Abdominal aorta

Common iliac artery

Internal iliac artery

External iliac artery

Colon

Bladder

Adipose (fat) tissue

Body cells

EVERYONE IS MADE UP OF BILLIONS OF CELLS, which are the basic structural units of the body. Bones, muscles, nerves, skin, blood, and all other body tissues are formed from different types of cells. Each cell has a specific function but works with other types of cells to perform the enormous number of tasks needed to sustain life. Most body cells have a similar basic structure. Each cell has an outer layer (called the cell membrane) and contains a fluid material (cytoplasm). Within the cytoplasm are many specialized structures (organelles). The most important organelle is the nucleus, which contains vital genetic material and acts as the cell's control center.

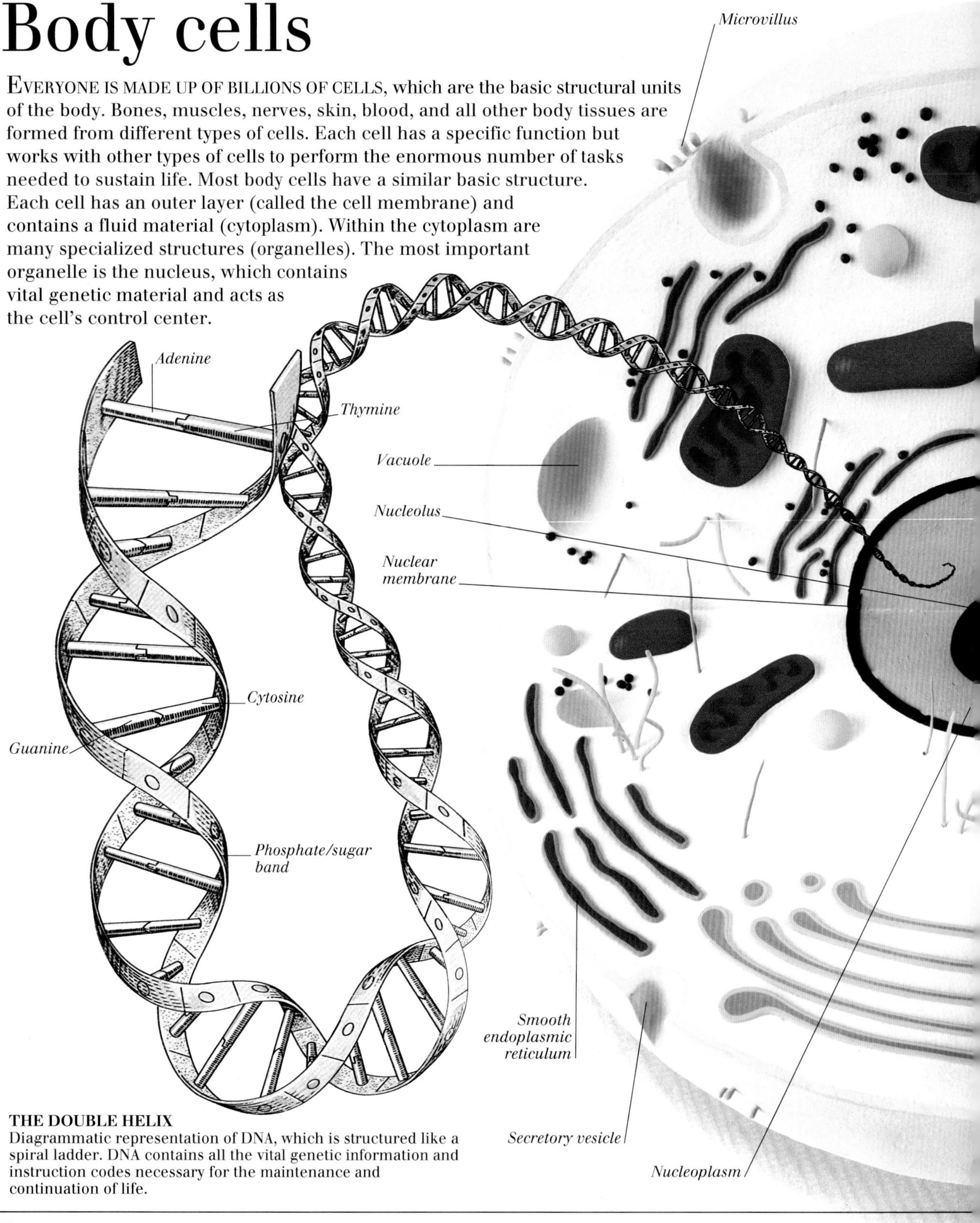

Microvillus

Adenine

Thymine

Vacuole

Nucleolus

Nuclear membrane

Cytosine

Guanine

Phosphate/sugar band

Smooth endoplasmic reticulum

THE DOUBLE HELIX
Diagrammatic representation of DNA, which is structured like a spiral ladder. DNA contains all the vital genetic information and instruction codes necessary for the maintenance and continuation of life.

Secretory vesicle

Nucleoplasm

GENERALIZED HUMAN CELL

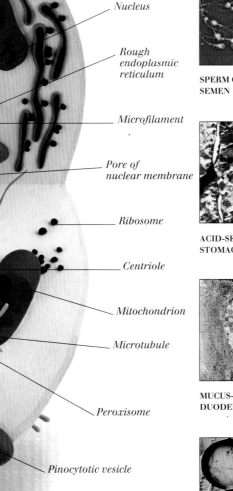

Cytoplasm

Lysosome

Cell membrane

Mitochondrial crista

Nucleus

Rough endoplasmic reticulum

Microfilament

Pore of nuclear membrane

Ribosome

Centriole

Mitochondrion

Microtubule

Peroxisome

Pinocytotic vesicle

Golgi complex (Golgi apparatus; Golgi body)

TYPES OF CELLS

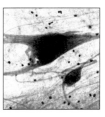

BONE-FORMING CELL

NERVE CELLS IN SPINAL CORD

SPERM CELLS IN SEMEN

SECRETORY THYROID GLAND CELLS

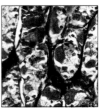

ACID-SECRETING STOMACH CELLS

CONNECTIVE TISSUE CELLS

MUCUS-SECRETING DUODENAL CELLS

RED AND TWO WHITE BLOOD CELLS

FAT CELLS IN ADIPOSE TISSUE

EPITHELIAL CELLS IN CHEEK

Skeleton

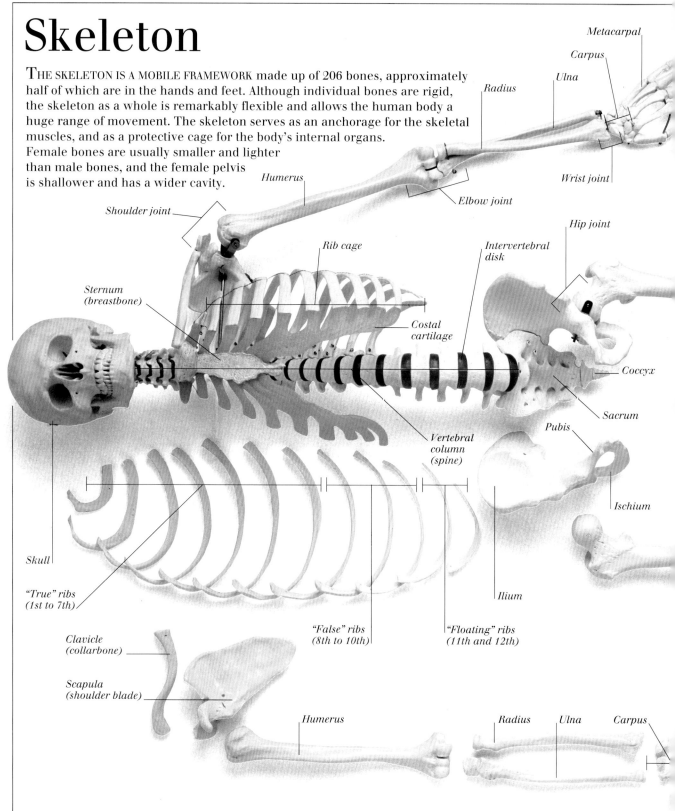

THE SKELETON IS A MOBILE FRAMEWORK made up of 206 bones, approximately half of which are in the hands and feet. Although individual bones are rigid, the skeleton as a whole is remarkably flexible and allows the human body a huge range of movement. The skeleton serves as an anchorage for the skeletal muscles, and as a protective cage for the body's internal organs. Female bones are usually smaller and lighter than male bones, and the female pelvis is shallower and has a wider cavity.

Metacarpal

Carpus

Ulna

Radius

Humerus

Shoulder joint

Elbow joint

Wrist joint

Hip joint

Rib cage

Intervertebral disk

Sternum (breastbone)

Costal cartilage

Coccyx

Vertebral column (spine)

Sacrum

Pubis

Ischium

Skull

"True" ribs (1st to 7th)

Ilium

Clavicle (collarbone)

"False" ribs (8th to 10th)

"Floating" ribs (11th and 12th)

Scapula (shoulder blade)

Humerus

Radius

Ulna

Carpus

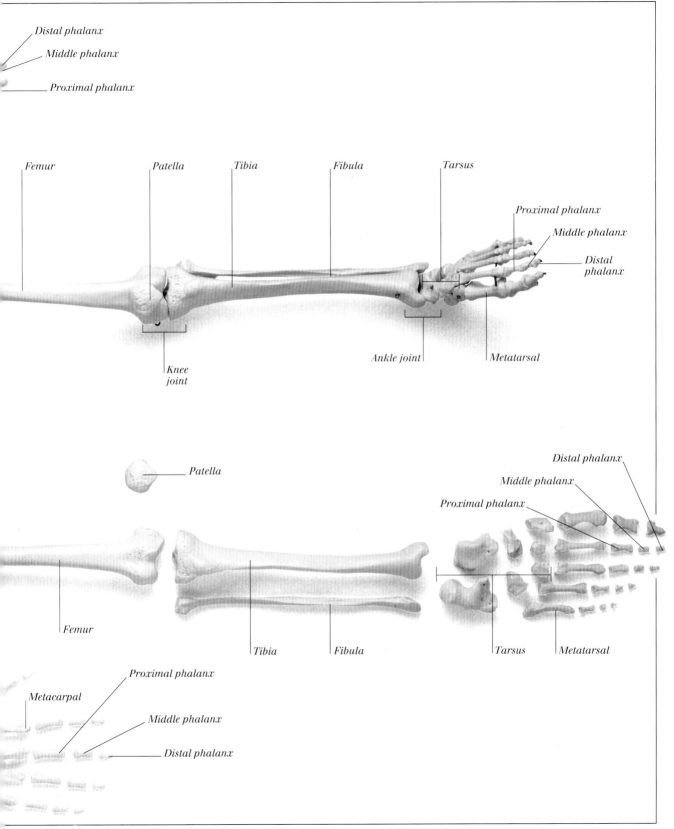

Distal phalanx

Middle phalanx

Proximal phalanx

Femur

Patella

Tibia

Fibula

Tarsus

Proximal phalanx

Middle phalanx

Distal phalanx

Knee joint

Ankle joint

Metatarsal

Patella

Distal phalanx

Middle phalanx

Proximal phalanx

Femur

Tibia

Fibula

Tarsus

Metatarsal

Metacarpal

Proximal phalanx

Middle phalanx

Distal phalanx

Skull

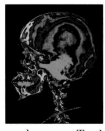

THE SKULL is the most complicated bony structure of the body—but every feature serves a purpose. Internally, the main hollow chamber of the skull has three levels that support the brain, with every bump and hollow corresponding to the shape of the brain. Underneath and toward the back of the skull is a large round hole, called the foramen magnum, through which the spinal cord passes. To the front of this are many smaller openings through which nerves, arteries, and veins pass to and from the brain. The roof of the skull is formed from four thin, curved bones that are firmly fixed together from the age of about two years. At the front of the skull are two orbits, which contain the eyeballs, and a central hole for the airway of the nose. The jawbone hinges on either side of the skull at ear level.

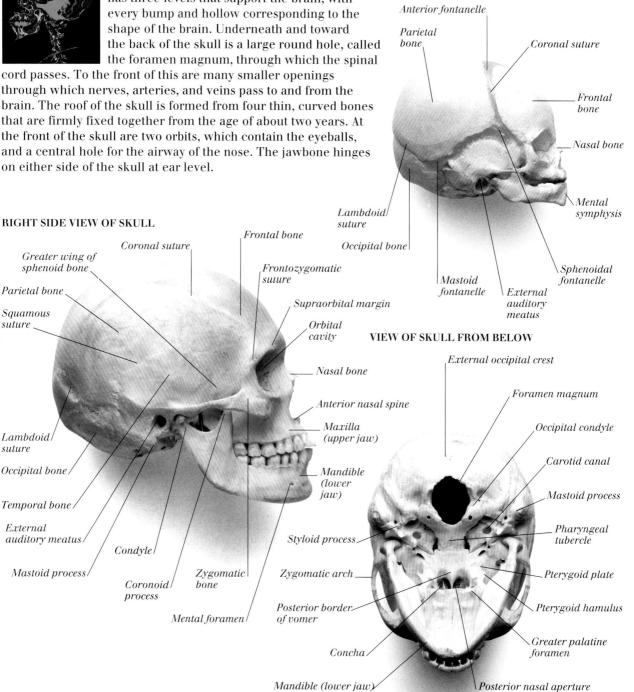

RIGHT SIDE VIEW OF A FETAL SKULL

Anterior fontanelle

Parietal bone

Coronal suture

Frontal bone

Nasal bone

Mental symphysis

Lambdoid suture

Occipital bone

Sphenoidal fontanelle

Mastoid fontanelle

External auditory meatus

RIGHT SIDE VIEW OF SKULL

Greater wing of sphenoid bone

Coronal suture

Frontal bone

Frontozygomatic suture

Parietal bone

Squamous suture

Supraorbital margin

Orbital cavity

Nasal bone

Anterior nasal spine

Maxilla (upper jaw)

Mandible (lower jaw)

Lambdoid suture

Occipital bone

Temporal bone

External auditory meatus

Mastoid process

Condyle

Coronoid process

Zygomatic bone

Mental foramen

VIEW OF SKULL FROM BELOW

External occipital crest

Foramen magnum

Occipital condyle

Carotid canal

Mastoid process

Pharyngeal tubercle

Pterygoid plate

Pterygoid hamulus

Greater palatine foramen

Styloid process

Zygomatic arch

Posterior border of vomer

Concha

Mandible (lower jaw)

Posterior nasal aperture

FRONT VIEW OF SKULL

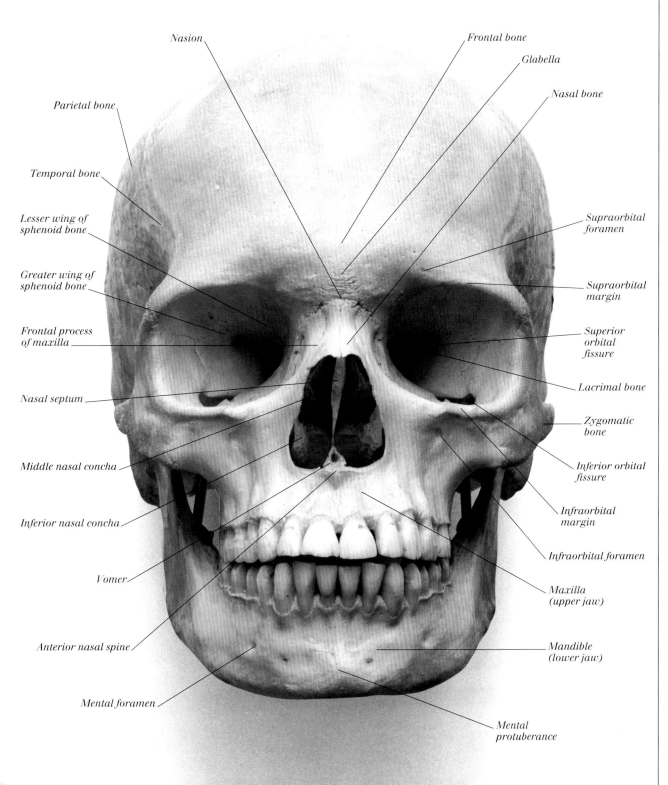

Nasion

Frontal bone

Glabella

Nasal bone

Parietal bone

Temporal bone

Lesser wing of
sphenoid bone

Greater wing of
sphenoid bone

Frontal process
of maxilla

Nasal septum

Middle nasal concha

Inferior nasal concha

Vomer

Anterior nasal spine

Mental foramen

Supraorbital
foramen

Supraorbital
margin

Superior
orbital
fissure

Lacrimal bone

Zygomatic
bone

Inferior orbital
fissure

Infraorbital
margin

Infraorbital foramen

Maxilla
(upper jaw)

Mandible
(lower jaw)

Mental
protuberance

Spine

THE SPINE (OR VERTEBRAL COLUMN) has two main functions: it serves as a protective surrounding for the delicate spinal cord and forms the supporting back bone of the skeleton. The spine consists of 24 separate differently shaped bones (vertebrae) with a curved, triangular bone (the sacrum) at the bottom. The sacrum is made up of fused vertebrae; at its lower end is a small tail-like structure made up of tiny bones collectively called the coccyx. Between each pair of vertebrae is a disc of cartilage that cushions the bones during movement. The top two vertebrae differ in appearance from the others and work as a pair: the first, called the atlas, rotates around a stout vertical peg on the second, the axis. This arrangement allows the skull to move freely up and down, and from side to side.

SPINE DIVIDED INTO VERTEBRAL SECTIONS

FRONT

Cervical vertebrae

Thoracic vertebrae

Lumbar vertebrae

Sacral vertebrae

Coccygeal vertebrae

TYPES OF VERTEBRAE (VIEWED FROM ABOVE)

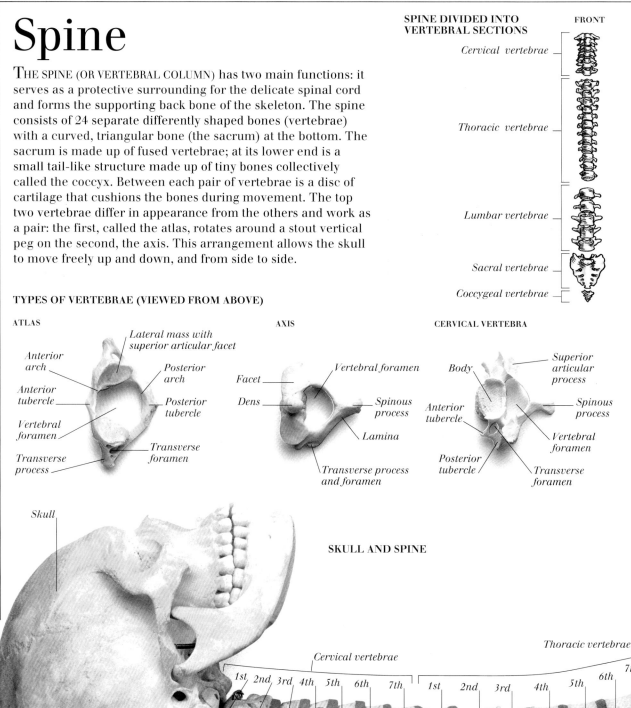

ATLAS

Lateral mass with superior articular facet

Anterior arch

Posterior arch

Anterior tubercle

Posterior tubercle

Vertebral foramen

Transverse process

Transverse foramen

AXIS

Facet

Dens

Vertebral foramen

Spinous process

Lamina

Transverse process and foramen

CERVICAL VERTEBRA

Body

Superior articular process

Anterior tubercle

Spinous process

Vertebral foramen

Posterior tubercle

Transverse foramen

SKULL AND SPINE

Skull

Cervical vertebrae

Thoracic vertebrae

1st 2nd 3rd 4th 5th 6th 7th

1st 2nd 3rd 4th 5th 6th 7th

Atlas

Axis

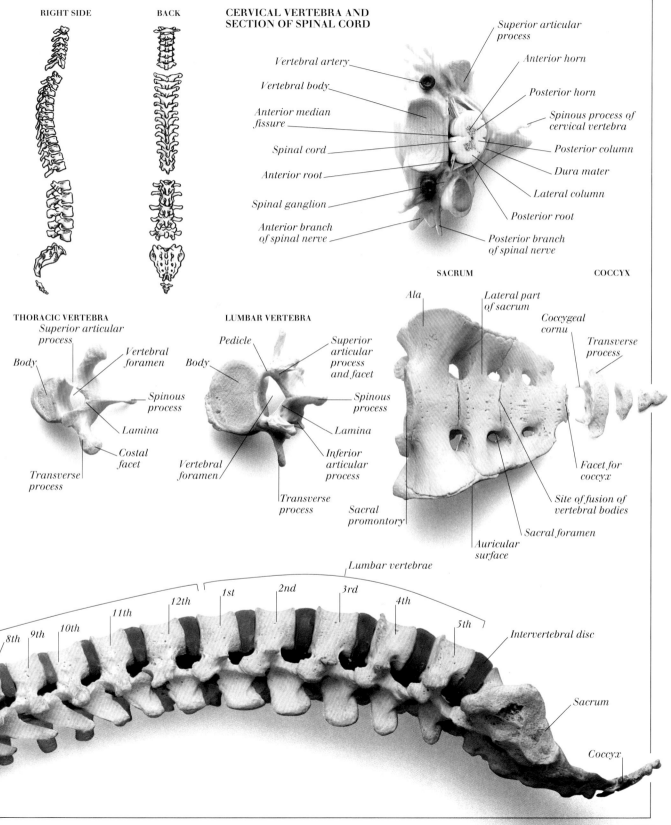

RIGHT SIDE

BACK

CERVICAL VERTEBRA AND SECTION OF SPINAL CORD

Superior articular process

Vertebral artery

Anterior horn

Vertebral body

Posterior horn

Anterior median fissure

Spinous process of cervical vertebra

Spinal cord

Posterior column

Anterior root

Dura mater

Spinal ganglion

Lateral column

Anterior branch of spinal nerve

Posterior root

Posterior branch of spinal nerve

SACRUM

COCCYX

Ala

Lateral part of sacrum

Coccygeal cornu

Transverse process

THORACIC VERTEBRA

Superior articular process

Vertebral foramen

Body

Spinous process

Lamina

Costal facet

Transverse process

LUMBAR VERTEBRA

Pedicle

Superior articular process and facet

Body

Spinous process

Lamina

Inferior articular process

Vertebral foramen

Transverse process

Sacral promontory

Auricular surface

Sacral foramen

Site of fusion of vertebral bodies

Facet for coccyx

Lumbar vertebrae

1st 2nd 3rd 4th 5th

12th

11th

10th

9th

8th

Intervertebral disc

Sacrum

Coccyx

Bones and joints

BONES FORM the body's hard, strong skeletal framework. Each bone has a hard, compact exterior surrounding a spongy, lighter interior. The long bones of the arms and legs, such as the femur (thigh bone), have a central cavity containing bone marrow. Bones are composed chiefly of calcium, phosphorus, and a fibrous substance known as collagen. Bones meet at joints, which are of several different types. For example, the hip is a ball-and-socket joint that allows the femur a wide range of movement, whereas finger joints are simple hinge joints that allow only bending and straightening. Joints are held in place by bands of tissue called ligaments. Movement of joints is facilitated by the smooth hyaline cartilage that covers the bone ends and by the synovial membrane that lines and lubricates the joint.

LIGAMENTS SURROUNDING HIP JOINT

Iliac crest

Iliac fossa

Pubofemoral ligament

Iliac spine

Obturator canal

Greater trochanter of femur

Superior ramus of pubis

Iliofemoral ligament

Body of pubis

Intertrochanteric line

Obturator membrane

Lesser trochanter of femur

Ischial tuberosity

Femur

Ischium

SECTION THROUGH LEFT FEMUR

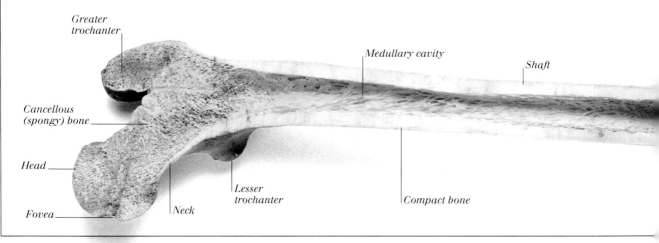

Greater trochanter

Medullary cavity

Shaft

Cancellous (spongy) bone

Head

Lesser trochanter

Compact bone

Fovea

Neck

224

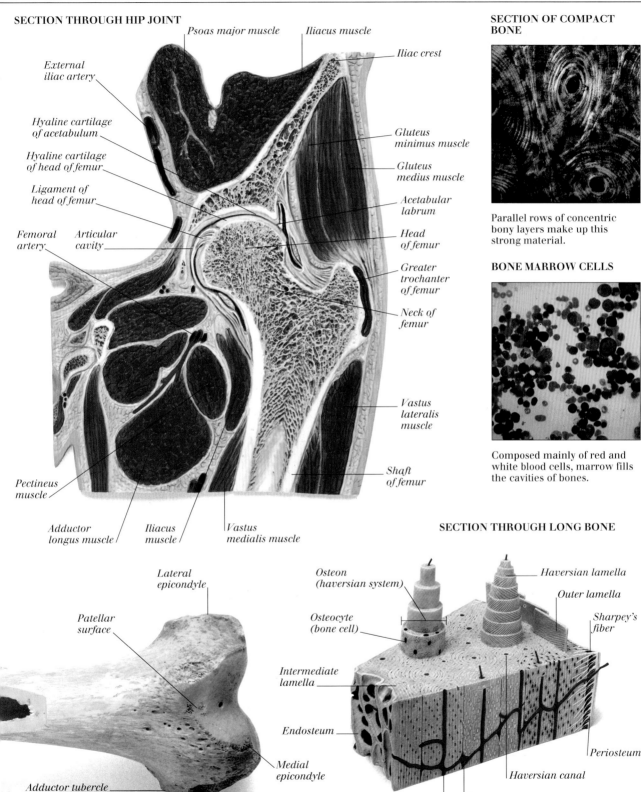

SECTION THROUGH HIP JOINT

Psoas major muscle

Iliacus muscle

Iliac crest

External
iliac artery

Hyaline cartilage
of acetabulum

Hyaline cartilage
of head of femur

Ligament of
head of femur

Femoral
artery

Articular
cavity

Gluteus
minimus muscle

Gluteus
medius muscle

Acetabular
labrum

Head
of femur

Greater
trochanter
of femur

Neck of
femur

Vastus
lateralis
muscle

Shaft
of femur

Pectineus
muscle

Adductor
longus muscle

Iliacus
muscle

Vastus
medialis muscle

SECTION OF COMPACT BONE

Parallel rows of concentric
bony layers make up this
strong material.

BONE MARROW CELLS

Composed mainly of red and
white blood cells, marrow fills
the cavities of bones.

SECTION THROUGH LONG BONE

Lateral
epicondyle

Patellar
surface

Osteon
(haversian system)

Osteocyte
(bone cell)

Intermediate
lamella

Endosteum

Haversian lamella

Outer lamella

Sharpey's
fiber

Periosteum

Adductor tubercle

Medial
epicondyle

Volkmann's vessel

Lacuna

Haversian canal

Muscles 1

THERE ARE THREE MAIN TYPES OF MUSCLE: skeletal
muscle (also called voluntary muscle because it can be
consciously controlled); smooth muscle (also called
involuntary muscle because it is not under voluntary
control); and the specialized muscle tissue of the heart.
Humans have more than 600 skeletal muscles, which
differ in size and shape according to the jobs they do.
Skeletal muscles are attached either directly or indirectly
(via tendons) to bones, and work in opposing pairs (one
muscle in the pair contracts while the other relaxes) to
produce body movements as diverse as walking, threading a
needle, and an array of facial expressions. Smooth muscles
occur in the walls of internal body organs and perform
actions such as forcing food through the intestines,
contracting the uterus (womb) in childbirth, and pumping
blood through the blood vessels.

SOME OTHER MUSCLES IN THE BODY

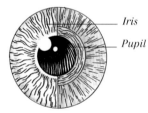

Iris

Pupil

IRIS
The muscle fibers contract and
dilate (expand) to alter pupil size.

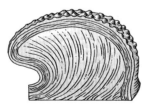

TONGUE
Interlacing layers of muscle
allow great mobility.

ILEUM
Opposing muscle layers
transport semidigested food.

SUPERFICIAL SKELETAL MUSCLES

FRONT VIEW

Brachioradialis

Flexors of forearm

Brachialis

Frontalis

Orbicularis oculi

Temporalis

Sternocleidomastoid

Trapezius

Pectoralis major

Deltoid

Serratus anterior

Biceps brachii

Rectus abdominis

Linea alba

External oblique

Tensor fasciae latae

Iliopsoas

Pectineus

Adductor longus

Rectus femoris

Sartorius

Vastus lateralis

Gracilis

Vastus medialis

Gastrocnemius

Tibialis anterior

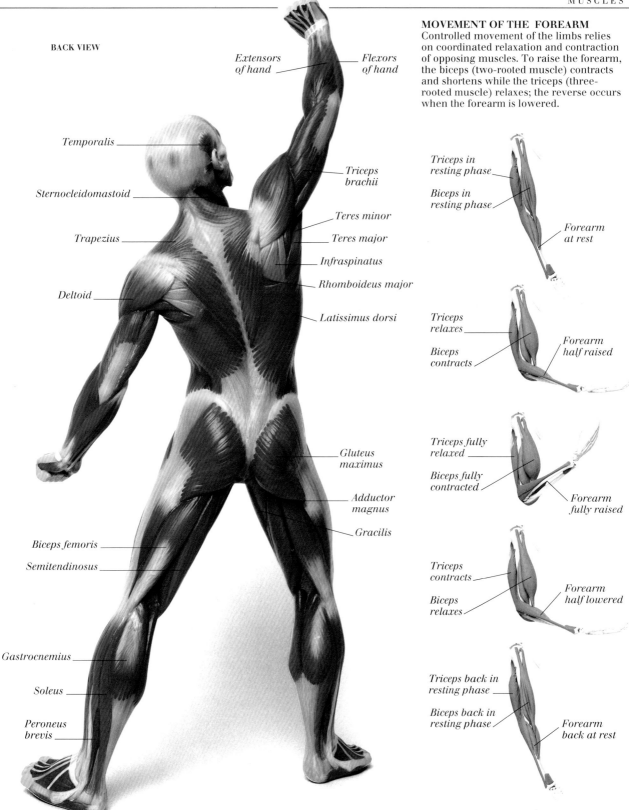

BACK VIEW

Extensors
of hand

Flexors
of hand

Temporalis

Sternocleidomastoid

Trapezius

Deltoid

Triceps
brachii

Teres minor

Teres major

Infraspinatus

Rhomboideus major

Latissimus dorsi

Gluteus
maximus

Adductor
magnus

Gracilis

Biceps femoris

Semitendinosus

Gastrocnemius

Soleus

Peroneus
brevis

MOVEMENT OF THE FOREARM
Controlled movement of the limbs relies
on coordinated relaxation and contraction
of opposing muscles. To raise the forearm,
the biceps (two-rooted muscle) contracts
and shortens while the triceps (three-
rooted muscle) relaxes; the reverse occurs
when the forearm is lowered.

Triceps in
resting phase

Biceps in
resting phase

Forearm
at rest

Triceps
relaxes

Biceps
contracts

Forearm
half raised

Triceps fully
relaxed

Biceps fully
contracted

Forearm
fully raised

Triceps
contracts

Biceps
relaxes

Forearm
half lowered

Triceps back in
resting phase

Biceps back in
resting phase

Forearm
back at rest

Muscles 2

SKELETAL MUSCLE FIBER

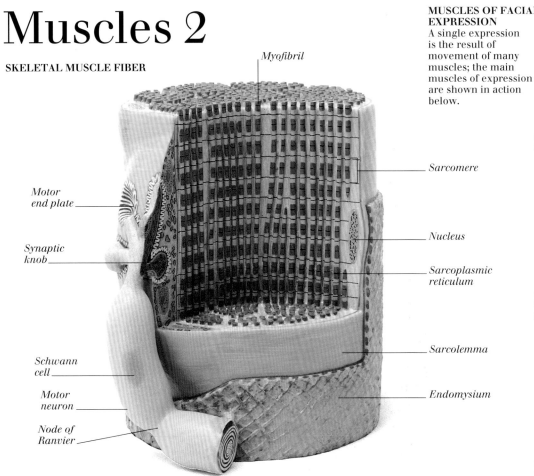

Myofibril

Sarcomere

Motor end plate

Synaptic knob

Nucleus

Sarcoplasmic reticulum

Sarcolemma

Schwann cell

Motor neuron

Node of Ranvier

Endomysium

MUSCLES OF FACIAL EXPRESSION
A single expression is the result of movement of many muscles; the main muscles of expression are shown in action below.

FRONTALIS

CORRUGATOR SUPERCILII

ORBICULARIS ORIS

ZYGOMATICUS MAJOR

DEPRESSOR ANGULI ORIS

TYPES OF MUSCLE

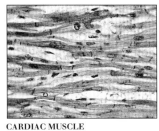

CARDIAC MUSCLE

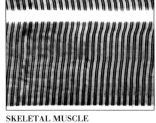

SKELETAL MUSCLE

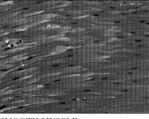

SMOOTH MUSCLE

CONTRACTION OF SKELETAL MUSCLE

RELAXED STATE

CONTRACTED STATE

**MUSCLES OF
HEAD AND NECK**

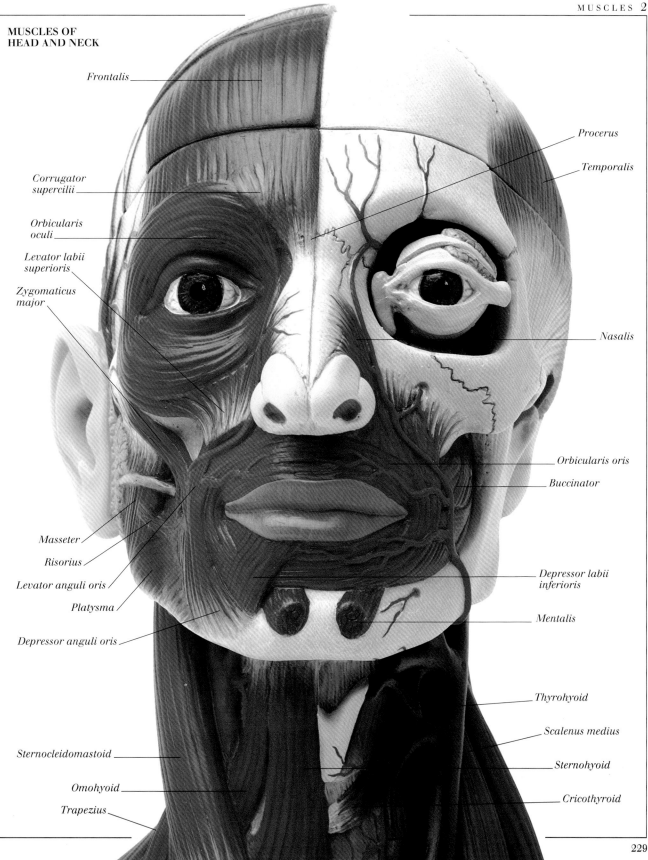

Frontalis

Procerus

Temporalis

Corrugator
supercilii

Orbicularis
oculi

Levator labii
superioris

Zygomaticus
major

Nasalis

Orbicularis oris

Buccinator

Masseter

Risorius

Levator anguli oris

Platysma

Depressor labii
inferioris

Mentalis

Depressor anguli oris

Thyrohyoid

Scalenus medius

Sternocleidomastoid

Sternohyoid

Omohyoid

Cricothyroid

Trapezius

Hands

THE HUMAN HAND is an extremely versatile tool, capable of delicate manipulation as well as powerful gripping actions. The arrangement of its 27 small bones, moved by 37 skeletal muscles that are connected to the bones by tendons, allows a wide range of movements. Our ability to bring the tips of our thumbs and fingers together, combined with the extraordinary sensitivity of our fingertips due to their rich supply of nerve endings, makes our hands uniquely dextrous.

X-RAY OF LEFT HAND OF A YOUNG CHILD

Area of ossification in phalanx

Area of ossification in metacarpal

Area of ossification in wrist

Epiphysis of ulna

Epiphysis of radius

Areas of cartilage in the wrist and at the ends of the finger bones are the sites of growth and have still to ossify.

BONES OF HAND

Ring finger

Middle finger

Index finger

Little finger

Distal phalanx

Middle phalanx

Proximal phalanx

2nd metacarpal

3rd metacarpal

4th metacarpal

5th metacarpal

Hamate

Pisiform

Capitate

Triquetral

Lunate

Ulna

Head

Shaft

Base

Distal phalanx of thumb

Proximal phalanx of thumb

1st metacarpal

Trapezium

Trapezoid

Scaphoid

Radius

230

STRUCTURES UNDERLYING SKIN OF PALM OF HAND

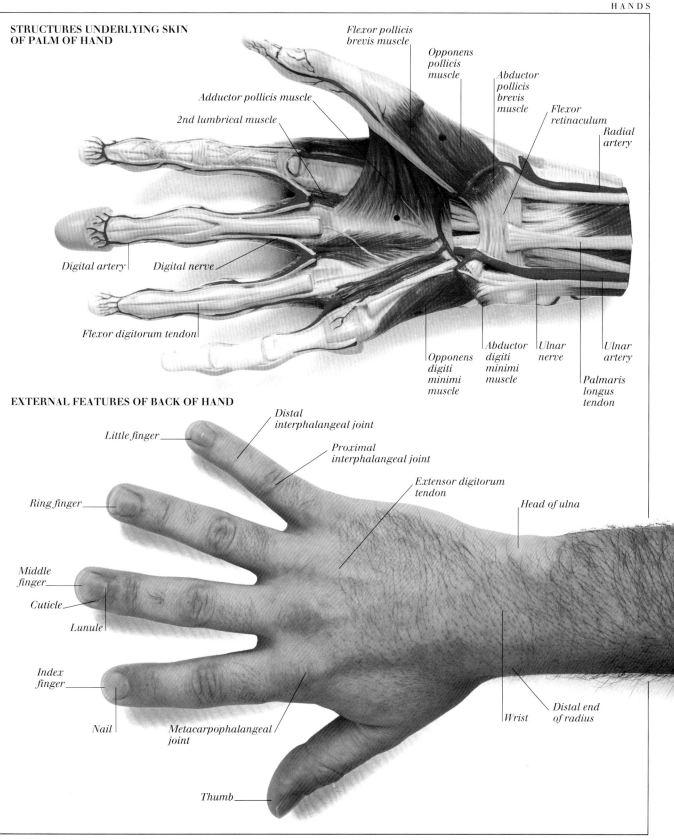

Flexor pollicis brevis muscle

Opponens pollicis muscle

Adductor pollicis brevis muscle

Flexor retinaculum

Radial artery

Adductor pollicis muscle

2nd lumbrical muscle

Digital artery

Digital nerve

Flexor digitorum tendon

Opponens digiti minimi muscle

Abductor digiti minimi muscle

Ulnar nerve

Ulnar artery

Palmaris longus tendon

EXTERNAL FEATURES OF BACK OF HAND

Distal interphalangeal joint

Little finger

Proximal interphalangeal joint

Extensor digitorum tendon

Head of ulna

Ring finger

Middle finger

Cuticle

Lunule

Index finger

Nail

Metacarpophalangeal joint

Wrist

Distal end of radius

Thumb

Feet

THE FEET AND TOES are essential elements in body movement. They bear and propel the weight of the body during walking and running, and also help to maintain balance during changes of body position. Each foot has 26 bones, more than 100 ligaments, and 33 muscles, some of which are attached to the lower leg. The heel pad and the arch of the foot act as shock absorbers, providing a cushion against the jolts that occur with every step.

BONES OF FOOT

LIGAMENTS OF FOOT

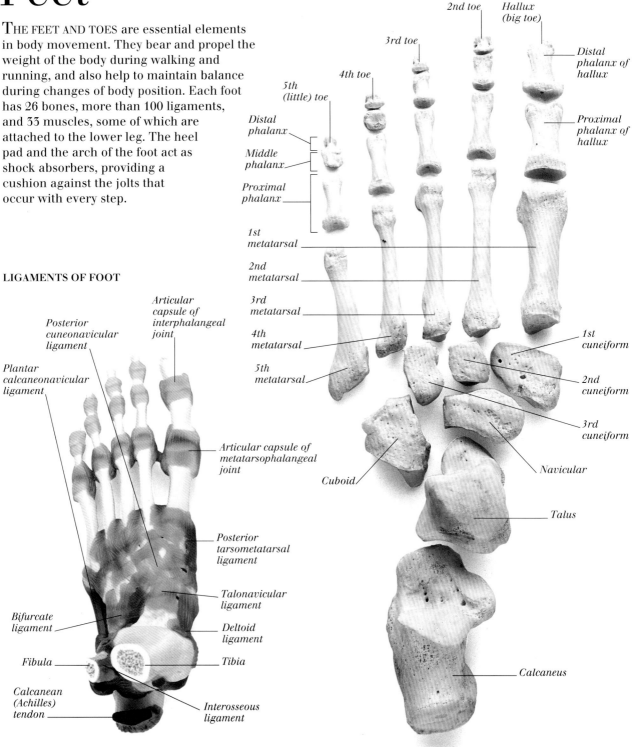

2nd toe

Hallux (big toe)

3rd toe

4th toe

Distal phalanx of hallux

5th (little) toe

Distal phalanx

Proximal phalanx of hallux

Middle phalanx

Proximal phalanx

1st metatarsal

2nd metatarsal

3rd metatarsal

4th metatarsal

5th metatarsal

1st cuneiform

2nd cuneiform

3rd cuneiform

Navicular

Cuboid

Talus

Calcaneus

Articular capsule of interphalangeal joint

Posterior cuneonavicular ligament

Plantar calcaneonavicular ligament

Articular capsule of metatarsophalangeal joint

Posterior tarsometatarsal ligament

Talonavicular ligament

Bifurcate ligament

Deltoid ligament

Fibula

Tibia

Calcanean (Achilles) tendon

Interosseous ligament

STRUCTURES UNDERLYING SKIN OF FOOT

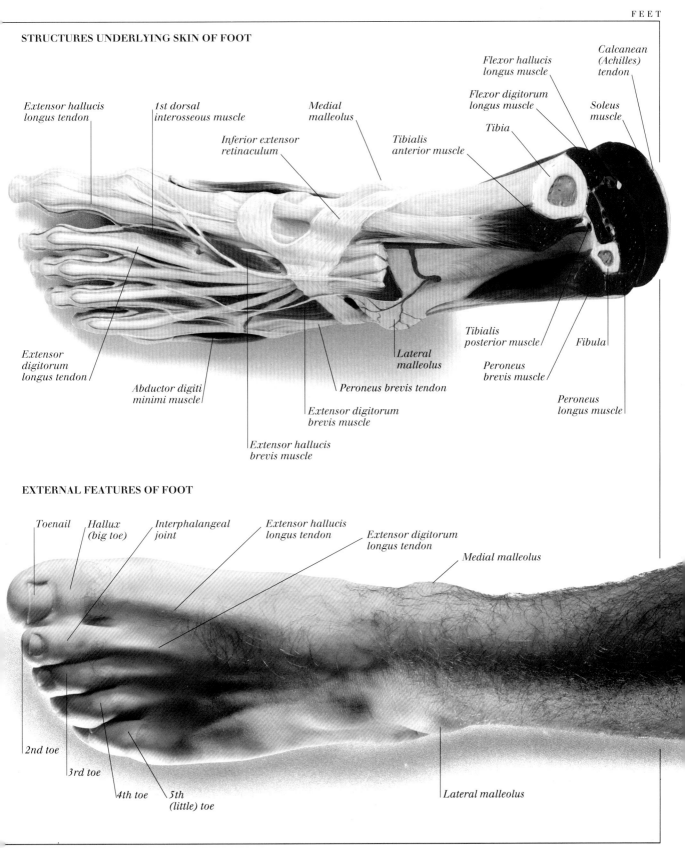

Extensor hallucis longus tendon

1st dorsal interosseous muscle

Medial malleolus

Inferior extensor retinaculum

Tibialis anterior muscle

Flexor hallucis longus muscle

Flexor digitorum longus muscle

Calcanean (Achilles) tendon

Tibia

Soleus muscle

Extensor digitorum longus tendon

Abductor digiti minimi muscle

Extensor hallucis brevis muscle

Extensor digitorum brevis muscle

Peroneus brevis tendon

Lateral malleolus

Tibialis posterior muscle

Peroneus brevis muscle

Fibula

Peroneus longus muscle

EXTERNAL FEATURES OF FOOT

Toenail

Hallux (big toe)

Interphalangeal joint

Extensor hallucis longus tendon

Extensor digitorum longus tendon

Medial malleolus

2nd toe

3rd toe

4th toe

5th (little) toe

Lateral malleolus

233

Skin and hair

SKIN IS THE BODY'S LARGEST ORGAN, a waterproof barrier that protects the internal organs against infection, injury, and harmful sun rays. The skin is also an important sensory organ and helps to control body temperature. The outer layer of the skin, known as the epidermis, is coated with keratin, a tough, horny protein that is also the chief constituent of hair and nails. Dead cells are shed from the skin's surface and are replaced by new cells from the base of the epidermis, the region that also produces the skin pigment, melanin. The dermis contains most of the skin's living structures, and includes nerve endings, blood vessels, elastic fibers, sweat glands that cool the skin, and sebaceous glands that produce oil to keep the skin supple. Beneath the dermis lies the subcutaneous tissue (hypodermis), which is rich in fat and blood vessels. Hair shafts grow from hair follicles situated in the dermis and subcutaneous tissue. Hair grows on every part of the skin apart from the palms of the hands and soles of the feet.

SECTION OF HAIR

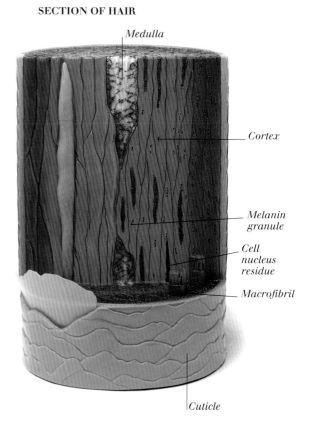

Medulla

Cortex

Melanin granule

Cell nucleus residue

Macrofibril

Cuticle

SECTIONS OF DIFFERENT TYPES OF SKIN

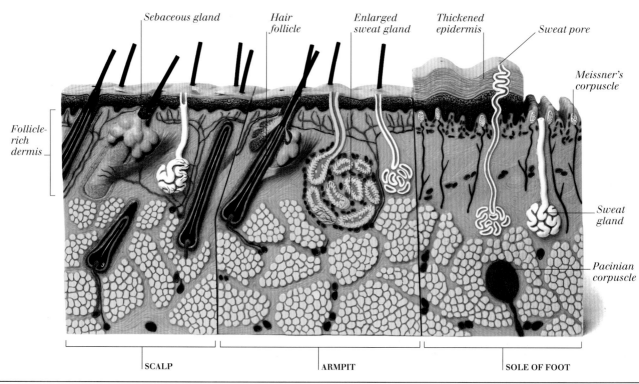

Sebaceous gland

Hair follicle

Enlarged sweat gland

Thickened epidermis

Sweat pore

Meissner's corpuscle

Follicle-rich dermis

Sweat gland

Pacinian corpuscle

SCALP

ARMPIT

SOLE OF FOOT

SECTION OF SKIN

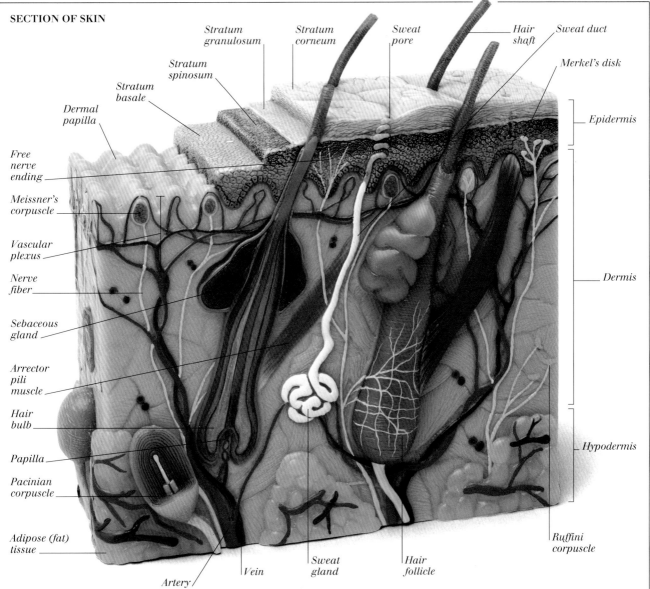

Stratum granulosum

Stratum corneum

Sweat pore

Hair shaft

Sweat duct

Merkel's disk

Stratum spinosum

Stratum basale

Dermal papilla

Free nerve ending

Meissner's corpuscle

Vascular plexus

Nerve fiber

Sebaceous gland

Arrector pili muscle

Hair bulb

Papilla

Pacinian corpuscle

Adipose (fat) tissue

Artery

Vein

Sweat gland

Hair follicle

Epidermis

Dermis

Hypodermis

Ruffini corpuscle

PHOTOMICROGRAPHS OF SKIN AND HAIR

SECTION OF SKIN
The flaky cells at the skin's surface are shed continuously.

SWEAT PORE
This allows loss of fluid as part of temperature control.

SKIN HAIR
Two hairs pushing through the outer layer of skin.

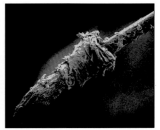

HEAD HAIR
The root and part of the shaft of a hair from the scalp.

Brain

THE BRAIN IS THE MAJOR ORGAN of the central nervous system and the control center for all the body's voluntary and involuntary activities. It is also responsible for the complexities of thought, memory, emotion, and language. In adults, this complex organ is a mere 3 lb (1.4 kg) in weight, containing over 10 thousand million nerve cells. Three distinct regions can easily be seen—the brainstem, the cerebellum, and the large cerebrum. The brainstem controls vital body functions, such as breathing and digestion. The cerebellum's main functions are the maintenance of posture and the coordination of body movements. The cerebrum, which consists of the right and left cerebral hemispheres joined by the corpus callosum, is the site of most conscious and intelligent activities.

MRI SCAN OF TRANSVERSE SECTION THROUGH BRAIN

White matter

Skull

Scalp

Gray matter

Lateral ventricle

Longitudinal fissure

Coronal section

Sagittal section

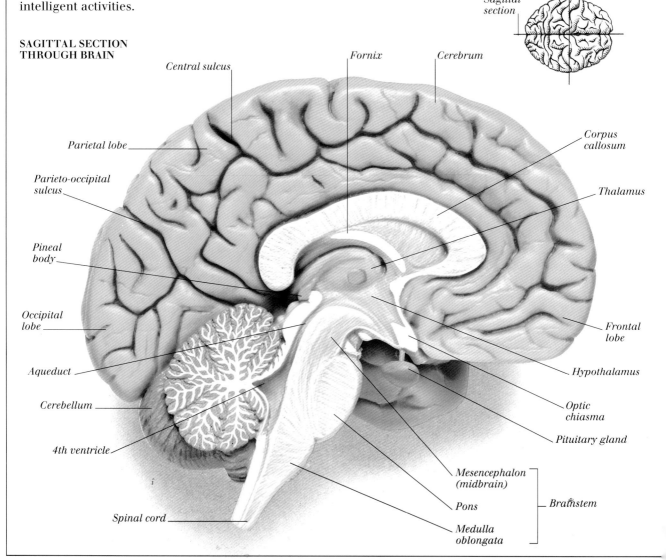

SAGITTAL SECTION THROUGH BRAIN

Central sulcus

Fornix

Cerebrum

Parietal lobe

Parieto-occipital sulcus

Pineal body

Occipital lobe

Aqueduct

Cerebellum

4th ventricle

Spinal cord

Corpus callosum

Thalamus

Frontal lobe

Hypothalamus

Optic chiasma

Pituitary gland

Mesencephalon (midbrain)

Pons

Medulla oblongata

Brainstem

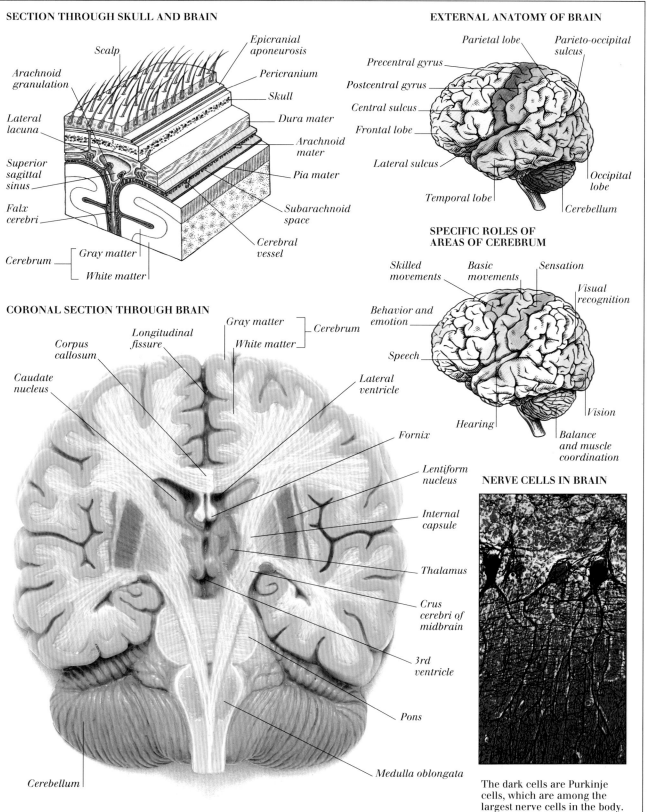

SECTION THROUGH SKULL AND BRAIN

Scalp

Epicranial aponeurosis

Arachnoid granulation

Pericranium

Skull

Lateral lacuna

Dura mater

Superior sagittal sinus

Arachnoid mater

Falx cerebri

Pia mater

Cerebral vessel

Cerebrum — Gray matter / White matter

Subarachnoid space

EXTERNAL ANATOMY OF BRAIN

Parietal lobe

Parieto-occipital sulcus

Precentral gyrus

Postcentral gyrus

Central sulcus

Frontal lobe

Lateral sulcus

Occipital lobe

Temporal lobe

Cerebellum

SPECIFIC ROLES OF AREAS OF CEREBRUM

Skilled movements

Basic movements

Sensation

Visual recognition

Behavior and emotion

Speech

Hearing

Vision

Balance and muscle coordination

CORONAL SECTION THROUGH BRAIN

Corpus callosum

Longitudinal fissure

Gray matter / White matter — Cerebrum

Caudate nucleus

Lateral ventricle

Fornix

Lentiform nucleus

Internal capsule

Thalamus

Crus cerebri of midbrain

3rd ventricle

Pons

Medulla oblongata

Cerebellum

NERVE CELLS IN BRAIN

The dark cells are Purkinje cells, which are among the largest nerve cells in the body.

257

Nervous system

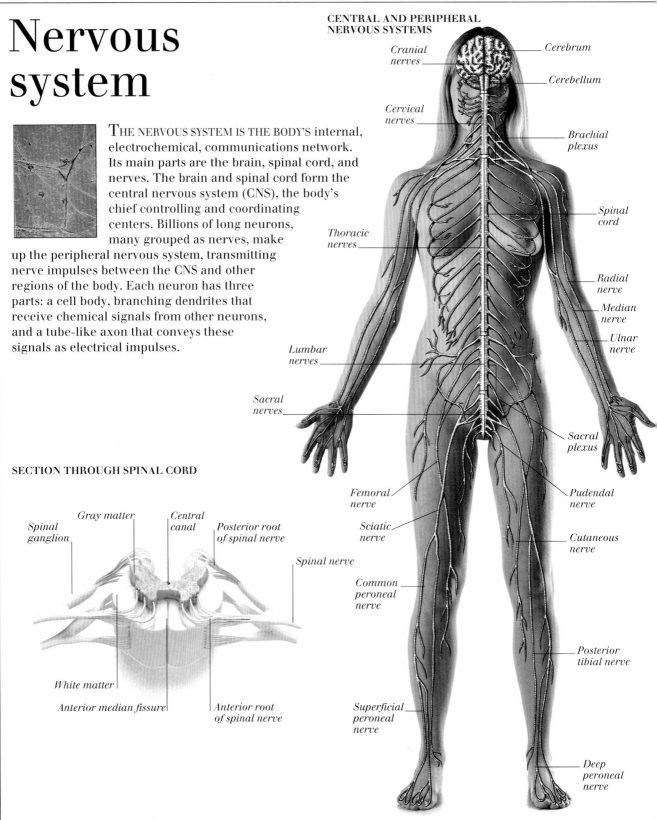

THE NERVOUS SYSTEM IS THE BODY'S internal, electrochemical, communications network. Its main parts are the brain, spinal cord, and nerves. The brain and spinal cord form the central nervous system (CNS), the body's chief controlling and coordinating centers. Billions of long neurons, many grouped as nerves, make up the peripheral nervous system, transmitting nerve impulses between the CNS and other regions of the body. Each neuron has three parts: a cell body, branching dendrites that receive chemical signals from other neurons, and a tube-like axon that conveys these signals as electrical impulses.

CENTRAL AND PERIPHERAL NERVOUS SYSTEMS

Cranial nerves

Cerebrum

Cerebellum

Cervical nerves

Brachial plexus

Spinal cord

Thoracic nerves

Radial nerve

Median nerve

Ulnar nerve

Lumbar nerves

Sacral nerves

Sacral plexus

SECTION THROUGH SPINAL CORD

Femoral nerve

Pudendal nerve

Sciatic nerve

Cutaneous nerve

Common peroneal nerve

Spinal ganglion

Gray matter

Central canal

Posterior root of spinal nerve

Spinal nerve

Posterior tibial nerve

White matter

Anterior median fissure

Anterior root of spinal nerve

Superficial peroneal nerve

Deep peroneal nerve

STRUCTURE OF A MOTOR NEURON

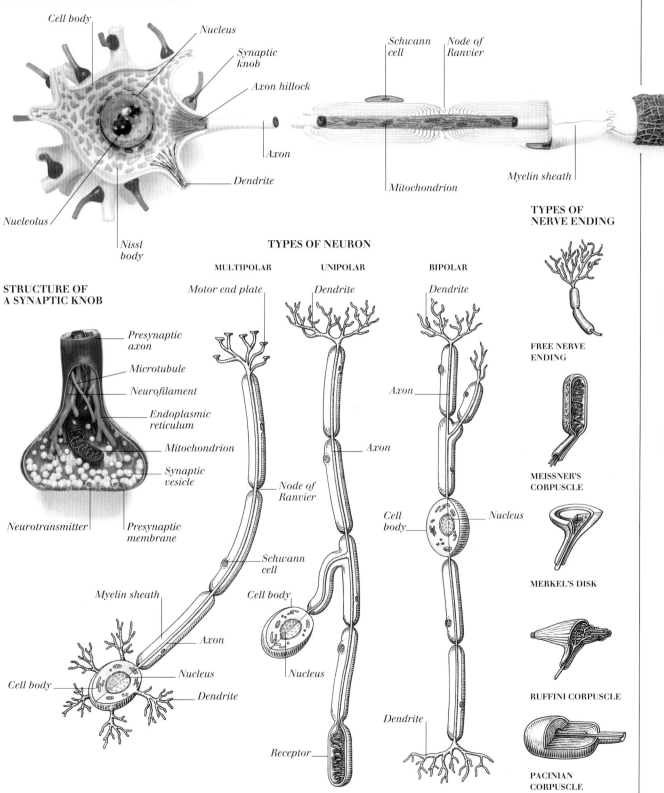

Cell body

Nucleus

Synaptic knob

Axon hillock

Axon

Dendrite

Nucleolus

Nissl body

Schwann cell

Node of Ranvier

Mitochondrion

Myelin sheath

STRUCTURE OF A SYNAPTIC KNOB

Presynaptic axon

Microtubule

Neurofilament

Endoplasmic reticulum

Mitochondrion

Synaptic vesicle

Neurotransmitter

Presynaptic membrane

Myelin sheath

Axon

Cell body

Nucleus

Dendrite

TYPES OF NEURON

MULTIPOLAR

Motor end plate

Node of Ranvier

Schwann cell

Cell body

Nucleus

UNIPOLAR

Dendrite

Axon

Cell body

Nucleus

Receptor

BIPOLAR

Dendrite

Axon

Cell body

Nucleus

Dendrite

TYPES OF NERVE ENDING

FREE NERVE ENDING

MEISSNER'S CORPUSCLE

MERKEL'S DISK

RUFFINI CORPUSCLE

PACINIAN CORPUSCLE

239

Eye

THE EYE IS THE ORGAN OF SIGHT. The two eyeballs, protected within bony sockets called orbits and on the outside by the eyelids, eyebrows, and tear film, are directly connected to the brain by the optic nerves. Each eye is moved by six muscles, which are attached around the eyeball. Light rays entering the eye through the pupil are focused by the cornea and lens to form an image on the retina. The retina contains millions of light-sensitive cells, called rods and cones, which convert the image into a pattern of nerve impulses. These impulses are transmitted along the optic nerve to the brain. Information from the two optic nerves is processed in the brain to produce a single coordinated image.

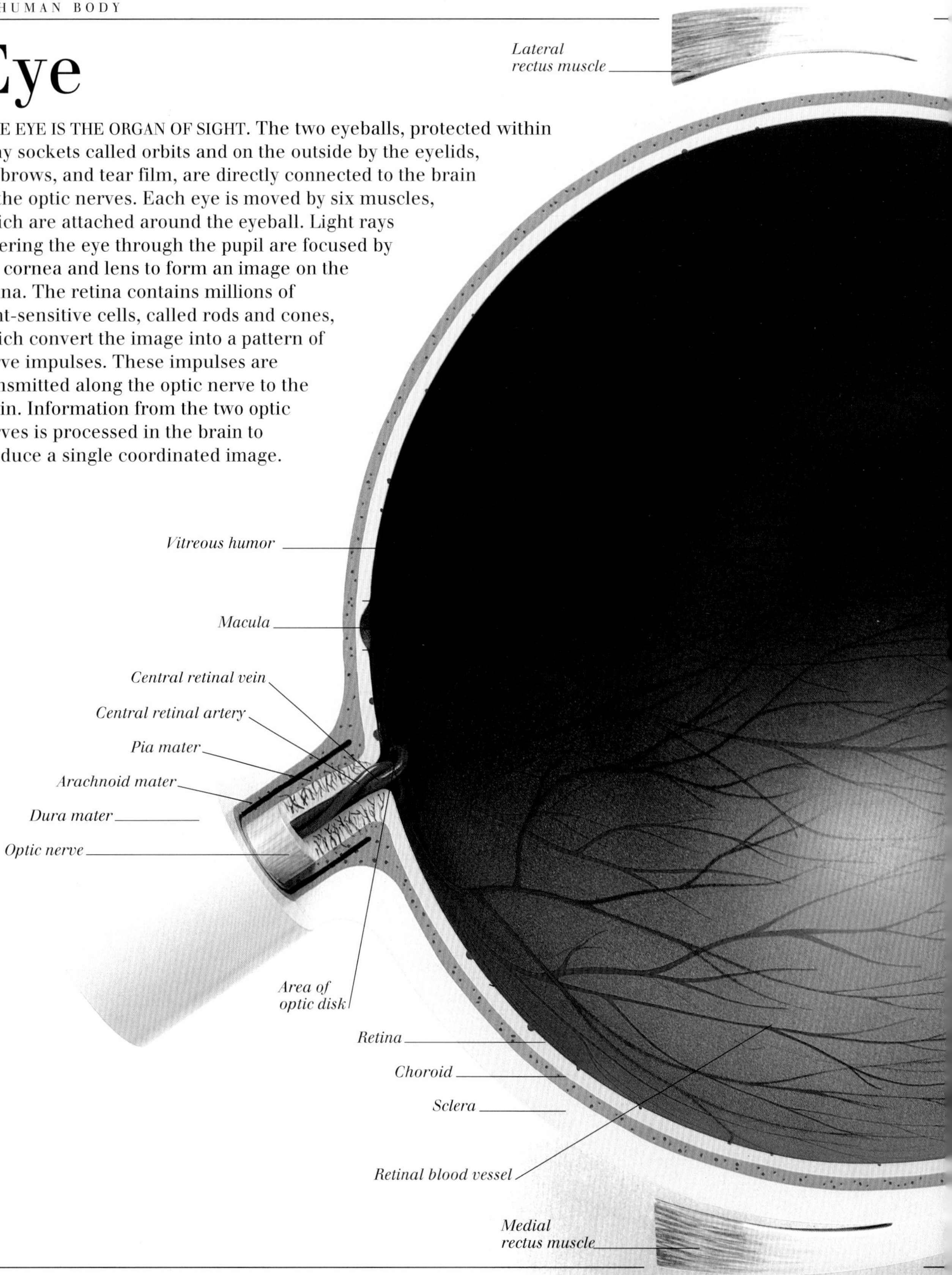

Lateral rectus muscle

Vitreous humor

Macula

Central retinal vein

Central retinal artery

Pia mater

Arachnoid mater

Dura mater

Optic nerve

Area of optic disk

Retina

Choroid

Sclera

Retinal blood vessel

Medial rectus muscle

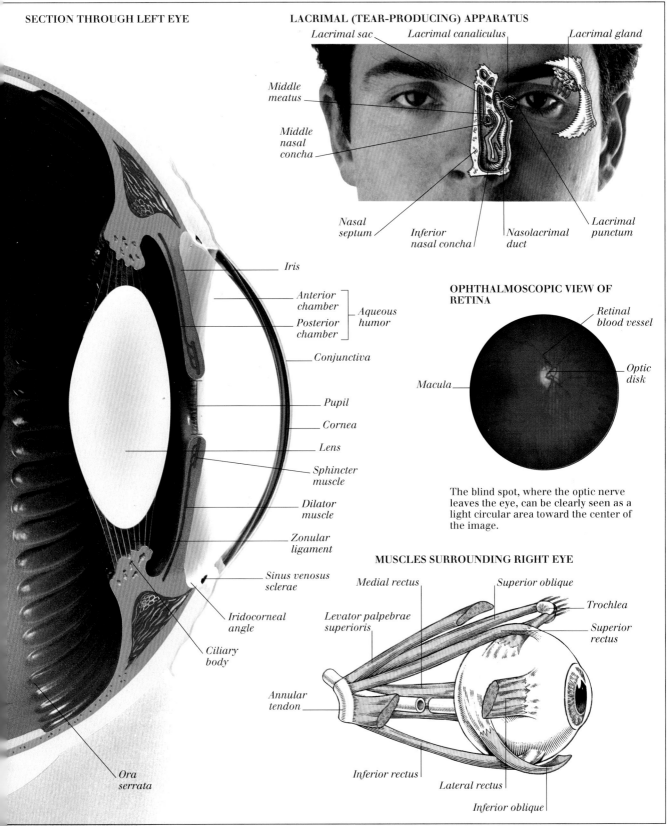

SECTION THROUGH LEFT EYE

LACRIMAL (TEAR-PRODUCING) APPARATUS

Lacrimal sac

Lacrimal canaliculus

Lacrimal gland

Middle meatus

Middle nasal concha

Nasal septum

Inferior nasal concha

Nasolacrimal duct

Lacrimal punctum

Iris

Anterior chamber

Posterior chamber

Aqueous humor

Conjunctiva

Pupil

Cornea

Lens

Sphincter muscle

Dilator muscle

Zonular ligament

Sinus venosus sclerae

Iridocorneal angle

Ciliary body

Ora serrata

OPHTHALMOSCOPIC VIEW OF RETINA

Retinal blood vessel

Optic disk

Macula

The blind spot, where the optic nerve leaves the eye, can be clearly seen as a light circular area toward the center of the image.

MUSCLES SURROUNDING RIGHT EYE

Medial rectus

Superior oblique

Trochlea

Levator palpebrae superioris

Superior rectus

Annular tendon

Inferior rectus

Lateral rectus

Inferior oblique

Ear

THE EAR IS THE ORGAN OF HEARING AND BALANCE. The outer ear consists of a flap called the auricle or pinna and the auditory canal. The main functional parts—the middle and inner ears—are enclosed within the skull. The middle ear consists of three tiny bones, known as auditory ossicles, and the eustachian tube, which links the ear to the back of the nose. The inner ear consists of the spiral-shaped cochlea, and also the semicircular canals and the vestibule, which are the organs of balance. Sound waves entering the ear travel through the auditory canal to the tympanic membrane (eardrum), where they are converted to vibrations that are transmitted via the ossicles to the cochlea. Here, the vibrations are converted by millions of microscopic hairs into electrical nerve signals to be interpreted by the brain.

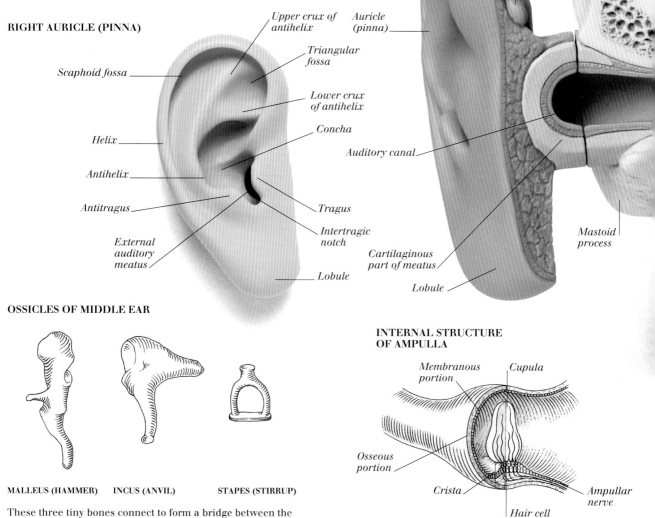

RIGHT AURICLE (PINNA)

- Upper crux of antihelix
- Auricle (pinna)
- Triangular fossa
- Scaphoid fossa
- Lower crux of antihelix
- Helix
- Concha
- Antihelix
- Auditory canal
- Antitragus
- Tragus
- Intertragic notch
- External auditory meatus
- Cartilaginous part of meatus
- Lobule
- Temporal bone
- Cartilage of auricle
- Mastoid process
- Lobule

OSSICLES OF MIDDLE EAR

MALLEUS (HAMMER)   INCUS (ANVIL)   STAPES (STIRRUP)

These three tiny bones connect to form a bridge between the tympanic membrane and the oval window. With a system of membranes they convey sound vibrations to the inner ear.

INTERNAL STRUCTURE OF AMPULLA

- Membranous portion
- Cupula
- Osseous portion
- Crista
- Hair cell of crista
- Ampullar nerve

242

LABYRINTH

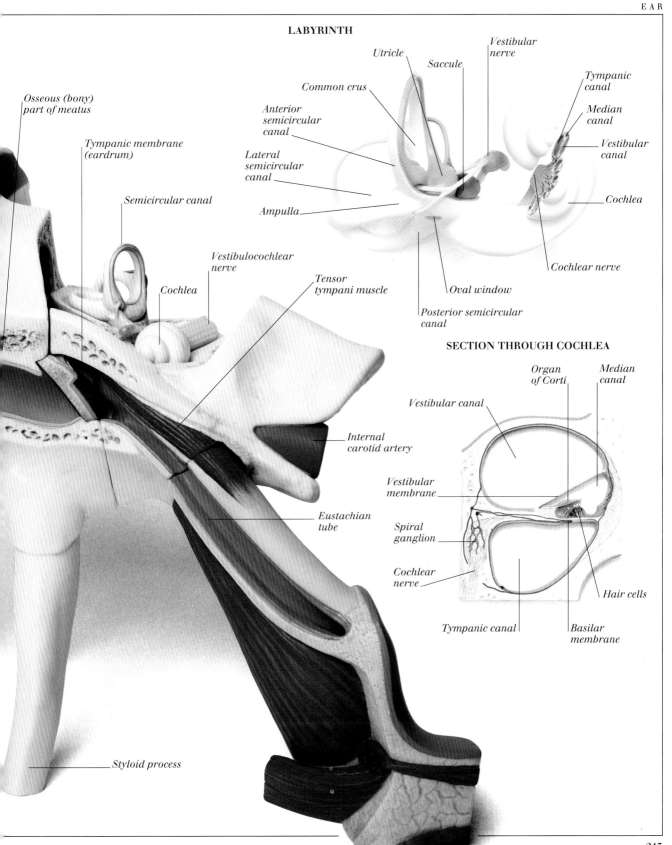

Osseous (bony) part of meatus

Tympanic membrane (eardrum)

Semicircular canal

Cochlea

Vestibulocochlear nerve

Tensor tympani muscle

Utricle

Saccule

Vestibular nerve

Common crus

Tympanic canal

Anterior semicircular canal

Median canal

Lateral semicircular canal

Vestibular canal

Ampulla

Cochlea

Cochlear nerve

Oval window

Posterior semicircular canal

Internal carotid artery

Eustachian tube

Styloid process

SECTION THROUGH COCHLEA

Organ of Corti

Median canal

Vestibular canal

Vestibular membrane

Spiral ganglion

Cochlear nerve

Hair cells

Tympanic canal

Basilar membrane

Nose, mouth, and throat

WITH EVERY BREATH, air passes through the nasal cavity down the pharynx (throat), larynx ("voice box"), and trachea (windpipe) to the lungs. The nasal cavity warms and moistens air, and the tiny layers in its lining protect the airway against damage by foreign bodies. During swallowing, the tongue moves up and back, the larynx rises, the epiglottis closes off the entrance to the trachea, and the soft palate separates the nasal cavity from the pharynx. Saliva, secreted from three pairs of salivary glands, lubricates food to make swallowing easier; it also begins the chemical breakdown of food, and helps to produce taste. The senses of taste and smell are closely linked. Both depend on the detection of dissolved molecules by sensory receptors in the olfactory nerve endings of the nose and in the taste buds of the tongue.

STRUCTURE OF TONGUE

Median glossoepiglottic fold

Epiglottis

Palatine tonsil

Sulcus terminalis

Palatoglossal arch

Foramen cecum

Vallate papilla

Median sulcus

Foliate papilla

Fungiform papilla

Filiform papilla

Apex

TASTE AREAS ON TONGUE

Bitter

Sour

Salt

Sweet

STRUCTURES SURROUNDING PHARYNX

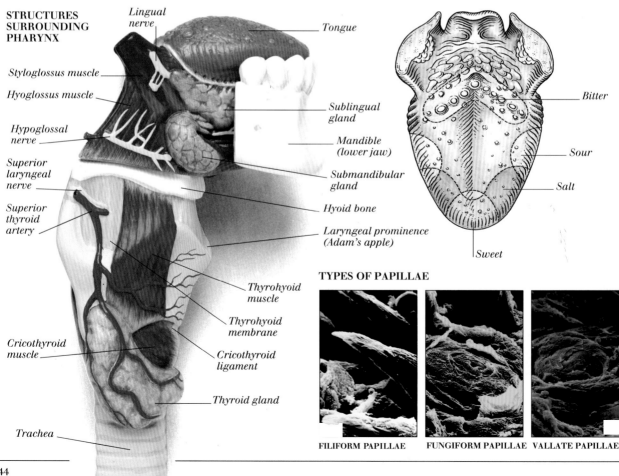

Lingual nerve

Tongue

Styloglossus muscle

Hyoglossus muscle

Sublingual gland

Hypoglossal nerve

Mandible (lower jaw)

Superior laryngeal nerve

Submandibular gland

Superior thyroid artery

Hyoid bone

Laryngeal prominence (Adam's apple)

Thyrohyoid muscle

Thyrohyoid membrane

Cricothyroid muscle

Cricothyroid ligament

Thyroid gland

Trachea

TYPES OF PAPILLAE

FILIFORM PAPILLAE   **FUNGIFORM PAPILLAE**   **VALLATE PAPILLAE**

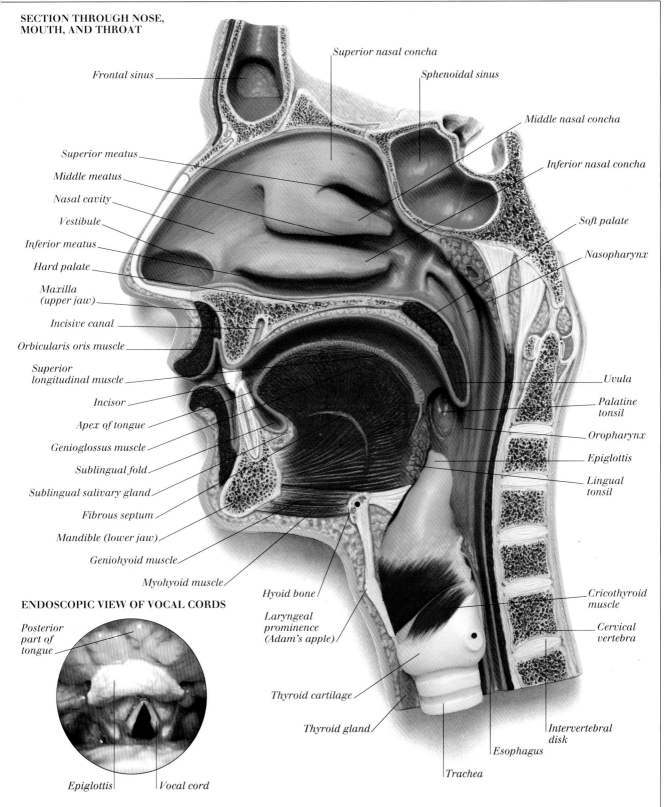

SECTION THROUGH NOSE, MOUTH, AND THROAT

Frontal sinus

Superior nasal concha

Sphenoidal sinus

Middle nasal concha

Inferior nasal concha

Superior meatus

Middle meatus

Nasal cavity

Vestibule

Inferior meatus

Hard palate

Soft palate

Nasopharynx

Maxilla (upper jaw)

Incisive canal

Orbicularis oris muscle

Superior longitudinal muscle

Incisor

Apex of tongue

Genioglossus muscle

Sublingual fold

Sublingual salivary gland

Fibrous septum

Mandible (lower jaw)

Geniohyoid muscle

Myohyoid muscle

Uvula

Palatine tonsil

Oropharynx

Epiglottis

Lingual tonsil

Hyoid bone

Laryngeal prominence (Adam's apple)

Thyroid cartilage

Thyroid gland

Cricothyroid muscle

Cervical vertebra

Intervertebral disk

Esophagus

Trachea

ENDOSCOPIC VIEW OF VOCAL CORDS

Posterior part of tongue

Epiglottis

Vocal cord

Teeth

THE 20 PRIMARY TEETH (also called deciduous or milk teeth) usually begin to erupt when a baby is about six months old. They start to be replaced by the permanent teeth when the child is about six years old. By the age of 20, most adults have a full set of 32 teeth although the third molars (commonly called wisdom teeth) may never erupt. While teeth help people to speak clearly and give shape to the face, their main function is the chewing of food. Incisors and canines shear and tear the food into pieces; premolars and molars crush and grind it further. Although tooth enamel is the hardest substance in the body, it tends to be eroded and destroyed by acid produced in the mouth during the breakdown of food.

DEVELOPMENT OF TEETH IN A FETUS

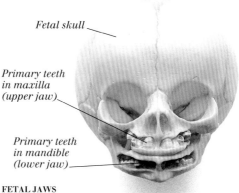

Fetal skull

Primary teeth in maxilla (upper jaw)

Primary teeth in mandible (lower jaw)

FETAL JAWS
By the sixth week of embryonic development areas of thickening occur in each jaw; these areas give rise to tooth buds. By the time the fetus is six months old, enamel has formed on the tooth buds.

DEVELOPMENT OF JAW AND TEETH

Maxilla (upper jaw)

Mandible (lower jaw)

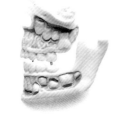

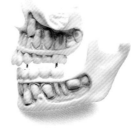

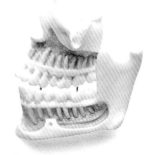

A NEWBORN BABY'S JAWS
The primary teeth can be seen developing in the jawbones; they begin to erupt around the age of six months.

A FIVE-YEAR-OLD CHILD'S TEETH
There is a full set of 20 erupted primary teeth; the permanent teeth can be seen developing in the upper and lower jaws.

A NINE-YEAR-OLD CHILD'S TEETH
Most of the teeth are primary teeth but the permanent incisors and first molars have now emerged.

AN ADULT'S TEETH
By the age of 20, the full set of 32 permanent teeth (including the wisdom teeth) should be in position.

THE PERMANENT TEETH

Molars | *Premolars* | *Canines* | *Incisors* | *Canines* | *Premolars* | *Molars*

UPPER

LOWER

3rd (wisdom) | 2nd | 1st | 2nd | 1st | Lateral | Central | Lateral | 1st | 2nd | 1st | 2nd | 3rd (wisdom)

STRUCTURE OF A TOOTH

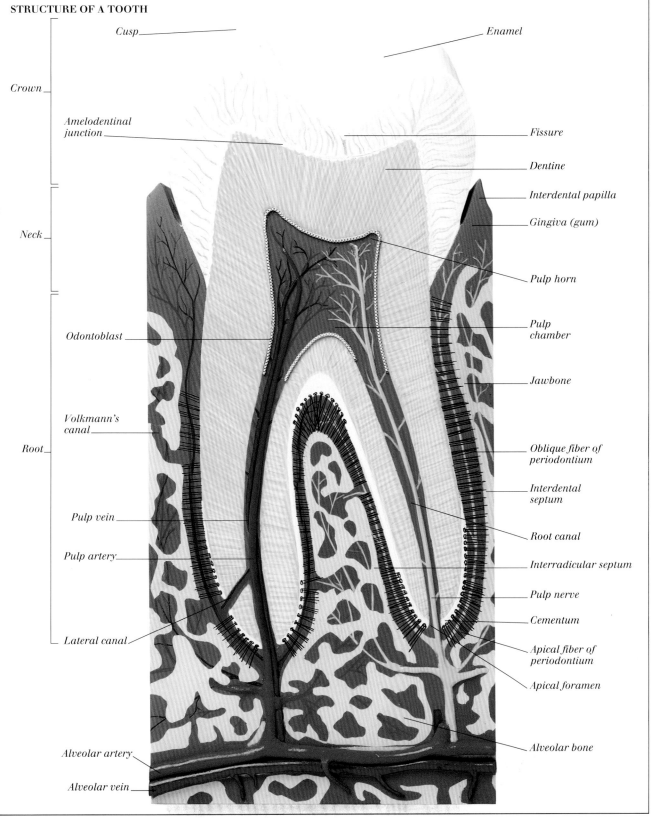

Cusp

Enamel

Crown

Ameledentinal junction

Fissure

Dentine

Interdental papilla

Neck

Gingiva (gum)

Pulp horn

Odontoblast

Pulp chamber

Jawbone

Volkmann's canal

Oblique fiber of periodontium

Root

Interdental septum

Pulp vein

Root canal

Pulp artery

Interradicular septum

Pulp nerve

Cementum

Lateral canal

Apical fiber of periodontium

Apical foramen

Alveolar artery

Alveolar bone

Alveolar vein

Digestive system

THE DIGESTIVE SYSTEM BREAKS DOWN FOOD into particles so tiny that blood can take nourishment to all parts of the body. The system's main part is a 30-foot (9 m) tube from mouth to rectum; muscles in this alimentary canal force food along. Chewed food first travels through the esophagus to the stomach, which churns and liquidizes food before it passes through the duodenum, jejunum, and ileum—the three parts of the long, convoluted small intestine. Here, digestive juices from the gallbladder and pancreas break down food particles; many filter out into the blood through tiny fingerlike villi that line the small intestine's inner wall. Undigested food in the colon forms feces that leave the body through the anus.

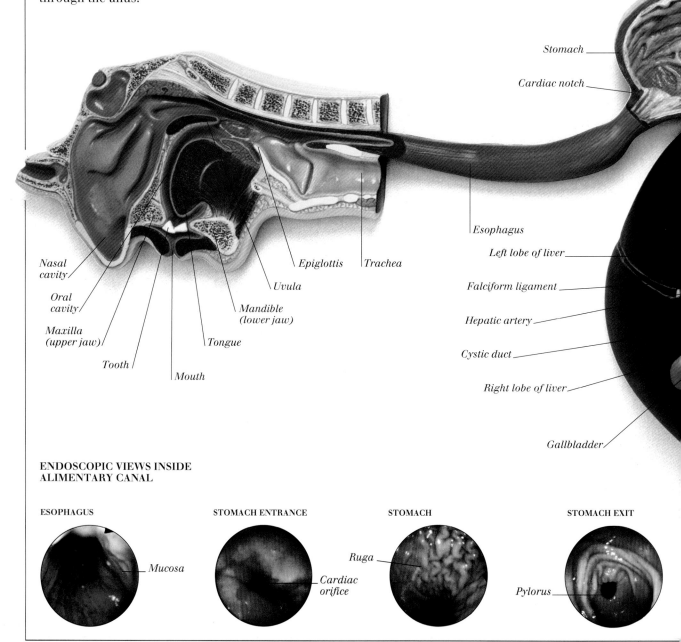

Stomach

Cardiac notch

Esophagus

Left lobe of liver

Falciform ligament

Hepatic artery

Cystic duct

Right lobe of liver

Gallbladder

Nasal cavity

Oral cavity

Maxilla (upper jaw)

Tooth

Mouth

Tongue

Mandible (lower jaw)

Uvula

Epiglottis

Trachea

ENDOSCOPIC VIEWS INSIDE ALIMENTARY CANAL

ESOPHAGUS

Mucosa

STOMACH ENTRANCE

Cardiac orifice

STOMACH

Ruga

STOMACH EXIT

Pylorus

ALIMENTARY CANAL

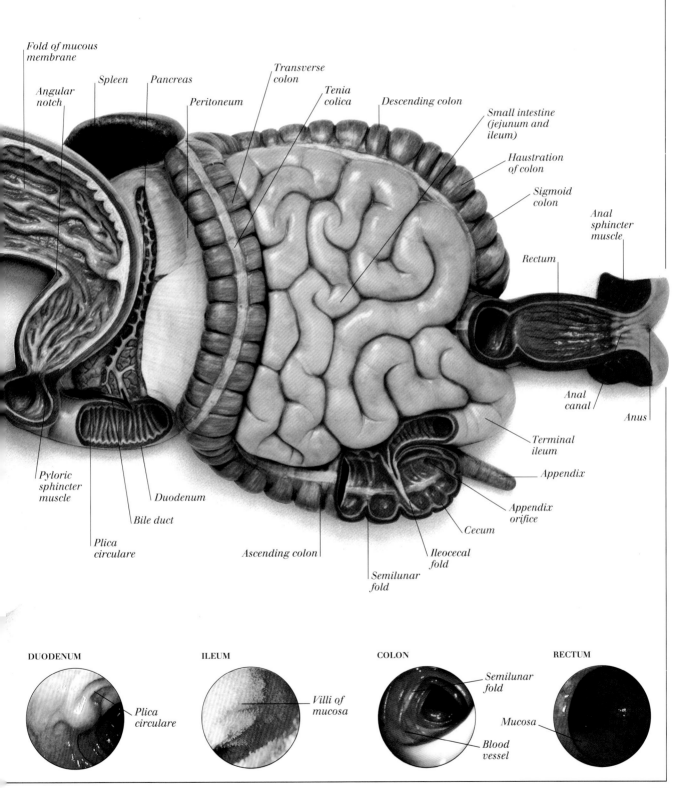

Fold of mucous membrane

Angular notch

Spleen

Pancreas

Peritoneum

Transverse colon

Tenia colica

Descending colon

Small intestine (jejunum and ileum)

Haustration of colon

Sigmoid colon

Anal sphincter muscle

Rectum

Anal canal

Anus

Terminal ileum

Appendix

Appendix orifice

Cecum

Ileocecal fold

Semilunar fold

Ascending colon

Pyloric sphincter muscle

Bile duct

Duodenum

Plica circulare

DUODENUM

Plica circulare

ILEUM

Villi of mucosa

COLON

Semilunar fold

Blood vessel

RECTUM

Mucosa

Heart

THE HEART IS A HOLLOW MUSCLE in the middle of the chest that pumps blood around the body, supplying cells with oxygen and nutrients. A muscular wall, called the septum, divides the heart lengthwise into left and right sides. A valve divides each side into two chambers: an upper atrium and a lower ventricle. When the heart muscle contracts, it squeezes blood through the atria and then through the ventricles. Oxygenated blood from the lungs flows from the pulmonary veins into the left atrium, through the left ventricle, and then out via the aorta to all parts of the body. Deoxygenated blood returning from the body flows from the vena cava into the right atrium, through the right ventricle, and then out via the pulmonary artery to the lungs for reoxygenation. At rest the heart beats between 60 and 80 times a minute; during exercise or at times of stress or excitement the rate may increase to 200 beats a minute.

ARTERIES AND VEINS SURROUNDING HEART

Aorta

Left coronary artery

Cardiac vein

Right coronary artery

Coronary sinus

Main branch of left coronary artery

SECTION THROUGH HEART WALL

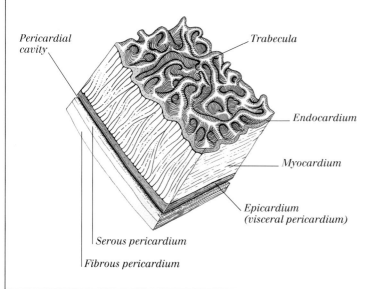

Pericardial cavity

Trabecula

Endocardium

Myocardium

Epicardium (visceral pericardium)

Serous pericardium

Fibrous pericardium

HEARTBEAT SEQUENCE

ATRIAL DIASTOLE

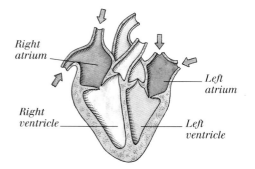

Right atrium

Left atrium

Right ventricle

Left ventricle

Deoxygenated blood enters the right atrium while the left atrium receives oxygenated blood.

STRUCTURE OF HEART

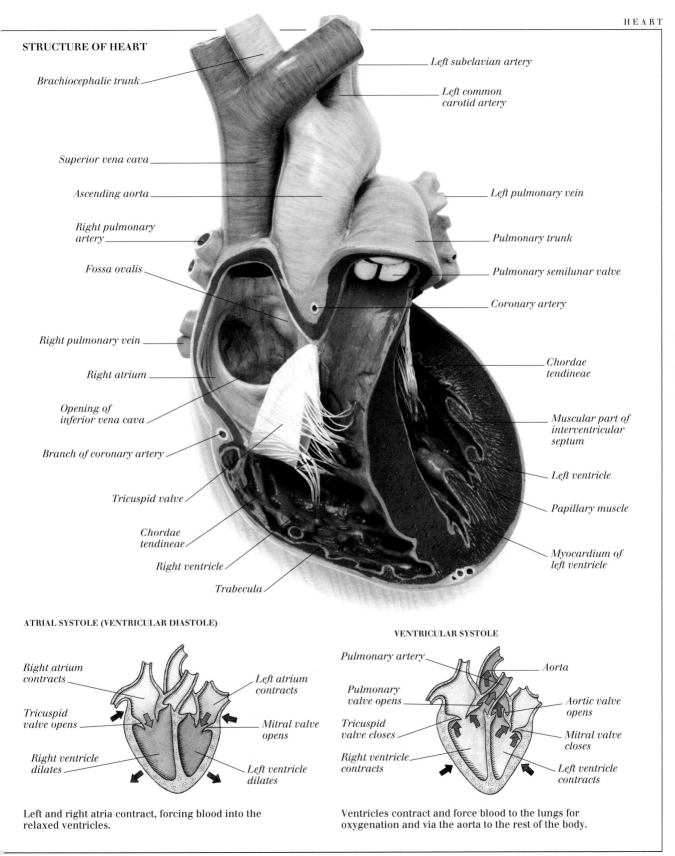

Brachiocephalic trunk

Left subclavian artery

Left common carotid artery

Superior vena cava

Ascending aorta

Left pulmonary vein

Right pulmonary artery

Fossa ovalis

Pulmonary trunk

Pulmonary semilunar valve

Coronary artery

Right pulmonary vein

Right atrium

Chordae tendineae

Opening of inferior vena cava

Muscular part of interventricular septum

Branch of coronary artery

Left ventricle

Tricuspid valve

Papillary muscle

Chordae tendineae

Right ventricle

Myocardium of left ventricle

Trabecula

ATRIAL SYSTOLE (VENTRICULAR DIASTOLE)

Right atrium contracts

Left atrium contracts

Tricuspid valve opens

Mitral valve opens

Right ventricle dilates

Left ventricle dilates

Left and right atria contract, forcing blood into the relaxed ventricles.

VENTRICULAR SYSTOLE

Pulmonary artery

Aorta

Pulmonary valve opens

Aortic valve opens

Tricuspid valve closes

Mitral valve closes

Right ventricle contracts

Left ventricle contracts

Ventricles contract and force blood to the lungs for oxygenation and via the aorta to the rest of the body.

Circulatory system

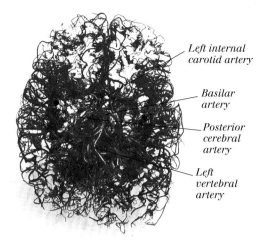

ARTERIAL SYSTEM OF BRAIN

Left internal carotid artery

Basilar artery

Posterior cerebral artery

Left vertebral artery

THE CIRCULATORY SYSTEM consists of the heart and blood vessels, which together maintain a continuous flow of blood around the body. The heart pumps oxygen-rich blood from the lungs to all parts of the body through a network of tubes called arteries, and smaller branches called arterioles. Blood returns to the heart via small vessels called venules, which lead in turn into larger tubes called veins. Arterioles and venules are linked by a network of tiny vessels called capillaries, where the exchange of oxygen and carbon dioxide between blood and body cells takes place. Blood has four main components: red blood cells, white blood cells, platelets, and liquid plasma.

CIRCULATORY SYSTEM OF HEART AND LUNGS

Superior vena cava

Aorta

CIRCULATORY SYSTEM OF LIVER

Inferior vena cava

Portal vein

Common bile duct

Hepatic artery

Gallbladder

Right ventricle

Left ventricle

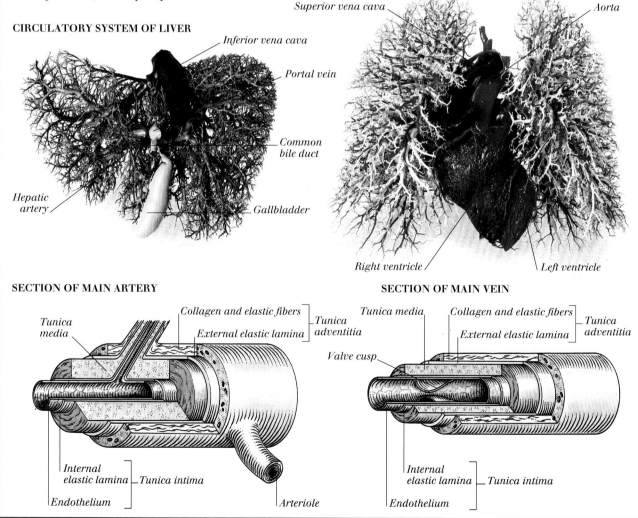

SECTION OF MAIN ARTERY

Tunica media

Collagen and elastic fibers

External elastic lamina

Tunica adventitia

Internal elastic lamina

Tunica intima

Endothelium

Arteriole

SECTION OF MAIN VEIN

Tunica media

Collagen and elastic fibers

External elastic lamina

Tunica adventitia

Valve cusp

Internal elastic lamina

Tunica intima

Endothelium

PRINCIPAL ARTERIES AND VEINS OF CIRCULATORY SYSTEM

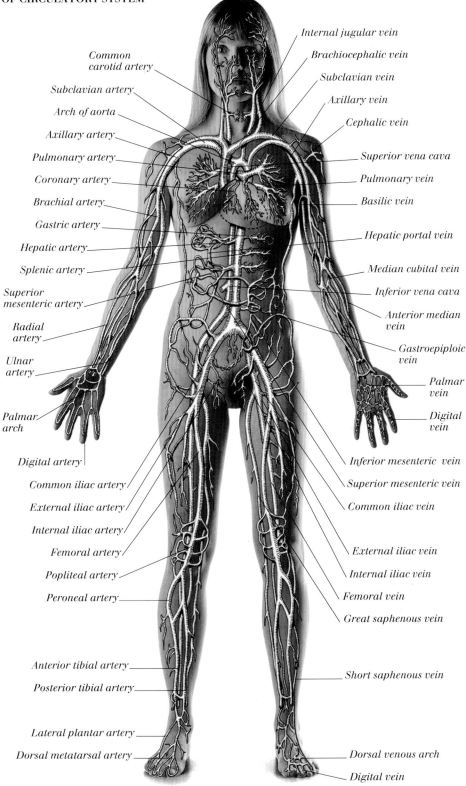

Common carotid artery

Subclavian artery

Arch of aorta

Axillary artery

Pulmonary artery

Coronary artery

Brachial artery

Gastric artery

Hepatic artery

Splenic artery

Superior mesenteric artery

Radial artery

Ulnar artery

Palmar arch

Digital artery

Common iliac artery

External iliac artery

Internal iliac artery

Femoral artery

Popliteal artery

Peroneal artery

Anterior tibial artery

Posterior tibial artery

Lateral plantar artery

Dorsal metatarsal artery

Internal jugular vein

Brachiocephalic vein

Subclavian vein

Axillary vein

Cephalic vein

Superior vena cava

Pulmonary vein

Basilic vein

Hepatic portal vein

Median cubital vein

Inferior vena cava

Anterior median vein

Gastroepiploic vein

Palmar vein

Digital vein

Inferior mesenteric vein

Superior mesenteric vein

Common iliac vein

External iliac vein

Internal iliac vein

Femoral vein

Great saphenous vein

Short saphenous vein

Dorsal venous arch

Digital vein

TYPES OF BLOOD CELLS

RED BLOOD CELLS
These cells are biconcave in shape to maximize their oxygen-carrying capacity.

WHITE BLOOD CELLS
Lymphocytes are the smallest white blood cells; they form antibodies against disease.

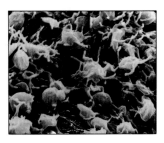

PLATELETS
Tiny cells that are activated whenever blood clotting or repair to vessels is necessary.

BLOOD CLOTTING

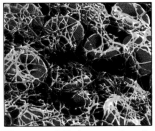

Filaments of fibrin enmesh red blood cells as part of the process of blood clotting.

Respiratory system

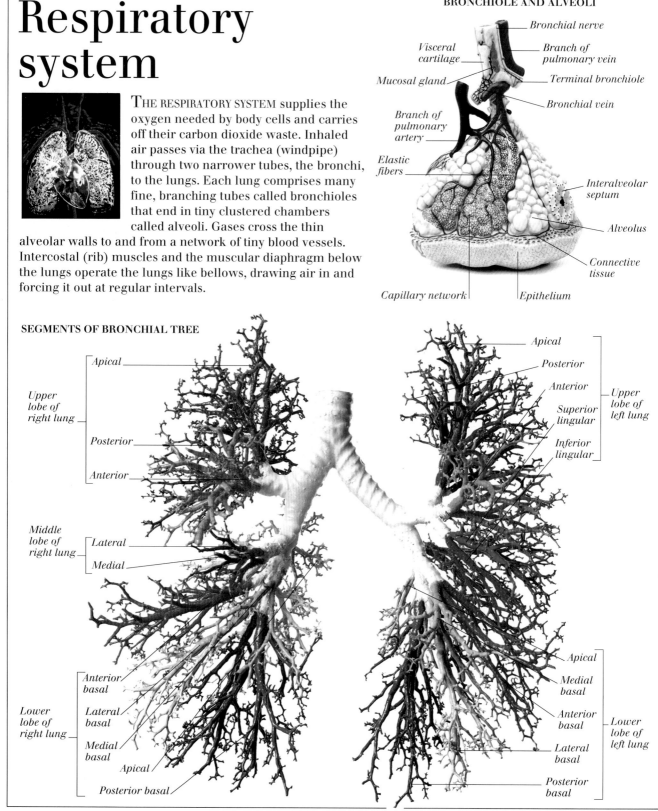

THE RESPIRATORY SYSTEM supplies the oxygen needed by body cells and carries off their carbon dioxide waste. Inhaled air passes via the trachea (windpipe) through two narrower tubes, the bronchi, to the lungs. Each lung comprises many fine, branching tubes called bronchioles that end in tiny clustered chambers called alveoli. Gases cross the thin alveolar walls to and from a network of tiny blood vessels. Intercostal (rib) muscles and the muscular diaphragm below the lungs operate the lungs like bellows, drawing air in and forcing it out at regular intervals.

BRONCHIOLE AND ALVEOLI

Bronchial nerve
Visceral cartilage
Branch of pulmonary vein
Mucosal gland
Terminal bronchiole
Bronchial vein
Branch of pulmonary artery
Elastic fibers
Interalveolar septum
Alveolus
Connective tissue
Capillary network
Epithelium

SEGMENTS OF BRONCHIAL TREE

Apical
Upper lobe of right lung
Posterior
Anterior

Middle lobe of right lung
Lateral
Medial

Lower lobe of right lung
Anterior basal
Lateral basal
Medial basal
Apical
Posterior basal

Apical
Posterior
Anterior
Superior lingular
Inferior lingular
Upper lobe of left lung

Apical
Medial basal
Anterior basal
Lower lobe of left lung
Lateral basal
Posterior basal

STRUCTURES OF THORACIC CAVITY

GASEOUS EXCHANGE IN ALVEOLUS

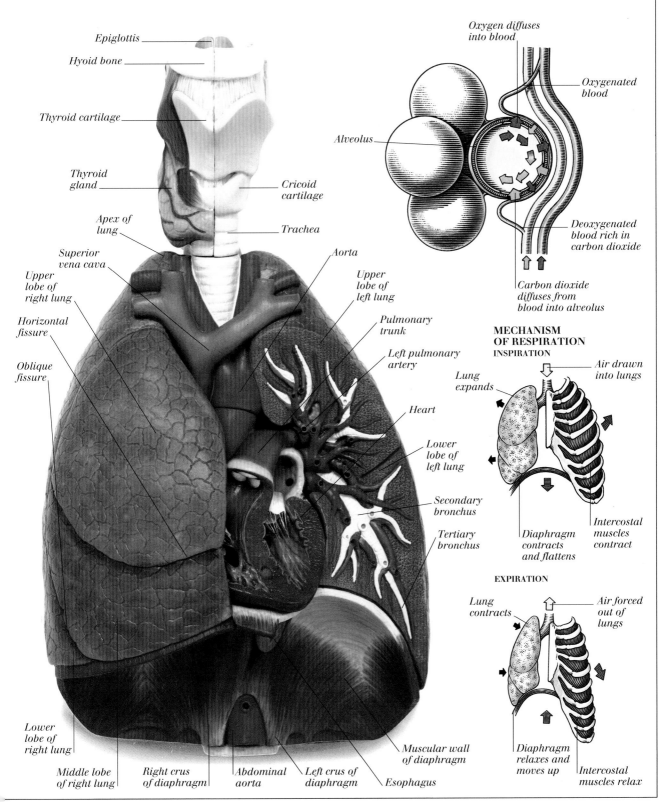

STRUCTURES OF THORACIC CAVITY

Epiglottis

Hyoid bone

Thyroid cartilage

Thyroid gland

Cricoid cartilage

Apex of lung

Trachea

Superior vena cava

Aorta

Upper lobe of right lung

Upper lobe of left lung

Horizontal fissure

Pulmonary trunk

Oblique fissure

Left pulmonary artery

Heart

Lower lobe of left lung

Secondary bronchus

Tertiary bronchus

Lower lobe of right lung

Muscular wall of diaphragm

Middle lobe of right lung

Right crus of diaphragm

Abdominal aorta

Left crus of diaphragm

Esophagus

GASEOUS EXCHANGE IN ALVEOLUS

Oxygen diffuses into blood

Oxygenated blood

Alveolus

Deoxygenated blood rich in carbon dioxide

Carbon dioxide diffuses from blood into alveolus

MECHANISM OF RESPIRATION

INSPIRATION

Lung expands

Air drawn into lungs

Diaphragm contracts and flattens

Intercostal muscles contract

EXPIRATION

Lung contracts

Air forced out of lungs

Diaphragm relaxes and moves up

Intercostal muscles relax

Urinary system

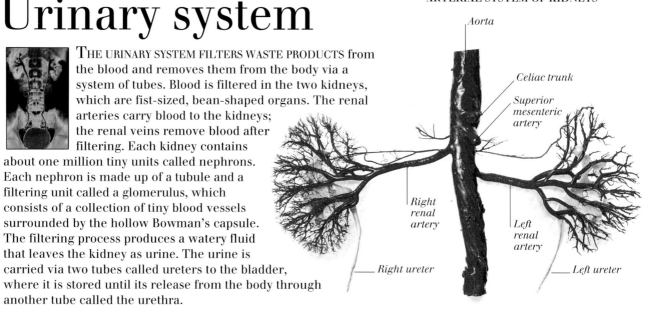

THE URINARY SYSTEM FILTERS WASTE PRODUCTS from the blood and removes them from the body via a system of tubes. Blood is filtered in the two kidneys, which are fist-sized, bean-shaped organs. The renal arteries carry blood to the kidneys; the renal veins remove blood after filtering. Each kidney contains about one million tiny units called nephrons. Each nephron is made up of a tubule and a filtering unit called a glomerulus, which consists of a collection of tiny blood vessels surrounded by the hollow Bowman's capsule. The filtering process produces a watery fluid that leaves the kidney as urine. The urine is carried via two tubes called ureters to the bladder, where it is stored until its release from the body through another tube called the urethra.

ARTERIAL SYSTEM OF KIDNEYS

- Aorta
- Celiac trunk
- Superior mesenteric artery
- Right renal artery
- Left renal artery
- Right ureter
- Left ureter

SECTION THROUGH LEFT KIDNEY

- Interlobular vein
- Collecting tubule
- Medullary pyramid
- Bowman's capsule
- Interlobular artery
- Nephron
- Cortex
- Medulla
- Loop of Henlé
- Renal artery
- Renal vein
- Renal pelvis
- Renal sinus
- Ureter
- Major calyx
- Minor calyx
- Renal papilla
- Fibrous capsule
- Renal column

SECTION OF KIDNEY

- Interlobular artery
- Collecting tubule
- Interlobular vein
- Distal convoluted tubule
- Nephron
- Cortex
- Glomerulus
- Bowman's capsule
- Proximal convoluted tubule
- Medulla
- Collecting duct
- Loop of Henlé
- Duct of Bellini
- Vasa recta

MALE URINARY TRACT

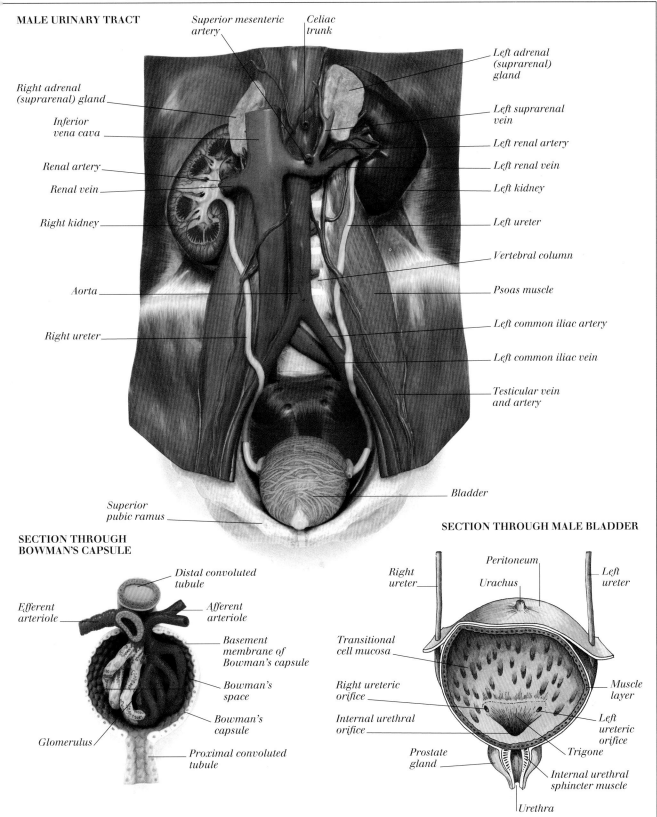

Superior mesenteric artery

Celiac trunk

Left adrenal (suprarenal) gland

Right adrenal (suprarenal) gland

Left suprarenal vein

Inferior vena cava

Left renal artery

Renal artery

Left renal vein

Renal vein

Left kidney

Right kidney

Left ureter

Vertebral column

Psoas muscle

Aorta

Left common iliac artery

Right ureter

Left common iliac vein

Testicular vein and artery

Bladder

Superior pubic ramus

SECTION THROUGH BOWMAN'S CAPSULE

Distal convoluted tubule

Efferent arteriole

Afferent arteriole

Basement membrane of Bowman's capsule

Bowman's space

Bowman's capsule

Glomerulus

Proximal convoluted tubule

SECTION THROUGH MALE BLADDER

Right ureter

Peritoneum

Urachus

Left ureter

Transitional cell mucosa

Muscle layer

Right ureteric orifice

Left ureteric orifice

Internal urethral orifice

Trigone

Prostate gland

Internal urethral sphincter muscle

Urethra

257

Reproductive system

SEX ORGANS LOCATED IN THE PELVIS create new human lives. Each month a ripe egg is released from one of the female's ovaries into a fallopian tube leading to the uterus (womb), a muscular pear-sized organ. A male produces minute tadpole-like sperm in two oval glands called testes. When the male is ready to release sperm into the female's vagina, many millions pass into his urethra and leave his body through the fleshy penis. The sperm travel up through the vagina into the uterus and one sperm may enter and fertilize an egg. The fertilized egg becomes embedded in the uterus wall and starts to grow into a new human being.

SECTION THROUGH OVARY

Corpus albicans

Fallopian tube

Corpus luteum

Mature ruptured follicle

Primary follicle

Germinal epithelium

Graffian follicle

Oocyte (egg)

Secondary follicle

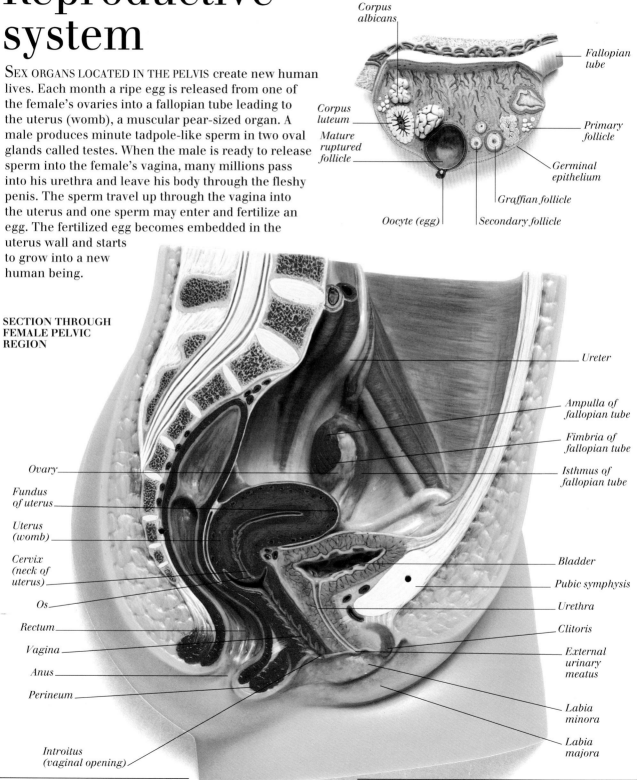

SECTION THROUGH FEMALE PELVIC REGION

Ureter

Ampulla of fallopian tube

Fimbria of fallopian tube

Isthmus of fallopian tube

Ovary

Fundus of uterus

Uterus (womb)

Cervix (neck of uterus)

Os

Rectum

Vagina

Anus

Perineum

Bladder

Pubic symphysis

Urethra

Clitoris

External urinary meatus

Labia minora

Labia majora

Introitus (vaginal opening)

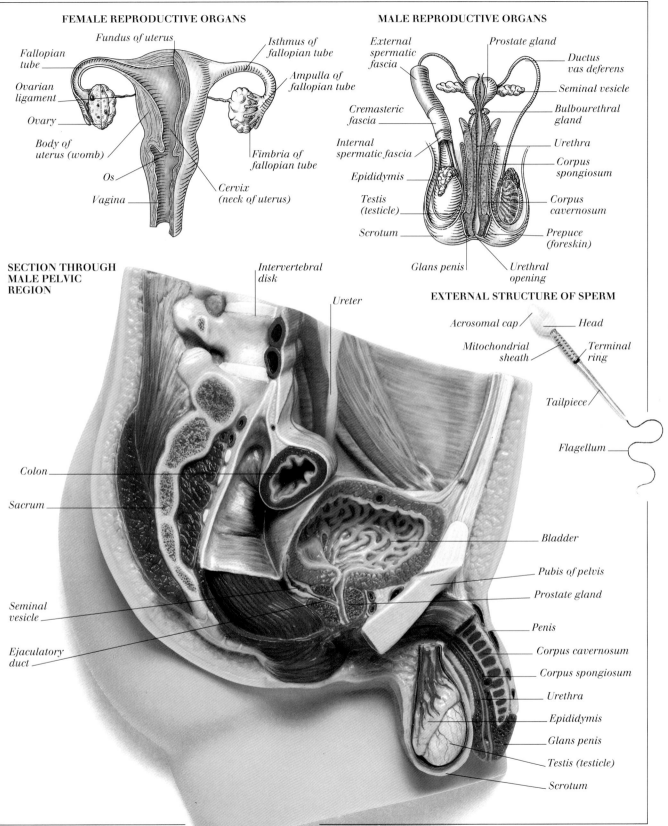

FEMALE REPRODUCTIVE ORGANS

Fundus of uterus

Isthmus of fallopian tube

Fallopian tube

Ampulla of fallopian tube

Ovarian ligament

Ovary

Body of uterus (womb)

Os

Vagina

Fimbria of fallopian tube

Cervix (neck of uterus)

MALE REPRODUCTIVE ORGANS

External spermatic fascia

Prostate gland

Ductus vas deferens

Seminal vesicle

Cremasteric fascia

Bulbourethral gland

Internal spermatic fascia

Urethra

Epididymis

Corpus spongiosum

Testis (testicle)

Corpus cavernosum

Scrotum

Prepuce (foreskin)

Glans penis

Urethral opening

SECTION THROUGH MALE PELVIC REGION

Intervertebral disk

Ureter

EXTERNAL STRUCTURE OF SPERM

Acrosomal cap

Head

Mitochondrial sheath

Terminal ring

Tailpiece

Flagellum

Colon

Bladder

Sacrum

Pubis of pelvis

Prostate gland

Penis

Seminal vesicle

Corpus cavernosum

Corpus spongiosum

Ejaculatory duct

Urethra

Epididymis

Glans penis

Testis (testicle)

Scrotum

259

Development of a baby

A FERTILIZED EGG IS NOURISHED AND PROTECTED as it
develops into an embryo and then a fetus during the 40
weeks of pregnancy. The placenta, a mass of blood vessels
implanted in the uterus lining, delivers nourishment and
oxygen, and removes waste through the umbilical cord.
Meanwhile, the fetus lies snugly in its amniotic sac, a bag of
fluid that protects it against any sudden jolts. In the last
weeks of the pregnancy, the rapidly growing fetus turns
head down: a baby ready to be born.

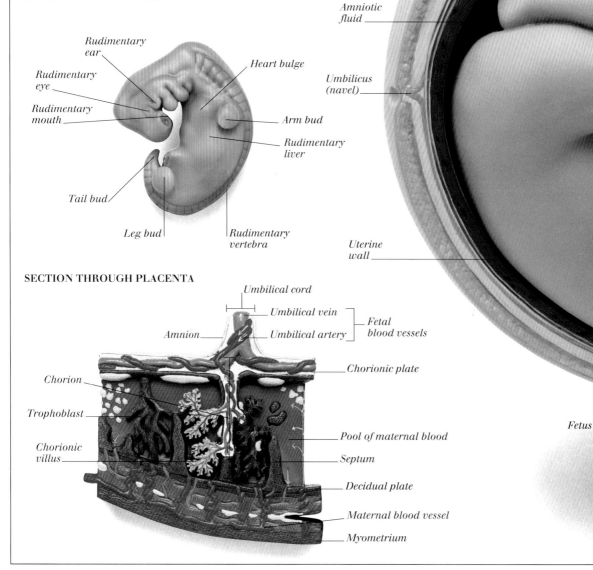

EMBRYO AT FIVE WEEKS

Rudimentary ear

Rudimentary eye

Rudimentary mouth

Tail bud

Leg bud

Heart bulge

Arm bud

Rudimentary liver

Rudimentary vertebra

Amniotic fluid

Umbilicus (navel)

Uterine wall

Fetus

SECTION THROUGH PLACENTA

Umbilical cord

Umbilical vein

Amnion

Umbilical artery

Fetal blood vessels

Chorionic plate

Chorion

Trophoblast

Chorionic villus

Pool of maternal blood

Septum

Decidual plate

Maternal blood vessel

Myometrium

SECTION THROUGH PELVIS IN NINTH MONTH OF PREGNANCY

THE DEVELOPING FETUS

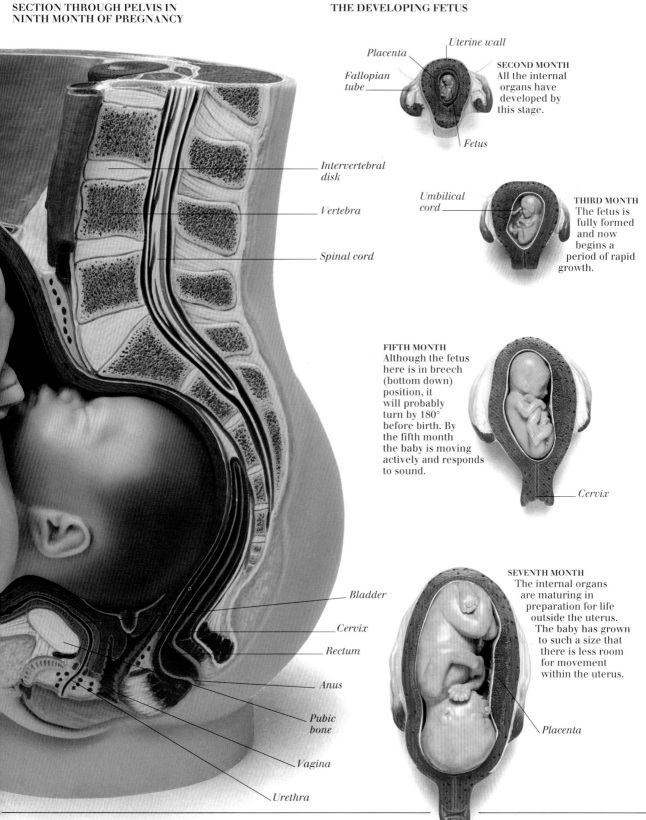

Placenta

Uterine wall

Fallopian tube

Fetus

SECOND MONTH
All the internal organs have developed by this stage.

Intervertebral disk

Vertebra

Spinal cord

Umbilical cord

THIRD MONTH
The fetus is fully formed and now begins a period of rapid growth.

FIFTH MONTH
Although the fetus here is in breech (bottom down) position, it will probably turn by 180° before birth. By the fifth month the baby is moving actively and responds to sound.

Cervix

SEVENTH MONTH
The internal organs are maturing in preparation for life outside the uterus. The baby has grown to such a size that there is less room for movement within the uterus.

Bladder

Cervix

Rectum

Anus

Pubic bone

Placenta

Vagina

Urethra

GEOLOGY, GEOGRAPHY, AND METEOROLGY

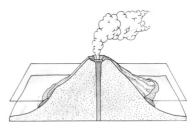

Earth's physical features

MOST OF THE EARTH'S SURFACE (about 70 percent) is covered with water. The largest single body of water, the Pacific Ocean, alone covers about 30 percent of the surface. Most of the land is distributed as seven continents; these are (from largest to smallest) Asia, Africa, North America, South America, Antarctica, Europe, and Australasia. The physical features of the land are remarkably varied. Among the most notable are mountain ranges, rivers, and deserts. The largest mountain ranges—the Himalayas in Asia and the Andes in South America—extend for thousands of miles. The Himalayas include the world's highest mountain, Mount Everest (29,029 feet). The longest rivers are the River Nile in Africa (4,160 miles) and the Amazon River in South America (4,000 miles). Deserts cover about 20 percent of the total land area. The largest is the Sahara, which covers nearly a third of Africa. The Earth's surface features can be represented in various ways. Only a globe can correctly represent areas, shapes, sizes, and directions, because there is always distortion when a spherical surface like the Earth's is projected onto the flat surface of a map. Each map projection is therefore a compromise: some aspects of global features are shown accurately by allowing others to be distorted. Even satellite mapping does not produce completely accurate maps, although they can show physical features with great clarity.

EXAMPLES OF MAP PROJECTIONS

CYLINDRICAL PROJECTION

CYLINDRICAL-PROJECTION MAP

SATELLITE MAPPING OF THE EARTH

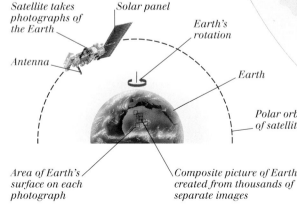

Satellite takes photographs of the Earth

Solar panel

Earth's rotation

Antenna

Earth

Polar orbit of satellite

Area of Earth's surface on each photograph

Composite picture of Earth created from thousands of separate images

180°
160°
120°
80°

Great Slave Lake
Great Bear Lake
Lake Superior
Greenland

Mackenzie-Peace River

Baffin Island

Bering Sea

Hudson Bay

Rocky Mountains

NORTH AMERICA

Mississippi-Missouri River

Lake Huron
Lake Ontario
Lake Erie
Lake Michigan

Sonoran Desert

Appalachian Mountains

Sierra Madre

Gulf of Mexico

ATLANTIC OCEAN

Chihuahuan Desert

Caribbean Sea

Guiana Highlands

Amazon River

Brazilian Highlands

PACIFIC OCEAN

Andes

Atacama Desert

Gran Chaco

Mato Grosso

Parana River

Pampas

Patagonia

180°
160°
120°
80°

WEST OF GREENWICH MERIDIAN

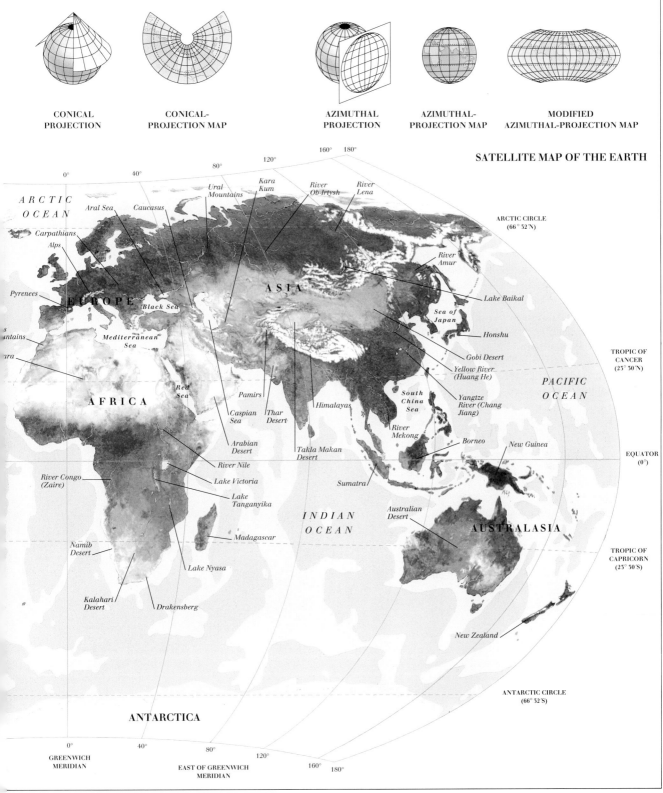

CONICAL
PROJECTION

CONICAL-
PROJECTION MAP

AZIMUTHAL
PROJECTION

AZIMUTHAL-
PROJECTION MAP

MODIFIED
AZIMUTHAL-PROJECTION MAP

SATELLITE MAP OF THE EARTH

160°   180°
120°
80°
40°
0°

*ARCTIC
OCEAN*

ARCTIC CIRCLE
(66° 52´N)

*Ural
Mountains*

*Kara
Kum*

*River
Ob-Irtysh*

*River
Lena*

Aral Sea

Caucasus

Carpathians

Alps

*River
Amur*

A S I A

Pyrenees

EUROPE

Black Sea

Lake Baikal

*Sea of
Japan*

ntains

*Mediterranean
Sea*

Honshu

TROPIC OF
CANCER
(25° 30´N)

ara

Gobi Desert

*PACIFIC
OCEAN*

Yellow River
(Huang He)

*Red
Sea*

Pamirs

AFRICA

*South
China
Sea*

Yangtze
River (Chang
Jiang)

*Caspian
Sea*

*Thar
Desert*

Himalayas

*River
Mekong*

*Arabian
Desert*

*Takla Makan
Desert*

Borneo

New Guinea

EQUATOR
(0°)

River Nile

Lake Victoria

*River Congo
(Zaire)*

Sumatra

Lake
Tanganyika

*INDIAN
OCEAN*

*Australian
Desert*

AUSTRALASIA

Madagascar

*Namib
Desert*

Lake Nyasa

TROPIC OF
CAPRICORN
(25° 50´S)

*Kalahari
Desert*

Drakensberg

New Zealand

ANTARCTIC CIRCLE
(66° 52´S)

ANTARCTICA

0°   40°   80°   120°   160°   180°

GREENWICH
MERIDIAN

EAST OF GREENWICH
MERIDIAN

265

The rock cycle

THE ROCK CYCLE IS A CONTINUOUS PROCESS through which old rocks are transformed into new ones. Rocks can be divided into three main groups: igneous, sedimentary, and metamorphic. Igneous rocks are formed when magma (molten rock) from the Earth's interior cools and solidifies (see pp. 274-275). Sedimentary rocks are formed when sediment (rock particles, for example) becomes compressed and cemented together in a process known as lithification (see pp. 276-277). Metamorphic rocks are formed when igneous, sedimentary, or other metamorphic rocks are changed by heat or pressure (see pp. 274-275). Rocks are added to the Earth's surface by crustal movements and volcanic activity. Once exposed on the surface, the rocks are broken down into rock particles by weathering (see pp. 282-283). The particles are then transported by glaciers, rivers, and wind and are deposited as sediment in lakes, deltas, deserts, and on the ocean floor. Some of this sediment undergoes lithification and forms sedimentary rock. This rock may be thrust back to the surface by crustal movements or forced deeper into the Earth's interior, where heat and pressure transform it into metamorphic rock. The metamorphic rock in turn may be pushed up to the surface or may be melted to form magma. Eventually, the magma cools and solidifies—below or on the surface—forming igneous rock. When the sedimentary, igneous, and metamorphic rocks are exposed once more on the Earth's surface, the cycle begins again.

HEXAGONAL BASALT
COLUMNS, ICELAND

THE ROCK CYCLE

Igneous rock

Weathering, transport, and deposition

Sediment

Cooling and solidification (crystallization)

Heat and pressure (metamorphism)

Weathering, transport, and deposition

Weathering, transport, and deposition

Compression and cementation (lithification)

Magma

Melting

Metamorphic rock

Heat and pressure (metamorphism)

Sedimentary rock

STAGES IN THE ROCK CYCLE

Magma extruded as lava, which solidifies to form igneous rock

Lava flow

Vent

Main conduit

Secondary conduit

Lava

Ash

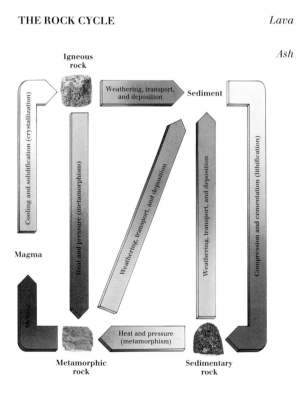

Rock surrounding magma changed by heat to form metamorphic rock

Intense heat of rising magma melts some of the surrounding rock

Sedimentary rock crushed and folded to form metamorphic rock

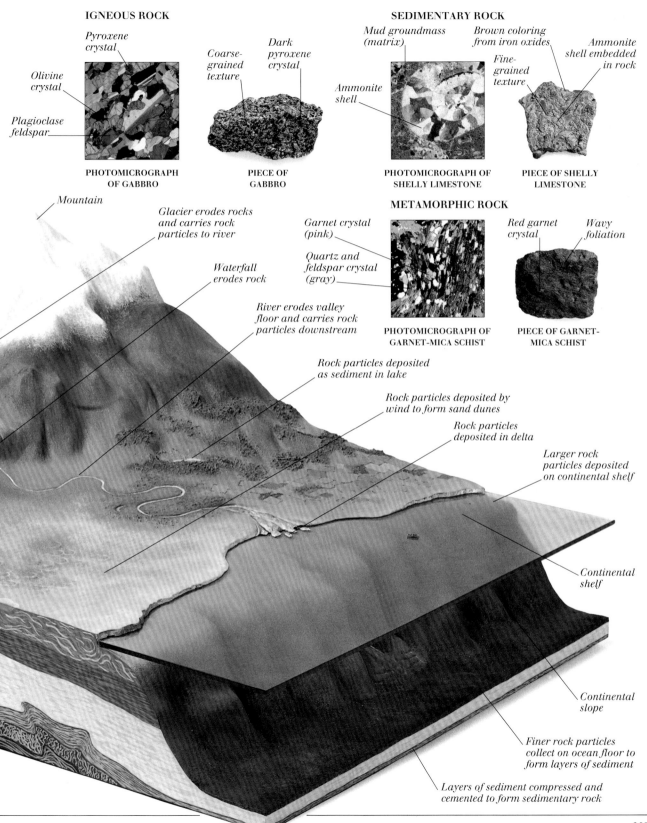

IGNEOUS ROCK

Pyroxene crystal

Olivine crystal

Plagioclase feldspar

Coarse-grained texture

Dark pyroxene crystal

PHOTOMICROGRAPH OF GABBRO

PIECE OF GABBRO

SEDIMENTARY ROCK

Mud groundmass (matrix)

Brown coloring from iron oxides

Fine-grained texture

Ammonite shell embedded in rock

Ammonite shell

PHOTOMICROGRAPH OF SHELLY LIMESTONE

PIECE OF SHELLY LIMESTONE

METAMORPHIC ROCK

Garnet crystal (pink)

Quartz and feldspar crystal (gray)

Red garnet crystal

Wavy foliation

PHOTOMICROGRAPH OF GARNET-MICA SCHIST

PIECE OF GARNET-MICA SCHIST

Mountain

Glacier erodes rocks and carries rock particles to river

Waterfall erodes rock

River erodes valley floor and carries rock particles downstream

Rock particles deposited as sediment in lake

Rock particles deposited by wind to form sand dunes

Rock particles deposited in delta

Larger rock particles deposited on continental shelf

Continental shelf

Continental slope

Finer rock particles collect on ocean floor to form layers of sediment

Layers of sediment compressed and cemented to form sedimentary rock

Minerals

A MINERAL IS A NATURALLY OCCURRING SUBSTANCE that has a characteristic chemical composition and specific physical properties, such as habit and streak (see pp. 270-271). A rock, by comparison, is an aggregate of minerals and need not have a specific chemical composition. Minerals are made up of elements (substances that cannot be broken down chemically into simpler substances), each of which can be represented by a chemical symbol. Minerals can be divided into two main groups: native elements and compounds. Native elements are made up of a pure element. Examples include gold (chemical symbol Au), silver (Ag), copper (Cu), and carbon (C); carbon occurs as a native element in two forms, diamond and graphite. Compounds are combinations of two or more elements. For example, sulfides are compounds of sulfur (S) and one or more other elements, such as lead (Pb) in the mineral galena, or antimony (Sb) in the mineral stibnite.

NATIVE ELEMENTS

Dendritic (branching) copper

Limonite groundmass (matrix)

COPPER
(Cu)

SULFIDES

Cubic galena crystal

GALENA
(PbS)

Dendritic (branching) gold

Kimberlite groundmass (matrix)

Quartz vein

GOLD
(Au)

White diamond

DIAMOND
(C)

Hexagonal graphite crystal

GRAPHITE
(C)

OXIDES/HYDROXIDES

Milky quartz groundmass (matrix)

Smoky quartz crystal

SMOKY QUARTZ
(SiO_2)

Rounded bauxite grains in groundmass (matrix)

BAUXITE
(FeO(OH) and $Al_2O_3.2H_2O$)

Mass of specular hematite crystals

SPECULAR HEMATITE
(Fe_2O_3)

Prismatic stibnite crystal

Quartz groundmass (matrix)

STIBNITE
(Sb_2S_3)

Perfect octahedral pyrites crystal

Quartz crystal

PYRITES
(FeS_2)

Parallel bands of onyx

ONYX
(SiO_2)

Kidney ore hematite

Specular crystals of hematite

KIDNEY ORE HEMATITE
(Fe_2O_3)

PHOSPHATES

Limonite groundmass (matrix)

Rock groundmass (matrix)

Radiating wavellite crystals

WAVELLITE
$(Al_3(PO_4)_2(OH,F)_3.5H_2O)$

Prismatic pyromorphite crystals

PYROMORPHITE
$(Pb_5(PO_4)_3Cl)$

CARBONATES

Striated cerussite crystal

Dog tooth calcite crystal

CERUSSITE
$(PbCO_3)$

CALCITE
$(CaCO_3)$

SULFATES

Rock groundmass (matrix)

Radiating crystal mass of daisy gypsum

Radiating cyanotrichite crystals

CYANOTRICHITE
$(Cu_4Al_2(SO_4)(OH)_{12}.2H_2O)$

DAISY GYPSUM
$(CaSO_4.2H_2O)$

MOLYBDATE

Tabular wulfenite crystal

Dark rock groundmass (matrix)

WULFENITE
$(PbMoO_4)$

SILICATES

Feldspar groundmass (matrix)

Transparent bicolored tourmaline crystal

Dodecahedral sodalite crystal

SODALITE
$(Na_8Al_6Si_6O_{24}Cl_2)$

Striated surface of olivine crystal

TOURMALINE
$(Na(Mg,Fe,Li,Mn,Al)_3Al_6(BO_3)_3Si_6.O_{18}(OH,F)_4)$

OLIVINE
$(Fe_2SiO_4 - Mg_2SiO_4)$

Striated prismatic epidote crystal

Tabular muscovite crystal

EPIDOTE
$(Ca_2(Al,Fe)_3(SiO_4)_3(OH))$

Orthoclase crystal

MUSCOVITE
$(KAl_2(Si_3Al)O_{10}(OH,F)_2)$

ORTHOCLASE
$(KAlSi_3O_8)$

HALIDES

Cubic rock salt crystal

Cubic fluorite crystal

GREEN FLUORITE
(CaF_2)

ORANGE HALITE (ROCK SALT)
$(NaCl)$

Mineral features

MINERALS CAN BE IDENTIFIED BY STUDYING features such as fracture, cleavage, crystal system, habit, hardness, color, and streak. Minerals can break in different ways. If a mineral breaks in an irregular way, leaving rough surfaces, it possesses fracture. If a mineral breaks along well-defined planes of weakness, it possesses cleavage. Specific minerals have distinctive patterns of cleavage. For example, mica cleaves along one plane. Most minerals form crystals that can be categorized into crystal systems according to their symmetry and number of faces. Within each system, several different but related forms of crystal are possible; for example, a cubic crystal can have six, eight, or twelve sides. A mineral's habit is the typical form taken by an aggregate of its crystals. Examples of habit include botryoidal (like a bunch of grapes) and massive (no definite form). The relative hardness of a mineral may be assessed by testing its resistance to scratching. This property is usually measured using Mohs' scale, which increases in hardness from 1 (talc) to 10 (diamond). The color of a mineral is not a dependable guide to its identity as some minerals have a range of colors. Streak (the color the powdered mineral makes when rubbed across an unglazed tile) is a more reliable indicator.

CLEAVAGE

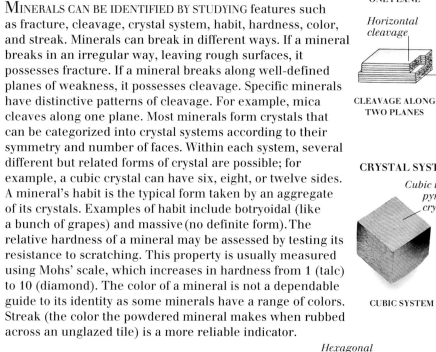

Cleavage in one direction

CLEAVAGE ALONG ONE PLANE

Cleavage in three directions, forming a block cube

CLEAVAGE ALONG THREE PLANES

Horizontal cleavage

Vertical cleavage

CLEAVAGE ALONG TWO PLANES

Cleavage in four directions, forming a double-pyramid crystal

CLEAVAGE ALONG FOUR PLANES

CRYSTAL SYSTEMS

Cubic iron pyrites crystal

CUBIC SYSTEM

Representation of cubic system

Tetragonal idocrase crystal

Representation of tetragonal system

TETRAGONAL SYSTEM

Hexagonal beryl crystal

Representation of hexagonal/trigonal system

HEXAGONAL/TRIGONAL SYSTEM

Orthorhombic barite crystal

Representation of orthorhombic system

ORTHORHOMBIC SYSTEM

Monoclinic selenite crystal

Representation of monoclinic system

MONOCLINIC SYSTEM

Representation of triclinic system

Triclinic axinite crystal

TRICLINIC SYSTEM

FRACTURE

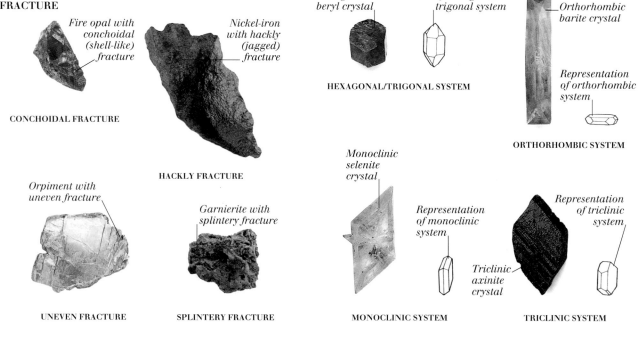

Fire opal with conchoidal (shell-like) fracture

CONCHOIDAL FRACTURE

Nickel-iron with hackly (jagged) fracture

HACKLY FRACTURE

Orpiment with uneven fracture

UNEVEN FRACTURE

Garnierite with splintery fracture

SPLINTERY FRACTURE

HABIT

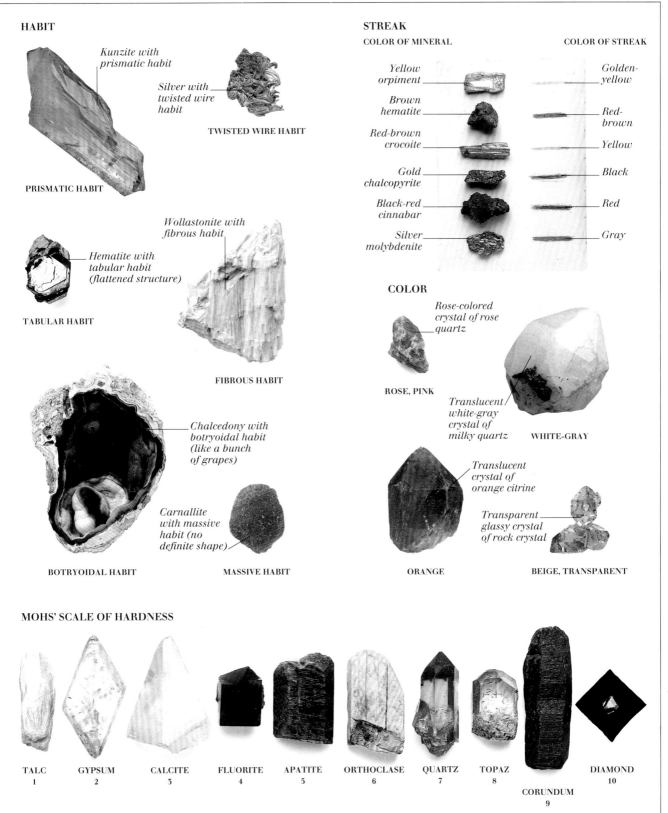

Kunzite with prismatic habit

Silver with twisted wire habit

TWISTED WIRE HABIT

PRISMATIC HABIT

Wollastonite with fibrous habit

Hematite with tabular habit (flattened structure)

TABULAR HABIT

FIBROUS HABIT

Chalcedony with botryoidal habit (like a bunch of grapes)

Carnallite with massive habit (no definite shape)

BOTRYOIDAL HABIT

MASSIVE HABIT

STREAK

COLOR OF MINERAL		COLOR OF STREAK
Yellow orpiment		*Golden-yellow*
Brown hematite		*Red-brown*
Red-brown crocoite		*Yellow*
Gold chalcopyrite		*Black*
Black-red cinnabar		*Red*
Silver molybdenite		*Gray*

COLOR

Rose-colored crystal of rose quartz

ROSE, PINK

Translucent white-gray crystal of milky quartz

WHITE-GRAY

Translucent crystal of orange citrine

Transparent glassy crystal of rock crystal

ORANGE

BEIGE, TRANSPARENT

MOHS' SCALE OF HARDNESS

| TALC 1 | GYPSUM 2 | CALCITE 3 | FLUORITE 4 | APATITE 5 | ORTHOCLASE 6 | QUARTZ 7 | TOPAZ 8 | CORUNDUM 9 | DIAMOND 10 |

Volcanoes

VOLCANOES ARE VENTS OR FISSURES IN THE EARTH'S crust through which magma (molten rock that originates from deep beneath the crust) is forced onto the surface as lava. They occur most commonly along the boundaries of crustal plates; most volcanoes lie in a belt called the "Ring of Fire," which runs along the edge of the Pacific Ocean. Volcanoes can be classified according to the violence and frequency of their eruptions.

Nonexplosive volcanic eruptions generally occur where crustal plates pull apart. These eruptions produce runny basaltic lava that spreads quickly over a wide area to form relatively flat cones. The most violent eruptions take place where plates collide. Such eruptions produce thick rhyolitic lava and may also blast out clouds of dust and pyroclasts (lava fragments). The lava does not flow far before cooling and therefore builds up steep-sided, conical volcanoes. Some volcanoes produce lava and ash eruptions, which build up composite volcanic cones. Volcanoes that erupt frequently are described as active, those that erupt rarely are termed dormant, and those that have stopped erupting altogether are termed extinct. Besides the volcanoes themselves, other features associated with volcanic regions include geysers, hot mineral springs, solfataras, fumaroles, and bubbling mud pools.

Folded, rope-like surface

PAHOEHOE
(ROPY LAVA)

HORU GEYSER,
NEW ZEALAND

VOLCANO TYPES

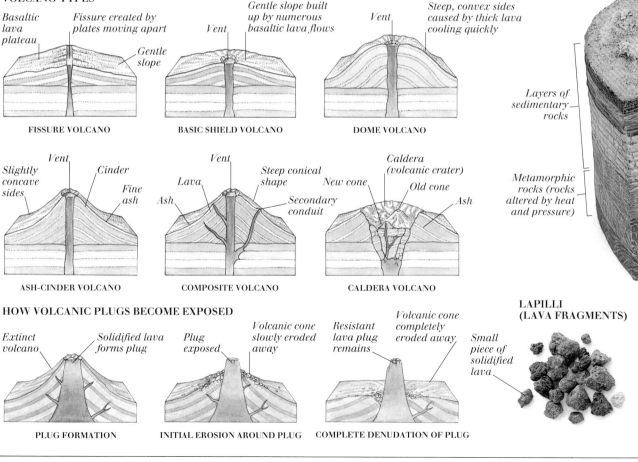

Basaltic lava plateau — Fissure created by plates moving apart — Gentle slope

FISSURE VOLCANO

Gentle slope built up by numerous basaltic lava flows — Vent

BASIC SHIELD VOLCANO

Steep, convex sides caused by thick lava cooling quickly — Vent

DOME VOLCANO

Slightly concave sides — Vent — Cinder — Fine ash

ASH-CINDER VOLCANO

Vent — Lava — Steep conical shape — Ash — Secondary conduit

COMPOSITE VOLCANO

Caldera (volcanic crater) — New cone — Old cone — Ash

CALDERA VOLCANO

Layers of sedimentary rocks

Metamorphic rocks (rocks altered by heat and pressure)

HOW VOLCANIC PLUGS BECOME EXPOSED

Extinct volcano — Solidified lava forms plug

PLUG FORMATION

Plug exposed — Volcanic cone slowly eroded away

INITIAL EROSION AROUND PLUG

Resistant lava plug remains — Volcanic cone completely eroded away

COMPLETE DENUDATION OF PLUG

LAPILLI
(LAVA FRAGMENTS)

Small piece of solidified lava

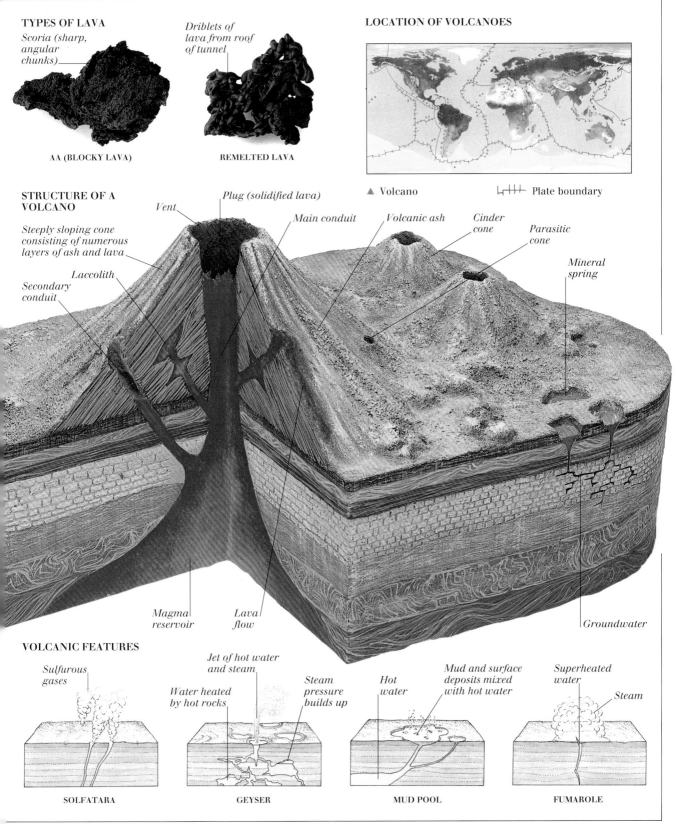

TYPES OF LAVA

Scoria (sharp, angular chunks)

Driblets of lava from roof of tunnel

AA (BLOCKY LAVA)

REMELTED LAVA

LOCATION OF VOLCANOES

▲ Volcano

╟╂╫ Plate boundary

STRUCTURE OF A VOLCANO

Steeply sloping cone consisting of numerous layers of ash and lava

Laccolith

Secondary conduit

Vent

Plug (solidified lava)

Main conduit

Volcanic ash

Cinder cone

Parasitic cone

Mineral spring

Magma reservoir

Lava flow

Groundwater

VOLCANIC FEATURES

Sulfurous gases

Jet of hot water and steam

Water heated by hot rocks

Steam pressure builds up

Hot water

Mud and surface deposits mixed with hot water

Superheated water

Steam

SOLFATARA

GEYSER

MUD POOL

FUMAROLE

Igneous and metamorphic rocks

IGNEOUS ROCKS ARE FORMED WHEN MAGMA (molten rock that originates from deep beneath the Earth's crust) cools and solidifies. There are two main types of igneous rock: intrusive and extrusive. Intrusive rocks are formed deep underground, where magma is forced into cracks or between rock layers to form structures including sills, dikes, and batholiths. The magma cools slowly to form coarse-grained rocks such as gabbro and pegmatite. Extrusive rocks are formed above the Earth's surface from lava (magma that has been ejected in a volcanic eruption). The molten lava cools quickly, producing fine-grained rocks such as rhyolite and basalt. Metamorphic rocks are those that have been altered by intense heat (contact metamorphism) or extreme pressure (regional metamorphism). Contact metamorphism occurs when rocks are changed by heat from, for example, an igneous intrusion or lava flow. Regional metamorphism occurs when rock is crushed in the middle of a folding mountain range. Metamorphic rocks can be formed from igneous rocks, sedimentary rocks, or even other metamorphic rocks.

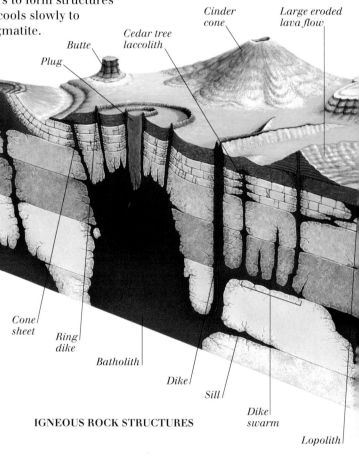

Cinder cone
Large eroded lava flow
Cedar tree laccolith
Butte
Plug
Cone sheet
Ring dike
Batholith
Dike
Sill
Dike swarm
Lopolith

IGNEOUS ROCK STRUCTURES

CONTACT METAMORPHISM

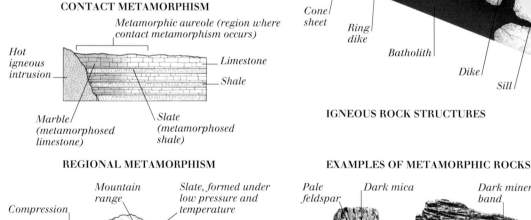

Metamorphic aureole (region where contact metamorphism occurs)
Hot igneous intrusion
Limestone
Shale
Marble (metamorphosed limestone)
Slate (metamorphosed shale)

REGIONAL METAMORPHISM

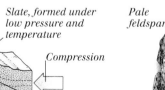

Mountain range
Slate, formed under low pressure and temperature
Compression
Compression
Schist, formed under medium pressure and temperature
Crust
Gneiss, formed under high pressure and temperature
Mantle
Magma

EXAMPLES OF METAMORPHIC ROCKS

Pale feldspar
Dark mica
Dark mineral band
Pale calcite

GNEISS
FOLDED SCHIST
SKARN

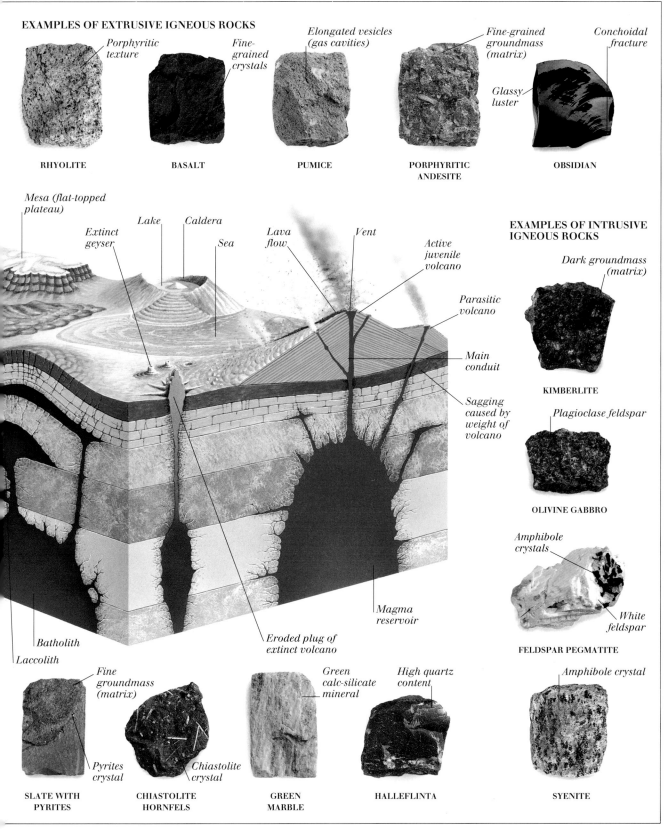

EXAMPLES OF EXTRUSIVE IGNEOUS ROCKS

Porphyritic texture

Fine-grained crystals

Elongated vesicles (gas cavities)

Fine-grained groundmass (matrix)

Conchoidal fracture

Glassy luster

RHYOLITE

BASALT

PUMICE

PORPHYRITIC ANDESITE

OBSIDIAN

Mesa (flat-topped plateau)

Extinct geyser

Lake

Caldera

Sea

Lava flow

Vent

Active juvenile volcano

Parasitic volcano

Main conduit

Sagging caused by weight of volcano

Batholith

Laccolith

Eroded plug of extinct volcano

Magma reservoir

EXAMPLES OF INTRUSIVE IGNEOUS ROCKS

Dark groundmass (matrix)

KIMBERLITE

Plagioclase feldspar

OLIVINE GABBRO

Amphibole crystals

White feldspar

FELDSPAR PEGMATITE

Amphibole crystal

Fine groundmass (matrix)

Pyrites crystal

Green calc-silicate mineral

High quartz content

Chiastolite crystal

SLATE WITH PYRITES

CHIASTOLITE HORNFELS

GREEN MARBLE

HALLEFLINTA

SYENITE

Sedimentary rocks

SEDIMENTARY ROCKS ARE FORMED BY THE ACCUMULATION and consolidation of sediments (see pp. 266-267). There are three main types of sedimentary rock: clastic sedimentary rocks, such as breccia or sandstone, are formed from other rocks that have been broken down into fragments by weathering (see pp. 282-283), which have then been transported and deposited elsewhere; organic sedimentary rocks, such as coal (see pp. 280-281), are derived from plant and animal remains; and chemical sedimentary rocks are formed by chemical processes. For example, rock salt is formed when salt dissolved in water is deposited as the water evaporates. Sedimentary rocks are laid down in layers called beds, or strata. Each new layer is laid down horizontally over older ones. There are usually some gaps in the sequence, called unconformities. These represent periods in which no new sediments were being laid down, or when earlier sedimentary layers were raised above sea level and eroded away.

THE GRAND CANYON, U.S.A.

EXAMPLES OF UNCONFORMITIES

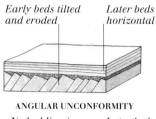

Early beds tilted and eroded   *Later beds horizontal*

ANGULAR UNCONFORMITY

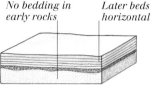

No bedding in early rocks   *Later beds horizontal*

NONCONFORMITY

Early beds folded and eroded   *Later beds horizontal*

DISCONFORMITY

SEDIMENTARY LAYERS OF THE GRAND CANYON REGION

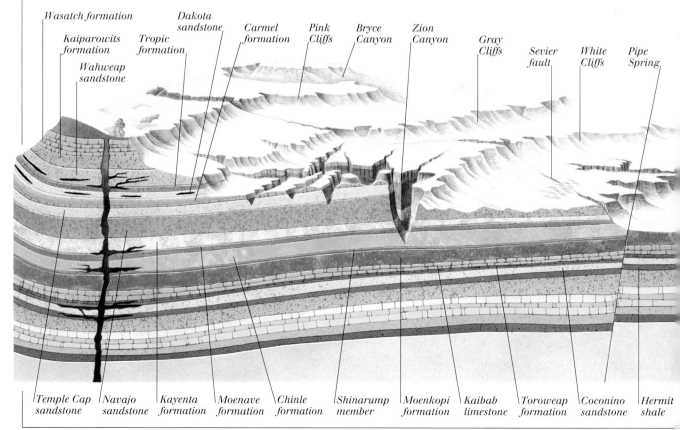

Wasatch formation

Kaiparowits formation

Wahweap sandstone

Tropic formation

Dakota sandstone

Carmel formation

Pink Cliffs

Bryce Canyon

Zion Canyon

Gray Cliffs

Sevier fault

White Cliffs

Pipe Spring

Temple Cap sandstone

Navajo sandstone

Kayenta formation

Moenave formation

Chinle formation

Shinarump member

Moenkopi formation

Kaibab limestone

Toroweap formation

Coconino sandstone

Hermit shale

EXAMPLES OF SEDIMENTARY ROCKS

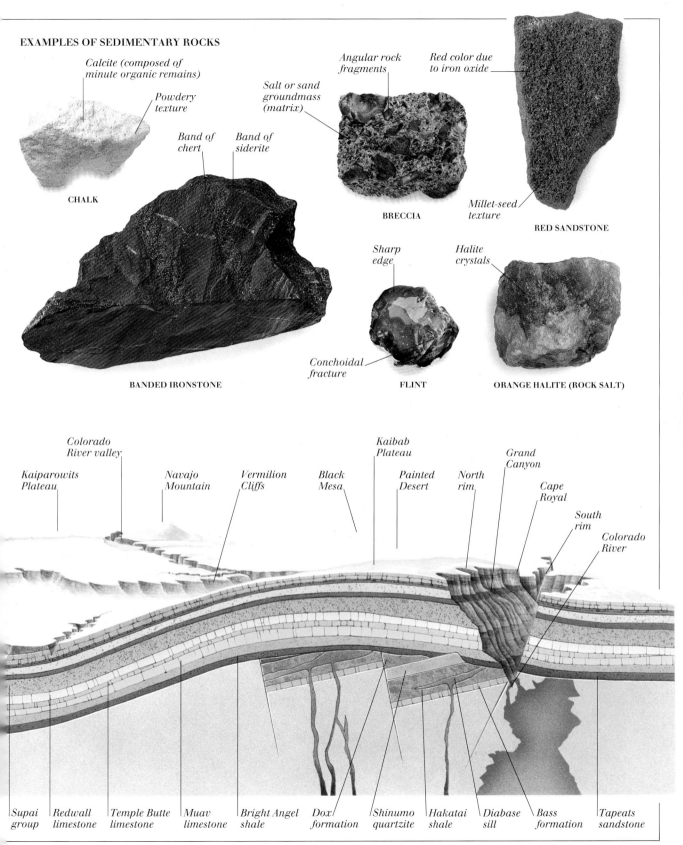

Calcite (composed of minute organic remains)

Powdery texture

CHALK

Band of chert

Band of siderite

BANDED IRONSTONE

Angular rock fragments

Salt or sand groundmass (matrix)

BRECCIA

Red color due to iron oxide

Millet-seed texture

RED SANDSTONE

Sharp edge

Conchoidal fracture

FLINT

Halite crystals

ORANGE HALITE (ROCK SALT)

Kaiparowits Plateau

Colorado River valley

Navajo Mountain

Vermilion Cliffs

Black Mesa

Kaibab Plateau

Painted Desert

North rim

Grand Canyon

Cape Royal

South rim

Colorado River

Supai group

Redwall limestone

Temple Butte limestone

Muav limestone

Bright Angel shale

Dox formation

Shinumo quartzite

Hakatai shale

Diabase sill

Bass formation

Tapeats sandstone

Fossils

FOSSILS ARE THE REMAINS of plants and animals that have been preserved in rock. A fossil may be the preserved remains of an organism itself, an impression of it in rock, or preserved traces (known as trace fossils) left by an organism while it was alive, such as organic carbon outlines, fossilized footprints, or droppings. Most dead organisms soon rot away or are eaten by scavengers. For fossilization to occur, rapid burial by sediment is necessary. The organism decays, but the harder parts—bones, teeth, and shells, for example—may be preserved and hardened by minerals from the surrounding sediment. Fossilization may also occur even when the hard parts of an organism are dissolved away to leave an impression called a mold. The mold is filled by minerals, thereby creating a cast of the organism. The study of fossils (paleontology) not only can show how living things have evolved, but can also help reveal the Earth's geological history—for example, by aiding in the dating of rock strata.

PROCESS OF FOSSILIZATION

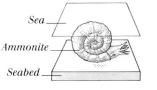

Sea

Ammonite

Seabed

ANIMAL DIES

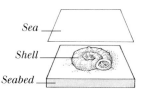

Sea

Shell

Seabed

SOFT PARTS ROT

Sea

Shell

Sediment

Seabed

SHELL BURIED

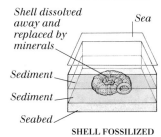

Shell dissolved away and replaced by minerals

Sea

Sediment

Sediment

Seabed

SHELL FOSSILIZED

EXAMPLES OF FOSSILS

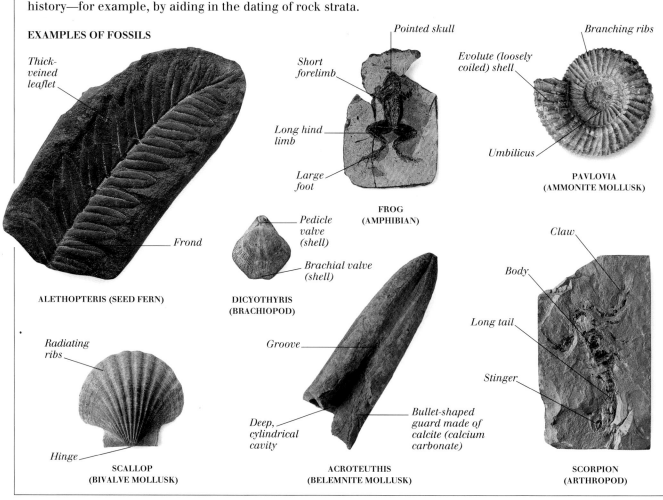

Thick-veined leaflet

Frond

ALETHOPTERIS (SEED FERN)

Radiating ribs

Hinge

SCALLOP (BIVALVE MOLLUSK)

Short forelimb

Pointed skull

Long hind limb

Large foot

FROG (AMPHIBIAN)

Pedicle valve (shell)

Brachial valve (shell)

DICYOTHYRIS (BRACHIOPOD)

Groove

Deep, cylindrical cavity

Bullet-shaped guard made of calcite (calcium carbonate)

ACROTEUTHIS (BELEMNITE MOLLUSK)

Evolute (loosely coiled) shell

Branching ribs

Umbilicus

PAVLOVIA (AMMONITE MOLLUSK)

Claw

Body

Long tail

Stinger

SCORPION (ARTHROPOD)

278

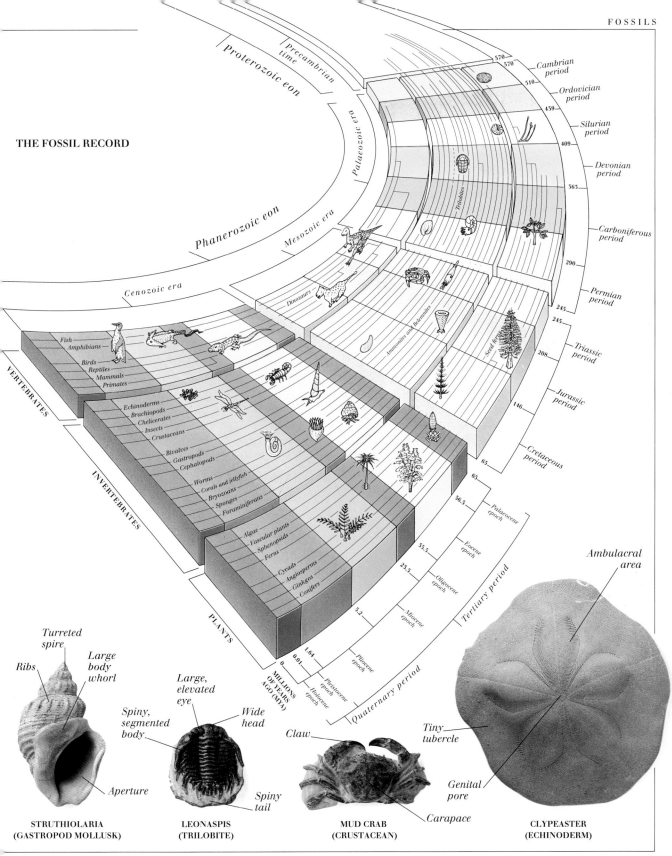

THE FOSSIL RECORD

Precambrian time

Proterozoic eon

Palaeozoic era

Phanerozoic eon

Mesozoic era

Cenozoic era

570
510
439
409
363
290
245

Cambrian period
Ordovician period
Silurian period
Devonian period
Carboniferous period
Permian period

Trilobita

Dinosaurs

Ammonites and Belemnites

Seed fern

245
208
146
65

Triassic period
Jurassic period
Cretaceous period

VERTEBRATES

Fish
Amphibians
Birds
Reptiles
Mammals
Primates

INVERTEBRATES

Echinoderms
Brachiopods
Chelicerates
Insects
Crustaceans
Bivalves
Gastropods
Cephalopods
Worms
Corals and jellyfish
Bryozoans
Sponges
Foraminiferans

PLANTS

Algae
Vascular plants
Sphenopsids
Ferns
Cycads
Angiosperms
Ginkgos
Conifers

65
36.5
35.5
25.5
5.2
1.64
0.01
0

Palaeocene epoch
Eocene epoch
Oligocene epoch
Miocene epoch
Pliocene epoch
Pleistocene epoch
Holocene epoch

Tertiary period

Quaternary period

MILLIONS OF YEARS AGO (MYA)

Turreted spire

Ribs

Large body whorl

Aperture

STRUTHIOLARIA
(GASTROPOD MOLLUSK)

Large, elevated eye

Spiny, segmented body

Wide head

Spiny tail

LEONASPIS
(TRILOBITE)

Claw

Carapace

MUD CRAB
(CRUSTACEAN)

Ambulacral area

Tiny tubercle

Genital pore

CLYPEASTER
(ECHINODERM)

279

Mineral resources

MINERAL RESOURCES CAN BE DEFINED AS naturally occurring substances that can be extracted from the Earth and are useful as fuels and raw materials. Coal, oil, and gas—collectively called fossil fuels—are commonly included in this group, but are not strictly minerals, because they are of organic origin. Coal formation begins when vegetation is buried and partly decomposed to form peat. Overlying sediments compress the peat and transform it into lignite (soft brown coal). As the overlying sediments accumulate, increasing pressure and temperature eventually transform the lignite into bituminous and hard anthracite coals. Oil and gas are usually formed from organic molecules that were deposited in marine sediments. Under the effects of heat and pressure, the compressed organic molecules undergo complex chemical changes to form oil and gas. The oil and gas percolate upward through water-saturated permeable rocks. They may rise to the Earth's surface, or accumulate below an impermeable layer of rock that has been folded or faulted to form a trap—an anticline (upfold) trap, for example. Minerals are inorganic substances that may consist of a single chemical element, such as gold, silver, or copper, or combinations of elements (see pp. 268-269). Some minerals are concentrated in mineralization zones in rock associated with crustal movements or volcanic activity. Others may be found in sediments as placer deposits—accumulations of high-density minerals that have been weathered out of rocks, transported, and deposited (on riverbeds, for example).

OIL RIG, NORTH SEA

PLANT MATTER

Stalk

Leaf

Decayed plant matter

About 60% carbon

PEAT

About 70% carbon

Crumbly texture

LIGNITE (BROWN COAL)

Powdery texture

About 80% carbon

Shiny surface

BITUMINOUS COAL

About 95% carbon

ANTHRACITE COAL

HOW COAL IS FORMED

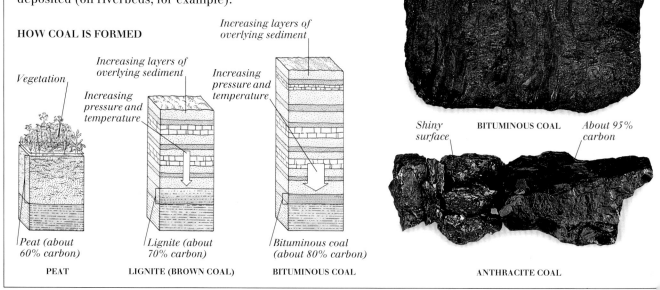

Vegetation

Increasing pressure and temperature

Increasing layers of overlying sediment

Increasing pressure and temperature

Increasing layers of overlying sediment

Increasing pressure and temperature

Peat (about 60% carbon)

PEAT

Lignite (about 70% carbon)

LIGNITE (BROWN COAL)

Bituminous coal (about 80% carbon)

BITUMINOUS COAL

EXAMPLES OF OIL AND GAS TRAPS

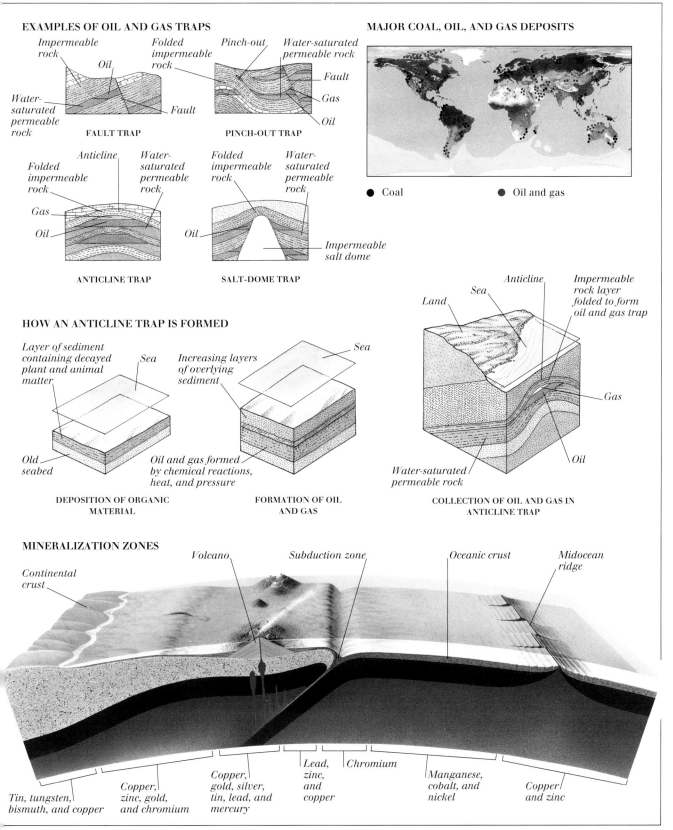

Impermeable rock

Oil

Folded impermeable rock

Pinch-out

Water-saturated permeable rock

Water-saturated permeable rock

Fault

FAULT TRAP

Fault

Gas

Oil

PINCH-OUT TRAP

Anticline

Water-saturated permeable rock

Folded impermeable rock

Gas

Oil

ANTICLINE TRAP

Folded impermeable rock

Water-saturated permeable rock

Oil

Impermeable salt dome

SALT-DOME TRAP

MAJOR COAL, OIL, AND GAS DEPOSITS

● Coal

● Oil and gas

HOW AN ANTICLINE TRAP IS FORMED

Layer of sediment containing decayed plant and animal matter

Sea

Old seabed

Increasing layers of overlying sediment

Sea

Oil and gas formed by chemical reactions, heat, and pressure

DEPOSITION OF ORGANIC MATERIAL

FORMATION OF OIL AND GAS

Land

Sea

Anticline

Impermeable rock layer folded to form oil and gas trap

Gas

Oil

Water-saturated permeable rock

COLLECTION OF OIL AND GAS IN ANTICLINE TRAP

MINERALIZATION ZONES

Continental crust

Volcano

Subduction zone

Oceanic crust

Midocean ridge

Tin, tungsten, bismuth, and copper

Copper, zinc, gold, and chromium

Copper, gold, silver, tin, lead, and mercury

Lead, zinc, and copper

Chromium

Manganese, cobalt, and nickel

Copper and zinc

281

Weathering and erosion

WEATHERING IS THE BREAKING DOWN of rocks on the Earth's surface. There are two main types: physical (or mechanical), and chemical. Physical weathering may be caused by temperature changes, such as freezing and thawing, or by abrasion from material carried by winds, rivers, or glaciers. Rocks may also be broken down by the actions of animals and plants, such as the burrowing of animals and the growth of roots. Chemical weathering causes rocks to decompose by changing their chemical composition. For example, rainwater may dissolve certain minerals in a rock. Erosion is the wearing away and removal of land surfaces by water, wind, or ice. It is greatest in areas of little or no surface vegetation, such as deserts, where sand dunes may form.

FORMATION OF A ROCK PAVEMENT (HAMADA)

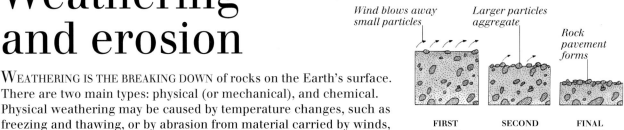

Wind blows away small particles

Larger particles aggregate

Rock pavement forms

FIRST STAGE **SECOND STAGE** **FINAL STAGE**

FEATURES PRODUCED BY WIND ACTION

Wind-blown sand

Mushroom-shaped rock

Neck

Rock base eroded by wind-blown sand

ROCK PEDESTAL

Wind-blown sand Widened joint Soft rock

Hard rock

ZEUGEN

Wind-blown sand Furrow

Hard rock

Soft rock eroded by wind-blown sand

YARDANG

FEATURES OF WEATHERING AND EROSION

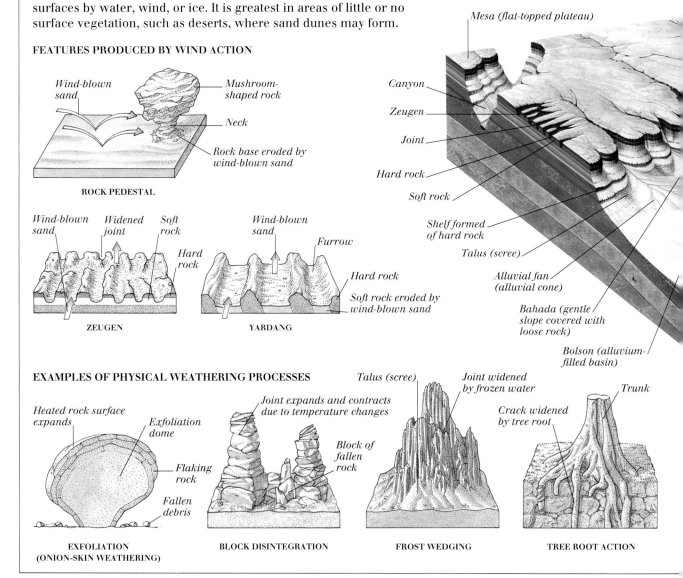

Mesa (flat-topped plateau)

Canyon

Zeugen

Joint

Hard rock

Soft rock

Shelf formed of hard rock

Talus (scree)

Alluvial fan (alluvial cone)

Bahada (gentle slope covered with loose rock)

Bolson (alluvium-filled basin)

EXAMPLES OF PHYSICAL WEATHERING PROCESSES

Heated rock surface expands

Exfoliation dome

Flaking rock

Fallen debris

EXFOLIATION (ONION-SKIN WEATHERING)

Joint expands and contracts due to temperature changes

Block of fallen rock

BLOCK DISINTEGRATION

Talus (scree)

Joint widened by frozen water

FROST WEDGING

Crack widened by tree root

Trunk

TREE ROOT ACTION

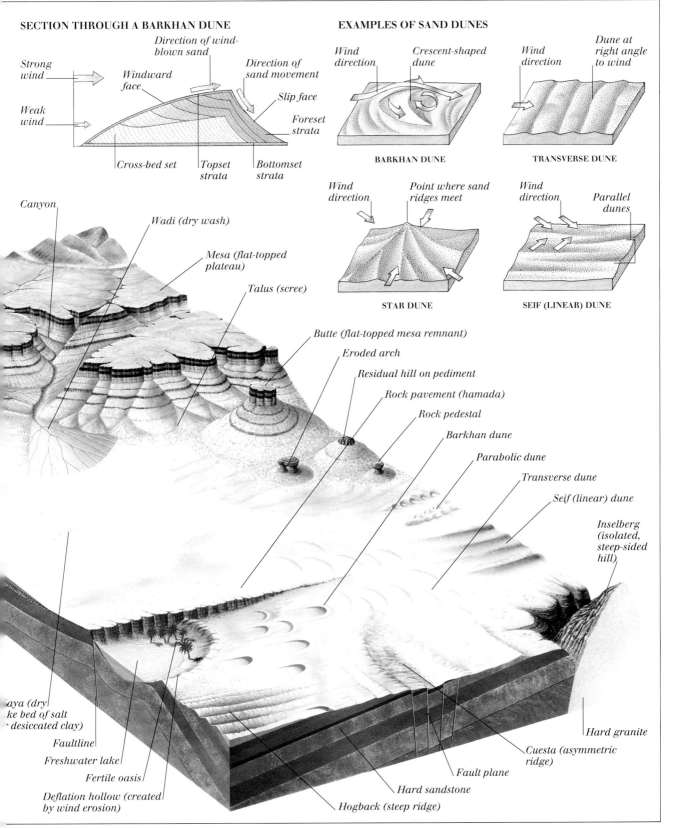

SECTION THROUGH A BARKHAN DUNE

Strong wind

Weak wind

Direction of wind-blown sand

Windward face

Direction of sand movement

Slip face

Foreset strata

Cross-bed set

Topset strata

Bottomset strata

EXAMPLES OF SAND DUNES

Wind direction

Crescent-shaped dune

BARKHAN DUNE

Wind direction

Dune at right angle to wind

TRANSVERSE DUNE

Wind direction

Point where sand ridges meet

STAR DUNE

Wind direction

Parallel dunes

SEIF (LINEAR) DUNE

Canyon

Wadi (dry wash)

Mesa (flat-topped plateau)

Talus (scree)

Butte (flat-topped mesa remnant)

Eroded arch

Residual hill on pediment

Rock pavement (hamada)

Rock pedestal

Barkhan dune

Parabolic dune

Transverse dune

Seif (linear) dune

Inselberg (isolated, steep-sided hill)

Playa (dry lake bed of salt or desiccated clay)

Faultline

Freshwater lake

Fertile oasis

Deflation hollow (created by wind erosion)

Hogback (steep ridge)

Hard sandstone

Fault plane

Cuesta (asymmetric ridge)

Hard granite

283

Caves

CAVES COMMONLY FORM in areas of limestone, although on coastlines they also occur in other rocks. Limestone is made of calcite (calcium carbonate), which dissolves in the carbonic acid naturally present in rainwater, and in humic acids from the decay of vegetation. The acidic water trickles down through cracks and joints in the limestone and between rock layers, breaking up the surface terrain into clints (blocks of rock), separated by grikes (deep cracks), and punctuated by sinkholes (also called swallow holes or potholes) into which surface streams may disappear. Underground, the acidic water dissolves the rock around crevices, opening up a network of passages and caves, which can become large caverns if the roofs collapse. Various features are formed when the dissolved calcite is redeposited. For example, it may be redeposited along an underground stream to form a gour (series of calcite ridges), or in caves and passages to form stalactites and stalagmites. Stalactites develop where calcite is left behind as water drips from the roof; where the drops land, stalagmites build up.

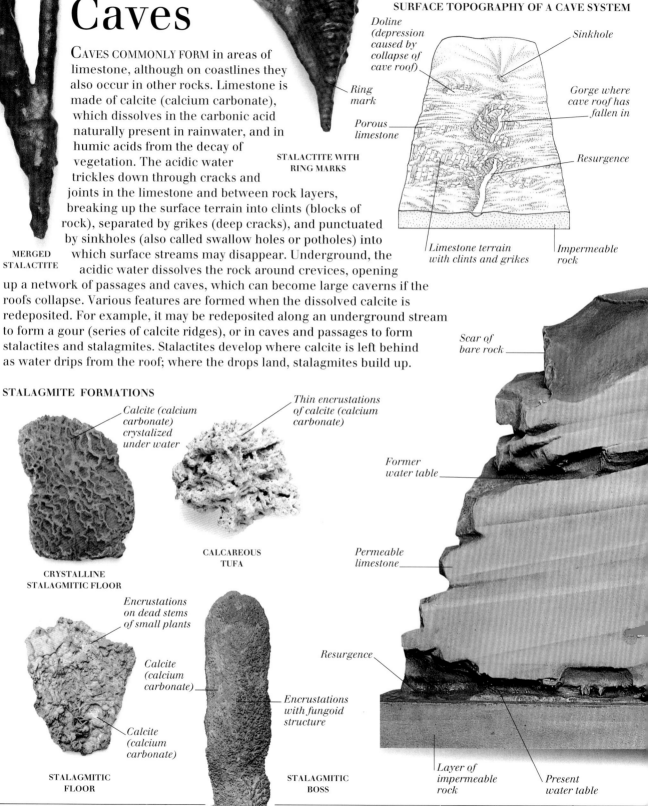

MERGED
STALACTITE

STALACTITE WITH
RING MARKS

Ring
mark

SURFACE TOPOGRAPHY OF A CAVE SYSTEM

Doline (depression caused by collapse of cave roof)

Sinkhole

Porous limestone

Gorge where cave roof has fallen in

Resurgence

Limestone terrain with clints and grikes

Impermeable rock

STALAGMITE FORMATIONS

Calcite (calcium carbonate) crystalized under water

Thin encrustations of calcite (calcium carbonate)

CRYSTALLINE
STALAGMITIC FLOOR

CALCAREOUS
TUFA

Encrustations on dead stems of small plants

Calcite (calcium carbonate)

Calcite (calcium carbonate)

STALAGMITIC
FLOOR

Encrustations with fungoid structure

STALAGMITIC
BOSS

Scar of bare rock

Former water table

Permeable limestone

Resurgence

Layer of impermeable rock

Present water table

DEVELOPMENT OF A CAVE SYSTEM

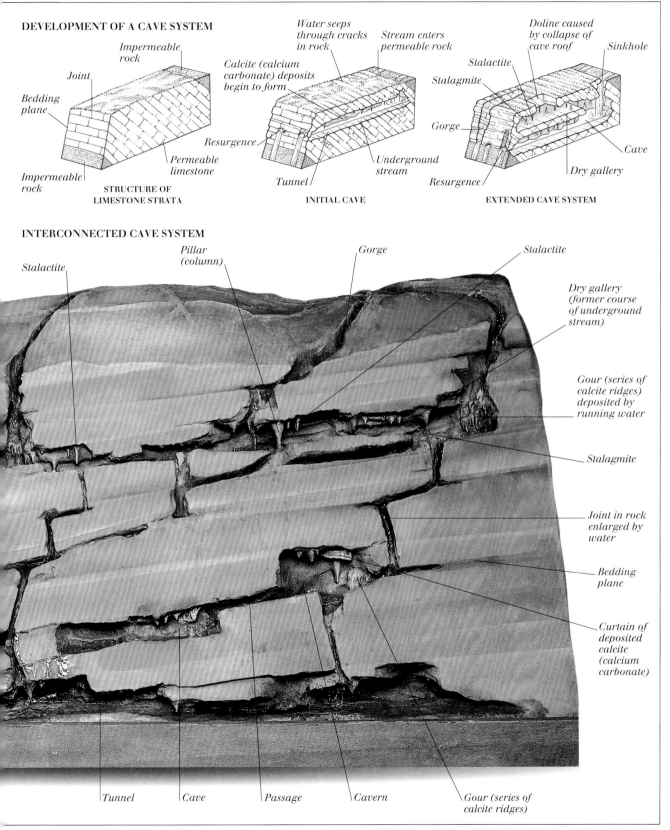

Impermeable rock

Joint

Bedding plane

Impermeable rock

Permeable limestone

STRUCTURE OF LIMESTONE STRATA

Water seeps through cracks in rock

Stream enters permeable rock

Calcite (calcium carbonate) deposits begin to form

Resurgence

Tunnel

Underground stream

INITIAL CAVE

Doline caused by collapse of cave roof

Sinkhole

Stalactite

Stalagmite

Gorge

Resurgence

Dry gallery

Cave

EXTENDED CAVE SYSTEM

INTERCONNECTED CAVE SYSTEM

Stalactite

Pillar (column)

Gorge

Stalactite

Dry gallery (former course of underground stream)

Gour (series of calcite ridges) deposited by running water

Stalagmite

Joint in rock enlarged by water

Bedding plane

Curtain of deposited calcite (calcium carbonate)

Tunnel

Cave

Passage

Cavern

Gour (series of calcite ridges)

285

Glaciers

GLACIER BAY, ALASKA

A VALLEY GLACIER IS A LARGE MASS OF ICE that forms on land and moves slowly downhill under its own weight. It is formed from snow that collects in cirques (mountain hollows also known as corries), compressing into ice as more and more snow accumulates. The cirque is deepened by frost wedging and abrasion (see pp. 282-283), and arêtes (sharp ridges) develop between adjacent cirques. Eventually, so much ice builds up that the glacier begins to flow. As the glacier moves it collects moraine (debris), which may range in size from particles of dust to large boulders. The rocks at the base of the glacier erode the glacial valley, giving it a U-shaped cross section. Under the glacier, *roches moutonnées* (eroded outcrops of hard rock) and drumlins (rounded mounds of rock and clay) are left behind on the valley floor. The glacier ends at a terminus (the snout), where the ice melts as fast as it arrives. If the temperature increases, the ice melts faster than it arrives, and the glacier retreats. The retreating glacier leaves behind its moraine and also erratics (isolated single boulders). Glacial streams from the melting glacier deposit eskers and kames (ridges and mounds of sand and gravel) but carry away the finer sediment to form a stratified outwash plain. Lumps of ice carried on to this plain melt, creating holes called kettles.

VALLEY GLACIER

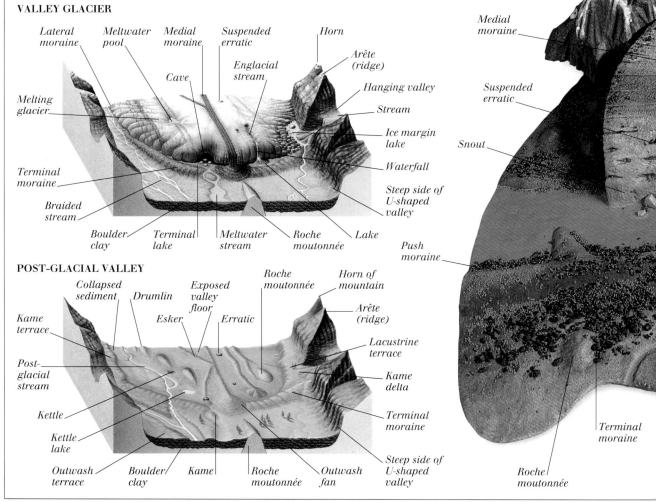

POST-GLACIAL VALLEY

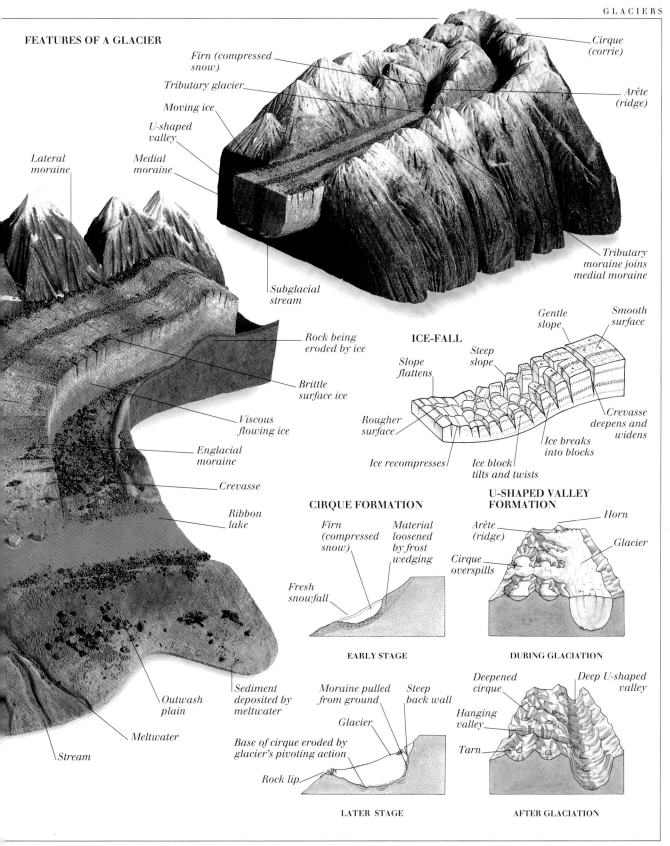

FEATURES OF A GLACIER

Cirque
(corrie)

Firn (compressed
snow)

Tributary glacier

Arête
(ridge)

Moving ice

U-shaped
valley

Lateral
moraine

Medial
moraine

Tributary
moraine joins
medial moraine

Subglacial
stream

Rock being
eroded by ice

ICE-FALL

Gentle
slope

Smooth
surface

Steep
slope

Slope
flattens

Brittle
surface ice

Viscous
flowing ice

Crevasse
deepens and
widens

Rougher
surface

Englacial
moraine

Ice recompresses

Ice block
tilts and twists

Ice breaks
into blocks

Crevasse

Ribbon
lake

CIRQUE FORMATION

**U-SHAPED VALLEY
FORMATION**

Firn
(compressed
snow)

Material
loosened
by frost
wedging

Arête
(ridge)

Horn

Glacier

Cirque
overspills

Fresh
snowfall

Outwash
plain

EARLY STAGE

DURING GLACIATION

Sediment
deposited by
meltwater

Moraine pulled
from ground

Steep
back wall

Deepened
cirque

Deep U-shaped
valley

Meltwater

Glacier

Hanging
valley

Stream

Base of cirque eroded by
glacier's pivoting action

Tarn

Rock lip

LATER STAGE

AFTER GLACIATION

287

Rivers

RIVERS FORM PART of the water cycle—the continuous
circulation of water between the land, sea, and
atmosphere. The source of a river may be a mountain
spring, or lake, or a melting glacier. The course that
the river subsequently takes depends on the slope of
the terrain and on the rock types and formations over
which it flows. In its early, upland stages, a river
tumbles steeply over rocks and boulders and cuts a
steep-sided V-shaped valley. Farther downstream, it
flows smoothly over sediments and forms winding
meanders, eroding sideways to create broad valleys
and plains. On reaching the coast, the river may deposit
sediment, forming an estuary or delta (see pp. 290-291).

RIVER CAPTURE

*Tributary erodes
headward*

River

River

EARLY STAGE

*Dry
valley*

*River captured
by tributary*

*River flow
decreases*

*River flow
increases*

LATER STAGE

THE WATER CYCLE

*Precipitation
falls on high
ground*

Wind

*Water
carried
downstream
by river*

*Water vapor released
into atmosphere by
trees and other plants*

Wind

*Water vapor
forms clouds*

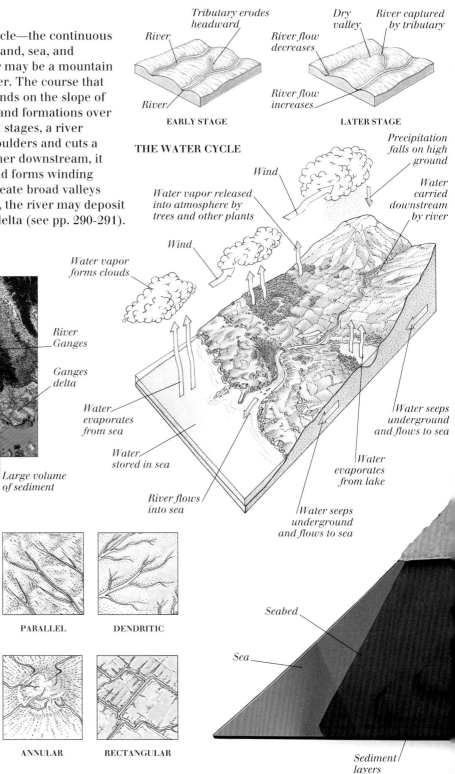

*Water
evaporates
from sea*

*Water
stored in sea*

*River flows
into sea*

*Water seeps
underground
and flows to sea*

*Water seeps
underground
and flows to sea*

*Water
evaporates
from lake*

SATELLITE IMAGE OF GANGES RIVER DELTA, BANGLADESH

*River
Ganges*

*Ganges
delta*

*Infertile
swampland*

Distributary

*Large volume
of sediment*

RIVER DRAINAGE PATTERNS

RADIAL

CENTRIPETAL

PARALLEL

DENDRITIC

DERANGED

TRELLISED

ANNULAR

RECTANGULAR

Seabed

Sea

*Sediment
layers*

STAGES IN A RIVER'S DEVELOPMENT

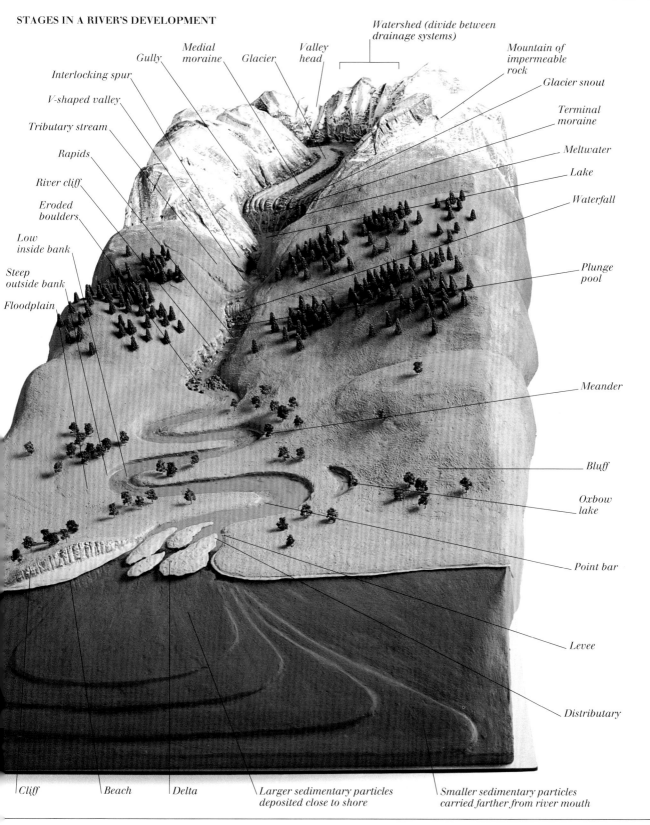

Watershed (divide between drainage systems)

Gully

Medial moraine

Glacier

Valley head

Mountain of impermeable rock

Glacier snout

Interlocking spur

Terminal moraine

V-shaped valley

Meltwater

Tributary stream

Lake

Rapids

Waterfall

River cliff

Eroded boulders

Plunge pool

Low inside bank

Steep outside bank

Floodplain

Meander

Bluff

Oxbow lake

Point bar

Levee

Distributary

Cliff   Beach   Delta   Larger sedimentary particles deposited close to shore

Smaller sedimentary particles carried farther from river mouth

River features

RIVERS ARE ONE OF THE MAJOR FORCES that shape the landscape. Near its source, a river is steep (see pp. 288-289). It erodes downward, carving out V-shaped valleys and deep gorges. Waterfalls and rapids are formed where the river flows from hard rock to softer, more easily eroded rock. Farther downstream, meanders may form and there is greater sideways erosion, resulting in a broad river valley. The river sometimes erodes through the neck of a meander to form an oxbow lake. Sediment deposited on the valley floor by meandering rivers and during floods helps to create a floodplain. Floods may also deposit sediment on the banks of the river to form levees. As a river spills into the sea or a lake, it deposits large amounts of sediment, and may form a delta. A delta is an area of sand bars, swamps and lagoons through which the river flows in several channels called distributaries—the Mississippi delta, for example. Often, a rise in sea level may have flooded the river mouth to form a broad estuary, a tidal section where seawater mixes with fresh water.

HOW WATERFALLS AND RAPIDS ARE FORMED

Plunge pool

Hard rock

Softer rock

WATERFALL

Hard rock

River erodes softer rocks to form rapids

Softer rock

Gently sloping rock strata

RAPIDS

A RIVER VALLEY DRAINAGE SYSTEM

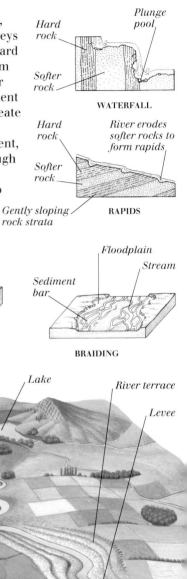

Headward erosion

Waterfall

Gorge

Steep gorge cut by river

Mountain

GORGE

Floodplain

Stream

Sediment bar

BRAIDING

Entrenched meander

Braiding

Lake

River terrace

Levee

River erodes headward

HEADWARD EROSION

River erodes downward

Natural bridge

Meander

Steep cliffs

ENTRENCHED MEANDER

Old meander

Bridge

River

NATURAL BRIDGE

Oxbow lake

Lake

River mouth

Sediment deposited on seabed

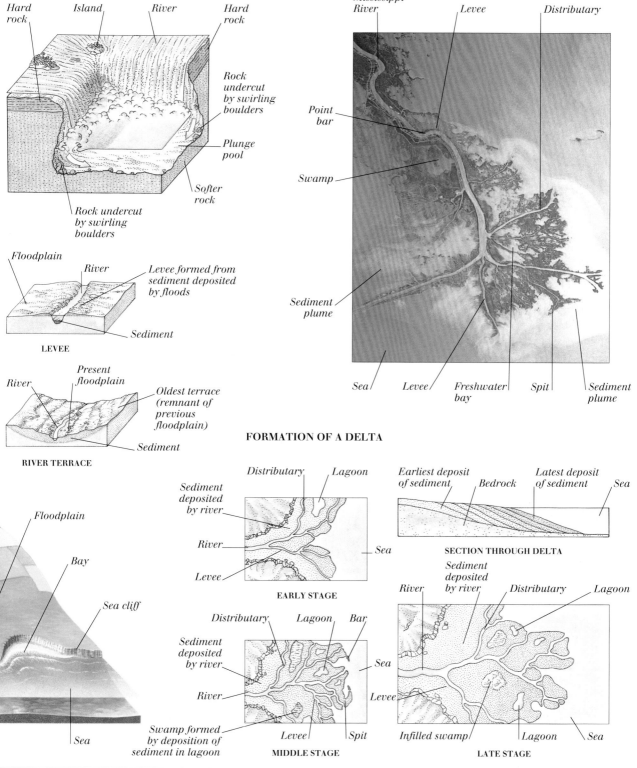

WATERFALL FEATURES

Hard rock
Island
River
Hard rock

Rock undercut by swirling boulders

Plunge pool

Softer rock

Rock undercut by swirling boulders

Floodplain
River
Levee formed from sediment deposited by floods

Sediment

LEVEE

River
Present floodplain
Oldest terrace (remnant of previous floodplain)

Sediment

RIVER TERRACE

Floodplain

Bay

Sea cliff

Sea

THE MISSISSIPPI DELTA

Mississippi River
Levee
Distributary

Point bar

Swamp

Sediment plume

Sea
Levee
Freshwater bay
Spit
Sediment plume

FORMATION OF A DELTA

Distributary
Lagoon

Sediment deposited by river

River

Levee

Sea

EARLY STAGE

Earliest deposit of sediment
Bedrock
Latest deposit of sediment
Sea

SECTION THROUGH DELTA

Distributary
Lagoon
Bar

Sediment deposited by river

River

Sea

Swamp formed by deposition of sediment in lagoon

Levee
Spit

MIDDLE STAGE

Sediment deposited by river

River
Distributary
Lagoon

Levee

Infilled swamp
Lagoon
Sea

LATE STAGE

291

Lakes and groundwater

NATURAL LAKES OCCUR WHERE a large quantity of water collects in a hollow in impermeable rock or is prevented from draining away by a barrier, such as moraine (glacial deposits) or solidified lava. Lakes are often relatively short-lived landscape features, because they tend to become silted up by sediment from the streams and rivers that feed them. Some of the more long-lasting lakes are found in deep rift valleys formed by vertical movements of the Earth's crust (see pp. 58-59)—for example, Lake Baikal in Russia, the world's largest freshwater lake, and the Dead Sea in the Middle East, one of the world's saltiest lakes. Where water is able to drain away, it sinks into the ground until it reaches a layer of impermeable rock, then accumulates in the permeable rock above it. This water-saturated permeable rock is called an aquifer. The saturated zone varies in depth according to seasonal and climatic changes. In wet conditions, the water stored underground builds up, while in dry periods it becomes depleted. Where the upper edge of the saturated zone—the water table—meets the ground surface, water emerges as springs. In an artesian basin, where the aquifer is below an aquiclude (layer of impermeable rock), the water table throughout the basin is determined by its height at the rim. At the center of such a basin, the water table is above ground level. The water in the basin is thus trapped below the water table and can rise under its own pressure along fault lines or well shafts.

LAKE BAIKAL, RUSSIA

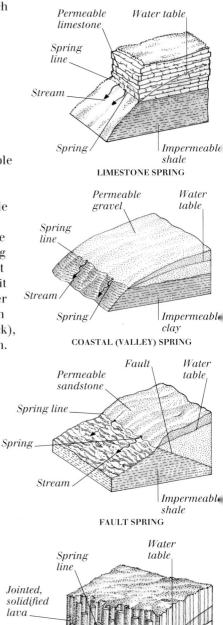

EXAMPLES OF SPRINGS

Permeable limestone
Water table
Spring line
Stream
Spring
Impermeable shale

LIMESTONE SPRING

Permeable gravel
Water table
Spring line
Stream
Spring
Impermeable clay

COASTAL (VALLEY) SPRING

Fault
Water table
Permeable sandstone
Spring line
Spring
Stream
Impermeable shale

FAULT SPRING

Water table
Spring line
Jointed, solidified lava
Spring
Jointed, solidified lava
Stream
Impermeable mudstone

LAVA SPRING

STRUCTURE OF AN ARTESIAN BASIN

Recharge area
Water table
Height of water table in recharge area
Artesian spring
Aquiclude (impermeable rock)
Artesian spring
Fault
Artesian well
Aquifer (saturated rock)
Aquiclude (impermeable rock)

FEATURES OF A GROUNDWATER SYSTEM

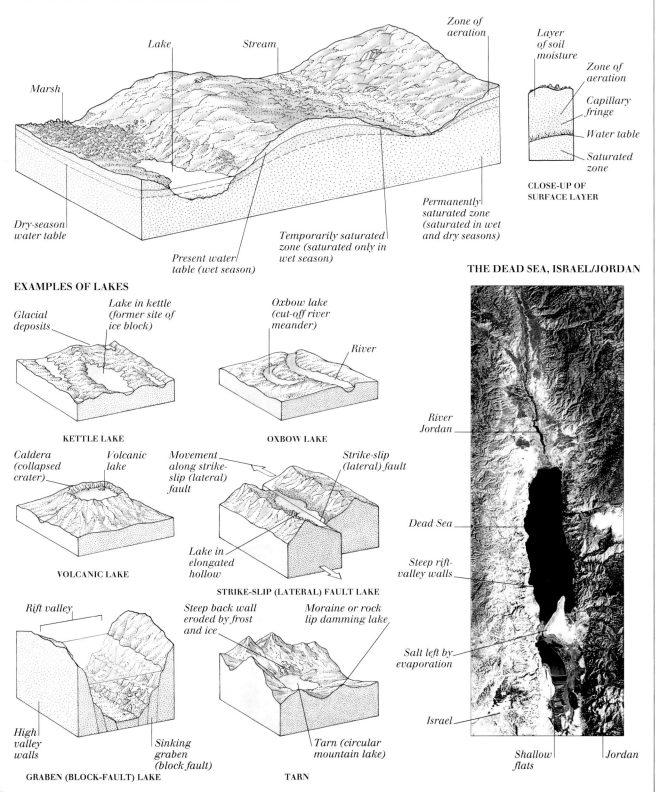

Zone of aeration

Lake

Stream

Marsh

Layer of soil moisture

Zone of aeration

Capillary fringe

Water table

Saturated zone

CLOSE-UP OF SURFACE LAYER

Dry-season water table

Present water table (wet season)

Temporarily saturated zone (saturated only in wet season)

Permanently saturated zone (saturated in wet and dry seasons)

EXAMPLES OF LAKES

Glacial deposits

Lake in kettle (former site of ice block)

Oxbow lake (cut-off river meander)

River

KETTLE LAKE

OXBOW LAKE

Caldera (collapsed crater)

Volcanic lake

Movement along strike-slip (lateral) fault

Strike-slip (lateral) fault

Lake in elongated hollow

VOLCANIC LAKE

STRIKE-SLIP (LATERAL) FAULT LAKE

Rift valley

Steep back wall eroded by frost and ice

Moraine or rock lip damming lake

High valley walls

Sinking graben (block fault)

Tarn (circular mountain lake)

GRABEN (BLOCK-FAULT) LAKE

TARN

THE DEAD SEA, ISRAEL/JORDAN

River Jordan

Dead Sea

Steep rift-valley walls

Salt left by evaporation

Israel

Shallow flats

Jordan

293

Coastlines

COASTLINES ARE AMONG THE MOST RAPIDLY changing landscape features. Some are eroded by waves, wind, and rain, causing cliffs to be undercut and caves to be hollowed out of solid rock. Others are built up by waves transporting sand and small rocks in a process known as longshore drift and by rivers depositing sediment in deltas. Additional influences include the activities of living organisms such as coral, crustal movements, and sea-level variations due to climatic changes. Rising land or a drop in sea level creates an emergent coastline, with cliffs and beaches standing above the new shoreline. Sinking land or a rise in sea level produces a drowned coastline, typified by fjords (submerged glacial valleys) or submerged river valleys.

FEATURES OF A SEA CLIFF

Cliff top

Cliff face

High tide level

Low tide level

Offshore deposits

Wave-cut platform

Undercut area of cliff

FEATURES OF WAVES

Wave height

Crest

Wavelength

Trough

Shorter wavelength near beach

Circular orbit of water and suspended particles

Orbit deformed into ellipse as water gets shallower

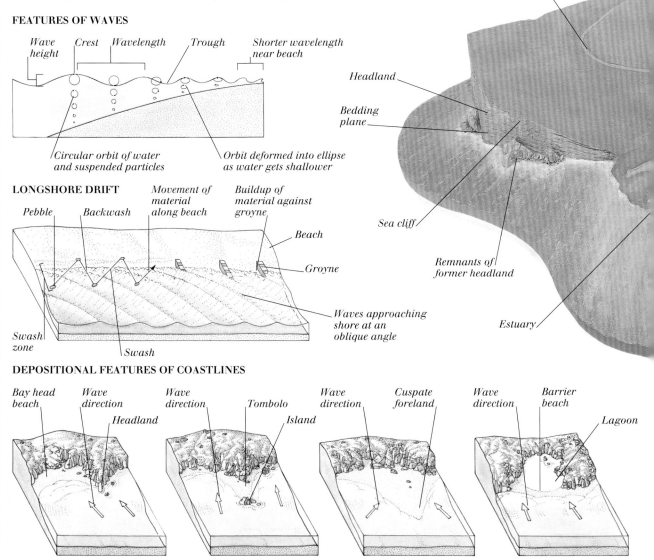

Mature river

Headland

Bedding plane

Sea cliff

Remnants of former headland

Estuary

LONGSHORE DRIFT

Pebble

Backwash

Movement of material along beach

Buildup of material against groyne

Beach

Groyne

Swash zone

Swash

Waves approaching shore at an oblique angle

DEPOSITIONAL FEATURES OF COASTLINES

Bay head beach

Wave direction

Headland

Wave direction

Tombolo

Island

Wave direction

Cuspate foreland

Wave direction

Barrier beach

Lagoon

BAY HEAD BEACH

TOMBOLO

CUSPATE FORELAND

BARRIER BEACH

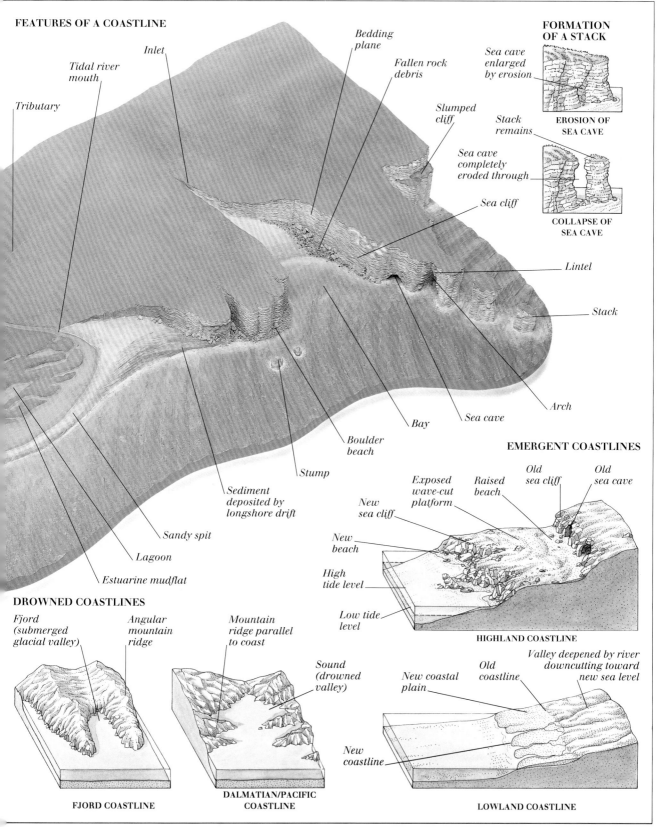

FEATURES OF A COASTLINE

Tidal river mouth

Inlet

Bedding plane

Fallen rock debris

Slumped cliff

Tributary

Sea cliff

Lintel

Stack

Arch

Sea cave

Bay

Boulder beach

Stump

Sediment deposited by longshore drift

Sandy spit

Lagoon

Estuarine mudflat

FORMATION OF A STACK

Sea cave enlarged by erosion

EROSION OF SEA CAVE

Stack remains

Sea cave completely eroded through

COLLAPSE OF SEA CAVE

EMERGENT COASTLINES

Exposed wave-cut platform

Raised beach

Old sea cliff

Old sea cave

New sea cliff

New beach

High tide level

Low tide level

HIGHLAND COASTLINE

DROWNED COASTLINES

Fjord (submerged glacial valley)

Angular mountain ridge

Mountain ridge parallel to coast

Sound (drowned valley)

FJORD COASTLINE

DALMATIAN/PACIFIC COASTLINE

New coastal plain

Old coastline

Valley deepened by river downcutting toward new sea level

New coastline

LOWLAND COASTLINE

Oceans and seas

OCEANS AND SEAS COVER ABOUT 70 PERCENT of the Earth's
surface and account for about 97 percent of its total
water. These oceans and seas play a crucial role
in regulating temperature variations and
determining climate. Their waters absorb
heat from the Sun, especially in tropical
regions, and the surface currents distribute
it around the Earth, warming overlying
air masses and neighboring land in
winter and cooling them in summer.
The oceans are never still. Differences
in temperature and salinity drive
deep current systems, while surface
currents are generated by winds
blowing over the oceans. All currents
are deflected—to the right in the
Northern Hemisphere, to the left in
the Southern Hemisphere—as a result
of the Earth's rotation. This deflective
factor is known as the Coriolis force.
A current that begins on the surface is
immediately deflected. This current in
turn generates a current in the layer of water
beneath, which is also deflected. As the movement
is transmitted downward, the deflections form an
Ekman spiral. The waters of the oceans and seas are
also moved by the constant ebb and flow of tides. These
are caused by the gravitational pull of the Moon and Sun.
The highest tides (Spring tides) occur at full and new Moon;
the lowest tides (neap tides) occur at first and last quarter.

SURFACE CURRENTS

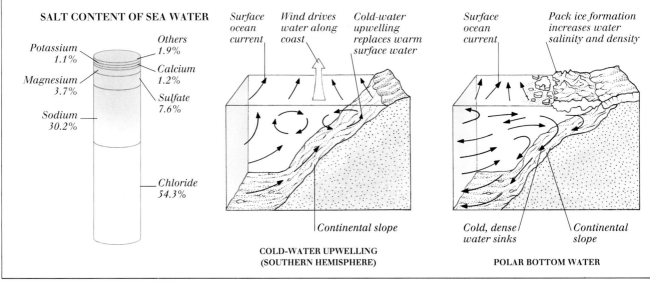

SALT CONTENT OF SEA WATER

Others
1.9%

Potassium
1.1%

Calcium
1.2%

Magnesium
3.7%

Sulfate
7.6%

Sodium
30.2%

Chloride
54.3%

Surface
ocean
current

Wind drives
water along
coast

Cold-water
upwelling
replaces warm
surface water

Continental slope

**COLD-WATER UPWELLING
(SOUTHERN HEMISPHERE)**

Surface
ocean
current

Pack ice formation
increases water
salinity and density

Cold, dense
water sinks

Continental
slope

POLAR BOTTOM WATER

OFFSHORE CURRENTS

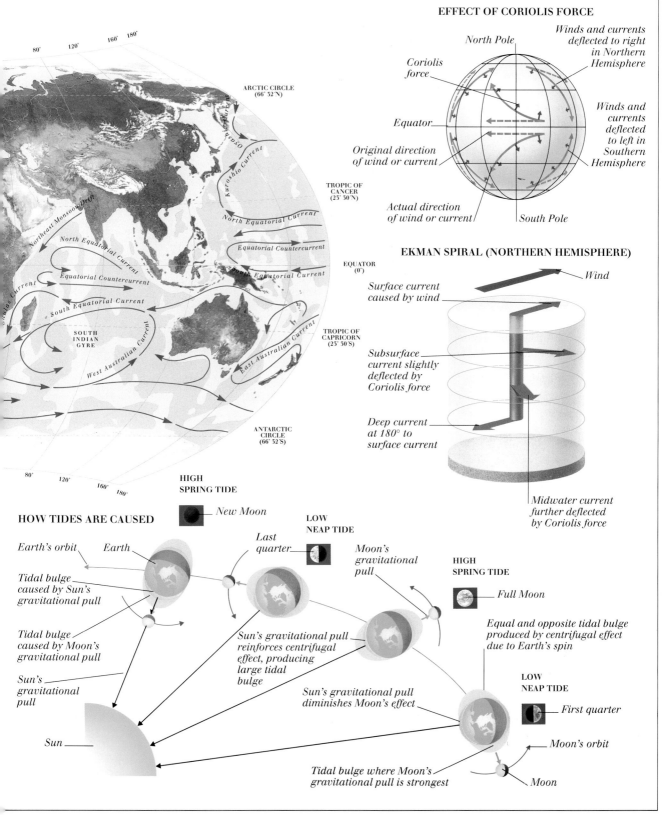

EFFECT OF CORIOLIS FORCE

North Pole

Coriolis force

Winds and currents deflected to right in Northern Hemisphere

Equator

Original direction of wind or current

Winds and currents deflected to left in Southern Hemisphere

Actual direction of wind or current

South Pole

EKMAN SPIRAL (NORTHERN HEMISPHERE)

EQUATOR (0°)

Wind

Surface current caused by wind

Subsurface current slightly deflected by Coriolis force

Deep current at 180° to surface current

Midwater current further deflected by Coriolis force

ARCTIC CIRCLE (66° 52'N)

Oyashio Current

Kuroshio Current

Northeast Monsoon Drift

North Equatorial Current

TROPIC OF CANCER (23° 30'N)

North Equatorial Current

Equatorial Countercurrent

South Equatorial Current

Equatorial Countercurrent

South Equatorial Current

Somalia Current

SOUTH INDIAN GYRE

East Australian Current

West Australian Current

TROPIC OF CAPRICORN (23° 30'S)

ANTARCTIC CIRCLE (66° 52'S)

80° 120° 160° 180°

HOW TIDES ARE CAUSED

Earth's orbit *Earth*

Tidal bulge caused by Sun's gravitational pull

Tidal bulge caused by Moon's gravitational pull

Sun's gravitational pull

Sun

HIGH SPRING TIDE

New Moon

Last quarter

LOW NEAP TIDE

Moon's gravitational pull

Sun's gravitational pull reinforces centrifugal effect, producing large tidal bulge

Sun's gravitational pull diminishes Moon's effect

Tidal bulge where Moon's gravitational pull is strongest

HIGH SPRING TIDE

Full Moon

Equal and opposite tidal bulge produced by centrifugal effect due to Earth's spin

LOW NEAP TIDE

First quarter

Moon's orbit

Moon

The ocean floor

THE OCEAN FLOOR INCLUDES TWO SECTIONS: the continental shelf and slope, and the deep-ocean floor. The continental shelf and slope are part of the continental crust, but may extend far into the ocean. Sloping quite gently to a depth of about 460 feet, the continental shelf is covered in sandy deposits shaped by waves and tidal currents. At the edge of the continental shelf, the seabed slopes down to the abyssal plain, which lies at an average depth of about 12,500 feet. On this deep-ocean floor is a layer of sediment made up of clays, fine oozes formed from the remains of tiny sea creatures, and occasional mineral-rich deposits. Echo-sounding and remote sensing from satellites has revealed that the abyssal plain is divided by a world-circling system of mountain ranges, far bigger than any on land—the midocean ridge. Here, magma (molten rock) wells up from the Earth's interior and solidifies, widening the ocean floor (see pp. 58-59). As the ocean floor spreads, volcanoes that have formed over hot spots in the crust move away from their magma source; they become extinct and are increasingly submerged and eroded. Volcanoes eroded below sea level remain as seamounts (underwater mountains). In warm waters, a volcano that projects above the ocean surface often acquires a fringing coral reef, which may develop into an atoll as the volcano becomes submerged.

CONTINENTAL-SHELF FLOOR

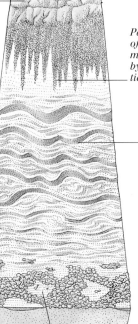

Bedrock exposed by tidal scour

Shoreline

Parallel strips of coarse material left by strong tidal currents

Sand deposited in wavy pattern by weaker currents

Irregular patches of fine sand deposited by weakest currents

FEATURES OF THE OCEAN FLOOR

Sediment

Submarine canyon

Continental shelf

Course of mud river

Continental rise

Continental slope

Guyot (flat-topped seamount)

Seamount (underwater mountain)

Abyssal plain

Continental crust

Ooze (sediment consisting of remains of tiny sea creatures)

Layer of volcanic rock

Pillow lava

Volcanic crystalline rock

Oceanic crust

DEEP-OCEAN FLOOR SEDIMENTS

KEY

☐ Calcareous ooze

☐ Pelagic clay

☐ Glacial sediments

☐ Siliceous ooze

☐ Terrigenous sediments

☐ Continental margin sediments

▨ Metalliferous muds

▧ Major nodule fields

ECHO-SOUND PROFILE OF OCEAN FLOOR

Sand wave

Event mark indicates synchronization of survey equipment

Sand wave

Seabed profile

Minor oscillations caused by ship's movement

Velocity of sound in water (1,493 m/sec; 4,898 ft/sec)

Reference code

Midocean ridge

Magma (molten rock)

Ocean trench

Sediment

DEVELOPMENT OF AN ATOLL

Volcanic island

Coral grows on shoreline

Sea level

FRINGING REEF

Lagoon

Eroded volcanic island subsides

Coral continues to grow, forming barrier reef

BARRIER REEF

Coral continues to grow where waves bring food

Lagoon

Dead coral

Volcanic island becomes submerged

ATOLL

Coral submerged too deeply to grow

Volcanic island is submerged further

SUBMERGED ATOLL

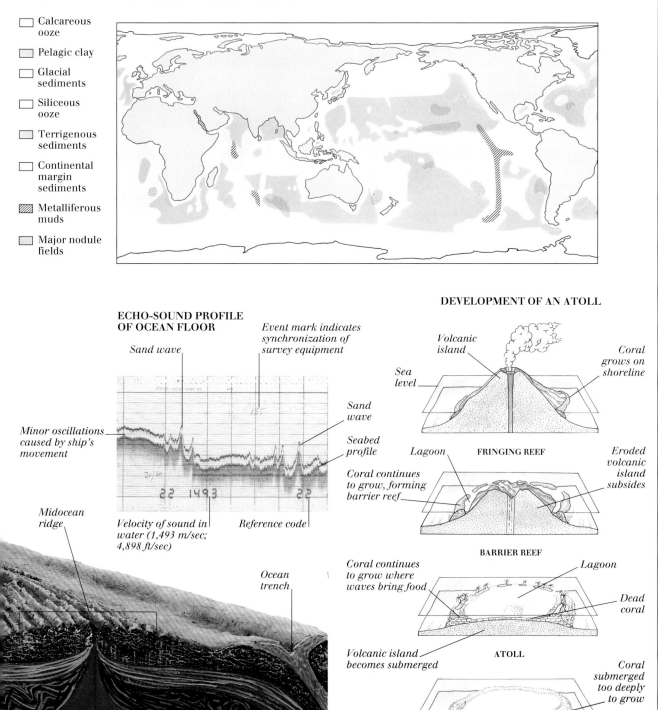

The atmosphere

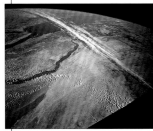

JET STREAM

THE EARTH IS SURROUNDED BY ITS ATMOSPHERE, a blanket of gases that enables life to exist on the planet. This layer has no definite outer edge, gradually becoming thinner until it merges into space, but over 80 percent of atmospheric gases are held by gravity within about 10 miles of the Earth's surface. The atmosphere blocks out much harmful ultraviolet solar radiation, and insulates the Earth against extremes of temperature by limiting both incoming solar radiation and the escape of re-radiated heat into space. This natural balance may be distorted by the greenhouse effect, as gases such as carbon dioxide have built up in the atmosphere, trapping more heat. Close to the Earth's surface, differences in air temperature and pressure cause air to circulate between the equator and poles. This circulation, together with the Coriolis force, gives rise to the prevailing surface winds and the high-level jet streams.

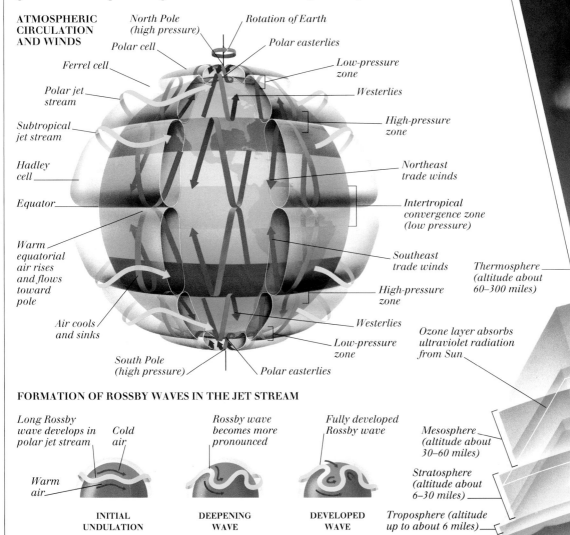

ATMOSPHERIC CIRCULATION AND WINDS

North Pole (high pressure)
Rotation of Earth
Polar cell
Polar easterlies
Ferrel cell
Low-pressure zone
Polar jet stream
Westerlies
Subtropical jet stream
High-pressure zone
Hadley cell
Northeast trade winds
Equator
Intertropical convergence zone (low pressure)
Warm equatorial air rises and flows toward pole
Southeast trade winds
High-pressure zone
Air cools and sinks
Westerlies
South Pole (high pressure)
Low-pressure zone
Polar easterlies

Exosphere (altitude above about 300 miles)
Corona
Thermosphere (altitude about 60–300 miles)
Ozone layer absorbs ultraviolet radiation from Sun

FORMATION OF ROSSBY WAVES IN THE JET STREAM

Long Rossby wave develops in polar jet stream
Cold air
Rossby wave becomes more pronounced
Fully developed Rossby wave
Warm air

INITIAL UNDULATION

DEEPENING WAVE

DEVELOPED WAVE

Mesosphere (altitude about 30–60 miles)
Stratosphere (altitude about 6–30 miles)
Troposphere (altitude up to about 6 miles)

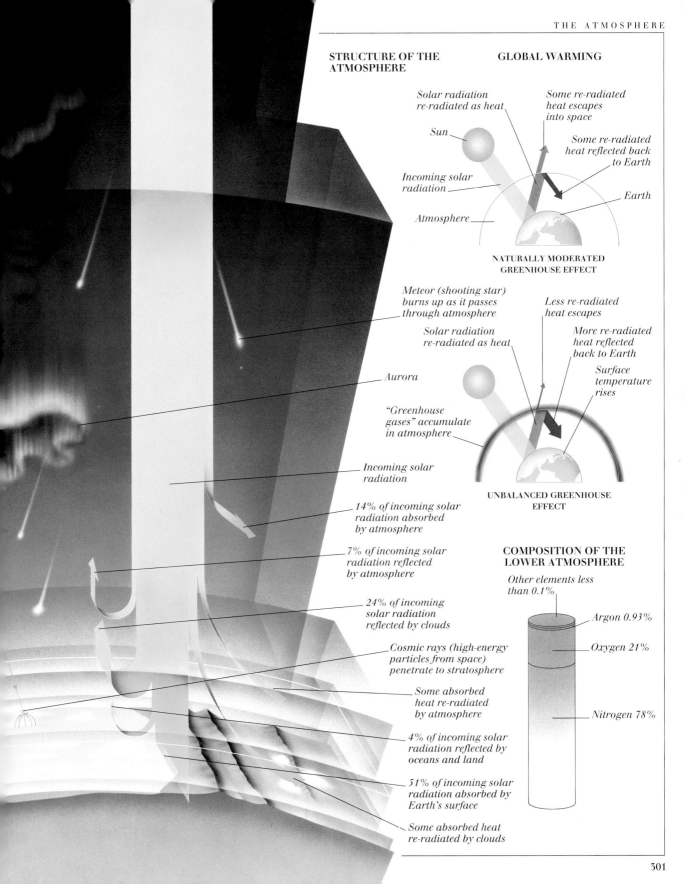

STRUCTURE OF THE ATMOSPHERE

GLOBAL WARMING

Solar radiation
re-radiated as heat

Some re-radiated
heat escapes
into space

Sun

Some re-radiated
heat reflected back
to Earth

Incoming solar
radiation

Earth

Atmosphere

**NATURALLY MODERATED
GREENHOUSE EFFECT**

Meteor (shooting star)
burns up as it passes
through atmosphere

Less re-radiated
heat escapes

Solar radiation
re-radiated as heat

More re-radiated
heat reflected
back to Earth

Aurora

Surface
temperature
rises

"Greenhouse
gases" accumulate
in atmosphere

Incoming solar
radiation

**UNBALANCED GREENHOUSE
EFFECT**

14% of incoming solar
radiation absorbed
by atmosphere

7% of incoming solar
radiation reflected
by atmosphere

COMPOSITION OF THE LOWER ATMOSPHERE

24% of incoming
solar radiation
reflected by clouds

Other elements less
than 0.1%

Cosmic rays (high-energy
particles from space)
penetrate to stratosphere

Argon 0.93%

Oxygen 21%

Some absorbed
heat re-radiated
by atmosphere

4% of incoming solar
radiation reflected by
oceans and land

Nitrogen 78%

51% of incoming solar
radiation absorbed by
Earth's surface

Some absorbed heat
re-radiated by clouds

Weather

WEATHER IS DEFINED AS THE ATMOSPHERIC CONDITIONS at a particular time and place; climate is the average weather conditions for a given region over time. Weather conditions include temperature, wind, cloud cover, and precipitation, such as rain or snow. Good weather is associated with high-pressure areas, where air is sinking. Cloudy, wet, changeable weather is common in low-pressure zones with rising, unstable air. Such conditions occur at temperate latitudes, where warm air meets cool air along the polar fronts. Here, spiraling low-pressure cells known as depressions (mid-latitude cyclones) often form. A depression usually contains a sector of warmer air, beginning at a warm front and ending at a cold front. If the two fronts merge, forming an occluded front, the warm air is pushed upward. An extreme form of low-pressure cell is a hurricane (also called a typhoon or tropical cyclone), which brings torrential rain, and exceptionally strong winds.

TYPES OF OCCLUDED FRONT

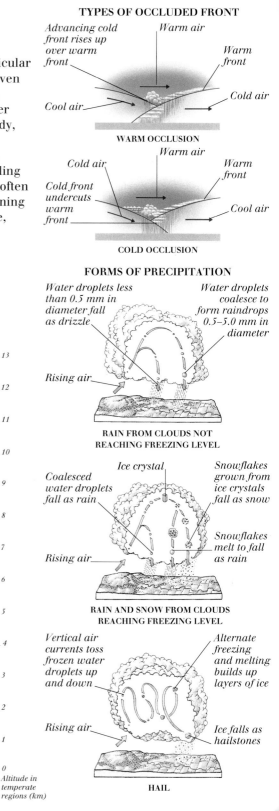

Advancing cold front rises up over warm front

Warm air

Warm front

Cool air

Cold air

WARM OCCLUSION

Cold air

Warm air

Warm front

Cold front undercuts warm front

Cool air

COLD OCCLUSION

FORMS OF PRECIPITATION

Water droplets less than 0.5 mm in diameter fall as drizzle

Water droplets coalesce to form raindrops 0.5–5.0 mm in diameter

Rising air

RAIN FROM CLOUDS NOT REACHING FREEZING LEVEL

Coalesced water droplets fall as rain

Ice crystal

Snowflakes grown from ice crystals fall as snow

Rising air

Snowflakes melt to fall as rain

RAIN AND SNOW FROM CLOUDS REACHING FREEZING LEVEL

Vertical air currents toss frozen water droplets up and down

Alternate freezing and melting builds up layers of ice

Rising air

Ice falls as hailstones

HAIL

TYPES OF CLOUD

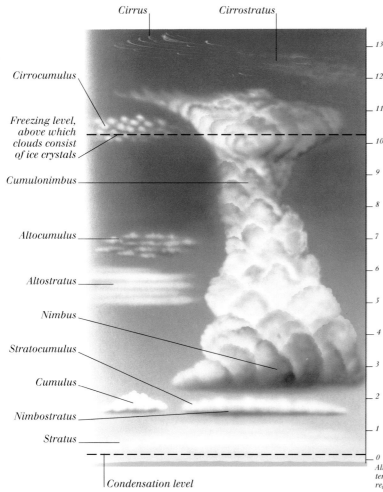

Cirrus

Cirrostratus

Cirrocumulus

Freezing level, above which clouds consist of ice crystals

Cumulonimbus

Altocumulus

Altostratus

Nimbus

Stratocumulus

Cumulus

Nimbostratus

Stratus

Condensation level

13

12

11

10

9

8

7

6

5

4

3

2

1

0

Altitude in temperate regions (km)

STRUCTURE OF A HURRICANE

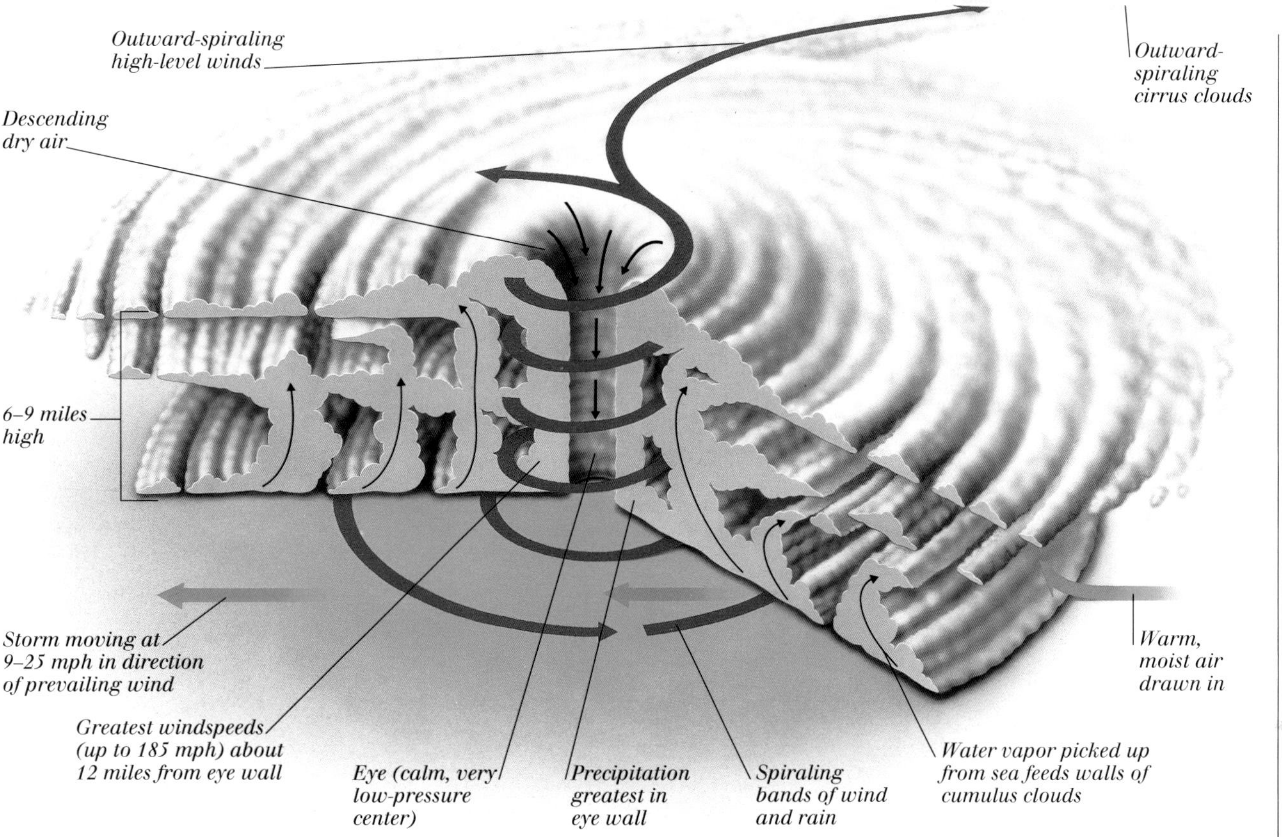

Outward-spiraling high-level winds
Outward-spiraling cirrus clouds
Descending dry air
6–9 miles high
Storm moving at 9–25 mph in direction of prevailing wind
Warm, moist air drawn in
Greatest windspeeds (up to 185 mph) about 12 miles from eye wall
Eye (calm, very low-pressure center)
Precipitation greatest in eye wall
Spiraling bands of wind and rain
Water vapor picked up from sea feeds walls of cumulus clouds

WEATHER MAP

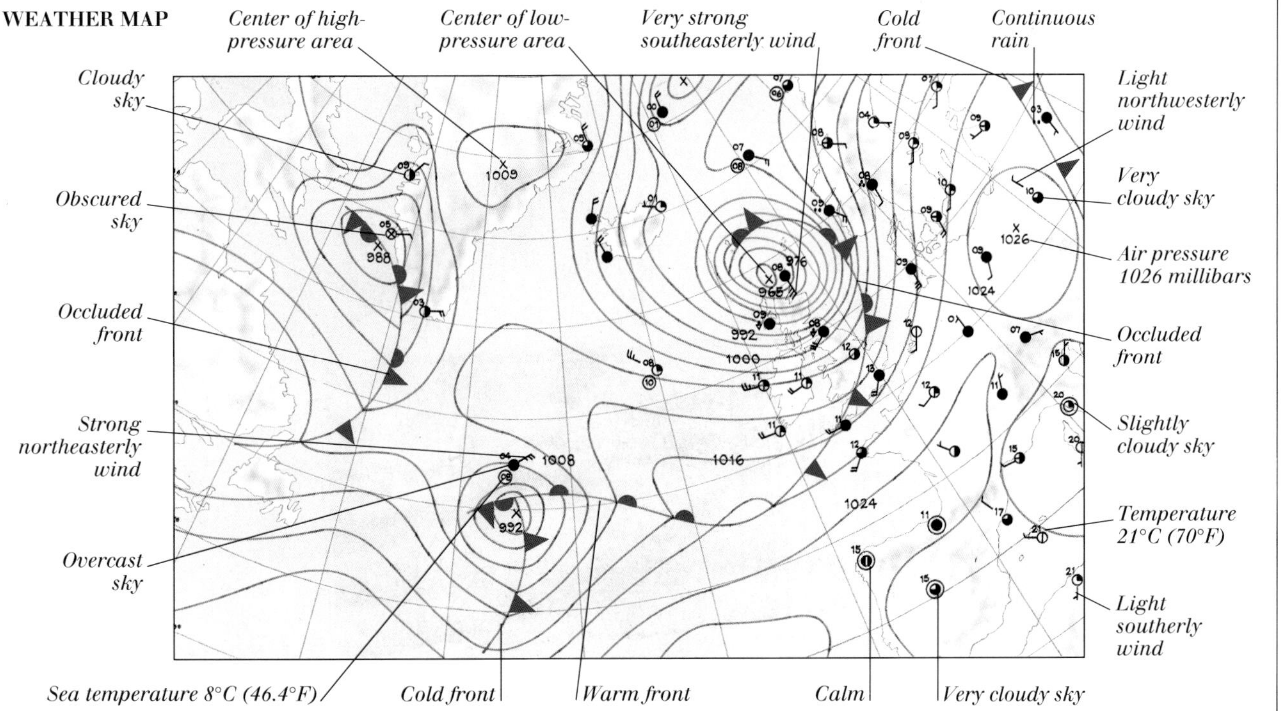

Center of high-pressure area
Center of low-pressure area
Very strong southeasterly wind
Cold front
Continuous rain
Cloudy sky
Light northwesterly wind
Very cloudy sky
Obscured sky
Air pressure 1026 millibars
Occluded front
Occluded front
Strong northeasterly wind
Slightly cloudy sky
Temperature 21°C (70°F)
Overcast sky
Light southerly wind
Sea temperature 8°C (46.4°F)
Cold front
Warm front
Calm
Very cloudy sky
1009
988
968
976
992
1000
1008
1016
1024
1026
992

Physics and Chemistry

The variety of matter

**PLANT AND INSECT
(LIVING MATTER)**

MATTER IS ANYTHING THAT OCCUPIES SPACE. It includes everything from natural substances, such as minerals or living organisms, to synthetic materials. Matter can exist in three distinct states—solid, liquid, and gas. A solid is rigid and retains its shape. A liquid is fluid, has a definite volume, and will take the shape of its container. A gas (also fluid) fills a space, so its volume will be the same as the volume of its container. Most substances can exist as a solid, a liquid, or a gas: the state is determined by temperature. At very high temperatures, matter becomes plasma, often considered to be a fourth state of matter. All matter is composed of microscopic particles, such as atoms and molecules (see pp. 308-309). The arrangement and interactions of these particles give a substance its physical and chemical properties, by which matter can be identified. There is a huge variety of matter because particles can arrange themselves in countless ways, in one substance or by mixing with others. Natural glass, for example, seems to be a solid but is, in fact, a supercool liquid: the atoms are not locked into a pattern and can flow. Pure substances known as elements (see p. 310) combine to form compounds or mixtures. Mixtures called colloids are made up of larger particles of matter suspended in a solid, liquid, or gas, while a solution is one substance dissolved in another.

TYPES OF COLLOID

HAIR GEL (SOLID IN LIQUID)

**SHAVING CREAM
(AIR IN LIQUID)**

**MIST
(LIQUID IN GAS)**

EXAMPLES OF MATTER

The element silicon in pure crystalline form

Polythene is made by combining natural materials in new ways

**POLYTHENE
(SYNTHETIC POLYMER)**

**PURE SILICON
(SEMICONDUCTOR)**

Low pressure gases

Central electrode

Streaks of plasma (mixture of electrons and charged atoms)

Voltage tears electrons from atoms of low pressure gases inside

**BALL CONTAINING
HIGH-TEMPERATURE GAS
(PLASMA)**

Obsidian is molten volcanic rock that cools quickly, so atoms cannot form a regular pattern

**OBSIDIAN
(NATURAL GLASS)**

Azurite is found naturally with deposits of copper ore

**AZURITE
(CRYSTALLINE MINERAL)**

Solid crystals dissolve in liquid water

Water

Potassium permanganate crystals

**POTASSIUM PERMANGANATE AND WATER
(SOLUTION)**

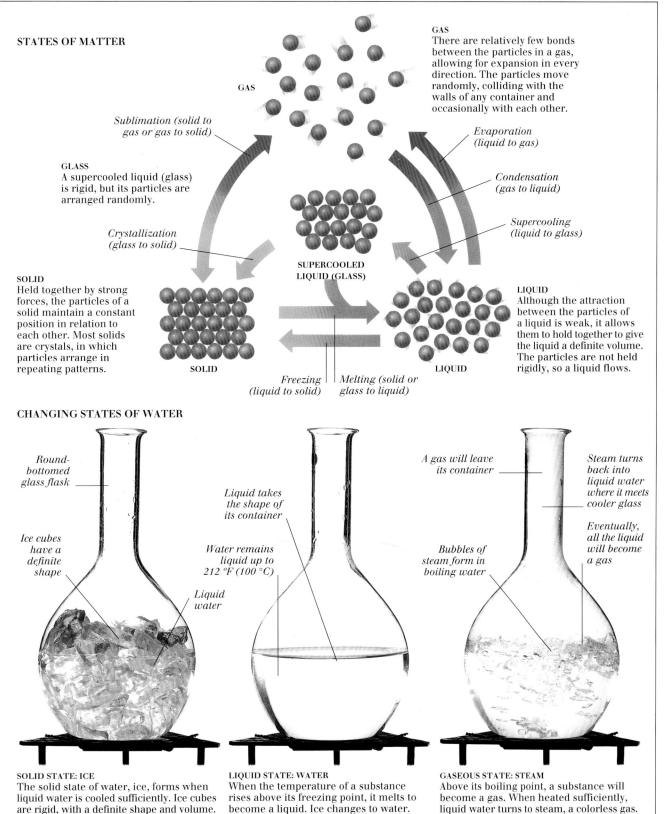

STATES OF MATTER

GAS
There are relatively few bonds between the particles in a gas, allowing for expansion in every direction. The particles move randomly, colliding with the walls of any container and occasionally with each other.

GAS

Sublimation (solid to gas or gas to solid)

Evaporation (liquid to gas)

Condensation (gas to liquid)

Supercooling (liquid to glass)

GLASS
A supercooled liquid (glass) is rigid, but its particles are arranged randomly.

Crystallization (glass to solid)

SUPERCOOLED LIQUID (GLASS)

SOLID
Held together by strong forces, the particles of a solid maintain a constant position in relation to each other. Most solids are crystals, in which particles arrange in repeating patterns.

SOLID

LIQUID
Although the attraction between the particles of a liquid is weak, it allows them to hold together to give the liquid a definite volume. The particles are not held rigidly, so a liquid flows.

LIQUID

Freezing (liquid to solid)

Melting (solid or glass to liquid)

CHANGING STATES OF WATER

Round-bottomed glass flask

Ice cubes have a definite shape

Liquid water

Liquid takes the shape of its container

Water remains liquid up to 212 °F (100 °C)

A gas will leave its container

Bubbles of steam form in boiling water

Steam turns back into liquid water where it meets cooler glass

Eventually, all the liquid will become a gas

SOLID STATE: ICE
The solid state of water, ice, forms when liquid water is cooled sufficiently. Ice cubes are rigid, with a definite shape and volume.

LIQUID STATE: WATER
When the temperature of a substance rises above its freezing point, it melts to become a liquid. Ice changes to water.

GASEOUS STATE: STEAM
Above its boiling point, a substance will become a gas. When heated sufficiently, liquid water turns to steam, a colorless gas.

Atoms and molecules

FALSE-COLOR IMAGE OF ACTUAL GOLD ATOMS

ATOMS ARE THE smallest individual parts of an element (see pp. 310-311). They are tiny, with diameters in the order of one ten-thousand-millionth of a meter (10^{-10} m). Two or more atoms join together (bond) to form a molecule of a substance known as a compound. For example, when atoms of the elements hydrogen and fluorine join together, they form a molecule of the compound hydrogen fluoride. So molecules are the smallest individual parts of a compound. Atoms themselves are not indivisible —they possess an internal structure. At their center is a dense nucleus consisting of protons, which have a positive electric charge (see p. 316), and neutrons, which are uncharged. Around the nucleus are negatively charged electrons. It is the electrons that give a substance most of its physical and chemical properties. They do not follow definite paths around the nucleus. Instead, electrons are said to be found within certain regions, called orbitals. These are arranged around the nucleus in "shells," each containing electrons of a particular energy. For example, the first shell (1) can hold up to two electrons, in a so-called s-orbital (1s). The second shell (2) can hold up to eight electrons in s-orbitals (2s) and p-orbitals (2p). If an atom loses an electron, it becomes a positive ion (cation). If an electron is gained, an atom becomes a negative ion (anion). Ions of opposite charges will attract and join together in a type of bonding known as ionic bonding. In covalent bonding, the atoms bond by sharing their electrons in what become molecular orbitals.

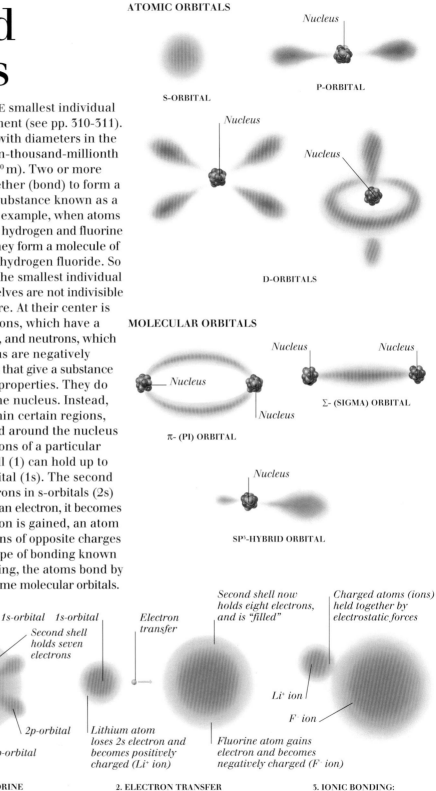

ATOMIC ORBITALS

Nucleus

S-ORBITAL

Nucleus

P-ORBITAL

Nucleus

Nucleus

D-ORBITALS

MOLECULAR ORBITALS

Nucleus

Nucleus

Nucleus

Nucleus

Σ- (SIGMA) ORBITAL

π- (PI) ORBITAL

Nucleus

SP⁵-HYBRID ORBITAL

EXAMPLE OF IONIC BONDING

1s-orbital

2s-orbital

2p-orbital

2s-orbital

1. NEUTRAL LITHIUM ATOM (Li)

1s-orbital   *1s-orbital*

Second shell holds seven electrons

2p-orbital

2p-orbital

NEUTRAL FLUORINE ATOM (F)

Electron transfer

Lithium atom loses 2s electron and becomes positively charged (Li⁺ ion)

2. ELECTRON TRANSFER

Second shell now holds eight electrons, and is "filled"

Fluorine atom gains electron and becomes negatively charged (F⁻ ion)

Charged atoms (ions) held together by electrostatic forces

Li⁺ ion

F⁻ ion

3. IONIC BONDING: LITHIUM FLUORIDE MOLECULE (LiF)

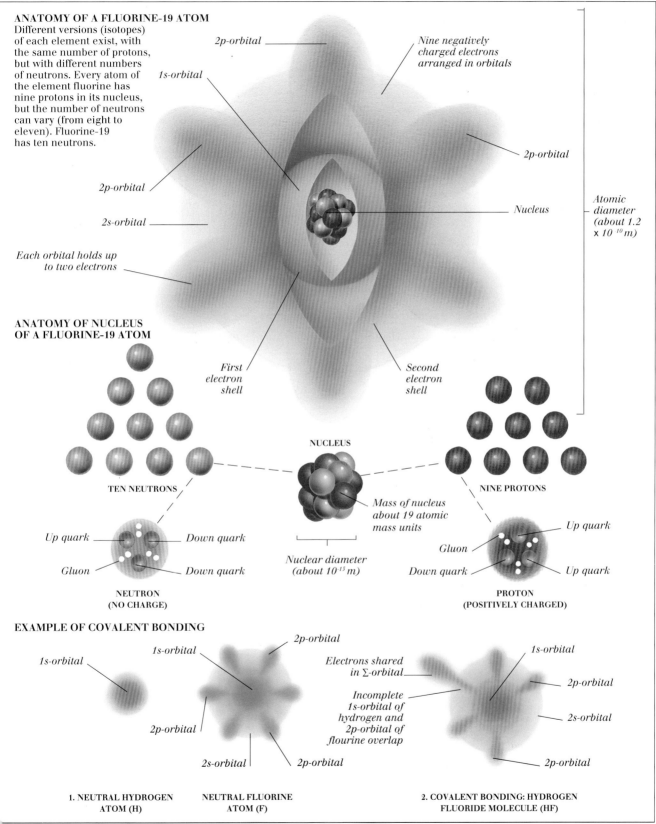

ANATOMY OF A FLUORINE-19 ATOM

Different versions (isotopes) of each element exist, with the same number of protons, but with different numbers of neutrons. Every atom of the element fluorine has nine protons in its nucleus, but the number of neutrons can vary (from eight to eleven). Fluorine-19 has ten neutrons.

2p-orbital

1s-orbital

Nine negatively charged electrons arranged in orbitals

2p-orbital

2p-orbital

2s-orbital

Nucleus

Atomic diameter (about 1.2 × 10 ^{10} m)

Each orbital holds up to two electrons

ANATOMY OF NUCLEUS OF A FLUORINE-19 ATOM

First electron shell

Second electron shell

NUCLEUS

TEN NEUTRONS

NINE PROTONS

Mass of nucleus about 19 atomic mass units

Up quark

Down quark

Gluon

Down quark

Up quark

Gluon

Down quark

Up quark

Nuclear diameter (about 10 $^{-15}$ m)

NEUTRON (NO CHARGE)

PROTON (POSITIVELY CHARGED)

EXAMPLE OF COVALENT BONDING

2p-orbital

1s-orbital

1s-orbital

1s-orbital

Electrons shared in Σ-orbital

2p-orbital

2s-orbital

Incomplete 1s-orbital of hydrogen and 2p-orbital of flourine overlap

2p-orbital

2s-orbital

2p-orbital

2p-orbital

1. NEUTRAL HYDROGEN ATOM (H)

NEUTRAL FLUORINE ATOM (F)

2. COVALENT BONDING: HYDROGEN FLUORIDE MOLECULE (HF)

The periodic table

AN ELEMENT is a substance that consists of atoms of one type only. The 92 elements that occur naturally, and the 17 elements created artificially, are often arranged into a chart called the periodic table. Each element is defined by its atomic number—the number of protons in the nucleus of each of its atoms (it is also the number of electrons present). Atomic numbers increase along each row (period) and down each column (group). The shape of the table is determined by the way in which electrons arrange themselves around the nucleus: the positioning of elements in order of increasing atomic number brings together atoms with a similar pattern of orbiting electrons (orbitals). These appear in blocks. Electrons occupy shells of a certain energy (see pp. 308-309). Periods are ordered according to the filling of successive shells with electrons, while groups reflect the number of electrons in the outer shell (valency electrons). These outer electrons are important—they decide the chemical properties of the atom. Elements that appear in the same group have similar properties because they have the same number of electrons in their outer shell. Elements in Group 0 have filled shells, where the outer shell holds its maximum number of electrons, and are stable. Atoms of Group I elements have just one electron in their outer shell. This makes them unstable—and ready to react with other substances.

METALS AND NON-METALS
Elements at the left-hand side of each period are metals. Metals easily lose electrons and form positive ions. Non-metals, on the right of a period, tend to become negative ions. Semi-metals, which have properties of both metals and non-metals, are between the two.

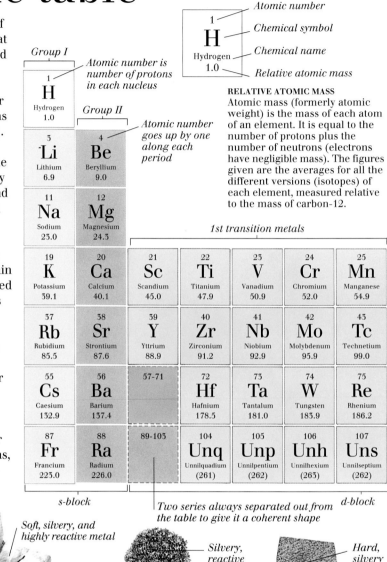

Atomic number is number of protons in each nucleus

Atomic number goes up by one along each period

Atomic number
Chemical symbol
Chemical name
Relative atomic mass

RELATIVE ATOMIC MASS
Atomic mass (formerly atomic weight) is the mass of each atom of an element. It is equal to the number of protons plus the number of neutrons (electrons have negligible mass). The figures given are the averages for all the different versions (isotopes) of each element, measured relative to the mass of carbon-12.

1st transition metals

s-block

Two series always separated out from the table to give it a coherent shape

d-block

Group I	Group II						
1 **H** Hydrogen 1.0							
3 **Li** Lithium 6.9	4 **Be** Beryllium 9.0						
11 **Na** Sodium 23.0	12 **Mg** Magnesium 24.3						
19 **K** Potassium 39.1	20 **Ca** Calcium 40.1	21 **Sc** Scandium 45.0	22 **Ti** Titanium 47.9	23 **V** Vanadium 50.9	24 **Cr** Chromium 52.0	25 **Mn** Manganese 54.9	
37 **Rb** Rubidium 85.5	38 **Sr** Strontium 87.6	39 **Y** Yttrium 88.9	40 **Zr** Zirconium 91.2	41 **Nb** Niobium 92.9	42 **Mo** Molybdenum 95.9	43 **Tc** Technetium 99.0	
55 **Cs** Caesium 132.9	56 **Ba** Barium 137.4	57-71	72 **Hf** Hafnium 178.5	73 **Ta** Tantalum 181.0	74 **W** Tungsten 183.9	75 **Re** Rhenium 186.2	
87 **Fr** Francium 223.0	88 **Ra** Radium 226.0	89-103	104 **Unq** Unnilquadium (261)	105 **Unp** Unnilpentium (262)	106 **Unh** Unnilhexium (263)	107 **Uns** Unnilseptium (262)	

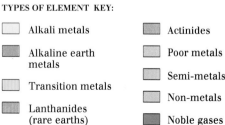

Soft, silvery, and highly reactive metal

SODIUM:
GROUP 1 METAL

Silvery, reactive metal

MAGNESIUM:
GROUP 2 METAL

Hard, silvery metal

CHROMIUM:
1ST TRANSITION METAL

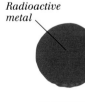

Radioactive metal

PLUTONIUM:
ACTINIDE SERIES METAL

TYPES OF ELEMENT KEY:

- Alkali metals
- Alkaline earth metals
- Transition metals
- Lanthanides (rare earths)
- Actinides
- Poor metals
- Semi-metals
- Non-metals
- Noble gases

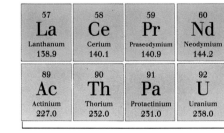

57 **La** Lanthanum 138.9	58 **Ce** Cerium 140.1	59 **Pr** Praseodymium 140.9	60 **Nd** Neodymium 144.2
89 **Ac** Actinium 227.0	90 **Th** Thorium 232.0	91 **Pa** Protactinium 231.0	92 **U** Uranium 238.0

ALLOTROPES OF CARBON
Some elements exist in more than one form —these are known as allotropes. Carbon powder, graphite, and diamond are allotropes of carbon. They all consist of carbon atoms, but have very different physical properties.

DIAMOND

GRAPHITE

CARBON POWDER

Bright yellow crystal

SULFUR: GROUP 6 SOLID NON-METAL

IODINE: GROUP 7 SOLID NON-METAL

Purple-black solid turns to gas easily

Boron and carbon groups

Nitrogen and oxygen groups

Halogens

Group 0

				2 **He** Helium 4.0

Period

Short period

Group III	Group IV	Group V	Group VI	Group VII	
5 **B** Boron 10.8	6 **C** Carbon 12.0	7 **N** Nitrogen 14.0	8 **O** Oxygen 16.0	9 **F** Fluorine 19.0	10 **Ne** Neon 20.2
13 **Al** Aluminum 27.0	14 **Si** Silicon 28.1	15 **P** Phosphorus 31.0	16 **S** Sulfur 32.1	17 **Cl** Chlorine 35.5	18 **Ar** Argon 40.0

2nd transition metals

3rd transition metals

Long period

26 **Fe** Iron 55.9	27 **Co** Cobalt 58.9	28 **Ni** Nickel 58.7	29 **Cu** Copper 63.5	30 **Zn** Zinc 65.4	31 **Ga** Gallium 69.7	32 **Ge** Germanium 72.6	33 **As** Arsenic 74.9	34 **Se** Selenium 79.0	35 **Br** Bromine 79.9	36 **Kr** Krypton 83.8
44 **Ru** Ruthenium 101.0	45 **Rh** Rhodium 102.9	46 **Pd** Palladium 106.4	47 **Ag** Silver 107.9	48 **Cd** Cadmium 112.4	49 **In** Indium 114.8	50 **Sn** Tin 118.7	51 **Sb** Antimony 121.8	52 **Te** Tellurium 127.6	53 **I** Iodine 126.9	54 **Xe** Xenon 131.3
76 **Os** Osmium 190.2	77 **Ir** Iridium 192.2	78 **Pt** Platinum 195.1	79 **Au** Gold 197.0	80 **Hg** Mercury 200.6	81 **Tl** Thallium 204.4	82 **Pb** Lead 207.2	83 **Bi** Bismuth 209.0	84 **Po** Polonium 210.0	85 **At** Astatine 210.0	86 **Rn** Radon 222.0

108 **Uno** Unniloctium (265)	109 **Une** Unnilennium (266)

d-block

p-block

Atomic mass is estimated, as element exists fleetingly

Shiny semi-metal

Unreactive, colorless gas glows red in discharge tube

NOBLE GASES
Group 0 contains elements that have a filled (complete) outer shell of electrons, which means the atoms do not need to lose or gain electrons by bonding with other atoms. This makes them stable and they do not easily form ions or react with other elements. Noble gases are also called rare or inert gases.

Yellow, unreactive precious metal

Soft, shiny, reactive metal

GOLD: 3RD TRANSITION METAL

TIN: GROUP 4 POOR METAL

ANTIMONY: GROUP 5 SEMI-METAL

NEON: GROUP 0 COLORLESS GAS

61 **Pm** Promethium 147.0	62 **Sm** Samarium 150.4	63 **Eu** Europium 152.0	64 **Gd** Gadolinium 157.3	65 **Tb** Terbium 158.9	66 **Dy** Dysprosium 162.5	67 **Ho** Holmium 164.9	68 **Er** Erbium 167.3	69 **Tm** Thulium 168.9	70 **Yb** Ytterbium 175.0	71 **Lu** Lutetium 175.0
93 **Np** Neptunium 237.0	94 **Pu** Plutonium 242.0	95 **Am** Americium 243.0	96 **Cm** Curium 247.0	97 **Bk** Berkelium 247.0	98 **Cf** Californium 251.0	99 **Es** Einsteinium 254.0	100 **Fm** Fermium 253.0	101 **Md** Mendelevium 256.0	102 **No** Nobelium 254.0	103 **Lr** Lawrencium 257.0

f-block

Chemical reactions

A CHEMICAL REACTION TAKES PLACE whenever bonds between atoms are broken or made. In each case, atoms or groups of atoms rearrange, making new substances (products) from the original ones (reactants). Reactions happen naturally, or can be made to happen; they may take years, or only an instant. Some of the main types are shown here. A reaction usually involves a change in energy (see pp. 314-315). In a burning reaction, for example, the making of new bonds between atoms releases energy as heat and light. This type of reaction, in which heat is given off, is an exothermic reaction. Many reactions, like burning, are irreversible, but some can take place in either direction, and are said to be reversible. Reactions can be used to form solids from solutions: in a double decomposition reaction, two compounds in solution break down and re-form into two new substances, often creating a precipitate (insoluble solid); in displacement, an element (eg. copper) displaces another element (eg. silver) from a solution. The rate (speed) of a reaction is determined by many different factors, such as temperature, and the size and shape of the reactants. To describe and keep track of reactions, internationally recognized chemical symbols and equations are used. Reactions are also used in the laboratory to identify matter. An experiment with candle wax, for example, demonstrates that it contains carbon and hydrogen.

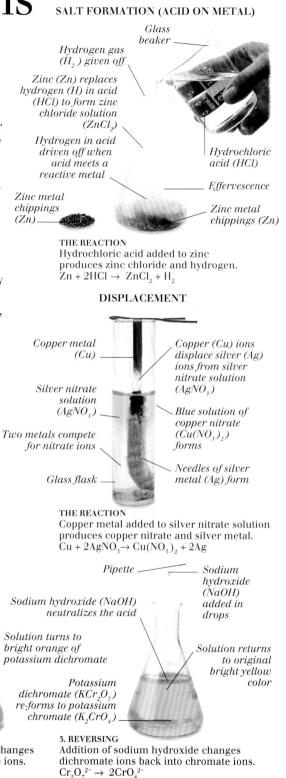

SALT FORMATION (ACID ON METAL)

Glass beaker

Hydrogen gas (H_2) given off

Zinc (Zn) replaces hydrogen (H) in acid (HCl) to form zinc chloride solution ($ZnCl_2$)

Hydrogen in acid driven off when acid meets a reactive metal

Hydrochloric acid (HCl)

Effervescence

Zinc metal chippings (Zn)

Zinc metal chippings (Zn)

THE REACTION
Hydrochloric acid added to zinc produces zinc chloride and hydrogen.
$Zn + 2HCl \rightarrow ZnCl_2 + H_2$

DISPLACEMENT

Copper metal (Cu)

Silver nitrate solution ($AgNO_3$)

Two metals compete for nitrate ions

Glass flask

Copper (Cu) ions displace silver (Ag) ions from silver nitrate solution ($AgNO_3$)

Blue solution of copper nitrate ($Cu(NO_3)_2$) forms

Needles of silver metal (Ag) form

THE REACTION
Copper metal added to silver nitrate solution produces copper nitrate and silver metal.
$Cu + 2AgNO_3 \rightarrow Cu(NO_3)_2 + 2Ag$

BURNING MATTER

Ammonium dichromate ((NH_4)$_2Cr_2O_7$)

Flame

In this burning reaction, atoms form simpler substances and give off heat and light

Ammonium dichromate ((NH_4)$_2Cr_2O_7$) converts to chromium oxide (Cr_2O_3)

Nitrogen monoxide (NO) and water vapor (H_2O) given off as colorless gases

THE REACTION
When lit, ammonium dichromate combines with oxygen from air.
$(NH_4)_2Cr_2O_7 + O_2 \rightarrow Cr_2O_3 + 4H_2O + 2NO$

A REVERSIBLE REACTION

Flat-bottomed glass flask

Potassium chromate solution (K_2CrO_4)

Bright yellow solution contains potassium and chromate ions

Pipette

Hydrochloric acid (HCl) added in drops

Acid causes reaction to take place

Chromate ions converted to orange dichromate ions

Potassium dichromate (KCr_2O_7) forms

Sodium hydroxide (NaOH) neutralizes the acid

Solution turns to bright orange of potassium dichromate

Potassium dichromate (KCr_2O_7) re-forms to potassium chromate (K_2CrO_4)

Pipette

Sodium hydroxide (NaOH) added in drops

Solution returns to original bright yellow color

1. THE REACTANT
Potassium chromate dissolves in water to form potassium ions and chromate ions.
$K_2CrO_4 \rightarrow 2K^+ + CrO_4^{2-}$

2. THE REACTION
Addition of hydrochloric acid changes chromate ions into dichromate ions.
$2CrO_4^{2-} \rightarrow Cr_2O_7^{2-}$

3. REVERSING
Addition of sodium hydroxide changes dichromate ions back into chromate ions.
$Cr_2O_7^{2-} \rightarrow 2CrO_4^{2-}$

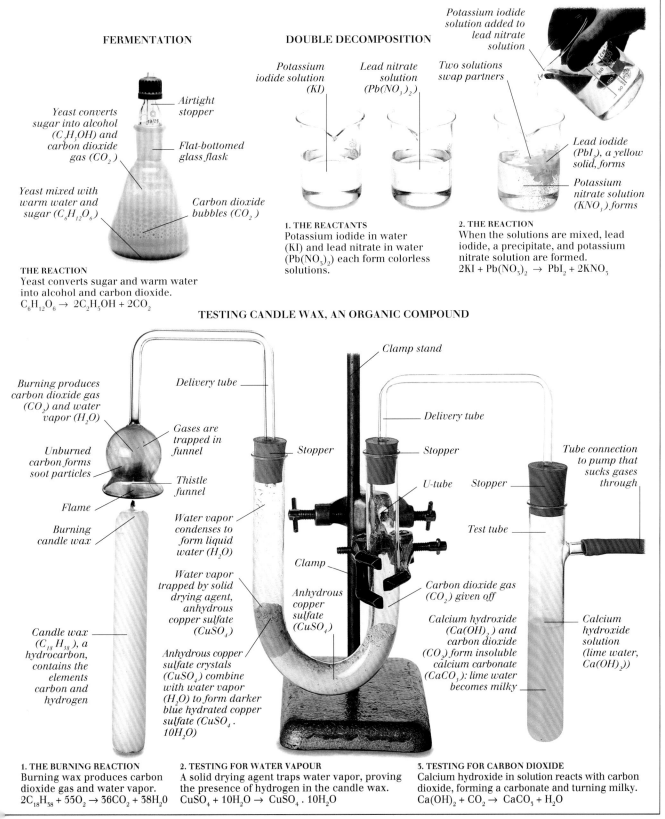

FERMENTATION

Yeast converts sugar into alcohol (C_2H_5OH) and carbon dioxide gas (CO_2)

Airtight stopper

Flat-bottomed glass flask

Yeast mixed with warm water and sugar ($C_6H_{12}O_6$)

Carbon dioxide bubbles (CO_2)

THE REACTION
Yeast converts sugar and warm water into alcohol and carbon dioxide.
$C_6H_{12}O_6 \rightarrow 2C_2H_5OH + 2CO_2$

DOUBLE DECOMPOSITION

Potassium iodide solution (KI)

Lead nitrate solution ($Pb(NO_3)_2$)

Two solutions swap partners

Potassium iodide solution added to lead nitrate solution

Lead iodide (PbI_2), a yellow solid, forms

Potassium nitrate solution (KNO_3) forms

1. THE REACTANTS
Potassium iodide in water (KI) and lead nitrate in water ($Pb(NO_3)_2$) each form colorless solutions.

2. THE REACTION
When the solutions are mixed, lead iodide, a precipitate, and potassium nitrate solution are formed.
$2KI + Pb(NO_3)_2 \rightarrow PbI_2 + 2KNO_3$

TESTING CANDLE WAX, AN ORGANIC COMPOUND

Clamp stand

Delivery tube

Burning produces carbon dioxide gas (CO_2) and water vapor (H_2O)

Delivery tube

Gases are trapped in funnel

Stopper

Stopper

Tube connection to pump that sucks gases through

Unburned carbon forms soot particles

U-tube

Stopper

Thistle funnel

Flame

Test tube

Burning candle wax

Water vapor condenses to form liquid water (H_2O)

Clamp

Carbon dioxide gas (CO_2) given off

Anhydrous copper sulfate ($CuSO_4$)

Calcium hydroxide solution (lime water, $Ca(OH)_2$)

Water vapor trapped by solid drying agent, anhydrous copper sulfate ($CuSO_4$)

Candle wax ($C_{18}H_{38}$), a hydrocarbon, contains the elements carbon and hydrogen

Anhydrous copper sulfate crystals ($CuSO_4$) combine with water vapor (H_2O) to form darker blue hydrated copper sulfate ($CuSO_4 . 10H_2O$)

Calcium hydroxide ($Ca(OH)_2$) and carbon dioxide (CO_2) form insoluble calcium carbonate ($CaCO_3$): lime water becomes milky

1. THE BURNING REACTION
Burning wax produces carbon dioxide gas and water vapor.
$2C_{18}H_{38} + 55O_2 \rightarrow 36CO_2 + 38H_2O$

2. TESTING FOR WATER VAPOUR
A solid drying agent traps water vapor, proving the presence of hydrogen in the candle wax.
$CuSO_4 + 10H_2O \rightarrow CuSO_4 . 10H_2O$

3. TESTING FOR CARBON DIOXIDE
Calcium hydroxide in solution reacts with carbon dioxide, forming a carbonate and turning milky.
$Ca(OH)_2 + CO_2 \rightarrow CaCO_3 + H_2O$

Energy

ANYTHING THAT HAPPENS—from a pin drop to an explosion
—requires energy. Energy is the capacity for doing work
(making something happen). Various forms of energy exist,
including light, heat, sound, electrical, chemical, nuclear,
kinetic, and potential energies. The Law of Conservation
of Energy states that the total amount of energy in the
Universe is fixed—energy cannot be created or destroyed,
it can only change from one form to another (energy
transfer). For example, potential energy is energy that
is stored, and can be used in the future. An object gains
potential energy when it is lifted; as the object is released,
potential energy changes into the energy of motion (kinetic
energy). During transference, some of the energy converts
into heat. A combined heat and power station can put some
of the "waste" heat to useful effect in local schools and
housing. Most of the Earth's energy is provided by the Sun,
in the form of electromagnetic radiation (see pp. 316-317).
Some of this energy transfers to plant and animal life, and
ultimately to fossil fuels, where it is stored in chemical
form. Our bodies obtain energy from the food we eat,
while energy needed for other tasks, such as heating and
transportation, can be obtained by burning fossil fuels
—or by harnessing natural forces like wind or moving
water—to generate electricity. Another source is nuclear
power, where energy is released by reactions in the nucleus
of an atom. All energy is measured by the international
unit, the joule (J). As a guide, one joule is about equal to
the amount of energy needed to lift an apple one yard.

SANKEY DIAGRAM SHOWING ENERGY FLOW IN A COAL-FIRED COMBINED HEAT AND POWER STATION

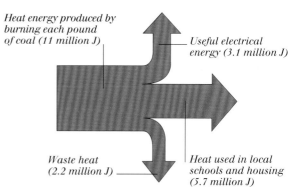

Heat energy produced by burning each pound of coal (11 million J)

Useful electrical energy (3.1 million J)

Waste heat (2.2 million J)

Heat used in local schools and housing (5.7 million J)

CROSS-SECTION OF HYDROELECTRIC POWER STATION WITH FRANCIS TURBINE

CROSS-SECTION OF NUCLEAR POWER STATION WITH PRESSURIZED WATER REACTOR

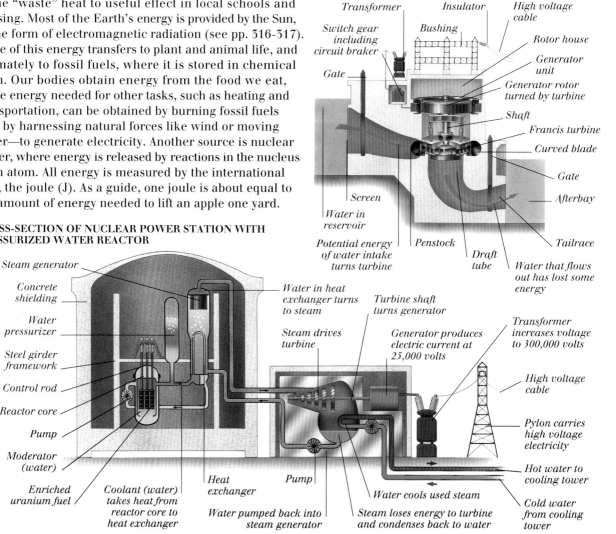

Transformer
Insulator
High voltage cable
Switch gear including circuit braker
Bushing
Rotor house
Generator unit
Gate
Generator rotor turned by turbine
Shaft
Francis turbine
Curved blade
Gate
Afterbay
Screen
Water in reservoir
Potential energy of water intake turns turbine
Penstock
Draft tube
Tailrace
Water that flows out has lost some energy

Steam generator
Water in heat exchanger turns to steam
Turbine shaft turns generator
Transformer increases voltage to 300,000 volts
Concrete shielding
Steam drives turbine
Generator produces electric current at 25,000 volts
Water pressurizer
Steel girder framework
High voltage cable
Control rod
Reactor core
Pump
Pylon carries high voltage electricity
Moderator (water)
Hot water to cooling tower
Enriched uranium fuel
Coolant (water) takes heat from reactor core to heat exchanger
Heat exchanger
Pump
Water cools used steam
Cold water from cooling tower
Water pumped back into steam generator
Steam loses energy to turbine and condenses back to water

ENERGY SYSTEMS

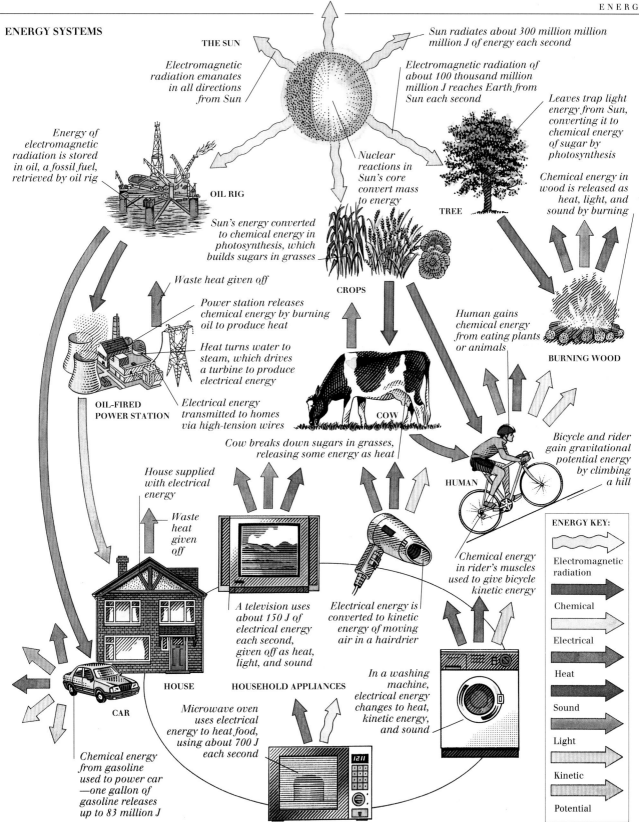

THE SUN

Electromagnetic radiation emanates in all directions from Sun

Sun radiates about 300 million million million J of energy each second

Electromagnetic radiation of about 100 thousand million million J reaches Earth from Sun each second

Leaves trap light energy from Sun, converting it to chemical energy of sugar by photosynthesis

Energy of electromagnetic radiation is stored in oil, a fossil fuel, retrieved by oil rig

OIL RIG

Nuclear reactions in Sun's core convert mass to energy

TREE

Chemical energy in wood is released as heat, light, and sound by burning

Sun's energy converted to chemical energy in photosynthesis, which builds sugars in grasses

CROPS

Waste heat given off

Power station releases chemical energy by burning oil to produce heat

Heat turns water to steam, which drives a turbine to produce electrical energy

OIL-FIRED POWER STATION

Electrical energy transmitted to homes via high-tension wires

Human gains chemical energy from eating plants or animals

BURNING WOOD

COW

Cow breaks down sugars in grasses, releasing some energy as heat

HUMAN

Bicycle and rider gain gravitational potential energy by climbing a hill

House supplied with electrical energy

Waste heat given off

Chemical energy in rider's muscles used to give bicycle kinetic energy

ENERGY KEY:

A television uses about 150 J of electrical energy each second, given off as heat, light, and sound

Electrical energy is converted to kinetic energy of moving air in a hairdrier

Electromagnetic radiation

Chemical

Electrical

Heat

Sound

Light

Kinetic

Potential

HOUSE

HOUSEHOLD APPLIANCES

In a washing machine, electrical energy changes to heat, kinetic energy, and sound

CAR

Microwave oven uses electrical energy to heat food, using about 700 J each second

Chemical energy from gasoline used to power car —one gallon of gasoline releases up to 83 million J

Electricity and magnetism

ELECTRICAL EFFECTS result from an imbalance of electric charge. There are two types of electric charge: positive (carried by protons) and negative (carried by electrons). If charges are opposite (unlike), they attract one another, while like charges repel. These forces of attraction and repulsion (electrostatic forces) exist between any two charged particles. Matter is normally uncharged, but if electrons are gained, an object will gain an overall negative charge; if they are removed, it becomes positive. Objects with an overall negative or positive charge are said to have an imbalance of charge, and exert the same forces as individual negative and positive charges. On this larger scale, the forces will always act to regain the balance of charge. This causes static electricity. Lightning, for example, is produced by clouds discharging a huge excess of negative electrons. If charges are free—in a wire or material that allows electrons to pass through it—the forces cause a flow of charge called an electric current. Some substances exhibit the strange phenomenon of magnetism—which also produces attractive and repulsive forces. Magnetic substances consist of small regions called domains. Normally unmagnetized, they can be magnetized by being placed in a magnetic field. Magnetism and electricity are inextricably linked, a fact put to use in motors and generators.

LIGHTNING

VAN DE GRAAFF (ELECTROSTATIC) GENERATOR

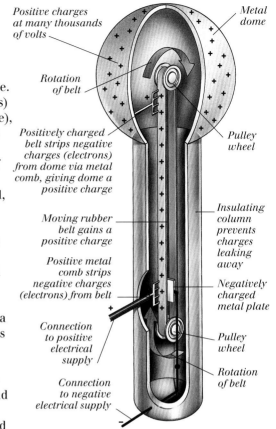

Positive charges at many thousands of volts

Metal dome

Rotation of belt

Positively charged belt strips negative charges (electrons) from dome via metal comb, giving dome a positive charge

Pulley wheel

Moving rubber belt gains a positive charge

Insulating column prevents charges leaking away

Positive metal comb strips negative charges (electrons) from belt

Negatively charged metal plate

Connection to positive electrical supply

Pulley wheel

Connection to negative electrical supply

Rotation of belt

CURRENT ELECTRICITY

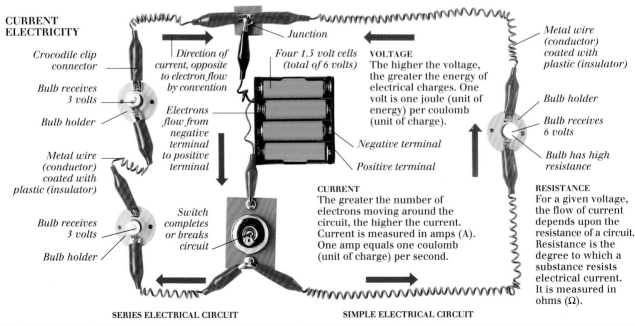

Crocodile clip connector

Junction

Direction of current, opposite to electron flow by convention

Four 1.5 volt cells (total of 6 volts)

Metal wire (conductor) coated with plastic (insulator)

Bulb receives 3 volts

Bulb holder

Electrons flow from negative terminal to positive terminal

Bulb holder

Bulb receives 6 volts

Metal wire (conductor) coated with plastic (insulator)

Negative terminal

Positive terminal

Bulb has high resistance

Bulb receives 3 volts

Bulb holder

Switch completes or breaks circuit

VOLTAGE
The higher the voltage, the greater the energy of electrical charges. One volt is one joule (unit of energy) per coulomb (unit of charge).

CURRENT
The greater the number of electrons moving around the circuit, the higher the current. Current is measured in amps (A). One amp equals one coulomb (unit of charge) per second.

RESISTANCE
For a given voltage, the flow of current depends upon the resistance of a circuit. Resistance is the degree to which a substance resists electrical current. It is measured in ohms (Ω).

SERIES ELECTRICAL CIRCUIT

SIMPLE ELECTRICAL CIRCUIT

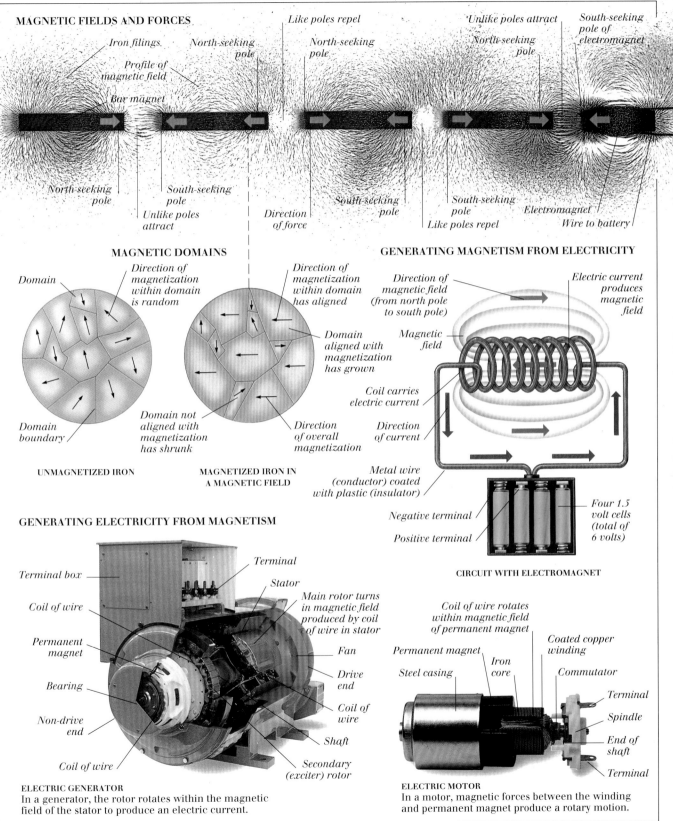

MAGNETIC FIELDS AND FORCES

Iron filings

North-seeking pole

Profile of magnetic field

Bar magnet

Like poles repel

North-seeking pole

North-seeking pole

Unlike poles attract

North-seeking pole

South-seeking pole of electromagnet

North-seeking pole

South-seeking pole

Unlike poles attract

Direction of force

South-seeking pole

South-seeking pole

Like poles repel

South-seeking pole

Electromagnet

Wire to battery

MAGNETIC DOMAINS

Domain

Direction of magnetization within domain is random

Direction of magnetization within domain has aligned

Domain aligned with magnetization has grown

Domain boundary

Domain not aligned with magnetization has shrunk

Direction of overall magnetization

UNMAGNETIZED IRON

MAGNETIZED IRON IN A MAGNETIC FIELD

GENERATING MAGNETISM FROM ELECTRICITY

Direction of magnetic field (from north pole to south pole)

Electric current produces magnetic field

Magnetic field

Coil carries electric current

Direction of current

Metal wire (conductor) coated with plastic (insulator)

Negative terminal

Positive terminal

Four 1.5 volt cells (total of 6 volts)

CIRCUIT WITH ELECTROMAGNET

GENERATING ELECTRICITY FROM MAGNETISM

Terminal box

Coil of wire

Permanent magnet

Bearing

Non-drive end

Coil of wire

Terminal

Stator

Main rotor turns in magnetic field produced by coil of wire in stator

Fan

Drive end

Coil of wire

Shaft

Secondary (exciter) rotor

ELECTRIC GENERATOR
In a generator, the rotor rotates within the magnetic field of the stator to produce an electric current.

Coil of wire rotates within magnetic field of permanent magnet

Permanent magnet

Steel casing

Iron core

Coated copper winding

Commutator

Terminal

Spindle

End of shaft

Terminal

ELECTRIC MOTOR
In a motor, magnetic forces between the winding and permanent magnet produce a rotary motion.

Light

INFRARED IMAGE OF A HOUSE

LIGHT IS A FORM OF ENERGY. It is a type of electromagnetic radiation, like X rays or radio waves. All electromagnetic radiation is produced by electric charges (see pp. 316-317): it is caused by the effects of oscillating electric and magnetic fields as they travel through space. Electromagnetic radiation is considered to have both wave and particle properties. It can be thought of as a wave of electricity and magnetism. In that case, the difference between the various forms of radiation is their wavelength. Radiation can also be said to consist of particles, or packets of energy, called photons. The difference between light and X rays, for instance, is the amount of energy that each photon carries. The complete range of radiation is referred to as the electromagnetic spectrum, extending from low energy, long wavelength radio waves to high energy, short wavelength gamma rays. Light is the only part of the electromagnetic spectrum that is visible. White light from the Sun is made up of all the visible wavelengths of radiation, which can be seen when it is separated by using a prism. Light, like all forms of electromagnetic radiation, can be reflected (bounced back) and refracted (bent). Different parts of the electromagnetic spectrum are produced in different ways. Sometimes visible light— and infrared radiation—is generated by the vibrating particles of warm or hot objects. The emission of light in this way is called incandescence. Light can also be produced by fluorescence, a phenomenon in which electrons gain and lose energy within atoms.

MAXWELLIAN DIAGRAM OF ELECTROMAGNETIC RADIATION AS WAVES

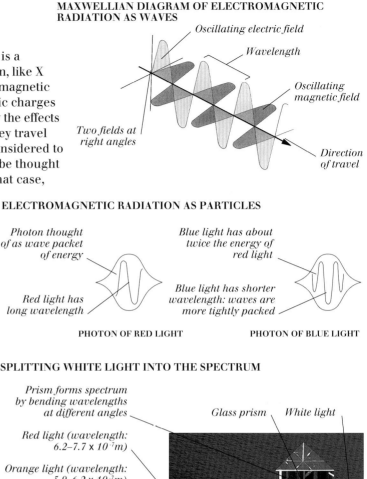

Oscillating electric field

Wavelength

Oscillating magnetic field

Two fields at right angles

Direction of travel

ELECTROMAGNETIC RADIATION AS PARTICLES

Photon thought of as wave packet of energy

Blue light has about twice the energy of red light

Red light has long wavelength

Blue light has shorter wavelength: waves are more tightly packed

PHOTON OF RED LIGHT   **PHOTON OF BLUE LIGHT**

SPLITTING WHITE LIGHT INTO THE SPECTRUM

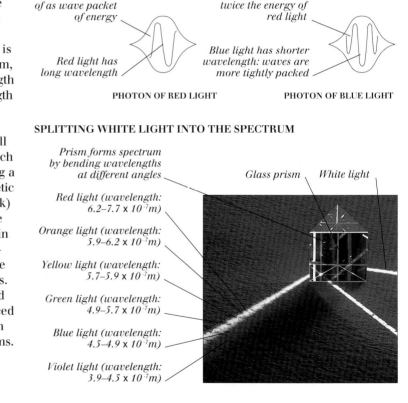

Prism forms spectrum by bending wavelengths at different angles

Glass prism   *White light*

Red light (wavelength: $6.2–7.7 \times 10^{-7}$m)

Orange light (wavelength: $5.9–6.2 \times 10^{-7}$m)

Yellow light (wavelength: $5.7–5.9 \times 10^{-7}$m)

Green light (wavelength: $4.9–5.7 \times 10^{-7}$m)

Blue light (wavelength: $4.5–4.9 \times 10^{-7}$m)

Violet light (wavelength: $3.9–4.5 \times 10^{-7}$m)

THE ELECTROMAGNETIC SPECTRUM

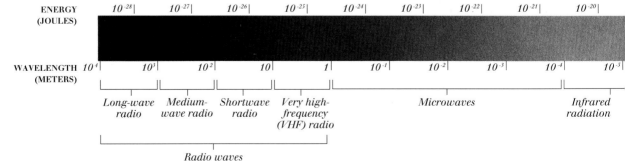

| ENERGY (JOULES) | 10^{-28} | 10^{-27} | 10^{-26} | 10^{-25} | 10^{-24} | 10^{-23} | 10^{-22} | 10^{-21} | 10^{-20} |

| WAVELENGTH (METERS) | 10^{4} | 10^{3} | 10^{2} | 10 | 1 | 10^{-1} | 10^{-2} | 10^{-3} | 10^{-4} | 10^{-5} |

Long-wave radio   *Medium-wave radio*   *Shortwave radio*   *Very high-frequency (VHF) radio*   *Microwaves*   *Infrared radiation*

Radio waves

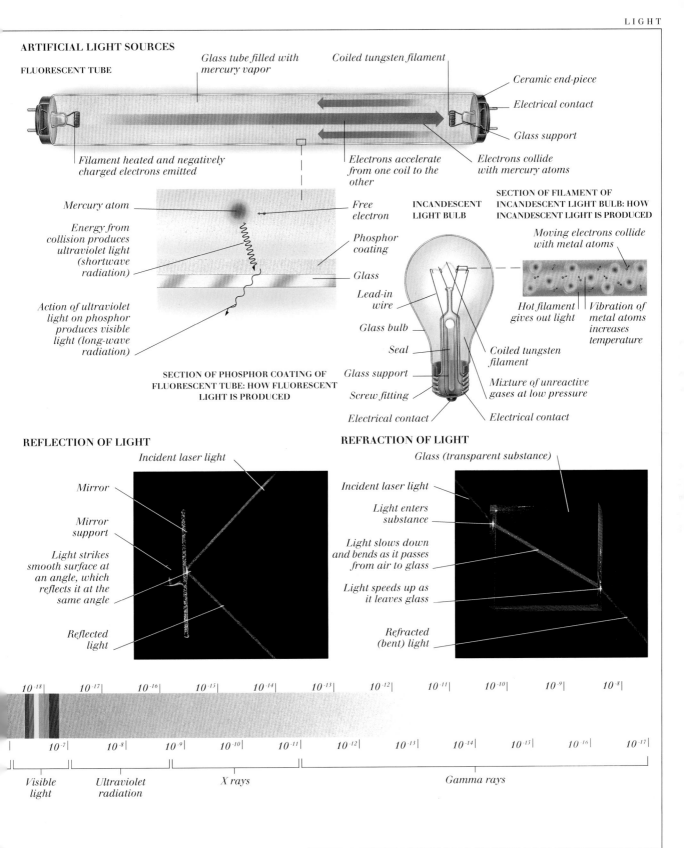

ARTIFICIAL LIGHT SOURCES

FLUORESCENT TUBE

Glass tube filled with mercury vapor

Coiled tungsten filament

Ceramic end-piece

Electrical contact

Glass support

Filament heated and negatively charged electrons emitted

Electrons accelerate from one coil to the other

Electrons collide with mercury atoms

Mercury atom

Free electron

Energy from collision produces ultraviolet light (shortwave radiation)

Phosphor coating

Glass

Action of ultraviolet light on phosphor produces visible light (long-wave radiation)

SECTION OF PHOSPHOR COATING OF FLUORESCENT TUBE: HOW FLUORESCENT LIGHT IS PRODUCED

INCANDESCENT LIGHT BULB

SECTION OF FILAMENT OF INCANDESCENT LIGHT BULB: HOW INCANDESCENT LIGHT IS PRODUCED

Moving electrons collide with metal atoms

Hot filament gives out light

Vibration of metal atoms increases temperature

Lead-in wire

Glass bulb

Seal

Coiled tungsten filament

Glass support

Mixture of unreactive gases at low pressure

Screw fitting

Electrical contact

Electrical contact

REFLECTION OF LIGHT

Incident laser light

Mirror

Mirror support

Light strikes smooth surface at an angle, which reflects it at the same angle

Reflected light

REFRACTION OF LIGHT

Glass (transparent substance)

Incident laser light

Light enters substance

Light slows down and bends as it passes from air to glass

Light speeds up as it leaves glass

Refracted (bent) light

10^{-18} | 10^{-17} | 10^{-16} | 10^{-15} | 10^{-14} | 10^{-13} | 10^{-12} | 10^{-11} | 10^{-10} | 10^{-9} | 10^{-8} |

10^{-7} | 10^{-8} | 10^{-9} | 10^{-10} | 10^{-11} | 10^{-12} | 10^{-13} | 10^{-14} | 10^{-15} | 10^{-16} | 10^{-17} |

Visible light

Ultraviolet radiation

X rays

Gamma rays

Force and motion

FORCES ARE PUSHES OR PULLS that change the motion of objects. To make a stationary object move, or a moving object stop, a force is needed. A force is also required to change the speed or direction of an object. This change in speed or direction is known as acceleration. Acceleration depends on the size (magnitude) of the force, and on the mass of the object. The effects of forces were first summarized by Isaac Newton in his three laws of motion. The international unit of force, named after him, is the newton (N), which is approximately equal to the weight of one apple. Gravity—the force of attraction between any two masses—can be measured using a newton meter (spring balance). Forces are put to useful effect in machines. A simple machine, such as a wheel and axle, is a device that changes the size or direction of an applied force. It allows an applied force (the effort) to produce another force (the load). A lever uses a bar that turns on a fulcrum to exert force. In all simple machines, there is a relationship between force and distance. A small force (in a compound pulley, for instance) moves through a large distance to lift a heavy object a small distance. This is called the Law of Simple Machines.

SIMPLE MACHINES

Single-pulley system (simple pulley)

Pulley wheel

Simple pulley only changes direction of a force

Effort is the same size as the load (10 N) and is pulled the same distance

One rope attached to load

Load of 10 N

Two-pulley system (simple pulley)

Pulley wheel

Effort is half the load (5 N), but the rope must be pulled twice the distance

Two ropes share the force and distance

Pulley wheel

Load of 10 N

Four-pulley system (compound pulley)

Two pulley wheels

Effort is one quarter of the load (2.5 N), but the rope must be pulled four times the distance

Four ropes share the force and distance

SIMPLE AND COMPOUND PULLEYS

Two pulley wheels

Load of 10 N

NEWTON METERS (SPRING BALANCES)

Weight is measured using a spring

When weight pulls downward, pointer moves along scale and measures force

Weight is 10 N

Weight is 20 N

Mass of 1 kg

Mass of 2 kg

WEIGHT AND MASS
The mass of an object is a measure of the quantity of matter that it possesses. Mass is usually measured in grams (g) or kilograms (kg). The weight of an object is the force exerted on the object's mass by gravity. Since weight is a force, its unit is the newton (N).

Wheel and axle multiplies the effort

Force is transmitted to the wheels by the chain

Pedal

Crank

A larger force, the load, is produced at the axle

Effort, provided by cyclist's muscles, is smaller than the load, but moves through a greater distance

WHEEL AND AXLE

A screw, acting like a wedge wrapped around a shaft, multiplies the effort

Effort, a turning force supplied through a screwdriver

Pitch (the angle of the screw thread)

The smaller the angle of pitch, the less force is required, but more turns are needed to move it through a greater distance

A larger force, the load, pulls the screw into wood

SCREW

Effort pushes axe into wood

Axe blade has wedge shape

Wedge multiplies effort

A larger force, the load, moves through a smaller distance to push wood apart

WEDGE

NEWTON'S THREE LAWS OF MOTION

NEWTON'S FIRST LAW
When no force acts on a body, it will
continue in a state of rest or uniform motion.

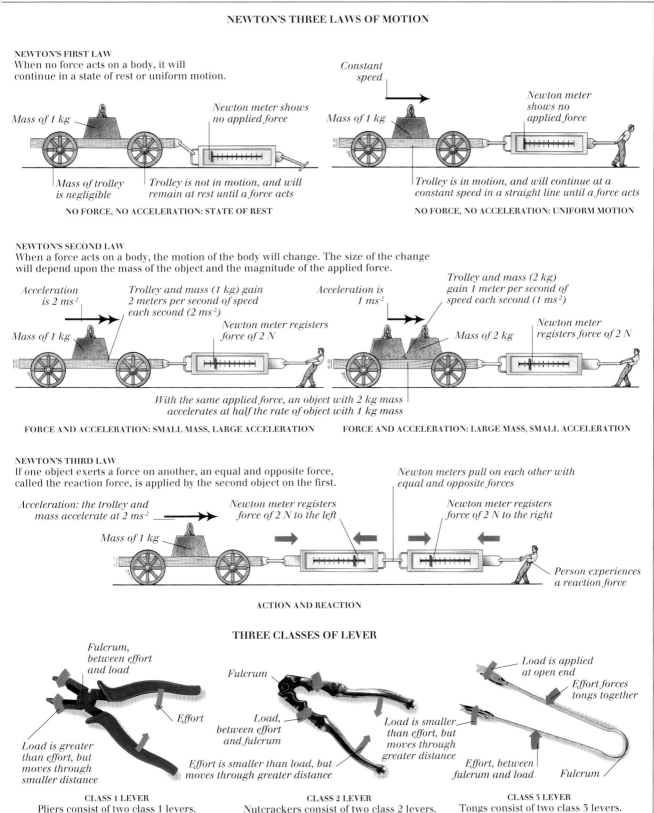

Mass of 1 kg

*Newton meter shows
no applied force*

*Mass of trolley
is negligible*

*Trolley is not in motion, and will
remain at rest until a force acts*

NO FORCE, NO ACCELERATION: STATE OF REST

*Constant
speed*

Mass of 1 kg

*Newton meter
shows no
applied force*

*Trolley is in motion, and will continue at a
constant speed in a straight line until a force acts*

NO FORCE, NO ACCELERATION: UNIFORM MOTION

NEWTON'S SECOND LAW
When a force acts on a body, the motion of the body will change. The size of the change
will depend upon the mass of the object and the magnitude of the applied force.

*Acceleration
is 2 ms⁻²*

*Trolley and mass (1 kg) gain
2 meters per second of speed
each second (2 ms⁻²)*

*Newton meter registers
force of 2 N*

Mass of 1 kg

*Acceleration is
1 ms⁻²*

*Trolley and mass (2 kg)
gain 1 meter per second of
speed each second (1 ms⁻²)*

*Newton meter
registers force of 2 N*

Mass of 2 kg

*With the same applied force, an object with 2 kg mass
accelerates at half the rate of object with 1 kg mass*

FORCE AND ACCELERATION: SMALL MASS, LARGE ACCELERATION

FORCE AND ACCELERATION: LARGE MASS, SMALL ACCELERATION

NEWTON'S THIRD LAW
If one object exerts a force on another, an equal and opposite force,
called the reaction force, is applied by the second object on the first.

*Newton meters pull on each other with
equal and opposite forces*

*Acceleration: the trolley and
mass accelerate at 2 ms⁻²*

*Newton meter registers
force of 2 N to the left*

*Newton meter registers
force of 2 N to the right*

Mass of 1 kg

*Person experiences
a reaction force*

ACTION AND REACTION

THREE CLASSES OF LEVER

*Fulcrum,
between effort
and load*

Effort

*Load is greater
than effort, but
moves through
smaller distance*

Fulcrum

*Load,
between effort
and fulcrum*

*Effort is smaller than load, but
moves through greater distance*

*Load is applied
at open end*

*Effort forces
tongs together*

*Load is smaller
than effort, but
moves through
greater distance*

*Effort, between
fulcrum and load*

Fulcrum

CLASS 1 LEVER
Pliers consist of two class 1 levers.

CLASS 2 LEVER
Nutcrackers consist of two class 2 levers.

CLASS 3 LEVER
Tongs consist of two class 3 levers.

Rail and Road

Steam locomotives

WAGONS THAT ARE PULLED along tracks have been used to transport material since the 16th century, but these trains were drawn by men or horses until the invention of the steam locomotive. Steam locomotives enabled the basic railroad system to realize its true potential. In 1804, Richard Trevithick built the world's first working steam locomotive in South Wales. It was not entirely successful, but it encouraged others to develop new designs. By 1829, the British engineer Robert Stephenson had built the Rocket, considered to be the forerunner of the modern locomotive. The Rocket was a self-sufficient unit, carrying coal to heat the boiler and a water supply for generating steam. Steam passed from the boiler to force the pistons back and forth, and this movement turned the driving wheels, propelling the train forward. Used steam was then expelled in characteristic puffs. Later steam locomotives, like Ellerman Lines and the Mallard, worked in a similar way, but on a much larger scale. The simple design and reliability of steam locomotives ensured that they changed very little in 120 years of use, before being replaced in the 1950s by more efficient diesel and electric power (see pp. 326-329).

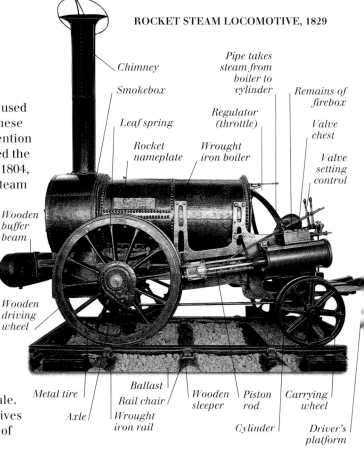

ROCKET STEAM LOCOMOTIVE, 1829

Chimney

Smokebox

Leaf spring

Rocket nameplate

Pipe takes steam from boiler to cylinder

Regulator (throttle)

Wrought iron boiler

Remains of firebox

Valve chest

Valve setting control

Wooden buffer beam

Wooden driving wheel

Metal tire

Axle

Ballast

Rail chair

Wrought iron rail

Wooden sleeper

Piston rod

Cylinder

Carrying wheel

Driver's platform

Stay

ELLERMAN LINES, 1949 (CUTAWAY VIEW)

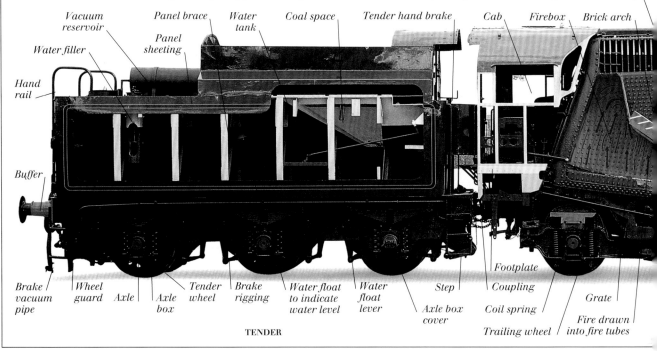

Vacuum reservoir

Panel brace

Water tank

Coal space

Tender hand brake

Cab

Firebox

Brick arch

Water filler

Panel sheeting

Hand rail

Buffer

Brake vacuum pipe

Wheel guard

Axle

Axle box

Tender wheel

Brake rigging

Water float to indicate water level

Water float lever

Step

Axle box cover

Footplate

Coupling

Coil spring

Trailing wheel

Grate

Fire drawn into fire tubes

TENDER

CAB INTERIOR OF MALLARD EXPRESS STEAM LOCOMOTIVE, 1938

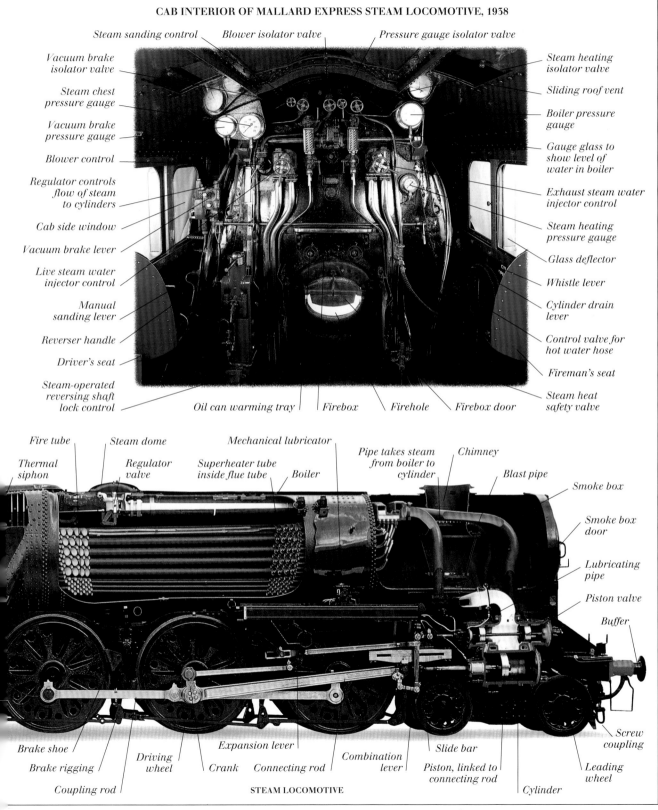

Steam sanding control

Blower isolator valve

Pressure gauge isolator valve

Vacuum brake isolator valve

Steam chest pressure gauge

Vacuum brake pressure gauge

Blower control

Regulator controls flow of steam to cylinders

Cab side window

Vacuum brake lever

Live steam water injector control

Manual sanding lever

Reverser handle

Driver's seat

Steam-operated reversing shaft lock control

Steam heating isolator valve

Sliding roof vent

Boiler pressure gauge

Gauge glass to show level of water in boiler

Exhaust steam water injector control

Steam heating pressure gauge

Glass deflector

Whistle lever

Cylinder drain lever

Control valve for hot water hose

Fireman's seat

Oil can warming tray

Firebox

Firehole

Firebox door

Steam heat safety valve

Fire tube

Steam dome

Mechanical lubricator

Thermal siphon

Regulator valve

Superheater tube inside flue tube

Boiler

Pipe takes steam from boiler to cylinder

Chimney

Blast pipe

Smoke box

Smoke box door

Lubricating pipe

Piston valve

Buffer

Brake shoe

Brake rigging

Coupling rod

Driving wheel

Crank

Expansion lever

Connecting rod

Combination lever

Slide bar

Piston, linked to connecting rod

Screw coupling

Leading wheel

Cylinder

STEAM LOCOMOTIVE

Diesel trains

RUDOLF DIESEL FIRST DEMONSTRATED the diesel engine in Germany in 1898, but it was not until the 1940s that diesel locomotives were successfully established on both passenger and freight services in the U.S. Early diesel locomotives like the Union Pacific were more expensive to build than steam locomotives, but were more efficient and cheaper to operate, especially where oil was plentiful. One feature of diesel engines is that the power output cannot be coupled directly to the wheels. To convert the mechanical energy produced by diesel engines, a transmission system is needed. Almost all diesel locomotives have electric transmissions, and are known as diesel-electric locomotives. The diesel engine works by drawing air into the cylinders and compressing it to increase its temperature; a small quantity of diesel fuel is then injected into it. The resulting combustion drives the generator (more recently an alternator) to produce electricity, which is fed to electric motors connected to the wheels. Diesel-electric locomotives are essentially electric locomotives that carry their own power plants, and are used worldwide today. The Deltic diesel-electric locomotive, similar to the one shown here, replaced classic express steam locomotives, and ran at speeds up to 100 mph.

FRONT VIEW OF UNION PACIFIC DIESEL-ELECTRIC LOCOMOTIVE, 1950s

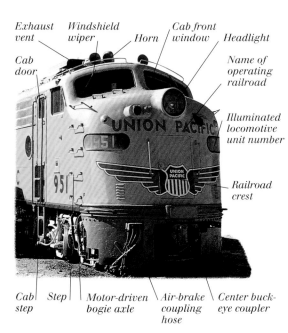

Exhaust vent
Windshield wiper
Cab door
Horn
Cab front window
Headlight
Name of operating railroad
Illuminated locomotive unit number
Railroad crest
Cab step
Step
Motor-driven bogie axle
Air-brake coupling hose
Center buck-eye coupler

PROTOTYPE DELTIC DIESEL-ELECTRIC LOCOMOTIVE, 1956

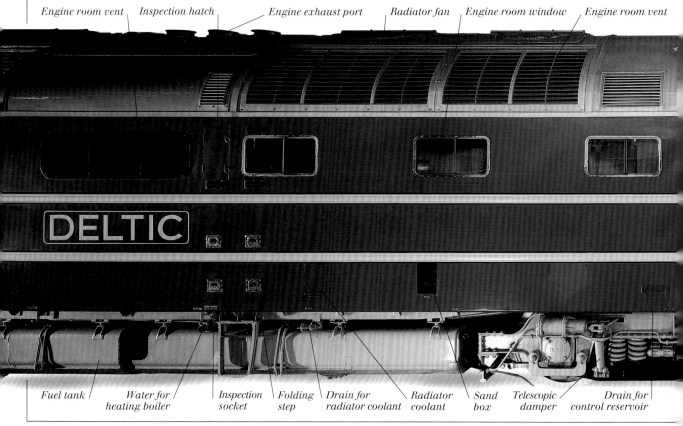

Engine room vent
Inspection hatch
Engine exhaust port
Radiator fan
Engine room window
Engine room vent

DELTIC

Fuel tank
Water for heating boiler
Inspection socket
Folding step
Drain for radiator coolant
Radiator coolant
Sand box
Telescopic damper
Drain for control reservoir

DIESEL ENGINE OF BRITISH RAIL CLASS 20
DIESEL-ELECTRIC LOCOMOTIVE

Exhaust vent

Cylinder head
(V-four configuration)

Turbo-charged diesel
engine drives generator

Generator
cooling fan

Generator
compartment
vent

Auxiliary
generator

Main generator
produces
electricity that
drives wheels

Main chassis
member

Innermost
wheel set on
cab-end bogie

Air brake pipe

Brake
rigging

Battery
box

Engine crankcase

Air reservoir and
isolator valves

Lubricating oil
primary pump and
fuel supply pump

Cab
door

Driver's seat

Cab

Warning horn

Windshield

Windshield wiper

Cab window

Manufacturer's
logo

Cab vent

Indicator
light

Sand box

Buffer

Brake cylinder

Roller-bearing
axle box

Brake
shoe

Brake
actuating chain

Transverse leaf spring
secondary suspension

Coil spring primary
suspension

EXAMPLES OF FREIGHT CARS

BOX CAR

HOPPER CAR

REFRIGERATOR CAR

LIVESTOCK CAR

FLAT CAR WITH BULKHEADS

AUTOMOBILE CAR

Electric and high-speed trains

THE FIRST ELECTRIC LOCOMOTIVE ran in 1879 in Berlin, Germany. In Europe, electric trains developed as a more efficient alternative to the steam locomotive and diesel-electric power. Like diesels, electric trains employ electric motors to drive the wheels but, unlike diesels, the electricity is generated externally at a power station. Electric current is picked up either from a catenary (overhead cable) via a pantograph, or from a third rail. Since it does not carry its own power-generating equipment, an electric locomotive has a better power-to-weight ratio and greater acceleration than its diesel-electric equivalent. This makes electric trains highly suitable for urban routes with many stops. They are also faster, quieter, and cause less pollution. The latest electric French TGV (Train à Grande Vitesse) reaches 186 mph; other trains, like the London to Paris and Brussels Eurostar, can run at several voltages and operate between different countries. Simpler electric trains perform special duties—the "People Mover" at Gatwick Airport, London, runs between terminals.

HOW ALTERNATING CURRENT (AC) ELECTRIC TRAINS WORK

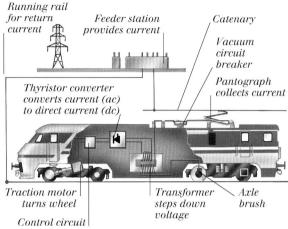

Running rail for return current
Feeder station provides current
Catenary
Vacuum circuit breaker
Pantograph collects current
Thyristor converter converts current (ac) to direct current (dc)
Traction motor turns wheel
Control circuit
Transformer steps down voltage
Axle brush

FRONT VIEW OF PARIS METRO

Route number
Windshield wiper
Unit number
Operator's initials (Régie Autonome des Transports Parisien)
Rubber running wheel
Guard for rubber wheel

124
031
RATP

Door open/shut indicator light
Driver's seat
Handle
Front light (white)
Rear light (red)
Buffing pad
Rubber guide wheel

FRONT VIEW OF ITALIAN STATE RAILWAYS CLASS 402 ELECTRIC LOCOMOTIVE

Collector strip for electric current
Double-arm pantograph
Headlight
Windshield wiper
Italian State Railways crest
Number of electric (E) locomotive (class 402 No. 5)
Buffer
Jumper cable
Conventional hook-screw coupling
Front light (white)
Rear light (red)

SIDE VIEW OF GATWICK EXPRESS "PEOPLE MOVER"

Gatwick
Gatwick

Pneumatic rubber wheel
Concrete track
Automatic door
No driver (train controlled by central computer)

EUROSTAR MULTI-VOLTAGE ELECTRIC TRAIN

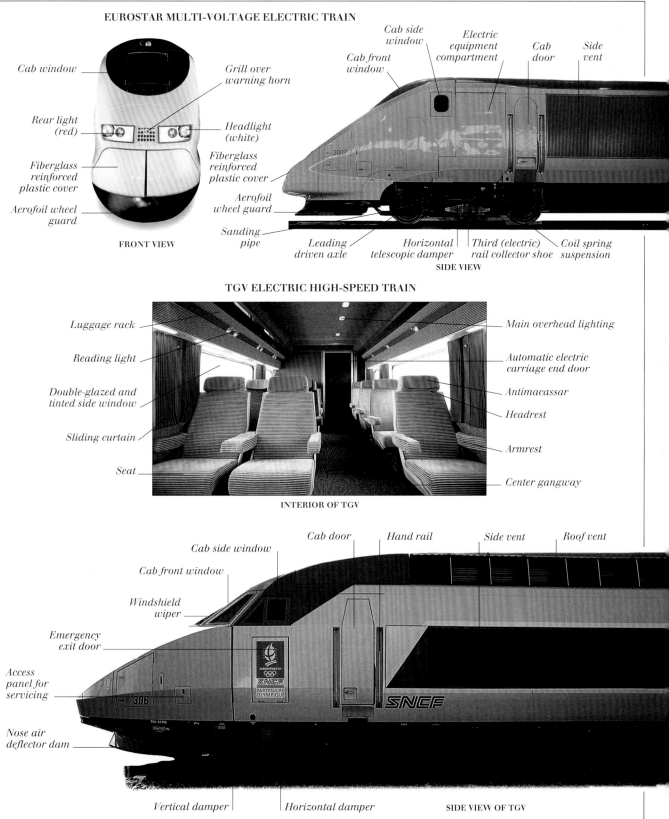

Cab window

Grill over warning horn

Rear light (red)

Headlight (white)

Fiberglass reinforced plastic cover

Fiberglass reinforced plastic cover

Aerofoil wheel guard

Aerofoil wheel guard

FRONT VIEW

Cab side window

Cab front window

Electric equipment compartment

Cab door

Side vent

Sanding pipe

Leading driven axle

Horizontal telescopic damper

Third (electric) rail collector shoe

Coil spring suspension

SIDE VIEW

TGV ELECTRIC HIGH-SPEED TRAIN

Luggage rack

Reading light

Double-glazed and tinted side window

Sliding curtain

Seat

Main overhead lighting

Automatic electric carriage end door

Antimacassar

Headrest

Armrest

Center gangway

INTERIOR OF TGV

Cab side window

Cab front window

Windshield wiper

Emergency exit door

Access panel for servicing

Nose air deflector dam

Cab door

Hand rail

Side vent

Roof vent

SNCF

Vertical damper

Horizontal damper

SIDE VIEW OF TGV

Train equipment

MODERN RAILROAD TRACK consists of two parallel steel rails clipped onto a support called a sleeper. Sleepers are usually made of reinforced concrete, although wood and steel are still used. The distance between the inside edges of the rails is the track gauge. It evolved in Britain, which uses a gauge of 4 ft 8½ in (1,435 mm), known as the standard gauge. As engineering grew more sophisticated, narrower gauges were adopted because they cost less to build. The loading gauge, which is equally important, determines the size of the largest loaded vehicle that may pass through tunnels and under bridges with adequate clearance. Safe train operation relies on following a signaling system. At first, signaling was based on a simple time interval between trains, but it now depends on maintaining a safe distance between successive trains traveling in the same direction. Most modern signals are colored lights, but older mechanical semaphore signals are still used. On the latest high-speed lines, train drivers receive control instructions by electronic means. Signaling depends on reliable control of the train by effective braking. For fast, modern trains, which have considerable momentum, it is essential that each vehicle in the train can be braked by the driver or by a train control system, such as Automatic Train Protection (ATP). Braking is achieved by the brake shoe acting on the wheel rim (rim brakes), by disc brakes, or, increasingly, by electrical braking.

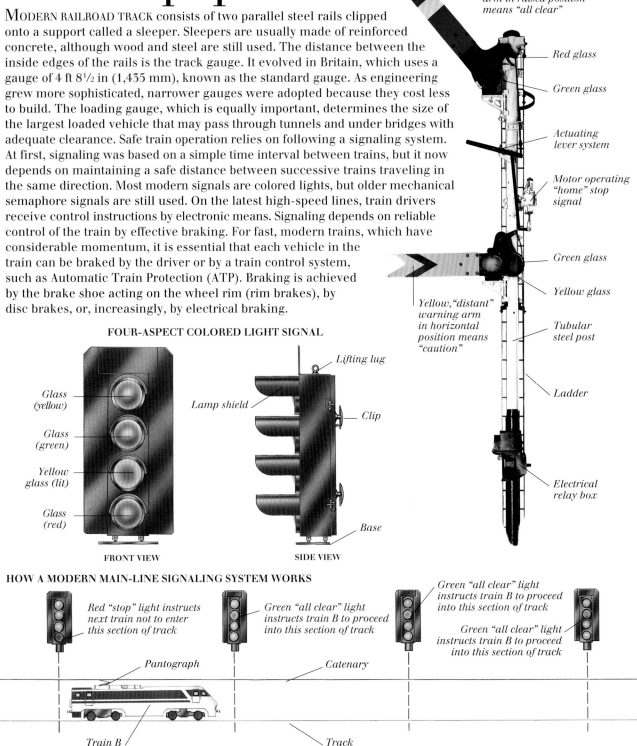

MECHANICAL SEMAPHORE SIGNAL

Red, square-ended arm in raised position means "all clear"

Red glass

Green glass

Actuating lever system

Motor operating "home" stop signal

Green glass

Yellow glass

Yellow, "distant" warning arm in horizontal position means "caution"

Tubular steel post

Ladder

Electrical relay box

FOUR-ASPECT COLORED LIGHT SIGNAL

Glass (yellow)

Glass (green)

Yellow glass (lit)

Glass (red)

Lamp shield

Lifting lug

Clip

Base

FRONT VIEW

SIDE VIEW

HOW A MODERN MAIN-LINE SIGNALING SYSTEM WORKS

Red "stop" light instructs next train not to enter this section of track

Green "all clear" light instructs train B to proceed into this section of track

Green "all clear" light instructs train B to proceed into this section of track

Green "all clear" light instructs train B to proceed into this section of track

Pantograph

Catenary

Train B

Track

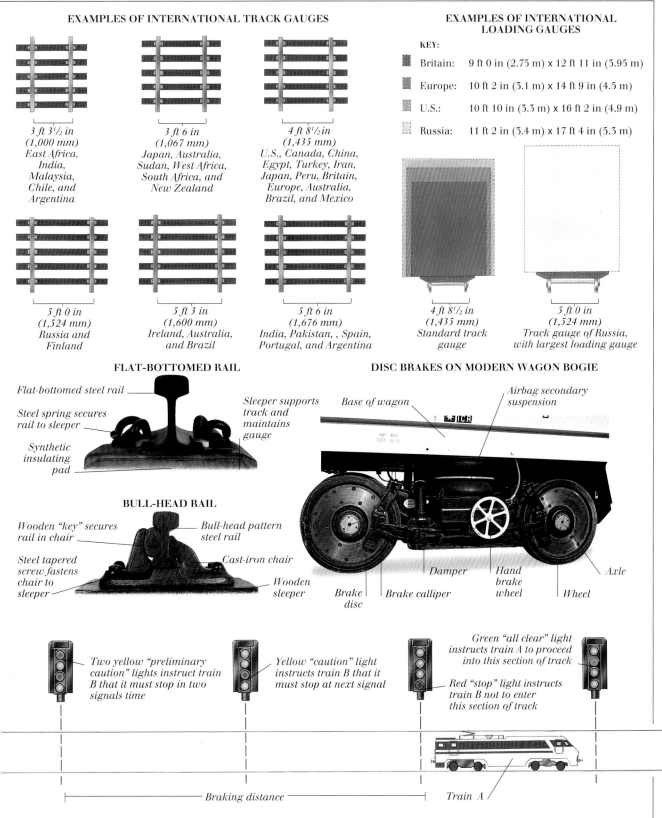

EXAMPLES OF INTERNATIONAL TRACK GAUGES

3 ft 3¹/₂ in
(1,000 mm)
East Africa,
India,
Malaysia,
Chile, and
Argentina

3 ft 6 in
(1,067 mm)
Japan, Australia,
Sudan, West Africa,
South Africa, and
New Zealand

4 ft 8¹/₂ in
(1,435 mm)
U.S., Canada, China,
Egypt, Turkey, Iran,
Japan, Peru, Britain,
Europe, Australia,
Brazil, and Mexico

5 ft 0 in
(1,524 mm)
Russia and
Finland

5 ft 3 in
(1,600 mm)
Ireland, Australia,
and Brazil

5 ft 6 in
(1,676 mm)
India, Pakistan, , Spain,
Portugal, and Argentina

EXAMPLES OF INTERNATIONAL LOADING GAUGES

KEY:
Britain: 9 ft 0 in (2.75 m) x 12 ft 11 in (3.95 m)
Europe: 10 ft 2 in (3.1 m) x 14 ft 9 in (4.5 m)
U.S.:   10 ft 10 in (3.3 m) x 16 ft 2 in (4.9 m)
Russia: 11 ft 2 in (3.4 m) x 17 ft 4 in (5.3 m)

4 ft 8¹/₂ in
(1,435 mm)
Standard track
gauge

5 ft 0 in
(1,524 mm)
Track gauge of Russia,
with largest loading gauge

FLAT-BOTTOMED RAIL

Flat-bottomed steel rail

Steel spring secures rail to sleeper

Synthetic insulating pad

Sleeper supports track and maintains gauge

BULL-HEAD RAIL

Wooden "key" secures rail in chair

Steel tapered screw fastens chair to sleeper

Bull-head pattern steel rail

Cast-iron chair

Wooden sleeper

DISC BRAKES ON MODERN WAGON BOGIE

Base of wagon

Airbag secondary suspension

HOT BOX TEST VALVE

Brake disc

Brake calliper

Damper

Hand brake wheel

Axle

Wheel

Two yellow "preliminary caution" lights instruct train B that it must stop in two signals time

Yellow "caution" light instructs train B that it must stop at next signal

Green "all clear" light instructs train A to proceed into this section of track

Red "stop" light instructs train B not to enter this section of track

Braking distance

Train A

Trolleys and buses

WHEN CITY POPULATIONS exploded in the 1800s, there was an urgent need for mass transportation. Trolleys were an early solution. The first trolleys, like buses, were horse-drawn, but in 1881, electric streetcars appeared in Berlin, Germany. Electric trolleys soon became widespread throughout Europe and North America. Trolleys run on rails along a fixed route, using electric motors that receive power from overhead cables. As road networks developed, motorized buses offered a flexible alternative to trolleys. By the 1930s, they had replaced trolley systems in many cities. City buses typically have doors at both the front and rear to make loading and unloading easier. Double-decker designs are popular, occupying the same amount of street space as single-decker buses but able to transport twice the number of people. Buses are also commonly used for inter-city travel and touring. Tour buses have reclining seats, large windows, luggage space, and toilets. Recently, as city traffic has become increasingly congested, many city planners have designed new electric streetcar routes to run alongside bus routes as part of an integrated transport system.

METROLINK TROLLEY, MANCHESTER, BRITAIN

EARLY TROLLEY, c.1900

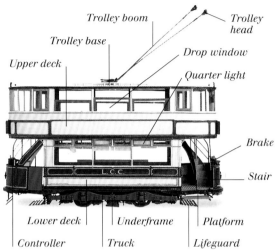

- Trolley boom
- Trolley head
- Trolley base
- Drop window
- Upper deck
- Quarter light
- Brake
- Stair
- Lower deck
- Underframe
- Platform
- Controller
- Truck
- Lifeguard
- L.C.C.

MCW METROBUS, LONDON, ENGLAND

- Square roof dome
- Upper deck air intake
- Window vent
- Mirror for driver to see upstairs
- Upper deck windshield
- Route number
- Operator's logo
- Route information
- Destination screen
- Destination screen
- Side mirror
- Side mirror
- Asymmetric windshield
- Windshield wiper
- Side mirror
- Sidelight
- Permit holder
- Headlight
- Grill
- Turning indicator
- Fog light
- Front bumper
- License plate
- Manufacturer's logo
- Entrance door
- Emergency door control
- Turning indicator

LONDON NORTHERN

Hornsey Rise · Crouch End
Turnpike Lane
West Green Road

41

ARCHWAY STN.

PAY DRIVER

mcw

KYV 739X

LONDON NORTHERN

FRONT VIEW

SINGLE-DECKER BUS, NEW YORK CITY, NEW YORK

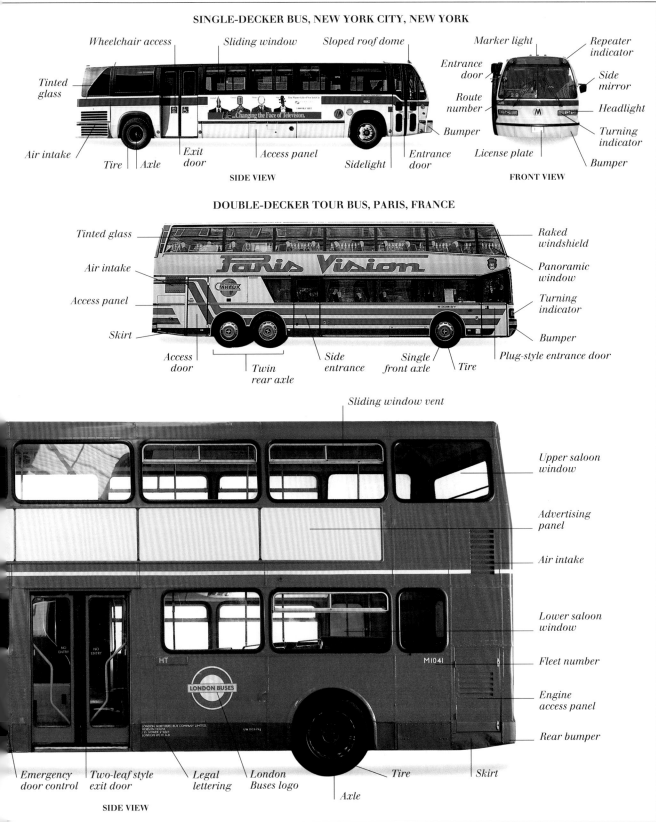

Wheelchair access

Sliding window

Sloped roof dome

Tinted glass

Marker light

Repeater indicator

Entrance door

Side mirror

Route number

Headlight

Air intake

Turning indicator

Tire

Axle

Exit door

Access panel

Sidelight

Entrance door

License plate

Bumper

SIDE VIEW

FRONT VIEW

DOUBLE-DECKER TOUR BUS, PARIS, FRANCE

Tinted glass

Raked windshield

Air intake

Panoramic window

Access panel

Turning indicator

Skirt

Bumper

Access door

Twin rear axle

Side entrance

Single front axle

Tire

Plug-style entrance door

Sliding window vent

Upper saloon window

Advertising panel

Air intake

Lower saloon window

Fleet number

Engine access panel

Rear bumper

Emergency door control

Two-leaf style exit door

Legal lettering

London Buses logo

Tire

Skirt

Axle

SIDE VIEW

HT

M1041

LONDON BUSES

333

The first cars

THE EARLIEST ROAD VEHICLE powered by an engine, the Cugnot steam traction engine, was built in 1770. More practical steam carriages, such as the Bordino, were available in the early 19th century, but they were heavy and cumbersome. Restrictive laws and the introduction of railways, faster and able to carry more passengers, saw the decline of "cars" powered by steam. It was not until 1860 that the first practical power unit for road vehicles was developed with the invention of the internal combustion engine by the Belgian Étienne Lenoir. By around 1890, Karl Benz and Gottlieb Daimler in Germany and Albert de Dion and Armand Peugeot in France were building cars for sale to the public. These early cars, despite being primitive, expensive, and produced in limited numbers, heralded the age of the automobile.

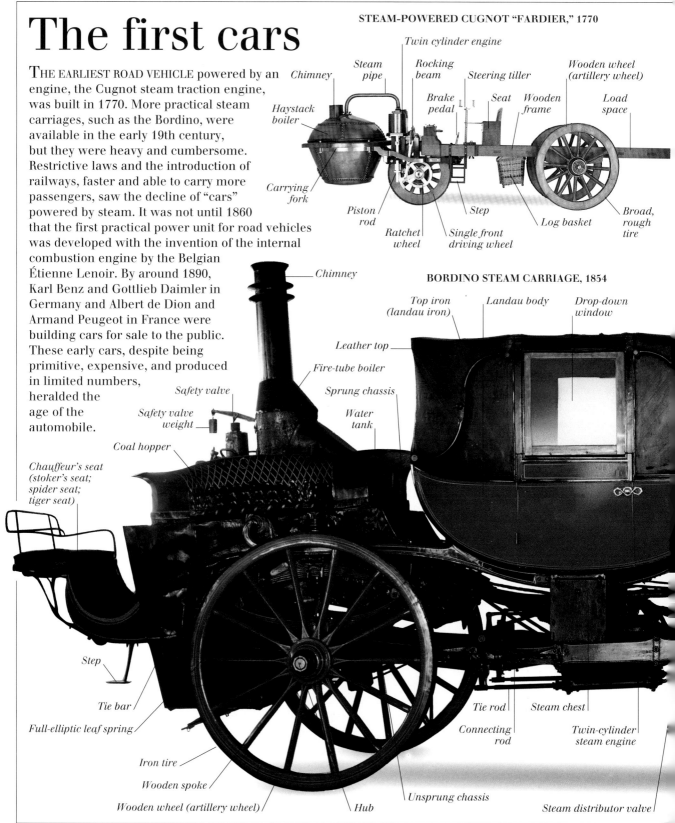

STEAM-POWERED CUGNOT "FARDIER," 1770

Twin cylinder engine

Steam pipe — Rocking beam — Steering tiller — Wooden wheel (artillery wheel)

Chimney

Brake pedal — Seat — Wooden frame — Load space

Haystack boiler

Carrying fork

Piston rod — Step — Log basket — Broad, rough tire

Ratchet wheel — Single front driving wheel

BORDINO STEAM CARRIAGE, 1854

Chimney

Top iron (landau iron) — Landau body — Drop-down window

Leather top

Fire-tube boiler

Safety valve — Sprung chassis

Safety valve weight — Water tank

Coal hopper

Chauffeur's seat (stoker's seat; spider seat; tiger seat)

Step

Tie bar

Full-elliptic leaf spring

Iron tire

Wooden spoke

Wooden wheel (artillery wheel)

Hub

Tie rod — Steam chest

Connecting rod — Twin-cylinder steam engine

Unsprung chassis

Steam distributor valve

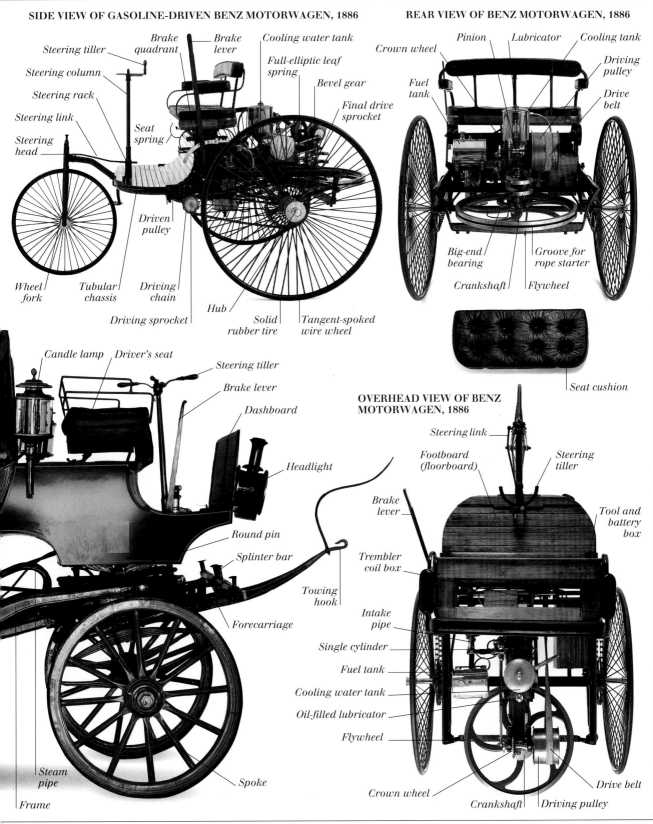

SIDE VIEW OF GASOLINE-DRIVEN BENZ MOTORWAGEN, 1886

Steering tiller
Brake quadrant
Brake lever
Cooling water tank
Full-elliptic leaf spring
Steering column
Bevel gear
Steering rack
Final drive sprocket
Steering link
Steering head
Seat spring
Driven pulley
Wheel fork
Tubular chassis
Driving chain
Driving sprocket
Hub
Solid rubber tire
Tangent-spoked wire wheel

REAR VIEW OF BENZ MOTORWAGEN, 1886

Pinion
Lubricator
Cooling tank
Crown wheel
Driving pulley
Fuel tank
Drive belt
Big-end bearing
Groove for rope starter
Crankshaft
Flywheel

Seat cushion

OVERHEAD VIEW OF BENZ MOTORWAGEN, 1886

Candle lamp
Driver's seat
Steering tiller
Brake lever
Dashboard
Headlight
Round pin
Splinter bar
Towing hook
Forecarriage

Steering link
Footboard (floorboard)
Steering tiller
Brake lever
Tool and battery box
Trembler coil box
Intake pipe
Single cylinder
Fuel tank
Cooling water tank
Oil-filled lubricator
Flywheel
Crown wheel
Crankshaft
Driving pulley
Drive belt

Steam pipe
Spoke
Frame

Elegance and utility

DURING THE FIRST DECADE OF THIS CENTURY, the motorist who could afford it had a choice of some of the finest cars ever made. These handbuilt cars were powerful and luxurious, using the finest wood, leather, and cloth, and bodywork made to the customer's individual requirements. Some had six-cylinder engines as big as 15 liters. The price of such cars was several times that of an average house, and their yearly running costs were also very high. As a result, basic, utilitarian cars became popular. Costing perhaps one-tenth of the price of a luxury car, these cars had very little trim and often had only single-cylinder engines.

1904 OLDSMOBILE SINGLE-CYLINDER ENGINE

Oil bottle dripfeed
Crankcase
Exhaust pipe
Starting handle bracket
Cylinder head
Cylinder
Starter cog
Carburetor
Engine timing gear
Crankshaft
Gear band
Flywheel

FRONT VIEW OF 1906 RENAULT

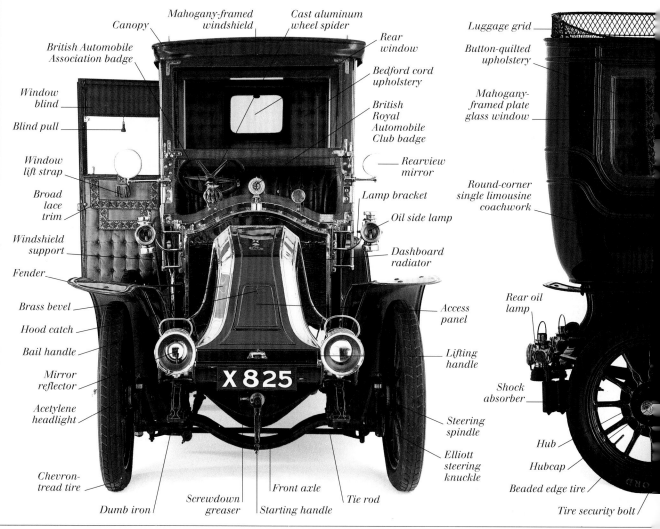

Canopy
Mahogany-framed windshield
Cast aluminum wheel spider
British Automobile Association badge
Rear window
Window blind
Bedford cord upholstery
Blind pull
British Royal Automobile Club badge
Window lift strap
Rearview mirror
Broad lace trim
Lamp bracket
Windshield support
Oil side lamp
Fender
Dashboard radiator
Brass bevel
Hood catch
Access panel
Bail handle
Lifting handle
Mirror reflector
Acetylene headlight
Steering spindle
Elliott steering knuckle
Chevron-tread tire
Dumb iron
Screwdown greaser
Front axle
Starting handle
Tie rod

SIDE VIEW OF 1906 RENAULT

Luggage grid
Button-quilted upholstery
Mahogany-framed plate glass window
Round-corner single limousine coachwork
Rear oil lamp
Shock absorber
Hub
Hubcap
Beaded edge tire
Tire security bolt

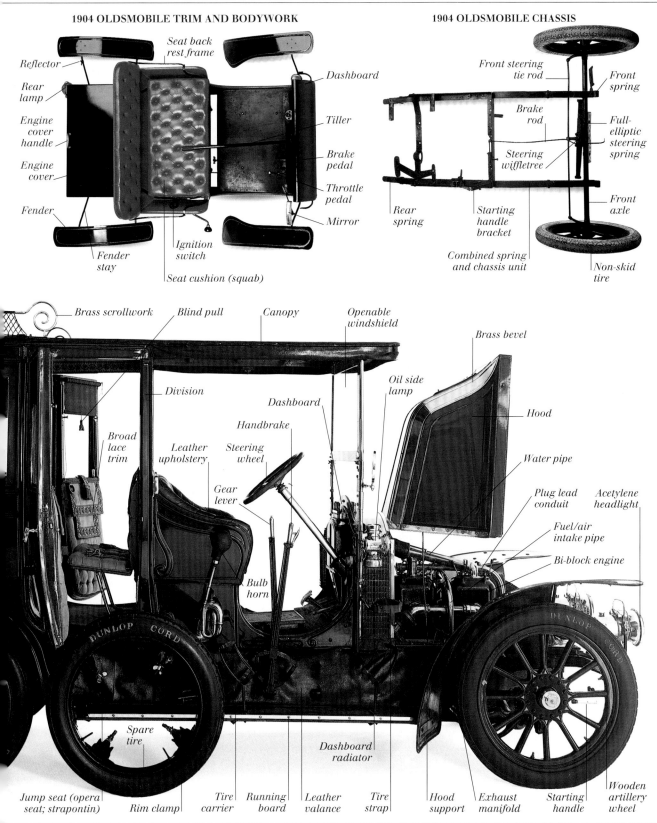

1904 OLDSMOBILE TRIM AND BODYWORK

Reflector
Rear lamp
Engine cover handle
Engine cover
Fender
Fender stay
Seat back rest frame
Ignition switch
Seat cushion (squab)
Dashboard
Tiller
Brake pedal
Throttle pedal
Mirror

1904 OLDSMOBILE CHASSIS

Front steering tie rod
Brake rod
Steering wiffletree
Front spring
Full-elliptic steering spring
Front axle
Rear spring
Starting handle bracket
Combined spring and chassis unit
Non-skid tire

Brass scrollwork
Blind pull
Canopy
Openable windshield
Brass bevel
Division
Oil side lamp
Hood
Dashboard
Handbrake
Broad lace trim
Leather upholstery
Steering wheel
Gear lever
Water pipe
Plug lead conduit
Acetylene headlight
Fuel/air intake pipe
Bi-block engine
Bulb horn
Spare tire
Jump seat (opera seat; strapontin)
Rim clamp
Tire carrier
Running board
Leather valance
Dashboard radiator
Tire strap
Hood support
Exhaust manifold
Starting handle
Wooden artillery wheel

Mass production

THE FIRST CARS WERE HAND-ASSEMBLED from individually built parts, a time-consuming procedure that required skilled mechanics and made cars very expensive. This problem was solved, in America, by a Detroit car manufacturer named Henry Ford. He introduced mass production by using standardized parts, and later combined these with a moving production line. The work was brought to the workers, each of whom performed one simple task in the construction process as the chassis moved along the line. The first mass-produced car, the Ford Model T, was launched in 1908. At first it was available in a limited range of body styles and colors. However, when the production line was introduced in 1914, the color range was cut back; the Model T became available, as Henry Ford said, in "any color you like, so long as it's black." Ford cut the production time for a car from several days to about 12 hours, and eventually to minutes, making cars much cheaper than before. As a result, half the cars in the world were Model T Fords by 1920.

Throttle lever
Openable windshield
Steering wheel
Ignition lever
Windshield stay
Dashboard
Side lamp
Bulb horn
Spring shock absorber
Fender
Headlight
Radiator
Front transverse leaf spring
License plate
Starting handle
Steering knuckle
Front axle
Steering spindle connecting-rod

STAGES OF FORD MODEL T PRODUCTION

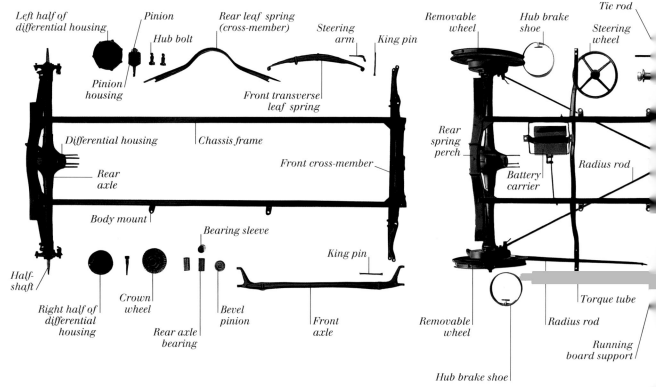

Left half of differential housing
Pinion
Rear leaf spring (cross-member)
Steering arm
King pin
Removable wheel
Hub brake shoe
Tie rod
Steering wheel
Hub bolt
Pinion housing
Front transverse leaf spring
Differential housing
Chassis frame
Rear spring perch
Radius rod
Rear axle
Front cross-member
Battery carrier
Body mount
Bearing sleeve
King pin
Half-shaft
Crown wheel
Bevel pinion
Front axle
Removable wheel
Torque tube
Right half of differential housing
Rear axle bearing
Radius rod
Running board support
Hub brake shoe

SIDE VIEW OF 1913 FORD MODEL T

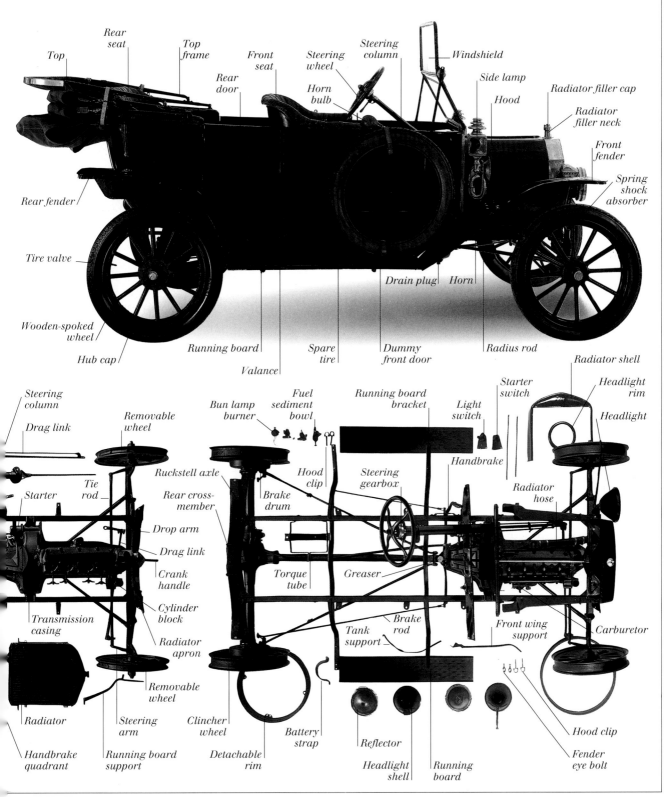

Top

Rear seat

Top frame

Rear door

Front seat

Steering wheel

Horn bulb

Steering column

Windshield

Side lamp

Hood

Radiator filler cap

Radiator filler neck

Front fender

Spring shock absorber

Rear fender

Tire valve

Drain plug

Horn

Wooden-spoked wheel

Hub cap

Running board

Valance

Spare tire

Dummy front door

Radius rod

Radiator shell

Steering column

Drag link

Removable wheel

Bun lamp burner

Fuel sediment bowl

Running board bracket

Light switch

Starter switch

Headlight rim

Headlight

Tie rod

Ruckstell axle

Hood clip

Steering gearbox

Handbrake

Radiator hose

Starter

Rear cross-member

Brake drum

Drop arm

Drag link

Crank handle

Cylinder block

Torque tube

Greaser

Brake rod

Front wing support

Carburetor

Transmission casing

Radiator apron

Tank support

Radiator

Steering arm

Removable wheel

Clincher wheel

Battery strap

Reflector

Hood clip

Fender eye bolt

Handbrake quadrant

Running board support

Detachable rim

Headlight shell

Running board

The "people's car"

WORKING PARTS OF VOLKSWAGEN BEETLE

THE MOST POPULAR CAR in the history of car manufacture is the Volkswagen Beetle, originally called the KdF Wagen. The car was developed in Germany in the 1930s by Dr. Ferdinand Porsche. At that time, Germany had only half the number of cars of Britain or France, and Adolf Hitler took a personal interest in the development of the Volkswagen ("people's car"). The intention was to provide a new industry, new jobs, and a car so inexpensive that anyone with a job could afford it. Dr. Porsche designed a car that was cheap to build and run; its rear-mounted, air-cooled engine cut down the number of parts needed and also reduced weight. However, few civilians managed to obtain the Beetle before the outbreak of the Second World War in 1939. After the war, the Beetle proved so popular that eventually more than 20 million were sold.

Fuel tank
Fuel tank sender unit
Steering tie-rod
Fuel filler neck
Windshield-wiper motor assembly
Steering box assembly
Steering idler
Frame head
Anti-roll bar
Suspension strut
Brake back plate
Track control arm
Pedal cluster
Strut cartridge (shock absorber)
Dust shroud
Front suspension top mount
Gear lever knob
Front road spring
Seat mount
Front suspension top mount
Handbrake
Floor pan (platform chassis)
Torsion bar cover
Rear brake drum
Trailing arm
Tire
Sports wheel
Rear shock absorber
Drive shaft
Transaxle (gearbox and final drive)
Heat exchanger
Clutch and flywheel
Starter motor
Flat-four engine
Air filter
Tail pipe

CUSTOMIZED VOLKSWAGEN BEETLE

Taillight
Air scoop
Vent window
Luggage compartment lid
Turn signal and parking light
Tail pipe
Pressed steel wheel
Fuel filler cap

FLAT-FOUR CYLINDER ARRANGEMENT

Counterweight
Piston
Crankshaft
Big end
Connecting rod (con-rod)

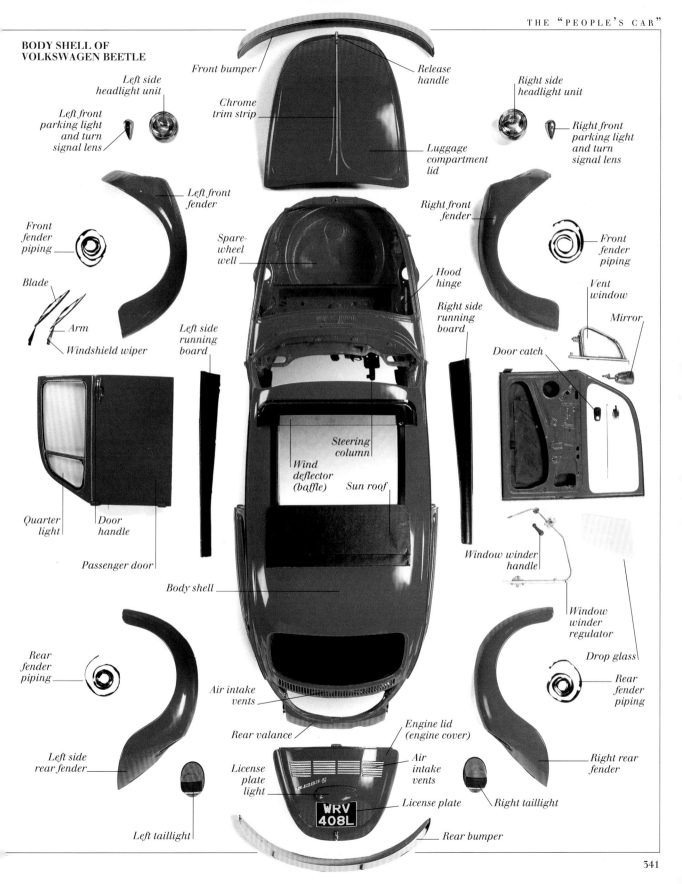

BODY SHELL OF VOLKSWAGEN BEETLE

Front bumper

Release handle

Left side headlight unit

Chrome trim strip

Right side headlight unit

Left front parking light and turn signal lens

Luggage compartment lid

Right front parking light and turn signal lens

Left front fender

Right front fender

Front fender piping

Spare-wheel well

Hood hinge

Front fender piping

Blade

Right side running board

Vent window

Arm

Mirror

Windshield wiper

Left side running board

Door catch

Quarter light

Steering column

Door handle

Wind deflector (baffle)

Sun roof

Passenger door

Window winder handle

Body shell

Window winder regulator

Rear fender piping

Drop glass

Rear fender piping

Air intake vents

Left side rear fender

Engine lid (engine cover)

Right rear fender

Rear valance

Air intake vents

License plate light

License plate

Left taillight

WRV 408L

Right taillight

Rear bumper

341

Early engines

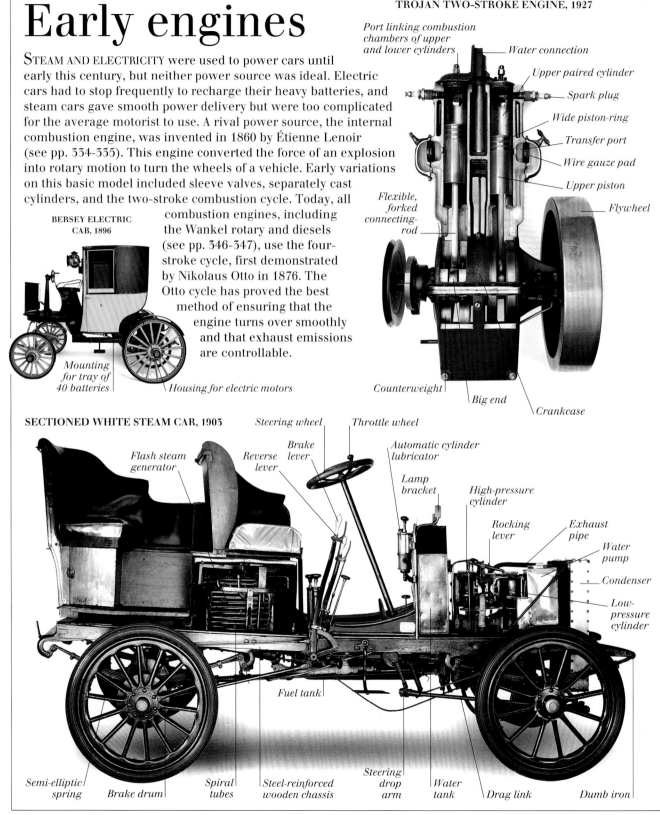

STEAM AND ELECTRICITY were used to power cars until early this century, but neither power source was ideal. Electric cars had to stop frequently to recharge their heavy batteries, and steam cars gave smooth power delivery but were too complicated for the average motorist to use. A rival power source, the internal combustion engine, was invented in 1860 by Étienne Lenoir (see pp. 334-335). This engine converted the force of an explosion into rotary motion to turn the wheels of a vehicle. Early variations on this basic model included sleeve valves, separately cast cylinders, and the two-stroke combustion cycle. Today, all combustion engines, including the Wankel rotary and diesels (see pp. 346-347), use the four-stroke cycle, first demonstrated by Nikolaus Otto in 1876. The Otto cycle has proved the best method of ensuring that the engine turns over smoothly and that exhaust emissions are controllable.

TROJAN TWO-STROKE ENGINE, 1927

Port linking combustion chambers of upper and lower cylinders

Water connection

Upper paired cylinder

Spark plug

Wide piston-ring

Transfer port

Wire gauze pad

Upper piston

Flywheel

Flexible, forked connecting-rod

Counterweight

Big end

Crankcase

BERSEY ELECTRIC CAB, 1896

Mounting for tray of 40 batteries

Housing for electric motors

SECTIONED WHITE STEAM CAR, 1903

Steering wheel

Throttle wheel

Brake lever

Reverse lever

Automatic cylinder lubricator

Flash steam generator

Lamp bracket

High-pressure cylinder

Rocking lever

Exhaust pipe

Water pump

Condenser

Low-pressure cylinder

Fuel tank

Semi-elliptic spring

Brake drum

Spiral tubes

Steel-reinforced wooden chassis

Steering drop arm

Water tank

Drag link

Dumb iron

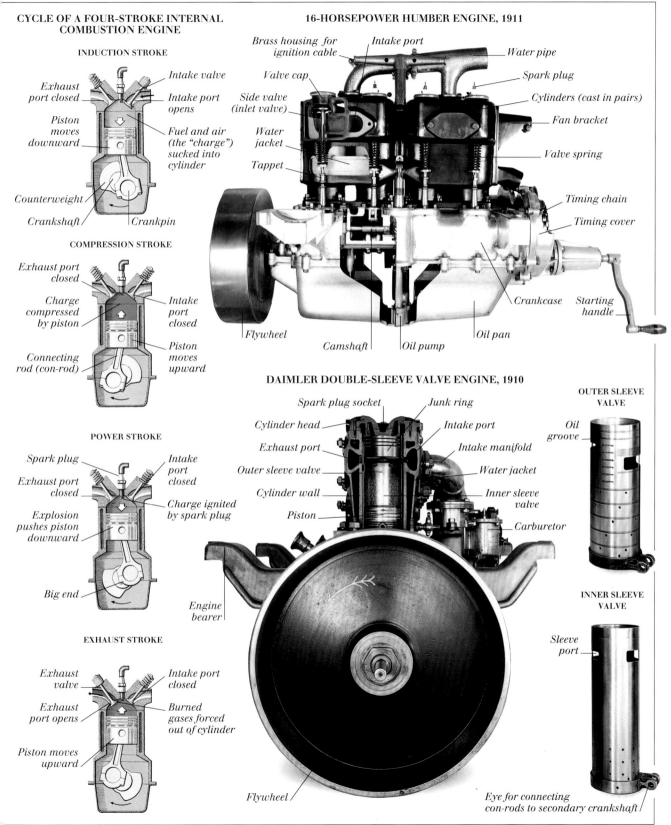

CYCLE OF A FOUR-STROKE INTERNAL COMBUSTION ENGINE

INDUCTION STROKE

Exhaust port closed

Intake valve

Intake port opens

Piston moves downward

Fuel and air (the "charge") sucked into cylinder

Counterweight

Crankshaft

Crankpin

COMPRESSION STROKE

Exhaust port closed

Charge compressed by piston

Intake port closed

Connecting rod (con-rod)

Piston moves upward

POWER STROKE

Spark plug

Intake port closed

Exhaust port closed

Explosion pushes piston downward

Charge ignited by spark plug

Big end

EXHAUST STROKE

Exhaust valve

Intake port closed

Exhaust port opens

Burned gases forced out of cylinder

Piston moves upward

16-HORSEPOWER HUMBER ENGINE, 1911

Brass housing for ignition cable

Intake port

Water pipe

Valve cap

Spark plug

Side valve (inlet valve)

Cylinders (cast in pairs)

Water jacket

Fan bracket

Tappet

Valve spring

Timing chain

Timing cover

Flywheel

Camshaft

Oil pump

Oil pan

Crankcase

Starting handle

DAIMLER DOUBLE-SLEEVE VALVE ENGINE, 1910

Spark plug socket

Junk ring

Cylinder head

Intake port

Exhaust port

Intake manifold

Outer sleeve valve

Water jacket

Cylinder wall

Inner sleeve valve

Piston

Carburetor

Engine bearer

Flywheel

OUTER SLEEVE VALVE

Oil groove

INNER SLEEVE VALVE

Sleeve port

Eye for connecting con-rods to secondary crankshaft

Modern engines

TODAY'S GASOLINE ENGINE WORKS on the same basic principles as the first car engines of a century ago, although it has been greatly refined. Modern engines, often made from special metal alloys, are much lighter than earlier engines. Computerized ignition systems, fuel injectors, and multi-valve cylinder heads achieve a more efficient combustion of the fuel/air mixture (the charge) so that less fuel is wasted. As a result of this greater efficiency, the power and performance of a modern engine are increased, and the level of pollution in the exhaust gases is reduced. Exhaust pollution levels today are also lowered by the increasing use of special filters called catalytic converters, which absorb many exhaust pollutants. The need to produce ever more efficient engines means that it can take up to seven years to develop a new engine for a family car, at a cost of many millions of dollars.

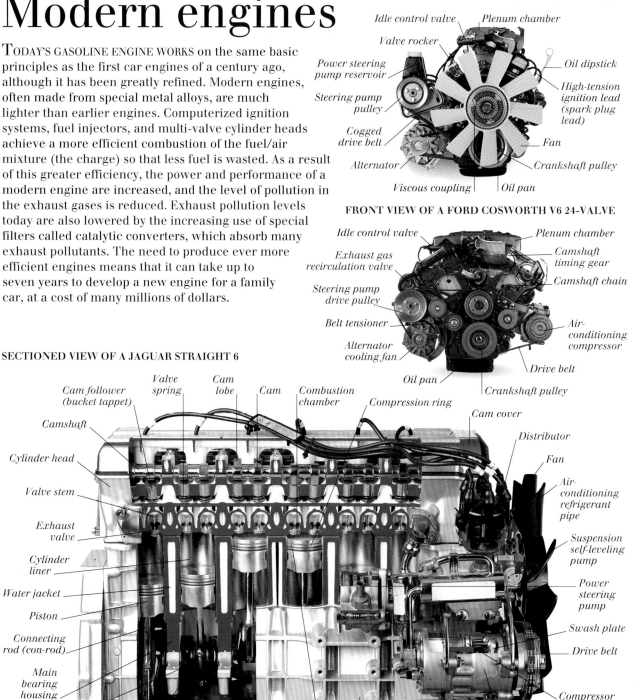

FRONT VIEW OF A FORD COSWORTH V6 12-VALVE

Idle control valve
Plenum chamber
Valve rocker
Power steering pump reservoir
Oil dipstick
Steering pump pulley
High-tension ignition lead (spark plug lead)
Cogged drive belt
Fan
Alternator
Crankshaft pulley
Viscous coupling
Oil pan

FRONT VIEW OF A FORD COSWORTH V6 24-VALVE

Idle control valve
Plenum chamber
Exhaust gas recirculation valve
Camshaft timing gear
Steering pump drive pulley
Camshaft chain
Belt tensioner
Air-conditioning compressor
Alternator cooling fan
Drive belt
Oil pan
Crankshaft pulley

SECTIONED VIEW OF A JAGUAR STRAIGHT 6

Cam follower (bucket tappet)
Valve spring
Cam lobe
Cam
Combustion chamber
Compression ring
Cam cover
Camshaft
Distributor
Cylinder head
Fan
Valve stem
Air-conditioning refrigerant pipe
Exhaust valve
Suspension self-leveling pump
Cylinder liner
Power steering pump
Water jacket
Swash plate
Piston
Drive belt
Connecting rod (con-rod)
Compressor piston
Main bearing housing
Big end
Air-conditioning compressor
Transmission adaptor plate
Crankshaft counterweight
Oil pan
Oil pick-up pipe
Anti-surge baffle
Crankcase
Oil-control ring (scraper ring)

FRONT VIEW OF A JAGUAR V12

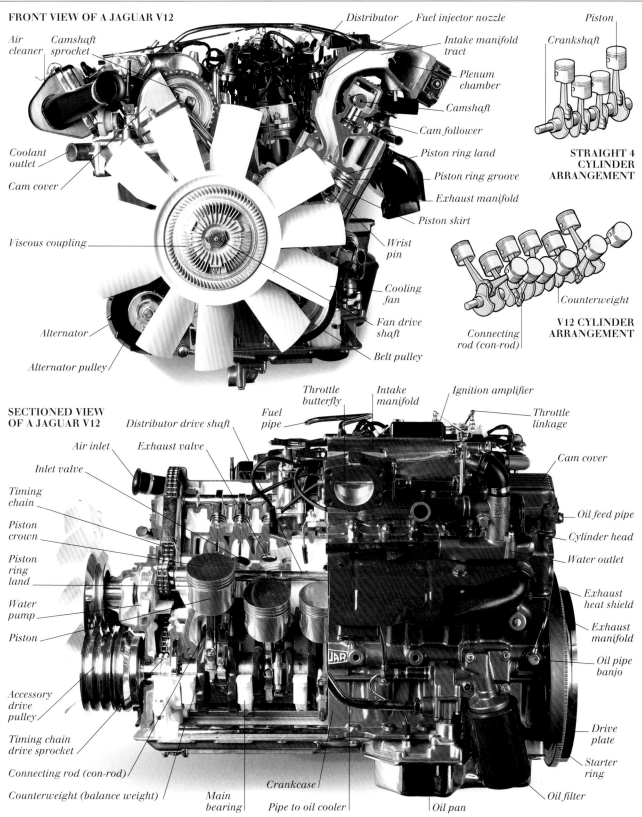

Distributor

Fuel injector nozzle

Piston

Air cleaner

Camshaft sprocket

Intake manifold tract

Crankshaft

Plenum chamber

Camshaft

Cam follower

Coolant outlet

Piston ring land

STRAIGHT 4 CYLINDER ARRANGEMENT

Cam cover

Piston ring groove

Exhaust manifold

Piston skirt

Viscous coupling

Wrist pin

Cooling fan

Fan drive shaft

Belt pulley

Alternator

Connecting rod (con-rod)

Counterweight

V12 CYLINDER ARRANGEMENT

Alternator pulley

SECTIONED VIEW OF A JAGUAR V12

Throttle butterfly

Intake manifold

Ignition amplifier

Throttle linkage

Distributor drive shaft

Fuel pipe

Cam cover

Air inlet

Exhaust valve

Inlet valve

Oil feed pipe

Timing chain

Cylinder head

Piston crown

Water outlet

Piston ring land

Exhaust heat shield

Water pump

Exhaust manifold

Piston

Oil pipe banjo

Accessory drive pulley

Drive plate

Timing chain drive sprocket

Starter ring

Connecting rod (con-rod)

Counterweight (balance weight)

Main bearing

Crankcase

Pipe to oil cooler

Oil filter

Oil pan

345

Alternative engines

THE MOST COMMON TYPE OF ALTERNATIVE ENGINE is the diesel engine. Instead of igniting the compressed fuel/air mixture with a spark, the diesel engine uses compression alone, which heats the mixture to the point where it explodes. A diesel engine's fuel consumption is low in comparison with similarly sized piston engines, despite its heavier, reinforced moving parts and cylinder block. Another type of engine is the rotary-combustion, first successfully developed by Felix Wankel in the 1950s. Its two trilobate (three-sided) rotors revolve in housings shaped in a fat figure eight. The four sequences of the four-stroke cycle, which occur consecutively in a piston engine, occur simultaneously in a rotary engine, producing power in a continuous stream.

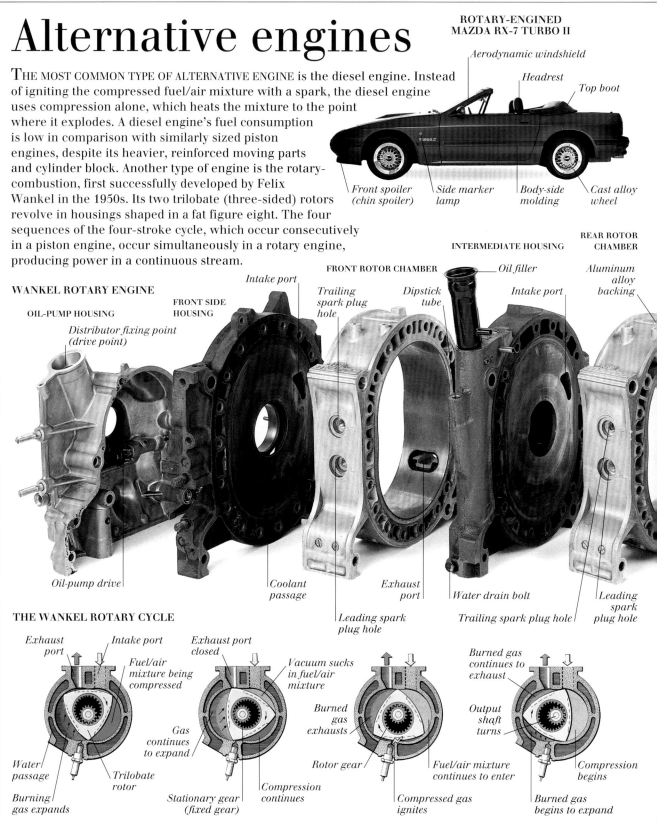

ROTARY-ENGINED MAZDA RX-7 TURBO II

Aerodynamic windshield
Headrest
Top boot
Front spoiler (chin spoiler)
Side marker lamp
Body-side molding
Cast alloy wheel

WANKEL ROTARY ENGINE

OIL-PUMP HOUSING
FRONT SIDE HOUSING
Distributor fixing point (drive point)
Intake port
FRONT ROTOR CHAMBER
Trailing spark plug hole
INTERMEDIATE HOUSING
Oil filler
Dipstick tube
Intake port
REAR ROTOR CHAMBER
Aluminum alloy backing

Oil-pump drive
Coolant passage
Leading spark plug hole
Exhaust port
Water drain bolt
Trailing spark plug hole
Leading spark plug hole

THE WANKEL ROTARY CYCLE

Exhaust port
Intake port
Fuel/air mixture being compressed
Water passage
Burning gas expands
Trilobate rotor
Gas continues to expand
Stationary gear (fixed gear)

Exhaust port closed
Vacuum sucks in fuel/air mixture
Burned gas exhausts
Rotor gear
Compression continues
Compressed gas ignites
Fuel/air mixture continues to enter

Burned gas continues to exhaust
Output shaft turns
Compression begins
Burned gas begins to expand

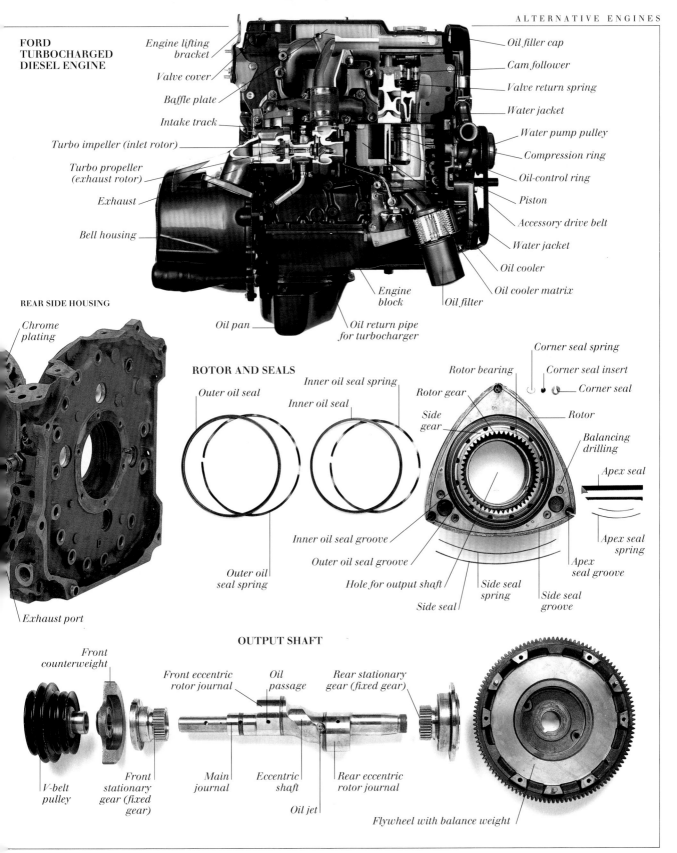

FORD TURBOCHARGED DIESEL ENGINE

Engine lifting bracket

Valve cover

Baffle plate

Intake track

Turbo impeller (inlet rotor)

Turbo propeller (exhaust rotor)

Exhaust

Bell housing

Oil filler cap

Cam follower

Valve return spring

Water jacket

Water pump pulley

Compression ring

Oil-control ring

Piston

Accessory drive belt

Water jacket

Oil cooler

Oil cooler matrix

Engine block

Oil filter

Oil pan

Oil return pipe for turbocharger

REAR SIDE HOUSING

Chrome plating

Exhaust port

ROTOR AND SEALS

Outer oil seal

Inner oil seal spring

Inner oil seal

Corner seal spring

Rotor bearing

Corner seal insert

Rotor gear

Corner seal

Side gear

Rotor

Balancing drilling

Apex seal

Inner oil seal groove

Outer oil seal groove

Outer oil seal spring

Hole for output shaft

Side seal spring

Side seal

Apex seal groove

Side seal groove

Apex seal spring

OUTPUT SHAFT

Front counterweight

Front eccentric rotor journal

Oil passage

Rear stationary gear (fixed gear)

V-belt pulley

Front stationary gear (fixed gear)

Main journal

Eccentric shaft

Rear eccentric rotor journal

Oil jet

Flywheel with balance weight

Modern bodywork

THE BODY OF A MODERN MASS-PRODUCED CAR is built on the monocoque (single-shell) principle, in which the roof, side panels, and floor are welded into a single integral unit. This bodyshell protects and supports the car's internal parts. Steel and glass are used to construct the bodyshell, creating a unit that is both light and strong. Its lightness helps to conserve energy, while its strength protects the occupants. Modern bodywork is designed with the aid of computers, which are used to predict factors such as aerodynamic efficiency and impact resistance. High technology is also employed on the production line, where robots are used to assemble, weld, and paint the body.

RENAULT
LOGO

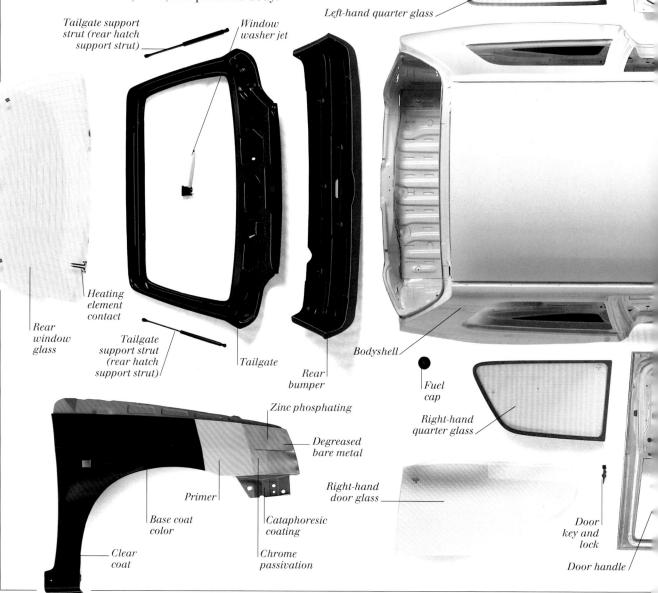

Door handle

Door lock

Left-hand door glass

Left-hand quarter glass

Tailgate support strut (rear hatch support strut)

Window washer jet

Heating element contact

Rear window glass

Tailgate support strut (rear hatch support strut)

Tailgate

Rear bumper

Bodyshell

Fuel cap

Right-hand quarter glass

Zinc phosphating

Degreased bare metal

Primer

Base coat color

Cataphoresic coating

Chrome passivation

Right-hand door glass

Clear coat

Door key and lock

Door handle

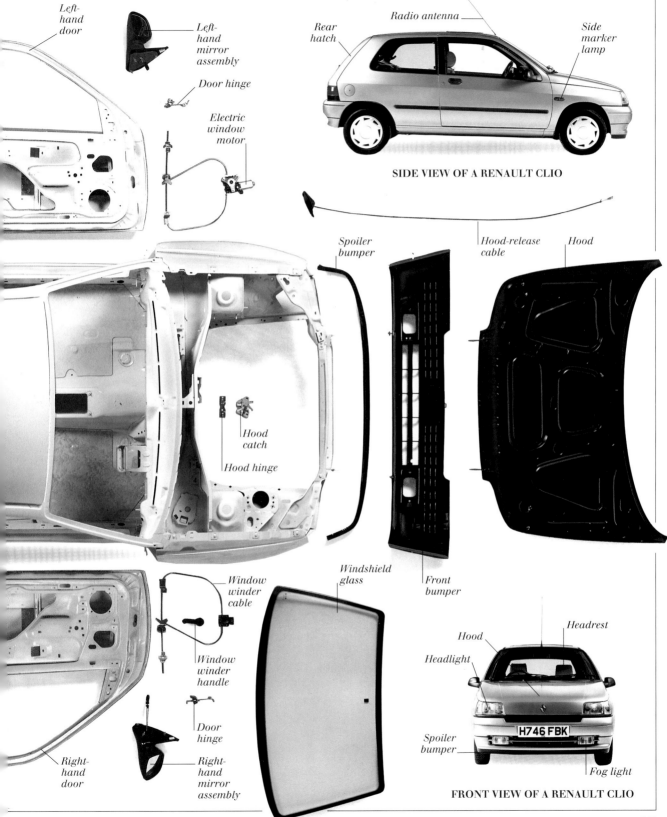

Left-hand door

Left-hand mirror assembly

Door hinge

Electric window motor

Radio antenna

Rear hatch

Side marker lamp

SIDE VIEW OF A RENAULT CLIO

Spoiler bumper

Hood-release cable

Hood

Hood catch

Hood hinge

Window winder cable

Windshield glass

Front bumper

Window winder handle

Door hinge

Right-hand door

Right-hand mirror assembly

Hood

Headrest

Headlight

Spoiler bumper

H746 FBK

Fog light

FRONT VIEW OF A RENAULT CLIO

Modern components

A TYPICAL MODERN CAR has several thousand individual mechanical components. These are assembled to form the car's various mechanical systems: engine and exhaust, transmission, steering, suspension, and brakes. To ensure that each system functions properly, components are manufactured to extremely fine tolerances—to within about one ten-thousandth of an inch in some cases.

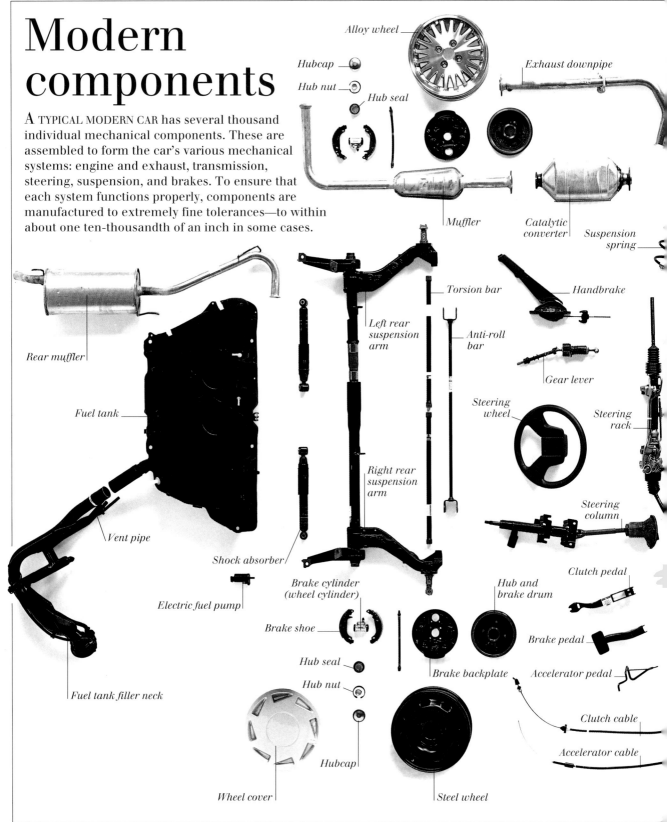

Alloy wheel

Hubcap

Hub nut

Hub seal

Exhaust downpipe

Muffler

Catalytic converter

Suspension spring

Torsion bar

Handbrake

Left rear suspension arm

Anti-roll bar

Gear lever

Steering wheel

Steering rack

Rear muffler

Fuel tank

Right rear suspension arm

Steering column

Vent pipe

Shock absorber

Brake cylinder (wheel cylinder)

Electric fuel pump

Hub and brake drum

Clutch pedal

Brake shoe

Brake pedal

Hub seal

Brake backplate

Accelerator pedal

Hub nut

Fuel tank filler neck

Clutch cable

Accelerator cable

Wheel cover

Hubcap

Steel wheel

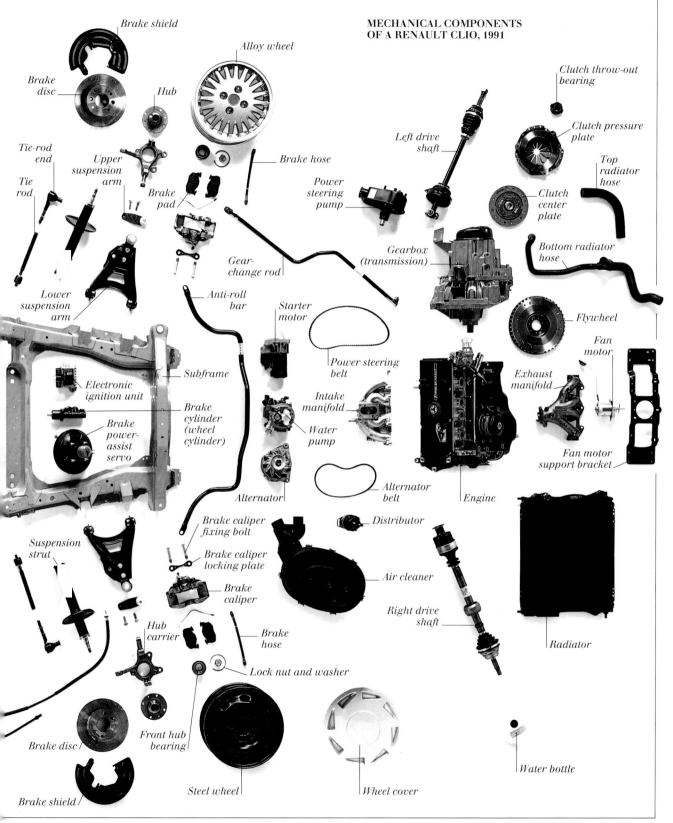

MECHANICAL COMPONENTS OF A RENAULT CLIO, 1991

Brake shield

Alloy wheel

Clutch throw-out bearing

Brake disc

Hub

Clutch pressure plate

Left drive shaft

Tie-rod end

Upper suspension arm

Brake hose

Top radiator hose

Tie rod

Brake pad

Power steering pump

Clutch center plate

Gearbox (transmission)

Bottom radiator hose

Lower suspension arm

Gear-change rod

Anti-roll bar

Starter motor

Flywheel

Subframe

Power steering belt

Fan motor

Electronic ignition unit

Brake cylinder (wheel cylinder)

Intake manifold

Exhaust manifold

Brake power-assist servo

Water pump

Alternator

Alternator belt

Engine

Fan motor support bracket

Brake caliper fixing bolt

Distributor

Suspension strut

Brake caliper locking plate

Air cleaner

Hub carrier

Brake caliper

Brake hose

Right drive shaft

Lock nut and washer

Radiator

Brake disc

Front hub bearing

Steel wheel

Wheel cover

Water bottle

Brake shield

Modern trim

A MODERN CAR HAS TWO TYPES OF TRIM, according to the materials used: hard (chrome and plastics) and soft (upholstered materials). Safety and comfort are priorities in the trim's design: seats help the occupants maintain a comfortable posture, rubber seals keep out dirt and moisture, and headlights light the way. Older cars had interior or leather paneling cut and fitted by craftsmen; modern cars use precisely molded plastics and seat fabrics cut by robot-controlled lasers to reduce costs and production time. Doors are now assembled off the production line so that complex wiring can be built in.

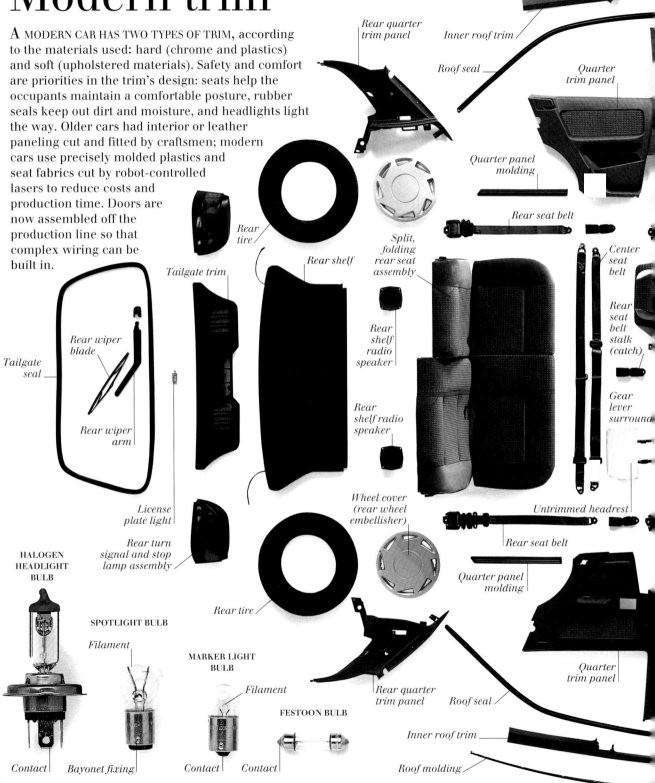

TRIM OF A RENAULT CLIO, 1991

Rear quarter trim panel

Inner roof trim

Roof seal

Quarter trim panel

Quarter panel molding

Rear seat belt

Center seat belt

Rear seat belt stalk (catch)

Gear lever surround

Untrimmed headrest

Rear seat belt

Quarter panel molding

Quarter trim panel

Rear quarter trim panel

Roof seal

Inner roof trim

Roof molding

Rear tire

Rear shelf

Split, folding rear seat assembly

Rear shelf radio speaker

Rear shelf radio speaker

Wheel cover (rear wheel embellisher)

Rear tire

Tailgate trim

Tailgate seal

Rear wiper blade

Rear wiper arm

License plate light

Rear turn signal and stop lamp assembly

HALOGEN HEADLIGHT BULB

Filament

SPOTLIGHT BULB

Contact

Bayonet fixing

MARKER LIGHT BULB

Filament

Contact

FESTOON BULB

Contact

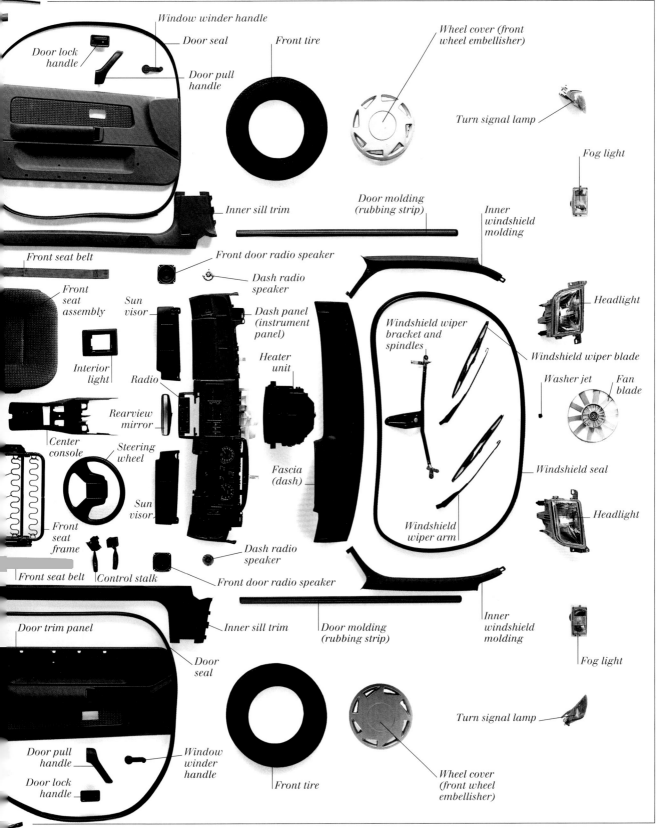

Window winder handle

Door lock handle

Door seal

Door pull handle

Front tire

Wheel cover (front wheel embellisher)

Turn signal lamp

Fog light

Inner sill trim

Door molding (rubbing strip)

Inner windshield molding

Front seat belt

Front door radio speaker

Dash radio speaker

Front seat assembly

Sun visor

Dash panel (instrument panel)

Headlight

Windshield wiper bracket and spindles

Windshield wiper blade

Interior light

Heater unit

Washer jet

Fan blade

Radio

Rearview mirror

Center console

Steering wheel

Fascia (dash)

Windshield seal

Front seat frame

Sun visor

Windshield wiper arm

Headlight

Front seat belt

Control stalk

Dash radio speaker

Front door radio speaker

Inner windshield molding

Door trim panel

Inner sill trim

Door molding (rubbing strip)

Door seal

Fog light

Door pull handle

Window winder handle

Door lock handle

Front tire

Turn signal lamp

Wheel cover (front wheel embellisher)

All-terrain vehicles

THE MODERN ALL-TERRAIN VEHICLE has its origins in the American military Jeep of the 1940s and the British Land Rover. Such vehicles have been used for a wide range of purposes, from safari travel to fire fighting. The principal special features of such cars—including four- or six-wheel drive, high ground clearance, and toughened braking, suspension, and transmission systems—are designed to enable driving under the most difficult off-road conditions. The vehicle shown here is equipped for safari travel and carries a comprehensive range of survival gear.

COOKING EQUIPMENT

TWO–BURNER
ALCOHOL STOVE

Handle
for all
pans

Flame
regulator

Wick

Zipper

Tie

Cooking
pot

Mosquito netting

Ventilation
flap

Locking
fuel filler
cap

Raised
air
intake

Dust
filter

Guard

**SIDE VIEW OF
PINZGAUER
TURBO D**

HAND WINCH

Folding
rooftop tent

Galvanized roof-rack

Steel body

Jerrycan

Spare wheel
and tire

Bodyside molding
(rub strip)

TIRE
PUMP

Pressure
gauge

TIRE IRON

Heavy-duty shovel

Tubular backbone chassis

Fuel tank

Metal jerrycan for fuel

Plastic
jerrycan
for water

LEFT-HAND TREAD PLATE · **RIGHT-HAND TREAD PLATE**

TOW STRAP · **HEAVY-DUTY SHACKLE**

SAFETY WINDSHIELD CLAMPS

WASHING BUCKET

Radio aerial · Observation roof hatch · Grab handle · Rearview mirror · Windshield washer bottle · Wrap-around bumper · Access step

SECURITY CHAIN

FRONT VIEW OF PINZGAUER TURBO D

Observation roof hatch · Radio aerial · Galvanized roof-rack · Laminated windshield · Rearview mirror · Air vent · Radiator grille · Indicator · Headlight · Headlight guard · External step · Independent swing axle · Locking differential · Towing loop · All-terrain tire

REAR VIEW OF PINZGAUER TURBO D

Roof-rack · Observation platform · External step for roof · Jerrycan · Jerrycan carrier · Spare wheel · Bodyside molding (rub strip) · Offset door hinge · Rear bumper · Rear light cluster · Mudflap · Door and wheel support frame · Off-road tire · Locking differential · Independent swing axle

355

Racing cars

SINCE MOTORING BEGAN, racing cars have been a major focus of innovation in car design. Features that are now commonplace, such as disc brakes, turbochargers, and even safety belts, were used first on competition cars. Research into racing cars has contributed to a new understanding of engine performance, aerodynamics, and tire adhesion, and has led to the development of ultra-light materials such as carbon-fiber for car bodies. Like the 1937 Bugatti Type 57S below, a modern Williams Formula One car has a low, streamlined body and an open cockpit. Unlike its forerunner, it also has a front wing that pushes the front wheels firmly onto the track, huge slick tires for extra grip, and electrical sensors that continually relay information to the pits about the car's performance.

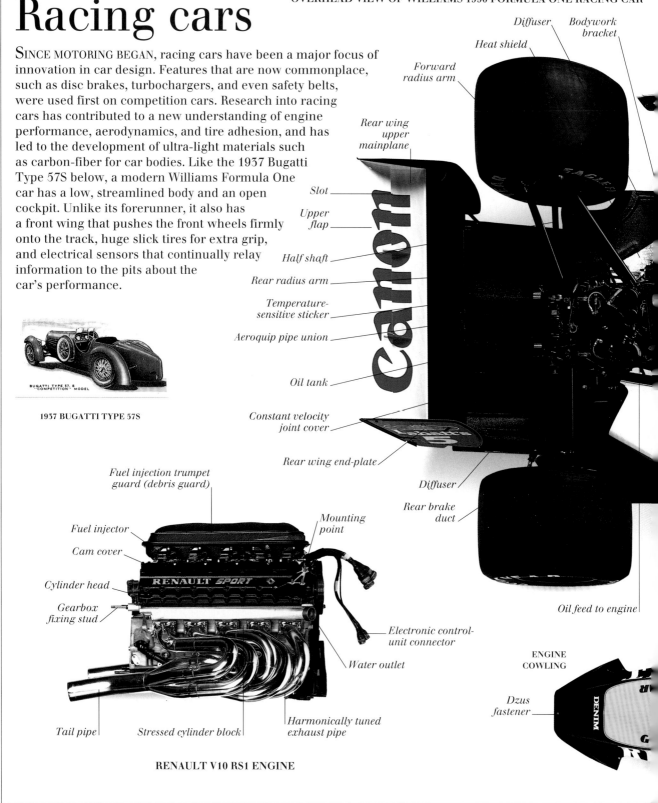

1937 BUGATTI TYPE 57S

Diffuser

Bodywork bracket

Heat shield

Forward radius arm

Rear wing upper mainplane

Slot

Upper flap

Half shaft

Rear radius arm

Temperature-sensitive sticker

Aeroquip pipe union

Oil tank

Constant velocity joint cover

Rear wing end-plate

Diffuser

Rear brake duct

Oil feed to engine

ENGINE COWLING

Dzus fastener

Fuel injection trumpet guard (debris guard)

Mounting point

Fuel injector

Cam cover

Cylinder head

Gearbox fixing stud

Electronic control-unit connector

Water outlet

Tail pipe

Stressed cylinder block

Harmonically tuned exhaust pipe

RENAULT V10 RS1 ENGINE

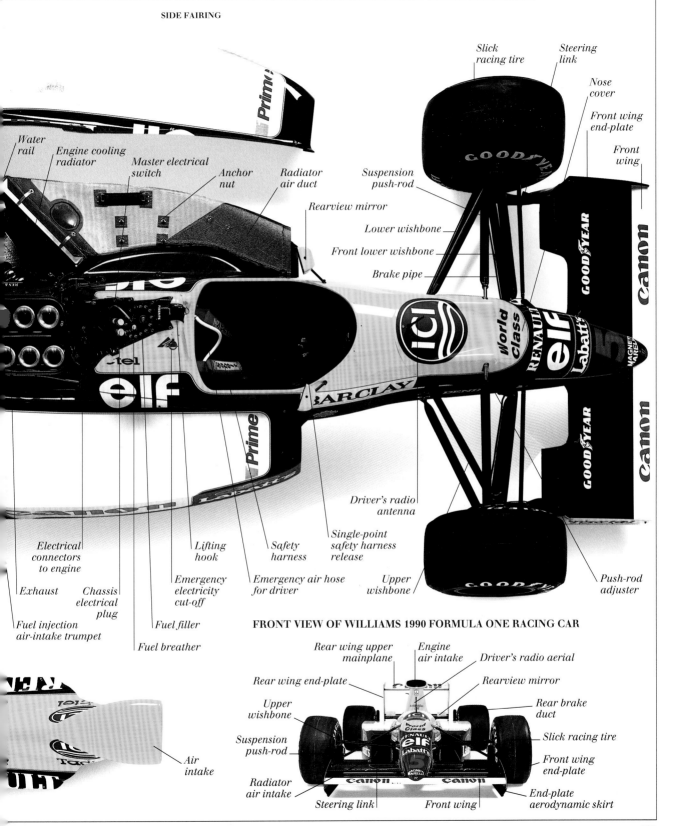

SIDE FAIRING

Slick racing tire

Steering link

Nose cover

Front wing end-plate

Front wing

Water rail

Engine cooling radiator

Master electrical switch

Anchor nut

Radiator air duct

Suspension push-rod

Rearview mirror

Lower wishbone

Front lower wishbone

Brake pipe

Driver's radio antenna

Single-point safety harness release

Upper wishbone

Push-rod adjuster

Electrical connectors to engine

Lifting hook

Safety harness

Exhaust

Chassis electrical plug

Emergency electricity cut-off

Emergency air hose for driver

Fuel injection air-intake trumpet

Fuel filler

Fuel breather

FRONT VIEW OF WILLIAMS 1990 FORMULA ONE RACING CAR

Rear wing upper mainplane

Engine air intake

Driver's radio aerial

Rear wing end-plate

Rearview mirror

Upper wishbone

Rear brake duct

Suspension push-rod

Slick racing tire

Radiator air intake

Front wing end-plate

Air intake

Steering link

Front wing

End-plate aerodynamic skirt

Bicycle anatomy

THE BICYCLE IS A TWO-WHEELED, lightweight machine, which is propelled by human power. It is efficient, cheap, easily manufactured, and one of the world's most popular forms of transportation. The first pedal-driven bicycle was built in Scotland in 1839. Since then the basic design—of a frame, wheels, brakes, handlebars, and a saddle—has been gradually improved, with the addition of a chain, gear system, and pneumatic tires (tires inflated with air). The recent invention of the mountain bike (all-terrain bike) has been an important development. With its strong, rugged frame, wide tires, and 21 gears, a mountain bike enables riders to reach rough and hilly areas that were previously inaccessible to cyclists.

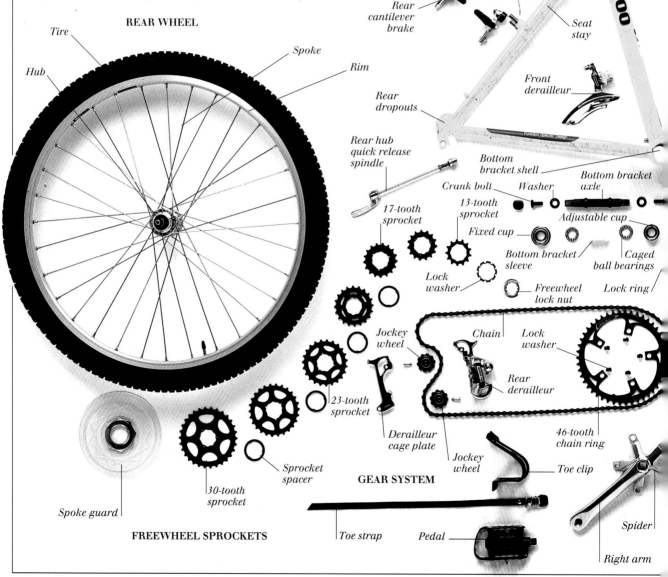

REAR WHEEL

Tire

Spoke

Hub

Rim

Saddle (seat)

Seat post

Seat post quick release bolt

Cable guide

Straddle wire

Seat tube

Rear cantilever brake

Seat stay

Rear dropouts

Front derailleur

Rear hub quick release spindle

Bottom bracket shell

Crank bolt

Washer

Bottom bracket axle

17-tooth sprocket

13-tooth sprocket

Fixed cup

Adjustable cup

Bottom bracket sleeve

Caged ball bearings

Lock washer

Freewheel lock nut

Lock ring

Jockey wheel

Chain

Lock washer

Rear derailleur

23-tooth sprocket

Derailleur cage plate

Jockey wheel

46-tooth chain ring

Toe clip

Sprocket spacer

GEAR SYSTEM

30-tooth sprocket

Spider

Spoke guard

FREEWHEEL SPROCKETS

Toe strap

Pedal

Right arm

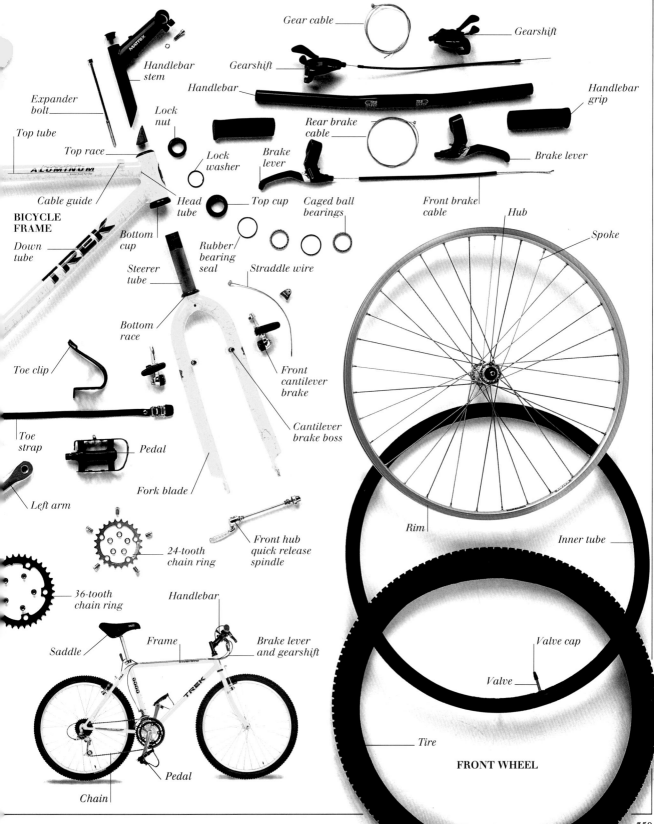

Gear cable

Gearshift

Gearshift

Handlebar
stem

Handlebar

Handlebar
grip

Expander
bolt

Lock
nut

Rear brake
cable

Top tube

Brake
lever

Brake lever

Top race

Lock
washer

Cable guide

Head
tube

Top cup

Caged ball
bearings

Front brake
cable

Hub

Spoke

**BICYCLE
FRAME**

Down
tube

Bottom
cup

Rubber
bearing
seal

Steerer
tube

Straddle wire

Bottom
race

Toe clip

Front
cantilever
brake

Cantilever
brake boss

Toe
strap

Pedal

Rim

Inner tube

Left arm

Fork blade

Front hub
quick release
spindle

24-tooth
chain ring

36-tooth
chain ring

Handlebar

Valve cap

Saddle

Frame

Brake lever
and gearshift

Valve

Pedal

Tire

FRONT WHEEL

Chain

Bicycles

ALTHOUGH ALL BICYCLES are made up of the same basic components, they can vary greatly in design. A racing bike, such as the Eddy Merckx model, with its light frame and steep head- and seat-angles, is built for speed. Its design forces the rider to adopt the aero tuck, a crouched, aerodynamic position. While a touring bike resembles a racing bike in many respects, it is designed for comfort and stability on long-distance journeys. Touring bikes are characterized by more relaxed frame angles, heavy chain stays that support the rear panniers, and a long wheelbase (the distance between the wheel axles) for reliable handling. All-purpose bicycles, known as hybrids, combine the light weight and speed of sports bikes with the rugged durability of mountain bikes (see pp. 358-359). Bicycles that are not designed for conventional road use include time-trial bikes, which have a short head tube, sloping top tube, aero handlebars, and aerodynamic tubing. Most Human Powered Vehicles (HPVs) are recumbents—the rider has a recumbent position—which maximize power output and minimize drag (resistance). Essential to the safety of all riders are helmets, and both front and rear lights; locks protect against theft.

FRONT AND REAR LIGHTS

White front light

Red rear light

HELMET

Hard outer shell

Air vent

Polystyrene padding

Quick-release strap

EDDY MERCKX RACING BICYCLE

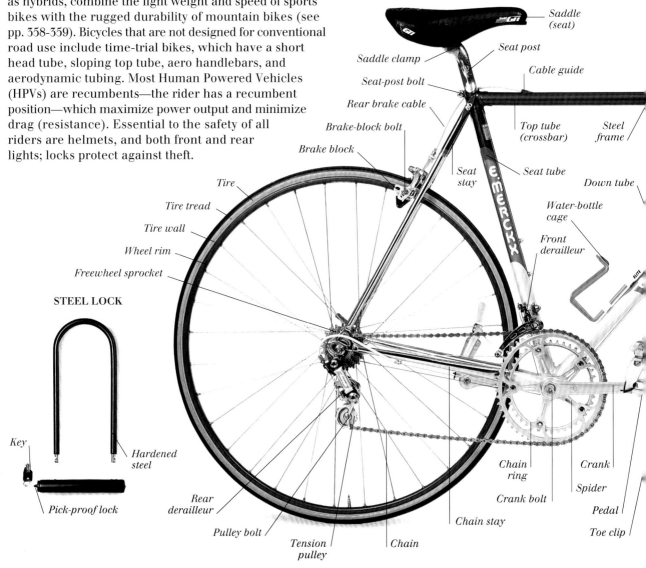

Saddle (seat)

Saddle clamp

Seat post

Cable guide

Seat-post bolt

Rear brake cable

Top tube (crossbar)

Steel frame

Brake-block bolt

Brake block

Seat stay

Seat tube

Down tube

Tire

Water-bottle cage

Tire tread

Front derailleur

Tire wall

Wheel rim

Freewheel sprocket

STEEL LOCK

Key

Hardened steel

Pick-proof lock

Rear derailleur

Pulley bolt

Tension pulley

Chain

Chain stay

Chain ring

Crank bolt

Crank

Spider

Pedal

Toe clip

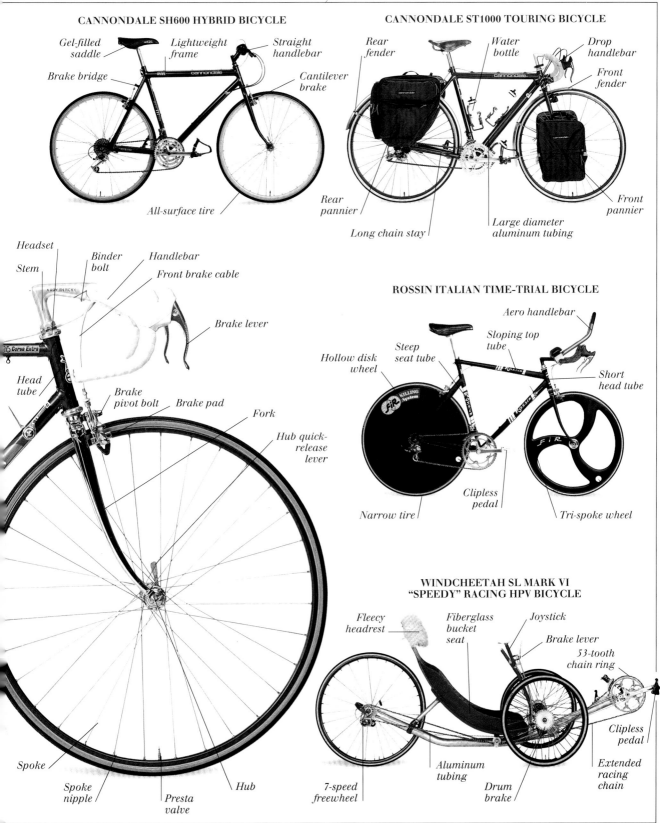

CANNONDALE SH600 HYBRID BICYCLE

Gel-filled saddle

Lightweight frame

Straight handlebar

Brake bridge

Cantilever brake

All-surface tire

CANNONDALE ST1000 TOURING BICYCLE

Rear fender

Water bottle

Drop handlebar

Front fender

Rear pannier

Long chain stay

Large diameter aluminum tubing

Front pannier

Headset

Stem

Binder bolt

Handlebar

Front brake cable

Brake lever

Head tube

Brake pivot bolt

Brake pad

Fork

Hub quick-release lever

Spoke

Spoke nipple

Presta valve

Hub

ROSSIN ITALIAN TIME-TRIAL BICYCLE

Aero handlebar

Sloping top tube

Steep seat tube

Hollow disk wheel

Short head tube

Clipless pedal

Narrow tire

Tri-spoke wheel

WINDCHEETAH SL MARK VI "SPEEDY" RACING HPV BICYCLE

Fleecy headrest

Fiberglass bucket seat

Joystick

Brake lever

53-tooth chain ring

Clipless pedal

Aluminum tubing

Extended racing chain

7-speed freewheel

Drum brake

The motorcycle

THE MOTORCYCLE HAS EVOLVED from a motorized cycle—a basic bicycle with an engine—into a sophisticated, high-performance machine. In 1901, the Werner brothers established the most viable location for the engine, positioning it low in the center of the chassis (see pp. 364-365): the new Werner became the basis for the modern motorcycle. Motorcycles are used for many purposes —for commuting, delivering messages, touring, and racing—and different machines have been developed to suit the demands of different types of riders. The Vespa scooter, for instance, which is small-wheeled, economical, and easy-to-ride, was designed to meet the needs of the commuter. Sidecars provided transportation for the family until the arrival of cheap cars caused their popularity to decline. Serious riders generally favor larger capacity machines that are capable of greater performance and offer more comfort. Four-cylinder machines have been common since the Honda CB750 appeared in 1969. Despite advances in motorcycle technology, many riders are attracted to the traditional look of motorcycles like the twin-cylinder Harley-Davidson. Harley-Davidson Glides exploit the style of the classic American V-twin engine, where the cylinders are placed in a V-formation.

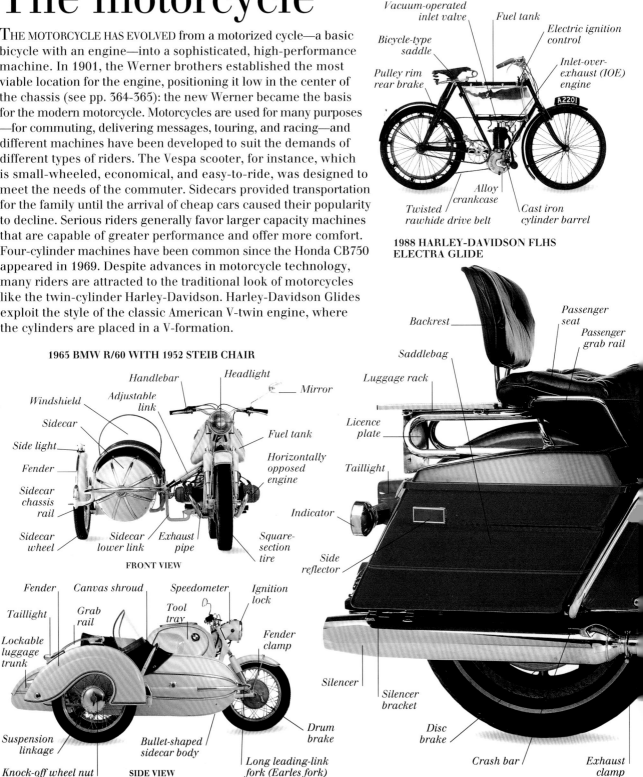

1901 WERNER MOTORCYCLE

Vacuum-operated inlet valve
Fuel tank
Bicycle-type saddle
Electric ignition control
Pulley rim rear brake
Inlet-over-exhaust (IOE) engine
A2201
Alloy crankcase
Twisted rawhide drive belt
Cast iron cylinder barrel

1988 HARLEY-DAVIDSON FLHS ELECTRA GLIDE

Backrest
Passenger seat
Passenger grab rail
Saddlebag
Luggage rack
Licence plate
Taillight
Indicator
Side reflector
Silencer
Silencer bracket
Disc brake
Crash bar
Exhaust clamp

1965 BMW R/60 WITH 1952 STEIB CHAIR

Handlebar
Headlight
Adjustable link
Mirror
Windshield
Sidecar
Fuel tank
Side light
Horizontally opposed engine
Fender
Sidecar chassis rail
Sidecar wheel
Sidecar lower link
Exhaust pipe
Square-section tire
FRONT VIEW

Fender
Canvas shroud
Speedometer
Ignition lock
Taillight
Grab rail
Tool tray
Fender clamp
Lockable luggage trunk
Silencer
Suspension linkage
Bullet-shaped sidecar body
Drum brake
Knock-off wheel nut
SIDE VIEW
Long leading-link fork (Earles fork)

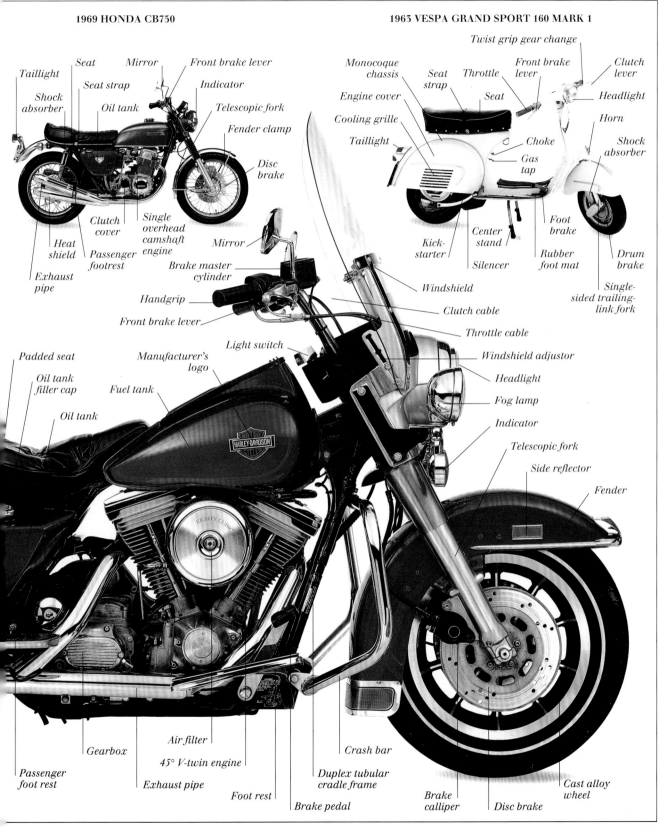

1969 HONDA CB750

Taillight
Seat
Mirror
Front brake lever
Shock absorber
Seat strap
Indicator
Oil tank
Telescopic fork
Fender clamp
Disc brake
Clutch cover
Single overhead camshaft engine
Mirror
Heat shield
Passenger footrest
Brake master cylinder
Exhaust pipe
Handgrip
Front brake lever

1963 VESPA GRAND SPORT 160 MARK 1

Twist grip gear change
Monocoque chassis
Seat strap
Throttle
Front brake lever
Clutch lever
Engine cover
Seat
Headlight
Cooling grille
Horn
Taillight
Choke
Shock absorber
Gas tap
Kick-starter
Center stand
Foot brake
Silencer
Rubber foot mat
Drum brake
Single-sided trailing-link fork
Windshield
Clutch cable
Throttle cable
Windshield adjustor
Light switch
Headlight
Padded seat
Manufacturer's logo
Fog lamp
Oil tank filler cap
Fuel tank
Indicator
Oil tank
Telescopic fork
Side reflector
Fender
HARLEY-DAVIDSON
EIGHTY CUBIC INCHES
Passenger foot rest
Gearbox
Air filter
45° V-twin engine
Exhaust pipe
Foot rest
Crash bar
Duplex tubular cradle frame
Brake pedal
Brake calliper
Disc brake
Cast alloy wheel

The motorcycle chassis

THE MOTORCYCLE CHASSIS is the main "body" of the motorcycle, to which the engine is attached. Consisting of the frame, wheels, suspension, and brakes, the chassis performs various functions. The frame, which is built from steel or alloy, keeps the wheels in line to maintain the handling of the motorcycle, and serves as a structure for mounting other components. The engine and gearbox unit is bolted into place, while items such as the seat, the fenders, and the fairing are more easily removable. Suspension cushions the rider from irregularities in the road surface. In most suspension systems, coil springs controlled by an oil damper separate the main mass of the motorcycle from the wheels. At the front, the spring and damper are usually incorporated in a telescopic fork; the rear employs a pivoted swing arm. The suspension also helps to retain maximum contact between the tires and the road, necessary to effective braking and steering. Drum brakes were common until the 1970s, but modern motorcycles use disc brakes, which are more powerful.

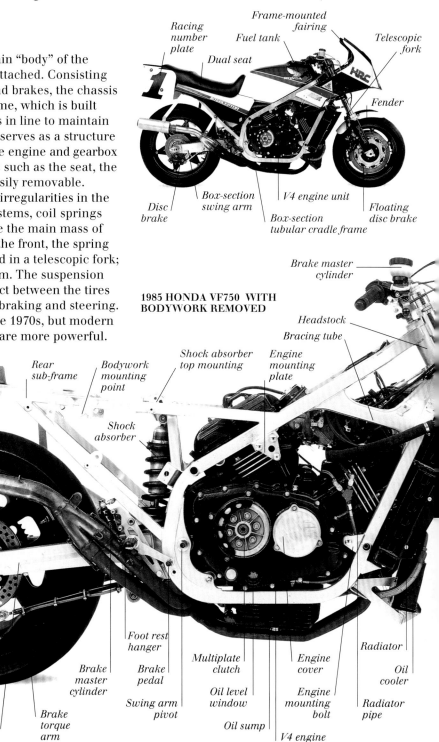

1985 HONDA VF750 WITH BODYWORK

Racing number plate
Frame-mounted fairing
Fuel tank
Dual seat
Telescopic fork
Fender
V4 engine unit
Floating disc brake
Box-section tubular cradle frame
Box-section swing arm
Disc brake

1985 HONDA VF750 WITH BODYWORK REMOVED

Brake master cylinder
Headstock
Bracing tube
Engine mounting plate
Shock absorber top mounting
Bodywork mounting point
Rear sub-frame
Square-section steel tubing
Exhaust mounting strap
Shock absorber
Exhaust pipe
Light alloy wheel
Radiator
Axle adjustor
Disc brake
Foot rest hanger
Multiplate clutch
Engine cover
Oil cooler
Disc brake calliper
Brake master cylinder
Brake pedal
Oil level window
Engine mounting bolt
Radiator pipe
Box-section swing arm
Brake torque arm
Swing arm pivot
Oil sump
V4 engine unit

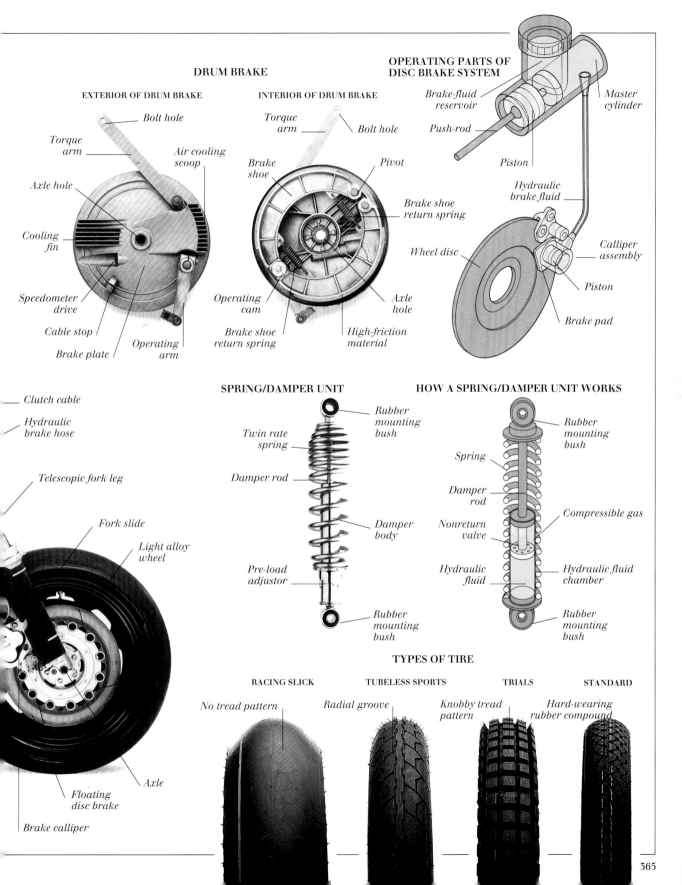

DRUM BRAKE

EXTERIOR OF DRUM BRAKE

Bolt hole

Torque arm

Air cooling scoop

Axle hole

Cooling fin

Speedometer drive

Cable stop

Brake plate

Operating arm

INTERIOR OF DRUM BRAKE

Torque arm

Bolt hole

Brake shoe

Pivot

Brake shoe return spring

Operating cam

Axle hole

Brake shoe return spring

High-friction material

OPERATING PARTS OF DISC BRAKE SYSTEM

Brake-fluid reservoir

Master cylinder

Push-rod

Piston

Hydraulic brake fluid

Wheel disc

Calliper assembly

Piston

Brake pad

Clutch cable

Hydraulic brake hose

Telescopic fork leg

Fork slide

Light alloy wheel

Axle

Floating disc brake

Brake calliper

SPRING/DAMPER UNIT

Rubber mounting bush

Twin rate spring

Damper rod

Damper body

Pre-load adjustor

Rubber mounting bush

HOW A SPRING/DAMPER UNIT WORKS

Rubber mounting bush

Spring

Damper rod

Nonreturn valve

Compressible gas

Hydraulic fluid

Hydraulic fluid chamber

Rubber mounting bush

TYPES OF TIRE

RACING SLICK

No tread pattern

TUBELESS SPORTS

Radial groove

TRIALS

Knobby tread pattern

STANDARD

Hard-wearing rubber compound

Motorcycle engines

MOTORCYCLE ENGINES must be lightweight and compact, and have a good power output. They have between one and six cylinders, can be cooled by air or water, and the capacity of the combustion chamber varies from 49cc (cubic centimeters) to 1500cc. Two types of internal combustion engine are common: the four-stroke, which is used in cars (see pp. 342-343), and the two-stroke. A basic two-stroke engine has only three moving parts—the crankshaft, the connecting rod, and the piston—but the power output is high. The engine fires every two strokes (rather than every four), giving a "power stroke" every revolution (see p. 343). Power is conveyed from the engine to the rear wheel by the transmission system. This usually consists of a clutch, a gearbox, and a final drive system. Clutches are multiplate devices, which run in oil. Gearboxes have five or six speeds and are operated by foot pedal. Shaft and belt drive systems are used in some cases, but chain drive to the rear wheel is most common.

EXTERIOR OF STANDARD TWO-STROKE ENGINE

Spark plug cap
Fuel tap
Carburetor mounting
Kick-starter
Carburetor
Cylinder head
Cooling fin
Exhaust port
Case screw
Clutch activating arm
Engine cover
Gear lever

TRANSMISSION SYSTEM

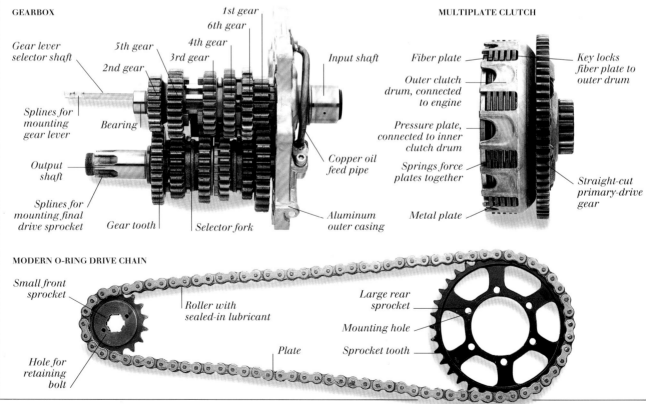

GEARBOX

Gear lever selector shaft
5th gear
2nd gear
4th gear
3rd gear
1st gear
6th gear
Input shaft
Splines for mounting gear lever
Bearing
Output shaft
Splines for mounting final drive sprocket
Gear tooth
Selector fork
Copper oil feed pipe
Aluminum outer casing

MULTIPLATE CLUTCH

Fiber plate
Outer clutch drum, connected to engine
Pressure plate, connected to inner clutch drum
Springs force plates together
Metal plate
Key locks fiber plate to outer drum
Straight-cut primary-drive gear

MODERN O-RING DRIVE CHAIN

Small front sprocket
Roller with sealed-in lubricant
Large rear sprocket
Mounting hole
Plate
Sprocket tooth
Hole for retaining bolt

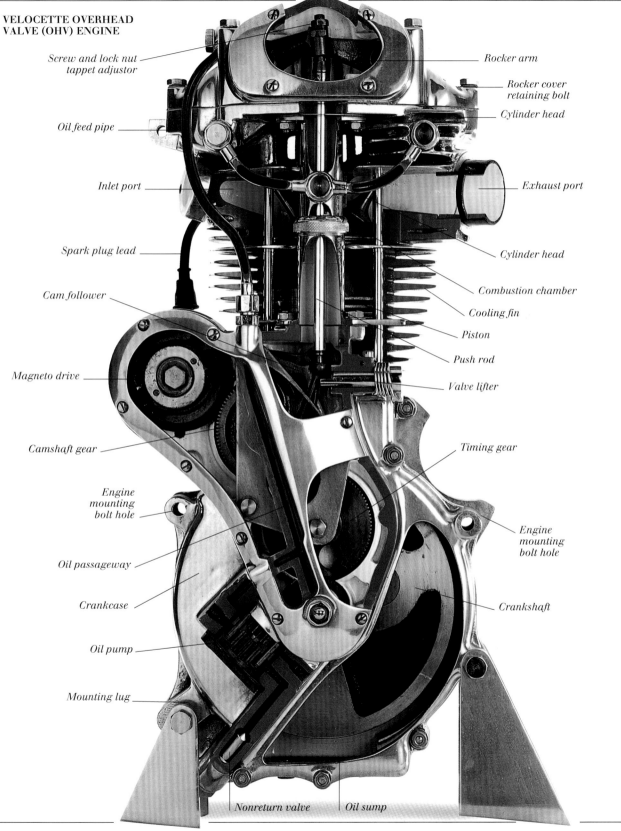

**VELOCETTE OVERHEAD
VALVE (OHV) ENGINE**

Screw and lock nut
tappet adjustor

Rocker arm

Rocker cover
retaining bolt

Cylinder head

Oil feed pipe

Inlet port

Exhaust port

Spark plug lead

Cylinder head

Combustion chamber

Cam follower

Cooling fin

Piston

Push rod

Magneto drive

Valve lifter

Camshaft gear

Timing gear

Engine
mounting
bolt hole

Engine
mounting
bolt hole

Oil passageway

Crankcase

Crankshaft

Oil pump

Mounting lug

Nonreturn valve

Oil sump

Competition motorcycles

THERE ARE MANY TYPES of motorcycle sports and in each, a special machine has evolved to perform to specific requirements. Races take place on roads or tracks or "off-road," in fields, dirt tracks, and even the desert. "Grand Prix" world championships in roadracing exist for 125cc, 250cc, and 500cc classes, as well as for sidecars. The latest racing sidecars have more in common with racing cars than motorcycles. The rider and passenger operate within an all-enclosing, aerodynamic fairing. The Suzuki RGV500 shown here, like other Grand Prix machines, carries advertising, which promotes the manufacturer and helps to cover the cost of developing motorcycle technology. In Speedway, which originated in the U.S. in 1902, motorcycles operate without brakes or a gearbox. Off-road competition motorcycles have less emphasis on high power output. In Motocross, for example, which is held on rough terrain, they must have high ground clearance, flexible long-travel suspension, and tires with a chunky tread pattern, to allow them to grip in sand or mud.

1992 HUSQVARNA MOTOCROSS TC610

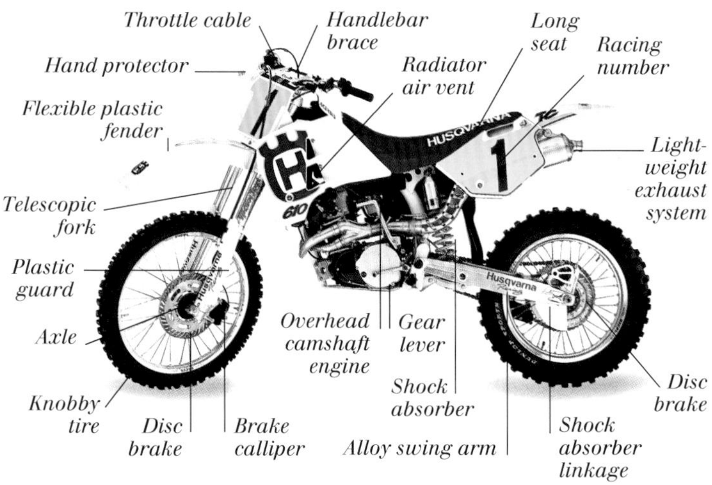

Throttle cable
Handlebar brace
Long seat
Racing number
Hand protector
Radiator air vent
Flexible plastic fender
Light-weight exhaust system
Telescopic fork
Plastic guard
Axle
Overhead camshaft engine
Gear lever
Shock absorber
Disc brake
Knobby tire
Disc brake
Brake calliper
Alloy swing arm
Shock absorber linkage

1992 SUZUKI RGV500
SIDE VIEW

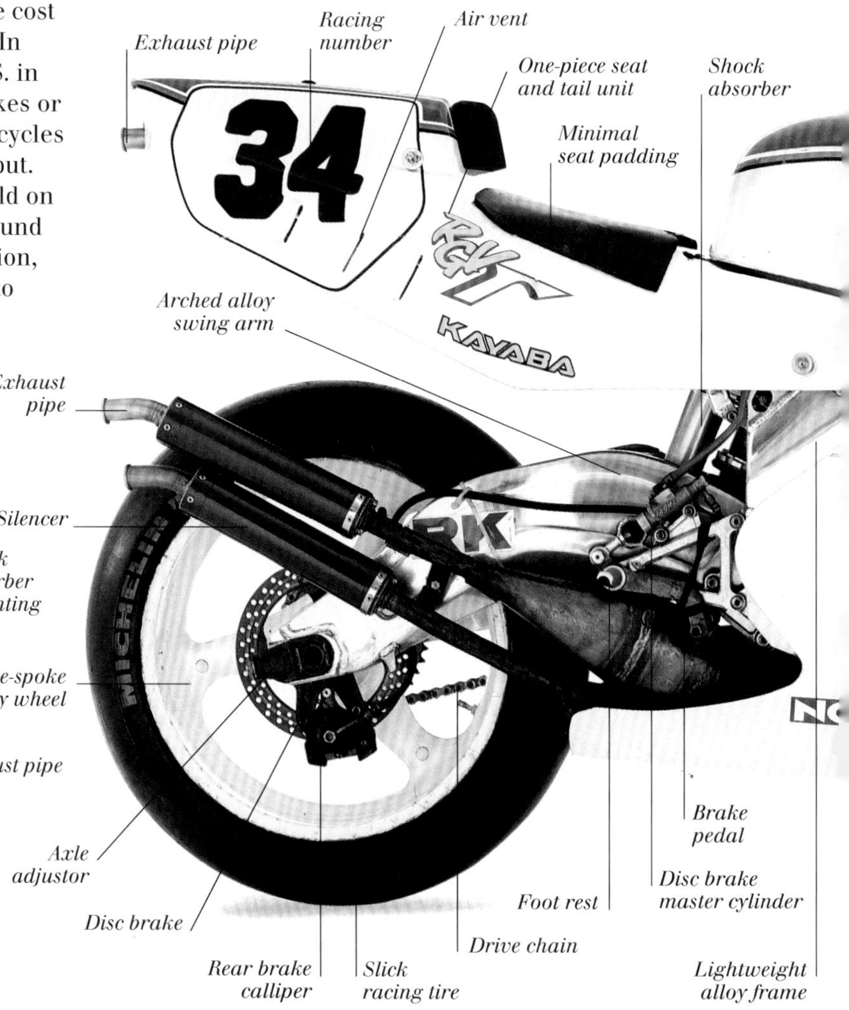

Exhaust pipe
Racing number
Air vent
One-piece seat and tail unit
Shock absorber
Minimal seat padding
34
Arched alloy swing arm

Exhaust pipe
Vent
Silencer
Shock absorber mounting
Three-spoke alloy wheel
Exhaust pipe
Axle adjustor
Disc brake
Rear brake calliper
Slick racing tire
Drive chain
Foot rest
Brake pedal
Disc brake master cylinder
Lightweight alloy frame

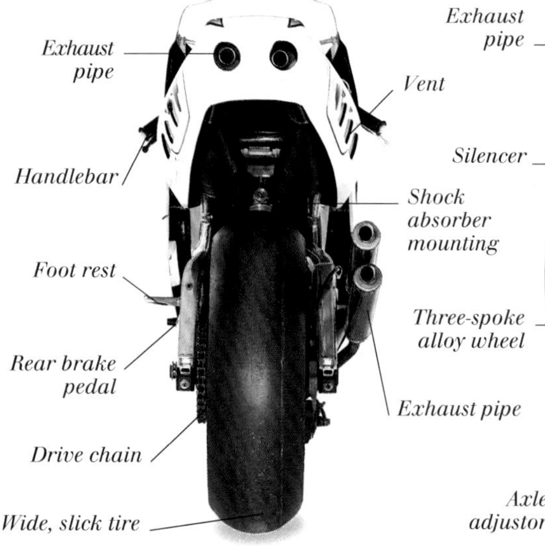

Exhaust pipe
Handlebar
Foot rest
Rear brake pedal
Drive chain
Wide, slick tire

REAR VIEW

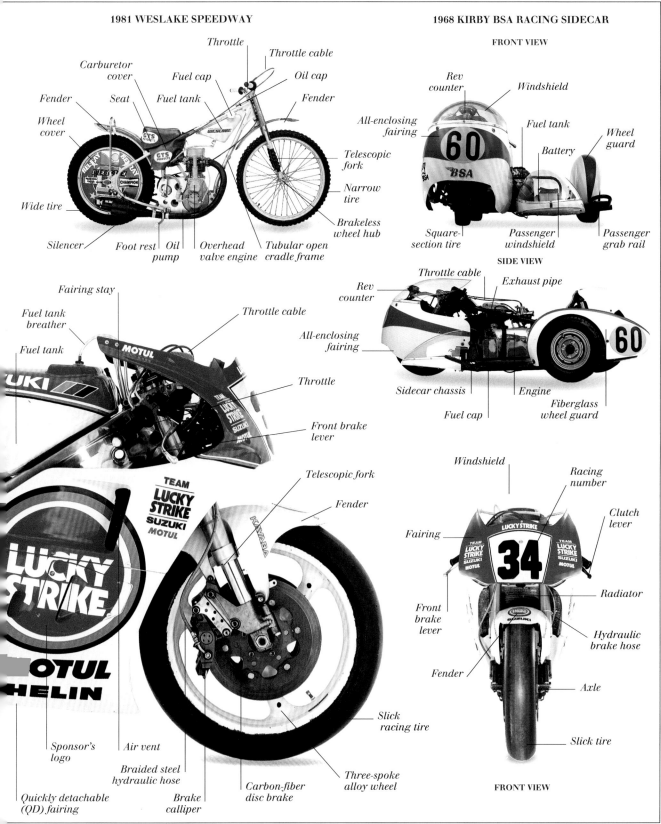

1981 WESLAKE SPEEDWAY

Throttle
Throttle cable
Carburetor cover
Fuel cap
Oil cap
Fender
Seat
Fuel tank
Fender
Wheel cover
Telescopic fork
Narrow tire
Wide tire
Brakeless wheel hub
Silencer
Foot rest
Oil pump
Overhead valve engine
Tubular open cradle frame

Fairing stay
Throttle cable
Fuel tank breather
Fuel tank
Throttle
Front brake lever
Telescopic fork
Fender
Slick racing tire
Sponsor's logo
Air vent
Braided steel hydraulic hose
Brake calliper
Carbon-fiber disc brake
Three-spoke alloy wheel
Quickly detachable (QD) fairing

MOTUL
TEAM LUCKY STRIKE SUZUKI MOTUL

1968 KIRBY BSA RACING SIDECAR

FRONT VIEW

Rev counter
Windshield
All-enclosing fairing
Fuel tank
Battery
Wheel guard
60
BSA
Square-section tire
Passenger windshield
Passenger grab rail

SIDE VIEW

Throttle cable
Exhaust pipe
Rev counter
All-enclosing fairing
60
Sidecar chassis
Engine
Fiberglass wheel guard
Fuel cap

Windshield
Racing number
Fairing
Clutch lever
34
Radiator
Front brake lever
Hydraulic brake hose
Fender
Axle
Slick tire

FRONT VIEW

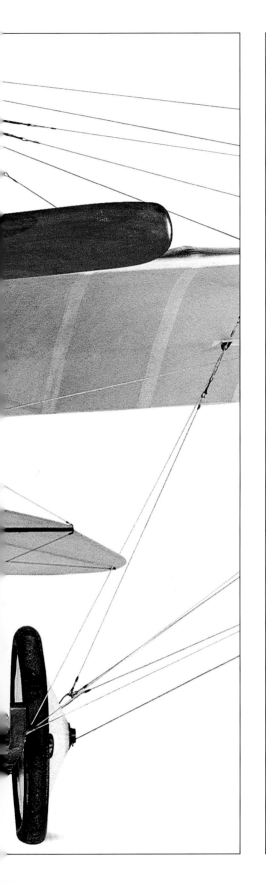

Sea and Air

Ships of Greece and Rome

ROMAN ANCHOR

IN THE EXPANSIVE EMPIRES OF GREECE AND ROME, powerful fleets were needed for battle, trade, and communication. Greek galleys were powered by a sail and many oars. A new armament, the embolos (ram), was fitted on to the galley bow. As ramming duels required fast and maneuverable boats, extra rows of oarsmen were added, culminating in the trireme. During the fifth and fourth centuries B.C., the trireme dominated the Mediterranean. It was powered by 170 oarsmen, each pulling one oar, and ranged on three levels, as the model opposite shows. The trireme also carried archers and soldiers for boarding enemy craft. Galleys were pulled out of the water when not in use, and were kept in dockyard ship-sheds. The merchant ships of the Greeks and Romans were mighty vessels, too. The full-bodied Roman corbita, for example, could hold up to 400 tons of cargo, such as spices, gems, silk, and animals. The construction of these boats was based on a stout hull with planking secured by mortice and tenon. Some of these ships made long trading voyages, sailing even as far as India. To make them easier to steer, corbitas set a foresail called an "artemon." It flew from a forward-leaning mast that was the forerunner of the long bowsprits carried by the great clipper ships of the 19th century.

Stock
Shank
Palm
Acutely angled arm
Ring
Crown

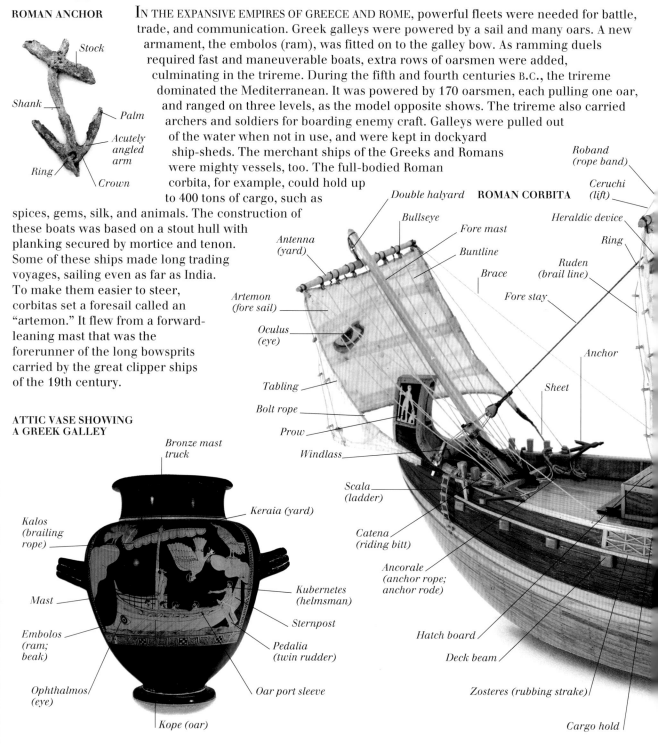

ROMAN CORBITA

Roband (rope band)
Ceruchi (lift)
Heraldic device
Ring
Ruden (brail line)
Fore stay
Double halyard
Bullseye
Fore mast
Buntline
Brace
Antenna (yard)
Artemon (fore sail)
Oculus (eye)
Anchor
Sheet
Tabling
Bolt rope
Prow
Windlass
Scala (ladder)
Catena (riding bitt)
Ancorale (anchor rope; anchor rode)
Hatch board
Deck beam
Zosteres (rubbing strake)
Cargo hold

ATTIC VASE SHOWING A GREEK GALLEY

Bronze mast truck
Keraia (yard)
Kalos (brailing rope)
Mast
Embolos (ram; beak)
Ophthalmos (eye)
Kubernetes (helmsman)
Sternpost
Pedalia (twin rudder)
Oar port sleeve
Kope (oar)

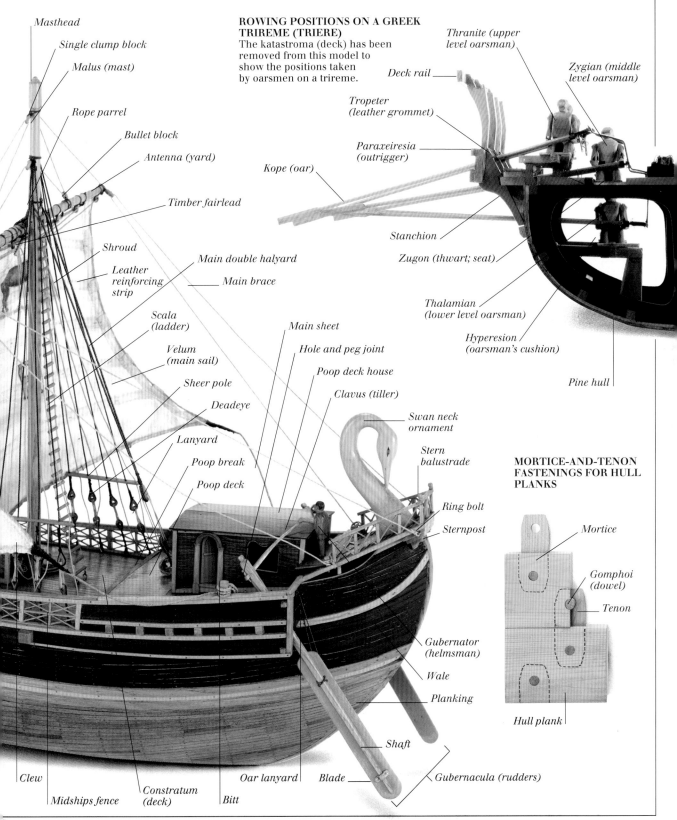

Masthead

Single clump block

Malus (mast)

Rope parrel

Bullet block

Antenna (yard)

Timber fairlead

Shroud

Leather reinforcing strip

Scala (ladder)

Velum (main sail)

Sheer pole

Deadeye

Lanyard

Poop break

Poop deck

Clew

Midships fence

Constratum (deck)

Bitt

ROWING POSITIONS ON A GREEK TRIREME (TRIERE)
The katastroma (deck) has been removed from this model to show the positions taken by oarsmen on a trireme.

Thranite (upper level oarsman)

Zygian (middle level oarsman)

Deck rail

Tropeter (leather grommet)

Paraxeiresia (outrigger)

Kope (oar)

Stanchion

Zugon (thwart; seat)

Thalamian (lower level oarsman)

Hyperesion (oarsman's cushion)

Pine hull

Main double halyard

Main brace

Main sheet

Hole and peg joint

Poop deck house

Clavus (tiller)

Swan neck ornament

Stern balustrade

Ring bolt

Sternpost

Gubernator (helmsman)

Wale

Planking

Shaft

Oar lanyard

Blade

Gubernacula (rudders)

MORTICE-AND-TENON FASTENINGS FOR HULL PLANKS

Mortice

Gomphoi (dowel)

Tenon

Hull plank

373

Viking ships

IN THE DARK AGES (roughly 500 A.D. to 1000 A.D.) the longships of Scandinavia were among the most feared sights for people of northern Europe. The Vikings launched raids from Scandinavia every summer in longships equipped with a single steering oar on the right, or "steerboard" side (hence, "starboard"). A longboat had one row of oars on each side and a single sail. The hull was clinker-built, with overlapping planks. Prowheads adorned fighting ships during war campaigns. The longship was also used for coastal travel. The karv below was probably built as transport for an important family, while the smaller faering was a rowing boat only. The fleet of William of Normandy that invaded England in 1066 owed much to the Viking boat building tradition, and has been depicted in the Bayeux Tapestry (right). Seals of port towns and royal courts through the ages provide a record of contemporary ship design. The seal opposite shows a European craft from somewhat later than the Viking period. Fighting platforms, or castles, and the addition of more masts and sails changed the character of the medieval ship. Note also that the steering oar has been replaced by a centered rudder.

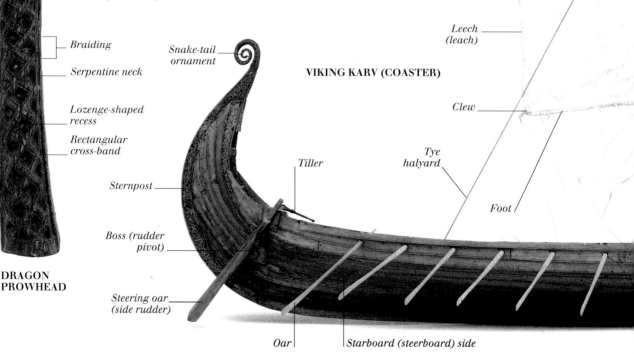

BOAT BUILDERS' TOOLS

Shave
Broad axe
Breast auger
Sheer
Master shipwright
Stempost
Hood end
Keel
T-handle auger
Axe
Strake
Tree cut for planking

Roband
Leather diagonal reinforcement
Square sail of homespun yarn
Leech (leach)
Clew
Tye halyard
Foot

Zoomorphic head
Eye
Tooth

Braiding
Serpentine neck
Lozenge-shaped recess
Rectangular cross-band

DRAGON PROWHEAD

Snake-tail ornament

VIKING KARV (COASTER)

Tiller
Sternpost
Boss (rudder pivot)
Steering oar (side rudder)
Oar
Starboard (steerboard) side

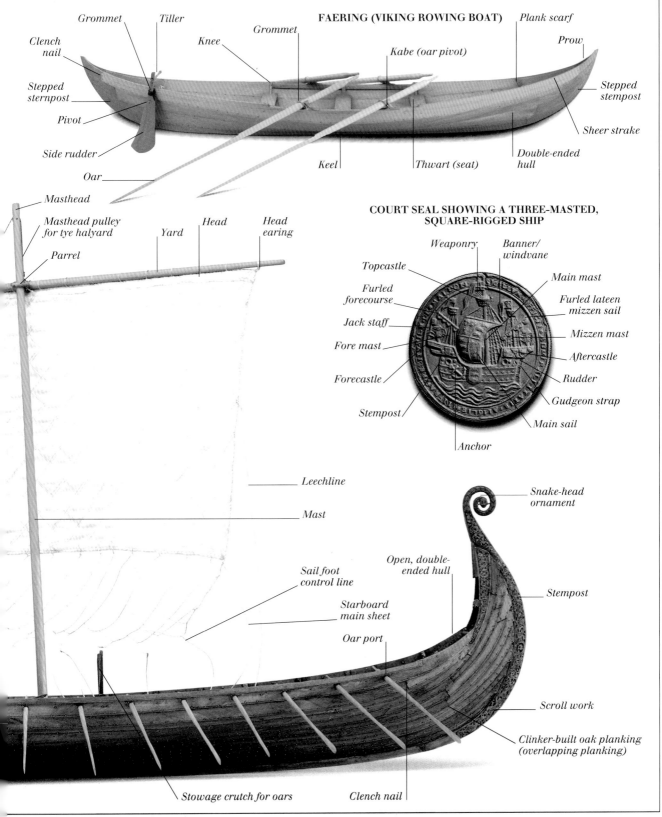

FAERING (VIKING ROWING BOAT)

Grommet

Tiller

Knee

Grommet

Kabe (oar pivot)

Plank scarf

Prow

Clench nail

Stepped sternpost

Pivot

Side rudder

Oar

Keel

Thwart (seat)

Double-ended hull

Stepped stempost

Sheer strake

Masthead

Masthead pulley for tye halyard

Parrel

Yard

Head

Head earing

COURT SEAL SHOWING A THREE-MASTED, SQUARE-RIGGED SHIP

Weaponry

Banner/windvane

Topcastle

Main mast

Furled forecourse

Furled lateen mizzen sail

Jack staff

Mizzen mast

Fore mast

Aftercastle

Forecastle

Rudder

Stempost

Gudgeon strap

Anchor

Main sail

Leechline

Mast

Snake-head ornament

Sail foot control line

Open, double-ended hull

Stempost

Starboard main sheet

Oar port

Scroll work

Clinker-built oak planking (overlapping planking)

Stowage crutch for oars

Clench nail

Medieval warships and traders

FROM THE 16TH CENTURY, SHIPS WERE BUILT WITH A NEW FORM OF HULL, constructed with carvel (edge-to-edge) planking. Warships of the time, like King Henry VIII of England's Mary Rose, boasted awesome fire power. This ship carried both long-range bronze cannon, and short-range, anti personnel guns in iron. Elsewhere, ships took on a multiformity of shapes. Dhows transported slaves from East Africa to Arabia, their fore-and-aft rigged lateen sails allowing them to sail close to the wind around the lands of the Indian Ocean. The Chinese sailed to East Africa and Arabia in junks, trading goods that were carried in watertight compartments. New astronomical tools helped medieval sailors to find their way. Cross-staves and astrolabes were used to measure the altitude of the sun or stars. One of the cross-pieces was slid along the staff of the cross-stave—which was graduated in degrees of altitude—until its top aligned with the celestial body and its base with the horizon. The sighting rule of the astrolabe was simply lined up with a known body, and its altitude read from marks on the metal disk. Sundials used the shadow of the sun to show sailors the time of day.

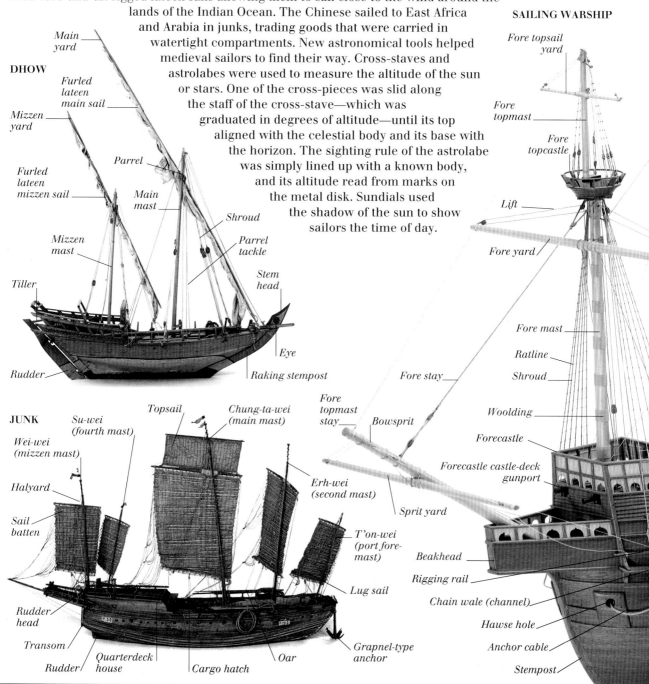

SAILING WARSHIP

Fore topsail yard
Fore topmast
Fore topcastle
Lift
Fore yard
Fore mast
Ratline
Shroud
Fore stay
Woolding
Forecastle
Forecastle castle-deck gunport
Beakhead
Rigging rail
Chain wale (channel)
Hawse hole
Anchor cable
Stempost

DHOW

Main yard
Furled lateen main sail
Mizzen yard
Parrel
Furled lateen mizzen sail
Main mast
Shroud
Parrel tackle
Mizzen mast
Stem head
Tiller
Rudder
Eye
Raking stempost

JUNK

Su-wei (fourth mast)
Topsail
Chung-ta-wei (main mast)
Fore topmast stay
Bowsprit
Wei-wei (mizzen mast)
Erh-wei (second mast)
Halyard
Sprit yard
Sail batten
T'on-wei (port fore-mast)
Rudder head
Lug sail
Transom
Grapnel-type anchor
Rudder
Quarterdeck house
Oar
Cargo hatch

Main topgallant mast

Main topgallant yard

Main top yard

Main topmast topcastle

Mizzen topmast

Mizzen top yard

Main topmast stay

Mizzen topcastle

Main topmast

Lift

Main topcastle

Bonaventure top yard

Lift

Bonaventure topmast

Main yard

Parrel

30 degree cross-piece

Tye

Bonaventure topcastle

Jeer

Brace

Bonaventure yard

Main stay

Bonaventure mast

Mizzen mast

Aftercastle

Mizzen yard

Gnomon

Main mast

Swifting tackle

Aftercastle castle-deck gunport

Outrigger

Pivot

Hour line

Dial

Upper deck gunport

Chain wale (channel)

Lid

Deadeye

Gangway

Gun carriage

Transom

Rudder

Sternpost

Keel

Blindage (removable archery screen)

Wale

Main deck gunport

Carvel planking

Port bower anchor

CROSS-STAVE (CROSS-STAFF)

90 degree cross-piece (transversary)

Clamp

Boxwood staff

60 degree cross-piece

Altitude scale in degrees and minutes

Ocular end

10 degree cross-piece (dutch shoe)

SUNDIAL

Style of the gnomon (edge)

Needle

Swivel suspension ring

Graduated ring

ASTROLABE

Scale of degrees

Pivot

Alidade (sighting rule)

Bottom ballast

Scribed arc decoration

The expansion of sail

BY THE 18TH CENTURY, SAILING SHIPS had become fast and effective floating fortresses. The navies of the north European powers competed with each other by building heavily-armed fighting ships called "men-of-war." The distinctive round stern of the ship below, with its open gallery, balcony, and elaborate wood carving is typical of the period. Hulls around this time were semicircular in cross section, although many boat designers were soon to return to the V-shaped hulls used by the Vikings. Ships of the period carried more sail than ever before. A labyrinth of rigging supported the masts and yards from which the profusion of square sails were set. Ships grew higher as extra masts were fitted above the lower masts, and the bowsprit became longer, to allow the ship to carry staysails, spritsails, and jibs. Ships went into battle in single file, so that broadsides from the multiple decks of guns would have maximum effect. Ships were classified by rates, the rating of a vessel depending on how many guns it had. A first rate ship had more than 100 guns. The guns fired solid round shot, usually made of iron.

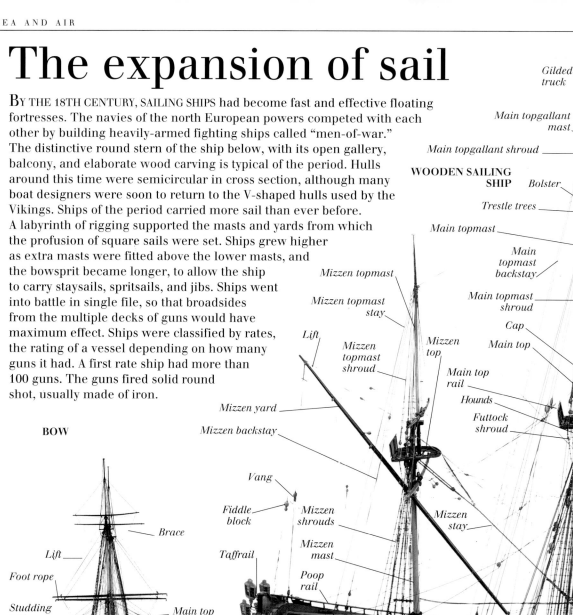

WOODEN SAILING SHIP

Gilded truck
Main topgallant mast
Main topgallant shroud
Bolster
Trestle trees
Main topmast
Main topmast backstay
Main topmast shroud
Cap
Main top
Masthead
Main top rail
Hounds
Futtock shroud
Mizzen topmast
Mizzen topmast stay
Lift
Mizzen topmast shroud
Mizzen top
Mizzen yard
Mizzen backstay
Vang
Fiddle block
Mizzen shrouds
Mizzen stay
Mizzen mast
Taffrail
Poop rail
Main shrouds
Main mast

BOW

Brace
Lift
Foot rope
Studding sail boom
Main top rail
Studding sail yard (stuns'l yard)
Jacob's ladder
Rope preventer
Rudder chain
Rudder
Sternpost
Pintle strap
Gudgeon strap
Wash cant
Knee of the head
Hawse hole
Ship's wheel
Binnacle box
Keel
Channel
Chains
Step
Boat slide

SAIL PATTERN OF A 74-GUN SHIP

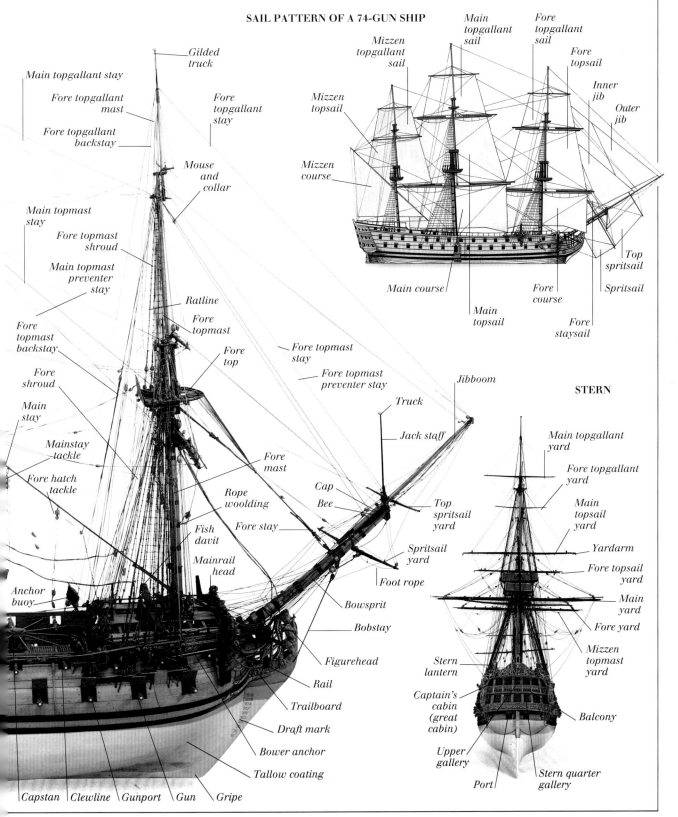

Main topgallant stay

Fore topgallant mast

Fore topgallant backstay

Gilded truck

Fore topgallant stay

Mouse and collar

Main topmast stay

Fore topmast shroud

Main topmast preventer stay

Fore topmast backstay

Fore shroud

Main stay

Mainstay tackle

Fore hatch tackle

Anchor buoy

Ratline

Fore topmast

Fore top

Fore mast

Rope woolding

Fore stay

Fish davit

Mainrail head

Fore topmast stay

Fore topmast preventer stay

Cap

Bee

Truck

Jack staff

Top spritsail yard

Spritsail yard

Foot rope

Bowsprit

Bobstay

Figurehead

Rail

Trailboard

Draft mark

Bower anchor

Tallow coating

Capstan   Clewline   Gunport   Gun   Gripe

Mizzen topgallant sail

Main topgallant sail

Fore topgallant sail

Fore topgallant stay

Mizzen topsail

Mizzen topgallant sail

Mizzen course

Main course

Main topsail

Fore course

Fore staysail

Fore topsail

Inner jib

Outer jib

Top spritsail

Spritsail

Jibboom

STERN

Main topgallant yard

Fore topgallant yard

Main topsail yard

Yardarm

Fore topsail yard

Main yard

Fore yard

Mizzen topmast yard

Stern lantern

Captain's cabin (great cabin)

Upper gallery

Port

Balcony

Stern quarter gallery

379

A ship of the line

THE 74-GUN THIRD-RATER WAS A MAINSTAY of British and French battlefleets in the late 18th and early 19th centuries. (The biggest ships in the fledgling American navy of the time were 44-gun frigates.) The length of such a man-of-war was determined by the number of guns needed for each deck, allowing room for crews to man them. The gun deck of this vessel was about 170 ft (52 m) long. Her decks had to be strong to carry the weight of the guns. The deck planks have been removed in the model below to illustrate the number of beams needed to make the hull strong enough. Only timber with perfect grain was used. The upper deck was open at the waist, but forward and aft were officers' cabins. The forecastle (foc's'l) and quarterdeck carried light guns and provided platforms for handling the rigging and for reconnaissance. The ship's longboats, or launches, were carried on skids between the gangways.

LONGBOAT

Truck
Mast
Jib halyard
Flag halyard
Backstay
Topping lift
Fore stay halyard
Shrouds
Peak halyard
Fore staysail halyard
Main sheet
Parrel
Gaff
Boom
Bowsprit
Traveler
Stem
Waterline
Deadeyes
Oar
Side bench

Thole pins
Windlass bar
Transom
Tiller
Planking
Rabbit line
Sheerplank
Frame
Keel
Rudder
Floor
Thwart (seat)

UPPER DECK OF A 74-GUN SHIP

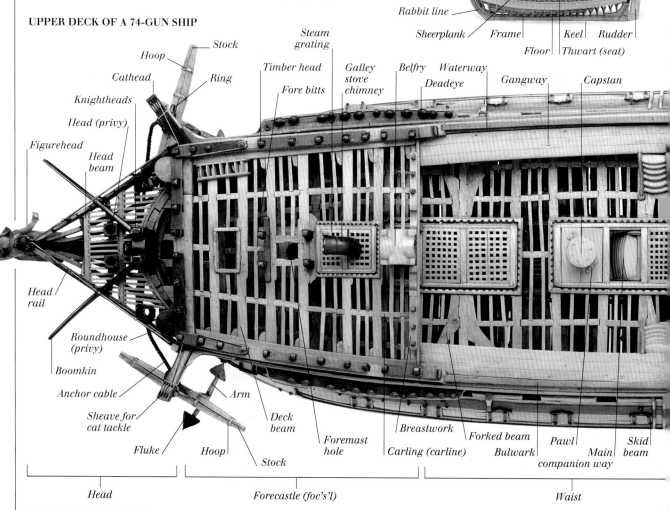

Stock
Hoop
Steam grating
Cathead
Ring
Timber head
Galley stove chimney
Belfry
Waterway
Gangway
Capstan
Knightheads
Fore bitts
Deadeye
Head (privy)
Figurehead
Head beam
Head rail
Roundhouse (privy)
Boomkin
Anchor cable
Arm
Sheave for cat tackle
Deck beam
Fluke
Hoop
Stock
Foremast hole
Breastwork
Forked beam
Pawl
Skid beam
Carling (carline)
Bulwark
Main companion way

Head
Forecastle (foc's'l)
Waist

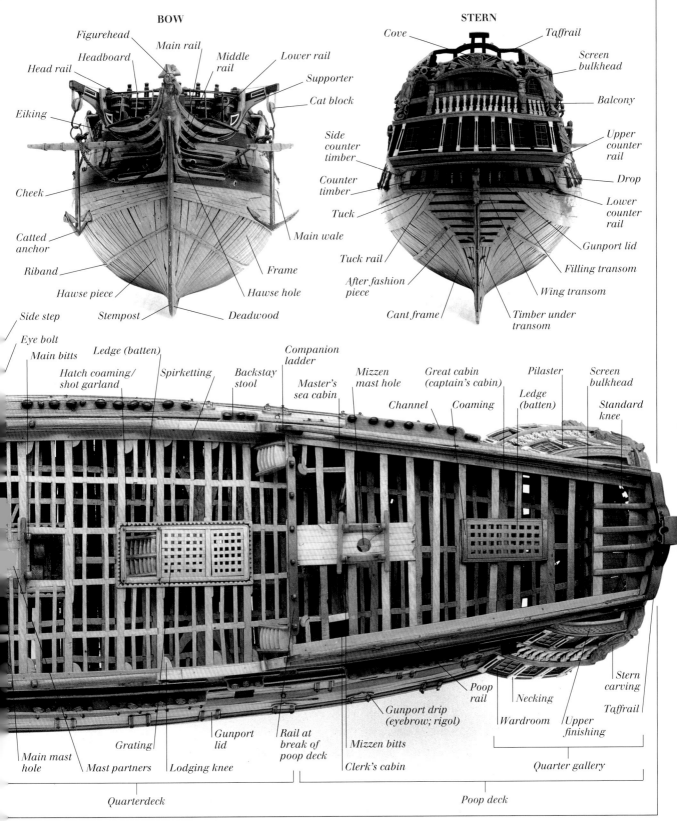

BOW

Figurehead
Headboard
Head rail
Main rail
Middle rail
Lower rail
Supporter
Cat block
Eiking
Cheek
Catted anchor
Riband
Hawse piece
Side step
Eye bolt
Main bitts
Stempost
Deadwood
Main wale
Frame
Hawse hole

STERN

Cove
Taffrail
Screen bulkhead
Balcony
Side counter timber
Counter timber
Upper counter rail
Drop
Tuck
Lower counter rail
Tuck rail
Gunport lid
After fashion piece
Filling transom
Cant frame
Wing transom
Timber under transom

Ledge (batten)
Hatch coaming/ shot garland
Spirketting
Backstay stool
Companion ladder
Master's sea cabin
Mizzen mast hole
Great cabin (captain's cabin)
Channel
Coaming
Pilaster
Ledge (batten)
Screen bulkhead
Standard knee
Main mast hole
Mast partners
Grating
Gunport lid
Lodging knee
Rail at break of poop deck
Mizzen bitts
Gunport drip (eyebrow; rigol)
Clerk's cabin
Poop rail
Necking
Wardroom
Upper finishing
Stern carving
Taffrail
Quarter gallery

Quarterdeck
Poop deck

Rigging

Most sailing ships have two types of rigging. Standing rigging—kept taut by turnbuckles or old-fashioned lanyards and deadeyes—refers to the ropes, wires, and chains that support the masts and yards (horizontal spars). Running rigging, which includes types of block and tackle, halyards, and sheets, is used to hoist, lower, or trim sails.

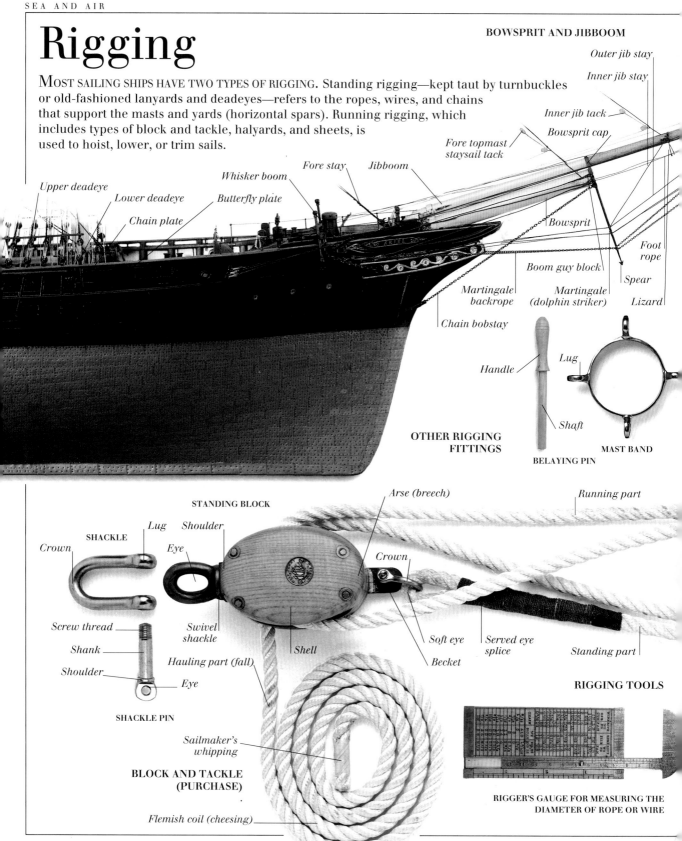

BOWSPRIT AND JIBBOOM

Outer jib stay

Inner jib stay

Inner jib tack

Bowsprit cap

Fore topmast staysail tack

Fore stay

Jibboom

Whisker boom

Upper deadeye

Lower deadeye

Butterfly plate

Chain plate

Bowsprit

Foot rope

Boom guy block

Spear

Martingale backrope

Martingale (dolphin striker)

Lizard

Chain bobstay

Handle

Lug

Shaft

OTHER RIGGING FITTINGS

MAST BAND

BELAYING PIN

Arse (breech)

Running part

STANDING BLOCK

Shoulder

SHACKLE

Lug

Eye

Crown

Crown

SHACKLE

Screw thread

Swivel shackle

Soft eye

Served eye splice

Shank

Shell

Shoulder

Becket

Standing part

Eye

SHACKLE PIN

Hauling part (fall)

RIGGING TOOLS

Sailmaker's whipping

BLOCK AND TACKLE (PURCHASE)

Flemish coil (cheesing)

RIGGER'S GAUGE FOR MEASURING THE DIAMETER OF ROPE OR WIRE

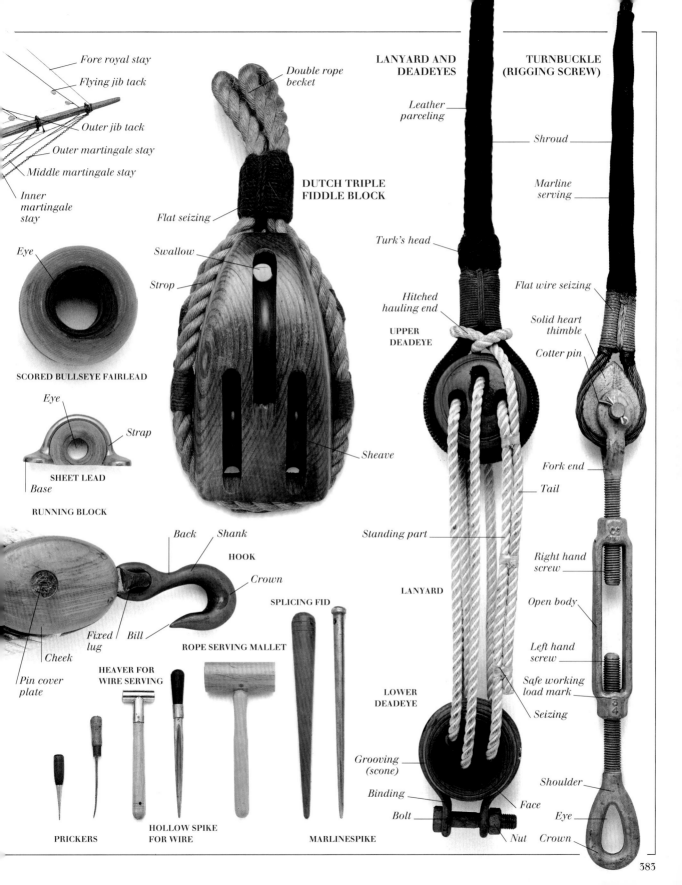

Fore royal stay

Flying jib tack

Outer jib tack

Outer martingale stay

Middle martingale stay

Inner martingale stay

Eye

SCORED BULLSEYE FAIRLEAD

Eye

Strap

SHEET LEAD

Base

RUNNING BLOCK

Cheek

Pin cover plate

Back   Shank

HOOK

Crown

Fixed lug   Bill

ROPE SERVING MALLET

HEAVER FOR WIRE SERVING

SPLICING FID

PRICKERS

HOLLOW SPIKE FOR WIRE

MARLINESPIKE

Double rope becket

DUTCH TRIPLE FIDDLE BLOCK

Flat seizing

Swallow

Strop

Sheave

LANYARD AND DEADEYES

Leather parceling

Turk's head

Hitched hauling end

UPPER DEADEYE

Standing part

LANYARD

LOWER DEADEYE

Grooving (scone)

Binding

Bolt

Face

Nut

TURNBUCKLE (RIGGING SCREW)

Shroud

Marline serving

Flat wire seizing

Solid heart thimble

Cotter pin

Fork end

Tail

Right hand screw

Open body

Left hand screw

Safe working load mark

Seizing

Shoulder

Eye

Crown

383

Sails

THERE ARE TWO MAIN TYPES OF SAILS: Old-fashioned square sails hang from yards at right angles to the mast, and are powerful drivers with following winds; fore-and-aft sails are set parallel to the length of the boat, with the luff (leading edge) of the sail attached to a mast or a stay. They are more efficient for all-round sailing, and almost all modern sailboats are rigged this way. Some fore-and-aft sails have a gaff at the head; Marconi-rig sails are pointed at the top (below). The bottom (foot) of the sail is on a boom. Sails are made of strips of cloth sewn together. Cotton and flax are traditional sail materials but synthetic fabrics are now more often used.

TOP OF A MARCONI SAIL

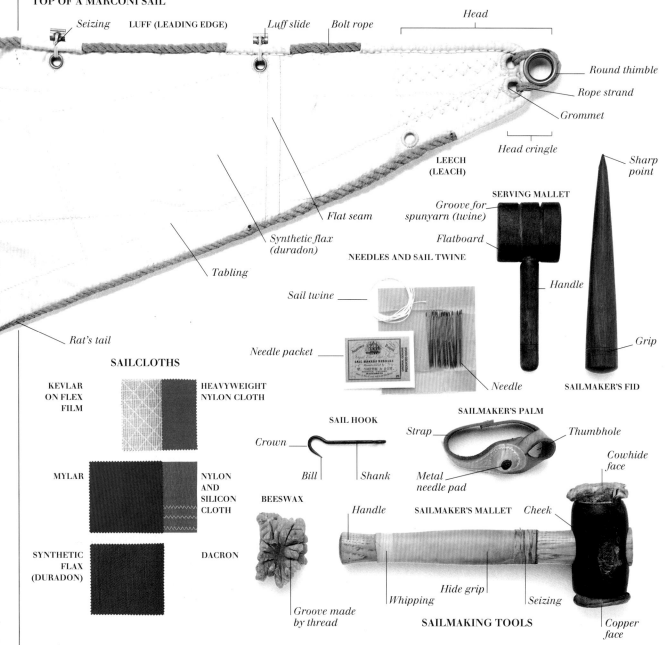

Seizing   LUFF (LEADING EDGE)   Luff slide   Bolt rope   Head

Round thimble

Rope strand

Grommet

Head cringle

LEECH
(LEACH)

Flat seam

Synthetic flax
(duradon)

Tabling

Rat's tail

SERVING MALLET

Groove for
spunyarn (twine)

Flatboard

Handle

Sharp
point

Grip

SAILMAKER'S FID

NEEDLES AND SAIL TWINE

Sail twine

Needle packet

Needle

SAILCLOTHS

KEVLAR
ON FLEX
FILM

HEAVYWEIGHT
NYLON CLOTH

MYLAR

NYLON
AND
SILICON
CLOTH

SYNTHETIC
FLAX
(DURADON)

DACRON

SAIL HOOK

Crown

Bill   Shank

BEESWAX

Groove made
by thread

SAILMAKER'S PALM

Strap

Metal
needle pad

Thumbhole

Cowhide
face

Handle   **SAILMAKER'S MALLET**   Cheek

Whipping   Hide grip   Seizing

Copper
face

SAILMAKING TOOLS

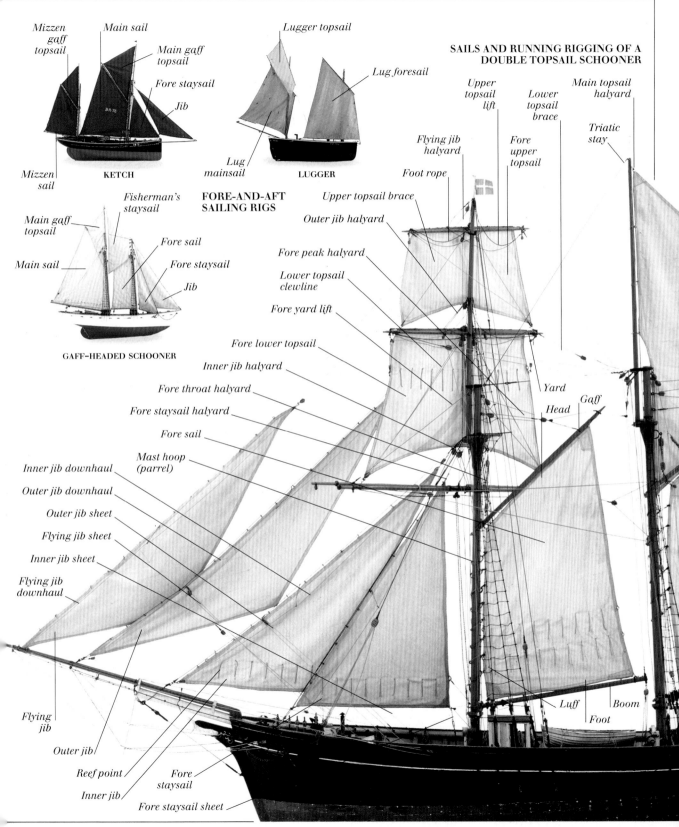

Mizzen gaff topsail

Main sail

Main gaff topsail

Fore staysail

Jib

Mizzen sail

KETCH

Lugger topsail

Lug foresail

Lug mainsail

LUGGER

Main gaff topsail

Fisherman's staysail

Fore sail

Main sail

Fore staysail

Jib

GAFF–HEADED SCHOONER

FORE-AND-AFT SAILING RIGS

SAILS AND RUNNING RIGGING OF A DOUBLE TOPSAIL SCHOONER

Upper topsail lift

Lower topsail brace

Main topsail halyard

Flying jib halyard

Foot rope

Fore upper topsail

Triatic stay

Upper topsail brace

Outer jib halyard

Fore peak halyard

Lower topsail clewline

Fore yard lift

Fore lower topsail

Inner jib halyard

Fore throat halyard

Fore staysail halyard

Fore sail

Mast hoop (parrel)

Inner jib downhaul

Outer jib downhaul

Outer jib sheet

Flying jib sheet

Inner jib sheet

Flying jib downhaul

Yard

Head

Gaff

Luff

Boom

Foot

Flying jib

Outer jib

Reef point

Fore staysail

Inner jib

Fore staysail sheet

Mooring and anchoring

IN MOST HARBORS AND PORTS, a ship can moor (tie up or "make fast") directly to a pier, wharf, or quay (pronounced "key"), using heavy hawsers and docking lines attached to bitts or bollards. Hawsers are tied to each other with knots called bends. In open water, however, ships that are not under way must drop an anchor, which attaches the ship securely to the seabed. The earliest anchors were simply heavy stones. Later, various anchor designs were developed for different uses. Most small vessels today use Danforth or plow anchors, which dig deeply into the sea bottom. A permanent mooring is an anchor set in the bottom to which a ship can tie up without using its own anchor. On old sailing ships, anchors were pulled up, or "weighed," by sailors pushing against bars that turned a capstan, which wound up the anchor cable. Now, most capstans are powered by electricity.

**STONE ANCHOR
(KILLICK)**

Rope hole

**TYPES
OF ANCHOR**

**CLOSE-
STOWING
ANCHOR**

**CQR ANCHOR
(PLOW ANCHOR)**

**BRITISH ADMIRALTY
ANCHOR TYPE ACII**

**YACHTSMAN'S
ANCHOR (KEDGE)**

**STOCKLESS
ANCHOR**

**MUSHROOM ANCHOR
(PERMANENT MOORING ANCHOR)**

ANCHOR CHAIN

End link

Common link

Patent link

**DANFORTH
ANCHOR**

Shank

Pea (bill)

Fluke (palm)

Stock

Tripping palm

Crown

Throat

SHACKLE, SWIVELS, AND LINK

Crown

Bolt

Lug

Screw thread

**GALVANIZED
"D" SHACKLE**

**MOORING
SWIVEL**

**CHAIN
SWIVEL**

SCREW LINK

**TWIN BOLLARDS
(BITTS), WITH RAKED
PILLARS AND A HAWSER
(HEAVY ROPE)**

Flat

Rim

Base

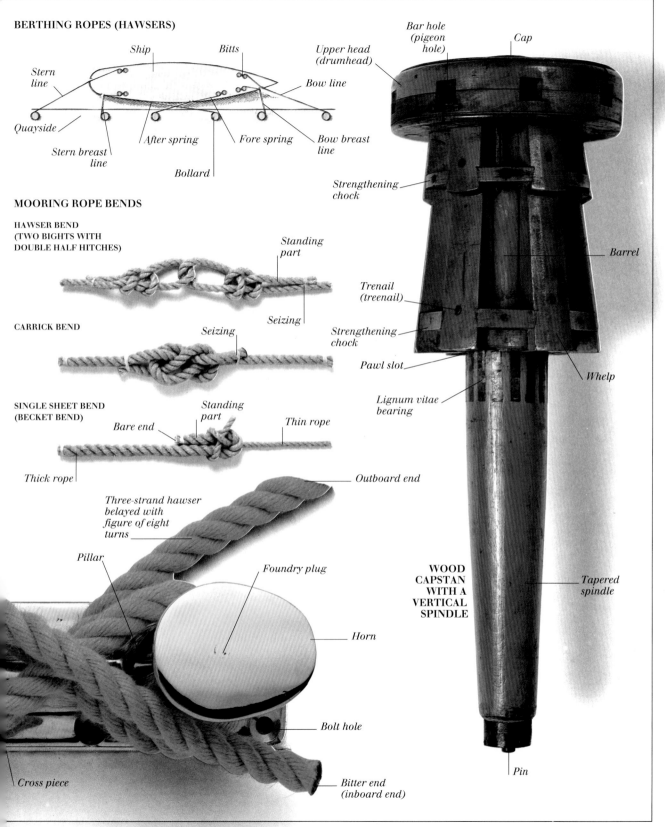

BERTHING ROPES (HAWSERS)

Stern line

Ship

Bitts

Bar hole (pigeon hole)

Cap

Upper head (drumhead)

Bow line

Quayside

Stern breast line

After spring

Fore spring

Bollard

Bow breast line

MOORING ROPE BENDS

HAWSER BEND (TWO BIGHTS WITH DOUBLE HALF HITCHES)

Standing part

Seizing

Strengthening chock

Barrel

CARRICK BEND

Seizing

Seizing

Trenail (treenail)

Strengthening chock

Pawl slot

Whelp

SINGLE SHEET BEND (BECKET BEND)

Standing part

Bare end

Thin rope

Lignum vitae bearing

Thick rope

Outboard end

Three-strand hawser belayed with figure of eight turns

Pillar

Foundry plug

WOOD CAPSTAN WITH A VERTICAL SPINDLE

Horn

Tapered spindle

Bolt hole

Cross piece

Bitter end (inboard end)

Pin

387

Ropes and knots

ALL KINDS OF ROPES ARE USED AT SEA, from thin twines and yarn to thick hawsers. Synthetic fibers are much in use today. Nylon ropes stretch, and so are ideal for anchoring; polyester (frequently called by the trade name Dacron) has little stretch and is used for halyards and sheets. Different knots have different uses. Knots that join two ropes are often called bends; hitches join a rope to another object. Ropes, usually called "lines" on board ship, can also be joined by seizing (lashing them together side by side) or splicing (unraveling the ends and weaving them together).

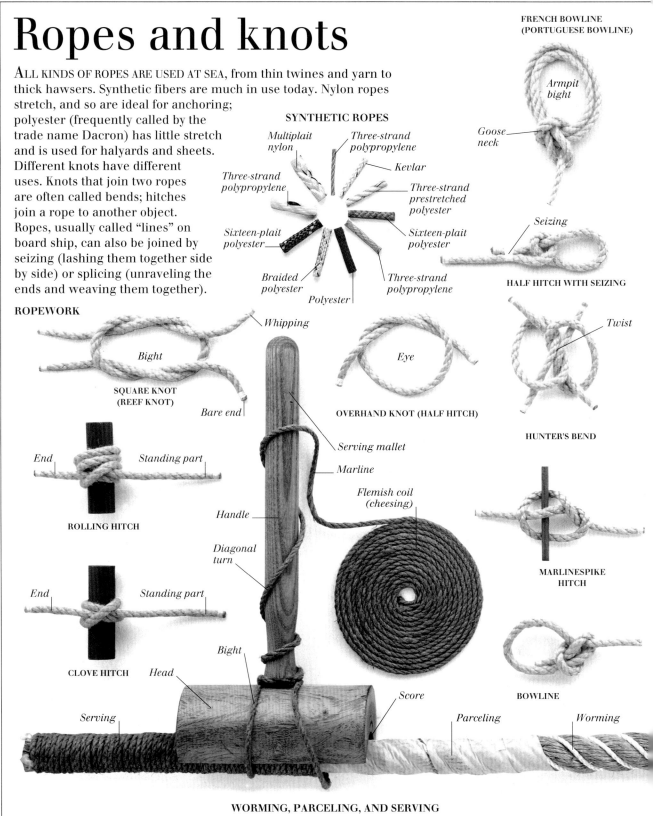

**FRENCH BOWLINE
(PORTUGUESE BOWLINE)**

Armpit bight

Goose neck

SYNTHETIC ROPES

Multiplait nylon

Three-strand polypropylene

Kevlar

Three-strand polypropylene

Three-strand prestretched polyester

Sixteen-plait polyester

Sixteen-plait polyester

Braided polyester

Three-strand polypropylene

Polyester

Seizing

HALF HITCH WITH SEIZING

ROPEWORK

Whipping

Bight

Eye

Twist

**SQUARE KNOT
(REEF KNOT)**

Bare end

OVERHAND KNOT (HALF HITCH)

HUNTER'S BEND

End *Standing part*

ROLLING HITCH

Serving mallet

Marline

Handle

*Flemish coil
(cheesing)*

**MARLINESPIKE
HITCH**

Diagonal turn

End *Standing part*

CLOVE HITCH

Head

Bight

Score

BOWLINE

Serving

Parceling

Worming

WORMING, PARCELING, AND SERVING

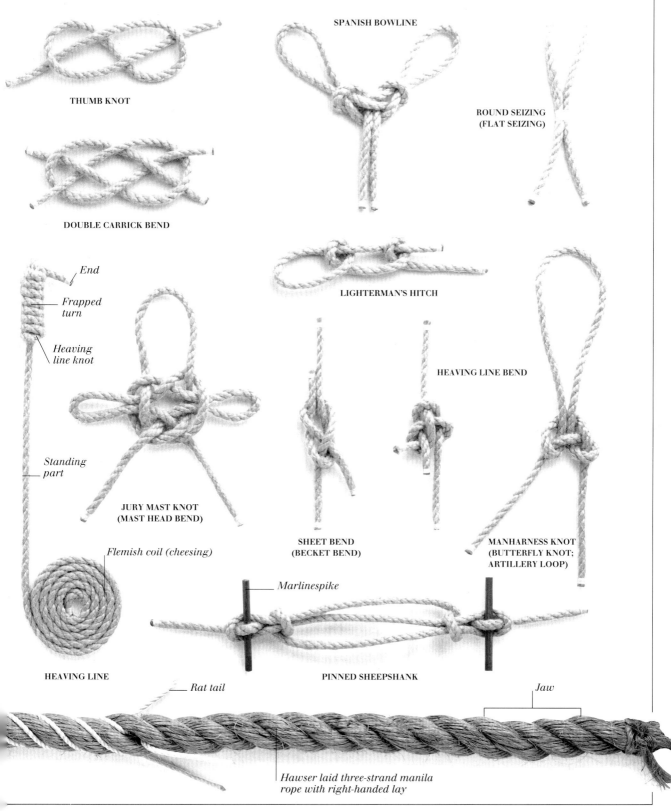

THUMB KNOT

DOUBLE CARRICK BEND

SPANISH BOWLINE

ROUND SEIZING
(FLAT SEIZING)

End

Frapped turn

Heaving line knot

LIGHTERMAN'S HITCH

HEAVING LINE BEND

Standing part

JURY MAST KNOT
(MAST HEAD BEND)

SHEET BEND
(BECKET BEND)

MANHARNESS KNOT
(BUTTERFLY KNOT;
ARTILLERY LOOP)

Flemish coil (cheesing)

Marlinespike

HEAVING LINE

PINNED SHEEPSHANK

Rat tail

Jaw

*Hawser laid three-strand manila
rope with right-handed lay*

Paddle wheels and propellers

THE INVENTION OF THE STEAM ENGINE IN THE 18TH CENTURY made mechanically driven ships fitted with paddle wheels or propellers a viable alternative to sails. Paddle wheels have fixed or feathered floats, and the model shown below features both types. Feathered floats give more propulsive power than fixed floats because they are almost upright at all times in the water. Paddle wheels were superseded by the propeller on oceangoing vessels in the mid-19th century. Propellers are more efficient, work better in rough water, and are less vulnerable in collisions. The first propellers were two-bladed, but later three- and four-bladed versions are more powerful; the shape and pitch of the blades have also been refined over the years. At the beginning of the 18th century, tillers were replaced on many larger ships by the ship's wheel as a means of steering.

SHIP'S WHEEL

- King spoke handle
- Handle
- Spoke
- Rim plate
- Felloe (rim section)
- Maker's name
- Nave plate
- Nave

PADDLE WHEEL WITH FIXED FLOATS

- Wrist pin
- Limb
- Fixed float
- Hub
- Deck beam

OSCILLATING STEAM ENGINE

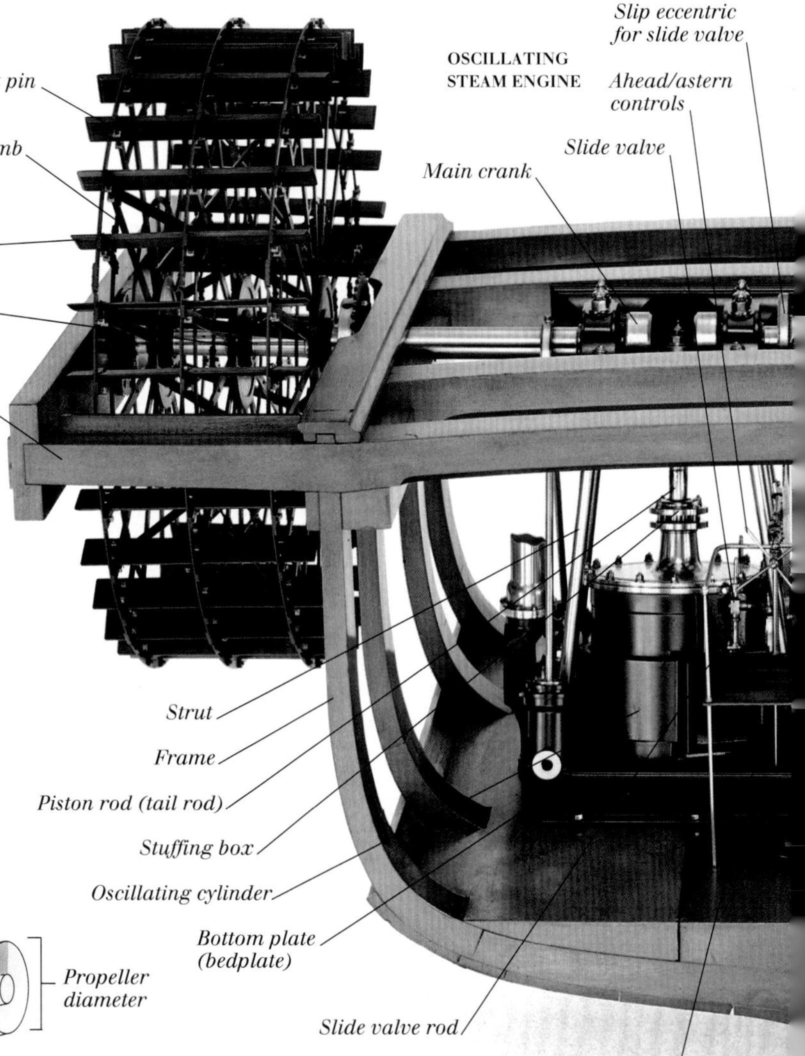

- Slip eccentric for slide valve
- Ahead/astern controls
- Main crank
- Slide valve

THREE-BLADED PROPELLER

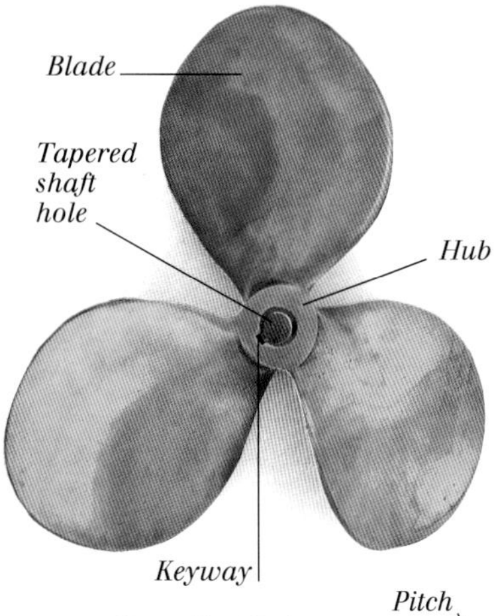

- Blade
- Tapered shaft hole
- Hub
- Keyway

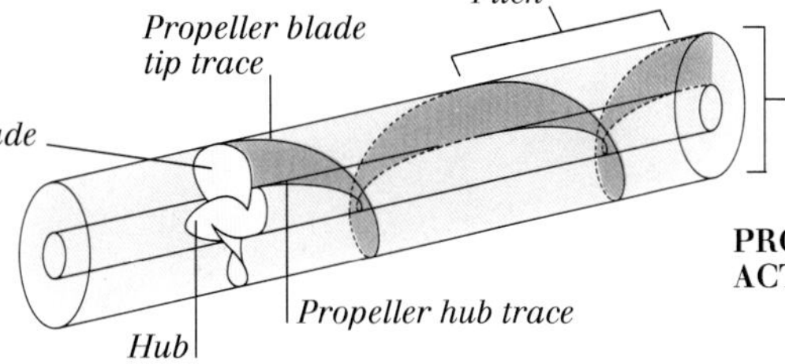

- Strut
- Frame
- Piston rod (tail rod)
- Stuffing box
- Oscillating cylinder
- Bottom plate (bedplate)
- Slide valve rod
- Control platform

- Pitch
- Propeller blade tip trace
- Blade
- Propeller diameter
- Hub
- Propeller hub trace

PROPELLER ACTION

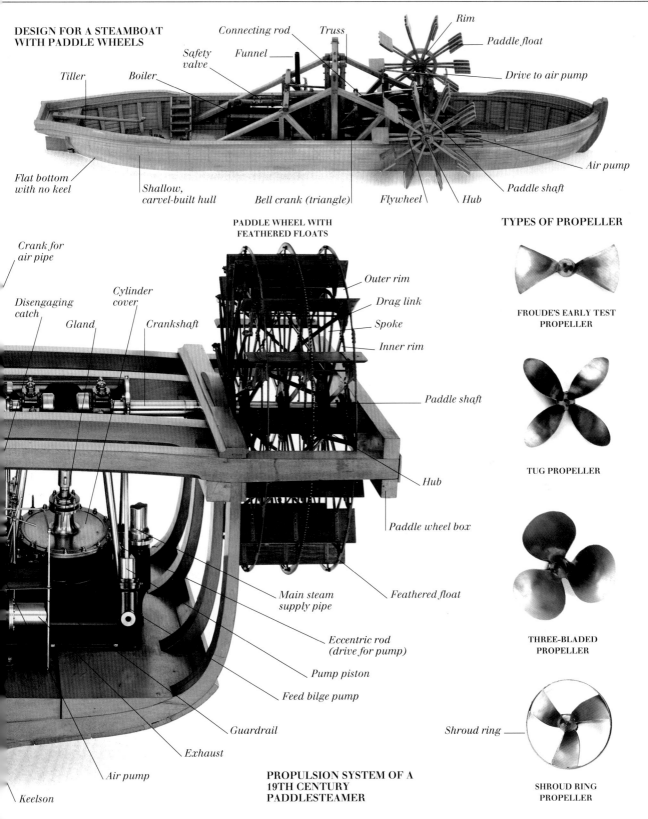

DESIGN FOR A STEAMBOAT WITH PADDLE WHEELS

Connecting rod

Truss

Rim

Paddle float

Safety valve

Funnel

Drive to air pump

Tiller

Boiler

Flat bottom with no keel

Shallow, carvel-built hull

Bell crank (triangle)

Flywheel

Hub

Air pump

Paddle shaft

PADDLE WHEEL WITH FEATHERED FLOATS

TYPES OF PROPELLER

Crank for air pipe

Outer rim

Drag link

Disengaging catch

Cylinder cover

Spoke

Gland

Crankshaft

Inner rim

Paddle shaft

Hub

Paddle wheel box

Main steam supply pipe

Feathered float

Eccentric rod (drive for pump)

Pump piston

Feed bilge pump

Guardrail

Exhaust

Air pump

Keelson

PROPULSION SYSTEM OF A 19TH CENTURY PADDLESTEAMER

FROUDE'S EARLY TEST PROPELLER

TUG PROPELLER

THREE-BLADED PROPELLER

Shroud ring

SHROUD RING PROPELLER

Anatomy of an iron ship

IRON PARTS WERE USED IN WOODEN SHIPS AS EARLY AS 1675, often in the same form as the wooden parts that they replaced. Eventually, as on the tea clipper Cutty Sark (below), iron standing rigging was found to be stronger than the traditional rope. The first "ironclads" were warships whose wooden hulls were protected by iron armor plates. Later ironclads actually had iron hulls. The model opposite is based on the British warship HMS Warrior, launched in 1860, the first battleship built entirely of iron. The plan of an iron paddlesteamer (bottom), built somewhat later, shows that the craft had the masts and bowsprit of a sailing ship; but it also boasted a steam propulsion plant amid ships that turned two side paddlewheels. Early iron plates were painstakingly riveted together (below), but by the 1940s, steel vessels were welded together, whole sections at a time. The Liberty ships built in America during World War II are prime examples of such "production-line" vessels.

TEA CLIPPER

Steel yard

Iron wire stay

Steel lower mast

Steel bowsprit

Forged iron anchor

Wooden planking with copper sheathing

RIVETED PLATES

Pan head rivet

Plate

Button head rivet (snap head)

Seam

LIBERTY SHIP

Gun section

Accommodation section

Cargo derrick

Weld line

Stern section

Midships section

Cargo hold

Bow section

PLAN OF AN IRON PADDLESTEAMER

Steering position

Steering gear

Stern

Vertical frame ladder

Mast step

Rudder

Rudder post

Heel of rudder post

Mizzen mast

Poop deck

Lounge

Guardrail

Deck lantern

Binnacle

Main mast

State room

Steam whistle

After funnel

Skylight

Eccentric

Crankshaft

Guardrail

Paddle wheel

Connecting rod

Bar keel

Afterpeak

Cabin

Tank

Main mast step

Donkey boiler

Box boiler

Foundation

Reversing wheel

Bottom plate

Side lever

Cylinder

Stern framing

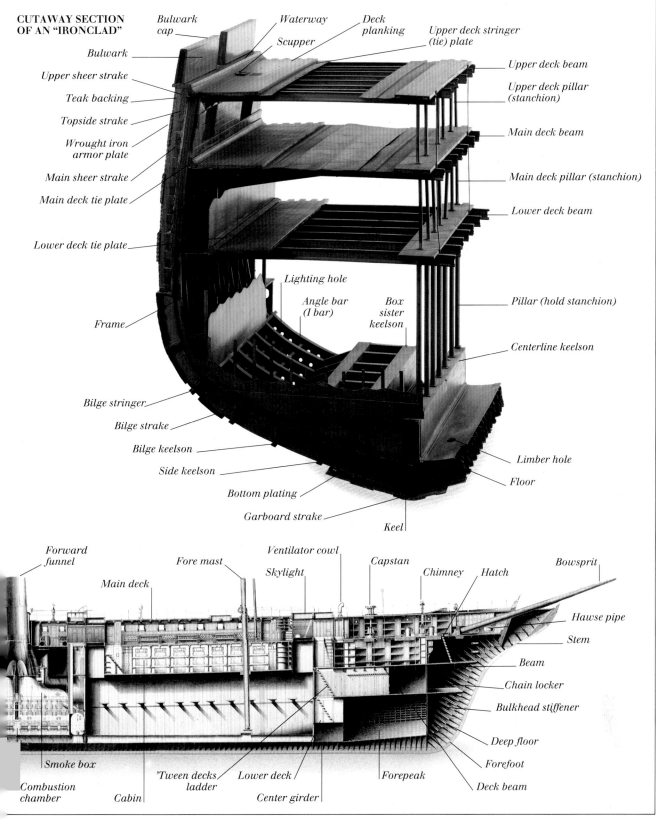

CUTAWAY SECTION OF AN "IRONCLAD"

Bulwark cap

Bulwark

Upper sheer strake

Teak backing

Topside strake

Wrought iron armor plate

Main sheer strake

Main deck tie plate

Lower deck tie plate

Frame

Bilge stringer

Bilge strake

Bilge keelson

Side keelson

Bottom plating

Garboard strake

Keel

Waterway

Scupper

Deck planking

Upper deck stringer (tie) plate

Upper deck beam

Upper deck pillar (stanchion)

Main deck beam

Main deck pillar (stanchion)

Lower deck beam

Pillar (hold stanchion)

Centerline keelson

Lighting hole

Angle bar (I bar)

Box sister keelson

Limber hole

Floor

Forward funnel

Fore mast

Main deck

Skylight

Ventilator cowl

Capstan

Chimney

Hatch

Bowsprit

Hawse pipe

Stem

Beam

Chain locker

Bulkhead stiffener

Deep floor

Forefoot

Deck beam

Forepeak

Center girder

Lower deck

'Tween decks ladder

Cabin

Combustion chamber

Smoke box

393

The battleship

IN THE EARLY YEARS OF THE 20TH CENTURY, sea warfare—
attacking enemy vessels or defending a ship—was
revolutionized by the introduction of Dreadnought-type
battleships like the Brazilian vessel below. These new
ships combined the latest advances in steam
propulsion, gunnery, and armor plating. Their gun
turrets, protected by armor up to 12 in (30 cm) thick,
were designed to fire shells over great distances.
The ship shown here, the Minas Geraes, was 500 ft
(152 m) long. It was built at Elswick, England, and
launched in 1908. Its chief armament was of 12 in (30 cm)
guns (firing shells with a 12 in diameter). Other naval
weapons developed in the 20th century include the torpedo—
as portrayed on the upper cigarette card (right). This was
a self-propelled underwater missile, often steered by
gyro-control. Depth charges were designed in the
First World War for use against submerged U-boats.
They are canisters filled with explosives that are
detonated by depth-sensitive pistols. The lower
cigarette card shows depth charges being
fired by a "thrower," fired from a
torpedo tube, and rolled from the
stern. Ship's shields were fitted to
warships from the late 19th century
onwards. The shield shown
opposite depicts a traditional
ship's cannon.

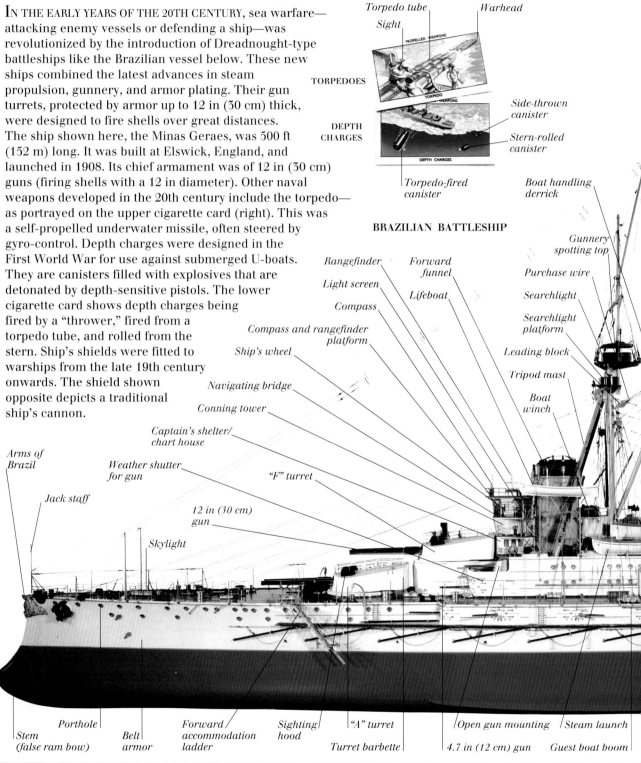

20TH CENTURY WEAPONRY

Torpedo tube

Sight

Warhead

TORPEDOES

DEPTH CHARGES

Side-thrown canister

Stern-rolled canister

Torpedo-fired canister

Boat handling derrick

BRAZILIAN BATTLESHIP

Rangefinder

Light screen

Compass

Compass and rangefinder platform

Ship's wheel

Navigating bridge

Conning tower

Captain's shelter/ chart house

Weather shutter for gun

Arms of Brazil

Jack staff

12 in (30 cm) gun

Skylight

Forward funnel

Lifeboat

Gunnery spotting top

Purchase wire

Searchlight

Searchlight platform

Leading block

Tripod mast

Boat winch

"F" turret

Stem (false ram bow)

Porthole

Belt armor

Forward accommodation ladder

Sighting hood

"A" turret

Turret barbette

Open gun mounting

4.7 in (12 cm) gun

Steam launch

Guest boat boom

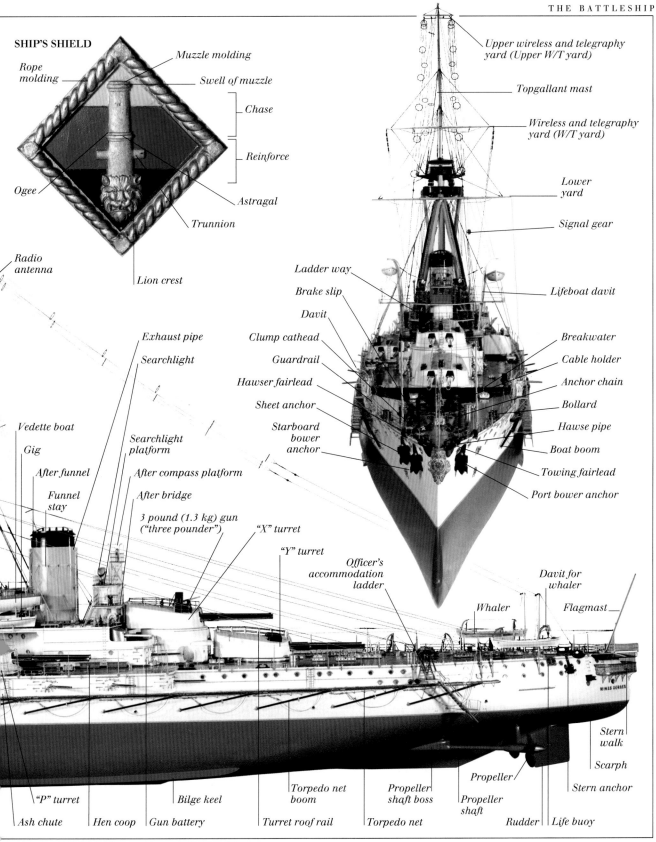

SHIP'S SHIELD

Rope molding

Muzzle molding

Swell of muzzle

Chase

Reinforce

Astragal

Ogee

Trunnion

Lion crest

Radio antenna

Upper wireless and telegraphy yard (Upper W/T yard)

Topgallant mast

Wireless and telegraphy yard (W/T yard)

Lower yard

Signal gear

Ladder way

Brake slip

Davit

Clump cathead

Guardrail

Hawser fairlead

Sheet anchor

Starboard bower anchor

Exhaust pipe

Searchlight

Lifeboat davit

Breakwater

Cable holder

Anchor chain

Bollard

Hawse pipe

Boat boom

Towing fairlead

Port bower anchor

Vedette boat

Gig

After funnel

Funnel stay

Searchlight platform

After compass platform

After bridge

3 pound (1.3 kg) gun ("three pounder")

"X" turret

"Y" turret

Officer's accommodation ladder

Davit for whaler

Whaler

Flagmast

Stern walk

Scarph

Stern anchor

"P" turret

Ash chute

Hen coop

Bilge keel

Gun battery

Torpedo net boom

Turret roof rail

Propeller shaft boss

Torpedo net

Propeller

Propeller shaft

Rudder

Life buoy

Frigates and submarines

FROM THE MID-19TH CENTURY, ARMORED SHIPS provided a new challenge to enemy craft. In response, huge revolving gun turrets were developed. These could shoot in any direction, were loaded quickly from the breech, and fired exploding shells. Today's fighting ships, like the Royal Navy frigate opposite, also carry missile launchers and helicopters. Submarines operate underwater, have great speed, and some can fire missiles while submerged. A nuclear sub can operate for several years without refueling.

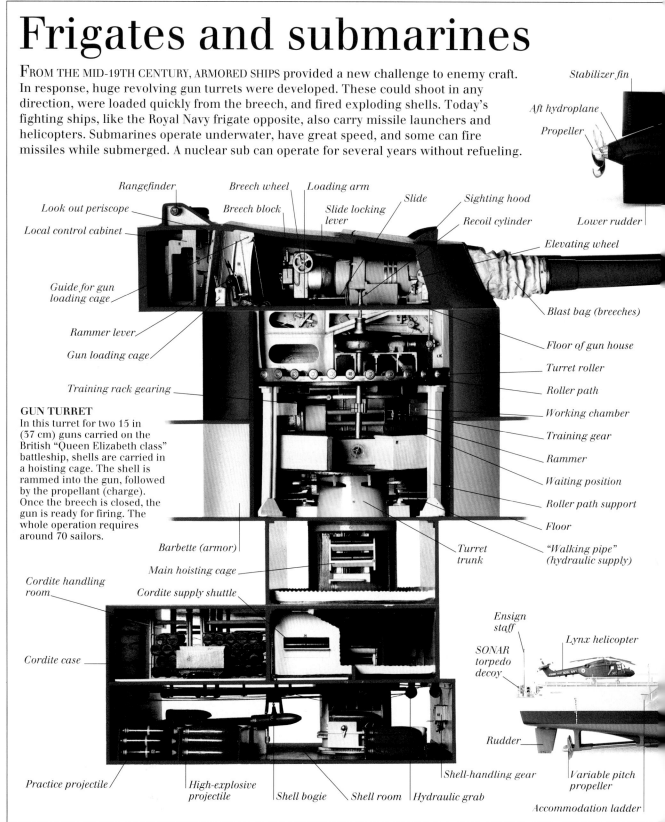

Stabilizer fin

Aft hydroplane

Propeller

Rangefinder

Look out periscope

Local control cabinet

Breech wheel

Breech block

Loading arm

Slide locking lever

Slide

Sighting hood

Recoil cylinder

Lower rudder

Elevating wheel

Guide for gun loading cage

Blast bag (breeches)

Rammer lever

Gun loading cage

Training rack gearing

Floor of gun house

Turret roller

Roller path

Working chamber

Training gear

Rammer

Waiting position

Roller path support

Floor

"Walking pipe" (hydraulic supply)

GUN TURRET

In this turret for two 15 in (37 cm) guns carried on the British "Queen Elizabeth class" battleship, shells are carried in a hoisting cage. The shell is rammed into the gun, followed by the propellant (charge). Once the breech is closed, the gun is ready for firing. The whole operation requires around 70 sailors.

Barbette (armor)

Main hoisting cage

Turret trunk

Cordite handling room

Cordite supply shuttle

Ensign staff

SONAR torpedo decoy

Lynx helicopter

Cordite case

Rudder

Practice projectile

High-explosive projectile

Shell bogie

Shell room

Shell-handling gear

Hydraulic grab

Variable pitch propeller

Accommodation ladder

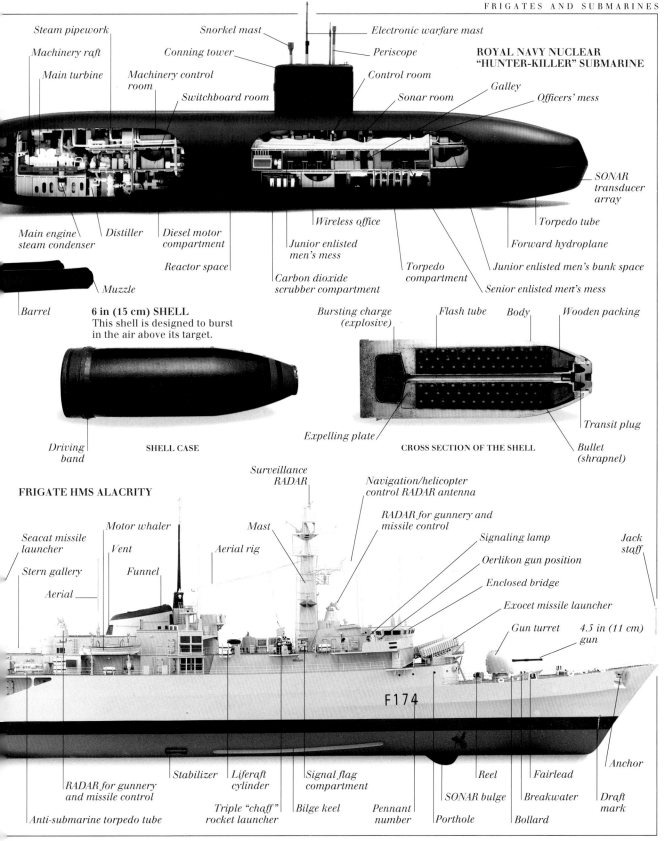

Steam pipework

Machinery raft

Main turbine

Snorkel mast

Conning tower

Machinery control room

Switchboard room

Electronic warfare mast

Periscope

ROYAL NAVY NUCLEAR "HUNTER-KILLER" SUBMARINE

Control room

Sonar room

Galley

Officers' mess

SONAR transducer array

Main engine steam condenser

Distiller

Diesel motor compartment

Reactor space

Wireless office

Junior enlisted men's mess

Carbon dioxide scrubber compartment

Torpedo compartment

Senior enlisted men's mess

Junior enlisted men's bunk space

Torpedo tube

Forward hydroplane

Barrel

Muzzle

6 in (15 cm) SHELL
This shell is designed to burst in the air above its target.

Bursting charge (explosive)

Flash tube

Body

Wooden packing

Expelling plate

Transit plug

Driving band

SHELL CASE

CROSS SECTION OF THE SHELL

Bullet (shrapnel)

FRIGATE HMS ALACRITY

Surveillance RADAR

Navigation/helicopter control RADAR antenna

RADAR for gunnery and missile control

Mast

Seacat missile launcher

Motor whaler

Vent

Aerial rig

Signaling lamp

Jack staff

Stern gallery

Funnel

Oerlikon gun position

Aerial

Enclosed bridge

Exocet missile launcher

Gun turret

4.5 in (11 cm) gun

F174

RADAR for gunnery and missile control

Stabilizer

Liferaft cylinder

Signal flag compartment

Reel

Fairlead

Anchor

Anti-submarine torpedo tube

Triple "chaff" rocket launcher

Bilge keel

Pennant number

SONAR bulge

Porthole

Breakwater

Bollard

Draft mark

Pioneers of flight

FLIGHT HAS FASCINATED MANKIND for centuries, and countless unsuccessful flying machines have been designed. The first successful flight was made by the French Montgolfier brothers in 1783, when they flew a balloon over Paris. The next major advance was the development of gliders, notably by the Englishman Sir George Cayley, who in 1845 designed the first glider to make a sustained flight, and by the German Otto Lilienthal, who became known as the world's first pilot because he managed to achieve controlled flights. However, powered flight did not become a practical possibility until the invention of lightweight, gas-driven internal-combustion engines at the end of the 19th century. Then, in 1903, the American brothers Orville and Wilbur Wright made the first powered flight in their Wright Flyer biplane, which used a four-cylinder, gas-driven engine. Aircraft design advanced rapidly, and in 1909 the Frenchman Louis Blériot made his pioneering flight across the English Channel (see pp. 400-401). The American Glenn Curtiss also achieved several "firsts" in his Model-D Pusher and its variants, most notably winning the world's first competition for airspeed at Reims in 1909.

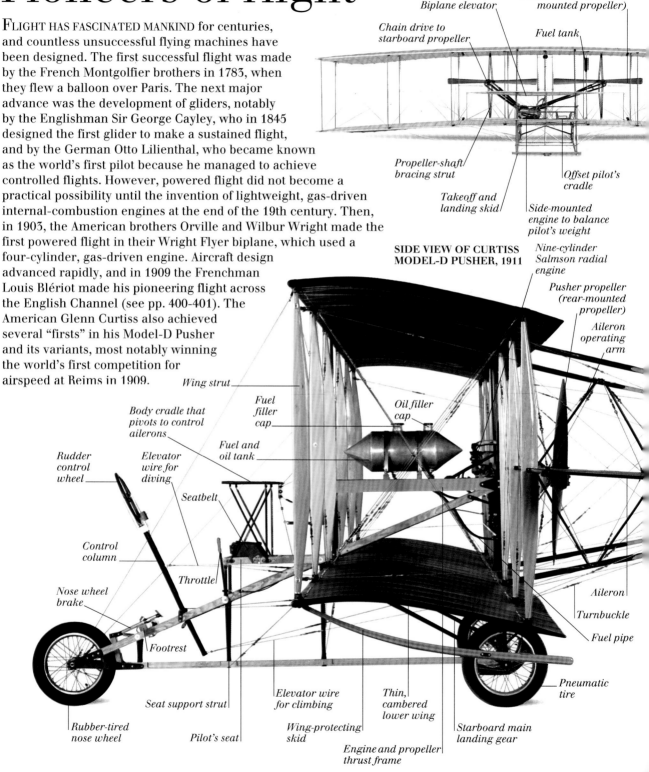

Biplane elevator

Chain drive to starboard propeller

Pusher propeller (rear-mounted propeller)

Fuel tank

Propeller-shaft bracing strut

Takeoff and landing skid

Offset pilot's cradle

Side-mounted engine to balance pilot's weight

SIDE VIEW OF CURTISS MODEL-D PUSHER, 1911

Nine-cylinder Salmson radial engine

Pusher propeller (rear-mounted propeller)

Aileron operating arm

Wing strut

Body cradle that pivots to control ailerons

Fuel filler cap

Oil filler cap

Fuel and oil tank

Rudder control wheel

Elevator wire for diving

Seatbelt

Control column

Throttle

Nose wheel brake

Footrest

Aileron

Turnbuckle

Fuel pipe

Pneumatic tire

Rubber-tired nose wheel

Seat support strut

Pilot's seat

Elevator wire for climbing

Wing-protecting skid

Thin, cambered lower wing

Engine and propeller thrust frame

Starboard main landing gear

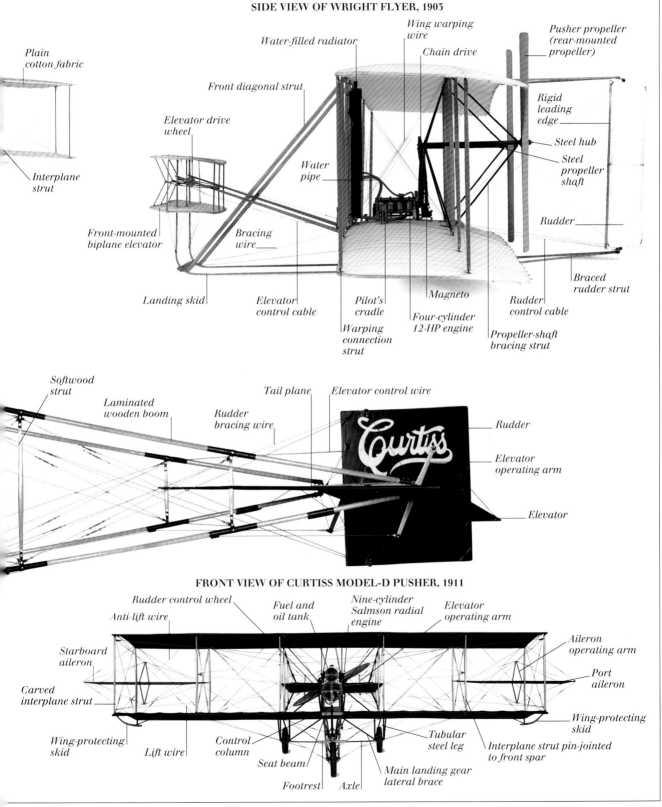

SIDE VIEW OF WRIGHT FLYER, 1903

Plain cotton fabric

Interplane strut

Water-filled radiator

Wing warping wire

Chain drive

Pusher propeller (rear-mounted propeller)

Front diagonal strut

Elevator drive wheel

Rigid leading edge

Water pipe

Steel hub

Steel propeller shaft

Front-mounted biplane elevator

Bracing wire

Rudder

Landing skid

Elevator control cable

Pilot's cradle

Magneto

Rudder control cable

Braced rudder strut

Warping connection strut

Four-cylinder 12-HP engine

Propeller-shaft bracing strut

Softwood strut

Tail plane

Elevator control wire

Rudder

Laminated wooden boom

Rudder bracing wire

Elevator operating arm

Elevator

FRONT VIEW OF CURTISS MODEL-D PUSHER, 1911

Rudder control wheel

Fuel and oil tank

Nine-cylinder Salmson radial engine

Elevator operating arm

Anti-lift wire

Aileron operating arm

Starboard aileron

Port aileron

Carved interplane strut

Wing-protecting skid

Wing-protecting skid

Lift wire

Control column

Seat beam

Footrest

Axle

Tubular steel leg

Main landing gear lateral brace

Interplane strut pin-jointed to front spar

Early monoplanes

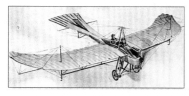

RUMPLER MONOPLANE, 1908

MONOPLANES HAVE ONE WING on each side of the fuselage. The principal disadvantage of this arrangement in early wooden-framed aircraft was that single wings were weak. They required strong wires to brace them to king posts above and below the fuselage. However, single wings also had advantages: they experienced less drag than multiple wings, allowing greater speed; they also made aircraft more maneuverable because single wings were easier to warp (twist) than double wings, and warping the wings was how pilots controlled the roll of early aircraft. By 1912, the French pilot Louis Blériot had used a monoplane to make the first flight across the English Channel, and the Briton Robert Blackburn and the Frenchman Armand Deperdussin had proved the greater speed of monoplanes. However, a spate of crashes caused by broken wings discouraged monoplane production, except in Germany, where all-metal monoplanes were developed in 1917. The wings of all-metal monoplanes did not need strengthening by struts or bracing wires, but despite this, such planes were not widely adopted until the 1930s.

FRONT VIEW OF BLACKBURN MONOPLANE, 1912

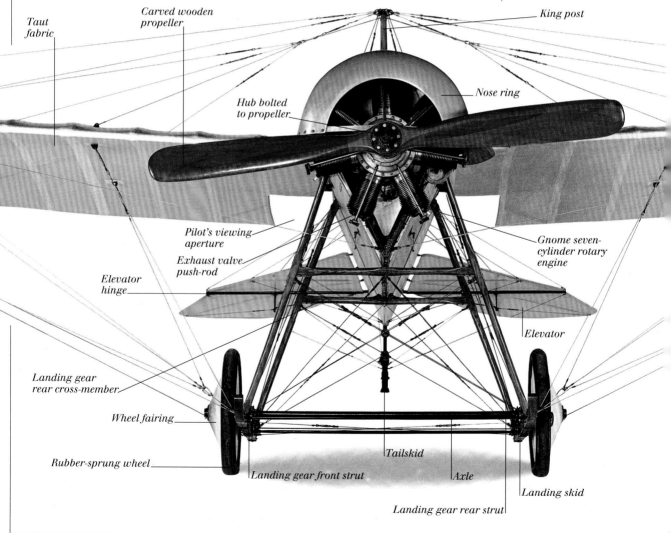

Taut fabric

Carved wooden propeller

King post

Hub bolted to propeller

Nose ring

Pilot's viewing aperture

Gnome seven-cylinder rotary engine

Exhaust valve push-rod

Elevator hinge

Elevator

Landing gear rear cross-member

Wheel fairing

Rubber-sprung wheel

Tailskid

Landing gear front strut

Axle

Landing skid

Landing gear rear strut

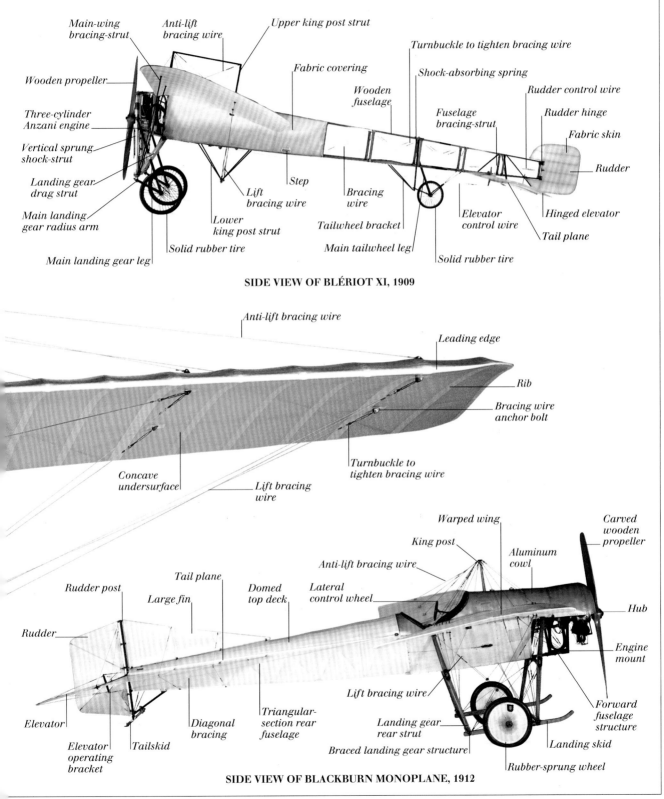

Main-wing bracing-strut

Anti-lift bracing wire

Upper king post strut

Wooden propeller

Fabric covering

Turnbuckle to tighten bracing wire

Shock-absorbing spring

Rudder control wire

Three-cylinder Anzani engine

Wooden fuselage

Rudder hinge

Fuselage bracing-strut

Fabric skin

Vertical sprung shock-strut

Rudder

Landing gear drag strut

Lift bracing wire

Step

Hinged elevator

Main landing gear radius arm

Bracing wire

Elevator control wire

Tail plane

Lower king post strut

Tailwheel bracket

Solid rubber tire

Main landing gear leg

Solid rubber tire

Main tailwheel leg

SIDE VIEW OF BLÉRIOT XI, 1909

Anti-lift bracing wire

Leading edge

Rib

Bracing wire anchor bolt

Concave undersurface

Lift bracing wire

Turnbuckle to tighten bracing wire

Warped wing

Carved wooden propeller

King post

Aluminum cowl

Anti-lift bracing wire

Rudder post

Tail plane

Domed top deck

Lateral control wheel

Large fin

Hub

Rudder

Engine mount

Elevator

Lift bracing wire

Forward fuselage structure

Diagonal bracing

Triangular-section rear fuselage

Landing gear rear strut

Landing skid

Elevator operating bracket

Tailskid

Braced landing gear structure

Rubber-sprung wheel

SIDE VIEW OF BLACKBURN MONOPLANE, 1912

Biplanes and triplanes

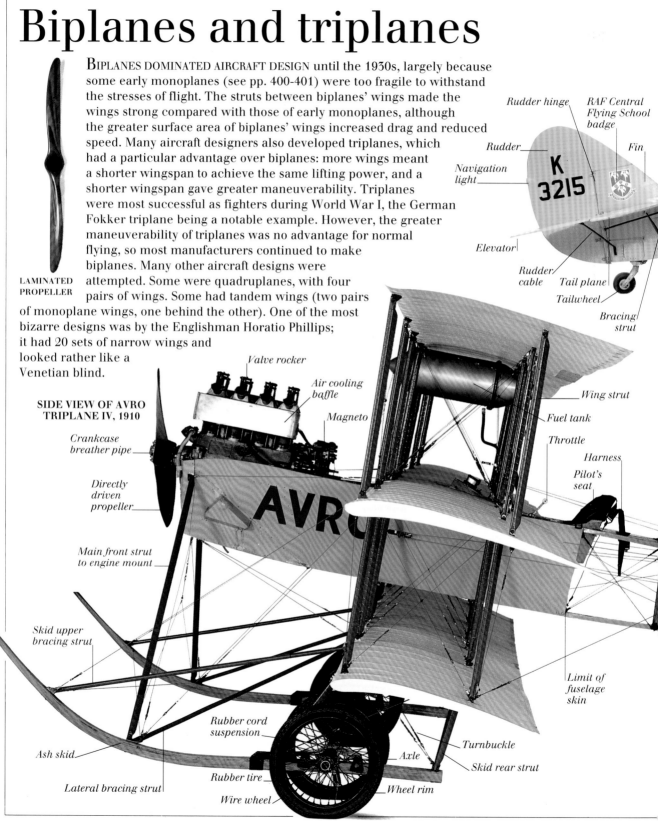

BIPLANES DOMINATED AIRCRAFT DESIGN until the 1930s, largely because some early monoplanes (see pp. 400-401) were too fragile to withstand the stresses of flight. The struts between biplanes' wings made the wings strong compared with those of early monoplanes, although the greater surface area of biplanes' wings increased drag and reduced speed. Many aircraft designers also developed triplanes, which had a particular advantage over biplanes: more wings meant a shorter wingspan to achieve the same lifting power, and a shorter wingspan gave greater maneuverability. Triplanes were most successful as fighters during World War I, the German Fokker triplane being a notable example. However, the greater maneuverability of triplanes was no advantage for normal flying, so most manufacturers continued to make biplanes. Many other aircraft designs were attempted. Some were quadruplanes, with four pairs of wings. Some had tandem wings (two pairs of monoplane wings, one behind the other). One of the most bizarre designs was by the Englishman Horatio Phillips; it had 20 sets of narrow wings and looked rather like a Venetian blind.

LAMINATED
PROPELLER

Rudder hinge

RAF Central
Flying School
badge

Rudder

Fin

Navigation
light

K
3215

Elevator

Rudder
cable

Tail plane

Tailwheel

Bracing
strut

Valve rocker

Air cooling
baffle

Magneto

Wing strut

Fuel tank

Throttle

Harness

Pilot's
seat

SIDE VIEW OF AVRO
TRIPLANE IV, 1910

Crankcase
breather pipe

Directly
driven
propeller

AVRO

Main front strut
to engine mount

Skid upper
bracing strut

Limit of
fuselage
skin

Rubber cord
suspension

Turnbuckle

Ash skid

Axle

Skid rear strut

Rubber tire

Lateral bracing strut

Wheel rim

Wire wheel

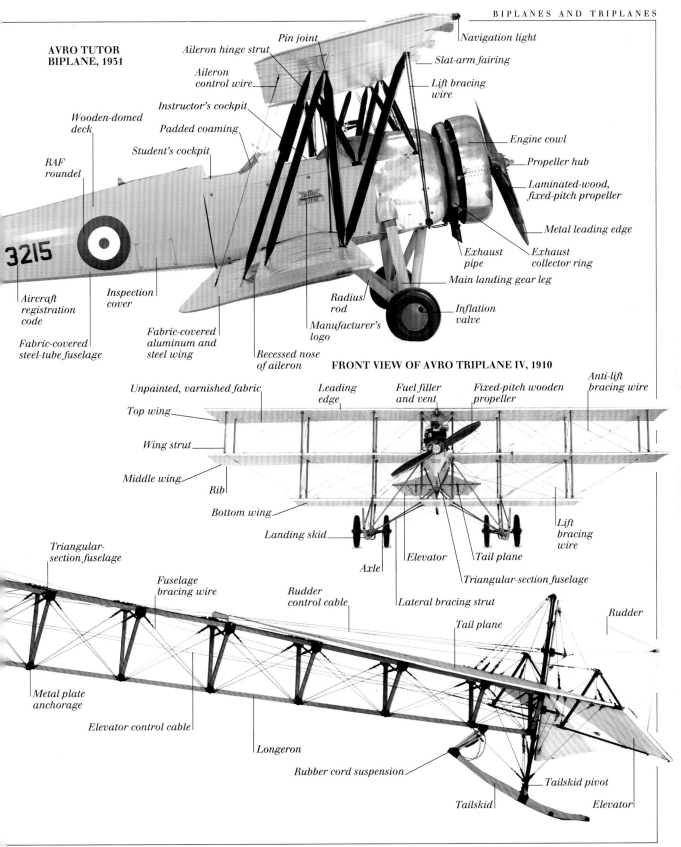

AVRO TUTOR BIPLANE, 1931

Pin joint

Aileron hinge strut

Navigation light

Aileron control wire

Slat-arm fairing

Lift bracing wire

Instructor's cockpit

Wooden-domed deck

Padded coaming

Engine cowl

RAF roundel

Student's cockpit

Propeller hub

Laminated-wood, fixed-pitch propeller

3215

Metal leading edge

Exhaust collector ring

Exhaust pipe

Main landing gear leg

Aircraft registration code

Inspection cover

Radius rod

Inflation valve

Fabric-covered steel-tube fuselage

Fabric-covered aluminum and steel wing

Manufacturer's logo

Recessed nose of aileron

FRONT VIEW OF AVRO TRIPLANE IV, 1910

Unpainted, varnished fabric

Leading edge

Fuel filler and vent

Fixed-pitch wooden propeller

Anti-lift bracing wire

Top wing

Wing strut

Middle wing

Rib

Bottom wing

Landing skid

Axle

Elevator

Tail plane

Lift bracing wire

Triangular-section fuselage

Fuselage bracing wire

Rudder control cable

Triangular-section fuselage

Tail plane

Rudder

Metal plate anchorage

Lateral bracing strut

Elevator control cable

Longeron

Rubber cord suspension

Tailskid pivot

Tailskid

Elevator

World War I aircraft

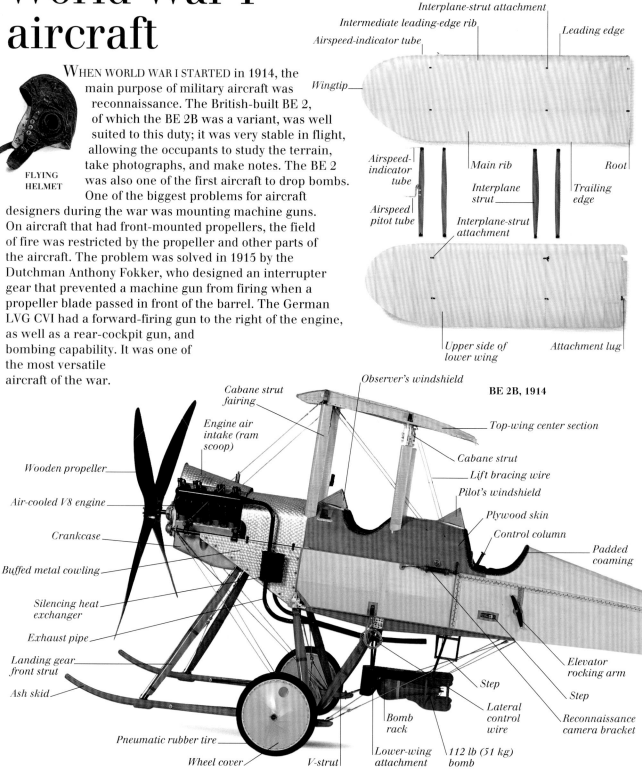

FLYING HELMET

WHEN WORLD WAR I STARTED in 1914, the main purpose of military aircraft was reconnaissance. The British-built BE 2, of which the BE 2B was a variant, was well suited to this duty; it was very stable in flight, allowing the occupants to study the terrain, take photographs, and make notes. The BE 2 was also one of the first aircraft to drop bombs. One of the biggest problems for aircraft designers during the war was mounting machine guns. On aircraft that had front-mounted propellers, the field of fire was restricted by the propeller and other parts of the aircraft. The problem was solved in 1915 by the Dutchman Anthony Fokker, who designed an interrupter gear that prevented a machine gun from firing when a propeller blade passed in front of the barrel. The German LVG CVI had a forward-firing gun to the right of the engine, as well as a rear-cockpit gun, and bombing capability. It was one of the most versatile aircraft of the war.

PORT WINGS FROM A BE 2B

Interplane-strut attachment
Intermediate leading-edge rib
Airspeed-indicator tube
Leading edge
Wingtip
Airspeed-indicator tube
Main rib
Root
Interplane strut
Trailing edge
Airspeed pitot tube
Interplane-strut attachment
Upper side of lower wing
Attachment lug

BE 2B, 1914

Cabane strut fairing
Observer's windshield
Engine air intake (ram scoop)
Top-wing center section
Cabane strut
Wooden propeller
Lift bracing wire
Air-cooled V8 engine
Pilot's windshield
Plywood skin
Crankcase
Control column
Buffed metal cowling
Padded coaming
Silencing heat exchanger
Exhaust pipe
Landing gear front strut
Elevator rocking arm
Ash skid
Step
Step
Lateral control wire
Reconnaissance camera bracket
Pneumatic rubber tire
Bomb rack
Wheel cover
V-strut
Lower-wing attachment
112 lb (51 kg) bomb

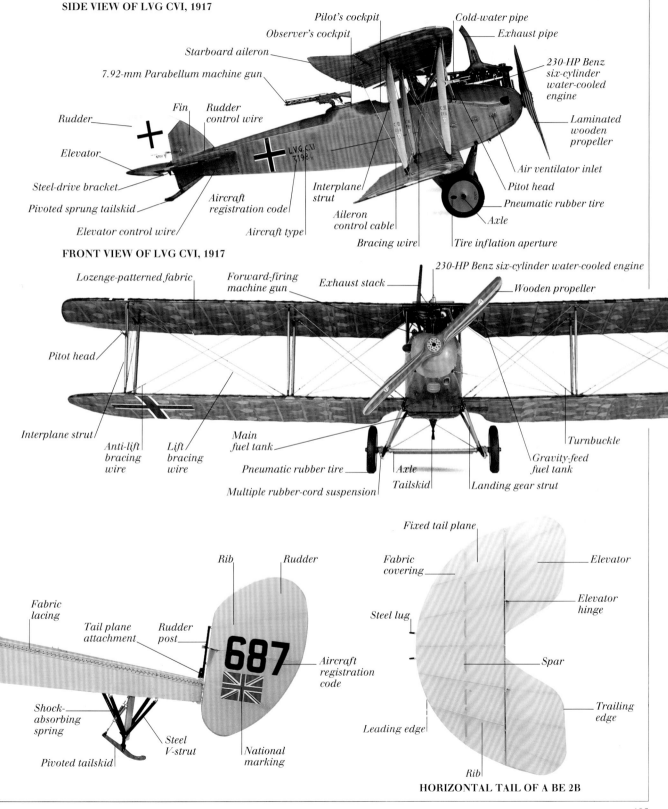

SIDE VIEW OF LVG CVI, 1917

Pilot's cockpit

Observer's cockpit

Cold-water pipe

Exhaust pipe

Starboard aileron

7.92-mm Parabellum machine gun

230-HP Benz six-cylinder water-cooled engine

Fin

Rudder control wire

Rudder

Elevator

Laminated wooden propeller

Steel-drive bracket

Air ventilator inlet

Pivoted sprung tailskid

Interplane strut

Pitot head

Pneumatic rubber tire

Aircraft registration code

Aileron control cable

Axle

Elevator control wire

Aircraft type

Bracing wire

Tire inflation aperture

FRONT VIEW OF LVG CVI, 1917

Lozenge-patterned fabric

Forward-firing machine gun

Exhaust stack

230-HP Benz six-cylinder water-cooled engine

Wooden propeller

Pitot head

Interplane strut

Anti-lift bracing wire

Lift bracing wire

Main fuel tank

Turnbuckle

Gravity-feed fuel tank

Pneumatic rubber tire

Axle

Tailskid

Landing gear strut

Multiple rubber-cord suspension

Fabric lacing

Rib

Rudder

Fixed tail plane

Fabric covering

Elevator

Tail plane attachment

Rudder post

Steel lug

Elevator hinge

Aircraft registration code

Spar

Shock-absorbing spring

Steel V-strut

National marking

Pivoted tailskid

Leading edge

Rib

Trailing edge

HORIZONTAL TAIL OF A BE 2B

Early passenger aircraft

FRONT VIEW OF LOCKHEED ELECTRA, 1934

UNTIL THE 1930s, most passenger aircraft were biplanes, with two pairs of wings and a wooden or metal framework covered with fabric or, sometimes, plywood. Such aircraft were restricted to low speeds and low altitudes because of the drag on their wings. Many had an open cockpit, situated behind or in front of an enclosed—but unpressurized—cabin that carried a maximum of 10 people. The passengers usually sat in wicker chairs that were not bolted to the floor, and the journey could be bumpy when flying through turbulence. Warm clothing, and earplugs to reduce the effects of prolonged noise, were often required. During the 1930s, powerful, streamlined, all-metal monoplanes, such as the Lockheed Electra shown here, became widespread. By 1939, the advent of pressurized cabins allowed fast flights at high altitudes, where there is less turbulence. Flying boats were still necessary on many routes until 1945 because of inadequate runways and the frequency of emergency sea landings. World War II, however, resulted in enough good runways being built for land planes to become standard on all major airline routes.

PASSENGER CABIN TRIM PANELS

SIDE VIEW OF LOCKHEED ELECTRA, 1934

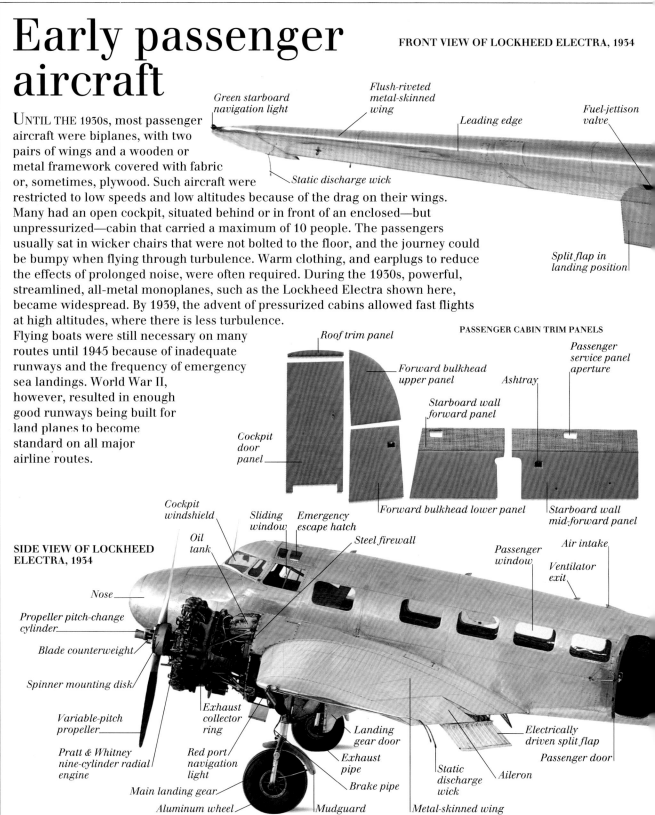

Green starboard navigation light

Flush-riveted metal-skinned wing

Leading edge

Fuel-jettison valve

Static discharge wick

Split flap in landing position

Roof trim panel

Forward bulkhead upper panel

Passenger service panel aperture

Ashtray

Starboard wall forward panel

Cockpit door panel

Forward bulkhead lower panel

Starboard wall mid-forward panel

Cockpit windshield

Sliding window

Emergency escape hatch

Steel firewall

Passenger window

Air intake

Ventilator exit

Oil tank

Nose

Propeller pitch-change cylinder

Blade counterweight

Spinner mounting disk

Variable-pitch propeller

Pratt & Whitney nine-cylinder radial engine

Exhaust collector ring

Red port navigation light

Landing gear door

Exhaust pipe

Electrically driven split flap

Passenger door

Static discharge wick

Aileron

Main landing gear

Brake pipe

Aluminum wheel

Mudguard

Metal-skinned wing

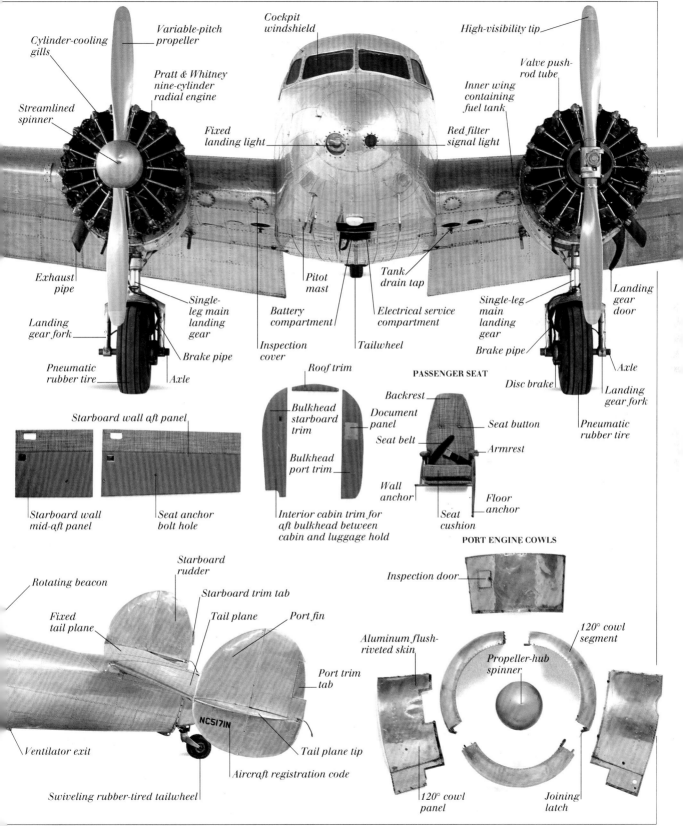

Cylinder-cooling gills

Variable-pitch propeller

Cockpit windshield

High-visibility tip

Pratt & Whitney nine-cylinder radial engine

Valve push-rod tube

Streamlined spinner

Inner wing containing fuel tank

Fixed landing light

Red filter signal light

Exhaust pipe

Single-leg main landing gear

Pitot mast

Tank drain tap

Single-leg main landing gear

Landing gear door

Landing gear fork

Battery compartment

Electrical service compartment

Brake pipe

Axle

Pneumatic rubber tire

Brake pipe

Inspection cover

Tailwheel

Disc brake

Pneumatic rubber tire

Axle

Landing gear fork

PASSENGER SEAT

Roof trim

Bulkhead starboard trim

Backrest

Document panel

Seat button

Starboard wall aft panel

Seat belt

Armrest

Bulkhead port trim

Wall anchor

Floor anchor

Starboard wall mid-aft panel

Seat anchor bolt hole

Interior cabin trim for aft bulkhead between cabin and luggage hold

Seat cushion

PORT ENGINE COWLS

Rotating beacon

Starboard rudder

Inspection door

Starboard trim tab

Fixed tail plane

Tail plane

Port fin

Aluminum flush-riveted skin

120° cowl segment

Propeller-hub spinner

Port trim tab

Ventilator exit

NC5171N

Tail plane tip

Swiveling rubber-tired tailwheel

Aircraft registration code

120° cowl panel

Joining latch

World War II aircraft

WHEN WORLD WAR II began in 1939, air forces had already replaced most of their fabric-skinned biplanes with all-metal stressed-skin monoplanes. Aircraft played a far greater role in military operations during World War II than ever before. The wide range of aircraft duties and the introduction of radar tracking and guidance systems put pressure on designers to improve aircraft performance. The main areas of improvement were speed, range, and engine power. Bombers became larger and more powerful—converting from two to four engines—in order to carry a heavier bomb load; the U.S. B-17 Flying Fortress could carry up to 6 tons of bombs over a distance of about 2,000 miles (3,200 km). Some aircraft increased their range by using drop tanks (fuel tanks that were jettisoned when empty to reduce drag). Fighters needed speed and maneuverability: the Hawker Tempest shown here had a maximum speed of 435 mph (700 kph) and was one of the few Allied aircraft capable of catching the German jet-powered V1 "flying bomb." By 1944, Britain had introduced its first turbojet-powered aircraft, the Gloster Meteor fighter, and Germany had introduced the fastest fighter in the world, the turbojet-powered Me 262, which had a maximum speed of 540 mph (868 kph).

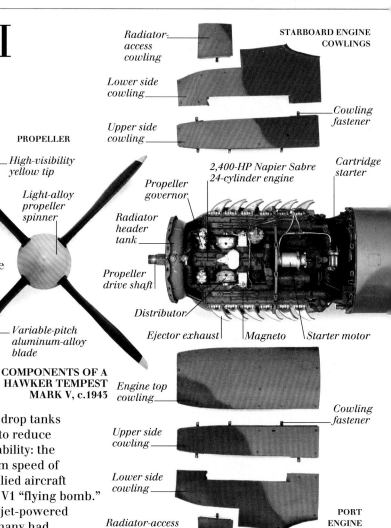

PROPELLER

High-visibility yellow tip

Light-alloy propeller spinner

Variable-pitch aluminum-alloy blade

COMPONENTS OF A HAWKER TEMPEST MARK V, c.1943

STARBOARD ENGINE COWLINGS

Radiator-access cowling

Lower side cowling

Upper side cowling

Cowling fastener

2,400-HP Napier Sabre 24-cylinder engine

Cartridge starter

Propeller governor

Radiator header tank

Propeller drive shaft

Distributor

Ejector exhaust

Magneto

Starter motor

Engine top cowling

Upper side cowling

Lower side cowling

Radiator-access cowling

Cowling fastener

PORT ENGINE COWLINGS

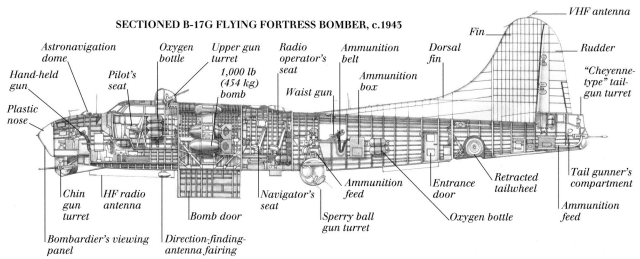

SECTIONED B-17G FLYING FORTRESS BOMBER, c.1943

Astronavigation dome

Hand-held gun

Plastic nose

Pilot's seat

Oxygen bottle

Upper gun turret

1,000 lb (454 kg) bomb

Radio operator's seat

Waist gun

Ammunition belt

Ammunition box

Dorsal fin

Fin

VHF antenna

Rudder

"Cheyenne-type" tail-gun turret

Chin gun turret

HF radio antenna

Bomb door

Navigator's seat

Ammunition feed

Sperry ball gun turret

Entrance door

Oxygen bottle

Retracted tailwheel

Tail gunner's compartment

Ammunition feed

Bombardier's viewing panel

Direction-finding-antenna fairing

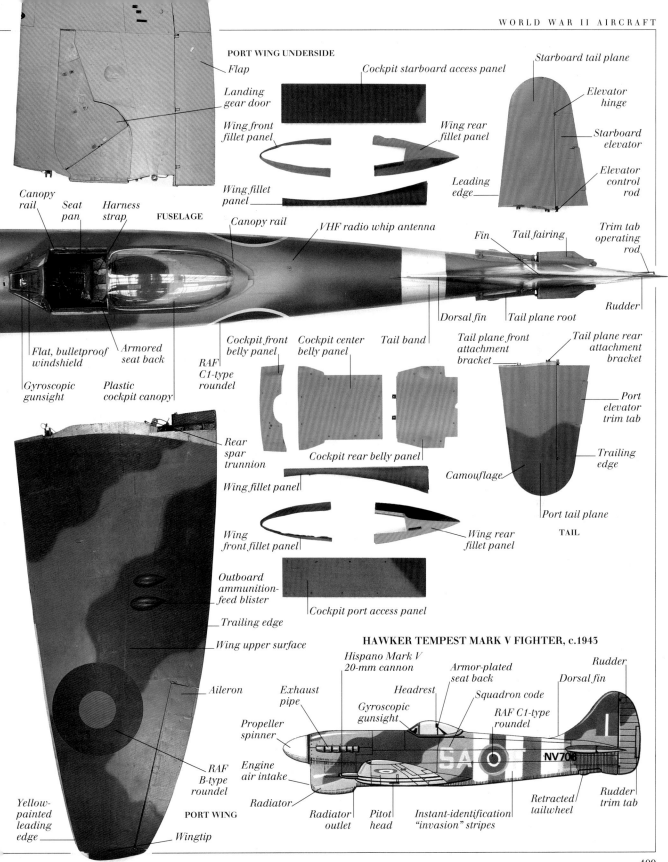

PORT WING UNDERSIDE

Flap

Cockpit starboard access panel

Starboard tail plane

Landing gear door

Elevator hinge

Wing front fillet panel

Wing rear fillet panel

Starboard elevator

Leading edge

Elevator control rod

Wing fillet panel

Canopy rail

Seat pan

Harness strap

FUSELAGE

Canopy rail

VHF radio whip antenna

Fin

Tail fairing

Trim tab operating rod

Dorsal fin

Tail plane root

Rudder

Flat, bulletproof windshield

Armored seat back

Cockpit front belly panel

Cockpit center belly panel

Tail band

Tail plane front attachment bracket

Tail plane rear attachment bracket

Gyroscopic gunsight

Plastic cockpit canopy

RAF C1-type roundel

Port elevator trim tab

Rear spar trunnion

Cockpit rear belly panel

Camouflage

Trailing edge

Wing fillet panel

Wing front fillet panel

Wing rear fillet panel

Port tail plane

TAIL

Outboard ammunition-feed blister

Cockpit port access panel

Trailing edge

Wing upper surface

HAWKER TEMPEST MARK V FIGHTER, c.1943

Aileron

Hispano Mark V 20-mm cannon

Armor-plated seat back

Rudder

Exhaust pipe

Headrest

Squadron code

Dorsal fin

Gyroscopic gunsight

RAF C1-type roundel

Propeller spinner

RAF B-type roundel

Engine air intake

SA

NV70

Yellow-painted leading edge

Radiator

Radiator outlet

Pitot head

Instant-identification "invasion" stripes

Retracted tailwheel

Rudder trim tab

PORT WING

Wingtip

Modern piston aircraft engines

PISTON ENGINES today are used mainly to power the vast numbers of light aircraft and ultralights, as well as crop sprayers and crop dusters, small helicopters, and fire-bombers (which dump water on large fires). Virtually all heavier aircraft are now powered by jet engines. Modern piston aircraft engines work on the same basic principles as the engine used by the Wright brothers in the first powered flight in 1903. However, today's engines are more sophisticated than earlier engines. For example, modern aircraft engines may use a two-stroke or a four-stroke combustion cycle; they may have from one to nine air- or liquid-cooled cylinders, which may be arranged horizontally, in-line, in V formation, or radially; and they may drive the aircraft's propeller either directly or through a reduction gearbox. One of the more unconventional types of modern aircraft engine is the rotary engine shown here, which has a trilobate (three-sided) rotor spinning in a chamber shaped like a fat figure-eight.

MID WEST TWO-STROKE, THREE-CYLINDER ENGINE

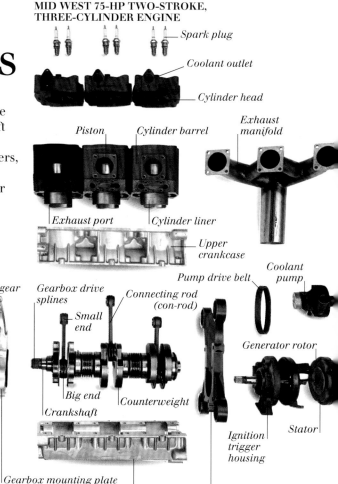

MID WEST 75-HP TWO-STROKE, THREE-CYLINDER ENGINE

Spark plug
Coolant outlet
Cylinder head
Piston
Cylinder barrel
Exhaust manifold
Exhaust port
Cylinder liner
Upper crankcase
Reduction gearbox
Driven gear
Gearbox drive splines
Connecting rod (con-rod)
Pump drive belt
Coolant pump
Small end
Propeller drive flange
Big end
Counterweight
Generator rotor
Torsional vibration damper
Sprag clutch
Crankshaft
Stator
Ignition trigger housing
Gearbox mounting plate
Lower crankcase
Engine mounting plate

ROTOR AND HOUSINGS OF A MID WEST SINGLE-ROTOR ENGINE

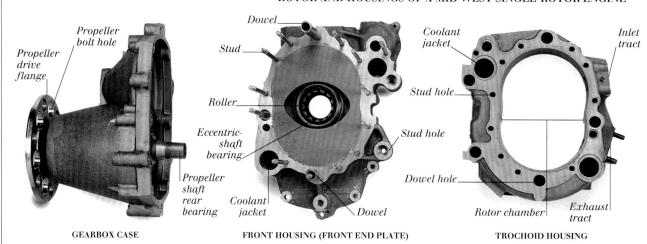

Propeller bolt hole
Propeller drive flange
Dowel
Stud
Coolant jacket
Inlet tract
Roller
Stud hole
Eccentric-shaft bearing
Stud hole
Propeller shaft rear bearing
Coolant jacket
Dowel hole
Dowel
Rotor chamber
Exhaust tract

GEARBOX CASE **FRONT HOUSING (FRONT END PLATE)** **TROCHOID HOUSING**

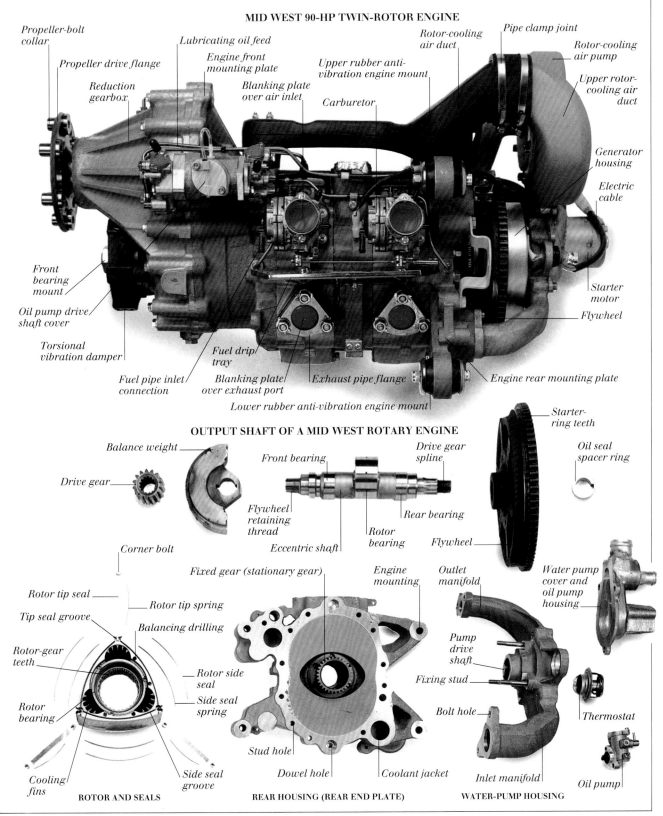

MID WEST 90-HP TWIN-ROTOR ENGINE

Propeller-bolt collar

Propeller drive flange

Reduction gearbox

Lubricating oil feed

Engine front mounting plate

Blanking plate over air inlet

Upper rubber anti-vibration engine mount

Carburetor

Rotor-cooling air duct

Pipe clamp joint

Rotor-cooling air pump

Upper rotor-cooling air duct

Generator housing

Electric cable

Front bearing mount

Oil pump drive shaft cover

Torsional vibration damper

Fuel pipe inlet connection

Fuel drip tray

Blanking plate over exhaust port

Exhaust pipe flange

Lower rubber anti-vibration engine mount

Starter motor

Flywheel

Engine rear mounting plate

OUTPUT SHAFT OF A MID WEST ROTARY ENGINE

Balance weight

Drive gear

Corner bolt

Front bearing

Drive gear spline

Flywheel retaining thread

Eccentric shaft

Rotor bearing

Rear bearing

Flywheel

Starter-ring teeth

Oil seal spacer ring

Rotor tip seal

Tip seal groove

Rotor-gear teeth

Rotor bearing

Cooling fins

Rotor tip spring

Balancing drilling

Rotor side seal

Side seal spring

Side seal groove

Fixed gear (stationary gear)

Engine mounting

Outlet manifold

Pump drive shaft

Fixing stud

Bolt hole

Stud hole

Dowel hole

Coolant jacket

Inlet manifold

Water pump cover and oil pump housing

Thermostat

Oil pump

ROTOR AND SEALS

REAR HOUSING (REAR END PLATE)

WATER-PUMP HOUSING

Modern jetliners 1

BAE 146 JETLINER

MODERN JETLINERS HAVE ENABLED ordinary people to travel to places where once only the wealthy could afford to go. Compared with the first jetliners (which were introduced in the 1940s), modern jetliners are much quieter, burn fuel more efficiently, and produce less air pollution. These advances are largely due to the replacement of turbojet engines with turbofan engines (see pp. 418-419). The greater power of turbofan engines at low speeds enables modern jetliners to carry more fuel and passengers than turbojet aircraft; a modern Boeing 747-400 (popularly known as a "jumbo jet") can fly 400 people for 8,500 miles (13,700 km) without needing to refuel. Jetliners fly at high altitudes, typically cruising at 26,000-36,000 ft (8,000-11,000 m), where they can use fuel efficiently and usually avoid bad weather. The pilot always controls the aircraft during takeoff and landing, but at other times the aircraft is usually controlled by an autopilot. Autopilots are complex onboard mechanisms that detect deviations from an aircraft's route and make appropriate adjustments to the flight controls. Flight decks are also equipped with radar that warns pilots of approaching hazards, such as mountain ranges, bad weather, and other aircraft.

Shoulder nacelle

Engine pylon

Hinged nacelle panel

Nose cowling

Fan duct nozzle

Fire extinguisher discharge indicator

Core-engine jet pipe

Oil-filler door

Push-in door for hand-held fire extinguisher

Drain mast

TURBOFAN ENGINE COWLING

Oil-filler door for integrated-drive generator

STRUCTURAL COMPONENTS OF A BAE 146 JETLINER

FUSELAGE NOSE-SECTION

FUSELAGE MID-SECTION

Electrically heated, birdproof windshield

Side window

Anchor for open door

Rain gutter

Hinge

Peephole

Finger recess

Static air-pressure plate

Forward main door aperture

VHF omni-range and instrument-landing-system antennas

Light-alloy door frame

Passenger window aperture

Main external operating handle

Multiple-pinned lock

Floor level

Radome

Toilet service connector

FORWARD MAIN DOOR

Anchor for open door

Air temperature probe

Stall-warning vane

Pitot head for dynamic air pressure

S02E000760 ESS

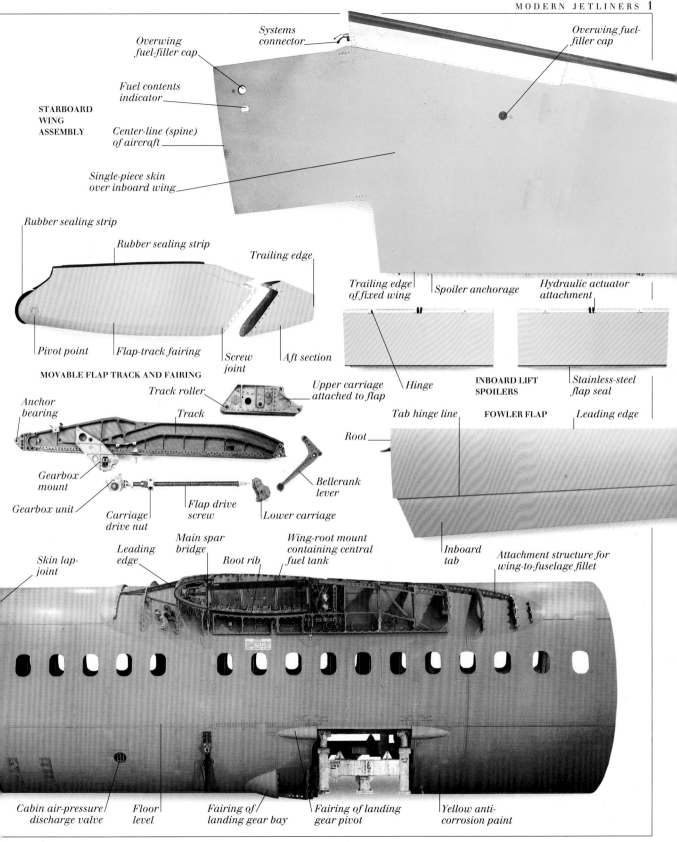

STARBOARD
WING
ASSEMBLY

Overwing
fuel-filler cap

Systems
connector

Overwing fuel-
filler cap

Fuel contents
indicator

Center-line (spine)
of aircraft

Single-piece skin
over inboard wing

Rubber sealing strip

Rubber sealing strip

Trailing edge

Trailing edge
of fixed wing

Spoiler anchorage

Hydraulic actuator
attachment

Pivot point

Flap-track fairing

Screw
joint

Aft section

Hinge

INBOARD LIFT
SPOILERS

Stainless-steel
flap seal

MOVABLE FLAP TRACK AND FAIRING

Track roller

Upper carriage
attached to flap

FOWLER FLAP

Leading edge

Anchor
bearing

Track

Tab hinge line

Root

Gearbox
mount

Bellcrank
lever

Gearbox unit

Carriage
drive nut

Flap drive
screw

Lower carriage

Inboard
tab

Main spar
bridge

Wing-root mount
containing central
fuel tank

Attachment structure for
wing-to-fuselage fillet

Skin lap-
joint

Leading
edge

Root rib

Cabin air-pressure
discharge valve

Floor
level

Fairing of
landing gear bay

Fairing of landing
gear pivot

Yellow anti-
corrosion paint

Modern jetliners 2

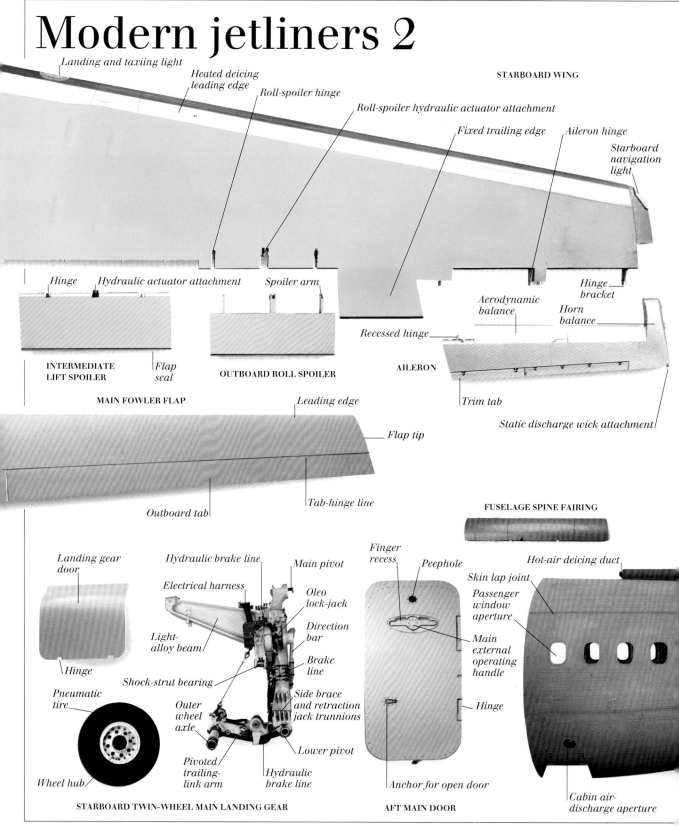

Landing and taxiing light

Heated deicing leading edge

Roll-spoiler hinge

Roll-spoiler hydraulic actuator attachment

STARBOARD WING

Fixed trailing edge

Aileron hinge

Starboard navigation light

Hinge

Hydraulic actuator attachment

Spoiler arm

Hinge bracket

Aerodynamic balance

Horn balance

Recessed hinge

INTERMEDIATE LIFT SPOILER

Flap seal

OUTBOARD ROLL SPOILER

AILERON

Trim tab

MAIN FOWLER FLAP

Leading edge

Flap tip

Static discharge wick attachment

FUSELAGE SPINE FAIRING

Outboard tab

Tab-hinge line

Landing gear door

Hydraulic brake line

Main pivot

Finger recess

Peephole

Hot-air deicing duct

Skin lap joint

Electrical harness

Oleo lock-jack

Passenger window aperture

Light-alloy beam

Direction bar

Main external operating handle

Shock-strut bearing

Brake line

Pneumatic tire

Outer wheel axle

Side brace and retraction jack trunnions

Hinge

Hinge

Wheel hub

Pivoted trailing-link arm

Hydraulic brake line

Lower pivot

Anchor for open door

Cabin air-discharge aperture

STARBOARD TWIN-WHEEL MAIN LANDING GEAR

AFT MAIN DOOR

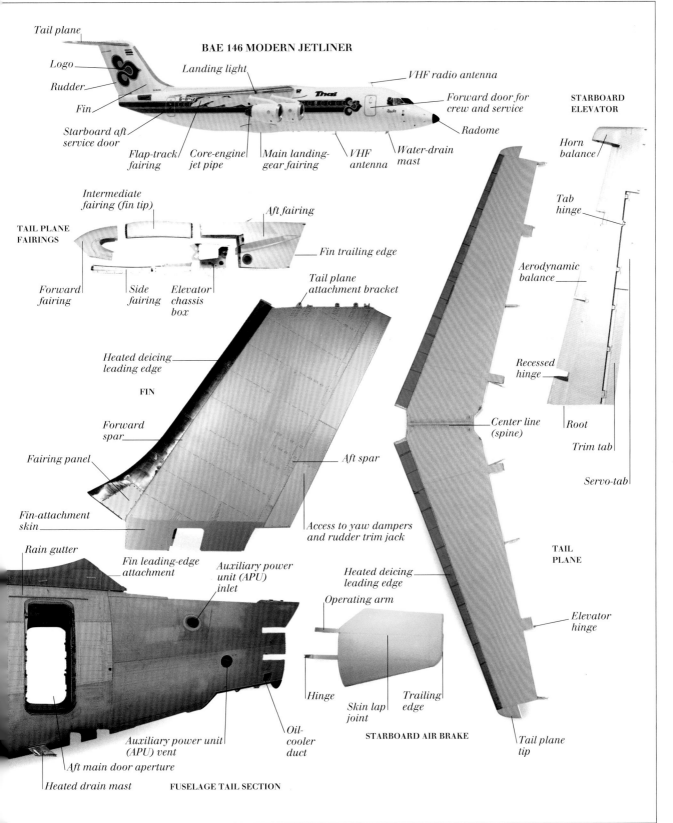

BAE 146 MODERN JETLINER

Tail plane

Logo

Rudder

Fin

Starboard aft service door

Landing light

Flap-track fairing

Core-engine jet pipe

Main landing-gear fairing

VHF antenna

VHF radio antenna

Forward door for crew and service

Radome

Water-drain mast

STARBOARD ELEVATOR

Horn balance

Tab hinge

Aerodynamic balance

Recessed hinge

Root

Trim tab

Servo-tab

TAIL PLANE FAIRINGS

Intermediate fairing (fin tip)

Aft fairing

Fin trailing edge

Forward fairing

Side fairing

Elevator chassis box

Tail plane attachment bracket

Center line (spine)

FIN

Heated deicing leading edge

Forward spar

Aft spar

Fairing panel

Fin-attachment skin

Access to yaw dampers and rudder trim jack

TAIL PLANE

Rain gutter

Fin leading-edge attachment

Auxiliary power unit (APU) inlet

Heated deicing leading edge

Operating arm

Elevator hinge

Auxiliary power unit (APU) vent

Oil-cooler duct

Hinge

Skin lap joint

Trailing edge

Tail plane tip

Aft main door aperture

Heated drain mast

FUSELAGE TAIL SECTION

STARBOARD AIR BRAKE

Supersonic jetliners

SUPERSONIC AIRCRAFT FLY FASTER than the speed of sound (Mach 1). There are many supersonic military aircraft, but only two supersonic passenger-carrying aircraft (also called SSTs, or supersonic transports) have been produced: the Russian Tu-144, and the Concorde, produced jointly by Britain and France. The Tu-144 had a greater maximum speed than the Concorde but was withdrawn in 1978, after only seven months in service. The Concorde has remained in service since 1976. It features many innovations, including a droop nose, which is lowered during takeoff and landing to aid visibility from the cockpit, and the pumping of fuel between forward and aft trim tanks to help stabilize the aircraft. The Concorde has a narrow fuselage and short-span wings to reduce drag during supersonic flight. Its noisy turbojet engines with afterburners enable it to carry 100 passengers at a cruising speed of Mach 2 at 50,000-60,000 ft (15,000-18,000 m). Once an aircraft is flying faster than Mach 1, it produces a continuous air-pressure wave, which is heard as a "sonic boom."

COMPUTER-DESIGNED SST

Strake

Fin

Standby pitot head

Inboard elevon-actuator fairing

Nose gear leg

Starboard outboard engine air intake

FRONT VIEW OF CONCORDE

Toilets

Electrothermal deicing panel

Starboard forward trim tank

Overhead luggage compartments

Passenger accommodation

Seat attachment rail

OVERHEAD VIEW OF CONCORDE

Underfloor air-conditioning duct

Life raft

VHF antenna

Wardrobe

Variable nozzle

Leading edge

Forward galley

Additional crew's seat

Aluminum-alloy layers and insulation

Flight engineer's seat

Erosion-resistant radome

Cockpit windshield

Retractable visor

"A" frame

Lateral bracing strut

Telescopic strut

Port forward trim tank

Nose gear leg

Steering actuator

Plug-type passenger door

Nose gear door

Multi-ply high-pressure tire

Machined skin panel

Standby flight-control hydraulic jack

Captain's seat

Upper rudder

Fin

Dorsal fin

Emergency exit

Weather radar

Visor jack

Droop-nose hinge

Cockpit air-conditioning duct

Pivoted retractable frame

G-BOAG

Tail cone

Aft door

Elevon (combined elevator and aileron)

Hot-section steel and titanium skin

Engine cowling

Landing gear door

Bogie main landing gear

SECTIONED VIEW OF CONCORDE

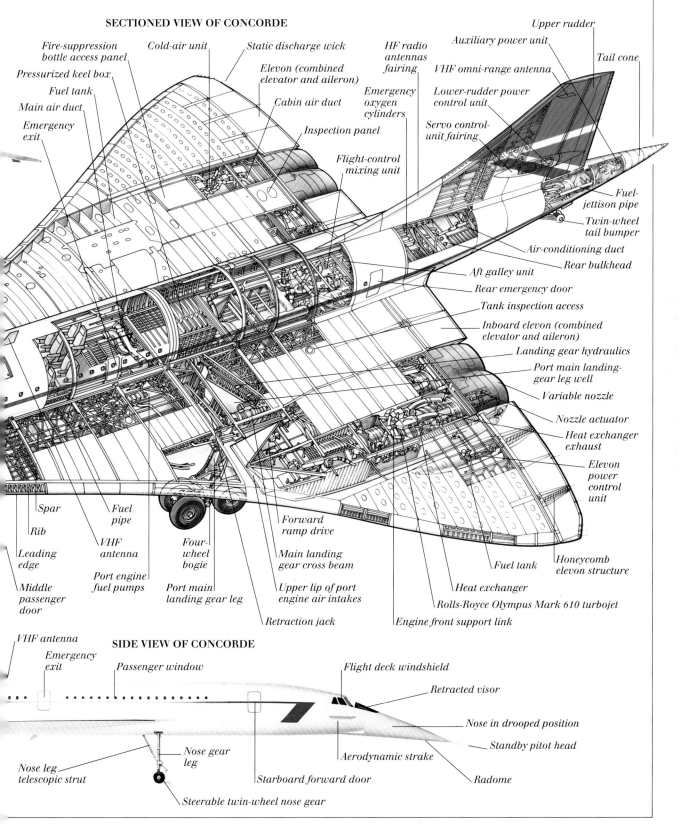

Fire-suppression bottle access panel

Cold-air unit

Static discharge wick

Elevon (combined elevator and aileron)

HF radio antennas fairing

Upper rudder

Auxiliary power unit

Tail cone

VHF omni-range antenna

Pressurized keel box

Fuel tank

Main air duct

Emergency exit

Cabin air duct

Emergency oxygen cylinders

Lower-rudder power control unit

Inspection panel

Servo control-unit fairing

Flight-control mixing unit

Fuel-jettison pipe

Twin-wheel tail bumper

Air-conditioning duct

Rear bulkhead

Aft galley unit

Rear emergency door

Tank inspection access

Inboard elevon (combined elevator and aileron)

Landing gear hydraulics

Port main landing-gear leg well

Variable nozzle

Nozzle actuator

Heat exchanger exhaust

Elevon power control unit

Spar

Rib

Fuel pipe

Leading edge

VHF antenna

Four-wheel bogie

Forward ramp drive

Main landing gear cross beam

Fuel tank

Honeycomb elevon structure

Middle passenger door

Port engine fuel pumps

Port main landing gear leg

Upper lip of port engine air intakes

Heat exchanger

Rolls-Royce Olympus Mark 610 turbojet

Retraction jack

Engine front support link

VHF antenna

SIDE VIEW OF CONCORDE

Emergency exit

Passenger window

Flight deck windshield

Retracted visor

Nose in drooped position

Standby pitot head

Nose gear leg

Aerodynamic strake

Nose leg telescopic strut

Starboard forward door

Radome

Steerable twin-wheel nose gear

Jet engines

JET ENGINES ARE USED BY MOST MILITARY and heavy aircraft and by many helicopters. The simplest type of jet engine, or gas turbine, is the turbojet. It works by continuously burning a mixture of fuel and air in a combustion chamber to produce a jet of hot exhaust gas that is expelled through a nozzle to produce thrust. The hot gas also spins turbine blades which, in turn, spin the blades of an air compressor; the compressor forces air into the combustion chamber. Many of the fastest aircraft use turbojets, with additional booster units called afterburners, but their use is restricted by their high noise emission. Most jetliners use quieter turbofan jet engines. An enormous fan, driven by a low-pressure turbine, feeds some air into the compressor but feeds most of it through bypass ducts to join the exhaust jetstream in the tail cone. The bypass stream produces most of the thrust. Many smaller, propeller-driven aircraft use turboprop jet engines, in which the engine powers a propeller.

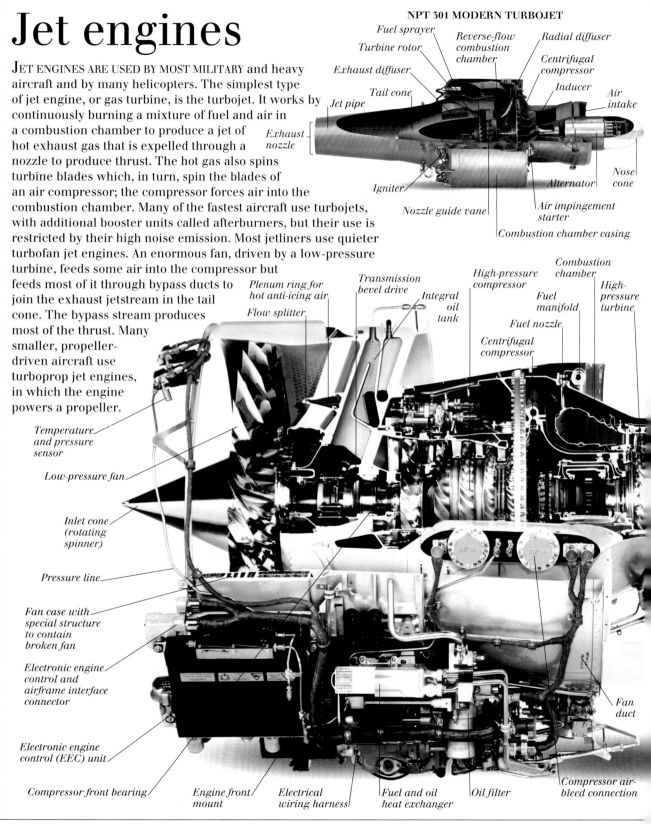

NPT 301 MODERN TURBOJET

Fuel sprayer
Turbine rotor
Reverse-flow combustion chamber
Radial diffuser
Centrifugal compressor
Exhaust diffuser
Inducer
Air intake
Tail cone
Jet pipe
Exhaust nozzle
Nose cone
Igniter
Alternator
Nozzle guide vane
Air impingement starter
Combustion chamber casing

Plenum ring for hot anti-icing air
Transmission bevel drive
High-pressure compressor
Combustion chamber
Flow splitter
Integral oil tank
Fuel manifold
High-pressure turbine
Fuel nozzle
Centrifugal compressor
Temperature and pressure sensor
Low-pressure fan
Inlet cone (rotating spinner)
Pressure line
Fan case with special structure to contain broken fan
Electronic engine control and airframe interface connector
Fan duct
Electronic engine control (EEC) unit
Compressor front bearing
Engine front mount
Electrical wiring harness
Fuel and oil heat exchanger
Oil filter
Compressor air-bleed connection

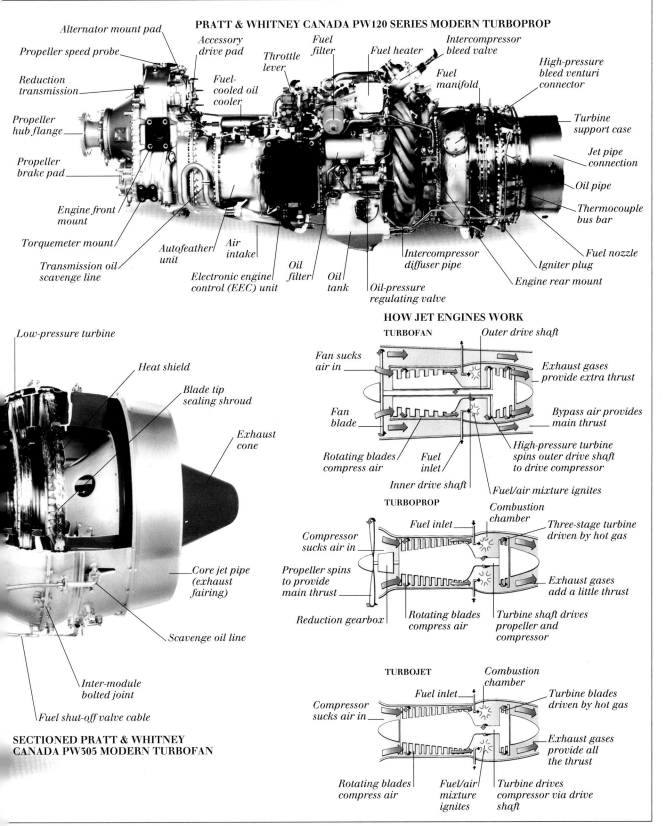

PRATT & WHITNEY CANADA PW120 SERIES MODERN TURBOPROP

Alternator mount pad

Propeller speed probe

Reduction transmission

Propeller hub flange

Propeller brake pad

Engine front mount

Torquemeter mount

Transmission oil scavenge line

Accessory drive pad

Throttle lever

Fuel-cooled oil cooler

Autofeather unit

Air intake

Electronic engine control (EEC) unit

Oil filter

Oil tank

Oil-pressure regulating valve

Fuel filter

Fuel heater

Fuel manifold

Oil filter

Intercompressor bleed valve

Intercompressor diffuser pipe

High-pressure bleed venturi connector

Turbine support case

Jet pipe connection

Oil pipe

Thermocouple bus bar

Fuel nozzle

Igniter plug

Engine rear mount

HOW JET ENGINES WORK

TURBOFAN

Fan sucks air in

Fan blade

Rotating blades compress air

Outer drive shaft

Fuel inlet

Inner drive shaft

Exhaust gases provide extra thrust

Bypass air provides main thrust

High-pressure turbine spins outer drive shaft to drive compressor

Fuel/air mixture ignites

TURBOPROP

Compressor sucks air in

Propeller spins to provide main thrust

Reduction gearbox

Fuel inlet

Rotating blades compress air

Combustion chamber

Three-stage turbine driven by hot gas

Exhaust gases add a little thrust

Turbine shaft drives propeller and compressor

TURBOJET

Compressor sucks air in

Rotating blades compress air

Fuel inlet

Fuel/air mixture ignites

Combustion chamber

Turbine blades driven by hot gas

Exhaust gases provide all the thrust

Turbine drives compressor via drive shaft

Low-pressure turbine

Heat shield

Blade tip sealing shroud

Exhaust cone

Core jet pipe (exhaust fairing)

Scavenge oil line

Inter-module bolted joint

Fuel shut-off valve cable

SECTIONED PRATT & WHITNEY CANADA PW305 MODERN TURBOFAN

419

Modern military aircraft

MODERN MILITARY AIRCRAFT ARE AMONG THE MOST SOPHISTICATED and expensive products of the 20th century. Fighters need computer-operated controls for maneuverability, powerful engines, and effective air-to-air weapons. Most modern fighters also have guided missiles, radar, and passive, infrared sensors. These developments enable today's fighters to engage in combat with adversaries who are outside visual range. Bombers carry a large weapon load and enough fuel for long-range flights. A few military aircraft, such as the Tornado and the F-14 Tomcat, have variable-sweep ("swing") wings. During takeoff and landing their wings are fully extended, but for high-speed flight and low-level attacks the wings are pivoted fully back. A recent development is the "stealth" bomber, which is designed to absorb or deflect enemy radar in order to remain undetected. Earlier bombers, such as the Tornado, use terrain-following radars to fly so close to the ground that they avoid enemy radar detection.

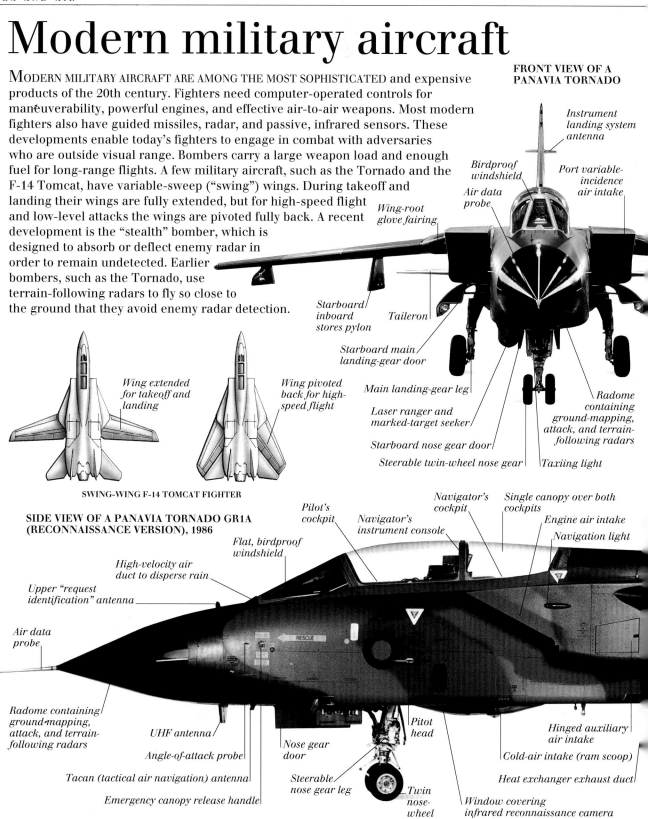

FRONT VIEW OF A PANAVIA TORNADO

Instrument landing system antenna

Birdproof windshield

Port variable-incidence air intake

Air data probe

Wing-root glove fairing

Starboard inboard stores pylon

Taileron

Starboard main landing-gear door

Main landing-gear leg

Laser ranger and marked-target seeker

Starboard nose gear door

Steerable twin-wheel nose gear

Radome containing ground-mapping, attack, and terrain-following radars

Taxiing light

Wing extended for takeoff and landing

Wing pivoted back for high-speed flight

SWING-WING F-14 TOMCAT FIGHTER

SIDE VIEW OF A PANAVIA TORNADO GR1A (RECONNAISSANCE VERSION), 1986

Pilot's cockpit

Navigator's cockpit

Navigator's instrument console

Single canopy over both cockpits

Engine air intake

Navigation light

Flat, birdproof windshield

High-velocity air duct to disperse rain

Upper "request identification" antenna

Air data probe

Radome containing ground-mapping, attack, and terrain-following radars

UHF antenna

Angle-of-attack probe

Tacan (tactical air navigation) antenna

Emergency canopy release handle

Nose gear door

Steerable nose gear leg

Pitot head

Twin nose-wheel

Hinged auxiliary air intake

Cold-air intake (ram scoop)

Heat exchanger exhaust duct

Window covering infrared reconnaissance camera

NORTHROP B-2 ("STEALTH" BOMBER), 1989

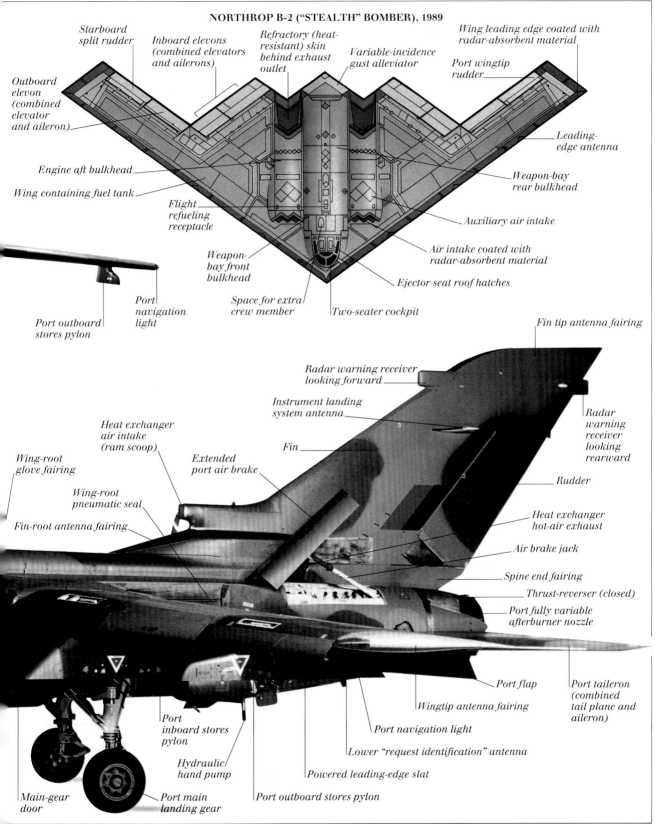

Starboard split rudder

Inboard elevons (combined elevators and ailerons)

Refractory (heat-resistant) skin behind exhaust outlet

Variable-incidence gust alleviator

Wing leading edge coated with radar-absorbent material

Port wingtip rudder

Outboard elevon (combined elevator and aileron)

Leading-edge antenna

Engine aft bulkhead

Wing containing fuel tank

Weapon-bay rear bulkhead

Flight refueling receptacle

Weapon-bay front bulkhead

Auxiliary air intake

Air intake coated with radar-absorbent material

Ejector-seat roof hatches

Space for extra crew member

Two-seater cockpit

Port navigation light

Port outboard stores pylon

Fin tip antenna fairing

Radar warning receiver looking forward

Instrument landing system antenna

Fin

Extended port air brake

Heat exchanger air intake (ram scoop)

Wing-root glove fairing

Wing-root pneumatic seal

Fin-root antenna fairing

Radar warning receiver looking rearward

Rudder

Heat exchanger hot-air exhaust

Air brake jack

Spine end fairing

Thrust-reverser (closed)

Port fully variable afterburner nozzle

Port flap

Port taileron (combined tail plane and aileron)

Wingtip antenna fairing

Port navigation light

Lower "request identification" antenna

Powered leading-edge slat

Port inboard stores pylon

Hydraulic hand pump

Main-gear door

Port main landing gear

Port outboard stores pylon

421

Helicopters

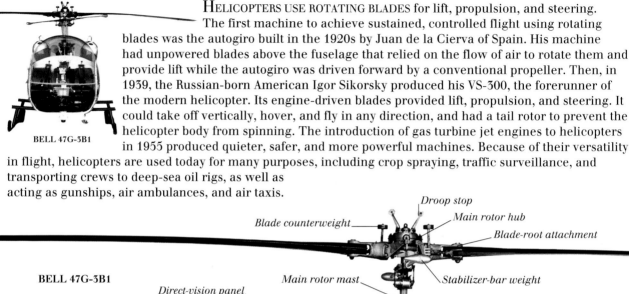

BELL 47G-3B1

HELICOPTERS USE ROTATING BLADES for lift, propulsion, and steering. The first machine to achieve sustained, controlled flight using rotating blades was the autogiro built in the 1920s by Juan de la Cierva of Spain. His machine had unpowered blades above the fuselage that relied on the flow of air to rotate them and provide lift while the autogiro was driven forward by a conventional propeller. Then, in 1939, the Russian-born American Igor Sikorsky produced his VS-300, the forerunner of the modern helicopter. Its engine-driven blades provided lift, propulsion, and steering. It could take off vertically, hover, and fly in any direction, and had a tail rotor to prevent the helicopter body from spinning. The introduction of gas turbine jet engines to helicopters in 1955 produced quieter, safer, and more powerful machines. Because of their versatility in flight, helicopters are used today for many purposes, including crop spraying, traffic surveillance, and transporting crews to deep-sea oil rigs, as well as acting as gunships, air ambulances, and air taxis.

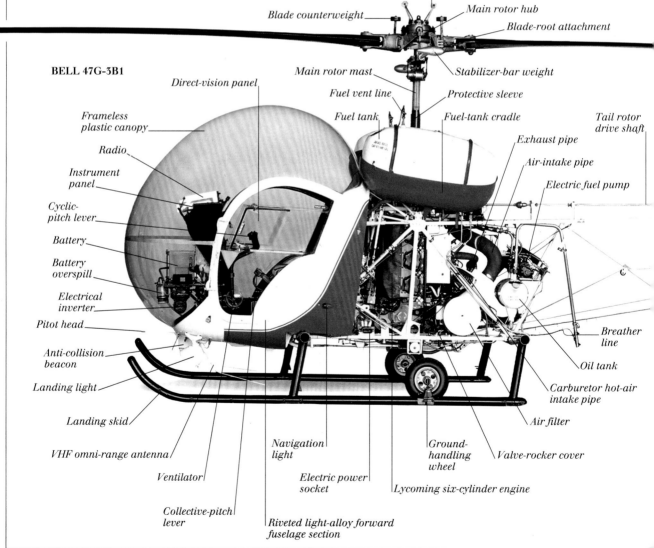

BELL 47G-3B1

Droop stop

Blade counterweight

Main rotor hub

Blade-root attachment

Direct-vision panel

Main rotor mast

Stabilizer-bar weight

Frameless plastic canopy

Fuel vent line

Protective sleeve

Fuel tank

Fuel-tank cradle

Tail rotor drive shaft

Radio

Exhaust pipe

Instrument panel

Air-intake pipe

Cyclic-pitch lever

Electric fuel pump

Battery

Battery overspill

Electrical inverter

Pitot head

Breather line

Anti-collision beacon

Oil tank

Landing light

Carburetor hot-air intake pipe

Landing skid

Air filter

VHF omni-range antenna

Navigation light

Ground-handling wheel

Valve-rocker cover

Ventilator

Electric power socket

Lycoming six-cylinder engine

Collective-pitch lever

Riveted light-alloy forward fuselage section

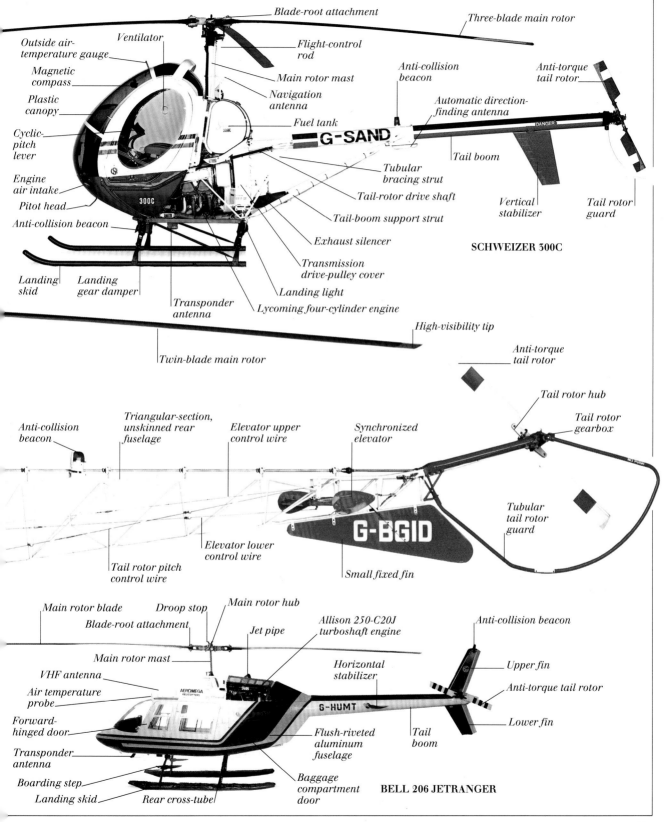

Blade-root attachment

Three-blade main rotor

Outside air-temperature gauge

Ventilator

Flight-control rod

Anti-collision beacon

Anti-torque tail rotor

Magnetic compass

Main rotor mast

Automatic direction-finding antenna

Plastic canopy

Navigation antenna

Cyclic-pitch lever

Fuel tank

G-SAND

DANGER

Engine air intake

Tubular bracing strut

Tail boom

Pitot head

Tail-rotor drive shaft

Anti-collision beacon

Tail-boom support strut

Vertical stabilizer

Tail rotor guard

Exhaust silencer

SCHWEIZER 300C

Transmission drive-pulley cover

Landing skid

Landing gear damper

Landing light

Transponder antenna

Lycoming four-cylinder engine

High-visibility tip

Twin-blade main rotor

Anti-torque tail rotor

Tail rotor hub

Anti-collision beacon

Triangular-section, unskinned rear fuselage

Elevator upper control wire

Synchronized elevator

Tail rotor gearbox

Tubular tail rotor guard

G-BGID

Elevator lower control wire

Tail rotor pitch control wire

Small fixed fin

Main rotor blade

Droop stop

Main rotor hub

Allison 250-C20J turboshaft engine

Anti-collision beacon

Blade-root attachment

Jet pipe

Main rotor mast

Horizontal stabilizer

Upper fin

VHF antenna

Anti-torque tail rotor

Air temperature probe

G-HUMT

Lower fin

Forward-hinged door

AEROMEGA HELICOPTERS

Flush-riveted aluminum fuselage

Tail boom

Transponder antenna

Boarding step

Baggage compartment door

BELL 206 JETRANGER

Landing skid

Rear cross-tube

Light aircraft

LIGHT AIRCRAFT, SUCH AS THE ARV SUPER 2 shown here, are small, lightweight, and of simple construction. More than a million have been built since World War I, mainly for recreational use by private owners. Virtually all light aircraft have piston engines, most of which are air-cooled, although some are liquid-cooled. Open cockpits, almost universal in the 1920s, have now been replaced by enclosed cabins. The cabins of high-wing aircraft have one or two doors, while those of low-wing aircraft usually have a sliding or hinged canopy. Most modern light aircraft are made of aluminum alloy, although some are made of wood or of fiber-reinforced materials. Light aircraft today also usually have navigational instruments, an electrical system, cabin heating, wheel brakes, and a two-way radio.

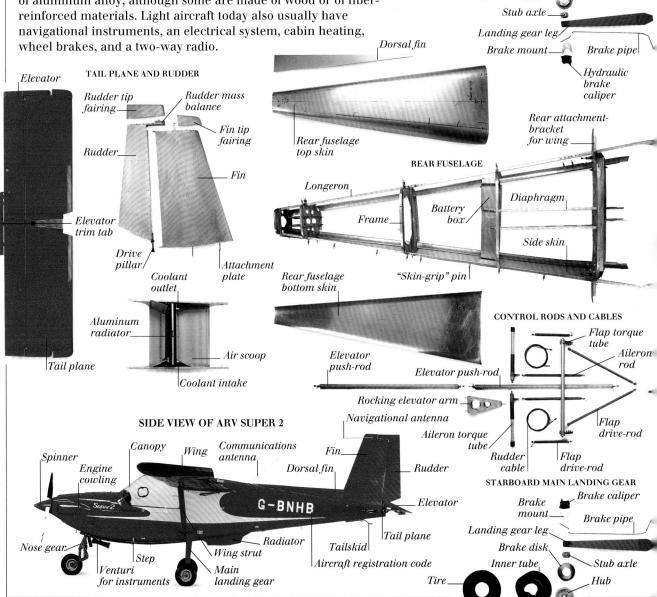

Port wingtip

Aileron mass balance

Aileron torque tube

Port aileron

PORT MAIN LANDING GEAR

Inner tube

Hub

Tire

Brake disk

Stub axle

Landing gear leg

Brake mount

Brake pipe

Hydraulic brake caliper

Dorsal fin

TAIL PLANE AND RUDDER

Elevator

Rudder tip fairing

Rudder mass balance

Fin tip fairing

Rudder

Fin

Rear fuselage top skin

Rear attachment-bracket for wing

REAR FUSELAGE

Longeron

Frame

Battery box

Diaphragm

Side skin

Elevator trim tab

Drive pillar

Attachment plate

Rear fuselage bottom skin

"Skin-grip" pin

Tail plane

Coolant outlet

Aluminum radiator

Air scoop

Coolant intake

Elevator push-rod

Elevator push-rod

Rocking elevator arm

Navigational antenna

Aileron torque tube

CONTROL RODS AND CABLES

Flap torque tube

Aileron rod

Flap drive-rod

Rudder cable

Flap drive-rod

SIDE VIEW OF ARV SUPER 2

Spinner

Engine cowling

Canopy

Wing

Communications antenna

Fin

Dorsal fin

Rudder

Elevator

Super 2

G-BNHB

Radiator

Tail plane

Nose gear

Step

Venturi for instruments

Wing strut

Main landing gear

Tailskid

Aircraft registration code

STARBOARD MAIN LANDING GEAR

Brake caliper

Brake mount

Brake pipe

Landing gear leg

Brake disk

Inner tube

Stub axle

Tire

Hub

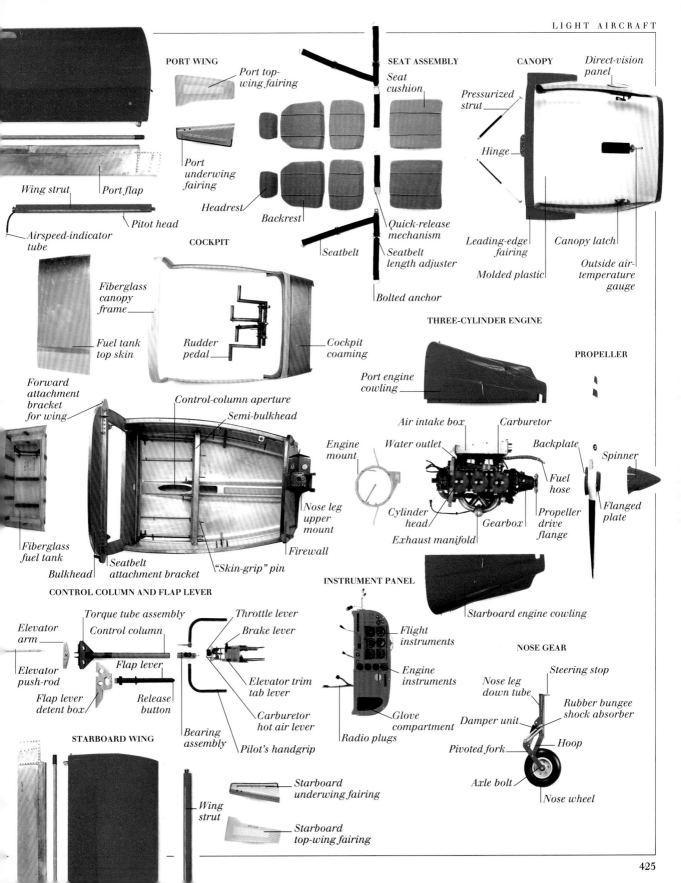

PORT WING

Port top-wing fairing

Port underwing fairing

Headrest

Backrest

Wing strut

Port flap

Pitot head

Airspeed-indicator tube

SEAT ASSEMBLY

Seat cushion

Seatbelt

Quick-release mechanism

Seatbelt length adjuster

Bolted anchor

CANOPY

Direct-vision panel

Pressurized strut

Hinge

Leading-edge fairing

Canopy latch

Molded plastic

Outside air-temperature gauge

COCKPIT

Fiberglass canopy frame

Fuel tank top skin

Rudder pedal

Cockpit coaming

Forward attachment bracket for wing

Control-column aperture

Semi-bulkhead

Engine mount

Nose leg upper mount

Firewall

"Skin-grip" pin

Fiberglass fuel tank

Bulkhead

Seatbelt attachment bracket

THREE-CYLINDER ENGINE

Port engine cowling

PROPELLER

Air intake box

Water outlet

Carburetor

Backplate

Spinner

Fuel hose

Cylinder head

Gearbox

Propeller drive flange

Flanged plate

Exhaust manifold

Starboard engine cowling

CONTROL COLUMN AND FLAP LEVER

Torque tube assembly

Control column

Elevator arm

Flap lever

Elevator push-rod

Flap lever detent box

Release button

Bearing assembly

Throttle lever

Brake lever

Elevator trim tab lever

Carburetor hot air lever

Pilot's handgrip

INSTRUMENT PANEL

Flight instruments

Engine instruments

Glove compartment

Radio plugs

NOSE GEAR

Steering stop

Nose leg down tube

Rubber bungee shock absorber

Damper unit

Hoop

Pivoted fork

Axle bolt

Nose wheel

STARBOARD WING

Wing strut

Starboard underwing fairing

Starboard top-wing fairing

Gliders, hang gliders, and ultralights

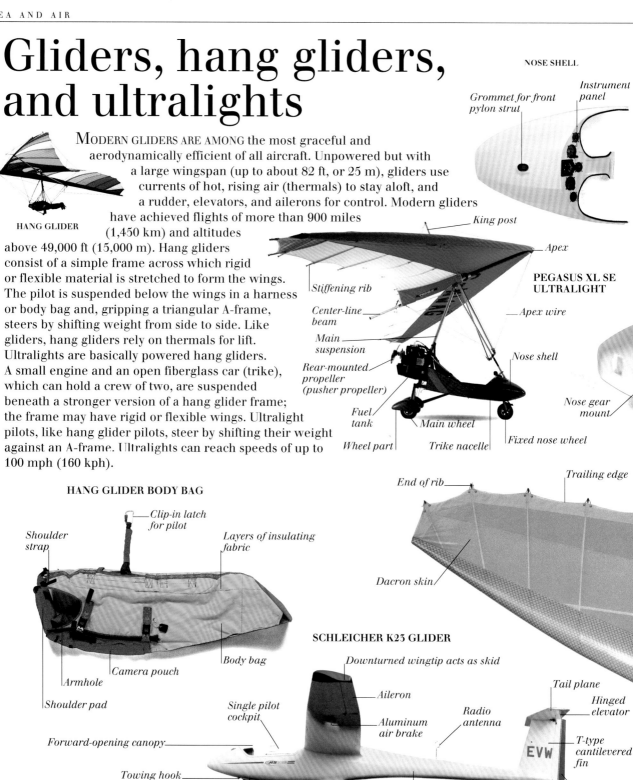

MODERN GLIDERS ARE AMONG the most graceful and aerodynamically efficient of all aircraft. Unpowered but with a large wingspan (up to about 82 ft, or 25 m), gliders use currents of hot, rising air (thermals) to stay aloft, and a rudder, elevators, and ailerons for control. Modern gliders have achieved flights of more than 900 miles (1,450 km) and altitudes above 49,000 ft (15,000 m). Hang gliders consist of a simple frame across which rigid or flexible material is stretched to form the wings. The pilot is suspended below the wings in a harness or body bag and, gripping a triangular A-frame, steers by shifting weight from side to side. Like gliders, hang gliders rely on thermals for lift. Ultralights are basically powered hang gliders. A small engine and an open fiberglass car (trike), which can hold a crew of two, are suspended beneath a stronger version of a hang glider frame; the frame may have rigid or flexible wings. Ultralight pilots, like hang glider pilots, steer by shifting their weight against an A-frame. Ultralights can reach speeds of up to 100 mph (160 kph).

HANG GLIDER

NOSE SHELL

Grommet for front pylon strut

Instrument panel

King post

Apex

PEGASUS XL SE ULTRALIGHT

Apex wire

Stiffening rib

Center-line beam

Main suspension

Rear-mounted propeller (pusher propeller)

Fuel tank

Wheel part

Main wheel

Trike nacelle

Nose shell

Nose gear mount

Fixed nose wheel

HANG GLIDER BODY BAG

Shoulder strap

Clip-in latch for pilot

Layers of insulating fabric

Armhole

Camera pouch

Body bag

Shoulder pad

End of rib

Trailing edge

Dacron skin

SCHLEICHER K23 GLIDER

Downturned wingtip acts as skid

Single pilot cockpit

Aileron

Aluminum air brake

Radio antenna

Tail plane

Hinged elevator

Forward-opening canopy

Towing hook

Nose wheel

Nonretractable main wheel

Fuselage of fiberglass and foam layers

T-type cantilevered fin

Rudder

Tailwheel

EVW

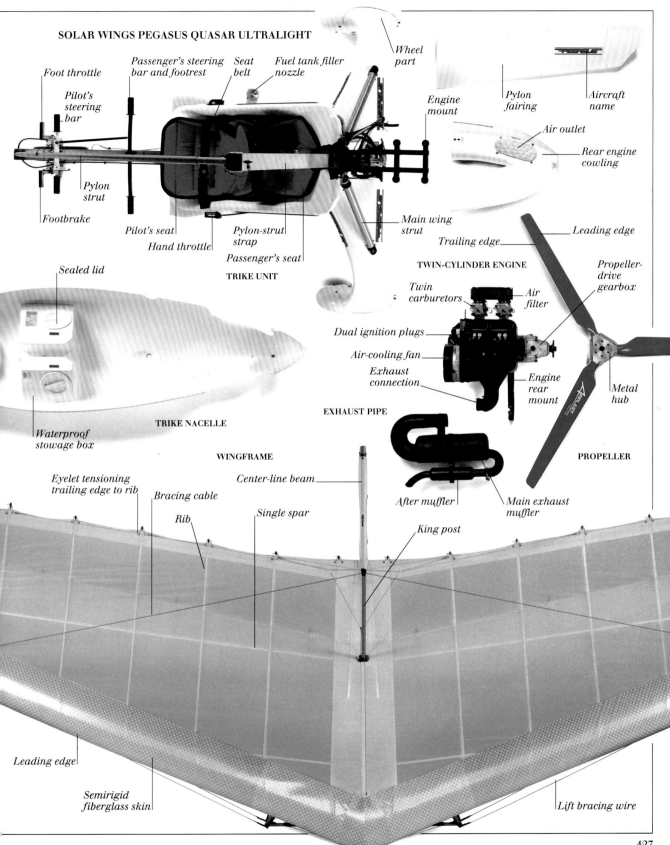

SOLAR WINGS PEGASUS QUASAR ULTRALIGHT

Foot throttle

Pilot's steering bar

Passenger's steering bar and footrest

Seat belt

Fuel tank filler nozzle

Wheel part

Engine mount

Pylon fairing

Aircraft name

Air outlet

Rear engine cowling

Pylon strut

Footbrake

Pilot's seat

Hand throttle

Pylon-strut strap

Passenger's seat

Main wing strut

TRIKE UNIT

Sealed lid

Waterproof stowage box

TRIKE NACELLE

WINGFRAME

TWIN-CYLINDER ENGINE

Twin carburetors

Air filter

Dual ignition plugs

Air-cooling fan

Exhaust connection

Engine rear mount

Leading edge

Trailing edge

Propeller-drive gearbox

Metal hub

EXHAUST PIPE

After muffler

Main exhaust muffler

PROPELLER

Eyelet tensioning trailing edge to rib

Bracing cable

Rib

Center-line beam

Single spar

King post

Leading edge

Semirigid fiberglass skin

Lift bracing wire

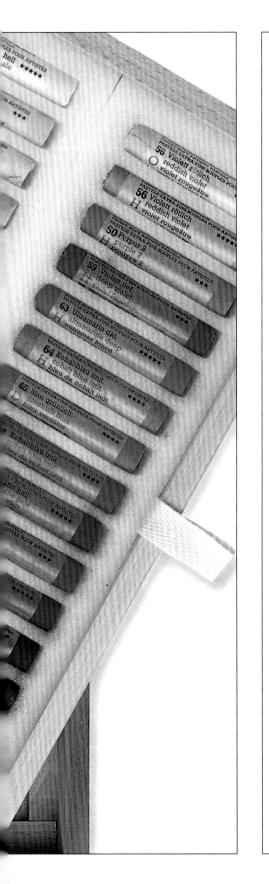

THE
VISUAL ARTS

Drawing

DRAWINGS CAN BE FINISHED WORKS OF ART, or preparatory studies for paintings and other visual arts. They can be made using a wide variety of drawing instruments such as pencils, graphite sticks, chalks, charcoal, pens and inks, and silver wires. The most common drawing instrument is the graphite pencil. A graphite pencil consists of a thin rod of graphite mixed with clay, encased in wood. Charcoal is one of the oldest drawing instruments. It is produced by firing twigs of willow, vine, or other woods at high temperatures in airtight containers. Erasers can be used to rub out marks made by drawing materials such as graphite pencils or charcoal, or to achieve a particular effect—such as smudging. Fixative is often applied—using a mouth diffuser or aerosol spray fixative—to prevent smudging once a drawing is finished. Silver lines can be produced by drawing silver wire across specially prepared paper— a technique known as silverpoint. The lines are permanent and cannot be erased. In time the silver lines oxidize and turn brown.

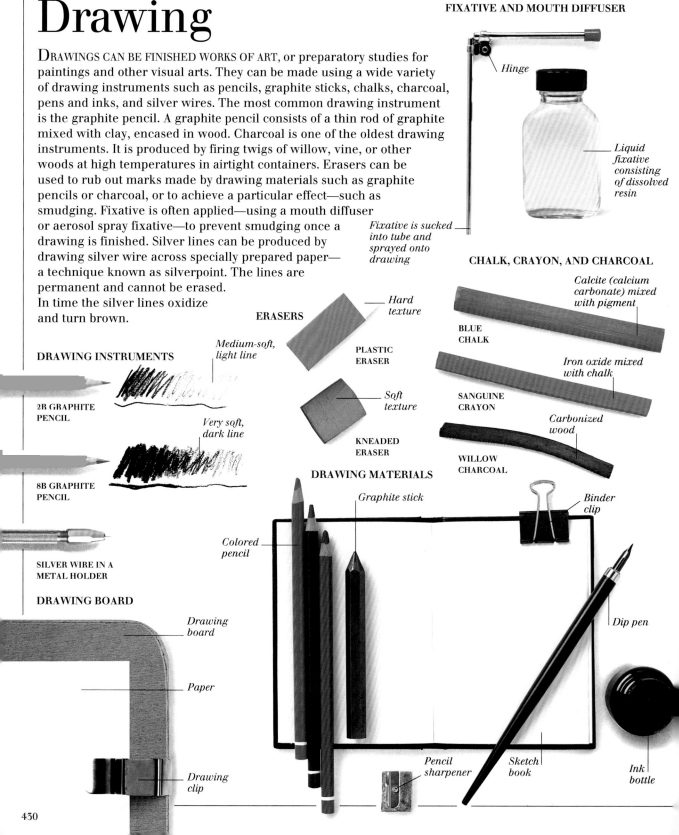

FIXATIVE AND MOUTH DIFFUSER

Hinge

Liquid fixative consisting of dissolved resin

Fixative is sucked into tube and sprayed onto drawing

CHALK, CRAYON, AND CHARCOAL

Calcite (calcium carbonate) mixed with pigment

BLUE CHALK

Iron oxide mixed with chalk

SANGUINE CRAYON

Carbonized wood

WILLOW CHARCOAL

ERASERS

Hard texture

PLASTIC ERASER

Medium-soft, light line

Soft texture

KNEADED ERASER

DRAWING INSTRUMENTS

2B GRAPHITE PENCIL

Very soft, dark line

8B GRAPHITE PENCIL

SILVER WIRE IN A METAL HOLDER

DRAWING BOARD

Drawing board

Paper

Drawing clip

DRAWING MATERIALS

Colored pencil

Graphite stick

Binder clip

Dip pen

Pencil sharpener

Sketch book

Ink bottle

Silver lines
oxidize to a
light brown
color

Figures drawn
in ink on top
of lines

Line drawn
in silverpoint
using a ruler

Vanishing
point located
on head of
man riding
rearing horse

Lines of
squared
pavement slabs
recede toward
a single
vanishing
point

Complex perspective
drawing done as a
preparatory study
for a painting

Paper prepared
with size (glue)
and pigment

EXAMPLE OF A SILVERPOINT DRAWING
The Adoration of the Magi, Leonardo da Vinci, 1481
Pen and ink over silverpoint on paper
6½ x 11½ in (16.5 x 29.2 cm)

Handmade, tinted
paper

One of a series
of drawings
recording
London during
1944–1945

Charcoal lines
softened by
rubbing and
smudging

Charcoal
gives strong,
expressive lines

Broad charcoal
mark

Lines rapidly
drawn on site

EXAMPLE OF A CHARCOAL DRAWING
St. Paul's and the River, David Bomberg, 1945
Charcoal on paper
20 x 25⅛ in (50.8 x 65.8 cm)

Tempera

ILLUMINATED MANUSCRIPT

THE TERM TEMPERA is applied to any paint in which pigment is tempered (mixed) with a water-based binding medium—usually egg yolk. Egg tempera is applied to a smooth surface such as vellum (for illuminated manuscripts) or more commonly to hardwood panels prepared with gesso—a mixture of chalk and size (glue). Bristle brushes are used to apply the gesso. A layer of gesso grosso (coarse gesso) is followed by successive layers of gesso sotile (fine gesso) that are sanded between coats to provide a smooth, yet absorbent ground. The paint is applied with fine sable brushes in thin layers, using light brushstrokes. Tempera dries quickly to form a tough skin with a satin sheen. The luminous white surface of the gesso combined with the overlaid paint produces the brilliant crispness and rich colors particular to this medium. Egg tempera paintings are frequently gilded with gold. Leaves of finely beaten gold are applied to a bole (reddish-brown clay) base and polished by burnishing.

MATERIALS FOR GILDING

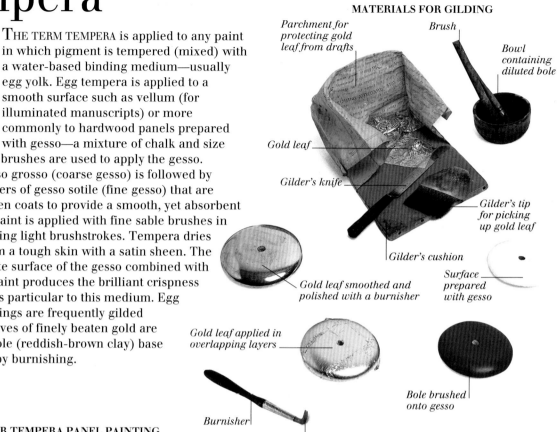

Parchment for protecting gold leaf from drafts

Brush

Bowl containing diluted bole

Gold leaf

Gilder's knife

Gilder's tip for picking up gold leaf

Gilder's cushion

Gold leaf smoothed and polished with a burnisher

Surface prepared with gesso

Gold leaf applied in overlapping layers

Bole brushed onto gesso

Burnisher

Agate tip

MATERIALS FOR TEMPERA PANEL PAINTING

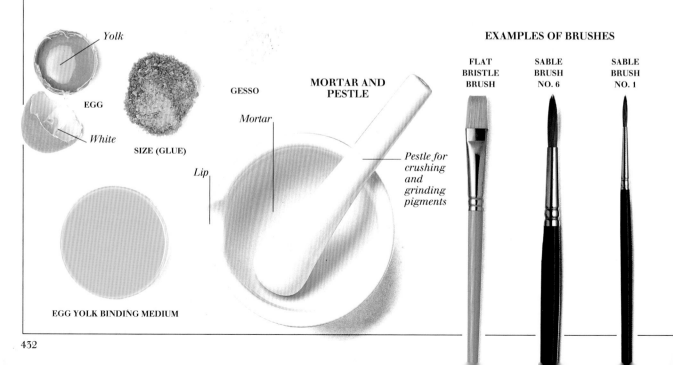

Yolk

EGG

White

SIZE (GLUE)

GESSO

MORTAR AND PESTLE

Mortar

Lip

Pestle for crushing and grinding pigments

EGG YOLK BINDING MEDIUM

EXAMPLES OF BRUSHES

FLAT BRISTLE BRUSH

SABLE BRUSH NO. 6

SABLE BRUSH NO. 1

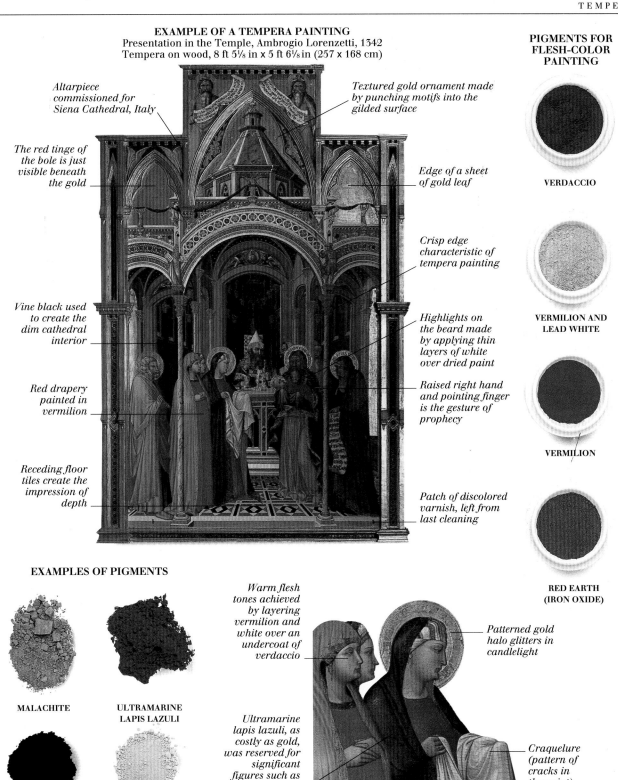

EXAMPLE OF A TEMPERA PAINTING
Presentation in the Temple, Ambrogio Lorenzetti, 1342
Tempera on wood, 8 ft 5⅛ in x 5 ft 6⅛ in (257 x 168 cm)

PIGMENTS FOR FLESH-COLOR PAINTING

Altarpiece commissioned for Siena Cathedral, Italy

Textured gold ornament made by punching motifs into the gilded surface

The red tinge of the bole is just visible beneath the gold

Edge of a sheet of gold leaf

Crisp edge characteristic of tempera painting

Vine black used to create the dim cathedral interior

Highlights on the beard made by applying thin layers of white over dried paint

Red drapery painted in vermilion

Raised right hand and pointing finger is the gesture of prophecy

Receding floor tiles create the impression of depth

Patch of discolored varnish, left from last cleaning

VERDACCIO

VERMILION AND LEAD WHITE

VERMILION

RED EARTH (IRON OXIDE)

EXAMPLES OF PIGMENTS

MALACHITE

ULTRAMARINE LAPIS LAZULI

VINE BLACK

LEAD TIN YELLOW

Warm flesh tones achieved by layering vermilion and white over an undercoat of verdaccio

Patterned gold halo glitters in candlelight

Ultramarine lapis lazuli, as costly as gold, was reserved for significant figures such as the Virgin Mary

Craquelure (pattern of cracks in the paint)

DETAIL FROM "PRESENTATION IN THE TEMPLE"

Fresco

FRESCO IS A METHOD OF WALL PAINTING. In buon fresco (true fresco), pigments are mixed with water and applied to an intonaco (layer of fresh, damp lime-plaster). The intonaco absorbs and binds the pigments as it dries making the picture a permanent part of the wall surface. The intonaco is applied in sections called giornate (daily sections). The size of each giornata depends on the artist's estimate of how much can be painted before the plaster sets. The junctions between giornate are sometimes visible on a finished fresco. The range of colors used in buon fresco are limited to lime-resistant pigments such as earth colors (below). Slaked lime (burnt lime mixed with water), bianco di San Giovanni (slaked lime that has been partly exposed to air), and chalk can be used to produce fresco whites. In fresco secco (dry fresco), pigments are mixed with a binding medium and applied to dry plaster. The pigments are not completely absorbed into the plaster and may flake off over time.

CROSS-SECTION SHOWING FRESCO LAYERS

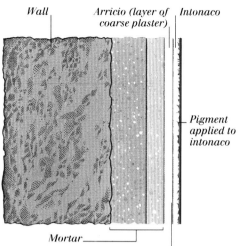

Wall

Arricio (layer of coarse plaster)

Intonaco

Pigment applied to intonaco

Mortar

Sinopia (design) drawn on surface of arricio

EXAMPLES OF EARTH COLOR PIGMENTS

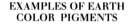

RAW UMBER

RED EARTH (IRON OXIDE)

GREEN EARTH

RAW SIENNA

EXAMPLES OF FRESCO BRUSHES

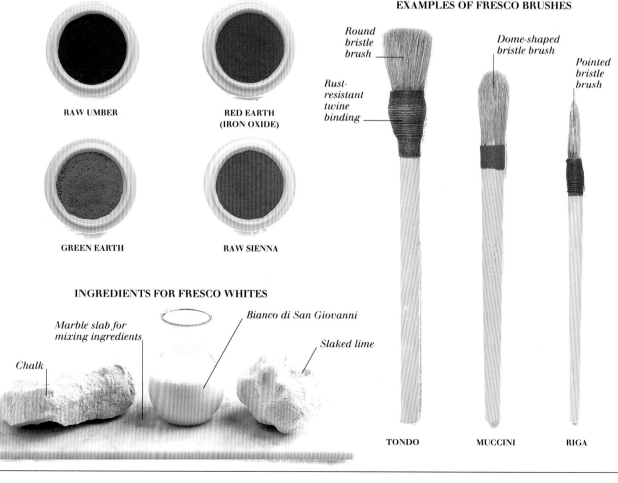

Round bristle brush

Dome-shaped bristle brush

Pointed bristle brush

Rust-resistant twine binding

INGREDIENTS FOR FRESCO WHITES

Marble slab for mixing ingredients

Bianco di San Giovanni

Slaked lime

Chalk

TONDO

MUCCINI

RIGA

EXAMPLE OF A FRESCO
The Expulsion of the Merchants from the Temple, Giotto, c.1306
Fresco, 78 x 72 in (200 x 185 cm)

One of a series of frescoes in the Arena Chapel, Padua, Italy

Temple acts as a backdrop for the action

Patches of azurite blue have turned green due to reaction with carbon dioxide

Bianco di San Giovanni often used for fresco whites

Gold leaf applied to apostle's halo

Hairline junction between giornate is visible

Green earth pigment applied to robe

Child painted on top of apostle's robe

Red earth pigment applied in buon fresco has retained rich hue

Azurite blue applied in fresco secco has flaked off to reveal the plaster beneath

Dry, matt surface characteristic of buon fresco

Paint applied in buon fresco to child's face

Artist has to finish giornata before plaster dries

Junction between giornate

A fresco was generally worked in zones from the top down

Area with little detail can be painted quickly, allowing a larger giornata to be completed

White dove represents the Holy Ghost

Paint applied in fresco secco to child's body has flaked off

Sinopia (design) sketched in red earth

Highly detailed area takes a longer time to paint, restricting the size of the giornata

DETAIL FROM "THE EXPULSION"

GIORNATE (DAILY SECTIONS) IN "THE EXPULSION"

Oils

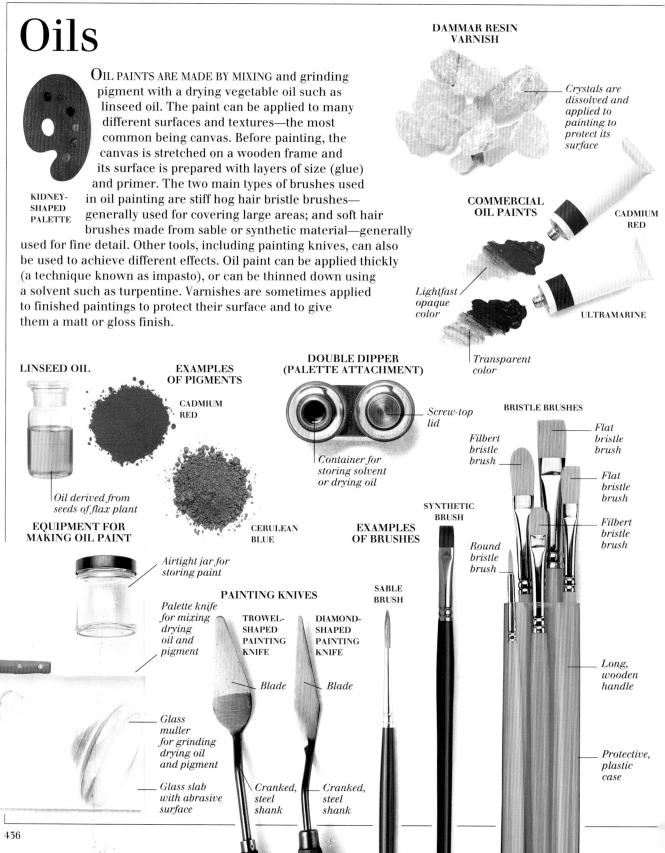

OIL PAINTS ARE MADE BY MIXING and grinding pigment with a drying vegetable oil such as linseed oil. The paint can be applied to many different surfaces and textures—the most common being canvas. Before painting, the canvas is stretched on a wooden frame and its surface is prepared with layers of size (glue) and primer. The two main types of brushes used in oil painting are stiff hog hair bristle brushes—generally used for covering large areas; and soft hair brushes made from sable or synthetic material—generally used for fine detail. Other tools, including painting knives, can also be used to achieve different effects. Oil paint can be applied thickly (a technique known as impasto), or can be thinned down using a solvent such as turpentine. Varnishes are sometimes applied to finished paintings to protect their surface and to give them a matt or gloss finish.

KIDNEY-SHAPED PALETTE

DAMMAR RESIN VARNISH

Crystals are dissolved and applied to painting to protect its surface

COMMERCIAL OIL PAINTS

CADMIUM RED

Lightfast opaque color

Transparent color

ULTRAMARINE

LINSEED OIL

Oil derived from seeds of flax plant

EXAMPLES OF PIGMENTS

CADMIUM RED

CERULEAN BLUE

EQUIPMENT FOR MAKING OIL PAINT

DOUBLE DIPPER (PALETTE ATTACHMENT)

Screw-top lid

Container for storing solvent or drying oil

EXAMPLES OF BRUSHES

SYNTHETIC BRUSH

BRISTLE BRUSHES

Filbert bristle brush

Flat bristle brush

Flat bristle brush

Filbert bristle brush

Round bristle brush

Airtight jar for storing paint

PAINTING KNIVES

Palette knife for mixing drying oil and pigment

TROWEL-SHAPED PAINTING KNIFE

DIAMOND-SHAPED PAINTING KNIFE

SABLE BRUSH

Blade

Blade

Long, wooden handle

Glass muller for grinding drying oil and pigment

Glass slab with abrasive surface

Cranked, steel shank

Cranked, steel shank

Protective, plastic case

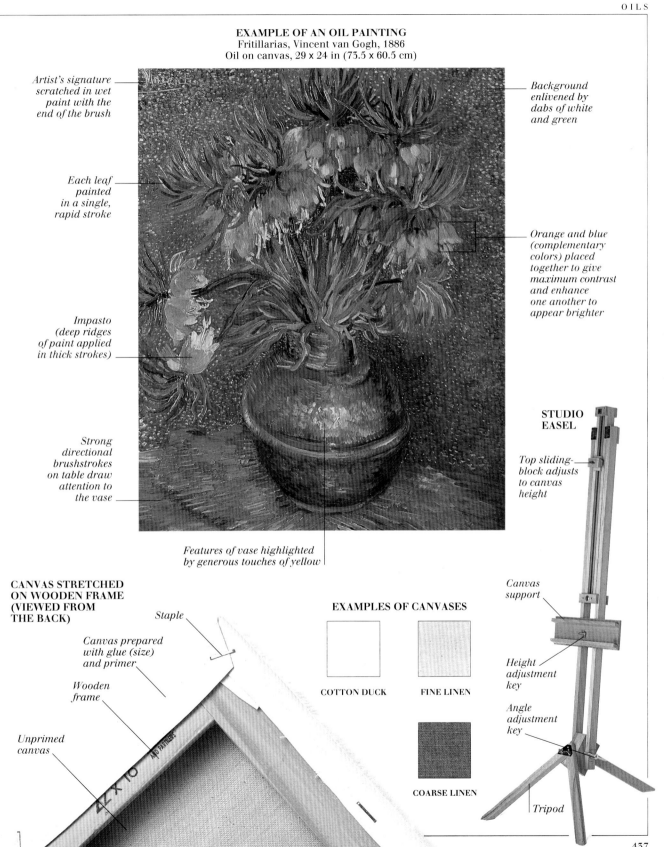

EXAMPLE OF AN OIL PAINTING
Fritillarias, Vincent van Gogh, 1886
Oil on canvas, 29 x 24 in (73.5 x 60.5 cm)

Artist's signature scratched in wet paint with the end of the brush

Each leaf painted in a single, rapid stroke

Impasto (deep ridges of paint applied in thick strokes)

Strong directional brushstrokes on table draw attention to the vase

Background enlivened by dabs of white and green

Orange and blue (complementary colors) placed together to give maximum contrast and enhance one another to appear brighter

Features of vase highlighted by generous touches of yellow

STUDIO EASEL

Top sliding-block adjusts to canvas height

Canvas support

Height adjustment key

Angle adjustment key

Tripod

CANVAS STRETCHED ON WOODEN FRAME (VIEWED FROM THE BACK)

Staple

Canvas prepared with glue (size) and primer

Wooden frame

Unprimed canvas

EXAMPLES OF CANVASES

COTTON DUCK

FINE LINEN

COARSE LINEN

437

Watercolor

WATERCOLOR PAINT IS MADE OF GROUND PIGMENT mixed with a water-soluble binding medium, usually gum arabic. It is usually applied to paper using soft hair brushes such as sable, goat hair, squirrel, and synthetic brushes. Watercolors are often diluted and applied as overlaying washes (thin, transparent layers) to build up depth of color. Washes can be laid in a variety of ways to create a range of different effects. For example, a wet-in-wet wash can be achieved by laying a wash on top of another wet wash. The two washes blend together to give a fused effect. Sponges are used to modify washes by soaking up paint so that areas of pigment are lightened or removed from the paper. Watercolors can also be applied undiluted—a technique known as dry brush—to create a broken-color effect. Watercolors are generally transparent and allow light to reflect from the surface of the paper through the layers of paint to give a luminous effect. They can be thickened and made opaque by adding body color (Chinese white).

GUM ARABIC

Natural sap from acacia tree

NATURAL SPONGE

ANATOMY OF A SABLE BRUSH

Soft red sable hair *Toe (tip)*

Wooden handle

SOFT HAIR BRUSHES

Hair trimmed and cemented into ferrule

ROUND SABLE BRUSH (NO. 6)

Round ferrule *Hair tied with clove hitch knot*

ROUND SABLE BRUSH (NO. 1)

TUBES OF WATERCOLOR PAINT

SYNTHETIC WASH BRUSH

WINSOR GREEN

Winsor Green
Vert Winsor
Winsorgrün
Verde Winsor
Verde Winsor
0102 720 SL Series 1 A

Cadmium Yellow
Kadmiumgelb
Amarillo de Cadmio
Giallo di cadmio
0102 108 SL Series 4 A

SQUIRREL MOP WASH BRUSH

CADMIUM YELLOW

PORTABLE BOX OF WATERCOLOR PAINTS

Painted color swatch *Chinese white* *Pan of watercolor paint*

Lid can be used for mixing colors

ARTISTS' WATER COLOUR
Chinese White
Blanc de Chine

LARGE GOAT HAKE WASH BRUSH

EXAMPLE OF A WATERCOLOR
Burning of the Houses of Parliament, Turner, 1834
Watercolor on paper, 11½ x 17½ in (29.2 x 44.5 cm)

Transparent washes laid on top of each other to create tonal depth

Transparent washes allow light to reflect off the surface of the paper to give a luminous effect

Highlight scratched out with a scalpel

Paper shows through thin wash to give flames added highlight

Crowd painted with thin strokes laid over a pale wash

Undiluted paint applied, then partly washed out, to create the impression of water

EXAMPLES OF WATERCOLOR PAPERS

SMOOTH-TEXTURED PAPER

MEDIUM-TEXTURED PAPER

ROUGH-TEXTURED PAPER

EXAMPLES OF WASHES

WASH OVER DRY BRUSH
Wash laid over paint applied with dry brush gives two-tone effect

GRADED WASH
Strong wash applied to tilted paper gives graded effect

DRY BRUSH
Undiluted paint dragged across surface of paper gives broken effect

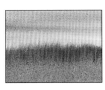

WET-IN-WET
Two diluted washes left to run together to give fused effect

COLOR WHEEL OF WATERCOLOR PAINTS

Yellow (primary color)

Secondary colors made by mixing yellow and blue

Secondary colors made by mixing red and yellow

Blue (primary color)

Red (primary color)

Secondary colors made by mixing blue and red

Pastels

PASTELS ARE STICKS OF PIGMENT made by mixing ground pigment with chalk and a binding medium, such as gum arabic. They vary in hardness depending on the proportion of the binding medium to the chalk. Soft pastel—the most common form of pastel—contains just enough binding medium to hold the pigment in stick form. Pastels can be applied directly to any support (surface) with sufficient tooth (texture). When a pastel is drawn over a textured surface, the pigment crumbles and lodges in the fibers of the support. Pastel marks have a particular soft, matt quality and are suitable for techniques such as blending, scumbling, and feathering. Blending is a technique of rubbing and fusing two or more colors on the support using fingers or various tools such as tortillons (paper stumps), soft hair brushes, kneaded erasers, and soft bread. Scumbling is a technique of building up layers of pastel colors. The side or blunted tip of a soft pastel is lightly drawn over an underpainted area so that patches of the color beneath show through. Feathering is a technique of applying parallel strokes of color with the point of a pastel, usually over an existing layer of pastel color. A thin spray of fixative can be applied— using a mouth diffuser (see pp. 430-431) or aerosol spray fixative—to a finished pastel painting, or in between layers of color, to prevent smudging.

EQUIPMENT FOR MAKING PASTELS

Glass muller

Chalk

Glass slab with abrasive surface | *Gum arabic* | *Ivory-black pigment* | *Cobalt-blue pigment*

EXAMPLES OF SOFT PASTELS

COBALT-BLUE HALF PASTEL

VERMILION HALF PASTEL

OLIVE-GREEN FULL PASTEL

MAUVE FULL PASTEL

BOXED PASTEL SET

EQUIPMENT USED WITH PASTELS

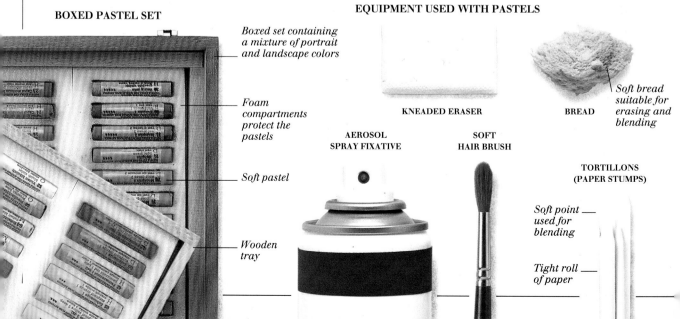

Boxed set containing a mixture of portrait and landscape colors

Foam compartments protect the pastels

Soft pastel

Wooden tray

KNEADED ERASER

AEROSOL SPRAY FIXATIVE

SOFT HAIR BRUSH

BREAD

Soft bread suitable for erasing and blending

TORTILLONS (PAPER STUMPS)

Soft point used for blending

Tight roll of paper

EXAMPLE OF A PASTEL PAINTING
Woman Drying her Neck, Edgar Degas, c.1898
Pastel on cardboard, 24½ x 25½ in (62.5 x 65.5 cm)

Pastels applied directly to support

Colors are blended together using fingers or tools such as tortillons

Built up layers of pastel

Rich color of fabric created by overlaying yellows and oranges

Broken colors, characteristic of scumbling technique

Toned color of paper visible beneath thinly applied pastels

Pure bright colors laid side by side produce strong contrasts

DETAIL FROM "WOMAN DRYING HER NECK"

Feathering technique used to produce skin tones

EXAMPLES OF TEXTURED PAPERS AND PASTEL BOARDS

WATERCOLOR PAPER (ROUGH TEXTURE)

GLASS PAPER

WATERCOLOR PAPER (MEDIUM TEXTURE)

INGRES PAPER

FLOCKED PASTEL BOARD

CANSON PAPER

EXAMPLES OF COLORED AND TINTED PAPERS

Acrylics

ACRYLIC PAINT IS MADE BY MIXING PIGMENT with a synthetic resin. It can be thinned with water but dries to become water insoluble. Acrylics are applied to many surfaces, such as paper and acrylic-primed board and canvas. A variety of brushes, painting knives, rollers, air-brushes, plastic scrapers, and other tools are used in acrylic painting. The versatility of acrylics makes them suitable for a wide range of techniques. They can be used opaquely or—by adding water—in a transparent, watercolor style. Acrylic mediums can be added to the paint to adjust its consistency for special effects such as glazing and impasto (ridges of paint applied in thick strokes) or to make it more matt or glossy. Acrylics are quick-drying, which allows layers of paint to be applied on top of each other almost immediately.

EXAMPLES OF BRUSHES

Sable brush

Bristle sash brush

Synthetic bristle brush

Synthetic sable brush

Bristle brush

Goat hair brush

Synthetic wash brush

Ox hair brush

EXAMPLES OF PAINTS USED IN ACRYLICS

Azo yellow

Phthalo green

Cerulean blue

Phthalo blue

Quinacridone red

Titanium white

Pad of disposable paper palettes

Yellow ochre

Burnt sienna

Burnt umber

Credit card

Paint spread evenly

Flexible, plastic blade

PAINTING TOOLS

Stippled effect achieved using thick paint

Striated effect

Glue spreader

PLASTIC PAINTING KNIFE

PLASTIC SCRAPERS

Plastic handle

Blended tones

Paint cup

Main lever

Nozzle

AIR-BRUSH

SPONGE ROLLER

Uniform tone

Air hose

EXAMPLE OF AN ACRYLIC PAINTING
A Bigger Splash, David Hockney, 1967
Acrylic on canvas, 95½ x 96 in (242.5 x 243.8 cm)

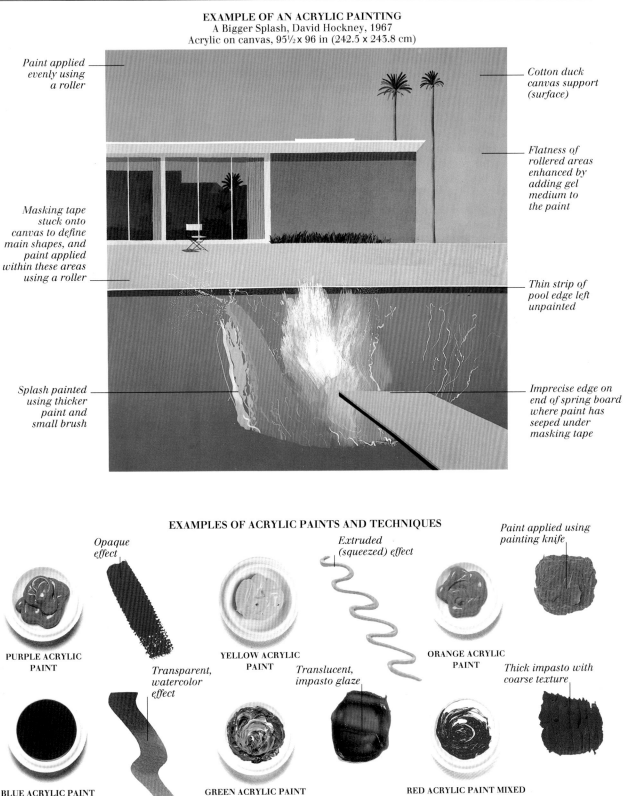

Paint applied evenly using a roller

Cotton duck canvas support (surface)

Flatness of rollered areas enhanced by adding gel medium to the paint

Masking tape stuck onto canvas to define main shapes, and paint applied within these areas using a roller

Thin strip of pool edge left unpainted

Splash painted using thicker paint and small brush

Imprecise edge on end of spring board where paint has seeped under masking tape

EXAMPLES OF ACRYLIC PAINTS AND TECHNIQUES

Opaque effect

Extruded (squeezed) effect

Paint applied using painting knife

PURPLE ACRYLIC PAINT

YELLOW ACRYLIC PAINT

ORANGE ACRYLIC PAINT

Transparent, watercolor effect

Translucent, impasto glaze

Thick impasto with coarse texture

BLUE ACRYLIC PAINT DILUTED WITH WATER

GREEN ACRYLIC PAINT MIXED WITH GEL MEDIUM

RED ACRYLIC PAINT MIXED WITH TEXTURE PASTE

Calligraphy

CALLIGRAPHY IS BEAUTIFULLY FORMED LETTERING. The term applies to written text and illumination (the decoration of manuscripts using gold leaf and color). The essential materials needed to practice calligraphy are a writing tool, ink, and a writing surface. Quills are among the oldest writing tools. They are usually made from goose or turkey feathers, and are noted for their flexibility and ability to produce fine lines. A quill point, however, is not very durable and constant recutting and trimming is required. The most commonly used writing instrument in western calligraphy is a detachable, metal nib held in a penholder. The metal nib is very durable, and there are a wide range of different types. Particular types of nibs—such as copperplate, speedball, and round-hand nibs—are used for specific styles of lettering. Some nibs have integral ink reservoirs and others have reservoirs that are detachable. Brushes are also used for writing, and for filling in outlined letters and painting decoration. Other writing tools used in calligraphy are fountain pens, felt-tipped pens, rotring pens, and reed pens. Calligraphy inks may come in liquid form, or as a solid ink stick. Ink sticks are ground down in distilled water to form a liquid ink. The most common writing surfaces for calligraphy are good quality, smooth -surfaced papers. To achieve the best writing position, the calligrapher places the paper on a drawing board set at an angle.

EQUIPMENT USED IN BRUSH LETTERING

Brush rest

Wolf hair brush

Goat hair brush

BRUSHES AND BRUSH REST

Liquid ink made by grinding down ink stick in distilled water

Solid carbon ink stick

Ink stone

INK STICK AND STONE

Feather

PENS, NIBS, AND BRUSHES USED IN CALLIGRAPHY

PENHOLDER

FELT-TIPPED PEN

ROTRING PEN

REED PEN

SQUARE SABLE BRUSH

POINTED SABLE BRUSH

COPPERPLATE NIB

SPEEDBALL NIB

ROUND-HAND NIB AND DETACHABLE INK RESERVOIR

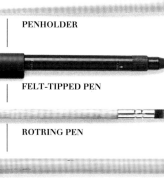

Feather stripped for better handling

Barrel

Hand-cut point

GOOSE-FEATHER QUILL

GOAT HAIR BRUSH

WOLF HAIR BRUSH

FOUNTAIN PEN AND INK

Bottle of permanent black ink

Barrel

Clip

Nib

Outer cap

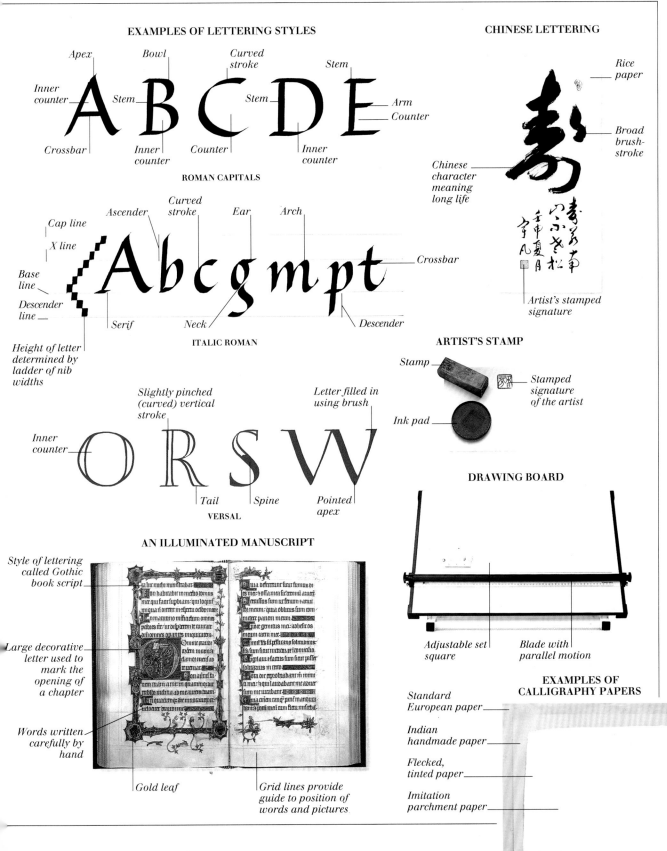

EXAMPLES OF LETTERING STYLES

Apex
Bowl
Curved stroke
Stem
Inner counter
Stem
Stem
Arm
Counter
Crossbar
Inner counter
Counter
Inner counter

ROMAN CAPITALS

Cap line
X line
Ascender
Curved stroke
Ear
Arch
Base line
Crossbar
Descender line
Serif
Neck
Descender
Height of letter determined by ladder of nib widths

ITALIC ROMAN

Slightly pinched (curved) vertical stroke
Letter filled in using brush
Inner counter
Tail
Spine
Pointed apex

VERSAL

CHINESE LETTERING

Rice paper
Broad brush-stroke
Chinese character meaning long life
Artist's stamped signature

ARTIST'S STAMP

Stamp
Stamped signature of the artist
Ink pad

DRAWING BOARD

Adjustable set square
Blade with parallel motion

AN ILLUMINATED MANUSCRIPT

Style of lettering called Gothic book script
Large decorative letter used to mark the opening of a chapter
Words written carefully by hand
Gold leaf
Grid lines provide guide to position of words and pictures

EXAMPLES OF CALLIGRAPHY PAPERS

Standard European paper
Indian handmade paper
Flecked, tinted paper
Imitation parchment paper

Printmaking 1

PRINTS ARE MADE BY FOUR BASIC printing processes – intaglio, lithographic, relief, and screen. In intaglio printing, lines are engraved or etched onto the surface of a metal plate. Lines are engraved using sharp metal tools. They are etched by corroding the metal plate with acid, using acid-resistant ground to protect the areas not to be etched. The plate is then inked and wiped, leaving the grooves filled with ink and the surface clean. Dampened paper is laid over the plate, and both paper and plate are passed through the rollers of an etching press. The pressure of the rollers forces the paper into the grooves, so that it takes up the ink, leaving an impression on the paper. Lithographic printing is based on the antipathy between grease and water. An image is drawn on a surface—usually a stone or metal plate—with a greasy medium, such as tusche (lihographic ink). The greasy drawing is fixed onto the plate by applying an acidic solution, such as gum arabic. The surface is then dampened and rolled with ink. The ink adheres only to the greasy areas and is repelled by the water. Paper is laid on the plate and pressure is applied by means of a press. In relief printing, the non-printing areas of a wood or linoleum block are cut away using gouges, knives, and other tools. The printing areas are left raised in relief and are rolled with ink. Paper is laid on the inked block and pressure is applied by means of a press or by burnishing (rubbing) the back of the paper. The most common forms of relief printing are woodcut, wood engraving, and linocut. In screen printing, the printing surface is a mesh stretched across a wooden frame. A stencil is applied to the mesh to seal the non-printing areas and ink is scraped through the mesh to produce an image.

THE FOUR MAIN PRINTING PROCESSES

Paper — — Printed image

Metal plate — — Engraved or etched image

— Inked area

INTAGLIO

Printed image — — Paper

Damp surface rejects ink

Ink adheres to greasy image — — Image drawn on stone with greasy medium

LITHOGRAPHIC

Paper — — Printed image

Raised figure

Wood block — — Inked surface

RELIEF

Ink forced through mesh — — Wooden frame

— Stencil

— Printed image

Paper —

SCREEN

LEATHER
INK DABBER

EQUIPMENT USED IN INTAGLIO PRINTING

ROCKER   SCRIBER   ROULETTE   SCRAPER   BURNISHER   CLAMP

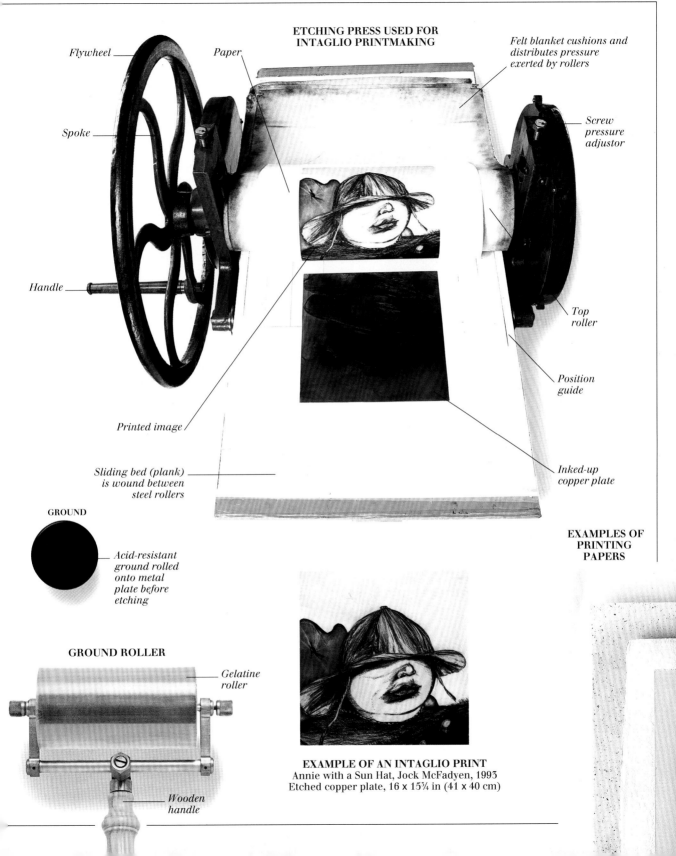

ETCHING PRESS USED FOR INTAGLIO PRINTMAKING

Flywheel

Paper

Felt blanket cushions and distributes pressure exerted by rollers

Spoke

Screw pressure adjustor

Handle

Top roller

Position guide

Printed image

Inked-up copper plate

Sliding bed (plank) is wound between steel rollers

GROUND

Acid-resistant ground rolled onto metal plate before etching

EXAMPLES OF PRINTING PAPERS

GROUND ROLLER

Gelatine roller

Wooden handle

EXAMPLE OF AN INTAGLIO PRINT
Annie with a Sun Hat, Jock McFadyen, 1993
Etched copper plate, 16 x 15¾ in (41 x 40 cm)

Printmaking 2

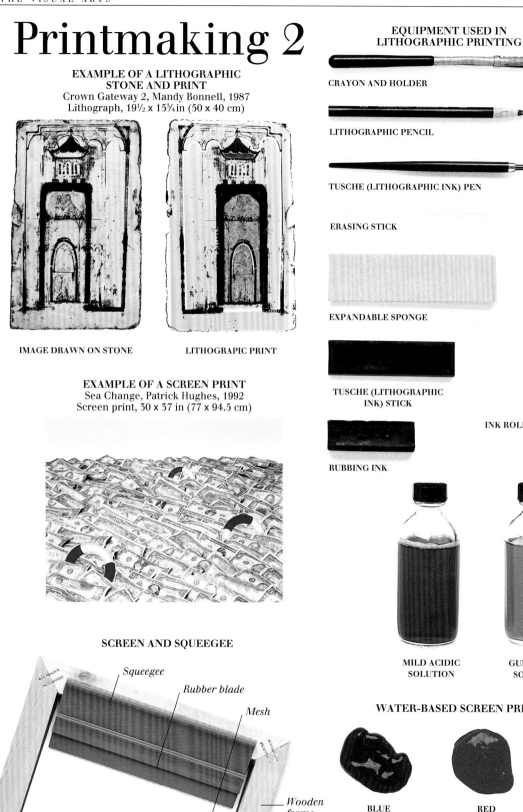

EXAMPLE OF A LITHOGRAPHIC STONE AND PRINT
Crown Gateway 2, Mandy Bonnell, 1987
Lithograph, 19½ x 15¾ in (50 x 40 cm)

IMAGE DRAWN ON STONE

LITHOGRAPIC PRINT

EXAMPLE OF A SCREEN PRINT
Sea Change, Patrick Hughes, 1992
Screen print, 30 x 37 in (77 x 94.5 cm)

SCREEN AND SQUEEGEE

Squeegee

Rubber blade

Mesh

Wooden frame

EQUIPMENT USED IN LITHOGRAPHIC PRINTING

CRAYON AND HOLDER

LITHOGRAPHIC PENCIL

TUSCHE (LITHOGRAPHIC INK) PEN

ERASING STICK

EXPANDABLE SPONGE

TUSCHE (LITHOGRAPHIC INK) STICK

INK ROLLER

RUBBING INK

MILD ACIDIC SOLUTION

GUM ARABIC SOLUTION

WATER-BASED SCREEN PRINTING INKS

BLUE ACRYLIC INK

RED ACRYLIC INK

BROWN TEXTILE INK

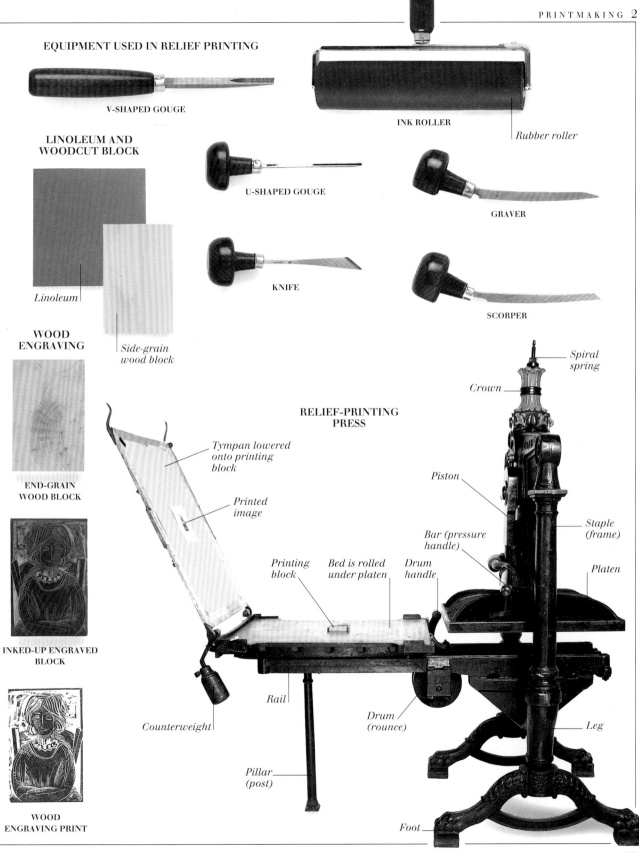

EQUIPMENT USED IN RELIEF PRINTING

V-SHAPED GOUGE

INK ROLLER

Rubber roller

LINOLEUM AND WOODCUT BLOCK

Linoleum

U-SHAPED GOUGE

GRAVER

KNIFE

SCORPER

Side-grain wood block

WOOD ENGRAVING

END-GRAIN WOOD BLOCK

INKED-UP ENGRAVED BLOCK

WOOD ENGRAVING PRINT

RELIEF-PRINTING PRESS

Spiral spring

Crown

Tympan lowered onto printing block

Printed image

Piston

Staple (frame)

Bar (pressure handle)

Platen

Printing block

Bed is rolled under platen

Drum handle

Rail

Counterweight

Drum (rounce)

Leg

Pillar (post)

Foot

Mosaic

MOSAIC IS THE ART OF MAKING patterns and pictures from tesserae (small, colored pieces of glass, marble, and other materials). Different materials are cut into tesserae using different tools. Smalti (glass enamel) and marble are cut into pieces using a hammer and a hardy (a pointed blade) embedded in a log. Vitreous glass is cut into pieces using a pair of pliers. Mosaics can be made using a direct or indirect method. In the direct method, the tesserae are laid directly into a bed of cement–based adhesive. In the indirect method, the design is drawn in reverse on paper or cloth. The tesserae are then stuck face down on the paper or cloth using water-soluble glue. Adhesive is spread with a trowel onto a solid surface—such as a wall—and the back of the mosaic is laid into the adhesive. Finally, the paper or cloth is soaked off to reveal the mosaic. Gaps between tesserae can be filled with grout. Grout is forced into gaps by dragging a grouting squeegee across the face of the mosaic. Mosaics are usually used to decorate walls and floors, but they can also be applied to smaller objects.

EQUIPMENT FOR BREAKING MARBLE

Strip of marble, ready for breaking into cubes

Mosaic hammer

Alicante (red marble) pieces

Hardy (pointed blade) embedded in a log

PLIERS

Hardwearing, tungsten carbide tip

Handle with rubber grip

SMALTI (GLASS ENAMEL)

EXAMPLE OF A MOSAIC (DIRECT METHOD)
Seascape, Tessa Hunkin, 1993
Smalti mosaic on board
31½ in (80 cm) diameter

RED SMALTI

MOSAIC TOOLS

CEMENT-BASED ADHESIVE

GROUT

YELLOW SMALTI

TROWEL

Notch

Steel blade

Wooden handle

BLUE SMALTI

GROUTING SQUEEGEE

Wooden handle

Rubber blade

Gold-leaf smalti

STAGES IN THE CREATION OF A MOSAIC (INDIRECT METHOD)

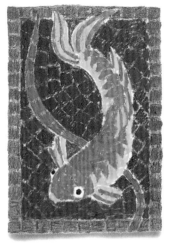

COLOR SKETCH
A color sketch is drawn in oil pastel to give a clear impression of how the finished mosaic will look.

REVERSE IMAGE
Tesserae are glued face down on reverse image on paper. Mosaic is then attached to solid surface and paper is removed.

MOSAIC POT

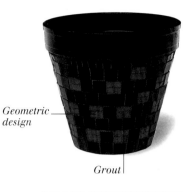

Geometric design

Grout

MOSAIC MOSQUE DESIGN

Floral design

Geometric border

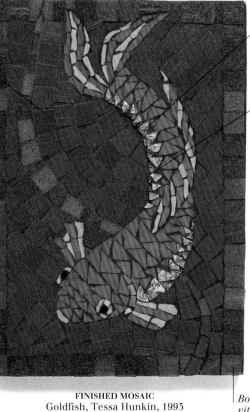

Andamenti (line along which tesserae are laid)

Gold tessera with ripple finish

Gold tessera placed upside-down

Grout fills the gaps between the tesserae

Mosaic mounted on board

Vitreous glass cut into triangular shape with pliers

FINISHED MOSAIC
Goldfish, Tessa Hunkin, 1993
Vitreous glass mosaic on board
14 x 10 in (35.5 x 25.5 cm)

Border of square vitreous glass

VITREOUS GLASS

GREEN VITREOUS GLASS WITH GOLD LEAF

RED VITREOUS GLASS

Plain finish

Ripple finish

SHEETS OF VITREOUS GLASS

BLUE VITREOUS GLASS

Sculpture 1

THE TWO TRADITIONAL SCULPTURE METHODS are carving and modeling. A carved sculpture is made by cutting away the surplus from a block of hard material such as stone, marble, or wood. The tools used for carving vary according to the material being carved. Heavy steel points, claws, and chisels that are struck with a lump hammer are generally used for stone and marble. Sharp gouges and chisels that are struck with a wooden mallet are used for wood. Sculptures formed from hard materials are generally finished by filing with rasps, rifflers, and other abrasive implements. Modeling is a process by which shapes are built up, using malleable materials such as clay, plaster, and wax. The material is cut with wire-ended tools and modeled with the fingers or a variety of hardwood and metal implements. For large or intricate modeled sculptures an armature (frame), made from metal or wood, is used to provide internal support. Sculptures formed in soft materials may harden naturally or can be made more durable by firing in a kiln. Modeled sculptures are often first designed in wax or another material to be cast later in a metal (see pp. 454-455) such as bronze. The development of many new materials in the 20th century has enabled sculptors to experiment with new techniques such as construction (joining preformed pieces of material such as machine components, mirrors, and furniture) and kinetic (mobile) sculpture.

EXAMPLES OF MARBLE-CARVING TOOLS

2½ lb (1.1 kg) iron head

Ash handle

LUMP HAMMER

WIDE MARBLE CLAW

NARROW MARBLE CLAW

POINT

FLAT CHISEL

BULLNOSE CHISEL

EXAMPLES OF WOOD-CARVING TOOLS

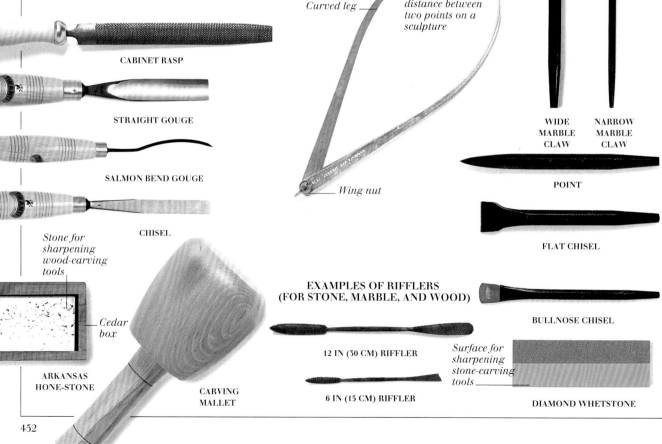

CABINET RASP

STRAIGHT GOUGE

SALMON BEND GOUGE

CHISEL

Stone for sharpening wood-carving tools

Cedar box

ARKANSAS HONE-STONE

CARVING MALLET

CALLIPERS

Curved leg

Gap measures distance between two points on a sculpture

Wing nut

EXAMPLES OF RIFFLERS (FOR STONE, MARBLE, AND WOOD)

12 IN (50 CM) RIFFLER

6 IN (15 CM) RIFFLER

Surface for sharpening stone-carving tools

DIAMOND WHETSTONE

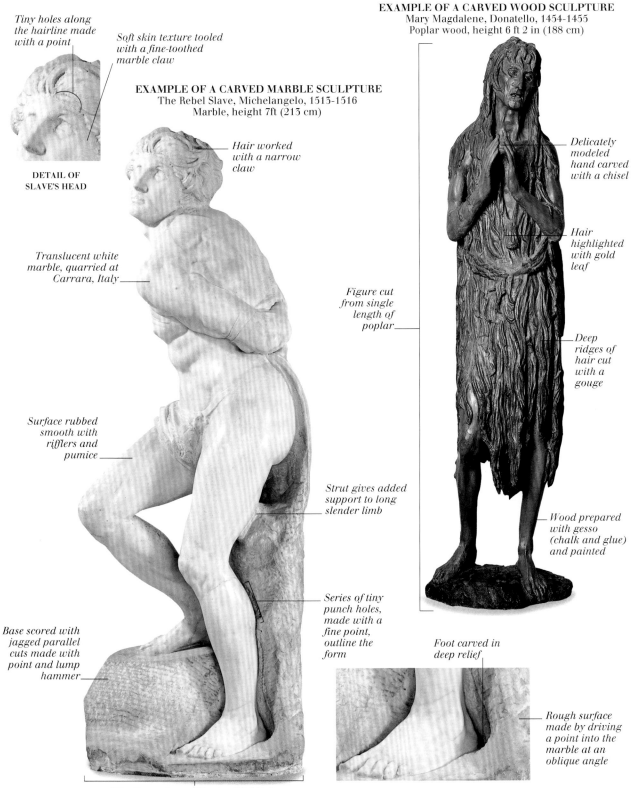

Tiny holes along the hairline made with a point

Soft skin texture tooled with a fine-toothed marble claw

DETAIL OF SLAVE'S HEAD

EXAMPLE OF A CARVED MARBLE SCULPTURE
The Rebel Slave, Michelangelo, 1513-1516
Marble, height 7ft (213 cm)

Hair worked with a narrow claw

Translucent white marble, quarried at Carrara, Italy

Surface rubbed smooth with rifflers and pumice

Strut gives added support to long slender limb

Base scored with jagged parallel cuts made with point and lump hammer

Series of tiny punch holes, made with a fine point, outline the form

The dimensions of the marble block determine the size of the sculpture

EXAMPLE OF A CARVED WOOD SCULPTURE
Mary Magdalene, Donatello, 1454-1455
Poplar wood, height 6 ft 2 in (188 cm)

Delicately modeled hand carved with a chisel

Hair highlighted with gold leaf

Figure cut from single length of poplar

Deep ridges of hair cut with a gouge

Wood prepared with gesso (chalk and glue) and painted

Foot carved in deep relief

Rough surface made by driving a point into the marble at an oblique angle

DETAIL OF SLAVE'S FOOT

Sculpture 2

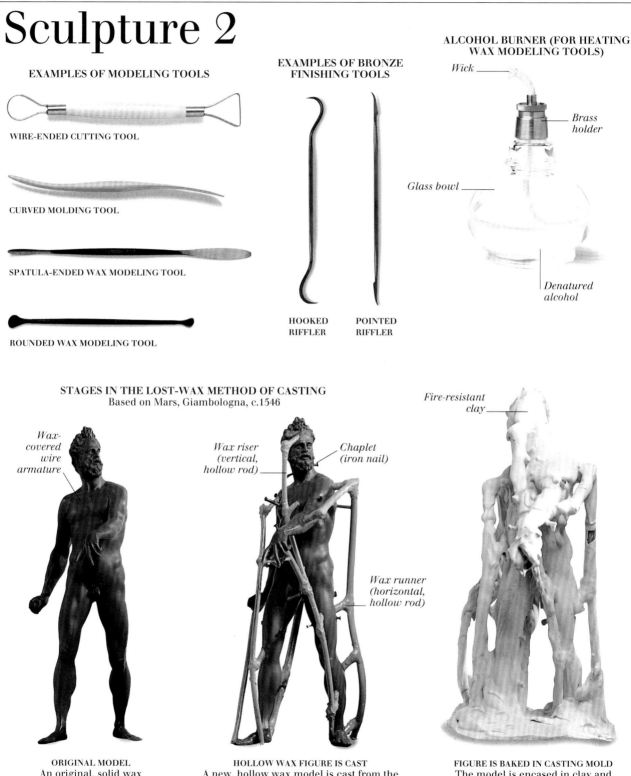

EXAMPLES OF MODELING TOOLS

WIRE-ENDED CUTTING TOOL

CURVED MOLDING TOOL

SPATULA-ENDED WAX MODELING TOOL

ROUNDED WAX MODELING TOOL

EXAMPLES OF BRONZE FINISHING TOOLS

HOOKED RIFFLER

POINTED RIFFLER

ALCOHOL BURNER (FOR HEATING WAX MODELING TOOLS)

Wick

Brass holder

Glass bowl

Denatured alcohol

STAGES IN THE LOST-WAX METHOD OF CASTING
Based on Mars, Giambologna, c.1546

Wax-covered wire armature

Wax riser (vertical, hollow rod)

Chaplet (iron nail)

Wax runner (horizontal, hollow rod)

Fire-resistant clay

ORIGINAL MODEL
An original, solid wax model is made and preserved so that numerous replicas can be cast.

HOLLOW WAX FIGURE IS CAST
A new, hollow wax model is cast from the original model. It is filled with a plaster core that is held in place with nails. Wax runners and risers are attached.

FIGURE IS BAKED IN CASTING MOLD
The model is encased in clay and baked. The wax melts away (through the channels made by the wax rods) and is replaced by molten bronze.

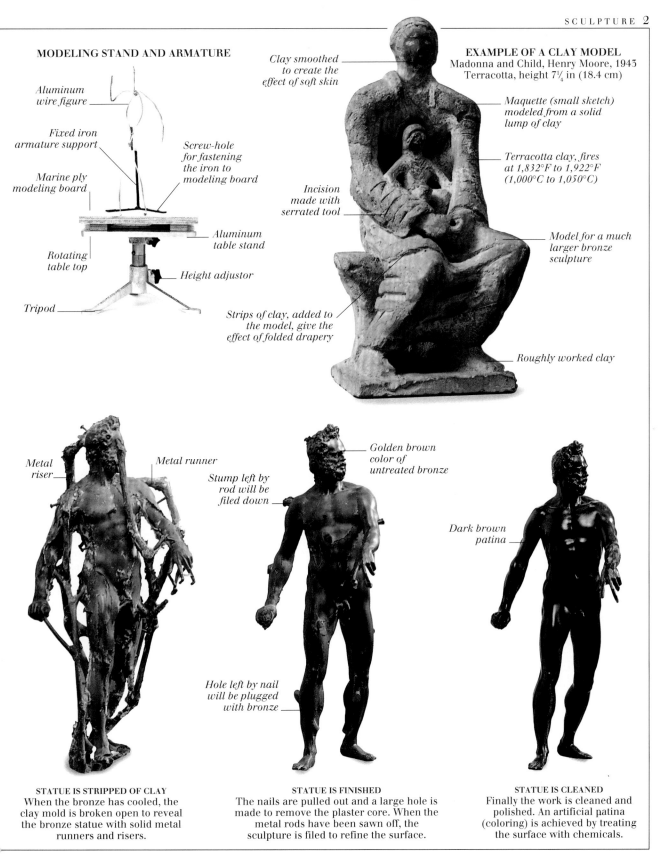

MODELING STAND AND ARMATURE

Aluminum wire figure

Fixed iron armature support

Screw-hole for fastening the iron to modeling board

Marine ply modeling board

Rotating table top

Aluminum table stand

Height adjustor

Tripod

EXAMPLE OF A CLAY MODEL
Madonna and Child, Henry Moore, 1943
Terracotta, height 7¼ in (18.4 cm)

Clay smoothed to create the effect of soft skin

Maquette (small sketch) modeled from a solid lump of clay

Terracotta clay, fires at 1,832°F to 1,922°F (1,000°C to 1,050°C)

Incision made with serrated tool

Model for a much larger bronze sculpture

Strips of clay, added to the model, give the effect of folded drapery

Roughly worked clay

Metal riser

Metal runner

Golden brown color of untreated bronze

Stump left by rod will be filed down

Dark brown patina

Hole left by nail will be plugged with bronze

STATUE IS STRIPPED OF CLAY
When the bronze has cooled, the clay mold is broken open to reveal the bronze statue with solid metal runners and risers.

STATUE IS FINISHED
The nails are pulled out and a large hole is made to remove the plaster core. When the metal rods have been sawn off, the sculpture is filed to refine the surface.

STATUE IS CLEANED
Finally the work is cleaned and polished. An artificial patina (coloring) is achieved by treating the surface with chemicals.

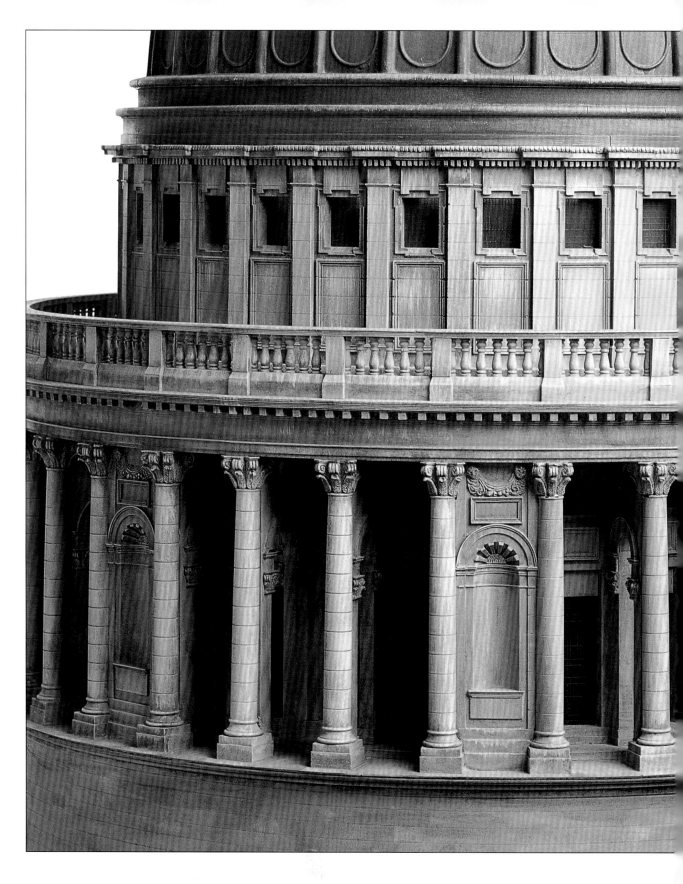

ARCHITECTURE

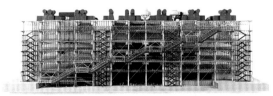

Ancient Egypt

THE CIVILIZATION OF THE ANCIENT EGYPTIANS (which lasted from about 3100 BC until it was finally absorbed into the Roman empire in 30 BC) is famous for its temples and tombs. Egyptian temples were often huge and geometric, like the Temple of Amon-Re (below and right). They were usually decorated with hieroglyphs (sacred characters used for picture writing) and painted reliefs depicting gods, Pharaohs (kings), and queens. Tombs were particularly important to the Egyptians, who believed that the dead were resurrected in the afterlife. The tombs were often decorated—for example, the surround of the false door opposite— in order to give comfort to the dead. The best-known ancient Egyptian tombs are the pyramids, which were designed to symbolize the rays of the sun. Many of the architectural forms used by the ancient Egyptians were later adopted by other civilizations. For example, columns and capitals were later used by the ancient Greeks (see pp. 460-461) and ancient Romans (see pp. 462-465).

SIDE VIEW OF HYPOSTYLE HALL, TEMPLE OF AMON-RE, KARNAK, EGYPT, c.1290 BC

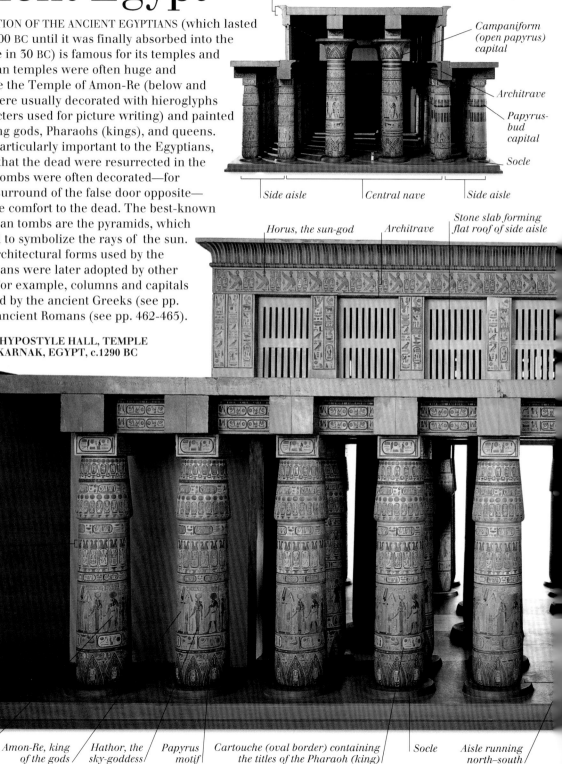

FRONT VIEW OF HYPOSTYLE HALL, TEMPLE OF AMON-RE

Cornice decorated with cavetto molding

Campaniform (open papyrus) capital

Architrave

Papyrus-bud capital

Socle

Side aisle

Central nave

Side aisle

Horus, the sun-god

Architrave

Stone slab forming flat roof of side aisle

Kepresh crown with disc

Chons, the moon-god

Amon-Re, king of the gods

Hathor, the sky-goddess

Papyrus motif

Cartouche (oval border) containing the titles of the Pharaoh (king)

Socle

Aisle running north–south

LIMESTONE FALSE DOOR WITH HIEROGLYPHS, TOMB OF KING TJETJI, GIZA, EGYPT, c.2400 BC

Lintel

Hieroglyph representing a house

Disc representing sun or light

Eroded image of Tjetji

Limestone stela (slab)

Hoe-shaped hieroglyph representing "mr" sound

Head of false door

Image of Tjetji's wife

Image of Tjetji's daughter

PLANT CAPITAL OF THE PTOLEMAIC-ROMAN PERIOD, EGYPT, 332-30 BC

Palm leaf

Papyrus flower

Papyrus leaf

Papyrus stem

Lotus bud

Lotus stem

Cornice decorated with cavetto molding

Bead molding

Trellis window

Rectangular pier decorated with hieroglyphs

Elevated roof of central nave

Clerestory

Disc representing sun or light

Architrave

Square abacus

Papyrus-bud capital

Papyriform column

Shaft

Scene depicting a Pharaoh (king) paying homage to the god Amon-Re

Central nave

ANCIENT EGYPTIAN BUILDING DECORATION

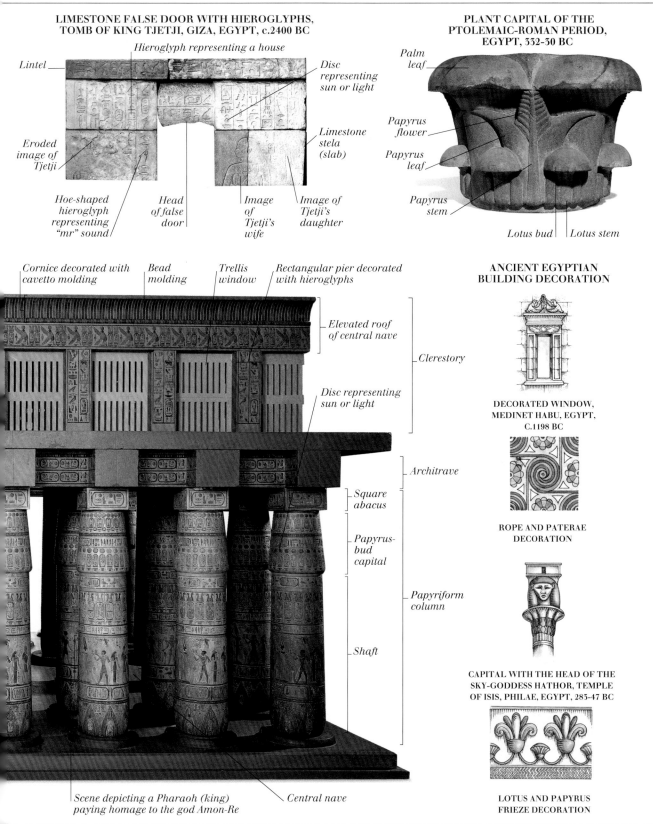

DECORATED WINDOW, MEDINET HABU, EGYPT, C.1198 BC

ROPE AND PATERAE DECORATION

CAPITAL WITH THE HEAD OF THE SKY-GODDESS HATHOR, TEMPLE OF ISIS, PHILAE, EGYPT, 283-47 BC

LOTUS AND PAPYRUS FRIEZE DECORATION

Ancient Greece

THE CLASSICAL TEMPLES OF ANCIENT GREECE were built according to the belief that certain forms and proportions were pleasing to the gods. There were three main ancient Greek architectural orders (styles), which can be distinguished by the decoration and proportions of their columns, capitals (column tops), and entablatures (structures resting on the capitals). The oldest is the Doric order, which dates from the seventh century BC and was used mainly on the Greek mainland and in the western colonies, such as Sicily and southern Italy. The Temple of Neptune, shown here, is a classic example of this order. It is hypaethral (roofless) and peripteral (surrounded by a single row of columns). About a century later, the more decorative Ionic order developed on the Aegean Islands. Features of this order include volutes (spiral scrolls) on capitals and acroteria (pediment ornaments). The Corinthian order was invented in Athens in the fifth century BC and is typically identified by an acanthus leaf on the capitals. This order was later widely used in ancient Roman architecture.

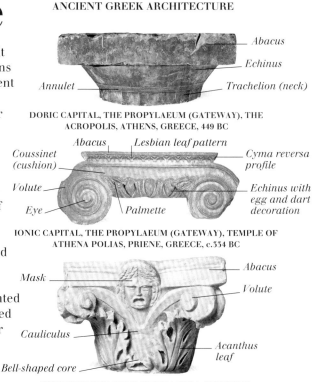

CAPITALS OF THE THREE ORDERS OF ANCIENT GREEK ARCHITECTURE

Abacus

Echinus

Annulet

Trachelion (neck)

DORIC CAPITAL, THE PROPYLAEUM (GATEWAY), THE ACROPOLIS, ATHENS, GREECE, 449 BC

Abacus

Lesbian leaf pattern

Coussinet (cushion)

Cyma reversa profile

Volute

Echinus with egg and dart decoration

Eye

Palmette

IONIC CAPITAL, THE PROPYLAEUM (GATEWAY), TEMPLE OF ATHENA POLIAS, PRIENE, GREECE, c.334 BC

Mask

Abacus

Volute

Cauliculus

Acanthus leaf

Bell-shaped core

CORINTHIAN CAPITAL FROM A STOA (PORTICO), PROBABLY FROM ASIA MINOR

TEMPLE OF NEPTUNE, PAESTUM, ITALY, c.460 BC

Raking cornice

Trachelion (neck)

Taenia

Triglyph

Metope

Glyph (channel)

Pediment

Doric entablature

Pteron (external colonnade)

Euthynteria

Drum

Stylobate

Column of the Doric order

PLAN OF THE TEMPLE OF NEPTUNE, PAESTUM

Pronaos (vestibule)

Naos wall

Anta (pilaster terminating naos wall)

Naos (cella)

Peristyle

Opisthodomos (rear portico)

Pteron (external colonnade)

Hexastyle pteron (colonnade of six columns)

ANCIENT GREEK BUILDING DECORATION

Volute

FACADE, TREASURY OF ATREUS, MYCENAE, GREECE, 1350-1250 BC

Meander

FRETWORK, PARTHENON, ATHENS, GREECE, 447-436 BC

ACROTERION, TEMPLE OF APHAIA, AEGINA, GREECE, 490 BC

Griffon (gryphon)

Raking cornice

ANTEFIXA, TEMPLE OF APHAIA, AEGINA, GREECE, 490 BC

Palmette

Volute

Regula (short fillet beneath taenia)

Eaves

Cornice

Frieze

Architrave

Capital

Shaft

Crepidoma (stepped base)

Entasis (slight curve of a column)

Intercolumniation

Fluting

461

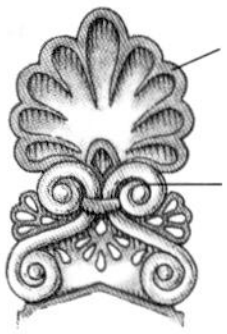

Ancient Rome 1

IN THE EARLY PERIOD OF THE ROMAN EMPIRE extensive use
was made of ancient Greek architectural ideas, particularly
those of the Corinthian order (see pp. 460-461). As a result,
many early Roman buildings—such as the Temple of Vesta
(opposite)—closely resemble ancient Greek buildings. A
distinctive Roman style began to evolve in the first century
AD. This style developed the interiors of buildings (the Greeks
had concentrated on the exterior) by wing arches, vaults, and
domes inside the buildings and by ornamenting internal walls;
many of these features can be seen in the Pantheon. Exterior
columns were often used for decorative rather than structural
purposes, as in the Colosseum and the Porta Nigra (see
pp. 464-465). Smaller buildings had timber frames with
wattle-and-daub walls, as in the mill (see pp. 464-465).
Roman architecture remained influential for many centuries,
with some of its principles being used in the 11th century in
Romanesque buildings (see pp. 468-469) and also in the 15th
and 16th centuries in Renaissance buildings (see pp. 474-477).

ANCIENT ROMAN BUILDING DECORATION

**FESTOON, TEMPLE OF VESTA,
TIVOLI, ITALY, C.80 BC**

**RICHLY DECORATED
ROMAN OVUM**

INTERIOR OF THE PANTHEON, ROME, ITALY, 118-c.128

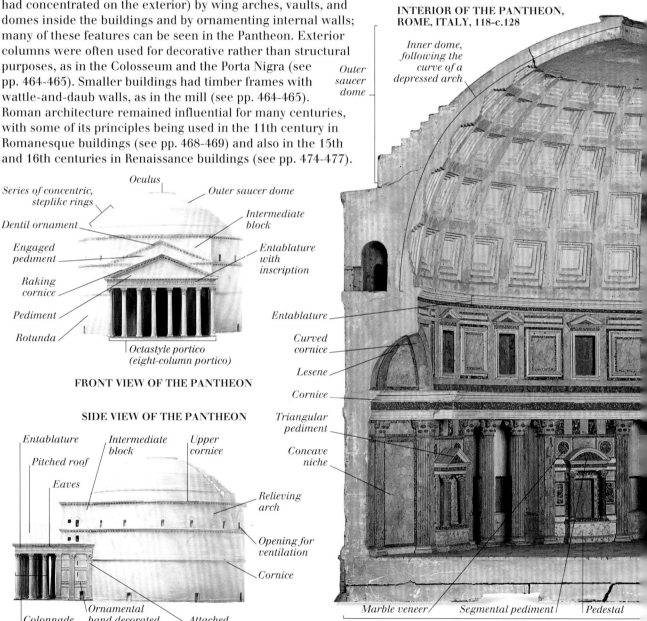

Outer saucer dome

Inner dome, following the curve of a depressed arch

Entablature

Curved cornice

Lesene

Cornice

Triangular pediment

Concave niche

Marble veneer

Segmental pediment

Pedestal

Oculus

Series of concentric, steplike rings

Outer saucer dome

Dentil ornament

Intermediate block

Engaged pediment

Entablature with inscription

Raking cornice

Pediment

Rotunda

Octastyle portico (eight-column portico)

FRONT VIEW OF THE PANTHEON

SIDE VIEW OF THE PANTHEON

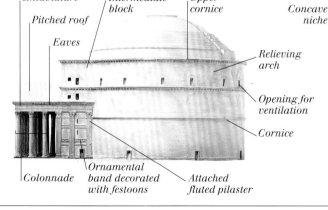

Entablature

Intermediate block

Upper cornice

Pitched roof

Eaves

Relieving arch

Opening for ventilation

Cornice

Colonnade

Ornamental band decorated with festoons

Attached fluted pilaster

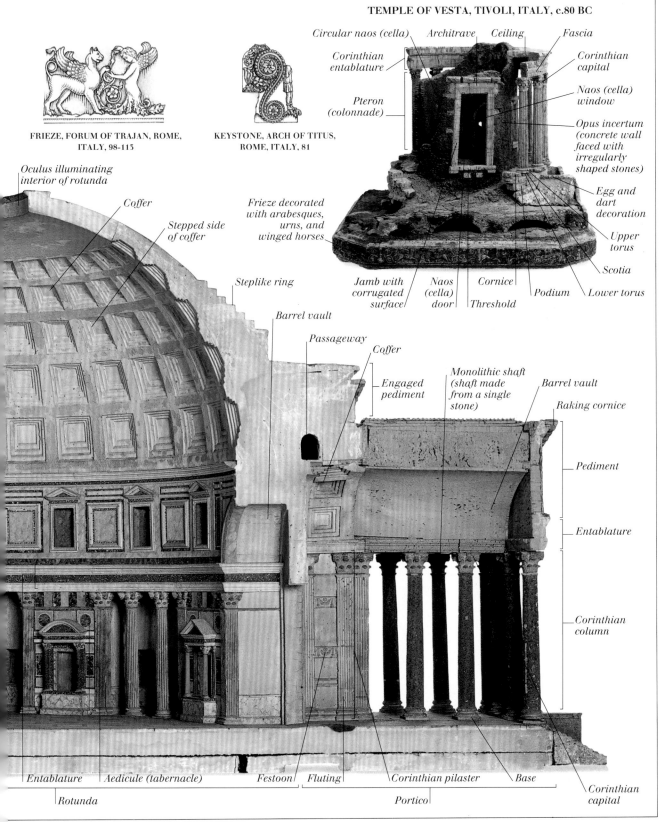

FRIEZE, FORUM OF TRAJAN, ROME, ITALY, 98-113

KEYSTONE, ARCH OF TITUS, ROME, ITALY, 81

TEMPLE OF VESTA, TIVOLI, ITALY, c.80 BC

Circular naos (cella)

Architrave

Ceiling

Fascia

Corinthian entablature

Corinthian capital

Pteron (colonnade)

Naos (cella) window

Opus incertum (concrete wall faced with irregularly shaped stones)

Egg and dart decoration

Upper torus

Scotia

Jamb with corrugated surface

Naos (cella) door

Cornice

Threshold

Podium

Lower torus

Oculus illuminating interior of rotunda

Coffer

Stepped side of coffer

Frieze decorated with arabesques, urns, and winged horses

Steplike ring

Barrel vault

Passageway

Coffer

Engaged pediment

Monolithic shaft (shaft made from a single stone)

Barrel vault

Raking cornice

Pediment

Entablature

Corinthian column

Corinthian capital

Entablature

Aedicule (tabernacle)

Festoon

Fluting

Corinthian pilaster

Base

Rotunda

Portico

Ancient Rome 2

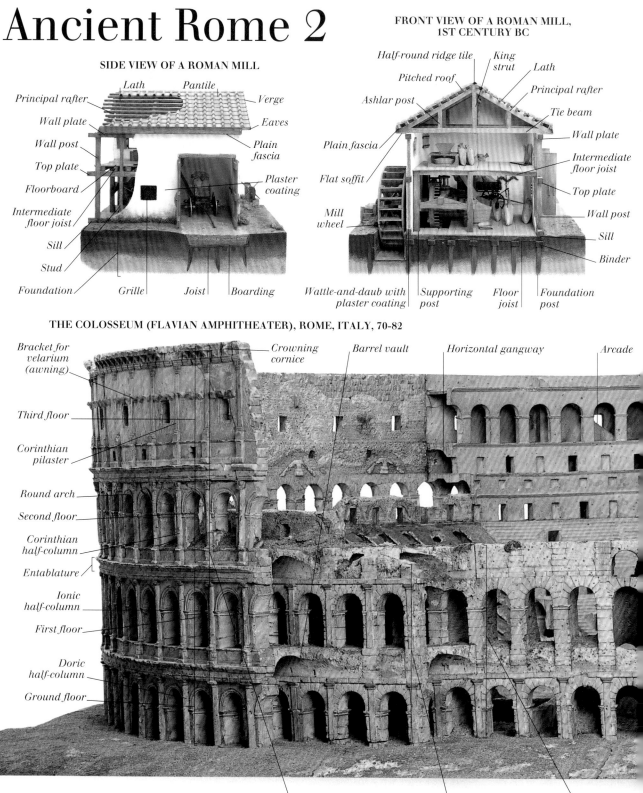

SIDE VIEW OF A ROMAN MILL

Lath
Pantile
Principal rafter
Verge
Wall plate
Eaves
Wall post
Plain fascia
Top plate
Plaster coating
Floorboard
Intermediate floor joist
Sill
Stud
Foundation
Grille
Joist
Boarding

FRONT VIEW OF A ROMAN MILL, 1ST CENTURY BC

Half-round ridge tile
King strut
Lath
Pitched roof
Principal rafter
Ashlar post
Tie beam
Plain fascia
Wall plate
Flat soffit
Intermediate floor joist
Top plate
Mill wheel
Wall post
Sill
Binder
Wattle-and-daub with plaster coating
Supporting post
Floor joist
Foundation post

THE COLOSSEUM (FLAVIAN AMPHITHEATER), ROME, ITALY, 70-82

Bracket for velarium (awning)
Crowning cornice
Barrel vault
Horizontal gangway
Arcade
Third floor
Corinthian pilaster
Round arch
Second floor
Corinthian half-column
Entablature
Ionic half-column
First floor
Doric half-column
Ground floor
External travertine shell
Intermediate shell
Inner shell

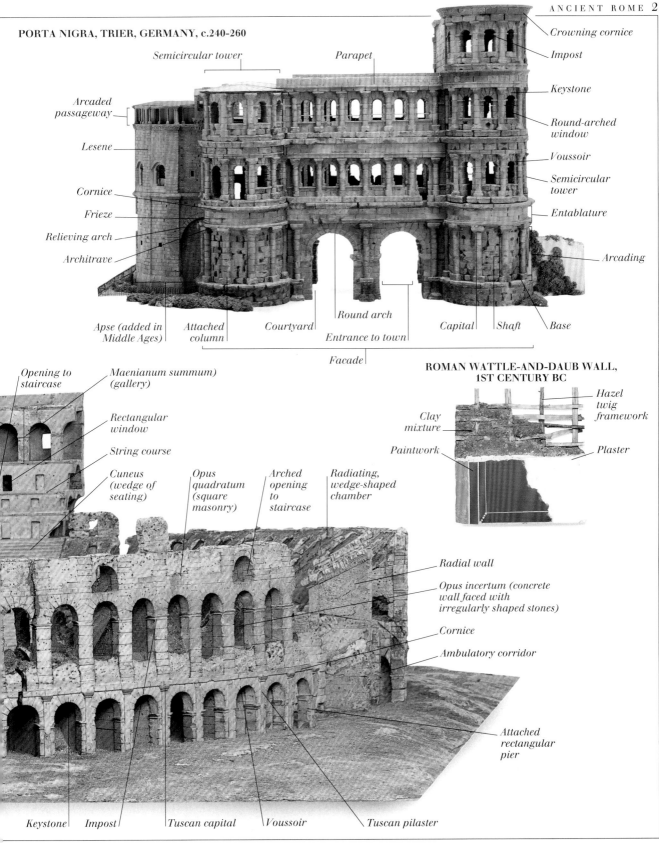

PORTA NIGRA, TRIER, GERMANY, c.240-260

Semicircular tower

Parapet

Crowning cornice

Impost

Arcaded passageway

Keystone

Lesene

Round-arched window

Voussoir

Semicircular tower

Cornice

Entablature

Frieze

Relieving arch

Architrave

Arcading

Apse (added in Middle Ages)

Attached column

Courtyard

Round arch

Entrance to town

Capital

Shaft

Base

Facade

ROMAN WATTLE-AND-DAUB WALL, 1ST CENTURY BC

Opening to staircase

Maenianum summum) (gallery)

Hazel twig framework

Clay mixture

Rectangular window

String course

Paintwork

Plaster

Cuneus (wedge of seating)

Opus quadratum (square masonry)

Arched opening to staircase

Radiating, wedge-shaped chamber

Radial wall

Opus incertum (concrete wall faced with irregularly shaped stones)

Cornice

Ambulatory corridor

Attached rectangular pier

Keystone

Impost

Tuscan capital

Voussoir

Tuscan pilaster

465

Medieval castles and houses

WARFARE WAS COMMON IN EUROPE in the Middle Ages, and many monarchs and nobles built castles as a form of defense. Typical medieval castles have outer walls surrounding a moat. Inside the moat is a bailey (courtyard), protected by a chemise (jacket wall). The innermost and strongest part of a medieval castle is the keep. There are two main types of keep: towers called donjons, such as the Tour de César and Coucy-le-Château in France, and rectangular keeps ("hall-keeps"), such as the Tower of London. Castles were often guarded by salients (projecting fortifications), like those of the Bastille. Medieval houses typically had timber cruck (tent-like) frames, wattle-and-daub walls, and pitched roofs, like those on medieval London Bridge (opposite).

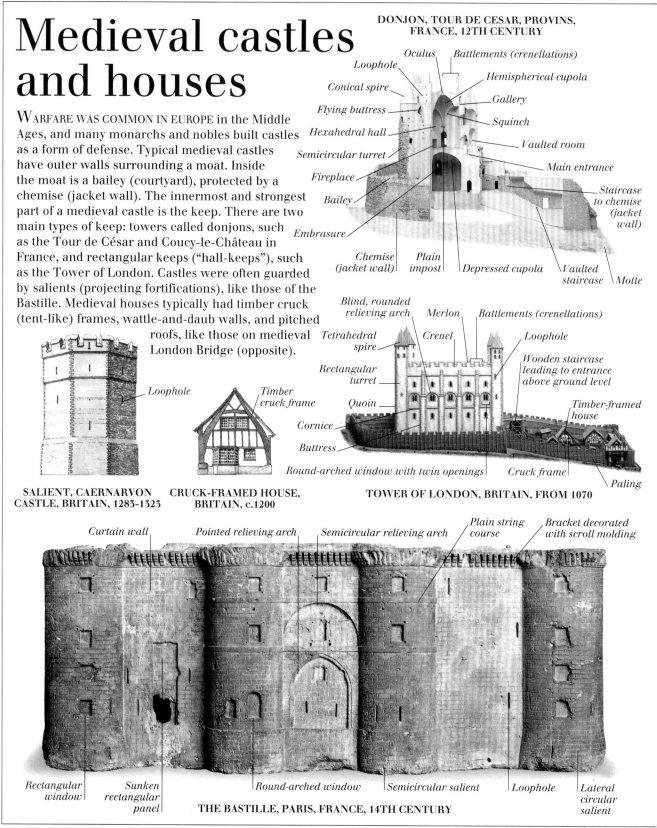

DONJON, TOUR DE CESAR, PROVINS, FRANCE, 12TH CENTURY

Oculus · Loophole · Battlements (crenellations) · Conical spire · Hemispherical cupola · Flying buttress · Gallery · Hexahedral hall · Squinch · Semicircular turret · Vaulted room · Fireplace · Main entrance · Bailey · Staircase to chemise (jacket wall) · Embrasure · Chemise (jacket wall) · Plain impost · Depressed cupola · Vaulted staircase · Motte

Loophole

SALIENT, CAERNARVON CASTLE, BRITAIN, 1283-1323

Timber cruck frame

CRUCK-FRAMED HOUSE, BRITAIN, c.1200

Blind, rounded relieving arch · Merlon · Battlements (crenellations) · Tetrahedral spire · Crenel · Loophole · Rectangular turret · Wooden staircase leading to entrance above ground level · Quoin · Timber-framed house · Cornice · Buttress · Round-arched window with twin openings · Cruck frame · Paling

TOWER OF LONDON, BRITAIN, FROM 1070

Curtain wall · Pointed relieving arch · Semicircular relieving arch · Plain string course · Bracket decorated with scroll molding

Rectangular window · Sunken rectangular panel · Round-arched window · Semicircular salient · Loophole · Lateral circular salient

THE BASTILLE, PARIS, FRANCE, 14TH CENTURY

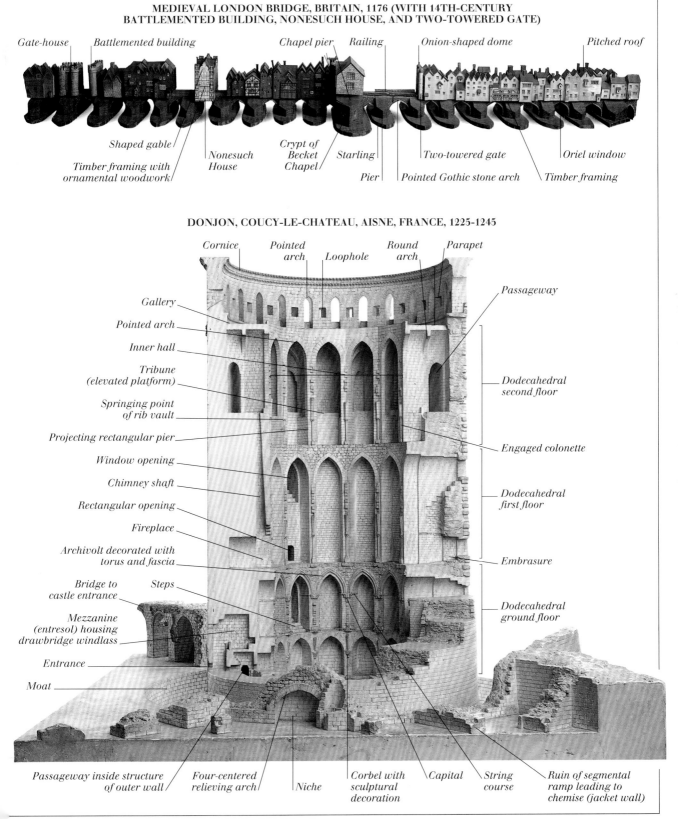

MEDIEVAL LONDON BRIDGE, BRITAIN, 1176 (WITH 14TH-CENTURY BATTLEMENTED BUILDING, NONESUCH HOUSE, AND TWO-TOWERED GATE)

Gate-house

Battlemented building

Chapel pier

Railing

Onion-shaped dome

Pitched roof

Shaped gable

Timber framing with ornamental woodwork

Nonesuch House

Crypt of Becket Chapel

Starling

Two-towered gate

Oriel window

Pier

Pointed Gothic stone arch

Timber framing

DONJON, COUCY-LE-CHATEAU, AISNE, FRANCE, 1225-1245

Cornice

Pointed arch

Loophole

Round arch

Parapet

Gallery

Passageway

Pointed arch

Inner hall

Tribune (elevated platform)

Springing point of rib vault

Projecting rectangular pier

Dodecahedral second floor

Engaged colonette

Window opening

Chimney shaft

Rectangular opening

Dodecahedral first floor

Fireplace

Archivolt decorated with torus and fascia

Embrasure

Bridge to castle entrance

Steps

Mezzanine (entresol) housing drawbridge windlass

Dodecahedral ground floor

Entrance

Moat

Passageway inside structure of outer wall

Four-centered relieving arch

Niche

Corbel with sculptural decoration

Capital

String course

Ruin of segmental ramp leading to chemise (jacket wall)

Medieval churches

LARGE NUMBERS OF CHURCHES were built in Europe in the Middle Ages. European churches of this period typically have high vaults supported by massive piers and columns. In the 10th century, the Romanesque style developed. Romanesque architects adopted many Roman or early Christian architectural ideas, such as cross-shaped ground plans—like that of Angoulême Cathedral (opposite)—and the basilican system of a nave with a central vessel and side aisles. In the mid-12th century, flying buttresses and pointed vaults appeared. These features later became widely used in Gothic architecture (see pp. 470-471). Bagneux Church (opposite) has both styles: a Romanesque tower and a Gothic nave and choir.

ABBEY OF ST. FOI, CONQUES, FRANCE, c.1050-c.1130

Finial

Incline

Circular staircase-turret

Loophole

Octahedral spire

Octahedral crossing tower

Round-arched window

Series of archivolts decorated with torus

Series of jambs decorated with colonettes

CHURCH ROOF BOSS, BRITAIN

ROMANESQUE CAPITALS

"THE FLIGHT INTO EGYPT" CAPITAL, CATHEDRAL OF ST. LAZARE, AUTUN, FRANCE, 1120-1130

"CHRIST IN MAJESTY" CAPITAL, BASILICA OF ST. MADELEINE, VEZELAY, FRANCE, 1120-1140

Pitched roof

Tribune (elevated platform)

Twin opening of gallery bays

Compound pier

Semicircular transverse arch

Vaulting shaft

Attached half-column

Round arcade arch

Romanesque capital

Arcade

Square central shaft

Barrel vault

Lean-to roof

Transept

Quadrant arch

Colonette

Round stilted arch

Attached half-column

Side aisle

Main vessel

Side aisle

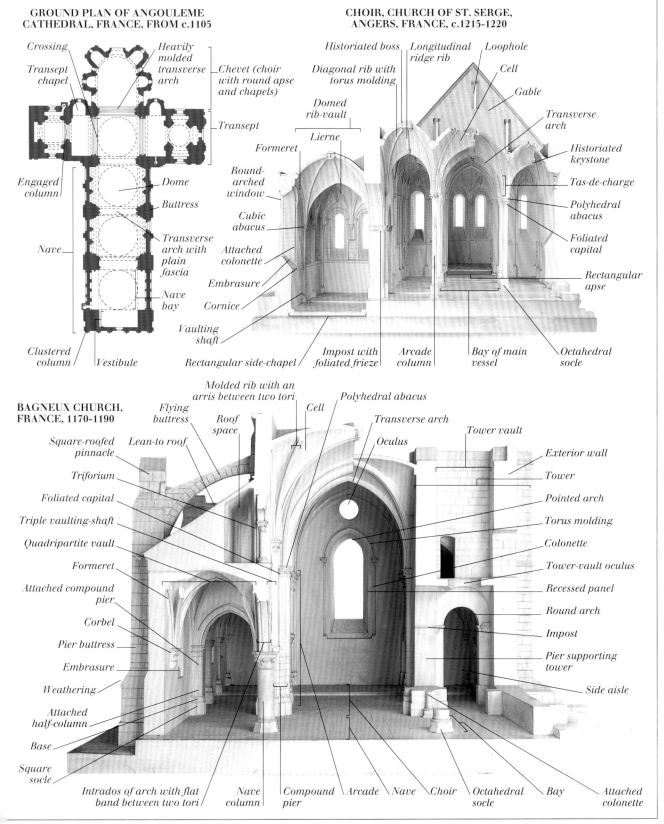

GROUND PLAN OF ANGOULEME CATHEDRAL, FRANCE, FROM c.1105

Crossing

Transept chapel

Heavily molded transverse arch

Chevet (choir with round apse and chapels)

Transept

Engaged column

Dome

Buttress

Transverse arch with plain fascia

Nave

Nave bay

Clustered column

Vestibule

CHOIR, CHURCH OF ST. SERGE, ANGERS, FRANCE, c.1215-1220

Historiated boss

Longitudinal ridge rib

Loophole

Diagonal rib with torus molding

Cell

Gable

Transverse arch

Domed rib-vault

Lierne

Historiated keystone

Formeret

Tas-de-charge

Round-arched window

Polyhedral abacus

Cubic abacus

Foliated capital

Attached colonette

Rectangular apse

Embrasure

Cornice

Vaulting shaft

Rectangular side-chapel

Impost with foliated frieze

Arcade column

Bay of main vessel

Octahedral socle

BAGNEUX CHURCH, FRANCE, 1170-1190

Square-roofed pinnacle

Lean-to roof

Molded rib with an arris between two tori

Flying buttress

Roof space

Cell

Polyhedral abacus

Transverse arch

Oculus

Tower vault

Exterior wall

Tower

Triforium

Foliated capital

Pointed arch

Triple vaulting-shaft

Torus molding

Quadripartite vault

Colonette

Formeret

Tower-vault oculus

Attached compound pier

Recessed panel

Corbel

Round arch

Pier buttress

Impost

Embrasure

Pier supporting tower

Weathering

Attached half-column

Side aisle

Base

Square socle

Intrados of arch with flat band between two tori

Nave column

Compound pier

Arcade

Nave

Choir

Octahedral socle

Bay

Attached colonette

Gothic 1

GOTHIC BUILDINGS are characterized by rib vaults, pointed or lancet arches, flying buttresses, decorative tracery and gables, and stained-glass windows. Typical Gothic buildings include the Cathedrals of Salisbury and old St. Paul's in England, and Notre Dame de Paris in France (see pp. 472-473). The Gothic style developed out of Romanesque architecture in France (see pp. 468-469) in the mid-12th century and then spread throughout Europe. The decorative elements of Gothic architecture became highly developed in buildings of the English Decorated style (late 13th-14th century) and the French Flamboyant style (15th-16th century). These styles are exemplified by the tower of Salisbury Cathedral and by the staircase in the Church of St. Maclou (see pp. 472-473), respectively. In both of these styles, embellishments such as ballflowers and curvilinear (flowing) tracery were used liberally. The English Perpendicular style (late 14th-15th century), which followed the Decorated style, emphasized the vertical and horizontal elements of a building. A notable feature of this style is the hammer-beam roof.

GROUND PLAN OF SALISBURY CATHEDRAL

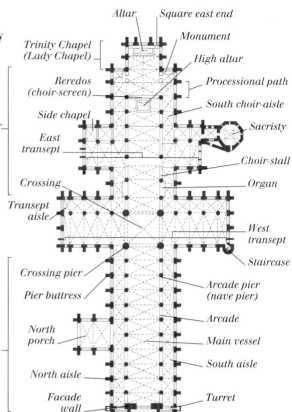

Altar
Square east end
Trinity Chapel (Lady Chapel)
Monument
High altar
Reredos (choir-screen)
Processional path
Side chapel
South choir-aisle
Choir
Sacristy
East transept
Choir-stall
Crossing
Organ
Transept aisle
West transept
Crossing pier
Staircase
Pier buttress
Arcade pier (nave pier)
North porch
Arcade
Nave
Main vessel
North aisle
South aisle
Facade wall
Turret

GOTHIC TORUS WITH BALLFLOWERS

Limestone block
Block members carved into rolls
Block members cut polygonally
Pencil guideline
Early stage of ballflower carving

BLOCK AFTER INITIAL CUTTING

BLOCK WITH MEMBERS CUT INTO ROLLS

Torus
Ballflower
Fillet
Mason's mark

FINISHED BLOCK

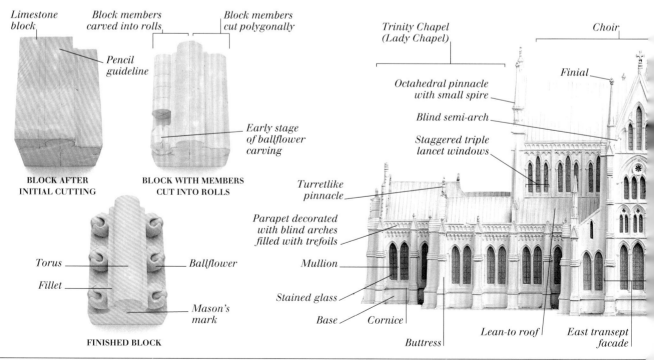

Trinity Chapel (Lady Chapel)
Choir
Octahedral pinnacle with small spire
Finial
Blind semi-arch
Staggered triple lancet windows
Turretlike pinnacle
Parapet decorated with blind arches filled with trefoils
Mullion
Stained glass
Base
Cornice
Lean-to roof
East transept facade
Buttress

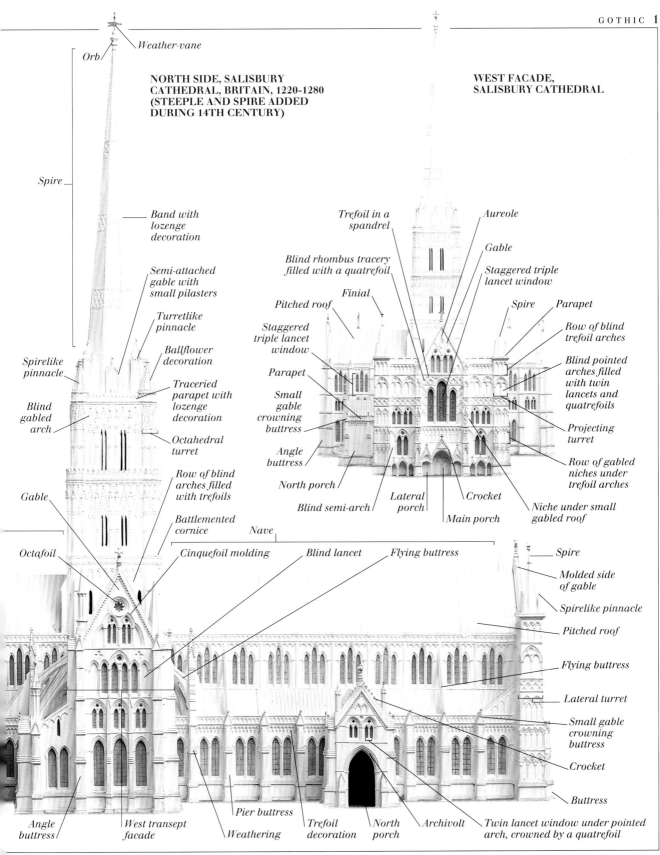

Weather-vane

Orb

**NORTH SIDE, SALISBURY
CATHEDRAL, BRITAIN, 1220-1280
(STEEPLE AND SPIRE ADDED
DURING 14TH CENTURY)**

**WEST FACADE,
SALISBURY CATHEDRAL**

Spire

Band with
lozenge
decoration

Semi-attached
gable with
small pilasters

Turretlike
pinnacle

Ballflower
decoration

Traceried
parapet with
lozenge
decoration

Spirelike
pinnacle

Blind
gabled
arch

Octahedral
turret

Gable

Row of blind
arches filled
with trefoils

Octafoil

Battlemented
cornice

Nave

Cinquefoil molding

Blind lancet

Flying buttress

Angle
buttress

West transept
facade

Weathering

Pier buttress

Trefoil
decoration

North
porch

Archivolt

Trefoil in a
spandrel

Aureole

Gable

Blind rhombus tracery
filled with a quatrefoil

Staggered triple
lancet window

Finial

Pitched roof

Spire

Parapet

Staggered
triple lancet
window

Row of blind
trefoil arches

Parapet

Blind pointed
arches filled
with twin
lancets and
quatrefoils

Small
gable
crowning
buttress

Angle
buttress

Projecting
turret

North porch

Blind semi-arch

Lateral
porch

Crocket

Main porch

Row of gabled
niches under
trefoil arches

Niche under small
gabled roof

Spire

Molded side
of gable

Spirelike pinnacle

Pitched roof

Flying buttress

Lateral turret

Small gable
crowning
buttress

Crocket

Buttress

Twin lancet window under pointed
arch, crowned by a quatrefoil

Gothic 2

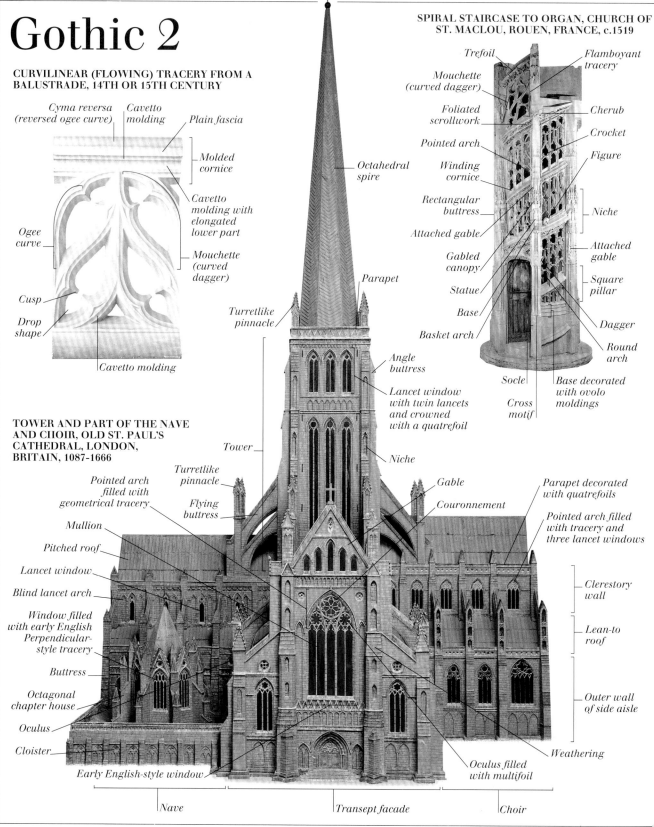

CURVILINEAR (FLOWING) TRACERY FROM A BALUSTRADE, 14TH OR 15TH CENTURY

Cyma reversa (reversed ogee curve)

Cavetto molding

Plain fascia

Molded cornice

Cavetto molding with elongated lower part

Mouchette (curved dagger)

Ogee curve

Cusp

Drop shape

Cavetto molding

TOWER AND PART OF THE NAVE AND CHOIR, OLD ST. PAUL'S CATHEDRAL, LONDON, BRITAIN, 1087-1666

Octahedral spire

Parapet

Turretlike pinnacle

Angle buttress

Lancet window with twin lancets and crowned with a quatrefoil

Niche

Tower

Turretlike pinnacle

Flying buttress

Gable

Couronnement

Parapet decorated with quatrefoils

Pointed arch filled with geometrical tracery

Pointed arch filled with tracery and three lancet windows

Mullion

Pitched roof

Lancet window

Blind lancet arch

Window filled with early English Perpendicular-style tracery

Clerestory wall

Lean-to roof

Buttress

Octagonal chapter house

Oculus

Outer wall of side aisle

Cloister

Weathering

Early English-style window

Oculus filled with multifoil

Nave

Transept facade

Choir

SPIRAL STAIRCASE TO ORGAN, CHURCH OF ST. MACLOU, ROUEN, FRANCE, c.1519

Trefoil

Flamboyant tracery

Mouchette (curved dagger)

Cherub

Foliated scrollwork

Crocket

Pointed arch

Figure

Winding cornice

Rectangular buttress

Niche

Attached gable

Attached gable

Gabled canopy

Square pillar

Statue

Base

Dagger

Basket arch

Round arch

Socle

Cross motif

Base decorated with ovolo moldings

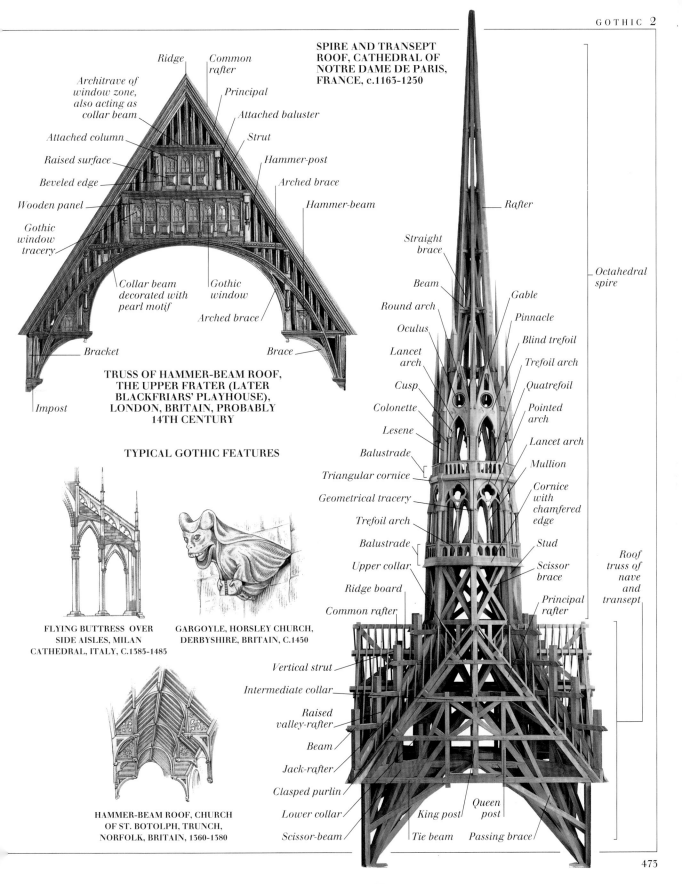

Ridge

Common rafter

Architrave of window zone, also acting as collar beam

Principal

Attached baluster

Attached column

Strut

Raised surface

Hammer-post

Beveled edge

Arched brace

Wooden panel

Hammer-beam

Gothic window tracery

Collar beam decorated with pearl motif

Gothic window

Arched brace

Bracket

Brace

Impost

TRUSS OF HAMMER-BEAM ROOF, THE UPPER FRATER (LATER BLACKFRIARS' PLAYHOUSE), LONDON, BRITAIN, PROBABLY 14TH CENTURY

TYPICAL GOTHIC FEATURES

FLYING BUTTRESS OVER SIDE AISLES, MILAN CATHEDRAL, ITALY, C.1385-1485

GARGOYLE, HORSLEY CHURCH, DERBYSHIRE, BRITAIN, C.1450

HAMMER-BEAM ROOF, CHURCH OF ST. BOTOLPH, TRUNCH, NORFOLK, BRITAIN, 1360-1380

SPIRE AND TRANSEPT ROOF, CATHEDRAL OF NOTRE DAME DE PARIS, FRANCE, c.1163-1250

Rafter

Straight brace

Beam

Gable

Round arch

Pinnacle

Oculus

Blind trefoil

Lancet arch

Trefoil arch

Cusp

Quatrefoil

Colonette

Pointed arch

Lesene

Lancet arch

Balustrade

Mullion

Triangular cornice

Cornice with chamfered edge

Geometrical tracery

Trefoil arch

Stud

Balustrade

Scissor brace

Upper collar

Ridge board

Principal rafter

Common rafter

Octahedral spire

Roof truss of nave and transept

Vertical strut

Intermediate collar

Raised valley-rafter

Beam

Jack-rafter

Clasped purlin

Queen post

Lower collar

King post

Scissor-beam

Tie beam

Passing brace

Renaissance 1

THE RENAISSANCE was a period in European history—lasting roughly from the 14th century to the mid-17th century—during which the arts and sciences underwent great changes. In architecture, these changes were marked by a return to the classical forms and proportions of ancient Roman buildings. The Renaissance originated in Italy, and the buildings most characteristic of its style can be found there, such as the Palazzo Strozzi shown here. Mannerism is a branch of the Renaissance style that distorts the classical forms; an example is the Laurentian Library staircase. As the Renaissance style spread to other European countries, many of its features were incorporated into the local architecture. For example, the Château de Montal in France (see pp. 476-477) incorporates aedicules (tabernacles).

FACADE ON TO PIAZZA, PALAZZO STROZZI

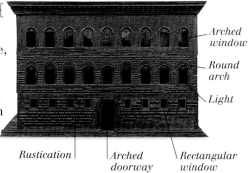

Crowning cornice

Arched window

Round arch

Light

Rustication

Arched doorway

Rectangular window

SIDE VIEW OF PALAZZO STROZZI, FLORENCE, ITALY, 1489 (BY G. DA SANGALLO, B. DA MAIANO, AND CRONACA)

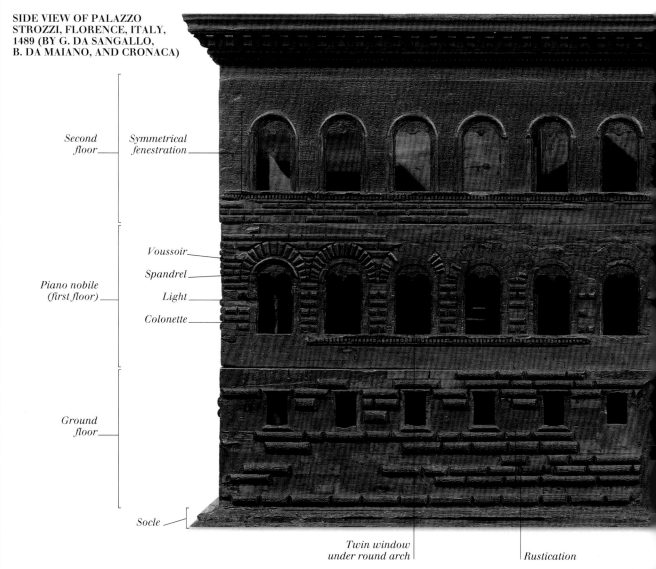

Second floor

Symmetrical fenestration

Piano nobile (first floor)

Voussoir

Spandrel

Light

Colonette

Ground floor

Socle

Twin window under round arch

Rustication

DETAILS FROM ITALIAN RENAISSANCE BUILDINGS

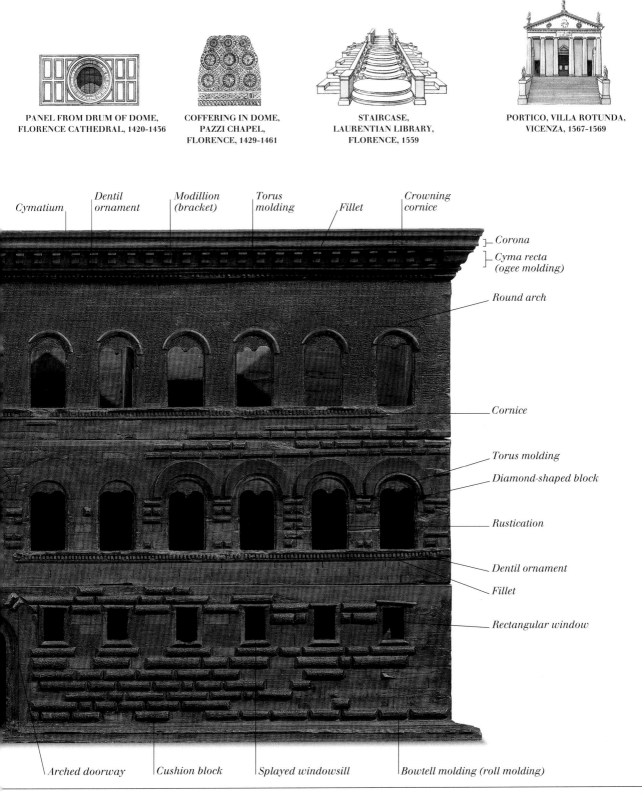

PANEL FROM DRUM OF DOME,
FLORENCE CATHEDRAL, 1420-1436

COFFERING IN DOME,
PAZZI CHAPEL,
FLORENCE, 1429-1461

STAIRCASE,
LAURENTIAN LIBRARY,
FLORENCE, 1559

PORTICO, VILLA ROTUNDA,
VICENZA, 1567-1569

Cymatium

Dentil ornament

Modillion (bracket)

Torus molding

Fillet

Crowning cornice

Corona

Cyma recta (ogee molding)

Round arch

Cornice

Torus molding

Diamond-shaped block

Rustication

Dentil ornament

Fillet

Rectangular window

Arched doorway

Cushion block

Splayed windowsill

Bowtell molding (roll molding)

Renaissance 2

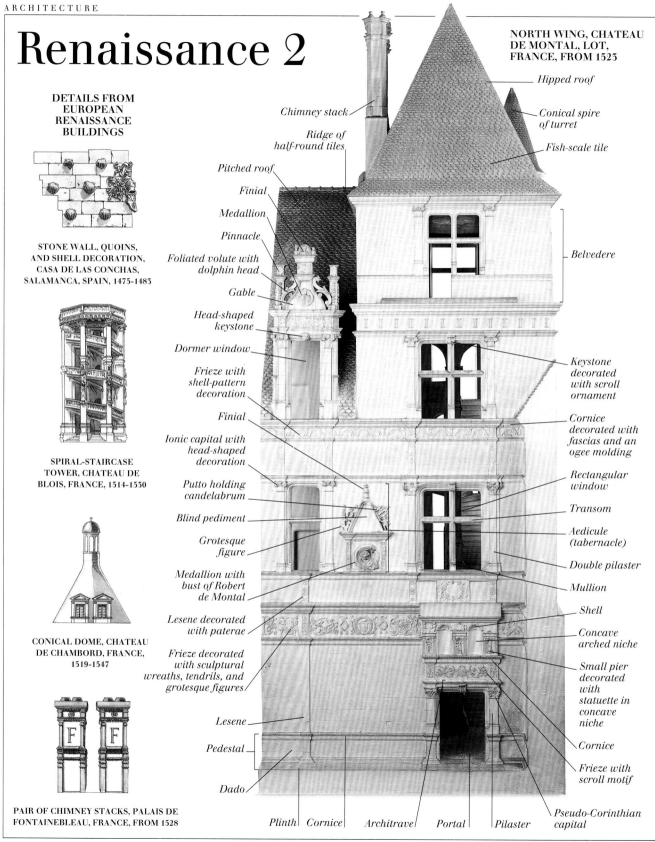

NORTH WING, CHATEAU DE MONTAL, LOT, FRANCE, FROM 1523

DETAILS FROM EUROPEAN RENAISSANCE BUILDINGS

STONE WALL, QUOINS, AND SHELL DECORATION, CASA DE LAS CONCHAS, SALAMANCA, SPAIN, 1475-1483

SPIRAL-STAIRCASE TOWER, CHATEAU DE BLOIS, FRANCE, 1514-1530

CONICAL DOME, CHATEAU DE CHAMBORD, FRANCE, 1519-1547

PAIR OF CHIMNEY STACKS, PALAIS DE FONTAINEBLEAU, FRANCE, FROM 1528

Chimney stack

Ridge of half-round tiles

Pitched roof

Finial

Medallion

Pinnacle

Foliated volute with dolphin head

Gable

Head-shaped keystone

Dormer window

Frieze with shell-pattern decoration

Finial

Ionic capital with head-shaped decoration

Putto holding candelabrum

Blind pediment

Grotesque figure

Medallion with bust of Robert de Montal

Lesene decorated with paterae

Frieze decorated with sculptural wreaths, tendrils, and grotesque figures

Lesene

Pedestal

Dado

Hipped roof

Conical spire of turret

Fish-scale tile

Belvedere

Keystone decorated with scroll ornament

Cornice decorated with fascias and an ogee molding

Rectangular window

Transom

Aedicule (tabernacle)

Double pilaster

Mullion

Shell

Concave arched niche

Small pier decorated with statuette in concave niche

Cornice

Frieze with scroll motif

Pseudo-Corinthian capital

Plinth | Cornice | Architrave | Portal | Pilaster

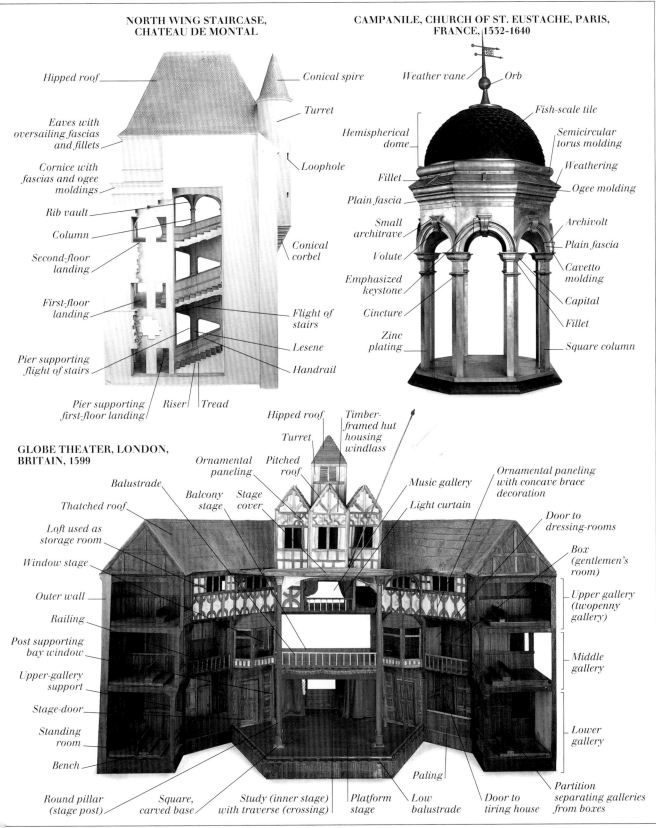

NORTH WING STAIRCASE, CHATEAU DE MONTAL

Hipped roof

Eaves with oversailing fascias and fillets

Cornice with fascias and ogee moldings

Rib vault

Column

Second-floor landing

First-floor landing

Pier supporting flight of stairs

Pier supporting first-floor landing

Riser

Tread

Conical spire

Turret

Loophole

Conical corbel

Flight of stairs

Lesene

Handrail

CAMPANILE, CHURCH OF ST. EUSTACHE, PARIS, FRANCE, 1532-1640

Weather vane

Orb

Fish-scale tile

Hemispherical dome

Semicircular torus molding

Fillet

Weathering

Plain fascia

Ogee molding

Small architrave

Archivolt

Volute

Plain fascia

Emphasized keystone

Cavetto molding

Cincture

Capital

Fillet

Zinc plating

Square column

GLOBE THEATER, LONDON, BRITAIN, 1599

Hipped roof

Timber-framed hut housing windlass

Turret

Pitched roof

Ornamental paneling

Balustrade

Balcony stage

Stage cover

Music gallery

Light curtain

Ornamental paneling with concave brace decoration

Thatched roof

Door to dressing-rooms

Loft used as storage room

Box (gentlemen's room)

Window stage

Upper gallery (twopenny gallery)

Outer wall

Railing

Middle gallery

Post supporting bay window

Upper-gallery support

Stage-door

Lower gallery

Standing room

Bench

Paling

Partition separating galleries from boxes

Round pillar (stage post)

Square, carved base

Study (inner stage) with traverse (crossing)

Platform stage

Low balustrade

Door to tiring house

Baroque and neoclassical 1

THE BAROQUE STYLE EVOLVED IN THE EARLY 17TH CENTURY in Rome. It is characterized by curved outlines and ostentatious decoration, as can be seen in the Italian church details (right). The baroque style was particularly widely favored in Italy, Spain, and Germany. It was also adopted in Britain and France, but with adaptations. The British architects Sir Christopher Wren and Nicholas Hawksmoor, for example, used baroque features—such as the concave walls of St. Paul's Cathedral and the curved buttresses of the Church of St. George in the East (see pp. 480-481)—but they did so with restraint. Similarly, the curved buttresses and volutes of the Parisian Church of St. Paul-St. Louis are relatively plain. In the second half of the 17th century, a distinct classical style (known as neoclassicism) developed in northern Europe as a reaction to the excesses of baroque. Typical of this new style were churches such as the Madeleine (a proposed facade is shown below), as well as secular buildings such as the Cirque Napoleon (opposite) and the buildings of the British architect Sir John Soane (see pp. 482-483). In early 18th century France, an extremely lavish form of baroque developed, known as rococo. The balcony from Nantes (see pp. 482-483) with its twisted ironwork and head-shaped corbels is typical of this style.

DETAILS FROM ITALIAN BAROQUE CHURCHES

SCROLLED BUTTRESS, CHURCH OF ST. MARIA DELLA SALUTE, VENICE, 1631-1682

STATUE OF THE ECSTASY OF ST. THERESA, CHURCH OF ST. MARIA DELLA VITTORIA, ROME, 1645-1652

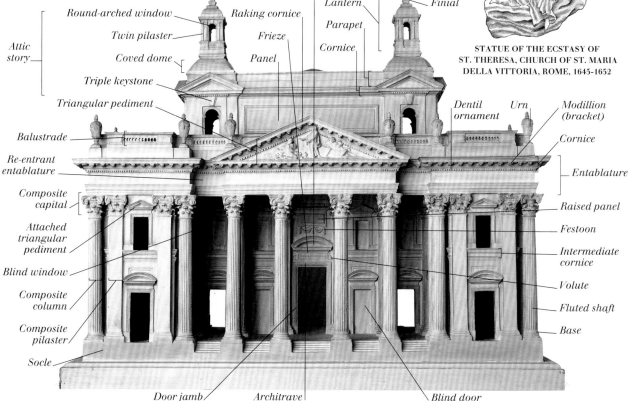

PROPOSED FACADE, THE MADELEINE (NEOCLASSICAL), PARIS, FRANCE, 1764 (BY P. CONTANT D'IVRY)

Attic story

Round-arched window

Twin pilaster

Coved dome

Triple keystone

Triangular pediment

Balustrade

Re-entrant entablature

Composite capital

Attached triangular pediment

Blind window

Composite column

Composite pilaster

Socle

Raking cornice

Frieze

Panel

Attached segmental pediment

Lantern

Parapet

Cornice

Finial

Dentil ornament

Urn

Modillion (bracket)

Cornice

Entablature

Raised panel

Festoon

Intermediate cornice

Volute

Fluted shaft

Base

Door jamb

Architrave

Blind door

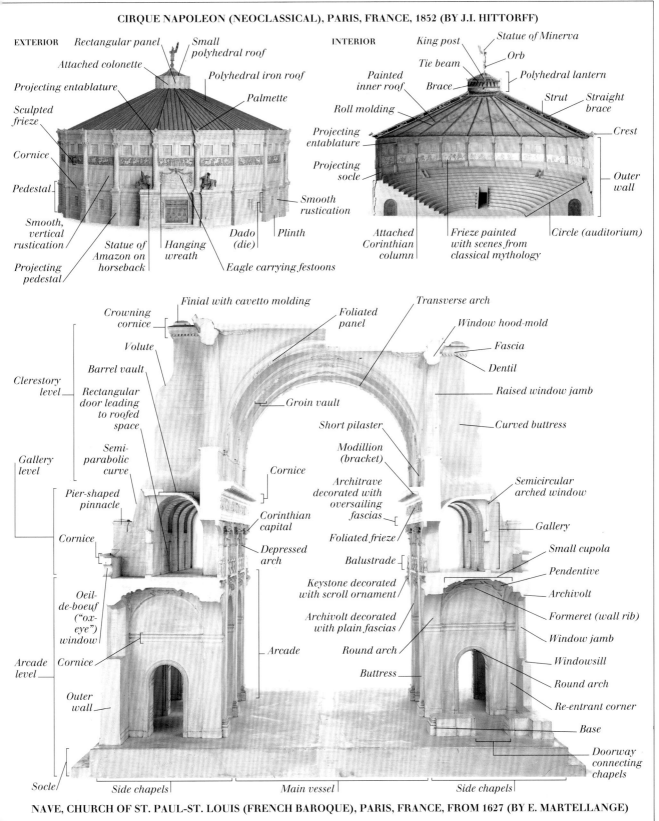

CIRQUE NAPOLEON (NEOCLASSICAL), PARIS, FRANCE, 1852 (BY J.I. HITTORFF)

EXTERIOR

Rectangular panel

Small polyhedral roof

Attached colonette

Polyhedral iron roof

Projecting entablature

Palmette

Sculpted frieze

Cornice

Pedestal

Smooth, vertical rustication

Statue of Amazon on horseback

Hanging wreath

Smooth rustication

Dado (die)

Plinth

Eagle carrying festoons

Projecting pedestal

INTERIOR

King post

Statue of Minerva

Tie beam

Orb

Painted inner roof

Polyhedral lantern

Brace

Roll molding

Strut

Straight brace

Projecting entablature

Crest

Projecting socle

Outer wall

Attached Corinthian column

Frieze painted with scenes from classical mythology

Circle (auditorium)

Finial with cavetto molding

Foliated panel

Transverse arch

Crowning cornice

Window hood-mold

Volute

Fascia

Barrel vault

Dentil

Clerestory level

Groin vault

Raised window jamb

Rectangular door leading to roofed space

Short pilaster

Curved buttress

Semi-parabolic curve

Modillion (bracket)

Gallery level

Cornice

Architrave decorated with oversailing fascias

Semicircular arched window

Pier-shaped pinnacle

Corinthian capital

Gallery

Cornice

Depressed arch

Foliated frieze

Balustrade

Small cupola

Pendentive

Oeil-de-boeuf ("ox-eye") window

Keystone decorated with scroll ornament

Archivolt

Formeret (wall rib)

Cornice

Archivolt decorated with plain fascias

Window jamb

Arcade level

Round arch

Windowsill

Arcade

Outer wall

Buttress

Round arch

Re-entrant corner

Base

Doorway connecting chapels

Socle

Side chapels

Main vessel

Side chapels

NAVE, CHURCH OF ST. PAUL-ST. LOUIS (FRENCH BAROQUE), PARIS, FRANCE, FROM 1627 (BY E. MARTELLANGE)

Baroque and neoclassical 2

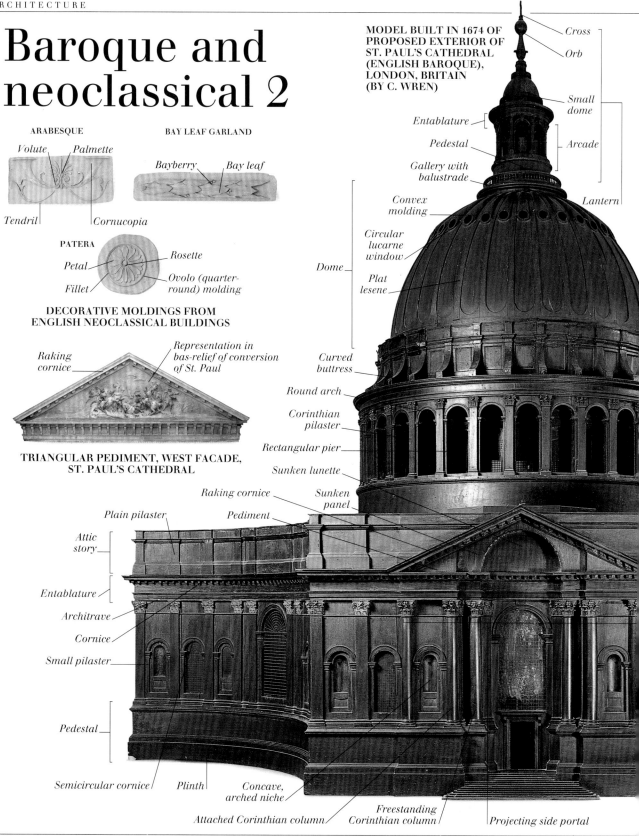

MODEL BUILT IN 1674 OF PROPOSED EXTERIOR OF ST. PAUL'S CATHEDRAL (ENGLISH BAROQUE), LONDON, BRITAIN (BY C. WREN)

Cross

Orb

Small dome

Entablature

Pedestal

Arcade

Gallery with balustrade

Lantern

Convex molding

Circular lucarne window

Dome

Plat lesene

Curved buttress

Round arch

Corinthian pilaster

Rectangular pier

Sunken lunette

ARABESQUE

Volute

Palmette

Tendril

Cornucopia

BAY LEAF GARLAND

Bayberry

Bay leaf

PATERA

Petal

Rosette

Fillet

Ovolo (quarter-round) molding

DECORATIVE MOLDINGS FROM ENGLISH NEOCLASSICAL BUILDINGS

Raking cornice

Representation in bas-relief of conversion of St. Paul

TRIANGULAR PEDIMENT, WEST FACADE, ST. PAUL'S CATHEDRAL

Plain pilaster

Raking cornice

Sunken panel

Pediment

Attic story

Entablature

Architrave

Cornice

Small pilaster

Pedestal

Semicircular cornice

Plinth

Concave, arched niche

Attached Corinthian column

Freestanding Corinthian column

Projecting side portal

CHURCH OF ST. GEORGE IN THE EAST (ENGLISH BAROQUE), LONDON, BRITAIN, 1714-1734 (BY N. HAWKSMOOR)

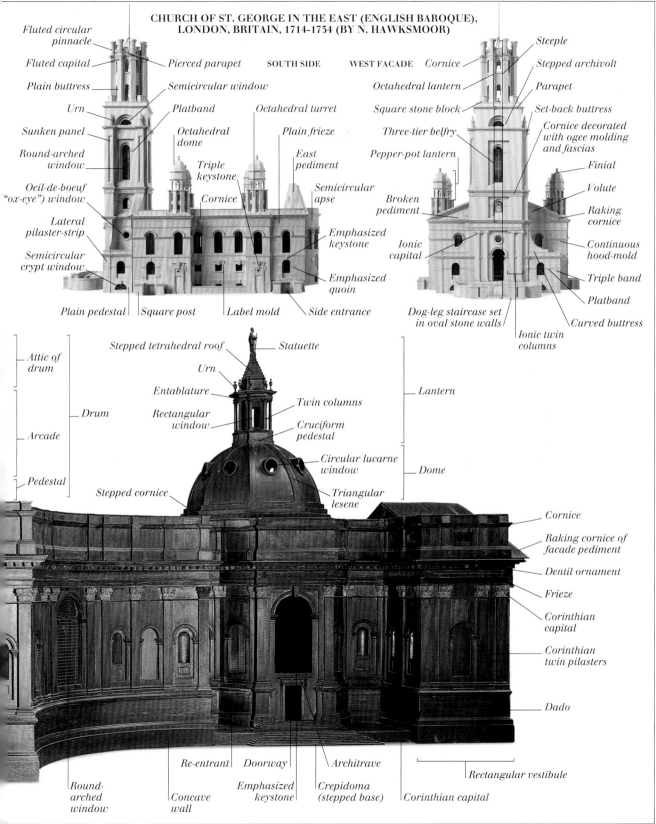

SOUTH SIDE

Fluted circular pinnacle
Fluted capital
Pierced parapet
Plain buttress
Semicircular window
Urn
Platband
Sunken panel
Octahedral dome
Octahedral turret
Round-arched window
Plain frieze
Octahedral dome
Triple keystone
East pediment
Oeil-de-boeuf ("ox-eye") window
Cornice
Semicircular apse
Lateral pilaster-strip
Emphasized keystone
Semicircular crypt window
Emphasized quoin
Plain pedestal
Square post
Label mold
Side entrance

WEST FACADE

Cornice
Steeple
Stepped archivolt
Octahedral lantern
Parapet
Square stone block
Set-back buttress
Three-tier belfry
Cornice decorated with ogee molding and fascias
Pepper-pot lantern
Finial
Volute
Broken pediment
Raking cornice
Ionic capital
Continuous hood-mold
Triple band
Platband
Dog-leg staircase set in oval stone walls
Curved buttress
Ionic twin columns

Attic of drum
Stepped tetrahedral roof
Statuette
Urn
Drum
Entablature
Lantern
Rectangular window
Twin columns
Arcade
Cruciform pedestal
Circular lucarne window
Pedestal
Dome
Stepped cornice
Triangular lesene
Cornice
Raking cornice of facade pediment
Dentil ornament
Frieze
Corinthian capital
Corinthian twin pilasters
Dado
Re-entrant
Doorway
Architrave
Rectangular vestibule
Round-arched window
Concave wall
Emphasized keystone
Crepidoma (stepped base)
Corinthian capital

Baroque and neoclassical 3

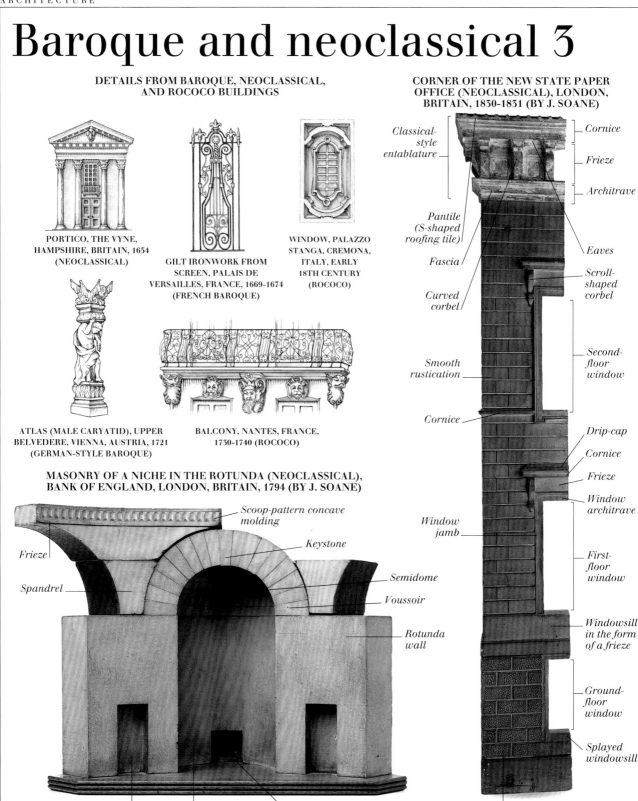

DETAILS FROM BAROQUE, NEOCLASSICAL, AND ROCOCO BUILDINGS

PORTICO, THE VYNE, HAMPSHIRE, BRITAIN, 1654 (NEOCLASSICAL)

GILT IRONWORK FROM SCREEN, PALAIS DE VERSAILLES, FRANCE, 1669-1674 (FRENCH BAROQUE)

WINDOW, PALAZZO STANGA, CREMONA, ITALY, EARLY 18TH CENTURY (ROCOCO)

ATLAS (MALE CARYATID), UPPER BELVEDERE, VIENNA, AUSTRIA, 1721 (GERMAN-STYLE BAROQUE)

BALCONY, NANTES, FRANCE, 1730-1740 (ROCOCO)

CORNER OF THE NEW STATE PAPER OFFICE (NEOCLASSICAL), LONDON, BRITAIN, 1830-1831 (BY J. SOANE)

Classical-style entablature

Cornice

Frieze

Architrave

Pantile (S-shaped roofing tile)

Fascia

Curved corbel

Eaves

Scroll-shaped corbel

Smooth rustication

Second-floor window

Cornice

Drip-cap

Cornice

Frieze

Window architrave

Window jamb

First-floor window

Windowsill in the form of a frieze

Ground-floor window

Splayed windowsill

Vermiculated rustication

MASONRY OF A NICHE IN THE ROTUNDA (NEOCLASSICAL), BANK OF ENGLAND, LONDON, BRITAIN, 1794 (BY J. SOANE)

Scoop-pattern concave molding

Keystone

Frieze

Semidome

Spandrel

Voussoir

Rotunda wall

Flat, rectangular niche

Rounded niche

Flat, square niche

TYRINGHAM HOUSE (NEOCLASSICAL), BUCKINGHAMSHIRE, BRITAIN, 1793-1797 (BY J. SOANE)

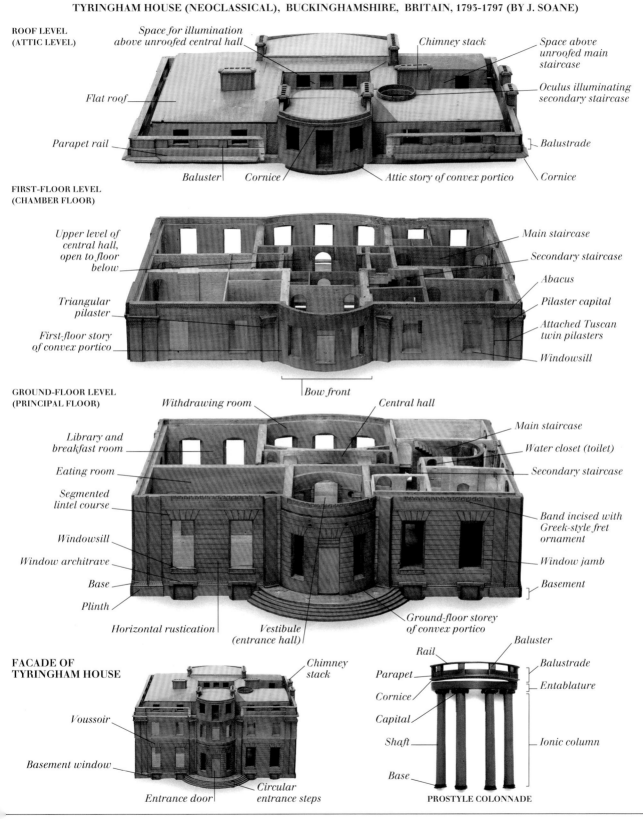

ROOF LEVEL (ATTIC LEVEL)

Space for illumination above unroofed central hall

Chimney stack

Space above unroofed main staircase

Oculus illuminating secondary staircase

Flat roof

Parapet rail

Balustrade

Cornice

Baluster

Cornice

Attic story of convex portico

FIRST-FLOOR LEVEL (CHAMBER FLOOR)

Upper level of central hall, open to floor below

Main staircase

Secondary staircase

Abacus

Pilaster capital

Attached Tuscan twin pilasters

Triangular pilaster

First-floor story of convex portico

Windowsill

Bow front

GROUND-FLOOR LEVEL (PRINCIPAL FLOOR)

Withdrawing room

Central hall

Library and breakfast room

Main staircase

Water closet (toilet)

Eating room

Secondary staircase

Segmented lintel course

Band incised with Greek-style fret ornament

Windowsill

Window architrave

Window jamb

Base

Basement

Plinth

Horizontal rustication

Vestibule (entrance hall)

Ground-floor storey of convex portico

FACADE OF TYRINGHAM HOUSE

Chimney stack

Voussoir

Basement window

Entrance door

Circular entrance steps

Baluster

Rail

Balustrade

Parapet

Entablature

Cornice

Capital

Shaft

Ionic column

Base

PROSTYLE COLONNADE

Arches and vaults

ARCHES ARE CURVED STRUCTURES used to bridge spans and to support the weight of upper parts of buildings, such as domes, as in St. Paul's Cathedral (below) and the historical temple (opposite). The voussoirs (wedge-shaped blocks) that form an arch (right) support each other and convert the downward force of the weight of the building into an outward force. This outward force is in turn transferred to buttresses, piers, or abutments. A vault is an arched roof or ceiling. There are four main types of vault (opposite). A barrel vault is a single vault, semicircular in cross-section; a groin vault consists of two barrel vaults intersecting at right angles; a rib vault is a groin vault reinforced by ribs; and a fan vault is a rib vault in which the ribs radiate from the springing point (where the arch begins) like a fan.

PARTS OF AN ARCH

Voussoir Keystone Crown Abutment

Keystone

Abutment

Extrados

Intrados (soffit) Haunch

Impost

Intrados (soffit)

Abutment

Springing point

Span

Abutment

FRONT **SIDE**

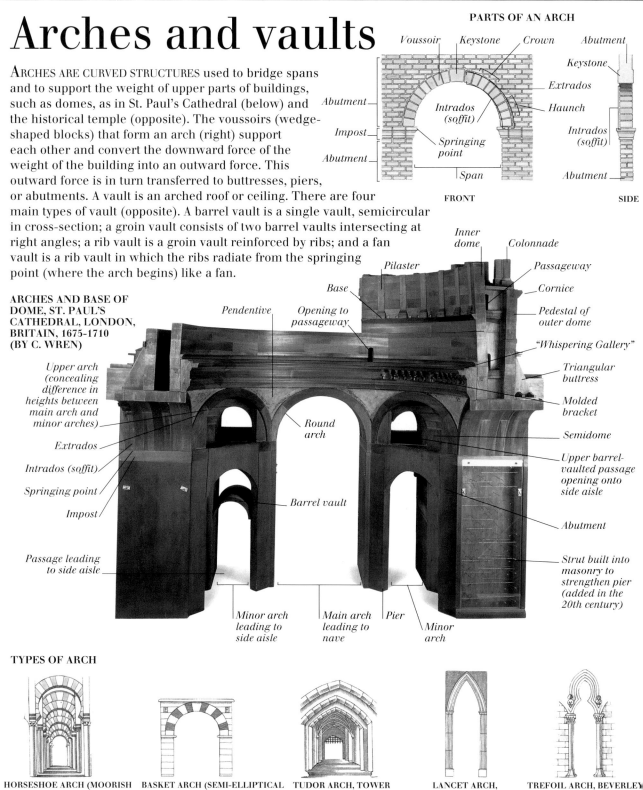

ARCHES AND BASE OF DOME, ST. PAUL'S CATHEDRAL, LONDON, BRITAIN, 1675-1710 (BY C. WREN)

Inner dome

Colonnade

Pilaster

Passageway

Base

Cornice

Pendentive

Opening to passageway

Pedestal of outer dome

"Whispering Gallery"

Upper arch (concealing difference in heights between main arch and minor arches)

Triangular buttress

Molded bracket

Round arch

Semidome

Extrados

Upper barrel-vaulted passage opening onto side aisle

Intrados (soffit)

Springing point

Impost

Barrel vault

Abutment

Passage leading to side aisle

Strut built into masonry to strengthen pier (added in the 20th century)

Minor arch leading to side aisle

Main arch leading to nave

Pier

Minor arch

TYPES OF ARCH

HORSESHOE ARCH (MOORISH ARCH), GREAT MOSQUE, CORDOBA, SPAIN, 785

BASKET ARCH (SEMI-ELLIPTICAL ARCH), PALATINE CHAPEL, AIX-LA-CHAPELLE, FRANCE, 790-798

TUDOR ARCH, TOWER OF LONDON, BRITAIN, C.1086-1097

LANCET ARCH, WESTMINSTER ABBEY, LONDON, BRITAIN, 1503-1519

TREFOIL ARCH, BEVERLEY MINSTER, YORKSHIRE, BRITAIN, C.1300

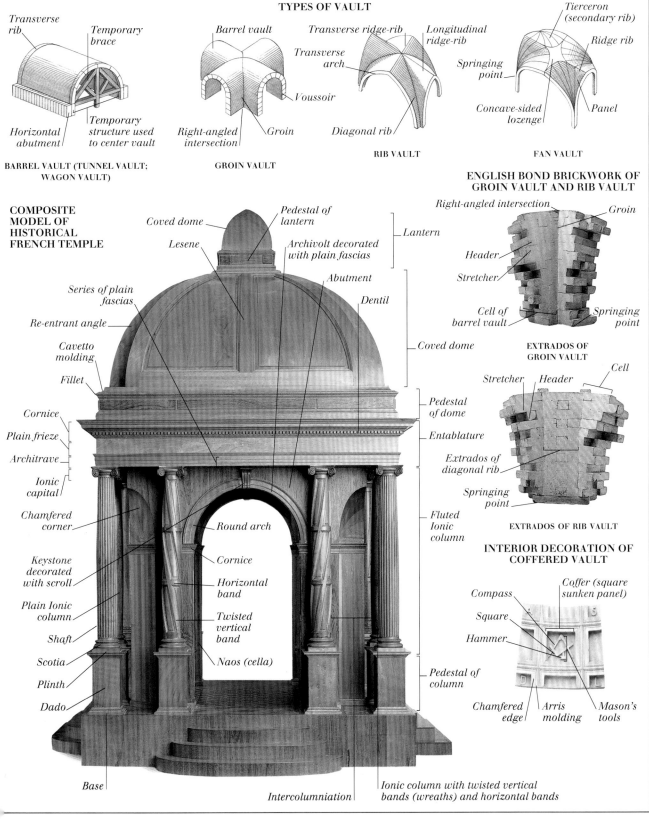

TYPES OF VAULT

Transverse rib

Temporary brace

Horizontal abutment

Temporary structure used to center vault

BARREL VAULT (TUNNEL VAULT; WAGON VAULT)

Barrel vault

Voussoir

Right-angled intersection

Groin

GROIN VAULT

Transverse ridge-rib

Transverse arch

Longitudinal ridge-rib

Diagonal rib

RIB VAULT

Tierceron (secondary rib)

Ridge rib

Springing point

Concave-sided lozenge

Panel

FAN VAULT

COMPOSITE MODEL OF HISTORICAL FRENCH TEMPLE

Coved dome

Lesene

Series of plain fascias

Re-entrant angle

Cavetto molding

Fillet

Cornice

Plain frieze

Architrave

Ionic capital

Chamfered corner

Keystone decorated with scroll

Plain Ionic column

Shaft

Scotia

Plinth

Dado

Base

Pedestal of lantern

Archivolt decorated with plain fascias

Abutment

Dentil

Round arch

Cornice

Horizontal band

Twisted vertical band

Naos (cella)

Intercolumniation

Lantern

Coved dome

Pedestal of dome

Entablature

Fluted Ionic column

Pedestal of column

Ionic column with twisted vertical bands (wreaths) and horizontal bands

ENGLISH BOND BRICKWORK OF GROIN VAULT AND RIB VAULT

Right-angled intersection

Groin

Header

Stretcher

Cell of barrel vault

Springing point

EXTRADOS OF GROIN VAULT

Stretcher

Header

Cell

Extrados of diagonal rib

Springing point

EXTRADOS OF RIB VAULT

INTERIOR DECORATION OF COFFERED VAULT

Compass

Square

Hammer

Coffer (square sunken panel)

Chamfered edge

Arris molding

Mason's tools

485

Domes

A DOME IS A CONVEX ROOF. Domes are categorized according to the shapes of both the base and the section through the center of the dome. The base may be circular, square, or polygonal (many-sided), depending on the plan of the drum (the walls on which the dome rests). The section of a dome may be the same shape as any arch (see pp. 484-485). Various types of dome are illustrated here: a hemispherical dome, which has a circular base and a semicircular section; a saucer dome, which has a circular base and a segmental (less than a semicircle) section; a polyhedral dome, which is a dome on a polygonal base whose sides meet at the top of the dome; and an onion dome, which has a circular or polygonal base and an ogee-shaped section. Many domes have a lantern (a turret with windows) to provide light inside.

LANTERN AND UPPER DOME TIMBERING, ST. PAUL'S CATHEDRAL

ROOF WITH LANTERN AND ONION DOME

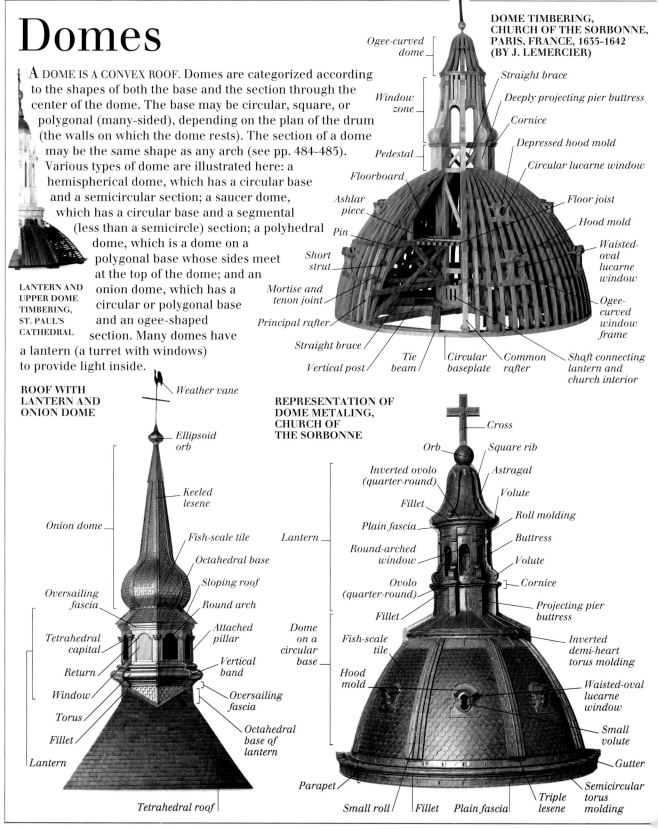

DOME TIMBERING, CHURCH OF THE SORBONNE, PARIS, FRANCE, 1635-1642 (BY J. LEMERCIER)

Ogee-curved dome
Straight brace
Window zone
Deeply projecting pier buttress
Cornice
Depressed hood mold
Pedestal
Circular lucarne window
Floorboard
Floor joist
Ashlar piece
Hood mold
Pin
Waisted-oval lucarne window
Short strut
Ogee-curved window frame
Mortise and tenon joint
Principal rafter
Shaft connecting lantern and church interior
Straight brace
Tie beam
Circular baseplate
Common rafter
Vertical post

Weather vane
Ellipsoid orb
Keeled lesene
Onion dome
Fish-scale tile
Octahedral base
Sloping roof
Round arch
Oversailing fascia
Attached pillar
Tetrahedral capital
Vertical band
Return
Window
Oversailing fascia
Torus
Octahedral base of lantern
Fillet
Lantern
Tetrahedral roof

REPRESENTATION OF DOME METALING, CHURCH OF THE SORBONNE

Cross
Orb
Square rib
Inverted ovolo (quarter-round)
Astragal
Fillet
Volute
Plain fascia
Roll molding
Lantern
Round-arched window
Buttress
Ovolo (quarter-round)
Volute
Fillet
Cornice
Dome on a circular base
Projecting pier buttress
Fish-scale tile
Inverted demi-heart torus molding
Hood mold
Waisted-oval lucarne window
Small volute
Gutter
Parapet
Semicircular torus molding
Small roll
Fillet
Plain fascia
Triple lesene

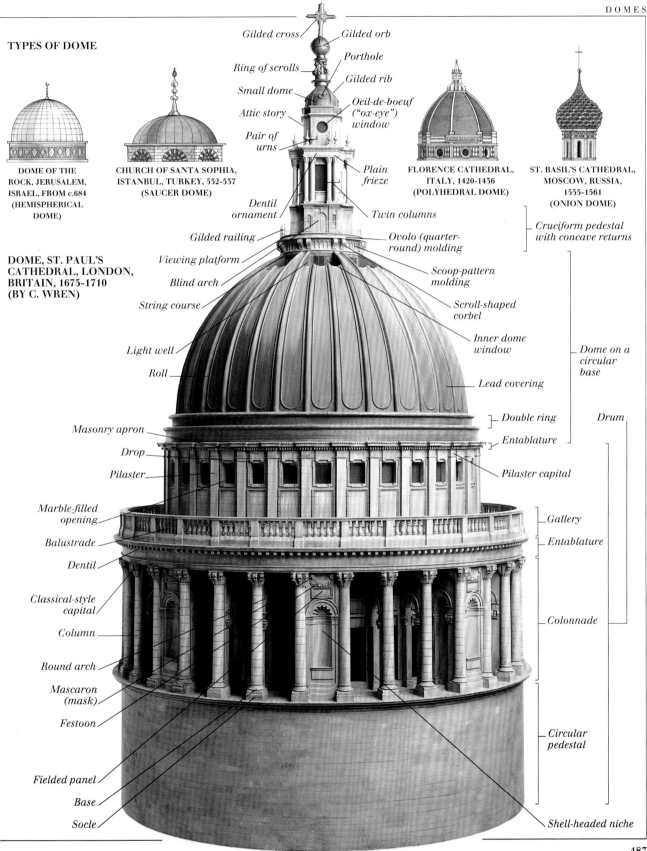

TYPES OF DOME

DOME OF THE
ROCK, JERUSALEM,
ISRAEL, FROM c.684
(HEMISPHERICAL
DOME)

CHURCH OF SANTA SOPHIA,
ISTANBUL, TURKEY, 532-537
(SAUCER DOME)

FLORENCE CATHEDRAL,
ITALY, 1420-1436
(POLYHEDRAL DOME)

ST. BASIL'S CATHEDRAL,
MOSCOW, RUSSIA,
1555-1561
(ONION DOME)

DOME, ST. PAUL'S
CATHEDRAL, LONDON,
BRITAIN, 1675-1710
(BY C. WREN)

Gilded cross
Gilded orb
Porthole
Ring of scrolls
Gilded rib
Small dome
Oeil-de-boeuf
("ox-eye")
window
Attic story
Pair of
urns
Plain
frieze
Dentil
ornament
Twin columns
Gilded railing
Ovolo (quarter-
round) molding
Viewing platform
Scoop-pattern
molding
Blind arch
Scroll-shaped
corbel
String course
Inner dome
window
Light well
Roll
Lead covering
Masonry apron
Double ring
Drop
Entablature
Pilaster
Pilaster capital
Marble-filled
opening
Gallery
Balustrade
Entablature
Dentil
Classical-style
capital
Column
Colonnade
Round arch
Mascaron
(mask)
Festoon
Circular
pedestal
Fielded panel
Base
Socle
Shell-headed niche

Cruciform pedestal
with concave returns
Dome on a
circular
base
Drum

487

Islamic buildings

**OPUS SECTILE
MOSAIC DESIGN**

THE ISLAMIC RELIGION was founded by
the prophet Mohammed, who was born in
Mecca (in present-day Saudi Arabia) about
570 AD. During the next three centuries,
Islam spread from Arabia to North Africa
and Spain, as well as into India and much
of the rest of Asia. The worldwide
influence of Islam remains strong today.
Common characteristics of Islamic buildings
include ogee arches and roofs, onion domes,
and walls decorated with carved stone, paintings,
inlays, or mosaics. The most important type of
Islamic building is the mosque—the place
of worship—which generally has a minaret
(tower) from which the muezzin (official crier)
calls Muslims to prayer. Most mosques have a
mihrab (decorative niche) that indicates the
direction of Mecca. As figurative art is not
allowed in Islam, buildings are ornamented
with geometric and arabesque motifs and
inscriptions (frequently Koranic verses).

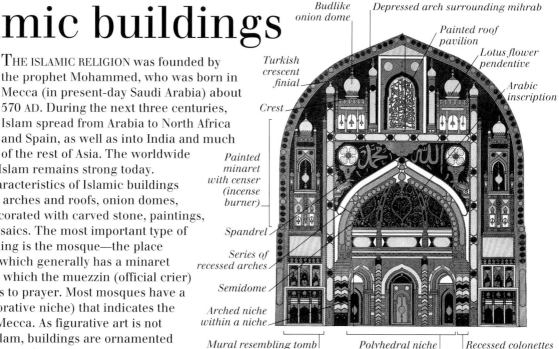

**MIHRAB, JAMI MASJID (PRINCIPAL OR CONGREGATIONAL
MOSQUE), BIJAPUR, INDIA, c.1636**

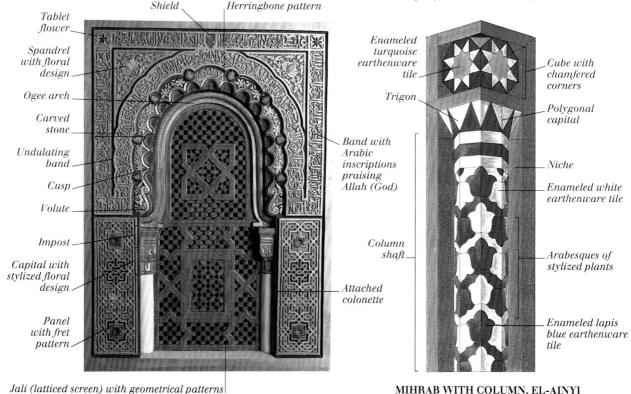

ARCH, THE ALHAMBRA, GRANADA, SPAIN, 1533-1354

**MIHRAB WITH COLUMN, EL-AINYI
MOSQUE, CAIRO, EGYPT, 15TH CENTURY**

EXAMPLES OF ISLAMIC MOSAICS, EGYPT AND SYRIA

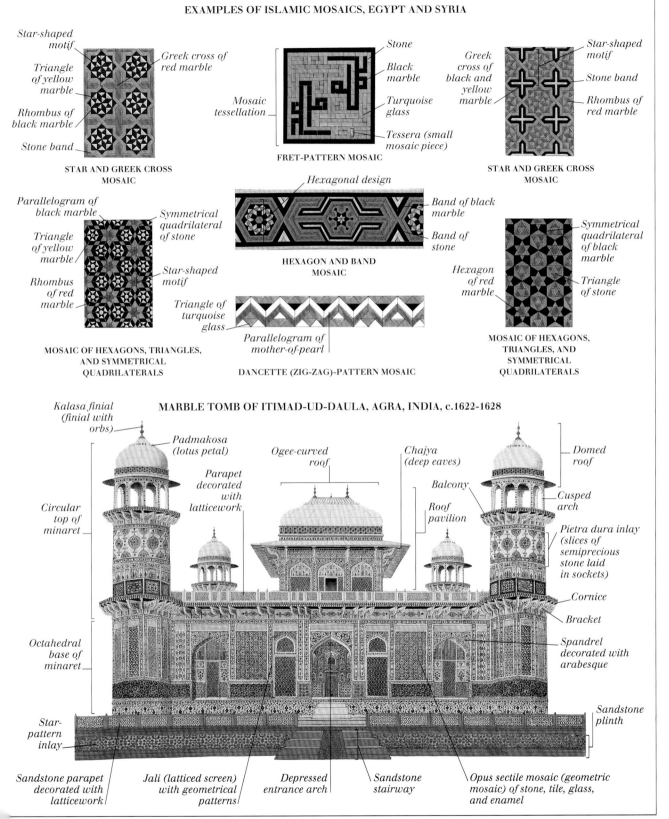

Star-shaped motif

Triangle of yellow marble

Rhombus of black marble

Stone band

Greek cross of red marble

STAR AND GREEK CROSS MOSAIC

Stone

Black marble

Turquoise glass

Mosaic tessellation

Tessera (small mosaic piece)

FRET-PATTERN MOSAIC

Greek cross of black and yellow marble

Star-shaped motif

Stone band

Rhombus of red marble

STAR AND GREEK CROSS MOSAIC

Parallelogram of black marble

Triangle of yellow marble

Rhombus of red marble

Symmetrical quadrilateral of stone

Star-shaped motif

MOSAIC OF HEXAGONS, TRIANGLES, AND SYMMETRICAL QUADRILATERALS

Hexagonal design

Band of black marble

Band of stone

HEXAGON AND BAND MOSAIC

Triangle of turquoise glass

Parallelogram of mother-of-pearl

DANCETTE (ZIG-ZAG)-PATTERN MOSAIC

Symmetrical quadrilateral of black marble

Hexagon of red marble

Triangle of stone

MOSAIC OF HEXAGONS, TRIANGLES, AND SYMMETRICAL QUADRILATERALS

MARBLE TOMB OF ITIMAD-UD-DAULA, AGRA, INDIA, c.1622-1628

Kalasa finial (finial with orbs)

Padmakosa (lotus petal)

Ogee-curved roof

Chajya (deep eaves)

Domed roof

Circular top of minaret

Parapet decorated with latticework

Balcony

Roof pavilion

Cusped arch

Pietra dura inlay (slices of semiprecious stone laid in sockets)

Cornice

Bracket

Octahedral base of minaret

Spandrel decorated with arabesque

Star-pattern inlay

Sandstone plinth

Sandstone parapet decorated with latticework

Jali (latticed screen) with geometrical patterns

Depressed entrance arch

Sandstone stairway

Opus sectile mosaic (geometric mosaic) of stone, tile, glass, and enamel

489

South and east Asia

THE TRADITIONAL ARCHITECTURE of south and east Asia has been profoundly influenced by the spread from India of Buddhism and Hinduism. This influence is shown by both the abundance and by the architectural styles of temples and shrines in the region. Many early Hindu temples consist of rooms carved from solid rock faces. However, freestanding structures began to be built in southern India from about the eighth century AD. Many were built in the Dravidian style, like the Temple of Virupaksha (opposite), with its characteristic antarala (terraced tower), perforated windows, and numerous arches, pilasters, and carvings. The earliest Buddhist religious monuments were Indian stupas, which consisted of a single hemispherical dome surmounted by a chattravali (shaft) and surrounded by railings with ornate gates. Later Indian stupas and those built elsewhere were sometimes modified. For example, in Sri Lanka, the dome became bell-shaped, and was called a dagoba. Buddhist pagodas, such as the Burmese example (right), are multistoried temples, each story having a projecting roof. The form of these buildings probably derived from the yasti (pointed spire) of the stupa. Another feature of many traditional Asian buildings is their imaginative roof forms, such as gambrel (mansard) roofs, and roofs with angle rafters (below).

DETAILS FROM EAST ASIAN BUILDINGS

KASUGA-STYLE ROOF WITH SUMIGI (ANGLE RAFTERS), KASUGADO SHRINE OF ENJOJI, NARA, JAPAN, 12TH-14TH CENTURY

TERRACES, TEMPLE OF HEAVEN, BEIJING, CHINA, 15TH CENTURY

GAMBREL (MANSARD) ROOF WITH UPSWEPT EAVES AND UNDULATING GABLES, HIMEJI CASTLE, HIMEJI, JAPAN, 1608-1609

CORNER CAPITAL WITH ROOF BEAMS, POPCHU-SA TEMPLE, POPCHU-SA, SOUTH KOREA, 17TH CENTURY

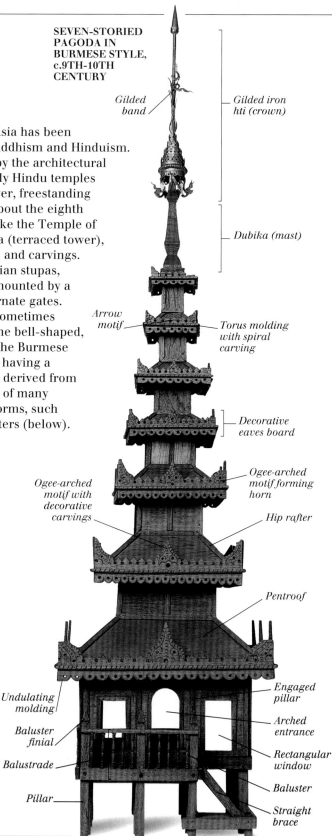

SEVEN-STORIED PAGODA IN BURMESE STYLE, c.9TH-10TH CENTURY

Gilded band

Gilded iron hti (crown)

Dubika (mast)

Arrow motif

Torus molding with spiral carving

Decorative eaves board

Ogee-arched motif with decorative carvings

Ogee-arched motif forming horn

Hip rafter

Pentroof

Engaged pillar

Arched entrance

Rectangular window

Baluster

Straight brace

Pillar

Balustrade

Baluster finial

Undulating molding

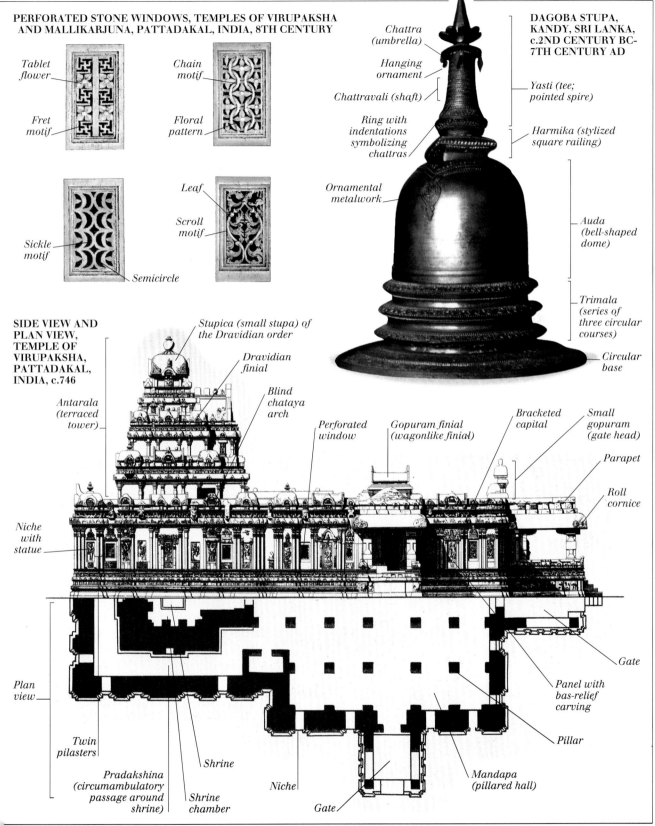

PERFORATED STONE WINDOWS, TEMPLES OF VIRUPAKSHA AND MALLIKARJUNA, PATTADAKAL, INDIA, 8TH CENTURY

Tablet flower

Fret motif

Chain motif

Floral pattern

Leaf

Scroll motif

Sickle motif

Semicircle

DAGOBA STUPA, KANDY, SRI LANKA, c.2ND CENTURY BC-7TH CENTURY AD

Chattra (umbrella)

Hanging ornament

Chattravali (shaft)

Ring with indentations symbolizing chattras

Yasti (tee; pointed spire)

Harmika (stylized square railing)

Ornamental metalwork

Auda (bell-shaped dome)

Trimala (series of three circular courses)

Circular base

SIDE VIEW AND PLAN VIEW, TEMPLE OF VIRUPAKSHA, PATTADAKAL, INDIA, c.746

Stupica (small stupa) of the Dravidian order

Dravidian finial

Blind chataya arch

Perforated window

Gopuram finial (wagonlike finial)

Bracketed capital

Small gopuram (gate head)

Parapet

Roll cornice

Antarala (terraced tower)

Niche with statue

Gate

Plan view

Panel with bas-relief carving

Pillar

Twin pilasters

Shrine

Niche

Mandapa (pillared hall)

Pradakshina (circumambulatory passage around shrine)

Shrine chamber

Gate

491

The 19th century

BUILDINGS OF THE 19TH CENTURY are characterized by the use of new materials and by a great diversity of architectural styles. From the end of the 18th century, iron and steel became widely used as alternatives to wood for the framework of buildings, as in the flax-spinning mill shown here. Built in Britain in 1796, this mill exemplifies an architectural style that became common throughout the industrialized world for more than a century. The Industrial Revolution also brought mass production of building parts—a development that enabled the British architect Sir Joseph Paxton to erect London's Crystal Palace (a building made entirely of iron and glass) in only nine months, ready for the Great Exhibition of 1851. The 19th century saw a widespread revival of older architectural styles. For example, in the United States and Germany, Neo-Greek architecture was fashionable; in Britain and France, Neo-Baroque, Neo-Byzantine, and Neo-Gothic styles (as seen in the Palace of Westminster and Tower Bridge, London) were dominant.

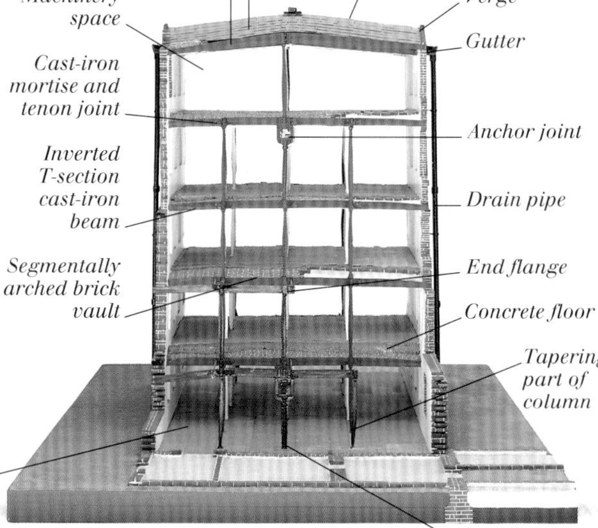

FLAX-SPINNING MILL, SHREWSBURY, BRITAIN, 1796 (BY C. BAGE)

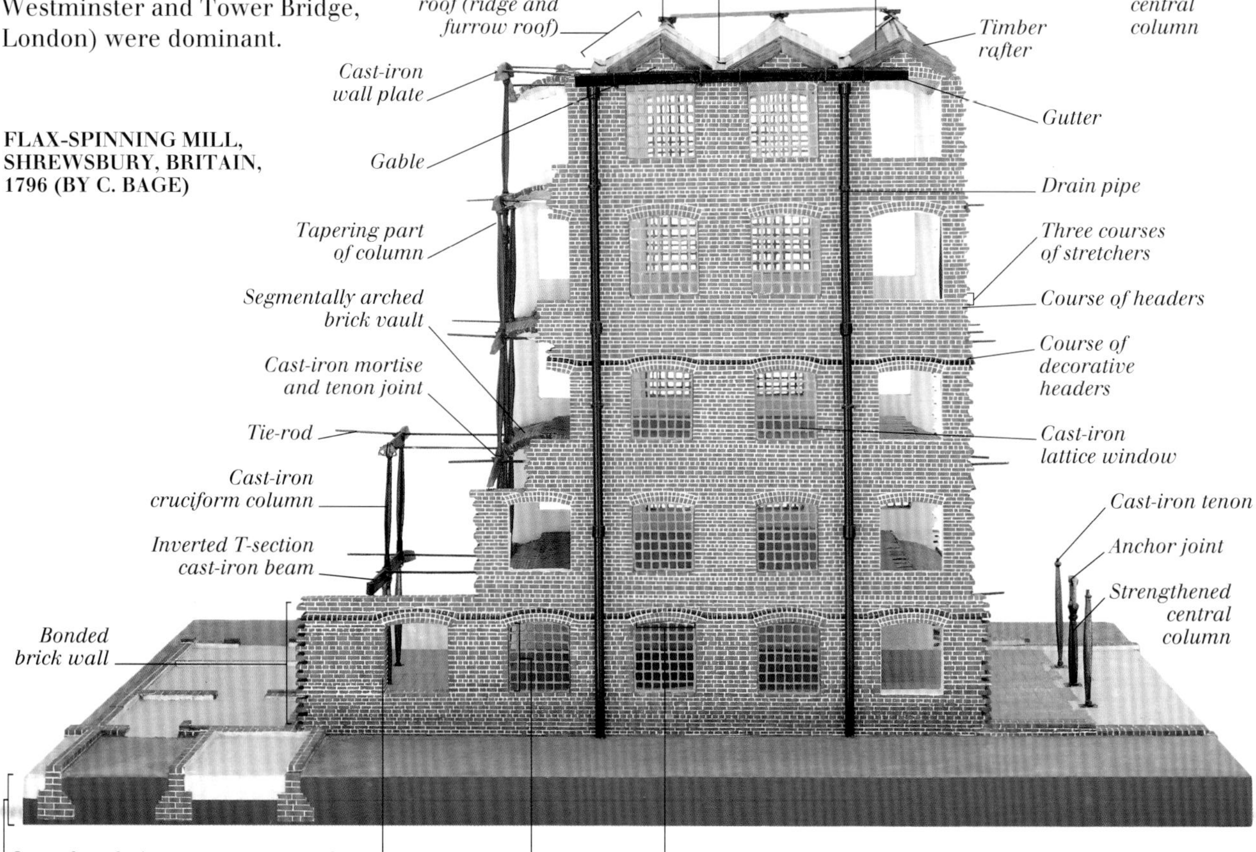

Cast-iron wall plate Pitched roof Ridge Verge Gutter
Machinery space
Cast-iron mortise and tenon joint
Inverted T-section cast-iron beam
Segmentally arched brick vault
Anchor joint
Drain pipe
End flange
Concrete floor
Tapering part of column
Paved ground floor
Strengthened central column

Multi-gabled roof (ridge and furrow roof) Ridge Furrow Verge
Timber rafter
Cast-iron wall plate
Gable
Gutter
Tapering part of column
Drain pipe
Three courses of stretchers
Segmentally arched brick vault
Course of headers
Cast-iron mortise and tenon joint
Course of decorative headers
Tie-rod
Cast-iron cruciform column
Cast-iron lattice window
Inverted T-section cast-iron beam
Cast-iron tenon
Anchor joint
Strengthened central column
Bonded brick wall
Stone foundation Quoin Jamb Gauged arch (segmental arch of tapered bricks)

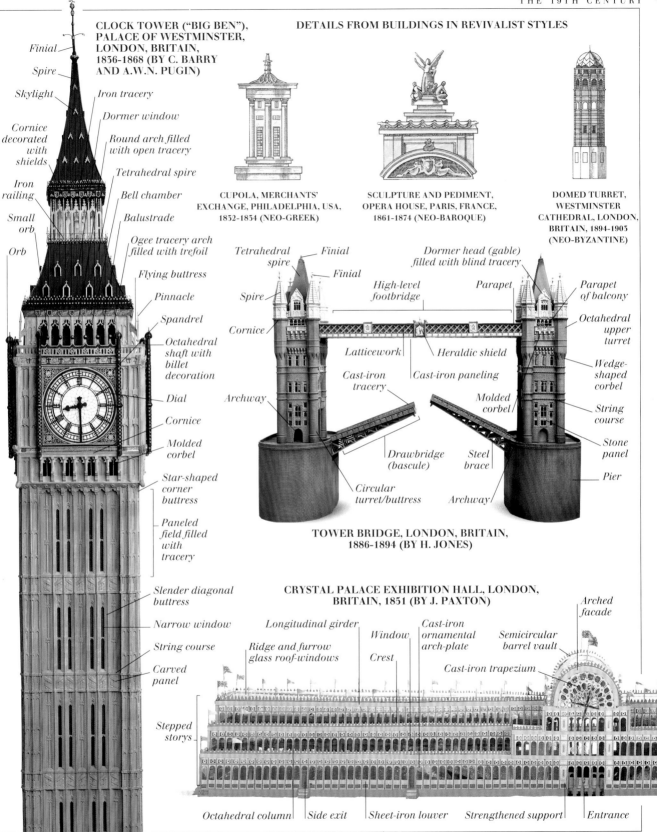

CLOCK TOWER ("BIG BEN"), PALACE OF WESTMINSTER, LONDON, BRITAIN, 1836-1868 (BY C. BARRY AND A.W.N. PUGIN)

Finial
Spire
Skylight
Cornice decorated with shields
Iron railing
Small orb
Orb
Iron tracery
Dormer window
Round arch filled with open tracery
Tetrahedral spire
Bell chamber
Balustrade
Ogee tracery arch filled with trefoil
Flying buttress
Pinnacle
Spandrel
Octahedral shaft with billet decoration
Dial
Cornice
Molded corbel
Star-shaped corner buttress
Paneled field filled with tracery
Slender diagonal buttress
Narrow window
String course
Carved panel
Stepped storys

DETAILS FROM BUILDINGS IN REVIVALIST STYLES

CUPOLA, MERCHANTS' EXCHANGE, PHILADELPHIA, USA, 1832-1834 (NEO-GREEK)

SCULPTURE AND PEDIMENT, OPERA HOUSE, PARIS, FRANCE, 1861-1874 (NEO-BAROQUE)

DOMED TURRET, WESTMINSTER CATHEDRAL, LONDON, BRITAIN, 1894-1903 (NEO-BYZANTINE)

Tetrahedral spire
Finial
Finial
Spire
Cornice
High-level footbridge
Latticework
Cast-iron tracery
Archway
Dormer head (gable) filled with blind tracery
Parapet
Heraldic shield
Cast-iron paneling
Parapet of balcony
Octahedral upper turret
Wedge-shaped corbel
String course
Stone panel
Pier
Molded corbel
Drawbridge (bascule)
Steel brace
Archway
Circular turret/buttress

TOWER BRIDGE, LONDON, BRITAIN, 1886-1894 (BY H. JONES)

CRYSTAL PALACE EXHIBITION HALL, LONDON, BRITAIN, 1851 (BY J. PAXTON)

Longitudinal girder
Window
Cast-iron ornamental arch-plate
Arched facade
Semicircular barrel vault
Ridge and furrow glass roof-windows
Crest
Cast-iron trapezium
Octahedral column
Side exit
Sheet-iron louver
Strengthened support
Entrance

The early 20th century

EMPIRE STATE
BUILDING, NEW
YORK, USA, 1929-1931
(BY R. H. SHREVE,
T. LAMB, AND
A. L. HARMON)

ARCHITECTURE OF THE EARLY 20TH CENTURY is notable for radical new types of steel and glass buildings—particularly skyscrapers—and the widespread use of steel-reinforced concrete. The steel-framed skyscraper was pioneered in Chicago in the 1880s but did not become widespread until the first decades of the 20th century. As construction techniques were refined, skyscrapers became higher and higher. For example, the Empire State Building (right) of 1929-1931 has 102 storys. Many buildings of this period were constructed from lightweight concrete slabs that could be supported by cantilever beams or by pilotis (stilts), as in the Villa Savoye (below). The early 20th century also produced a great variety of architectural styles, some of which are illustrated opposite. Despite their diversity, the styles of this period generally had one thing in common: they were completely new, with few links to past architectural styles. This originality is in marked contrast to 19th-century architecture (see pp. 492-493), much of which was revivalist.

VILLA SAVOYE, POISSY, FRANCE, 1929-1931 (BY LE CORBUSIER)

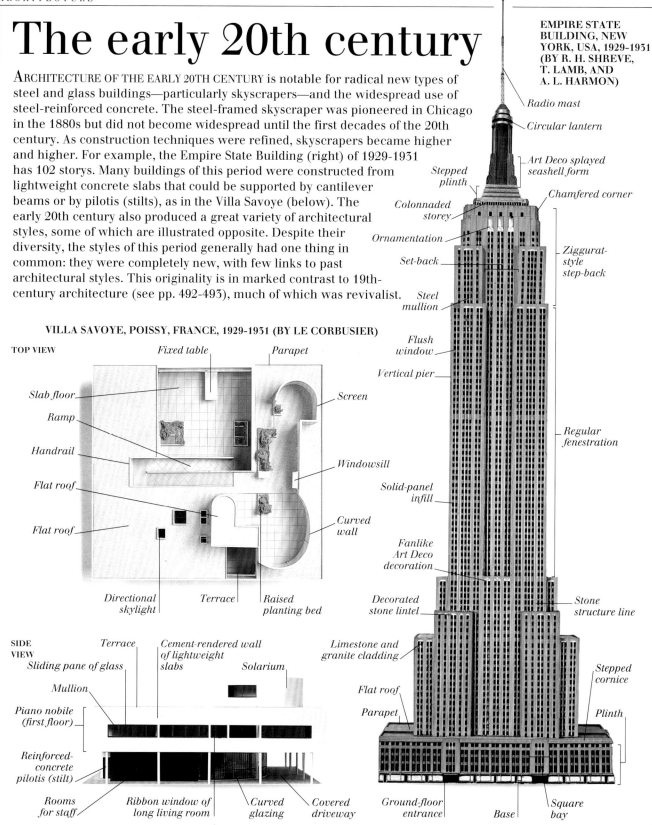

TOP VIEW

Fixed table · Parapet · Screen · Windowsill · Curved wall

Slab floor · Ramp · Handrail · Flat roof · Flat roof

Directional skylight · Terrace · Raised planting bed

SIDE VIEW

Terrace · Cement-rendered wall of lightweight slabs · Solarium

Sliding pane of glass · Mullion · Piano nobile (first floor) · Reinforced-concrete pilotis (stilt)

Rooms for staff · Ribbon window of long living room · Curved glazing · Covered driveway

Radio mast · Circular lantern · Art Deco splayed seashell form · Chamfered corner · Ziggurat-style step-back

Stepped plinth · Colonnaded storey · Ornamentation · Set-back · Steel mullion · Flush window · Vertical pier · Regular fenestration · Solid-panel infill · Fanlike Art Deco decoration · Decorated stone lintel · Limestone and granite cladding · Flat roof · Parapet · Stone structure line · Stepped cornice · Plinth · Ground-floor entrance · Base · Square bay

MIDWAY GARDENS, CHICAGO, USA, 1914 (BY F. L. WRIGHT)

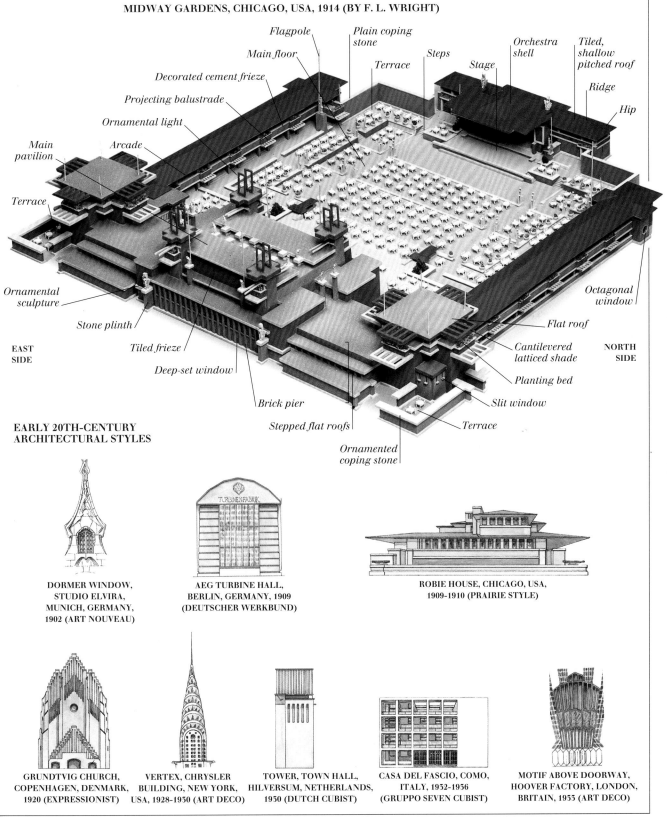

Flagpole

Plain coping stone

Main floor

Terrace

Steps

Stage

Orchestra shell

Tiled, shallow pitched roof

Ridge

Hip

Decorated cement frieze

Projecting balustrade

Ornamental light

Arcade

Main pavilion

Terrace

Ornamental sculpture

Stone plinth

Tiled frieze

Deep-set window

Brick pier

Stepped flat roofs

Ornamented coping stone

Terrace

Slit window

Planting bed

Cantilevered latticed shade

Flat roof

Octagonal window

EAST SIDE

NORTH SIDE

EARLY 20TH-CENTURY ARCHITECTURAL STYLES

DORMER WINDOW, STUDIO ELVIRA, MUNICH, GERMANY, 1902 (ART NOUVEAU)

AEG TURBINE HALL, BERLIN, GERMANY, 1909 (DEUTSCHER WERKBUND)

ROBIE HOUSE, CHICAGO, USA, 1909-1910 (PRAIRIE STYLE)

GRUNDTVIG CHURCH, COPENHAGEN, DENMARK, 1920 (EXPRESSIONIST)

VERTEX, CHRYSLER BUILDING, NEW YORK, USA, 1928-1930 (ART DECO)

TOWER, TOWN HALL, HILVERSUM, NETHERLANDS, 1930 (DUTCH CUBIST)

CASA DEL FASCIO, COMO, ITALY, 1932-1936 (GRUPPO SEVEN CUBIST)

MOTIF ABOVE DOORWAY, HOOVER FACTORY, LONDON, BRITAIN, 1933 (ART DECO)

Modern buildings 1

ARCHITECTURE SINCE ABOUT THE 1950s is generally known as modern architecture. One of its main influences has been functionalism—a belief that a building's function should be apparent in its design. Both the Centre Georges Pompidou (below and opposite) and the Hong Kong and Shanghai Bank (see pp. 498-499) are functionalist buildings. On each, elements of engineering and the building's services are clearly visible on the outside. In the 1980s, some architects rejected functionalism in favor of postmodernism, in which historical styles—particularly neoclassicism—were revived, using modern building materials and techniques. In many modern buildings, walls are made of glass or concrete hung from a frame, as in the Kawana House (right); this type of wall construction is known as curtain walling. Other modern construction techniques include the intricate interlocking of concrete vaults—as in the Sydney Opera House (see pp. 498-499)—and the use of high-tension beams to create complex roof shapes, such as the paraboloid roof of the Church of St. Pierre de Libreville (see pp. 498-499).

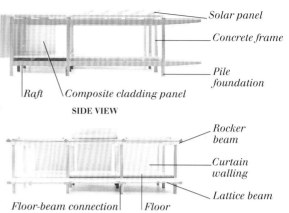

Solar panel
Concrete frame
Pile foundation
Raft
Composite cladding panel

SIDE VIEW

Rocker beam
Curtain walling
Lattice beam
Floor-beam connection
Floor

FRONT VIEW

SERVICES FACADE, CENTRE GEORGES POMPIDOU, PARIS, FRANCE, 1977 (BY R. PIANO AND R. ROGERS)

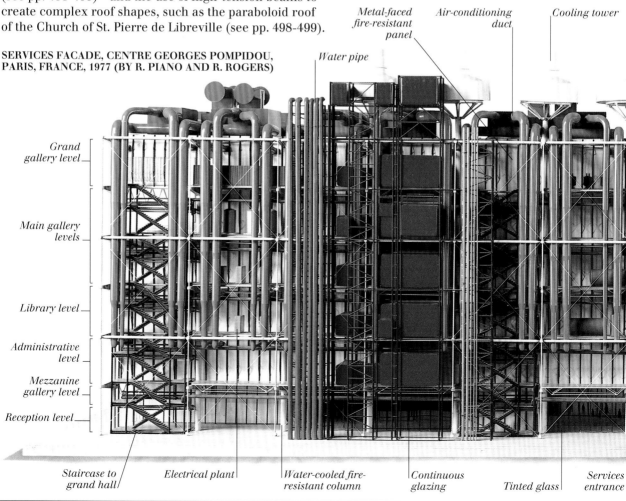

Metal-faced fire-resistant panel
Air-conditioning duct
Cooling tower
Water pipe

Grand gallery level

Main gallery levels

Library level

Administrative level

Mezzanine gallery level

Reception level

Staircase to grand hall
Electrical plant
Water-cooled fire-resistant column
Continuous glazing
Tinted glass
Services entrance

PRINCIPAL FACADE, CENTRE GEORGES POMPIDOU

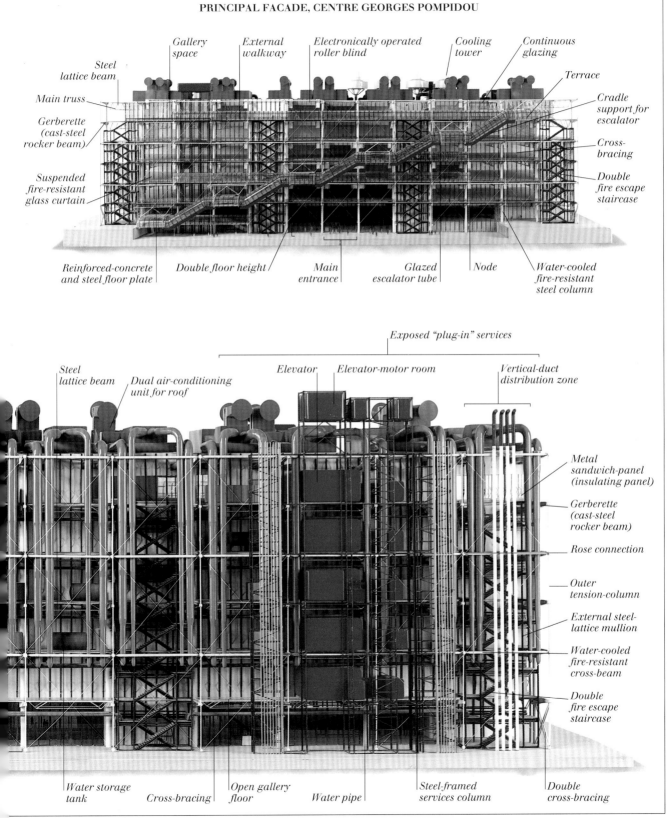

Gallery space

External walkway

Electronically operated roller blind

Cooling tower

Continuous glazing

Steel lattice beam

Main truss

Terrace

Cradle support for escalator

Gerberette (cast-steel rocker beam)

Cross-bracing

Double fire escape staircase

Suspended fire-resistant glass curtain

Reinforced-concrete and steel floor plate

Double floor height

Main entrance

Glazed escalator tube

Node

Water-cooled fire-resistant steel column

Exposed "plug-in" services

Steel lattice beam

Dual air-conditioning unit for roof

Elevator

Elevator-motor room

Vertical-duct distribution zone

Metal sandwich-panel (insulating panel)

Gerberette (cast-steel rocker beam)

Rose connection

Outer tension-column

External steel-lattice mullion

Water-cooled fire-resistant cross-beam

Double fire escape staircase

Water storage tank

Cross-bracing

Open gallery floor

Water pipe

Steel-framed services column

Double cross-bracing

Modern buildings 2

HONG KONG AND SHANGHAI BANK, HONG KONG, 1981-1985 (BY N. FOSTER)

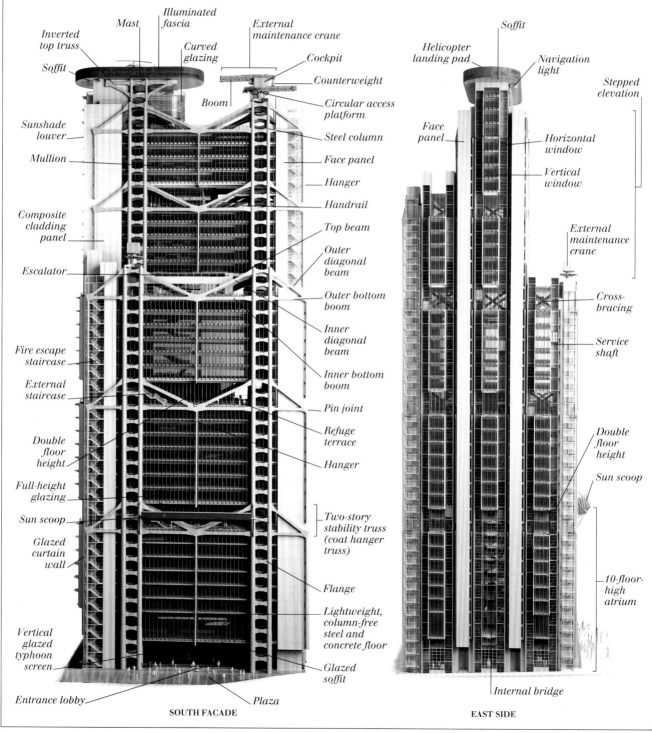

Inverted top truss
Mast
Illuminated fascia
Curved glazing
External maintenance crane
Cockpit
Soffit
Counterweight
Boom
Circular access platform
Sunshade louver
Steel column
Mullion
Face panel
Hanger
Handrail
Composite cladding panel
Top beam
Outer diagonal beam
Escalator
Outer bottom boom
Inner diagonal beam
Inner bottom boom
Fire escape staircase
Pin joint
External staircase
Refuge terrace
Double floor height
Hanger
Full-height glazing
Sun scoop
Two-story stability truss (coat hanger truss)
Glazed curtain wall
Flange
Lightweight, column-free steel and concrete floor
Vertical glazed typhoon screen
Glazed soffit
Entrance lobby
Plaza

SOUTH FACADE

Soffit
Helicopter landing pad
Navigation light
Stepped elevation
Face panel
Horizontal window
Vertical window
External maintenance crane
Cross-bracing
Service shaft
Double floor height
Sun scoop
10-floor-high atrium
Internal bridge

EAST SIDE

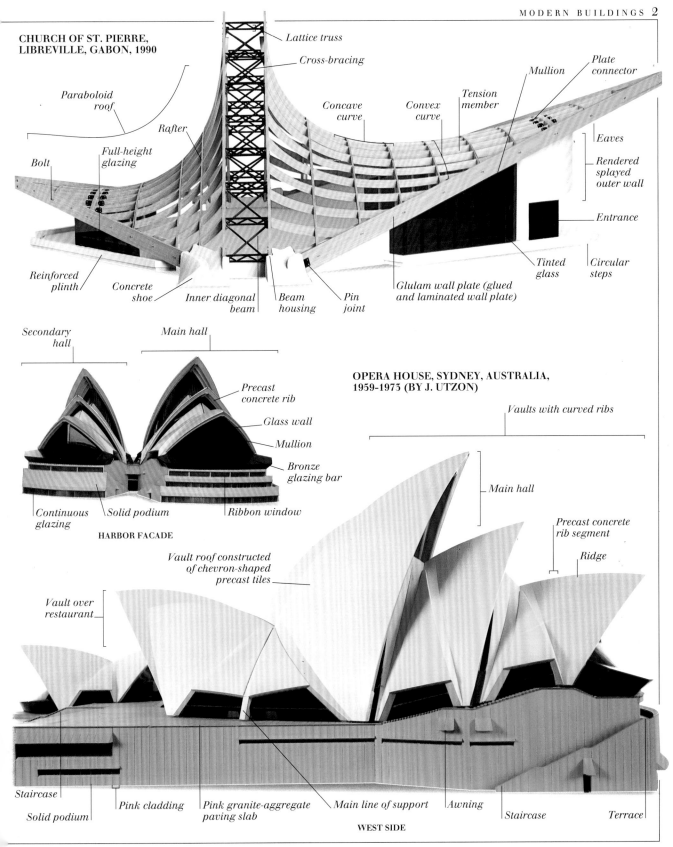

CHURCH OF ST. PIERRE, LIBREVILLE, GABON, 1990

Lattice truss

Cross-bracing

Paraboloid roof

Rafter

Concave curve

Convex curve

Tension member

Mullion

Plate connector

Eaves

Rendered splayed outer wall

Full-height glazing

Bolt

Entrance

Reinforced plinth

Concrete shoe

Inner diagonal beam

Beam housing

Pin joint

Glulam wall plate (glued and laminated wall plate)

Tinted glass

Circular steps

Secondary hall

Main hall

OPERA HOUSE, SYDNEY, AUSTRALIA, 1959-1973 (BY J. UTZON)

Precast concrete rib

Glass wall

Mullion

Bronze glazing bar

Vaults with curved ribs

Continuous glazing

Solid podium

Ribbon window

HARBOR FACADE

Main hall

Precast concrete rib segment

Ridge

Vault roof constructed of chevron-shaped precast tiles

Vault over restaurant

Staircase

Solid podium

Pink cladding

Pink granite-aggregate paving slab

Main line of support

Awning

Staircase

Terrace

WEST SIDE

499

Music

Musical notation

MUSICAL NOTATION IS ANY METHOD by which sounds are written down so that they can be read and performed by others. The present-day conventional system of notation uses a five-line stave (staff)—divided by vertical lines into sections known as bars—on which notes, rests, clefs, key signatures, time signatures, accidentals, and other symbols are written. A note indicates the duration of a sound and, according to its position on the stave, its pitch. Notes can be arranged on the stave in order of pitch to form a scale. A silence in the music is indicated by a rest. The clef, which is placed at the begininng of a stave, fixes the pitch. The key signature, which is placed after the clef, indicates the key. The time signature, placed after the key signature, shows the number of beats in a bar. Accidentals are used to indicate the raising or lowering of the pitch of a note.

ELEMENTS OF MUSICAL NOTATION

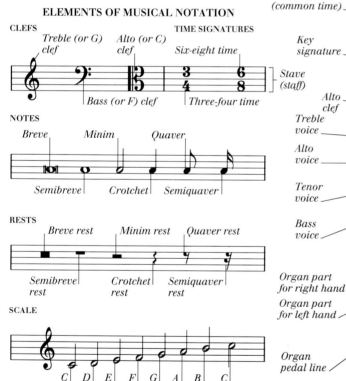

CLEFS

Treble (or G) clef

Alto (or C) clef

Bass (or F) clef

TIME SIGNATURES

Six-eight time

$\frac{3}{4}$ $\frac{6}{8}$

Three-four time

Stave (staff)

NOTES

Breve Minim Quaver

Semibreve Crotchet Semiquaver

RESTS

Breve rest Minim rest Quaver rest

Semibreve rest Crotchet rest Semiquaver rest

SCALE

C D E F G A B C

ACCIDENTALS

Sharp Natural Double sharp

Flat Double flat Key signature

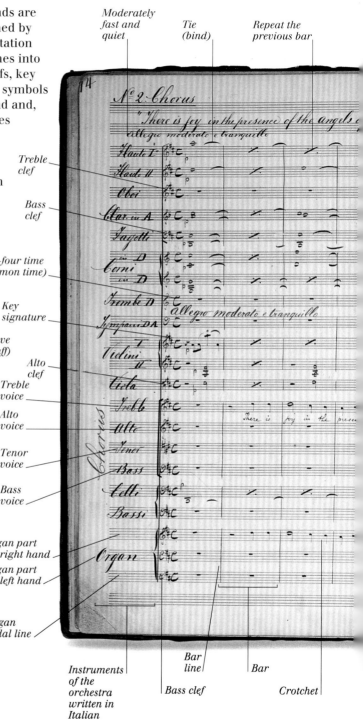

Moderately fast and quiet

Tie (bind)

Repeat the previous bar

Treble clef

Bass clef

Four-four time (common time)

Key signature

Alto clef

Treble voice

Alto voice

Tenor voice

Bass voice

Organ part for right hand

Organ part for left hand

Organ pedal line

Instruments of the orchestra written in Italian

Bar line

Bass clef

Bar

Crotchet

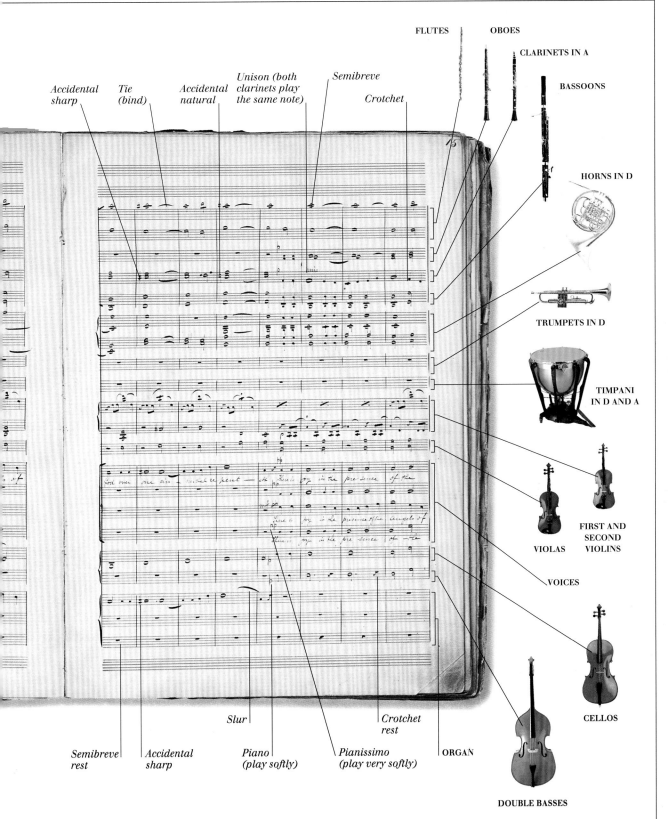

FLUTES

OBOES

CLARINETS IN A

BASSOONS

Accidental sharp

Tie (bind)

Accidental natural

Unison (both clarinets play the same note)

Semibreve

Crotchet

HORNS IN D

TRUMPETS IN D

TIMPANI IN D AND A

FIRST AND SECOND VIOLINS

VIOLAS

VOICES

CELLOS

Slur

Crotchet rest

ORGAN

Semibreve rest

Accidental sharp

Piano (play softly)

Pianissimo (play very softly)

DOUBLE BASSES

Orchestras

AN ORCHESTRA IS A GROUP of musicians that
plays music written for a specific combination of
instruments. The number and type of instruments
included in the orchestra depends on the style of
music being played. The modern orchestra (also
known as a symphony orchestra) is made up
of four sections of instruments—stringed,
woodwind, brass, and percussion. The
stringed section consists of violins, violas,
cellos (violoncellos), double basses, and
sometimes a harp (see pp. 510-511). The main
instruments of the woodwind section are flutes,
oboes, clarinets, and bassoons—the piccolo, cor
anglais, bass clarinet, saxophone, and double
bassoon (contrabassoon) can also be included
if the music requires them (see pp. 508-509).
The brass section usually consists of horns,
trumpets, trombones, and the tuba (see
pp. 506-507). The main instruments of
the percussion section are the timpani
(see pp. 518-519). The snare drum,
bass drum, cymbals, tambourine,
triangle, tubular bells, xylophone,
vibraphone, gong (tam-tam),
castanets, and maracas can
also be included in the
percussion section (see
pp. 516-517). The musicians
are usually arranged in a semi-
circle—strings spread along the
front, woodwind and brass in the
center, and percussion at the back.
A conductor stands in front of the
musicians and controls the tempo
(speed) of the music and the overall
balance of the sound, ensuring
that no instruments are too
loud or too soft in relation
to the others.

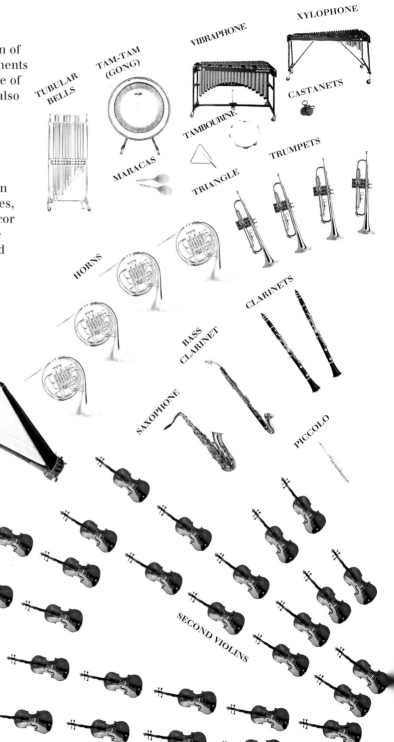

TUBULAR BELLS

TAM-TAM (GONG)

VIBRAPHONE

XYLOPHONE

CASTANETS

TAMBOURINE

MARACAS

TRIANGLE

TRUMPETS

HORNS

CLARINETS

BASS CLARINET

HARP

SAXOPHONE

PICCOLO

SECOND VIOLINS

FIRST VIOLINS

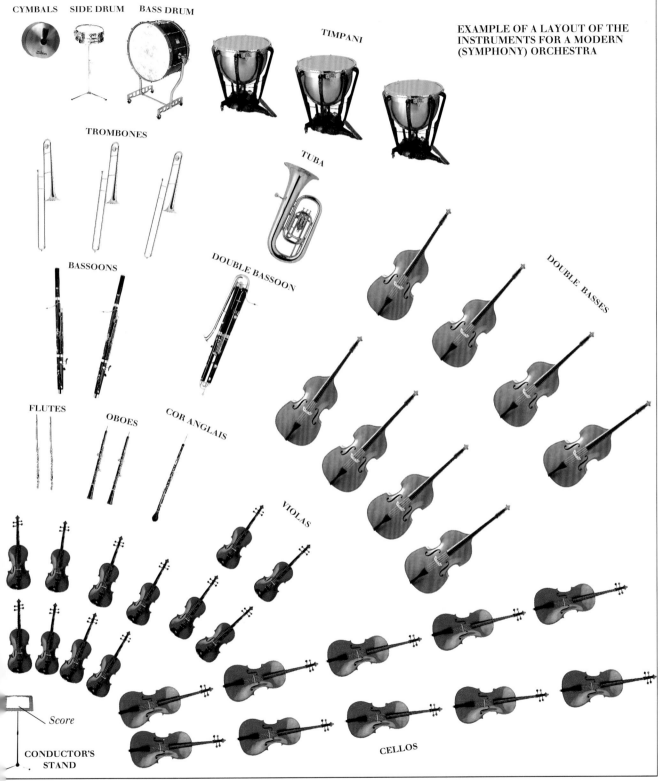

CYMBALS **SIDE DRUM** **BASS DRUM**

TIMPANI

EXAMPLE OF A LAYOUT OF THE INSTRUMENTS FOR A MODERN (SYMPHONY) ORCHESTRA

TROMBONES

TUBA

BASSOONS

DOUBLE BASSOON

DOUBLE BASSES

FLUTES

OBOES

COR ANGLAIS

VIOLAS

Score

CONDUCTOR'S STAND

CELLOS

Brass instruments

BRASS INSTRUMENTS ARE WIND INSTRUMENTS that are made of metal, usually brass. Although they appear in many different shapes and sizes, all brass instruments have a mouthpiece, a length of hollow tube, and a flared bell. The mouthpiece of a brass instrument may be cup-shaped, as in the cornet, or cone-shaped, as in the horn. The tube may be wide or narrow, mainly conical, as in the horn and tuba, or mainly cylindrical, as in the trumpet and trombone. The sound of a brass instrument is made by the player's lips vibrating against the mouthpiece, so that the air vibrates in the tube. By changing lip tension, the player can vary the vibrations and produce notes of different pitches. The range of notes produced by a brass instrument can be extended by means of a valve system. Most brass instruments, such as the trumpet, have piston valves that divert the air in the instrument along an extra piece of tubing (known as a valve slide) when pressed down. The total length of the tube is increased and the pitch of the note produced is lowered. Instead of valves, the trombone has a movable slide that can be pushed away from or drawn toward the player. The sound of a brass instrument can also be changed by inserting a mute into the bell of the instrument.

BUGLE

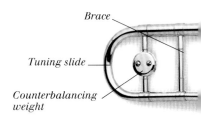

Brace

Tuning slide

Counterbalancing weight

SIMPLIFIED DIAGRAM SHOWING HOW A PISTON VALVE SYSTEM WORKS

Piston valves at rest

Air bypasses piston valves

PISTON VALVES AT REST

First piston valve pressed down

Second and third piston valves at rest

Air diverted through first valve slide

PISTON VALVE PRESSED DOWN

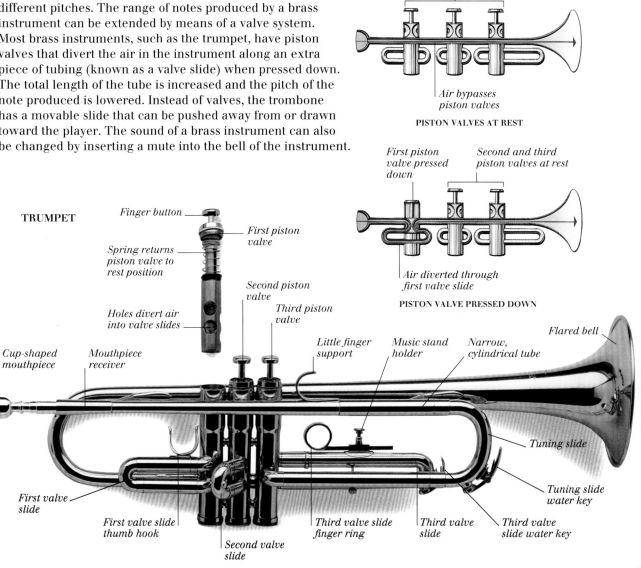

TRUMPET

Finger button

First piston valve

Spring returns piston valve to rest position

Second piston valve

Third piston valve

Holes divert air into valve slides

Cup-shaped mouthpiece

Mouthpiece receiver

Little finger support

Music stand holder

Narrow, cylindrical tube

Flared bell

Tuning slide

Tuning slide water key

First valve slide

First valve slide thumb hook

Second valve slide

Third valve slide finger ring

Third valve slide

Third valve slide water key

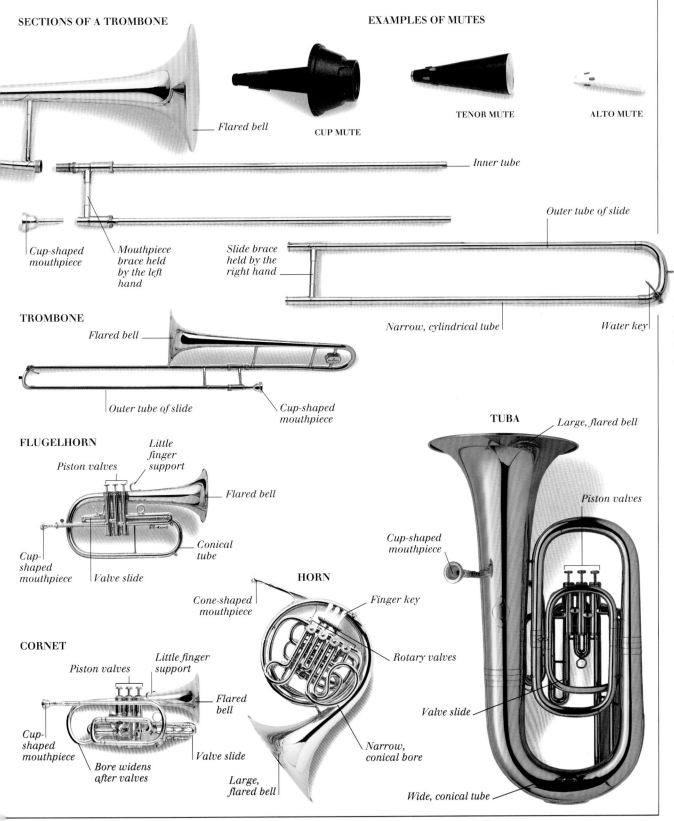

SECTIONS OF A TROMBONE

Flared bell

EXAMPLES OF MUTES

CUP MUTE

TENOR MUTE

ALTO MUTE

Inner tube

Outer tube of slide

Cup-shaped mouthpiece

Mouthpiece brace held by the left hand

Slide brace held by the right hand

Narrow, cylindrical tube

Water key

TROMBONE

Flared bell

Outer tube of slide

Cup-shaped mouthpiece

FLUGELHORN

Little finger support

Piston valves

Flared bell

Cup-shaped mouthpiece

Conical tube

Valve slide

TUBA

Large, flared bell

Piston valves

Cup-shaped mouthpiece

Valve slide

HORN

Cone-shaped mouthpiece

Finger key

Rotary valves

Narrow, conical bore

Large, flared bell

CORNET

Piston valves

Little finger support

Flared bell

Cup-shaped mouthpiece

Bore widens after valves

Valve slide

Wide, conical tube

507

Woodwind instruments

WOODWIND INSTRUMENTS ARE wind instruments that are generally made of wood, although some are made of metal or plastic. The sound of a woodwind instrument is produced by the vibration of air in a hollow tube. The air is made to vibrate by blowing across a blow hole—as in the flute and piccolo— or by blowing through a single reed— as in the clarinet and saxophone— or a double reed—as in the bassoon, cor anglais, and oboe. The pitch of a woodwind instrument can be changed by opening or closing holes cut into the tube of the instrument.

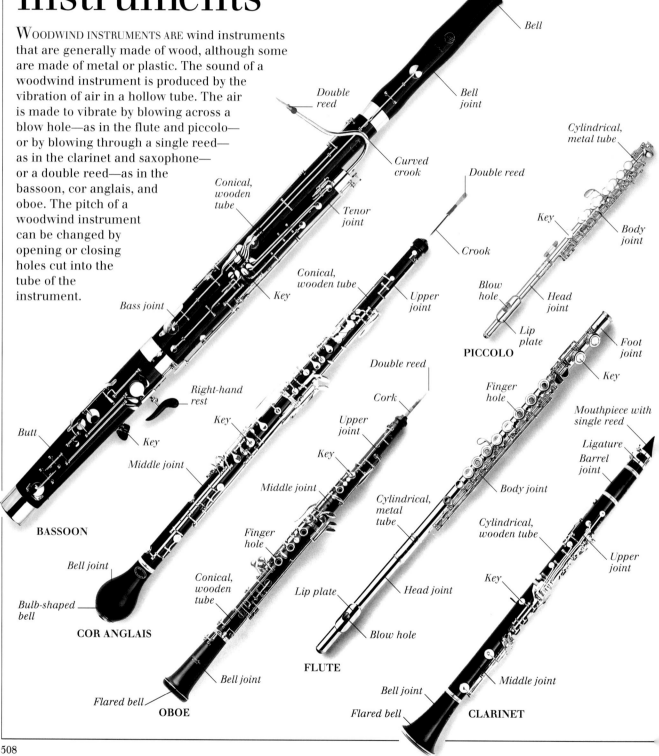

Bell

Double reed

Bell joint

Curved crook

Cylindrical, metal tube

Double reed

Conical, wooden tube

Tenor joint

Key

Body joint

Conical, wooden tube

Upper joint

Crook

Blow hole

Head joint

Bass joint

Key

Lip plate

PICCOLO

Double reed

Cork

Foot joint

Finger hole

Key

Right-hand rest

Upper joint

Key

Mouthpiece with single reed

Butt

Key

Key

Middle joint

Ligature

Barrel joint

Body joint

BASSOON

Middle joint

Cylindrical, metal tube

Cylindrical, wooden tube

Bell joint

Finger hole

Key

Upper joint

Bulb-shaped bell

Conical, wooden tube

Head joint

COR ANGLAIS

Finger hole

Key

Lip plate

Bell joint

Blow hole

FLUTE

Bell joint

Middle joint

Flared bell

OBOE

Flared bell

CLARINET

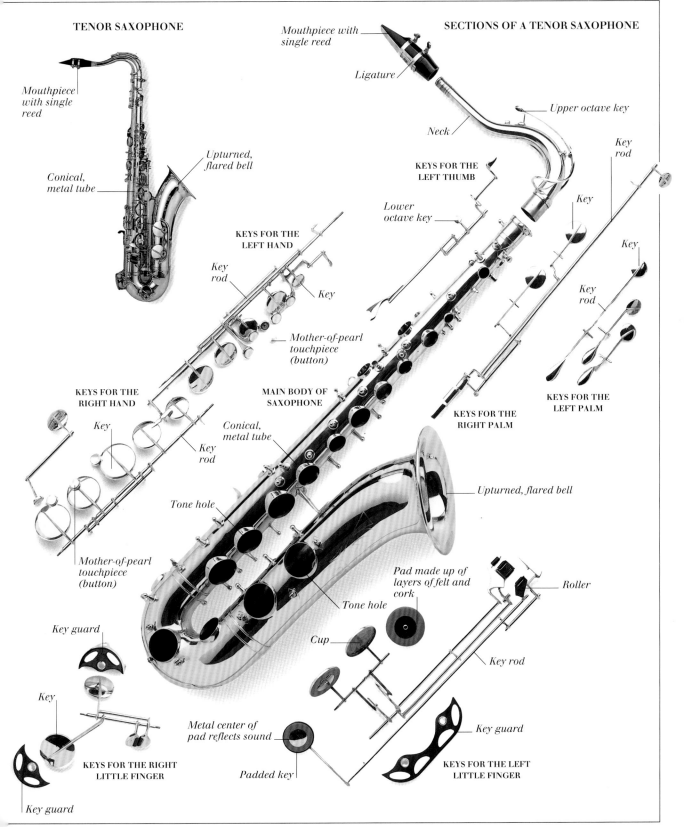

TENOR SAXOPHONE

SECTIONS OF A TENOR SAXOPHONE

Mouthpiece with single reed

Ligature

Upper octave key

Neck

Key rod

Mouthpiece with single reed

Conical, metal tube

Upturned, flared bell

KEYS FOR THE LEFT THUMB

Lower octave key

Key

KEYS FOR THE LEFT HAND

Key rod

Key

Key

Mother-of-pearl touchpiece (button)

Key rod

KEYS FOR THE RIGHT HAND

MAIN BODY OF SAXOPHONE

KEYS FOR THE RIGHT PALM

KEYS FOR THE LEFT PALM

Key

Conical, metal tube

Key rod

Tone hole

Upturned, flared bell

Mother-of-pearl touchpiece (button)

Tone hole

Pad made up of layers of felt and cork

Roller

Key guard

Cup

Key rod

Key

Metal center of pad reflects sound

Key guard

KEYS FOR THE RIGHT LITTLE FINGER

Padded key

KEYS FOR THE LEFT LITTLE FINGER

Key guard

Stringed instruments

STRINGED INSTRUMENTS PRODUCE SOUND by the vibration of stretched strings. This may be done by drawing a bow across the strings, as in the violin; or by plucking the strings, as in the harp and guitar (see pp. 512-513). The four modern members of the bowed string family are the violin, viola, cello (violoncello), and double bass. Each consists of a hollow, wooden body, a long neck, and four strings. The bow is a wooden stick with horsehair stretched across its length. The vibrations made by drawing the bow across the strings are transmitted to the hollow body, and this itself vibrates, amplifying and enriching the sound produced. The harp consists of a set of strings of different lengths stretched across a wooden frame. The strings are plucked by the player's thumbs and fingers—except the little finger of each hand—which produces vibrations that are amplified by the harp's sound board. The pitch of the note produced by any stringed instrument depends on the length, weight, and tension of the string. A shorter, lighter, or tighter string gives a higher note.

Scroll eye

Scroll

Peg hole

Ebony tuning pegs

Neck made of maple wood

Fingerboard

Strings

Rounded shoulder

Belly (sound board)

Head

Point

Stick

Scroll

Waist

Horsehair

Peg box

Scroll eye

Tuning peg

Nut

Bridge

String

Fingerboard

Rounded shoulder

Sound hole

Belly (sound board)

Purfling

Rib

Waist

Sound hole

Purfling

Bridge

Frog

Tuning adjustor

Screw

Tailpiece

Chin rest

Tailpiece

Chin rest

Tailpiece loop fits around end pin

VIOLIN BOW

VIOLIN

SECTIONS OF A VIOLIN

End pin (tail pin)

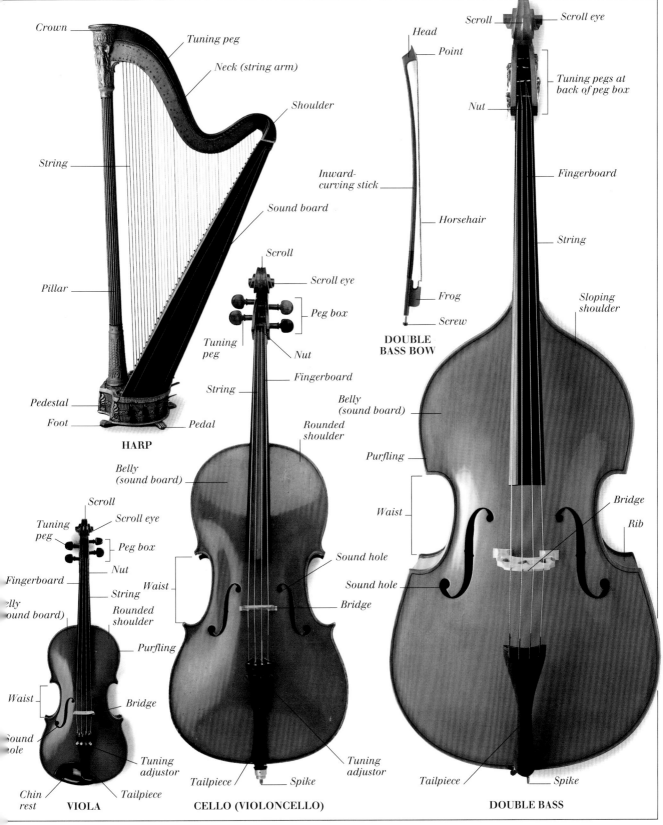

Crown

Tuning peg

Neck (string arm)

Shoulder

String

Sound board

Pillar

Pedestal

Foot

Pedal

HARP

Scroll

Scroll eye

Peg box

Tuning peg

Nut

Fingerboard

String

Rounded shoulder

Belly (sound board)

Waist

Sound hole

Bridge

Tailpiece

Spike

Tuning adjustor

CELLO (VIOLONCELLO)

Head

Point

Inward-curving stick

Horsehair

Frog

Screw

DOUBLE BASS BOW

Scroll

Scroll eye

Tuning pegs at back of peg box

Nut

Fingerboard

String

Sloping shoulder

Belly (sound board)

Purfling

Waist

Sound hole

Bridge

Rib

Tailpiece

Spike

DOUBLE BASS

Scroll

Tuning peg

Scroll eye

Peg box

Nut

Fingerboard

String

Belly (sound board)

Rounded shoulder

Purfling

Waist

Bridge

Sound hole

Tuning adjustor

Tailpiece

Chin rest

VIOLA

511

Guitars

THE GUITAR IS A PLUCKED stringed instrument (see pp. 510-511). There are two types of guitar—acoustic and electric. Acoustic guitars have hollow bodies and six or twelve strings. Plucking or strumming the strings produces vibrations that are amplified by their hollow bodies. Electric guitars usually have solid bodies and six strings. Pick-ups placed under the strings convert vibrations into electronic signals that are magnified by an amplifier, and sent to a loudspeaker where they are converted into sounds (see pp. 520-521). Electric bass guitars are very similar in structure to electric guitars, and produce sound in the same way, but have four heavier-gage strings and play lower pitched notes.

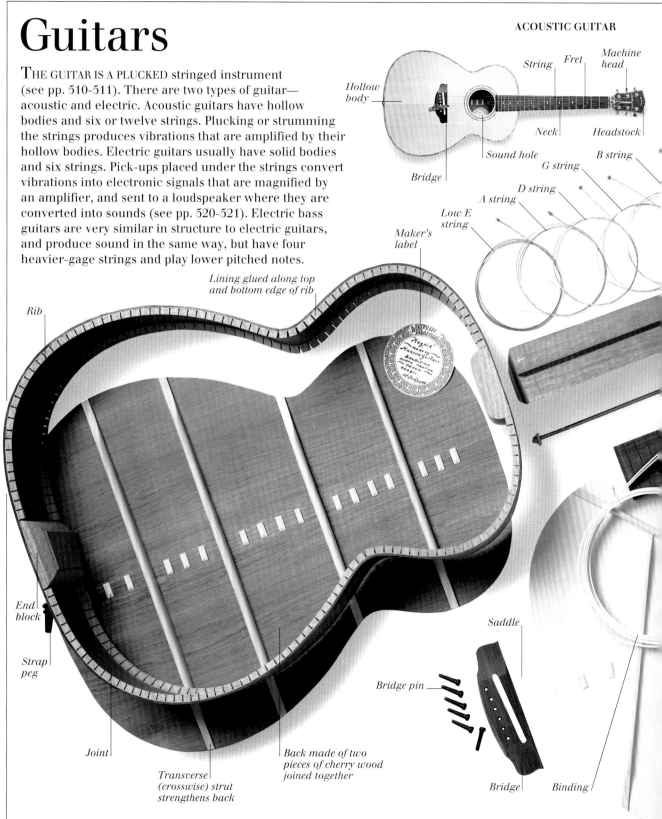

ACOUSTIC GUITAR

Machine head

String

Fret

Hollow body

Neck

Headstock

Sound hole

Bridge

B string

G string

D string

A string

Low E string

Maker's label

Lining glued along top and bottom edge of rib

Rib

End block

Strap peg

Joint

Transverse (crosswise) strut strengthens back

Back made of two pieces of cherry wood joined together

Bridge pin

Saddle

Bridge

Binding

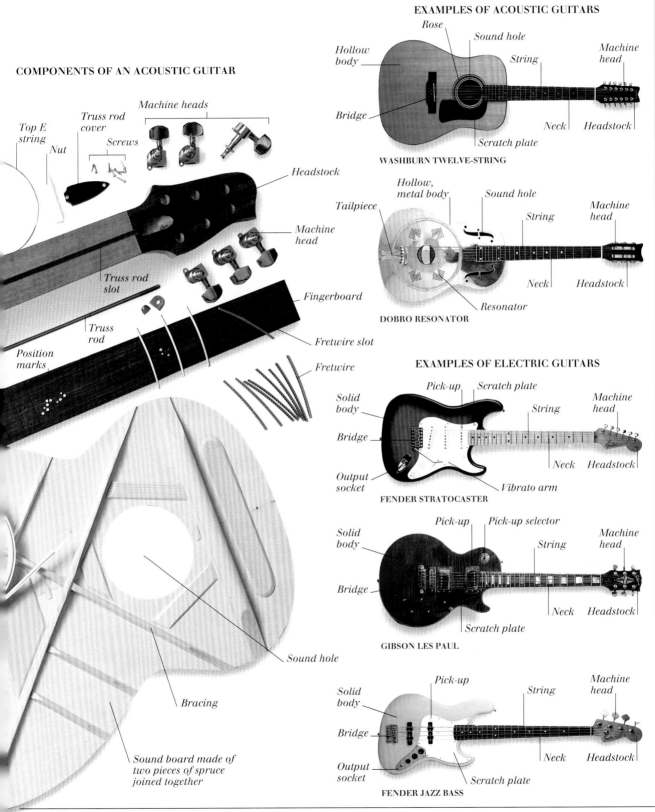

EXAMPLES OF ACOUSTIC GUITARS

Rose

Sound hole

Hollow body

String

Machine head

Bridge

Neck

Headstock

Scratch plate

WASHBURN TWELVE-STRING

Hollow, metal body

Sound hole

Tailpiece

String

Machine head

Neck

Headstock

Resonator

DOBRO RESONATOR

COMPONENTS OF AN ACOUSTIC GUITAR

Machine heads

Top E string

Truss rod cover

Nut

Screws

Headstock

Machine head

Truss rod slot

Fingerboard

Truss rod

Fretwire slot

Position marks

Fretwire

EXAMPLES OF ELECTRIC GUITARS

Pick-up

Scratch plate

Solid body

String

Machine head

Bridge

Neck

Headstock

Output socket

Vibrato arm

FENDER STRATOCASTER

Solid body

Pick-up

Pick-up selector

String

Machine head

Bridge

Neck

Headstock

Scratch plate

GIBSON LES PAUL

Bracing

Solid body

Pick-up

String

Machine head

Bridge

Neck

Headstock

Sound hole

Sound board made of two pieces of spruce joined together

Output socket

Scratch plate

FENDER JAZZ BASS

Keyboard instruments

K<small>EYBOARD INSTRUMENTS</small> are instruments that are sounded by means of a keyboard. The organ and piano are two of the principal members of the keyboard family. The organ consists of pipes which are operated by one or more keyboards and foot pedals. The pipes are lined up in rows (known as ranks or registers) on top of a wind chest. The sound of the organ is made when air is admitted into a pipe by pressing a key or pedal. The piano consists of wire strings stretched over a metal frame, and a keyboard and pedals that operate hammers and dampers. The piano frame is either vertical—as in the upright piano—or horizontal—as in the grand piano. When a key is at rest, a damper lies against the string to keep it from vibrating. When a key is pressed down, the damper moves away from the string as the hammer strikes it, causing the string to vibrate and sound a note.

ORGAN
PIPE

UPRIGHT PIANO

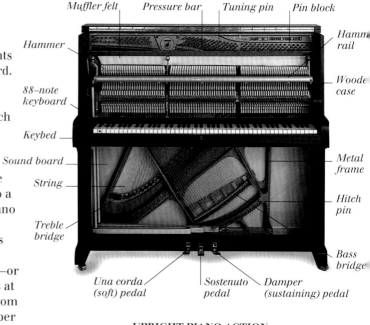

Muffler felt
Pressure bar
Tuning pin
Pin block
Hammer
Hamm[er] rail
88–note keyboard
Woode[n] case
Keybed
Sound board
String
Metal frame
Hitch pin
Treble bridge
Bass bridge
Una corda (soft) pedal
Sostenuto pedal
Damper (sustaining) pedal

UPRIGHT PIANO ACTION

KEY AT REST

String
Hammer
Damper lies against string, and keeps it from vibrating
Hammer rest
Back check
Damper lever
Action lever
Jack
Capstan screw
Key released

ORGAN CONSOLE

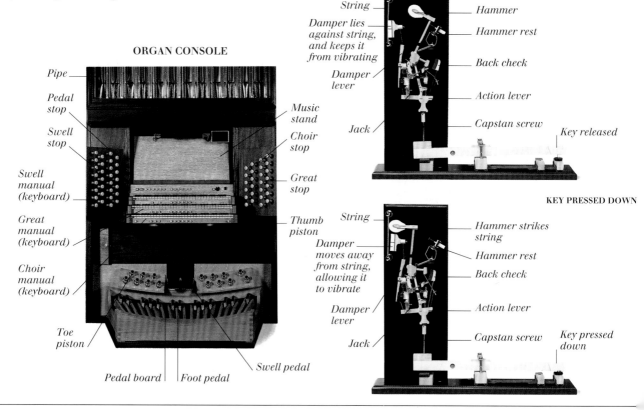

Pipe
Pedal stop
Music stand
Swell stop
Choir stop
Swell manual (keyboard)
Great stop
Great manual (keyboard)
Thumb piston
Choir manual (keyboard)
Toe piston
Pedal board
Foot pedal
Swell pedal

KEY PRESSED DOWN

String
Hammer strikes string
Damper moves away from string, allowing it to vibrate
Hammer rest
Back check
Damper lever
Action lever
Jack
Capstan screw
Key pressed down

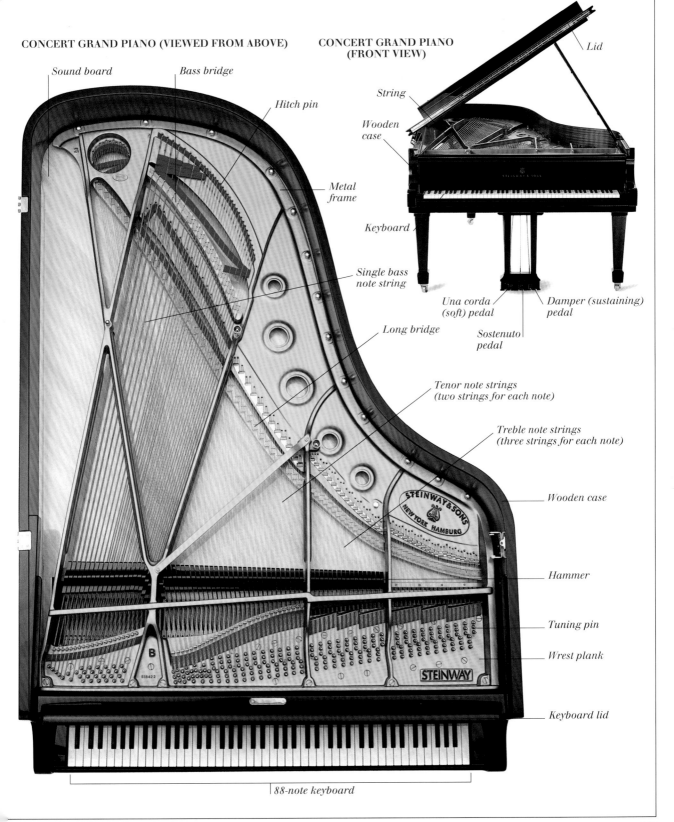

CONCERT GRAND PIANO (VIEWED FROM ABOVE)

CONCERT GRAND PIANO (FRONT VIEW)

Sound board

Bass bridge

Hitch pin

Lid

String

Wooden case

Metal frame

Keyboard

Single bass note string

Una corda (soft) pedal

Damper (sustaining) pedal

Sostenuto pedal

Long bridge

Tenor note strings (two strings for each note)

Treble note strings (three strings for each note)

Wooden case

STEINWAY & SONS
NEW YORK HAMBURG

Hammer

Tuning pin

Wrest plank

STEINWAY

Keyboard lid

88-note keyboard

Percussion instruments

PERCUSSION INSTRUMENTS are a large group of instruments that produce sound by being struck, shaken, scraped, or clashed together. Some percussion instruments—such as the gong (tam-tam), cymbals, and maracas—do not have a definite pitch and are used for rhythm and impact, and the distinctive

TEMPLE BLOCKS

timber (color) of their sound. Other percussion instruments—such as the xylophone, vibraphone, and tubular bells—are tuned to a definite pitch and can play melody, harmony, and rhythms. The xylophone and vibraphone each have two rows of bars that are arranged in a similar way to the black and white keys of a piano. Metal tubes are suspended below the bars to amplify the sound. The vibraphone has electrically operated fans that rotate in the tubes and produce a vibrato (wavering pitch) effect.

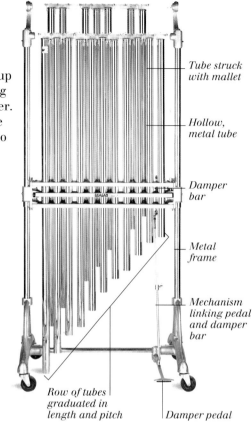

Tube struck with mallet

Hollow, metal tube

Damper bar

Metal frame

Mechanism linking pedal and damper bar

Row of tubes graduated in length and pitch

Damper pedal

EXAMPLES OF MALLETS

SOFT-HEADED MALLET

Felt-covered head

HARD-HEADED MALLET

Rosewood head

HAMMER MALLET

Leather-covered head

Tam-tam struck in center with soft-headed mallet

GONG (TAM-TAM)

Cord

Metal frame

Row of bars graduated in length and pitch

XYLOPHONE

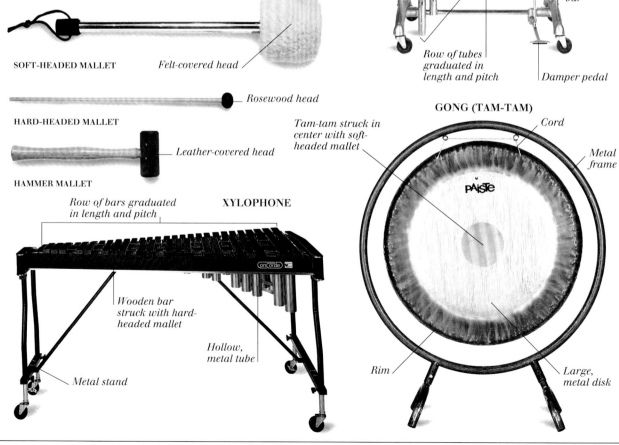

Wooden bar struck with hard-headed mallet

Hollow, metal tube

Metal stand

Rim

Large, metal disk

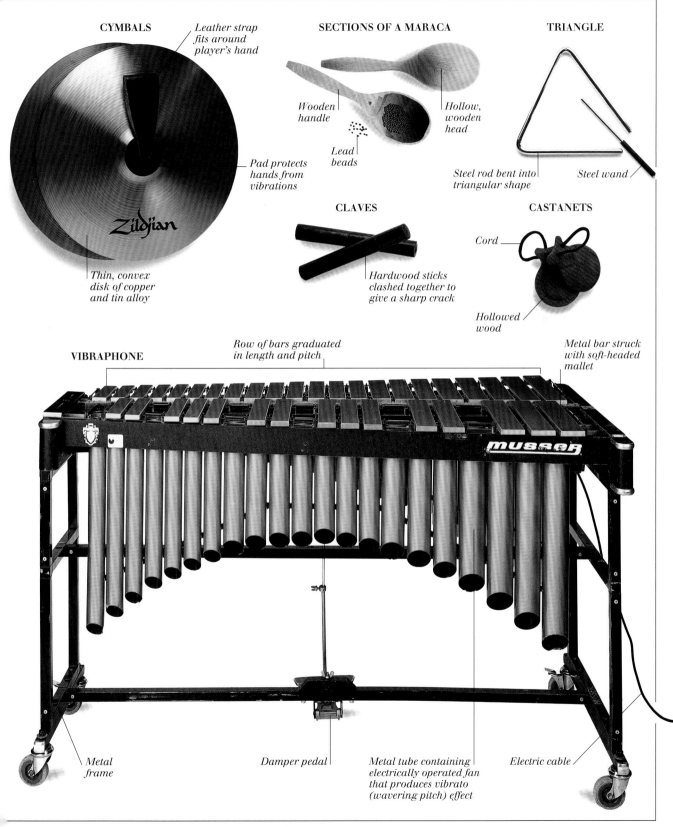

CYMBALS

Leather strap fits around player's hand

Pad protects hands from vibrations

Thin, convex disk of copper and tin alloy

SECTIONS OF A MARACA

Wooden handle

Lead beads

Hollow, wooden head

TRIANGLE

Steel rod bent into triangular shape

Steel wand

CLAVES

Hardwood sticks clashed together to give a sharp crack

CASTANETS

Cord

Hollowed wood

VIBRAPHONE

Row of bars graduated in length and pitch

Metal bar struck with soft-headed mallet

Metal frame

Damper pedal

Metal tube containing electrically operated fan that produces vibrato (wavering pitch) effect

Electric cable

Drums

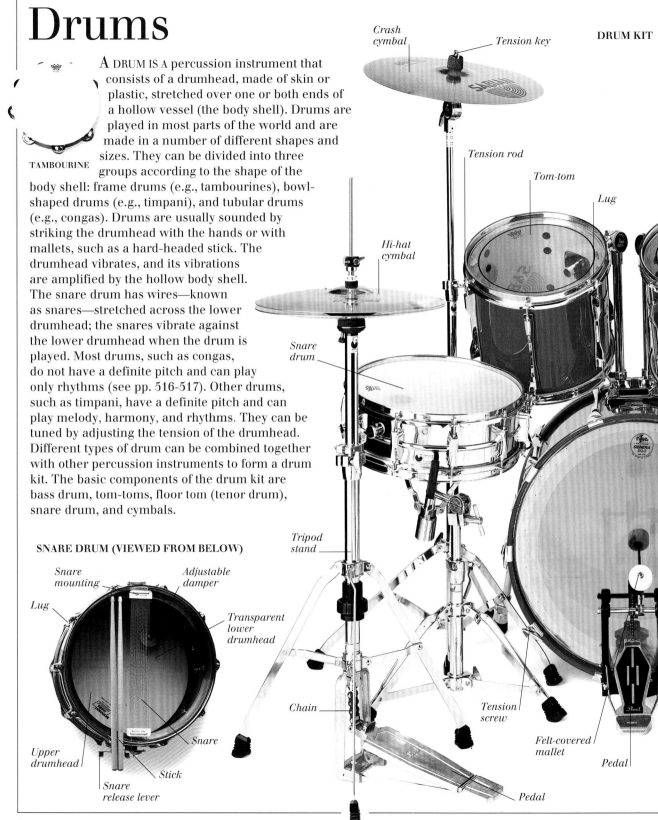

TAMBOURINE

A DRUM IS A percussion instrument that consists of a drumhead, made of skin or plastic, stretched over one or both ends of a hollow vessel (the body shell). Drums are played in most parts of the world and are made in a number of different shapes and sizes. They can be divided into three groups according to the shape of the body shell: frame drums (e.g., tambourines), bowl-shaped drums (e.g., timpani), and tubular drums (e.g., congas). Drums are usually sounded by striking the drumhead with the hands or with mallets, such as a hard-headed stick. The drumhead vibrates, and its vibrations are amplified by the hollow body shell. The snare drum has wires—known as snares—stretched across the lower drumhead; the snares vibrate against the lower drumhead when the drum is played. Most drums, such as congas, do not have a definite pitch and can play only rhythms (see pp. 516-517). Other drums, such as timpani, have a definite pitch and can play melody, harmony, and rhythms. They can be tuned by adjusting the tension of the drumhead. Different types of drum can be combined together with other percussion instruments to form a drum kit. The basic components of the drum kit are bass drum, tom-toms, floor tom (tenor drum), snare drum, and cymbals.

DRUM KIT

Crash cymbal

Tension key

Tension rod

Tom-tom

Lug

Hi-hat cymbal

Snare drum

Tripod stand

Chain

Tension screw

Felt-covered mallet

Pedal

Pedal

SNARE DRUM (VIEWED FROM BELOW)

Snare mounting

Adjustable damper

Lug

Transparent lower drumhead

Snare

Upper drumhead

Stick

Snare release lever

EXAMPLES OF STICKS

Acorn

HARD-HEADED STICK

Taper

SOFT-HEADED STICK

Felt-covered head

WIRE BRUSH

Wire bristles

Ride cymbal

Tension key

Tom-tom

Tension rod

Lug

Height adjustment key

Floor tom (tenor drum)

Tension rod

Lug

Wooden body shell

Bass drum

Height adjustment key

Leg

Rubber foot

CONGAS

Metal hoop

Drumhead

Tension rod

Wooden body shell

Tripod stand

Leg

TIMPANUM (KETTLE DRUM)

Drumhead

Tension rod

Metal hoop

Tuning gauge

Copper body shell

Strut

Crown

Tension rod

Tuning pedal

Castor

Electronic instruments

ELECTRONIC INSTRUMENTS generate electronic signals that are magnified by an amplifier, and sent to a loudspeaker where they are converted into sounds. Synthesizers, and other electronic instruments, simulate the characteristic sounds of conventional instruments, and also create entirely new sounds. Most electronic instruments are keyboard instruments, but electronic wind and percussion instruments are also popular. A digital sampler records and stores sounds from musical instruments or other sources. When the sound is played back, the pitch of the original sound can be altered. A keyboard can be connected to the sampler so that a tune can be played using the sampled sounds. With a MIDI (Musical Instrument Digital Interface) system, a computer can be linked with other electronic instruments, such as keyboards and electronic drums, to make sounds together or in sequence. It is also possible, using music software, to compose and play music on a home computer.

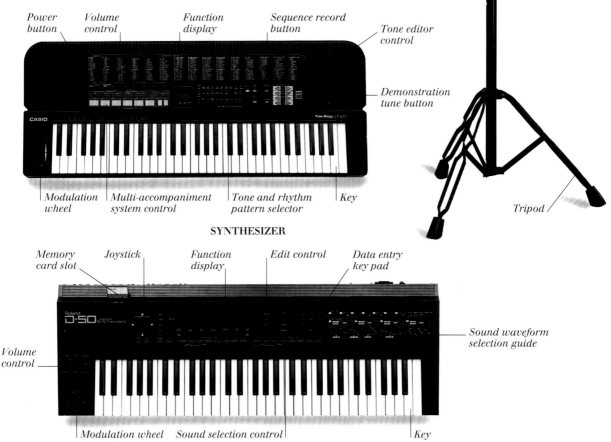

ELECTRONIC DRUMS

Drum pad

Height adjustment key

Tripod

HOME KEYBOARD

Power button

Volume control

Function display

Sequence record button

Tone editor control

Demonstration tune button

Modulation wheel

Multi-accompaniment system control

Tone and rhythm pattern selector

Key

SYNTHESIZER

Memory card slot

Joystick

Function display

Edit control

Data entry key pad

Sound waveform selection guide

Volume control

Modulation wheel

Sound selection control

Key

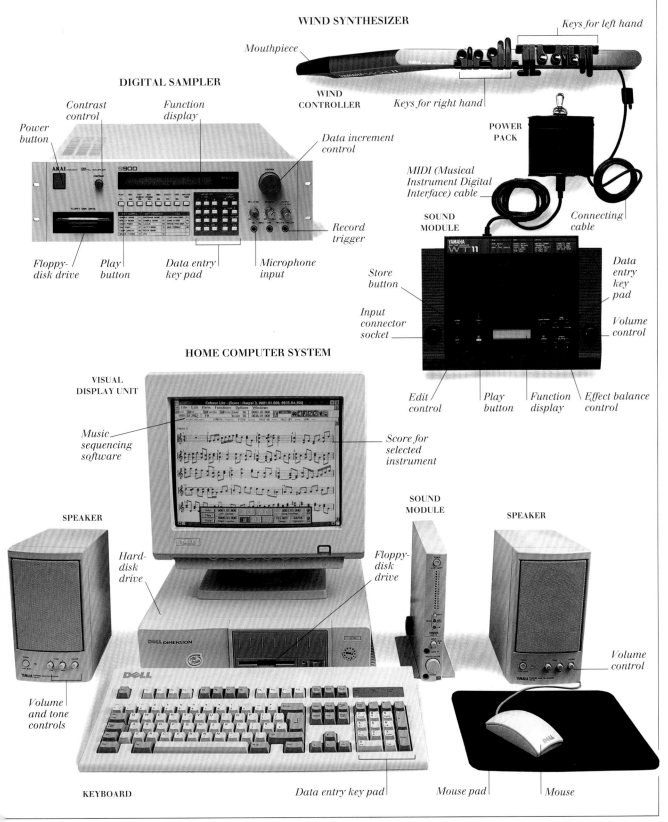

WIND SYNTHESIZER

Keys for left hand

Mouthpiece

WIND
CONTROLLER

Keys for right hand

DIGITAL SAMPLER

Contrast
control

Function
display

Power
button

Data increment
control

POWER
PACK

MIDI (Musical
Instrument Digital
Interface) cable

Connecting
cable

SOUND
MODULE

Record
trigger

Floppy-
disk drive

Play
button

Data entry
key pad

Microphone
input

Store
button

Data
entry
key
pad

Input
connector
socket

Volume
control

HOME COMPUTER SYSTEM

VISUAL
DISPLAY UNIT

Edit
control

Play
button

Function
display

Effect balance
control

Music
sequencing
software

Score for
selected
instrument

SPEAKER

SOUND
MODULE

SPEAKER

Hard-
disk
drive

Floppy-
disk
drive

Volume
control

Volume
and tone
controls

KEYBOARD

Data entry key pad

Mouse pad

Mouse

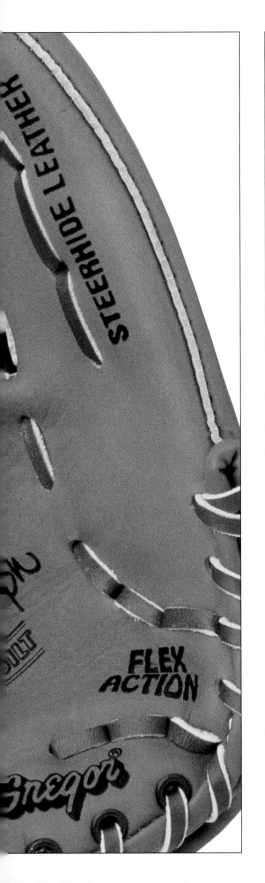

SPORTS

Soccer

GAMES INVOLVING KICKING A BALL have a long history and were recorded in China as early as 300 BC; in medieval Europe, street football was banned as a menace to the public; only in 1863 were the rules established, specifically banning carrying the ball for all players except the goalkeeper, and separating rugby from soccer. Soccer, also known as association football, is a team sport in which players attempt to score goals by passing and dribbling the ball down the field past opposing defenders, and kicking or heading the ball into the goal net, outwitting the defending goalkeeper or "goalie." Each team consists of ten outfield players (defenders, midfielders, and strikers) and a goalkeeper. Players from the opposing team may challenge the player in possession of the ball, but an illegal or foul tackle results in a penalty if a foul occurs inside the penalty area or a free kick if outside the penalty area. The round ball used in soccer is more easily controlled than the oval balls used in American, Canadian, and Australian rules football and in rugby. The result is a more "open" or flowing game which is played and watched by millions of people worldwide.

LINESMAN'S FLAG

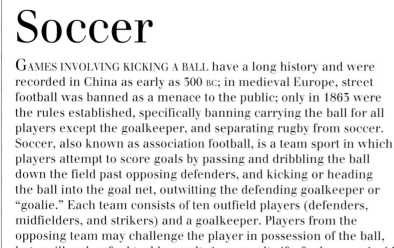

Lightweight, brightly colored fabric

Handle with rubber grip

REFEREE'S EQUIPMENT

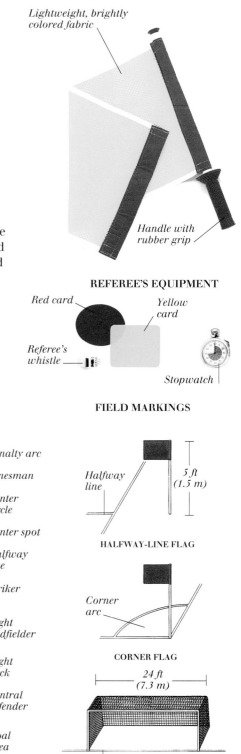

Red card

Yellow card

Referee's whistle

Stopwatch

FIELD MARKINGS

Halfway line

5 ft (1.5 m)

HALFWAY-LINE FLAG

Corner arc

CORNER FLAG

24 ft (7.3 m)

Goal line

GOAL

SOCCER FIELD

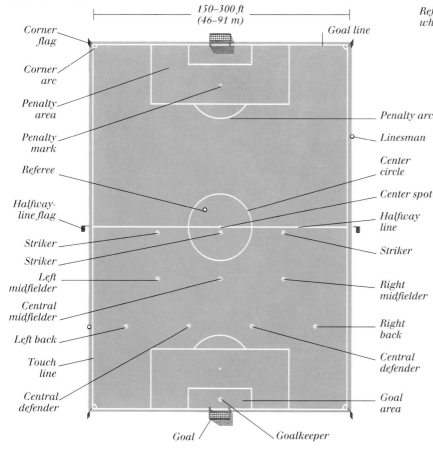

150–300 ft (46–91 m)

Corner flag

Goal line

Corner arc

Penalty area

Penalty arc

Penalty mark

Linesman

Referee

Center circle

Center spot

Halfway-line flag

Halfway line

Striker

Striker

Striker

Left midfielder

Right midfielder

Central midfielder

Left back

Right back

Touch line

Central defender

Central defender

Goal area

Goal

Goalkeeper

GOALKEEPER

Goalkeeper's shirt

Glove

Shin guard

Shorts

Sock

Soccer shoe

SOCCER UNIFORM

Open-neck collar

Lightweight, man-made fabric team shirt

Team logo

Manufacturer's logo

Ribbed welt

lotto

Motta

Sponsor's logo

Manufacturer's name

Edge cut to fit perfectly

MAKING A SOCCER BALL

Hole punched in panel for stitching

Mitre

F.I.F.A. APPROVED

MULTIPLEX

Waxed thread

Ball size number

5

Mitre

MULTIPLEX®

8¹/₂–9 in (22–23 cm)

Needle

Bladder valve

Bladder made from latex rubber

Panels sewn together with ball inside out

Laminated panel

Long cotton sock

Club crest

Synthetic shoelace

Interchangeable nylon stud

Team shorts

SOCCER SHOE

Football

IN AMERICAN AND CANADIAN FOOTBALL, the object of the game is to get the ball across the opponent's goal line, either by passing or carrying it across (a touchdown), or by kicking it between their goalposts (a field goal). An American football team has 11 players on the field at a time, although up to 40 players can appear for each side in a single game. The agile offense tries to score points, and the heavy hitting defense holds back the opposition. When in possession of the ball, a team has four chances (downs), to move it at least ten yards up the field to make a first down. The opposition gains possession if they fail, or by tackling and intercepting the ball. Canadian football is played on a larger field, with 12 men on each side. A team has only three chances, instead of four, to achieve a first down. Otherwise, the game is very similar to American football. Helmets, face masks, and layers of body padding are worn by the players for protection.

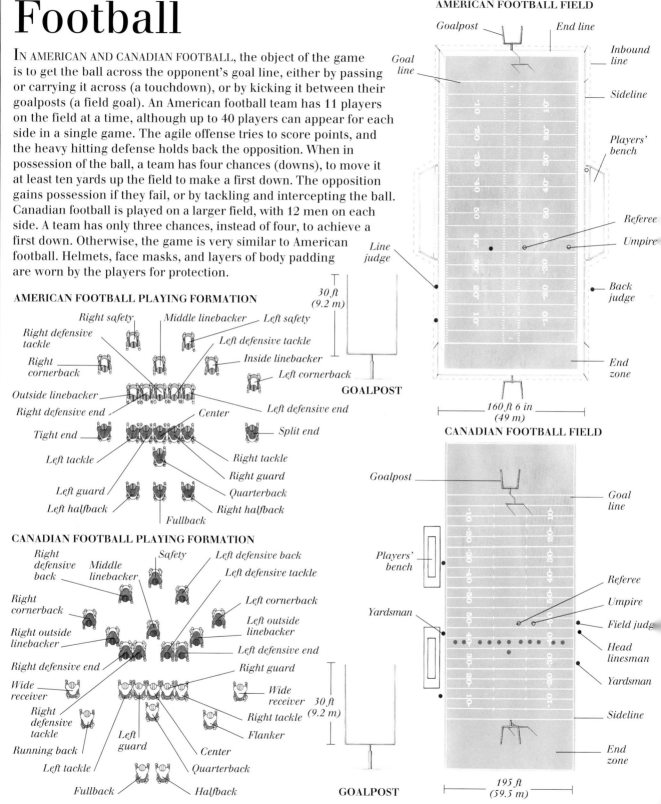

AMERICAN FOOTBALL FIELD

Goalpost
End line
Goal line
Inbound line
Sideline
Players' bench
Referee
Umpire
Line judge
Back judge
End zone

30 ft (9.2 m)

GOALPOST

160 ft 6 in (49 m)

AMERICAN FOOTBALL PLAYING FORMATION

Right safety
Middle linebacker
Left safety
Right defensive tackle
Left defensive tackle
Right cornerback
Inside linebacker
Left cornerback
Outside linebacker
Left defensive end
Right defensive end
Center
Tight end
Split end
Left tackle
Right tackle
Right guard
Left guard
Quarterback
Left halfback
Right halfback
Fullback

CANADIAN FOOTBALL PLAYING FORMATION

Right defensive back
Middle linebacker
Safety
Left defensive back
Left defensive tackle
Right cornerback
Left cornerback
Left outside linebacker
Right outside linebacker
Left defensive end
Right defensive end
Right guard
Wide receiver
Wide receiver
Right defensive tackle
Right tackle
Running back
Left guard
Flanker
Center
Left tackle
Quarterback
Fullback
Halfback

30 ft (9.2 m)

GOALPOST

CANADIAN FOOTBALL FIELD

Goalpost
Goal line
Players' bench
Referee
Umpire
Yardsman
Field judge
Head linesman
Yardsman
Sideline
End zone

195 ft (59.5 m)

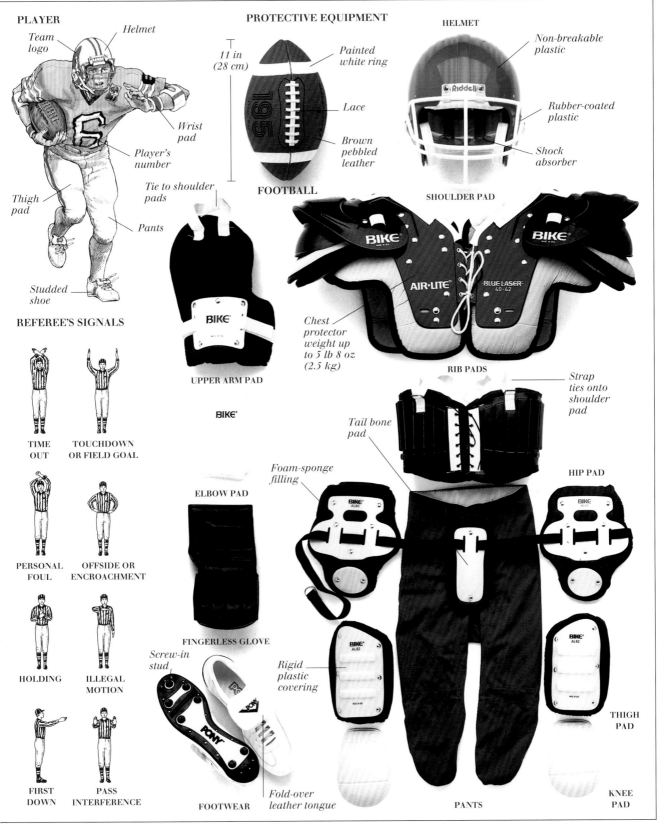

PLAYER

- Team logo
- Helmet
- Wrist pad
- Player's number
- Thigh pad
- Pants
- Tie to shoulder pads
- Studded shoe

PROTECTIVE EQUIPMENT

FOOTBALL

11 in (28 cm)

- Painted white ring
- Lace
- Brown pebbled leather

HELMET

- Non-breakable plastic
- Rubber-coated plastic
- Shock absorber

Riddell

SHOULDER PAD

BIKE

AIR·LITE

BLUE·LASER 40-42

Chest protector weight up to 5 lb 8 oz (2.5 kg)

UPPER ARM PAD

BIKE

RIB PADS

Strap ties onto shoulder pad

HIP PAD

Tail bone pad

ELBOW PAD

Foam-sponge filling

BIKE AL80

BIKE AL80

FINGERLESS GLOVE

Screw-in stud

PONY

Rigid plastic covering

BIKE AL82

BIKE AL82

THIGH PAD

KNEE PAD

Fold-over leather tongue

FOOTWEAR

PANTS

REFEREE'S SIGNALS

TIME OUT	TOUCHDOWN OR FIELD GOAL
PERSONAL FOUL	OFFSIDE OR ENCROACHMENT
HOLDING	ILLEGAL MOTION
FIRST DOWN	PASS INTERFERENCE

Australian rules and Gaelic football

VARIETIES OF FOOTBALL have developed all over the world and Australian rules football is considered to be one of the roughest versions, allowing full body tackles although participants wear no protective padding. Two teams of 18 players play on a large, oval pitch. Players can kick or punch the ball, which is shaped like a rugby ball, but cannot throw it. Running with the ball is permitted, as long as the ball touches the ground at least once every ten meters. The full backs defend two sets of posts. Teams try to score goals (six points) between the inner posts or behinds (one point) inside the outer posts. Each game has four quarters of 25 minutes, and the team with the most points at the end of the allotted time is the winner. In Gaelic football, an Irish version of soccer (see pp. 524–525), a size 5 association football is used. Each team can have 15 players on the field at a time. Players are allowed to catch, fist, and kick the ball, or dribble it using their hands or feet, but cannot throw it. Teams are awarded three points for getting the ball into the net, and one point for getting it through the posts above the crossbar. Gaelic football is rarely played outside of Ireland.

START OF PLAY

Field umpire

Center circle

SCORING

GOAL
(6 POINTS)

BEHIND
(1 POINT)

AUSTRALIAN RULES FOOTBALL FIELD

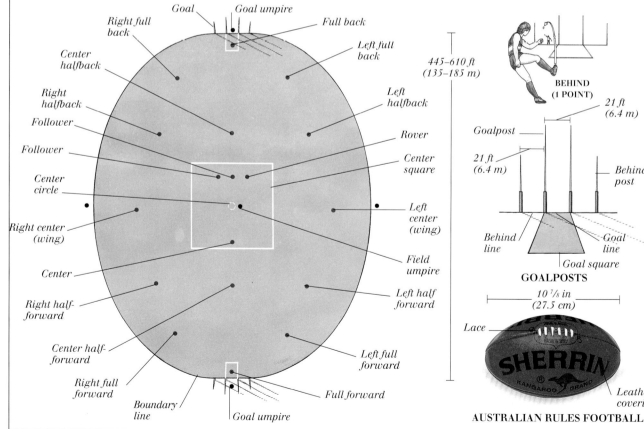

Goal

Goal umpire

Right full back

Full back

Center halfback

Left full back

Right halfback

Left halfback

Follower

Follower

Rover

Center square

Center circle

Right center (wing)

Left center (wing)

Center

Field umpire

Right half-forward

Left half forward

Center half-forward

Left full forward

Right full forward

Full forward

Boundary line

Goal umpire

445–610 ft
(135–185 m)

21 ft
(6.4 m)

Goalpost

21 ft
(6.4 m)

Behind post

Behind line

Goal line

Goal square

GOALPOSTS

10 7/8 in
(27.5 cm)

Lace

Leather covering

AUSTRALIAN RULES FOOTBALL

528

AUSTRALIAN RULES FOOTBALL SKILLS

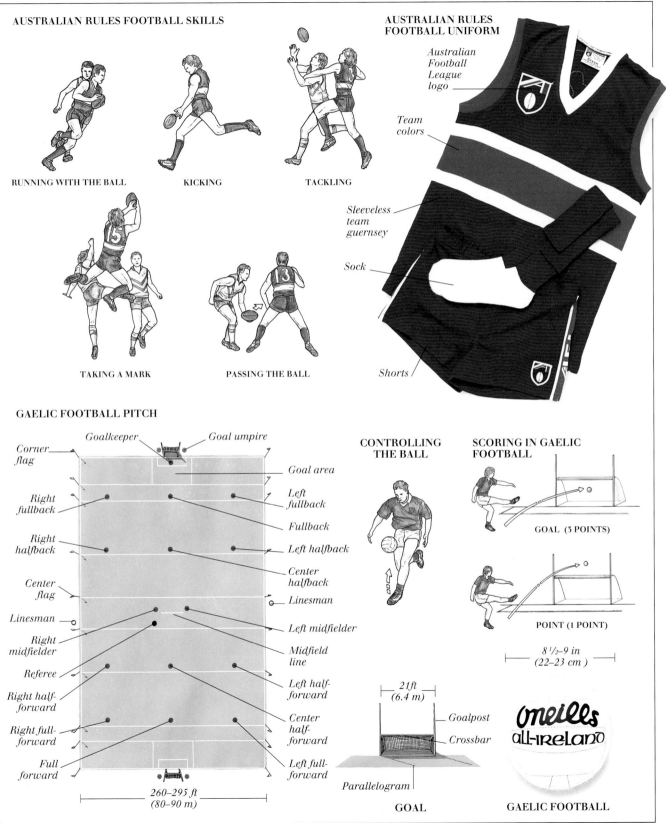

RUNNING WITH THE BALL

KICKING

TACKLING

TAKING A MARK

PASSING THE BALL

AUSTRALIAN RULES FOOTBALL UNIFORM

Australian Football League logo

Team colors

Sleeveless team guernsey

Sock

Shorts

GAELIC FOOTBALL PITCH

Goalkeeper

Goal umpire

Corner flag

Goal area

Right fullback

Left fullback

Fullback

Right halfback

Left halfback

Center halfback

Center flag

Linesman

Linesman

Left midfielder

Right midfielder

Midfield line

Referee

Right half-forward

Left half-forward

Right full-forward

Center half-forward

Full forward

Left full-forward

260–295 ft
(80–90 m)

CONTROLLING THE BALL

SCORING IN GAELIC FOOTBALL

GOAL (3 POINTS)

POINT (1 POINT)

8 1/2–9 in
(22–23 cm)

21ft
(6.4 m)

Goalpost

Crossbar

Parallelogram

GOAL

o'neills
all-ireland

GAELIC FOOTBALL

Rugby

RUGBY IS PLAYED WITH AN OVAL BALL which may be carried, thrown, or kicked. There are two types of rugby. Rugby Union is an amateur game played by two teams of 15 players. Players can score points in two ways: by placing the ball behind the opponents' goal line (a try, scoring four points) or by kicking it over the crossbar of the opponent's goal (a conversion, scoring two points; a penalty kick, scoring three points; or a drop-kick, scoring three points). Rugby League developed from the Union game but is played by 13 players at amateur and professional levels. In League games, a try scores four points; a conversion scores two points; a drop goal scores three points, and a penalty kick scores two points. In both forms of the game, whenever a rule is broken, play is resumed with a scrum. In a scrum, each team's forwards bind together facing each other and fight for possession of the ball.

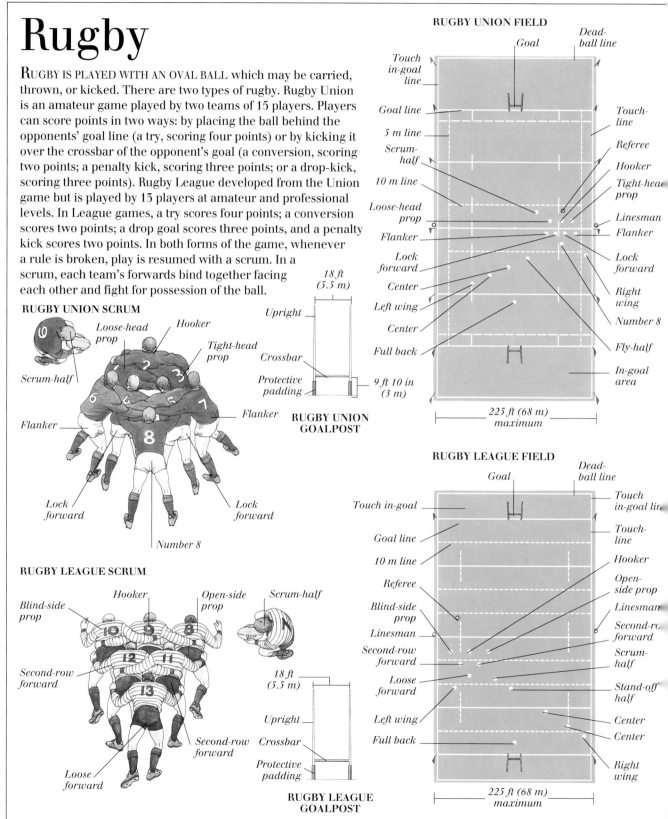

RUGBY UNION FIELD

Touch in-goal line
Goal
Dead-ball line
Goal line
Touch-line
5 m line
Scrum-half
Referee
10 m line
Hooker
Loose-head prop
Tight-head prop
Flanker
Linesman
Lock forward
Flanker
Center
Lock forward
Left wing
Right wing
Center
Number 8
Full back
Fly-half
In-goal area
225 ft (68 m) maximum

RUGBY UNION SCRUM

Loose-head prop
Hooker
Tight-head prop
Scrum-half
Flanker
Flanker
Lock forward
Lock forward
Number 8

RUGBY UNION GOALPOST

18 ft (5.5 m)
Upright
Crossbar
Protective padding
9 ft 10 in (3 m)

RUGBY LEAGUE FIELD

Goal
Dead-ball line
Touch in-goal
Touch in-goal line
Goal line
Touch-line
10 m line
Hooker
Referee
Open-side prop
Blind-side prop
Linesman
Linesman
Second-row forward
Second-row forward
Scrum-half
Loose forward
Stand-off half
Left wing
Center
Full back
Center
Right wing
225 ft (68 m) maximum

RUGBY LEAGUE SCRUM

Hooker
Open-side prop
Scrum-half
Blind-side prop
Second-row forward
Second-row forward
Loose forward

RUGBY LEAGUE GOALPOST

18 ft (5.5 m)
Upright
Crossbar
Protective padding

RUGBY SCORING AND SKILLS

GOAL

Goal line

TRY

PASS

PLACE KICK

FLYING TACKLE

RUGBY UNION PLAYER

Shirt in team color

Knee-high sock

Team shorts

Studded boot

RUGBY UNION BALL

Four-panel construction

Laminated leather panel covered with textured plastic

Mitre

MULTIPLEX

11–12 in (28–30 cm)

RUGBY LEAGUE BALL

Four-panel construction

Laminated leather panel covered with smooth plastic

Mitre

MULTIPLEX E

11 in (28 cm)

RUGBY LEAGUE SHIRT

Team crest

Official logo of the British Rugby Football League

Three-quarter sleeve

RUGBY UNION SHIRT

Button-up collar

Ankle support

Circular stud

RUGBY SHOE

Team crest

Team color

Long sleeve

RUGBY SHIRTS

Basketball

BASKETBALL IS A BALL GAME for two teams of five players, originally devised in 1890 by James Naismath for the Y.M.C.A. in Springfield, Massachusetts. The object of the game is to take possession of the ball and score points by throwing the ball into the opposing team's basket. A player moves the ball up and down the court by bouncing it along the ground or "dribbling"; the ball may be passed between players by throwing, bouncing, or rolling. Players may not run with or kick the ball, although pivoting on one foot is allowed. The game begins with the referee throwing the ball into the air and a player from each team jumping up to try and "tip" the ball to a teammate. The length of the game and the number of periods played varies at different levels. There are amateur, professional, and international rules. No game ends in a draw. As many extra periods as necessary are played to break the tie. In addition to the five players on court, each team has up to seven substitutes, but players may only leave the court with the permission of the referee. Basketball is a noncontact sport and fouls on other players are penalized by a throw-in awarded against the offending team; a free throw at the basket is awarded when a player is fouled in the act of shooting. Basketball is a fast-moving game, requiring both physical and mental coordination. Skillful tactical play matters more than simple physical strength and the agility of the players makes the game an excellent spectator sport.

INTERNATIONAL BASKETBALL COURT

Backboard

End-line

Restraining circle

Player's bench

Referee

Timekeeper

Clock operator

Scorer

Referee

Right forward

Three-point line

Basket

Semi-circle

Right guard

Left guard

Center

Centerline

Left forward

Center circle

Free-throw line

Sideline

49 ft 3 in (15 m)

BASKET AND BACKBOARD

Backboard

Metal rim

Cord net

6 ft
(1.8 m)

BASKET AND BACKBOARD STRUCTURE

10 ft
(3.05 m)

BASKETBALL SKILLS

CHEST PASS

DRIBBLE

OVERHEAD PASS

LAY-UP SHOT

JUMP SHOT

LONG PASS

ZONE DEFENSES

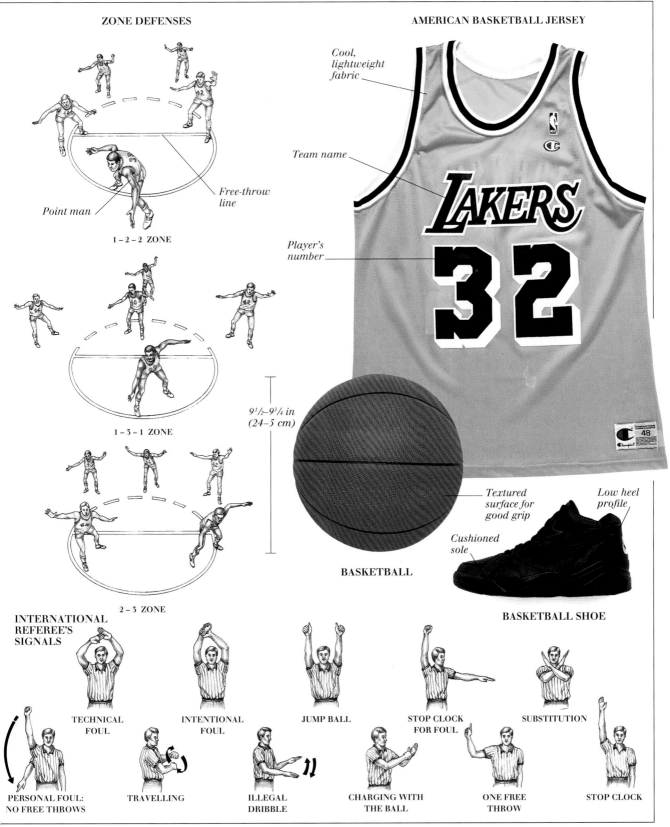

Point man

Free-throw line

1 – 2 – 2 ZONE

1 – 3 – 1 ZONE

2 – 3 ZONE

$9\frac{1}{2}$–$9\frac{3}{4}$ in (24–5 cm)

AMERICAN BASKETBALL JERSEY

Cool, lightweight fabric

Team name

Player's number

LAKERS

32

Champion 48

BASKETBALL

Textured surface for good grip

Cushioned sole

Low heel profile

BASKETBALL SHOE

INTERNATIONAL REFEREE'S SIGNALS

TECHNICAL FOUL

INTENTIONAL FOUL

JUMP BALL

STOP CLOCK FOR FOUL

SUBSTITUTION

PERSONAL FOUL: NO FREE THROWS

TRAVELLING

ILLEGAL DRIBBLE

CHARGING WITH THE BALL

ONE FREE THROW

STOP CLOCK

Volleyball, netball, and handball

VOLLEYBALL, NETBALL, AND HANDBALL are fast-moving team sports played with balls, usually on courts with a hard surface. In volleyball, the object of the game is to hit the ball over a net strung across the center of the court so that it touches the ground on the opponent's side. The team of six players can take three hits to direct the ball over the net, although the same player cannot hit the ball twice in a row. Players can hit the ball with their arms, hands or any other part of their upper body. Teams score points only while serving. The first team to score 15 points, with a two-point margin over their opponent, wins the game. Netball is similar to basketball (see pp. 532–533), but is played on a slightly larger court with seven players instead of five. A team moves the ball toward the goal by throwing, passing, and catching it with the aim of throwing the ball through the opponents' goal net. Players are confined by their playing position to specific areas of the court. Team handball is one of the world's fastest games. Each side has seven players. A team moves the ball by dribbling, passing, or bouncing it as they run. Players may stop, catch, throw, bounce, or strike the ball with any part of the body above the knees. Each team tries to score goals by directing the ball past the opposition's goalkeeper into the net, which is similar to a soccer goal net (see pp. 524–525).

VOLLEYBALL SHOTS

OVERHAND SERVE   SPIKE (SMASH)

UNDERHAND SERVE   FOREARM PASS (DIG)

VOLLEYBALL KIT

Team colors

Ribbed cuff

Cotton-knit jersey

Elastic waist

Shorts

Elastic knit fabric

Injected molded padding

VOLLEYBALL COURT

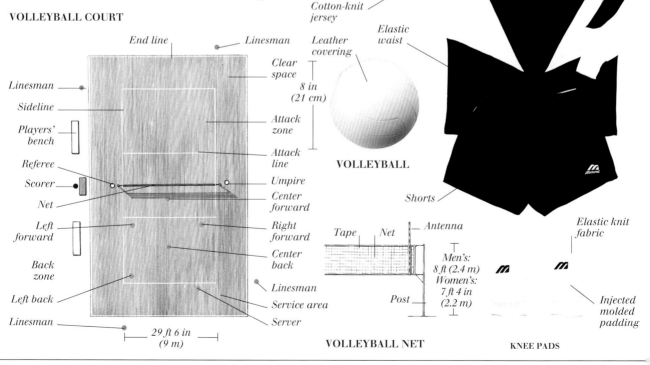

End line
Linesman
Linesman
Sideline
Players' bench
Referee
Scorer
Net
Left forward
Back zone
Left back
Linesman

Clear space
Leather covering
8 in (21 cm)
Attack zone
Attack line
VOLLEYBALL

Umpire
Center forward
Right forward
Center back
Linesman
Service area
Server

29 ft 6 in (9 m)

Tape   Net   Antenna
Men's: 8 ft (2.4 m)
Women's: 7 ft 4 in (2.2 m)
Post

VOLLEYBALL NET

KNEE PADS

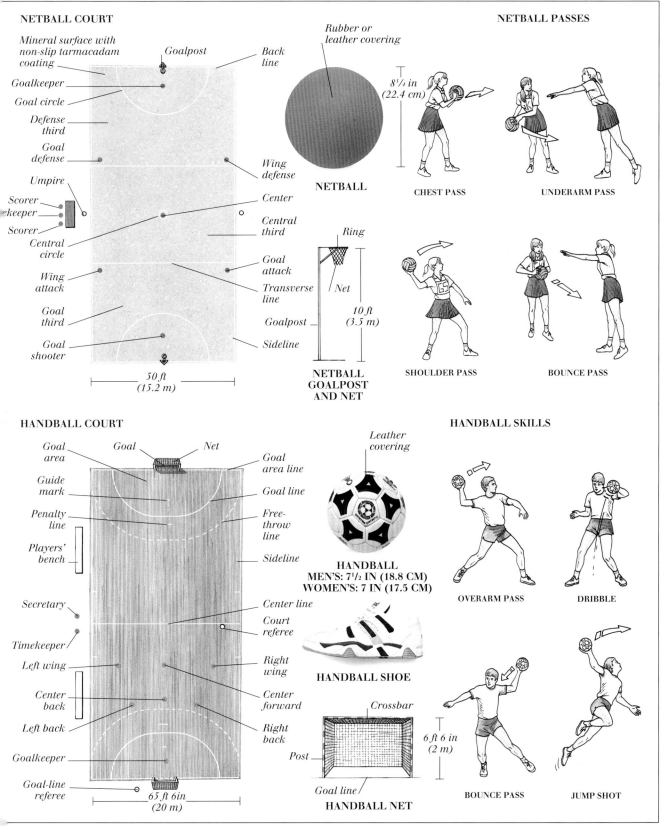

NETBALL COURT

Mineral surface with non-slip tarmacadam coating

Goalpost

Back line

Goalkeeper

Goal circle

Defense third

Goal defense

Wing defense

Umpire

Scorer

keeper

Center

Scorer

Central third

Central circle

Wing attack

Goal attack

Transverse line

Goal third

Goal shooter

Sideline

50 ft (15.2 m)

NETBALL PASSES

Rubber or leather covering

8³/₄ in (22.4 cm)

NETBALL

CHEST PASS

UNDERARM PASS

Ring

Net

10 ft (3.5 m)

Goalpost

NETBALL GOALPOST AND NET

SHOULDER PASS

BOUNCE PASS

HANDBALL COURT

Goal area

Goal

Net

Goal area line

Guide mark

Goal line

Penalty line

Free-throw line

Players' bench

Sideline

Secretary

Center line

Court referee

Timekeeper

Right wing

Left wing

Center back

Center forward

Left back

Right back

Goalkeeper

Goal-line referee

65 ft 6in (20 m)

HANDBALL SKILLS

Leather covering

HANDBALL
MEN'S: 7¹/₂ IN (18.8 CM)
WOMEN'S: 7 IN (17.5 CM)

OVERARM PASS

DRIBBLE

HANDBALL SHOE

Crossbar

6 ft 6 in (2 m)

Post

Goal line

HANDBALL NET

BOUNCE PASS

JUMP SHOT

Baseball

BASEBALL IS A BALL GAME for two teams of nine players. The batter hits the ball thrown by the opposing team's pitcher, into the area between the foul lines. He then runs round all four fixed bases in order to score a run, touching or "tagging" each base in turn. The pitcher must throw the ball at a height between the batter's armpits and knees, a height which is called the strike zone. A ball pitched in this area that crosses over the home plate is called a "strike" and the batter has three strikes in which to try to hit the ball (otherwise he has "struck out"). The fielding team tries to get the batting team out by catching the ball before it bounces, tagging a player of the batting team who is running between bases with the ball, or by tagging a base before the player has reached it. Members of the batting team may stop safely at a base as long as it is not occupied by another member of their team. When the batter runs to first base, his teammate at first base must run onto second – this is called a force play. A game consists of nine innings and each team will bat once during an inning. When three members of the batting team are out, the teams swap roles. The team with the most runs wins the game.

BATTER'S HELMET

Plastic shell

Peak

Foam padding

Wire coated in strong nylon

Plastic-coated foam padding

CATCHER'S MASK

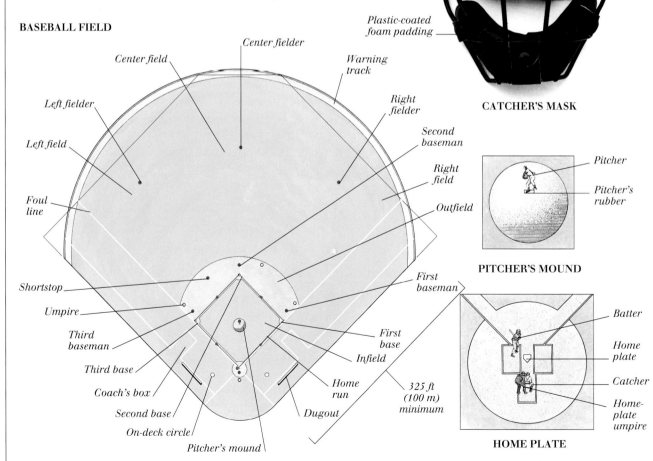

BASEBALL FIELD

Center fielder

Center field

Warning track

Left fielder

Right fielder

Left field

Second baseman

Foul line

Right field

Outfield

Shortstop

First baseman

Umpire

First base

Third baseman

Infield

Third base

Home run

Coach's box

325 ft (100 m) minimum

Second base

Dugout

On-deck circle

Pitcher's mound

PITCHER'S MOUND

Pitcher

Pitcher's rubber

HOME PLATE

Batter

Home plate

Catcher

Home-plate umpire

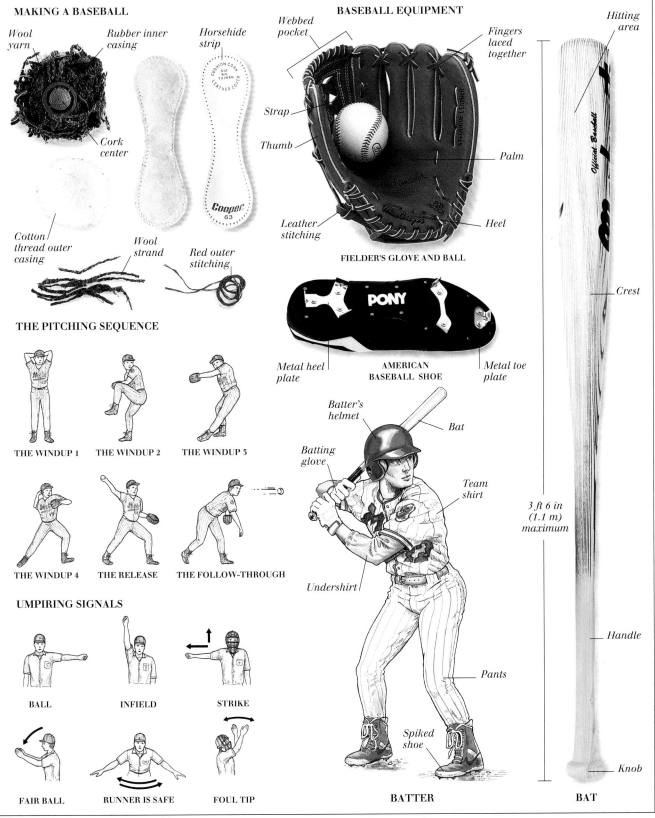

MAKING A BASEBALL

Wool yarn

Rubber inner casing

Horsehide strip

CUSHION CORK
.801
TAIWAN
LEATHER COVER

Cork center

Cooper
63

Cotton thread outer casing

Wool strand

Red outer stitching

THE PITCHING SEQUENCE

THE WINDUP 1

THE WINDUP 2

THE WINDUP 3

THE WINDUP 4

THE RELEASE

THE FOLLOW-THROUGH

UMPIRING SIGNALS

BALL

INFIELD

STRIKE

FAIR BALL

RUNNER IS SAFE

FOUL TIP

BASEBALL EQUIPMENT

Webbed pocket

Fingers laced together

Strap

Thumb

Palm

Leather stitching

Heel

SPEERIDE LEATHER

Official Baseball

FIELDER'S GLOVE AND BALL

PONY

Metal heel plate

AMERICAN BASEBALL SHOE

Metal toe plate

Batter's helmet

Bat

Batting glove

Team shirt

Undershirt

Pants

Spiked shoe

BATTER

Hitting area

Crest

3 ft 6 in (1.1 m) maximum

Handle

Knob

BAT

Cricket

CRICKET IS A BALL GAME PLAYED by two teams of eleven players on a pitch with two sets of three stumps (wickets). The bowler bowls the ball down the pitch to the batsman of the opposing team, who must defend the wicket in front of which he stands. The object of the game is to score as many runs as possible. Runs can be scored individually by running the length of the playing strip, or by hitting a ball which lands outside the boundary (six), or which lands inside the boundary but bounces or rolls outside (four); the opposing team will bowl and field, attempting to dismiss the batsmen. A batsman can be dismissed in one of several ways: by the bowler hitting the wicket with the ball ("bowled"); by a fielder catching the ball hit by the batsman before it touches the ground ("caught"); by the wicket-keeper or another fielder breaking the wicket while the batsman is attempting a run and is therefore out of his ground ("stumped" or "run out"); by the batsman breaking the wicket with his own bat or body ("hit wicket"); by a part of the batsman's body being hit by a ball that would otherwise have hit the wicket ("leg before wicket" ["lbw"]). A match consists of one or two innings and each innings ends when the tenth batsman of the batting team is out, when a certain number of overs (a series of six balls bowled) have been played, or when the captain of the batting team "declares" ending the innings voluntarily.

FORWARD DEFENSIVE STROKE   **BACKWARD DEFENSIVE STROKE**

ON-DRIVE   **OFF-DRIVE**

PULL   **HOOK**

SQUARE CUT   **LEG GLANCE**

CRICKET BALL AND WICKET

Leather skin — — Seam
BALL

Bail —
WICKET

Stump —

CRICKET PITCH

Wicket-keeper

Batsman

Wicket

Bowling crease

66 ft (20 m)

Bowler

Return crease

Umpire   *Non-striking batsman*

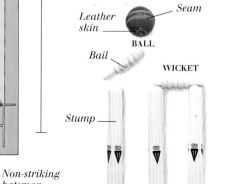

POSSIBLE FIELD POSITIONS FOR AN AWAY SWING BOWLER TO A RIGHT-HANDED BATSMAN (IN RED) AND OTHER FIELD POSITIONS

Umpire
Long on   Long off
Boundary line   Bowler
Deep mid-wicket   Non-striking batsman
Mid-on
Silly mid-on   Extra cover
Forward short leg   Mid-off
Square leg   Silly mid-off
Deep square leg   Cover
Square-leg umpire   Point
Batsman   Gulley
Long leg   Third man
Leg slip   Second slip
Wicket-keeper   First slip
Fine leg   Sight screen   Bowler

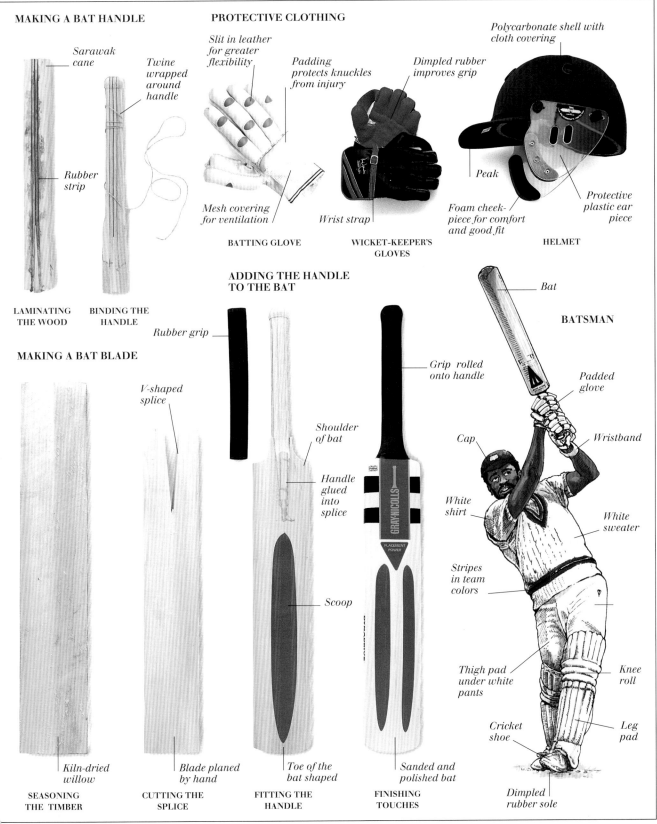

MAKING A BAT HANDLE

Sarawak cane

Twine wrapped around handle

Rubber strip

LAMINATING THE WOOD

BINDING THE HANDLE

PROTECTIVE CLOTHING

Slit in leather for greater flexibility

Padding protects knuckles from injury

Dimpled rubber improves grip

Polycarbonate shell with cloth covering

Mesh covering for ventilation

Wrist strap

Peak

Foam cheek-piece for comfort and good fit

Protective plastic ear piece

BATTING GLOVE

WICKET-KEEPER'S GLOVES

HELMET

ADDING THE HANDLE TO THE BAT

Rubber grip

Shoulder of bat

Handle glued into splice

Grip rolled onto handle

Scoop

Bat

BATSMAN

Padded glove

Cap

Wristband

White shirt

White sweater

Stripes in team colors

MAKING A BAT BLADE

V-shaped splice

Kiln-dried willow

Blade planed by hand

Toe of the bat shaped

Sanded and polished bat

Thigh pad under white pants

Knee roll

Cricket shoe

Leg pad

Dimpled rubber sole

SEASONING THE TIMBER

CUTTING THE SPLICE

FITTING THE HANDLE

FINISHING TOUCHES

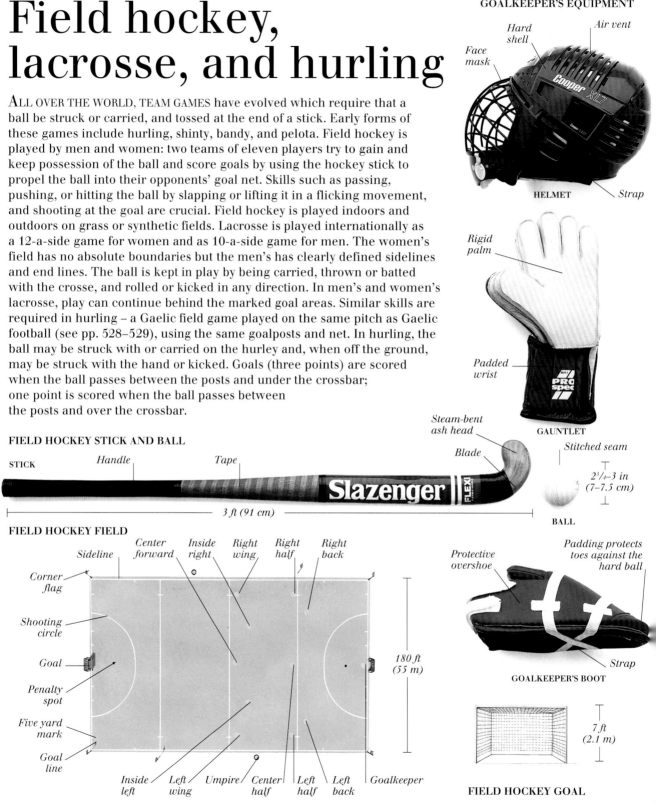

Field hockey, lacrosse, and hurling

ALL OVER THE WORLD, TEAM GAMES have evolved which require that a ball be struck or carried, and tossed at the end of a stick. Early forms of these games include hurling, shinty, bandy, and pelota. Field hockey is played by men and women: two teams of eleven players try to gain and keep possession of the ball and score goals by using the hockey stick to propel the ball into their opponents' goal net. Skills such as passing, pushing, or hitting the ball by slapping or lifting it in a flicking movement, and shooting at the goal are crucial. Field hockey is played indoors and outdoors on grass or synthetic fields. Lacrosse is played internationally as a 12-a-side game for women and as 10-a-side game for men. The women's field has no absolute boundaries but the men's has clearly defined sidelines and end lines. The ball is kept in play by being carried, thrown or batted with the crosse, and rolled or kicked in any direction. In men's and women's lacrosse, play can continue behind the marked goal areas. Similar skills are required in hurling – a Gaelic field game played on the same pitch as Gaelic football (see pp. 528–529), using the same goalposts and net. In hurling, the ball may be struck with or carried on the hurley and, when off the ground, may be struck with the hand or kicked. Goals (three points) are scored when the ball passes between the posts and under the crossbar; one point is scored when the ball passes between the posts and over the crossbar.

GOALKEEPER'S EQUIPMENT

Hard shell
Air vent
Face mask
HELMET
Strap

Rigid palm
Padded wrist
GAUNTLET

FIELD HOCKEY STICK AND BALL

STICK
Handle
Tape
Steam-bent ash head
Blade
Slazenger FLEXI
3 ft (91 cm)

Stitched seam
2 1/4–3 in (7–7.5 cm)
BALL

FIELD HOCKEY FIELD

Sideline
Corner flag
Shooting circle
Goal
Penalty spot
Five yard mark
Goal line
Center forward
Inside right
Right wing
Right half
Right back
Inside left
Left wing
Umpire
Center half
Left half
Left back
Goalkeeper
180 ft (55 m)

Protective overshoe
Padding protects toes against the hard ball
Strap
GOALKEEPER'S BOOT

7 ft (2.1 m)
FIELD HOCKEY GOAL

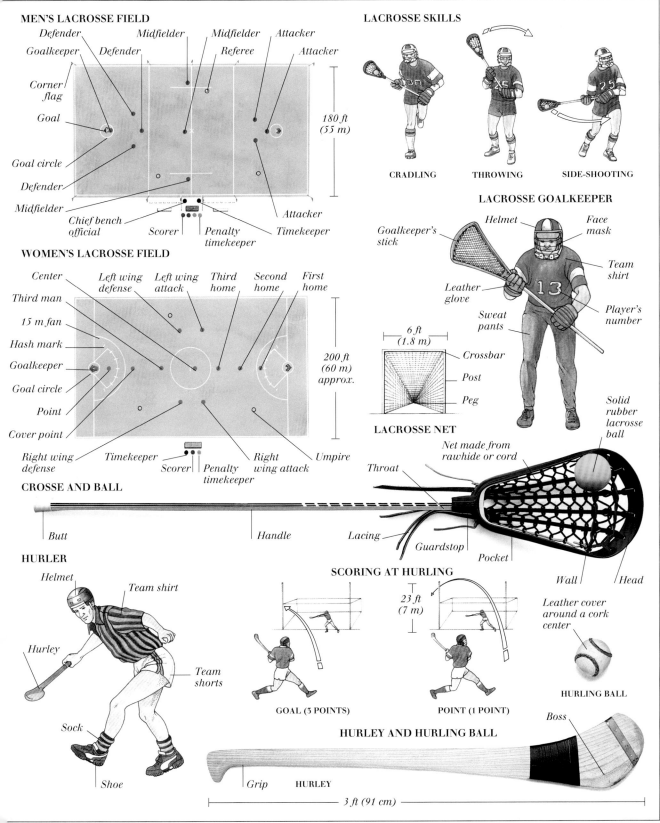

MEN'S LACROSSE FIELD

Defender
Midfielder
Midfielder
Attacker
Goalkeeper
Defender
Referee
Attacker
Corner flag
Goal
180 ft (55 m)
Goal circle
Defender
Midfielder
Attacker
Chief bench official
Scorer
Penalty timekeeper
Timekeeper

WOMEN'S LACROSSE FIELD

Center
Left wing defense
Left wing attack
Third home
Second home
First home
Third man
15 m fan
Hash mark
Goalkeeper
200 ft (60 m) approx.
Goal circle
Point
Cover point
Right wing defense
Timekeeper
Scorer
Penalty timekeeper
Right wing attack
Umpire

CROSSE AND BALL

Butt
Handle
Throat
Lacing
Guardstop
Pocket

HURLER

Helmet
Team shirt
Hurley
Team shorts
Sock
Shoe

LACROSSE SKILLS

CRADLING
THROWING
SIDE-SHOOTING

LACROSSE GOALKEEPER

Helmet
Face mask
Goalkeeper's stick
Team shirt
Leather glove
Player's number
Sweat pants
6 ft (1.8 m)
Crossbar
Post
Peg
Solid rubber lacrosse ball

LACROSSE NET

Net made from rawhide or cord
Wall
Head

SCORING AT HURLING

23 ft (7 m)
GOAL (3 POINTS)
POINT (1 POINT)

Leather cover around a cork center

HURLING BALL

HURLEY AND HURLING BALL

Boss
Grip
HURLEY
3 ft (91 cm)

Track and field

THE SPORTS that make up athletics are divided into two main groups: track events – which include sprinting, middle, and long distance running, relay running, hurdling, and walking – and field events which require jumping and throwing skills. Contests designed to test the speed, strength, agility, and stamina of athletes were held by the ancient Greeks over 4,000 years ago. However, the abolition of the Olympic Games in 393 AD meant that track and field events were neglected until the revival of large-scale competitions in the mid-nineteenth century. Modern stadiums offer areas reserved for the long jump, triple jump, and pole vault usually situated outside the running track. The javelin, shot, hammer, and discus are thrown within the track area. Most athletes specialize in one or two events but, in the heptathlon, women compete in seven events, held over two days: 200 m and 800 m races, 100 m hurdles, javelin, shot put, high jump, and long jump. In the decathlon, men compete in ten events over two days: 100 m, 400 m, and 1,500 m races, 110 m hurdles, javelin, discus, shot put, pole vault, high jump, and long jump.

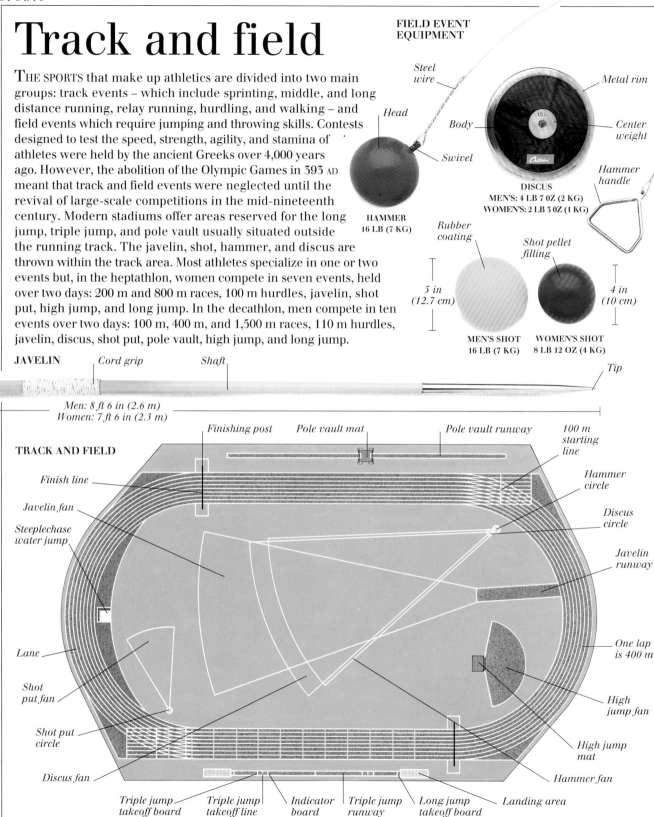

FIELD EVENT EQUIPMENT

Steel wire

Head

Body

Swivel

Metal rim

Center weight

HAMMER
16 LB (7 KG)

DISCUS
MEN'S: 4 LB 7 OZ (2 KG)
WOMEN'S: 2 LB 3 OZ (1 KG)

Hammer handle

Rubber coating

Shot pellet filling

5 in (12.7 cm)

4 in (10 cm)

MEN'S SHOT
16 LB (7 KG)

WOMEN'S SHOT
8 LB 12 OZ (4 KG)

JAVELIN

Cord grip

Shaft

Tip

Men: 8 ft 6 in (2.6 m)
Women: 7 ft 6 in (2.3 m)

TRACK AND FIELD

Finishing post

Pole vault mat

Pole vault runway

100 m starting line

Finish line

Javelin fan

Steeplechase water jump

Hammer circle

Discus circle

Javelin runway

Lane

One lap is 400 m

Shot put fan

High jump fan

Shot put circle

High jump mat

Discus fan

Hammer fan

Triple jump takeoff board

Triple jump takeoff line

Indicator board

Triple jump runway

Long jump takeoff board

Landing area

542

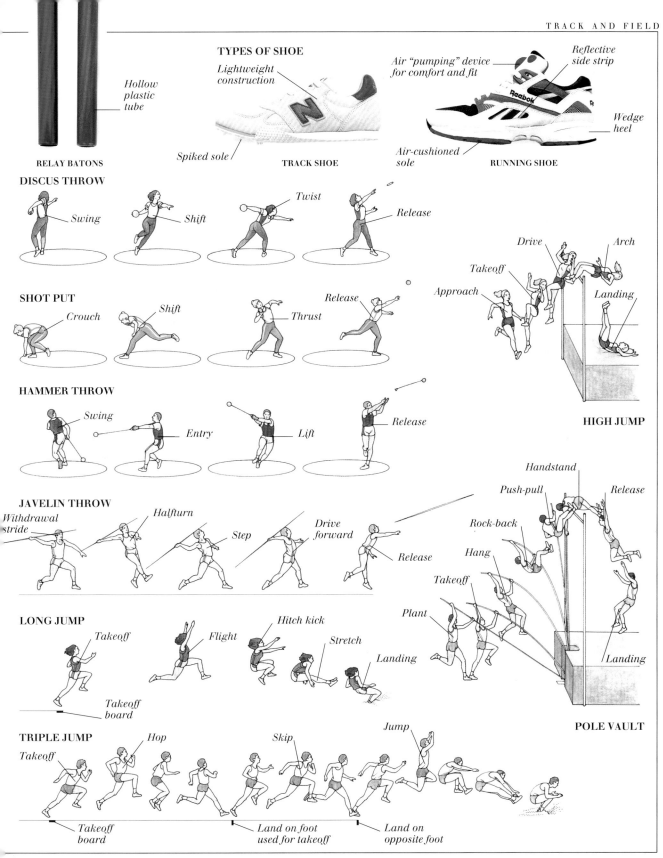

TYPES OF SHOE

Hollow plastic tube

Lightweight construction

Spiked sole

RELAY BATONS

TRACK SHOE

Air "pumping" device for comfort and fit

Reflective side strip

Reebok

Wedge heel

Air-cushioned sole

RUNNING SHOE

DISCUS THROW

Swing

Shift

Twist

Release

SHOT PUT

Crouch

Shift

Thrust

Release

Drive

Arch

Takeoff

Landing

Approach

HIGH JUMP

HAMMER THROW

Swing

Entry

Lift

Release

JAVELIN THROW

Withdrawal stride

Halfturn

Step

Drive forward

Release

Handstand

Push-pull

Release

Rock-back

Hang

Takeoff

Plant

Landing

LONG JUMP

Takeoff

Flight

Hitch kick

Stretch

Landing

Takeoff board

POLE VAULT

TRIPLE JUMP

Takeoff

Hop

Skip

Jump

Takeoff board

Land on foot used for takeoff

Land on opposite foot

543

Racket sports

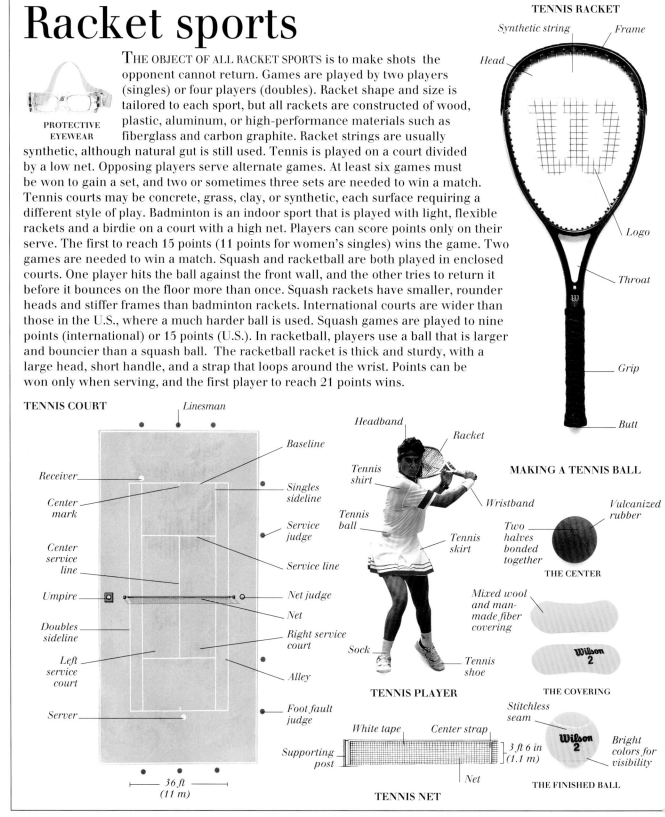

THE OBJECT OF ALL RACKET SPORTS is to make shots the opponent cannot return. Games are played by two players (singles) or four players (doubles). Racket shape and size is tailored to each sport, but all rackets are constructed of wood, plastic, aluminum, or high-performance materials such as fiberglass and carbon graphite. Racket strings are usually synthetic, although natural gut is still used. Tennis is played on a court divided by a low net. Opposing players serve alternate games. At least six games must be won to gain a set, and two or sometimes three sets are needed to win a match. Tennis courts may be concrete, grass, clay, or synthetic, each surface requiring a different style of play. Badminton is an indoor sport that is played with light, flexible rackets and a birdie on a court with a high net. Players can score points only on their serve. The first to reach 15 points (11 points for women's singles) wins the game. Two games are needed to win a match. Squash and racketball are both played in enclosed courts. One player hits the ball against the front wall, and the other tries to return it before it bounces on the floor more than once. Squash rackets have smaller, rounder heads and stiffer frames than badminton rackets. International courts are wider than those in the U.S., where a much harder ball is used. Squash games are played to nine points (international) or 15 points (U.S.). In racketball, players use a ball that is larger and bouncier than a squash ball. The racketball racket is thick and sturdy, with a large head, short handle, and a strap that loops around the wrist. Points can be won only when serving, and the first player to reach 21 points wins.

PROTECTIVE EYEWEAR

TENNIS RACKET

Synthetic string
Frame
Head
Logo
Throat
Grip
Butt

TENNIS COURT

Linesman
Baseline
Receiver
Singles sideline
Center mark
Service judge
Center service line
Service line
Umpire
Net judge
Net
Doubles sideline
Right service court
Left service court
Alley
Server
Foot fault judge

36 ft
(11 m)

TENNIS PLAYER

Headband
Racket
Tennis shirt
Wristband
Tennis ball
Tennis skirt
Tennis shoe
Sock

TENNIS NET

White tape
Center strap
Supporting post
Net
3 ft 6 in
(1.1 m)

MAKING A TENNIS BALL

Two halves bonded together
Vulcanized rubber

THE CENTER

Mixed wool and man-made fiber covering

THE COVERING

Stitchless seam
Wilson 2
Bright colors for visibility

THE FINISHED BALL

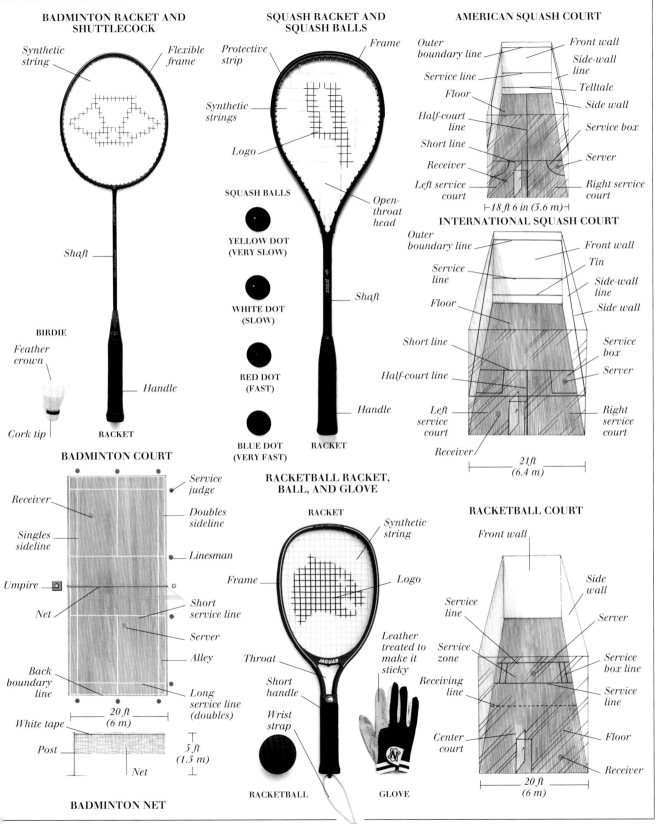

BADMINTON RACKET AND SHUTTLECOCK

Synthetic string

Flexible frame

Shaft

BIRDIE

Feather crown

Handle

Cork tip

RACKET

SQUASH RACKET AND SQUASH BALLS

Protective strip

Frame

Synthetic strings

Logo

Open-throat head

SQUASH BALLS

YELLOW DOT (VERY SLOW)

WHITE DOT (SLOW)

RED DOT (FAST)

BLUE DOT (VERY FAST)

Shaft

Handle

RACKET

AMERICAN SQUASH COURT

Outer boundary line

Front wall

Service line

Side-wall line

Floor

Telltale

Half-court line

Side wall

Short line

Service box

Receiver

Server

Left service court

Right service court

⊢18 ft 6 in (5.6 m)⊣

INTERNATIONAL SQUASH COURT

Outer boundary line

Front wall

Service line

Tin

Floor

Side-wall line

Side wall

Short line

Service box

Half-court line

Server

Left service court

Right service court

Receiver

21ft (6.4 m)

BADMINTON COURT

Receiver

Service judge

Singles sideline

Doubles sideline

Linesman

Umpire

Short service line

Net

Server

Alley

Back boundary line

Long service line (doubles)

20 ft (6 m)

White tape

Post

5 ft (1.5 m)

Net

BADMINTON NET

RACKETBALL RACKET, BALL, AND GLOVE

RACKET

Synthetic string

Frame

Logo

Leather treated to make it sticky

Throat

Short handle

Wrist strap

RACKETBALL

GLOVE

RACKETBALL COURT

Front wall

Side wall

Service line

Server

Service zone

Service box line

Receiving line

Service line

Center court

Floor

Receiver

20 ft (6 m)

Golf

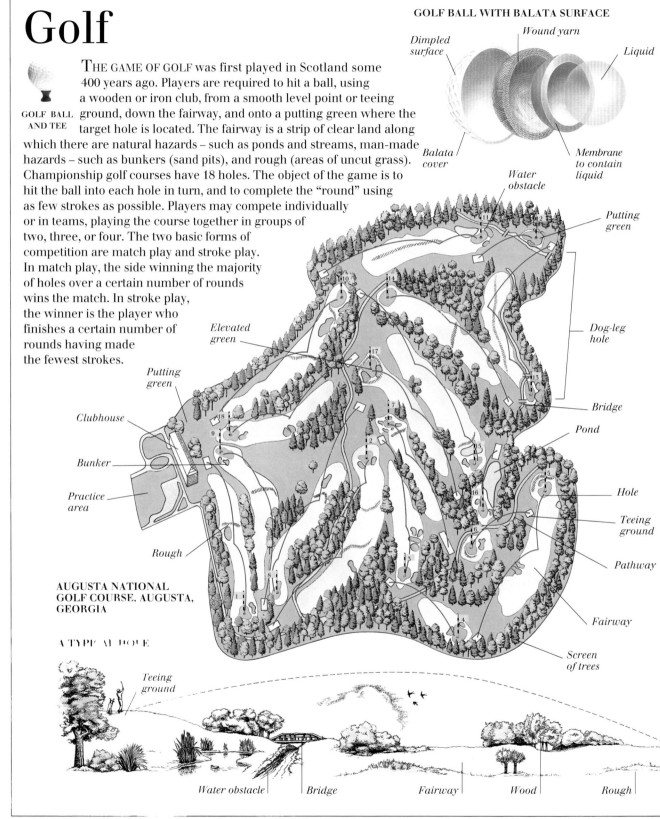

GOLF BALL AND TEE

THE GAME OF GOLF was first played in Scotland some 400 years ago. Players are required to hit a ball, using a wooden or iron club, from a smooth level point or teeing ground, down the fairway, and onto a putting green where the target hole is located. The fairway is a strip of clear land along which there are natural hazards – such as ponds and streams, man-made hazards – such as bunkers (sand pits), and rough (areas of uncut grass). Championship golf courses have 18 holes. The object of the game is to hit the ball into each hole in turn, and to complete the "round" using as few strokes as possible. Players may compete individually or in teams, playing the course together in groups of two, three, or four. The two basic forms of competition are match play and stroke play. In match play, the side winning the majority of holes over a certain number of rounds wins the match. In stroke play, the winner is the player who finishes a certain number of rounds having made the fewest strokes.

GOLF BALL WITH BALATA SURFACE

Dimpled surface

Wound yarn

Liquid

Balata cover

Membrane to contain liquid

Water obstacle

Putting green

Dog-leg hole

Elevated green

Bridge

Putting green

Pond

Clubhouse

Bunker

Hole

Practice area

Teeing ground

Rough

Pathway

Fairway

AUGUSTA NATIONAL GOLF COURSE, AUGUSTA, GEORGIA

Screen of trees

A TYPICAL HOLE

Teeing ground

Water obstacle

Bridge

Fairway

Wood

Rough

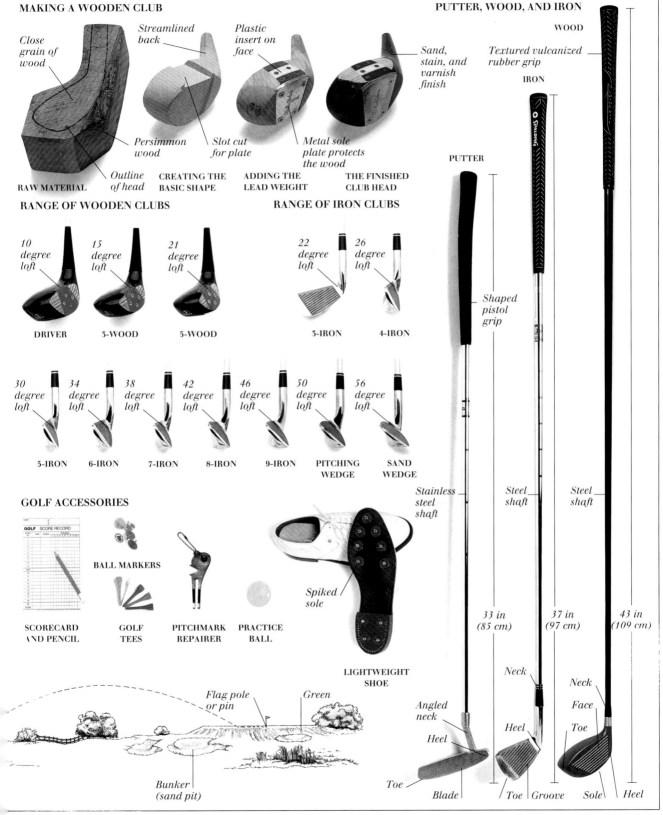

MAKING A WOODEN CLUB

Close grain of wood

Streamlined back

Plastic insert on face

Sand, stain, and varnish finish

Persimmon wood

Slot cut for plate

Metal sole plate protects the wood

Outline of head

RAW MATERIAL

CREATING THE BASIC SHAPE

ADDING THE LEAD WEIGHT

THE FINISHED CLUB HEAD

PUTTER, WOOD, AND IRON

WOOD

Textured vulcanized rubber grip

IRON

PUTTER

RANGE OF WOODEN CLUBS

10 degree loft

15 degree loft

21 degree loft

DRIVER

3-WOOD

5-WOOD

RANGE OF IRON CLUBS

22 degree loft

26 degree loft

3-IRON

4-IRON

30 degree loft

34 degree loft

38 degree loft

42 degree loft

46 degree loft

50 degree loft

56 degree loft

5-IRON

6-IRON

7-IRON

8-IRON

9-IRON

PITCHING WEDGE

SAND WEDGE

Shaped pistol grip

GOLF ACCESSORIES

GOLF SCORE RECORD

BALL MARKERS

Spiked sole

Stainless steel shaft

Steel shaft

Steel shaft

SCORECARD AND PENCIL

GOLF TEES

PITCHMARK REPAIRER

PRACTICE BALL

LIGHTWEIGHT SHOE

33 in (85 cm)

37 in (97 cm)

43 in (109 cm)

Flag pole or pin

Green

Neck

Neck

Angled neck

Face

Heel

Toe

Heel

Toe

Bunker (sand pit)

Toe

Blade

Toe

Groove

Sole

Heel

Archery and shooting

TARGET SHOOTING AND ARCHERY EVOLVED as practice for hunting and battle skills. Modern bows, although designed according to the principles of early hunting bows, use laminates, fiberglass, dacron, and carbon, and are equipped with sights and stabilizers. Competitors in target archery shoot over distances of 100 ft (30 m), 165 ft (50 m), 230 ft (70 m), and 300 ft (90 m) for men, and 100 ft (30 m), 165 ft (50 m), 200 ft (60 m), and 230 ft (70 m) for women. The closer the shot is to the center of the target, the higher the score. The individual scores are added up, and the archer with the highest total wins the competition. Crossbows are used in match competitions over 33 ft (10 m), and 100 ft (30 m). Rifle shooting is divided into three categories: smallbore, bigbore, and air rifle. Contests take place over a variety of distances and further subdivisions are based on the type of shooting position used; prone, kneeling, or standing. The Olympic biathlon combines cross-country skiing and rifle shooting over a course of approximately 12½ miles (20 km). Additional magazines of ammunition are carried in the butt of the rifles. Bigbore rifles fitted with a telescopic sight can be used for hunting and running game target shooting. Pistol shooting events, using rapid-fire pistols, target pistols, and air pistols, take place over 33 ft (10 m), 82 ft (25 m), and 165 ft (50 m) distances. In rapid-fire pistol shooting, a total of 60 shots are fired from a distance of 82 ft (25 m).

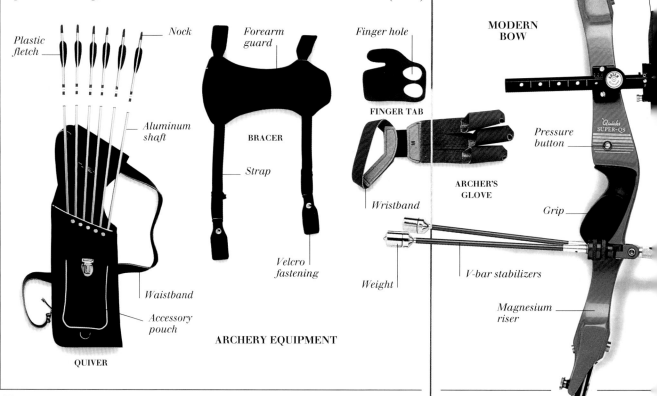

CROSSBOW AND BOLT

Laminated fiberglass bow

Bolt

Bolt rest

1¾ in (45 mm)

Stirrup held between feet when drawing bow

Sight

CROSSBOW TARGET

Hardwood laminate limb

Dacron string

Sight

MODERN BOW

Pressure button

Quicks SUPER-QS

Grip

V-bar stabilizers

Magnesium riser

Plastic fletch

Nock

Forearm guard

Finger hole

Aluminum shaft

FINGER TAB

BRACER

Strap

ARCHER'S GLOVE

Wristband

Weight

Waistband

Velcro fastening

Accessory pouch

ARCHERY EQUIPMENT

QUIVER

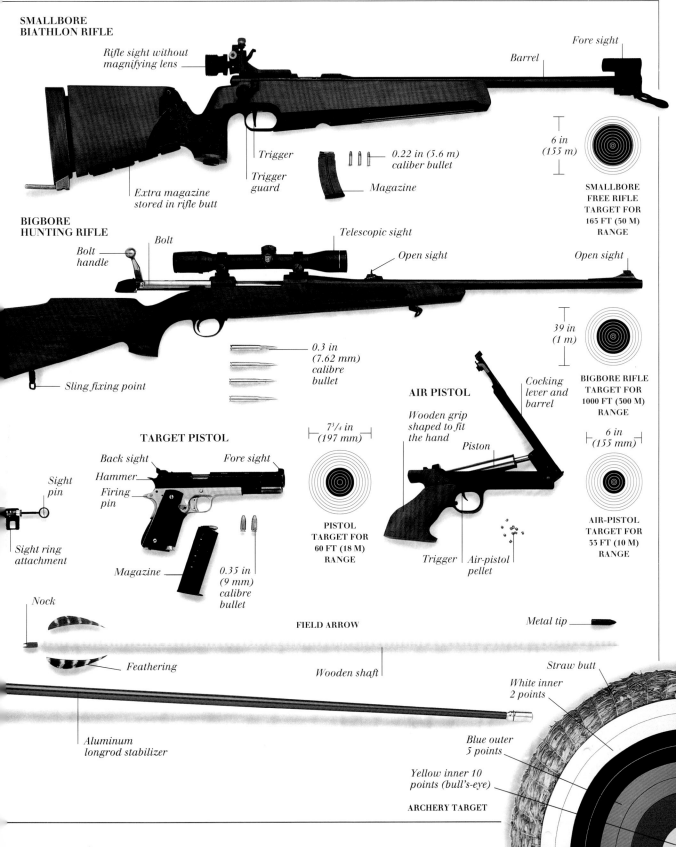

**SMALLBORE
BIATHLON RIFLE**

Rifle sight without magnifying lens

Fore sight

Barrel

Trigger

0.22 in (5.6 m) caliber bullet

Trigger guard

Magazine

Extra magazine stored in rifle butt

6 in (155 m)

SMALLBORE FREE RIFLE TARGET FOR 165 FT (50 M) RANGE

**BIGBORE
HUNTING RIFLE**

Bolt handle

Bolt

Telescopic sight

Open sight

Open sight

0.3 in (7.62 mm) calibre bullet

Sling fixing point

39 in (1 m)

Cocking lever and barrel

BIGBORE RIFLE TARGET FOR 1000 FT (500 M) RANGE

AIR PISTOL

Wooden grip shaped to fit the hand

Piston

6 in (155 mm)

TARGET PISTOL

Back sight

Fore sight

Hammer

Firing pin

Sight pin

7³/₄ in (197 mm)

AIR-PISTOL TARGET FOR 33 FT (10 M) RANGE

Sight ring attachment

Magazine

0.35 in (9 mm) calibre bullet

PISTOL TARGET FOR 60 FT (18 M) RANGE

Trigger

Air-pistol pellet

Nock

FIELD ARROW

Metal tip

Feathering

Wooden shaft

Straw butt

White inner 2 points

Aluminum longrod stabilizer

Blue outer 5 points

Yellow inner 10 points (bull's-eye)

ARCHERY TARGET

Ice hockey

ICE HOCKEY IS PLAYED by two teams of six players on an ice rink, with a goal net at each end. The object of this fast, and often dangerous, game is to hit a frozen rubber puck into the opposing team's net with an ice hockey stick. The game begins when the referee drops the puck between the sticks of two players from opposing teams, who face off. The rink is divided into three areas: defending, neutral, and attacking zones. Players may move with the puck and pass it to one another along the ice, but the puck should not travel more than two zones across the rink markings. A goal is scored when the puck entirely crosses the goal-line between the posts and under the crossbar of the goal. A team may field up to 20 players although only six players are allowed on the ice at one time; substitutions occur frequently. Each game consists of three periods of 20 minutes, divided by breaks of 15 minutes.

GOALKEEPER

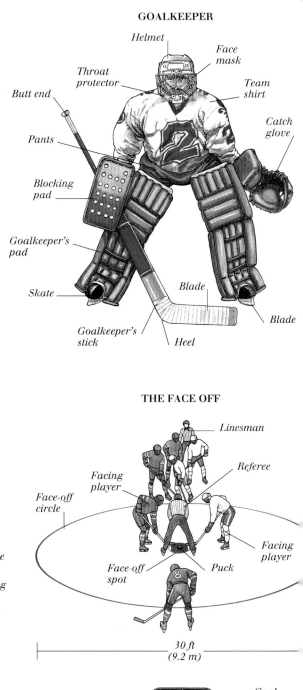

Helmet
Face mask
Throat protector
Team shirt
Butt end
Pants
Catch glove
Blocking pad
Goalkeeper's pad
Blade
Skate
Goalkeeper's stick
Heel
Blade

ICE HOCKEY RINK

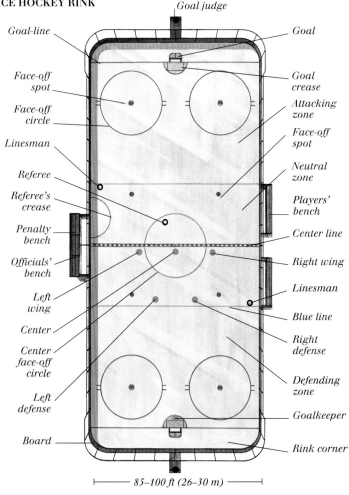

Goal judge
Goal-line
Goal
Face-off spot
Goal crease
Face-off circle
Attacking zone
Linesman
Face-off spot
Referee
Neutral zone
Referee's crease
Players' bench
Penalty bench
Center line
Officials' bench
Right wing
Left wing
Linesman
Center
Blue line
Center face-off circle
Right defense
Left defense
Defending zone
Board
Goalkeeper
Rink corner

|— 85–100 ft (26–30 m) —|

THE FACE OFF

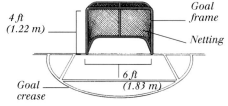

Linesman
Facing player
Referee
Face-off circle
Facing player
Face-off spot
Puck

|— 30 ft (9.2 m) —|

4 ft (1.22 m)
Goal frame
Netting
6 ft (1.83 m)
Goal crease

ICE HOCKEY GOAL

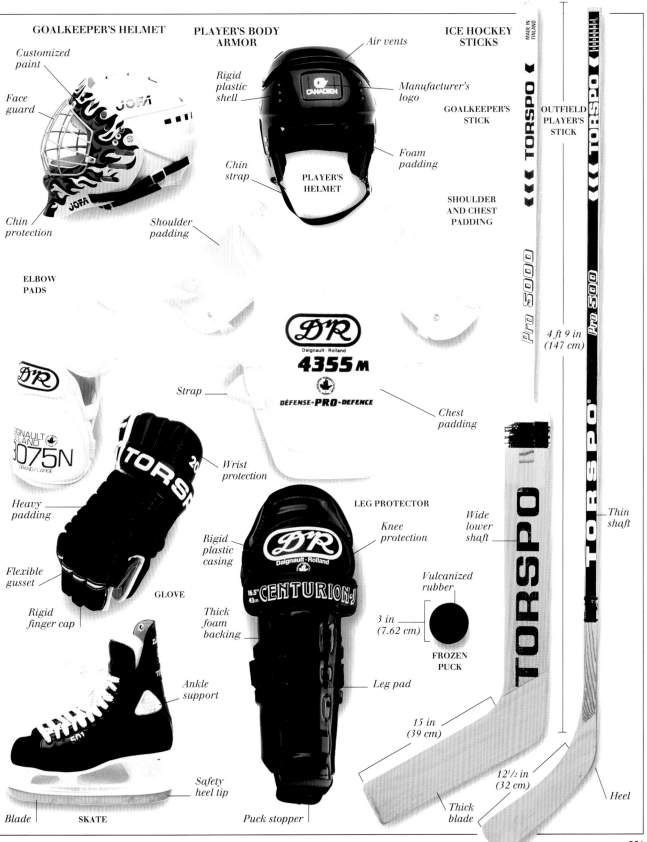

GOALKEEPER'S HELMET

Customized paint

Face guard

Chin protection

PLAYER'S BODY ARMOR

Air vents

Rigid plastic shell

Manufacturer's logo

Chin strap

PLAYER'S HELMET

Foam padding

Shoulder padding

ICE HOCKEY STICKS

MADE IN FINLAND

GOALKEEPER'S STICK

SHOULDER AND CHEST PADDING

OUTFIELD PLAYER'S STICK

4 ft 9 in (147 cm)

ELBOW PADS

4355 M

DÉFENSE-**PRO**-DEFENCE

Strap

Chest padding

Wrist protection

Heavy padding

Flexible gusset

Rigid finger cap

GLOVE

LEG PROTECTOR

Rigid plastic casing

Knee protection

CENTURION-J

Thick foam backing

Leg pad

Wide lower shaft

Thin shaft

Vulcanized rubber

3 in (7.62 cm)

FROZEN PUCK

Ankle support

Safety heel tip

Blade SKATE

Puck stopper

15 in (39 cm)

12 1/2 in (32 cm)

Thick blade

Heel

Alpine skiing

COMPETITIVE ALPINE SKIING is divided into four disciplines: downhill, slalom, giant slalom, and super-giant slalom (Super-G). Each one tests different skills. In downhill skiing, competitors race down a slope marked out by control flags, known as "gates," and are timed on a single run only. Competitors wear crash helmets, one-piece Lycra suits, and long skis with flattened tips to minimize air resistance. Slalom and giant slalom skiers negotiate a twisting course requiring balance, agility, and quick reactions. Courses are defined by pairs of gates. Racers must pass through each pair of gates to complete the course successfully. Competitors are timed on two runs over different courses, and the skier who completes the courses in the shortest time wins. The equipment and protective guards used by slalom skiiers are shown opposite. In Super-G races, competitors ski a single run that combines the technical challenge of slalom with the speed of downhill. The course requires skiers to complete medium-to-long radius turns at high speed, and contain up to two jumps. Clothing is the same as for downhill, but slightly shorter skis are used.

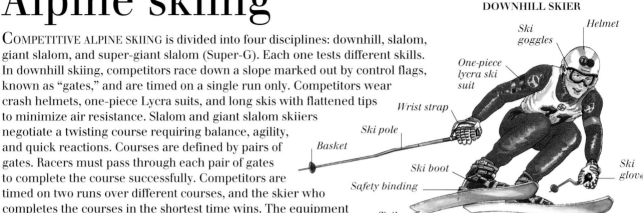

DOWNHILL SKIER

Ski goggles
Helmet
Ski
One-piece lycra ski suit
Wrist strap
Ski pole
Basket
Ski boot
Safety binding
Tail
Ski glove

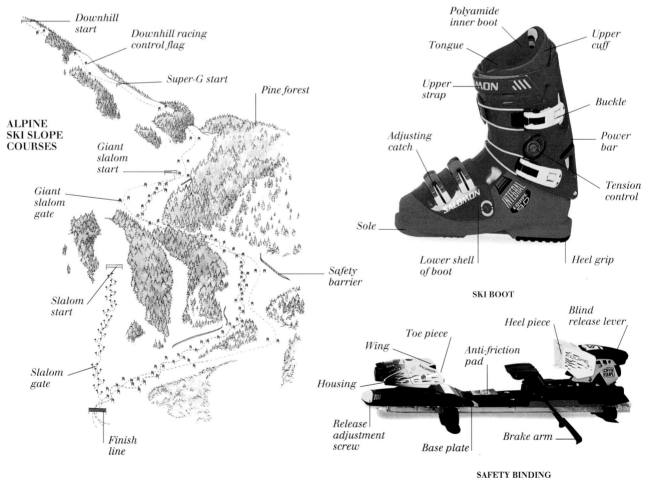

ALPINE SKI SLOPE COURSES

Downhill start
Downhill racing control flag
Super-G start
Pine forest
Giant slalom start
Giant slalom gate
Safety barrier
Slalom start
Slalom gate
Finish line

Polyamide inner boot
Tongue
Upper cuff
Upper strap
Buckle
Adjusting catch
Power bar
Tension control
Sole
Lower shell of boot
Heel grip

SKI BOOT

Toe piece
Heel piece
Blind release lever
Wing
Anti-friction pad
Housing
Release adjustment screw
Base plate
Brake arm

SAFETY BINDING

SLALOM CLOTHING AND EQUIPMENT

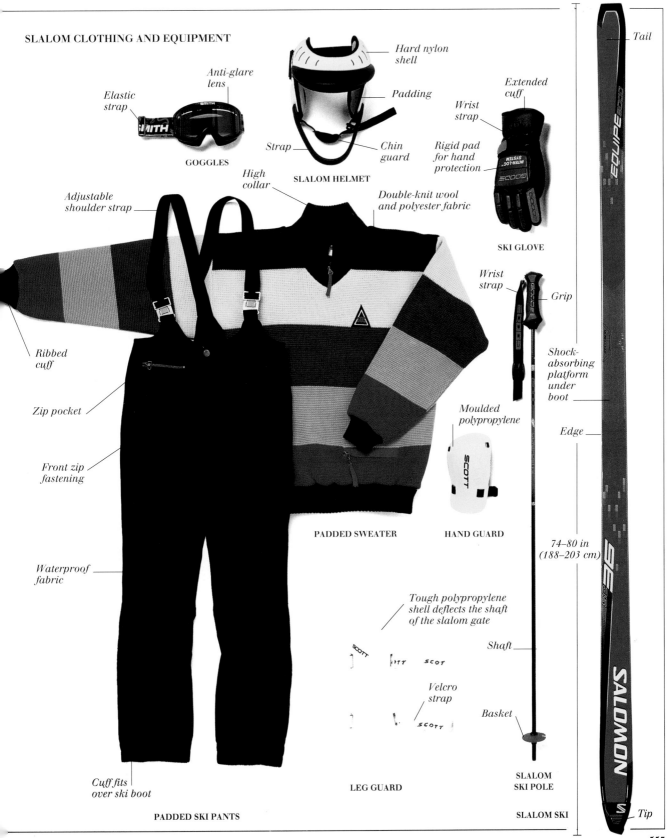

GOGGLES

Elastic strap

Anti-glare lens

SLALOM HELMET

Hard nylon shell

Padding

Strap

Chin guard

SKI GLOVE

Extended cuff

Wrist strap

Rigid pad for hand protection

Double-knit wool and polyester fabric

High collar

Adjustable shoulder strap

Ribbed cuff

Zip pocket

Front zip fastening

Waterproof fabric

Cuff fits over ski boot

PADDED SKI PANTS

PADDED SWEATER

HAND GUARD

Moulded polypropylene

LEG GUARD

Tough polypropylene shell deflects the shaft of the slalom gate

Velcro strap

SLALOM SKI POLE

Wrist strap

Grip

Shock-absorbing platform under boot

Shaft

Basket

74–80 in (188–203 cm)

SLALOM SKI

Tail

Edge

Tip

Equestrian sports

EQUESTRIAN SPORTS HAVE TAKEN place throughout the world for centuries: events involving mounted horses were recorded in the Olympic Games of 642 BC. Show jumping, however, is a much more recent innovation, and the first competitions were held at the beginning of the 1900s. In this sport, horse and rider must negotiate a course of variable, unfixed obstacles, making as few mistakes as possible. Show-jumping fences consist of wooden stands, known as standards or wings, that support planks or poles. Parts of the fence are designed to collapse on impact, preventing injury to the horse and rider. Judges penalize competitors for errors, such as knocking down obstacles, refusing jumps, or deviating from the course. Depending on the type of competition, the rider with the fewest faults, most points, or fastest time wins. There are two basic forms of horse racing – flat races and races with jumps, such as steeplechase or hurdle races. Thoroughbred horses are used in this sport, because they have great strength and stamina and can achieve speeds of up to 40 mph (65 kph). Jockeys wear silks – caps and jackets designed in distinctive colors and patterns which help identify the horses. In harness racing, the horse is driven from a light, two-wheeled carriage called a sulky. Horses are trained to trot and to pace, and different races are held for each of these types of gait. In pacing races, the horses wear hobbles to prevent them from breaking into a trot or gallop. Breeds such as the Standard-bred and the French Trotter have been developed especially for this sport.

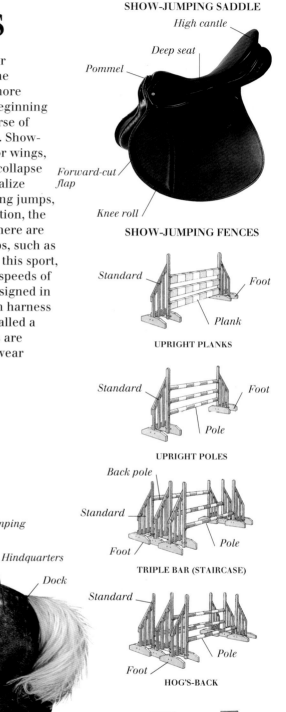

SHOW-JUMPING SADDLE

High cantle
Deep seat
Pommel
Forward-cut flap
Knee roll

SHOW-JUMPING FENCES

Standard — Foot
Plank
UPRIGHT PLANKS

Standard — Foot
Pole
UPRIGHT POLES

Back pole
Standard
Foot — Pole
TRIPLE BAR (STAIRCASE)

Standard
Pole
Foot
HOG'S-BACK

Pillar
Wooden block painted to resemble a brick
WALL

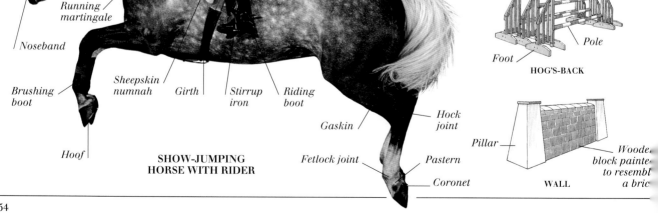

Hard hat
Browband
Throat-latch
Rein
Riding jacket
Jodhpurs
Cheek-piece
Show-jumping saddle
Hindquarters
Dock
Running martingale
Noseband
Brushing boot
Sheepskin numnah
Girth
Stirrup iron
Riding boot
Gaskin
Hock joint
Hoof
Fetlock joint
Pastern
Coronet

SHOW-JUMPING HORSE WITH RIDER

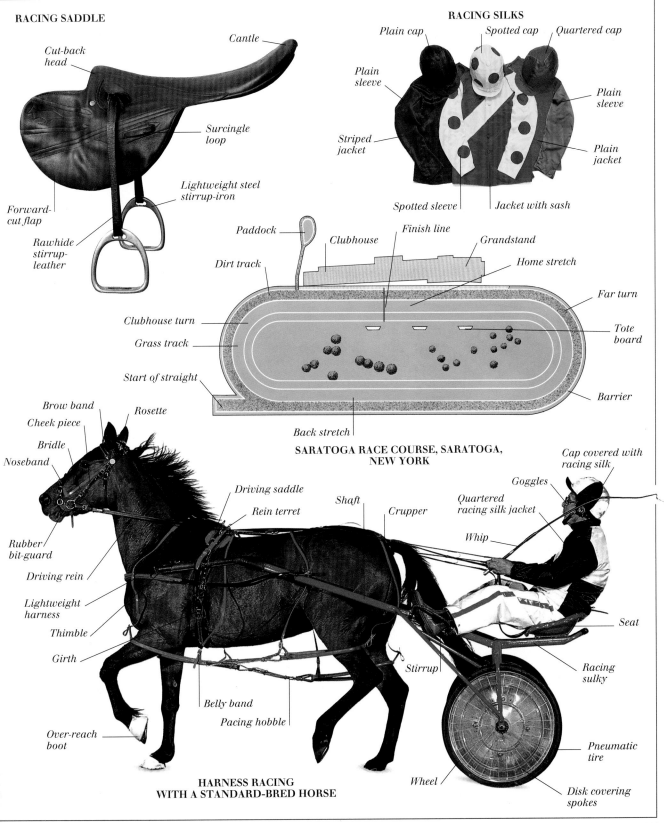

RACING SADDLE

Cut-back head
Cantle
Surcingle loop
Lightweight steel stirrup-iron
Forward-cut flap
Rawhide stirrup-leather

RACING SILKS

Plain cap
Spotted cap
Quartered cap
Plain sleeve
Plain sleeve
Striped jacket
Plain jacket
Spotted sleeve
Jacket with sash

Paddock
Clubhouse
Finish line
Grandstand
Dirt track
Home stretch
Far turn
Clubhouse turn
Tote board
Grass track
Start of straight
Barrier
Back stretch

**SARATOGA RACE COURSE, SARATOGA,
NEW YORK**

Brow band
Rosette
Cheek piece
Bridle
Noseband
Driving saddle
Rein terret
Shaft
Crupper
Cap covered with racing silk
Goggles
Quartered racing silk jacket
Whip
Rubber bit-guard
Driving rein
Lightweight harness
Thimble
Girth
Seat
Racing sulky
Belly band
Pacing hobble
Stirrup
Over-reach boot
Pneumatic tire
Wheel
Disk covering spokes

**HARNESS RACING
WITH A STANDARD-BRED HORSE**

Judo and fencing

COMBAT SPORTS ARE BASED ON THE SKILLS used in fighting. In these sports, the competitors may be unarmed – as in judo and boxing – or armed – as in fencing and kendo. Judo is a system of unarmed combat developed in the East. Translated from the Japanese the name means "the gentle way." Students learn how to turn an opponent's force to their own advantage. The usual uniform is loose white pants and a jacket, fastened with a cloth belt. The color of belt indicates the student's level of expertise, from white-belted novices to the expert black belts. Competitions take place on a mat or "shiaijo," 30 or 33 ft (9 or 10 m) square in size, bounded by "danger" and "safety" areas to prevent injury. Competitors try to throw, pin, or master their opponent by applying pressure to the arm joints or neck. Judo matches are strictly monitored, and competitors receive points for superior technique, not for injuring their opponent. Fencing is a combat sport using swords, which takes place on a narrow piste or strip 46 ft (14 m) long. Competitors try to hit specific target areas on their opponent with their sword or foil while avoiding being touched themselves. The winner is the one who scores the greatest number of hits. Fencers wear uniforms made from strong white material, which affords maximum protection while allowing freedom of movement, steel mesh masks with padded bibs to protect the fencer's neck, and a long white glove on their sword hand. Fencing foils do not have sharpened blades, and their tips end in a blunt button to prevent injuries. Three types of swords are used – foils, épées, and sabres. Official foil and épée competitions always use an electric scoring system. The sword tips are connected to lights by a long wire that passes underneath each fencer's jacket. A bulb flashes when a hit is made.

JUDO HOLDS AND THROWS

SIDE FOUR QUARTER HOLD

SINGLE WING

BODY DROP

ONE ARM SHOULDER THROW

SHOULDER WHEEL

SWEEPING LOW THROW

STOMACH THROW

KNEE WHEEL

JUDO KIT

Drawstring

Black belt

Heavy-duty cotton jacket

Cotton pants

JUDO MAT

52 ft 6 in
(16 m)

Judge

Scorer

Holding timekeeper

Timekeeper

Contestant

Referee

Contest area

Safety area

Danger area

Contestant

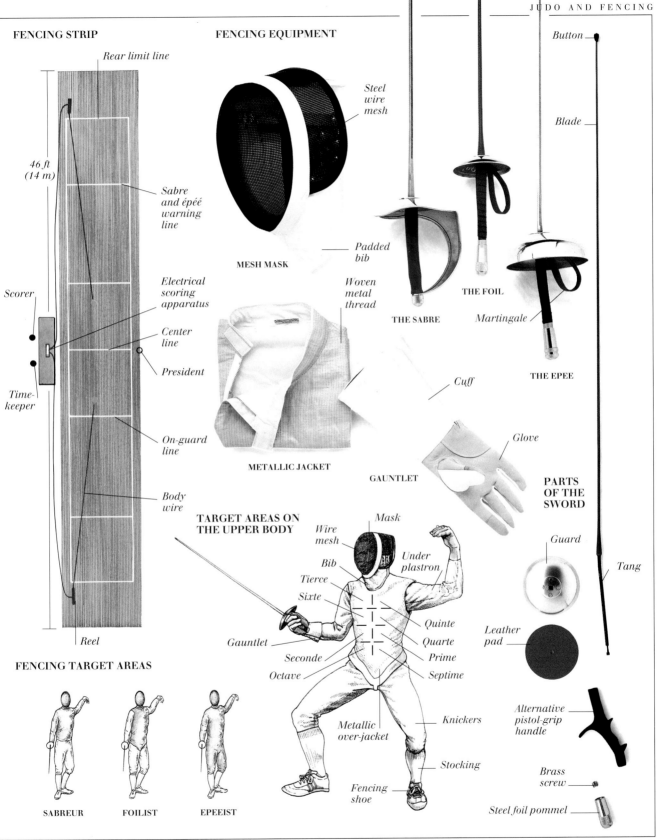

FENCING STRIP

Rear limit line

46 ft
(14 m)

Sabre
and épéé
warning
line

Scorer

Electrical
scoring
apparatus

Center
line

President

Time-
keeper

On-guard
line

Body
wire

Reel

FENCING TARGET AREAS

SABREUR

FOILIST

EPEEIST

FENCING EQUIPMENT

Steel
wire
mesh

MESH MASK

Padded
bib

Woven
metal
thread

Electrical
scoring
apparatus

METALLIC JACKET

Cuff

GAUNTLET

Glove

**TARGET AREAS ON
THE UPPER BODY**

Mask

Wire
mesh

Bib

Tierce

Sixte

Gauntlet

Seconde

Octave

Under
plastron

Quinte

Quarte

Prime

Septime

Metallic
over-jacket

Knickers

Stocking

Fencing
shoe

THE SABRE

THE FOIL

Martingale

THE EPEE

Button

Blade

**PARTS
OF THE
SWORD**

Guard

Tang

Leather
pad

Alternative
pistol-grip
handle

Brass
screw

Steel foil pommel

Swimming and diving

SWIMMING GOGGLES

SWIMMING WAS INCLUDED in the first modern Olympic Games in 1896 and diving events were added in 1904. Swimming is both an individual and a team sport and races take place over a predetermined distance in one of the four major categories of stroke – freestyle (usually front crawl), butterfly, breaststroke, and backstroke. Competition pools are clearly marked for racing and anti-turbulence lane lines are used to separate the swimmers and help keep the water calm. The first team or individual to finish the race is the winner. Competitive diving is divided into men's and women's springboard and platform (highboard) events. There are six official groups of dives: forward dives, backward dives, armstand dives, twist dives, reverse dives, and inward dives. Competitors perform a set number of dives and after each one a panel of judges awards marks according to the quality of execution and the degree of difficulty.

STYLES OF DIVES

Starting position
Hands above head
Legs fully stretched
Flight
Arched back
Toes pointed
Entry
Feet together
Hands close together

FORWARD DIVE

BACKWARD DIVE

Latex rubber molds to shape of head

CAPS

SPEEDO

Rubber-covered wire

NOSE CLIP

Molded rubber

EARPLUG

SWIMWEAR

High neckline

Man-made stretch fabric

Drawstring

High-cut leg

Strong seam

SWIMSUIT

TRUNKS

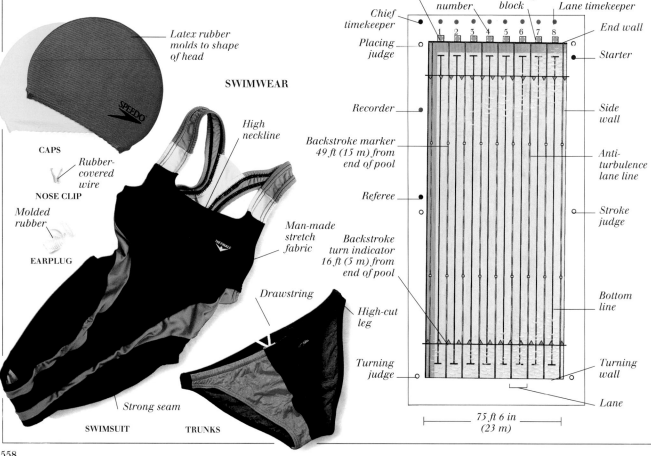

SWIMMING POOL

Swimmer
Lane number
Starting block
Lane timekeeper
Chief timekeeper
End wall
Placing judge
Starter
Recorder
Side wall
Backstroke marker 49 ft (15 m) from end of pool
Anti-turbulence lane line
Referee
Stroke judge
Backstroke turn indicator 16 ft (5 m) from end of pool
Bottom line
Turning judge
Turning wall
Lane

75 ft 6 in (23 m)

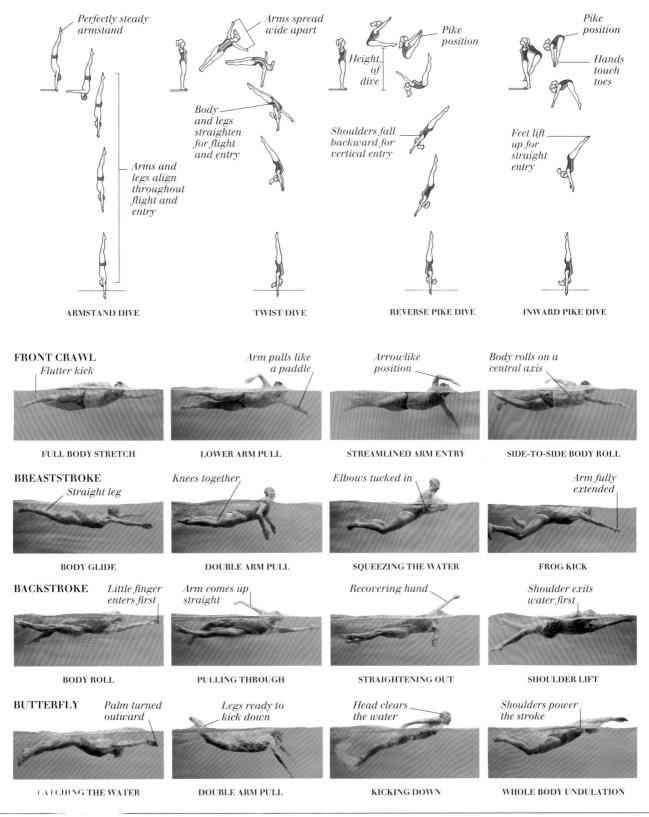

Perfectly steady armstand

Arms and legs align throughout flight and entry

ARMSTAND DIVE

Arms spread wide apart

Body and legs straighten for flight and entry

TWIST DIVE

Pike position

Height of dive

Shoulders fall backward for vertical entry

REVERSE PIKE DIVE

Pike position

Hands touch toes

Feet lift up for straight entry

INWARD PIKE DIVE

FRONT CRAWL
Flutter kick

Arm pulls like a paddle

Arrowlike position

Body rolls on a central axis

FULL BODY STRETCH   LOWER ARM PULL   STREAMLINED ARM ENTRY   SIDE-TO-SIDE BODY ROLL

BREASTSTROKE
Straight leg

Knees together

Elbows tucked in

Arm fully extended

BODY GLIDE   DOUBLE ARM PULL   SQUEEZING THE WATER   FROG KICK

BACKSTROKE
Little finger enters first

Arm comes up straight

Recovering hand

Shoulder exits water first

BODY ROLL   PULLING THROUGH   STRAIGHTENING OUT   SHOULDER LIFT

BUTTERFLY
Palm turned outward

Legs ready to kick down

Head clears the water

Shoulders power the stroke

CATCHING THE WATER   DOUBLE ARM PULL   KICKING DOWN   WHOLE BODY UNDULATION

Kayaking, rowing, and sailing

WATERBORNE SPORTS are as varied as the crafts used. There are two disciplines in rowing; sweep rowing, in which each rower has one oar, and sculling, in which rowers use two oars. There are a number of different Olympic and competitive rowing events for both men and women. The number of rowers and weight classes vary. Some rowing events use a coxswain; a steersman who does not row but directs the crew. Kayaks are used in straight sprint and slalom races. Slalom races take place over a course consisting of 20 to 25 gates, including at least six upstream gates. In yacht racing, competitors must complete prescribed courses, organized by the race committees, in the shortest possible time, using sail power only. Olympic events include classes for keel boats, dinghies, catamarans, and windsurfers.

SAILING GEAR

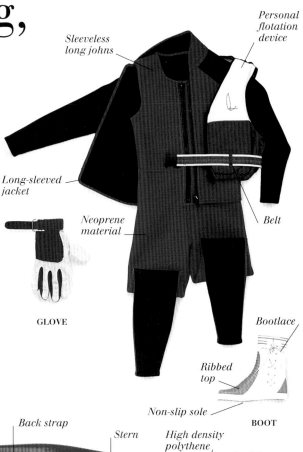

- Sleeveless long johns
- Personal flotation device
- Long-sleeved jacket
- Neoprene material
- Belt
- GLOVE
- Bootlace
- Ribbed top
- Non-slip sole
- BOOT

ONE-PERSON KAYAK AND PADDLE

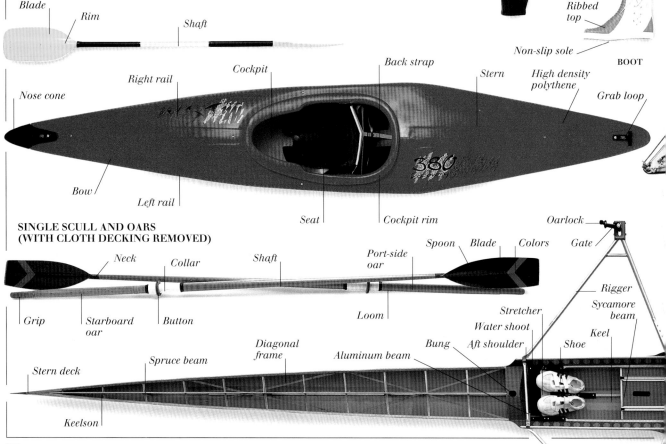

- Blade
- Rim
- Shaft
- Cockpit
- Back strap
- Stern
- High density polythene
- Nose cone
- Right rail
- Grab loop
- Bow
- Left rail
- Seat
- Cockpit rim

SINGLE SCULL AND OARS (WITH CLOTH DECKING REMOVED)

- Neck
- Collar
- Shaft
- Port-side oar
- Spoon
- Blade
- Colors
- Oarlock
- Gate
- Grip
- Starboard oar
- Button
- Loom
- Rigger
- Sycamore beam
- Stretcher
- Water shoot
- Keel
- Stern deck
- Spruce beam
- Diagonal frame
- Aluminum beam
- Bung
- Aft shoulder
- Shoe
- Keelson

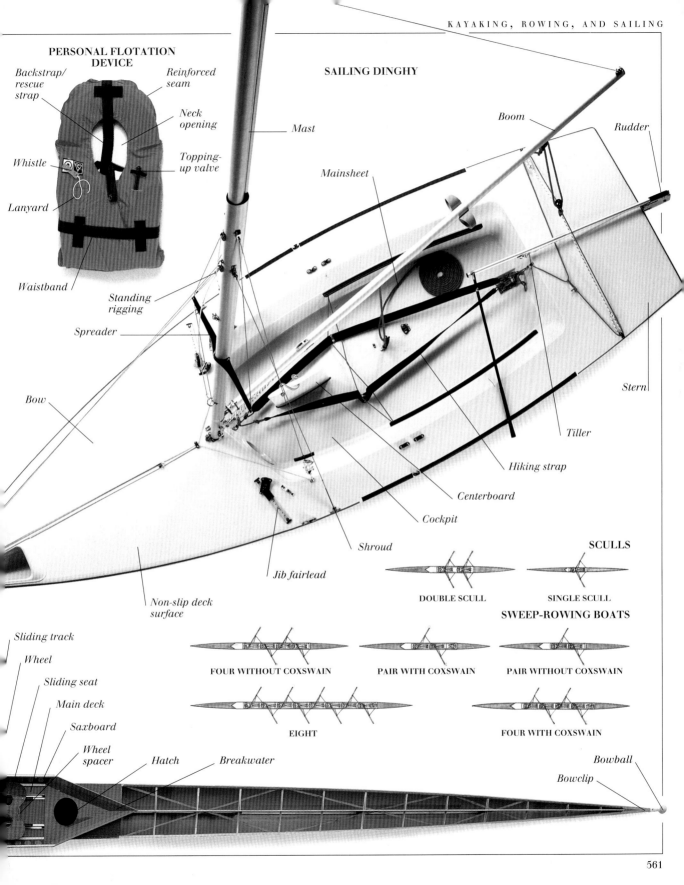

PERSONAL FLOTATION DEVICE

Backstrap/ rescue strap

Reinforced seam

Neck opening

Whistle

Topping-up valve

Lanyard

Waistband

Standing rigging

Spreader

Bow

SAILING DINGHY

Mast

Boom

Rudder

Mainsheet

Stern

Tiller

Hiking strap

Centerboard

Cockpit

Shroud

Jib fairlead

Non-slip deck surface

SCULLS

DOUBLE SCULL

SINGLE SCULL

SWEEP-ROWING BOATS

FOUR WITHOUT COXSWAIN

PAIR WITH COXSWAIN

PAIR WITHOUT COXSWAIN

EIGHT

FOUR WITH COXSWAIN

Sliding track

Wheel

Sliding seat

Main deck

Saxboard

Wheel spacer

Hatch

Breakwater

Bowball

Bowclip

Angling

ANGLING MEANS FISHING WITH A ROD, reel, line, and lure. There are several different types of angling: freshwater coarse angling, for members of the carp family and pike; freshwater game angling, for salmon and trout; and sea angling, for sea fish such as flatfish, bass, and mackerel. Anglers use a variety of methods of catching fish. These include bait fishing, in which bait (food to allure the fish) is placed on a hook and cast into the water; fly fishing, in which a natural or artificial fly is used to lure the fish; and spinning, in which a lure that looks like a small fish revolves as it is pulled through the water. The angler uses the rod, reel, and line to cast the lure over the water. The reel controls the line as it spills off the spool and as it is wound back. Weights may be fixed to the line so that it will sink. Swivels are attached to prevent the line from twisting. When a fish bites, the hook must become embedded in its mouth and remain there while the catch is reeled in.

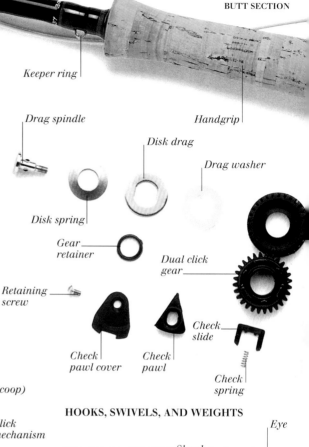

BUTT SECTION

Keeper ring

Drag spindle

Handgrip

Disk drag

Drag washer

Disk spring

Gear retainer

Dual click gear

Retaining screw

Check slide

Check pawl cover

Check pawl

Check spring

REELS

Spool-release button

Reel foot (reel scoop)

Plate-nut

Click mechanism

Mechanical brake

Side plate

Centrifugal brake

Spool

Handle

Star drag

Level-wind system

BAITCASTER

HOOKS, SWIVELS, AND WEIGHTS

Eye

Shank

Gap

ANATOMY OF A HOOK

Bend

Throat

Point

TREBLE HOOK

Barb

ABERDEEN HOOK

REVERSED BEND HOOK

Reel foot (reel scoop)

Unskirted spool

Handle

Line

Tension nut (drag adjustment)

Ratchet (anti-reverse device)

Handgrip

Reel

Bail arm

SPINNING REEL

EXAMPLES OF BARREL SWIVELS

HILLMAN ANTI-KINK WEIGHT

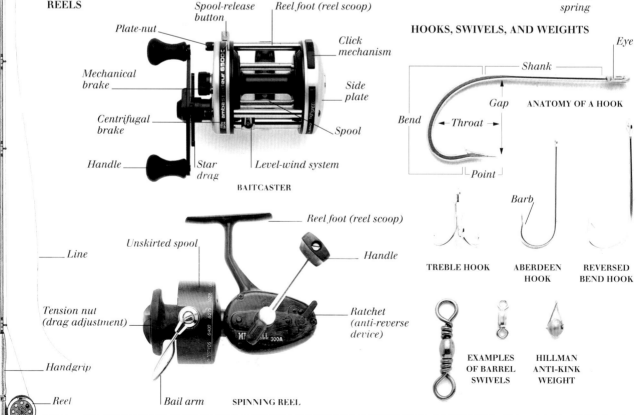

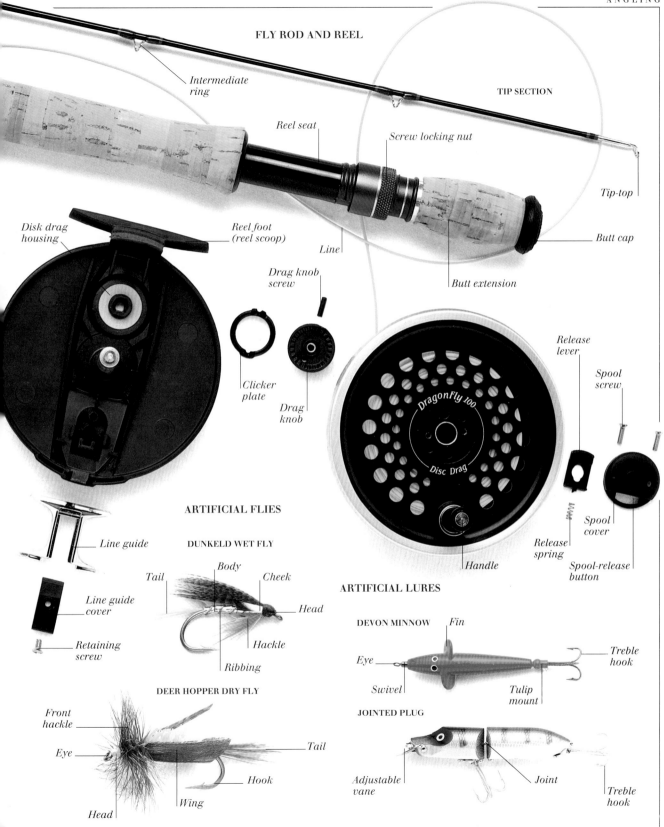

FLY ROD AND REEL

Intermediate
ring

TIP SECTION

Reel seat

Screw locking nut

Tip-top

Disk drag
housing

Reel foot
(reel scoop)

Butt cap

Line

Drag knob
screw

Butt extension

Release
lever

Spool
screw

Clicker
plate

DragonFly 100

Disc Drag

Drag
knob

Spool
cover

Line guide

ARTIFICIAL FLIES

Release
spring

Spool-release
button

Handle

Line guide
cover

DUNKELD WET FLY

Body

Tail

Cheek

ARTIFICIAL LURES

Retaining
screw

Head

DEVON MINNOW

Fin

Hackle

Eye

Treble
hook

Ribbing

Swivel

Tulip
mount

DEER HOPPER DRY FLY

JOINTED PLUG

Front
hackle

Eye

Tail

Adjustable
vane

Joint

Hook

Treble
hook

Head

Wing

563

EVERYDAY THINGS

Drills

THE ELECTRICALLY POWERED MOTOR OF A POWER DRILL, cooled by a fan, turns a shaft at high speed. The shaft connects, in turn, to a system of gears that rotates a chuck even faster. Clamped by the chuck, a sharp drill bit cuts out the hole, and at the same time the bit's screw-shaped grooves channel the waste out of the hole. For drilling hard materials, many power drills have a hammer mechanism; when this is operated a ratchet in the gearcase causes the chuck and bit to pound in and out as they drill. A hand drill, although slower and less forceful than a power drill, is easier to control. For cutting wide holes, carpenters often prefer a brace-and-bit. This acts like a lever: the bowed handle of the brace moves a larger distance than the bit, turning the bit with extra force.

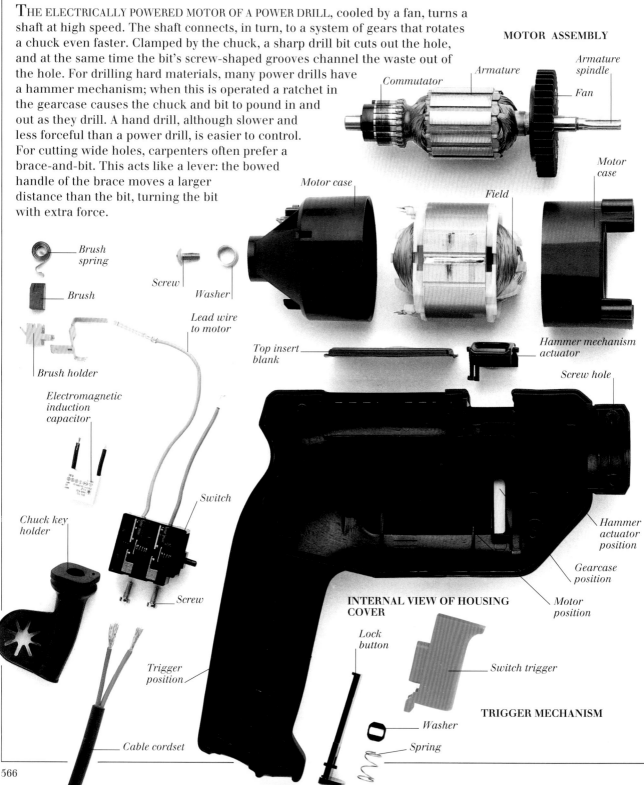

MOTOR ASSEMBLY

Armature

Armature spindle

Commutator

Fan

Motor case

Motor case

Field

Brush spring

Screw

Washer

Brush

Lead wire to motor

Brush holder

Hammer mechanism actuator

Electromagnetic induction capacitor

Top insert blank

Screw hole

Chuck key holder

Switch

Hammer actuator position

Gearcase position

Screw

Motor position

INTERNAL VIEW OF HOUSING COVER

Trigger position

Lock button

Switch trigger

Cable cordset

Washer

Spring

TRIGGER MECHANISM

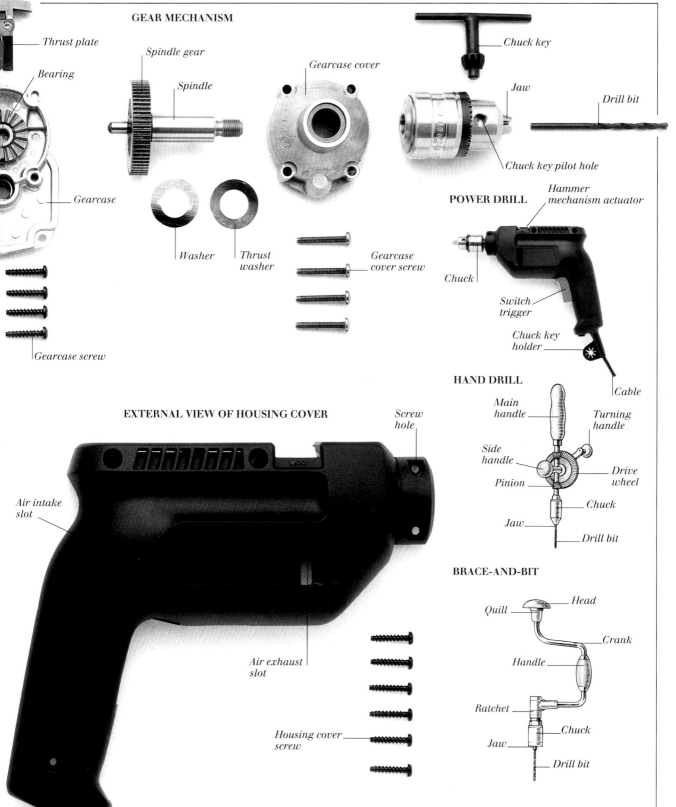

GEAR MECHANISM

Thrust plate

Bearing

Spindle gear

Spindle

Gearcase cover

Chuck key

Jaw

Drill bit

Gearcase

Washer

Thrust washer

Gearcase cover screw

Chuck key pilot hole

POWER DRILL

Hammer mechanism actuator

Chuck

Switch trigger

Chuck key holder

Cable

Gearcase screw

HAND DRILL

Main handle

Turning handle

Side handle

Drive wheel

Pinion

Chuck

Jaw

Drill bit

EXTERNAL VIEW OF HOUSING COVER

Screw hole

Air intake slot

Air exhaust slot

Housing cover screw

BRACE-AND-BIT

Quill

Head

Crank

Handle

Ratchet

Chuck

Jaw

Drill bit

Shoes

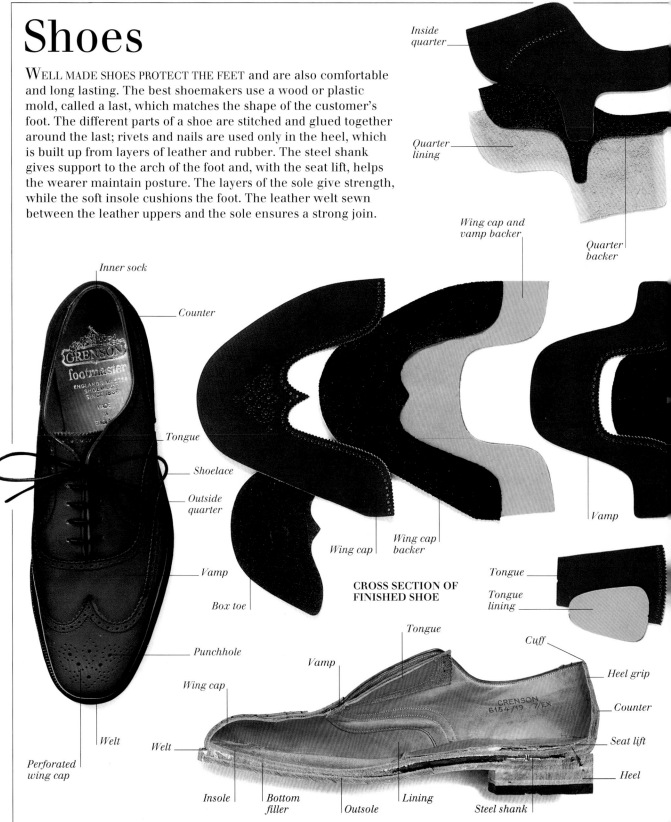

WELL MADE SHOES PROTECT THE FEET and are also comfortable and long lasting. The best shoemakers use a wood or plastic mold, called a last, which matches the shape of the customer's foot. The different parts of a shoe are stitched and glued together around the last; rivets and nails are used only in the heel, which is built up from layers of leather and rubber. The steel shank gives support to the arch of the foot and, with the seat lift, helps the wearer maintain posture. The layers of the sole give strength, while the soft insole cushions the foot. The leather welt sewn between the leather uppers and the sole ensures a strong join.

Inside quarter

Quarter lining

Wing cap and vamp backer

Quarter backer

Inner sock

Counter

GRENSON
footmaster
ENGLAND'S MASTER
SHOEMAKERS
SINCE 1896
MADE
IN
ENGLAND

Tongue

Shoelace

Outside quarter

Wing cap

Wing cap backer

Vamp

Vamp

Box toe

Wing cap

CROSS SECTION OF FINISHED SHOE

Tongue

Tongue lining

Punchhole

Tongue

Cuff

Heel grip

Vamp

Wing cap

CRENSON
6154/19 . 7/EX

Counter

Welt

Welt

Seat lift

Heel

Perforated wing cap

Insole

Bottom filler

Outsole

Lining

Steel shank

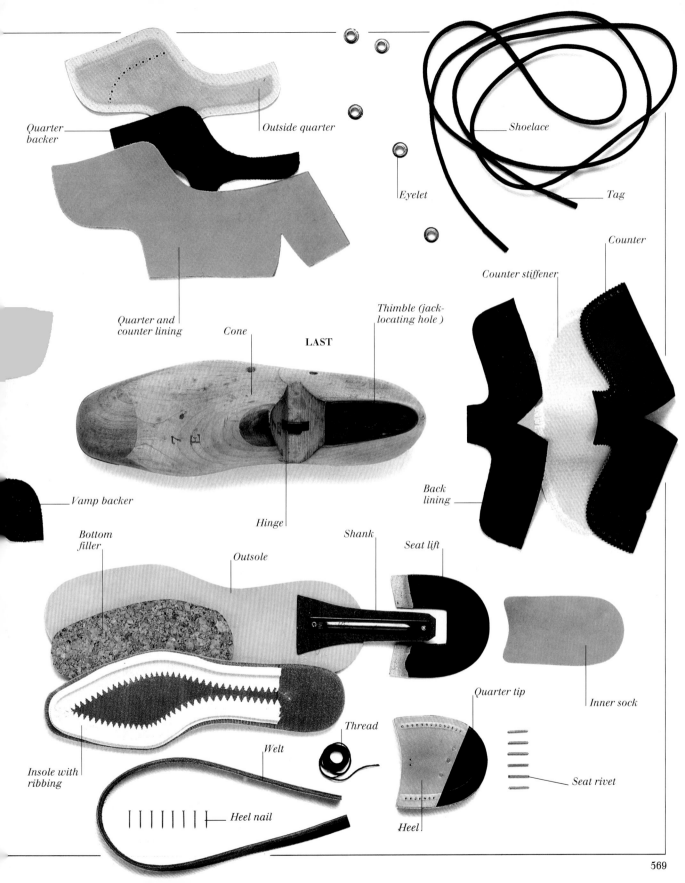

Quarter backer

Outside quarter

Shoelace

Eyelet

Tag

Quarter and counter lining

Counter stiffener

Counter

Cone

LAST

Thimble (jack-locating hole)

Back lining

Vamp backer

Hinge

Bottom filler

Outsole

Shank

Seat lift

Quarter tip

Inner sock

Thread

Insole with ribbing

Welt

Seat rivet

Heel nail

Heel

Clock

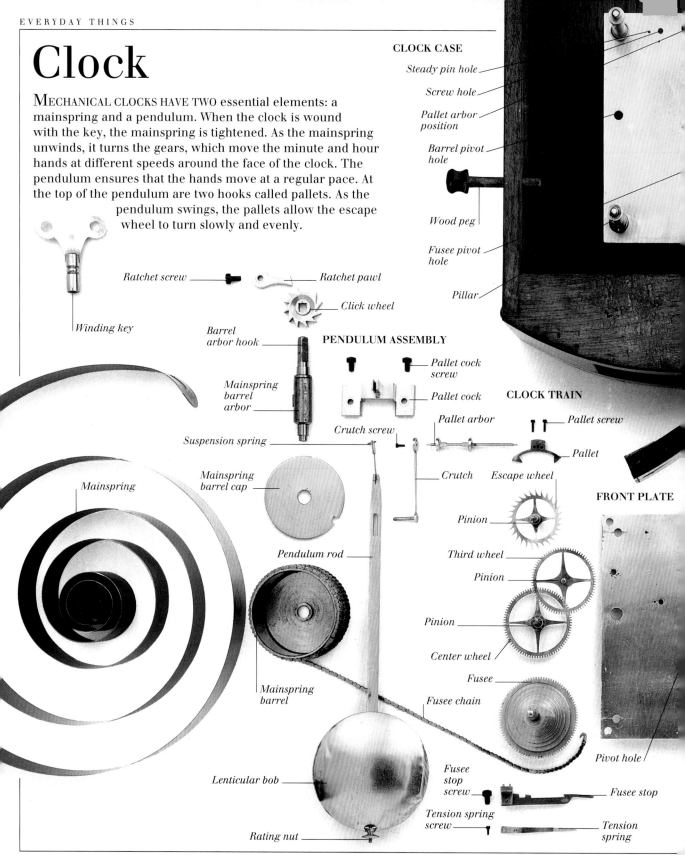

MECHANICAL CLOCKS HAVE TWO essential elements: a mainspring and a pendulum. When the clock is wound with the key, the mainspring is tightened. As the mainspring unwinds, it turns the gears, which move the minute and hour hands at different speeds around the face of the clock. The pendulum ensures that the hands move at a regular pace. At the top of the pendulum are two hooks called pallets. As the pendulum swings, the pallets allow the escape wheel to turn slowly and evenly.

CLOCK CASE

Steady pin hole

Screw hole

Pallet arbor position

Barrel pivot hole

Wood peg

Fusee pivot hole

Pillar

Ratchet screw

Ratchet pawl

Click wheel

Winding key

Barrel arbor hook

PENDULUM ASSEMBLY

Pallet cock screw

Mainspring barrel arbor

Pallet cock

CLOCK TRAIN

Suspension spring

Crutch screw

Pallet arbor

Pallet screw

Pallet

Mainspring

Mainspring barrel cap

Crutch

Escape wheel

FRONT PLATE

Pinion

Pendulum rod

Third wheel

Pinion

Pinion

Center wheel

Mainspring barrel

Fusee

Fusee chain

Lenticular bob

Fusee stop screw

Pivot hole

Fusee stop

Tension spring screw

Rating nut

Tension spring

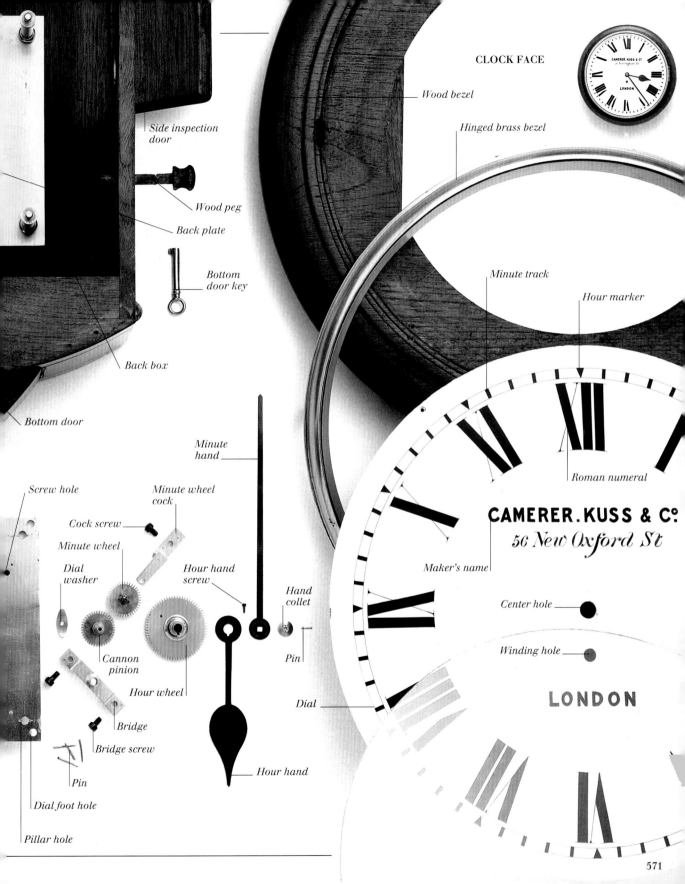

Side inspection door

Wood peg

Back plate

Bottom door key

Back box

Bottom door

CLOCK FACE

Wood bezel

Hinged brass bezel

Minute track

Hour marker

Roman numeral

CAMERER. KUSS & Co.

56 New Oxford St

Maker's name

Center hole

Winding hole

LONDON

Dial

Minute hand

Minute wheel cock

Cock screw

Minute wheel

Dial washer

Hour hand screw

Hand collet

Pin

Screw hole

Cannon pinion

Hour wheel

Bridge

Bridge screw

Pin

Dial foot hole

Hour hand

Pillar hole

Lamp

THE FIRST SPRING-TENSIONED, adjustable work lamp was designed in 1934 by George Carwardine. This type of lamp imitates the human arm in the way that it can be kept in a fixed position or moved easily and precisely. In the arm, such control is achieved by coordinating the opposing action of paired muscles (e.g., when the biceps contracts, the triceps relaxes and the arm bends). In the work lamp, one muscle of a pair is represented by the springs that pull on the rigid bars of the lamp; the other muscle is represented by the nuts, bolts, screws, and washers in the lamp's joints that resist the pull of the springs. By balancing the pull of the springs against the resistance in the joints, the lamp's height and angle can be adjusted with minimal pressure.

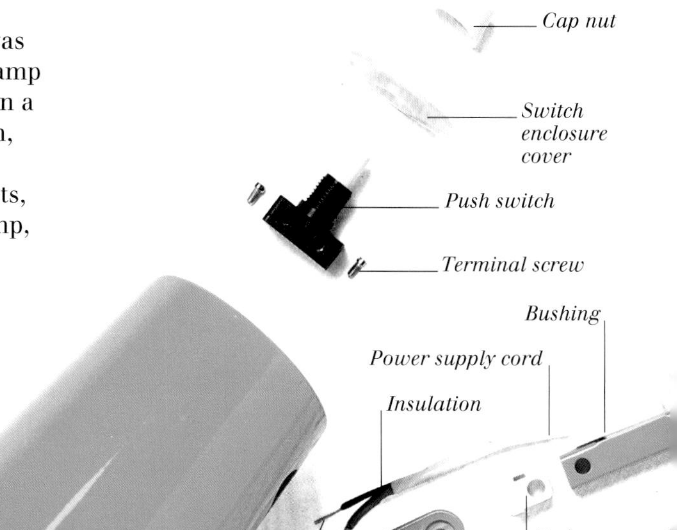

Cap nut

Switch enclosure cover

Push switch

Terminal screw

Bushing

Power supply cord

Insulation

End cap

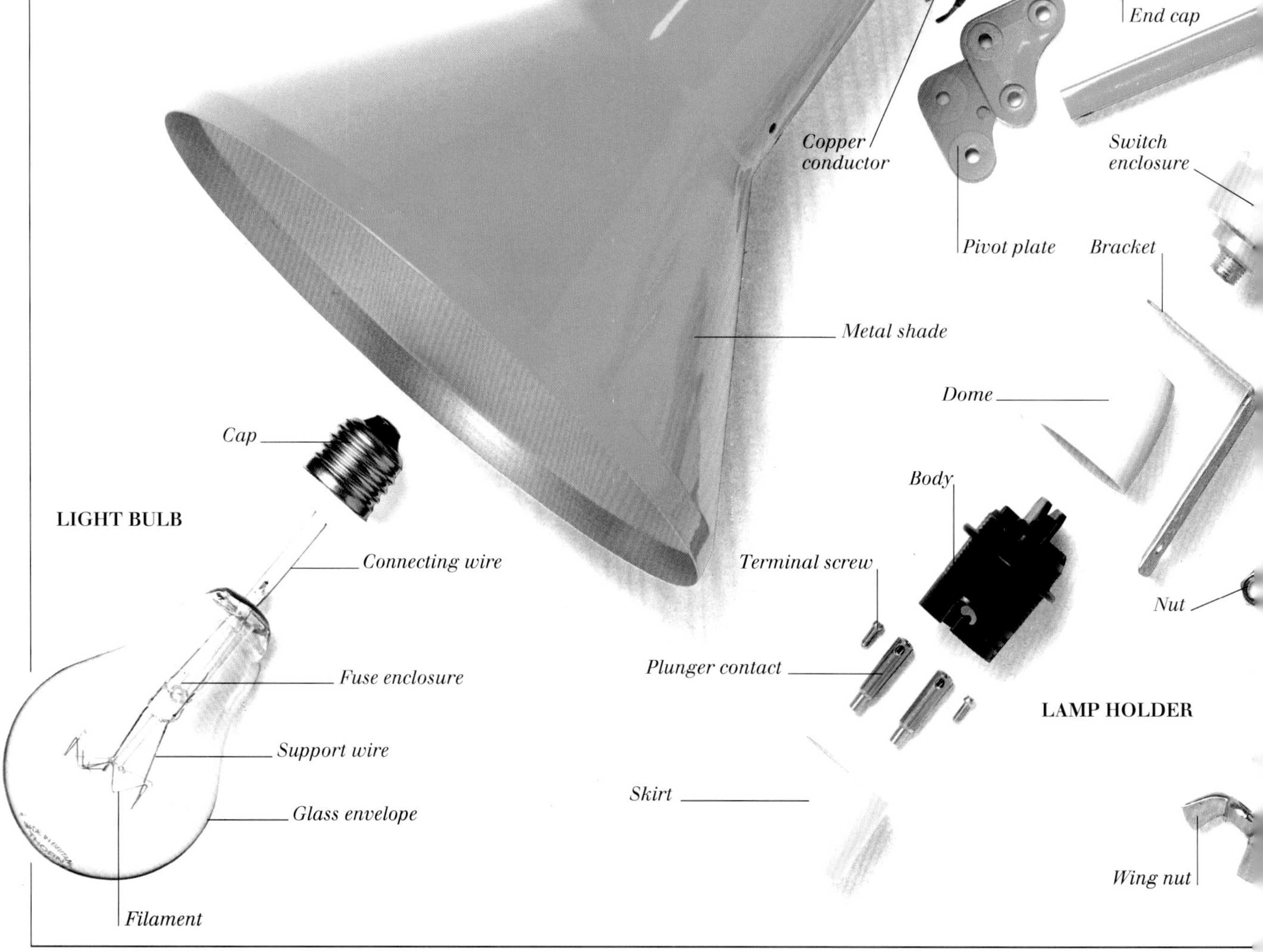

Copper conductor

Switch enclosure

Pivot plate

Bracket

Metal shade

Dome

Body

Cap

LIGHT BULB

Connecting wire

Terminal screw

Nut

Plunger contact

LAMP HOLDER

Fuse enclosure

Support wire

Skirt

Glass envelope

Wing nut

Filament

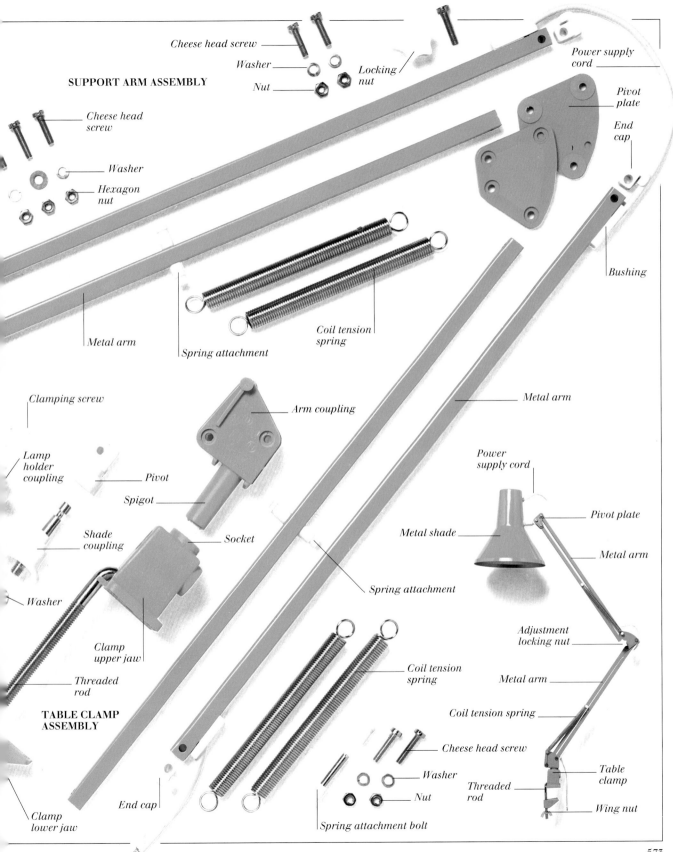

SUPPORT ARM ASSEMBLY

Cheese head screw

Washer

Nut

Locking nut

Power supply cord

Cheese head screw

Pivot plate

End cap

Washer

Hexagon nut

Metal arm

Spring attachment

Coil tension spring

Bushing

Clamping screw

Arm coupling

Metal arm

Lamp holder coupling

Pivot

Power supply cord

Spigot

Pivot plate

Shade coupling

Socket

Metal shade

Metal arm

Spring attachment

Washer

Adjustment locking nut

Clamp upper jaw

Metal arm

TABLE CLAMP ASSEMBLY

Coil tension spring

Coil tension spring

Threaded rod

Cheese head screw

Washer

Table clamp

Clamp lower jaw

End cap

Nut

Threaded rod

Wing nut

Spring attachment bolt

573

Mini television

MINIATURIZED TELEVISION SETS are small enough to be held in the hand while being watched. A signal sent by a broadcast transmitter is picked up by the television antenna and passed to an electron gun at the back of the television set. In response to the signal this gun produces an electron beam that is passed through a deflection yoke. The yoke contains magnets and coils that cause the beam to scan across the screen in a series of lines. The screen is coated with phosphor, which glows when hit by the beam. As the beam scans the screen, its strength is varied so that the phosphor glows with different intensities in different parts of the screen. A continuous sequence of 25 black-and-white pictures per second appears on the screen so rapidly that the illusion of a moving picture is created.

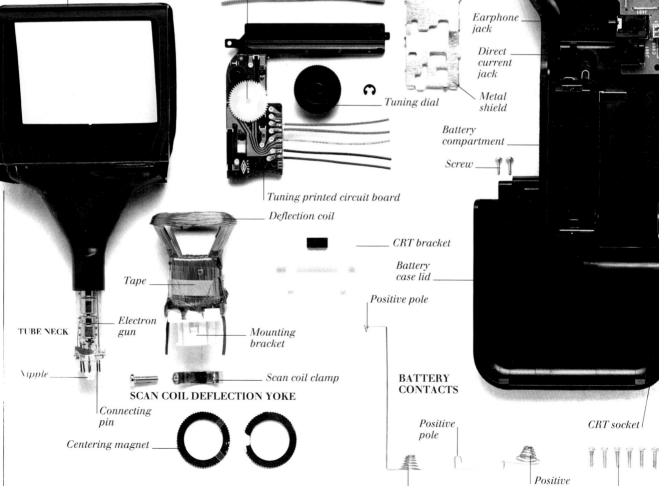

CATHODE RAY TUBE (CRT)

CRT cover

Dial pointer

Tuning drive gear

Antenna connector

Tuner

Rear cabinet

Electrolytic capacitor

Keystone (East-West) amplifier integrated circuit

Earphone jack

Direct current jack

Tuning dial

Metal shield

Battery compartment

Screw

Tuning printed circuit board

Deflection coil

CRT bracket

Battery case lid

Positive pole

Tape

Electron gun

TUBE NECK

Mounting bracket

Nipple

Scan coil clamp

BATTERY CONTACTS

SCAN COIL DEFLECTION YOKE

Connecting pin

Centering magnet

Positive pole

CRT socket

Negative pole

Positive pole

Screw

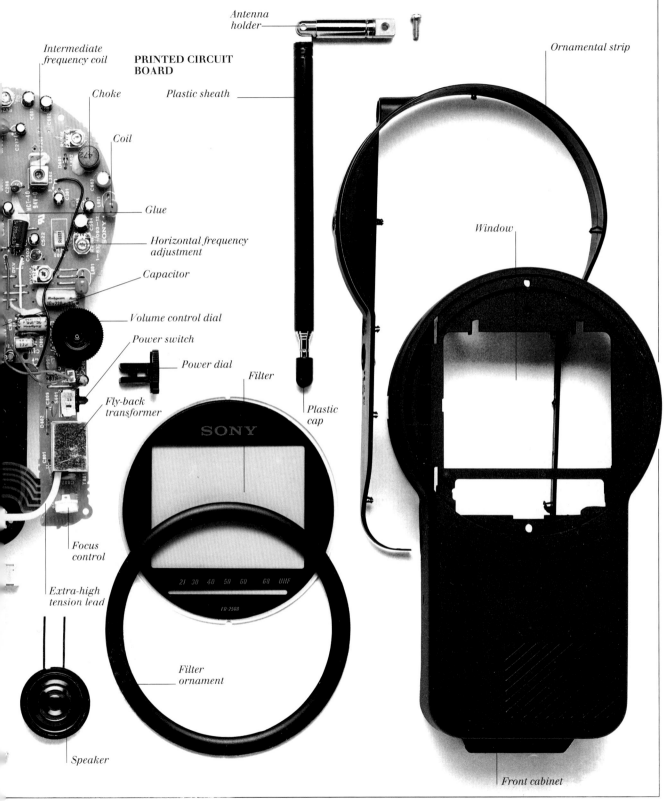

*Intermediate
frequency coil*

**PRINTED CIRCUIT
BOARD**

Choke

Coil

Glue

*Horizontal frequency
adjustment*

Capacitor

Volume control dial

Power switch

Power dial

*Fly-back
transformer*

*Focus
control*

*Extra-high
tension lead*

Speaker

*Antenna
holder*

Plastic sheath

Filter

*Plastic
cap*

SONY

21 30 40 50 60 68 UHF

FD-250B

*Filter
ornament*

Ornamental strip

Window

Front cabinet

Chair

A TRADITIONALLY MADE DINING CHAIR, such as the Regency-style carver shown here, is held together, not by nails or bolts, but by snugly fitting joints, screws, dowels, and glue. Its curved arms and top splats, as well as its tapering legs, are cut from seasoned—that is, dried—mahogany. Mortice slots in the back legs receive the tenon tongues of the top and bottom splats; angled grooves at the top of the back legs, called rebates, take the curved arm rail. Though the various joints are so tight-fitting that they could produce a solid frame on their own, screws and glue are used to give the joints added strength. The comfortable, upholstered seat pad shown here consists of a patterned cover, calico lining, and foam padding that has been treated for fire safety; it is supported by webbing stretched across a wood frame.

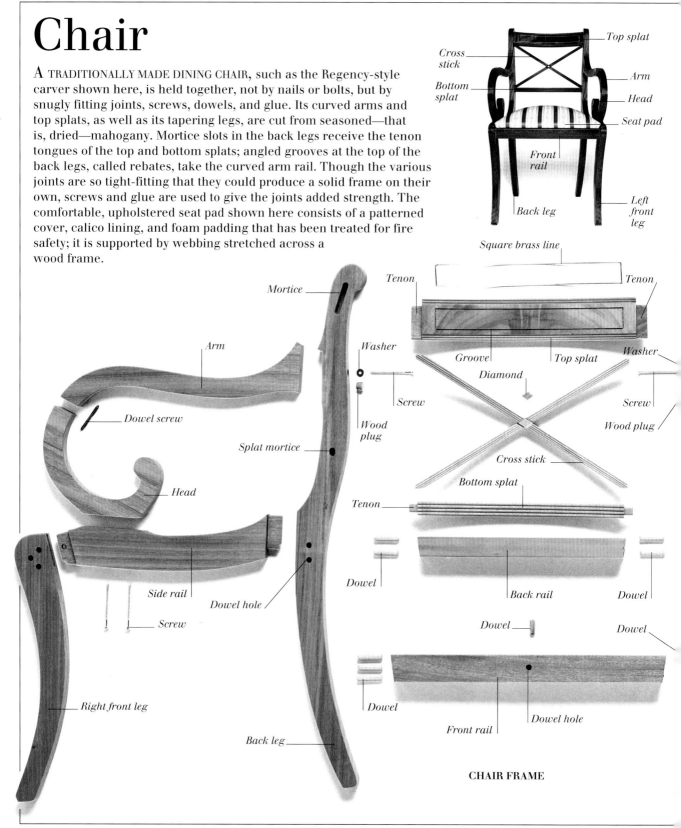

Top splat

Cross stick

Bottom splat

Arm

Head

Seat pad

Front rail

Back leg

Left front leg

Mortice

Arm

Dowel screw

Splat mortice

Head

Side rail

Screw

Right front leg

Back leg

Dowel hole

Washer

Screw

Wood plug

Tenon

Dowel

Square brass line

Tenon

Groove

Top splat

Diamond

Washer

Screw

Wood plug

Cross stick

Bottom splat

Dowel

Back rail

Dowel

Dowel

Dowel

Dowel

Front rail

Dowel hole

CHAIR FRAME

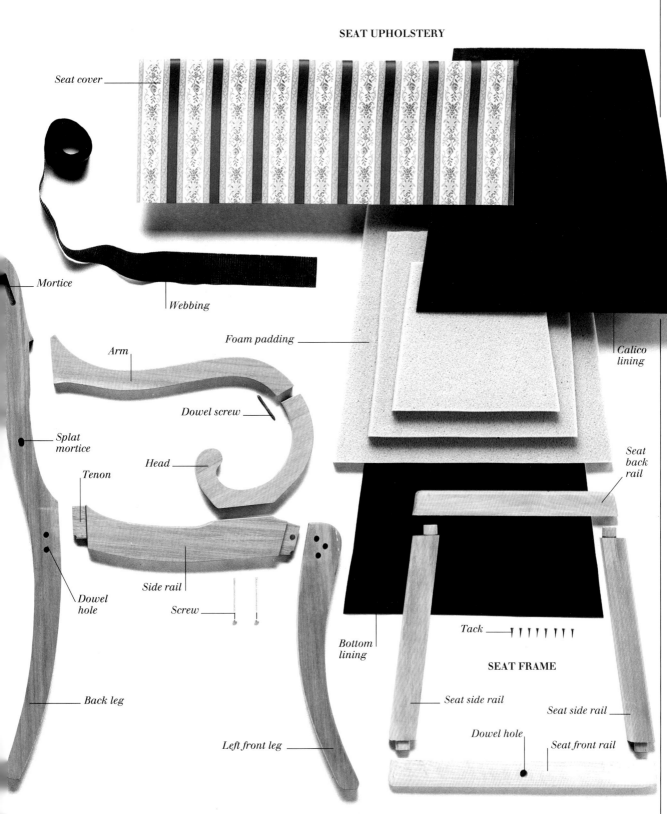

SEAT UPHOLSTERY

Seat cover

Mortice

Webbing

Arm

Dowel screw

Foam padding

Calico lining

Splat mortice

Head

Tenon

Seat back rail

Side rail

Dowel hole

Screw

Bottom lining

Tack

SEAT FRAME

Back leg

Seat side rail

Seat side rail

Left front leg

Dowel hole

Seat front rail

Toaster

MOST ELECTRIC TOASTERS NOT ONLY GRILL slices of bread, they also pop them up when ready. While the slices rest on a spring-loaded rack, electric heating elements toast the bread. At the same time, a bimetallic strip heats and expands. One of the two metals in this strip expands more quickly than the other, causing the strip to curve. As it bends, it completes an electrical circuit and activates an electromagnet. The magnet attracts a catch, releasing the spring that holds the rack down in the toaster. The elements switch off, and the toasted slices pop up.

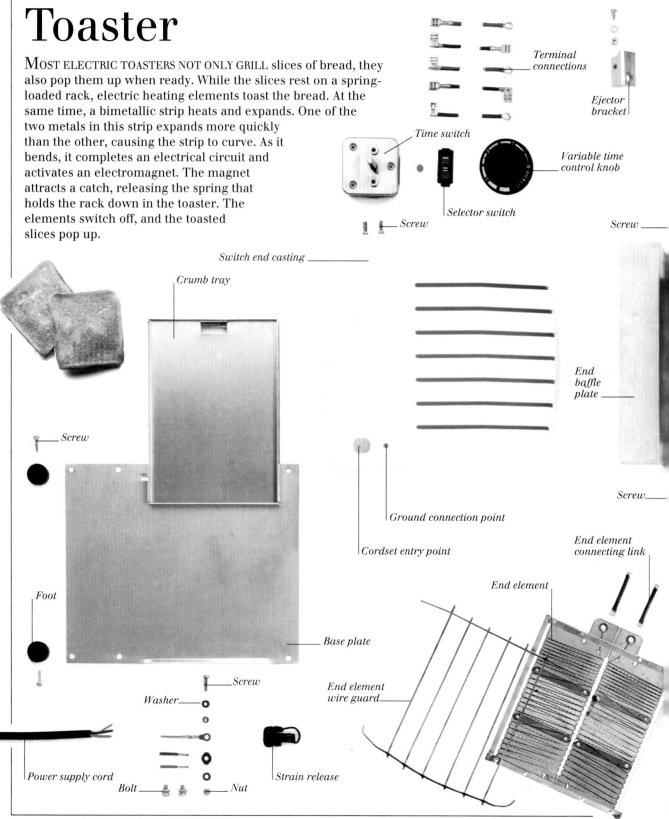

Terminal connections

Ejector bracket

Time switch

Variable time control knob

Selector switch

Screw

Screw

Switch end casting

Crumb tray

End baffle plate

Screw

Screw

Ground connection point

Cordset entry point

End element connecting link

End element

Foot

Base plate

End element wire guard

Screw

Washer

Power supply cord

Bolt

Nut

Strain release

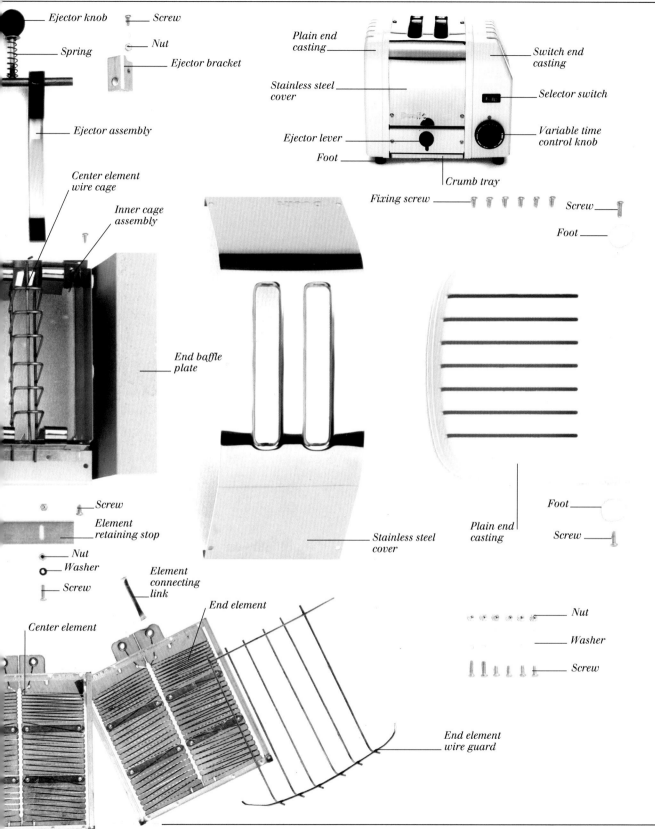

Ejector knob

Screw

Nut

Spring

Ejector bracket

Ejector assembly

Center element
wire cage

Inner cage
assembly

Plain end
casting

Switch end
casting

Stainless steel
cover

Selector switch

Ejector lever

Variable time
control knob

Foot

Crumb tray

Fixing screw

Screw

Foot

End baffle
plate

Screw

Element
retaining stop

Nut

Washer

Screw

Element
connecting
link

End element

Stainless steel
cover

Plain end
casting

Foot

Screw

Nut

Washer

Screw

Center element

End element
wire guard

Lawnmower

THE SHARP BLADES OF A LAWNMOWER—whether driven by electrical, gasoline, or human power—shave grass close to the ground. The gasoline-powered type shown here has a small engine that is electrically ignited by a battery and spark plug. This engine rotates a horizontal blade at the base of the lawnmower, which then slices the grass against a fixed blade. A grass bag at the back of the machine collects the cuttings. As the engine rotates the blades, it also turns the rear wheels, moving the lawnmower forward. Gears ensure that the horizontal blade spins faster than the wheels so that all of the grass is cut neatly before the lawnmower moves on.

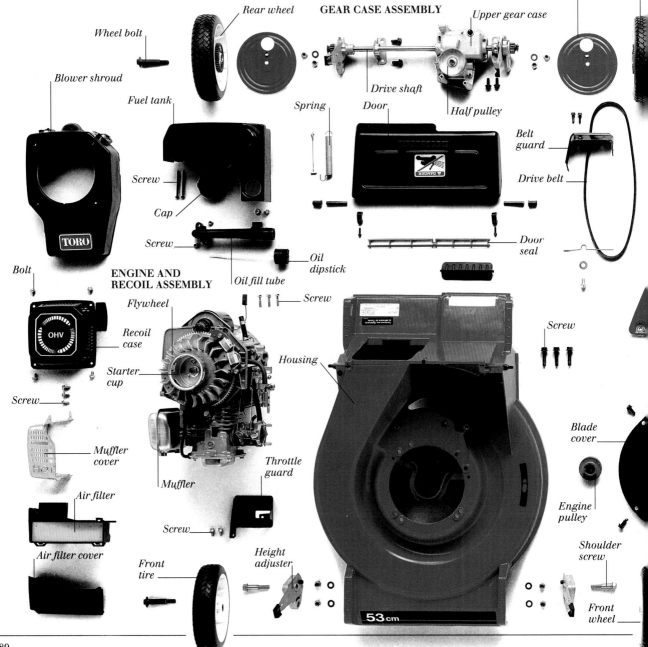

Rear tire

Wheel cover

Rear wheel

GEAR CASE ASSEMBLY

Upper gear case

Wheel bolt

Blower shroud

Drive shaft

Fuel tank

Spring

Door

Half pulley

Belt guard

Screw

Drive belt

Cap

Screw

Door seal

Oil dipstick

Bolt

ENGINE AND RECOIL ASSEMBLY

Oil fill tube

Screw

Screw

Flywheel

Recoil case

Housing

Screw

Starter cup

Screw

Blade cover

Muffler cover

Air filter

Throttle guard

Muffler

Engine pulley

Screw

Air filter cover

Front tire

Height adjuster

Shoulder screw

53 cm

Front wheel

TORO

OHV

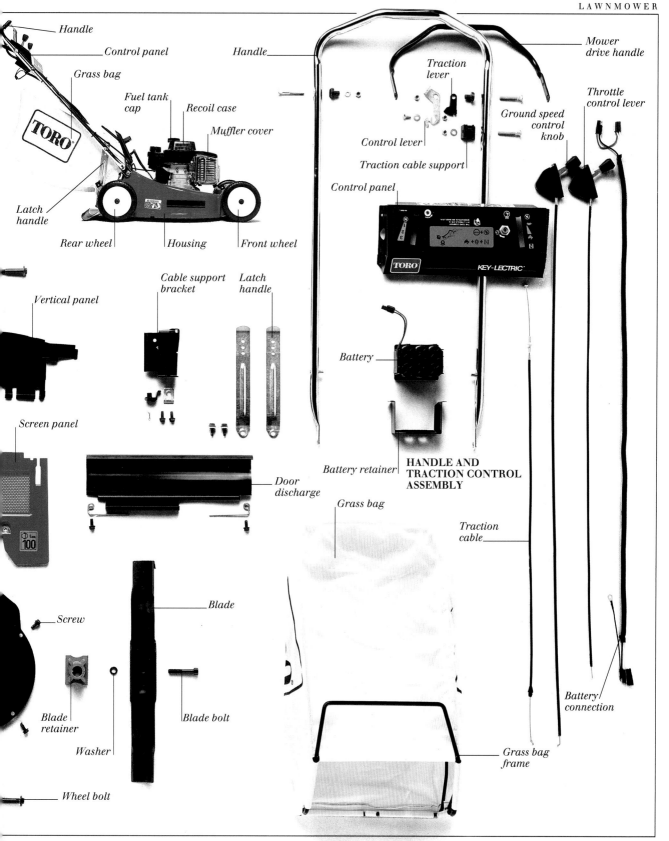

Handle

Control panel

Grass bag

Fuel tank cap

Recoil case

Muffler cover

Latch handle

Rear wheel

Housing

Front wheel

Handle

Traction lever

Mower drive handle

Control lever

Traction cable support

Ground speed control knob

Throttle control lever

Control panel

TORO

KEY-LECTRIC

Battery

Vertical panel

Cable support bracket

Latch handle

Screen panel

Door discharge

Battery retainer

HANDLE AND TRACTION CONTROL ASSEMBLY

Grass bag

Traction cable

Screw

Blade

Blade retainer

Washer

Blade bolt

Battery connection

Grass bag frame

Wheel bolt

Saddle

THE FIRST HORSEBACK RIDERS HAD NO SADDLES; they sat bareback, clinging to the animal's mane. Next came a simple cloth saddle. The leather saddle, which was invented about 2,000 years ago by the warriors of the Asian steppes, revolutionized horseback riding. On this saddle, horsemen could gallop toward the enemy, fire arrows in all directions, and stay on their horses. Modern saddles are of two main types. The Western saddle is a heavy, working saddle used mainly by ranch hands in the United States. It has a metal horn at the front for securing a lasso and a high cantle at the back to keep the rider on the horse. The English saddle is much lighter. Designed for sport, it allows the horse to gallop fast. Its drawback is that it provides less stability; to stay on the horse, the rider must grip the animal with the knees.

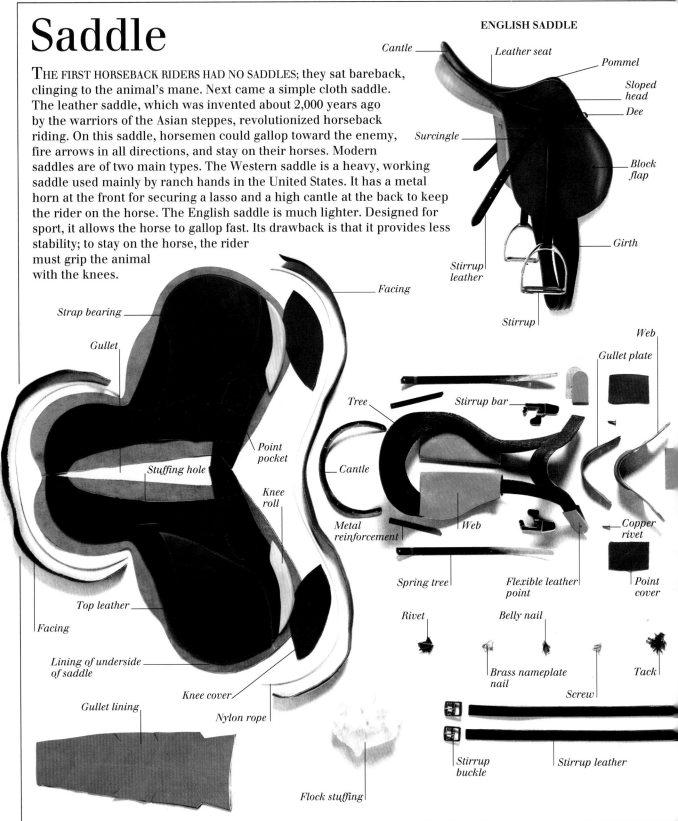

ENGLISH SADDLE

Cantle
Leather seat
Pommel
Sloped head
Dee
Surcingle
Block flap
Girth
Stirrup leather
Stirrup

Facing
Strap bearing
Gullet
Point pocket
Stuffing hole
Knee roll
Cantle
Tree
Stirrup bar
Web
Gullet plate
Metal reinforcement
Web
Copper rivet
Top leather
Spring tree
Flexible leather point
Point cover
Facing
Rivet
Belly nail
Lining of underside of saddle
Brass nameplate nail
Screw
Tack
Knee cover
Gullet lining
Nylon rope
Stirrup buckle
Stirrup leather
Flock stuffing

SHAPED GIRTH

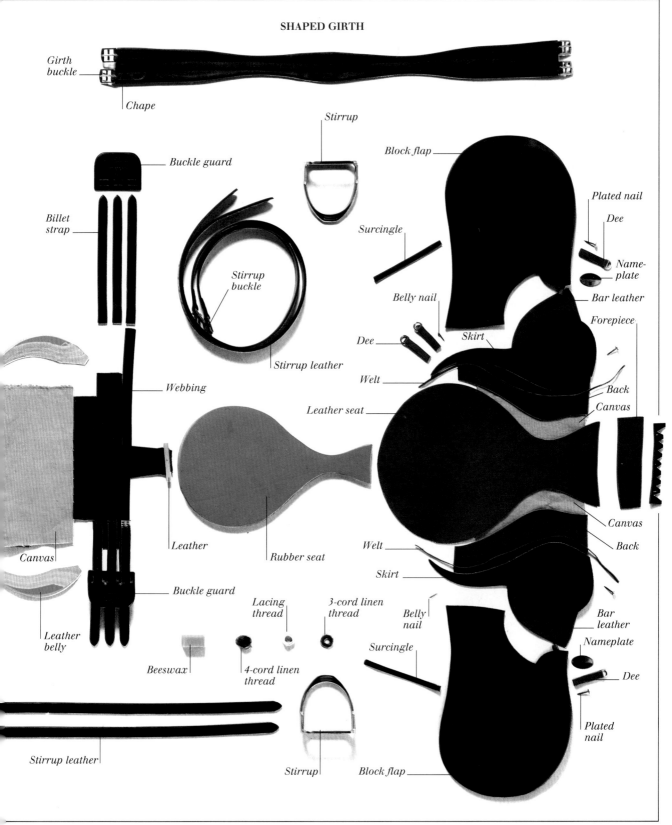

Girth buckle

Chape

Stirrup

Block flap

Buckle guard

Plated nail

Dee

Billet strap

Surcingle

Name-plate

Stirrup buckle

Belly nail

Bar leather

Forepiece

Dee

Skirt

Back

Welt

Canvas

Webbing

Leather seat

Canvas

Back

Leather

Welt

Skirt

Bar leather

Canvas

Rubber seat

Belly nail

Nameplate

Buckle guard

Surcingle

Dee

Leather belly

Lacing thread

3-cord linen thread

Beeswax

4-cord linen thread

Plated nail

Stirrup leather

Stirrup

Block flap

CD-ROM

CD-ROM _____
drive

A CD-ROM IS A TYPE OF COMPACT DISC (CD) that can be used to produce
images on a computer screen. ROM stands for Read Only Memory,
which means that the digitally recorded data registered in pits on the
surface of the disc is fixed and cannot be altered or replaced. The CD
is loaded into the CD-ROM player, where the data on the spinning
disc is read by a laser. CD-ROMs are different from vinyl records in that
they are not read along a spiral groove, from outer circumference
to inner edge: instead each image or piece of information has a
coordinate on the disc, which is located by the laser. Information
picked up by the laser is relayed to the computer, where it is
translated into the text and images that appear on screen. The
information is relayed through a SCSI (Small Computer System
Interface), which processes the electronic impulses between the
disc drive and the computer system. The user can move around the
program by clicking on different parts of the screen with a mouse
(a hand-held tool with a clicking button whose movement on its pad is
mimicked by an icon on the screen). The image in the viewing area
(see opposite) can be changed by clicking on the active scrolling
button: this moves a rectangular panel down the scrolling figure
in the navigational panel. Clicking on active text will provide
a new screen with more information, either in the form of text
and diagrams, or as narrated animated sequences.

CD
loading
tray

Caddy
cover flap

Front bezel

Push
button

CD-ROM CASING

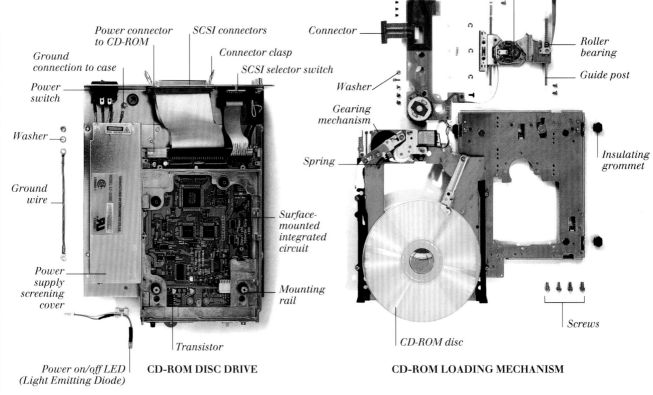

CD-ROM
drive motor

Film strip
connector

Laser

Connector

Roller
bearing

Guide post

Washer

Gearing
mechanism

Spring

Insulating
grommet

Power connector
to CD-ROM

SCSI connectors

Connector clasp

SCSI selector switch

Ground
connection to case

Power
switch

Washer

Ground
wire

Surface-
mounted
integrated
circuit

Power
supply
screening
cover

Mounting
rail

Screws

Transistor

CD-ROM disc

Power on/off LED
(Light Emitting Diode)

CD-ROM DISC DRIVE

CD-ROM LOADING MECHANISM

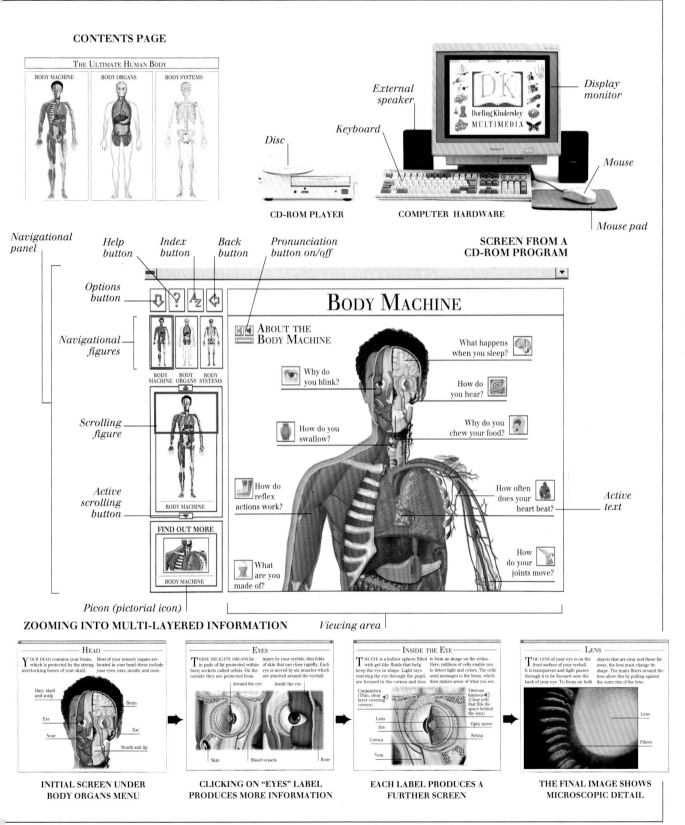

CONTENTS PAGE

THE ULTIMATE HUMAN BODY

BODY MACHINE | BODY ORGANS | BODY SYSTEMS

External speaker

Keyboard

Disc

Display monitor

Dorling Kindersley MULTIMEDIA

Mouse

CD-ROM PLAYER

COMPUTER HARDWARE

Mouse pad

SCREEN FROM A CD-ROM PROGRAM

Navigational panel

Help button

Index button

Back button

Pronunciation button on/off

Options button

Navigational figures

BODY MACHINE | BODY ORGANS | BODY SYSTEMS

Scrolling figure

Active scrolling button

BODY MACHINE

FIND OUT MORE

BODY MACHINE

Picon (pictorial icon)

ZOOMING INTO MULTI-LAYERED INFORMATION

BODY MACHINE

ABOUT THE BODY MACHINE

Why do you blink?

How do you swallow?

How do reflex actions work?

What are you made of?

What happens when you sleep?

How do you hear?

Why do you chew your food?

How often does your heart beat?

How do your joints move?

Active text

Viewing area

HEAD

YOUR HEAD contains your brain, which is protected by the strong interlocking bones of your skull. Most of your sensory organs are located in your head: these include your eyes, ears, mouth, and nose.

Hair, skull and scalp
Brain
Eye
Nose
Ear
Mouth and lip

INITIAL SCREEN UNDER BODY ORGANS MENU

EYES

THESE DELICATE ORGANS lie in pads of fat protected within bony sockets called orbits. On the outside they are protected from injury by your eyelids, thin folds of skin that can close rapidly. Each eye is moved by six muscles which are attached around the eyeball.

Around the eye
Inside the eye
Skin
Blood vessels
Bone

CLICKING ON "EYES" LABEL PRODUCES MORE INFORMATION

INSIDE THE EYE

THE EYE is a hollow sphere filled with gel-like fluids that help keep the eye in shape. Light rays entering the eye through the pupil, are focused by the cornea and lens to form an image on the retina. Here, millions of cells enable you to detect light and colors. The cells send messages to the brain, which then makes sense of what you see.

Conjunctiva (Thin, clear layer covering cornea)
Lens
Iris
Cornea
Vein
Vitreous humous (Clear jelly that fills the space behind the lens)
Optic nerve
Retina

EACH LABEL PRODUCES A FURTHER SCREEN

LENS

THE LENS of your eye is on the front surface of your eyeball. It is transparent and light passes through it to be focused onto the back of your eye. To focus on both objects that are near and those far away, the lens must change its shape. The many fibers around the lens allow this by pulling against the outer rim of the lens.

Lens
Fibers

THE FINAL IMAGE SHOWS MICROSCOPIC DETAIL

Books

THOUGH THE PROCESS OF BOOKBINDING today is usually mechanized, some books are still bound by hand. The pages of a book are printed on large sheets of paper called sections, or signatures. When folded, sections usually make 8, 16, or 32 pages. To assemble a hand-bound hardback book, the binder first places the folded sections in the correct order within the endpapers. Next, he or she sews the sections together along the spine edge using strong thread and then pastes them with glue for extra strength. After trimming the pages, the binder puts the book in a press and hammers the spine to shape it. The binder then glues one or more linings on the spine. The cover, or case, comes last. To make this, the bookbinder sticks cover boards to the endpapers, front and back, and then covers them with cloth or leather.

HALF-BOUND BOOK

LEATHER-BOUND BOOK

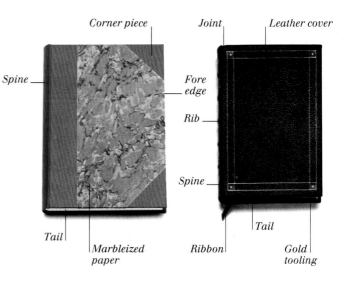

Corner piece

Spine

Fore edge

Rib

Spine

Tail

Marbleized paper

Joint

Leather cover

Tail

Ribbon

Gold tooling

HALF-BOUND BOOK

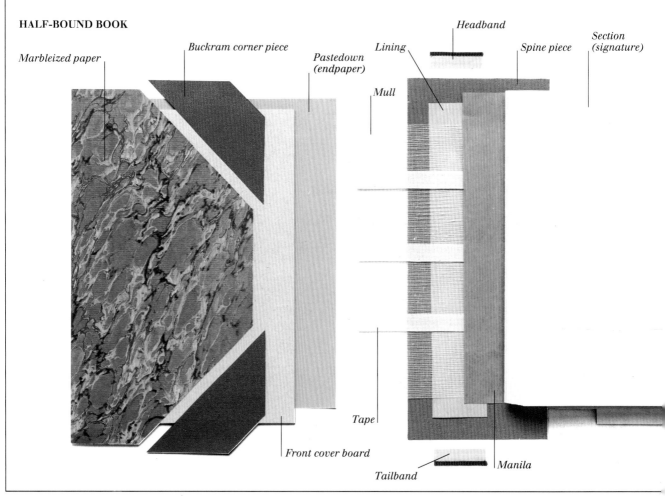

Marbleized paper

Buckram corner piece

Pastedown (endpaper)

Lining

Headband

Spine piece

Section (signature)

Mull

Tape

Front cover board

Tailband

Manila

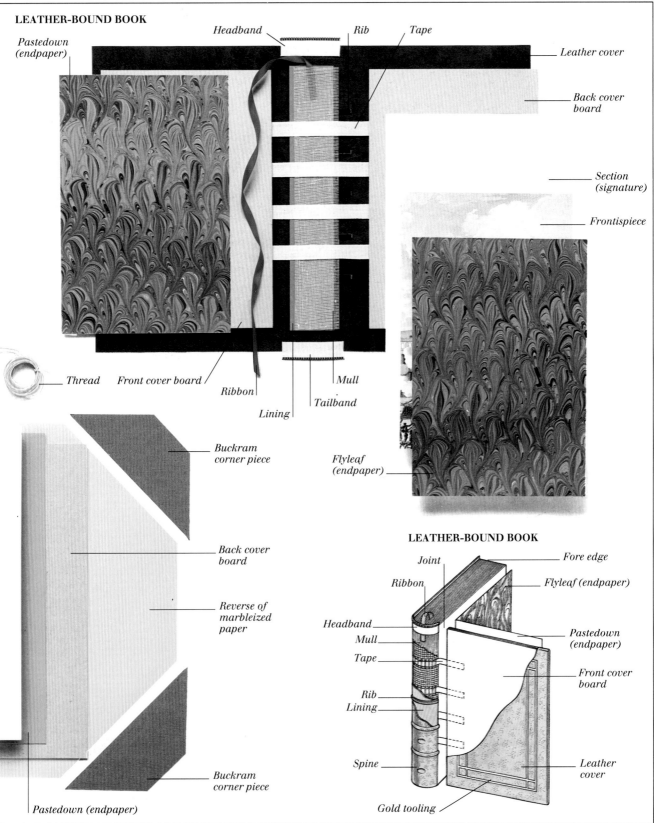

LEATHER-BOUND BOOK

Pastedown (endpaper)

Headband

Rib

Tape

Leather cover

Back cover board

Section (signature)

Frontispiece

Thread

Front cover board

Ribbon

Lining

Mull

Tailband

Flyleaf (endpaper)

Buckram corner piece

Back cover board

Reverse of marbleized paper

Buckram corner piece

Pastedown (endpaper)

LEATHER-BOUND BOOK

Joint

Ribbon

Headband

Mull

Tape

Rib

Lining

Spine

Fore edge

Flyleaf (endpaper)

Pastedown (endpaper)

Front cover board

Leather cover

Gold tooling

Camera

A CAMERA IS AN INSTRUMENT used for recording images on photographic film. It consists of a light-tight box with a shutter, a lens containing a diaphragm, and a viewing system. When the shutter is released, the film is exposed to light from the subject that is being photographed. Adjusting the shutter speed alters the time for which the film is exposed to light. The diaphragm, by altering the aperture of the lens, controls the intensity of light entering the camera. The total amount of light entering the camera is called the exposure. The lens focuses the light onto the film. When there is insufficient light to produce an adequate image, a flashgun may be used to give extra light.

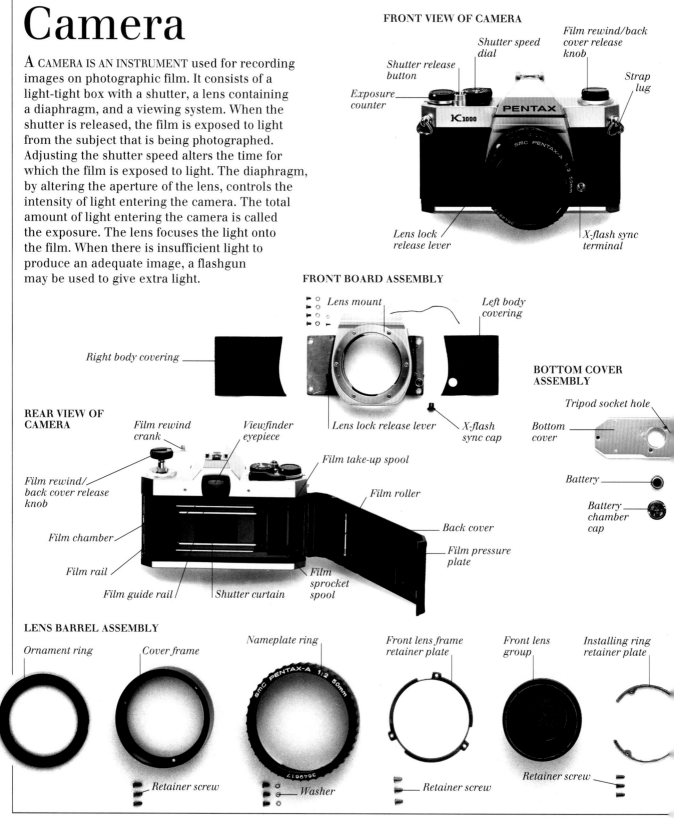

FRONT VIEW OF CAMERA

Shutter speed dial

Shutter release button

Film rewind/back cover release knob

Exposure counter

Strap lug

Lens lock release lever

X-flash sync terminal

FRONT BOARD ASSEMBLY

Lens mount

Left body covering

Right body covering

BOTTOM COVER ASSEMBLY

Tripod socket hole

Bottom cover

Lens lock release lever

X-flash sync cap

Battery

Battery chamber cap

REAR VIEW OF CAMERA

Film rewind crank

Viewfinder eyepiece

Film take-up spool

Film rewind/back cover release knob

Film roller

Film chamber

Back cover

Film rail

Film pressure plate

Film guide rail

Shutter curtain

Film sprocket spool

LENS BARREL ASSEMBLY

Ornament ring

Cover frame

Nameplate ring

Front lens frame retainer plate

Front lens group

Installing ring retainer plate

Retainer screw

Washer

Retainer screw

Retainer screw

TOP COVER ASSEMBLY

Shutter dial knob spring

Film speed indicator

Speed dial knob

Shutter speed dial

Retainer screw

Counter dial housing

Film wind lever

Counter dial cover

Exposure counter dial

Wind lever install spring

Wind lever collar

Top cover

X-contact

Hot shoe

Rewind shaft

Film rewind/ back cover release knob

Retainer screw

Washer

Window

Prism retainer spring

Prism retainer plate

Shutter release button

Shutter speed index

Rewind shaft bushing

Film rewind crank

MAIN BODY

Pentaprism

Cover frame

Retainer screw

Strap lug

Viewfinder eyepiece

TOP VIEW OF CAMERA

Focusing ring

Aperture/distance index

Subject distance scale

Hole for film rewind button

Depth-of-field guide

Lens alignment node

Aperture auto-lock button

Lens lock release lever

Shutter release button

Shutter cocked indicator

Exposure counter

Retainer screw

Film rewind crank

Film rewind/back cover release knob

Hot shoe

X-contact

Shutter speed index

Film speed indicator

Film wind lever

Shutter speed dial

Supporter ring retainer plate

Supporter ring

Diaphragm blade

Installing ring

Main barrel assembly

Rear lens group

Opening and closing plate

Appendix: useful data

UNITS OF MEASUREMENT

U.S. unit	Equivalent
Length	
1 foot (ft)	12 inches (in)
1 yard (yd)	3 feet
1 rod (rd)	5.5 yards
1 mile (mi)	1,760 yards
Mass	
1 dram (dr)	27.344 grains (gr)
1 ounce (oz)	16 drams
1 pound (lb)	16 ounces
1 hundredweight (cwt) (long)	112 pounds
1 hundredweight (cwt) (short)	100 pounds
1 ton (long)	2,240 pounds
1 ton (short)	2,000 pounds
Area	
1 square foot (ft²)	144 square inches (in²)
1 square yard (yd²)	9 square feet
1 acre	4,840 square yards
1 square mile	640 acres
Volume	
1 cubic foot	1,728 cubic inches
1 cubic yard	27 cubic feet
Capacity (liquid and dry measures)	
1 fluidram (fl dr)	60 minims (min)
1 fluid ounce (fl oz)	8 fluidrams
1 gill (gi)	4 fluid ounces
1 pint (pt)	4 gills
1 quart (qt)	2 pints
1 gallon (gal)	4 quarts
1 peck (pk)	2 gallons
1 bushel (bu)	4 pecks

Metric unit	Equivalent
Length	
1 centimeter (cm)	10 millimeters (mm)
1 meter (m)	100 centimeters
1 kilometer (km)	1,000 meters
Mass	
1 kilogram (kg)	1,000 grams (g)
1 tonne (t)	1,000 kilograms
Area	
1 square centimeter (cm²)	100 square millimeters (mm²)
1 square meter (m²)	10,000 square centimeters
1 hectare	10,000 square meters
1 square kilometer (km²)	1,000,000 square meters
Volume	
1 cubic centimeter (cc)	1 milliliter (ml)
1 liter (l)	1,000 milliliters
1 cubic meter (m³)	1,000 liters
Capacity (liquid and dry measures)	
1 centiliter (cl)	10 milliliters (ml)
1 deciliter (dl)	10 centiliters
1 liter (l)	10 deciliters
1 decaliter (dal)	10 liters
1 hectoliter (hi)	10 decaliters
1 kiloliter (kl)	10 hectoliters

TEMPERATURE SCALES

To convert from Celsius (C) to Fahrenheit (F): $F = (C \times 9 \div 5) + 32$
To convert from Fahrenheit to Celsius: $C = (F - 32) \times 5 \div 9$
To convert from Celsius to Kelvin (K): $K = C + 273$
To convert from Kelvin to Celsius: $C = K - 273$

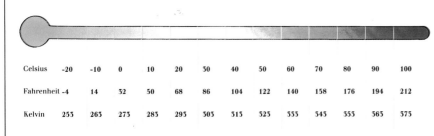

Celsius	-20	-10	0	10	20	30	40	50	60	70	80	90	100
Fahrenheit	-4	14	32	50	68	86	104	122	140	158	176	194	212
Kelvin	253	263	273	283	293	303	313	323	333	343	353	363	373

AREAS AND VOLUMES

CIRCLE
Radius r
Diameter $d = 2 \times r$
Circumference = $2 \times \pi \times r$
Area = $\pi \times r^2$
($\pi = 3.1416$)

TRIANGLE
Height h
Sides a, b, c
Perimeter = $a + b + c$
Area = $\frac{1}{2} \times b \times h$

RECTANGLE
Sides a, b
Perimeter = $2 \times (a + b)$
Area = $a \times b$

CYLINDER
Height h
Radius r
Surface area = $2 \times \pi \times r \times h$ (excluding ends)
Volume = $\pi \times r^2 \times h$

CONE
Height h
Radius r
Side l
Surface area = $\pi \times r \times l$ (excluding base)
Volume = $\frac{1}{3} \times \pi \times r^2 \times l$

RECTANGULAR BLOCK
Sides a, b, c
Surface area = $2 \times (a \times b + b \times c + a \times c)$
Volume = $a \times b \times c$

U.S. – METRIC CONVERSIONS

To convert	Into	Multiply by
Length		
Inches	centimeters	2.5400
Feet	meters	0.3048
Miles	kilometers	1.6090
Yards	meters	0.9144
Mass		
Ounces	grams	28.3500
Pounds	kilograms	0.4536
Long tons	tonnes	1.0160
Short tons	tonnes	0.9070
Area		
Square inches	square centimeters	6.4520
Square feet	square meters	0.0929
Acres	hectares	0.4047
Square miles	square kilometers	2.5900
Square yards	square meters	0.8361
Volume		
Cubic inches	cubic centimeters	16.3900
Cubic feet	cubic meters	0.0283
Capacity		
Pints (liquid)	liters	0.4730
Gallons (liquid)	liters	3.7850

METRIC – U.S. CONVERSIONS

To convert	Into	Multiply by
Length		
Centimeters	inches	0.3937
Meters	feet	3.2810
Kilometers	miles	0.6214
Meters	yards	1.0940
Mass		
Grams	ounces	0.0352
Kilograms	pounds	2.2050
Tonnes	long tons	0.9843
Tonnes	short tons	1.1025
Area		
Square centimeters	square inches	0.1550
Square meters	square feet	10.7600
Hectares	acres	2.4710
Square kilometers	square miles	0.3861
Square meters	square yards	1.1960
Volume		
Cubic centimeters	cubic inches	0.0610
Cubic meters	cubic feet	35.3100
Capacity		
Liters	pints (liquid)	2.1142
Liters	gallons (liquid)	0.2642

NUMBER SYSTEMS

Roman	Arabic
I	1
II	2
III	3
IV	4
V	5
VI	6
VII	7
VIII	8
IX	9
X	10
XI	11
XII	12
XIII	13
XIV	14
XV	15
XX	20
XXI	21
XXX	30
XL	40
L	50
LX	60
LXX	70
LXXX	80
XC	90
C	100
CI	101
CC	200
CCC	300
CD	400
D	500
DC	600
DCC	700
DCCC	800
CM	900
M	1,000
MM	2,000

PHYSICS SYMBOLS

Symbol	Meaning
α	alpha particle
β	beta ray
γ	gamma ray; photon
ε	electromotive force
η	efficiency; viscosity
λ	wavelength
μ	micro-; permeability
ν	frequency; neutrino
ρ	density; resistivity
σ	conductivity
c	velocity of light
e	electronic charge

MATHEMATICS SYMBOLS

Symbol	Meaning
$+$	plus
$-$	minus
$\pm$	plus or minus
$\times$	multiplied by
$\div$	divided by
$=$	equals
$>$	is greater than
$<$	is less than
$\geq$	is greater than or equal to
$\leq$	is less than or equal to
$\%$	per cent
$\sqrt{}$	root
π	pi (3.1416)
$°$	degree
∞	infinity
$\approx$	is approximately equal to
$\angle$	angle

CHEMISTRY SYMBOLS

Symbol	Meaning
$+$	plus; together with
$-$	single bond
$\cdot$	single bond; single unpaired electron; two separate parts or compounds regarded as loosely joined
$=$	double bond
$\equiv$	triple bond
R	group
X	halogen atom
Z	atomic number

BIOLOGY SYMBOLS

Symbol	Meaning
○	female individual (used in inheritance charts)
□	male individual (used in inheritance charts)
♀	female
♂	male
$\times$	crossed with; hybrid
$+$	wild type
F_1	offspring of the first generation
F_2	offspring of the second generation

POWERS OF TEN USED WITH SCIENTIFIC UNITS

Factor	Name	Prefix	Symbol
10^{18}	quintillion	exa-	E
10^{15}	quadrillion	peta-	P
10^{12}	trillion	tera-	T
10^{9}	billion	giga-	G
10^{6}	million	mega-	M
10^{3}	thousand	kilo-	k
10^{2}	hundred	hecto-	h
10^{1}	ten	deca-	da
10^{-1}	one tenth	deci-	d
10^{-2}	one hundredth	centi-	c
10^{-3}	one thousandth	milli-	m
10^{-6}	one millionth	micro-	μ
10^{-9}	one billionth	nano-	n
10^{-12}	one trillionth	pico-	p
10^{-15}	one quadrillionth	femto-	f
10^{-18}	one quintillionth	atto-	a

Index

615

621

623

Acknowledgments

Dorling Kindersley would like to thank (in order of sections):

**The Universe
(consultant editors – Sue Becklake, Gevorkyan Tatyana Alekseyevna):**
John Becklake; the Memorial Museum of Cosmonautics, Moscow; The Cosmos Pavilion, Moscow; The United States Space and Rocket Center, Alabama; Broadhurst, Clarkson and Fuller Ltd; Susannah Massey

**Prehistoric Earth
(consultant editors – William Lindsay, Martyn Bramwell, Dr. Ralph E. Molnar, David Lambert):**
Dr. Monty Reid, Andrew Neuman, and the staff of the Royal Tyrrell Museum of Palaeontology, Drumheller, Alberta; Dr. Angela Milner and the staff of the Department of Palaeontology, the Natural History Museum, London; Professor W. Ziegler and the staff, in particular Michael Loderstaedt, of the Naturmuseum Senckenburg, Frankfurt; Dr. Alexander Liebau, Axel Hunghrebüller, Reiner Schoch, and the staff of the Institut und Museum für Geologie und Paläontologie der Universität, Tübingen; Rupert Wild of the Institut für Paläontologie, Staatliches Museum für Naturkunde, Stuttgart; Dr. Scheiber of the Stadtmuseum, Nördlingen; Professor Dr. Dietrich Herm of Staatssammlung für Paläontologie und Historische Geologie, München; Dr. Michael Keith-Lucas of the Department of Botany, University of Reading; Richard Walker; American Museum of Natural History, New York

**Plants
(consultant editor – Richard Walker):**
Diana Miller; Lawrie Springate; Karen Sidwell; Chris Thody; Michelle End; Susan Barnes and Chris Jones of the EMU Unit of the Natural History Museum, London; Jenny Evans of Kew Gardens, London; Kate Biggs of the Royal Horticultural Society Gardens, Wisley, Surrey; Spike Walker of Microworld Services; Neil Fletcher; John Bryant of Bedgebury Pinetum, Kent; Dean Franklin

**Animals
(consultant editor – Richard Walker):**
David Manning's Animal Ark; Intellectual Animals; Howletts Zoo, Canterbury; John Dunlop; Alexander O'Donnell; Sue Evans of the Royal Veterinary College, London; Dr. Geoff Potts and Fred Frettsome of the Marine Biological Association of the United Kingdom, Plymouth; Jeremy Adams of the Booth Museum of Natural History, Brighton; Derek Telling of the Department of Anatomy, University of Bristol; the Natural History Museum, London; Andy Highfield of the Tortoise Trust; Brian Harris of the Aquarium, London Zoo; the Invertebrate Department, London Zoo; Dr. Harold McClure of the Yerkes Regional Primate Research Center, Emory University, Atlanta, Georgia; Nielson Lausen of the Harvard Medical

School, New England Regional Primates Research Center, Southborough, Massachusetts; Dr. Paul Hopwood of the Department of Veterinary Anatomy, University of Sydney; Dean Franklin

**The Human Body
(consultant editors – Dr. Frances Williams, Dr. Fiona Payne, Richard Cummins FRCS):**
Derek Edwards and Dr Martin Collins, British School of Osteopathy; Dr. M.C.E. Hutchinson of the Department of Anatomy, United Medical and Dental Schools of Guy's and St. Thomas' Hospitals, London. Models – Barry O'Rorke (Bodyline Agency) and Pauline Swaine (MOT Model Agency)

**Geology, Geography, and Meteorology
(consultant editor – Martyn Bramwell):**
Dr. John Nudds of the Manchester Museum, Manchester; Dr. Alan Wooley and Dr. Andrew Clark of the Natural History Museum, London; Graham Bartlett of the National Meteorological Library and Archive, Bracknell; Tony Drake of BP Exploration, Uxbridge; Jane Davies of the Royal Society of Chemistry, Cambridge; Dr. Tony Waltham of Nottingham Trent University, Nottingham; staff of the Smithsonian Institute, Washington; staff of the United States Geological Survey, Washington; staff of the National Geographic Society, Washington; staff of Edward Lawrence Associates (Export Ltd), Midhurst; John Farndon; David Lambert

**Rail and Road
Rail (consultant editor – John Coiley)**
Michael Ashworth of the London Transport Museum

Road (consultant editors – David Burgess-Wise, Hugo Wilson)
The National Motor Museum, Beaulieu; Alf Newell of Renault UK Ltd; David Suter of Cheltenham Cutaway Exhibits Ltd; Francesca Riccini of the Science Museum, London. Signore Amadelli of the Museo dell' Automobile Carlo Biscaretti di Ruffia; Paul Bolton of the Mazda MCL Group; Duncan Bradford of Reg Mills Wire Wheels; John and Leslie Brewster of Autocavan; David Burgess-Wise; Trevor Cass of Garrett Turbo Service; John Corbett of The Patrick Collection; Gary Crumpler of Williams Grand Prix Engineering Ltd; Mollie Easterbrooke and Duncan Gough of Overland Ltd; Arthur Fairley of the Vauxhall Motor Co; Paul Foulkes-Halbard of Filching Manor Motor Museum; Frank Gilbert of I. Wilkinson and Son Ltd; Paolo Gratton of Gratton Museum; Colvin Gunn of Gunn and Son; Judy Hogg of Ecurie Bertelli; Milton Holman of Dream Cars; Ian Matthews of IMAT Electronics; Eric Neal of Jaguar Cars Ltd; Paul Niblett, Keith Davidson, Mark Reumel, and David Woolf of Michelin Tyre plc; Doug Nye; Kevin O'Keefe of O'Keefe Cars; Seat UK; Roger Smith; Jim Stirling of Ironbridge Gorge Museum, Staffordshire; Jon Taylor; Doug Thompson; Martyn Watkins of Ford Motor Co Ltd; John Cattermole, Customer Services Manager, at London Northern Buses; F. W. Evans Cycles Ltd; Trek UK Ltd (Bicycle); Sam Grimmer

**Physics and Chemistry
(consultant editor – Jack Challoner)**

**Sea and Air
Sea (consultant editors – Geoff Hales and Harvey B. Loomis):**
David Spence, Gillian Hutchinson, David Topliss, Simon Stephens, Robert Baldwin, Jonathan Betts, all of the National Maritime Museum, London; Ian Friel; Simon Turnage of Captain O.M. Watts of London Ltd; Davey and Co Ltd, Great Dunmow; Avon Inflatables Ltd, Llanelli; Musto Ltd, Benfleet; Peter Martin of Spencer Rigging Ltd, Southampton; Peter Rowson of Ratseys Sailmakers, Southampton; Swiftech Ltd, Wallingford; Colin Scattergood of the Barrow Boat Co Ltd, Colchester; Professor J.S. Morrison of the Trireme Trust, Cambridge; The Cutty Sark Maritime Trust; Adrian Daniels of Kelvin Hughes Marine Instruments, London; Arthur Credland of Hull City Council Museums and Art Galleries; The Hull Maritime Society; Gerald Clark; Peter Fitzgerald of the Science Museum, London; Alec Michael of HMB Subwork Ltd, Great Yarmouth, and Ray Ward of the OSEL Group, Great Yarmouth; Richard Bird of UWI, Weybridge; Walker Marine Instruments, Birmingham; The International Sailing Craft Association; The Exeter Maritime Museum; Jane Wilson of the Trinity Lighthouse Co, London; The Imperial War Museum Collections; Thorn Security Ltd; Michael Bach

Air (consultant editor – Bill Gunston):
Aeromega Helicopters, Stapleford; Aero Shopping, London; Avionics Mobile Services Ltd, Watford; Roy Barber and John Chapman of the RAF Museum, Hendon; Mitch Barnes Aviation, London; Mike Beach; British Caledonian Flight Training Ltd; Fred Coates of Helitech (Luton) Ltd; Michael Cuttell and CSE Aviation Ltd, Oxford; Dowty Aerospace Landing Gear, Gloucester; Guy Hartcup of the Airship Association; Anthony Hooley, Chris Walsh, and David Cord of British Aerospace Regional Aircraft Ltd; Ken Huntley of Mid-West Aero Engines Ltd; Imperial War Museum, Duxford; The London Gliding Club, Dunstable; Musée des Ballons, Calvados; Noel Penny Turbines Ltd; Andy Pavey of Aviation Scotland Ltd; Tony Pavey of Thermal Aircraft Developments, London; the Commanding Officer and personnel of RAF St Athan; the Commanding Officer and personnel of RAF Wittering; The Science Museum, London; Ross Sharp of the Science Museum, Wroughton; The Shuttleworth Collection; Skysport Engineering; Mike Smith; Solar Wings Ltd, Marlborough; Julian Temple of Brooklands Museum Trust Ltd; Kelvin Wilson of Flying Start

**Architecture
(consultant editor – Alexandra Kennedy):**
Stephen Cutler for advice and text; Gavin Morgan of the Museum of London, London; Chris Zeuner of the Weald and Downland Museum, Singleton, Sussex; Alan Hills and James Putnam of the British Museum, London; Dr. Simon Penn and Michael Thomas of the Avoncroft Museum of Buildings, Bromsgrove,

Worcestershire; Christina Scull of Sir John Soane's Museum, London; Paul Kennedy and John Williamson of the London Door Co, London; Lou Davis of The Original Box Sash Window Co, Windsor; Goddard and Gibbs Studios Ltd, London, for access to stained glass windows; The Royal Courts of Justice, Strand, London; Charles Brooking and Peter Dalton for access to the doors and windows in the Charles Brooking Collection, University of Greenwich, Dartford, Kent; Clare O'Brien of the Shakespeare Globe Trust, Shakespeare's Globe Museum, Bear Gardens, Southwark, London; Ken Teague of the Horniman Museum, London; Canon Haliburton, Mike Payton, Ken Stones, and Anthony Webb of St. Paul's Cathedral, London; Roy Spring of Salisbury Cathedral; Reverend Gillean Craig of the Church of St. George in the East, London; the Science Museum, London; Dr. Neil Bingham; Lin Kennedy of Historic Royal Palaces; Katy Harris of Sir Norman Foster and Partners; Production Design, Thames Television plc, London, for supplying models; Dominique Reynier of Le Centre Georges Pompidou, Paris; Denis Roche of Le Musée National des Monuments Français, Paris; Franck Gioria and students of Les Compagnons du Devoir, Paris, for access to construction models; Frank Folliot of Le Musée Carnavalet, Paris; Dr Martina Harms of Hessische Landesmuseums, Darmstadt; Jefferson Chapman of the University of Tennessee, Knoxville, for access to the model of the Hypostyle Hall, Temple of Amon-Re; staff of the Palazzo Strozzi, Florence; staff of the Sydney Opera House, Sydney; staff of the Empire State Building, New York; Nick Jackson; Ann Terrell

The Visual Arts
(consultant editor – Pip Seymour):
Rosemary Simmons; Michael Taylor of Paupers Press, London; Tessa Hunkin and Emma Biggs of Mosaic Workshop, London; John Tiranti, Jonathan Lyons of Alec Tiranti Ltd, London; Chris Hough; Dr. Ashok Roy; Satwinder Sehmi of Alphabet Soup, London; Phillip Poole of Cornelissens, London; George Weil and Sons Ltd, London; The National Gallery, London; Chris Webster of the Tate Gallery, London; China Art Cultural Centre, London; London Graphic Centre, London; A.P. Fitzpatrick, London; Flowers Graphics, London; Intaglio Printmaker, London; Falkiner Papers, London; Edgar Udny and Co, London; John Green

Music
(consultant editor – Susan Sturrock):
Boosey and Hawkes Music Publishers Ltd, London, for permission to reproduce extract from The Prodigal Son by Arthur Sullivan; The Bass and Drum Cellar, London; Empire Drums and Percussion, London; Argents (part of World of Music), London; Bill Lewington Ltd, London; Frobenius organ at Kingston Parish Church, Kingston-upon-Thames, Surrey; Yamaha-Kemble Music (UK) Ltd, Tilbrook, Milton Keynes; Yamaha Atelier, London; Akai (UK) Ltd, Hounslow, Middlesex; Casio Electronics Co Ltd, London; Roland (UK) Ltd, Fleet, Hampshire; Richard Schulman

Sports
The Sports Council Information Centre, London; The British Olympic Games Committee; Brian Crennell of Black's Leisure Group (First Sport); Lillywhites of Piccadilly, London; Mitre Sports International Ltd, Huddersfield; David Bloomfield of the Football Association; Denver Athletics Ltd, Norfolk; Greg Everest and Keith Birley of the British League of Australian Rules Football; Peter McNally of the Gaelic Athletic Association; Rex King of the Rugby Football Union, Twickenham; Neil Tunnicliffe of the Rugby Football League, Leeds; Wayne Patterson of the Basketball Hall of Fame, Springfield, Connecticut; Brian Coleman of the English Basketball Association; All American Imports, Northampton; George Bulman of the English Volleyball Association; Julie Longdon of Mizuno Mallory (UK) Ltd; Juliet Stanford of the All-England Netball Association; Jeff Rowland of the British Handball Association; Cally Melin of Adidas UK Ltd; Patrick Donnely of the Baseball Hall of Fame, Cooperstown, New York; Ian Lepage and Stephen Barlow of the Hockey Association, Milton Keynes; Alison Taylor and Anita Mason of the All England Women's Lacrosse Association, Birmingham; David Shuttleworth of the English Lacrosse Union; Les Barnett and Jock Bentley of the British Athletic Federation Ltd, Birmingham; Mike Gilks of the Badminton Association of England; Gurinder Purewall for advice on archery; Chris McCartney of the US Archery Association; Geoff Doe of the National Smallbore Rifle Association, Bisley, Surrey, for information and reference material on shooting; Fagan Sports Goods Distributors, Surrey; Konrad Bartelski for advice on skiing; The British Ski Federation, Edinburgh; Mike Barnett of Snow and Rock of London; Sally Spurway of Mast-Co. Ltd, Reading; Sarah Morgan for advice on equestrian sports; Steve Brown and the New York Racing Association Inc, New York; Danrho of London; Alan Skipp and James Chambers of the Amateur Fencing Association, London; Carla Richards of the US Fencing Association; Hamilton Bland and John Dryer of the Amateur Swimming Association, Loughborough; Cotswold Camping Ltd, London; Tim Spalton of Glyn Locke (Racing Shells) Ltd, Chalgrove; Terry Friel of the US Rowing Association; House of Hardy; Leeda Fishing Tackle

Everyday Things
City Clocks (Clocks); Christopher Cullen of Babber Electronics; Sony UK Ltd (Mini-television); Black and Decker Ltd (Drills); British Footwear Manufacturing Federation; Grenson Shoes Ltd (Shoes); The Folio Society; R S Bookbinders (Books); Pentax UK Ltd (Camera); F E Murdin of the Decorative Lighting Association; Habitat (Lamp); Chingford Reproductions Ltd (Chair); Dualit Ltd (Toaster); J B Dove; Toro Wheelhorse UK Ltd (Lawnmower); WandH Gidden Ltd (Saddle)

PHOTOGRAPHY:
M. Alexander; Peter Anderson; Charles Brooks; Jane Burton; Peter Chadwick; Simon Clay; John Coiley; Andy Crawford; Geoff Dann; Philip Dowell; John Downs; Mike Dunning; Torla Evans; David Exton; Robert and Anthony Fretwell of Fretwell Photography Ltd.; Philip Gatward; Anna Hodgson; Gary Kevin; J. Heseltine; Cyril Laubscher; John Lepine; Lynton Gardiner (American Museum of Natural History, New York); Steve Gorton; Michelangelo Gratton; Judith Harrington; Peter Hayman; Anna Hodgson; Colin Keates; Gary Kevin; Dave King; Bob Langrish; Brian D.Morgan; Nick Nicholls; Nick Parfitt; Tim Parmenter and Colin Keates (Natural History Museum, London); Tim Ridley; Dave Rudkin; Philippe Sebert; James Stevenson; Clive Streeter; Harry Taylor; Matthew Ward; Jerry Young

PHOTOGRAPHIC ASSISTANCE:
Kevin Zak; Gary Ombler

ILLUSTRATORS:
Julian Baum; Rick Blakeley; Kuo Kang Chen; Karen Cochrane; Simone End; Ian Fleming; Roy Flooks; Mark Franklin; David Gardner; Will Giles; Mick Gillah; David Hopkins; Selwyn Hutchinson; Mei Lim; Linden Artists; Nick Loates; Chris Lyon; Kathleen McDougall; Coral Mula; Sandra Pond; Dave Pugh; Colin Rose; Graham Rosewarne; John Temperton; John Woodcock; Chris Woolmer

MODEL MAKERS:
Roby Braun; David Donkin; Morrison Frederick; Gordon Models; John Holmes; Graham High and Jeremy Hunt of Centaur Studios; Richard Kemp; Kelvin Thatcher; Paul Wilkinson

ADDITIONAL DESIGN ASSISTANCE:
Stefan Morris; Ulysses Santos; Suchada Smith

ADDITIONAL EDITORIAL ASSISTANCE:
Helen Castle; Colette Connolly; Camela Decaire; Nick Harris; Andrea Horth; Stewart McEwen; Damien Moore; Melanie Tham;

INDEX: Kay Wright